Windows Server® 2008
Inside Out

William R. Stanek

PUBLISHED BY
Microsoft Press
A Division of Microsoft Corporation
One Microsoft Way
Redmond, Washington 98052-6399

Library of Congress Control Number: 2007942102

Printed and bound in the United States of America.

4 5 6 7 8 9   QGT   3 2 1 0

Distributed in Canada by H.B. Fenn and Company Ltd.

A CIP catalogue record for this book is available from the British Library.

Microsoft Press books are available through booksellers and distributors worldwide. For further information about international editions, contact your local Microsoft Corporation office or contact Microsoft Press International directly at fax (425) 936-7329. Visit our Web site at www.microsoft.com/mspress. Send comments to mspinput@microsoft.com.

Microsoft, Microsoft Press, Active Directory, Authenticode, BitLocker, ClearType, Excel, IntelliMirror, Internet Explorer, Jscript, MS-DOS, Outlook, RemoteApp, SharePoint, SideShow, SQL Server, Visio, Win32, Windows, Windows Media, Windows NT, Windows PowerShell, Windows Server, and Windows Vista are either registered trademarks or trademarks of Microsoft Corporation in the United States and/or other countries. Other product and company names mentioned herein may be the trademarks of their respective owners.

The example companies, organizations, products, domain names, e-mail addresses, logos, people, places, and events depicted herein are fictitious. No association with any real company, organization, product, domain name, e-mail address, logo, person, place, or event is intended or should be inferred.

This book expresses the author's views and opinions. The information contained in this book is provided without any express, statutory, or implied warranties. Neither the authors, Microsoft Corporation, nor its resellers, or distributors will be held liable for any damages caused or alleged to be caused either directly or indirectly by this book.

Acquisitions Editor: Martin DelRe
Developmental Editor: Karen Szall
Project Editor: Victoria Thulman
Editorial Production: Publishing.Com
Technical Reviewer: Randall Galloway; Technical Review services provided by Content Master, a member of CM Group, Ltd.
Cover: Tom Draper Design

Body Part No. X14-40131

Contents at a Glance

Table of Contents

What do you think of this book? We want to hear from you!

Microsoft is interested in hearing your feedback so we can continually improve our books and learning resources for you. To participate in a brief online survey, please visit:

www.microsoft.com/learning/booksurvey/

Part 2: Managing Windows Server 2008 Systems

Part 3: Managing Windows Server 2008 Storage and File Systems

Part 4: Managing Windows Server 2008 Networking and Print Services

Part 5: Managing Active Directory and Security

Part 6: Windows Server 2008 Disaster Planning and Recovery

Acknowledgments

Few projects have ever been as challenging or as fun as writing *Windows Server 2008 Inside Out*. Why? When I set out to write *Windows Server 2008 Inside Out*, I decided I would try to detail every quirk, every insider secret, and every sticky detail that I've learned about Windows Server 2008 since I started working with it in 2002—back when Windows Server 2008 was known as Windows Longhorn. As nearly six years have passed since I began working with Windows Server 2008, it is my sincere hope that the book you hold in yours hands is the best of its class when it comes to managing a Windows Server 2008 implementation and handling everyday administration. I also hope the result of all the hard work is that *Windows Server 2008 Inside Out* is something unique. It takes into account all the experiences I've had while consulting, conducting training courses, and writing books about Windows Vista and Windows Server 2008. As this is my 35th Windows-related book and I've helped millions of people learn Windows over my 20+-year career, I hope that counts for an awful lot. But no man is an island and this book couldn't have been written without help from some very special people.

Without the support of my wife and children, this book would not have been possible. As I literally was writing every day since I signed on to this project—holidays included—my wife had to manage everything else and the little ones had a lot more responsibilities around the house. Thank you for your support and your extraordinary ability to put up with the clackety-clackety of my keyboard.

As I've stated in *Windows Server 2008 Administrator's Pocket Consultant* and in *Windows Vista Administrator's Pocket Consultant*, the team at Microsoft Press is top-notch. Karen Szall was instrumental throughout the writing process. Martin DelRe was the acquisitions editor for the project. He believed in the book and my unique approach and was really great to work with. Completing and publishing the book wouldn't have been possible without their help! Thanks also to Lucinda Rowley!

Curt Philips headed up the editorial process for Publishing.com. As the project manager for this and other Pocket Consultants I've written, he wore many hats and helped out in many ways. Thank you! I'd also like to add that everyone was very understanding—writing a book of this length is very fun but also very exhausting.

Unfortunately for the writer (but fortunately for readers), writing is only one part of the publishing process. Next came editing and author review. I must say, Microsoft Press has the most thorough editorial and technical review process I've seen anywhere—and I've written a lot of books for many different publishers. Randall Galloway was the technical editor for the book. Rozanne Whalen served as the copyeditor and was particularly thorough in her edits, which was much appreciated. I also want to thank Andrea Fox for her careful proofreading of the pages.

I want to thank a number of other people at Microsoft who provided technical reviews and insights, including Jose Luis Auricchio, Craig Threadgill, Jackson Robinson, Sasa Vidanovic, Anders Brabæk, Chris Gregory, Pat Telford, Monica Ene-Pietrosanu, Jose Renato Roda, Robert Hoover, Deepak Shenoy, Akshat Kesarwani, Shawn Travers, Heath Aubin, David Kennedy, Greg Cottingham, Sanjay Pandit, Lesley Kipling, Bernardo Castaneda Leon, Mark Kradel, and Robert Mitchell. Robert Mitchell in particular went above and beyond. Thank you!

I'd also like to thank Valerie DeGiulo and the Microsoft Press Creative Team for their contributions.

Hopefully, I haven't forgotten anyone but if I have, it was an oversight. *Honest.* ;-)

About the CD

The companion CD that ships with this book contains many tools and resources to help you get the most out of your *Inside Out* book.

What's on the CD

The companion CD is loaded with useful tools and links to help you with your Windows Server 2008 installation. The CD includes:

- **Complete e-book** An electronic version of *Windows Server 2008 Inside Out* in PDF format.

- **Product information** Links to information about the features and capabilities of Windows Server 2008 as well as product guides to help you optimize Windows Server 2008 in your enterprise.

- **Resources** Links to white papers, guides, webcasts, test labs and more to help you use and troubleshoot the features of Windows Server 2008.

- **Scripts** More than 700 sample scripts to help you automate management and maintenance tasks.

- **Tools** Many links to tools for IIS, PowerShell, System Center Data Operations, and more that you can put to use right away.

- **Sample chapters** Chapters from 15 other Windows Server 2008 books contain a wealth of information and provide a preview look at books that were recently published or will be published in the near future.

System Requirements

The following are the minimum system requirements necessary to run the CD:

- Microsoft Windows Vista, Windows XP with Service Pack (SP) 2, Windows Server 2003 with SP1, or newer operating system

- 500 megahertz (MHz) processor or higher

- 2 gigabyte (GB) storage space (a portion of this disk space will be freed after installation if the original download package is removed from the hard drive)

- 256 megabytes (MB) RAM

- CD-ROM or DVD-ROM drive

- 1024×768 or higher resolution monitor

- Microsoft Windows or Windows Vista–compatible sound card and speakers
- Microsoft Internet Explorer 6 or newer
- Microsoft Mouse or compatible pointing device

> **Digital Content for Digital Book Readers:** If you bought a digital-only edition of this book, you can enjoy select content from the print edition's companion CD.
> Visit **http://go.microsoft.com/fwlink/?LinkId=107443&clcid=0x409** to get your downloadable content. This content is always up-to-date and available to all readers.

Viewing the E-Book

The electronic version of the book and some of the other documentation included on this CD is provided in Portable Document Format (PDF). To view these files, you will need Adobe Acrobat or Acrobat Reader. For more information about these products or to download the Acrobat Reader, visit the Adobe Web site at *http://www.adobe.com.*

Support Information

Every effort has been made to ensure the accuracy of the contents of the book and of this CD. As corrections or changes are collected, they will be added to a Microsoft Knowledge Base article. Microsoft Press provides support for books and companion CDs at the following Web site:

http://www.microsoft.com/learning/support/books/

If you have comments, questions, or ideas regarding the book or this CD, or questions that are not answered by visiting the site above, please send them via e-mail to:

mspinput@microsoft.com

You can also click the Feedback or CD Support links on the Welcome page. Please note that Microsoft software product support is not offered through the above addresses. If your question is about the software, and not about the content of this book, please visit the Microsoft Help and Support page or the Microsoft Knowledge Base at:

http://support.microsoft.com

In the United States, Microsoft software product support issues not covered by the Microsoft Knowledge Base are addressed by Microsoft Product Support Services. Location-specific software support options are available from:

http://support.microsoft.com/gp/selfoverview/

Microsoft Press provides corrections for books through the World Wide Web at *http://www.microsoft.com/mspress/support/*. To connect directly to the Microsoft Press Knowledge Base and enter a query regarding a question or issue that you may have, go to *http://www.microsoft.com/mspress/support/search.htm*.

Find Additional Content Online

As new or updated material becomes available that complements your book, it will be posted online on the Microsoft Press Online Windows Server and Client Web site. Based on the final build of Windows Server 2008, the type of material you might find includes updates to book content, articles, links to companion content, errata, sample chapters, and more. This Web site will be available soon at *www.microsoft.com/learning/books/online/serverclient*, and will be updated periodically.

How to Reach the Author

E-mail: williamstanek@aol.com

Web: *http://www.williamstanek.com/*

Conventions and Features Used in This Book

This book uses special text and design conventions to make it easier for you to find the information you need.

Text Conventions

Convention	Meaning
Abbreviated menu commands	For your convenience, this book uses abbreviated menu commands. For example, "Click Tools, Track Changes, Highlight Changes" means that you should click the Tools menu, point to Track Changes, and click the Highlight Changes command.
Boldface type	**Boldface** type is used to indicate text that you enter or type.
Initial Capital Letters	The first letters of the names of menus, dialog boxes, dialog box elements, and commands are capitalized. Example: the Save As dialog box.
Italicized type	*Italicized* type is used to indicate new terms.
Plus sign (+) in text	Keyboard shortcuts are indicated by a plus sign (+) separating two key names. For example, Ctrl+Alt+Delete means that you press the Ctrl, Alt, and Delete keys at the same time.

Design Conventions

INSIDE OUT **This statement illustrates an example of an "Inside Out" heading**

These are the book's signature tips. In these tips, you'll get the straight scoop on what's going on with the software—inside information about why a feature works the way it does. You'll also find helpful hints, timesaving tricks, and handy workarounds to deal with software problems or alternative procedures related to the task being discussed.

TROUBLESHOOTING

This statement illustrates an example of a "Troubleshooting" problem statement

Look for these sidebars to find solutions to common problems you might encounter. Troubleshooting sidebars appear next to related information in the chapters. You can also use the Troubleshooting Topics index at the back of the book to look up problems by topic.

CAUTION

Cautions identify potential problems that you should look out for when you're completing a task or problems that you must address before you can complete a task.

Note

Notes offer additional information related to the task being discussed.

Sidebars

The sidebars sprinkled throughout these chapters provide ancillary information on the topic being discussed. Go to the sidebars to learn more about the technology or a feature.

Cross-references point you to other locations in the book that offer additional information about the topic being discussed.

PART 1

Windows Server 2008 Overview and Planning

Neo from the *Matrix* trilogy might not be impressed, but I certainly am. Windows Server 2008 is a powerful, versatile, and fully featured server operating system, and if you've been using Windows server operating systems for a while, I think you'll be impressed as well. Why? For starters, Windows Server 2008 includes a significantly enhanced operating system kernel, the NT 6.1 kernel. As this kernel is also used by Windows Vista with Service Pack 1 or later, the two operating systems share a common code base and many common features, allowing you to readily apply what you know about Windows Vista to Windows Server 2008.

In Windows Server 2008, Microsoft delivers a server operating system that is some-thing more than the sum of its parts. Windows Server 2008 isn't just a server operat-ing system or a network operating system. It is a best-of-class operating system with the foundation technologies necessary to provide networking, application, and online services that can be used anywhere within your organization. From top to bottom, Windows Server 2008 is dramatically different from earlier releases of Windows Server operating systems. Windows Server 2008 is in fact so different from its predecessors that Microsoft considers earlier releases of Windows Server to be legacy operating sys-tems—or admittedly at the very least to have legacy components.

The way you approach Windows Server 2008 will depend on your background and your implementation plans. If you are moving to Windows Server 2008 from an earlier Windows server operating system or switching from UNIX, you'll find that Windows Server 2008 is a significant change that requires a whole new way of thinking about the networking, application services, and the interoperations between clients and servers. The learning curve will be steep, but you will find clear transition paths to Windows Server 2008. You will also find that Windows Server 2008 has an extensive command-line interface that makes it easier to manage servers, workstations, and, indeed, the entire network using both graphical and command-line administration tools.

If you are moving from Windows Server 2003 to Windows Server 2008, you'll find the changes are no less significant but easier to understand. You are already familiar with administration tools such as Active Directory Users And Computers and the core tech-nologies and administration techniques. Your learning curve might still be steep, but in only some areas, not all of them.

You can adopt Windows Server 2008 incrementally as well. For example, you might add Windows Server 2008 Print Services and Windows Server 2008 File Services to allow the organization to take advantage of the latest enhancements and capabilities without having to implement a full transition of existing servers. In most, but not all, cases, incremental adoption has little or no impact on the network, while allowing the organization to test new technologies and incrementally roll out features to users as part of a standard continuance or upgrade process.

Regardless of your deployment plans and whether you are reading this book to prepare for implementation of Windows Server 2008 or to manage existing implementations, my mission in this book is to help you take full advantage of all the new features in Windows Server 2008. You will find the detailed inside information you need to get up to speed quickly with Windows Server 2008 changes and technologies, to make the right setup and configuration choices the first time, and to work around the rough edges, annoyances, and faults of this complex operating system. If the default settings are less than optimal, I'll show you how to fix them so things work the way you want them to work. If something doesn't function like it should, I'll let you know and I'll also show you the fastest, surest way to work around the issue. You'll find plenty of hacks and secrets, too.

To pack as much information as possible into the 1,500-plus pages of this book, I am assuming that you have basic networking skills and some experience managing Windows-based networks but that you don't need me to explain the basic structure and architecture of an operating system. So, I'm not going to waste your time answering such questions as, "What's the point of networks?" "Why use Windows Server 2008?" or "What's the difference between the GUI and the command line?" Instead, I'm going to start with a discussion of what Windows Server 2008 has to offer so that you can learn about changes that will most affect you, and then I'm going to follow this discussion with a comprehensive, informative look at Windows Server 2008 planning and installation.

What's New in Windows Server 2008

Windows Server 2008 brings together the best of Windows Server 2003 Release 2 (R2) and Windows Vista, building on the network services and directory features of Windows Server 2003 R2 and expanding the support services and automated help systems of Windows Vista. This means Windows Server 2008 is more manageable, reliable, and scalable than previous versions of the Windows operating system. It also means the operating system has improved usability, especially when it comes to remote management and administration from the command line. Add in enhancements to performance, availability, and security; a rewrite of the operating system kernel; and many additional features, and you have many reasons to adopt Windows Server 2008—or at the very least deploy it in engineering or development labs so that you can be ready for full implementation when the bosses say, "We gotta have it now."

A primary purpose of Windows Server 2008 is to ensure that the operating system can be optimized for use in any networking scenario. An edition of the server operating system is available to meet your organization's needs whether you want to deploy a basic server for hosting applications, a network server for hosting domain services, a robust enterprise server for hosting essential applications, or a highly available datacenter server for hosting critical business solutions.

Microsoft produced multiple editions of the operating system with varying features to match the needs of any organization. In addition to offering 32-bit, 64-bit, and embedded versions of the operating system, Microsoft introduced Windows Web Server as a low-cost server operating system for providing basic Web application hosting services, Windows Server Standard as the domain services operating system, Windows Server Enterprise as the robust solution for essential applications and large organizations, and Windows Server Datacenter as the solution for critical business operations. Thus, the four main product editions are these:

- **Windows Server 2008 Standard** Available in 32-bit and 64-bit versions, this is the replacement for Windows Server 2003, Standard Edition.
- **Windows Server 2008 Enterprise** Available in 32-bit and 64-bit versions, this is the replacement for Windows Server 2003, Enterprise Edition.
- **Windows Server 2008 Datacenter** Available in 32-bit and 64-bit versions, this is the replacement for Windows Server 2003, Datacenter Edition.
- **Windows Web Server 2008** Available in 32-bit and 64-bit versions, this is the replacement for Windows Server 2003, Web Edition.

The various features of each edition are discussed in the sections that follow.

Note

For more information about the minimum and recommended system requirements for each server edition, see "Determining Which Windows Edition to Use" on page 61.

Windows Server 2008 Standard

Windows Server 2008 Standard is the workhorse version of the operating system. It comes with a bunch of new features that are exclusive to Windows Server 2008, as you'd expect, and it also includes a few unexpected surprises, including many enhancements for storage area networks (SANs), storage reporting, and improved access services. Servers running Windows Server Standard can host a single distributed file system (DFS) namespace, which can be either a stand-alone namespace or a domain-based namespace. They can also act as Active Directory Federation Services (ADFS) Web agents.

Windows Server Standard is optimized to provide domain services, such as name resolution with DNS, automatic IP address assignments with Dynamic Host Configuration Protocol (DHCP), Transmission Control Protocol/Internet Protocol (TCP/IP) networking, printing, and faxing, in a small to moderately sized network environment. This edition supports two-way and four-way symmetric multiprocessing (SMP) and up to 4 gigabytes (GB) of memory on 32-bit systems and 32 GB on 64-bit systems.

Windows Server 2008 Enterprise

Windows Server 2008 Enterprise is the robust medium to large enterprise solution specifically designed for multidepartmental use. Unlike Windows Server Standard, Windows Server Enterprise supports clustering with up to eight-node clusters and very large memory (VLM) configurations of up to 32 GB on 32-bit systems and 2 TB on 64-bit systems. It allows you to use the Federation Service and Federation Service Proxy with ADFS. It also allows you to use multiple DFS namespaces.

Windows Server 2008 Datacenter

If Windows Server 2008 Standard is plain vanilla ice cream served with a spoon, Windows Server 2008 Datacenter is more like an ice cream sundae made with five different flavors, nuts, and whipped cream and served with a cherry on top and spoons for everyone at your table. This edition is designed to host business-critical systems and solutions using a minimum of 1 processor and a maximum of 64 and includes all the features of Windows Server Enterprise. Plus, it supports clustering for up to eight nodes and it increases VLM support, allowing for configurations of up to 64 GB of memory on 32-bit systems and 2 TB on 64-bit systems.

INSIDE OUT   **Obtaining Windows Server Datacenter Edition**

> You cannot purchase a retail edition of Windows Server 2008, Datacenter Edition. The x86/32-bit and X64/64-bit versions of Windows Server 2008 Datacenter Edition are only available through the Volume Licensing program or directly from hardware vendors. The IA64 version of Windows Server 2008 Datacenter Edition must be obtained through hardware vendors.

Windows Web Server 2008

Windows Web Server 2008 is the fourth option. It supports up to 2 GB of RAM and two CPUs and is designed, as the name implies, to provide Web services, primarily for hosting Web sites and Web-based applications on the Internet and intranets. As with all the other editions of Windows Server 2008, it supports Internet Information Services (IIS) 7.0, ASP.NET, and the Windows .NET Framework. These technologies work together to make the sharing of application services in Web environments possible.

However, Windows Web Server doesn't include many of the other common features of Windows Server 2008. The biggest feature missing is Active Directory, which means that servers running Windows Web Server cannot be domain controllers. Other servers in the datacenter can provide this functionality, however; and so servers running Windows Web Server can be part of an Active Directory domain. In addition, although Network Load Balancing support is included in Windows Web Server, the only other features it has in common with the other editions of Windows Server 2008 are the following:

- Distributed file system (DFS) (single namespace only)
- Encrypting File System (EFS)
- Remote Desktop for Administration

Because of this, Windows Web Server cannot provide Internet connection sharing, network bridging, or faxing services, and although it includes the Remote Desktop, it doesn't include Terminal Services. This means you can access a server running Windows Web Server using Remote Desktop, but cannot run applications on it remotely using Terminal Services.

> **Note**
>
> In a licensing change, Windows Web Server 2008 is no longer available only to Microsoft customers with Enterprise and Select licensing agreements or to service providers. An important security note for Windows Web Server is that Windows Firewall is not included. Because of this, there is no built-in firewall protection. Microsoft assumes the datacenter will have its own firewall that restricts access to servers as appropriate.

64-Bit Computing

64-bit computing has changed substantially since it was first introduced for Windows operating systems. Not only do computers running 64-bit versions of Windows perform better and run faster than their 32-bit counterparts, they are also more scalable, as they can process more data per clock cycle, address more memory, and perform numeric calculations faster. Windows Server 2008 supports two different 64-bit architectures:

- The first architecture is based on 64-bit extensions to the *x*86 instruction set, which is implemented in AMD Opteron (AMD64) processors, Intel Xeon processors with 64-bit extension technology, and other processors. This architecture offers native 32-bit processing and 64-bit extension processing, allowing simultaneous 32-bit and 64-bit computing.

- The second architecture is based on the Explicitly Parallel Instruction Computing (EPIC) processor architecture, which is implemented in Intel Itanium (IA-64) processors and other processors. This architecture offers native 64-bit processing, allowing 64-bit applications to achieve optimal performance.

INSIDE OUT   Running 32-bit applications on 64-bit hardware

In most cases, 64-bit hardware is compatible with 32-bit applications; however, 32-bit applications will perform better on 32-bit hardware. Windows Server 2008 64-bit editions support both 64-bit and 32-bit applications using the Windows on Windows 64 (WOW64) *x*86 emulation layer. The WOW64 subsystem isolates 32-bit applications from 64-bit applications. This prevents file system and Registry problems. The operating system provides interoperability across the 32-bit/64-bit boundary for the Component Object Model (COM) and basic operations, such as cut, copy, and paste from the Clipboard. However, 32-bit processes cannot load 64-bit dynamic-link libraries (DLLs), and 64-bit processes cannot load 32-bit DLLs.

64-bit computing is designed for performing operations that are memory-intensive and that require extensive numeric calculations. With 64-bit processing, applications can load large data sets entirely into physical memory (that is, RAM), which reduces the need to page to disk and increases performance substantially. The EPIC instruction set enables Itanium-based processors to perform up to 20 operations simultaneously.

Itanium-based computers differ in many fundamental ways from *x*86- and *x*64-based computers. Itanium-based computers use the Extensible Firmware Interface (EFI) and the GUID partition table (GPT) disk type. *x*86- and *x*64-based computers use the BIOS and the master boot record (MBR) disk type. This means there are differences in the way you manage computers with these architectures, particularly when it comes to setup and disk configuration. For details on setting up Itanium-based, *x*86-based and *x*64-based computers, see "Getting a Quick Start" on page 69. Techniques for using MBR and GPT disks are covered in detail in Chapter 14, "Storage Management."

Note

In this text, I typically will refer to 32-bit systems designed for *x*86 architecture as 32-bit and 64-bit systems designed for *x*64 architecture as 64-bit systems. Support for Itanium 64-bit (IA-64) processors is no longer standard in Windows operating systems. Microsoft has developed a separate edition for computers with IA-64 processors. This edition is called Windows Server 2008 for Itanium-Based Systems. If a feature is specific to chip architecture, I will specify the chip architecture, such as *x*86 (IA-32) or Itanium (IA-64). Keep in mind that the Windows Server 2008 64-bit extended system versions run on *x*86 chip architectures.

Virtualized Computing

Windows Server 2008 Hyper-V is a virtual machine technology that allows multiple guest operating systems to run concurrently on one computer and provide separate applications and services to client computers as shown in Figure 1-1. As part of the Hyper-V feature, which can be installed on servers with x64-based processors that implement hardware-assisted virtualization and hardware data execution protection, the Windows hypervisor acts as the virtual machine engine, providing the necessary layer of software for installing guest operating systems. You can, for example, use this technology to concurrently run UNIX, Linux, and Windows Server 2008 on the same computer.

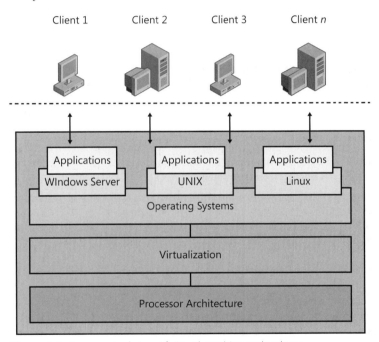

Figure 1-1 A conceptual view of virtual machine technology.

The number of virtual machines you can run on any individual computer depends on the computer's hardware configuration and workload. During setup, you specify the amount of memory available to a virtual machine. Although that memory allocation can be changed, the amount of memory actively allocated to a virtual machine cannot be otherwise used. Although Hyper-V is based on Virtual PC and Virtual Server technology, you cannot install this feature on a computer that has Virtual PC or Virtual Server installed. If you are familiar with Virtual PC or Virtual Server technology, you'll find that working with Hyper-V is similar.

Virtualization can offer performance improvements, reduce the number of servers, and reduce the total cost of ownership (TCO). AMD Virtualization (AMD-V) technology is included in second and later generation AMD Opteron processors as well as other next generation AMD processors. Third generation AMD Opteron processors feature Rapid Virtualization Indexing to accelerate the performance of virtualized applications. Intel Virtualization Technology (Intel VT) is included in Intel Xeon 3000, 5000, and 7000 sequence processors, Intel Itanium 2 processors, and next generation Intel processors with the Intel vPro label.

Windows Vista and Windows Server 2008

In Windows Vista, Microsoft brings the Windows family of operating systems for business and home users together and puts the operating systems on similar paths.

Windows Vista Editions

Like Windows Server 2008, Windows Vista has several main editions. These editions include:

- **Windows Vista Starter** The budget operating system designed for emerging markets
- **Windows Vista Home Basic** The entry-level operating system designed for home users with basic entertainment features
- **Windows Vista Home Premium** The enhanced operating system designed for home users with premium entertainment features
- **Windows Vista Business** The basic operating system designed for use in Windows domains
- **Windows Vista Enterprise** The enhanced operating system designed for use in Windows domains with extended management features
- **Windows Vista Ultimate** The enhanced operating system designed with all the available home user and business user features

Windows Vista and Active Directory

Windows Vista Business, Enterprise, and Ultimate are the only editions intended for use in Active Directory domains. These editions include extensions to Group Policy that require updating the Group Policy objects (GPOs) in a domain using servers running Windows 2000 or Windows Server 2003. In a domain upgraded to domain controllers running Windows Server 2008, however, you are not required to update the GPOs for these Windows Vista business editions.

> **Note**
>
> For more information about Group Policy and Windows Vista compatibility, see "Updating Group Policy Objects for Windows Vista" in Chapter 8, "Configuring User and Computer Policies" of *Microsoft Windows Vista Administrator's Pocket Consultant, 2nd Edition* (Microsoft Press, 2008).

Architecture Improvements

If you want to truly know how Windows Server 2008 works and what makes it tick, you need to dig under the hood. Digging under the hood means taking a look at:

- The NT kernel
- The boot environment
- The support architecture

All of these are discussed in the sections that follow.

Kernel Architecture

Windows Vista SP1 or later uses the NT 6.1 kernel, the same kernel that Windows Server 2008 uses. Sharing the same kernel means that Windows Vista SP1 or later and Windows Server 2008 share the following components as well as others:

- **Automatic Updates** Responsible for performing automatic updates to the operating system. This ensures that the operating system is up to date and has the most recent security updates. If you update a server from the standard Windows Update to Microsoft Update, you can get updates for additional products. By default, automatic updates are installed but not enabled on servers running Windows Server 2008. You can configure automatic updates using the Windows Update utility in Control Panel. Click Start, click Control Panel\Security, and then click Windows Update to start this utility.

- **BitLocker Drive Encryption** Provides an extra layer security for a server's hard disks. This protects the disks from attackers who have physical access to the server. BitLocker encryption can be used on servers with or without a Trusted Platform Module (TPM). When you add this feature to a server using the Add Features Wizard, you can manage it using the BitLocker Drive Encryption utility in Control Panel. Click Start, click Control Panel\Security, and then click BitLocker Drive Encryption. See Chapter 15, "TPM and BitLocker Drive Encryption," to learn how to work with and manage BitLocker Drive Encryption.

> **Note**
>
> Only computers with TPM have BitLocker Drive Encryption enabled by default. If you want to use BitLocker with non-TPM computers, you must enable this using the Control Panel Setup: Enable The Advanced Startup Options policy setting under Computer Configuration\Administrative Templates\Windows Components\BitLocker Drive Encryption.

- **Remote Assistance** Provides an assistance feature that allows an administrator to send a remote assistance invitation to a more senior administrator. The senior administrator can then accept the invitation to view the user's desktop and temporarily take control of the computer to resolve a problem. When you add this feature to a server using the Add Features Wizard, you can manage it using options on the Remote tab of the System Properties dialog box. In Control Panel\System And Maintenance, click System and then click Remote Settings under Tasks to view the related options.

- **Remote Desktop** Provides a remote connectivity feature that allows you to remotely connect to and manage a server from another computer. By default, Remote Desktop is installed but not enabled on servers running Windows Server 2008. You can manage the Remote Desktop configuration using options on the Remote tab of the System Properties dialog box. In Control Panel\System And Maintenance, click System and then click Remote Settings under Tasks to view the related options. You can establish remote connections using the Remote Desktop Connection utility. Click Start, click All Programs, click Accessories, and then click Remote Desktop Connection. See Chapter 19, "Using Remote Desktop for Administration" to learn how to configure and work with Remote Desktop.

- **Task Scheduler** Allows you to schedule execution of one-time and recurring tasks, such as tasks used for performing routine maintenance. Like Windows Vista, Windows Server 2008 makes extensive use of the scheduled task facilities. You can view and work with scheduled tasks in Server Manager. Expand the Configuration, Task Scheduler, and Task Scheduler Library nodes to view the currently configured scheduled tasks.

- **Windows Defender** Helps protect a server from spyware and other potentially unwanted software. You can run Windows Defender manually as necessary or configure it to run automatically according to a predefined schedule. By default, Windows Defender is not enabled on server installations. When Windows Defender is installed as part of the Desktop Experience feature, you can start it from the All Programs menu.

- **Desktop Experience** Installs additional Windows Vista desktop functionality on the server. You can use this feature when you use Windows Server 2008 as your desktop operating system. When you add this feature using the Add Features Wizard, the server's desktop functionality is enhanced and these programs are installed as well: Windows Calendar, Windows Defender, Windows Mail, Windows Media Player, Windows Photo Gallery, and Windows SideShow.

- **Windows Firewall** Helps protect a computer from attack by unauthorized users. Windows Server 2008 included a basic firewall called Windows Firewall and an advanced firewall called Windows Firewall With Advanced Security. By default, the firewalls are not enabled on server installations. To access the basic firewall, click Windows Firewall in Control Panel\Network And Internet. To access the advanced firewall, select Windows Firewall With Advanced Security on the Administrative Tools menu.

- **Windows Time** Synchronizes the system time with world time to ensure that the system time is accurate. You can configure computers to synchronize with a specific time server. The way Windows Time works depends on whether a computer is a member of a domain or a workgroup. In a domain, domain controllers are used for time synchronization and you can manage this feature through Group Policy. In a workgroup, you use Internet time servers for time synchronization and you can manage this feature through the Date And Time utility.

- **Wireless Networking** Installs the Wireless Networking feature to enable wireless connections. Wireless networking with Windows Server 2008 works the same as it does with Windows Vista. If a server has a wireless adapter, you can enable this feature using the Add Features Wizard.

In most instances, you can configure and manage these core components in exactly the same way on both Windows Vista and Windows Server 2008.

Boot Environment

Windows Server 2008 is the first truly hardware independent version of the Windows Server operating systems. Unlike earlier releases, Windows Server 2008 doesn't boot from an initialization file. Instead, the operating system uses the Windows Boot Manager to initialize and start the operating system.

The boot environment dramatically changes the way the operating system starts. The boot environment was created by Microsoft to resolve several prickly problems related to boot integrity, operating system integrity, and firmware abstraction. The boot environment is loaded prior to the operating system, making it a pre-operating system environment. As such, the boot environment can be used to validate the integrity of the startup process and the operating system itself before actually starting the operating system.

The boot environment is an extensible abstraction layer that allows the operating system to work with multiple types of firmware interfaces without requiring the operating system to be specifically written to work with these firmware interfaces. Rather than updating the operating system each time a new firmware interface is developed, the firmware interface developers can use the standard programming interfaces of the boot environment to allow the operating system to communicate as necessary through the firmware interfaces.

The two prevalent firmware interfaces currently are:

- Basic input/output system (BIOS)
- Extensible Firmware Interface (EFI)

Firmware interface abstraction makes it possible for Windows Server 2008 to work with BIOS-based and EFI-based computers in exactly the same way, and this is one of the primary reasons Windows Server 2008 achieves hardware independence. You'll learn more about the boot environment in Chapter 13, "Boot Configuration."

The next secret ingredient for Windows Server 2008's hardware independence is Windows Imaging Format (WIM). Microsoft distributes Windows Server 2008 on media using WIM disk images. WIM uses compression and single-instance storage to dramatically reduce the size of image files. Using compression reduces the size of the image in much the same way as Zip compression reduces the size of files. Using single-instance storage reduces the size of the image because only one physical copy of a file is stored for each instance of that file in the disk image.

Because WIM is hardware independent, Microsoft can use a single binary for each supported architecture:

- One binary for 32-bit architectures
- One binary for 64-bit architectures
- One binary for Itanium architectures

The final secret ingredient for Windows Server 2008's hardware independence is modularization. Windows Server 2008 uses modular component design so that each component of the operating system is defined as a separate independent unit or module. As modules can contain other modules, various major features of the operating system can be grouped together and described independently of other major features. Because modules are independent from each other, modules can be swapped in or out to customize the operating system environment. You'll learn more about adding components to Windows Server 2008 in Chapter 7, "Configuring Roles, Role Services, and Features."

Support Architecture

Windows Server 2008 includes extensive support architecture. At the heart of this architecture is built-in diagnostics—the next generation automated help system. Microsoft designed built-in diagnostics to be self-correcting and self-diagnosing, and failing that, to provide troubleshooting assistance while you are diagnosing problems.

Built-in diagnostics are primarily implemented through:

- Network Diagnostics Framework (NDF)
- Windows Diagnostics Infrastructure (WDI)

NDF is complementary to WDI. NDF diagnoses connectivity and networking issues. WDI diagnoses device, memory, and performance issues. Windows Server 2008 includes several related diagnostics tools as well.

Network Diagnostics Framework

As you'll learn more about in Chapter 20, "Networking with TCP/IP," Windows Server 2008 implements network awareness and network discovery features. Network awareness tracks changes in network configuration and connectivity. Network discovery controls a computer's ability to detect other computers and devices on a network.

Network awareness is a key component in the Network Diagnostics Framework. It allows Windows Server 2008 to detect the current network configuration and connectivity status. This is important because many networking and security settings depend on the type of network to which a computer running Windows Server 2008 is connected. Windows Server 2008 has separate configurations for domain networks, private networks, and public networks, and is able to detect when you change a network connection as well as whether or not the computer has a connection to the Internet.

If you disconnect a computer from one network switch or hub and plug it into a new network switch or hub, you may inadvertently cause the computer to think it is on a different network, and depending on the Group Policy configuration, this could cause the computer to enter a lockdown state where additional network security settings are applied. As shown in Figure 1-2, you can view the network connection status in Network And Sharing Center. In Control Panel\Network And Internet, click Network And Sharing Center to access this management console.

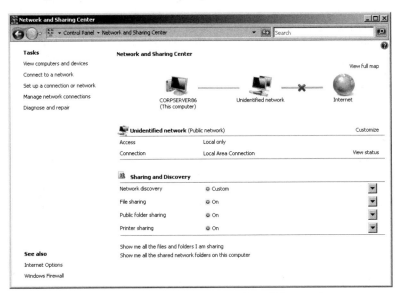

Figure 1-2 Examine the network state in Network And Sharing Center.

Chapter 1

Windows Server 2008 tracks the identification status of all networks to which the server has been connected. When Windows Server 2008 is in the process of identifying a network, Network And Sharing Center shows the Identifying Networks state. This is a temporary state for a network that is being identified. After Windows Server 2008 identifies a network, the network becomes an Identified Network and is listed by its network or domain name in Network And Sharing Center.

If Windows Server 2008 is unable to identify the network, the network is listed with the Unidentified Network status in Network And Sharing Center. In Group Policy under Computer Configuration\Windows Settings\Security Settings\Network List Manager Policies, you can set default location types and user permissions for each network state as well as for all networks (see Figure 1-3).

When you are working with Network And Sharing Center, you can attempt to diagnose a warning status using Windows Network Diagnostics—another key component of the Network Diagnostics Framework. To start diagnostics, click the warning icon or alternatively, click Diagnose And Repair under Tasks. Windows Network Diagnostics will then attempt to identify the network problem and provide a possible solution as shown in Figure 1-4.

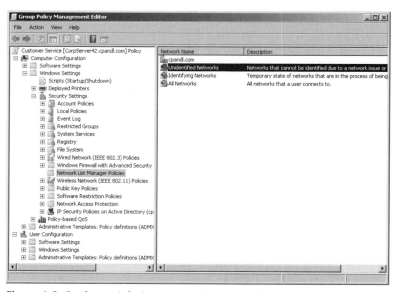

Figure 1-3 Configure default awareness settings in Group Policy.

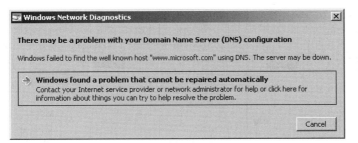

Figure 1-4 Review the proposed solution.

Windows Vista with SP1 or later and Windows Server 2008 have several networking enhancements that affect networking and NDF in general, including:

- **Support for Server Message Block (SMB) version 2** SMB is the file sharing protocol used by Windows operating systems. Windows Vista and Windows Server 2008 support SMB version 2, which enhances the performance of the original SMB protocol. Windows Vista with SP1 or later and Windows Server 2008 support the SMB Helper Class as part of the Network Diagnostics Framework (NDF). This helper class provides diagnostics information users will find useful when they are having problems connecting to file shares. Specifically, this helper class can help diagnose failures including when a user is trying to access a server that does not exist, when a user is trying to access a nonexisting share on existing server, and when a user misspells a share name and there is a similarly named share available.

> **Note**
>
> When working with Windows Vista SP1 or later and Windows Server 2008, file access and remote copy performance is increased significantly. SMB v2 offers significant file transfer improvements, as do improved file transfer algorithms. Additionally, network share thumbnails are cached for all users, allowing faster display of thumbnails when working with network shares.

- **Implementation of extensions to network awareness** Improvements in network selection algorithms allow a computer connected to one or more networks via two or more interfaces (regardless of whether they are wired or wireless) to select the route with the best performance for a particular data transfer. As part of the best route selection, Windows chooses the best interface (either wired or wireless) for the transfer and this improves the selection of wireless over wired networks when both interfaces are present.

- **Changes to network management policies** Network management policies are available for both wired (IEEE 802.3) networks and wireless (IEEE 802.11) networks under Computer Configuration\Windows Settings\Security Settings in Group Policy. If you right-click the Wired Network (IEEE 802.3) node, you can create a policy for Windows Vista or later computers that enables the use of IEEE 802.3 authentication on wired networks. If you right-click the Wireless Network (IEEE 802.11) node, you can create separate policies for Windows XP computers and Windows Vista or later computers that enable WLAN autoconfiguration, define the specific networks that can be used, and set network permissions.

- **Changes to wired and wireless single sign on (SSO)** SSO changes allow users to change their passwords when connecting to a wired or wireless network (as opposed to using the Winlogon change password feature), to correct a wrong password entered during sign on, and to reset an expired password—all as part of the network logon process.

Windows Vista with SP1 or later and Windows Server 2008 also support many network security enhancements, including:

- **Secure Socket Tunneling Protocol (SSTP) and Secure Remote Access (SRA)** SSTP allows data transmission at the data-link layer over a Hypertext Transfer Protocol over Secure Sockets Layer (HTTPS) connection. SRA enables secure access to remote networks over HTTPS. Together these technologies enable users to securely access a private network using an Internet connection. SSTP and SRA represent improvements over the Point-to-Point Tunneling Protocol (PPTP) and Layer Two Tunneling Protocol/Internet Protocol Security (L2TP/IPSec) protocols because they use the standard TCP/IP ports for secure Web traffic and this allows them to traverse most firewalls as well as Network Address Translation (NAT) and Web proxies. Because SSTP supports both IPv4 and IPv6, users can establish secure tunnels using either IP technology. Essentially, you get VPN technology that works everywhere, which should mean far fewer support calls.

- **CryptoAPI version 2 (CAPI2) and Online Certificate Status Protocol (OCSP) extensions** CAPI2 extends support for PKI and X.509 certificates and implements additional functionality for certificate path validation, certificate store designation, and signature verification. One of the steps during certificate path validation is revocation checking. This step involves verifying the certificate status to ensure that it has not been revoked by its issuer and OCSP is used to check the revocation status of certificates. CAPI2 also supports independent OCSP signer chains and additional OCSP download locations on a per-issuer basis. Independent OCSP signer chains modify the original OCSP implementation so that it can work with OCSP responses that are signed by trusted OCSP signers that are separate from the issuer of the certificate being validated. Additional OCSP download locations make it possible to specify OCSP download locations for issuing CA certificates as URLs that are added as a property to the CA certificate.

Windows Diagnostics Infrastructure

Windows Diagnostics Infrastructure (WDI) is an extensive diagnostics and problem resolution architecture that offers improved diagnostics guidance, additional error reporting details, expanded event logging, and extensive recovery policies. Although earlier versions of Windows include some help and diagnostics features, those features are, for the most part, not self-correcting or self-diagnosing. Windows Server 2008, on the other hand, can detect many types of hardware, memory, and performance issues and either resolve them automatically or help users through the process of resolving them.

WDI is divided into 10 broad diagnostics areas as shown in Table 1-1.

Many other enhancements in conjunction with WDI help to improve the overall performance of Windows Server 2008. These enhancements include:

- **Changes to device drivers and I/O management** Windows Server 2008 includes more reliable and better performing device drivers, which help prevent many common causes of hangs and crashes. Improved input/output (I/O) cancellation for device drivers ensures that the operating system can recover gracefully from blocking calls and that there are fewer blocking disk I/O operations.

- **Modifications to the application update process** During an update, Windows Server 2008 can use the update process to mark in-use files for update and then automatically replace the files the next time an application is started. This reduces the number of restarts required.

- **Optimized memory and process usage** Windows Server 2008 uses memory more efficiently, provides ordered execution for groups of threads, and provides new process scheduling mechanisms. By optimizing memory and process usage, Windows Server 2008 ensures that background processes have less performance impact on system performance.

- **Enhanced recovery from service failures** Windows Server 2008 uses service recovery policies more extensively than its predecessors do. When recovering a failed service, Windows Server 2008 automatically handles both service and nonservice dependencies as well. Any necessary dependent services and system components are started prior to starting the failed service.

Table 1-1 **Key Diagnostics Areas in the Windows Diagnostics Infrastructure**

Diagnostic Area	Description	Requirements
Application compatibility	Introduces the Program Compatibility Assistant (PCA) for diagnosing drivers blocked due to compatibility issues. PCA can detect failures caused by applications trying to load legacy Windows DLLs or trying to create COM objects that have been removed by Microsoft. PCA can detect several types of application installation failures. These install failures can be related to applications that do not have privileges to run as administrator but must be installed with elevated privileges as well as applications that fail to launch child processes that require elevation. In this case, PCA provides you with the option to restart the installer or update process as an administrator.	Diagnostic Policy Service, Program Compatibility Assistant Service
Corrupted file recovery	Introduces automatic detection, troubleshooting, and recovery of corrupted files. If Windows detects that an important operating system file is corrupted, Windows will attempt notification and recovery, which requires a restart in most cases for full resolution.	Diagnostic Policy Service
Disk reporting	Introduces customized alerts when a disk reports a Self-Monitoring And Reporting Technology (SMART) fault. SMART faults can indicate that a disk needs to be serviced or replaced. Alerts are logged in the event log by default and can also be displayed in a warning prompt.	Disks with SMART fault reporting, Diagnostic Policy Service, Desktop Experience feature. Server cannot be configured with Terminal Services role.
External support	Introduces Microsoft Support Diagnostic Tool (MSDT) for collecting and sending diagnostic data to a support professional to resolve a problem. MSDT.exe is stored in the %SystemRoot%\System32 folder and through policy settings can be configured for local and remote troubleshooting or remote troubleshooting only.	Diagnostic Policy Service
Boot performance	Introduces automatic detection and troubleshooting of issues that affect boot performance. Root causes of boot performance issues are logged to the event logs. Can also assist you in resolving related issues.	Diagnostic Policy Service

Diagnostic Area	Description	Requirements
Memory leak	Introduces automatic detection and troubleshooting of memory leak issues. A memory leak occurs if an application or system component doesn't completely free areas of physical memory after it is done with them.	Diagnostic Policy Service
Resource exhaustion	Introduces automatic detection and troubleshooting to resolve issues related to running out of virtual memory. Can also alert you if the computer is running low on virtual memory and identify the processes consuming the largest amount of memory, allowing you to close any or all of these high resource-consuming applications directly from the Close Programs To Prevent Information Loss dialog box provided. An alert is also logged in the event log.	Diagnostic Policy Service
Shutdown performance	Introduces automatic detection and troubleshooting of issues that affect shutdown performance. Root causes of shutdown performance issues are logged to the event logs. Can also assist you in resolving related issues.	Diagnostic Policy Service
Standby/resume performance	Introduces automatic detection and troubleshooting of issues that affect standby/resume performance on desktop computers. Root causes of standby/resume performance issues are logged to the event logs. Can also assist you in resolving related issues.	Diagnostic Policy Service
System responsiveness	Introduces automatic detection and troubleshooting of issues that affect the overall responsive of the operating system. Root causes of responsiveness issues are logged to the event logs. Can also assist you in resolving related issues.	Diagnostic Policy Service

Other Diagnostics Enhancements

Windows Server 2008 includes several new or enhanced diagnostics features, including:

- Restart Manager
- Problem Reports And Solutions
- Startup Repair Tool

- Performance Diagnostics console

- Windows Memory Diagnostics

In earlier versions of Windows, an application crash or hang is marked as not responding, and it is up to the user to exit and then restart the application. Windows Server 2008 attempts to automatically resolve the issues related to unresponsive applications by using Restart Manager. Restart Manager can shut down and restart unresponsive applications automatically. In many cases, this means that you may not have to intervene to try to resolve issues with frozen applications.

Failed installation and nonresponsive conditions of applications and drivers are also tracked through Problem Reports And Solutions. Should this occur, the built-in diagnostics displays a "Check For Solutions" balloon message. If you click the balloon, Windows Server 2008 opens the Problem Reports And Solutions console, which enables you to check on the Internet for solutions to selected problems. You can view a list of current problems at any time by following these steps:

1. In Control Panel, click System And Maintenance and then click Problem Reports And Solutions.

2. In the Problem Reports And Solutions console, click See Problems To Check in the left pane. The Problem Reports And Solutions console displays a list of known problems as shown in Figure 1-5.

3. Select the check box for a problem and then click Check For Solutions to search the Microsoft Web site for possible solutions.

To resolve startup problems, Windows Server 2008 uses the Startup Repair Tool (StR), which is installed automatically and started when a system fails to boot. After it is started, StR attempts to determine the cause of the startup failure by analyzing startup logs and error reports. Then StR attempts to fix the problem automatically. If StR is unable to resolve the problem, it restores the system to the last known working state and then provides diagnostic information and support options for further troubleshooting.

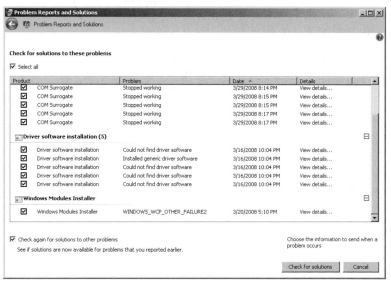

Figure 1-5 Review known problems and check for solutions.

Startup Repair performs many tests during diagnostics and troubleshooting. These tests can take anywhere from 5 to 30 minutes or more depending on the configured hardware, and include these specific tests:

- **Check for updates** Determines whether newly applied updates are affecting startup.

- **System disk test** Determines whether there is a problem with the system disk that is preventing startup. If so, StR can attempt to repair any missing or corrupt files.

- **Disk failure diagnosis** Determines whether any of the configured disks have failed.

- **Disk metadata test** Determines whether any of the available disks have a problem with their metadata that is preventing startup. As discussed in Chapter 16, "Managing Windows Server 2008 File Systems," the metadata associated with a disk depends on how a disk is partitioned and the file system format of disk partitions.

- **Target OS test** Determines whether the operating system you are attempting to start has a specific issue that is preventing startup.

- **Volume content check** Examines the content of disk volumes to ensure that volumes are accessible.

- **Boot manager diagnosis** Determines whether there is a problem with the boot manager or boot manager entries that are preventing startup.

- **System boot log diagnosis** Examines system boot log entries from previous startups to see if there are specific errors that might be related to the startup issue.

- **Event log diagnosis** Examines event log entries to see if there are specific errors that might be related to the startup issue.
- **Internal state check** Checks the current internal state of the pre-boot environment.
- **Boot status test** Checks the current boot status in the pre-boot environment.
- **Setup state check** Determines whether the computer is in a Setup state.
- **Registry hives test** Checks the computer's Registry hives.
- **Windows boot log diagnostics** Examines the Windows boot log entries to see if there are specific errors that might be related to the startup issue.
- **Bug check analysis** Performs a basic bug check analysis of the operating system.
- **File system test (chkdsk)** Performs a basic file system test using ChkDsk.
- **Software install log diagnostics** Examines software install log entries to see if there are specific errors that might be related to the startup issue.
- **Fallback diagnostics** Determines whether any flags have been set that indicate the computer should fall back to a previous state to correct the startup issue. If so, StR will attempt to restore the previous state.

Error detection for devices and failure detection for disk drives also is automated. If a device is having problems, hardware diagnostics can detect error conditions and either repair the problem automatically or guide the user through a recovery process. With disk drives, hardware diagnostics can use fault reports provided by disk drives to detect potential failure and alert you before this happens. Hardware diagnostics can also help guide you through the backup process after alerting you that a disk might be failing.

Windows Server 2008 can automatically detect performance issues, which include slow application startup, slow boot, slow standby/resume, and slow shutdown. If a computer is experiencing degraded performance, Performance Diagnostics can detect the problem and provide possible solutions for resolving the problem. For advanced performance issues, you can track related performance and reliability data in the Reliability And Performance Diagnostics console. As shown in Figure 1-6, this includes Performance Monitor and Reliability Monitor. You'll learn all about optimizing performance and improving reliability in Chapter 11, "Performance Monitoring and Tuning," and Chapter 12, "Comprehensive Performance Analysis and Logging."

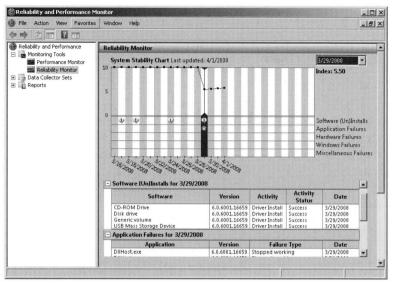

Figure 1-6 Check the computer's reliability details.

Windows Server 2008 can also detect issues related to memory leaks and failing memory. If you suspect that a computer has a memory problem that is not being automatically detected, you can run Windows Memory Diagnostics manually by completing the following steps:

1. Click Start, type **mdsched.exe** in the Search box, and then press Enter.

2. Choose whether to restart the computer and run the tool immediately or schedule the tool to run at the next restart.

3. Windows Memory Diagnostics runs automatically after the computer restarts and performs a standard memory test automatically. If you want to perform fewer or more tests, press F1, use the Up and Down Arrow keys to set the Test Mix as Basic, Standard, or Extended, and then press F10 to apply the desired settings and resume testing.

4. When testing is completed, the computer restarts automatically. You'll see the test results when you log on.

If a computer crashes because of failing memory, and Memory Diagnostics detects this, you are prompted to schedule a memory test the next time the computer is restarted.

Deploying Windows Server 2008 is a substantial undertaking, even on a small network. Just the task of planning a Windows Server 2008 deployment can be a daunting process, especially in a large enterprise. The larger the business, however, the more important it is that the planning process be thorough and fully account for the proposed project's goals, as well as lay out exactly how those goals will be accomplished.

Accommodating the goals of all the business units in a company can be difficult, and it is best accomplished with a well-planned series of steps that includes checkpoints and plenty of opportunity for management participation. The organization as a whole will benefit from your thorough preparation and so will the information technology (IT) department. Careful planning can also help you avoid common obstacles by helping you identify potential pitfalls and then determine how best to avoid them, or at least be ready for any unavoidable complications.

Overview of Planning

A clear road map can help with any complex project, and deploying Windows Server 2008 in the enterprise is certainly a complex project. A number of firms have developed models to describe IT processes such as planning and systems management—often used by their consulting group—each of which offers its own structured method of approaching a complex project. This detailed description of the people who should be involved, the tasks they will perform, and the order in which they should perform the tasks can be useful when approaching a large-scale project.

These models all share a largely common path for walking through the planning process—they divide it into different phases and describe it using different phrases. The *Microsoft Solutions Framework Process Model*, described in the next section, provides an illustration of one approach.

The Microsoft Solutions Framework Process Model

Microsoft has defined its own formalized processes for implementing IT solutions and network management. Two models are used: the *Microsoft Solutions Framework (MSF)*, which defines deployment project methods, and the *Microsoft Operations Framework (MOF)*, which has operations administration as its focus. Like any other process models, the MSF and MOF models have gone through several evolutions. At the time of this writing Microsoft has gone to a team system approach.

The MSF version 4 process model defines the following phases:

- **Envisioning** During the first phase, project goals are defined and clarified. Using this information, you create a vision/scope document stating the overall vision, goals, and scope of the project. You also create an initial risk assessment document. The final step in this phase is approval of these documents.

- **Planning** After the goals and scope have been agreed upon, you have to translate that information into functional specifications that document the specific features, services, and configuration options that are required to achieve the goals. A master project plan, which describes how the implementation will proceed, and a master project schedule, which sets the overall schedule, are approved at the end of this phase.

- **Building** During this phase, the Windows Server 2008 infrastructure, any required custom code (applications or scripting), and documentation are developed. Management marketing materials and end-user communications are developed with a goal of selling the idea of the project to the end user, whether the end user is an employee of the organization or a consumer. Test specifications, cases, metrics, scripts, and data are also developed as are the initial operations guides, support procedures, knowledge base, and troubleshooting documentation.

- **Stabilizing** When the new environment has been created in the lab, it is thoroughly tested prior to deployment. This is your chance to ensure that the platform is stable and ready to go before you begin the pilot deployment. You'll also work toward finalization of installation documentation, end-user communications, operations documents, and release notes.

- **Deploying** Finally, you deploy Windows Server 2008 into the production environment. IT staff first perform a small pilot project; after that is successfully completed, Windows Server 2008 is rolled out across the rest of the environment. During this phase, you will revise processes and procedures as necessary, perform end-user and administrator training, and document your configurations. You'll also create a repository for all final documentation.

- **Governing** From project inception to completion and beyond, one or more individuals on the IT management team will be responsible for developing the overall project charter and team orientation guidance. These individuals will track the overall project status, the status of project deliverables, and user satisfaction after the project is deployed. They'll also be responsible for closing out the project, developing a road map of next steps, and documenting the lessons learned.

These stages are seen as occurring more or less linearly, but not exclusively so, in that stages are commonly revisited at multiple points along the way.

> **Note**
>
> For more information about the MSF, visit *http://www.microsoft.com/msf/*.

> **Note**
>
> Keep in mind that every company has its own internal politics, which can introduce quirks into many projects and processes, even those in the IT department.

Your Plan: The Big Picture

The Microsoft model is an interesting one, but it is useful to get a bit more specific. This is especially true when working with people from other departments, who might not be familiar with IT processes. For our purposes, the deployment process can be broken down into a roughly sequential set of tasks:

- **Identify the team** For all but the smallest rollouts of a new operating system, a team of people will be involved in both the planning and deployment processes. The actual size and composition of this team will be different in each situation. Collecting the right mixture of skills and expertise will help ensure the success of your project.

- **Assess your goals** Any business undertaking the move to Windows Server 2008 has many reasons for doing so, only some of which are obvious to the IT department. It is important to carefully identify the goals of the *entire* company before determining the scope of the project to ensure that all critical goals are met.

- **Analyze the existing environment** Examine the current network environment, even if you think that you know *exactly* how everything works—you will often find you are only partially correct. Gather hardware and software inventories, network maps, and lists of which servers are providing which services. Also, identify critical business processes, and examine the administrative and security approaches that are currently in place. Windows Server 2008 offers a number of security and management improvements, and it is useful to know which ones are particularly important in your environment.

- **Define the project scope** Project scope is often one of the more difficult areas to pin down, and one that deserves particular attention in the planning process. Defining scope requires prioritizing the goals of the various groups within the organization and then realistically assessing what can be accomplished within an acceptable budget and timeframe. It's not often that the wish list of features and capabilities from the entire company can be fulfilled in the initial, or even later, deployment.

- **Design the new network environment**   After you have pinned down the project scope, you must develop a detailed design for the new operating system deployment and the affected portions of the network. During this time, you should create documentation describing the end state of the network, as well as the process of getting there. This design document serves as a road map for the people building the testing environment and, with refinements during the testing process, for the IT department later on.

- **Test the design**   Thorough testing in the lab is an often overlooked, but critically important, phase of deploying a new network operating system. By building a test lab and putting a prototype environment through its paces, you can identify and solve many problems in a controlled environment rather than in the field.

- **Install Windows Server 2008**   After you have validated your design in the lab and management has approved the deployment, you can begin to install Windows Server 2008 in your production environment. The installation process has two phases:

    ○ *Pilot phase*–During the pilot phase, you will deploy and test a small group of servers running Windows Server 2008 (and perhaps clients running Microsoft Windows Vista) in a production environment. You should pick a pilot group that is comfortable working with new technology, and for whom minor interruptions will not pose significant problems. In other words, this is not a good thing to do to the president of the company or the finance department just before taxes are due.

    ○ *Rollout*–After you have determined that the pilot phase was a success, you can begin the rollout to the rest of the company. Make sure you schedule adequate downtime, and allow for ongoing minor interruptions and increased support demands as users encounter changed functionality.

As mentioned, these steps are generally sequential, but not exclusively so. You are likely to find that as you work through one phase of planning, you must return to activities that are technically part of an earlier phase. This is actually a good thing, because it means you are refining your plan dynamically as you discover new factors and contingencies.

INSIDE OUT   **Getting off to a quick start**

People need not be assigned to all these tasks at the beginning of the planning process. If you have people who can take on the needs analysis and research on the current and new network environment (these are roughly the program management, product management, and development assignments from the MSF model), you can get the project under way while recruiting the rest of the project team.

Identifying Your Organizational Teams

A project like this requires a lot of time and effort as well as a broad range of knowledge, expertise, and experience. Unless you are managing a very small network, this project is likely to require more than one person to plan and implement. Team members are assigned to various roles, each of which is concerned with a different aspect of the project.

Each of these roles may be filled by one or more persons, devoting all or part of their workday—and beyond in some cases—to the project. No direct correlation exists between a team role and a single individual who performs it. In a large organization, a team of individuals might fulfill each of these roles, while in a small organization one person can fill more than one role.

Microsoft Solutions Framework Team Model

As with IT processes, a number of vendors and consultants have put together team models, which you can leverage in designing your own team. One such model is the *Microsoft Solutions Framework Team Model*, which uses seven teams to plan and deploy an IT project.

- **Architecture team** In increasingly complex IT environments, there needs to be someone responsible for overall project architecture and providing guidance for integrating the project into existing architecture. This role is filled by the architecture team. Specific deliverables include the architecture design and guidance for the integration solution.

- **Product management team** Program management's primary responsibility is ensuring that project goals are met within the constraints set forth at the beginning of the project. Program management handles the functional design, budget, schedule, and reporting. Specific deliverables include vision/scope document, functional specifications, master project plan, master project schedule, and status reports.

- **Program management team** This team is responsible for identifying the business and user needs of the project and ensuring that the final plan meets those needs. Specific deliverables include the project charter and team orientation guidance as well as documents for project structure documents and initial risk assessment.

- **User experience team** This team manages the transition of users to the new environment. This includes developing and delivering user training, as well as analysis of user feedback during testing and the pilot deployment. Specific deliverables include user reference manuals, usability test scenarios, and user interface graphic elements.

- **Development team** The development team is responsible for defining the physical design and feature set of the project and estimating the budget and time needed for project completion. Specific deliverables include any necessary source code/binaries as well as necessary integrated solution components.

- **Testing team** The testing team is critical in ensuring that the final deployment is successful. It designs and builds the test environment, develops a testing plan, and then performs the tests and resolves any issues it discovers before the pilot deployment occurs. Specific deliverables include test specifications, test cases with expected results, test metrics, test scripts, test data, and test reports.

- **Release management team** The release management team designs the test deployment and then performs that deployment as a means of verifying the reliability of the deployment before widespread adoption. Specific deliverables include deployment processes and procedures, installation scripts and configuration settings for deployment, operations guides, help desk and support procedures, knowledge base, help and training materials, operations documentation, and troubleshooting documentation.

Working together, these teams cover the various aspects of a significant project, such as rolling out Windows Server 2008.

Your Project Team

The Microsoft model is just that: a model. It serves as an example, yet you will not necessarily implement it, or any other model, exactly as designed by someone else. Although all IT projects share some things in common, and therefore need someone to handle those areas of the project, that's where the commonality stops.

Each company is in a different business and has IT needs related to its specific business activities. This might mean additional team members are needed to manage those aspects of the project. For example, if external clients and/or the public also access some of your IT systems as users, you have a set of user acceptance and testing requirements different than many other businesses.

The project team needs business managers who understand, and who can represent, the needs of the various business units. This requires knowledge of both the business operations and a clear picture of the daily tasks performed by line staff.

Representatives of the IT department bring their technical expertise to the table, not only to detail the inner workings of the network, but also to help business managers realistically assess how technology can help their departments and sort out the impractical goals from the realistic ones.

Make sure that all critical aspects of business operations are covered—include representatives from all departments that have critical IT needs, and the team must take the needs of the entire company into account. This means that people on the project team must collect information from line-of-business managers and the people actually doing the work. (Surprisingly enough, the latter escapes many a project team.)

After you have a team together, management must ensure that team members have adequate time and resources to fulfill the tasks required of them for the project. This can mean shifting all or part of their usual workload to others for the project duration, or providing resources such as Internet access, project-related software, and so on. Any project is easier, and more likely to be successful, with this critical real-time support from management.

INSIDE OUT   Hiring talent

Sometimes you don't have people available in-house with all the needed skills and must look to consultants or contracted workers. Examine which tasks should be outsourced and exactly what you must receive from the relationship. Pay particular attention to highly specialized or complex areas—the Active Directory Domain Services architecture, for example—and those with a high rate of change.

One-time tasks, such as creating user training programs and documentation, are also good candidates for outsourcing. For areas in which there will be an ongoing need for the lacking expertise, such as security, it might be a better idea to send a staff member to get additional training instead.

Assessing Project Goals

Carefully identifying the goals behind moving to Windows Server 2008 is an important part of the planning process. Without a clear list of objectives, you are unlikely to achieve them. Even with a clear set of goals in mind, it is unlikely you will accomplish them all. Most large business projects involve some compromise, and the process of deploying Windows Server 2008 is unlikely to be an exception.

Although deploying a new operating system is ultimately an IT task, most of the reasons behind the deployment won't be coming from the IT department. Computers are, after all, tools used by business to increase productivity, enhance communications, facilitate business tasks, and so on; the IT department is concerned with making sure that the computer environment needed by the business is implemented.

INSIDE OUT   Creating documentation almost painlessly

During the planning process, and as you begin to use the new network environment, you'll be creating numerous documents describing the current state of the network, the planned changes, IT standards, administrative procedures, and the like. It's a good idea to take advantage of all of this up-to-date information to create policies and procedures documents, which will help ensure that the network stays in compliance with your new standards and administration is accomplished as intended.

The same set of documents can also serve as a basis for user guides, as well as administrator and user training, and can be made available through the corporate intranet. If the people working on the project, especially those performing testing, take notes about any error conditions they encounter and the resolutions to them, you'll also have a good start on frequently asked questions (FAQs) and other technical support data.

The Business Perspective

Many discussions of the business reasons for new software deployments echo common themes: enhance productivity, eliminate downtime, reduce costs, and the like. Translating these often somewhat vague (and occasionally lofty) aspirations into concrete goals sometimes takes a bit of effort. It is well worth taking the time, however, to refine the big picture into specific objectives before moving on. An IT department should serve the needs of the business, not the other way around; if you don't understand those needs clearly, you'll have a hard time fulfilling them.

Be sure to ask for the input of people close to where the work is being done—department managers from each business area should be asked about what they need from IT, what works now, and what doesn't. These people care about the day-to-day operations of their computing environment; that is, will the changes help their staff do their work? Ask about work patterns, both static and burst—the Finance department's workflow is not the same in July as it is in April. Make sure to include all departments, as well as any significant subsets—human resources (HR), finance, sales, business units, executive management, and so on.

You should also identify risks that lie at the business level, such as resistance to change, lack of commitment (frequently expressed as inadequate resources: budget, staff, time, and so on), or even the occasional bit of overt opposition. At the same time, look for positives to exploit—enthusiastic staff can help energize others, and a manager in your corner can smooth many bumps along the way. By getting people involved, you can gain allies who are vested in the success of the project.

INSIDE OUT **Talk to the people who will use the technology**

Not to put too fine a point on it, but make sure that the team members who will be handling aspects of the user experience actually talk with users. The only way to adequately assess what the people doing the work need in critical areas such as usability, training, and support is to get in the trenches and see what they are doing. If possible, have meetings at the user's workstation, because it can provide additional insight into daily operations. If passwords are visible on sticky notes stuck to monitors—a far too common practice—you know you have security issues.

Identifying IT Goals

IT goals are often fairly obvious: improve network reliability, provide better security, deliver enhanced administration, and maybe even implement a particular new feature. They are also easier to identify than those of other departments—after all, they are directly related to technology.

When you define your goals, make sure that you are specific. It is easy to say you will improve security, but how will you know when you have done so? What's improved, and how much? In many cases, IT goals map to implementation of features or procedures; for example, to improve security you will implement Internet Protocol Security (IPSec) and encrypt all traffic to remote networks.

Don't overpromise either—eliminating downtime is a laudable goal, but not one you are likely to achieve on your network, and certainly not one on which you want your next review based.

Get to Know Each Other

Business units often seem to have little idea of the IT department's capabilities and operations—or worse, they have an idea, but it is an *extremely* unrealistic one. This can lead to expectations ranging from improbable to absurd, which is bad for everyone involved.

A major project like this brings together people from all over the company, some from departments that seldom cross paths. This is a great opportunity for members of the various areas of the company to become familiar with IT operations, and vice versa. A clearer understanding of both the big picture of the business and the workings of other departments will help smooth the interactions of IT and the rest of the company.

Chapter 2

Examining IT–Business Interaction

A number of aspects of your business should be considered when evaluating your overall IT requirements and the business environment in which you operate. Consider things such as the following:

- **Business organization** How large is the business? Are there offices in more than one location? Does the business operate across international, legal, or other boundaries? What sorts of departmental or functional boundaries exist?

- **Stability** Does the business undergo a lot of change? Are there frequent reorganizations, acquisitions, changes, and the like in business partnerships? What is the expected growth rate of the organization? Conversely, are substantial downsizings planned in the future?

- **External relationships** Do you need to provide access to vendors, partners, and so on? Are there external networks that people operating on your network must access?

- **Impact of Windows Server 2008 deployment** How will this deployment affect the various departments in your company? Are there any areas of the company that are particularly intolerant of disruption? Are there upcoming events that must be taken into consideration in scheduling?

- **Adaptability** Is management easily adaptable to change? If not, make sure you get every aspect of your plan right the first time. Having an idea of how staff might respond to new technologies and processes can help you plan for education and support.

Predicting Network Change

Part of planning is projecting into the future and predicting how future business needs will influence the activities of the IT department. Managing complicated systems is easier when done from a proactive stance, rather than a reactive one. Predicting network change is an art, not a science, but it will behoove you to hone your skills at it.

This is primarily a business assessment, based on things such as expected growth, changes in business focus, or possible downsizing and outsourcing—each of which provides its own challenges to the IT department. Being able to predict what will happen in the business and what those changes will mean to the IT department allows you to build in room for expansion in your network design.

When attempting to predict what will happen, look at the history of the company: are mergers, acquisitions, spin-offs, and so on common? If so, this indicates a considerable need for flexibility from the IT department, as well as the need to keep in close contact with people on the business side to avoid being blindsided by a change in the future.

As people meet to discuss the deployment, talk about what is coming up for the business units. Cultivate contacts in other parts of the company, and talk with those people regularly about what's going on in their departments, such as upcoming projects, as well as what's happening with other companies in the same business sector. Reading the company's news releases and articles in outside sources can also provide valuable hints of what's to come. By keeping your ear to the ground, doing a little research, and thinking through the potential impact of what you learn, you can be much better prepared for whatever is coming up next.

The Impact of Growth on Management

Many networks start out with a single administrator (or a small team), which only makes sense because many networks are small when first implemented. As those networks grow, it is not uncommon for a few administrative tasks to be delegated to others in the company who, although it is not their job, know how to assist the highly limited IT staff. This can lead to a haphazard approach to management, where who is doing what isn't always clear, and the methods for basics (such as data backups) vary from one department to the next, leading to potential problems as time goes by and staff moves on. If this sounds familiar to you, this is a good time to remedy the situation.

Analyzing the Existing Network

Before you can determine the path to your new network environment, you must determine where you are right now in terms of your existing network infrastructure. This requires determining a baseline for network and system hardware, software installation and configuration, operations, management, and security. Don't rely on what you think is the case; actually verify what is in place.

Project Worksheets Consolidate Information

A large network environment, with a lot of architectural and configuration information to be collected, can require juggling enormous amounts of data. If this is the case, you might find it useful to utilize project worksheets of some sort. If your company has not created customized worksheets, you can use those created by Microsoft to aid in the upgrade process. Typically, these are available in the operating system deployment kit.

Evaluating the Network Infrastructure

You should get an idea of what the current network looks like before moving to a new operating system. You will require configuration information while designing the modifications to the network and deploying the servers. In addition, some aspects of Windows Server 2008, such as the sites used in Active Directory replication, are based upon your physical network configuration. (A *site* is a segment of the network with good connectivity, consisting of one or more Internet Protocol [IP] subnets.)

For reasons such as this, you'll want to assess a number of aspects related to your physical network environment. Consider such characteristics as the following:

- **Network topology** Document the systems and devices on your network, including link speeds, wide area network (WAN) connections, sites using dial-up connections, and so on. Include devices such as routers, switches, servers, and clients, noting all forms of addressing, such as both NetBIOS names and IP addresses for Windows systems.

- **Network addressing** Are you currently employing Transmission Control Protocol/Internet Protocol (TCP/IP)? Is the address space private or public? Which TCP/IP subnets are in use at each location?

- **Remote locations** How many physical locations does the organization have? Are they all using broadband connections, or are there remote offices that connect sporadically by dial-up? What is the speed of those links?

- **Traffic patterns** Monitoring network traffic can provide insights into current performance, as well as help you to identify potential bottlenecks and other problems before they occur. Examine utilization statistics, paying attention to both regularly occurring patterns and anomalous spikes or lulls, which might indicate a problem.

- **Special cases** Are there any portions of the network that have out-of-the-ordinary configuration needs, such as test labs that are isolated from the rest of the network?

INSIDE OUT   Mapping the territory

Create a network map illustrating the location of all your current resources—this is easier using tools such as Microsoft Visio. Collect as much detailed information as possible about those resources, starting with basics, such as what is installed on each server, the services it's providing, and so on. Additional information, such as critical workflow processes and traffic patterns between servers, can also be very useful when it comes time to consolidate servers or deploy new ones. The easier it is to cross-reference all of this information, the better.

Assessing Systems

As part of planning, you should inventory the existing network servers, identifying each system's operating system version, IP address, and Domain Name System (DNS) names, as well as the services provided by that system. Collect such information by performing the following tasks:

- **Inventory hardware** Conduct a hardware inventory of the servers on your network, noting central processing unit (CPU), random access memory (RAM), disk space, and so on. Pay particular attention to older machines that might present compatibility issues if upgraded.

- **Identify network operating systems** Determine the current operating system on each computer, including the entire version number (even if it runs to many digits), as well as service packs, hot fixes, and other post-release additions.

- **Assess your current Microsoft Windows domains** Do you have Windows domains on the network? Microsoft Windows NT 4.0 or Active Directory? If multiple, detail the trust relationships. List the name of each domain, what it contains (users, resources, or both), and which servers are acting as domain controllers.

- **Identify localization factors** If your organization crosses international and/or language boundaries, identify the localized versions in use and the locations in which they are used. This is critical when upgrading to Windows Server 2008, because attempting an upgrade using a different localized version of Windows Server 2008 might fail.

- **Assess software licenses** Evaluate licenses for servers and client access. This will help you select the most appropriate licensing program.

- **Identify file storage** Review the contents and configuration of existing file servers, identifying partitions and volumes on each system. Identify existing distributed file system (DFS) servers and the contents of DFS shares. Don't forget shares used to store user data.

Chapter 2

INSIDE OUT   Where is the data?

Locating file shares that are maintained at a departmental, team, or even individual level can take a little bit of investigation, but it can well be worth it to allow you to centralize the management of data that is important to individual groups, while providing valuable services such as ensuring that regular data backups are performed.

You can gather hardware and software inventories of computers that run the Windows operating system by using tools such as Microsoft System Center Configuration Manager or HP Enterprise Discovery software. Review the types of clients that must be supported so that you can configure servers appropriately. This is also a good time to determine any client systems that must be upgraded (or replaced) to use Windows Server 2008 functionality.

> **Note**
>
> You can also gather this information with command-line scripts. To find more informa-
> tion on scripting, I recommend *Microsoft Windows Command-Line Administrator's Pocket
> Consultant 2nd Edition* by William R. Stanek (Microsoft Press, 2008).

Identify Network Services and Applications

Look at your current network services, noting which services are running on which
servers, and the dependencies of these services. Do this for all domain controllers and
member servers that you'll be upgrading. You'll use this information later to plan for
server placement and service hosting on the upgraded network configuration. Some
examples of services to document are as follows:

- **DNS services** You must assess your current DNS configuration. If you're currently
  using a non-Microsoft DNS server, you'll want to carefully plan DNS support
  because Active Directory relies on Windows Server 2008 DNS. See Chapter 23,
  "Architecting DNS Infrastructure," for guidance and be sure to review "Deploying
  Global Names" on page 803.

- **WINS services** You should assess the use of NetBIOS by legacy applications and
  computers running earlier versions of the Windows operating system to deter-
  mine whether NetBIOS support (such as Windows Internet Naming Service
  [WINS]) will be needed in the new network configuration. See "Understanding
  Name Resolution" on page 652 to review important changes, including Link-Local
  Multicast Name Resolution (LLMNR).

- **Print services** List printers and the print server assigned to each one. Consider
  who is assigned to the various administrative tasks and whether the printer will
  be published in Active Directory. Also determine whether all of the print servers
  will be upgraded in place or whether some will be consolidated. See "Migrating
  Printers and Print Queues" on page 873 to learn how you can easily move printers and their print queues from one print server to another.

- **Network applications** Inventory your applications, creating a list of the applications that are currently on the network, including version number (as well as
  post-release patches and such), which server hosts it, and how important each
  application is to your business. Use this information to determine whether
  upgrades or modifications are needed. Also watch for software that is never used
  and thus need not be purchased or supported—every unneeded application you
  can remove represents savings of both time and money.

This list is only the beginning. Your network will undoubtedly have many more services that you must take into account.

CAUTION

Make sure that you determine any dependencies in your network configuration. Discovering after the fact that a critical process relied upon the server that you just decommissioned is not going to make your job any easier. You can find out which Microsoft and third-party applications are certified to be compatible with Windows Server 2008 in the Windows Server Catalog (*http://www.windowsservercatalog.com/*).

Identifying Security Infrastructure

When you document your network infrastructure, you will need to review many aspects of your network security. In addition to security concerns that are specific to your network environment, the following factors should be addressed:

- Consider exactly who has access to what and why. Identify network resources, security groups, and assignment of access permissions.

- Determine which security protocols and services are in place. Are adequate virus protection, firewall protection, e-mail filtering, and so on in place? Do any applications or services require legacy NTLM authentication? Have you implemented a public key infrastructure (PKI) on your network?

- Examine auditing methods and identify the range of tracked access and objects.

- Determine which staff members have access to the Internet and which sorts of access they have. Look at the business case for access that crosses the corporate firewall—does everyone that has Internet access actually need it, or has it been provided across the board because it was easier to provide blanket access than to provide access selectively? Such access might be simpler to implement, but when you look at Internet access from the security perspective, it presents many potential problems.

- Consider inbound access as well; for example, can employees access their information from home? If so, examine the security that is in place for this access.

Note
Security is one area in which well-established methods matter—pay particular attention to all established policies and procedures, what has been officially documented, and what isn't documented as well.

Depending upon your existing network security mechanisms, the underlying security methods can change upon deployment of Windows Server 2008. The Windows NT 4.0 security model (using NTLM authentication), for instance, is initially supported upon upgrade to Windows Server 2008, but is no longer supported when the forest and domain functional levels are raised to Windows Server 2003 level or higher.

INSIDE OUT   Thinking about Internet access

From an IT perspective, the fewer employees that have Internet access, the better. When employees have access to the Internet, their activities can open the business to potential liability. You must balance the needs of employees who require Internet access to do their jobs with the potential risks to the company of an employee doing something irresponsible or, worse, illegal.

Employee Internet access also means more work for both IT staff and management, requiring that policies be defined and enforced, requiring auditing and constant vigilance against the various problems that are introduced. When you add in lost productivity caused by Web surfing, chatting, online shopping, and so on, it becomes clear that allowing Internet access is more complicated than just reconfiguring a firewall.

Reviewing Network Administration

Examining the administrative methods currently in use on your network provides you with a lot of information about what you are doing right, as well as identifying those areas that could use some improvement. Using this information, you can tweak network procedures where needed to optimize the administration of the new environment.

How Did You Get Here?

Some networks are entirely designed—actually considered, discussed, planned, and so forth—while other networks grow. At one extreme is a formally designed and carefully implemented administration scheme, complete with its supporting documentation set, training, and ongoing compliance monitoring. At the other end of the spectrum is the network for which administrative methods just sort of happen organically; someone did it that way once, it worked, that person kept doing it that way and maybe even taught others to do it that way—not surprisingly, this occurs most often on small networks. In the middle, and perhaps more typically, is a looser amalgamation of policies and procedures, some of which were formally implemented, while others were created ad hoc.

Depending on the path that led to your current administrative methods, you might have more or less in the way of documentation, or actual idea, of the detailed workings of day-to-day administration. Even if you have fully documented policies and procedures, you should still assess how management tasks are actually performed—you might be surprised at what you learn.

Network Administrative Model

Each company has its own sort of approach to network administration—some are very centralized, with even the smallest changes being made by the IT department, while others are partially managed by the business units, which control aspects such as user management. Administrative models fit into these categories:

- **Centralized** Administration of the entire network is handled by one group, perhaps in one location, although not necessarily. This provides a high degree of control at the cost of requiring IT staff for every change to the network, no matter how small.

- **Decentralized** This administrative model delegates more of the control of day-to-day operations to local administrators of some sort, often departmental. Certain aspects of network management might still be managed by a central IT department, in that a network with decentralized administration often has well-defined procedures controlling exactly *how* each administrative task is performed.

- **Hybrid** On many networks, a blend of these two methods is used: A centralized IT department performs many tasks (generally, the more difficult, delicate operations, and those with the broadest impact on the network), while delegating simpler tasks (such as user management) to departmental or group administrators.

Disaster Recovery

The costs of downtime caused by service interruption or data loss can be substantial, especially in large enterprise networks. As part of your overall planning, determine whether a comprehensive IT disaster recovery plan is in place. If one is in place, this is the time to determine its scope and effectiveness, as well as to verify that it is being followed. If one isn't in place, this is the time to create and implement one.

Document the various data sets being archived, schedules, backup validation routine, staff assignments, and so on. Make sure there are provisions for offsite data storage to protect your data in the case of a catastrophic event, such as a fire, earthquake, or flood.

Examine the following:

- **Systems and servers** Are all critical servers backed up regularly? Are secondary and/or backup servers available in case of system failure?

- **Enterprise data** Are regular backups made of core enterprise data stores such as databases, Active Directory, and the like?

- **User information** Where is user data stored? Is it routinely archived? Does the backup routine get *all* of the information that is important to individuals or is some of it stored on their personal machines and thus not archived?

CAUTION !

Whatever your current disaster recovery plan, make sure that it is being followed *before* you start making major changes to your network. Although moving to Windows Server 2008 should not present any major problems on the network, it's always better to have your backups and not need them than the other way around.

Network Management Tools

This is an excellent time to assess your current suite of network management tools. Pay particular attention to those that are unnecessary, incompatible, redundant, inefficient, or otherwise not terribly useful. You might find that some of the functionality of those tools is present natively in Windows Server 2008. Assess the following aspects of your management tools:

- Identify the tools currently in use, which tasks they perform, who uses them, and so on. Make note of administrative tasks that could be eased with additional tools.

- Decide whether the tools you identified are actually used. A lot of software ends up sitting on a shelf (or on your hard disk drive) and never being used. Identifying which tools are truly needed and eliminating those that aren't can save you money and simplify the learning curve for network administrators.

- Disk management and backup tools deserve special attention because of file system changes in Windows Server 2008. These tools are likely to require upgrading to function correctly under Windows Server 2008.

INSIDE OUT   Think about compatibility issues early

Dealing with compatibility issues can take a lot of time, so examine them early in the process. The time needed to determine whether your current hardware and software will work and what changes must be made to allow them to work with Windows Server 2008 can be lengthy. When you add to that the time necessary to requisition, obtain, install, and configure new software—especially if you must write custom code—you can see why you don't want to leave this until the end of the project.

Defining Objectives and Scope

A key aspect of planning any large-scale IT deployment of an operating system is determining the overall objectives for the deployment and the scope of users, computers, networks, and organization divisions that are affected. The fundamental question of scope is: What can you realistically expect to accomplish in the given time within existing project constraints, such as staffing and budget?

Some of the objectives that you identified in the early stages of the project are likely to change as constraints become more apparent and new needs and requirements emerge. To start with, you must identify who will be affected—which organizational subdivisions, which personnel, and who will be doing what? These are questions that map to the business goals that must be accomplished.

You also must identify the systems that will be affected—which WANs, local area networks (LANs), subnets, servers, and client systems? In addition, you must determine the software that will be changed—which server software, client software, and applications?

INSIDE OUT   Planning for scope creep

Projects grow, it's inevitable, and although the scope of some projects creeps, others gallop. Here are a few tips to help you keep it to a manageable level:

- When an addition to the project is proposed, never say yes right away. Think through the consequences thoroughly, examining the impact on the rest of the project and the project team, before agreeing to any proposed changes.

- Insist on management buyoff on changes to the plan. In at least some cases, you won't get approval, automatically deferring the requested changes.

- Argue for trade-offs in the project when possible, so that adding one objective means removing another, rather than just adding tasks to your to-do list.

- Try to defer any noncritical proposed changes to a future project.

Specifying Organizational Objectives

Many goals of the various business units and IT department are only loosely related, while others are universal—everyone wants security, for example. Take advantage of the places where goals converge to engage others in the project. If people can see that their needs are met, they are more likely to be supportive of others' goals and the project in general.

You have business objectives at this point; now they must be prioritized. You should make lists of various critical aspects of projects, as well as dependencies within the project plan, as part of the process of winnowing the big picture out into a set of realistic objectives. Determine what you can reasonably accomplish within the constraints of the current project. Also, decide what is outside the practical scope of this Windows Server 2008 deployment but is still important to implement at some later date.

The objectives that are directly related to the IT department will probably be clearer, and more numerous, after completing the analysis of the current network. These objectives should be organized to conform to existing change management procedures within your enterprise network.

When setting goals, be careful not to promise too much. Although it's tempting and sometimes easier in the short run to try to do everything, you can't. It's unlikely that you will implement every single item on every person's wish list during the first stage of this project, if at all. Knowing what you can't do is as important as knowing what you can.

INSIDE OUT   Gauging deployment success

It is difficult to gauge the success of a project without clearly defined goals. Make sure that you define specific, measurable goals that you can use to determine when each portion of the project is complete. Everyone on the project team, particularly management, should agree on these milestones *before* the rollout gets under way.

Some goals should map to user functionality (that is, the XYZ department is able to do ABC), while others will correspond to administrative tasks. Be granular in your goals: "Security policies will be followed" is difficult to quantify; however, "Virus definition files are updated daily" or "Operating system patches will be installed within 48 hours of release" is easy.

Setting the Schedule

You should create a project schedule, laying out the time line, tasks, and staff assignments. Including projected completion dates for milestones helps you keep on top of significant portions of the project and ensure that dependencies are managed.

It is critical that you are realistic when considering time lines; not just a little bit realistic, *really realistic*. This is, after all, your time you are allocating. Estimate too short a time and you are likely to spend evenings and weekends at the office with some of your closest coworkers.

A number of tasks will be repeated many times during the rollout of Windows Server 2008, which should make estimating the time needed for some things fairly simple: a 1-hour process repeated 25 times takes 25 hours. If, for example, you are building 25 new servers in-house, determine the actual time needed to build one and do the math.

When you have a rough idea of the time required, do the following:

- Assign staff members to the various tasks to make sure you have adequate staff to complete the project.

- Add some time to your estimates—IT projects always seem to take more time than you thought they would. This is the only buffer you are likely to get, so make sure you build in some "extra" time from the start.

- As much as possible, verify how long individual tasks take; you might be surprised at how much time you spend doing a seemingly simple task, and if your initial estimate is significantly off, you could end up running significantly short on time.

- Develop a schedule that clearly shows who is doing what and when.

- Get drop-dead dates, which should be later than the initial target date.

- Post the schedule in a place where the team, and perhaps other staff, can view it. Keep this schedule updated with milestones reached, changes to deliverable dates, and so on.

> **Note**
>
> You might want to use a project management tool, such as Microsoft Project, to develop the schedule. This sort of tool is especially useful when managing a project with a number of staff members working on a set of interdependent tasks.

Shaping the Budget

Determining the budget is a process constrained by many factors, including, but not limited to, IT-related costs for hardware and licensing. In addition to fixed IT costs, you also must consider the project scope and the non-IT costs that can come from the requirements of other departments within the organization. Thus, to come up with the budget, you will need information and assistance from all departments within the organization and with consideration for all aspects of the project.

Many projects end up costing more than is initially budgeted. Sometimes this is predictable and preventable with proper research and a bit of attention to ongoing expenses. As with time lines, pad your estimates a little bit to allow for the unexpected. Even so, it helps if you can find out how much of a buffer you have for any cost overruns.

In planning the budget, also keep in mind fiscal periods. If your project is crossing budget periods, is next year's budget for the project allocated and approved?

Chapter 2

> **Budget for Project Changes**
>
> Keep in mind that there are likely to be changes as the project is under way. Each change will probably have a cost associated with it, and you might have to fight for additional budget or go back to the department or individuals that want the change and ask them to allocate moneys from their budget to cover the requested change.

Allowing for Contingencies

No matter how carefully you plan any project, it is unlikely that everything will go exactly as planned. Accordingly, you should plan for contingencies that might present themselves; by having a number of possible responses to unforeseen events ready, you can better manage the vagaries of the project.

Start with perhaps the most common issue encountered during projects: problems in getting the assigned people to do the work. This all too common problem can derail any project, or at least cause the project manager a great deal of stress. After all, the ultimate success of any project relies upon people doing their assigned tasks. Many of these people are already stretched pretty thin, however, and you might encounter times when they aren't quite getting everything done. Your plan should include what to do in this circumstance—is the person's manager brought in, or is a backup person automatically assigned to complete the job?

Another possibility to plan for is a change in the feature set being implemented. Should such shifts occur, you must decide how to adjust to compensate for the reallocated time and money required. To make this easier, identify and prioritize the following:

- Objectives that could slip off this project and onto a later one should the need arise
- Objectives that you want to slip *into* the project if the opportunity presents itself

Items on both of these lists should be relatively small and independent of other processes and services. Avoid incurring additional expenses; you are more likely to encounter extra time than extra funding during your deployment.

In general, ask yourself what could happen to cause significant problems along the way. Then, more important, consider what you would do in response. By thinking through potential problems ahead of time, and planning what you might do in response, you can be prepared for many of the inevitable bumps along the way.

INSIDE OUT **Padding project estimates**

Many consultants pad their project estimates, primarily as a means of ensuring that the inevitable project scope creep isn't problematic later on. After all, it's preferable to have a client who is happy that the project came in early and under budget rather than one who is unhappy at the cost and time overruns. You might want to use this approach by adding in a little extra time and not allocating quite all of the available money. If you come in early and under budget, so much the better—but you probably won't.

Finalizing Project Scope

You have goals, know the time line, and have a budget pinned down—now it's time to get serious. Starting with the highest-priority aspects of the project, estimate time and budget needed to complete each portion. Work your way through the planned scope, assessing the time and costs associated with each portion of the project. This will help ensure that you have enough time and budget to successfully complete the project as designed.

As you finalize the project plan, each team member should review the final project scope, noting any concerns or questions he or she has about the proposal. Encourage the team to look for weak spots, unmet dependencies, and other places where the plan might break down. Although it is tempting to ignore potential problems that are noted this late in the game, you do so at your own peril. Avoiding known risks is much easier than recovering from unforeseen ones.

INSIDE OUT **Get management approval for your plan**

Executive business and IT management should approve the deployment plan, especially if they are not on the planning team. This executive sign-off on the plan should occur at a number of points along the way. After the project team agrees upon initial goals is a good time to get approval, as are critical junctures, such as after the plan has been validated in the lab and again after a successful pilot. In any case, make sure you have management sign-off before you perform *any* installations in a production environment.

Defining the New Network Environment

When you have determined the overall scope of your Windows deployment project and the associated network changes, you must develop the technical specifications for the project, detailing server configuration, changes to the network infrastructure, and so on. As much as possible, describe the process of transitioning to the new configuration. Care should be taken while developing this document because it will serve as the road map for the actual transition, much of which is likely to be done by staff members who were not in the planning meetings.

Defining Domain and Security Architecture

In defining the new (updated) network environment, you must review the current and projected infrastructure for your network. Analyze the domains in use on your network, and evaluate the implications for security operations and network performance.

Assess Domain Architecture and Changes

If you are implementing Active Directory for the first time, designing the domain architecture is probably going to take a substantial amount of work. Businesses already using Microsoft Windows Server 2003 to manage their network, on the other hand, will probably not have to change much, if they change anything at all. The amount of planning involved varies widely, depending on the current state of your network:

- **No Windows domains** If you are starting from scratch, you have a bit of work ahead of you. You should plan DNS and Active Directory carefully, taking plenty of time to consider the implications of your design before implementing it.

- **Windows NT 4.0 domains** This move will still entail quite a bit of change, yet it does provide the opportunity to rethink the current domain configuration before you start configuring Active Directory. Decide whether Active Directory will use existing DNS namespaces or new ones.

- **Windows 2000 or later domains** Changes required are minimal, although you are free to make additional changes if you wish. Any changes to the domain structure will likely be made to optimize operations or support additional functionality.

Also, consider whether you are going to be changing the number of domains you currently have. Will you be getting rid of any domains through consolidation?

Impact on Network

You also must assess the impact of the projected changes on your current network operations. Consider issues such as the following:

- Will network traffic change in ways that require modifications to the network infrastructure? Assess additional loads on each network segment as well as across WAN links.

- Do you need to make changes to network naming or addressing schemes? Are new DNS namespaces needed, and, if so, have the DNS names been registered?

- Will you use Read-Only Domain Controllers (RODCs) in remote offices? If so, will you also use Read-Only DNS (RO DNS)?

- Can you phase out NetBIOS and WINS reliance completely? If so, will you use LLMNR and DNS global names?

Identify Security Requirements

This is a good time to seriously review the security measures implemented on your network. Scrutinize the security devices, services, and protocols, as well as administrative procedures to ensure that they are adequate, appropriate, well documented, and adhered to rigorously.

Security in Windows Server 2008 is not the same as in earlier versions of Windows server operating systems—the security settings for the default (new) installation of Windows Server 2008 are much tighter than in previous versions. This might mean that services that were functioning perfectly prior to an upgrade don't work the same way afterward. Some services that were previously started by default are now disabled when first installed.

Assign staff members to be responsible for each aspect of your security plan and have them document completion of tasks. Among the tasks that should be assigned are the following:

- **Applying regular updates of virus software** Antivirus software is only as good as its virus definition files, so make sure yours are current. This means checking the vendor site every single day, even on weekends if possible. Many antivirus packages can perform automatic updates, yet you should verify that the updates are occurring.

- **Reviewing security alerts** Someone should read the various sites that post security alerts on a regular basis and/or receive their newsletters and alerts. The sites should include Microsoft (*http://www.microsoft.com/security/*), vendors of your other software (*http://www.symantec.com/*), network device vendors (*http://www.cisco.com/*), and at least one non-vendor site (such as *http://www.SANS.org/*).

- **Checking for system software updates** IT staff should consider implementing the Windows Server Update Services (WSUS) to help keep up-to-date on security updates, service packs, and other critical updates for both servers and clients. WSUS enables administrators to automatically scan and download updates to a centralized server and then configure Group Policy so client computers get automatic updates from WSUS. WSUS is available as an optional download for Windows Server 2008.

- **Checking for hardware firmware updates** It is important that the various devices on the network, especially security-related ones such as firewalls, have up-to-date firmware.

Changing the Administrative Approach

While you are rolling out Windows Server 2008 is an excellent time to fine-tune your administration methods and deal with any issues introduced by the growth and

Chapter 2

change. Well-designed administrative methods with clearly documented procedures can make a huge difference in both the initial rollout and ongoing operations.

Management Tools

Active Directory provides the framework for flexible, secure network management, allowing you to implement the administration method that works best in your environment. There are mechanisms that support both centralized and distributed administration; group policies offer centralized control, while selected administrative capabilities can be securely delegated at a highly granular level. The combination of these methods allows administration to be handled in the method that works best for each individual business in its unique circumstances.

> **Note**
> Make sure that all administrative tasks and processes are clearly defined and that each task has a person assigned to it.

Some administrative changes will be required because of the way Windows Server 2008 works. You might find that existing administration tools no longer work or are no longer needed. So, be sure to question the following:

- Whether your existing tools work under the new operating system. A number of older tools are incompatible with Windows Server 2008—management utilities must be Active Directory–aware, work with NTFS, and so on.

- Whether current tools will be needed once you move to Windows Server 2008. If a utility such as PKZIP, for example, is in use now, it might not be required for operations under Windows Server 2008, which has incorporated the functionality of ZIP into the operating system. Eliminating unneeded tools could well be one goal of the Windows Server 2008 deployment project, and it will have a definite payoff for the IT department as well in terms of simplified management, lower costs, and so forth.

Select and Implement Standards

You will also want to select and implement standards. If your IT department has not implemented standards for naming and administration procedures, this is a good time to do so. You'll be gathering information about your current configuration, which will show you the places where standardization is in place, as well as places where it would be useful.

Make sure that any standards you adopt allow for likely future growth and changes in the business. Using an individual's first name and last initial is a very simple scheme for creating user names and works well in a very small business. Small businesses, however, don't necessarily stay small forever—even Microsoft initially used this naming scheme, although it has been modified greatly over the years.

You can also benefit from standardization of system hardware and software configuration. Supporting 100 servers (or clients) is much easier if they share a common set of hardware, are similarly configured, and have largely the same software installed. This is, of course, possible only to a limited degree and dependent upon the services and applications that are required from each system. Still, it's worth considering.

When standardizing server hardware, keep in mind that the minimum functional hardware differs for various types of servers; that is, application servers have very different requirements than file servers. Also consider the impact of the decisions the IT department makes on other parts of the company and individual employees. There are some obvious things to watch for, such as unnecessarily exposing anyone's personal data—although surprising numbers of businesses and agencies still do.

> **Note**
>
> Standardization is especially important for networks that are still running Windows NT 4.0, because many of those environments use an eclectic, and sometimes downright odd, collection of computer and device names.

INSIDE OUT   Personal information is private!

The amount of personal information that businesses have about individuals is something that should give us all pause. What's even more alarming is the casual disregard with which much of this information is treated.

Consider the use of social security numbers in the United States; they show up as student ID numbers (and are posted on professors' doors) and health insurance policy numbers (and are printed on dozens of things from insurance cards to driver's licenses), to name two of the more common and egregious misuses. If that weren't enough, portions of your social security number are used as the default "secret PIN" for some accounts at financial institutions. The same social security number that you give to several people each time anyone in your family seeks medical care. How *secret*.

This might start to change, however. For example, social security numbers are part of what is protected under the Health Information Portability and Privacy Act (HIPPA), which carries severe penalties for inadvertent or negligent exposure of the data. HIPPA has specific data management requirements that are of concern to any IT department working with patient information. Even without the threat of federal penalties, all IT departments, not just those in the medical industry, would be well served by an inspection of which sorts of personal information they are managing and how they are protecting it.

Change Management

Formalized change management processes are very useful, especially for large organizations and those with distributed administrative models. By creating structured change control processes and implementing appropriate auditing, you can control the ongoing management of critical IT processes. This makes it easier to manage the network and reduces the opportunity for error.

Although this is particularly important when dealing with big-picture issues such as domain creation or Group Policy implementation, some organizations define change control mechanisms for every possible change, no matter how small. You'll have to determine for which IT processes you must define change management processes, finding a balance between managing changes effectively and over-regulating network management.

Even if you're not planning on implementing a formal change control process, make sure that the information about the initial configuration is collected in one spot. By doing this, and collecting brief notes about any changes that are made, you will at least have data about the configuration and the changes that have been made to it. This will also help later on, if you decide to put more stringent change control mechanisms in place, by providing at least rudimentary documentation of the current network state.

Thinking About Active Directory

Active Directory is an extremely complicated, and critical, portion of Windows Server 2008, and you should plan for it with appropriate care. This book goes into detail on doing this in Part 5, "Managing Active Directory and Security;" you should read this information if you are going to be designing a new Active Directory tree.

The following section discusses, in abbreviated form, some high-level aspects of Active Directory that you must consider. It is meant to offer perspective on how Active Directory fits in the overall planning picture, not to explain how to plan for a new Active Directory installation.

Designing the Active Directory Namespace

The Active Directory tree is based on a DNS domain structure, which must be implemented prior to, or as part of, installing the first Active Directory server in the forest. Each domain in the Active Directory tree is both a DNS and Windows domain, with the associated security and administrative functionality. DNS is thoroughly integrated with Active Directory, providing location services (also called *name resolution services*) for domains, servers, sites, and services, as well as constraining the structure of the Active Directory tree. It is wise to keep Active Directory in mind as you are designing the DNS namespace and vice versa, because they are immutably linked.

> **Note**
> Active Directory trees exist within a *forest*, which is a collection of one or more domain trees. The first domain installed in an Active Directory forest functions as the *forest root*.

The interdependence of Active Directory and DNS brings some special factors into play. For example, if your organization has outward-facing DNS servers, you must decide whether you will be using your external DNS name or another DNS domain name for Active Directory. Many organizations choose not to use their external DNS name for Active Directory, unless they want to expose the directory to the Internet for a business reason, such as an Internet service provider (ISP) that uses Active Directory logon servers.

Within a domain, another sort of hierarchy exists in the form of container objects called *organizational units* (OU), which are used to organize and manage users, network resources, and security. An OU can contain related users, groups, or computers, as well as other OUs.

> ### Note
>
> Designing the Active Directory namespace requires the participation of multiple levels of business and IT management, so be sure to provide adequate time for a comprehensive review and sign-off on domain architecture.

Managing Domain Trusts

Domain trusts allow automatic authentication and access to resources across domains. Active Directory automatically configures trust relationships such that each domain in an Active Directory forest trusts every other domain within that forest.

Active Directory domains are linked by a series of such transitive trust relationships between all domains in a domain tree, and between all domain trees in the forest. By using Windows Server 2008, you can also configure transitive trust relationships between forests.

> ### Understand Explicit Trust Relationships
>
> Explicit trusts between domains can speed up authentication requests. An explicit trust relationship allows authentication queries to go directly to the domain in question rather than having to search the domain tree and/or forest to locate the domain in which to authenticate a user.

Identifying Domain and Forest Functional Levels

Active Directory now has multiple domain and forest functional levels, each constraining the types of domain controllers that can be in use and the available feature set.

The domain functional levels are as follows:

- **Windows 2000 native** If you have only Windows 2000, Windows Server 2003, and Windows Server 2008 domain controllers, select this mode, which offers additional features. It provides full universal group functionality, group-nesting operations for security and distribution groups, and the ability to convert security groups to distribution groups. In addition, security principals can be migrated from one domain to another by the security identifier (SID) history.

- **Windows Server 2003** This mode supports Windows Server 2003 and Windows Server 2008 domain controllers and enables additional Active Directory domain-level features. In addition to the group features specified for the Windows 2000 native functional level, this mode supports the renaming of Active Directory domains, logon time stamp updates, and passwords for InetOrgPerson users. InetOrgPersons are a special type of user, discussed in Chapter 35, "Managing Users, Groups, and Computers."

- **Windows Server 2008** This mode supports only Windows Server 2008 domain controllers and enables all Active Directory domain-level features. In addition to the features specified for the other domain functional levels, this mode supports Distributed File System Replication for Sysvol for more robust and granular replication of Sysvol, Advanced Encryption Services (AES) 128-bit or AES 256-bit encryption for the Kerberos protocol, allows the display of the last interactive logon details for users, and fine-grained password policies for applying separate password and account lockout policies to users and groups.

The forest functional levels are as follows:

- **Windows 2000** Supports domains at the Windows 2000 native functional level

- **Windows Server 2003** Supports domains at the Windows Server 2003 and Windows Server 2008 functional levels

- **Windows Server 2008** Supports domains at Windows Server 2008 functional level.

When a forest is operating at Windows Server 2003 or Windows Server 2008 functional level, all Active Directory features, including the following, are enabled:

- *Replication enhancements*–Each changed value of a multi-valued attribute is now replicated separately–eliminating the possibility for data conflict and reducing replication traffic. Additional changes include enhanced global catalog replication and application partitions (which segregate data, and thus the replication of that data).

- *Schema*–Schema objects can be deactivated, and dynamic auxiliary classes are supported.

- *Management*–Forest trusts allow multiple forests to easily share resources. Active Directory domains can be renamed, and thus the Active Directory tree can be reorganized.

- *User management*–Last logon time is now tracked, and enhancements to InetOrgPerson password handling are enabled.

> **Note**
>
> In forests with the Windows 2000 functional level, the replication enhancements discussed for the Windows Server 2008 functional level are supported but only between two domain controllers running Windows Server 2008.

Selecting your domain and forest functional levels is generally a straightforward choice. Ultimately, the decision regarding the domain and forest functional levels at which to operate mostly comes down to choosing the one that supports the domain controllers you have in place now and expect to have in the future. In most circumstances, you will want to operate at the highest possible level because it enables more functionality. Also, keep in mind that all changes to functional level are one-way and cannot be reversed.

Defining Active Directory Server Roles

In addition to serving as domain controllers, a number of domain controllers fulfill special roles within Active Directory. Some of these roles provide a service to the entire forest, although others are specific to a domain or site. The Active Directory setup routine assigns and configures these roles, although you can change them later.

The Active Directory server roles are as follows:

- **Operations masters** A number of Active Directory operations must be carefully controlled to maintain the integrity of the directory structure and data. A specific domain controller serves as the *operations master* for each of these functions. That server is the only one that can perform certain operations related to that area. For example, you can make schema changes only on the domain controller serving as the schema master; if that server is unavailable, no changes can be made to the schema. There are two categories of operations masters:

  - **Forest-level operations masters** The schema master manages the schema and enforces schema consistency throughout the directory.

    The domain naming master controls domain creation and deletion, guaranteeing that each domain is unique within the forest.

  - **Domain-level operations masters** The RID master manages the pool of *relative identifiers* (RIDs). (A RID is a numeric string used to construct SIDs for security principals.)

    The infrastructure master handles user-to-group mappings, changes in group membership, and replication of those changes to other domain controllers.

    The PDC emulator is responsible for processing password changes and replicating password changes to other domain controllers. The PDC emulator must be available to reset and verify external trusts.

- **Global catalogs** A global catalog server provides a quick index of Active Directory objects, which is used by a variety of network clients and processes to locate directory objects. Global catalog servers can be heavily used, yet must be highly available to clients, especially for user logon, because the global catalog provides membership information for universal groups. Accordingly, each site in the network should have at least one global catalog server, or you should have a Windows Server 2003 or later domain controller with universal group caching enabled.

- **Bridgehead servers** Bridgehead servers manage intersite replication over low-bandwidth WAN links. Each site replicating with other sites usually has at least one bridgehead server, although a single site can have more than one if required for performance reasons.

> **Note**
>
> Active Directory replication depends on the concept of sites, defined as a collected set of subnets with good interconnectivity. Replication differs depending on whether it is within a site or between sites; intrasite replication occurs automatically every 15 seconds, while intersite replication is scheduled and usually quite a bit slower.

Planning for Server Usage

When planning for server usage, consider the workload of each server: which services it is providing, the expected user load, and so on. In small network environments, it is common for a single server to act as a domain controller and to provide DNS and Dynamic Host Configuration Protocol (DHCP) services and possibly even additional services. In larger network environments, one or more stand-alone servers might provide each of these services rather than aggregating them on a single system.

Server Roles

Windows Server 2008 employs a number of *server roles*, each of which corresponds to one or more services. You can manage many Windows Server 2008 services by these roles, although not all services are included in a role.

Your plan should detail which roles (and additional services) are needed and the number and placement of servers, as well as define the configuration for each service. When planning server usage, be sure to keep expected client load in mind and account for remote sites that might require additional servers to support local operations.

Key Windows Server 2008 server roles are as follows:

- **Domain controller** Active Directory domain controllers are perhaps the most important type of network server on a Windows network. Domain controllers are also one of most intensively used servers on a Windows network, so it is important to realistically assess operational requirements and server performance for each one. Remember to take into account any secondary Active Directory–related roles the server will be performing (such as global catalog, operations masters, and so on).

- How many domain controllers are required, and which ones will fulfill which roles?
- Which domains must be present at which sites?
- Where should global catalogs be placed?
- What remote offices (if any) will use RODCs?

- **DNS server** DNS is an integral part of a Windows network, with many important features (such as Active Directory) relying on it. Accordingly, DNS servers are now a required element of your suite of network services. Plan for enough DNS servers to service client requests, with adequate redundancy for fault tolerance and performance and distributed throughout your network to be available to all clients. Factor in remote sites with slow links to the main corporate network and those that might be only intermittently connected by dial-up.

- Define both internal and external namespaces.
- Plan name resolution path (forwarders and so on).
- Determine the storage of DNS information (zone files, Active Directory–integrated, application partitions).
- Determine whether you need read-only DNS servers at remote offices with RODCs.

Note

Microsoft DNS is the recommended method of providing domain name services on a network with Active Directory deployed, although some other DNS servers provide the required functionality. In practice, however, the intertwining of Active Directory and DNS, along with the complexity of the DNS records used by Active Directory, has meant that Microsoft DNS is the one most often used with Active Directory.

Note

DNS information can be stored in traditional zone files, Active Directory–integrated zones, or in application partitions, which are new to Windows Server 2008. An application partition contains a subset of directory information used by a single application. In the case of DNS, this partition is replicated only to domain controllers that are also providing DNS services, minimizing network traffic for DNS replication. There is one application partition for the forest (ForestDnsZones) and another for each domain (DomainDnsZones).

- **DHCP server** DHCP simplifies management of the IP address pool used by both server and client systems. A number of operational factors regarding use of DHCP should be considered:

    ○ Determine whether DNS servers are going to act as DHCP servers also, and, if so, will all of them or only a subset?

    ○ Define server configuration factors such as DHCP scopes and assignment of scopes to servers, as well as client settings such as DHCP lease length.

- **WINS server** First, determine whether you still need WINS on your network. If you have legacy applications in your network environment, WINS might be required to translate NetBIOS names to IP addresses. If so, consider the following:

    ○ Which clients need to access the WINS servers?

    ○ What WINS replication configuration is required?

- **Network Policy and Access Services** Network Policy and Access Services provides integrated protection, routing, and remote access services that facilitate secure, protected access by remote users. Consider the following:

    ○ Do you need protection policies?

    ○ Do you need to provide routing between networks?

    ○ Do you want to replace existing routers?

    ○ Do you have external users that need access to the internal network?

- **Application server** A Windows Server 2008 application server hosts distributed applications built using ASP.NET, Enterprise Services, and .NET Framework 3.0. Includes more than a dozen role services, which are discussed in detail in *Internet Information Server 7.0 Administrator's Pocket Consultant* (Microsoft Press, 2007).

- **File services** The file services role provides essential services for managing files and the way they are made available and replicated on the network. A number of server roles require some type of file service. Includes these role services and sub-services: File Server, Distributed File System, DFS Namespace, DFS Replication, File Server Resource Manager, Services for Network File System (NFS), Windows Search Service, Windows Server 2003 File Services, File Replication Service (FRS), and Indexing Service.

- **Print services** The print services role fulfills the needed role of managing printer operations on the network. Windows Server 2008 enables publishing printers in Active Directory, connecting to network printers using a Uniform Resource Locator (URL), and enhanced printer control through Group Policy.

- **Terminal services** The terminal services role supports thin client access, allowing for a single server to host network access for many users. A client with a Web browser, a Windows terminal, or a Remote Desktop client can access the terminal server to gain access to network resources.

- **Web server** Web servers host Web sites and Web-based applications. Web sites hosted on a Web server can have both static content and dynamic content. You can build Web applications hosted on a Web server using ASP.NET and .NET Framework 3.0.

INSIDE OUT   **Servers with multiple roles**

It is common for a single server to fill more than one role, especially on smaller networks. When selecting which roles to put on a single server, try to select ones with different needs. For instance, putting one processor-intensive role (for example, an application server) and a role (such as a file server) that does a lot of network input/output (I/O) on a single system makes more sense than putting two roles that stress the same subsystem on the same machine.

Determining Which Windows Edition to Use

As discussed in Chapter 1, "Introducing Windows Server 2008," there are several versions of Windows Server 2008 and each is intended for a particular sort of usage. Which version you select for each server depends upon both the required functionality and, in the case of upgrades, the operating system that is in place.

Using Windows Server 2008 Standard

This is the general-purpose version of Windows Server 2008, designed for a variety of purposes. The 32-bit version supports up to four processors and 4 gigabytes (GB) of RAM. The 64-bit version supports up to four processors and 32 GB of RAM. It functions well as a domain controller; Web, application, file, or print server; or for providing other network services (such as DNS or remote access services). Some advanced features are not supported, including the Windows System Resource Manager feature and clustering (although Network Load Balancing is included).

Because it is general purpose, and less expensive than most of the specialized versions, Windows Server 2008 Standard is the choice for many small and medium-sized businesses. Servers running Windows 2000 Server or Windows Server 2003, Standard Edition can be upgraded to Windows Server 2008 Standard.

Using Windows Server 2008 Enterprise

Windows Server 2008 Enterprise provides all the same services as Windows Server 2008 Standard, with a few additions, as well as improved performance, scalability, and reliability. Windows Server 2008 Enterprise is available in both 32-bit and 64-bit versions. Servers running Windows 2000 Server, Windows 2000 Advanced Server, Windows Server 2003, Standard Edition, and Windows Server 2003, Enterprise Edition can be upgraded to Windows Server 2008 Enterprise.

Hardware support is enhanced from Windows Server 2008 Standard, with support for eight processors and 64 GB of RAM on 32-bit platforms (up to 2 TB of RAM on 64-bit platforms), along with additional functionality such as the capability to use eight-node clusters. It allows you to use Active Directory Federated Services (AD FS) as well as multiple DFS namespaces.

With Active Directory Certificate Services (AD CS), it includes additional components and features, as shown in Table 2-1.

Table 2-1 Supported AD CS Options by Windows Server 2008 Editions

Support Option	Web Server	Standard	Enterprise	Datacenter
Can act as CA	no	yes	yes	yes
Network device enrollment	no	no	yes	yes
Online responder service	no	no	yes	yes
CA Web enrollment	no	yes	yes	yes
Customizable v2/v3 certificates	no	no	yes	yes
Key archival	no	no	yes	yes
Role separation	no	no	yes	yes
Certificate manager restrictions	no	no	yes	yes
Delegated enrollment agent restrictions	no	no	yes	yes

Additionally, as you probably know, Windows Server 2003 includes Windows System Resource Manager, but only in Windows Server 2003, Datacenter Edition—now you can get this feature in Windows Server 2008 Enterprise without shelling out any extra cash. Windows System Resource Manager allows you to specify the amount of system resources, including processors and memory, that is available to each application and to prioritize the resources. This permits tuning applications for optimal responsiveness. For example, you can specify that Microsoft Exchange Server can use up to 50 percent of the available central processing units (CPUs) and up to 75 percent of the available memory, while Microsoft SQL Server, also running on the server, can use only up to 33 percent of the available CPUs and up to 50 percent of the available memory. By further specifying that Exchange Server has priority over SQL Server, you can ensure that Exchange Server will always be optimally responsive.

Using Windows Server 2008 Datacenter

Windows Server 2008 Datacenter is the appropriate choice if you have mission-critical, high-volume applications or services that must be available 24/7. If you are running a largely e-commerce site, for example, this is the version of the Windows operating system for you. Windows Server 2008 Datacenter supports up to 64 GB of RAM with 32-bit platforms and up to 2 TB of RAM on 64-bit platforms. It even has a *minimum* number of processors, requiring at least 8, and can scale to 64 processors.

Only Windows 2000 Datacenter Server or Windows Server 2003, Datacenter Edition can be upgraded to Windows Server 2008 Datacenter.

INSIDE OUT   **IA64 Datacenter isn't a do-it-yourself project**

The hardware support provided by the IA64 Datacenter Edition requires that each server manufacturer create a custom *hardware abstraction layer* (HAL). IA64 Datacenter Edition, in fact, is available only directly from a hardware vendor as part of a new server purchase. Once the vendor configures the server, you may not be allowed to make any changes to the hardware without the vendor's authorization, and the vendor provides all support.

Using Windows Web Server 2008

Windows Web Server 2008 provides the advancements of Internet Information Services (IIS) 7.0, along with many standard Windows services and features at a lower cost than Windows Server 2008 Standard. Designed to appeal to administrators running dedicated Web servers, Windows Web Server is optimized for providing Web and application services.

Because of its focus, this edition is missing a number of features used in a corporate environment. For example, a Windows Web Server 2008 server cannot be a domain controller (although it can join a domain), services for other operating systems (such as UNIX and Macintosh) are not available, and Windows Web Server 2008 servers cannot be part of a server cluster, although they can be part of a Web farm using Network Load Balancing.

Selecting a Software Licensing Program

Product licensing is, in most ways, tertiary to your daily work—it is, after all, largely a matter of tracking paperwork. You need only select a licensing program, ensure that you purchase the appropriate number of licenses, and keep track of the proof of those purchases. Just because it's simple, however, don't take it lightly; the consequences for not tracking this particular set of paperwork can be expensive, time-consuming, and awkward to deal with.

There are two kinds of licenses associated with a Windows server product. Your planning should take into consideration how you handle both sorts of licenses.

- **Server License** This license is straightforward; each system running Windows Server 2008 requires a single Server License.

- **Client Access License** Each client or device accessing a Windows server also requires a license. Client Access Licenses (CALs) are in addition to the client operating system license and can represent a significant expense for most networks, so carefully assess your client access needs.

Chapter 2

> **Note**
>
> For more information about current Microsoft product licensing, see the following URL: *http://www.microsoft.com/licensing/.*

Retail Product Licenses

If your business is very small, and you don't purchase much software, buying retail products might be the most straightforward option for you. Indeed, it can be the only option. Even when you are at a large business that is taking advantage of one of Microsoft's volume-licensing options, you might encounter an immediate need that sends you to your local computer store for software.

Volume-Licensing Programs

Microsoft has several volume-licensing options, one (or more) of which could save you a substantial amount of money when it comes time to purchase software. You should examine these licensing programs carefully and compare your options before making a commitment.

Open License Program

The Open License program allows you to purchase software licenses for a number of Microsoft programs at a discount. These agreements last two years. Open License discounts are fixed and don't get larger if you purchase more software, either as an initial purchase or during the two-year term of the agreement.

The Open License program has several subprograms:

- **Open Business** This is the easiest volume licensing to qualify for because you must buy only five Microsoft products to qualify. A fixed discount is applied to your initial purchases and all covered purchases during the two-year term. You can add Software Assurance as an option, but you are severely limited in how you can use it.

- **Open Volume** This program assigns points to each Microsoft product and requires the purchase of software representing a certain number of points. To qualify for the Open Volume program, you must purchase 500 points worth of software from a single category: server, application, or system. The volume purchase price applies only to the categories of software for which you have fulfilled the minimum purchase requirement.

- **Open Value** This program is designed for organizations with at least five desktops that want to use Software Assurance. It gives you the ability to spread payments annually and gives a fixed discount to your initial purchases and all covered purchases during the three-year term. Company-wide and subscription options can be added for additional flexibility, though specific restrictions and limitations apply.

Interestingly enough, the Open License program does not include any physical items corresponding to your software purchase. You can purchase product media and documentation separately, for a nominal fee, plus shipping, of course.

Select License

Larger companies that don't want Software Assurance can opt to use the Select License program, which is designed for companies with 250 or more computers and a predictable pattern of software purchases. Select License uses the same sort of points-based model as the Open Volume program, with a minimum purchase of 1,500 points of software from at least one category. With 1,500 points, you must have purchases for 500 points at the end of the first year, 1,000 points at the end of the second year, and 1,500 points at the end of the third year.

If you are willing to commit to buying more software over the 3-year license term, you can get a greater discount. There are several levels of commitment to ongoing software purchases, each with its own discount amount. For example, if you commit to a Level B Select License you get a better discount over Level A but must have purchases worth a minimum of 12,000 points over three years (4,000 points at the end of the first year, 8,000 points at the end of the second year, and 12,000 points at the end of the third year).

> ### Note
>
> Although you must meet the minimum points required for each price level throughout the three-year term, Microsoft will make an adjustment annually to ensure that the price levels fairly reflect actual purchases. If the total points acquired per product pool are less than the necessary milestone quantity, Microsoft will adjust the price level for those product pools downward, meaning your future licenses will cost more. If points acquired total one-third or two-thirds of a higher pricing level at the 12-month or 24-month point in the term, Microsoft will adjust the price level for those product pools upward, meaning software licenses in those product pools will cost less.

Enterprise Agreement License

Large business organizations that want to use Software Assurance can take advantage of an Enterprise Agreement License, which provides a way to standardize on a set of Microsoft products and purchase all of those products at a discount. This includes the right to upgrade to new versions of software during the agreement period, as well as home use privileges for employees.

Chapter 2

Products covered under this agreement are those that Microsoft considers to be enterprise-class, such as Microsoft Windows Vista Enterprise, Microsoft Office Professional, and core CALs. The agreement is for three years and can be extended for one or three years at the end of the initial term.

Your organization must have at least 250 desktop PCs to qualify for the Enterprise Agreement License. This license program doesn't use points and instead, the pricing level is set based on the number of desktop PCs in the organization. For example, organizations with 250 to 2,399 desktop PCs have pricing level A while organizations with 2,400 to 5,999 desktop PCs have pricing level B.

> **Note**
> A subscription option can be added for additional flexibility. However, as with Open Value subscriptions, specific restrictions and limitations apply.

Software Assurance

Open Value and Enterprise Agreement licenses include Software Assurance. Software Assurance (SA) provides rolling upgrades for covered products, as well as many other benefits for both the corporation and its employees. Businesses will appreciate the access to support during "business hours," self-paced training, and special newsgroups, while employees can purchase Microsoft software at special discounts.

This program has some potential "gotchas," such as limitations on who can call for support. It's also important to remember that you must have both the server and all of the CALs that access that server covered under SA to gain the program benefits for the server.

INSIDE OUT   Windows Product Activation

How, or even if, *Windows Product Activation* (WPA) is implemented is determined by your licensing method. If you purchase retail products, standard product activation is required. If you have a volume license agreement of some sort, you do not have to deal with WPA. A reusable *volume license key* is provided for software licensed under the Open License program, although both Enterprise Agreement and Select License customers are provided with special product CDs with embedded product keys.

Final Considerations for Planning and Deployment

If you are doing a new installation—perhaps for a new business or a new location of an existing one—you have a substantial amount of additional planning to do. This extends well beyond your Windows Server 2008 systems to additional computers (clients, for a start), devices, services, applications, and so on.

The details of such a project are far beyond the scope of this book; indeed, entire books have been written on the topic. If you have to implement a network from the ground up, you might want to pick one up—the *Microsoft Windows Server 2008 Deployment Kit* is worth a serious review.

You must plan the entire network, including areas such as the following:

- Infrastructure architecture (including network topology, addressing, DNS, and so on)
- Active Directory design
- Servers and services
- Administration methods
- Network applications
- Clients
- Client applications
- Client devices (printers, scanners, and the like)

This is a considerable undertaking and requires educated, dedicated staff, as well as adequate time and other resources.

INSIDE OUT   Good news, bad news

Having the responsibility for deploying a new Windows-based network is both a good thing and a not-so-good thing.

- The not-so-good part is straightforward: It can be a staggering amount of work.
- The good thing—and it is a *very* good thing—is that you are starting with a clean slate and you have a chance to get it (at least mostly) right the first time. Many a network administrator would envy the chance to do a clean deployment, to start fresh with no existing problems, no legacy hardware or applications to maintain, no kludges or workarounds.

If you are faced with creating a new network, take advantage of this opportunity and do lots of research before you touch the first computer. With the abundance of technical information available, you should be able to avoid most problems and quickly resolve the few you encounter.

Installing Windows Server 2008

Y ou are likely to find yourself installing Windows Server 2008 in various circum-stances—a new installation for a new system, an upgrade of an existing Microsoft Windows installation, or perhaps even a new installation into a multiboot environment. You might need to install just a few systems, or you might need to deploy hundreds—or even thousands—in a diverse network environment.

Windows Server 2008 supports both interactive and automated setup processes, pro-viding flexibility in how you install and configure the operating system. You can even fully automate the installation of a basic or fully configured operating system onto a brand new computer to ease the administrative burden in large deployments.

In this chapter, I discuss the things you should know to help you prepare for and perform installations. There are three methods of performing a new installation of Windows Server 2008: interactive, unattended using only answer files, and unattended using answer files with Windows Deployment Services (WDS). By using one of these three options, you can deploy Windows Server 2008 to one system or a hundred—although the latter requires a lot more planning.

Getting a Quick Start

To install Windows Server 2008, you can boot from the Windows distribution media, run Setup from within your current Windows operating system, perform a command-line installation, or use one of the automated installation options.

In performing the installation, there are two basic approaches to setting up Windows Server 2008—interactively or as an automated process. An interactive installation is what many people regard as the regular Windows installation: the kind where you walk through the setup process and enter a lot of information during setup. It can be performed from distribution media (by booting from the distribution media or run-ning Windows Setup from a command line). The default Windows setup process when booting from the retail Windows Server 2008 DVD is interactive, prompting you for configuration information throughout the process.

There are several types of automated setup, which actually have administrator-configurable amounts of user interaction. The most basic form of unattended setup you can perform is an unattended installation using only answer files. To take unattended setup a step further, you can use your unattended answer files with Windows Deployment Services. In either case, the answer file contains all or part of the configuration information usually prompted for during a standard installation process. You can author unattended answer files using Windows System Image Manager.

The standard setup program for Windows Server 2008 is Setup.exe. You can run Setup.exe from within the Windows operating system to upgrade the existing operating system or to install Windows Server 2008 to a different partition. On BIOS-based (*x*86) systems, you can boot from the distribution media to initiate the setup process. Unlike 32-bit Intel systems that boot from a DVD-ROM, the Intel Architecture 64-bit (IA-64) Itanium-based systems do not—starting Setup is accomplished through the Extensible Firmware Interface (EFI) shell. To start Windows Setup, run the \IA64\ Setupldr.efi Setup boot loader on the DVD, and other than the partitioning method, Setup for an IA-64 system works the same as the 32-bit version.

The command-line switches on the Windows Setup programs offer you additional options for configuring the installation process. The general installation parameters include the following:

- **Setup /m:folder_name** The /m:*folder_name* option sets an alternate location for files to be used by Setup during the installation process—during setup, the alternate location is searched first, and files in the default location are used only if the installation files are not found in the specified alternate location.

- **Setup /noreboot** The /**noreboot** parameter prevents the rebooting of the system upon completion of the file copy phase. This is used to allow other commands or operations to be performed after the files have been copied, but prior to further Setup phases.

- **Setup /tempdrive:*drive_letter*** The /**tempdrive:*drive_letter*** parameter designates the hard disk drive location where the temporary installation files will be placed.

- **Setup /unattend:*answer_file*** The /**unattend:*answer_file*** parameter, when used with an answer file, instructs Setup to do an unattended new installation (a fresh installation as opposed to an upgrade) based on the values specified in the answer file. The answer file can contain all or part of the configuration information for which the installation process would normally prompt the user.

- **Setup /emsport:{com1|com2|usebiossettings|off}** The /**emsport** parameter is used to specify and enable or disable the Emergency Management Services. The default value for /**emsport** is **usebiossettings**, which draws its information from the Serial Port Console Redirection (SPCR) in the basic input/output system (BIOS) (for 32-bit systems) or the console device path in the EFI of Itanium-based (64-bit) systems. If this is specified on a system that does not support SPCR or EFI, the command will be ignored.

> **Note**
>
> The COM1 and COM2 parameters can be used only on the 32-bit *x*86-based platforms and are not supported on Itanium-based systems. If EMS is disabled from the command line, it can be reenabled by the boot settings—you configure EMS boot settings by using the Bootcfg command. Type **bootcfg /ems /?** at the command line to display all EMS configuration parameters. You can enable EMS, for example, on COM1 by using the following command line: `bootcfg /ems on /port com1 /baud 115200`.

- **Setup /emsbaudrate:*baudrate*** The baud rate used in Emergency Management Services is set by using the **/emsbaudrate:*baudrate*** parameter, with the slowest rate (9600 baud) as the default—accepted baud rates include 19200, 57600, and 115200. The **/emsbaudrate** option is used in conjunction with the **/emsport: com1** (or **com2**) parameter. The **/emsbaudrate** parameter settings can be used only on 32-bit *x*86-based platforms.

Product Licensing

Licensing for Windows Server 2008 has two aspects: server licenses and client access licenses (CALs). Each installation of Windows Server 2008 on a computer requires a server license. In addition to ensuring that you have the required licenses for Windows Server 2008, you must decide on the client access licensing scheme you will use before installing Windows Server 2008. Your choices are as follows:

- **Per server** One CAL is required for each concurrent connection to the server. This usually means one CAL for every connection to that server.

- **Per device or per user** A CAL is purchased for each user or device connecting to the server—this usually corresponds to one CAL for every user or computer that will access the server.

Your licensing program determines how you handle both the product key and product activation. Table 3-1 describes how each type of licensing affects installation.

Table 3-1 Overview of Windows Server 2008 Product Keys and Activation

Product License	Product Key	Product Activation
Retail Product License	Unique product key needed	WPA
Open License program	Reusable product key	No WPA
Select License	On volume license CD	No WPA
Enterprise Agreement License	On volume license CD	No WPA

Chapter 3

Matching Product Keys to Products

The product ID used during installation of a retail version is for a specific Windows Server 2008 edition and can be used only with the retail DVD. Likewise, Open License keys are only usable with the media issued by Microsoft as part of obtaining the volume license. In enterprises using both types of software, knowing which keys go with which software makes the installation process easier.

Preparing for Windows Server 2008 Installation

Installing a server operating system requires some assessment and preparation before you actually do the work. You'll want to review the server hardware and installation details, check the latest technical notes, verify backups, and have more than a few discussions with other information technology (IT) staff and managers.

System Hardware Requirements

Most versions of Windows Server 2008 share baseline requirements, such as a minimum of a 1-gigahertz (GHz) CPU, 512 megabytes (MB) of random access memory (RAM), and 10 gigabytes (GB) of hard disk drive space (for three of the x86-based servers). Yet, there are differences in recommended hardware for each edition—Web Server, Standard, Enterprise, and Datacenter—and further differences to support the 64-bit versions on Itanium-based servers. Table 3-2 shows the hardware requirements for Windows Server 2008 on 32-bit x86 platforms, while Table 3-3 describes the requirements on the Itanium-based platform. For 64-bit extended systems, refer to Table 3-4.

Note

These hardware guidelines are published by Microsoft and are subject to change as the technology landscape changes. If your computer doesn't meet the minimum requirements, you will not be able to install Windows Server 2008. If your computer doesn't meet the recommended requirements, you will experience performance issues.

Table 3-2 **Hardware Requirements for *x*86-Based Computers (32-Bit)**

Version	Min. CPU Speed	Recommended CPU Speed	# of CPUs	Min.–Max. RAM	Recommended RAM	Minimum Disk Space
Web Server	1 GHz	2 GHz	1–2	512 MB–4 GB	2 GB	10 GB
Standard	1 GHz	2 GHz	1–4	512 MB–4 GB	2 GB	10 GB
Enterprise	1 GHz	2 GHz	1–8	512 MB–64 GB	4 GB	20 GB
Datacenter	1 GHz	2 GHz	1–32	2 GB–64 GB	16 GB	20 GB

Table 3-3 **Hardware Requirements for Itanium-Based Computers (64-Bit)**

Version	Min. CPU Speed	Recommended CPU Speed	# of CPUs	Min.–Max. RAM	Recommended RAM	Minimum Disk Space
Web Server	N/A	N/A	N/A	N/A	N/A	10 GB
Standard	1.4 GHz	2 GHz	1–4	512 MB–32 GB	2 GB	10 GB
Enterprise	1.4 GHz	2 GHz	1–8	512 MB–64 GB	4 GB	20 GB
Datacenter	1.4 GHz	2 GHz	1–64	2 GB–2 TB	16 GB	20 GB

Table 3-4 **Hardware Requirements for 64-Bit Extended Systems**

Version	Min. CPU Speed	Recommended CPU Speed	# of CPUs	Min.–Max. RAM	Recommended RAM	Minimum Disk Space
Web Server	N/A	N/A	N/A	N/A	N/A	N/A
Standard	1.4 GHz	2 GHz	1–4	512 MB–32 GB	2 GB	4 GB
Enterprise	1.4 GHz	2 GHz	1–8	512 MB–64 GB	2 GB	4 GB
Datacenter	1.4 GHz	2 GHz	1–64	2 GB–2 TB	16 GB	20 GB

How a Clean Installation and an Upgrade Differ

If you have existing servers running the Windows operating system, you must decide which servers, if any, you will upgrade. The major differences between a clean installation and an upgrade are the following:

- **Upgrade** With an upgrade, the Windows Server 2008 Setup program performs a clean installation of the operating system followed by a migration of user settings, documents, and applications from the earlier version of Windows. During an upgrade, user settings are retained, existing applications and their settings are kept, and basic system configuration is not required. An upgrade installation should be used when you have existing servers running the Windows operating system that support upgrading to Windows Server 2008 and you want to minimize disruption by maintaining the existing settings, user information, and application configuration.

- **Clean installation** In contrast, a clean installation does not retain any user or system settings or knowledge of any installed applications, and you must configure all aspects of the hardware and software. You should use a clean installation when the operating system cannot be upgraded, the system must boot to multiple operating systems, a standardized configuration is required, or (obviously) when no operating system is currently installed.

Supported Upgrade Paths

Before performing an upgrade, you should make sure the server's installed software and hardware support Windows Server 2008. You can download tools for testing compatibility and documentation at the Windows Server Catalog Web site (*http://www. windowsservercatalog.com/*).

Microsoft Server operating systems from Windows 2000 and later can be upgraded to Windows Server 2008. In general, servers can be upgraded to a product with equal or greater capabilities, thus:

- Windows Server 2003 Standard or Enterprise editions can be upgraded to Standard or Enterprise editions of Windows Server 2008.

- Windows Server 2003, Datacenter Edition, can be upgraded to Windows Server 2008 Datacenter.

- Windows Server 2003, Web Edition, can be upgraded Windows Web Server 2008.

- Windows Server 2008 Standard can be upgraded to Enterprise or Datacenter editions of Windows Server 2008.

- Windows Server 2008 Enterprise can be upgraded to Windows Server 2008 Datacenter.

Using Windows Update

Windows Update is a convenient way of ensuring that the most recently updated driver and system files are always used during server installation. Windows Update connects to a distribution server containing updated files used during Windows installation. The files in Windows Update include setup information files, dynamic libraries used during setup, file assemblies, device drivers, and system files.

The Windows Update files can be obtained by using two methods:

- Windows Update files can be obtained directly from the Windows Update site during setup, ensuring that the absolute latest setup files are used during the installation.

- Windows Update files can be downloaded to a server on your local network and then shared to provide clients with access to a consistent local copy of the files.

Getting Windows Updates from the update site online is recommended for consumer use and small businesses that do not have a full-time Windows administrator. Otherwise, your organization probably should centralize the functionality locally using Windows Server Update Services (WSUS) in a client/server configuration. WSUS is available as an optional download for Windows Server 2008. Hosting Windows Update files on a local network provides you with additional security and the advantage of being able to ensure that important operating system updates are applied to all systems within your network environment.

> **Note**
>
> During setup of the operating system, the Windows Update process does not provide new installation files, but rather supplies only updated files that replace existing files used during setup. Windows Update might, however, provide device drivers that are not a replacement for device drivers existing on the distribution media (in-box device drivers) but that are new device drivers supplying additional support of devices or system hardware.

INSIDE OUT   Using Windows Server Update Services

WSUS (previously called Windows Update Services) has both a server and client component. Each managed client requires a Windows Server CAL. The WSUS server component uses a data store that runs with MSDE, WMSDE, or SQL Server. With SQL Server, every device managed by WSUS requires a SQL Server CAL or a per-processor license.

WSUS requires Internet Information Services (IIS), Background Intelligent Transfer Service (BITS) 2.0, and the Microsoft .NET Framework 3.0. The WSUS server component uses IIS to obtain updates over the Internet using HTTP port 80 and HTTPS port 443. WSUS can also use IIS to automatically update client computers with the necessary client software for WSUS.

For performance and network load balancing, large enterprises may want to have an extended WSUS environment with multiple WSUS servers. In a multiple WSUS server environment configuration, one WSUS server can be used as the central server for downloading updates and others WSUS servers can connect to this server to obtain settings and updates to distribute to clients.

WSUS is a supplement to the Windows Server 2008 operating system. As such, WSUS is not included in Windows Server 2008 and must be installed separately. After you've downloaded the installer packages from Microsoft and double-clicked each to install, you can configure the related role using Server Manager.

Preinstallation Tasks

You will want to assess the specifics of an installation and identify any tasks that must be done prior to the installation taking place. The following is a partial list—a general set of pointers to the installation-related tasks that must be performed.

- Check for firmware updates
- Check requirements for OS version
- Review the release notes on OS media
- Determine whether upgrade/new installation
- Check your system hardware compatibility
- Configure how the target computer boots
- Determine installation type: interactive or automated
- Determine license mode
- Choose installation partition
- Determine network connectivity and settings
- Identify domain/workgroup membership account information
- Disconnect uninterruptible power supply (UPS)
- Disable virus scanning

> **Note**
>
> When doing a clean installation on old hardware, check to see whether an OS exists, and if so, check event or system logs for hardware errors, consider multiboot, uncompress drives, and resolve any partition upgrade issues.

> **Plan for Windows Update**
>
> Hosting Windows Update on a local network server—as opposed to downloading updates directly from Microsoft each time you install the operating system—can speed updates and ensure consistency of driver versions across the network environment.

You must also assess your installation requirements and plan the configuration of the drives and partitions on the target computers. If you must create a new partition, modify the system partition, or format the system partition before installation, you can use configuration tools such as the DiskPart, Format, and Convert commands to manage partitions (prior to beginning the automated installation).

Installing Windows Server 2008

For many situations in which you're about to install Windows Server 2008 onto a new computer system—a bare-metal or a clean installation to a computer you can sit in front of—booting from the Windows Server 2008 distribution media is certainly the simplest. You need only configure the server to boot from the DVD-ROM by setting the boot device order in the firmware and provide information when prompted. The exception to this is when you must specify command-line switches or run the command line from within Setup. Alternatively, if you work in an environment that maintains standing images of operating systems in use, you can do an interactive installation from a distribution folder on the network.

Installation on *x86*-Based Systems

When you are working with Windows Server 2008 on *x86*-based systems, you should be aware of the special types of drive sections used by the operating system.

Active The active partition or volume is the drive section for system cache and startup. Some devices with removable storage may be listed as having an active partition.

Boot The boot partition or volume contains the operating system and its support files. The system and boot partition or volume can be the same.

Crash dump The partition to which the computer attempts to write dump files in the event of a system crash. By default, dump files are written to the %SystemRoot% folder, but can be located on any desired partition or volume.

Page file A partition containing a paging file used by the operating system. Because a computer can page memory to multiple disks, according to the way you configure virtual memory, a computer can have multiple page file partitions or volumes.

System The system partition or volume contains the hardware-specific files needed to load the operating system. As part of software configuration, the system partition or volume can't be part of a striped or spanned volume.

> **Note**
>
> Partitions and volumes are essentially the same thing. We use two different terms at times, however, because you create partitions on basic disks and you create volumes on dynamic disks. On an *x86*-based computer, you can mark a partition as active using Disk Management.
>
> Yes, the definitions of boot partition and system partition are backward from what you'd expect. The boot partition does in fact contain the \Windows directory—that's just the way it is. Hey, you have to click Start to stop the computer, so what'd you expect?

Chapter 3

Although these volumes or partitions can be the same, they are required nonetheless. When you install Windows Server 2008, the Setup program assesses all hard disk drive resources available. Typically, Windows Server 2008 puts boot and system on the same drive and partition and marks this partition as the active partition. The advantage of this configuration is that you don't need multiple drives for the operating system and can use an additional drive as a mirror of the operating system partitions. Contrary to some documentation, you can mirror operating system partitions—you do this by using dynamic disks as discussed in "Mirroring Boot and System Volumes" on page 459.

Installation on 64-Bit Systems

There are a number of differences when installing to the Intel Architecture 64 (IA-64) Itanium-based hardware platform. The IA-64 Extended Firmware Interface starts up loading a firmware-based boot menu (instead of Boot.ini).

IA-64 disks have a partition structure, called a globally unique identifier (GUID) partition table (part of the Extensible Firmware Interface, or EFI), that differs substantially from the 32-bit platform master boot record–based partitions. A GUID partition table (GPT)–based disk has two required partitions and one or more optional (original equipment manufacturer [OEM] or data) partitions (up to 128 total):

- EFI system partition (ESP)
- Microsoft Reserved partition (MSR)
- At least one data partition

The IA-64 boot menu presents a set of options, one of which is the EFI shell. The EFI shell provides an operating environment supporting the FAT and FAT32 file systems, as well as configuration and file management commands.

To view a list of partitions on an IA-64-based computer, use the Map command. The following appears in the resultant display:

- blk designates partition blocks
- fs# designates readable file systems

Changing to a partition is like changing a logical drive—enter the partition block number followed by a colon, press Enter, and then type **Dir** and press Enter to view the files.

EFI has a boot maintenance manager that allows you to configure the boot menu. By using the boot maintenance manager, you can choose to do any of the following:

- Add or remove a boot option
- Set timeout delay and the boot option to run automatically
- Define standard console devices
- Boot from a (selected) file
- Perform cold reboot

> **Note**
>
> You can modify any of the boot configuration settings for Windows Server 2008 by using the Bootcfg command or by using the System utility in Control Panel.

Intel's 64-bit systems do not boot from a DVD-ROM; thus, you must start Setup through the EFI shell. To do this, go to the fs# alias that maps to the DVD-ROM and run the \Setupldr.efi Setup boot loader.

The rest of setup for an IA-64 system is the same as the 32-bit version of Setup, with the exception of the IA-64 partitioning method. Setup determines whether there is an EFI partition—if one is not present, Setup creates (and formats) the EFI and the MSR partitions and asks you to create a data partition for the operating system.

CAUTION

> Because EFI does not have password protection, you must provide physical security for all IA-64 servers.

Chapter 3

Planning Partitions

Now that you know how Windows Server 2008 uses disks on both x86-based and Itanium-based systems, consider carefully how you want to partition the hard disk drives. The boot and system files require about 10 GB of space. To allow for flexibility, you should create a partition for the operating system with at least 40 GB minimum. This allows for the addition of service packs and other system files later. Don't forget that you should also have enough disk space for the page file and crash dump; I recommend reserving additional disk space equivalent to twice the installed RAM for this purpose.

Although on a 32-bit system you could have a single hard disk with a single partition, it is better to have multiple partitions, even if the computer has only one drive. By using multiple partitions, you can separate operating system files from application data. Not only does this enhance security, it permits the use of services that require installation on nonsystem partitions.

> **Create Additional Partitions**
>
> If you plan to create multiple partitions, you don't have to worry about doing it when installing the operating system. You can configure the Windows operating system to use a partition of the correct size, such as 40 GB or more, and then create the other partitions that you want to use after the installation is finished.

For systems with multiple disks, this is a good time to think about whether you want to use a redundant array of independent disks (RAID) to add fault tolerance for the operating system. RAID options are discussed in "Managing Volumes on Dynamic Disks" on page 452 and include the following:

- Disk striping (RAID 0)
- Disk mirroring or duplexing (RAID 1)
- Disk striping with parity (RAID 5)

As part of software configuration, you cannot use RAID 0 with system or boot volumes. More typically, operating system files are mirrored, and application data is striped with parity. If you plan to mirror the operating system, you will need two disks. If you plan to create a RAID-5 volume for your data, you'll need at least three disks.

RAID can be performed at the hardware level or at the operating system level. You will find that the hardware-based RAID provides the best performance and the easiest solution. Windows Server 2008 also provides software-based RAID. Software-based RAID is implemented by using dynamic disks. For a bare-metal installation, the disks on the computer should be formatted as basic disks, and then after installation, you upgrade to dynamic disks so you can implement software-based RAID. On existing installations, the computer might already have dynamic disks, such as would happen if a computer is currently using Windows Server 2003 and you are performing a new installation of Windows Server 2008.

Installation Type

You can deploy servers using one of two installation types:

- Full-server installation
- Core-server installation

The full-server installation type is a full-feature installation option of Windows Server 2008 Standard, Windows Server 2008 Enterprise, and Windows Server 2008 Datacenter that provides full functionality. You can configure a server using any allowed combination of roles, role services, and features, and a full user interface is provided for management of the server. This installation option provides the most dynamic solution and is recommended for deployments of Windows Server 2008 in which the server role may change over time.

The core-server installation type is a minimal installation option of Windows Server 2008 Standard, Enterprise, and Datacenter that provides a fixed subset of roles. You can configure a server using only a limited set of roles and a minimal user interface is provided for management of the server. This installation option is ideally suited to situations in which you want to dedicate servers to a specific server role or combination of roles. Because additional functionality is not installed, this reduces the overhead caused by other services and provides more resources for the dedicated role or roles.

You choose the installation type during installation of the operating system. At times you might want to dedicate a server to specific a role or combination of roles, and at other times a server's role may change over time. Therefore both installation options have a place in the typical enterprise.

INSIDE OUT   Choosing between full-server and core-server installations

With a full-server installation, you have a full working version of Windows Server 2008 that you can deploy with any permitted combination of roles, role services, and features. With a core-server installation, on the other hand, you have a minimal install of Windows Server 2008 that supports a limited set of roles and role combinations. The supported roles include Active Directory Domain Services, DNS Server, DHCP Server, File Services, and Print Services. Additionally, in its current implementation, a core-server installation is not an application platform for running server applications.

Although both types of installations use the same licensing rules and can be managed remotely using any available and permitted remote administration technique, full-server and core-server installations are completely different when it comes to local console administration. With a full-server installation, you have a full user interface that includes a full desktop environment for local console management of the server. With a core-server installation, you have a minimal user interface that includes a limited desktop environment for local console management of the server.

Naming Computers

It is surprising how few organizations take the time to plan out the names they're going to use for their computers. Sure, it is fun to have servers named Lefty, Curly, Moe, Ducky, Ruddy, and Aardvark, but just what do the names say about the role and location of those servers? You guessed it—nothing, which can make it difficult for users and even other administrators to find resources they need. Not to mention the management nightmare that happens when your 6 cutely named servers grow to number 50 or 500.

Rather than using names that are cute or arbitrary, decide on a naming scheme that is meaningful to both administrators and users—and this doesn't mean naming servers after the Seven Dwarfs or Lord of the Rings characters. Okay, it might be cool—way cool—to have servers named Bilbo, Gandalf, Frodo, and Gollum. But pretty soon you'd have Galadriel, Boromir, Theoden, Eowyn, and all the rest of the cast. And at that point, you'd better be ready to field lots of questions, such as, "How do you spell Aeyowin, anyway?" or "What's Thedding and where is it again?"

To help users and ease the administration burden, you might decide to use a naming scheme that helps identify what the computer does and where it is located. For example, you could name the first server in the Engineering department EngServer01 and the first server in the Technical Services department TechServer01. These names identify the computers as servers and specify the departments in which they are located.

Chapter 3

You might also have servers named CorpMail01 and CorpIntranet01, which identify the corporate mail and intranet servers, respectively.

Although naming conventions can be helpful, don't go overboard. The names Eng-Server01, TechServer01, CorpMail01, and CorpIntranet01 help identify computers by role and location, but they aren't overly complex. Keeping things simple should help ensure that computer names are easy to remember and easy to work with. Stay away from overly complex names, such as SeattleSrvBldg48DC17 or SvrSeaB48F15-05, if at all possible. Overly complex names are unnecessary in most instances and probably contain information that most users don't need. For example, users won't care that a server is in building 48 or that it is on floor 15. In fact, that information might be too specific and could actually help someone who wants to break into or sabotage the corporate network. Instead of putting exact mapping information in the computer name, keep a spreadsheet that maps computer locations for administration use, and include only general information about location or department in the computer name.

Finally, keep in mind that computer names must be unique in the domain and must be 64 characters or less in length. The first 15 characters of the computer name are used as the pre–Windows 2000 computer name for NetBIOS communications and must be unique in the domain as well. Further, for DNS compatibility, the name should consist of only alphanumeric characters (A–Z, a–z, and 0–9) and the hyphen.

Network and Domain Membership Options

During installation, you must decide on several important network and domain membership options, such as the following:

- Which protocols the server will use
- Whether the server will be a member of the domain
- What networking components will be installed

Protocols

The only protocols that Windows Server 2008 installs by default are Transmission Control Protocol/Internet Protocol version 4 (TCP/IPv4) and Transmission Control Protocol/Internet Protocol version 6 (TCP/IPv6). Throughout this book, I'll refer to TCP/IPv4 and TCP/IPv6 collectively as TCP/IP. To correctly install TCP/IP, you must decide whether you want to use static IP addressing or dynamic IP addressing. For static IP addresses, you need the following information:

- IP address
- Subnet mask/subnet prefix length
- Default gateway
- Preferred DNS server

For dynamic IP addressing, the IP information is assigned automatically by an available Dynamic Host Configuration Protocol (DHCP) server. If no DHCP server is available, the server will autoconfigure itself. Autoconfigured addressing is typically nonroutable, so you must correct this issue after installation.

Domain Membership

Just about every server you install will be a member of a domain rather than a member of a workgroup (unless your company has a datacenter or you work exclusively in an isolated development lab). You can join a computer to a domain after installation. If you want to do that, you should have a computer account created in the domain (or create one while joining the domain using an account with Administrator or Account Operator rights). A computer account is similar to a user account in that it resides in the accounts database held in Active Directory Domain Services and is maintained by domain controllers.

If a server is a member of a domain, users with domain memberships or permissions can access the server and its resources based on, of course, their individual rights and permissions without having to have a separate logon. This means that users can log on once to the domain and work with resources for which they have permissions to access, and they won't be prompted to log on separately for each server they work with. In contrast, however, if a server is a member of a workgroup, users must log on each time they want to work with a server and its resources.

Networking Components

During installation, you have the opportunity to install networking components. The common networking components for servers are selected automatically. They include the following:

- **Client for Microsoft Networks** Allows the computer to access resources on Windows-based networks

- **File and Printer Sharing for Microsoft Networks** Allows other Windows-based computers to access resources on the computer (required for remote logon)

- **Internet Protocol version 4 (TCP/IPv4)** Allows the computer to communicate over the network by using TCP/IPv4

- **Internet Protocol version 6 (TCP/IPv6)** Allows the computer to communicate over the network by using TCP/IPv6

- **QoS Packet Scheduler** Helps the computer manage the flow of network traffic and prioritize services

- **Link-Layer Topology Discovery Mapper I/O Driver** Allows the computer to discover and locate other computers, devices, and networking components on the network.

- **Link-Layer Topology Discovery Responder** Allows the computer to be discovered and located on the network by other computers.

You can install additional clients, services, and protocols during installation, including Network Load Balancing and Reliable Multicast Protocol. However, try to keep additional component installation to a minimum. Install the components that you know must be installed. Don't install components you think you might need. Remember, not only will the additional components use disk space, they might also run as services. Services use system processing time and memory, and in some cases, they also could lower the security of the system by providing an additional way for someone to break into it.

Performing a Clean Installation

To perform a clean installation of Windows Server 2008, complete the following steps:

1. Start the Setup program using one of the following techniques:

○ For a new installation, turn on the computer and insert the Windows Server 2008 distribution media into the computer's DVD-ROM drive. Press a key to start Setup from your media when prompted.

○ For a clean installation over an existing installation, start the computer and log on using an account with administrator privileges. Insert the Windows Server 2008 distribution media into the computer's DVD-ROM drive. Setup should start automatically. If Setup doesn't start automatically, use Windows Explorer to access the distribution media and then double-click Setup.exe.

> **Note**
>
> When you try to install Windows Server 2008, you may find that your computer doesn't recognize the installation media. If the media is damaged, you'll need to obtain replacement media. Otherwise, make sure that the DVD drive is configured as a startup device and that you are inserting the media into the appropriate DVD drive.

> **Note**
>
> If Windows Setup encounters a problem during installation, you can select the Rollback option on the boot menu to start the Rollback wizard (*x*:\Sources\Rollback.exe). You can use this wizard to subsequently attempt to restore the previous version of Windows. If the Rollback wizard is successful, the previous version of Windows is completely restored. If the Rollback wizard is unsuccessful, the server typically is left in an unbootable state and you must either perform a full restore of the previous installation or a clean installation of Windows Server 2008.

2. On the next Setup page, note that you have several options:

○ **Install Now** By clicking Install Now, you can start the installation.

○ **What To Know Before Installing Windows Server 2008** By clicking What To Know Before Installing Windows Server 2008 you can review helpful information about installing Windows Server 2008.

3. If you are starting the installation from an existing operating system and are connected to a network or the Internet, choose whether to get updates during the installation. Click either Go Online To Get The Latest Updates For Installation or Do Not Get The Latest Updates For Installation.

4. With volume and enterprise licensed editions of Windows Server 2008, you might not need to provide a product key during installation of the operating system. With retail editions, however, you'll be prompted to enter a product key, and then click Next to continue. Keep the following in mind:

○ When entering the product key, be sure to enter a key for the server edition you want to install. You don't need to worry about using the correct letter case or entering dashes. Setup enters all letters you type in uppercase. When a dash is needed, Setup enters the dash automatically.

○ On the Type Your Product Key For Activation page, the Next button is available for clicking only when the Product Key box is empty or when you've entered all 29 of the required characters. If you want to enter a product key, you must type the full product key before the Next button is available for clicking. If you don't want to enter a product key at this time, leave the Product Key box blank and then click Next.

○ The Automatically Activate Windows When I'm Online check box is selected by default to ensure that you are prompted to activate the operating system next time you connect to the Internet. Windows Server 2008 must be activated within the first 30 days after installation. If you don't activate Windows Server 2008 in the allotted time, you see an error stating "Your activation period has expired" or that you have a "non-genuine version of Windows Server 2008 installed." Windows Server 2008 will then run in a reduced functionality mode. You'll need to activate and validate Windows Server 2008 as necessary to resume full functionality mode.

5. If you enter an invalid product key, Setup will continue to display the Type Your Product Key For Activation page. To let you know there's a problem with the product key, Setup displays the following warning in the lower portion of the page: "Your product key cannot be validated. Review your product key and make sure you have entered it correctly." Before you can continue, you'll need to change the product key so that it exactly matches the product key sticker. If you don't see the discrepancy causing the problem, you may want to delete the previously entered product key and then retype the product key. After you've reentered the product key, click Next to continue. As long as you've entered a valid product key, you'll continue to the next page. Otherwise, you'll have to repeat this step.

Chapter 3

6. If you did not enter a product key, you'll then see the warning prompt, asking whether you want to enter a product key at this time. If you click Yes, you'll return to the Type Your Product Key For Activation page. If you click No, you'll be allowed to continue with the installation without entering a product key.

7. You'll need to choose whether to perform a full-server installation or a core-server installation. If you selected to continue without entering a product key, you'll next need to select the edition of Windows Server 2008 to install as well. Although Setup will allow you to choose any edition, it is important to choose the edition that you purchased. If you choose the wrong edition, you will need to purchase that edition or you will need to reinstall the correct edition.

> **Note**
>
> If you entered a product key and the server edition you want to install is not listed, click the Back arrow and enter the correct product key for that server edition. Keep in mind that you can continue without entering a product key and this will allow you to choose any available edition. However, if you choose the wrong edition, you will need to purchase that edition or you will need to reinstall/upgrade to the correct edition.

8. If you are prompted for language and keyboard settings, choose your language, time and currency format, and your keyboard layout. Only one keyboard layout is available during installation. If your keyboard language and the language of the edition of Windows Server 2008 you are installing are different, you might see unexpected characters as you type. Ensure that you select the correct keyboard language to avoid this. When you are ready to continue with the installation, click Next.

9. The license terms for Windows Server 2008 have changed from previous releases of Windows. When prompted, review the license terms. Select the I Accept The License Terms check box and then click Next.

10. On the Which Type Of Installation Do You Want? page, you'll need to select the type of installation you want Setup to perform. Because you are performing a clean installation to completely replace an existing installation or configure a new computer, select Custom (Advanced) as the installation type. If you started Setup from the boot prompt rather than from within Windows itself, the upgrade option is disabled. In order to upgrade rather than perform a clean install, you'll need to restart the computer and boot the currently installed operating system. After you log on, you'll then need to start the installation.

11. On the Where Do You Want To Install Windows? page, you'll need to select the disk or disk and partition on which you want to install the operating

system. Windows Server 2008 requires between 8 and 40 GB of disk space for installation. Keep the following in mind:

- ○ When a computer has a single hard disk with a single partition encompassing the whole disk, the whole disk partition is selected by default and you could click Next to choose this as the install location. With a disk that is completely unallocated, you'll need to create the necessary partition for installing the operating system as discussed in "Creating, Deleting, and Extending Disk Partitions During Installation" on page 95.

- ○ When a computer has multiple disks or a single disk with multiple partitions, you'll need to either select an existing partition to use for installing the operating system or create one. You can create and manage partitions as discussed in "Creating, Deleting, and Extending Disk Partitions During Installation" on page 95.

- ○ You might see a warning message stating "This computer's hardware may not support booting to this disk." This can occur if the disk has not been initialized for use or if the firmware of the computer does not support starting the operating system from the selected disk. To resolve this problem, create one or more partitions on all the hard disks that are not initialized.

- ○ You cannot select or format a hard disk partition that uses FAT or FAT32 or has other incompatible settings. To work around this issue, you might want to convert the partition to NTFS. As the inability to select a disk or partition could also be due to a problem with the drivers for the hard disk, you might need to install the device drivers required by a hard disk.

- ○ When working with this page, you can access a command prompt to perform any necessary preinstallation tasks, to forcibly remove a disk partition that is locked, or to load device drivers to support hard disks that aren't listed as available but should be available. To learn more see "Performing Additional Administration Tasks During Installations" on page 90.

12. If the partition you've selected contains a previous Windows installation, Setup provides a prompt stating that existing user and application settings will be moved to a folder named Windows.old and that you must copy these settings to the new installation to use them. Click OK.

13. Click Next. Setup starts the installation of the operating system. During this procedure, Setup copies the full disk image of Windows Server 2008 to the location you've selected and then expands it. Afterward, Setup installs features based on the computer's configuration and detected hardware. This process requires several automatic restarts. When Setup finishes the installation, the operating system will be loaded and you'll see the logon screen. After you enter and confirm a password for the administrator account, you can log on.

14. You'll then see the Initial Configuration Tasks console. Use this console to perform initial configuration tasks, such as setting the computer name.

> **Use a Strong Password for the Administrator Account**
>
> A strong password uses a combination of uppercase letters, lowercase letters, numbers, and special characters. If your administrator password does not meet the Windows server criteria for strong passwords, a dialog box explaining the criteria for the administrator password appears and you are given the opportunity to change the password or continue with it as is. The use of a strong password for the Administrator account is a security step well worth taking. Weak passwords remain one of the more significant ways that security of a Windows network is compromised, yet they are one of the easiest to correct.

Performing an Upgrade Installation

Although Windows Server 2008 provides an upgrade option during installation, an upgrade with Windows Server 2008 isn't what you think it is. With an upgrade, the Windows Server 2008 Setup program performs a clean installation of the operating system followed by a migration of user settings, documents, and applications from the earlier version of Windows.

During the migration portion of the upgrade, Setup moves folders and files for the previous installation to a folder named Windows.old. As a result, the previous installation will no longer run. Settings are migrated because Windows Server 2008 doesn't store user and application information in the same way as earlier versions of Windows do. See Chapter 1, "Introducing Windows Server 2008," for more information on where Windows Server 2008 stores user data.

The steps you perform for an upgrade installation of Windows Server 2008 are nearly identical to those you follow for a clean installation. The key difference is that in step 10, you'll need to select the installation type as Upgrade. If you started Setup from the boot prompt rather than from within Windows itself, the upgrade option is disabled. In order to upgrade rather than perform a clean install, you'll need to restart the computer and boot the currently installed operating system. After you log on, you'll then need to start the installation.

Because you are upgrading the operating system, you do not need to choose an installation location. During this process, Setup copies the full disk image of Windows Server 2008 to the system disk. Afterward, Setup installs features based on the computer's configuration and detected hardware.

When Setup finishes the installation, the operating system will be loaded and you'll see the logon screen. After you log on, you'll see the Initial Configuration Tasks console, which you can use to perform initial configuration tasks.

Activation Sequence

After you install Windows Server 2008, you should configure TCP/IP networking as discussed in Chapter 21, "Managing TCP/IP Networking." If the type of licensing you are using requires product activation after installation, you should activate Windows within 30 days of installation. You have several activation options.

Activate Windows over the Internet

Before you activate Windows over the Internet, you should ensure that the Enhanced Security Configuration settings in Internet Explorer allow members of the Administrators group to use Internet content. This is currently the default setting. You can confirm this by performing the following steps:

1. In Server Manager, select the Server Manager node and then in the main pane scroll down until you see the Security Information section.

2. In the Security Information section, click the Configure IE ESC link.

3. In the Internet Explorer Enhanced Security Configuration dialog box, ensure that the Administrators On option is selected and then click OK. Optionally, you can also ensure that the Users On option is selected before clicking OK.

You can now activate Windows over the Internet without being restricted by the security configuration. To do this, perform the following steps:

1. Click Start, and then click Control Panel.

2. Click System And Maintenance\System and then click the Activate Windows Now link under Windows Activation.

3. In the Windows Activation dialog box, click Activate Windows Online Now. The computer then checks its Internet connection and attempts to activate the operating system. If this process fails, you'll need to resolve any issues that are preventing your computer from connecting to the Internet and then click Activate Windows Online Now again.

Activate Windows by Telephone

With activation over the telephone, you can go straight to product activation by performing the following steps:

1. Click Start, and then click Control Panel.

2. Click System And Maintenance\System and then click the Activate Windows Now link under Windows Activation.

3. In the Windows Activation dialog box, click Show Me Other Ways To Activate and then click Use The Automated Phone System.

4. Select a geographic or country location and then click Next to obtain a telephone number for your area. You will also get an installation ID, which is a very long string of numbers that you will need to enter into the automated customer service phone system.

Chapter 3

5. After you call the phone number and give the installation ID, you will get an activation code, which is another long string of numbers that you have to enter on the Activate Windows page before you can continue with the activation.

6. Click Next and follow the prompts to complete activation.

Performing Additional Administration Tasks During Installation

Sometimes, you forget to perform a preinstallation task prior to starting the installation. Rather than restarting the operating system, you can access a command prompt from within Setup or use advanced drive options to perform the necessary administrative tasks.

Accessing a Command Prompt During Installation

When you access a command prompt from within Setup, you access the MINWINPC environment used by Setup to install the operating system. During installation on the Where Do You Want To Install Windows? page, you can access a command prompt by pressing Shift+F10. As Table 3-5 shows, the mini Windows PC environment gives you access to many of the same command-line tools that are available in a standard installation of Windows Server 2008.

Table 3-5 Commands Available in the Mini Windows PC Environment

Command	Description
Arp	Displays and modifies the IP to physical address translation tables used by the Address Resolution Protocol (ARP).
Assoc	Displays and modifies file extension associations.
Attrib	Displays and changes file attributes.
Cacls	Displays or modifies access control lists of files.
Call	Calls a script or script label as a procedure.
CD/Chdir	Displays the name of or changes the current directory.
Chcp	Displays or sets the active code page number.
Chkdsk	Checks a disk for errors and displays a report.
Chkntfs	Displays the status of volumes. Sets or excludes volumes from automatic system checking when the computer is started.
Choice	Creates a selection list from which users can select a choice in batch scripts.
Cls	Clears the console window.
Cmd	Starts a new instance of the Windows command shell.
Color	Sets the colors of the command-shell window.

Command	Description
Comp	Compares the contents of two files or sets of files.
Compact	Displays or modifies the compression of files or sets of files.
Convert	Converts FAT volumes to NTFS.
Copy	Copies or combines files.
Date	Displays or sets the system date.
Del	Deletes one or more files.
Dir	Displays a list of files and subdirectories within a directory.
Diskcomp	Compares the contents of two floppy disks.
Diskcopy	Copies the contents of one floppy disk to another.
Diskpart	Invokes a text-mode command interpreter so that you can manage disks, partitions, and volumes using a separate command prompt and commands that are internal to Diskpart.
Doskey	Edits command lines, recalls Windows commands, and creates macros.
Echo	Displays messages, or turns command echoing on or off.
Endlocal	Ends localization of environment changes in a batch file.
Erase	See Del.
Exit	Exits the command interpreter.
Expand	Uncompresses files.
FC	Compares two files and displays the differences between them.
Find/Findstr	Searches for a text string in files.
For	Runs a specified command for each file in a set of files.
Format	Formats a floppy disk or hard drive.
Ftp	Transfers files.
Ftype	Displays or modifies file types used in file extension associations
Goto	Directs the Windows command interpreter to a labeled line in a script.
Graftabl	Enables Windows to display extended character sets in graphics mode.
Hostname	Prints the computer's name.
IF	Performs conditional processing in batch programs.
Ipconfig	Displays TCP/IP configuration.
Label	Creates, changes, or deletes the volume label of a disk.
Md/Mkdir	Creates a directory or subdirectory.
Mode	Configures a system device.
More	Displays output one screen at a time.
Mountvol	Manages a volume mount point.

Chapter 3

Command	Description
Move	Moves files from one directory to another directory on the same drive.
Nbtstat	Displays status of NetBIOS.
Net Accounts	Manages user account and password policies.
Net Computer	Adds or removes computers from a domain.
Net Config Server	Displays or modifies configuration of Server service.
Net Config Workstation	Displays or modifies configuration of Workstation service.
Net Continue	Resumes a paused service.
Net File	Displays or manages open files on a server.
Net Group	Displays or manages global groups.
Net Localgroup	Displays or manages local group accounts.
Net Pause	Suspends a service.
Net Print	Displays or manages print jobs and shared queues.
Net Session	Lists or disconnects sessions.
Net Share	Displays or manages shared printers and directories.
Net Start	Lists or starts network services.
Net Statistics	Displays workstation and server statistics.
Net Stop	Stops services.
Net Time	Displays or synchronizes network time.
Net Use	Displays or manages remote connections.
Net User	Displays or manages local user accounts.
Net View	Displays network resources or computers.
Netsh	Invokes a separate command prompt that allows you to manage the configuration of various network services on local and remote computers.
Netstat	Displays status of network connections.
Path	Displays or sets a search path for executable files in the current command window.
Pathping	Traces routes and provides packet loss information.
Pause	Suspends processing of a script and waits for keyboard input.
Ping	Determines if a network connection can be established.
Popd	Changes to the directory stored by Pushd.
Print	Prints a text file.
Prompt	Changes the Windows command prompt.

Command	Description
Pushd	Saves the current directory then changes to a new directory.
Rd/Rmdir	Removes a directory.
Recover	Recovers readable information from a bad or defective disk.
Reg Add	Adds a new subkey or entry to the Registry.
Reg Compare	Compares Registry subkeys or entries.
Reg Copy	Copies a Registry entry to a specified key path on a local or remote system.
Reg Delete	Deletes a subkey or entries from the Registry.
Reg Query	Lists the entries under a key and the names of subkeys (if any).
Reg Restore	Writes saved subkeys and entries back to the Registry.
Reg Save	Saves a copy of specified subkeys, entries, and values to a file.
Regsvr32	Registers and unregisters DLLs.
Rem	Adds comments to scripts.
Ren	Renames a file.
Replace	Replaces a file.
Route	Manages network routing tables.
Set	Displays or modifies Windows environment variables. Also used to evaluate numeric expressions at the command line.
Setlocal	Begins localization of environment changes in a batch file.
Sfc	Scans and verifies protected operating system files.
Shift	Shifts the position of replaceable parameters in scripts.
Start	Starts a new command-shell window to run a specified program or command.
Subst	Maps a path to a drive letter.
Time	Displays or sets the system time.
Title	Sets the title for the command-shell window.
Tracert	Displays the path between computers.
Tree	Graphically displays the directory structure of a drive or path.
Type	Displays the contents of a text file.
Ver	Displays the Windows version.
Verify	Tells Windows whether to verify that your files are written correctly to a disk.
Vol	Displays a disk volume label and serial number.
Xcopy	Copies files and directories.

Chapter 3

Forcing Disk Partition Removal During Installation

During installation, you may be unable to select the hard disk you want to use. This issue can occur if the hard disk partition contains an invalid byte offset value. To resolve this issue, you'll need to remove the partitions on the hard disk (which destroys all associated data) and then create the necessary partitions using the advanced options in the Setup program. During installation on the Where Do You Want To Install Windows? page, you can remove unrecognized hard disk partitions by following these steps:

1. Press Shift+F10 to start a command prompt. At the command prompt, type **diskpart**. This starts the DiskPart utility.

2. To view a list of disks on the computer, type **list disk**. Select a disk by typing **select disk *DiskNumber*** where *DiskNumber* is the number of the disk you want to work with.

3. To permanently remove the partitions on the selected disk, type **clean**. When the cleaning process finishes, type **create partition primary size=N** where *N* is the size of the space you want to allocate to the partition in megabytes.

4. When the create partition process finishes, click the back arrow button in the Install Windows dialog box. This will return you to the previous window.

5. On the Which Type Of Installation Do You Want? page, click Custom (Advanced) to start a custom install.

6. On the Where Do You Want To Install Windows? page, click the disk you previously cleaned to select it as the install partition. You can then continue with the installation as discussed previously.

Loading Disk Device Drivers During Installation

During installation, on the Where Do You Want To Install Windows? page, you can use the Load Drivers option to load the device drivers for a hard disk drive. Typically, you use this option when a disk drive you want to use for installing the operating system isn't available for selection because the device drivers aren't available.

To load the device drivers and make the hard disk available for use during installation, follow these steps:

1. During installation, on the Where Do You Want To Install Windows? page, click Load Drivers.

2. When prompted, insert the installation media into a floppy disk, CD, DVD, or USB flash drive, and then click OK. Setup will then search the computer's removable media drives for the device drivers.

    a. If Setup finds multiple device drivers, select the driver to install and then click Next.

b. If Setup doesn't find the device driver, click Browse to use the Browse For Folder dialog box to select the device driver to load, click OK, and then click Next.

You can use the Rescan button to have Setup rescan the computer's removable media drives for the device drivers. If you are unable to successfully install a device driver, click the back arrow button in the upper-left corner of the Install Windows dialog box to go back to the previous page.

Creating, Deleting, and Extending Disk Partitions During Installation

During installation, on the Where Do You Want To Install Windows? page, you can access a command prompt by pressing Shift+F10. At the command prompt, you can use DiskPart to perform disk management tasks. Creating a partition is the key task you'll need to perform, but you can also delete and extend partitions as necessary. You generally don't need to format partitions as Setup will handle this for you.

To create, delete, or extend disk partitions, follow these steps:

1. Press Shift+F10 to open a command prompt. At the command prompt, type **diskpart**. This starts the DiskPart utility.

2. To view a list of disks on the computer, type **list disk**.

3. Select a disk by typing **select disk *DiskNumber*** where *DiskNumber* is the number of the disk you want to work with.

4. List the existing partitions on the disk by typing **list partition**. You can now:

   ○ **Create a partition** Use available space to create a partition by typing **create partition primary size=N** where *N* is the size of the space to allocate in megabytes.

   ○ **Delete a partition** Select the partition to delete by typing **select partition** followed by the partition number and then delete it by typing **delete partition**.

   ○ **Extend a partition** Select the partition to extend by typing **select partition** followed by the partition number and then extend it by typing **extend size=N** where *N* is the size of the additional space to allocate in megabytes.

5. When you are finished working with disks, click the back arrow button in the Install Windows dialog box. This will return you to the previous window.

6. On the Which Type Of Installation Do You Want? page, click Custom (Advanced) to start a custom install.

7. On the Where Do You Want To Install Windows? page, click the disk you previously cleaned to select it as the install partition. You can then continue with the installation as discussed previously.

Chapter 3

Troubleshooting Installation

Most of the time, installation completes normally and the Windows operating system starts without any problems. Some of the time, however, installation won't complete or, after installation, the server won't start up, and you must troubleshoot to figure out what's happening. The good news is that installation problems are usually the result of something simple. The bad news is that simple problems are sometimes the hardest to find.

> **Note**
>
> For more information about troubleshooting and recovery, see Chapter 41, "Backup and Recovery." Beyond that, you'll also find troubleshooters in the Help And Support console and in the Microsoft Knowledge Base, which is available online at *http://support.micro-soft.com/*. Both are good resources for troubleshooting.

Start with the Potential Points of Failure

Setup can fail for a variety of reasons, but more often than not it's because of incompatible hardware components or failure of the system to meet the minimum requirements for Windows Server 2008 installation. With this in mind, start troubleshooting by looking at the potential points of failure and how these failure points can be resolved.

Setup Refuses to Install or Start

If a hardware component is incompatible with Windows Server 2008, this could cause failure of the installation or failure to start up after installation. Make sure that Windows Server 2008 is detecting the system hardware and that the hardware is in the Windows Server Catalog or on the Hardware Compatibility List (HCL). As discussed previously, you can perform a compatibility check prior to installing Windows Server 2008.

After you've started installation, however, it's too late. At this point, you have several choices. You can reboot to a working operating system and then restart the installation from the command prompt using Setup and one of the following debugging options:

- **/1394debug:<*channel*>** Enables kernel debugging over a FireWire (IEEE 1394) port on a specific channel.

- **/debug:<*port*>** Enables kernel debugging over a COM1 or COM2 port.

- **/usbdebug:<*target*>** Enables kernel debugging over a USB port to a specific target device.

These options put Setup in debug mode, which can help identify what is going wrong. If Setup determines you have hardware conflicts, you can try to configure the hardware and server firmware to eliminate the conflicts. Troubleshooting firmware involves booting the server to the firmware and then completing the following steps:

- **Examine the boot order of disk devices** You might want to configure the system so that it boots first from DVD-ROM. Watch out, though; after installation, don't keep booting to DVD-ROM thinking you are booting to the operating system—hey, we all get tired and sometimes we just have to stop and think for a moment. If the installation problem is that you keep going back to the installation screen after installing the operating system, you are probably inadvertently booting from DVD-ROM—and you're probably way too tired by now to realize it.

- **Check Plug and Play device configuration and interrupt reservations** If a system has older components or components that aren't Plug and Play compatible, you might have a device conflict for a hard-coded interrupt. For example, a non–Plug and Play sound card could be hard-coded to use interrupt 13, which is already in use by a Plug and Play device. To work around this, you must configure interrupt 13 under your Plug and Play BIOS settings to be reserved for a non–Plug and Play device. This ensures that Plug and Play does not attempt to use that interrupt and resolves the issue in most cases.

> **Note**
>
> The only sure way to avoid problems with non–Plug and Play devices is to avoid using them altogether.

Rather than spending time—which could run into several hours—trying to troubleshoot a hardware conflict, you might consider removing the hardware component if it's non-essential—and you might be surprised at what I consider nonessential at this stage. By nonessential, I mean almost anything that isn't needed to start up and give you a display for logon. You probably don't need a network card, a sound card, a multimedia controller card, a video coder/decoder (codec), or a removable media drive. If these items are incompatible, you might resolve the problem simply by removing them. You can always try to install the components again after installation is complete.

Setup Reports a Media or DVD-ROM Error

When you install directly from the Windows Server 2008 DVD-ROM or perform a network install from a distribution share, you might encounter a media error that causes Setup to fail. With an actual DVD-ROM, you might need to clean the DVD-ROM so that it can be read or use a different DVD drive. If a computer's sole DVD-ROM drive is the problem, you must replace the drive or install from a distribution share. If you are working with a distribution share, the share might not have all the necessary files, or you might encounter problems connecting to the share. Try using an actual DVD-ROM.

Chapter 3

Setup Reports Insufficient System Resources

Windows Server 2008 requires a minimum of 512 MB of RAM and about 10 GB of disk space. If the system doesn't have enough memory, Setup won't start. If Setup starts and detects that there isn't enough space, it might not continue or you might need to create a new partition or delete an existing partition to get enough free space to install the operating system.

Continue Past Lockups and Freezes

If you can get past the potential points of failure, you still might find that the installation locks up or freezes. In this case, you might get a Stop error; then again, you might not.

Most Stop errors have cryptic error codes rather than clear messages telling you what's wrong. If you get a Stop error, write down the error number or code, then refer to the Microsoft Knowledge Base (available online at *http://support.microsoft.com/*) for help troubleshooting the problem. To break out of the stop, you most likely will have to press Ctrl+Alt+Del (sometimes several times) to get the server to restart. If this doesn't break out of the stop, press and hold the power button on the server until it reboots. Alternatively, disconnect the system power, wait a few seconds, and then connect it again.

The Windows operating system should start up and go directly back to Setup. In some cases, you will see a boot menu. If so, choose the Windows Setup option to allow the Setup program to attempt to continue the installation. Setup could freeze again. If it does, stay with it, and repeat this process—sometimes it takes several tries to get completely through the installation process.

RAM and CPUs can also be the source of problems. Issues to watch out for include the following:

- **Incompatible RAM** Not all RAM is compatible, and you can't mix and match RAM of different speeds and types. Ensure that all RAM modules are the same type and speed. Further, RAM modules from different manufacturers could in some cases perform differently (read incompatibly), and in such a case, try changing the RAM so that all modules have the same manufacturer.

- **Malfunctioning RAM** Static discharges can ruin RAM faster than anything else. If you didn't ground yourself and use a static discharge wire before working with the RAM modules, you could have inadvertently fried the RAM so that the modules don't work at all or are malfunctioning. RAM could have also arrived in this condition from the manufacturer or distributor. There are several troubleshooting techniques for determining this. You could update firmware to add a wait state to the RAM so that if the RAM is partially faulty the system will still boot (but you still must replace the RAM eventually). You can also try removing some RAM modules or changing their order.

- **Incompatible processors** Not all processors are created equal, and I'm not just talking about their speed in megahertz (which you generally want to be the same for all processors on a server). Some processors might have a cache or configuration that is incompatible with the server hardware or other processors. Check the processor speed and type to ensure that it is compatible with the server. In some cases, you might need to change hardware jumpers, depending on the speed and type of your processors.

- **Misconfigured processors** Adding additional processors to a server isn't a simple matter of inserting them. Often, you must change jumpers on the hardware, remove several terminators (one for a power subcomponent and one for the processor—save them because, trust me, you might find that you need them), and then insert the new components. Check the hardware jumpers (even if you think there aren't any), and ensure that the processors and the power subcomponents you've added are seated properly. If you can't get the installation to continue or the server to start up, you might need to remove the components you've added. Watch out, though; you probably don't want to continue the installation until the processor issue is resolved—single-processor systems have a different threading and default configuration than multiprocessor systems, meaning this situation might not be a simple matter of adding the processor after installation and making it all work properly.

- **System processor cache problems** Sometimes there can be an issue with the system processor cache and compatibility with Windows Server 2008. Consult the server documentation to read the correct configuration settings available and how the cache can be disabled. If you suspect a problem with this, boot to firmware and temporarily disable the system processor cache, following the server documentation. After the installation is complete, you should be able to enable the cache to avoid a performance hit. Be sure to check both the hardware vendor support site and the Microsoft Knowledge Base to see whether any known issues with your server's processor cache exist.

TROUBLESHOOTING

RAM and CPUs are incompatible

You might be surprised at how common it is for incompatible RAM or CPUs to present problems, especially when installing enterprise-class servers. We had a problem once when we ordered all the components from a single hardware vendor that had verified the compatibility of every element down to the last detail only to find that the wrong processors and RAM were shipped for the systems ordered. The result was that every time we added the additional processors and RAM modules, the server wouldn't start up. The only recourse was to continue installation with the minimum processor and RAM configurations shipped or wait until replacements arrived. Electing to wait for replacements added time to the project but ultimately proved to be the right decision. You can bet that we were glad that we padded the project schedule to allow for the unexpected—because the unexpected usually happens.

Most of the time the installation or setup problem is caused by a compatibility issue with the Windows operating system, and that problem can be fixed by making changes to firmware settings. Sometimes, however, the problem is the firmware, and you'll find that you must upgrade the firmware to resolve the problem.

Check with the hardware vendor to see whether a firmware upgrade is available. If so, install it as the hardware vendor directs. If a new firmware version isn't available, you might be able to disable the incompatible option prior to setup. If this doesn't work, the option you changed wasn't the source of the problem and you should reenable it before continuing.

> **Note**
>
> Reenabling the option might be necessary because some hardware-specific firmware settings cannot be changed after the installation. Thus, the only way to enable the option would be to reinstall the operating system.

Finally, hard disk drive settings could also cause lockups or freezes, particularly if you are using Integrated Device Electronics (IDE) drives. When using IDE drives and controllers, you want to ensure that the system recognizes both the drives and the controllers and that both are enabled and configured properly in firmware. You might have to check jumper settings on the drives and the cables that connect the drives. As discussed previously, check for conflicts between the drives, controllers, and other system components. You might need to temporarily remove unnecessary components, such as the sound card, to see whether this resolves a conflict. If a DVD drive is on the same channel as the disk drives, try moving it to the secondary channel and configuring it as a master device. You can also try lowering the data transfer rate for the IDE drives.

Postinstallation

After you've installed a server and logged on, you might be ready to call it a day. Don't do this yet because you should first perform a few final postinstallation procedures:

- **Check devices** Use Device Manager, as discussed in "Viewing Device and Driver Details" on page 219, to look for undetected or malfunctioning hardware components. If you find problems, you might need to download and install updated drivers for the computer—you can download from another system and then transfer the files to the new server using a USB key or by burning the files to a CD/ DVD-ROM. If you removed any system hardware prior to installation, you might want to add it back in and then check again for conflicts and issues that must be corrected. You aren't finished with Device Manager until every piece of hardware is working properly.

- **Check the TCP/IP configuration** Ensure that the TCP/IP configuration is correct and that any additional settings are applied as necessary for the network. Test TCP/IP networking from the command line using Ping or Tracert and in the Windows operating system by trying to browse the network. See Chapter 21 for details.

- **Check event logs** Use Event Viewer to check the Windows event logs. Any startup warnings or errors will be written to the logs. See Chapter 11, "Performance Monitoring and Tuning," for details.

- **Check disk partitioning** Use the Computer Management console to check and finalize the disk partitions. Often, you must create the server's application partition or configure software RAID. See Chapter 14, "Storage Management," for details.

- **Optimize system configuration** Follow the techniques discussed in Chapter 4, "Managing Windows Server 2008," and Chapter 5, "Configuring Windows Server 2008," for tuning the operating system. For example, you might need to change the display settings, virtual memory page file usage, or the Server service configuration. You might also need to add local group and user accounts to the server per standard IT procedures.

- **Reboot for good measure** After you've configured the server and optimized its settings, perform a final reboot to ensure that (1) the server starts, (2) all the server services start, and (3) no other errors occur. You should reboot even if the changes you made don't require it—better to find out about problems now rather than at 3 A.M. on a Saturday night.

- **Prepare backup and recovery** You're almost done, but not quite. Don't forget about creating a full backup of the server. For details on backing up servers and creating recovery discs, see Chapter 41.

These postinstallation procedures are not only important, they're essential to ensuring that the server performs as well as can be expected. After these procedures are completed, you should have a server that is nearly ready for its role in a production environment. Don't make the server available to users just yet. To finish the job, you'll need to install and configure any necessary roles, role services, features, and applications. For certain, configuring these components requires quite a bit of extra work beyond installing the operating system. The installation of these additional components and applications could require one or more reboots or might require several time periods in which users are blocked from accessing the server or are requested not to connect to it as well. Remember, from the users' perspective, it's usually better to not have a resource than to be given one and then have it taken away (even temporarily). Finalize the server, then deploy it, and you'll have happier users.

Chapter 3

PART 2
Managing Windows Server 2008 Systems

Managing Windows Server 2008

Systems that run Windows Server 2008 are the heart of any Microsoft Windows network. These are the systems that provide the essential services and applications for users and the network as a whole. As an administrator, it is your job to keep these systems running, and to do this, you must understand the administration options available and put them to the best use possible. Your front-line defense in managing systems running Windows Server 2008 is the administration and support tools discussed in this chapter.

To run most of the administration tools, you must have administrator privileges. If these aren't included with your current account, you'll need to provide the credentials for the Administrator account when you see the User Account Control prompt. You'll find detailed information about User Account Control (UAC) in Chapter 10, "Software and User Account Control Administration."

Working with the Administration Tools

Any explanation of how to manage Windows Server 2008 systems must involve the administration and support tools that are included with the operating system. These are the tools you will use every day, so you might as well learn a bit more about them.

Many utilities are available for administering Windows Server 2008 systems. The tools you'll use the most include the following:

- **Control Panel** A collection of tools for managing system configuration. You can organize Control Panel in different ways according to the view you're using. A view is simply a way of organizing and presenting options. Category Control Panel view is the default view and it provides access to tools by category, tool, and key tasks. Classic Control Panel view is an alternative view that lists each tool separately by name.

- **Graphical administrative tools** The key tools for managing network computers and their resources. You can access these tools by selecting them individually on the Administrative Tools submenu.

- **Administrative wizards** Tools designed to automate key administrative tasks. You can access many administrative wizards in Server Manager—the central administration console for Windows Server 2008.

- **Command-line utilities** You can launch most administrative utilities from the command line. In addition to these utilities, Windows Server 2008 provides others that are useful for working with Windows Server 2008 systems.

The following sections provide brief introductions to these administrative utilities. Additional details for key tools are provided throughout this book. Keep in mind that to use these utilities you might need an account with administrator privileges.

Using Control Panel Utilities

Control Panel contains utilities for working with a system's setup and configuration. With Classic Start Menu, you can access these tools by clicking Start, pointing to Settings, and then selecting Control Panel. With Simple Start Menu, you can access these tools by clicking Start and then selecting Control Panel.

Many Control Panel tools and related Properties dialog boxes can be opened directly by clicking Start, entering the name of the Control Panel Item with the .cpl extension, and pressing Enter. In the Windows\System32 folder these items are listed with the Control Panel Item type. For example, enter inetcpl.cpl to open the Internet Properties dialog box.

Some common utilities previously found in Control Panel have been moved. Windows Server 2008 does not use Add Or Remove Programs. The available services and components on the server are managed through roles, role services, and features discussed in Chapter 7, "Configuring Roles, Role Services, and Features." Installed programs are managed through the Programs And Features utility. Scheduled Tasks has been renamed Task Scheduler and is accessible in the Computer Management and Server Manager consoles and is also an option on the Administrative Tools menu.

Using Graphical Administrative Tools

Most administration tools are found on the Administrative Tools menu and can be run by clicking Start, pointing to All Programs, and then selecting Administrative Tools. As Table 4-1 shows, dozens of administration tools are available for working with Windows Server 2008. The tool you use depends on what you want to do and sometimes on how much control you want over the aspect of the operating system you are seeking to manage. Several tools, including Server Manager and Computer Management, are discussed later in this section. Other tools are discussed later in this chapter or in other appropriate chapters of this book.

Table 4-1 **Tools for Administration**

Administrative Tool	Description
Active Directory Domains And Trusts	Used to manage trust relationships between domains.
Active Directory Rights Management Services	Used to view and change configuration settings for Active Directory Rights Management Services (RMS) clusters in the enterprise.
Active Directory Sites And Services	Used to create sites and to manage the replication of Active Directory information.
Active Directory Users And Computers	Used to manage users, groups, contacts, computers, organizational units (OUs), and other objects in Active Directory Domain Services.
Certification Authority	Used to create and manage server certificates for servers and users on the network. Certificates are used to support Public Key Infrastructure (PKI) encryption and authentication.
Computer Management	Used to manage services, devices, disks, and the system hardware configuration. It is also used to access other system tools.
Data Sources (ODBC)	Used to add, remove, and configure Open Database Connectivity (ODBC) data sources and drivers.
DFS Management	Used to create and manage distributed file systems (DFS) that connect shared folders from different computers.
DHCP	Used to configure and manage the Dynamic Host Configuration Protocol (DHCP) service.
DNS	Used to configure and manage the Domain Name System (DNS) service, which can be integrated with Active Directory.
Event Viewer	Used to view the system event logs and manage event log configurations.
Failover Cluster Management	Used to manage failover clustering available with Windows Server 2008 Enterprise and Windows Server 2008 Datacenter. Clustering allows groups of computers to work together, providing failover support and additional processing capacity.
Fax Service Manager	Used to manage fax services and servers.
File Server Resource Manager	Used to manage directory quotas, file screening, and reports.
Group Policy Management	Used to configure and manage Group Policy objects (GPOs).
Internet Information Services (IIS) 6.0 Manager	Used to manage Windows Web servers running IIS 6.0.
Internet Information Services (IIS) Manager	Used to manage Windows Web servers running IIS 7.0 or later.
iSCSI Initiator	Used to connect to iSCSI targets and configure connection settings.
Local Security Policy	Used to view and manage settings for local security policy.

Chapter 4

Administrative Tool	Description
Memory Diagnostics Tool	Used to perform diagnostics testing on a computer's physical memory.
Network Load Balancing Manager	Used to manage Network Load Balancing (NLB) configuration settings and clusters.
Network Policy Server	Used to manage Network Access Policy (NAP) client settings, policies, and policy servers.
Print Management	Used to manage Windows 2000 or later print servers as well as related printers, print queues, print drivers, and so on.
Reliability And Performance Monitor	Used to display details on system reliability and performance. Configure traces and data collectors to obtain diagnostics and performance reports.
Remote Desktops	Used to connect to multiple remote desktops.
Routing and Remote Access	Used to configure and manage the Routing and Remote Access service, which controls routing interfaces, dynamic Internet Protocol (IP) routing, and remote access.
Security Configuration Wizard	Used to create security policies based on server roles.
Server Manager	Used to manage roles, role services, and features. Access diagnostics, configuration, and storage.
Services	Used to manage the startup and configuration of Windows services.
Services for Network File System (NFS)	Used to configure and maintain Services for NFS.
Share and Storage Management	Used to manage network shares and volumes. Provision storage for storage area networks (SANs).
Storage Explorer	Used to view and manage storage on SANs.
System Configuration	Used to perform startup troubleshooting and manage the system startup configuration.
Task Scheduler	Used to view and manage scheduled tasks.
Terminal Services Configuration	Used to manage Terminal Service protocol configurations and server settings.
Terminal Services Manager	Used to manage and monitor Terminal Service users, sessions, and processes.
Windows Deployment Services	Used to manage servers, devices, and system images used for deployments.
Windows Firewall with Advanced Security	Used to configure and manage firewall and IP Security (IPSec) policies.
Windows Server Backup	Used to manage backup and recovery. Also allows you to schedule automatic backups.

Chapter 4

Administrative Tool	Description
Windows System Resource Manager	Used to manage resource usage on a per-processor basis.
WINS	Used to manage WINS. This service resolves NetBIOS names to IP addresses and is used with computers running versions earlier than Microsoft Windows 2000.

Usually you can use graphical administrative tools to manage the system that you're currently logged on to, as well as systems throughout Windows Server 2008 domains. For example, in the Event Viewer console you specify the computer you want to work with by right-clicking the Event Viewer node in the left pane and then choosing Connect To Another Computer. This opens the Select Computer dialog box shown in Figure 4-1. You can then choose Another Computer and type the name of the computer, as shown.

> **Note**
>
> You can now connect to another server using alternate credentials. To do this, select the Connect As Another User check box and then click Set User. After you select or type the account name to use in the form *DOMAIN\UserName*, such as CPANDL\WilliamS, type the account password and then click OK.

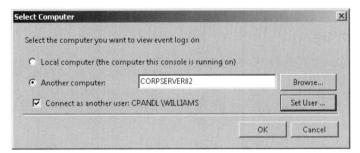

Figure 4-1 Connecting to another computer allows you to manage remote resources.

Which administrative tools are available on a server depends on its configuration. When you add roles, role services, and features, the related management tools are installed on the server. With Windows Server 2008, remote management is made possible by installing the Remote Server Administration Tools. If you want to manage a role, role service, or feature on another server and the management tool isn't available, you can install the related management tool by following these steps:

1. Click the Server Manager button on the Quick Launch toolbar. Alternatively, click Start, point to Administrative Tools, and then click Server Manager.

2. In Server Manager, select the Features node and then click Add Features.

3. In the Select Features dialog box, you'll find the administration tools under Remote Server Administration Tools. Tools are organized into two general categories: Role Administration Tools and Feature Administration Tools. Expand Remote Server Administration Tools.

4. To install an administration tool, select the check box for the related feature. When you select the first tool, Windows Server 2008 displays a warning prompt about additional features required to manage resources remotely. Click Add Required Features.

5. Click Next and then click Install.

The Microsoft Remote Server Administration Tools for Windows Vista are available on the Microsoft Download Center and Windows Update Web sites as optional updates to Windows Vista Business. These tools enable you to remotely manage roles and features in Windows Server 2008 from a computer running Windows Vista with Service Pack 1 or later. These tools are a replacement for the Windows Server 2003 Administration Tools Pack. The tools are compatible with both 32-bit and 64-bit versions of Windows Vista and can be used to manage both 32-bit and 64-bit versions of Windows Server 2008 whether servers are running full-server or core-server installations.

You should not install the Microsoft Remote Server Administration Tools for Windows Vista on a computer that has the Windows Server 2003 Administration Tools Pack or the Window 2000 Administration Tools Pack installed. You must remove all versions of earlier Administration Tools Pack tools from the computer before installing the Microsoft Remote Server Administration Tools for Windows Vista.

Using Command-Line Utilities

Many command-line utilities are included with Windows Server 2008. Most of the utilities you'll work with as an administrator rely on TCP/IP. Because of this, you should install TCP/IP networking before you experiment with these tools.

Utilities to Know

As an administrator, you should familiarize yourself with the following command-line utilities:

- **Appcmd** Displays and manages the configuration of IIS.

- **Arp** Displays and manages the IP to physical address mappings used by Windows Server 2008 to send data on the TCP/IP network.

- **Bcdedit** Displays and manages boot configuration data on the local system.

- **Dnscmd** Displays and manages the configuration of DNS services.

- **Diskpart** Displays and manages disk partitions on local and remote systems.

- **Ftp** Starts the built-in FTP client.

- **Hostname** Displays the computer name of the local system.

- **Ipconfig** Displays the TCP/IP properties for network adapters installed on the system. You can also use it to renew and release DHCP information.

- **Nbtstat** Displays statistics and current connections for NetBIOS over TCP/IP.

- **Net** Displays a family of useful networking commands.

- **Netsh** Displays and manages the network configuration of local and remote computers.

- **Netstat** Displays current TCP/IP connections and protocol statistics.

- **Nslookup** Checks the status of a host or IP address when used with DNS.

- **Pathping** Traces network paths and displays packet loss information.

- **Ping** Tests the connection to a remote host.

- **Route** Manages the routing tables on the system.

- **Schtasks** Displays and manages scheduled tasks on local and remote systems.

- **ServerManagerCmd** Displays and manages the roles, roles services, and features on the system.

- **Tracert** During testing, determines the network path taken to a remote system.

- **Wbadmin** Performs backup and recovery operations, including system state recovery and recovery of any type of disk to an alternate location. Also gets disk details including name, GUID, available space, and related volumes.

- **Wevtutil** Displays and manages event logs on local and remote systems.

To learn how to use these command-line tools, type the name at a command prompt followed by /?. Windows Server 2008 then provides an overview of how the command is used (in most cases).

Using Net Tools

You can more easily manage most of the tasks performed with the Net commands by using graphical administrative tools and Control Panel utilities. However, some of the Net tools are very useful for performing tasks quickly or for obtaining information, especially during telnet sessions to remote systems. These commands include the following:

- **Net Start** Starts a service on the system.

- **Net Stop** Stops a service on the system.

- **Net Time** Displays the current system time or synchronizes the system time with another computer.

Chapter 4

- **Net Use** Connects and disconnects from a shared resource.

- **Net View** Displays a list of network resources available to the system.

To learn how to use any of the Net command-line tools, type **net help** at a command prompt followed by the command name, such as **net help start**. Windows Server 2008 then provides an overview of how the command is used.

Using Windows PowerShell

For additional flexibility in your command-line scripting, you might want to install and use Windows PowerShell. PowerShell is a full-featured command shell that can use built-in commands called *cmdlets* and built-in programming features as well as standard command-line utilities. Although PowerShell is not installed by default, you can install PowerShell by completing the following steps:

1. Click the Server Manager button on the Quick Launch toolbar. Alternatively, click Start, point to Administrative Tools, and then click Server Manager.

2. In Server Manager, select the Features node and then click Add Features.

3. In the Select Features dialog box, scroll down and then select Windows PowerShell.

4. Click Next and then click Install.

As the included version of PowerShell might not be the most recent, however, you might want to check the Microsoft Download Center Web site for a more recent version. After you've installed PowerShell, you'll find a program shortcut on the Start menu. If you want to invoke PowerShell from a command prompt, keep in mind that the related executable (powershell.exe) is in the %SystemRoot%\System32\WindowsPowerShell\ *Version* directory, where *Version* is the version of PowerShell you installed, such as v1.0 or v2.0. The directory path for the most recently installed version should be in your command path by default. This ensures that you can start PowerShell from a command prompt without first having to change to the related directory.

After starting the Windows PowerShell, you can enter the name of a cmdlet at the prompt and it will run in much the same way as a command-line command. You can also execute cmdlets from within scripts. Cmdlets are named using verb-noun pairs. The verb tells you what the cmdlet does in general. The noun tells you what specifically the cmdlet works with. For example, the get-variable cmdlet either gets all Windows PowerShell environment variables and returns their values or gets a specifically named environment variable and returns its values. The common verbs associated with cmdlets are:

- **Get-** Queries a specific object or a subset of a type of object, such as a specified mailbox or all mailbox users.

- **Set-** Modifies specific settings of an object.

- **Enable-** Enables a setting or mail-enables a recipient.

- **Disable-** Disables an enabled setting or mail-disables a recipient.

- **New-** Creates a new instance of an item, such as a new mailbox.

- **Remove-** Removes an instance of an item, such as a mailbox.

At the Windows PowerShell prompt, you can get a complete list of cmdlets available by typing **help *-***. To get help documentation on a specific cmdlet, type **help** followed by the cmdlet name, such as **help get-variable**.

All cmdlets have configurable aliases as well that act as shortcuts for executing cmdlets. To list all aliases available, type **get-item -path alias:** at the PowerShell prompt. You can create an alias that invokes any command using the following syntax:

```
new-item -path alias:AliasName -value:FullCommandPath
```

where *AliasName* is the name of the alias to create and *FullCommandPath* is the full path to the command to run, such as:

```
new-item -path alias:sm -value:c:\windows\system32\compmgmtlauncher.exe
```

This example creates the alias *sm* for starting Server Manager. To use this alias, you would simply type **sm** and then press Enter when you are working with the PowerShell.

Using the Initial Configuration Tasks Console

The Initial Configuration Tasks console (shown on the next page) can help you quickly set up a new server. Windows Server 2008 automatically starts this console after you complete the installation of the operating system. If you do not want the console to start each time you log on, select the Do Not Show This Window At Logon check box in the lower-left corner of the console window. If you've closed the console and want to reopen it, or you've configured the console so that it doesn't start automatically, you can start the console at any time by clicking Start, typing **oobe** in the Search box, and then pressing Enter.

You can use the Initial Configuration Tasks console to perform initial configuration tasks, including those listed in Table 4-2. I'll discuss the related configuration tasks and technologies in more detail throughout this and other chapters in this book.

Chapter 4

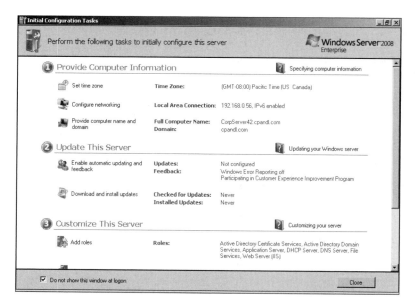

Table 4-2 **Initial Configuration Tasks**

Configuration Option	Description
Add Features	Use this option to start the Add Features Wizard, which you can then use to install features on the server. By default, servers have no configured features.
Add Roles	Use this option to start the Add Roles Wizard, which you can then use to install roles on the server. By default, servers have no configured roles.
Configure Networking	Use this option to display the Network Connections console. You can then configure available network connections.
Configure Windows Firewall	Use this option to display the basic Windows Firewall utility. You can then configure the basic Windows Firewall.
Download And Install Updates	Use this option to display the Windows Update utility in Control Panel, which you can then use to enable automatic updating or check for updates.
Enable Automatic Updating And Feedback	Use this option to enable Windows automatic updating and feedback. By default, servers are not configured for automatic updating but are configured to provide automatic feedback.
Enable Remote Desktop	Use this option to display the System Properties dialog box with the Remote tab selected. You can then configure Remote Desktop.
Provide Computer Name And Domain	Use this option to display the System Properties dialog box with the Computer Name tab selected. You can then change a computer's name and domain information.
Set Time Zone	Use this option to display the Date And Time dialog box. You can then configure the server's time zone.

Working with Computer Management

Computer Management provides tools for managing local and remote systems. The tools available through the console tree provide the core functionality and are divided into the following three categories as shown in the accompanying screen:

- System Tools

- Storage

- Services And Applications

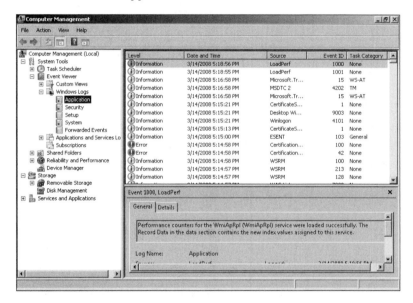

Computer Management System Tools

The Computer Management System Tools are designed to manage systems and view system information. The available system tools are these:

- **Task Scheduler** Used to view the Task Scheduler Library as well as to create and manage tasks.

- **Event Viewer** Used to view the event logs on the selected computer. Event logs are covered in Chapter 11, "Performance Monitoring and Tuning."

- **Shared Folders** Used to manage the properties of shared folders as well as sessions for users working with shared folders and the files the users are working with. Managing shared folders is covered in Chapter 17, "File Sharing and Security."

- **Local Users And Groups** On non–domain controller (DC) computers, used to manage local users and local user groups on the currently selected computer.

Chapter 4

Local users and local user groups aren't a part of Active Directory and are managed instead through the Local Users And Groups view. Domain controllers don't have local users or groups, and because of this there isn't a Local Users And Groups view. Local users and groups are discussed in Chapter 35, "Managing Users, Groups, and Computers."

- **Reliability And Performance** Used to monitor system reliability and performance through charts and logs. You can also use this tool to alert users of adverse performance conditions. For more information on performance logging and alerting, see "Performance Logging" on page 363.

- **Device Manager** Used as a central location for checking the status of any device installed on a computer and for updating the associated device drivers. You can also use it to troubleshoot device problems. Managing devices is covered in Chapter 8, "Managing and Troubleshooting Hardware."

Computer Management Storage Tools

The Computer Management Storage tools display drive information and provide access to drive management tools. The available Storage tools include:

- **Removable Storage** Used to manage removable media devices and tape libraries. It can also help you track work queues and operator requests related to removable media devices. Removable Storage is discussed further in Chapter 19, "Using Removable Media."

- **Disk Management** Used to manage hard disks and the way they are partitioned. You can also use it to manage volume sets and redundant array of independent disks (RAID) arrays. Disk Management is discussed in "Configuring Storage" on page 419.

Computer Management Services And Applications Tools

The Computer Management Services And Applications tools help you manage services and applications installed on the server. Any application or service-related task that can be performed in a separate tool can be performed through the Services And Applications node as well. For example, if the currently selected system has DHCP installed, you can manage DHCP through the server Applications And Services node. You could also use the DHCP tool in the Administrative Tools folder, and either way, you can perform the same tasks.

Working with Server Manager

The Server Manager console (shown in the next screen) is designed to handle core system-administration tasks. You'll spend a lot of time working with this tool, and you should get to know every detail. Start the Server Manager console with either of the following techniques:

- Choose Start, point to Administrative Tools, and then select Server Manager.

- Click Server Manager on the Quick Launch toolbar.

The main window has a two-pane view similar to Computer Management. You use the console tree in the left pane for navigation and tool selection. In the left pane, the primary nodes are divided into five broad categories:

- **Roles** Provides an overview of the status of the roles installed on a server as well as options for managing the roles. For each installed role, you'll find a node that you can select to view a detailed status of the role. Expand a role's node to display related management tools.

- **Features** Provides an overview of the status of the features installed on the server as well as options for managing features. Features that you add—such as Windows Server Backup—are included in Server Manager.

- **Diagnostics** Provides access to general-purpose tools for managing services and devices, monitoring performance, and viewing events.

- **Configuration** Provides access to general-purpose configuration tools.

- **Storage** Provides access to drive management tools.

The right pane is the details pane. When you select the top-level Server Manager node in the left pane, you get an overview of the server configuration in the right pane. Under Server Summary, you'll find the following sections:

- **Computer Information** The Computer Information section details list the computer name, workgroup/domain name, local administrator account name, network configuration, and product ID. You'll also find the options for changing system properties, viewing network connections, and configuring Remote Desktop.

Chapter 4

- **Security Information** The Security Information section details list the state of the Windows Firewall, the Windows Update configuration, the last time updates were checked for and installed, and the status of Internet Explorer Enhanced Security Configuration (IE ESC). You'll also find the options for accessing Windows Firewall With Advanced Security, configuring updates, running the Security Configuration Wizard, and configuring Internet Explorer Enhanced Security Configuration.

> **Note**
>
> When IE ESC is enabled, Internet security zones are configured as follows: the Internet zone is set to Medium-High, the Trusted Sites zone is set to Medium, the Local Intranet zone is set to Medium-Low, and the Restricted zone is set to High. When IE ESC is enabled, the following Internet settings are changed: the Enhanced Security Configuration dialog box is on, third-party browser extensions are off, sounds in Web pages are off, animations in Web pages are off, signature checking for downloaded programs is on, server certificate revocation is on, encrypted pages are not saved, temporary Internet files are deleted when the browser is closed, warnings for secure and nonsecure mode changes are on, and memory protection is on.

- **Roles Summary** The Roles Summary section lists the roles installed on the server. In this section, you'll also find options for going to roles, adding roles, and removing roles.

- **Features Summary** The Features Summary section lists the features installed on the server. In this section, you'll also find options for adding and removing features.

- **Resources And Support** The Resources And Support section lists the current settings for the Customer Experience Improvement Program and Windows Error Reporting. You'll also find options for participating in the Customer Experience Improvement Program (CEIP), configuring Windows Error Reporting (WER), and accessing the Windows Server TechCenter online at the Microsoft Web site.

In addition to roles and features that are included with Windows Server 2008 by default, Server Manager enables integration of additional roles and features that are available on the Microsoft Download Center and Windows Update Web sites as optional updates to Windows Server 2008.

Using Control Panel

Clicking the taskbar's Start button and then clicking Control Panel displays Control Panel. Control Panel contains consoles and utilities for managing server hardware and operating system settings. Control Panel in Windows Server 2008 has two views:

- Category Control Panel, shown in the following screen, is the default view that provides access to system utilities by category, utility, and key tasks. Category Control Panel view is also referred to simply as Control Panel.

- Classic Control Panel is an alternate view that provides the look and functionality of Control Panel in Windows 2000 and earlier versions of Windows. With Classic Control Panel, each Control Panel utility is listed separately by name.

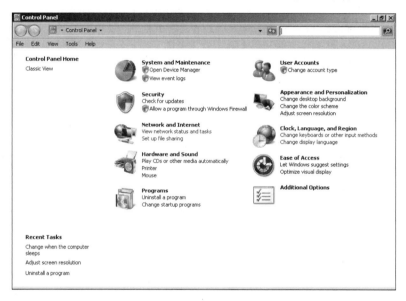

Because Category Control Panel provides quick access to frequent tasks, it is the view you typically will use most often. With this view, Control Panel opens as a console on which categories of utilities are listed. For each category, there's a top-level link and under this are several of the most frequently performed tasks for the category.

Clicking a category link provides a list of utilities in that category. For each utility listed within a category there's a link to open the utility and under this are several of the most frequently performed tasks for the utility.

In Category Control Panel view, all utilities and tasks run with a single click. The left pane of the console has a link to take you to the Control Panel Home page, links for each category, and links for recently performed tasks. Not only is this very efficient, but it's very easy to use.

As you might already know, some Control Panel utilities offer a fairly simple interface and are easy to work with, while others are fairly complex. Utilities that require little or no explanation are not discussed in this text; you will find a discussion of some of the more complex utilities later in this section.

Note

When you are working with Category Control Panel view, you'll see a Search box in the upper-right corner. To quickly find what you are looking for, type in part of the tool or task name. Consider the following example: Normally, you access the Change The Display Setting task under Control Panel\Appearance And Personalization\Personalization, which requires you to navigate through several Control Panel pages. If you type **display** in the Search box instead, you can quickly display this task and click it.

Using the Appearance And Personalization Console

In Windows Server 2008, you can access Personalization settings by clicking Start, Control Panel, Appearance And Personalization, and then Personalization. As Figure 4-2 shows, this displays the Personalization page in Control Panel.

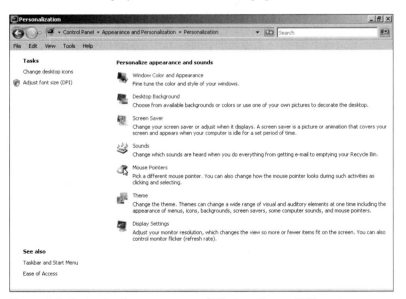

Figure 4-2 Customize the appearance of Windows Server 2008.

The available personalization settings are:

- **Window Color And Appearance** Sets the user experience level and color scheme for your computer. On the Personalization page, click Window Color And Appearance. In the Color Scheme list, choose the desired color scheme. Click OK to save your settings or continue with the next procedure. While you are working with the Appearance Settings dialog box, you may want to set appearance effects for screen fonts, shadows under menus, and display of window contents while dragging. In the Appearance Settings dialog box, click the Effects button and then use the options available to manage the display effects. By default, Windows Server 2008 smoothes the edges of screen fonts to make them easier to read. Typically, this is the desired behavior. For CRT monitors, you'll want to use the Standard setting. For LCD monitors, you'll want to use the ClearType setting.

- **Desktop Background** Controls the desktop background colors and pictures used. With Windows Server 2008, a solid color is generally what you want to ensure that server performance is not affected by displaying user backgrounds. On the Personalization page in Control Panel, click Desktop Background. Solid Colors is selected by default in the Location list, allowing you to choose from over 50 background colors or create your own background color by clicking More and then using the Color dialog box to select or mix your color. After you've located the color you want to use, click it to select it and then click OK.

- **Screen Saver** Controls the screen saver and when it is displayed. Screen savers turn on when a computer has been idle for a specified period, and offer the ability to password-lock your computer automatically when the screen saver turns on. Windows Server 2008 performs many housekeeping tasks in the background when the computer is idle. On the Personalization page in Control Panel, click Screen Saver. Use the Screen Saver list box to select a screen saver and then click OK. Although you can install additional screen savers, the standard screen savers are the best. None turns off the screen saver. Blank displays a blank screen, that is, a screen with a black background and no text or images. Windows Logo intermittently displays the Windows logo and arcing bands of lines against a black background.

- **Sounds** Controls the system sounds used by Windows Server 2008. On the Personalization page in Control Panel, click Sounds. Use the Sound Scheme list box to choose the sound scheme to use, and then click OK. Use the No Sounds scheme to turn off system sounds and the Windows Default scheme to turn on system sounds. Generally, you do not want to enable the Windows Audio Service, so click No if prompted to enable this service.

- **Mouse Pointers** Controls the mouse pointers used by Windows Server 2008. On the Personalization page in Control Panel, click Mouse Pointers. Use the Scheme list box to choose the pointer scheme to use and then click OK to save your settings.

- **Theme** Sets the theme used by Windows Server 2008. A theme is a collection of appearance settings that includes the desktop background, sounds, and mouse pointers used by Windows Server 2008. On the Personalization page in Control Panel, click Theme. In the Theme Settings dialog box, click Save As and then use the Save As dialog box to save your current appearance settings as a theme. If you want to use a theme saved to an alternate location, select Browse in the Theme list

Chapter 4

and then use the Open Theme dialog box to select the .theme file that contains the saved theme.

- **Display Settings** Controls monitors used by Windows Server 2008, their display resolution, and their refresh rate. Also allows you to extend your desktop onto a second monitor. On the Personalization page in Control Panel, click Display Settings. This opens the Display Settings dialog box. Use the Resolution slider to set the display size, such as 1600 × 1200 pixels. Use the Colors list box to select a color quality, such as Highest (32 Bit). Click OK.

Using the Date And Time Utility

Date And Time, as shown in Figure 4-3, is used to view or set a system's date, time, and time zone. You can manually set a computer's date and time by completing the following steps:

1. On the desktop taskbar, click the clock in the system tray and then click Change Date And Time Settings. This displays the Date And Time Settings dialog box.

2. To change the date and time, click Change Date And Time. Use the options shown in Figure 4-3 to set the system date and time as appropriate, and then click OK.

Figure 4-3 Set the computer's date and time.

4. To change the time zone, click Change Time Zone. Use the options shown in Figure 4-4 to set the time zone for the computer. Some time zones within the United States and abroad use daylight saving time. If you select a time zone where this is applicable, you'll be able to select the Automatically Adjust Clock For Daylight Saving Time check box. Use daylight saving time or clear this check box so that daylight saving time is not used.

Figure 4-4 Change the computer's time zone.

5. When you configure your computer to use daylight saving time, the Date And Time dialog box tells you the date and time when daylight saving time starts and ends as well as how the clock will be adjusted. If you want to be reminded one week before this occurs, select the Remind Me One Week Before This Change Occurs check box.

6. Click OK to save your settings.

Maintain Accurate System Time to Ensure Logon

Don't overlook the importance of the Date And Time settings. In a domain, the system time is checked during logon, and a discrepancy of more than a few minutes between the domain controller and the computer to which you are logging on can result in logon failure. Keep in mind that domain controllers do all their internal work in universal time and, though, they don't care about the time zone, an incorrect time zone setting can lead to denial of logon. Instead of setting the time on individual computers in the domain manually, you can use the Windows Time Service to synchronize time automatically on the network.

Using the Folder Options Utility

The Folder Options utility, shown in the following screen, is used to control how Windows Explorer displays files and folders and to set a wide variety of folder and file options, including the type of desktop used, the folder views used, whether offline files are used, and whether you must single-click or double-click to open items.

Chapter 4

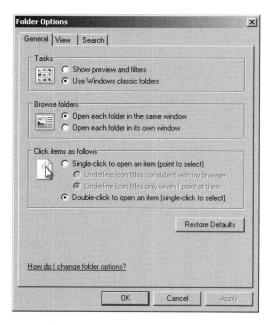

In Windows Server 2008, you can access the Folder Options utility by clicking Start, Control Panel, Appearance And Personalization, and then clicking Folder Options. As an administrator, you will probably want to set the following options on the General tab:

- **Single-Click To Open An Item (Point To Select)** Select this option to enable single-click to open and point to select.

> **Note**
>
> Because menu options and Control Panel options open with a single click by default, you might want to configure your computer to use single-click to open items such as documents as well. This might help you avoid confusion as to whether you need to click or double-click. When you have single-click open configured, pointing to an item selects it.

- **Show Hidden Files And Folders** Select this option to see hidden files and folders.

- **Hide Extensions For Known File Types** Clear this check box to see file names as well as file extensions.

- **Hide Protected Operating System Files** Clear this check box so that you can see and work with operating system files, which are otherwise hidden.

Using the Regional and Language Options Utility

The Regional and Language Options utility is used to set country-specific standards and formats, as shown in the following screen. In different countries, the unit of measurement, currency, and date formatting can be different. To change the settings, access the Control Panel, click Clock, Language, And Region, and then click Regional And Language Options. By choosing a language (country) in the Current Format list, you choose all the appropriate settings for numbers, currency, dates, and times. Examples of the formatting standards for the selected region are displayed as well.

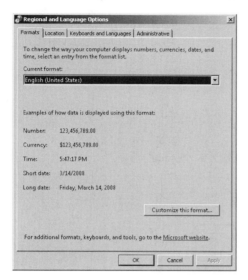

You can customize these settings by clicking Customize This Format and then using the Customize Regional Options dialog box to modify the basic number, currency, time, and date settings for the region. Regional settings are also used to specify your present location for the purposes of presenting local information in dialog boxes and within Help And Support Services windows. You set the system location by using the Location list on the Location tab. You'll want to keep track of localized versions in use and the locations in which they are used.

To configure support for additional display and input languages, access the Regional And Language Options utility as discussed previously. On the Keyboards And Languages tab, click Install/Uninstall Languages. Click Install Languages. Select the languages to install or click Browse For Folder to locate the folder that contains the language files. Click Next and then click Finish.

Using the System Console

You use the System console to view system information and perform basic configuration tasks. To access the System console, click System And Maintenance and then System in Control Panel. As Figure 4-5 shows, the System console is divided into four basic areas that provide links for performing common tasks and a system overview:

Windows Edition Shows the operating system edition and version. In addition, lists any service packs that you've applied.

System Lists the processor, memory, and type of operating system installed on the computer. The type of operating system is listed as 32-bit or 64-bit.

Computer Name, Domain, And Workgroup Settings Provides the computer name, description, domain, and workgroup details. If you want to change any of this information, click Change Settings and then click Change in the System Properties dialog box.

Windows Activation Shows whether you have activated the operating system and the product key. If Windows Server 2008 isn't activated yet, click the link provided to start the activation process and then follow the prompts. If you want to change the product key, click Change Product Key and then provide the new product key.

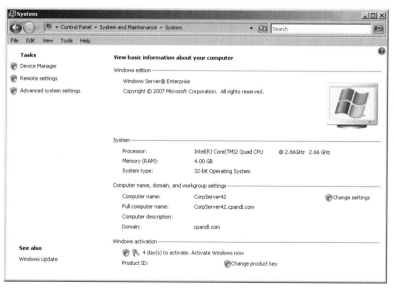

Figure 4-5 Use the System console to view and manage system properties.

When you're working in the System console, links in the left pane provide quick access to key support tools, including the following:

- Device Manager

- Remote Settings

- Advanced System Settings

Although volume-licensed versions of Windows Server 2008 might not require activation or product keys, retail versions of Windows Server 2008 require both activation and product keys. If Windows Server 2008 has not been activated, you can activate the operating system by clicking Click Here To Activate Windows Now under Windows Activation.

Unlike earlier versions of Windows, you can change the product key provided during installation as necessary to stay in compliance with your licensing plan. To change the product key, follow these steps:

1. Click System And Maintenance and then System in Control Panel.

2. In the System console, under Windows Activation, click Change Product Key.

3. In the Windows Activation wizard, type the product key.

4. When you click Next, the product key is validated. You'll then need to reactivate the operating system.

From within the System console, you can access the System Properties dialog box and use this dialog box to manage system properties. Click Change Settings under Computer Name, Domain, And Workgroup Settings.

The System Properties dialog box allows you to configure system properties, including properties for managing the operating system configuration, startup, shutdown, hardware profiles, and user profiles. System is the most advanced Control Panel utility, and its options are organized into several tabs.

The Computer Name tab displays the full computer name of the system and the domain membership, if applicable. The full computer name is essentially the DNS name of the computer, which also identifies the computer's place within the Active Directory hierarchy. To change the computer name or move a computer to a new domain, use one of the following procedures:

- For member servers (not domain controllers), you can click Change to change the system name and domain associated with the computer. This displays the Computer Name/Domain Changes dialog box (as shown in the screen on the next page). If you want to change the computer's name, type a new name in the Computer Name field. If you want to change the computer's domain or workgroup membership, select Domain or Workgroup as appropriate, and then enter the new domain or workgroup name. Click OK. If you change the computer's domain, the computer will be moved to that domain and, in which case, you might be prompted to provide the appropriate credentials for joining the computer to that domain.

- For domain controllers, you can click Change to modify the name of the computer, but doing so will make the domain controller temporarily unavailable to other computers in the domain. You cannot use this feature to change the domain in which the domain controller is running. To change the domain, you must demote the domain controller using Dcpromo to make it a member server, change the computer's network ID by using the System utility, and then promote the server using Dcpromo so that it is once again a domain controller.

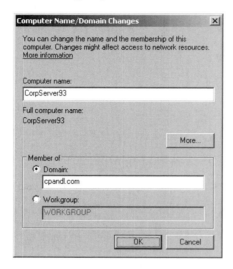

The other tabs in the System Properties dialog box are as follows:

- **Hardware** Used to configure a computer's Windows Update Driver Settings. If you enable these settings, Windows Server 2008 checks for driver updates as part of the normal update process. On the Hardware tab, click the Windows Update Driver Settings button. Select the desired update setting. The options available are: Check For Drivers Automatically (Recommended), Ask Me Each Time I Connect A New Device Before Checking For Drivers, or Never Check For Drivers When I Connect A Device. Click OK to save your settings.

- **Advanced** Used to control many of the key features of the Windows operating system, including application performance, user profiles, startup and recovery, environment variables, and error reporting. User profiles are discussed in Chapter 35, and application performance is discussed in Chapter 11.

- **Remote** Used to control Remote Assistance invitations and Remote Desktop connections. Remote Assistance invitations are primarily used with workstations and not servers. Remote Desktop is discussed in Chapter 19, "Using Remote Desktop for Administration."

Configuring Windows Server 2008

When you set out to work with Windows Server 2008, one of the first things you'll notice is that the desktop and Start menu are different from previous editions of the Windows operating system. For starters, there's a new search feature built into the Start menu and you have many new options. If you use Windows Server 2008 as your daily desktop operating system, you might want to install the Desktop Experience feature using the Add Features Wizard. This installs additional desktop functionality normally found only on Windows Vista, including these additional programs: Windows Calendar, Windows Defender, Windows Mail, Windows Media Player, Windows Photo Gallery, and Windows SideShow.

Although most system functions still are controlled through Control Panel, many administrative functions are accessed by using the Microsoft Management Console (MMC). You'll find there are many prepackaged administration tools for the MMC, many of which are accessible from the Administrative Tools menu. But the true power of the MMC is in its extensible framework that lets you build your own administration tools.

This chapter is the first of two that focus on customizing the configuration of Windows Server 2008. In this chapter, you'll learn how to customize the operating system interface. In Chapter 6, "Windows Server 2008 MMC Administration," you'll learn how to use and customize the MMC using the extensible framework provided by Microsoft. As you'll see, after you optimize the environment, you'll be well on your way to mastering Windows Server 2008.

Optimizing the Menu System

The Start menu allows you to run programs, open folders, search your computer, get help, and more. As with Windows Server 2003, the Start menu in Windows Server 2008 has two views:

- **Standard** The standard Start menu is the default view, which provides easy access to programs, folders, and search.

- **Classic** The Classic Start menu is an alternative view, which provides the look of the Start menu in Windows 2000 and earlier releases of Windows.

In most cases, you'll want to use the standard Start menu rather than the Classic Start menu because the standard Start menu includes enhancements that make it easier to access programs and folders on your computer. The standard Start menu is also more customizable.

To switch between the menu views, you right-click the Start button, select Properties to display the Taskbar And Start Menu Properties dialog box, and then select either Start Menu (for the standard Start menu) or Classic Start Menu. That is one way to change the interface. Now let's look at other ways you can change the interface, starting with how you can control the content of the Start menu.

Navigating the Start Menu Options

With standard Start menu, the right pane provides access to commonly used folders and features. Although at first glance it might seem that this part of the Start menu is similar to the Start menu in Windows Server 2003, this is deceiving because there are major changes in the locations accessed by these buttons.

In Windows Server 2003, your documents are stored by default in personal folders under %SystemDrive%\Documents and Settings\%UserName%. Your personal folder contains a My Documents folder, which in turn contains other folders, such as My Pictures and My Music. Windows Server 2003 also has folders named My Computer, My Recent Documents, and My Network Places.

In Windows Server 2008, these familiar folders don't exist. The only way your computer might have references to these folders is if you performed an in-place upgrade of the operating system. In this case, your main profile folder might include shortcuts to the locations where these folders were stored when your old settings were migrated. Generally, these shortcuts would point to locations under %SystemDrive%\Windows.old.

In Windows Server 2008, your documents are stored by default in personal folders under %SystemDrive%\Users\%UserName%. As shown in Figure 5-1, your personal folder contains the following folders:

- **Contacts** Stores your contacts for use in your mail programs
- **Desktop** Stores your desktop configuration
- **Documents** Stores your word processing documents
- **Downloads** Stores programs and data you've downloaded from the Internet
- **Favorites** Stores your Internet favorites
- **Links** Stores your Internet links
- **Music** Stores your music files
- **Pictures** Stores your pictures

- **Saved Games** Stores your saved game data

- **Searches** Stores your saved searches

- **Videos** Stores your video files

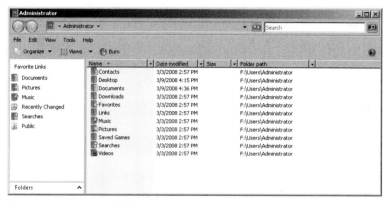

Figure 5-1 A personal folder in Windows Server 2008

With these folders in mind, you can put the Start menu's common folder options into perspective. From top to bottom, the option buttons are as follows:

- **Personal Folder** Shows your logon name. Selecting this option opens your personal folder.

- **Documents** Opens the Documents folder within your personal folder in Windows Explorer.

- **Computer** Opens the Computer view in Windows Explorer. This allows you to access hard disk drives and devices with removable storage.

- **Network** Opens Network Explorer. This allows you to browse the computers and devices on your network.

- **Control Panel** Opens Control Panel, which provides access to system configuration and management tools.

- **Default Programs** Displays the default programs in Control Panel. This lets you choose the programs that Windows Server 2008 uses by default for documents, pictures, and more.

- **Administrative Tools** Displays the Administrative Tools menu or window. This lets you access your computer's administrative tools.

- **Help And Support** Displays the Help And Support console. This lets you browse or search help topics.

- **Run** Displays the Run dialog box. This lets you run commands.

Chapter 5

> **Note**
>
> Although you might have used the Run options previously, you'll find the Search box to be much easier to work with. Not only can you use the Search box to open and run commands quicker, but you can also run commands with fewer clicks.

You can add features to the Start menu's right pane using the Customize Start Menu dialog box. Right-click the Start button and then select Properties. In the Taskbar And Start Menu Properties dialog box, click the Customize button on the Start Menu tab. In the Customize Start Menu dialog box, select or clear options as appropriate and then click OK twice.

Options you can add include:

- **Favorites** Displays your favorite links as a menu. This lets you quickly access favorite locations.

- **Games** Opens the Microsoft Games folder in Windows Explorer.

- **Music** Opens the Music folder within your personal folder in Windows Explorer.

- **Pictures** Opens the Pictures folder within your personal folder in Windows Explorer.

- **Printers** Opens the Printers window. This lets you access currently configured printers.

Below the Start menu's programs list in the left pane you'll find the Search box. The Search box allows you to quickly search your computer or the Internet. You can work with the Search box using the following techniques:

- To use the Search box, simply click the Start button and type your search text. Search results are displayed in the left pane of the Start menu. Select a result to run a program or open a folder or file.

- To clear the search results and return to the normal view, click the Clear button with the blue X to the right of the Search box, or press the Escape key.

You don't need to click in the Search box before you begin typing. Just type your search text and you'll see any matching results.

INSIDE OUT **Customizing search**

You can customize the way search works using the search-related options in the Customize Start Menu dialog box. Right-click the Start button and then select Properties. In the Taskbar And Start Menu Properties dialog box, click the Customize button on the Start Menu tab. In the Customize Start Menu dialog box, scroll down until you see the Search Communications option. You can then use these options to control how the search function works:

- **Search Communications** Determines whether Windows searches e-mail messages created using Windows Mail.

- **Search Favorites And History** Determines whether Windows searches Internet favorites and history.

- **Search Files** Determines whether Windows searches all indexed file locations, only the currently logged on user's file location, or no additional locations.

- **Search Programs** Determines whether Windows searches installed program locations.

Modifying the Start Menu Content

Regardless of whether you choose to use the standard or Classic Start menu, you can customize the menu by adding, removing, moving, copying, sorting, and renaming menu items. The standard Start menu does have a slight advantage over the Classic Start menu in the area of customization, however. As Figure 5-2 shows, this menu has the following features:

- **Pinned items list** Appears in the upper-left corner of the menu and allows you to add items that should always appear on the menu. If you no longer want an item to appear in the list, you can remove it as well.

- **Frequently used programs list** Appears below the pinned items list and shows the most frequently used programs. The Windows operating system manages this list automatically based on your program usage, but you can control the number of items that appear here and can remove items from the list. You can't add items to this list, however.

- **All Programs button** Appears in the lower-left corner of the menu and provides access to the program menus. The items that appear here are the same as you see when you are using the Classic Start menu and select Programs, including any items that normally appear above the Programs menu. You can rearrange the items to meet your needs and preferences.

Chapter 5

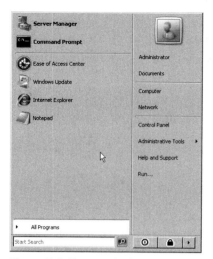

Figure 5-2 The standard Start menu has two customizable areas: the pinned items list and the most frequently used programs list.

> **Note**
>
> Items in the pinned items list and most frequently used programs list do not appear on the Classic Start menu. You can, however, add items to the top of the Start menu above the Programs folder.

Adding, Copying, and Moving Menu Items

To add an item to the pinned items list, navigate the menu system until you get to the program you want to work with. When you find it, right-click it, and then select Pin To Start Menu. Now you have a program shortcut pinned to the Start menu. Alternatively, if you drag a shortcut, folder, or program icon to the Start button and release the mouse button before the menu appears, the shortcut is added to the pinned items list. Keep in mind that these techniques are for the standard Start menu—the Classic Start menu doesn't have a pinned items list.

You can add a program to the top of the Classic Start menu, above the Programs folder. To do this, you drag a shortcut to the top of the menu from any location on the menu, the desktop, or in a Windows Explorer window. When you do this, you'll create a copy of the item rather than move the shortcut. This ensures that the shortcut remains in its original location and if you later delete the item from above the Programs menu, you'll still be able to access the item in its original location.

Chapter 5

TROUBLESHOOTING

No shortcut menus appear when I right-click

The appearance of the shortcut menu when you right-click a menu item is controlled by the drag and drop menu configuration option. If you don't see a shortcut menu when you right-click an item, the Enable Dragging And Dropping menu option has been disabled. To enable shortcut menus, right-click the Start button, choose Properties, and then click Customize. Select the Enable Context Menus And Dragging And Dropping check box.

The standard Start menu supports drag and drop, too. In fact, you can drag an item from any part of the menu to any other part of the menu, regardless of which menu you are using. This is how you add an item to any part of the menu. So, click the item you want to work with, hold down the mouse button, and navigate to where you'd like to add the item on the menu. A dark line shows where the new item will appear when you release the button.

You can use drag and drop to move items from the desktop or Windows Explorer to the menu as well. When you do this, the Windows operating system leaves the item where you got it and creates a copy on the Start menu. If the item you're dragging and dropping isn't a shortcut, that's okay as well. The operating system creates a shortcut to represent the item on the Start menu automatically. This allows you to drag a file or folder to the menu, providing a quick-access shortcut to the file or folder.

> **Note**
>
> The Windows operating system creates a shortcut only if you drag and drop a file or folder to a location within the menu. If you drag a file or folder onto the menu and then drop it into one of the document links, such as Documents, Windows Server 2008 moves the selected item to the document folder instead of creating a shortcut.

TROUBLESHOOTING

I'm unable to drag and drop items

All this talk about dragging and dropping items is fine as long as the drag and drop feature for the Start menu is enabled. If this feature is disabled, however, you won't be able to drag items to, from, or within the Start menu. To enable drag and drop, right-click Start, choose Properties, and then click Customize. Select Enable Context Menu And Dragging And Dropping.

To copy an item to a new location, press Ctrl, click the item, then hold the mouse button while dragging the item to the new location. A plus sign (+) appears next to the mouse pointer, indicating that you are copying the item, not moving it. Release the mouse button and then release the Ctrl key. You can copy items from the menu to the desktop, a folder, or a toolbar using the same technique.

> **Note**
>
> Keep in mind that when you drag an item from the left side of the standard Start menu to the All Programs menu, Windows Server 2008 always copies the item. Therefore, you don't need to hold down the Ctrl key. The same is true when you drag an item from the All Programs menu to the pinned items list.

Highlighting and Hiding Menu Items

When you work with the Start menu, you should be aware of two additional features, which you might or might not like: automatic highlighting and hiding of menu items.

For the standard Start menu, when you install new programs, by default the Windows operating system highlights the additional menus and menu items that have been created. These highlights last until you run the item (or for several days) and are designed to make it easier for you to find the new items and also ensure that you know what changes have been made to the Start menu. Some users love this feature; some users hate it. If you find the highlights distracting, you can remove them. To do this, right-click the Start button, choose Properties, and then click Customize. Clear the Highlight Newly Installed Programs check box, as shown in the following screen:

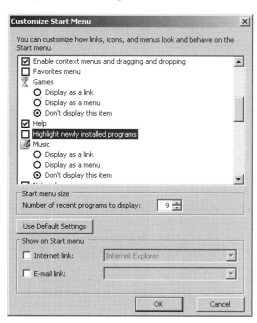

For the Classic Start menu, by default the Windows operating system displays the most frequently used items and hides the others. This feature is designed to reduce menu clutter by giving you shorter menus that make it easier for you to find the items you use the most. A double arrow at the bottom of a submenu indicates the presence of additional items that are not shown. To display these items, click the double arrow or wait a few seconds and the menu will expand automatically.

The newly displayed items are shown on a light-colored background to make them easier to see. Again, this is a feature you probably either love or hate. Don't worry; you can turn this feature off. To do this, right-click the Start button, choose Properties, and then click Customize. Clear the Use Personalized Menus check box, as shown in the following screen:

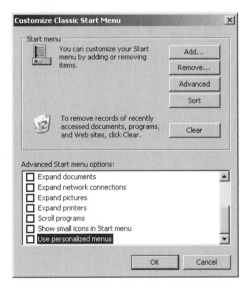

> **Note**
>
> The Use Personalized Menus option is only for the Start menu. It doesn't affect other programs that might use this feature, such as Microsoft Internet Explorer or Microsoft Office. To enable or disable personalized menus for these programs, you must do so within each individual program.

Controlling the Frequently Used Programs List

For the default Start menu, the Windows operating system manages the frequently used programs list based on your program usage. The list includes only shortcuts to .exe files; any other executable files that you use are not shown in the list regardless of

Chapter 5

how often you use them. There are many exceptions as well. For example, if the name of the shortcut that starts the program contains any of the following strings, it is not displayed in the list:

- Documentation
- Help
- Install
- More Info
- Readme
- Read Me
- Read First
- Setup
- Support
- What's New
- Remove

The list of excluded names or partial names is controlled by the AddRemoveNames value in the Registry location HKEY_LOCAL_MACHINE\SOFTWARE\Microsoft\ Windows\CurrentVersion\Explorer\FileAssociation. Further, the following program executables are specifically excluded from appearing in the list:

- Setup.exe
- Install.exe
- Isuninst.exe
- Unwise.exe
- Unwise32.exe
- St5unst.exe
- Rundll32.exe
- Msoobe.exe
- Lnkstub.exe
- Msascui.exe

The list of excluded programs is controlled by the AddRemoveApps value in the same Registry location mentioned previously. Additional programs can be registered to be excluded from the list by adding them to the KillList value in this Registry location. The following programs are in the Kill list by default:

- Explorer.exe
- Dvdplay.exe
- Mplay32.exe
- Msohtmed.exe
- Quickview.exe
- Rundll.exe
- Rundll32.exe
- Taskman.exe
- Bck32api.dll

The Windows operating system uses these Registry values to control the items that appear on the frequently used programs list. You can customize these values, particularly the Kill list, if you desire. You can also control whether and how the list is configured. By default, the Windows operating system shows up to six frequently used programs in the list. You can change this behavior by setting the number of programs to display using a value from 0 to 30. If you use a value of 0, no frequently used programs are displayed and you essentially disable this feature. Any other value sets the maximum number, up to and including that number, of frequently used programs that the operating system can display on the Start menu.

To disable the frequently used programs feature, right-click Start and choose Properties. Clear the Store And Display A List Of Recently Opened Programs check box and then click OK.

To specify the maximum number of programs that can appear in the frequently used programs list, right-click Start, choose Properties, and click Customize. Enter the value you want to use in the Number Of Recent Programs To Display text box, as shown in Figure 5-3. If you want to clear the program usage statistics, follow these steps:

1. Right-click Start and then choose Properties. Clear the Store And Display A List Of Recently Opened Programs check box and then click OK. After you click OK, the Windows operating system clears out any existing program usage statistics.

2. Right-click Start and then choose Properties. Select the Store And Display A List Of Recently Opened Programs check box and then click OK. After you click OK, the Windows operating system starts over, adding programs to the list each time you use them.

Chapter 5

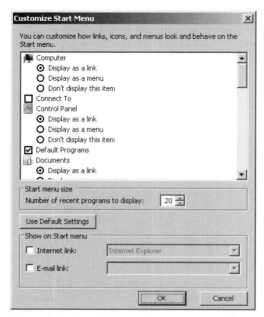

Figure 5-3 Control the maximum number of frequently used programs that is displayed by using a value from 0 to 30.

Sorting and Renaming Menu Items

As you add new programs, the Windows operating system typically adds the shortcuts for the programs to the menu in alphabetical order. This is an improvement over earlier behavior, which helps to ensure that programs aren't listed in a seemingly random order. With the standard Start menu, the Sort All Programs Menu By Name option is selected by default to ensure that menus are automatically alphabetized.

If you are using the Classic Start menu, menus aren't automatically alphabetized though you can manually sort all the submenus within the Programs menu at once. To do this, right-click Start, choose Properties, and then click Customize. In the Customize Classic Start Menu dialog box, click Sort.

> Note
>
> The Windows operating system maintains many menu settings separately for the Classic and standard Start menus, including drag and drop settings and sort order. This means if you change the order of a menu using the Classic Start menu, the changes don't appear if you change to using the standard Start menu.

While we're talking about sorting items, a related topic is renaming items. To rename a menu item, right-click the menu item you want to rename, and choose Rename. Edit the name of the item, and then click OK. Renaming an item can change the way the item is sorted, and Windows Server 2008 will re-sort the menu automatically by default.

Removing Items from the Start Menu

Windows Server 2008 gives you several options for removing items from the Start menu. If the item is in the pinned items list, you can remove it from the list by right-clicking it and choosing Unpin From Start Menu. Unfortunately, if you do this and the program is also one of your most frequently used programs, it could immediately reappear in the frequently used programs list. To ensure that the program doesn't show up in either location, right-click the item, and choose Remove From This List. This is the same option you choose to remove an item from the frequently used programs list. (Unfortunately, this isn't permanent, however. If you continue to use a program, it can show up again in the frequently used programs list. So, if you really want to block a program from the frequently used programs list, exclude it as discussed in "Controlling the Frequently Used Programs List" on page 137.)

Other types of menu items can be removed as well. To remove a regular menu item, right-click it, and choose Delete. Confirm that you want to remove the item by clicking Yes when prompted.

> **Note**
> Keep in mind that deleting an item from the menu doesn't uninstall the related program. It only deletes the shortcut to the program.

Customizing the Desktop and the Taskbar

By default the only items on the Windows Server 2008 desktop are the Recycle Bin and the taskbar. That's it. Everything else has been cleared away to allow you to customize the desktop any way you want. The problem is that some of the missing items, such as Computer, Network, and Internet Explorer, were pretty useful, or at least most of us have grown so accustomed to having the items on the desktop that we expect them to be there. So, if you're like me, the first thing you'll want to do to customize the desktop is to add frequently accessed programs, files, and folders and to restore the missing items. Another thing you might want to do is to customize the taskbar so that it works the way you want it to. By default, the taskbar doesn't automatically hide or lock, and it might include items that you don't want.

Chapter 5

Configuring Desktop Items

Windows Server 2008 allows you to drag program shortcuts, files, and folders from a Windows Explorer window onto the desktop. Simply click the item you want to move, hold down the mouse button, and drag the item to a location on the desktop. When you release the mouse button, the item is moved from its original location to the desktop. If you want to copy the item instead of moving it, press Ctrl, click the item, then hold the mouse button while dragging the item to the new location. On the desktop, release the mouse button, and then release the Ctrl key.

You can, in fact, use the copy and move techniques to add shortcuts for your personal folder, Computer, Network, and Control Panel to the desktop. But there's another way to add these items to the desktop so that they appear as standard desktop icons instead of shortcuts. Right-click an empty area of the desktop, and choose Personalize. In the left pane of the Personalization window, click Change Desktop Icons under the Tasks heading. This opens the Desktop Icon Settings dialog box, shown in the following screen.

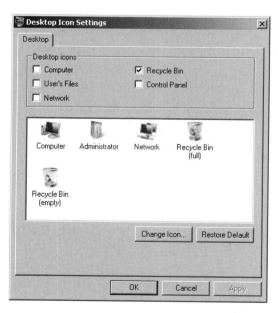

In the Desktop Icon Settings dialog box, select the items that you want to display on the desktop, for instance, Computer, Network, and Control Panel. Several uses for Computer and Network aren't obvious but are great time-savers.

Use Computer in the following ways:

- Right-click and choose Manage to start Server Manager.

- Right-click and choose Properties to display the System console in Control Panel.

- Right-click and choose Map Network Drive or Disconnect Network Drive to manage network shares.

Use Network as follows:

- Right-click and choose Explorer to find computers on the network.

- Right-click and choose Properties to display the Network And Sharing Center.

- Right-click and choose Map Network Drive or Disconnect Network Drive to manage network shares.

Configuring the Taskbar

The taskbar is one of those areas of the desktop that most people take for granted. It's sort of like people think, "Hey, there's the taskbar, what can I click?" when they should be thinking, "Hey, there's a taskbar. It tracks all the running programs for quick access and I can customize it to work the way I want it to." Beyond the Start button, the taskbar has three main areas:

- **Quick Launch** Provides quick access to the desktop and commonly used applications. Technically, it is a type of toolbar, and it is fully customizable.

- **Programs/Toolbars** Shows icons for running programs, which can be grouped according to type, as well as the toolbars that are selected for display.

- **Notification** Shows the system clock and programs that were loaded automatically at startup and that are running in the background.

You can change the behavior and properties of these taskbar areas in many ways.

Changing the Taskbar Size and Position

In the default configuration, the taskbar appears at the bottom of the screen and is sized so that one row of options is visible. As long as the taskbar position isn't locked, you can move it to any edge of the Windows desktop and resize it as necessary. To move the taskbar, simply click it and hold the mouse button while dragging it to a different edge of the desktop. When you move the mouse toward the left, right, top, or bottom edge of the desktop, you'll see a gray outline that shows you where the taskbar will appear. When you release the mouse button, the taskbar will appear in the new location.

With a left-docked or right-docked taskbar, you'll often have to resize the taskbar so that it is wider than usual to ensure that you can read the program names. I've found this approach useful when I am troubleshooting a system and I have lots of programs running and want to be able to switch quickly between them. In contrast, a top-docked taskbar seems to remove the clutter from the desktop, and I've found it useful when I don't want to use the Auto Hide feature.

To resize the taskbar, move the mouse pointer over the taskbar edge, and then drag it up or down, left or right, as appropriate. If you resize the taskbar so that it isn't visible (different from Auto Hide), you should still see a gray bar on the edge of the screen where the taskbar is docked. When you move the mouse pointer over the gray bar, the arrow pointer should change to the resize pointer, allowing you to resize the taskbar so that it is visible. On computers with a Windows key, you can press the Windows key and the Start menu will pop out from the edge of the screen that has the minimized taskbar, revealing the location of the taskbar as well.

> **Note**
>
> If the taskbar appears to get stuck in one location when you are trying to move it, simply log off and then log back on. As long as the taskbar isn't locked, you should then be able to move the taskbar.

Using Auto Hide and Locking

Windows Server 2008 has several features that control the visibility of the taskbar. You can enable the Auto Hide feature to hide the taskbar from view when it is not in use. You can lock the taskbar so that it cannot be resized or repositioned. You can also make the taskbar appear on top of other windows when you point to it. After the taskbar is positioned and sized the way you want it, I recommend enabling all three of these options. In this way, the taskbar has a fixed location and is visible when it is pointed to, ensuring that it isn't accidentally hidden behind other windows.

You can enable these options as shown in the following screen by right-clicking the taskbar and then choosing Properties from the shortcut menu. Afterward, select the Lock The Taskbar, Auto-Hide The Taskbar, and Keep The Taskbar On Top Of Other Windows check boxes as appropriate. Then click OK.

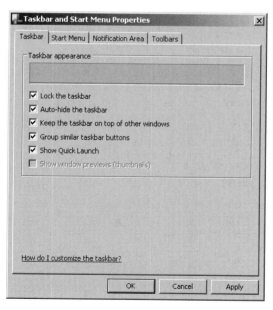

> **Note**
>
> Locking the taskbar doesn't prevent you from changing the taskbar in the future. If you want to change the taskbar, simply right-click the taskbar and then clear the Lock The Taskbar check box. You can then make any necessary changes and, if desired, relock the taskbar to ensure that the settings are protected from being accidentally changed.

Grouping Similar Taskbar Items

Windows can group similar taskbar items together to reduce taskbar clutter. For example, if you open multiple MMCs and the taskbar needs additional room for other items, these consoles are grouped under a single button and are then accessible by clicking the button and selecting the individual MMC you want to use. In some ways, this is a good thing, but it can be confusing.

You can control whether similar items are grouped together by right-clicking the taskbar and then choosing Properties from the shortcut menu. Afterward, select the Group Similar Taskbar Buttons check box to enable this option or clear the Group Similar Taskbar Buttons check box to disable this option.

Controlling Programs in the Notification Area

The notification area, also referred to as the system tray, is the area on the far right side of the taskbar. It shows the system clock as well as icons for programs that were loaded automatically by the operating system at startup and that are running in the background. Notifications for the operating system and programs behave in different ways:

- If you move the pointer over a system notification icon, you'll see a status window that provides information about the notification.

- If you move the pointer over a system notification icon and click, you'll see a control window that provides information about the notification and allows you to configure the related feature.

- If you move the pointer over a program notification icon and then click, you'll see a shortcut menu (provided one is available).

- If you move the pointer over a program notification icon and then double-click, you'll open the related program or window.

User-specified programs that run in the background are managed through the Startup folder. The Startup folder is configured at two levels. Under the %SystemDrive%\ProgramData\Microsoft\Windows\Start Menu\Programs folder, there is a Startup folder for all users of a given system. Any program referenced in this folder is run in the background regardless of which user logs on. Within the profile data for individual users, there is a Startup folder specific to each user's logon under %SystemDrive%\ Users\%UserName%\AppData\Roaming\Microsoft\Windows\Start Menu\Programs. Programs referenced in a personal Startup folder are run only when that user logs on.

Chapter 5

You can add or remove startup programs for all users by right-clicking Start and then selecting Explore All Users from the shortcut menu. This opens Windows Explorer with the Start Menu folder selected, as shown in Figure 5-4.

In the left pane, double-click the Programs folder under Start Menu, and then select the Startup folder. You can now add or remove startup programs for all users as follows:

● To add startup programs, create a shortcut to the program that you want to run.

● To remove a startup program, delete its shortcut from the Startup folder.

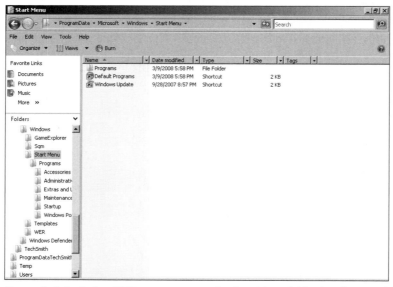

Figure 5-4 Exploring All Users gets you to the Start Menu folder for all users of the computer; then you must work your way down to the Startup folder under Programs.

You can add or remove startup programs for individual users as well, such as the administrator. To do this, log on as the user whose startup applications you want to manage. Right-click Start, and then select Explore from the shortcut menu. This opens Windows Explorer with the Start Menu folder in the user profile selected. In the left pane, double-click the Programs folder under Start Menu, and then select the Startup folder. You can now add or remove startup programs for this user as discussed previously.

Chapter 5

INSIDE OUT   Why log on as the user to access the Startup folder?

You might be wondering why I told you to log on as the user whose startup applications you want to control. Technically, you don't need to do this, but it is easier if you do. Why? Because when you select Explore, you'll be taken to that user's Start Menu folder—sometimes getting the right user profile folder is half the battle, especially on a system that has been upgraded or renamed or reinstalled and that contains several different profile entries for each user. If you can't log on as the user, access the user folder on the system drive, and work your way down through the user's profile data folders. These are listed by account name.

User-specified programs that run in the background are only one type of program that is displayed in the notification area. Some programs, such as Windows Update, are managed by the Windows operating system. For example, Windows Update runs periodically to check for updates to the operating system. When an update is detected, the user can be notified and given the opportunity to apply the update. Other types of programs are configured during installation to run in the background at startup, such as an antivirus program. You can typically enable or disable the display of notification area icons related to these programs through the setup options in the related applications. Windows Server 2008 also provides a common interface for controlling whether the icons for these programs are displayed in the notification area. This allows you to specify whether and how icons are displayed on a per-program basis.

To control the display of icons in the notification area, right-click the taskbar, and then choose Properties from the shortcut menu. In the Taskbar And Start Menu Properties dialog box, click the Notification Area tab. If you want all icons to be displayed, clear the Hide Inactive Icons check box, and then click OK. If you want to customize the appearance of icons, select the Hide Inactive Icons check box, and then click Customize. This displays the Customize Notifications dialog box shown in Figure 5-5.

You can now optimize the notification behavior for current items displayed in the notification area as well as items that were displayed in the past but aren't currently active. The Icon column shows the name of the program. The Behavior column shows the currently selected notification behavior, which is typically Hide When Inactive, but which can also be set to Hide or Show.

Note

When the Hide Inactive Icons check box is selected in the Taskbar And Start Menu Properties dialog box, you can right-click in the notification area and then select Customize Notifications to directly access the Customize Notifications Icons dialog box.

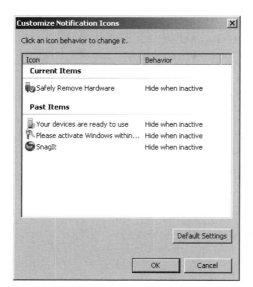

Figure 5-5 You can customize notifications for notification area items.

Optimizing Toolbars

Several custom toolbars are available for the taskbar. The toolbar that most people are familiar with is the Quick Launch toolbar, which provides quick access to commonly used programs and the Windows desktop. The taskbar can display other toolbars that come with Windows Server 2008, and you can create you own toolbars as well.

Customizing the Quick Launch Toolbar

The Quick Launch toolbar includes buttons that provide quick access to Server Manager and the Windows desktop. If your organization has custom applications or a preferred suite of applications, you can add buttons for these applications on the Quick Launch toolbar. If applications are no longer used, you can later remove the additional buttons.

You can add a button to the Quick Launch toolbar by clicking the item or existing shortcut that you want to place on the toolbar, holding the mouse button, and dragging the item or shortcut onto the Quick Launch toolbar. When you are in the location where you want to place the item or shortcut, release the mouse button. To remove a button from the Quick Launch toolbar, right-click the button on the toolbar, and then choose Delete from the shortcut menu. When prompted to confirm the action, click Yes.

INSIDE OUT   Restoring the Show Desktop button

Show Desktop is the most useful button on the Quick Launch toolbar. The first time you click this button, the operating system brings the Windows desktop to the foreground in front of all open windows. The second time you click this button, the operating system restores the original view, sending the desktop to the background. If this button is accidentally deleted, you can re-create it, but the process is not like creating a regular shortcut. This is because Show Desktop is a special button that must be created by using a Windows Explorer command file called Show Desktop.scf.

As with other aspects of the menu system, the Quick Launch toolbar options have a representation in the file system. You'll find Quick Launch options in the %System-Drive%\Users\%UserName%\AppData\Roaming\Microsoft\Internet Explorer\Quick Launch folder. Thus, the full file path to the necessary Show Desktop file would be %SystemDrive%\Users\%UserName%\AppData\Roaming\Microsoft\Internet Explorer\Quick Launch\Show Desktop.scf. To restore the button to the toolbar, you have several options. You can copy the Show Desktop shortcut from another user's profile, or you can create the Show Desktop.scf file. To create the Show Desktop.scf file, follow these steps:

1. Start Notepad, and then add the following lines of text:

   [Shell]
   Command=2
   IconFile=explorer.exe,3
   [Taskbar]
   Command=ToggleDesktop

2. Select Save from the File menu, and then save the file in the %SystemDrive%\Users\%UserName%\AppData\Roaming\Microsoft\Internet Explorer\Quick Launch folder. Use the file name Show Desktop.scf.

If you don't know the actual location for the current user's profile, open a command prompt, and type **set userprofile**. The command prompt then displays the variable value.

Displaying Other Custom Toolbars

In addition to the Quick Launch toolbar discussed previously, three other customizable toolbars are available for the taskbar:

- **Address** Provides an Address text box into which you can type Uniform Resource Locators (URLs) and other addresses that you want to access, either on the World Wide Web, on the local network, or on the local computer. When full file paths are specified, the default application for the file is launched automatically to display the specified file, such as Internet Explorer or Microsoft Office Word. One of the things you might not realize about the Address toolbar is that it retains the

Chapter 5

same URL history as the Address bar in Internet Explorer, meaning if you previously opened a document on a network share, you could quickly access it again through the history.

- **Links** Provides access to the Links folder on the Favorites menu of Internet Explorer. To add links to files, Web pages, or other resources, drag shortcuts onto the Links toolbar. To remove links, right-click the link, and select Delete. When prompted, confirm the action by clicking Yes.

- **Desktop** Provides access to all the shortcuts on the local desktop so that you don't have to minimize windows or click Show Desktop on the Quick Launch toolbar to access them.

You can display or hide individual toolbars by right-clicking the taskbar to display the shortcut menu, pointing to Toolbars, and then selecting the toolbar you want to use. This toggles the toolbar on and off.

> **Have Toolbars Use Less Space by Turning Off the Title**
>
> By default, a name label is displayed for all toolbars except Quick Launch. This label wastes taskbar space, and you can turn it off. Right-click the toolbar and then choose Show Title to clear the option. The option is a toggle; if you want to see the title again, repeat this procedure.

Creating Personal Toolbars

In addition to the custom toolbars that are available, you can create personal toolbars as well. Personal toolbars are based on existing folders, and their buttons are based on the folder contents. The most common toolbars you might create are ones that point to folders on the computer or shared folders on the network. For example, if you routinely access the C:\Windist, C:\Windows\System32\LogFiles, and C:\Windows\System32\Inetsvr folders, you could add a toolbar to the taskbar that provides quick access buttons to these resources. Then you could access one of the folders simply by clicking the corresponding toolbar button.

You can create personal toolbars by right-clicking the taskbar to display the shortcut menu, pointing to Toolbars, and then choosing New Toolbar. This displays the New Toolbar – Choose A Folder dialog box, as shown in the following screen:

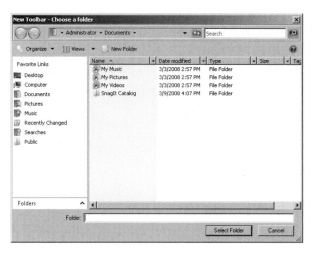

Next use the Folder list box to choose the folder you want to make into a toolbar. When you click Select Folder, the folder is displayed as a new toolbar on the taskbar. If you add shortcuts to the folder, the shortcuts automatically appear on the toolbar as buttons that can be selected. Keep in mind that if you decide that you don't want to use the toolbar anymore and close it, you must reselect the folder before it can be viewed on the taskbar again.

Windows Server 2008 MMC Administration

In this chapter, you'll learn how to work with and customize the Microsoft Management Console (MMC). You'll also find a discussion of administration tools that use the MMC. You can learn many techniques to help you better understand Windows Server 2008, and indeed, as mentioned in the previous chapter, you must master the MMC before you can truly master Windows Server 2008.

Introducing the MMC

The MMC, and the prepackaged administration tools that use it, help you more readily manage computers, users, and other aspects of the network environment. Not only does the MMC simplify administration, it also helps to integrate the many disparate tools in the Window operating system.

The advantages of having a unified interface are significant because after you learn the structure of one MMC tool, you can apply what you've learned to all the other MMC tools. Equally as significant is the capability to build your own consoles and customize existing consoles. You can in fact combine administrative components to build your own console configuration, and then store this console for future use. You would then have quick access to the tools you use the most through a single console.

For selected snap-ins, the MMC supports:

- Multiple-item selecting and editing. These features allow you to select multiple objects and perform the same operations on them, including editing.

- Drag-and-drop functionality. This allows you to perform such tasks as dragging a user, computer, or group from one organizational unit (OU) to another in Active Directory Users And Computers.

For the Active Directory Users And Computers snap-in, you can:

- Reset access permissions to the default values for objects, show the effective permission for an object, and show the parent of an inherited permission.

- Save Active Directory queries and reuse them so that you can easily perform common or complex queries.

If you've used the MMC in Microsoft Windows Server 2003, you might be wondering what's new in Windows Server 2008. For starters, the MMC in Windows Server 2008 has a new version number. It is MMC 3.0 and it offers several enhancements:

- In all of the console tools and in the MMC framework, the Action pane has been added as a complement to the Action menu. This was done to make it easier to determine the available actions for selected items.

- A Show/Hide Action Pane button has been added to the toolbar. This allows you to display or hide the Action pane.

- The Add/Remove Snap-Ins dialog box has been redesigned to make it easier to add or remove snap-ins. Additional features have been added to allow you to control snap-in extensions that are available and to organize snap-ins using nesting.

- Error notification has been improved and you are now given troubleshooting options regarding errors that could cause MMC to fail.

MMC 3.0 is available as an update for Windows 2000 and later. MMC 3.0 is designed to support snap-ins created for MMC 2.0 and MMC 1.2. You can add these snap-ins to an MMC 3.0 console, and they will run as they do in the versions of MMC for which they were designed. You can use MMC 3.0 to open a console created using MMC 2.0 or 1.2. If you then save the console, you will be prompted to save the console in MMC 3.0 format. Doing so will update the console so that it uses the MMC 3.0 framework. However, you will not be able to open the console on computers running previous versions of MMC. The reason for this is that MMC 2.0 and 1.2 do not support MMC 3.0 snap-ins or consoles.

Keep in mind that the MMC isn't a one-size-fits-all approach to administration. Some administrative functions aren't implemented for use with the MMC. You configure many system and operating system properties using Control Panel utilities. Many other system and administrative functions are accessed using wizards. Most administrative tools regardless of type have command-line counterparts that run as separate executables from the command line.

The really good news, however, is that you can integrate all non-MMC tools and even command-line utilities into a custom console by creating links to them. In this way, your custom console remains the central interface for administration, and you can use it to access quickly any type of tool with which you routinely work. For more information, see "Building Custom MMCs" on page 163.

Using the MMC

The MMC is a framework for management applications that offers a unified interface for administration. It is not designed to replace management applications; rather, it is designed to be their central interface. As such, the MMC doesn't have any inherent management functions. It uses add-in components, called *snap-ins*, to provide the necessary administrative functionality.

MMC Snap-Ins

To take advantage of what the MMC framework has to offer, you add any of the available stand-alone snap-ins to a console. A *console* is simply a container for snap-ins that uses the MMC framework. Dozens of preconfigured snap-ins are available from Microsoft, and they provide the functionality necessary for administration. Third-party tools from independent software vendors now use MMC snap-ins as well.

> **Note**
>
> The terms *console* and *tool* are often used interchangeably. For example, in the text, I often refer to such and such as a tool when technically it is a preconfigured console containing a snap-in. For example, Active Directory Users And Computers is a tool for managing users, groups, and computers. Not all tools are consoles, however. The System tool in Control Panel is a tool for managing system properties, but it is not a console.

Although you can load multiple snap-ins into a single console, most of the preconfigured consoles have only a single snap-in. For example, most of the tools on the Administrative Tools menu consist of a preconfigured console with a single snap-in—even the Computer Management tool, as shown in Figure 6-1, consists of a preconfigured console with the Computer Management snap-in added to it.

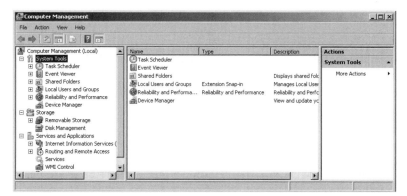

Figure 6-1 The Computer Management tool consists of a preconfigured console with the Computer Management snap-in added to it.

The many features of the Computer Management snap-in are good examples of how snap-ins can have nodes and extension components. A *node* defines a level within the console or within a snap-in. Computer Management has a root node, which is labeled Computer Management, and three top-level nodes, which are labeled System Tools, Storage, and Services And Applications. An *extension component* is a type of snap-in that is used to extend the functionality of an existing snap-in. Computer Management has many extensions. In fact, each entry under the top-level nodes is an extension—and many of these extensions can themselves have extensions.

These particular extensions are also implemented as stand-alone snap-ins, and when you use them in your own console, they add the same functionality as they do in the preconfigured administration tools. You'll find that many extensions are implemented as both extensions and stand-alone snap-ins. Many doesn't mean all: Some extensions are meant only to add functionality to an existing snap-in and they are not also implemented as stand-alone snap-ins.

Keep in mind that extensions are optional and can be included or excluded from a snap-in by changing options within the console when you are authoring it. For example, if you didn't want someone to be able to use Disk Management from within Computer Management, you could edit the extension options for Computer Management on that user's computer to remove the entry for Disk Management. The user would then be unable to manage disks from within Computer Management. The user would still, however, be able to manage disks using other tools.

MMC Modes

An MMC has two operating modes: author mode and user mode. In author mode, you can create and modify a console's design by adding or removing snap-ins and setting console options. In user mode, the console design is frozen, and you cannot change it. By default, the prepackaged console tools for administration open in user mode, and this is why you are unable to make changes to these console tools.

When you open a console that is in author mode, you have additional options on the File menu that help you design the interface. You can use these options to create new consoles, open existing consoles, save the current console, add or remove snap-ins, and set console options. In contrast, when you are working with one of the preconfigured console tools or any other tool in user mode, you have a limited File menu. With user mode, you can access a limited set of console options or exit the console—that's it.

In author mode, you also have a Favorites menu, which you can use to add and organize favorites. The Favorites menu does not appear in user mode.

When you are finished designing a console tool, you should change to user mode. Console tools should be run in user mode, and author mode should be used only for configuring console tools. Three user-mode levels are defined:

- **User mode—full access** Users can access all window management commands in the MMC but can't add or remove snap-ins or change console properties.

- **User mode—limited access, multiple window** Users can access only the areas of the console tree that were visible when the console was saved. Users can create new windows but cannot close existing windows.

- **User mode—limited access, single window** Users can access only the areas of the console tree that were visible when the console was saved and are prevented from opening new windows.

INSIDE OUT
Group Policy settings can control authoring and snap-in availability

Remember that, at any time, a user with appropriate permissions can enter author mode by right-clicking the console and selecting Author or by running the console tool from the command line with the /A switch. In author mode, users could change the configuration of the tool. One way to prevent this is to restrict authoring in Group Policy.

You can restrict all authoring by users at the local machine, OU, or domain level by enabling Restrict The User From Entering Author Mode in User Configuration\Administrative Templates\Windows Components\Microsoft Management Console within Group Policy.

You can set specific restricted and permitted snap-ins and extensions as well. One way to do this is first to prohibit the use of all snap-ins by enabling the Restrict Users To The Explicitly Permitted List Of Snap-Ins policy setting in User Configuration\Administrative Templates\Windows Components\Microsoft Management Console within Group Policy. Then specifically enable the snap-ins and extensions that are permitted using the policy settings under User Configuration\Administrative Templates\Windows Components\ Microsoft Management Console within Group Policy. All other snap-ins and extensions would then be prohibited.

Alternatively, you can disable Restrict Users To The Explicitly Permitted List Of Snap-Ins and then explicitly prohibit snap-ins by disabling them using the policy settings under User Configuration\Administrative Templates\Windows Components\Microsoft Management Console within Group Policy. All other snap-ins and extensions would then be permitted.

Be sure to read Chapter 36, "Managing Group Policy," before you try to implement Group Policy or make changes to Group Policy objects. If you get into trouble, such as could happen if you prohibit all snap-ins but neglect to enable snap-ins needed for management, you can reset Group Policy to its default configuration by using the Dcgpofix command-line utility as discussed in "Fixing Default Group Policy," on page 1282.

A console's mode is stored when you save the console and is applied when you open the console. In author mode, you can change the console mode by using the Options dialog box, which you display by selecting Options from the File menu. You cannot change the mode when a console is running in user mode. That doesn't mean you can't change back to author mode, however, and then make further changes as necessary.

To open any existing console tool in author mode, right-click the tool's icon and choose Author. This works for the preconfigured administration tools as well. Simply right-click the related menu item on the Administrative Tools menu, and then choose Author. You will then have full design control over the console, but remember that if you make changes, you probably don't want to overwrite the existing .msc file for the console. So, instead of choosing Save from the File menu after you make changes, choose Save As, and save the console with a different name, location, or both.

> **Note**
>
> Another way to enter author mode is to use the /A parameter when starting the console tool from the command line or the Run dialog box.

MMC Windows and Startup

As Figure 6-2 shows, the MMC window consists of three panes: console tree, the main pane, and the actions pane. The left pane is the console tree. It provides a hierarchical list of nodes available in the console. At the top of the tree is the console root, which could be specifically labeled Console Root, or, as with the preconfigured tools, it is simply the snap-in name. Generally, snap-ins appear as nodes below the console root. Snap-ins can also have nodes, as is the case with Computer Management. In any case, if there are nodes below the console root, you can expand them by clicking the plus sign to the left of the node label or by double-clicking the node.

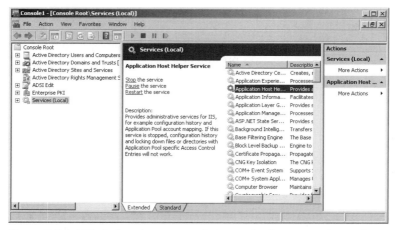

Figure 6-2 MMC windows have a console tree, a details pane, and an actions pane.

The main pane is also referred to as the details pane, and its contents change depending on the item you've selected in the console tree. When you are working with one of the lowest-level nodes in the console tree, you'll sometimes have two views to choose from in the details pane: standard or extended view. The difference between the two is that the extended view typically provides quick access links to related, frequently performed tasks and a detailed description of the selected item. These are not displayed in the standard view.

One way to start a console tool is to select it on the Administrative Tools menu or double-click its icon on the desktop or in Windows Explorer. You can also start console tools from the Search box on the Start menu and the command prompt. The executable for the MMC is Mmc.exe, and you can run it by clicking Start, typing **mmc** in the

Search box, and then pressing Enter, or by entering **mmc** at the command prompt. Either way, you'll end up with a blank (empty) console that you can use to design your custom administration tool.

To use an existing console, you can specify the console file to open when the MMC runs. This is, in fact, how the preconfigured tools and any other tools that you create are launched. For example, if you right-click Computer Management on the Administrative Tools menu, and then select Properties, you'll see that the target (the command that is run) for the menu item is as follows:

```
%SystemRoot%\System32\Compmgmt.msc /s
```

The first part of the target (%SystemRoot%\System32\Compmgmt.msc) is the file path to the associated Microsoft Saved Console (.msc) file. The second part of the target (/S) is a command parameter to use when running the MMC. It follows that you can run the MMC by specifying the file path to the .msc file to use and any necessary command parameters as well using the following syntax:

```
mmc FilePath Parameter(s)
```

where *FilePath* is the file path to the .msc file to use and *Parameter(s)* can include any of the following parameters:

- **/A** Enables author mode, which lets you make changes to preconfigured consoles as well as other consoles previously set in user mode.

- **/S** Prevents the console from displaying the splash screen that normally appears when the MMC starts in earlier versions of the Windows operating system. This parameter isn't needed when running on Windows Server 2008.

- **/32** Starts the 32-bit version of the MMC, which is needed only if you explicitly want to run the 32-bit version of the MMC on a 64-bit Windows system.

- **/64** Starts the 64-bit version of the MMC, which is available only on 64-bit Windows versions.

Most console tools are found in the %SystemRoot%\System32 directory. This puts them in the default search path for executables. Because there is a file type association for .msc files, specified files of this type are opened using Mmc.exe; you can open any of the preconfigured tools stored in %SystemRoot%\System32 by specifying the file name followed by the .msc extension. For example, you can start Event Viewer by typing the following:

eventvwr.msc

This works because of the file association that specifies .msc files are executed using Mmc.exe. (You can examine file associations using the ASSOC and FTYPE commands at the command prompt.)

Some console tools aren't in the %SystemRoot%\System32 directory, or the search path for that matter. For these tools, you must type the complete file path.

Chapter 6

INSIDE OUT   Using 32-bit and 64-bit versions of the MMC

The /32 and /64 parameters for the mmc command are meaningful only on 64-bit Windows versions. The 64-bit versions of the Windows operating system can run both 32-bit and 64-bit versions of the MMC. For 32-bit versions of the MMC, you use 32-bit snap-ins. For 64-bit versions of the MMC, you use 64-bit snap-ins. You can't mix and match MMC and snap-in versions, though. The 32-bit version of the MMC can be used only to work with 32-bit snap-ins. Similarly, the 64-bit version of the MMC can be used only to work with 64-bit snap-ins. In most cases, if you aren't sure which version to use, don't use the /32 or /64 parameter. This lets the Windows operating system decide which version to use based on the snap-ins contained in the .msc file you are opening.

When a console contains both 32-bit and 64-bit snap-ins and you don't specify the /32 or /64 parameter, Windows will open a subset of the configured snap-ins. If the console contains more 32-bit snap-ins, Windows will open the 32-bit snap-ins. If the console contains more 64-bit snap-ins, Windows will open the 64-bit snap-ins. If you explicitly use /32 or /64 with a console that contains both 32-bit and 64-bit snap-ins, Windows will open only the snap-ins for that bitness. On 64-bit systems, 32-bit versions of snap-ins are stored in the %SystemRoot%\SysWow64 folder and 64-bit versions of snap-ins are stored in the %SystemRoot%\System32 folder. By examining the contents of these folders, you can determine when 32-bit and 64-bit versions of snap-ins are available.

MMC Tool Availability

Generally, the preconfigured MMC consoles available on a server depend on the roles, role services, and features that are installed. As you install additional roles, role services, and features, additional tools for administration are installed, and these tools can be both console tools and standard tools. You don't have to rely on roles, role services, and features installation for tool availability, however. You can, in fact, install the complete administrative tool set on any full-server installation regardless of the roles, role services, or features being used.

Follow these steps to install the complete administrative tool set:

1. In Server Manager, select the Features node in the left pane and then click Add Features. This starts the Add Features Wizard.

2. On the Select Features page, select the Remote Server Administration Tools check box. This selects all the available tools under the Role Administration Tools and Feature Administration Tools nodes. If you are prompted to add the Web Server (IIS) role, follow the prompts to add this role to your server. Click Next.

3. Click Install. When the wizard finishes installing the administration tools, click Close.

These tools are then available from the Administrative Tools menu and can also be started quickly in the Search box or at the command prompt by typing only their file name (in most cases). At times, you might find it quicker to open consoles from the command line. For example, on a server optimized for handling background services and not programs being run by users, you might find that navigating the menu is too slow. To help you in these instances, Table 6-1 provides a list of the key console tools and their .msc file names.

Table 6-1 Key Console Tools and Their .msc File Names

Tool Name	.msc File Name
Active Directory Domain And Trusts	domain.msc
Active Directory Rights Management Services	AdRmsAdmin.msc
Active Directory Sites And Services	dssite.msc
Active Directory Users And Computers	dsa.msc
ADSI Edit	adsiedit.msc
Certification Authority	certsrv.msc
Computer Management	compmgmt.msc
DFS Management	dfsmgmt.msc
DHCP Manager	dhcpmgmt.msc
DNS Manager	dnsmgmt.msc
Event Viewer	eventvwr.msc
Failover Cluster Management	cluadmin.msc
Fax Service Manager	fxsadmin.msc
File Server Resource Manager	fsrm.msc
Group Policy Management	gpmc.msc
Health Registration Authority	hcscfg.msc
Local Security Policy	secpol.msc
Network Policy Server	nps.msc
Online Responder Manager	ocsp.msc
Print Management	printmanagement.msc
Reliability And Performance Monitor	perfmon.msc
Remote Desktops	tsmmc.msc
Routing And Remote Access	rrasmgmt.msc
Services	services.msc
Services For Network File System	nfsmgmt.msc
Share And Storage Management	storagemgmt.msc
Storage Explorer	storexpl.msc
Storage Manager For SANs	sanmmc.msc
Task Scheduler	taskschd.msc

Chapter 6

Tool Name	.msc File Name
Terminal Services Configuration	tsconfig.msc
Terminal Services Manager	tsadmin.msc
TS Gateway Manager	tsgateway.msc
TS Remote App Manager	remoteprograms.msc
UDDI Services	uddi.msc
Windows Deployment Services	wdsmgmt.msc
Windows Firewall With Advanced Security	wf.msc
Windows Server Backup	wbadmin.msc
Windows System Resource Manager	wsrm.msc
WINS Manager	winsmgmt.msc

MMC and Remote Computers

Some snap-ins can be set to work with local or remote systems. If this is the case, you'll see the name of the computer with focus in parentheses after the snap-in name in the console tree. When the snap-in is working with the local computer, you'll see (Local) after the snap-in name. When the snap-in is working with a remote computer, you'll see the remote computer name in parentheses after the snap-in name, such as (CORPSERVER01).

Generally, regardless of which type of snap-in you are using, you can specify the computer with which you want to work in one of two ways. Within the MMC, you can right-click the snap-in node in the console tree and then select Connect To Another Computer. This displays the Select Computer dialog box, as shown in the following screen:

If you want the snap-in to work with the computer the console is running on, select Local Computer. Otherwise, select Another Computer, and then type the computer name or Internet Protocol (IP) address of the computer you want to use. If you don't know the computer name or IP address, click Browse to search for the computer you want to work with.

Just about any snap-in that can be set to work with local and remote systems can be started from the command line with the focus set on a specific computer. This is a hidden feature that many people don't know about or don't understand. Simply set the focus when you start a console from the command line using the following parameter:

```
/computer=RemoteComputer
```

where *RemoteComputer* is the name or IP address of the remote computer you want the snap-in to work with, such as

```
eventvwr.msc /computer=corpserver01
```

Several different hidden options are available with the Active Directory-related snap-ins. For Active Directory Users And Computers, Active Directory Sites And Services, and Active Directory Domains And Trusts, you can use the */Server* parameter to open the snap-in and connect to a specified domain controller. For example, if you wanted to start Active Directory Users And Computers and connect to the CORPSVR02 domain controller, you could do this by typing the following:

```
dsa.msc /server=CorpSvr02
```

For Active Directory Users And Computers and Active Directory Sites And Services, you can use the */Domain* parameter to open the snap-in and connect to a domain controller in the specified domain. For example, if you wanted to start Active Directory Users And Computers and connect to the cpandl.com domain, you could do this by typing the following:

```
dsa.msc /domain=cpandl.com
```

Building Custom MMCs

If you find that the existing console tools don't meet your needs or you want to create your own administration tool with the features you choose, you can build your own custom console tools. This allows you to determine which features the console includes, which snap-ins it uses, and which additional commands are available.

The steps for creating custom console tools are as follows:

1. Create the console for the tool.

2. Add snap-ins to the console. Snap-ins you use can include Microsoft console tools as well as console tools from third-party vendors.

3. When you are finished with the design, save the console in user mode so that it is ready for use.

Each step is examined in detail in the sections that follow. Optionally, you can create one or more taskpad views containing shortcuts to menu commands, shell commands, and navigation components that you want to include in your custom tool. Techniques for creating taskpad views are discussed in "Designing Custom Taskpads for the MMC" on page 173.

Chapter 6

Step 1: Creating the Console

The first step in building a custom console tool is to create the console that you'll use as the framework. To get started, open a blank MMC in author mode. Click Start, type **mmc** in the Search box, and then press Enter. This opens a blank console titled Console1 that has a default console root as shown in Figure 6-3.

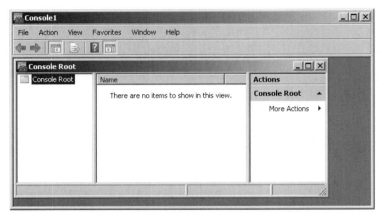

Figure 6-3 Open a blank console with the default console root.

If you want your custom tool to be based on an existing console, you can open its .msc file and add it to the new console. Select Open on the File menu, and then use the Open dialog box to find the .msc file you want to work with. As discussed previously, most .msc files are in the %SystemRoot%\System32 directory. Any existing console you choose will open in author mode automatically. Keep in mind that you generally don't want to overwrite the existing .msc file with the new .msc file you are creating. Because of this, when you save the custom console, be sure to choose Save As rather than Save on the File menu.

If you want to start from scratch, you'll work with the blank console you just opened. The first thing you'll want to do is rename the console root to give it and the related window a more meaningful name. For example, if you are creating a console tool to help you manage the Active Directory Domain Services, you could rename the console root Active Directory Management. To rename the console root and the related window, right-click the console root, and select Rename. Type the name you want to use, and then press Enter.

The next thing you'll want to do is to consider how many windows the console tool must have. Most console tools have a single window, but as shown in Figure 6-4, a console can have multiple windows, each with its own view of the console root. You add windows to the console by using the New Window option on the Window menu. After you add a window, you'll probably want the MMC to automatically tile the windows as shown in the figure. You can tile windows by selecting Tile Horizontally on the Window menu. You don't have to do this, however; anytime there are multiple windows, you can use the options on the Window menu to switch between them.

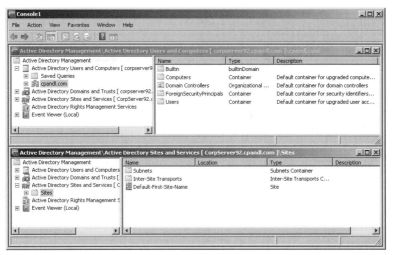

Figure 6-4 Although consoles can have multiple windows, most consoles have a single window.

INSIDE OUT   **Using multiple windows in consoles**

Most console tools have a single window for a good reason: The tool creators wanted to keep the interface as simple as possible. When you introduce multiple windows, you create additional views of the console root, making the interface more complex, and often unnecessarily so. Still, there are times when a console tool with multiple windows could come in handy. For example, you might want to have multiple views of the console root where different areas of the tool are featured, and you could do this by using multiple windows.

Step 2: Adding Snap-Ins to the Console

While you are thinking about the organization of the tool and the possibility of using additional views of the console root, you should also consider the types of snap-ins that you want to add to the console. Each of the tools listed in Table 6-1 is available as a stand-alone snap-in that you can add to the console. If you've installed any third-party tools on the computer, these tools might have stand-alone snap-ins that you can use. Many other snap-ins are available from Microsoft as well.

Again, think of snap-in types or categories, not necessarily specific snap-ins that you want to use. You might want to organize the snap-ins into groups by creating folders for storing snap-ins of a specific type or category. For example, if you are creating a console tool for managing Active Directory, you might find that there are four general types of snap-ins that you want to work with: General, Policy, Security, and Support. You would then create four folders in the console with these names.

Chapter 6

Folders are implemented as a snap-in that you add to the console root. To add folders to the console root, follow these steps:

1. In your MMC, choose Add/Remove Snap-In from the File menu in the main window. As shown in Figure 6-5, this displays the Add Or Remove Snap-Ins dialog box.

2. The Available Snap-Ins list shows all the snap-ins that are available. Scroll through the list until you see the Folder snap-in. Select Folder, and then click Add. The Folder snap-in is added to the Selected Snap-Ins list. Repeat this for each folder that you want to use. If you are following the example and want to use four folders, you would click Add three more times so that four Folder snap-ins appear in the Selected Snap-Ins list.

3. Now close the Add Or Remove Snap-Ins dialog box by clicking OK and return to the console you are creating.

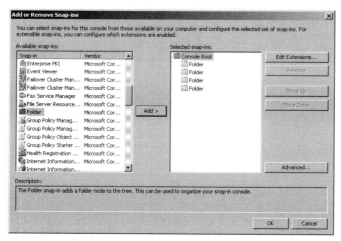

Figure 6-5 Added snap-ins are listed in the Selected Snap-Ins list.

After you add folders, you must rename them. Right-click the first folder, and choose Rename. Type a new name, and then press Enter. If you are following the example, rename the folders: General, Policy, Security, and Support. When you are finished renaming the folders, follow a similar process to add the appropriate snap-ins to your console:

1. Choose Add/Remove Snap-In on the File menu in the main window. This displays the Add Or Remove Snap-Ins dialog box shown previously in Figure 6-5.

2. Click Advanced. Select the Allow Changing The Parent Snap-In check box. When you click OK, the Add Or Remove Snap-Ins dialog box is updated to include a Parent Snap-In drop-down list.

3. In the Parent Snap-In drop-down list, choose the folder to use. In the Available Snap-Ins list, choose a snap-in to add as a subnode of the selected folder and then click Add. When you are finished adding snap-ins to the selected folder, repeat this step to add snap-ins to other folders.

4. When you are finished adding snap-ins to folders, click OK to close the Add Or Remove Snap-Ins dialog box and return to the console you are creating.

Some snap-ins prompt you to select a computer to manage, as shown in the following screen:

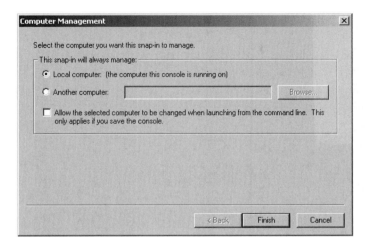

If you want the snap-in to work with whichever computer the console is running on, select Local Computer. Otherwise, select Another Computer, and then type the computer name or IP address of the computer you want to use. If you don't know the computer name or IP address, click Browse to search for the computer you want to work with.

Specify Which Computer to Manage

To ensure you can specify which computer to manage when running the console from the command line, you must select the Allow The Selected Computer To Be Changed When Launching From The Command Line check box. When you select this option and save the console, you can set the computer to manage using the /Computer=*RemoteComputer* parameter.

Some snap-ins are added by using wizards with several configuration pages, so when you select these snap-ins you start the associated wizard and the wizard helps you configure how the snap-in is used. One snap-in in particular that uses a wizard is Link To Web Address. When you add this snap-in, you start the Link To Web Address Wizard, as shown in the following screen, and the wizard prompts you to create an Internet shortcut. Here, you type the Uniform Resource Locator (URL) you want to use, click Next, enter a descriptive name for the URL, then click Finish. Then, when you select the related snap-in in the console tree, the designated Web page appears in the details pane.

Chapter 6

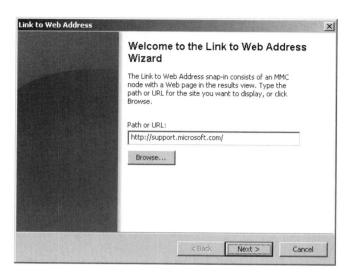

While you are adding snap-ins, you can also examine the available extensions for snap-ins. In the Add Or Remove Snap-Ins dialog box, choose a previously selected snap-in and then click Edit Extensions. In the Extensions For ... dialog box, all available extensions are enabled by default, as shown in the following screen. So, if you want to change this behavior, you can select the Enable Only Selected Extensions option and then clear the individual check boxes for extensions you want to exclude.

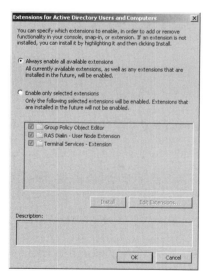

Figure 6-6 shows the example console with snap-ins organized using the previously discussed folders:

- **General** Containing Active Directory Users And Computers, Active Directory Sites And Services, and Active Directory Domains Aand Trusts

- **Policy** Containing Group Policy Management and Resultant Set of Policy

- **Security** Containing Security Templates and Security Configuration And Analysis

- **Support** Containing links to Microsoft Knowledge Base, Microsoft Tech Support, and Windows Server Home Page

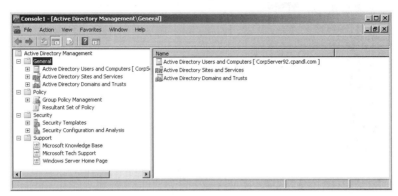

Figure 6-6 A custom console with snap-ins organized into four folders.

Step 3: Saving the Finished Console

When you are finished with the design, you are ready to save your custom console tool. Before you do this, however, there are a couple of final design issues you should consider:

- What you want the initial console view to be

- Which user mode you want to use

- Which icon you want to use

- What you want to name the console tool and where you want it to be located

Setting the Initial Console View Before Saving

By default, the MMC remembers the last selected node or snap-in and saves this as the initial view for the console. In the example tool created, if you expand the General folder, select Active Directory Users And Computers, and then save the console, this selection is saved when the console is next opened.

Keep in mind that subsequent views depend on user selections.

> **Note**
>
> Only the folder with the selected snap-in is expanded in the saved view. If you use folders and select a snap-in within a folder, the expanded view of the folder is saved with the snap-in selected. If you expand other folders, the console is not saved with these folders expanded.

Setting the Console Mode Before Saving

When you are finished authoring the console tool, select Options on the File menu. In the Options dialog box, as shown in the screen on the following page, you can change the console mode so that it is ready for use.

In most cases, you'll want to use User Mode–Full Access. Full access has the following characteristics:

- Users have a Window menu that allows them to open new windows, and they can also right-click a node or snap-in and choose New Window From Here to open a new window.

- Users can right-click and choose New Taskpad View to create a new taskpad view.

With user mode set to Limited Access, Multiple Window, the console has the following characteristics:

- Users have a Window menu that allows them to arrange windows, and they can also right-click a node or snap-in and choose New Window From Here to open a new window.

- Users cannot right-click and choose New Taskpad View to create a new taskpad view.

User mode set to Limited Access, Single Window has the following characteristics:

- Users do not have a Window menu and cannot right-click a node or snap-in and choose New Window From Here to open a new window.

- Users cannot right-click and choose New Taskpad View to create a new taskpad view.

To prevent user selections from changing the view, you'll find two handy options when you select Options from the File menu:

- **Do Not Save Changes To This Console** Select this check box to prevent the user from saving changes to the console. Clear this check box to change the view automatically based on the user's last selection in the console before exiting.

- **Allow The User To Customize Views** Select this check box to allow users to add windows focused on a selected item in the console. Clear this check box to prevent users from adding customized views.

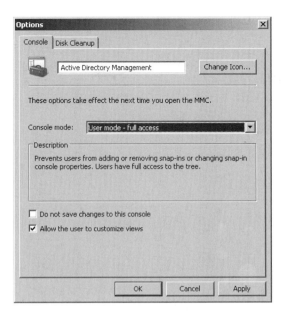

Setting the Console Icon Before Saving

While you are working in the Options dialog box, you might consider setting custom icons for your console tools. All the console tools developed by Microsoft have their own icons. You can use these icons for your console tools as well, or you could use icons from other Microsoft programs quite easily. In the Options dialog box (which is displayed when you select Options on the File menu), click Change Icon. This displays the Change Icon dialog box, as shown in the following screen:

In the Change Icon dialog box, click Browse. By default, the Open dialog box should open with the directory set to %SystemRoot%\System32. In this case, type **shell32.dll** as the File Name, and click Open. You should now see the Change Icon dialog box with the Shell32.dll selected, which will allow you to choose one of several hundred icons registered for use with the operating system shell (see the following screen). Choose an icon, click OK, and then click OK to close the Options dialog box. From then on, the icon will be associated with your custom console tool.

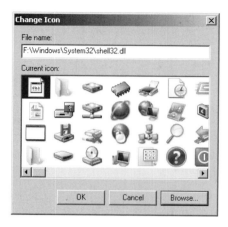

Saving the Console Tool to the Desktop, the Start Menu, or a Folder

After you set the user mode, you can save the console tool. The console tool can appear as one of the following:

- **A desktop icon** Select Save As on the File menu, and then navigate the folder structure to %SystemRoot%\Users\%UserName%\Desktop. Here, %UserName% is the name of the user who will work with the tool. After you type a name for the console, click Save.

- **A menu option on the Start menu for all users** Select Save As on the File menu, and then navigate the folder structure to %SystemRoot%\ProgramData\Microsoft\Windows\Start Menu\Programs\Administrative Tools. After you type a name for the console, click Save.

- **A menu option on the Start menu for a specific user** Select Save As on the File menu, and then navigate the folder structure to %SystemRoot%\Users\%UserName%\AppData\Roaming\Microsoft\Windows\Start Menu\Programs\Administrative Tools. Here, %UserName% is the name of the user who will work with the tool. After you type a name for the console, click Save.

- **A folder icon** Select Save As on the File menu, and then navigate to the folder where you want the console tool to reside. After you type a name for the console, click Save.

> ### Change Tool Names Using the Options Dialog Box
>
> By default, the name shown on the console tool's title bar is set to the file name you designate when saving it. As long as you are in author mode, you can change the console tool name using the Options dialog box. Select Options on the File menu, and then type the name in the box provided at the top of the Console tab.

Designing Custom Taskpads for the MMC

When you want to simplify administration or limit the available tasks for junior administrators or Power Users, you might want to consider adding a taskpad to a console tool. By using taskpads, you can create custom views of your console tools that contain shortcuts to menu commands, shell commands, and navigation components.

Getting Started with Taskpads

Basically, taskpads let you create a page of tasks that you can perform quickly by clicking the associated shortcut links rather than using the existing menu or interface provided by snap-ins. You can create multiple taskpads in a console, each of which is accessed as a taskpad view. If you've worked with Windows XP or Windows Vista, you've probably seen the revised Control Panel, which is a taskpad view of Control Panel. As with most taskpads, Control Panel has two purposes: It provides direct access to the commands or tasks so that you don't have to navigate menus, and it limits your options to a set of predefined tasks that you can perform.

You create taskpads when you are working with a console tool in author mode. Taskpads can contain the following items:

- **Menu commands** Menu commands are used to run the standard menu options of included snap-ins.

- **Shell commands** Shell commands are used to run scripts or programs or to open Web pages.

- **Navigation components** Navigation components are used to navigate to a saved view on the Favorites menu.

Taskpad commands are also called *tasks*. You run tasks simply by clicking their links. In the case of menu commands, clicking the links runs the menu commands. For shell commands, clicking the links runs the associated scripts or programs. For navigation components, clicking the links displays the designated navigation views. If you have multiple levels of taskpads, you must include navigation components to allow users to get back to the top-level taskpad. The concept is similar to having to create a home link on Web pages.

Figure 6-7 shows a taskpad created for the Active Directory Users And Computers snap-in that has been added to the custom tool created earlier in the chapter.

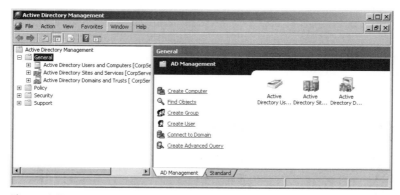

Figure 6-7 A custom console with a taskpad that uses a vertical list.

As you can see, the task page view is labeled AD Management, and it provides the following commands:

- **Create Computer** Used to start the New Object–Computer Wizard

- **Find Objects** Used to open the Find Users, Contacts, And Groups dialog box

- **Create Group** Used to start the New Object–Group Wizard

- **Create User** Used to start the New Object–User Wizard

- **Connect To Domain** Used to select the domain to work with

- **Create Advanced Query** Used to define an Active Directory query and save it so that it can be reused

> **Note**
>
> You could also add a Connect To Domain Forest option that would be used to select the domain forest to work with. We haven't used the taskpad to limit the options; rather, we've simply provided quick access shortcuts to commonly run tasks. In the next section, you'll learn how to limit user options.

Understanding Taskpad View Styles

Taskpads can be organized in several different ways. By default, they will have two views: an extended taskpad view and a standard view. The extended view contains the list of tasks that you've defined and can also contain the console items being managed. The standard view contains only the console items being managed. When you create the taskpad, you have the option of hiding the standard view simply by selecting the Hide Standard Tab check box.

The extended view of the taskpad can be organized using a vertical list, a horizontal list, or no list. In a vertical list as shown previously in Figure 6-7, taskpad commands are listed to the left of the console items they are used to manage. This organization approach works well when you have a long list of tasks and you still want users to be able to work with the related snap-ins.

With a horizontal list, as shown in Figure 6-8, the console items managed by the taskpad are listed above the taskpad commands. This organization style is best when you want to display multiple columns of taskpad commands and still be able to work with the related snap-ins.

Figure 6-8 A custom console with a taskpad that uses a horizontal list.

In some cases, you might not want to show the console items being managed by the taskpad in the same view as the tasks. In this case, you can specify that no list should be used. When you choose the No List option, the taskpad commands are shown by themselves on the taskpad tab (AD Management in the example), and users can click the Standard tab to access the related console items.

INSIDE OUT   Limiting user options in taskpads

As discussed, you can limit the options users have in console tools by selecting both the No List option and the Hide Standard Tab check box. Keep in mind that if the console tool doesn't include a taskpad for a snap-in, users will still be able to manage the snap-in in the usual way. For example, the taskpad shown in Figure 6-8 doesn't define any tasks that manage policy or security, so the snap-ins in these folders will be fully accessible. To make it so users can't work with these snap-ins directly, you must define taskpads for those snap-ins or add tasks that use menu commands from those snap-ins to the current taskpad or another taskpad.

Chapter 6

When you select the No List option, you can limit users' options to the tasks you've defined and not allow users to access the console items being managed. To do this, you specify that the Standard tab should be hidden. From then on, when working with the console items being managed, users can perform only the tasks defined on the taskpad, such as those shown in Figure 6-9.

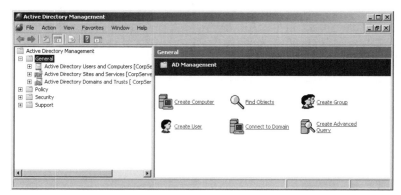

Figure 6-9. By using the No List style and hiding the Standard tab, you can limit user options.

Creating and Managing Taskpads

Any console tool that has at least one snap-in can have an associated taskpad. To create a taskpad, you must open the console in author mode, then follow these steps:

1. In your custom MMC, right-click the folder or console item that you want to work with, choose Action, and then choose New Taskpad View to start the New Taskpad View Wizard. Keep in mind that a single taskpad can be used to manage multiple console items.

2. In the New Taskpad View Wizard, click Next, and then configure the taskpad display (see Figure 6-10 for an example). Select the style for the details page as Vertical List, Horizontal List, or No List, and set the task description style as Text or InfoTip. You can also choose to hide the Standard tab (which only limits the tasks that can be performed if you also select the No List style). As you make selections, the wizard provides a depiction of what the results will look like as a finished taskpad. Click Next to continue.

3. On the Taskpad Reuse page (shown in Figure 6-11), you must decide whether to apply the taskpad view to the selected tree item only (the item you right-clicked) or to any other tree item of the same type. If you choose the latter option, you also have the option to change the default display for any items used in the taskpad to the taskpad view. Typically, you'll want to do this to standardize the view, especially if you've hidden the Standard tab and don't want users to have other options. Click Next.

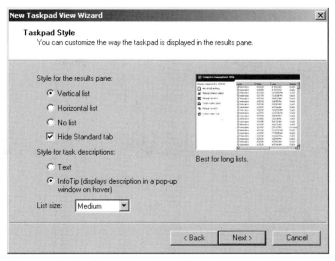

Figure 6-10 Configure the taskpad display in the New Taskpad View Wizard.

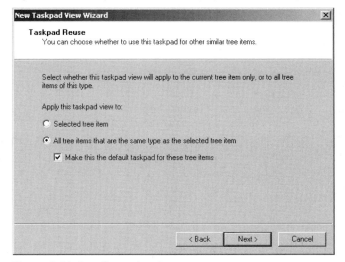

Figure 6-11 Specify a taskpad target.

Note

Basically, all snap-ins are of the same type. So, if you apply the taskpad to any other tree item of the same type, the taskpad view can include any snap-in that you have added to the console.

4. Next, you set the name and description for the taskpad. The name appears at the top of the taskpad and on the tab at the bottom of the taskpad. The description appears at the top of the taskpad under the taskpad name. Click Next.

5. On the final wizard page, you can click Finish to create the taskpad. The Add New Tasks To This Taskpad After The Wizard Closes check box is selected by default, so if you click Finish without clearing this option, the New Task Wizard starts and helps you create tasks for the taskpad.

If you want to create multiple taskpads, you can repeat this procedure. For the example console, you might want to have a taskpad for each folder and so in that case would create three additional taskpads. Any additional taskpads you create can be placed at the same place in the console tree or at a different part of the console tree. You access multiple taskpads placed at the same part of the console tree by using the tabs provided in the details pane.

As long as you are in author mode, any taskpad you created can easily be edited or removed. To edit a taskpad view, right-click the item where you defined the taskpad, and then select Edit Taskpad View from the shortcut menu. This opens a Properties dialog box containing two tabs:

- **General** Use the options on the General tab shown in the following screen to control the taskpad style as well as to display or hide the Standard tab. Click Options to specify to which items the taskpad view is applied.

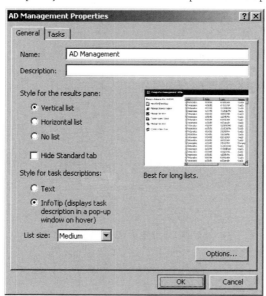

- **Tasks** Use the Tasks tab to list current tasks defined for the taskpad. Use the related options to create new tasks or manage the existing tasks.

Creating and Managing Tasks

You create tasks by using the New Task Wizard. By default, this wizard starts automatically when you finish creating a taskpad view. You can start the wizard using the taskpad Properties dialog box as well. On the Tasks tab, click New. Alternatively, in your MMC, right-click the folder or console item where you defined the taskpad, and then select Edit Taskpad View from the shortcut menu.

After the New Task Wizard is started, click Next, and then select the command type as follows:

- Choose Menu Command to run the standard menu options of included snap-ins.
- Choose Shell Command to run scripts or programs or to open Web pages.
- Choose Navigation to navigate to a saved view on the Favorites menu.

The subsequent screens you see depend on the type of task you are creating.

Creating Menu Command Tasks

After choosing to create a menu command, select a source for the command, as shown in Figure 6-12. You specify the source of the command as a node from the console tree or from the list in the results pane for the item selected when you started the wizard. If you choose Node In The Tree as the source, select a snap-in in the console tree, and then choose one of the available commands for that snap-in. The commands available change based on the snap-in you've selected.

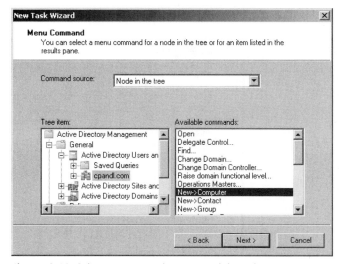

Figure 6-12 Select a command source and then choose a command from the list of available commands.

Next, you set the name and description for the task. The name is used as the shortcut link designator for the task. The description is displayed as text under the shortcut link or as an InfoTip, depending on the way you configured the taskpad.

On the Task Icon page, you can choose an icon for the task. Select Icons Provided By MMC to choose any of the icons provided by the MMC. Click an icon to select it and to display what the icon symbolizes and its alternate meanings. If you want to use a different set of icons, select Custom Icon, and then click Browse. This displays the Change Icon dialog box. Click Browse to display the Open dialog box. By default, the Open dialog box should open with the directory set to %SystemRoot%\System32. In this case, type **shell32.dll** as the File Name, and click Open. You should now see the Change Icon dialog box with the Shell32.dll selected, which will allow you to choose one of several hundred icons registered for use with the operating system shell.

When you click Next again, the wizard confirms the task creation and shows a current list of tasks on the taskpad provided you click Finish to finalize the creation of the current task. If you want to create another task, select the When I Click Finish, Run This Wizard Again check box, and then repeat this process. Otherwise, just click Finish.

Creating Shell Command Tasks

After choosing to create a shell command, specify the command line for the task, as shown in Figure 6-13.

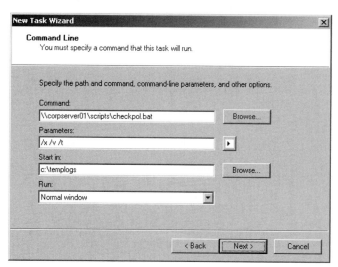

Figure 6-13 Set the command line for the script or program you want to run.

The options are as follows:

- **Command** The full file or Universal Naming Convention (UNC) path to the command you've chosen to run, such as C:\Scripts\Checkpol.bat or \\Corpserver01\Scripts\Checkpol.bat. The command can be a shell or batch script or a program. If you don't know the path to use, click Browse, and then use the Open dialog box to find the program that you want to run.

- **Parameters** The command-line parameters you want to pass to the script or program. Click the right arrow beside the Parameters field to display variables that you can use (these are related to the snap-in you selected originally when creating the taskpad). Select a variable to add it to the list of command-line parameters.

- **Start In** The startup (or base) directory for the script or program you've chosen, such as C:\Temp.

- **Run** The type of window the script or program should run within, either a normal, minimized, or maximized window.

Next, you set the name and description for the task. The name is used as the shortcut link designator for the task. The description is displayed as text under the shortcut link or as an InfoTip, depending on the way you configured the taskpad.

Next, you can choose an icon for the task. As discussed previously, you can select Icons Provided By MMC or Custom Icon. If you use custom icons, you probably want to use the Shell32.dll in the %SystemRoot%\System32 directory to provide the custom icon.

When you click Next again, the wizard confirms the task creation and shows a current list of tasks on the taskpad provided you click Finish to finalize the creation of the current task. If you want to create another task, select the When I Click Finish, Run This Wizard Again check box, and then repeat this process. Otherwise, just click Finish.

Creating Navigation Tasks

Navigation tasks are used to create links from one taskpad to another or from a taskpad to a saved console view. Before you can create navigation tasks, you must save a console view or a view of a particular taskpad to the Favorites menu. To do this, while in author mode, navigate down the console tree until the taskpad or item to which you want to navigate is selected, and then select Add To Favorites on the Favorites menu. In the Add To Favorites dialog box, shown in Figure 6-14, type a name for the favorite, and then click OK. Then you can create a navigation task on a selected taskpad that uses that favorite.

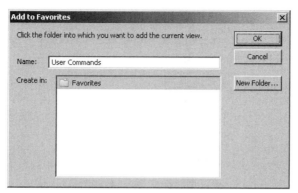

Figure 6-14 Save the current view of the console tool to the Favorites menu.

You create the navigation task using the New Task Wizard. In the New Task Wizard, choose Navigation as the task type. Next, select the favorite to which you want users to navigate when they click the related link. As shown in Figure 6-15, the only favorites available are the ones you've created as discussed previously.

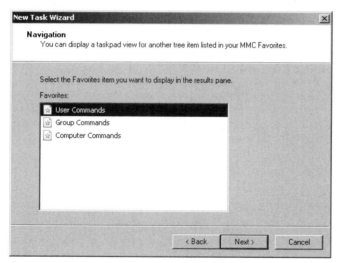

Figure 6-15 Select the previously defined favorite that you want to use.

Next, you set the name and description for the task. The name is used as the shortcut link designator for the task. The description is displayed as text under the shortcut link or as an InfoTip, depending on the way you configured the taskpad. If you are creating a link to the main console tool page, you might want to call it Home.

Next, you can choose an icon for the task. As discussed previously, you can select Icons Provided By MMC or Custom Icon. If you created a link called Home, there is a Home icon provided by the MMC to use. If you use custom icons, you probably want to use the Shell32.dll in the %SystemRoot%\System32 directory to provide the custom icon.

When you click Next again, the wizard confirms the task creation and shows a current list of tasks on the taskpad provided you click Finish to finalize the creation of the current task. If you want to create another task, select the When I Click Finish, Run This Wizard Again check box, and then repeat this process. Otherwise, just click Finish.

Arranging, Editing, and Removing Tasks

As long as you are in author mode, you can edit tasks and their properties by using the taskpad Properties dialog box. To display this dialog box, right-click the folder or item where you defined the taskpad, and then select Edit Taskpad View from the shortcut menu. On the Tasks tab shown in Figure 6-16, you can do the following:

- **Arrange tasks** To arrange tasks in a specific order, select a task, and then click Move Up or Move Down to set the task order.

- **Create new tasks** To create a new task, click New, and then use the New Task Wizard to define the task.

- **Edit existing tasks** To edit a task, select it, and then click Modify.

- **Remove tasks** To remove a task, select it, and then click Remove.

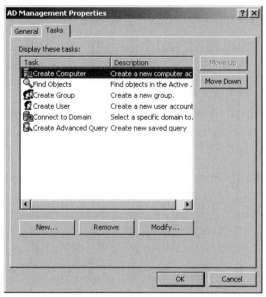

Figure 6-16 Use the Tasks tab in the taskpad Properties dialog box to arrange, create, edit, and remove tasks.

Publishing and Distributing Your Custom Tools

As you've seen, the MMC provides a complete framework for creating custom tools that can be tailored to the needs of a wide range of users. For administrators, you could create custom consoles tailored for each individual specialty, such as security administration, network administration, or user administration. For junior administrators or advanced users with delegated privileges, you could create custom consoles that include taskpads that help guide them by providing lists of common commands, and you can even restrict this list so that these individuals can perform only these commands.

Because custom consoles are saved as regular files, you can publish and distribute them as you would any other file. You could put the consoles on a network file server in a shared folder. You could e-mail the consoles directly to those who will use them. You could use Active Directory to publish the tools. You could even copy them directly to the Start menu on the appropriate computer as discussed previously.

In any case, users need appropriate access permissions to run the tasks and access the snap-ins. These permissions must be granted for a particular computer or the network. Keep in mind also that the MMC version shipped with Windows Server 2003 and previous versions of the Windows operating system will not run tools created using the MMC version that ships with Windows Server 2008 (MMC 3.0). Unless a computer has been updated specifically to use MMC 3.0, this version runs on only Windows Server 2008 and Windows Vista.

Configuring Roles, Role Services, and Features

Windows Server 2008 has different configuration architecture than its predecessors. You prepare servers for use by installing and configuring the following components:

- **Server roles** Server roles are related sets of software components that allow servers to perform a specific function for users and other computers on networks. A computer can be dedicated to a single role, such as Active Directory Domain Services, or a computer can provide multiple roles.

- **Role services** Role services are software components that provide the functionality of server roles. Each server role has one or more related role services. Some server roles, such as Domain Name Service (DNS) and Dynamic Host Configuration Protocol (DHCP), have a single function and installing the role installs this function. Other roles, such as Network Policy And Access Services and Active Directory Certificate Services, have multiple role services that you can install. With these server roles, you can choose which role services to install.

- **Features** Features are software components that provide additional functionality. Features, such as WINS and Windows Server Backup, are installed and removed separately from roles and role services. A computer can have multiple features installed or none, depending on its configuration.

You configure roles, role services, and features using the Server Manager console. Server Manager has a command-line counterpart, called ServerManagerCmd.exe, which you can install as a feature.

Using Roles, Role Services, and Features

Before modifying a server's configuration, you should carefully plan how adding or removing a role, role service, or feature will affect a server's overall performance. Although you typically want to combine complementary roles, doing so increases the workload on the server, so you'll need to optimize the server hardware accordingly. Also, keep in mind that roles, role services, and features can be dependent on other roles, role services, and features. When you install roles, role services, and features, Server Manager prompts you to install any additional roles, role services, or features that are required. If you try to remove a required component of an installed role, role service, or feature, Server Manager warns that you cannot remove the component unless you also remove the other role, role service, or feature.

Table 7-1 provides an overview of the primary roles and the related role services that you can deploy on a server running Windows Server 2008. In addition to roles and features that are included with Windows Server 2008 by default, Server Manager enables integration of additional roles and features that are available on the Microsoft Download Center as optional updates to Windows Server 2008.

Table 7-1 Primary Roles and Related Role Services for Windows Server 2008

Role	Description
Active Directory Certificate Services (AD CS)	AD CS provides functions necessary for issuing and revoking digital certificates for users, client computers, and servers. Includes these role services: Certification Authority, Certification Authority Web Enrollment, Online Certificate Status Protocol, and Microsoft Simple Certificate Enrollment Protocol (MSCEP).
Active Directory Domain Services (AD DS)	AD DS provides functions necessary for storing information about users, groups, computers, and other objects on the network and makes this information available to users and computers. Domain controllers give network users and computers access to permitted resources on the network.
Active Directory Federation Services (AD FS)	AD FS complements the authentication and access management features of AD DS by extending them to the World Wide Web. Includes these role services and subservices: Federation Service, Federation Service Proxy, AD FS Web Agents, Claims-Aware Agent, and Windows Token-Based Agent.
Active Directory Lightweight Directory Services (AD LDS)	AD LDS provides a data store for directory-enabled applications that do not require AD DS and do not need to be deployed on domain controllers. Does not include additional role services.
Active Directory Rights Management Services (AD RMS)	AD RMS provides controlled access to protected e-mail messages, documents, intranet Web pages, and other types of files. Includes these role services: Active Directory Rights Management Server and Identity Federation Support.
Application Server	Application Server allows a server to host distributed applications built using ASP.NET, Enterprise Services, and .NET Framework 3.0. Includes more than a dozen role services, which are discussed in detail in *Internet Information Services (IIS) 7.0 Administrator's Pocket Consultant* (Microsoft Press, 2007).
DHCP Server	DHCP provides centralized control over Internet Protocol (IP) addressing. DHCP servers can assign dynamic IP addresses and essential TCP/IP settings to other computers on a network. Does not include additional role services.
DNS Server	DNS is a name resolution system that resolves computer names to IP addresses. DNS servers are essential for name resolution in Active Directory domains. Does not include additional role services.
Fax Server	Fax Server provides centralized control over sending and receiving faxes in the enterprise. A fax server can act as a gateway for faxing and allows you to manage fax resources, such as jobs and reports, and fax devices on the server or on the network. Does not include additional role services.

Role	Description
File Services	File Services provide essential services for managing files and the way they are made available and replicated on the network. A number of server roles require some type of file service. Includes these role services and subservices: File Server, Distributed File System, DFS Namespace, DFS Replication, File Server Resource Manager, Services for Network File System (NFS), Windows Search Service, Windows Server 2003 File Services, File Replication Service (FRS), and Indexing Service.
Network Policy And Access Services (NPAS)	NPAS provides essential services for managing routing and remote access to networks. Includes these role services: Network Policy Server (NPS), Routing And Remote Access Services (RRAS), Remote Access Service, Routing, Health Registration Authority, and Host Credential Authorization Protocol (HCAP).
Print Services	Print Services provide essential services for managing network printers and print drivers. Includes these role services: Print Server, LPD Service, and Internet Printing.
Terminal Services	Terminal Services provide services that allow users to run Windows-based applications that are installed on a remote server. When users run an application on a terminal server, the execution and processing occur on the server, and only the data from the application is transmitted over the network. Includes these role services: Terminal Server, TS Licensing, TS Session Broker, TS Gateway, and TS Web Access.
Universal Description Discovery Integration (UDDI) Services	UDDI provides capabilities for sharing information about Web services both within an organization and between organizations. Includes these role services: UDDI Services Database and UDDI Services Web Application.
Web Server (IIS)	Web Server (IIS) is used to host Web sites and Web-based applications. Web sites hosted on a Web server can have both static content and dynamic content. You can build Web applications hosted on a Web server using ASP.NET and .NET Framework 3.0. When you deploy a Web server, you can manage the server configuration using IIS 7.0 modules and administration tools. Includes several dozen role services, which are discussed in detail in *Internet Information Services (IIS) 7.0 Administrator's Pocket Consultant*.
Windows Deployment Services (WDS)	WDS provides services for deploying Windows computers in the enterprise. Includes these role services: Deployment Server and Transport Server.
Windows SharePoint Services	Windows SharePoint Services enable team collaboration by connecting people and information. A SharePoint server is essentially a Web server running a full installation of IIS and using managed applications that provide the necessary collaboration functionality.
Windows Server Update Services	Microsoft Windows Server Update Services (WSUS) allows you to distribute updates that are released through Microsoft Update to computers in your organization using centralized servers rather than individual updates.

Table 7-2 provides an overview of the primary features that you can deploy on a server running Windows Server 2008. Unlike earlier releases of Windows, some important server features are not installed automatically. For example, you must add Windows Server Backup to use the built-in backup and restore features of the operating system.

Table 7-2 Primary Features for Windows Server 2008

Feature	Description
.NET Framework 3.0	Provides .NET Framework 3.0 APIs for application development. Additional subfeatures include .NET Framework 3.0 Features, XPS Viewer, and Windows Communication Foundation (WCF) Activation Components.
BitLocker Drive Encryption	Provides hardware-based security to protect data through full-volume encryption that prevents disk tampering while the operating system is offline. Computers that have Trusted Platform Module (TPM) can use BitLocker Drive Encryption in Startup Key or TPM-only mode. Both modes provide early integrity validation.
Background Intelligent Transfer Service (BITS) Server Extensions	Provides intelligent background transfers. When this feature is installed, the server can act as a BITS server that can receive file uploads by clients. This feature isn't necessary for downloads to clients using BITS.
Connection Manager Administration Kit (CMAK)	Provides functionality for generating Connection Manager profiles.
Desktop Experience	Provides additional Windows Vista desktop functionality on the server. Windows Vista features added include Windows Media Player, desktop themes, and Windows Photo Gallery. Although these features allow a server to be used like a desktop computer, they can reduce the server's overall performance.
Failover Clustering	Provides clustering functionality that allows multiple servers to work together to provide high availability for services and applications. Many types of services can be clustered, including file and print services. Messaging and database servers are ideal candidates for clustering.
Group Policy Management	Installs the Group Policy Management Console (GPMC), which provides centralized administration of Group Policy.
Internet Printing Client	Provides functionality that allows clients to use HTTP to connect to printers on Web print servers.
Internet Storage Name Server (iSNS)	Provides management and server functions for Internet SCSI (iSCSI) devices, allowing the server to process registration requests, de-registration requests, and queries from iSCSI devices.
Line Printer Remote (LPR) Port Monitor	Installs the LPR Port Monitor, which allows printing to devices attached to UNIX-based computers.

Feature	Description
Message Queuing	Provides management and server functions for distributed message queuing. A group of related subfeatures is available as well.
Multipath I/O (MPIO)	Provides functionality necessary for using multiple data paths to a storage device.
Network Load Balancing (NLB)	NLB provides failover support and load balancing for IP-based applications and services by distributing incoming application requests among a group of participating servers. Web servers are ideal candidates for load balancing.
Peer Name Resolution Protocol (PNRP)	Provides Link-Local Multicast Name Resolution (LLMNR) functionality that allows peer-to-peer name-resolution services. When you install this feature, applications running on the server can register and resolve names using LLMNR.
Remote Assistance	Allows a remote user to connect to the server to provide or receive Remote Assistance.
Remote Server Administration Tools (RSAT)	Installs role- and feature-management tools that can be used for remote administration of other Windows Server 2008 systems. Options for individual tools are provided or you can install tools by top-level category or subcategory.
Removable Storage Manager (RSM)	Installs the Removable Storage Manager tool, which you can use to manage removable media and removable media devices.
Remote Procedure Call (RPC) over HTTP Proxy	Installs a proxy for relaying RPC messages from client applications over HTTP to the server. RPC over HTTP is an alternative to having clients access the server over a VPN connection.
Simple TCP/IP Services	Installs additional TCP/IP services, including Character Generator, Daytime, Discard, Echo, and Quote of the Day.
Simple Mail Transfer Protocol (SMTP) Server	SMTP is a network protocol for controlling the transfer and routing of e-mail messages. When this feature is installed, the server can act as a basic SMTP server. For a full-featured solution, you'll need to install a messaging server such as Microsoft Exchange Server 2007.
Simple Network Management Protocol (SNMP) Services	SNMP is a protocol used to simplify management of TCP/IP networks. You can use SNMP for centralized network management if your network has SNMP-compliant devices. You can also use SNMP for network monitoring via network management software.
Storage Manager For SANs	Installs the Storage Manager For SANs console. This console provides a central management interface for storage area network (SAN) devices. You can view storage subsystems, create and manage logical unit numbers (LUNs), and manage iSCSI target devices. The SAN device must support Visual Disk Services (VDS).

Feature	Description
Subsystem for UNIX-based Applications (SUA)	Provides functionality for running UNIX-based programs. You can download additional management utilities from the Microsoft Web site.
Windows Internal Database	Installs SQL Server 2005 Embedded Edition. This allows the server to use relational databases with Windows roles and features that require an internal database, such as AD RMS, UDDI Services, Windows Server Update Services (WSUS), Windows SharePoint Services, and Windows System Resource Manager.
Windows PowerShell	Installs Windows PowerShell, which provides an enhanced command-line environment for managing Windows systems.
Windows Process Activation Service	Provides support for distributed Web-based applications that use HTTP and non-HTTP protocols.
Windows Recovery Environment	You can use the recovery environment to restore a server using recovery options if you cannot access recovery options provided by the server manufacturer.
Windows Server Backup	Allows you to back up and restore the operating system, system state, and any data stored on a server.
Windows System Resource Manager (WSRM)	Allows you to manage resource usage on a per-processor basis.
WINS Server	WINS is a name-resolution service that resolves computer names to IP addresses. Installing this feature allows the computer to act as a WINS server.
Wireless Networking	Allows the server to use wireless networking connections and profiles.

Making Supplemental Components Available

Microsoft designed Server Manager and the underlying framework for managing components to be extensible. This makes it easier to provide supplemental roles, role services, and features for the operating system. Some additional components are available as downloads from the Microsoft Web site, including Windows Media Server 2008 and Windows SharePoint Server 2008.

You can make these components available for installation and configuration by completing the following steps:

1. Download the installer package or packages from the Microsoft Web site. Typically, these are provided as a set of Microsoft Update Standalone Packages (.msu) files.

2. Double-click each installer package to register it for use.

3. If Server Manager is running on the server, restart or refresh Server Manager to make the new components available.

4. In Server Manager, use the appropriate wizard to install and configure the supplemental role, role service, or feature.

Installing Components with Server Manager

Server Manager is the primary tool you'll use to manage roles, role services, and features. Not only can you use Server Manager to add or remove roles, role services, and features, but you can also use Server Manager to view the configuration details and status for these software components.

Viewing Configured Roles and Role Services

When you select Roles in the left pane, Server Manager lists roles you've installed. The main view of the Roles node displays a Roles Summary entry that lists the number and names of roles installed. In the case of error-related events for a particular server role, Server Manager displays a warning icon to the left of the role name.

In the Roles window, the name of a role is a clickable link that accesses the related role details, as shown in Figure 7-1. The role details provide the following information:

- Summary information about the status of related system services. If applicable, Server Manager lists the number of related services that are running or stopped, such as "System Services: 9 Running, 1 Stopped." You can manage a service by selecting it and then clicking Stop, Start, or Restart. In many cases, if a service isn't running as you think it should, you can click Restart to resolve the issue by stopping and then starting the service.

- Summary information about events the related services and components have generated in the last 24 hours, including details on whether any errors have occurred, such as "Events: 31 warning(s), 191 informational in the last 24 hours." If you select an event and then click View Properties, you can get detailed information about the event.

- Summary information about the role services installed, including the number of role services installed and the status (Installed or Not Installed) of each individual role service that you can use with the role.

You can refresh the details manually by selecting Refresh on the Action menu. If you want to set a different default refresh interval, click Configure Refresh at the bottom of the main pane, use the options provided to set a new refresh interval, and then click OK. Otherwise, Server Manager refreshes the details periodically for you.

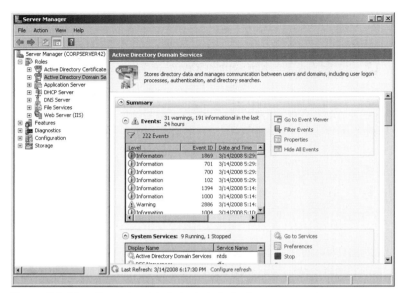

Figure 7-1 View the status details for installed roles.

Managing Server Roles

When you select Roles in Server Manager, the Roles Summary pane provides details on the current roles that you've installed. In the Roles Summary section, you'll find options for adding and removing roles. Keep in mind that some roles cannot be added at the same time as other roles, and you'll have to install each role separately. Other roles cannot be combined with existing roles, and you'll see warning prompts about this.

Adding a Server Role

You can add a server role by following these steps:

1. In Server Manager, select Roles in the left pane and then click Add Roles. This starts the Add Roles Wizard. If the wizard displays the Before You Begin page, read the introductory text and then click Next. You can avoid seeing the Before You Begin page the next time you start this wizard by selecting the Skip This Page By Default check box before clicking Next.

2. On the Select Server Roles page, select the check box for the role or roles to install (see Figure 7-2).

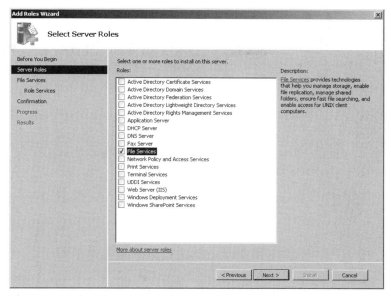

Figure 7-2 Select the roles to install.

Chapter 7

Note

Adding the Active Directory Domain Services role does not configure the server as a domain controller. To configure the server as a domain controller, you must run Dcpromo.exe as discussed in Chapter 33, "Implementing Active Directory." Additionally, if you plan to have a domain controller also act as a DNS server, Microsoft recommends that you install the Active Directory Domain Services role and then use Dcpromo to configure the server as a DNS server and domain controller. A server running a core server installation can act as a domain controller and can also hold any of the Flexible Single Master Operations (FSMO) roles for Active Directory.

---

3. If additional features are required to install a role, as shown in Figure 7-3, you'll then see the Add Features Required For dialog box. Click Add Required Features to close the dialog box and add the required components to the server installation. Click Next twice to continue.

> **Note**
>
> Occasionally, you'll need to install additional role services to install a role or role service. The procedure is similar to installing additional features. If so, you'll see an Add Role Services Required For dialog box. Click Add Required Role Services to close the dialog box and add the required components to the server installation.

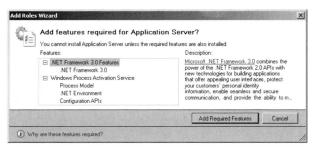

Figure 7-3 Confirm that required features can also be installed.

4. For each of the roles you are adding, you'll see a series of related pages that let you configure the associated role services as well as any other required configuration details. When selecting or clearing role services, keep the following in mind before you click Next to continue:

   ○ If you select a role service with additional required features or role services, you'll see a dialog box listing the additional required features or roles. After you review the required feature or roles, accept the additions and close the dialog box. If you click Cancel instead, the Add Roles Wizard will clear the role service you previously selected.

   ○ If you try to remove a role service that is required based on a previous role service, you'll see a warning prompt about dependent services that the Add Roles Wizard must also remove. In most cases, you'll want to click Cancel to preserve the previous selection. If you click the Remove Dependent Role Services button, the Add Roles Wizard will also remove the previously selected dependent services, which could cause the server to not function as expected.

5. On the Confirm Installation Selections page, click the Print, E-Mail, Or Save This Information link to generate an installation report and display it in Internet Explorer. You can then use standard Internet Explorer features to print or save the report. After you've reviewed the installation options and saved them as necessary, click Install to begin the installation process.

6. When the Add Roles Wizard finishes installing the server with the features you've selected, you'll see the Installation Results page. Review the installation details to ensure that all phases of the installation completed successfully. If any portion of the installation failed, note the reason for the failure and then use these troubleshooting techniques:

    a. Click the Print, E-Mail, Or Save The Installation Report link to create or update the installation report and display it in Internet Explorer.

    b. Scroll down to the bottom of the installation report in Internet Explorer and then click Full Log (Troubleshooting Only) to display the Server Manager log in Notepad.

    c. In Notepad, press Ctrl+F, enter the current date in the appropriate format for your language settings (such as 2009-08-30), and then click Find Next. Notepad will then move through the log to the first entry for the current date.

    d. Review the Server Manager entries for installation problems and take corrective actions as appropriate.

> **Note**
>
> In some cases, you might need to restart the server before installation or removal of a role, role service, or feature can be completed. In this case, you'll be prompted to restart the server when the Add Roles Wizard finishes. When you restart the server and log on, Server Manager will complete the installation or removal process.

Removing a Server Role

You can remove a server role by following these steps:

1. In Server Manager, select Roles in the left pane and then click Remove Roles. This starts the Remove Roles Wizard. If the wizard displays the Before You Begin page, read the introductory text and then click Next. You can avoid seeing the Before You Begin page the next time you start this wizard by selecting the Skip This Page By Default check box before clicking Next.

2. On the Remove Server Roles page, the wizard selects the currently installed roles as shown in Figure 7-4. Clear the check box for the role you want to remove and then click Next.

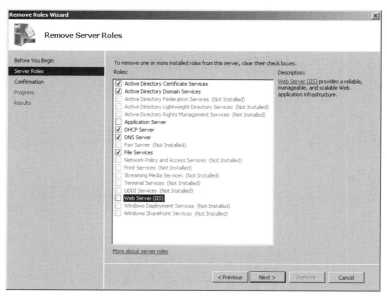

Figure 7-4 Clear selected roles to remove them.

3. If you try to remove a role that another role depends on, as shown in Figure 7-5, you'll see a warning prompt stating that you cannot remove the role unless you also remove the other role as well. If you click the Remove Dependent Role Services button, the Remove Roles Wizard will remove both roles.

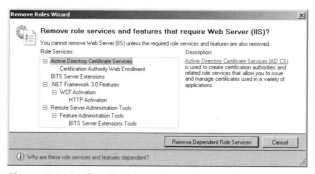

Figure 7-5 Confirm that dependent roles can also be removed.

4. On the Confirm Removal Selections page, review the related role services that the Remove Roles Wizard will remove based on your previous selections and then click Remove.

5. When the Remove Roles Wizard finishes modifying the server configuration, you'll see the Removal Results page. Review the modification details to ensure that all phases of the removal process completed successfully. If any portion of the removal process failed, note the reason for the failure and then use the previously discussed troubleshooting techniques to help resolve the problem.

Managing Role Services

In Server Manager, you can view the role services configured for a role by selecting Roles in the left pane and then scrolling down to the details section for the role that you want to work with. In the details section, you'll find a list of role services that you can install as well as their current Installed or Not Installed status. You can manage role services for servers by clicking Add Role Services or Remove Role Services for the related role details entry. Some roles, however, do not have individual role services that you can manage in this way. With these roles, you can modify the server role or remove the role only.

Adding a Role Service

You can add role services by following these steps:

1. In Server Manager, select Roles in the left pane and then scroll down until you see the details section for the role you want to manage. In the details section for the role, click Add Role Services. This starts the Add Role Services wizard.

2. On the Select Role Services page, the wizard dims the currently installed role services so that you cannot select the associated check box (see Figure 7-6). To add a role service, select its check box in the Role Services list. When you are finished selecting role services to add, click Next and then click Install.

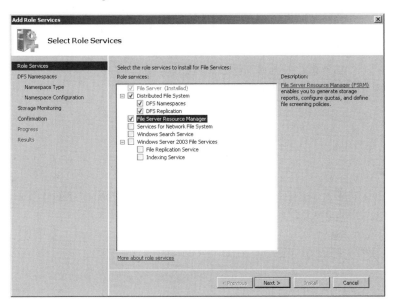

Figure 7-6 Select the role services to add.

Chapter 7

Removing a Role Service

You can remove role services by following these steps:

1. In Server Manager, select Roles in the left pane and then scroll down until you see the details section for the role you want to manage. In the details section for the role, click Remove Role Services. This starts the Remove Role Services wizard.

2. On the Select Role Services page, the wizard selects the currently installed role services as shown in Figure 7-7. To remove a role service, clear the related check box. If you try to remove a role service that another role service depends on, you'll see a warning prompt stating that you cannot remove the role service unless you also remove the other role service as well. If you click the Remove Dependent Role Service button, the Remove Role Services wizard will remove both role services.

3. When you are finished selecting role services to remove, click Next and then click Remove.

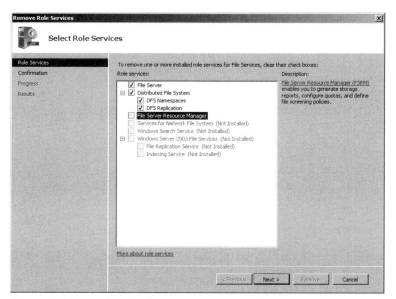

Figure 7-7 Clear selected role services to remove them.

Managing Windows Features

In earlier versions of Windows, you used the Add/Remove Windows Components option of the Add Or Remove Programs utility to add or remove operating system components. In Windows Server 2008, you configure operating system components as Windows features that you can turn on or off rather than add or remove.

Adding a Feature

You can add server features by following these steps:

1. In Server Manager, select Features in the left pane and then click Add Features. This starts the Add Features Wizard. If the wizard displays the Before You Begin page, read the introductory text and then click Next. You can avoid seeing the Before You Begin page the next time you start this wizard by selecting the Skip This Page By Default check box before clicking Next.

2. On the Select Features page, select the check boxes for the feature or features to install as shown in Figure 7-8. If additional features are required to install a feature, you'll then see the Add Features Required For dialog box. Click Add Required Features to close the dialog box and add the required components to the server installation.

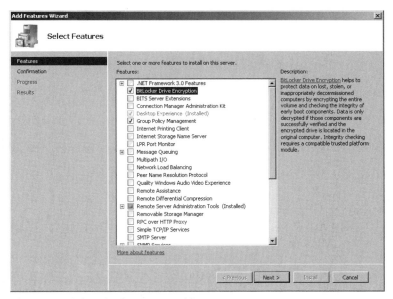

Figure 7-8 Select the features to add.

3. When you are finished selecting features to add, click Next and then click Install.

Removing a Feature

You can remove server features by following these steps:

1. In Server Manager, select Features in the left pane and then click Remove Features. This starts the Remove Features Wizard. If the wizard displays the Before You Begin page, read the introductory text and then click Next. You can avoid seeing the Before You Begin page the next time you start this wizard by selecting the Skip This Page By Default check box before clicking Next.

2. On the Select Features page, the Remove Features Wizard selects the currently installed features as shown in Figure 7-9. To remove a feature, clear the related check box. If you try to remove a feature that another feature depends on, you'll see a warning prompt stating that you cannot remove the feature unless you also remove the other feature as well. If you click the Remove Dependent Feature button, the Remove Features Wizard will remove both features.

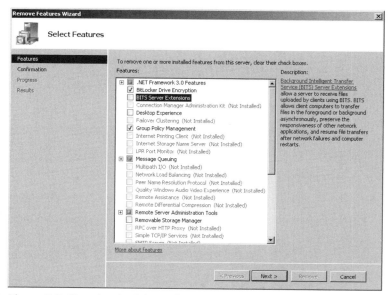

Figure 7-9 Clear the check boxes for selected features to remove them.

3. When you are finished selecting features to remove, click Next and then click Remove.

Installing Components at the Command Line

Server Manager's command-line counterpart is ServerManagerCmd.exe. When you work with ServerManagerCmd, you can:

- View the current configuration

- Add roles, role services, and features

- Remove roles, role services, and features

> **Note**
>
> You can't use ServerManagerCmd at the same time you are using one of Server Manager's add or remove wizards. Only one instance of either ServerManagerCmd or Server Manager can add or remove components at the same time.

Getting Started with ServerManagerCmd

You can manage roles, role services, and features using the following commands and command-line syntaxes:

- **-query** Obtains a detailed list of the server's current state with regard to roles, role services, and features. If *SaveFile.xml* is specified, the query results are displayed and saved to the named file, in XML format. Optionally, you can use -q instead of -query.

  ```
  ServerManagerCmd -query [SaveFile.xml] [-logPath LogFile.txt]
  ```

- **-install** Installs the named role, role service, or feature. The -allSubFeatures or -a parameter allows you to install all subordinate role services and features of the named component. The -setting or -s parameter allows you to configure required settings to specific values. Optionally, you can use -i instead of -install.

  ```
  ServerManagerCmd -install ComponentName [-setting SettingName=SettingValue]
  [-allSubFeatures] [-resultPath Results.xml] [-restart] | -whatIf]
  [-logPath LogFile.txt]
  ```

- **-inputPath** Adds or removes roles, role services, and features as specified in an XML answer file. Optionally, you can use -ip instead of -inputPath.

  ```
  ServerManagerCmd -inputPath AnswerFile.xml [-resultPath Results.xml] [-restart]
  | -whatIf] [-logPath LogFile.txt]
  ```

- **-remove** Removes the named role, role service, or feature. Optionally, you can use -r instead of -remove.

  ```
  ServerManagerCmd -remove ComponentName [-resultPath Results.xml]
  [-restart] | -whatIf] [-logPath LogFile.txt]
  ```

- **-version** Lists the version of the Server Manager command-line utility being used. Optionally, you can use -v instead of -version.

  ```
  ServerManagerCmd -version
  ```

Each of the commands accepts additional parameters and parameter values. Most commands and parameters have short forms that can be used instead of the full name. You can use the -logPath or -l parameter to log error details to a named log file. With the -install and -remove commands, you can use the -whatif or -w command to display the operations that would be performed if the command were executed. With the -install and -remove commands, you can use the -resultPath or -rp command to write standard output results to a named file in XML format. With the -install and -remove commands, you also can use the -restart command to restart the computer automatically (if restarting is necessary to complete the operation).

The parameter values that can be used with commands include:

- **AnswerFile.xml** Uses the XML-formatted answer file to determine what components to add or remove.

- **SaveFile.xml**   Saves the standard output results to a named file in XML format. The results are still displayed and it is important to note that results do not include errors, which are written separately to standard error output.

- **ComponentName**   Identifies the role, role service, or feature to work with.

- **SettingName**   Identifies a required setting by its name.

- **SettingValue**   Sets the configuration value for a setting.

- **LogFile**   Sets the name of the text file to which log error details should be written.

- **Results.xml**   Saves the results of the install or remove operation to a named file in XML format. Results are still displayed.

Table 7-3 provides a quick reference for the long and short form parameters for ServerManagerCmd.

Table 7-3 Long and Short Form Parameters for ServerManagerCmd

Operation	Parameter	Short Form
Change log path	-logPath	-l
Determine what if	-whatif	-w
Display version	-version	-v
Install component	-install	-i
Install from answer file	-inputPath	-ip
Query current state	-query	-q
Remove component	-remove	-r
Restart if necessary	-restart	
Saves the results	-resultPath	-rp
Specify required setting	-setting	-s

Understanding Component Names

Just about every installable role, role service, and feature has a component name. This name identifies the component so it can be manipulated from the command-line. Remember, supplemental components are made available by downloading and installing their installer packages from the Microsoft Web site.

Table 7-4 provides a hierarchical listing of the component names associated with roles, related role services, and related subcomponents. When you are installing a role, you can use the -allSubFeatures parameter to install all the subordinate role services and features listed under the role. When you are installing a role service, you can use the -allSubFeatures parameter to install all the subordinate features listed under the role service.

Table 7-4 **Component Names for Key Roles and Role Services**

Component Name	Role	Service	Feature
AD-Certificate	Active Directory Certificate Services		
ADCS-Cert-Authority		Certification Authority	
ADCS-Web-Enrollment		Certification Authority Web Enrollment	
ADCS-Online-Cert		Online Responder	
ADCS-Device-Enrollment		Network Device Enrollment Service	
	Active Directory Domain Services		
ADDS-Domain-Controller		Active Directory Domain Controller	
ADDS-Identity-Mgmt		Identity Management For UNIX	
ADDS-NIS			Server For Network Information Services
ADDS-NIS			Password Synchronization
ADDS-IDMU-Tools			Administration Tools
	Active Directory Federation Services		
ADFS-Federation		Federation Service	
ADFS-Proxy		Federation Service Proxy	
ADFS-Web-Agents		AD FS Web Agents	
ADFS-Claims			Claims-Aware Agent
ADFS-Windows-Token			Windows Token-Based Agent
ADLDS	Active Directory Lightweight Directory Services		
DHCP	DHCP Server		
DNS	DNS Server		
Fax	Fax Server		
	File Services		
FS-FileServer		File Server	
FS-DFS		Distributed File System	
FS-DFS-Namespace			DFS Namespaces
FS-DFS-Replication			DFS Replication
FS-Resource-Manager		File Server Resource Manager	
FS-NFS-Services		Services For Network File System	
FS-Search-Service		Windows Search Service	
FS-Win2003-Services		Windows Server 2003 File Services	
FS-Replication			File Replication Service

Component Name	Role	Service	Feature
FS-Indexing-Service			Indexing Service
NPAS	Network Policy And Access Services		
NPAS-Policy-Server		Network Policy Server	
NPAS-RRAS-Services		Routing And Remote Access Services	
NPAS-RRAS			Remote Access Service
NPAS-Routing			Routing
NPAS-Health		Health Registration Authority	
NPAS-Host-Cred		Host Credential Authorization Protocol	
Print-Services	Print Services		
Print-Server		Print Server	
Print-LPD-Service		LPD Service	
Print-Internet		Internet Printing	
Terminal-Services	Terminal Services		
TS-Terminal-Server		Terminal Server	
TS-Licensing		TS Licensing	
TS-Session-Broker		TS Session Broker	
TS-Gateway		TS Gateway	
TS-Web-Access		TS Web Access	
WDS	Windows Deployment Services		
WDS-Deployment		Deployment Server	
WDS-Transport		Transport Server	

Table 7-5 provides a hierarchical listing of the component names associated with features and related subfeatures. When you are installing a feature, you can use the -allSubFeatures parameter to install all the subordinate second-level and third-level features listed under the feature. When you are installing a second-level feature, you can use the -allSubFeatures parameter to install all the subordinate third-level features listed under the second-level feature.

> **Note**
> An asterisk following the feature command indicates the feature has unlisted subordinate features that generally are installed together by adding the -allSubFeatures parameter.

Table 7-5 **Component Names for Features and Subfeatures**

Component Name	Feature	Second-Level Feature	Third-Level Feature
NET-Framework*	.NET Framework 3.0 Features		
BitLocker	BitLocker Drive Encryption		
BITS	BITS Server Extensions		
CMAK	Connection Manager Administration Kit		
Desktop-Experience	Desktop Experience		
Failover-Clustering	Failover Clustering		
GPMC	Group Policy Management		
Internet-Print-Client	Internet Printing Client		
ISNS	Internet Storage Name Server		
LPR-Port-Monitor	LPR Port Monitor		
MSMQ*	Message Queuing		
Multipath-IO	Multipath I/O		
NLB	Network Load Balancing		
PNRP	Peer Name Resolution Protocol		
qWave	Quality Windows Audio Video Experience		
Remote-Assistance	Remote Assistance		
RDC	Remote Differential Compression		
RSAT	Remote Server Administration Tools		
RSAT-Role-Tools		Role Administration Tools	
RSAT-ADCS*			Active Directory Certificate Services Tools
RSAT-ADDS*			Active Directory Domain Services Tools
RSAT-ADLDS			Active Directory Lightweight Directory Services Tools
RSAT-RMS			Active Directory Rights Management Services Tools
RSAT-DHCP			DHCP Server Tools
RSAT-DNS-Server			DNS Server Tools
RSAT-Fax			Fax Server Tools
RSAT-File-Services*			File Services Tools
RSAT-NPAS*			Network Policy And Access Services Tools

Chapter 7

Component Name	Feature	Second-Level Feature	Third-Level Feature
RSAT-Print-Services			Print Services Tools
RSAT-TS*			Terminal Services Tools
RSAT-UDDI			UDDI Services Tools
RSAT-Web-Server			Web Server (IIS) Tools
RSAT-WDS			Windows Deployment Services Tools
RSAT-Feature-Tools		Feature Administration Tools	
RSAT-BitLocker			BitLocker Drive Encryption Tools
RSAT-Bits-Server			BITS Server Extensions Tools
RSAT-Clustering			Failover Clustering Tools
RSAT-NLB			Network Load Balancing Tools
RSAT-SMTP			SMTP Server Tools
RSAT-WINS			WINS Server Tools
Removable-Storage	Removable Storage Manager		
RPC-over-HTTP-Proxy	RPC over HTTP Proxy		
Simple-TCPIP	Simple TCP/IP Services		
SMTP-Server	SMTP Server		
SNMP-Services	SNMP Services		
SNMP-Service		SNMP Service	
SNMP-WMI-Provider		SNMP WMI Provider	
Storage-Mgr-SANS	Storage Manager For SANs		
Subsystem-UNIX-Apps	Subsystem For UNIX-Based Applications		
Telnet-Client	Telnet Client		
Telnet-Server	Telnet Server		
TFTP-Client	TFTP Client		
Windows-Internal-DB	Windows Internal Database		
PowerShell	Windows PowerShell		
Backup-Features	Windows Server Backup Features		
Backup		Windows Server Backup	
Backup-Tools		Command-Line Tools	

Component Name	Feature	Second-Level Feature	Third-Level Feature
WSRM	Windows System Resource Manager		
WINS-Server	WINS Server		
Wireless-Networking	Wireless LAN Service		

Determining the Installed Roles, Role Services, and Features

You can determine the roles, roles services, and features that are installed on a server by typing **servermanagercmd -query** at an elevated command prompt. Each installed role, role service, and feature is highlighted and marked as such, and following the display name of each role, role service, and feature is the management naming component in brackets. In the output, roles and role services are listed before features as shown in the following example:

```
----- Roles -----
[X] Active Directory Certificate Services  [AD-Certificate]
    [X] Certification Authority  [ADCS-Cert-Authority]
    [X] Certification Authority Web Enrollment  [ADCS-Web-Enrollment]
    [ ] Online Responder  [ADCS-Online-Cert]
    [ ] Network Device Enrollment Service  [ADCS-Device-Enrollment]
[X] Active Directory Domain Services
    [X] Active Directory Domain Controller  [ADDS-Domain-Controller]
    [ ] Identity Management for UNIX  [ADDS-Identity-Mgmt]
        [ ] Server for Network Information Services  [ADDS-NIS]
        [ ] Password Synchronization  [ADDS-Password-Sync]
        [ ] Administration Tools  [ADDS-IDMU-Tools]

...


----- Features -----
[X] .NET Framework 3.0 Features  [NET-Framework]
    [X] .NET Framework 3.0  [NET-Framework-Core]
    [ ] XPS Viewer  [NET-XPS-Viewer]
    [X] WCF Activation  [NET-Win-CFAC]
        [X] HTTP Activation  [NET-HTTP-Activation]
        [X] Non-HTTP Activation  [NET-Non-HTTP-Activ]
[X] BitLocker Drive Encryption  [BitLocker]
[X] BITS Server Extensions  [BITS]
```

For the purposes of documenting a server's configuration, you can save the output in a file as standard text using the redirection symbol (>) as shown in this example:

```
servermanagercmd -query > MySavedResults.txt
```

Here, you save the output to a file named MySavedResults.txt. If you want to save the results as an XML-formatted file, simply follow the -query command with the name of the XML file, such as:

```
servermanagercmd -query MySaveFile.xml
```

Saving the output to an XML file makes the file easier to manipulate using automation techniques.

Installing Components Using ServerManagerCmd

You can install roles, role services, and features by typing **servermanagercmd -install** **_ComponentName_** at an elevated command prompt, where _ComponentName_ is the name of the component to install as listed in Table 7-4 or Table 7-5. You can install subordinate components by including the -allSubFeatures parameter as shown in the following example:

```
servermanagercmd -install fs-dfs -allsubfeatures
```

Here, you install the Distributed File System role service as well as the subordinate DFS Namespaces and DFS Replication role services. The output for a successful installation should look similar to the following:

```
Start Installation...
[Installation] Succeeded: [File Services] Distributed File System.
[Installation] Succeeded: [File Services] DFS Namespaces.
[Installation] Succeeded: [File Services] DFS Replication.
<100/100>

Success: Installation succeeded.
```

Should a restart be required to complete an installation, you can have ServerManager-Cmd restart the computer by including the -restart parameter. To test the installation prior to performing that actual operation, you can use the -whatif parameter. If you are trying to install components that are already installed you'll see a note stating that no changes were made, such as:

```
NoChange: No changes were made because the roles, role services and features speci-
fied are already installed, or have already been removed from the local computer.
```

If an error occurs and ServerManagerCmd is not able to perform the operation specified, you'll see an error. Generally, error text is shown in red and includes an error flag and error text, such as:

```
WriteError: Failed to write the log file: . Access to the path 'C:\Windows\logs\
ServerManager.log' is denied.
```

This error indicates that ServerManagerCmd couldn't perform the operation because it couldn't gain write access to the log file. Other common errors you'll see are related to invalid arguments passed on the command line, such as:

```
ArgumentNotValid: Invalid parameters. Only specify either -install or -remove.
ArgumentNotValid: Invalid role, role service, or feature: 'fs-dfsd'. The name was not
found.
```

> **Note**
>
> If you forget to run the command prompt as an administrator, you'll see an error stating that Server Manager can be run only by a member of the built-in Administrators group on the local computer. You'll need to run the command prompt with elevated permissions to resolve this error.

When you install components, ServerManagerCmd writes extended logging information to %SystemRoot%\Logs\Servermanager.log. This logging information details every operation performed by ServerManagerCmd. You can write the detailed information to an alternate location by including the -logPath or -l parameter. In this example, you write the logging information to C:\Logs\Install.log:

```
servermanagercmd -install fs-dfs -allsubfeatures -logPath c:\logs\install.log
```

Removing Components Using ServerManagerCmd

You can uninstall roles, role services, and features by typing **servermanagercmd -remove** *ComponentName* at an elevated command prompt, where *ComponentName* is the name of the component to uninstall as listed in Table 7-4 or Table 7-5. You can uninstall subordinate components by including the -allSubFeatures parameter as shown in the following example:

```
servermanagercmd -remove fs-dfs -allsubfeatures
```

Here, you uninstall the Distributed File System role service as well as the subordinate DFS Namespaces and DFS Replication role services, and the output for a successful removal should look similar to the following:

```
Start Removal...
[Removal] Succeeded: [File Services] Distributed File System.
[Removal] Succeeded: [File Services] DFS Namespaces.
[Removal] Succeeded: [File Services] DFS Replication.
<100/100>

Success: Removal succeeded.
```

Should a restart be required to complete a removal, you can have ServerManagerCmd restart the computer by including the -restart parameter. As with installation, you can test the removal prior to performing that actual operation using the -whatif parameter. If you are trying to remove components that aren't installed, you'll see a note stating that no changes were made, such as:

```
NoChange: No changes were made because the roles, role services and features speci-
fied are already installed, or have already been removed from the local computer.
```

If an error occurs and ServerManagerCmd is not able to perform the operation specified, you'll see an error. During the removal process, ServerManagerCmd writes extended logging information to %SystemRoot%\Logs\Servermanager.log. As with the installation process, you can write the detailed information to an alternate location by including the -logPath or -l parameter.

Chapter 7

Managing and Troubleshooting Hardware

Unless you've standardized on a particular hardware platform, most servers that you'll work with will have different hardware components. This means different servers will probably have different motherboards, disk controllers, graphics cards, and network adapters. Fortunately, Windows Server 2008 is designed to work with an extensive list of hardware devices. When you install new hardware, Windows tries to detfect the device automatically and then install the correct driver software so that you can use the device. If Windows has a problem with a device, you must troubleshoot the installation, which usually means finding the correct device drivers for the hardware component and installing them.

One thing to keep in mind when working with devices is that, like other software, driver software can contain bugs. These bugs can cause a variety of problems on your servers, and not only could the hardware stop working, but the server could freeze as well. Because of this, you'll want to monitor routinely for hardware problems and take corrective actions as necessary. It is also helpful to maintain a hardware inventory for servers so that you know which devices are installed and who the manufacturers are.

Understanding Hardware Installation Changes

Hardware installation from Windows Server 2003 to Windows Server 2008 hasn't changed much. What has changed significantly since Windows Server 2003 was introduced, however, are the available options when it comes to hardware devices. All computers can use internal and external hardware devices.

Choosing Internal Devices

Internal hardware devices are devices you install inside your computer. Typically, you'll need to power down and unplug your computer, and then remove the computer case before you can install an internal device.

Although many workgroup and enterprise class server systems continue to use serial attached SCSI devices, servers aren't always built using such robust server systems. Increasingly, for general use, desktop class computers are being configured with server operating systems and most of these computers use internal devices with Enhanced Integrated Drive Electronics (EIDE) or Serial ATA (SATA).

EIDE, also called Parallel ATA (PATA), devices have been used for many years with desktop class computers. Although EIDE is still in use as of the time this book was written, you might find that most newer computers use SATA devices instead. As of the time this book was written, most motherboard manufacturers include SATA input ports on their boards. Because SATA cables are significantly smaller than EIDE cables, this results in less clutter inside your computer and improved airflow for better cooling.

With EIDE and SATA, there are some feature differences that you should know about. Typical EIDE devices support a maximum data transfer rate of 100 megabits per second (Mbps) and allow two devices to be connected per cable. Most EIDE devices have a 10-pin jumper block, which is used to configure whether the device is being used in a single device or Primary (Master)/Secondary (Subordinate) configuration. The pins on the jumper block are also used to configure cable selection settings.

On the other hand, typical SATA devices have a maximum data transfer rate of 150 or 300 Mbps and allow you to connect only one device per cable. Most SATA devices have an 8-pin jumper block and there are no Primary (Master)/Secondary (Subordinate) configurations.

Although Windows Server 2008 can be used with SCSI, EIDE, and SATA hardware devices, your computer must be configured specifically to work with these devices. For example, your computer will need a SCSI controller card to use SCSI devices. Although some older computer system motherboards don't have SATA input ports, you can install a PCI SATA controller card to add support for SATA drives.

Choosing External Devices

External hardware devices are devices you connect to your computer. Because you don't have to open your computer's case to connect external devices, you typically don't need to power down or unplug your computer before installing an external device. This makes external devices easier to install and also means you can attach most external devices without having to reboot your computer.

Most current computers use external devices with USB, FireWire, external SATA (eSATA), or a combination of these interfaces. An example of each interface is shown in the following illustration.

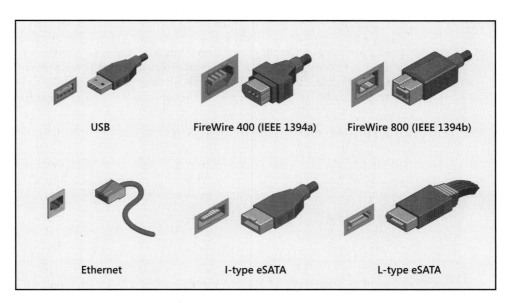

USB   FireWire 400 (IEEE 1394a)   FireWire 800 (IEEE 1394b)

Ethernet   I-type eSATA   L-type eSATA

USB 2.0 is the industry standard peripheral connection for most Windows-based computers. This connection transfers data at a maximum rate of 480 Mbps with sustained data transfer rates usually from 10 to 30 Mbps. The actual sustainable transfer rate depends on many factors including the type of device, the data you are transferring, and the speed of your computer. Each USB controller on your computer has a fixed amount of bandwidth, which all devices attached to the controller must share. If your computer's USB port is an earlier version, USB 1.0 or 1.1, you can use USB 2.0 devices, but the transfer rates will be significantly slower.

FireWire, also called IEEE 1394, is a high-performance connection standard for most Windows-based computers. This interface uses a peer-to-peer architecture in which peripherals negotiate bus conflicts to determine which device can best control a data transfer. FireWire has several configurations, including FireWire 400 and FireWire 800. FireWire 400, also called IEEE 1394a, has maximum sustained transfer rates of up to 400 Mbps. FireWire 800, also called IEEE 1394b, has maximum sustained transfer rates of up to 800 Mbps.

eSATA is an ultra-high-performance connection standard, primarily used with high-performance external devices. With external hard drives, eSATA provides a secure, reliable, and ultra-fast connection. eSATA has maximum sustained transfer rates of up to 3000 Mbps. It is important to note that there are several types of eSATA connectors and cables, and that eSATA and internal SATA cables and connectors cannot be used interchangeably.

INSIDE OUT   Using USB and FireWire devices

Although Windows Server 2008 can be used with both USB and FireWire hardware devices, your computer must be configured specifically to work with these devices. To support USB 2.0, a computer needs a USB 2.0 controller card. To support FireWire, a computer needs a FireWire controller card.

When working with USB, there are some important things to know. First of all, USB 1.0, 1.1, and 2.0 ports all look very similar. For your computer, the best way to determine which types of USB ports are available is to refer to the documentation that came with your computer; this documentation should list the types of USB ports and their locations. There are several different types of USB connectors. For devices that use connector cords, the USB 1.0/1.1 connector typically is U-shaped while the USB 2.0 connector typically is smaller and looks like a chubby letter T.

It is important to point out that newer LCD monitors will have USB 2.0 ports to which you can connect devices as well. When you have USB devices connected to a monitor, the monitor acts like a USB hub device. As with any USB hub device, all devices attached to the hub share the same bandwidth and the total available bandwidth is determined by the speed of the USB input to which the hub is connected on your computer. Generally speaking, never connect devices through a server's monitor when end-user performance is a concern.

When working with FireWire, keep in mind that FireWire ports and cables have different shapes and connectors, making it easy to tell the difference between them—if you know what you're looking for. Early FireWire implementations, which I'll call standard FireWire (as opposed to FireWire 400 or FireWire 800), have a different number of pins on their connector cables and a different number of connectors on their ports. Because of this, you can tell standard FireWire and FireWire 400 apart by looking closely at the cables and ports. If you look closely at standard FireWire cables and ports, you'll see four pins or four connectors. If you look closely at FireWire 400 cables and ports, you'll see six pins or six connectors. Although standard FireWire and FireWire 400 cables have rectangular-shaped connectors with one short flat end and the other rounded, FireWire 800 cables are square with one of the long sides having a notch.

When you are purchasing external devices, you might want to get a device with dual or triple interfaces. A device with dual or triple interfaces will give you more configuration options. Most devices with dual interfaces support USB 2.0 and FireWire 400, where a device with a triple interface might support USB 2.0, FireWire 400, and FireWire 800. Some have all of the previously mentioned interfaces as well as an eSATA interface.

Installing Devices

Every hardware component installed on a system has an associated device driver. Drivers are used to handle the low-level communications tasks between the operating system and hardware components. When you install a hardware component through the operating system, you tell the operating system about the device driver it uses. From then on, the device driver loads automatically and runs as part of the operating system.

Understanding Device Installation

Unlike earlier versions of Windows, Windows Server 2008 is very good at detecting devices that were not installed after upgrading or installing the operating system. If a device wasn't installed because Windows Server 2008 didn't include the driver, the built-in hardware diagnostics will, in many cases, detect the hardware and then use the automatic update framework to retrieve the required driver the next time Windows Update runs, provided that Windows Update is enabled and you've allowed driver updating as well as operating system updating.

After upgrading or installing the operating system, you should check for driver updates and apply them as appropriate before trying other techniques to install device drivers. Windows Update Driver Settings control whether Windows Server 2008 checks for drivers automatically. To access these settings, open the System Properties dialog box, click the Hardware tab, and then click Windows Update Driver Settings. If you want Windows to check for drivers automatically when you connect a new device, select Check For Drivers Automatically (Recommended) and then click OK. If you don't want a computer to check for drivers automatically, select either Ask Me Each Time I Connect A New Device Before Checking For Drivers or Never Check For Drivers When I Connect A Device, and then click OK twice.

Typically, device driver updates are seen as optional updates. The exceptions are for essential drivers, such as those for video, network adapters, and hard disk controllers. Because of these exceptions, you'll want to view all available updates on a computer, rather than only the important updates, to determine whether device driver updates are available. To install available device driver updates, follow these steps:

1. In Control Panel\System And Maintenance, double-click Windows Update. In Windows Update, click View Available Updates. If the computer has installed the updates it last downloaded, the View Available Updates option isn't available. In this case, you can click Check For Updates to see if there are new updates for the computer and then view the available updates (if any).

2. In the View Available Updates dialog box, you can review the available updates. By default, optional updates are not selected for installation. To ensure that an update is installed, select its corresponding check box.

3. Click Install to download and install the selected updates.

After you've installed the device driver, Windows Server 2008 should both detect the hardware within several minutes and install the device automatically. If Windows

Server 2008 detects the device but isn't able to install the device automatically, Windows Server 2008 starts the Driver Software Installation component, which in turn starts the Found New Hardware Wizard. In the Found New Hardware Wizard, you can then click Locate And Install Driver Software (Recommended) to continue with the installation. The Driver Software Installation component will then search for preconfigured drivers.

The Driver Software Installation component should use the driver that you've just made available on the computer to complete the installation. If for some reason this doesn't happen, you'll see a wizard page asking you to insert the disc that came with the hardware device. Continue with the installation manually as discussed in the next section.

Installing New Devices

After you install or connect a new hardware device, you must set up the device so that it is available for use. Most available new devices are plug and play compatible. Windows Server 2008 Plug and Play is optimized to support USB, FireWire, Personal Computer Memory Card International Association (PCMCIA, or PC Card), Peripheral Component Interconnect (PCI), and PCI Express devices. When you connect a Plug and Play device for the first time, Windows Server 2008 reads the Plug and Play identification tag contained in the device's firmware and then searches its master list of identification tags (which is created from the Setup Information files in the Inf folder). If the operating system finds a signed driver with a matching identification tag, it installs the driver and makes the device available for use automatically.

Windows Server 2008 provides pop-up balloon tips in the notification area that tell you about major steps in the Plug and Play installation process, such as device detection and finalization. For example, when installing a new disk drive, Windows Server 2008 might display Found New Hardware: Disk Drive, as shown in the following screen.

Then a balloon message is displayed to tell you that your new hardware is installed and ready to use, as shown in the following screen:

In this example, Plug and Play worked as expected. Windows Server 2008 detected the device, used the Plug and Play identification to determine which driver should be installed, and then set up the device. Because there are so many factors involved, detection and setup don't always work so smoothly, however. Sometimes the Windows operating system will warn you about something that you might need to take action to correct.

One of the more common warnings you'll see is related to you connecting Hi-Speed USB devices to non-Hi-Speed USB ports, as shown in the following screen. This is important because if you are connecting an external hard disk drive or other Hi-Speed USB device, the device won't operate at the rated speed. It will in fact operate at a much slower speed.

> ⚠ **HI-SPEED USB Device Plugged into non-HI-SPEED USB Hub** [×]
> A HI-SPEED USB device is plugged into a non-HI-SPEED USB hub.
> For assistance in solving this problem, click this message.

USB 1.0 is the original USB specification. USB 2.0 is the newer USB specification, and it is referred to as Hi-Speed USB. Although you can connect USB 2.0 devices to USB 1.0 ports, the devices operate at the USB 1.0 speed (which is many times slower than USB 2.0). If you want to achieve high-speed USB transfers, you must connect to a USB 2.0 port, if available. You might also want to consider adding a PCI expansion card with USB 2.0 ports.

Because of Plug and Play, you should be able to install new devices easily by using one of the following techniques:

- For a non-USB or non-FireWire device, simply shut down the computer, insert the card into the appropriate slot or connect the device to the computer, restart the computer, and then let Windows Server 2008 automatically detect the new device.

- For a USB or FireWire device, simply insert the device into the appropriate slot or connect it to the computer, restart the computer, and then let Windows Server 2008 automatically detect the new device.

Depending on the device, Windows Server 2008 should automatically detect the new device and install a built-in driver to support it as discussed previously. The device should then function immediately without any problems. Well, that's the idea, but it doesn't always work out that way. The success of an automatic detection and installation depends on the device being plug and play compatible and a device driver being available.

Windows Server 2008 includes many device drivers in a standard installation, and in this case, it should install the device automatically. If driver updating is allowed through Windows Update, Windows Server 2008 checks for drivers automatically using Windows Update either when you connect a new device or when it first detects the device. Because Windows Update does not automatically install device drivers, you'll need to check for available updates to install the driver.

Chapter 8

INSIDE OUT **Installing new drivers**

All device drivers provided through Windows Update have been thoroughly tested in the Windows Hardware Quality Labs (WHQL), and you should be able to count on them not to cause your system to crash or become unstable. However, just because driver updates are available doesn't mean you should install them. In a production environment, you'll rarely want to download and install new device drivers without thoroughly testing them yourself first. Better safe than sorry—always. Typically, you install new device drivers because you are experiencing problems with the old drivers or looking for new functionality. If you aren't experiencing problems or don't require the additional functionality, you might not want to update the drivers.

If Windows Server 2008 detects a Plug and Play device after you've connected it but cannot locate a suitable driver, it displays a warning that a problem occurred during installation, as shown in the following screen:

Sometimes when this happens, you must install the hardware device manually as you do with non–Plug and Play devices. See "Adding Non–Plug and Play Hardware" on page 235 for details.

More typically, Windows Server 2008 starts the Driver Software Installation component, which in turn starts the Found New Hardware Wizard. In this case, you can complete the installation by following these steps:

1. In the Found New Hardware Wizard, click Locate And Install Driver Software (Recommended) to continue with the installation.

2. The Driver Software Installation component will then search for preconfigured drivers. If it doesn't find a preconfigured driver, you are prompted to insert the disc that came with the hardware device.

3. Use one of the following techniques to continue:
   - If you have an installation disc for the device, insert it and then follow the prompts. The device should then be installed properly. Skip the remaining steps.
   - If you don't have an installation disc, click I Don't Have The Disk. Show Me Other Options and then follow the remaining steps in this procedure.

4. On the next wizard page, click Browse My Computer For Driver Software.

5. Click Browse to select a search location.

6. In the Browse For Folder dialog box, select the start folder for the search and then click OK. Because all subfolders of the selected folder are searched automatically, you can select the drive root path, such as C, to search an entire drive.

7. Click Next. The wizard will search for and install any appropriate driver. If the wizard can't find an appropriate driver, you'll need to obtain one and then follow the procedure in "Installing and Updating Device Drivers" on page 228 to complete the installation.

> **Note**
>
> If the wizard is fails to install the device, there might be a problem with the device itself or the driver, or a conflict with existing hardware. For additional details on adding hardware and troubleshooting, see "Managing Hardware" on page 235.

After you've successfully installed a device, you'll need to perform maintenance tasks periodically for the device and its drivers. When new drivers for a device are released, you might want to test them in a development or support environment to see whether the drivers resolve problems that users have been experiencing or include the new functionality you are looking for. If the drivers install without problems and resolve outstanding issues, you might then want to install the updated drivers on computers that use this device. On a server operating system, you can implement the driver update procedure as follows:

1. Check the device and driver information on each system prior to installing the new driver. Note the location, version, and file name of the existing driver.

2. Install the updated driver and reboot the computer. If the computer and the device function normally after the reboot, consider the update a success.

3. If the computer or the device malfunctions after the driver installation, roll back to the previously installed driver using the standard Device Manager utilities. If you cannot restart the computer and restore the driver, you might need to start the computer in Safe Mode or use Startup Repair to restore the system.

Viewing Device and Driver Details

You use Device Manager to view and configure hardware devices. You'll spend a lot of time working with this tool, so you should get to know it before working with devices.

To open Device Manager and obtain a detailed list of all the hardware devices installed on a system, follow these steps:

1. Click Server Manager on the Quick Launch toolbar, or click Start, then Administrative Tools, and then Server Manager.

Chapter 8

2. In Server Manager, expand the Diagnostics node. This expands the node to display its tools.

3. Select the Device Manager node. As shown in Figure 8-1, you should now see a complete list of devices installed on the system. By default, this list is organized by device type.

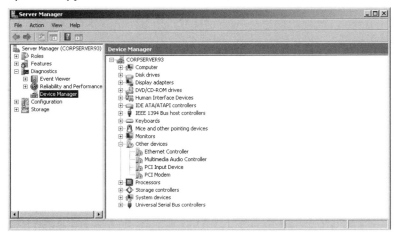

Figure 8-1 Use Device Manager to work with hardware devices.

4. Expand a device type to see a list of the specific instances of that device type.

After you access Device Manager, you can work with any of the installed devices. If you right-click a device entry, a shortcut menu is displayed. The available options depend on the device type, but they include the following:

Properties Displays the Properties dialog box for the device

Uninstall Uninstalls the device and its drivers

Disable Disables the device but doesn't uninstall it

Enable Enables a device if it's disabled

Update Driver Software Starts the Hardware Update Wizard, which you can use to update the device driver

Scan For Hardware Changes Tells Windows Server 2008 to check the hardware configuration and determine whether there are any changes

---

Note

The device list shows warning symbols if there are problems with a device. A yellow warning symbol with an exclamation point indicates a problem with a device. A red X indicates a device that was improperly installed or disabled by the user or the administrator for some reason.

You can use the options on the View menu in Server Manager to change the defaults for which types of devices are displayed and how the devices are listed. The options are as follows:

Devices By Type Displays devices by the type of device installed, such as disk drive or printer. The connection name is listed below the type. This is the default view.

Devices By Connection Displays devices by connection type, such as audio and video codecs.

Resources By Type Displays the status of allocated resources by type of device using the resource. Resource types are direct memory access (DMA) channels, input/output (I/O) ports, interrupt requests (IRQ), and memory addresses.

Resources By Connection Displays the status of all allocated resources by connection type rather than device type.

Show Hidden Devices Displays non–plug and play devices as well as devices that have been physically removed from the computer but haven't had their drivers uninstalled.

INSIDE OUT   View and save device settings for local and remote computers

You can use Computer Management to view and work with settings on remote computers. Right-click Computer Management in the console tree and then select Connect To Another Computer on the shortcut menu. In the Select Computer dialog box, choose Another Computer, and then type the fully qualified name of the computer you want to work with, such as **entdc01.microsoft.com**, where entdc01 is the computer name and microsoft.com is the domain name. If you don't know the computer name, click Browse to search for the computer you want to work with.

If you want detailed driver lists for multiple computers, you can do this using the Driverquery command-line utility. Use the /V parameter to get verbose output about all drivers or the /SI parameter to display properties only for signed drivers, such as **driverquery /v** or **driverquery /si**. If you want to write the information to a file, use the output redirection symbol (>) followed by the name of the file, such as **driverquery /si > systemdevices.txt**.

To list devices on remote computers, use the /S parameter followed by a computer name or Internet Protocol (IP) address to specify a remote computer to query. You can also specify the Run As permissions by using /U followed by the user name and /P followed by the user's password. Here's an example: **driverquery /v /s corpserver01 /u wrstanek /p 49iners**.

Working with Device Drivers

Each hardware component installed on a computer has an associated device driver. The job of the device driver is to describe how the operating system uses the hardware abstraction layer (HAL) to work with a hardware component. The HAL handles the low-level communication tasks between the operating system and a hardware component. By installing a hardware component through the operating system, you are telling the operating system about the device driver it uses. From then on, the device driver loads automatically and runs as part of the operating system.

Device Driver Essentials

Windows Server 2008 includes an extensive library of device drivers. In the base installation of the operating system, these drivers are maintained in the file repository of the driver store. Some service packs you install will also include updates to the driver store. You can find drivers in the FileRepository folder under %SystemRoot%\System32\DriverStore. The DriverStore folder also contains subfolders for localized driver information. You'll find a subfolder for each language component configured on the system. For example, for localized U.S. English driver information, you'll find a subfolder called en-US.

Every device driver in the driver store is certified to be fully compatible with Windows Server 2008 and is also digitally signed by Microsoft to assure the operating system of its authenticity. When you install a new Plug andPlay compatible device, Windows Server 2008 checks the driver store for a compatible device driver. If one is found, the operating system automatically installs the device.

Every device driver has an associated Setup Information file. This file, which ends with the .inf extension, is a text file containing detailed configuration information about the device being installed. The information file identifies any source files used by the driver as well. Source files have the .sys extension. Drivers are also associated with a component manifest (component.man) file. The manifest file is written in Extensible Markup Language (XML), includes details on the driver's digital signature, and might also include plug and play information used by the device to configure itself automatically.

Every driver installed on a system has a source (.sys) file in the %SystemRoot%\System32\Drivers folder. When you install a new device driver, the driver is written to a subfolder of %SystemRoot%\System32\Drivers, and configuration settings are stored in the Registry. The driver's .inf file is used to control the installation and write the Registry settings. If the driver doesn't already exist in the driver store, it does not already have an .inf file or other related files on the system. In this case, the driver's .inf file and other related files are written to a subfolder of %SystemRoot%\System32\DriverStore\FileRepository when you install the device.

Using Signed and Unsigned Device Drivers

Speaking of new device drivers, Microsoft recommends that you use signed device drivers whenever possible. Every device driver in the driver cache is digitally signed, which certifies the driver as having passed extensive testing by the Windows Hardware Quality Lab (WHQL). A device driver with a digital signature signed by Microsoft should not cause your system to crash or become unstable. The presence of a digital signature signed by Microsoft also ensures that the device driver hasn't been tampered with. If a device driver doesn't have a digital signature signed by Microsoft, it hasn't been approved for use through testing, or its files might have been modified from the original installation by another program. This means that unsigned drivers are much more likely than any other program you've installed to cause the operating system to freeze or the computer to crash.

The assurances you get with digitally signed drivers aren't applicable to unsigned device drivers. When you install an unsigned driver, there is no guarantee that it has been tested, and if the driver is poorly written, it is much more likely to cause the operating system to freeze or the server to crash than any other program you've installed. That said, there are times when you might have to use an unsigned device driver. In some situations, you might find that a particular device doesn't have a signed device driver. Here, you should check the manufacturer's Web site to see whether a signed driver is available because sometimes there is a signed driver, but it's just not distributed with the device or on the Windows Server 2008 distribution discs. If a signed driver isn't available, you might find that you have to use an unsigned driver.

> **Note**
>
> If you have to install an unsigned driver, proceed cautiously and remember to monitor the system closely. If you find that the system is inexplicably freezing or crashing, the unsigned driver is probably to blame and should be rolled back or uninstalled. Remember, any type of faulty driver can cause the system to fail, even a driver for a display adapter, a network adapter, or a sound card.

To prevent problems with unsigned drivers, Windows Server 2008 warns you by default when you try to install an unsigned device driver. You can also configure Windows to eliminate this warning or to prevent unsigned drivers from being installed altogether. To manage device driver settings for computers throughout the organization, you can use Group Policy. When you do this, Group Policy specifies the least secure setting using one of three configuration settings:

Ignore Use this setting to allow users to install any unsigned driver without having to see and respond to a warning prompt.

Warn Use this setting to prompt users each time either to continue with the installation of an unsigned driver or to stop the installation.

Block Use this setting to prevent users from installing unsigned driver software.

> **Note**
>
> When Group Policy is set to Ignore or Warn, you can install unsigned drivers. When Group Policy is set to Block, unsigned device drivers can't be installed without first overriding Group Policy.

You can configure device driver–signing settings on a per-user basis using the Code Signing For Device Drivers policy. This policy is located in User Configuration\Administrative Templates\System\Driver Installation. When you enable this policy, you can specify the action to take as Ignore, Warn, or Block. After you enable it, the system doesn't implement any setting less secure than the established setting.

Viewing Driver Information

To view detailed information about a device, right-click the device and select Properties or simply double-click the related entry in Device Manager. This opens the device's Properties dialog box, as shown in Figure 8-2. Most devices have at least two tabs, either General and Properties or General and Driver.

The most important information on the General tab is the device status. If the device is working properly, this is specifically stated. Otherwise, the error status of the device is shown, and you can click Check For Solutions to start the device troubleshooter. If the device is disabled, you have an option to enable the device instead (as shown in Figure 8-3).

You can temporarily disable a device by selecting Disable on the Driver tab. If you later want to enable the device, click the Enable Device button on the General tab and then when the troubleshooting wizard starts, click Next and then click Finish.

The Driver tab, shown in Figure 8-4, provides basic information about the driver provider, creation date, version, and digital signature. You should be wary of any drivers that list the provider as Unknown as well as drivers that are listed as Not Digitally Signed. Drivers signed by Microsoft are listed as being signed by Microsoft Windows or Microsoft Windows Hardware Compatibility Publisher.

You can view additional information about the driver by clicking Driver Details. If no driver files are required or have been loaded for the device, you'll see a message stating this. Otherwise, you'll see the names and locations of all associated files, including an icon that indicates the signing status of each individual file. Selecting a file in this list displays details for that file in the lower section of the dialog box, as shown in Figure 8-5.

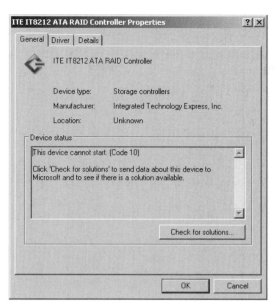

Figure 8-2 Use the device's Properties dialog box to obtain essential information about a device, including whether it is functioning properly.

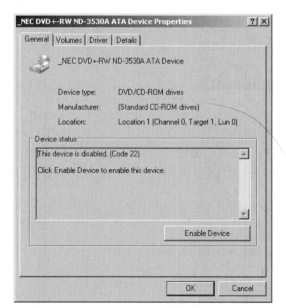

Figure 8-3 Disabled devices are listed with an error status because they aren't functioning; you can enable them by clicking Enable Device.

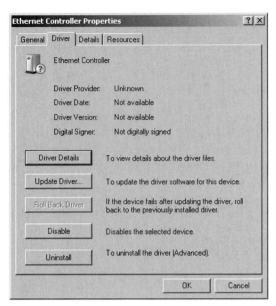

Figure 8-4 Use the Driver tab to determine the driver provider, creation date, version, and digital signature.

Figure 8-5 The Driver File Details dialog box displays information on the driver file locations, the provider, and the file versions.

Viewing Advanced, Resources, and Other Settings

Devices often have other tabs, such as Advanced, Resources, and Power Management. Most network adapters have an Advanced tab. As shown in Figure 8-6, these options can control transmission options. You should change these options only if you are trying to resolve specific performance or connectivity issues as directed by the device manufacturer or a Microsoft Knowledge Base article. The setting that causes the most problems is Speed & Duplex. Most of the time, you'll want this set to Auto Detect or Auto Negotiation. Sometimes, however, to correct a specific problem, you must use a preset speed and duplex setting, such as 100 Mbps Half Duplex or 1000 Mbps Full Duplex. You should do this, however, only when this setting is recommended based on your network configuration or the issue you are trying to troubleshoot.

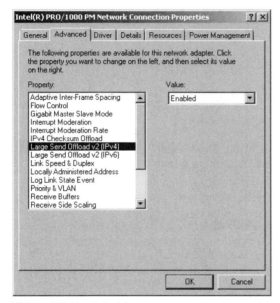

Figure 8-6 You'll find that most network adapters have an Advanced tab for setting transmission options.

Any device that uses system resources will have a Resources tab like the one shown in Figure 8-7.

The Resources tab options show the device resources that are currently assigned and their settings. There are four types of device resources:

- **DMA** The DMA channel used by the device. Values are shown as integers, such as 02.

- **Memory Range** The range of memory addresses used by the device. Values are shown in hexadecimal format, such as E8206000–E8206FFF.

- **I/O Range** The range of I/O ports used by the device. Values are shown in hexadecimal format, such as 5400–543F.

- **IRQ Line** IRQ line used by the device. Values are shown as integers, such as 10.

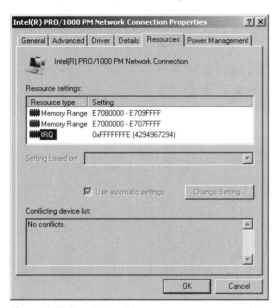

Figure 8-7 Any device that uses system resources has a Resources tab.

Devices can use multiple I/O and memory ranges. For example, the Video Graphics Adapter (VGA) adapter on one of our computers used three I/O ranges and three memory ranges. Additionally, multiple PCI devices can share the same IRQs when using the Advanced Configuration and Power Interface (ACPI) BIOS. This is because the ACPI BIOS allows IRQ sharing. To learn more about resource sharing and configuration options, see "Resolving Resource Conflicts" on page 240.

Installing and Updating Device Drivers

Device drivers are essential to the proper operation of Windows Server 2008. A faulty device driver can cause many problems on your systems—everything from unexpected restarts to application hangs to blue screens. To make it easier to detect and diagnose problems, you should maintain an inventory of all installed device drivers on systems you manage. Previously, we talked about using the Driverquery command to obtain a list of drivers for computers throughout the network. Ideally, the driver information should be stored on a centralized network share rather than on individual computers or could be printed out and placed in a binder where it is easily accessible. You should then periodically check manufacturer Web sites for known problems with related device drivers and for updated drivers. Windows Update can also help you because driver updates are made available through this service and can be installed automatically.

Although you can be fairly certain drivers obtained through Windows Update are newer than installed versions, this isn't the case for drivers you download yourself, and you should always double-check the driver version information before installation. As discussed previously, the current driver version is displayed in the driver's Properties dialog box, as shown in the following screen. Double-click the device in Device Manager to display the driver's Properties dialog box, then select the Driver tab. Be sure to check the driver date as well as the driver version.

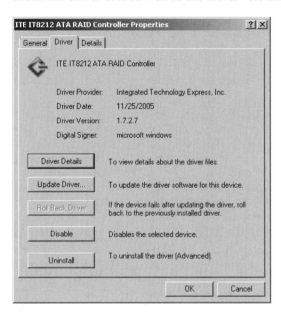

Next, check the driver version information for the driver you downloaded. To do this, extract the downloaded driver files to a folder. In the folder, you should find .dll or .sys files. Right-click one of these files, and choose Properties. Then in the Properties dialog box, click the Version tab to find the version information.

To continue with the installation of downloaded drivers, check to see whether the driver download includes a Setup program. If it does, run this program so that the proper files are copied to your system. After you do this, you can install the driver. You install and update drivers using the Found New Hardware, Add Hardware, and Update Driver Software Wizards. By default, these wizards can search for updated device drivers in the following locations:

- On the local computer

- On a hardware installation CD

- On the Windows Update site or your organization's Windows Update server

In Group Policy, several policies control the search possibilities:

Turn Off Access To All Windows Update Features under Computer Configuration\ Administrative Templates\System\Internet Communication Management\Internet Communication Settings If this policy setting is enabled, all Windows Update features are blocked and not available to users. Users will also be unable to access the Windows Update Web site.

Turn Off Windows Update Device Driver Searching under Computer Configuration\ Administrative Templates\System\Internet Communication Management\Internet Communication Settings By default, Windows Update searching is optional when installing a device. If you enable this setting, Windows Update will not be searched when you install a new device. If you disable this setting, Windows Update will always be searched when a new device is installed if no local drivers are present.

Turn Off Windows Update Device Driver Search Prompt under Computer Configuration\Administrative Templates\System\Driver Installation If you disable or do not configure the Turn Off Windows Update Device Driver Searching setting, this policy setting affects whether a search prompt is displayed for Windows Update of device drivers. If this policy setting is enabled, administrators aren't prompted to search Windows Update and the search will or will not take place automatically based on the Turn Off Windows Update Device Driver Searching setting. Otherwise, administrators will be prompted before Windows Update is searched.

Configure Driver Search Locations under User Configuration\Administrative Templates\ System\Driver Installation If you enable this policy setting, you can restrict users from searching floppy disk drives, CD drives, Windows Update, or any combination of these locations.

You can install and update device drivers by following these steps:

1. In Device Manager, select the Device Manager node. You should now see a complete list of devices installed on the system. By default, this list is organized by device type.

2. Right-click the device you want to manage and then select Update Driver. This starts the Update Driver Software wizard.

3. You can specify whether you want to install the drivers automatically or manually by selecting the driver from a list or specific location (see Figure 8-8).

Note

Updated drivers can add functionality to a device, improve performance, and resolve device problems. However, you should rarely install the latest drivers on a user's computer without first testing them in a test environment. Test first, then install.

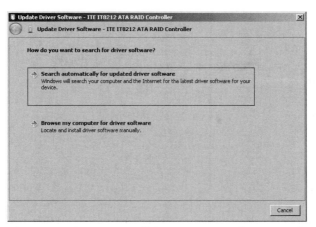

Figure 8-8 Choose to install drivers automatically or manually.

4. If you elect to install the driver automatically, Windows Server 2008 looks for a more recent version of the device driver and installs the driver if found. If a more recent version of the driver is not found, Windows Server 2008 keeps the current driver. In either case, click Close to complete the process and then skip the remaining steps.

5. If you chose to install the driver manually, you'll have the opportunity to do one of the following, as shown in Figure 8-9:

   Search for the driver If you want to search for drivers, click Browse to select a search location. Use the Browse For Folder dialog box to select the start folder for the search and then click OK. Because all subfolders of the selected folder are searched automatically, you can select the drive root path, such as C, to search an entire drive.

   Choose the driver to install If you want to choose the driver to install, click Let Me Pick From A List Of Device Drivers On My Computer. The wizard then displays a list of common hardware types. Select the appropriate hardware type, such as Modems or Network Adapters, and then click Next. Scroll through the list of manufacturers to find the manufacturer of the device and then choose the appropriate device in the right pane.

> **Note**
> If the manufacturer or device you want to use isn't listed, insert the media containing the device driver into the floppy drive, CD-ROM drive, or USB flash drive, and then click Have Disk. Follow the prompts. Afterward, select the appropriate device.

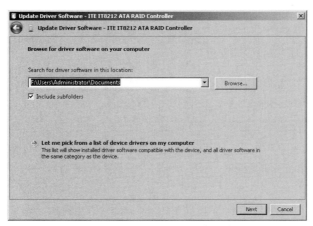

Figure 8-9 Search for or select a driver to install.

6. After selecting a device driver through a search or a manual selection, continue through the installation process by clicking Next. Click Close when the driver installation is completed. If the wizard can't find an appropriate driver, you'll need to obtain one and then repeat this procedure. Keep in mind that in some cases you'll need to reboot the system to activate the newly installed or updated device driver.

Restricting Device Installation Using Group Policy

In addition to code signing and search restrictions, you can use Group Policy settings to allow or prevent installation of devices based on device type. The related policy settings are found under Computer Configuration\Administrative Templates\System\Device Installation\Device Installation Restrictions and include the following:

- Allow Administrators To Override Device Installation Restriction Policies

- Allow Installation Of Devices Using Drivers That Match These Device Setup Classes

- Prevent Installation Of Drivers Matching These Device Setup Classes

- Allow Installation Of Devices That Match Any Of These Device IDs

- Prevent Installation Of Devices That Match Any Of These Device Ids

- Prevent Installation Of Removable Devices

- Prevent Installation Of Devices Not Described By Other Policy Settings

You can configure these policies by following these steps:

1. Access the policy for the appropriate site, domain, or organizational unit (OU).

2. Expand Computer Configuration, then Administrative Templates, then System, then Device Installation, and then Device Installation Restrictions.

3. Double-click the appropriate policy to view its Properties dialog box.

4. Set the state of the policy as Not Configured if you don't want the policy to be applied, Enabled if you want the policy to be applied, or Disabled if you want to block the policy from being used (all as permitted by the Group Policy configuration).

5. If you are enabling the policy and it has a Show option, click Show to use the Show Contents dialog box to specify which device IDs should be matched to this policy. Click OK twice.

Rolling Back Drivers

Occasionally, you'll find that an updated driver doesn't work as expected. It could cause problems, such as device failure or system instability. In most cases, this should occur only when you've installed unsigned device drivers as a last resort or beta versions of new drivers that might have improved performance or some other benefit that outweighs their potential to crash the system. However, it can sometimes occur with signed device drivers—even those published through Windows Update.

If you suspect that an updated driver is causing the system or device problems you are experiencing, you can attempt to recover the system to the previously installed device driver. To do this, follow these steps:

1. If you are having problems starting the system, you will need to boot the system in Safe Mode as discussed in "Resolving Startup Issues" on page 1416.

2. In Device Manager, select the Device Manager node. You should now see a complete list of devices installed on the system. By default, this list is organized by device type.

3. Right-click the device you want to manage and then select Properties. This opens the Properties dialog box for the device.

4. Click the Driver tab and then click Roll Back Driver. When prompted to confirm the action, click Yes.

5. Click Close to close the driver's Properties dialog box.

> **Note**
> If the driver file hasn't been updated, a backup drive file won't be available. In this case, the Roll Back Driver button will be disabled and you will not be able to click it. In this case, you should check the manufacturer's Web site for available versions of the driver for the device.

Chapter 8

Removing Device Drivers for Removed Devices

Windows device drivers for Plug and Play devices are loaded and unloaded dynamically. You can remove the driver for a device only when the device is plugged in. This means the proper way to remove a device from a system is first to uninstall its related device driver and then to remove the device from the system.

One reason for uninstalling a device is to remove a device that you no longer use or need. Start by uninstalling the related device driver. Access Device Manager, and then select the Device Manager node. Right-click the device you want to remove and then select Uninstall. When prompted, click OK to confirm that you want to remove the driver. Windows Server 2008 will then remove the related files and Registry settings.

At this point, you can shut down the system and remove the related hardware component if you want to. However, you might first want to check to see how the computer operates without the device in case some unforeseen problem or error occurs. So, rather than removing the device, you'll want to disable it. Disabling the device prevents Windows from reinstalling the device automatically the next time you restart the system. You disable a device by right-clicking it in Device Manager and then selecting Disable.

Sometimes when you are troubleshooting and trying to get a device to work properly, you might want to uninstall or unplug the device temporarily. Here, you could disable the device and then monitor the system to see whether problems previously experienced reoccur, or you could reinstall the device to see whether normal operations are restored. Uninstalling and then reinstalling the device forces Windows to go back to the device's original device and Registry settings, which can sometimes recover the device.

After you've uninstalled a device driver, one way to get Windows Server 2008 to reinstall the device is to reboot the computer. You can also try to rescan for devices using Device Manager by choosing Scan For Hardware Changes on the Action menu. Either way, the operating system should detect the uninstalled device as new hardware and then automatically reinstall the necessary device driver. If this doesn't happen, you must reinstall the device manually using the Add Hardware Wizard as discussed later in this chapter.

Uninstalling, Reinstalling, and Disabling Device Drivers

Uninstalling a device driver uninstalls the related device. When a device isn't working properly, sometimes you can completely uninstall the device, restart the system, and then reinstall the device driver to restore normal operations. You can uninstall and then reinstall a device by following these steps:

1. Access Device Manager, and then select the Device Manager node. You should now see a complete list of devices installed on the system. By default, this list is organized by device type.

2. Right-click the device you want to manage and then select Uninstall. When prompted to confirm the action, click OK.

3. Reboot the system. Windows Server 2008 should detect the presence of the device and automatically reinstall the necessary device driver. If the device isn't automatically reinstalled, reinstall it manually as discussed in "Installing and Updating Device Drivers" on page 228.

To prevent a device from being reinstalled automatically, disable the device instead of uninstalling it. You disable a device by right-clicking it in Device Manager and then selecting Disable.

Managing Hardware

Windows Plug and Play technology does a good job of detecting and automatically configuring new hardware. However, if the hardware doesn't support plug and play or it isn't automatically detected, you'll need to enter information about the new hardware into the Windows Server 2008 system. You do this by using the Add Hardware Wizard to install the hardware device and its related drivers on the system. You can also use this wizard to troubleshoot problems with existing hardware.

Adding Non–Plug and Play Hardware

Although Windows Server 2008 doesn't detect or set up non–Plug and Play devices automatically, it does maintain a driver cache for these devices. This driver cache has hundreds of drivers, any one of which you might be able to use. You might also be able to use an older driver if a Windows Server 2008 device driver isn't available. In either case, you install the device using the Add Hardware Wizard. Follow these steps:

1. If the device has a CD or a downloadable Setup program, run it to copy the driver files to your hard disk.

2. Connect the device to the computer. For internal devices, you must shut down the computer, add the device, and then restart the computer.

3. In Control Panel, click Classic View and then double-click Add Hardware.

> **Note**
>
> You can also start the Add Hardware Wizard from within Device Manager. Simply select the Add Legacy Hardware option on the Action menu.

4. In the Add Hardware Wizard, read the introductory message and then click Next.

5. Determine whether the wizard should search for new hardware or whether you want to select the hardware from a list (see Figure 8-10).

   ○ If you choose the search option, the wizard searches for and attempts to automatically detect the new hardware. The process takes a few minutes to go through all the device types and options. When the search is complete, any new devices found are displayed, and you can select one.

   ○ If you choose the manual option, or if no new devices are found in the automatic search, you'll have to select the hardware type yourself. Select the type of hardware, such as Modems or Network Adapters, and then click Next. Scroll through the list of manufacturers to find the manufacturer of the device and then choose the appropriate device in the right pane.

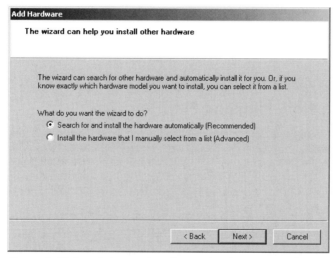

Figure 8-10 Search for or select the new hardware to install.

6. After you complete the selection and installation process, click Next, and then click Next again to confirm that you want to install the hardware.

7. After the wizard installs the drivers for the hardware device, click Finish. The new hardware should now be available.

Enabling and Disabling Hardware

When a device isn't working properly, sometimes you'll want to uninstall or disable it. Uninstalling a device removes the driver association for the device so that it temporarily appears that the device has been removed from the system. The next time you restart the system, Windows Server 2008 might try to reinstall the device. Typically, Windows Server 2008 reinstalls plug and play devices automatically, but does not automatically reinstall non–plug and play devices.

Disabling a device turns it off and prevents Windows Server 2008 from using it. Because a disabled device doesn't use system resources, you can be sure that it isn't causing a conflict on the system.

You can uninstall or disable a device by following these steps:

1. Access Device Manager, and then select the Device Manager node. You should now see a complete list of devices installed on the system. By default, this list is organized by device type.

2. Right-click the device you want to manage and then select Enable, Uninstall, or Disable depending on what you want to do with the device.

3. If prompted to confirm the action, click Yes or OK as appropriate.

Troubleshooting Hardware

Windows Server 2008's built-in hardware diagnostics can detect many types of problems with hardware devices. If a problem is detected, you might see a Problem Reports And Solutions balloon informing you of a problem. Click this balloon to open the Problem Reports And Solutions console. You can also access the Problem Reports And Solutions console in Control Panel by clicking the System And Maintenance link and then clicking Problem Reports And Solutions. In Problem Reports And Solutions, click See Problems To Check to display a list of known problems or click Check For Solutions to search the Microsoft Web site for possible solutions to known problems.

You can also access troubleshooting help for devices directly by following these steps:

1. Access Device Manager, and then select the Device Manager node.

2. Right-click the device that you want to troubleshoot and then select Properties.

3. On the General tab, click Check For Solutions. Click the Show Problem Details option to get more detailed information about the problem, as shown in Figure 8-11.

4. To send data about the device to Microsoft and see if there is a solution available, click Check Online For A Solution Later.

> **Note**
>
> Keep in mind that if the device drivers aren't installed properly, you won't have a Check For Solutions option. Instead, you'll have a Reinstall Driver button. Clicking Reinstall Driver starts the Hardware Update Wizard discussed in "Uninstalling, Reinstalling, and Disabling Device Drivers" on page 234.

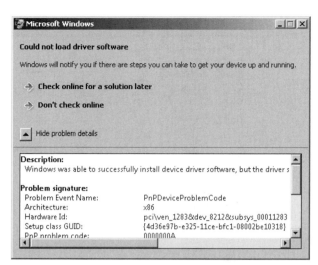

Figure 8-11 Review the problem details and then optionally check for solutions.

Whenever a device is installed incorrectly or has another problem, Device Manager displays a warning icon indicating that the device has a problem. If you double-click the device, an error code is displayed on the General tab of the device's Properties dialog box. As Table 8-1 shows, this error code can be helpful when trying to solve device problems as well. Most of the correction actions assume that you've selected the General tab from the device's Properties dialog box.

Table 8-1 Common Device Errors and Techniques to Resolve Them

Error Message	Correction Action
This device is not configured correctly. (Code 1)	Obtain a compatible driver for the device and click Update Driver to start the Hardware Update Wizard.
The driver for this device might be corrupted, or your system might be running low on memory or other resources. (Code 3)	Click Update Driver on the Driver tab to run the Hardware Update Wizard. You might see an "Out of Memory" message at startup because of this.
This device cannot start. (Code 10)	Click Update Driver on the Driver tab to run the Hardware Update Wizard. Don't try to find a driver automatically. Instead, choose the manual install option, and select the device driver you want to use.
This device cannot find enough free resources that it can use. (Code 12)	Resources assigned to this device conflict with another device, or the BIOS is incorrectly configured. Check the BIOS, and check for resource conflicts on the Resources tab of the device's Properties dialog box.
This device cannot work properly until you restart your computer. (Code 14)	Typically, the driver is installed correctly, but will not be started until you restart the computer.

Error Message	Correction Action
Windows cannot identify all the resources this device uses. (Code 16)	Check whether a signed driver is available for the device. If one is available and you've already installed it, you might need to manage the resources for the device. Check the Resources tab of the device's Properties dialog box.
This device is asking for an unknown resource type. (Code 17)	Reinstall or update the driver using a valid, signed driver.
Reinstall the drivers for this device. (Code 18)	After an upgrade, you might need to log on as an administrator to complete device installation. If this is not the case, click Update Driver on the Driver tab to reinstall the driver.
Your Registry might be corrupted. (Code 19)	Remove and reinstall the device. This should clear out incorrect or conflicting Registry settings.
Windows is removing this device. (Code 21)	The system will remove the device. The Registry might be corrupted. If the device continues to display this message, restart the computer.
This device is disabled. (Code 22)	This device has been disabled using Device Manager. To enable it, select Use This Device (Enable) under Device Usage on the General tab of the device's Properties dialog box.
This device is not present, is not working properly, or does not have all its drivers installed. (Code 24)	This may indicate a bad device or bad hardware. This error code can also occur with legacy ISA devices; upgrade the driver to resolve.
The drivers for this device are not installed. (Code 28)	Obtain a compatible driver for the device and then click Update Driver to start the Hardware Update Wizard.
This device is disabled because the firmware of the device did not give it the required resources. (Code 29)	Check the device documentation on how to assign resources. You might need to upgrade the BIOS or enable the device in the system BIOS.
This device is not working properly because Windows cannot load the drivers required for this device. (Code 31)	The device driver might be incompatible with Windows Server 2008. Obtain a compatible driver for the device and click Update Driver to start the Hardware Update Wizard.
A driver for this device was not required and has been disabled. (Code 32)	A dependent service for this device has been set to Disabled. Check the event logs to determine which services should be enabled and started.
Windows cannot determine which resources are required for this device. (Code 33)	This might indicate a bad device or bad hardware. This error code can also occur with legacy ISA devices; upgrade the driver and/or refer to the device documentation on how to set resource usage.

Chapter 8

Error Message	Correction Action
Windows cannot determine the settings for this device. (Code 34)	The legacy device must be manually configured. Verify the device jumpers or BIOS settings and then configure the device resource usage using the Resources tab of the device's Properties dialog box.
Your computer's system firmware does not include enough information to properly configure and use this device. (Code 35)	This error occurs on multiprocessor systems. Update the BIOS; check for a BIOS option to use MPS 1.1 or MPS 1.4. Usually you want MPS 1.4.
This device is requesting a PCI interrupt but is configured for an ISA interrupt (or vice versa). (Code 36)	ISA interrupts are nonshareable. If a device is in a PCI slot but the slot is configured in BIOS as "reserved for ISA," the error might be displayed. Change the BIOS settings.
Windows cannot initialize the device driver for this hardware. (Code 37)	Run the Hardware Update Wizard by clicking Update Driver on the Driver tab.
Windows cannot load the device driver for this hardware because a previous instance of the device driver is still in memory. (Code 38)	A device driver in memory is causing a conflict. Restart the computer.
Windows cannot load the device driver for this hardware. The driver might be corrupted or missing. (Code 39)	Check to ensure that the hardware device is properly installed and connected and that it has power. If it is properly installed and connected, look for an updated driver or reinstall the current driver.
Windows cannot access this hardware because its service key information in the Registry is missing or recorded incorrectly. (Code 40)	The Registry entry for the device driver is invalid. Reinstall the driver.
Windows has stopped this device because it has reported problems. (Code 43)	The device was stopped by the operating system. You might need to uninstall and then reinstall the device. The device might have problems with the no-execute processor feature. In this case, check for a new driver.
An application or service has shut down this hardware device. (Code 44)	The device was stopped by an application or service. Restart the computer. The device might have problems with the no-execute processor feature. In this case, check for a new driver.

Resolving Resource Conflicts

Anyone who remembers IRQ conflicts will be thankful that current computers support the ACPI BIOS. With the ACPI BIOS, resources are allocated automatically by the operating system at startup, and multiple devices can share the same IRQ settings. These changes mean IRQ conflicts are largely a thing of the past. However, the ACPI depends on Plug and Play, and devices that are not fully compatible can sometimes cause problems, particularly legacy ISA devices.

TROUBLESHOOTING

Check the device slot configuration

Some conflicts occur because PCI interrupts are shareable, while ISA interrupts are nonshareable. Typically, this is a BIOS problem. If a device is in a PCI slot but the slot is configured in BIOS as "reserved for ISA," a conflict can occur. You must change the BIOS settings rather than the resource configuration to resolve the problem.

If you suspect a device conflict is causing a problem with the current device, check the Conflicting Device list in the lower portion of the Resources tab. It will either list No Conflicts or the specific source of a known conflict. In Device Manager, you can quickly check resource allocations by choosing Resources By Type or Resources By Connection on the View menu.

In Figure 8-12, both ISA and PCI devices are using IRQ settings. You'll note that each ISA device has a separate IRQ setting, while multiple PCI devices share the same IRQ settings. This is very typical. Note also that several devices have a warning icon with an exclamation point. This is because the device isn't configured properly, not because there's a conflict. In this example, there are no conflicts.

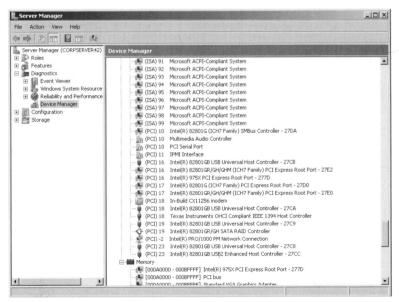

Figure 8-12 View resources by type or resources by connection to check resource settings in Device Manager.

Another way to check for conflicts is to use the System Information utility (Msinfo32.exe). Start the System Information utility by clicking All Programs, Accessories, System Tools, and then System Information. In System Information, expand Hardware Resources, and then select Conflicts/Sharing.

As shown in Figure 8-13, a list of all resources that are in use is displayed. Again, keep in mind that devices can share IRQ settings thanks to the ACPI, so what you are looking for are two unrelated devices sharing the same memory addresses or I/O ports, which would cause a conflict. Keep in mind that related devices *can* share memory addresses and I/O ports. In the example, the Intel 975X PCI Express Root Port shares the same I/O port as the Standard VGA Graphics Adapter and the PCI Bus shares the same memory addresses as the Motherboard Resources. That's okay because they are related.

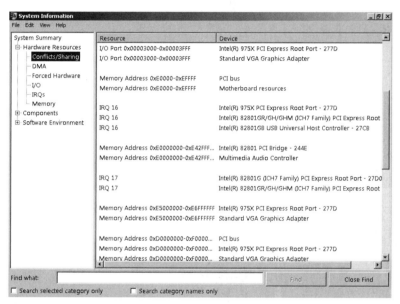

Figure 8-13 Use System Information to check for resource conflicts.

You can try to resolve resource conflicts in several different ways. Some devices use jumpers to manage resource settings, and in this case, the operating system cannot control the resource settings. To make changes, you must shut down the computer, remove the device, change the jumper settings, and then replace the device. In some cases, the jumpers are managed through software rather than an actual jumper switch. Here, you would use the device setup or configuration utility to change the resource settings.

For PCI devices, you can try swapping the cards between PCI slots. This will help if the IRQ or other resource settings are assigned on a per-slot basis, as is the case with some motherboards. You might be able to check the motherboard documentation to see which IRQ interrupts are assigned to which slots. In any case, you'll need to experiment to see which card configuration works.

For PCI devices, a conflict could also be caused by the device driver and the way it works with the ACPI BIOS. You should check to see whether an updated device driver and a BIOS update are available. Installing one or both should resolve the conflict.

As a last resort, you can change the resource settings manually for some devices in Device Manager. On the Resources tab, shown in Figure 8-14, select the resource type that you want to work with. If you can make a change, you should be able to clear the Use Automatic Settings check box and then see whether any of the alternate configurations in the Setting Based On box resolve the conflict. Keep in mind that you are now manually managing the resource settings. To allow the Windows operating system again to manage the settings automatically, you must select the Use Automatic Settings check box.

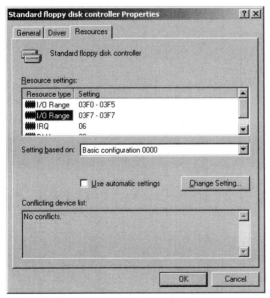

Figure 8-14 For legacy devices, you can use a different configuration to see whether this resolves a conflict.

Everyone who accesses a computer, whether in a workgroup or on a domain, at one time or another has worked with the Windows Registry whether the person realizes it or not. Whenever you log on, your user preferences are read from the Registry. Whenever you make changes to the system configuration, install applications or hardware, or make other changes to the working environment, the changes are stored in the Registry. Whenever you uninstall hardware, applications, or system components, these changes are recorded in the Registry as well.

The Registry is the central repository for configuration information in Microsoft Windows. Applications, system components, device drivers, and the operating system kernel all use the Registry to store settings and to obtain information about user preferences, system hardware configuration, and system defaults. The Registry also stores information about security settings, user rights, local accounts, and much more. Unlike Microsoft Windows NT, in domains, later versions of Windows do not store information about domain accounts or network objects in the Registry; these settings are managed by Active Directory Domain Services as discussed in Part 5, "Managing Active Directory and Security."

With so much information being read from and written to the Registry, it is not only important for administrators to understand its structures and uses, it is essential. You should know the types of data the Registry works with, what type of data is stored where, and how to make changes if necessary. This is important because often when you must fine-tune system configuration or correct errors to stabilize systems, you may be instructed to access the Registry and make such and such a change. Generally, the instructions assume you know what you're doing. Unfortunately, if you attempt such a change and really don't know what you're doing, you could make it so the system won't boot at all. So, with this in mind, let's look at how the Registry works and how you can work with it.

Chapter 9

Introducing the Registry

The Registry is written as a binary database with the information organized in a hierarchy. This hierarchy has a structure much like that used by a file system and is an inverted tree with the root at the top of the tree. Any time the Windows operating system must obtain system default values or information about your preferences, it obtains this information from the Registry. Any time you install programs or make changes in Control Panel, these changes usually are written to the Registry.

> **Note**
>
> I say "usually" because in Windows domains some configuration information is written to Active Directory directory service. For example, beginning with Microsoft Windows 2000, information about user accounts and network objects is stored in Active Directory. In addition, when you promote a member server to a domain controller, key Registry settings that apply to the server, such as the default configuration values, are transferred to Active Directory and thereafter managed through Active Directory. If you were later to demote the domain controller, the original Registry settings would not be restored either. Instead, the default settings are restored as they would appear on a newly installed server.

The Registry's importance is that it stores most of a system's state. If you make preference and settings changes to a system, these changes are stored in the Registry. If a system dies and cannot be recovered, you don't have to install a new system and then configure it to look like the old one. You could instead install Windows Server 2008 and then restore a backup of the failed system's Registry. This restores all the preferences and settings of the failed system on the new system.

Although it's great that the Registry can store settings that you've made, you might be wondering what else the Registry is good for. Well, in addition to storing settings that you've made, the Registry stores settings that the operating system makes as well. For example, the operating system kernel stores information needed by device drivers in the Registry, including the driver initialization parameters, which allows the device drivers to configure themselves to work with the system's hardware.

Many other system components make use of the Registry as well. When you install Windows Server 2008, the setup choices you make are used to build the initial Registry database. Setup modifies the Registry whenever you add or remove hardware from a system. Similarly, application setup programs modify the Registry to store the application installation settings and to determine whether components of the application are already installed. Then, when you run applications, the applications make use of the Registry settings.

Unlike previous releases of Windows, however, Windows Vista and Windows Server 2008 don't always store application settings directly in the Registry and may in fact read some settings from a user's profile. This behavior is new and occurs because of User Account Control (UAC). Of the many features UAC implements, there are two key features that change the way Windows installs and runs applications: application run levels and application virtualization.

To support run levels and virtualization, all applications that run on Windows Vista and Windows Server 2008 have a security token. The security token reflects the level of privileges required to run the application. Applications written for Windows Vista and Windows Server 2008 can have either an *administrator* token or a *standard user* token. Applications with administrator tokens require elevated privileges to run and perform core tasks. After it's started in elevated mode, an application with an administrator token can perform tasks that require administrator privileges and can also write to system locations of the Registry and the file system.

On the other hand, applications with standard user tokens do not require elevated privileges to run and perform core tasks. After it's started in standard user mode, an application with a standard user token must request elevated privileges to perform administration tasks. For all other tasks, the application should not run using elevated privileges. Further, the application should write data only to nonsystem locations of the Registry and the file system.

Standard user applications run in a special compatibility mode and use file system and Registry virtualization to provide virtualized views of resources. When an application attempts to write to a system location, Windows Vista and Windows Server 2008 give the application a private copy of the file or Registry value. Any changes are then written to the private copy and this private copy is in turn stored in the user's profile data. If the application attempts to read or write to this system location again, it is given the private copy from the user's profile to work with. By default, if an error occurs when working with virtualized data, the error notification and logging information show the virtualized location rather than the actual location the application was trying to work with.

INSIDE OUT   **The Transactional Registry**

Windows Server 2008 implements transactional technology in the kernel to preserve data integrity and handle error conditions when writing to the NTFS file system and the Registry. Applications that are written to take advantage of the Transactional Registry can use transactions to manage Registry changes as discrete operations that can be committed if successful or rolled back if unsuccessful. While a transaction is active, Registry changes are not visible to users or other applications—it is only when Windows Server 2008 commits the transaction that the changes are applied fully and become visible. Transactions used with the Registry can be coordinated with any other transactional resource, such as Microsoft Message Queuing (MSMQ). If the operating system fails during a transaction, work that has started to commit is written to the disk and incomplete transactional work is rolled back.

INSIDE OUT Controlling virtualization

In Local Security Policy, Security Options can enable or disable Registry virtualization. With Windows Vista and Windows Server 2008, a new security setting is provided for this purpose: User Account Control: Virtualize File And Registry Write Failures To Per-User Locations. This security setting enables the redirection of legacy application write failures to defined locations in the Registry and file system. This feature is designed to allow legacy programs that require administrator privileges to run. When enabled as per the default setting, this setting allows redirection of application write failures to defined user locations for both the file system and the Registry. When you disable this setting, applications that write data to protected locations silently fail.

To view or modify this setting in the Local Security Settings console, click Start, click Administrative Tools, and then click Local Security Policy. This opens the Local Security Policy console. Expand the Local Policies node in the left pane and then select the Security Options node. In the main pane, you should now see a list of policy settings. Scroll down through the list of security settings. Double-click User Account Control: Virtualize File And Registry Write Failures To Per-User Locations. On the Local Policy Setting tab of the dialog box, you'll see the current enabled or disabled state of the setting. To change the state of the setting select Enabled or Disabled as appropriate and then click OK.

Understanding the Registry Structure

Many administrative tools are little more than friendly user interfaces for managing the Registry, especially when it comes to Control Panel. So, rather than having you work directly with a particular area of the Registry, Microsoft provides tools that you can use to make the necessary changes safely and securely. Use these tools—that's what they are for.

CAUTION

The importance of using the proper tools to make Registry changes cannot be overstated. If there's a tool that lets you manage an area of the Registry, you should use it. Don't fool around with the Registry just because you can. Making improper changes to the Registry can cause a system to become unstable, and in some cases, it could even make it so the system won't boot.

As you can see, nearly everything you do with the operating system affects the Registry in one way or another. That's why it's so important to understand what the Registry is used for, how you can work with it, how you can secure it, and how you can maintain it.

The Registry is first a database. Like any other database, the Registry is designed for information storage and retrieval. Any Registry value entry can be identified by specifying the path to its location. For example, the path HKEY_LOCAL_MACHINE\ SOFTWARE\Microsoft\ServerManager\DoNotOpenServerManagerAtLogon specifies a Registry value that you can use to enable or disable the automatic display of Server Manager at log on.

Figure 9-1 shows this value in the Registry. Because of its hierarchical structure, the Registry appears to be organized much like a file system. In fact, its structure is often compared to that of a file system. However, this is a bit misleading because there is no actual folder/file representation on a system's hard disk to match the structure used by the Registry. The Registry's actual physical structure is separate from the way Registry information is represented. Locations in the Registry are represented by a logical structure that has little correlation to how value entries are stored.

Unlike Windows 2000 and Windows NT, Windows Server 2003 and Windows Server 2008 support larger Registry sizes than were previously possible and no longer keep the entire Registry in paged pool memory. Instead, 256-kilobyte (KB) views of the Registry are mapped into system cache as needed. This is an important change from the original architecture of the Registry, which effectively limited the Registry to about 80 percent of the total size of paged pool memory. The new Registry implementation is limited only by available space in the paging file.

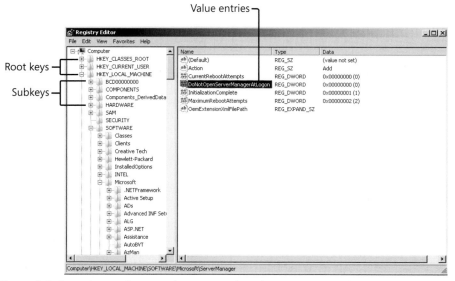

Figure 9-1 Accessing a value according to its path in the Registry.

At startup, 256-KB mapped views of the Registry are loaded into system cache so that Windows Server 2008 can quickly retrieve configuration information. Some of the Registry's information is created dynamically based on the system hardware configuration at startup and doesn't exist until it is created. For the most part, however, the Registry is stored in persistent form on disk and read from a set of files called hives. *Hives* are binary files that represent a grouping of keys and values. You'll find the hive files in the %SystemRoot%\System32\Config directory. Within this directory, you'll also find .sav, .log files, which serve as backup files for the Registry.

INSIDE OUT   Windows Server 2008 manages the Registry size and memory use

Windows NT and Windows 2000 store the entire Registry in paged, pooled memory. For 32-bit systems, this limits the Registry to approximately 160 megabytes (MB) because of the layout of the virtual address space in the operating system kernel. Unfortunately, in this configuration as the Registry grows in size it uses a considerable amount of paged, pooled memory and can leave too little memory for other kernel-mode components.

Windows Server 2003 and Windows Server 2008 resolve this problem by changing the way the Registry is stored in memory. Under the new implementation, 256-KB mapped views of the Registry are loaded into the system cache as necessary by the Cache Manager. The rest of the Registry is stored in the paging file on disk. Because the Registry is written to system cache, it can exist in system random access memory (RAM) and be paged to and from disk as needed. In previous versions of the Windows operating system, the operating system allowed you to control the maximum amount of memory and disk space that could be used by the Registry. With the improved memory management features, the operating system has now taken over control of managing how much memory the Registry uses. Most member servers use between 20 and 25 MB of memory for the Registry. Domain controllers or servers that have many configuration components, services, and applications can use considerably more. That said, however, one of my key domain controllers uses only 25 to 30 MB of memory for the Registry. This represents quite a change from the old architecture, when the in-memory requirements of the Registry could be up to 160 MB.

To read the Registry you need a special editor. The editor provided in Windows Server 2008 is Registry Editor. By using Registry Editor, you can navigate the Registry's logical structure from the top of the database to the bottom. From the top down, the levels of the database are defined as root keys, subkeys, and value entries.

INSIDE OUT   Regedit replaces Regedt32

Unlike previous versions of the Windows operating system that included two versions of Registry Editor, Windows Server 2003 and Windows Server 2008 ship with a single version. This version, Regedit.exe, integrates all of the features of both the previous Registry editors. From the original Regedit.exe it gets its core features. From Regedt32.exe, which is no longer available, it gets its security and Favorites features. By using the Permissions feature, you can view and manage permissions for Registry values. By using the Favorites feature, you can create and use favorites to quickly access stored locations within the Registry.

Regedt32 *really* is gone—although I, like many administrators, still refer to it. It is, after all, the editor administrators used because it gave us the ability to manage Registry security and it is the one that was recommended for administrators over Regedit. Because old habits die hard, Windows Server 2008 still has a stub file for Regedt32. However, if you run Regedt32, the operating system in fact starts Regedit.

At the top of the Registry hierarchy are the root keys. Each root key contains several subkeys, which contain other subkeys and value entries. The names of value entries must be unique within the associated subkey, and the value entries correspond to specific configuration parameters. The settings of those configuration parameters are the values stored in the value entry. Each value has an associated data type that controls the type of data it can store. For example, some value entries are used to store only binary data, while others are used to store only strings of characters, and the value's data type controls this.

We can now break down the Registry path HKEY_LOCAL_MACHINE\SOFTWARE\ Microsoft\Windows NT\CurrentVersion\Winlogon\AllowMultipleTSSessions so that it is more meaningful. Here, *HKEY_LOCAL_MACHINE* is the root key. Each entry below the root key until we get to *AllowMultipleTSSessions* represents a subkey level within the Registry hierarchy. Finally, *AllowMultipleTSSessions* is the actual value entry.

The Registry is very complex and it is often made more confusing because documentation on the subject uses a variety of different terms beyond those already discussed. When reading about the Registry in various sources, you might see references to the following:

- **Subtrees** A *subtree* is a name for the tree of keys and values stemming from a root key down the Registry hierarchy. In documentation, you often see root keys referred to as subtrees. What the documentation means when it refers to a subtree is the branch of keys and values contained within a specified root key.

- **Keys** Technically, root keys are the top of the Registry hierarchy, and everything below a root key is either a subkey or a value entry. In practice, subkeys are often referred to as keys. It's just easier to refer to such and such a key—sort of like when we refer to "such and such a folder" rather than saying "subfolder."

- **Values** A *value* is the lowest level of the Registry hierarchy. For ease of reference, value entries are often simply referred to as values. Technically, however, a value entry comprises three parts: a name, a data type, and a value. The name identifies the configuration setting. The data type identifies the format for the data. The value is the actual data within the entry.

Now that you know the basics of the Registry's structure, let's dig deeper, taking a closer look at the root keys, major subkeys, and data types.

Registry Root Keys

The Registry is organized into a hierarchy of keys, subkeys, and value entries. The root keys are at the top of the hierarchy and form the primary branches, or subtrees, of Registry information. There are two physical root keys, HKEY_LOCAL_MACHINE and HKEY_USERS. These physical root keys are associated with actual files stored on the disk and are divided into additional logical groupings of Registry information. As shown in Table 9-1, the logical groupings are simply subsets of information gathered from HKEY_LOCAL_MACHINE and HKEY_USERS.

Table 9-1 **Registry Subtrees**

Subtree	Description
Physical Subtree	
HKEY_LOCAL_MACHINE (HKLM)	Stores all the settings that pertain to the hardware currently installed on the machine.
HKEY_USERS (HKU)	Stores user profile data for each user who has previously logged on to the computer locally as well as a default user profile.
Logical Subtree	
HKEY_CLASSES_ROOT (HKCR)	Stores all file associations and object linking and embedding (OLE) class identifiers. This subtree is built from HKEY_LOCAL_MACHINE\SOFTWARE\ Classes and HKEY_CURRENT_USER\SOFTWARE\ Classes.
HKEY_CURRENT_CONFIG (HKCC)	Stores information about the hardware configuration with which you started the system. This subtree is built from HKEY_LOCAL_MACHINE\ SYSTEM\CurrentControlSet\Hardware Profiles\ Current, which in turn is a pointer to a numbered subkey that has the current hardware profile.
HKEY_CURRENT_USER (HKCU)	Stores information about the user currently logged on. This key has a pointer to HKEY_USERS\UserSID, where UserSID is the security identifier for the current user as well as for the default profile discussed previously.

INSIDE OUT   The Registry on 64-bit Windows systems

The Registry on 64-bit Windows systems is divided into 32-bit and 64-bit keys. Many keys are created in both 32-bit and 64-bit versions, and although the keys belong to different branches of the Registry, they have the same name. On these systems, Registry Editor (Regedit.exe) is designed to work with both 32-bit and 64-bit keys. The 32-bit keys, however, are represented with the WOW64 Registry redirector and appear under the HKEY_LOCAL_MACHINE\SOFTWARE\WOW6432Node key. If you want to work directly with the 32-bit keys, you can do so by using the 32-bit Registry editor located in the file path %SystemRoot%\Syswow64\Regedit.

To support both 32-bit and 64-bit interoperability through the Component Object Model (COM) and the use of 32-bit programs, the WOW64 redirector mirrors COM-related Registry keys and values between the 64-bit and 32-bit Registry views. In some cases, the keys and values are modified during the reflection process to adjust path-names and other values that might be version-dependent. This, in turn, means that the 32-bit and 64-bit values might differ.

HKEY_LOCAL_MACHINE

HKEY_LOCAL_MACHINE, abbreviated as HKLM, contains all the settings that pertain to the hardware currently installed on a system. It includes settings for memory, device drivers, installed hardware, and startup. Applications are supposed to store settings in HKLM only if the related data pertains to everyone who uses the computer.

As Figure 9-2 shows, HKLM contains the following major subkeys:

- COMPONENTS
- HARDWARE
- SAM
- SECURITY
- SOFTWARE
- SYSTEM

These subkeys are discussed in the sections that follow.

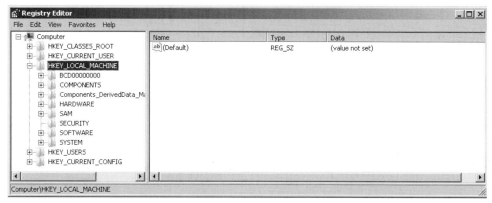

Figure 9-2 Accessing HKEY_LOCAL_MACHINE in the Registry.

HKLM\COMPONENTS

Windows Vista and Windows Server 2008 store information about updates and Windows features in a data store. These operating systems use the HKLM\COMPO-NENTS key to store information regarding the configuration and state of the data store, including the store architecture and format version. Windows Vista and Windows Server 2008 make changes to this data store whenever you download or install updates as well as when you add or remove features.

> **Note**
>
> If the component data store becomes corrupted you may see error code 0x80073712 whenever you try to install an update using the Windows Update Web site or you may find that Windows Features are not listed when you try to add or remove features. In this case, you can tell Windows that the store has become corrupted and should be rebuilt by typing the following command at an elevated command prompt: **reg delete HKLM\ COMPONENTS /v StoreDirty**. See Microsoft Knowledge Base article 931712 for more information (*http://support.microsoft.com/kb/931712*).

HKLM\HARDWARE

HKLM\HARDWARE stores information about the hardware configuration for the computer. This key is re-created by the operating system each time you start Windows Server 2008, and it exists only in memory, not on disk. To build this key, the operating system enumerates every device it can find by scanning the system buses and by searching for specific classes of devices, such as serial ports, keyboards, and pointer devices.

Under HKLM\HARDWARE, you'll find four standard subkeys that are dynamically created at startup and contain the information gathered by the operating system. These subkeys are as follows:

- **ACPI** Contains information about the Advanced Configuration Power Interface (ACPI), which is a part of system BIOS that supports Plug and Play and advanced power management. This subkey doesn't exist on non-ACPI-compliant computers.

- **DESCRIPTION** Contains hardware descriptions including those for the system's central processor, floating-point processor, and multifunction adapters. For portable computers, one of the multifunction devices lists information about the docking state. For any computer with multipurpose chip sets, one of the multifunction devices lists information about the controllers for disks, keyboards, parallel ports, serial ports, and pointer devices. There's also a catchall category for other controllers, such as when a computer has a PC Card controller.

- **DEVICEMAP** Contains information that maps devices to device drivers. You'll find device mappings for keyboards, pointer devices, parallel ports, Small Computer System Interface (SCSI) ports, serial ports, and video devices. Of particular note is that within the VIDEO subkey is a value entry for the VGA-compatible video device installed on the computer. This device is used when the computer must start in VGA display mode.

- **RESOURCEMAP** Contains mappings for the hardware abstraction layer (HAL), for the Plug and Play Manager, and for available system resources. Of particular note is the Plug and Play Manager. It uses this subkey to record information about devices it knows how to handle.

Additional nonstandard subkeys can exist under HKLM\HARDWARE. The subkeys are specific to the hardware used by the computer.

HKLM\SAM

HKLM\SAM stores the Security Accounts Manager (SAM) database. When you create local users and groups on member servers and workstations, the accounts are stored in HKLM\SAM as they were in Windows NT. This key is also used to store information about built-in user and group accounts, as well as group membership and aliases for accounts.

By default, the information stored in HKLM\SAM is inaccessible through Registry Editor. This is a security feature designed to help protect the security and integrity of the system.

HKLM\SECURITY

HKLM\SECURITY stores security information for the local machine. It contains information about cached logon credentials, policy settings, service-related security settings, and default security values. It also has a copy of the HKLM\SAM. As with the HKLM\SAM subkey, this subkey is inaccessible through Registry Editor. This is a security feature designed to help protect the security and integrity of the system.

HKLM\SOFTWARE

HKLM\SOFTWARE stores machine-wide settings for every application and system component installed on the system. This includes setup information, executable paths, default configuration settings, and registration information. Because this subkey resides under HKLM, the information here is applied globally. This is different from the HKCU\SOFTWARE configuration settings, which are applied on a per-user basis.

As Figure 9-3 shows, you'll find many important subkeys within HKLM\SOFTWARE, including the following:

- **Classes** Contains all file associations and OLE class identifiers. This is also the key from which HKEY_CLASSES_ROOT is built.

- **Clients** Stores information about protocols and shells used by every client application installed on the system. This includes the calendar, contacts, mail, media, and news clients.

- **Microsoft** Contains information about every Microsoft application and component installed on the system. This includes their complete configuration settings, defaults, registration information, and much more. You'll find most of the graphical user interface (GUI) preferences in HKLM\SOFTWARE\Microsoft\Windows\CurrentVersion. You'll find the configuration settings for most system components, language packs, hot fixes, and more under HKLM\SOFTWARE\Microsoft\Windows NT\CurrentVersion.

- **ODBC** Contains information about the Open Database Connectivity (ODBC) configuration on the system. It includes information about all ODBC drives and ODBC file Data Source Names (DSNs).

- **Policies** Contains information about local policies for applications and components installed on the system.

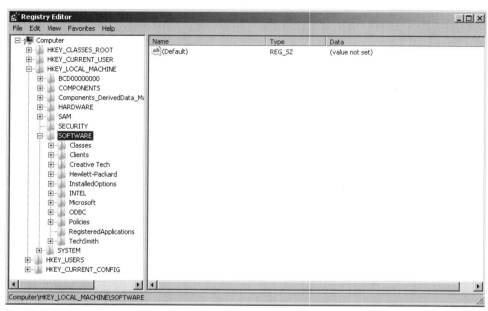

Figure 9-3 Accessing HKEY_LOCAL_MACHINE\SOFTWARE in the Registry.

HKLM\SYSTEM

HKLM\SYSTEM stores information about device drivers, services, startup parameters, and other machine-wide settings. You'll find several important subkeys within HKLM\SYSTEM. One of the most important is HKLM\SYSTEM\CurrentControlSet, as shown in Figure 9-4.

CurrentControlSet contains information about the set of controls and services used for the last successful boot of the system. This subkey always contains information on the set of controls actually in use and represents the most recent successful boot. The operating system writes the control set as the final part of the boot process so that it updates the Registry as appropriate to reflect which set of controls and services were last used for a successful boot. This is, in fact, how you can boot a system to the Last Known Good Configuration after it crashes or experiences a Stop error.

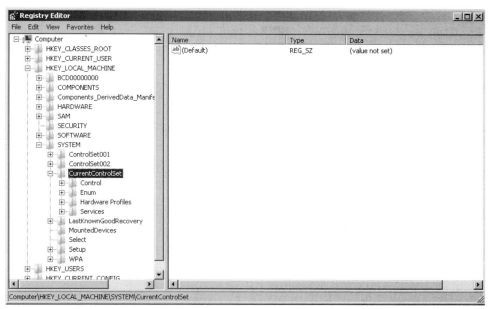

Figure 9-4 Accessing HKEY_LOCAL_MACHINE\SYSTEM\CurrentControlSet in the Registry.

HKLM\SYSTEM also contains previously created control sets. These are saved under the subkeys named ControlSet001, ControlSet002, and so forth. Within the control sets, you'll find four important subkeys:

- **Control** Contains control information about key operating system settings, tools, and subcomponents, including the HAL, keyboard layouts, system devices, interfaces, and device classes. Under BackupRestore, you'll find the saved settings for Backup, which include lists of Automated System Recovery (ASR) keys, files, and Registry settings not to restore. Under the SafeBoot subkey, you'll find the control sets used for minimal and network-only boots of the system.

- **Enum** Contains the complete enumeration of devices found on the computer when the operating system scans the system buses and searches for specific classes of devices. This represents the complete list of devices present during startup of the operating system.

- **Hardware Profiles** Contains a subkey for each hardware profile available on the system. The first hardware profile, 0000, is an empty profile. The other numbered profiles, beginning with 0001, represent profiles that are available for use on the system. The profile named Current always points to the profile being used currently by the operating system.

- **Services** Contains a subkey for each service installed on the system. These subkeys store the necessary configuration information for their related services, which can include startup parameters as well as security and performance settings.

Another interesting subkey is HKLM\SYSTEM\MountedDevices. The operating system creates this key and uses it to store the list of mounted and available disk devices. Disk devices are listed according to logical volume configuration and drive letter designator.

HKEY_USERS

HKEY_USERS, abbreviated as HKU, contains user profile data for every user who has previously logged on to the computer locally, as well as a default user profile. Each user's profile is owned by that user unless you change permissions or move profiles. Profile settings include the user's desktop configuration, environment variables, folder options, menu options, printers, and network connections.

User profiles are saved in subkeys of HKEY_USERS according to their security identifiers (SIDs). There is also a *SecurityID*_Classes subkey that represents file associations that are specific to a particular user. For example, if a user sets Adobe Photoshop as the default program for .jpeg and .jpg files and this is different from the system default, there are entries within this subkey that show this association.

When you use Group Policy as discussed in Part 5, the policy settings are applied to the individual user profiles stored in this key. The default profile specifies how the machine behaves when no one is logged on and is also used as the base profile for new users who log on to the computer. For example, if you wanted to ensure that the computer used a password-protected screen saver when no one was logged on, you would modify the default profile accordingly. The subkey for the default user profile is easy to pick out because it is named HKEY_USERS\.DEFAULT.

> **Note**
>
> The profile information stored in HKU is loaded from the profile data stored on disk. The default location for profiles is %SystemDrive%\Users*UserName*, where *UserName* is the user's pre–Windows 2000 logon name.

HKEY_CLASSES_ROOT

HKEY_CLASSES_ROOT, abbreviated as HKCR, stores all file associations that tell the computer which document file types are associated with which applications, as well as which action to take for various tasks, such as open, edit, close, or play, based on a specified document type. For example, if you double-click a .doc file, the document typically is opened for editing in Microsoft Word. This file association is added to HKCR when you install Microsoft Office or Microsoft Word. If Microsoft Office or Microsoft

Word isn't installed, a .doc file is opened instead in WordPad because of a default file association created when the operating system is installed.

HKCR is built from HKEY_LOCAL_MACHINE\SOFTWARE\Classes and HKEY_CUR-RENT_USER\SOFTWARE\Classes. The former provides computer-specific class registration, and the latter, user-specific class registration. Because the user-specific class registrations have precedence, this allows for different class registrations for each user of the machine. This is different from previous versions of the Windows operating system for which the same class registration information was provided for all users of a particular machine.

HKEY_CURRENT_CONFIG

HKEY_CURRENT_CONFIG, abbreviated as HKCC, contains information about the hardware configuration with which you started the system, which is also referred to as the machine's boot configuration. This key contains information about the current device assignments, device drivers, and system services that were present at boot time.

HKCC is built from HKEY_LOCAL_MACHINE \SYSTEM\CurrentControlSet\Hardware Profiles\Current, which in turn is a pointer to a numbered subkey that contains the current hardware profile. If a system has multiple hardware profiles, the key points to a different hardware profile, depending on the boot state or the hardware profile selection made at startup.

HKEY_CURRENT_USER

HKEY_CURRENT_USER, abbreviated as HKCU, contains information about the user currently logged on. This key has a pointer to HKEY_USERS*UserSID*, where *UserSID* is the security identifier for the current user as well as for the default profile discussed previously. Microsoft requires that applications store user-specific preferences under this key. For example, Microsoft Office settings for individual users are stored under this key. Additionally, as discussed previously, HKEY_CURRENT_USER\SOFTWARE\ Classes stores the user-specific settings for file associations.

Chapter 9

> **Note**
>
> If you don't want users to be able to set their own file associations, you could change the permissions on HKLM\SOFTWARE\Classes so users can't alter the global settings you want them to have. For more information about Registry permissions, see "Securing the Registry" on page 276.

Registry Data: How It Is Stored and Used

Now that you know more about the Registry's structure, let's take a look at the actual data within the Registry. Understanding how Registry data is stored and used is just as important as understanding the Registry structure.

Where Registry Data Comes From

As mentioned previously, some Registry data is created dynamically during startup of the operating system and some is stored on disk so it can be used each time you boot a computer. The dynamically created data is volatile, meaning that when you shut down the system, it is gone. For example, as part of the startup process, the operating system scans for system devices and uses the results to build the HKEY_LOCAL_MACHINE\ HARDWARE subkey. The information stored in this key exists only in memory and isn't stored anywhere on disk.

On the other hand, Registry data stored on disk is persistent. When you shut down a system, this Registry data remains on disk and is available the next time you boot the system. Some of this stored information is very important, especially when it comes to recovering from boot failure. For example, by using the information stored in HKEY_ LOCAL_MACHINE\SYSTEM\CurrentControlSet, you can boot using the Last Known Good Configuration. If the Registry data was corrupted, however, this information might not be available and the only way to recover the system would be to try repairing the installation or reinstalling the operating system.

To help safeguard the system and ensure that one section of bad data doesn't cause the whole Registry to fail to load, Windows Server 2008 has several built-in redundancies and fail safes. For starters, the Registry isn't written to a single file. Instead, it is written to a set of files called hives. There are six main types of hives, each representing a group of keys and values. Most of the hives are written to disk in the %SystemRoot%\System32\Config directory. Within this directory, you'll find these hive files:

- .DEFAULT, which corresponds to the HKEY_USERS\.DEFAULT subkey

- SAM, which corresponds to the HKEY_LOCAL_MACHINE\SAM subkey

- SECURITY, which corresponds to the HKEY_LOCAL_MACHINE\SECURITY subkey

- SOFTWARE, which corresponds to the HKEY_LOCAL_MACHINE\SOFTWARE subkey

- SYSTEM, which corresponds to the HKEY_LOCAL_MACHINE\SYSTEM subkey

The remaining hive files are stored in individual user profile directories with the default name of Ntuser.dat. These files are in fact hive files that are loaded into the Registry and used to set the pointer for the HKEY_CURRENT_USER root key. When no user is logged on to a system, the user profile for the default user is loaded into the Registry. When an actual user logs on, this user's profile is loaded into the Registry.

> **Note**
>
> The root keys not mentioned are HKEY_CURRENT_CONFIG and HKEY_CLASSES_ROOT. The on-disk data for HKEY_CURRENT_CONFIG comes from the subkey from which it is built: HKEY_LOCAL_MACHINE \SYSTEM\CurrentControlSet\Hardware Profiles\Current. Similarly, the on-disk data for HKEY_CLASSES_ROOT comes from HKEY_LOCAL_MACHINE \SOFTWARE\Classes and HKEY_CURRENT_USER\SOFTWARE\Classes.

Every hive file has associated log files—even Ntuser.dat. Windows Server 2008 uses the log files to help protect the Registry during updates. When a hive file is to be changed, the operating system writes the change to a log file and stores this log file on disk. The operating system then uses the change log to write the changes to the actual hive file. If the operating system were to crash while a change is being written to a hive file, the change log could later be used by the operating system to roll back the change, resetting the hive to its previous configuration.

INSIDE OUT   How Windows Server 2008 starts over with a clean Registry

Examine %SystemRoot%\System32\Config closely and you'll see several files with the .sav extension. These files represent the postinstallation state of the Registry. If you ever wonder how Windows Server 2008 can reset the Registry to that of a clean install after you demote a domain controller, this is the answer. By loading these files into the Registry and then writing them to disk as the original hive files, the server is returned to its postinstallation state with a clean Registry.

Types of Registry Data Available

When you work your way down to the lowest level of the Registry, you see the actual value entries. Each value entry has a name, a data type, and a value associated with it. Although value entries have a theoretical size limit of 1024 KB, most value entries are less than 1 KB in size. In fact, many value entries contain only a few bits of data. The type of information stored in these bits depends on the data type of the value entry.

The data types defined include the following:

- **REG_BINARY** Raw binary data without any formatting or parsing. You can view binary data in several forms, including standard binary and hexadecimal. In some cases, if you view the binary data, you will see the hexadecimal values as well as the text characters these values define.

- **REG_DWORD** A binary data type in which 32-bit integer values are stored as 4-byte-length values in hexadecimal. REG_DWORD is often used to track values that can be incremented, 4-byte status codes, or Boolean flags. With Boolean flags, a value of 0 means the flag is off (false) and a value of 1 means the flag is on (true).

- **REG_QWORD** A binary data type in which 64-bit integer values are stored as 8-byte-length values in hexadecimal. REG_QWORD is often used to track large values that can be incremented, 8-byte status codes, or Boolean flags. With Boolean flags, a value of 0 means the flag is off (false) and a value of 1 means the flag is on (true).

- **REG_SZ** A fixed-length string of Unicode characters. REG_SZ is used to store values that are meant to be read by users and can include names, descriptions, and so on, as well as stored file system paths.

- **REG_EXPAND_SZ** A variable-length string that can include environment variables that are to be expanded when the data is read by the operating system, its components, or services, as well as installed applications. Environment variables are enclosed in percentage signs (%) to set them off from other values in the string. For example, %SystemDrive% refers to the SystemDrive environment variable. A REG_EXPAND_SZ value that defines a path to use could include this environment variable, such as %SystemDrive%\Program Files\Common Files.

- **REG_MULTI_SZ** A multiple-parameter string that can be used to store multiple string values in a single entry. Each value is separated by a standard delimiter so that the individual values can be picked out as necessary.

- **REG_FULL_RESOURCE_DESCRIPTOR** A value with an encoded resource descriptor, such as a list of resources used by a device driver or a hardware component. REG_FULL_RESOURCE_DESCRIPTOR values are associated with hardware components, such as a system's central processors, floating-point processors, or multifunction adapters.

The most common data types you'll see in the Registry are REG_SZ and REG_DWORD. The vast majority of value entries have this data type. The most important thing to know about these data types is that one is used with strings of characters and the other is used with binary data that is normally represented in hexadecimal format. And don't worry, if you have to create a value entry—typically you do so because you are directed to by a Microsoft Knowledge Base article in an attempt to resolve an issue—you are usually told which data type to use. Again, more often than not, this data type is either REG_SZ or REG_DWORD.

Working with the Registry

Windows Server 2008 provides several tools for working with the Registry. The main tool, of course, is Registry Editor, which you start by typing **regedit** or **regedt32** at the command line or in the Run dialog box. Another tool for working with the Registry is the REG command. Both tools can be used to view and manage the Registry. Keep in mind that although both tools are considered editors, Windows Server 2008 applies any changes you make immediately. Thus, any change you make is applied automatically to the Registry without you having to save the change.

CAUTION

As an administrator, you have permission to make changes to most areas of the Registry. This allows you to make additions, changes, and deletions as necessary. However, before you do this, you should always make a backup of the system state along with the Registry first, as discussed in "Backing Up and Restoring the Registry" on page 272. This helps ensure that you can recover the Registry in case something goes wrong when you are making your modifications.

Searching the Registry

One of the common tasks you'll want to perform in Registry Editor is to search for a particular key. You can search for keys, values, and data entries using the Find option on the Edit menu (see the following screen).

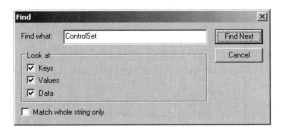

Don't let the simplicity of the Find dialog box fool you—there is a bit more to searching the Registry than you might think. So, if you want to find what you're looking for, do the following:

- The Find function in Registry Editor searches from the current node forward to the last value in the final root key branch. So, if you want to search the complete Registry, you must select the Computer node in the left pane before you select Find on the Edit menu or press Ctrl+F.

- Type the text you want to find in the Find What box. You can search only for standard American Standard Code for Information Interchange (ASCII) text. So, if you're searching for data entries, Registry Editor searches only string values (REG_SZ, REG_EXPAND_SZ, and REG_MULTI_SZ) for the specified text.

- Use the Look At options to control where Registry Editor looks for the text you want to find. You can search on key names, value names, and text within data entries. If you want to match only whole strings instead of searching for text within longer strings, select the Match Whole String Only check box.

After you make your selections, click Find Next to begin the search. If Registry Editor finds a match before reaching the end of the Registry, it selects and displays the matching item. If the match isn't what you'tre looking for, press F3 to search again from the current position in the Registry.

Chapter 9

Modifying the Registry

When you want to work with keys and values in the Registry, you typically are working with subkeys of a particular key. This allows you to add a subkey and define its values and to remove subkeys and their values. You cannot, however, add or remove root keys or insert keys at the root node of the Registry. Default security settings within some subkeys might also prohibit you from working with their keys and values. For example, by default you cannot create, modify, or remove keys or values within HKLM\SAM and HKLM\SECURITY.

Modifying Values

The most common change you'll make to the Registry is to modify an existing value. For example, a Knowledge Base article might recommend that you change a value from 0 to 1 to enable a certain feature in Windows Server 2008 or from 1 to 0 to disable it. To change a value, locate the value in Registry Editor, and then in the right pane double-click the value name. This opens an Edit dialog box, the style of which depends on the type of data you are modifying.

The most common values you'll modify are REG_SZ, REG_MULTI_SZ, and REG_DWORD. Figure 9-5 shows the Edit String dialog box, which is displayed when you modify REG_SZ values. In the dialog box, you would typically replace the existing value shown in the Value Data box with the value you need to enter.

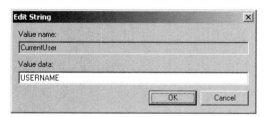

Figure 9-5   Using the Edit String dialog box.

Figure 9-6 shows the Edit Multi-String dialog box, which is displayed when you modify REG_MULTI_SZ values. In this example, there are three separate string values. In the dialog box, each value is separated by a new line to make the values easier to work with. If directed to change a value, you would typically need to replace an existing value, making sure you don't accidentally modify the entry before or after the entry you are working with. If directed to add a value, you would begin typing on a new line following the last value.

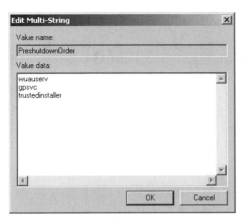

Figure 9-6 Using the Edit Multi-String dialog box.

Figure 9-7 shows the Edit DWORD Value dialog box, which is displayed when you modify REG_DWORD values. In this example, the value is displayed in hexadecimal format. Typically, you won't need to worry about the data format. You simply enter a new value as you've been directed. For example, if the Current value entry represents a flag, the data entry of 1 indicates the flag is on (or true). To turn off the flag (switch it to false), you would replace the 1 with a 0.

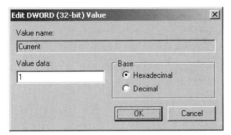

Figure 9-7 Using the Edit DWORD Value dialog box.

Note

The Windows Clipboard is available when you are working with Registry Editor. This means you can use the Copy, Cut, and Paste commands just as you do with other Windows programs. If there is a value in a Knowledge Base article that's difficult to type, you might want to copy it to the Clipboard and then paste it into the Value Data box of the Edit dialog box.

Chapter 9

Adding Keys and Values

As noted previously, you can add or remove keys in most areas of the Registry. The exceptions pertain to the root node, the root keys, and areas of the Registry where permissions prohibit modifications.

You add new keys as subkeys of a selected key. Access the key with which you want to work, and then add the subkey by right-clicking the key and selecting Edit, New, and then Key. Registry Editor creates a new key and selects its name so that you can set it as appropriate. The default name is New Key #1.

The new key has a default value entry associated with it automatically. The data type for this default value is REG_SZ. Just about every key in the Registry has a similarly named and typed value entry, so don't delete this value entry. Either set its value by double-clicking it to display the Edit String dialog box, or create additional value entries under the selected key.

To create additional value entries under a key, right-click the key, then select New followed by one of these menu options:

- **String Value** Used to enter a fixed-length string of Unicode characters; type REG_SZ

- **Binary Value** Used to enter raw binary data without any formatting or parsing; type REG_BINARY

- **DWORD (32-bit) Value** Used to enter binary data type in which 4-byte integer values are stored; type REG_DWORD

- **QWORD (64-bit) Value** Used to enter binary data type in which 8-byte integer values are stored; type REG_QWORD

- **Multi-String Value** Used to enter a multiple-parameter string; type REG_MULTI_SZ

- **Expandable String Value** Used to enter a variable-length string that can include environment variables that are to be expanded when the data is read; type REG_EXPAND_SZ

Creating a new value adds it to the selected key and gives it a default name of New Value #1, New Value #2, and so on. The name of the value is selected for editing so that you can change it immediately. After you change the value name, double-click the value name to edit the value data.

Removing Keys and Values

Removing keys and values from the Registry is easy but should never be done without careful forethought to the possible consequences. That said, you delete a key or value by selecting it, and then pressing the Delete key. Registry Editor will ask you to confirm the deletion. After you do this, the key or value is permanently removed from the Registry. Keep in mind that when you remove a key, Registry Editor removes all subkeys and values associated with the key.

Modifying the Registry of a Remote Machine

You can modify the Registry of remote computers without having to log on locally. To do this, select Connect Network Registry on the File menu in Registry Editor, then use the Select Computer dialog box to specify the computer with which you want to work. In most cases, all you must do is type the name of the remote computer and then click OK. If prompted, you might need to enter the user name and password of a user account that is authorized to access the remote computer.

After you connect, you get a new icon for the remote computer under your Computer icon in the left pane of Registry Editor. Double-click this icon to access the physical root keys on the remote computer (HKEY_LOCAL_MACHINE and HKEY_USERS). The logical root keys aren't available because they are either dynamically created or simply pointers to subsets of information from within HKEY_LOCAL_MACHINE and HKEY_USERS. You can then edit the computer's Registry as necessary. When you are done, you can select Disconnect Network Registry on the File menu and then choose the computer from which you want to disconnect. Registry Editor then closes the Registry on the remote computer and breaks the connection.

When working with remote computers, you can also load or unload hives as discussed in "Loading and Unloading Hive Files" on page 270. If you're wondering why you would do this, the primary reason is to work with a specific hive, such as the hive that points to Dianne Prescott's user profile because she inadvertently changed the display mode to an invalid setting and can no longer access the computer locally. With her user profile data loaded, you could then edit the Registry to correct the problem and then save the changes so that she can once again log on to the system.

Importing and Exporting Registry Data

Sometimes you might find that it is necessary or useful to copy all or part of the Registry to a file. For example, if you've installed a service or component that requires extensive configuration, you might want to use it on another computer without having to go through the whole configuration process again. So, instead, you could install the service or component baseline on the new computer, then export the application's Registry settings from the previous computer, copy them over to the other computer, and then import the Registry settings so that the service or component is properly configured. Of course, this technique works only if the complete configuration of the service or component is stored in the Registry, but you can probably see how useful being able to import and export Registry data can be.

By using Registry Editor, it is fairly easy to import and export Registry data. This includes the entire Registry, branches of data stemming from a particular root key, and individual subkeys and the values they contain. When you export data, you create a .reg file that contains the designated Registry data. This Registry file is a script that can then be loaded back into the Registry of this or any other computer by importing it.

> **Note**
>
> Because the Registry script is written as standard text, you could view it and, if necessary, modify it in any standard text editor as well. Be aware, however, that double-clicking the .reg file launches Registry Editor, which prompts you as to whether you want to import the data into the Registry. If you are concerned about this, save the data to a file with the .hiv extension because double-clicking files with this extension won't start Registry Editor. Files with the .hiv extension must be manually imported (or you could simply change the file extension to .reg when it is time to use the data).

To export Registry data, right-click the branch or key you want to export, and then select Export. You can also right-click the root node for the computer you are working with, such as Computer for a local computer, to export the entire Registry. Either way, you'll see the Export Registry File dialog box as shown in Figure 9-8. Use the Save In selection list to choose a save location for the .reg file, and then type a file name. The Export Range panel shows you the selected branch within the Registry that will be exported. You can change this as necessary or select All to export the entire Registry. Then click Save to create the .reg file.

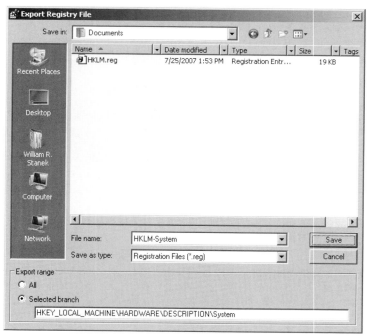

Figure 9-8 Exporting Registry data to a .reg file so that it can be saved and, if necessary, imported on this or another computer.

INSIDE OUT   **Want to export the entire Registry quickly?**

You can export the entire Registry at the command line by typing **regedit /e SaveFile**, where *SaveFile* is the complete file path to the location where you want to save the copy of the Registry. For example, if you wanted to save a copy of the Registry to C:\ Corpsvr06-regdata.reg, you would type **regedit /e C:\corpsvr06-regdata.reg**.

You can also extend this technique to rapidly determine the exact Registry values the operating system modifies when you make a change to a system or application setting. Start by opening the application of the System utility you want to work with as well as a command prompt window. Next, export the Registry prior to making the change you want to track. Then immediately and without doing anything else, make the change that you want to track and export the Registry to a different file using the command prompt window you opened previously. Finally, use the file comparison tool (fc.exe) to compare the two files. For example, if you saved the original Registry to orig.reg and the changed Registry to new.reg, you could type the following command at a command prompt to write the changes to a file called changes.txt: **fc /u orig.reg new.reg > changes.txt**. When you examine the changes.txt file in a text editor, you'll see a comparison of the Registry files and the exact differences between the files.

Importing Registry data adds the contents of the Registry script file to the Registry of the computer you are working with, either creating new keys and values if they don't already exist or overwriting keys and values if they do exist. You can import Registry data in one of two ways. You can double-click the .reg file, which starts Registry Editor and prompts you as to whether you want to import the data. Or you can select Import on the File menu, then use the Import Registry File dialog box to select and open the Registry data file you want to import.

INSIDE OUT   **Using export and import processes to distribute Registry changes**

The export and import processes provide a convenient way to distribute Registry changes to users. You could, for example, export a subkey with an important configuration change and then mail the associated .reg file to users so they could import it simply by double-clicking it. Alternatively, you could copy the .reg file to a network share where users could access and load it. Either way, you have a quick and easy way to distribute Registry changes. Officially, however, distributing Registry changes in this manner is frowned upon because of the potential security problems associated with doing so. The preferred technique is to distribute Registry changes through Group Policy as discussed in Part 5.

Chapter 9

Loading and Unloading Hive Files

Just as you sometimes must import or export Registry data, you'll sometimes need to work with individual hive files. The most common reason for doing this, as discussed previously, is when you must modify a user's profile to correct an issue that prevents the user from accessing or using a system. Here, you would load the user's Ntuser.dat file into Registry Editor and then make the necessary changes. Another reason for doing this would be to change a particular part of the Registry on a remote system. For example, if you needed to repair an area of the Registry, you could load the related hive file into the Registry of another machine and then repair the problem on the remote machine.

Loading and unloading hives affects only HKEY_LOCAL_MACHINE and HKEY_USERS, and you can perform these actions only when you select one of these root keys. Rather than replacing the selected root key, the hive you are loading then becomes a subkey of that root key. HKEY_LOCAL_MACHINE and HKEY_USERS are of course used to build all the logical root keys used on a system, so you could in fact work with any area of the Registry.

After you select either HKEY_LOCAL_MACHINE or HKEY_USERS in Registry Editor, you can load a hive for the current machine or another machine by selecting Load Hive on the File menu. Registry Editor then prompts you for the location and name of the previously saved hive file. Select the file, and then click Open. Afterward, enter a name for the key under which you want the hive to reside while it is loaded into the current system's Registry, and then click OK.

> **Note**
>
> You can't work with hive files that are already being used by the operating system or another process. You could, however, make a copy of the hive and then work with it. At the command line, type **reg save** followed by the abbreviated name of the root key to save and the file name to use for the hive file. For example, you could type **reg save hkcu c:\curr-hkcu.hiv** to save HKEY_CURRENT_USER to a file called Curr-hkcu.hiv on drive C. Although you can save the logical root keys (HKCC, HKCR, HKCU) in this manner, you can save only subkeys of HKLM and HKU using this technique.

When you are finished working with a hive, you should unload it to clear it out of memory. Unloading the hive doesn't save the changes you've made—as with any modifications to the Registry, your changes are applied automatically without the need to save them. To unload a hive, select it, and choose Unload Hive on the File menu. When prompted to confirm, click Yes.

Working with the Registry from the Command Line

If you want to work with the Registry from the command line, you can do so using the REG command. REG is run using the permissions of the current user and can be used to access the Registry on both local and remote systems. As with Registry Editor, you can work only with HKEY_LOCAL_MACHINE and HKEY_USERS on remote computers. These keys are, of course, used to build all the logical root keys used on a system, so you can in fact work with any area of the Registry on a remote computer.

REG has different subcommands for performing various Registry tasks. These commands include the following:

- **REG ADD** Adds a new subkey or value entry to the Registry

- **REG COMPARE** Compares Registry subkeys or value entries

- **REG COPY** Copies a Registry entry to a specified key path on a local or remote system

- **REG DELETE** Deletes a subkey or value entries from the Registry

- **REG EXPORT** Exports Registry data and writes it to a file

> **Note**
>
> These files have the same format as files you export from Registry Editor. Typically, however, they are saved with the .hiv extension so double-clicking files with this extension won't start Registry Editor.

- **REG IMPORT** Imports Registry data and either creates new keys and value entries or overwrites existing keys and value entries

- **REG LOAD** Loads a Registry hive file

- **REG QUERY** Lists the value entries under a key and the names of subkeys (if any)

- **REG RESTORE** Writes saved subkeys and entries back to the Registry

- **REG SAVE** Saves a copy of specified subkeys and value entries to a file

- **REG UNLOAD** Unloads a Registry hive file

You can learn the syntax for using each of these commands by typing **reg** followed by the name of the subcommand you want to learn about and then /?. For example, if you wanted to learn more about REG ADD, you would type **reg add** /? at the command line.

Chapter 9

Backing Up and Restoring the Registry

By now it should be pretty clear how important the Registry is and that it should be protected. I'll go so far as to say that part of every backup and recovery plan should include the Registry. Backing up and restoring the Registry normally isn't done from within Registry Editor, however. It is handled through the Windows Server Backup utility or through your preferred third-party backup software. Either way, you have an effective means to minimize downtime and ensure that the system can be recovered if the Registry becomes corrupted.

You can make a backup of the entire Registry very easily at the command line. Simply type **regedit /e** *SaveFile*, where *SaveFile* is the complete file path to the save location for the Registry data. Following this, you could save a copy of the Registry to C:\Backups\Regdata.reg by typing **regedit /e c:\backups\regdata.reg**. You would then have a complete backup of the Registry.

You can also easily make backups of individual root keys. To do this, you use REG SAVE. Type **reg save** followed by the abbreviated name of the root key you want to save and the file name to use. For example, you could type **reg save hkcu c:\backups\hkcu.hiv** to save HKEY_CURRENT_USER to a file in the C:\Backups directory. Again, although you can save the logical root keys (HKCC, HKCR, HKCU) in this manner, you can save only subkeys of HKLM and HKU using this technique.

Okay, so now you have your fast and easy backups of Registry data. What you do not have, however, is a sure way to recover a system in the event the Registry becomes corrupted and the system cannot be booted. Partly this is because you have no way to boot the system to get at the Registry data.

In Windows Server 2008, you create a system state backup to help you recover the Registry and get a system to a bootable state. The system state backup includes essential system files needed to recover the local system as well as Registry data. All computers have system state data, which must be backed up in addition to other files to restore a complete working system.

Normally, you back up the system state data when you perform a normal (full) backup of the rest of the data on the system. Thus, if you are performing a full recovery of a server rather than a repair, you use the complete system backup as well as system state data to recover the server completely. Techniques for performing full system backups and recovery are discussed in Chapter 41, "Backup and Recovery."

That said, you can create separate system state backups. The fastest and easiest way to do so is to use Wbadmin, the command-line counterpart to Windows Server Backup. You create a system state backup using Wbadmin by entering the following command at an elevated command prompt:

```
wbadmin start systemstatebackup -backuptarget StorageDrive
```

where *StorageDrive* is the drive letter for the storage location, such as:

```
wbadmin start systemstatebackup -backuptarget d:
```

Maintaining the Registry

The Registry is a database, and like any other database it works best when it is optimized. Optimize the Registry by reducing the amount of clutter and information it contains. This means uninstalling unnecessary system components, services, and applications. One way to uninstall components, services, and applications is to use the Uninstall Or Change A Program utility in Control Panel. This utility allows you to remove Windows components and their related services safely as well as applications installed using the Windows Installer. In Control Panel, click the Uninstall A Program link under the Programs heading to access the Uninstall Or Change A Program utility.

Most applications include uninstall utilities that attempt to remove the application, its data, and its Registry settings safely and effectively as well. Sometimes, however, applications either do not include an uninstall utility or for one reason or another do not fully remove their Registry settings, and this is where Registry maintenance utilities come in handy.

At the Microsoft Download Center on the Web, you'll find a download package for the Windows Installer Clean Up Utility. This download package includes several files as well as a helper application called Windows Installer Zapper. The Windows Installer Clean Up Utility calls Windows Installer Zapper to perform clean up operations on the Windows Installer configuration management information. Although not to be used by novice administrators, you can also work directly with Windows Installer Zapper.

Before you download and work with these utilities, you should refer to Microsoft Knowledge Base Article 29031 (*http://support.microsoft.com/kb/290301/en-us*). This article also includes a download link for obtaining the installer package. After you download the installer package, right-click it and then select Run As Administrator. You can then follow the prompts to install the Clean Up utilities. In the %SystemDrive%\ Program Files\Windows Installer Clean Up folder, you'll find Windows Installer Clean Up Utility (msicuu.exe), Windows Installer Zapper (msizap.exe), and a read me file (readme.txt).

> **Note**
> There are two versions of Windows Installer Zapper: MsiZapA.exe is for use in Windows 95, Windows 98, and Windows Me, and MsiZapU.exe is for use in all other versions of Windows. When you install the Windows Installer Clean Up Utility, the installation process installs the correct version automatically and renames the .exe as Msizap.exe.

Both tools are designed to work with programs installed using the Windows Installer and must be run using an account with Administrator permissions. In addition to being able to clear out Registry settings for programs you've installed and then uninstalled, you can use these utilities to recover the Registry to the state it was in prior to a failed or inadvertently terminated application installation. This works as long as the application used the Windows Installer.

Using the Windows Installer Clean Up Utility

Windows Installer Clean Up Utility removes Registry settings for applications that were installed using the Windows Installer. It is most useful for cleaning up Registry remnants of applications that were partially uninstalled or whose uninstall failed. It is also useful for cleaning up applications that can't be uninstalled or reinstalled because of partial or damaged settings in the Registry. It isn't, however, intended to be used as an uninstaller because it won't clean up the application's files or shortcuts and will make it necessary to reinstall the application to use it again.

> **Note**
>
> Keep in mind that the profile of the current user is part of the Registry. Because of this, the Windows Installer Clean Up Utility will remove user-specific installation data from this profile. It won't, however, remove this information from other profiles.

If you've already run the installer package, you can start this utility by clicking Start, All Programs, Windows Installer Clean Up. When the Windows Installer Clean Up Utility dialog box is displayed, select the program or programs to clean up, and then click Remove. The Windows Installer Clean Up Utility keeps a log file to record the applications that users delete in this manner. The log is stored in the %SystemDrive%\Users\ *UserName*\AppData\Local \Temp directory and is named Msicuu.log.

> **Note**
>
> The Windows Installer Clean Up Utility is a GUI for the Windows Installer Zapper discussed in the next section. When you use this utility, it runs the Windows Installer Clean Up Utility with the /T parameter to delete an application's Registry entries. It has an added benefit because it creates a log file, which is not used with Windows Installer Zapper.

> **CAUTION**
>
> The Windows Installer Clean Up Utility is meant to be used as a last resort only. Don't use this program if you can uninstall programs by other means.

Using the Windows Installer Zapper

The Windows Installer Zapper (Msizap.exe) is an advanced command-line utility for removing Registry settings for applications that were installed using the Windows Installer. Like the Windows Installer Clean Up Utility, it can be used to clean up Registry settings for applications that were partially uninstalled or for which the uninstall failed, as well as applications that can't be uninstalled or reinstalled because of partial or damaged settings in the Registry. Additionally, it can be used to remove Registry settings related to failed installations or failed rollbacks of installations. It can also be used to correct failures related to multiple instances of a setup program running simultaneously and in cases when a setup program won't run. Because you can inadvertently cause serious problems with the operating system, only experienced administrators should use this utility.

You'll find the Windows Installer Zapper in the %SystemDrive%\Program Files\Windows Installer Clean Up folder. The complete syntax for the Windows Installer Zapper is as follows:

```
msizap [*] [!] [A] [M] [P] [S] [W] [T] [G] [AppToZap]
```

where

- **AppToZap** Specifies an application's product code or the file path to the application Windows Installer (.msi) program

- ***** Deletes all Windows Installer configuration information on the computer, including information stored in the Registry and on disk. Must be used with the ALLPRODUCTS flag

- **!** Turns off warning prompts asking you to confirm your actions

- **A** Gives administrators Full Control permissions on the applicable Windows Installer data so that it can be deleted even if the administrator doesn't have specific access to the data

- **M** Deletes Registry information related to managed patches

- **P** Deletes Registry information related to active installations

- **S** Deletes Registry information saved for rollback to the previous state

- **T** Used when you are specifying a specific application to clean up

- **W** Examines all user profiles for data that should be deleted

- **G** Removes orphaned Windows Installer files that have been cached for all users

CAUTION

Windows Installer Zapper is meant as a last resort only. Don't use this program if you can uninstall programs by other means.

Chapter 9

Removing Registry Settings for Active Installations That Have Failed

Application installations can fail during installation or after installation. When applications are being installed, an InProgress key is created in the Registry under the HKLM\SOFTWARE\Microsoft\Windows\CurrentVersion\Installer subkey. In cases when installation fails, the system might not be able to edit or remove this key, which could cause the application's setup program to fail the next time you try to run it. Running Windows Installer Zapper with the P parameter clears out the InProgress key, which should allow you to run the application's setup program.

After installation, applications rely on their Registry settings to configure themselves properly. If these settings become damaged or the installation becomes damaged, the application won't run. Some programs have a repair utility that can be accessed simply by rerunning the installation. During the repair process, the Windows Installer might attempt to write changes to the Registry to repair the installation or roll it back to get back to the original state. If this process fails for any reason, the Registry can contain unwanted settings for the application. Running Windows Installer Zapper with the S parameter clears out the rollback data for the active installation. Rollback data is stored in the HKLM\SOFTWARE\Microsoft\Windows\CurrentVersion\Installer\Rollback key.

Any running installation also has rollback data, so you typically use the P and S parameters together. This means you would type **msizap ps** at an elevated command line.

Removing Partial or Damaged Settings for Individual Applications

When an application can't be successfully uninstalled you can attempt to clean up its settings from the Registry using the Windows Installer Zapper. To do this, you need to know the product code for the application or the full path to the Windows Installer file used to install the application. The installer file ends with the .msi extension and usually is found in one of the application's installation directories.

You then type **msizap t** followed by the product code or .msi file path. For example, if the installer file path is C:\Apps\KDC\KDC.msi, you would type **msizap t c:\apps\kdc\kdc.msi** at the command line to clear out the application's settings. Because the current user's profile is a part of the Registry, user-specific settings for the application will be removed from this profile. If you want to clear out these settings for all user profiles on the system, add the W parameter, such as **msizap wt c:\apps\kdc\kdc.msi**.

Securing the Registry

The Registry is a critical area of the operating system. It has some limited built-in security to reduce the risk of settings being inadvertently changed or deleted. Additionally, some areas of the Registry are available only to certain users. For example, HKLM\SAM and HKLM\SECURITY are available only to the LocalSystem user. This security in some cases might not be enough, however, to prevent unauthorized access to the

Registry. Because of this, you might want to set tighter access controls than the default permissions, and you can do this from within the Registry. You can also control remote access to the Registry and configure access auditing.

Preventing Access to the Registry Utilities

One of the best ways to protect the Registry from unauthorized access is to make it so users can't access the Registry in the first place. For a server, this means tightly controlling physical security and allowing only administrators the right to log on locally. For other systems or when it isn't practical to prevent users from logging on locally to a server, you can configure the permissions on Regedit.exe and Reg.exe so that they are more secure. You could also remove Registry Editor and the REG command from a system, but this can introduce other problems and make managing the system more difficult, especially if you also prevent remote access to the Registry.

To modify permissions on Registry Editor, access the %SystemRoot% folder, right-click Regedit.exe, and then select Properties. In the Regedit Properties dialog box, click the Security tab, as shown in Figure 9-9. Add and remove users and groups as necessary, then set permissions as appropriate. Permissions work the same as with other types of files. You select an object and then allow or deny specific permissions. See Chapter 14, "File Sharing and Security," for details.

Figure 9-9 Tighten controls on Registry Editor to limit access to it.

To modify permissions on the REG command, access the %SystemRoot%\System32 folder, right-click Reg.exe, and then select Properties. In the Reg Properties dialog box, click the Security tab. As Figure 9-10 shows, this command by default can be used by users as well as administrators. Add and remove users and groups as necessary, then set permissions as appropriate.

Chapter 9

Figure 9-10 Reg.exe is designed to be used by users as well as administrators and to be run from the command line; its permissions reflect this.

> **Note**
> I'm not forgetting about Regedt32. It's only a link to Regedit.exe, so you don't really need to set its access permissions. The permissions on Regedit.exe will apply regardless of whether users attempt to run Regedt32 or Regedit.exe.

Applying Permissions to Registry Keys

Keys within the Registry have access permissions as well. Rather than editing these permissions directly, I recommend you use an appropriate security template as discussed in Chapter 36, "Managing Group Policy." Using the right security template locks down access to the Registry for you, and you won't have to worry about making inadvertent changes that will prevent systems from booting or applications from running.

That said, you might in some limited situations want to or have to change permissions on individual keys in the Registry. To do this, start Registry Editor and then navigate to the key you want to work with. When you find the key, right-click it, and select Permissions, or select the key, then choose Permissions on the Edit menu. This displays a Permissions For dialog box similar to the one shown in Figure 9-11. Permissions work the same as for files. You can add and remove users and groups as necessary. You can select an object and then allow or deny specific permissions.

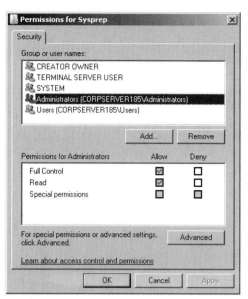

Figure 9-11 Use the Permissions For dialog box to set permissions on specific Registry keys.

Many permissions are inherited from higher-level keys and are unavailable. To edit these permissions, you must access the Advanced Security Settings dialog box by clicking the Advanced button. As Figure 9-12 shows, the Advanced Security Settings dialog box has four tabs:

- **Permissions** The Inherited From column on the Permissions tab shows from where the permissions are inherited. Usually, this is the root key for the key branch you are working with, such as CURRENT_USER. You can use the Add and Edit buttons on the Permissions tab to set access permissions for individual users and groups. Table 9-2 shows the individual permissions you can assign.

CAUTION

Before you click OK to apply changes, consider whether you should clear the Include Inheritable Permissions From This Object's Parent option. If you don't do this, you'll change permissions on the selected key and all its subkeys.

- **Auditing** Allows you to configure auditing for the selected key. The actions you can audit are the same as the permissions listed in Table 9-2. See "Registry Root Keys" on page 251.

Chapter 9

- **Owner** Shows the current owner of the selected key and allows you to reassign ownership. By default, only the selected key is affected, but if you want the change to apply to all subkeys of the currently selected key, choose Replace Owner On Subcontainers And Objects.

CAUTION

Be sure you understand the implications of taking ownership of Registry keys. Changing ownership could inadvertently prevent the operating system or other users from running applications, services, or application components.

- **Effective Permissions** Lets you see which permissions would be given to a particular user or group based on the current settings. This is helpful because permission changes you make on the Permissions tab aren't applied until you click OK or Apply.

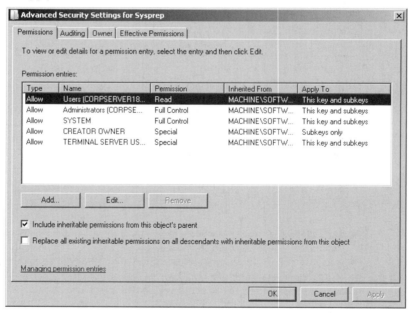

Figure 9-12 Use the Advanced Security Settings dialog box to change the way permissions are inherited or set and to view auditing settings, ownership, and effective permissions.

Table 9-2 **Registry Permissions and Their Meanings**

Permission	Meaning
Full Control	Allows user or group to perform any of the actions related to any other permission
Query Value	Allows querying the Registry for a subkey value
Set Value	Allows creating new values or modifying existing values below the specified key
Create Subkey	Allows creating a new subkey below the specified key
Enumerate Subkeys	Allows getting a list of all subkeys of a particular key
Notify	Allows registering a callback function that is triggered when the select value changes
Create Link	Allows creating a link to a specified key
Delete	Allows deleting a key or value
Write DAC	Allows writing access controls on the specified key
Write Owner	Allows taking ownership of the specified key
Read Control	Allows reading the discretionary access control list (DACL) for the specified key

Controlling Remote Registry Access

Hackers and unauthorized users can attempt to access a system's Registry remotely just like you do. If you want to be sure they are kept out of the Registry, you can prevent remote Registry access. One way remote access to a system's Registry can be controlled is through the Registry key HKLM\SYSTEM\CurrentControlSet\Control\SecurePipe-Servers\Winreg. If you want to limit remote access to the Registry, you can start by changing the permissions on this key.

If this key exists, then the following occurs:

1. Windows Server 2008 uses the permissions on the key to determine who can access the Registry remotely, and by default any authenticated user can do so. In fact, authenticated users have Query Value, Enumerate Subkeys, Notify, and Read Control permissions on this key.

2. Windows Server 2008 then uses the permissions on the keys to determine access to individual keys.

If this key doesn't exist, Windows Server 2008 allows all users to access the Registry remotely and uses the permissions on the keys only to determine which keys can be accessed.

INSIDE OUT   Services might need remote access to the Registry

Some services require remote access to the Registry to function correctly. This includes the Directory Replicator service and the Spooler service. If you restrict remote access to the Registry, you must bypass the access restrictions. Either add the account name of the service to the access list on the Winreg key or list the keys to which services need access in the Machine or Users value under the AllowedPaths key. Both values are REG_MULTI_ SZ strings. Paths entered in the Machine value allow machine (LocalSystem) access to the locations listed. Paths entered in the Users value allow users access to the locations listed. As long as there are no explicit access restrictions on these keys, remote access is granted. After you make changes, you must restart the computer so that Registry access can be reconfigured on startup.

Windows Vista and Windows Server 2008 disable remote access to all Registry paths by default. As a result, the only Registry paths remotely accessible are those explicitly permitted as part of the default configuration or by an administrator. In Local Security Policy, you can use Security Options to enable or disable remote Registry access. With Windows Vista and Windows Server 2008, two new security settings are provided for this purpose:

- Network Access: Remotely Accessible Registry Paths

- Network Access: Remotely Accessible Registry Paths And Sub-Paths

These security settings determine which Registry paths and subpaths can be accessed over the network, regardless of the users or groups listed in the access control list (ACL) of the Winreg Registry key. A number of default paths are set, and you should not modify these default paths without carefully considering the damage that changing this setting may cause.

You can follow these steps to access and modify these settings in the Local Security Policy console:

1. Click Start, click Administrative Tools, and then click Local Security Policy. This opens the Local Security Policy console.

2. Expand the Local Policies node in the left pane and then select the Security Options node.

3. In the main pane, you should now see a list of policy settings. Scroll down through the list of security settings. As appropriate, double-click Network Access: Remotely Accessible Registry Paths or Network Access: Remotely Accessible Registry Paths And Sub-Paths.

4. On the Local Policy Setting tab of the Properties dialog box, you'll see a list of remotely accessible Registry paths or a list of remotely accessible Registry paths and subpaths depending on which security setting you are working with. You can

now add or remove paths or subpaths as necessary. Note that the default settings are listed on the Explain tab.

> **Note**
>
> Windows Server 2008 has an actual service called Remote Registry service. This service does in fact control remote access to the Registry. You want to disable this service only if you are trying to protect isolated systems from unauthorized access, such as when the system is in a perimeter network and is accessible from the Internet. If you disable Remote Registry service before starting the Routing and Remote Access service, you cannot view or change the Routing and Remote Access configuration. Routing and Remote Access reads and writes configuration information to the Registry, and any action that requires access to configuration information could cause Routing and Remote Access to stop functioning. To resolve this, stop the Routing and Remote Access service, start the Remote Registry service, and then restart the Routing and Remote Access service.

Auditing Registry Access

Access to the Registry can be audited as can access to files and other areas of the operating system. Auditing allows you to track which users access the Registry and what they're doing. All the permissions listed previously in Table 9-1 can be audited. However, you usually limit what you audit to only the essentials to reduce the amount of data that is written to the security logs and to reduce the resource burden on the affected server.

Before you can enable auditing of the Registry, you must enable the auditing function on the system you are working with. You can do this either through the server's local policy or through the appropriate Group Policy Object. The policy that controls auditing is Computer Configuration\Windows Settings\Security Settings\Local Policies\ Audit Policy. For more information on auditing and Group Policy, see Chapter 14 and Chapter 36, respectively.

After auditing is enabled for a system, you can configure how you want auditing to work for the Registry. This means configuring auditing for each key you want to track. Thanks to inheritance, this doesn't mean you have to go through every key in the Registry and enable auditing for it. Instead, you can select a root key or any subkey to designate the start of the branch for which you want to track access and then ensure the auditing settings are inherited for all subkeys below it (this is the default setting).

Say, for example, you wanted to audit access to HKLM\SAM and its subkeys. To do this, you would follow these steps:

1. After you locate the key in Registry Editor, right-click it, and select Permissions, or select the key, then choose Permissions on the Edit menu. This displays the Permissions For SAM dialog box.

2. In the Permissions For SAM dialog box, click the Advanced button.

3. In the Advanced Security Settings dialog box, click the Auditing tab.

4. Click Add to select a user or group whose access you want to track.

5. After you select the user or group, click OK. The Auditing Entry For SAM dialog box is displayed, as shown in Figure 9-13.

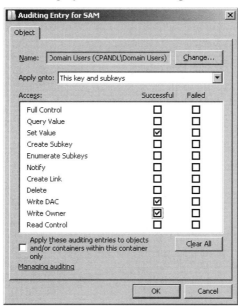

Figure 9-13 Use the Auditing Entry For dialog box to specify the permissions you want to track.

6. For each permission, select the type of auditing you want to track. If you want to track successful use of the permission, select the adjacent Successful check box. If you want to track failed use of the permission, select the adjacent Failed check box. Click OK to close the dialog box.

7. Repeat Step 6 to audit other users or groups.

8. If you want auditing to apply to subkeys, ensure the Include Inheritable Auditing Entries From This Object's Parent check box is selected.

9. Click OK twice.

Software and User Account Control Administration

Compared to earlier releases of Windows, the processes of installing, configuring, running, and maintaining software work differently in Windows Server 2008. Primarily, this is because of an enhanced security architecture that changes the way accounts are used and the way applications are installed and run.

Windows Server 2008 has two general types of user accounts, standard user accounts and administrator user accounts. Standard users can perform any general computing tasks, such as starting programs, opening documents, and creating folders, and any support tasks that do not affect other users or the security of the computer. Administrators, on the other hand, have complete access to the computer and can make changes that affect other users and the security of the computer.

Understanding Software Installation Changes

In Windows Server 2008, software installation, configuration, and maintenance are processes that require elevated privileges. As discussed in "Mastering User Account Control" on page 288, elevation is a feature of User Account Control (UAC). Because of User Account Control, Windows Server 2008 is able to detect software installation. When Windows Server 2008 detects a software installation related process, it prompts for permission or consent prior to allowing you to install, configure, or maintain software on your computer. This means you must either install software using an account with administrator privileges or provide administrator permissions when prompted. It also means administrator privileges are required to perform the following software maintenance tasks:

- Change/update
- Repair/reinstall
- Uninstall/remove

Windows Server 2008 does not include an Add/Remote Programs utility. Instead, Windows Server 2008 relies completely on the software itself to provide the necessary installation features through a related setup program. As discussed in "Maintaining Application Integrity" on page 294, Windows Server 2008 also provides new architecture for software that fundamentally changes the way software access tokens are used and the way software programs write to system locations. These changes are so far reaching that software not specifically designed to support the new architecture guidelines are considered legacy applications. Thus, software is either Windows Server 2008 compliant or it is legacy.

Part of the installation process involves validating your credentials and checking the software's compatibility with Windows Server 2008. Most software applications have a setup program that uses Windows Installer, InstallShield, or Wise Install. The job of the installer program is to track the installation process and make sure the installation completes successfully. If the installation fails, the installer is also responsible for restoring your computer to its original state by reversing all the changes made by the setup program. Although this works great in theory, you can encounter problems, particularly when you are installing older programs. Older programs won't have and won't be able to use the features of the latest versions of installer programs, and as a result, they sometimes are unable to uninstall a program completely.

As a partially uninstalled program can spell disaster for your computer, you should protect yourself by backing up a server prior to installing any software. By backing up a server as discussed in Chapter 41, "Backup and Recovery," you can be sure that you can fully recover the server to the state it was in prior to installing the software. This way, if you run into problems, you'll have an effective recovery strategy.

Before installing any software, you should do the following:

- Check to see whether it is compatible with Windows Server 2008. You can determine compatibility in several ways. You can check the software packaging, which should specify whether the program is compatible or provide a Windows Server 2008 logo. Alternatively, you can check the software developer's Web site for a list of compatible operating systems.

- Check the software developer's Web site for updates for the program. If available, download the updates prior to installing the software and then install them immediately after completing the software installation. Some software programs have automated update processes that you can use to check for updates after installing the software. In this case, after installation, run the software and then use the built-in update feature to check for updates.

Diagnosing a problem you are having as a compatibility issue isn't always easy. For deeper compatibility issues, you might need to contact the software developer's technical support staff. To avoid known compatibility issues with legacy applications, Windows Server 2008 includes an automated detection feature known as the Program Compatibility Assistant.

If the Program Compatibility Assistant detects a known compatibility issue when you run a legacy application, it notifies you about the problem and provides possible solutions for resolving the problem automatically. You can then allow the Program Compatibility Assistant to reconfigure the application for you. Although the Program Compatibility Assistant is helpful, it can't detect or avoid all compatibility issues. You might have to configure compatibility manually. One way to do this is to right-click the software shortcut, select Properties, and then use the options on the Compatibility tab to configure software compatibility options.

> **Note**
>
> Don't use the Program Compatibility Assistant or similar compatibility features to install older virus detection, backup, or system programs. These programs may attempt to modify your computer's file systems in a way that is incompatible with Windows Server 2008 and this could prevent Windows Server 2008 from starting.

Installation using a software application CD or DVD is fairly straightforward. Not all programs have distribution media discs. If you download a program from the Internet, it'll probably be in a .zip or self-extracting executable file and you can install the program by following these steps:

1. Start Windows Explorer. Extract the program's setup files using one of the following techniques:

   o If the program is distributed in a .zip file, right-click the file and select Extract All. This displays the Extract Compressed (Zipped) Folders dialog box. Click Browse, select a destination folder, and then click OK. Click Extract.

   o If the program is distributed in a self-extracting executable file, double-click the .exe file to extract the setup files. You'll see one of several types of prompts. If prompted to run the file, click Run. If prompted to extract the program files or select a destination folder, click Browse, select a destination folder, and then click OK. Click Extract or OK as appropriate.

2. In Windows Explorer, browse the setup folders and find the necessary setup program file. Double-click the setup file to start the installation process.

3. When Setup starts, follow the prompts to install the software.

If software installation fails and the software used an installer, follow the prompts to allow the installer to restore your computer to its original state. Otherwise, exit Setup and then try rerunning Setup to either complete the installation or uninstall the program. If this doesn't work, you can use the techniques discussed in "Maintaining the Registry" on page 273 to clean up the installer settings.

Installing software is only one part of software management. Often after you install software, you'll need to make configuration changes to your computer or the software itself. You might need to reconfigure, repair, or uninstall the software, or you might need to resolve problems with the way the software starts or runs.

After you install software, you can manage its installation using the Programs And Features page in Control Panel. More than any other versions of Windows, Windows Server 2008 takes advantage of the features of the installer program used with your software. This means you'll have more configuration options than you otherwise would. For example, previously, most software allowed you to rerun Setup to uninstall the program, but didn't necessarily allow you to rerun Setup to change or repair the

Chapter 10

software. Windows Server 2008 provides these features to make it easier to manage your software.

You can use the Programs And Features page to reconfigure, repair, or uninstall software by following these steps:

1. In Control Panel, click Uninstall A Program under Programs.

2. In the Name list, select the program you want to work with and then select one of the following options on the toolbar:
   - Change to modify the program's configuration
   - Repair to repair the program's installation
   - Uninstall to uninstall the program
   - Uninstall/Change to uninstall or change a program with an older installer program.

When you install the Desktop Experience feature, you can use Software Explorer within Windows Defender to work with running programs. To access Software Explorer, follow these steps:

1. In Control Panel\Security, click Windows Defender.

2. In Windows Defender, click Tools and then click Software Explorer.

3. In Software Explorer, use the Category list to select the type of program you want to work with. Your choices are:
   - Startup Programs
   - Currently Running Programs
   - Network Connected Programs
   - Winsock Service Providers

When you are working with Software Explorer, you can view details about a running program's configuration by selecting Currently Running Programs in the Category list and then clicking the program in the left pane. When you select a program or process in the left pane, you can terminate the process by clicking End Process and then clicking Yes when prompted to confirm the action. When you click the Task Manager button, Windows Server 2008 opens Task Manager. You can also open Task Manager by pressing Ctrl+Alt+Delete. You'll learn more about Task Manager in Chapter 11, "Performance Monitoring and Tuning."

Mastering User Account Control

User Account Control seeks to improve usability while at the same time enhancing security by redefining how standard user and administrator user accounts are used. User Account Control represents a fundamental shift in computing by providing a framework that limits the scope of administrator-level access privileges and that requires all applications to run in a specific user mode. In this way, UAC prevents users from making inadvertent changes to system settings and locks down the computer to prevent unauthorized applications from installing or performing malicious actions.

Elevation, Prompts, and the Secure Desktop

Unlike earlier releases of Windows, Windows Server 2008 and Windows Vista make it easy to determine which tasks standard users can perform and which tasks administrators can perform. You might have noticed the multicolored shield icon next to certain options in windows, wizards, and dialog boxes of Windows Server 2008. This is the Permissions icon. It indicates that the related option requires administrator permissions to run.

In Windows Server 2008, regardless of whether you are logged on as a standard user or an administrator, you see a User Account Control (UAC) prompt whenever you attempt to perform a task that requires administrator permissions by default. The way the prompt works depends on whether you are logged on with a standard user account or an administrator account.

When you are logged on with a standard user account in a workgroup, you are prompted to provide administrator credentials as shown in the following screen. In a domain, the prompt shows the logon domain and provides user name and password boxes. To proceed, you must enter the name of an administrator account, type the account's password, and then click OK. The task or application will then run with administrator permissions.

When you are logged on with an administrator account, you are prompted for consent to continue as shown the following screen. The consent prompt asks your approval to continue. The task or application will then run with administrator permissions.

The process of getting approval prior to running an application in administrator mode and prior to performing actions that change system-wide settings is known as *elevation*. Elevation enhances security by reducing the exposure and attack surface of the operating system. It does this by providing notification when you are about to perform an action that could impact system settings, such as installing an application, and eliminates the ability for malicious programs to invoke administrator privileges without your knowledge and consent.

Prior to elevation and display of the User Account Control prompt, Windows Server 2008 performs several background tasks. The key task you need to know about is that Windows Server 2008 switches to a secure, isolated desktop prior to displaying the prompt. The purpose of switching to the secure desktop is to prevent other processes or applications from providing the required permissions or consent. All other running programs and processes continue to run on the interactive user desktop and only the prompt itself runs on the secure desktop.

Elevation, prompts, and the secure desktop are aspects of User Account Control that affect you the most. Although they seem restrictive at first, these features prevent users from making inadvertent changes to system settings and lock down the computer to prevent unauthorized applications from installing or performing malicious actions.

The key component of UAC that determines whether and how administrators are prompted is Admin Approval Mode. By default, all administrators except the built-in local administrator account, run in, and are subject to, Admin Approval Mode. Because they are running in and subject to Admin Approval Mode, all administrators, except the built-in local administrator account, see the elevation prompt whenever they run administrator applications.

Configuring UAC and Admin Approval Mode

In Group Policy under Local Policies\Security Options, five security settings determine how Admin Approval Mode and elevation prompting works. Table 10-1 summarizes these security settings.

Table 10-1 **Security Settings Related to Admin Approval Mode**

Security Setting	Description
User Account Control: Admin Approval Mode For The Built-In Administrator Account	Determines whether users and processes running as the built-in local administrator account are subject to Admin Approval Mode. By default, this feature is disabled, which means the built-in local administrator account is not subject to Admin Approval Mode or to the elevation prompt behavior stipulated for other administrators in Admin Approval Mode. If you enable this setting, users and processes running as the built-in local administrator will be subject to Admin Approval and also subject to the elevation prompt behavior stipulated for other administrators in Admin Approval Mode.
User Account Control: Behavior Of The Elevation Prompt For Administrators In Admin Approval Mode	Determines whether administrators subject to Admin Approval Mode see an elevation prompt when running administrator applications and also determines how the elevation prompt works. By default, administrators are prompted for consent when running administrator applications. You can configure this option so administrators are prompted for credentials, as is the case with standard users. You can also configure this option so administrators are not prompted at all, in which case the administrator will not be able to elevate privileges. This doesn't prevent administrators from right-clicking an application shortcut and selecting Run As Administrator.
User Account Control: Behavior Of The Elevation Prompt For Standard Users	Determines whether users logged on with a standard user account see an elevation prompt when running administrator applications. By default, users logged on with a standard user account are prompted for the credentials of an administrator when running administrator applications. You can also configure this option so users are not prompted, in which case the users will not be able to elevate privileges by supplying administrator credentials. This doesn't prevent users from right-clicking an application shortcut and selecting Run As Administrator.
User Account Control: Run All Administrators In Admin Approval Mode	Determines whether users logged on with an administrator account are subject to Admin Approval Mode. By default, this feature is enabled, which means administrators are subject to Admin Approval Mode and further subject to the elevation prompt behavior stipulated for administrators in Admin Approval Mode. If you disable this setting, users logged on with an administrator account are not subject to Admin Approval and therefore not subject to the elevation prompt behavior stipulated for administrators in Admin Approval Mode.
User Account Control: Switch To The Secure Desktop When Prompting For Elevation	Determines whether Windows Server 2008 switches to the secure desktop before prompting for elevation. As the name implies, the secure desktop restricts the programs and processes that have access to the desktop environment and in this way reduces the possibility that a malicious program or user could gain access to the process being elevated. By default, this security option is enabled. If you don't want Windows Server 2008 to switch to the secure desktop prior to prompting for elevation, you can disable this setting. However, if you do this, you'll make the computer more susceptible to malware and attack.

Chapter 10

In a domain environment, you can use Microsoft Active Directory–based Group Policy to apply the desired security configuration to a particular set of computers. Simply configure the desired settings to a Group Policy object (GPO) that applies to those computers.

For workgroup configurations or for a special case, you can configure these security settings on a per-computer basis using local security policy. To access local security policy and configure UAC settings, follow these steps:

1. Click Start, All Programs, Administrative Tools, Local Security Policy. This starts the Local Security Policy console.

2. In the console tree, under Security Settings, expand Local Policies and then select Security Options, as shown in Figure 10-1.

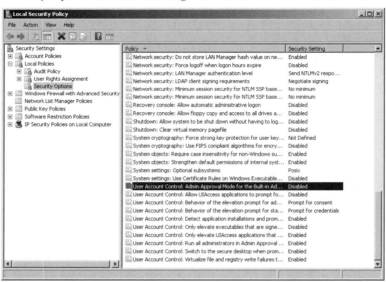

Figure 10-1 Configure UAC options through local security policy.

3. Double-click User Account Control: Admin Approval Mode For The Built-In Administrator Account. This opens the related Properties dialog box shown in Figure 10-2. Select Enabled to turn on this setting or Disabled to turn off this setting. Click OK.

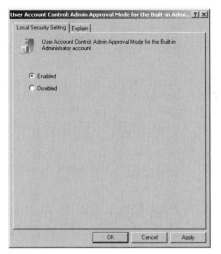

Figure 10-2 Configure Admin Approval Mode for the built-in Administrator account

4. Double-click User Account Control: Behavior Of The Elevation Prompt For Administrators In Admin Approval Mode. To turn off this setting, clear the Define This Policy Setting check box and then click OK. To turn on and configure this setting, select the Define This Policy Setting check box, make a prompt selection, and then click OK. The available options are Elevate Without Prompting, Prompt For Credentials, and Prompt For Consent.

6. Double-click User Account Control: Behavior Of The Elevation Prompt For Standard Users. To turn off this setting, clear the Define This Policy Setting check box and then click OK. To turn on and configure this setting, select the Define This Policy Setting check box, make a prompt selection, and then click OK. The available options are Automatically Deny Elevation Requests and Prompt For Credentials.

> **Note**
> If you deny elevation requests, elevation prompts will not be presented to users. This includes Remote Assistance users who might be trying to assist a user remotely.

7. Double-click User Account Control: Run All Administrators In Admin Approval Mode. Select Enabled to turn on this setting or Disabled to turn off this setting. Click OK.

8. Double-click User Account Control: Switch To The Secure Desktop When Prompting For Elevation. Select Enabled to turn on this setting or Disabled to turn off this setting. Click OK.

Chapter 10

Maintaining Application Integrity

To help maintain internal consistency and application integrity, Windows Server 2008 defines two run levels for applications: standard and administrator. Windows Server 2008 determines whether a user needs elevated privileges to run a program by supplying most applications and processes with a security token. If an application has a standard token, or an application cannot be identified as an administrator application, elevated privileges are not required to run the application, and Windows Server 2008 starts it as a standard application by default. If an application has an administrator token, elevated privileges are required to run the application, and Windows Server 2008 prompts the user for permission or confirmation prior to running the application.

Application Access Tokens

With Windows Server 2008, applications are said to be either Windows Server 2008–compliant or legacy. Any application written specifically for Windows Server 2008 is considered to be a compliant application. Applications that have been certified as compliant with the new Windows Server 2008 architecture have the Windows Server 2008–Compliant logo. Any application written for an earlier version of Windows or not certified as compliant is considered to be a legacy application.

Distinguishing between compliant and legacy applications is important because of the architecture changes required to support UAC. Windows Server 2008–compliant applications use UAC to reduce the attack surface of the operating system. They do this by preventing unauthorized programs from installing or running without the user's consent and by restricting the default privileges granted to applications. This in turn makes it harder for malicious programs to take over a computer.

In Windows Server 2008, the Application Information service facilitates the running of interactive applications with an administrator access token. By default, this service is stopped and configured for manual startup. When this service is stopped, you will be unable to start interactive applications with the additional administrator privileges you might require to perform tasks.

All applications that run on Windows Server 2008 derive their security context from the current user's access token. By default, UAC turns all users into standard users even if they are members of the Administrators group. If an administrator user has consented to use their administrator privileges, a new access token is created for the user that contains all of the user's privileges and this access token is used to start an application or process rather than the user's standard access token.

INSIDE OUT   Examining administrator and standard user access tokens

You can see the difference between the administrator user and standard user access tokens by opening two Command Prompt windows. Run the first command prompt with elevation by right-clicking and selecting Run As Administrator. Run the other command prompt as a standard user.

In the administrator Command Prompt window, type the following:

1. `cd %UserProfile%`
2. `whoami /all > admin.txt`

In the standard Command Prompt window, type the following:

1. `whoami /all > user.txt`
2. `fc user.txt admin.txt`

The resulting output is a comparison of the differences between your standard access token and your administrator access token. Both access tokens will have the same security identifiers (SIDs), but the elevated administrator access token will have more privileges than the standard user access token.

Most applications can run using a standard user access token. Whether applications need to run with standard or administrator privileges depends on the actions the applications perform. Applications that require administrator privileges, referred to as *administrator applications*, differ from user applications that require standard user privileges, referred to as *user applications*, in several ways.

Administrator applications require elevated privileges to run and perform core tasks. When started in elevated mode, an application with a user's administrator access token can perform tasks that require administrator privileges and can also write to system locations of the Registry and the file system.

Standard user applications do not require elevated privileges to run and perform core tasks. When started in standard user mode, an application with a user's standard access token must request elevated privileges to perform administration tasks. For all other tasks, the application should not run using elevated privileges. Further, the application should write data only to nonsystem locations of the Registry and the file system.

Chapter 10

INSIDE OUT   Virtualization for legacy applications

You configure any applications not specifically written for or certified compatible with Windows Server 2008 as legacy applications. Legacy applications run using a user's standard access token by default. To prevent legacy applications from making changes to the operating system that could cause problems, legacy applications run in a special compatibility mode. In this mode, the operating system uses file system and Registry virtualization to provide "virtualized" views of file and Registry locations.

When a legacy application attempts to write to a system location, the operating system gives the application a private copy of the file or Registry value. Any changes the application makes are then written to the private copy, and this private copy is in turn stored in the user's profile data. If the application attempts to read or write to this system location again, the operating system gives it the private copy from the user's profile to work with.

By default, if an error occurs when the application is working with virtualized data, the error notification and logging information shows the virtualized location rather than the actual location that the application is trying to work with. This ensures that there is consistency between how virtualization is used and how related errors are reported.

Application Run Levels

Because of UAC, the processes related to installing and running applications have also changed. In earlier versions of Windows, the Power Users group gave users specific administrator privileges to perform basic system tasks when installing and running applications. Applications written for Windows Server 2008 do not require the use of the Power Users group; Windows Server 2008 maintains it only for legacy application compatibility.

Windows Server 2008 detects application installations and prompts users for elevation to continue the installation by default. Installation packages for Windows Server 2008–compliant applications use application manifests that contain run level designations to help track required privileges. Application manifests define the application's desired privileges as one of the following:

RunAsInvoker   Runs the application with the same privileges as the user. Any user can run the application. For a standard user or a user who is a member of the Administrators group, the application runs with a standard access token. The application would run with higher privileges only if the parent process from which it is started has an administrator access token. For example, if you start an elevated Command Prompt window and then launch an application from this window, the application will run with an administrator access token.

RunAsHighest Runs the application with the highest privileges of the user. The application can be run by both administrator users and standard users. The tasks that can be performed by the application depend on the user's privileges. For a standard user, the application runs with a standard access token. For a user who is a member of a group with additional privileges, such as the Backup Operators, Server Operators, or Account Operators group, the application runs with a partial administrator access token that contains only the privileges the user has been granted. For a user who is a member of the Administrators group, the application runs with a full administrator access token.

RunAsAdmin Runs the application with administrator privileges. Only administrators can run the application. For a standard user or a user who is a member of a group with additional privileges, the application runs only if the user can be prompted for credentials required to run in elevated mode or if the application is started from within an elevated process, such as an elevated Command Prompt window. For a user who is a member of the Administrators group, the application runs with an administrator access token.

Windows Server 2008 protects application processes by labeling them with integrity levels ranging from high to low. Applications that modify system data, such as Disk Management, are considered "high" integrity, while those performing tasks that could compromise the operating system, such as Microsoft Internet Explorer, are considered "low" integrity. Applications with lower integrity levels cannot modify data in applications with higher integrity levels.

Windows Server 2008 identifies the publisher of any application that attempts to run with an administrator's full access token. Then, depending on that publisher, Windows Server 2008 marks the application as being a Windows Server 2008 application, a publisher verified (signed) application, or a publisher not verified (unsigned) application. When you are installing or running an application, the elevation prompt is designed to help identify the potential security risk of installing or running the application. First of all the prompt is color-coded. Secondly, the elevation prompt displays a unique message depending on the category to which the application belongs.

When working with the elevation prompt, keep the following in mind:

- Red is a strong warning, representing likely danger. If the application is from a blocked publisher or is blocked by Group Policy, the elevation prompt has a red background and displays the message "The application is blocked from running."

- Yellow is a general warning, indicating potential danger. If the application is unsigned (or is signed but not yet trusted), the elevation prompt has a yellow background and red shield icon and displays the message "An unidentified program wants access to your computer."

Chapter 10

- Blue/green is for administrative elevation. If the application is administrative (such as Server Manager), the elevation prompt has a blue/green background and displays the message "Windows needs your permission to continue."

- Gray is for general elevation. If the application has been signed by Authenticode and is trusted by the local computer, the elevation prompt has a gray background and displays the message "A program needs your permission to continue."

Only core Windows processes can access the secure desktop prompt. This serves to further secure the elevation process by preventing spoofing of the elevation prompt. The secure desktop is enabled by default in Group Policy.

Configuring Run Levels

By default, only applications running with a user's administrator access token run in elevated mode. Sometimes, you'll want an application running with a user's standard access token to be in elevated mode. For example, you might want to start the Command Prompt window in elevated mode so you can perform administrator tasks.

In addition to application manifests discussed previously, Windows Server 2008 provides three different ways to set the run level for applications. You can choose to perform one of the following:

Running an application once as an administrator You can run an application once as an administrator by right-clicking the application's shortcut or menu item and then selecting Run As Administrator as shown in the following screen. If you are using a standard account and prompting is enabled, you are prompted for consent before the application is started. If you are using a standard account and prompting is disabled, the application will fail to run. If you are using an administrator account and prompting for consent is enabled, you are prompted for consent before the application is started.

Always running an application as an administrator Windows Server 2008 also enables you to mark an application so that it always runs with administrator privileges. This is useful for resolving compatibility issues with legacy applications that require administrator privileges. It is also useful for Windows Server 2008–compliant applications that normally run in standard mode but that you use to perform administrative tasks. You cannot mark system applications or processes to always run as an administrator. Only nonsystem applications and processes can be marked to always run as an administrator. You can mark an application to always run as an administrator by right-clicking the application's shortcut and then selecting Properties. In the Properties dialog box, click the Compatibility tab. Under Privilege Level, select the Run This Program As An Administrator check box, as shown in the following screen, and then click OK.

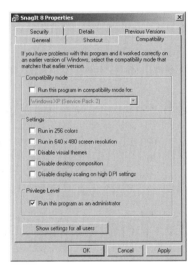

> **Note**
>
> If the Run This Program As An Administrator option is unavailable, it means that the application is blocked from always running as elevated, the application does not require administrative credentials to run, or you are not logged on as an administrator.

Controlling Application Installation and Run Behavior

In Group Policy under Local Policies\Security Options, five security settings determine how application installation and run behavior works. Table 10-2 summarizes these security settings.

Table 10-2 **Security Settings Related to Application Installation and Run Behavior**

Security Setting	Description
User Account Control: Allow UIAccess Applications To Prompt For Elevation Without Using The Secure Desktop	Determines whether User Interface Accessibility (UIAccess) applications can bypass the secure desktop to increase usability in certain instances. By default, this setting is disabled. When enabled, UIAccess programs are allowed to respond to elevation prompts on the user's behalf (which increases the risk that the prompt could be manipulated by a malicious program). This setting primarily applies to Remote Assistance scenarios, as this is the key UIAccess program in use. To avoid problems, be sure to have users select Allow IT Expert To Respond To User Account Control Prompts when making a Remote Assistance request.
User Account Control: Detect Application Installations And Prompt For Elevation	Determines whether Windows Server 2008 automatically detects application installation and prompts for elevation or consent. Because this setting is enabled by default, Windows Server 2008 automatically detects application installations and prompts users for elevation or consent to continue the installation. If you disable this setting, users are not prompted, in which case the users will not be able to elevate permissions by supplying administrator credentials.
User Account Control: Only Elevate Executables That Are Signed And Validated	Determines whether Windows Server 2008 allows running of only executables that are signed and validated. By default, this setting is disabled. When enabled, Windows enforces the public key certificate change validation of an executable before permitting it to run.
User Account Control: Only Elevate UIAccess Applications That Are Installed In Secure Locations	Determines whether Windows Server 2008 validates that UIAccess applications are secure before allowing them to run. By default, this setting is disabled. When enabled, only UIAccess applications in secure locations on the file system are allowed to run. Secure locations are limited to subdirectories of Program Files, including Program Files directories specifically for *x*86 or *x*64.
User Account Control: Virtualize File And Registry Write Failures To Per-User Locations	Determines how Windows Server 2008 notifies users about application write errors. Because this setting is enabled by default, error notifications and error logging related to virtualized files and Registry values show the virtualized location rather than the actual location to which the application was trying to write. If you disable this setting, error notifications and error logging related to virtualized files and Registry values show the actual location to which the application was trying to write.

For workgroup configurations or for a special case, you can configure these security settings on a per-computer basis using local security policy. To access local security policy and configure UAC settings, follow these steps:

1. Click Start, All Programs, Administrative Tools, Local Security Policy. This starts the Local Security Policy console.

2. In the console tree, under Security Settings, expand Local Policies and then select Security Options.

3. Double-click the setting you want to work with to display its Properties dialog box.

4. All settings related to application installation and run behavior can be defined and then configured. Make any necessary changes, and then click OK. Repeat this procedure to modify the related security settings as necessary.

In a domain environment, you can use Active Directory–based Group Policy to apply the desired security configuration to a particular set of computers. Simply apply the desired settings to a Group Policy object (GPO) that applies to those computers.

Chapter 10

Performance Monitoring and Tuning

Performance monitoring and tuning is the process of tracking system performance to establish baselines and to identify and resolve problems. When you install a server, you should create a performance baseline to see how the server is performing given its current resources and typical usage. If a server isn't performing as expected, is unresponsive, or is generating errors, you'll want to try to investigate. Many tools are designed to help you monitor server performance and troubleshoot performance issues. This chapter discusses the key tools for fine-tuning the system configuration, tracking system health, and troubleshooting the event logs. In the next chapter, you'll learn more about comprehensive monitoring techniques you can use for establishing performance baselines and pinpointing performance bottlenecks.

Tuning Performance, Memory Usage, and Data Throughput

Out of the box, Windows Server 2008 is optimized for general network environments. The operating system might not, however, be optimized for the way a particular system is being used in your organization. You can often improve Windows operating system and application performance considerably simply by fine-tuning the way a system uses resources.

Tuning Windows Operating System Performance

One of the reasons the Windows operating system no longer ships with 3D screen savers is that when these screen savers turn on, they use a considerable amount of processing power to render the 3D art. In some cases, the screen saver alone put the processor at 99 percent utilization, and you can probably imagine how well servers performed when the processor was maxed out. Similarly, you don't want the Windows operating system to tie up too much processing power displaying visual effects when administrators or other users are logged on to a server. So, if you're wondering why all the fancy visuals are turned off in the standard configuration of Windows Server 2008, this is why—the processing power is better used supporting the server's roles and applications than displaying fancy visuals to users who log on.

In most cases, you want to keep the visual effects to the bare minimum as per the default configuration after installation. This ensures that users who log on either locally or remotely won't severely impact the performance of the system just by logging on and displaying menus and dialog boxes. You can check or change the visual effects options by using the Performance Options dialog box. In Control Panel, click System And Maintenance, System, and then Advanced System Settings under Tasks. Then on the Advanced tab in the System Properties dialog box, click the Settings button in the Performance panel to display the Visual Effects tab in the Performance Options dialog box, as shown in the following screen:

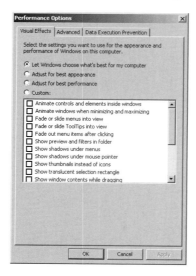

Tuning Processor Scheduling

The way the Windows operating system performs for applications and installed services is determined by the processor-scheduling configuration. Processor-scheduling options control how much processor resources are allocated to applications running on a server, which in turn determines the responsiveness of applications. You can optimize processor scheduling for the following application types:

- **Programs**   When processor scheduling is optimized for programs, the active (foreground) application running on the system gets the best response time and the greatest share of available resources. Generally, you'll want to use this option only on development servers or when you are using Windows Server 2008 as your desktop operating system.

- **Background services**   When processor scheduling is optimized for background services, all applications receive equal amounts of processor resources, and the active application doesn't get the best response time. Generally, you'll want to use this option for production servers.

You can check or change processor-scheduling configuration by using the Advanced tab of the Performance Options dialog box. In Control Panel, click System And Maintenance, System, and then Advanced System Settings under Tasks. Then on the Advanced tab in the System Properties dialog box, click the Settings button in the Performance panel to display the Performance Options dialog box. Finally, select the Advanced tab, as shown in the following screen, in the Performance Options dialog box.

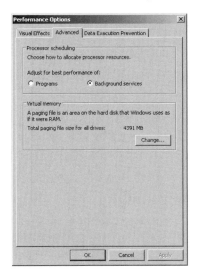

Tuning Virtual Memory

Windows Server 2008 uses virtual memory to allow a system to page parts of memory to disk. This makes it possible for a system to create a paging file on disk and use more memory space than is physically available. All servers have an initial paging file. It is created automatically on the drive containing the operating system during installation and setup, and written as a file named Pagefile.sys.

In some cases, you can improve a server's performance by optimizing the way the paging file is used. You can configure the size of the paging file so that it is optimal given the server's RAM and usage. Although Windows Server 2008 can expand paging files incrementally as needed, you'll want to size the paging file so that it is as large as it needs to be for average usage conditions. This helps reduce fragmentation of data within the paging file and also keeps the server from having to expand the paging file continually.

You can also fix the paging file size so that the server needn't spend any resources expanding the paging file. This helps to ensure that paging files don't become fragmented, which can result in poor system performance. If you want to manage virtual memory manually, you use a fixed virtual memory size in most cases. To do this, set the initial size and the maximum size to the same value. This ensures that the paging file is consistent and can be written to a single contiguous file (if possible given the amount of space on the volume).

Chapter 11

If a server has multiple hard disk drives, you might consider creating a paging file for each physical hard disk drive on the system. Multiple paging files can incrementally improve the performance of virtual memory on symmetric multiprocessing (SMP) machines with eight or more processors and a large amount of RAM. When you use multiple paging files, you create several smaller paging files rather than one big one. For example, if the paging file should be set to 4096 MB and the system has two disk drives, you could configure both drives to use a paging file 2048 MB in size.

> ## INSIDE OUT
> ### Consider the RAID configuration of disks when setting the paging file location
>
> You should always consider the redundant array of independent disks (RAID) configuration of disks when setting the paging file location. RAID configurations can slow down read/write performance for the paging file. By using RAID 1, you typically get better write performance than RAID 5. By using RAID 5, you typically get better read performance than RAID 1. So, there's a trade-off to be made with either RAID configuration.

In most cases for computers with 8 GB or less of RAM, I recommend setting the total paging file size so that it's twice the physical RAM size on the system. For instance, on a computer with 2048 MB of RAM, you would ensure that the Total Paging File Size For All Drives setting is at least 4096 MB. On systems with more than 8 GB of RAM, you should follow the hardware manufacturer's guidelines for configuring the paging file. Typically, this means setting the paging file to be the same size as physical memory.

You can manage the paging file configuration by using the Virtual Memory dialog box, shown in the screen on the next page. To access this dialog box, click the Advanced tab in the System Properties dialog box, and then click the Settings button in the Performance panel to display the Performance Options dialog box. Finally select the Advanced tab in the Performance Options dialog box, and then click Change in the Virtual Memory panel.

Windows Server 2008 automatically manages virtual memory much better than its predecessors do. Typically, Windows Server 2008 will allocate virtual memory at least as large as the total physical memory installed on the computer. You control whether Windows automatically manages virtual memory using the Automatically Manage Paging File Size For All Drives check box. When this check box is selected, Windows automatically manages virtual memory. When this check box is cleared, you can manually manage memory.

The upper section of the Virtual Memory dialog box shows the current paging file location and size. Each volume is listed with information about its associated paging file (if any). When a volume has a page file managed by the operating system, the paging file is listed as System Managed. When a volume has a page file, the initial and maximum size values set for the paging file are shown. If the paging file has a size that can be incremented, the initial and maximum sizes will be different, such as 768–1536 MB. If the paging file has a fixed size (recommended), the initial and maximum sizes will be the same, such as 1024–1024 MB.

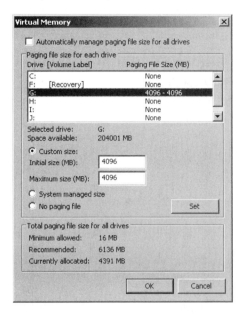

Selecting a disk drive in the top portion of the Virtual Memory dialog box allows you to configure whether and how the paging file is used. Usually, you want to select Custom Size and then set the Initial Size and Maximum Size options. Then click Set to apply the changes before you configure another disk drive. When you are finished configuring paging file usage, click OK. You then will be prompted to restart the server for the changes to take effect. Click OK. When you close the System utility, you will be prompted to restart the system for the changes to take effect. Click Yes to restart the computer now, or click No if you plan to restart the server later.

CAUTION

Don't set the total paging file size to 0 MB. As you set the paging file for individual drives, pay particular attention to the Total Paging File Size For All Drives information. You don't want to configure a server so that the Currently Allocated value is 0 MB. This means no paging file is configured, and it will drastically reduce the server's performance.

Chapter 11

TROUBLESHOOTING

Be careful when setting or moving the paging file

Some documentation recommends that you move the paging file from the system drive to a different drive to improve performance. Don't do this without understanding the implications of doing so. The paging file is also used for debugging purposes when a Stop error occurs. On the system volume, the initial size of the paging file must be as large as the current physical RAM. If it isn't, Windows Server 2008 won't be able to write Stop information to the system drive when fatal errors occur. Because of this, my recommendation is to leave the paging file on the system drive.

Tracking a System's General Health

The fastest, easiest way to track a system's general health is to use Task Manager or Process Resource Monitor. Unlike some of the other performance tools that require some preparation before you can use them, you can start and use these tools without any preparation. This makes them very useful when you want to see what's going on with a system right now.

Monitoring Essentials

By using Task Manager, you can track running applications and processes and determine resource usage. This can help you understand how a server is performing and whether there are any problems, such as applications that aren't running or processes that are hogging system resources. You can open Task Manager by pressing Ctrl+Shift+Esc or by clicking Start, typing **taskmgr** in the Search box, and then pressing Enter.

To work with Task Manager, the key issue you must understand is the distinction between an application, an image name, and a process. Basically, the executable name of an application, such as Taskmgr.exe, is known to the operating system as its *image name,* and any time that you start an application the operating system starts one or more processes to support it. As Figure 11-1 shows, Task Manager has six tabs:

- **Applications** Shows programs that run in a user context on the system and displays whether they're running or not responding. Also allows you to interact with applications and halt their execution.

- **Processes** Lists the image name of the processes running on the system, including those run by the operating system and users. Includes usage statistics for system resources allocated to each process and allows you to interact with and stop processes.

- **Services** Shows the system services configured on the server. Includes their status, such as running or stopped.

- **Performance** Displays current processor and memory usage. Includes graphs as well as detailed statistics.

- **Networking** Displays current network usage for each of the system's connections to the network.

- **Users** Details the users currently logged on to the system. Includes local users as well as users connected through Remote Desktop sessions and allows you to disconnect, log off, and send console messages to these users.

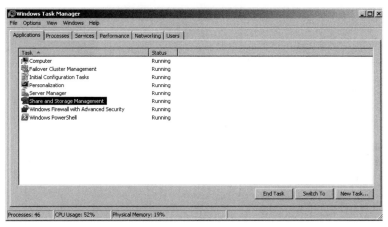

Figure 11-1 Use Task Manager to track resource usage.

CAUTION

Task Manager uses system resources while it's running. Because of this, you should run it only while you are tracking performance.

No single command-line tool performs all the same functions as Task Manager. The closest tools in functionality are the PowerShell cmdlets get-process and get-service. You obtain detailed information about running processes using get-process and detailed information about configured services using get-service.

As Figure 11-2 shows, get-process's standard output is much more detailed than the default Task Manager view, especially when it comes to current per-process resource usage and activity. To run get-process, access a Windows PowerShell prompt, and then enter **get-process**. If you've installed the Windows PowerShell feature, this prompt is available by entering **powershell** in a command prompt or by clicking Start, All Programs, Windows PowerShell, Windows PowerShell.

Chapter 11

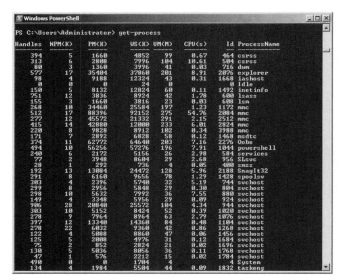

Figure 11-2 Use get-process to track running applications and processes and to determine resource usage.

Use Get-Process to Reduce Resource Usage

Because get-process is text-based rather than a graphical utility, it will, in most cases, use fewer system resources than Task Manager. On systems for which you are very concerned about resource usage and the possibility of bogging down a system by tracking performance information, you might initially want to start tracking performance by using get-process.

As Figure 11-3 shows, get-service's standard output shows the status of each configured service along with its internal name and display name. To run get-service, access a Windows PowerShell prompt and then enter **get-service**.

The sections that follow discuss how to use these tools to gather information about systems and resolve problems. The focus of the discussion is on Task Manager, get-process, and get-service, which should be your primary tools for tracking a system's general health.

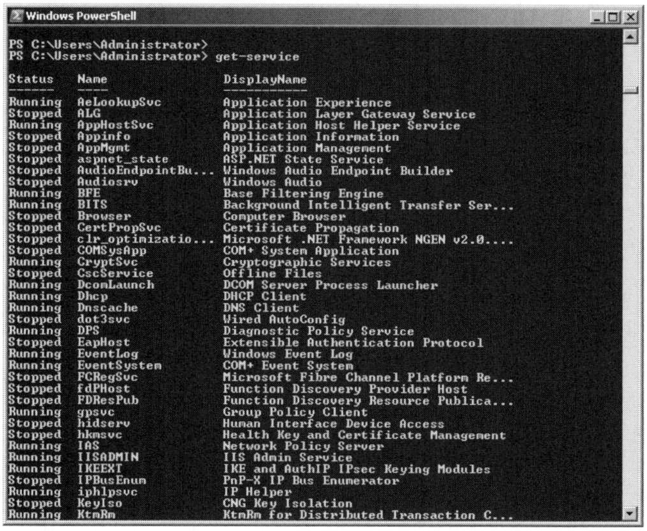

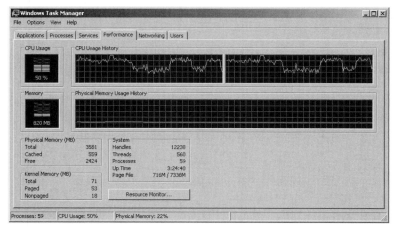

Figure 11-3 Use get-service to track the status of configured services.

Getting Processor and Memory Usage for Troubleshooting

The Performance tab in Task Manager, shown in Figure 11-4, should be the first tab you check if you suspect a performance issue with a system. It shows current processor and memory usage and also graphs some historical usage statistics based on data collected since you started Task Manager.

Figure 11-4 The Performance tab provides a summary of current processor and memory usage as well as some historical usage statistics based on data collected since you started Task Manager.

Some of the performance data is fairly self-explanatory. The CPU Usage and CPU Usage History graphs show the percentage of processor resources being used. If a system has multiple CPUs, you'll see a history graph for each CPU by default. In Figure 11-4, the server has two CPUs, so there are two history graphs.

> **Note**
>
> For multiprocessor systems, you can configure the CPU history to show one graph per CPU or one graph for all CPUs. To change this behavior, click View, point to CPU History, and then choose a viewing style.

The Memory and Physical Memory Usage History graphs show the physical memory being used by the system. The physical memory usage does not include the paging file, which is an area of memory written to disk also referred to as virtual memory. The tough data to interpret here is the information below the graphs.

System shows summary statistics for handles, threads, processes, up time, and page file usage. Handles shows the number of input/output (I/O) file handles in use. Because each handle requires system memory to maintain, this is important to note. Threads shows the number of threads in use. Threads allow concurrent execution of process requests. Processes shows the number of processes in use. Up Time shows you the total amount of time the system has been up since it was last started. Page File shows you the current size of the page file in megabytes followed by the maximum possible size for the page file. The maximum page file size is determined by the virtual memory configuration of the server.

Physical Memory shows the total RAM on the system. Total shows the amount of physical RAM. Cached shows the amount of memory used for system caching. Free shows the RAM not currently being used and available for use.

Kernel Memory shows the memory used by the operating system kernel. Total lists all memory being used by the operating system kernel, including physical memory (RAM) and virtual memory. Nonpaged reflects memory used by the operating system kernel that can't be written to disk. Paged reflects memory that can be paged to virtual memory if necessary.

In Figure 11-4, you see an example of a system with moderate to fairly high central processing unit (CPU) usage but with very little ongoing paging file activity. A system with CPU usage consistently at these levels would warrant some additional monitoring to determine whether you should add resources to the system. Basically, you'd want to determine whether these were average usage conditions or whether you were seeing peak usage.

If these are average usage conditions, increasing the processor speed or adding processors could improve performance and allow for better handling of peak usage situations. If these statistics represent peak usage conditions, the system probably wouldn't need additional resources. Sometimes the CPU usage can be high if the system has too little memory as well. A quick check of the memory usage of the server, including its current and peak usage, shows, however, that this isn't the case for this particular system.

Figure 11-5 shows performance data for the same system. In this example, the system has high CPU usage and in many cases, CPU usage is at 100 percent. If CPU usage were consistent at 100 percent, I might suspect a runaway process and look for a process that is causing the problem. Here, however, there are times when CPU usage isn't maxed out, and you'd definitely want to take a closer look at what's going on starting with memory usage. One thing to note right away is that the system has quite a bit of available RAM—around 2400 MB—and the paging file really isn't very large—only 721 MB.

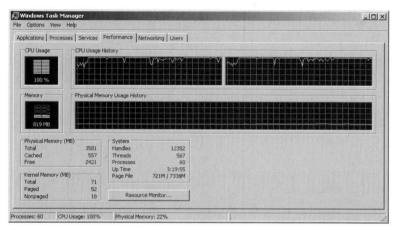

Figure 11-5 Heavy activity on the system is causing CPU usage to soar and in many cases to max out.

Such a large amount of available RAM and such little use of the paging file tells me that processes, disk I/O, or both activities are using up CPU resources. If this level of usage were consistent, you have a problem that needs investigating. Here, increasing the server's RAM or virtual memory will not solve the problem. Instead, you would need to start by checking for system processes that have high CPU usage time, which will tell you what activities are causing the strain on the server's processors. If the high CPU usage activities are related to installed applications, roles, or role services, you might want to consider adding CPUs to the server. Generally, you add CPUs to a server in matched pairs. In this example, the server has two CPUs so you would want to consider upgrading to four CPUs. You might also consider offloading some of the system's load. For example, you could move one of its roles or applications to a different server.

Another scenario you might encounter is one where the server has little available RAM and a large page file. A small amount of available RAM would be a concern, and if this level of usage were consistent, you might consider changing the way applications use RAM, adding RAM, or both. A large amount of virtual memory being used (relative to available physical RAM) is also an area of possible concern that might make you consider adding physical RAM. Although increasing the amount of RAM could offer some relief to the CPU, it might not be enough, so you could consider increasing the processor speed or adding processors. You might also consider offloading some of the system's load. For example, you could move one of its roles or applications to a different server.

Chapter 11

Getting Information on Running Applications

The Applications tab in Task Manager, shown in Figure 11-6, lists applications being run by users on the computer along with status details that show whether the applications are running or not responding. If an application has an open file, such as a Microsoft Word document, the name of the file is shown as well.

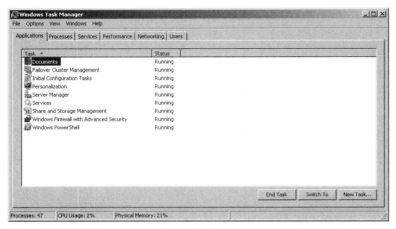

Figure 11-6 Task Manager tracks applications users are running on the Applications tab.

To work with an application, select it by clicking it in the Task list. You can then right-click the application name to select the Switch To, Bring To Front, Minimize, or Maximize option. Don't overlook the usefulness of the Go To Process option when you right-click: Use this when you're trying to find the primary process for a particular application because selecting this option highlights the related process on the Processes tab. Select Create Dump File to create a dump file for debugging an application.

If you see an application with a status of Not Responding, that's an indicator that the application might be frozen, and you might want to select it and then click End Task. Keep in mind that the Not Responding message can also be an indicator that an application is busy and should be left alone until it finishes. Generally, don't use End Task to stop an application that is running without errors. Instead, click the Switch To button to switch to the application and then exit as you normally would.

Monitoring and Troubleshooting Processes

You can view information about processes running on a system by using the Processes tab of Task Manager or by running get-process. The Task Manager display differs greatly from the output provided by get-process. By default, the Processes tab shows all processes that are running, including those run by the operating system, local services, network services, the interactive user, and remote users. The interactive user is the user account logged on to the local console. If you don't want to see processes from remote users, such as those users connecting by using Remote Desktop Connection, clear the Show Processes From All Users check box.

The default view of the Processes tab shows each running process by image name and user name. The CPU column shows the percentage of processor utilization for each process. The Memory column shows the amount of memory the process is currently using. By default, processes are sorted by user name, but you can change this by clicking any of the available column headers to sort the information based on that column. Clicking again on the same column reverses the sort order. For example, click Image Name to alphabetically sort the image names. Click Image Name again to reverse sort the image names.

TROUBLESHOOTING

Isolate 32-bit or 64-bit processes

By default, 32-bit Windows systems show both 16-bit and 32-bit tasks that are running on the system, and 64-bit systems show both 32-bit and 64-bit tasks that are running on the system. To show only 32-bit tasks on 32-bit systems, click Options and then select Show 16-Bit Tasks. To show only 64-bit tasks on 64-bit systems, click Options and then select Show 32-Bit Tasks. This should clear the option for the related item on the Option menu.

As you may recall from Figure 11-2, get-process shows much more detailed information for each process. This information is useful for troubleshooting. If you click View and choose Select Columns, you'll see a dialog box that allows you to add columns to the Processes tab. To get the additional information shown by get-process, the following columns should be selected:

- CPU Usage
- CPU Time
- Memory – Working Set
- Memory – Working Set Delta
- Memory – Private Working Set
- Memory – Commit Size
- Page Faults
- Page Fault Delta
- Base Priority
- Handles
- Threads

Chapter 11

You will then have a process display like the one shown in Figure 11-7.

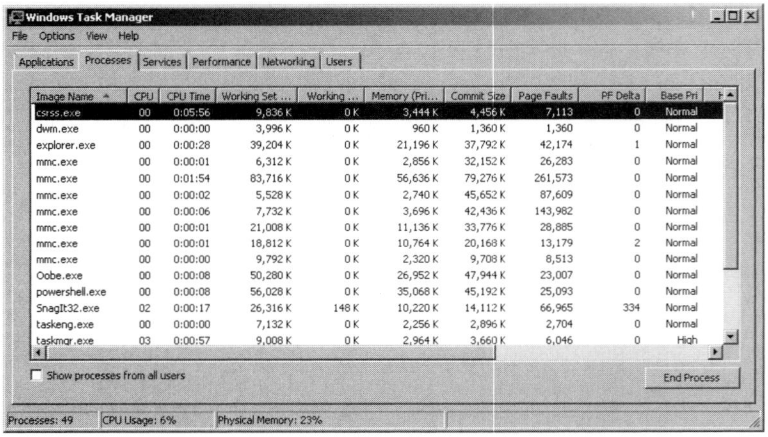

Figure 11-7 The Processes tab provides detailed information on running processes according to image name and user name.

Okay, so now that you've added all these extra columns of information, you are probably wondering what it all means and why you want to track it. As stated previously, you primarily use this information for troubleshooting. It helps you pinpoint which processes are hogging system resources and the type of resources the resource hogs are using. When you know what's going on with processes, you can modify the system or its applications accordingly to resolve a performance problem.

Table 11-1 summarizes the information provided by these and other process-related statistics. The value in parentheses following the Task Manager column name is the name of the corresponding get-process property (if available). If by monitoring processes you notice what looks like a problem, you will probably want to start more detailed monitoring of the system. One tool to consider is System Monitor, which is discussed in Chapter 12, "Comprehensive Performance Analysis and Logging."

> **Note**
> For formatting purposes, the get-process property names are shown with hyphens where necessary. The actual property names do not contain hyphens.

Table 11-1 **Process Statistics and How They Can Be Used**

Column Name	Description
Base Priority (BasePriority)	Shows the priority of the process. Priority determines how much of the system resources are allocated to a process. The standard priorities are Low (4), Below Normal (6), Normal (8), Above Normal (10), High (13), and Real-Time (24). Most processes have a Normal priority by default, and the highest priority is given to real-time processes.
CPU Time (TotalProcessor-Time)	Shows the total amount of CPU time used by the process since it was started. Click the column header to quickly see the processes that are using the most CPU time. If a process is using a lot of CPU time, the related application might have a configuration problem. This could also indicate a runaway or nonresponsive process that is unnecessarily tying up the CPU.
CPU Usage (CPU)	Shows the percentage of CPU utilization for the process. The System Idle Process shows what percentage of CPU power is idle. A 99 in the CPU column for the System Idle Process means 99 percent of the system resources currently aren't being used. If the system has low idle time (meaning high CPU usage) during peak or average usage, you might consider upgrading to faster processors or adding processors.
Handles (HandleCount)	Shows the number of file handles maintained by the process. The number of handles used is an indicator of how dependent the process is on the file system. Some processes have thousands of open file handles. Each file handle requires system memory to maintain.
Image Name (ProcessName)	Shows the name of the process.
Image Path Name (Path)	Shows the full path to the executable for the process.
Memory – Commit Size (Virtual-MemorySize)	Shows the amount of virtual memory allocated to and reserved for a process. Virtual memory is memory on disk and is slower to access than pooled memory. By configuring an application to use more physical RAM, you might be able to increase performance. To do this, however, the system must have available RAM. If it doesn't, other processes running on the system might slow down.
Memory – Non-Paged Pool (NonpagedSystem-MemorySize)	Shows the amount of virtual memory for a process that cannot be written to disk. The nonpaged pool is an area of RAM for objects that can't be written to disk. You should note processes that require a high amount of nonpaged pool memory. If there isn't enough free memory on the server, these processes might be the reason for a high level of page faults.
Memory – Paged Pool (PagedSystem-MemorySize)	Shows the amount of committed virtual memory for a process that can be written to disk. The paged pool is an area of RAM for objects that can be written to disk when they aren't used. As process activity increases, so does the amount of pool memory the process uses. Most processes have more paged pool than nonpaged pool requirements.

Column Name	Description
Memory – Peak Working Set (PeakWorkingSet)	Shows the maximum amount of memory the process used, including both the private working set and the non-private working set. If peak memory is exceptionally large, this can be an indicator of a memory leak.
Memory – Working Set (WorkingSet)	Shows the amount of memory the process is currently using, including both the private working set and the non-private working set. The private working set is memory the process is using that cannot be shared with other processes. The non-private working set is memory the process is using that can be shared with other processes. If memory usage for a process slowly grows over time and doesn't go back to the baseline value, this can be an indicator of a memory leak.
Memory – Working Set Delta	Shows the change in memory usage for the process recorded since the last update. A constantly changing memory delta can be an indicator that a process is in use, but it could also indicate a problem. Generally, the memory delta might show increasing memory usage when a process is being used and then show a negative delta (indicated by parentheses in Task Manager) as activity slows.
Page Fault Delta	Shows the change in the number of page faults for the process recorded since the last update. As with memory usage, you might see an increase in page faults when a process is active and then a decrease as activity slows.
Page Faults	Shows page faults caused by the process. Page faults occur when a process requests a page in memory and the system can't find it at the requested location. If the requested page is elsewhere in memory, the fault is called a *soft page fault*. If the requested page must be retrieved from disk, the fault is called a *hard page fault*. Most processors can handle large numbers of soft faults. Hard faults, on the other hand, can cause significant delays. If there are a lot of hard faults, you might need to increase the amount of memory or reduce the system cache size.
PID (Id)	Shows the run-time identification number of the process.
Session ID (SessionId)	Shows the identification number user (session) within which the process is running. This corresponds to the ID value listed on the Users tab.
Threads (Threads)	Shows the number of threads that the process is using. Most server applications are multithreaded, which allows concurrent execution of process requests. Some applications can dynamically control the number of concurrently executing threads to improve application performance. Too many threads, however, can actually reduce performance, because the operating system has to switch thread contexts too frequently.

At a Windows PowerShell prompt, you can get key stats for all processes by following these steps:

1. Get all the processes running on the server and store them in the $a variable by entering:

```
$a = get-process
```

2. Use the InputObject parameter to pass the process objects stored in $a to get-process and then pass the objects to the format-table cmdlet along with the list of properties you want to see by entering:

```
get-process -inputobject $a | format-table –property ProcessName,
BasePriority, HandleCount, Id, NonpagedSystemMemorySize,
PagedSystemMemorySize, PeakPagedMemorySize, PeakVirtualMemorySize,
PeakWorkingSet, SessionId, Threads, TotalProcessorTime,
VirtualMemorySize, WorkingSet, CPU, Path
```

> **Note**
>
> The order of the properties in the comma-separated list determines the display order. If you want to change the display order, simply move the property to a different position in the list.

When you know the process you want to examine, you don't need to use this multistep procedure. Simply enter the name of the process without the .exe or .dll instead of using -inputobject $a. In this example, you list details about the explorer process:

```
get-process explorer | format-table –property ProcessName, BasePriority,
HandleCount, Id, NonpagedSystemMemorySize, PagedSystemMemorySize,
PeakPagedMemorySize, PeakVirtualMemorySize, PeakWorkingSet, SessionId,
Threads, TotalProcessorTime, VirtualMemorySize, WorkingSet, CPU, Path
```

You can enter part of a process name as well using an asterisk as a wildcard to match a partial name. In this example, get-process lists any process with a name that starts with exp:

```
get-process exp* | format-table –property ProcessName, BasePriority,
HandleCount, Id, NonpagedSystemMemorySize, PagedSystemMemorySize,
PeakPagedMemorySize, PeakVirtualMemorySize, PeakWorkingSet, SessionId,
Threads, TotalProcessorTime, VirtualMemorySize, WorkingSet, CPU, Path
```

Some interesting additional properties you can use with get-process include:

- **MinWorkingSet** The minimum amount of working set memory used by the process

- **Modules** The executables and dynamically linked libraries used by the process

- **PeakVirtualMemorySize** The peak amount of virtual memory used by the process

Chapter 11

- **PriorityBoostEnabled** A Boolean value that indicates whether the process has the PriorityBoost feature enabled

- **PriorityClass** The priority class of the process

- **PrivilegedProcessorTime** The amount of kernel-mode usage time for the process

- **ProcessorAffinity** The processor affinity setting for the process

- **Responding** A Boolean value that indicates whether the process responded when tested

- **StartTime** The date and time the process was started

- **UserProcessorTime** The amount of user-mode usage time for the process

- **Description** A description of the process

- **FileVersion** The file version of the process's executable

In Task Manager, you can stop processes that you suspect aren't running properly. To do this, right-click the process, and choose End Process to stop the process or End Process Tree to stop the process as well as any other processes it started. To stop a process at the Windows PowerShell prompt, you can use stop-process. The best way to use stop-process is to identity the process ID of the process that you want to stop rather than a process name. This ensures that you stop only the intended process rather than all instances of processes with a particular process name. You should also have stop-process prompt you to confirm how you want to proceed using the -confirm parameter. In the following example, you stop the process with the process ID 4524:

```
stop-process -id 4524 -confirm
```

As you are confirming this action and passing through the output, you'll see a prompt asking you to confirm. You can then:

- Press Y to answer Yes and confirm that you want to perform the action and continue.

- Press A to answer Yes to all prompts and confirm that you want to perform all actions without further prompting.

- Press N to answer No and skip the action and continue to the next action.

- Press L to answer No to all prompts and confirm that you do not want to perform any actions.

- Press N to answer No and confirm that you do not want to perform the action.

- Press S to suspend the pipeline and return to the command prompt. To later return to the pipeline, type **exit**.

Monitoring and Troubleshooting Services

You can view information about services running on a system by using the Services tab of Task Manager or by running get-service. By default, the Services tab shows all services configured on the system whether they are running, stopped, or in a different state. As shown in Figure 11-8, services are listed by name, process ID (PID), description, status, and group.

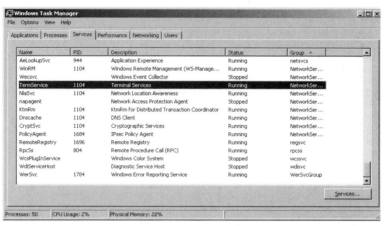

Figure 11-8 The Services tab provides detailed information on configured services.

As multiple services typically run under the same process ID, you can quickly sort services by their associated process ID by clicking the related column heading. You can click the Status column heading to sort services according to their status as Running or Stopped. If you right-click a service's listing in Task Manager, you display a shortcut menu that allows you to start a stopped service, stop a started service, or go to the related process on the Processes tab.

The Group column provides additional information about related identities or service host contexts under which a service runs. Services running an identity with a restriction have the restriction appended. For example, a service running under the Local Service identity may be listed as LocalServiceNoNetwork to indicate that the service has no network access, or as LocalSystemNetworkRestricted to indicate that the service has restricted access to the network.

Services that have svchost.exe list their associated context for the -k parameter. For example, the RemoteRegistry service runs with the command line svchost.exe -k regsvc and you'll see an entry of regsvc in the Group column for this service.

At a Windows PowerShell prompt, you can get the status of configured services simply by entering **get-service**. By default, only the service status, internal name, and display name are shown. Additional properties that you can display include:

- **CanPauseAndContinue** Indicates whether the service can be paused and resumed

- **CanStop** Indicates whether you can stop the service

- **DependentServices** Lists the services that depend on this service
- **ServicesDependedOn** Lists the services on which this service depends

At a Windows PowerShell prompt, you can get the available details for all services by following these steps:

1. Get all the services running on the server and store them in the $a variable by entering:

   ```
   $a = get-service
   ```

2. Use the InputObject parameter to pass the service objects stored in $a to get-service and then pass the objects to the format-table cmdlet along with the list of properties you want to see by entering:

   ```
   get-service -inputobject $a | format-table -property Name, DisplayName,
   CanPauseAndContinue, CanStop, DependentServices, ServicesDependedOn, Status
   ```

When you know the service you want to examine, you don't need to use this multistep procedure. Simply enter the internal name of the process instead of using -inputobject $a. In this example, you list details about the TermService process:

```
get-service TermService | format-table -property Name, DisplayName,
CanPauseAndContinue, CanStop, DependentServices, ServicesDependedOn, Status
```

You can enter part of a service name as well using an asterisk as a wildcard to match a partial name. In this example, get-service lists any service with a name that starts with term:

```
get-service Term* | format-table -property Name, DisplayName,
CanPauseAndContinue, CanStop, DependentServices, ServicesDependedOn, Status
```

To list services by display name, use the -displayname parameter and enclose the display name in quotation marks, such as:

```
get-service -displayname "Terminal Services" | format-table -property Name,
DisplayName, CanPauseAndContinue, CanStop, DependentServices,
ServicesDependedOn, Status
```

You can use the following cmdlets to manage services:

- **Suspend-Service** Pauses a service
- **Resume-Service** Resumes a paused service
- **Start-Service** Starts a stopped service
- **Stop-Service** Stops a started service
- **Restart-Service** Stops and then starts a service

Typically, you'll use Restart-Service when you suspect a service is having a problem and you want to reset it.

Getting Network Usage Information

As Figure 11-9 shows, the Networking tab in Task Manager displays current network usage for each of the system's connections to the network.

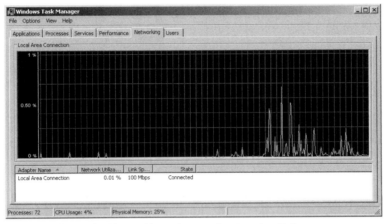

Figure 11-9 Use the Networking tab to track network activity.

You can use the information provided to determine the following quickly:

- The number of network adapters installed on the computer

- The percentage of utilization of each network adapter

- The link speed of each network adapter

- The state of each network adapter

The network activity graph shows traffic going to and from the computer as well as how much of the network capacity is in use. If a system has one network adapter, the graph details network traffic on this adapter over time. If a system has multiple network adapters, the graph displays a composite index of all network connections, which represents all network traffic.

TROUBLESHOOTING

Get separate views of bytes received and sent for troubleshooting

For troubleshooting, it is sometimes useful to have separate views of traffic going to the computer (Bytes Received) and traffic going from the computer (Bytes Sent). To do this, click View, choose Network Adapter History, and then select Bytes Sent. Then click View, choose Network Adapter History, and then select Bytes Received. Afterward, Bytes Sent are shown in red, Bytes Received in yellow, and Bytes Total in green.

You can also get more detailed information for each adapter. This information is useful for troubleshooting. If you click View and choose Select Columns, you'll see a dialog box that will let you add columns for summary statistics to the Networking tab. Table 11-2 summarizes the key network statistics available.

Table 11-2 **Network Statistics and How They Can Be Used**

Column Name	Description
Bytes Sent Throughput	Shows percentage of current connection bandwidth used by traffic sent from the system.
Bytes Received Throughput	Shows percentage of current connection bandwidth used by traffic received by the system.
Bytes Throughput	Shows percentage of current connection bandwidth used for all traffic on the network adapter. If this shows 50 percent or more utilization consistently, you'll want to monitor the system more closely and consider adding network adapters.
Bytes Sent	Shows cumulative total bytes sent on the connection since the system booted.
Bytes Received	Shows cumulative total bytes received on the connection since the system booted.
Bytes	Shows cumulative total bytes on the connection since the system booted.
Unicasts	Shows cumulative number of unicast packets received or sent since the system booted.
Unicasts Sent	Shows total packets sent by unicast since the system booted.
Unicasts Received	Shows total packets received by unicast since the system booted.
Nonunicasts	Shows total number of broadcast packets sent or received since the system booted. Too much broadcast traffic on the network can be an indicator of networking problems. If you see a lot of nonunicast traffic, monitor the amount received during the refresh interval.
Nonunicasts Sent	Shows total broadcast packets sent since the system booted.
Nonunicasts Received	Shows total broadcast packets received since the system booted.

Getting Information on User and Remote User Sessions

Members of the Administrators group and any users to which you specifically grant remote access can connect to systems using Terminal Services or Remote Desktop Connection. Both techniques allow users to access systems remotely and use the systems as if they were sitting at the keyboard. In the standard configuration, however, remote access is disabled. You can enable the remote access feature by using the System utility in Control Panel, System And Maintenance. Open the System Properties dialog box by clicking Advanced System Settings, and then click the Remote tab. In the Remote Desktop panel, select one of the following options and then click OK:

- Allow Connections From Computers Running Any Version Of Remote Desktop (Less Secure)

- Allow Connections Only From Computers Running Remote Desktop With Network Level Authentication (More Secure)

> **NOTE**
> Windows Vista, Windows Server 2008, and later releases of Windows have Network Level Authentication. Most earlier releases of Windows do not.

With Remote Desktop, Windows Server 2008 allows one console session and two remote administration sessions. Most remote sessions are created as console sessions. The reason for this is that the console session provides full functionality for administration. If you log on locally to the console and someone is logged on remotely to the console, you will be prompted to end his or her user session so that you can log on. If you click Yes, the user's session is disconnected, halting all user-started applications without saving application data. If you click No, you will not be allowed to log on. See Chapter 19, "Using Remote Desktop for Administration," for details on how you can use Remote Desktop to configure remote sessions for administration rather than console sessions.

If you configure a server by using Terminal Services, multiple users can log on to a system up to the maximum allowed by licensing. To keep track of sessions after you've configured Terminal Services, you can use the Users tab of Task Manager. As shown in Figure 11-10, the Users tab lists user connections according to the following factors:

- **User** The pre–Windows 2000 logon name of the user account, such as Wrstanek or Administrator. If you want to see the logon domain as well as the logon name, select Show Full Account Name on the Options menu.

- **ID** The session ID. All user connections have a unique session ID. The session ID for any user logged on locally is 0.

- **Status** The status of the connection (Active or Disconnected).

- **Client Name** The name of the computer from which the user is connecting. This field is blank for console sessions.

- **Session** The type of session. Console is used for users logged on locally. Otherwise, indicates the connection type and protocol, such as RDP-TCP for a connection using the Remote Desktop Protocol (RDP) with Transmission Control Protocol (TCP) as the transport protocol.

Chapter 11

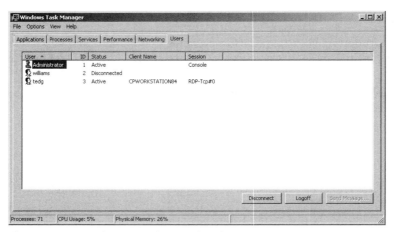

Figure 11-10 Use the Users tab to track and manage remote user sessions.

The Users tab can help you determine who is logged on and whether that user's status is either Active or Inactive. Right-click an active session and you can choose Send Message to send a console message to the user. This message is displayed on the screen of that user's session.

If you must end a user session, you can do this in one of two ways. Right-clicking the session and choosing Log Off logs the user off using the normal logoff process. This allows application data and system state information to be saved as during a normal logoff. Right-clicking the session and choosing Disconnect forcibly ends a user's session without saving application data or system state information.

You can also connect to an inactive session. Right-click the inactive session, and then choose Connect. When prompted, provide the user's password.

Finally, by default the shortcut keys used to end a remote control session are Ctrl+* (Ctrl+Shift+8). If you want a session to use different shortcut keys, right-click the session you want to work with, and then select Remote Control. You can then set the shortcut keys to end the remote control session.

Tracking Events and Troubleshooting by Using Event Viewer

The Windows operating system defines an event as any significant occurrence in the operating system or an application that should be recorded for tracking purposes. Informational events can be tracked as well as events that record warnings, errors, and auditing. Critical errors that deserve immediate attention, such as when the server has run out of disk space or memory, are recorded in the logs and displayed on screen.

Understanding the Event Logs

The Windows service that controls event logging is the Event Log service. When this service is started, events are recorded in one of the available event logs. Two general types of log files are used:

Windows logs Logs that the operating system uses to record general system events related to applications, security, setup, and system components.

Applications and Services logs Logs that specific applications and services use to record application-specific or service-specific events.

Windows logs you'll see include:

- **Application** Contains events logged by applications. You'll find events in this log for Microsoft Exchange Server, SQL Server, Internet Information Services (IIS), and other installed applications. It is also used to record events from printers and, if you've configured alert logging, alerts. The default location is %SystemRoot%\System32\Winevt\Logs\Application.evtx. The default log size is 20480 MB.

- **Forwarded Events** When you configure event forwarding, this log records forwarded events from other servers. The default location is %SystemRoot%\System32\Config\FordwardedEvents.evtx. The default log size is 20480 MB.

- **Security** Contains events you've set for auditing with local or global group policies. Depending on the auditing configuration, you'll find events for logon, logoff, privilege use, and shutdown, as well as general system events, such as the loading of the authentication package by the Local Security Authority (LSA). The default location is %SystemRoot%\System32\Winevt\Logs\Security.evtx. The default log size is 131072 MB on domain controllers and 20480 MB on member servers.

> **Note**
>
> Only administrators are granted access to the Security log by default. If other users need to access the Security log, you must specifically grant them the Manage Auditing and the Security Log user rights. You can learn more about assigning user rights in Chapter 35, "Managing Users, Groups, and Computers."

- **Setup** This log records events logged by the operating system or its components during setup and installation. The default location is %SystemRoot%\System32\Winevt\Logs\Setup.evtx. The default log size is 1028 MB.

- **System** Contains events logged by Windows Server 2008 and its components. You should routinely check this log for warnings and errors, especially those related to the failure of a service to start at bootup or the improper configuration of a service. The default location is %SystemRoot%\System32\Winevt\Logs\System.evtx. The default log size is 20480 MB.

Applications and Services logs you'll see include:

- **DFS Replication** This log records distributed file system (DFS) replication activities. The default location is %SystemRoot%\System32\Winevt\Logs\DfsReplication.evtx. The default log size is 15168 MB.

- **Directory Service** Contains events logged by Active Directory. The primary events relate to the Active Directory database and global catalogs. You'll find details on database consistency checks, online defragmentation, and updates. The default location is %SystemRoot%\System32\Winevt\Logs\Directory Service.evtx.

- **DNS Server** Contains Domain Name System (DNS) queries, responses, and other DNS activities. You might also find details on activities that relate to DNS integration with Active Directory. The default location is %SystemRoot%\System32\Winevt\Logs\DNS Server.evtx. The default log size is 16384 MB.

- **File Replication Service** Contains events logged by the File Replication Service, a service used to replicate Active Directory changes to other domain controllers. You'll find details on any important events that took place while a domain controller attempted to update other domain controllers. The default location is %SystemRoot%\System32\Winevt\Logs\File Replication Service.evtx. The default log size is 20480 MB.

- **Hardware Events** When hardware subsystem event reporting is configured, this log records hardware events reported to the operating system. The default location is %SystemRoot%\System32\Config\HardwareEvents.evtx. The default log size is 20480 MB.

- **Microsoft\Windows** Logs that track events related to specific Windows services and features. Logs are organized by component type and event category. Operational logs track events generated by the standard operations of the related component. In some cases, you'll see supplemental logs for analysis, debugging, and recording administration-related tasks. Most of the related logs have a fixed default log size of 1028 MB.

By default, the logs are sized as appropriate for the type of system you are working with and its configuration. In a standard configuration of Windows Server 2008, most logs are sized as listed previously. As shown, most logs have a fairly large maximum size. This includes the DNS Server, System, and Application logs. Because they are less critical, the Directory Service and File Replication Service logs on domain controllers have a maximum size of 1028 MB. Because the Security log is so important, it is usually configured with a maximum size of 131072 MB on domain controllers and 20480 MB on member servers. Primarily, this is to allow the server to record a complete security audit trail for situations in which the server is under attack and a large number of security events are generated.

Windows Server 2008 logs are configured to overwrite old events as needed by default. So, when the log reaches its maximum size, the operating system overwrites old events with new events. If desired, you can have Windows automatically archive logs. In this configuration, when the maximum file size is reached, Windows archives the events by saving a copy of the current log in the default directory. Windows then creates a new log for storing current events.

You can also configure logs so that Windows never overwrites events. However, the problem with doing it that way is, when the maximum size is reached, events can't be overwritten and the system will generate an error message telling you that such and such an event log is full each time it tries to write an event—and you can quickly get to where there are dozens of these errors being displayed.

> **Note**
>
> You can control the log configuration through Group Policy as well. This means changes you make in Group Policy could in turn change the maximum log size and which action to take when the maximum log size is reached. For more information about Group Policy, see Chapter 36, "Managing Group Policy."

Accessing the Event Logs and Viewing Events

You can view the event logs using Event Viewer, as shown in Figure 11-11. Event Viewer is a Microsoft Management Console (MMC) snap-in that can be started from the Administrative Tools menu or by typing **eventvwr** at the command line.

Event Viewer has custom views as well as standard views of logs. Using the custom Administrative Events view, you can view all errors and warnings for all logs. Using your own custom views, you can create views to surface particular types and categories of events from any logs you want to track. You can also access event logs directly to view all the events they contain.

You can use the following techniques to work with logs and custom views:

- To view all errors and warnings for all logs, expand Custom Views and then select Administrative Events. In the main pane, you should see a list of all warning and error events for the server.

- To view all errors and warnings for a specific server role, expand Custom Views, expand Server Roles, and then select the role to view. In the main pane, you should now see a list of all events for the selected role.

- To view summary information for Windows logs, select the Windows Logs node. You'll then see a list of available logs by name and type along with the number of events and log size.

- To view summary information for Applications and Services logs, select the Applications And Services Logs node. You'll then see a list of available logs by name and type along with the number of events and log size.

- To view events in a specific log, expand the Windows Logs node, the Applications And Services Logs node, or both nodes. Select the log you want to view, such as Application or System.

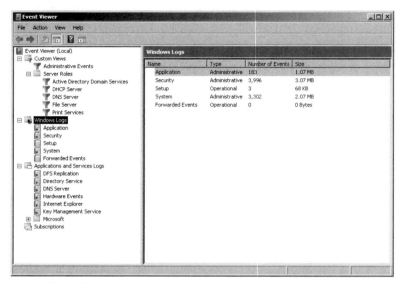

Figure 11-11 The main view in Event Viewer lists the available logs and shows their current size.

As Figure 11-12 shows, individual event entries provide an overview of the event that took place. Each event is recorded according to the date and time the event took place as well as the event level. For all the logs except Security, the event levels are classified as Information, Warning, or Error. For the Security log, the event levels are classified as Audit Success or Audit Failure. These event levels have the following meanings:

- **Information** Generally relates to a successful action, such as the success of a service starting up. If you've configured alert logging, the alerts are also recorded with this event type to show they've been triggered.

- **Warning** Describes events that aren't critical but could be useful in preventing future system problems. Most warnings should be examined to determine whether a preventative measure should be taken.

- **Error** Indicates a fatal error or significant problem occurred, such as the failure of a service to start. All errors should be examined to determine what corrective measure should be taken to prevent the error from reoccurring.

- **Audit Success** Describes an audited security event that completed as requested, such as when a user logs on or logs off successfully.

- **Audit Failure** Describes an audited security event that didn't complete as requested, such as when a user tries to log on and fails. Audit failure events can be useful in tracking down security issues.

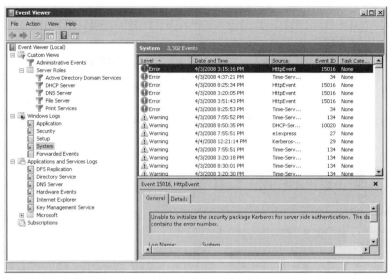

Figure 11-12 Events are logged according to the date and time they occurred as well as by type.

> **Note**
>
> Any attempt by users, services, or applications to perform a task for which they don't have appropriate permissions can be recorded as an audit failure. If someone is trying to break into a system, you might see a large number of audit failure events. If a service or application doesn't have the permissions it needs to perform certain tasks, you might also see a large number of audit failure events.

Other pertinent information recorded with an event includes the event source, event ID, task category, user, and computer. The Source column lists the application, service, or component that logged the event. The Task Category column details the category of the event and is sometimes used to further describe the event. The Event ID column provides an identifier for the specific event that occurred. You can sometimes look up events in the Microsoft Knowledge Base to get more detailed information.

When you select an event, Event Viewer shows additional details in the lower pane, including a general description of the event and other fields of information. The User field shows the name of the user who was logged on when the event occurred (if applicable). If a server process triggered the event, the user name usually is that of the special identity that caused the event. This includes the special identities Anonymous Logon, Local Service, Network Service, and System. Although events can have no user associated with them, they can also be associated with a specific user who was logged on at the time the event occurred.

Chapter 11

The Computer field shows the name of the computer that caused the event to occur. Because you are working with a log from a particular computer, this is usually the account name of that computer. However, this is not always the case. Some events can be triggered because of other computers on the network. Some events triggered by the local machine are stored with the computer name as MACHINENAME. For some events, any binary data or error code generated by the event is available on the Details tab.

You can double-click any event to open its Properties dialog box (see Figure 11-13). The Properties dialog box provides the information that is available in the details pane as well as an option to copy the event data to the Clipboard. Most of the event descriptions aren't easy to understand, so if you need a little help deciphering the event, click Copy. You can then paste the event description into an e-mail message to another administrator.

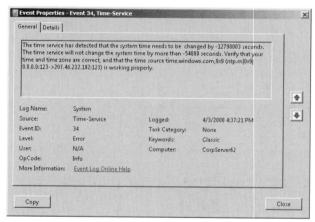

Figure 11-13 Event details include a description of the event and in some cases binary data generated by the event.

> **Note**
>
> Within every event description is a Help And Support Center link that you can click. This link provides access to the Microsoft Web site where you can query for any additional information that might be available on the event.

Viewing Event Logs on Remote Systems

You can use Event Viewer to view events on other computers on your network. Start Event Viewer, right-click Event Viewer (Local) in the left pane, and then choose Connect To Another Computer. In the Select Computer dialog box, shown in Figure 11-14, type the domain name or Internet Protocol (IP) address of the computer for which you want to view the event log and then click OK. Or you can click Browse to search for the computer you want to use. If you need to specify logon credentials, select the Connect As Another User check box and then click the Set User button. Afterward, type the user name and password to use for logon, and then click OK.

> **Note**
>
> Keep in mind that you must be logged on as an administrator or be a member of the Administrators group to view events on a remote computer. You must also configure Windows Firewall on the local computer to allow your outbound connection and the remote computer to allow your inbound connection.

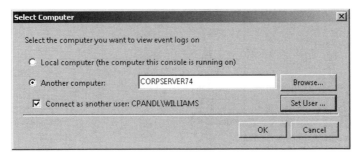

Figure 11-14 Connect to a remote computer.

Sorting, Finding, and Filtering Events

Event Viewer provides several ways for you to organize and search for events in the logs. You can sort events based on date or other stored information. You can search a particular event log for specific events and view events one at a time. You can also filter events so that only the specific events you want to see are shown.

Sorting the Event Logs

By default, logs are sorted so that the newest events are listed first. If you'd rather see the oldest events first, you can do this by clicking View, pointing to Sort By, and then selecting Date And Time. Or you can simply click the Date And Time column header. This change must be made for each log in which you want to see the oldest events first.

You can also sort events based on information in other columns. For example, if you wanted to sort the events based on the event level, you would click the Level column header.

Searching the Event Logs

By using the Find feature, you can search for events within a selected log and view matching events one at a time. Say, for instance, a Microsoft Knowledge Base article says to look for an event with such and such an event source and you want to search for it quickly. You can use the Find feature to do this.

To search, right-click an event log and select Find. In the Find dialog box, type the search text to match and then click Find Next. The first event that matches the search criteria is highlighted in the log. You can double-click the event to get more detailed information or click Find Next to find the next match.

Filtering the Event Logs

The Find option works well if you want to perform quick searches, such as for a single event of a specific type. If you want to perform an extended search, however, such as when you want to review all events of a particular type, there's a better way to do it and that's to create a filtered view so that only the specific events you want to see are shown.

Windows creates several filtered views of the event logs for you automatically. In Event Viewer, filtered views are listed under the Custom Views node. When you select the Administrative Events node, you'll see a list of all errors and warnings for all logs. When you expand the Server Roles node and then select a role-specific view, you'll see a list of all events for the selected role.

You can create and work with filtered views in several different ways. You can:

- Create a custom view by filtering the events in a specific log and saving this filtered view for later use. Simply right-click the log and select Create Custom View. This displays the Create Custom View dialog box, as shown in the following screen. Choose the filter options you want to use, as described in Table 11-3, and then click OK. In the Save Filter To Custom View dialog box, type a name and description for the view. Select where to save the custom view. By default, custom views are saved under the Custom Views node. You can create a new node by clicking New Folder, entering the name of the new folder, and then clicking OK. Click OK to close the Save Filter To Custom View dialog box.

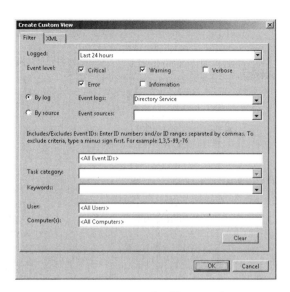

- Create a temporary view by filtering the events in a specific log. Simply select the log and then right-click and select Filter Current Log. This displays the Filter Current Log dialog box, as shown in the following screen. Choose the filter options you want to use, as described in Table 11-3, and then click OK. After you've applied the filter, only events with the options you specify are displayed in the selected event log. For the rest of the current Event Viewer session, the filter is applied to the selected log and you know this because the upper portion of the main pane shows you are working with a filtered log.

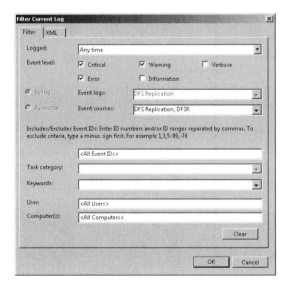

Set Filter Options

You can set as many filter options as you want to narrow the results. Keep in mind, however, that each filter option you apply sets a search criterion that must be matched for an event to be displayed. The options are cumulative so that an event must match all filter options.

Table 11-3 **Find and Filter Options for Event Logging**

Option	Description
Computer	Includes all events associated with a particular computer. Usually this is the name of the computer whose logs you are working with.
Event ID	Includes or excludes events with the event IDs you specify. Enter ID numbers or ID ranges separated by commas. To exclude an event, enter a minus sign before the event ID.
Event Level	Allows you to include or exclude events by level. The most important event levels are warnings, which indicate that something might pose a future problem and might need to be examined, and errors, which indicate a fatal error or significant problem occurred.
Event Sources	Includes events only from specified sources, such as an application, service, or component that logged the event.
Event Logs	Includes events only from specified logs. When working with a custom log view, the log you right-clicked is selected automatically and you can't choose additional logs.
Logged	With filters, all events from the first to the last are displayed by default. You can choose to include events from the Last Hour, Last 12 Hours, Last 24 Hours, Last 7 Days, Last 30 Days, or a custom range.
Task Category	Includes events only within a given category. The categories available change based on the event source you choose.
User	Includes events associated with a particular user account that was logged on when the event was triggered. Server processes can log events with the special identities Anonymous Logon, Local Service, Network Service, and System. Not all events have a user associated with them.

You can apply a filter to a custom view as well as to a log. To filter a custom view, right-click the view and then select Filter Current Custom View. Choose the filter options you want to use and then click OK. For the rest of the current Event Viewer session, the filter is applied to the selected view and you know this because the upper portion of the main pane shows you are working with a filtered view.

If you later want to clear a filter that is applied to a view or log, right-click the log and select Clear Filter. Another option is to save the filtered view as a custom view so you can access it next time you open Event Viewer. To do this, right-click the filtered log or custom view and select Save Filter To Custom View. Afterward, type a name and description for the view. Select where to save the custom view. By default, custom views are saved under the Custom Views node. You can create a new node by clicking New Folder, entering the name of the new folder, and then clicking OK. Click OK to close the Save Filter To Custom View dialog box.

Archiving Event Logs

In most cases, you'll want to have several months' worth of log data available in case you must go back through the logs to troubleshoot a problem. One way to do this, of course, is to set the log size so that it is large enough to accommodate this. However, this usually isn't practical because individual logs can grow quite large. So, as part of your routine, you might want to archive the log files on critical systems periodically, such as for domain controllers or application servers.

To archive logs automatically, right-click the log and select Properties. In the Properties dialog box, select Archive The Log When Full, Do Not Overwrite Events. To create a log archive manually, right-click the log in the left pane of Event Viewer, and then select Save Events As. In the Save As dialog box, select a directory and a log file name. In the Save As Type dialog box, Event Log (*.evtx) is the default file type. This saves the file in event log format for access in Event Viewer. You can also select .txt to save the log in tab-delimited text format, such as for accessing it in a text editor. For importing the log data into a spreadsheet or database, select .csv to save the log in comma-delimited text format. Select .xml to save the log in Extensible Markup Language (XML) format. After you select a log format, click Save.

Logs saved in Event Log format (.evtx) can be reopened in Event Viewer at any time. To do this, right-click the Event Viewer node in the left pane of Event Viewer and choose Open Saved Log. Use the Open Saved Log dialog box to select a directory and a log file. By default, the Event Log Files format is selected in the File Name list. This ensures that logs saved as .evtx, .evt, and .etl are listed. You can also filter the list by selecting a specific file type. When you click Open, Windows displays the Open Saved Log dialog box. Type a name and description for the saved log. Select where to open the log in Event Viewer. By default, saved logs are listed under Saved Logs. You can create a new node by clicking New Folder, entering the name of the new folder, and then clicking OK. Click Open to close the Open Saved Log dialog box. Windows loads the saved event log into Event Viewer and adds a related entry to the list of available logs in the left pane, as shown in Figure 11-15.

If you later want to remove the saved log from Event Viewer, right-click the log and select Delete. When prompted to confirm, click Yes. The saved log file still exists in its original location on the hard disk but is no longer displayed in Event Viewer.

Chapter 11

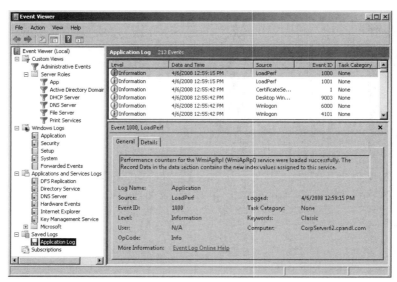

Figure 11-15 Archived logs can be reopened in Event Viewer.

Tracking Events Using PowerShell

When you are working with a specific system or trying to track down issues, Event Viewer is an excellent tool to use and should be your tool of choice. As you've seen, Event Viewer can also be used to access logs on remote systems. No single command-line tool included with Windows Server 2008 provides the same level of functionality, though the PowerShell cmdlet get-eventlog does come close. You can use get-eventlog to obtain detailed information from the event logs.

Because get-eventlog is a text-based rather than graphical utility, it will, in most cases, use fewer system resources than Event Viewer. On systems for which you are very concerned about resource usage and the possibility of bogging down a system through your interactive logon, you might initially want to track events by using get-eventlog.

As Figure 11-16 shows, get-eventlog's standard output provides the essential information about events. To run get-eventlog, access a Windows PowerShell prompt, and then enter **get-eventlog** followed by the name of the event log you want to examine, such as application. If the log name contains spaces, you must enclose the log name in quotation marks, such as **get-eventlog "directory service"**.

Figure 11-16 Use get-eventlog to work with event logs at the command line.

Any Windows log or Applications and Services log that you can work with in Event Viewer is accessible at the command line. When you follow get-eventlog with the log name, the -logname parameter is implied. You can also specify the -logname parameter directly as shown in this example:

```
get-eventlog –logname security
```

By default, get-eventlog returns every event in the specified event log from newest to oldest. In most cases, this is simply too much information and you'll need to filter the events to get a usable amount of data. One way to filter the event logs is to specify that you want to see details about only the newest events. For example, you might want to see only the 50 or 500 newest events in a log.

Using the -newest parameter, you can return only the newest events. The following example lists the 50 newest events in the security log:

```
get-eventlog security -newest 50
```

As shown in Figure 11-16, get-eventlog displays several properties in column format, including: Index, TimeGenerated (listed with the column heading Time), Source, EventID, EntryType (listed with the column heading Type), and Message. To help make sense of the logs, you might want to group events by type, source, or event ID. When you group events by type, you can more easily separate informational events from critical, warning, and error events. When you group by source, you can more easily track events from specific sources. When you group by event ID, you can more easily correlate the recurrence of specific events.

Chapter 11

You can group events by source, eventid, entrytype, and timegenerated using the following technique:

1. Get the events you want to work with and store them in the $e variable by entering:

```
$e = get-eventlog -newest 500 -logname application
```

2. Use the group-object cmdlet to group the event objects stored in $e by a specified property. In this example, you group by eventid:

```
$e | group-object -property eventid
```

Another way to work with events is to sort them according to a specific property. You can sort by source, eventid, entrytype, or timegenerated using the following technique:

1. Get the events you want to work with and store them in the $e variable by entering:

```
$e = get-eventlog -newest 100 -logname application
```

2. Use the sort-object cmdlet to sort the event objects stored in $e by a specified property. In this example, you sort by event type:

```
$e | sort-object -property entrytype
```

Finally, you might also want to match specific text in a specified property. For example, you may only want to return error events. To do this, you would search the EntryType property for occurrences of the word *error*. Here is an example:

1. Get the events you want to work with and store them in the $e variable by entering:

```
$e = get-eventlog -newest 500 -logname application
```

2. Use the where-object cmdlet to search for specific text in a named property of the event objects stored in $e. In this example, you match events with the error entry type:

```
$e | where-object {$_.EntryType -match "error"}
```

The where-object cmdlet uses a search algorithm that is not case-sensitive, meaning you could enter Error, error, or ERROR to match error events. You can also search for warning, critical, and information events. Because where-object considers partial text matches to be valid, you don't want to enter the full event type. You could also search for warn, crit, or info, such as:

```
$e = get-eventlog -newest 500 -logname application
$e | where-object {$_.EntryType -match "warn"}
```

You can use where-object with other event object properties as well. The following example searches for event sources containing the text .NET:

```
$e = get-eventlog -newest 500 -logname application
$e | where-object {$_.Source -match ".NET"}
```

The following example searches for event ID 1101:

```
$e = get-eventlog -newest 500 -logname application
$e | where-object {$_.Source -match "1101"}
```

Using Subscriptions and Forwarded Events

In an enterprise, you might also want servers to forward specific events to central event logging servers. To do this, you configure and enable event forwarding on the applicable servers and then you create subscriptions to the forwarded events on your central event logging server or servers.

In a domain, you can configure forwarding and collection of forwarded events by following these steps:

1. To configure forwarding, log on to all source computers and type **winrm quickconfig** at an elevated command prompt. This creates a WinRM listener on HTTP://* to accept WS-Man requests to any IP address on the source computer. When prompted to confirm, press Y.

2. To configure collection, type **wecutil qc** at an elevated command prompt. This starts the Windows Event Collector Service and configures this service to use the delayed-start mode.

3. Add the computer account of the collector computer to the local Administrators group on each of the source computers. In Local Users And Computers, right-click Administrators and select Add To Group. In the Properties dialog box, click Add. In the Select Users, Computers, Or Groups dialog box, click Object Types. In the Object Types dialog box, select Computers and then click OK. In the Select Users, Computers, Or Groups dialog box, type the account name of the collector computer and then click OK twice. Repeat this process as necessary.

You can create subscriptions on the central event logging server by following these steps:

1. Open Event Viewer and connect to the central event logging server. Afterward, right-click the Subscriptions node and select Create Subscription.

2. In the Subscription Properties dialog box, shown in Figure 11-17, type a name for the subscription, such as All File Servers. Optionally, enter a description.

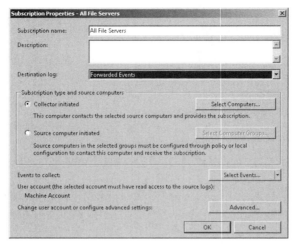

Figure 11-17 Collect the forwarded events.

3. The Forwarded Events log is selected as the destination log by default. Generally, this is the log you'll want to use.

4. Collector initiated event forwarding is the easiest to configure and the default setting. To specify the computers that forward events to the server, click Select Computers. In the Computers dialog box, click Add Domain Computers. In the Select Computer dialog box, type the account name of a computer that is forwarding events and then click OK twice. Repeat this process as necessary.

5. Click Select Events. In the Query Filter dialog box, select the filter options and logs to use and then click OK.

6. Click OK to create the subscription. Now when you access the destination log, you'll see the forwarded events.

Comprehensive Performance Analysis and Logging

Windows Server 2008 provides many tools to help you track performance. In the previous chapter, we looked at tuning performance through configuration settings; using Task Manager to track running processes, users, and network utilization; and using the event logs to track important occurrences recorded by the operating system. Although these tools are excellent and do their jobs well, you might need to dig deeper to establish comprehensive performance baselines, diagnose complex system problems, and optimize system performance.

The key comprehensive monitoring and optimization tools and features available include the following:

- **Performance Monitor** Performance Monitor can be used to track and display performance information in real time. It gathers information on any performance parameters you've configured for monitoring and presents it using a graphical display.

- **Reliability Monitor** Tracks changes to the system and compares them to changes in system stability, thus giving you a graphical representation of the relationship between changes in the system configuration and changes in system stability.

- **Data Collector Sets and Reports** Data collector sets can be considered to be the logging counterpart to Performance Monitor. By using Data Collector Sets, you can record performance information in real time and store it in a log so that it can be analyzed in a report later.

- **Performance Counter Alerts** Performance counter alerts can be used to notify users when certain events occur or when certain performance thresholds are reached. For example, you could configure a performance alert that lets you know when the C drive is running low on free space or the central processing unit (CPU) is operating at 95 percent or more of capacity.

Before discussing each of these tools in turn, let's look at how you can establish performance baselines.

Establishing Performance Baselines

One of the key reasons for tracking performance information is to establish a baseline for a computer that allows you to compare past performance with current performance. There are several types of baselines you can use, including the following:

- **Postinstallation baselines** A postinstallation baseline is a performance level that is meant to represent the way a computer performs after installing all the roles, role services, features, and applications that will be used on the system.

- **Typical usage baselines** A typical usage baseline is a performance level that is meant to represent average usage conditions and serve as a starting point against which you can measure future performance.

- **Test baselines** A test baseline is a performance level that you use during testing of a system. In the test lab, you might want to simulate peak usage loads and test how the system performs under these conditions.

Although it is important to obtain postinstallation and typical usage baseline values, the more important of the two is the typical usage baseline. This is the baseline you get when you simulate user loads or when users actually start working with a server. Ideally, it represents typical or average loads. After you have a typical usage baseline, you can gather information in the future to try to determine how resource usage has changed and how the computer is performing comparatively.

To be able to establish a baseline, you must collect a representative set of performance statistics. By that I mean collect the data that you actually need to determine resource usage and performance in future scenarios. If possible, you should also collect several data samples at the same time each day over a period of several days. This will give you a more meaningful data sample.

You must work to keep the baseline in sync with how the server is used. As you install new roles, role services, features, and applications, you must establish new baselines. This ensures that future comparisons with the baseline are accurate and that they use the most current system configuration to determine how resource usage has changed and how the computer is performing comparatively.

Monitoring Reliability and Performance

The Reliability And Performance Monitor console is the tool of choice for monitoring a system's reliability and performance. You can start Reliability And Performance Monitor by clicking Start, selecting All Programs, Administrative Tools, and then Reliability And Performance Monitor, or you can type **perfmon** at the command line. With the Reliability And Performance node selected, you see an overview of resource usage. As

Figure 12-1 shows, the resource usage statistics are broken down into four utilization categories:

CPU Shows the current CPU utilization and the maximum CPU utilization. If you expand the CPU entry below the graph (by clicking the options button), you'll see a list of currently running executables by name, process ID, description, number of threads used, current CPU utilization, and average CPU utilization.

Disk Shows the number of kilobytes per second being read from or written to disk and the highest percentage usage. If you expand the Disk entry below the graph (by clicking the options button), you'll see a list of currently running executables that are performing or have performed I/O operations by name, process ID, description, file being read or written, number of bytes being read per minute, number of bytes being written per minute, I/O priority, and the associated disk response time.

Network Shows the current network bandwidth utilization in kilobytes and the percentage of total bandwidth utilization. If you expand the Network entry below the graph (by clicking the options button), you see a list of currently running executables that are transferring or have transferred data on the network by name, process ID, IP address being contacted, number of bytes being sent per minute, number of bytes received per minute, and total bytes sent or received per minute.

Memory Shows the current memory utilization and the number of hard faults occurring per second. If you expand the Memory entry below the graph (by clicking the options button), you'll see a list of currently running executables by name, process ID, hard faults per minute, commit memory in KB, working set memory in KB, shareable memory in KB, and private (non-shareable) memory in KB.

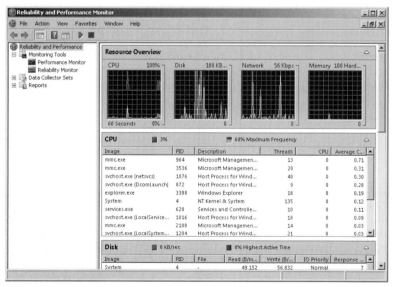

Figure 12-1 Reliability And Performance provides an overview of the resource usage.

In Reliability And Performance, you'll find Performance Monitor and Reliability Monitor under the Monitoring Tools node. Performance Monitor graphically displays statistics for the set of performance parameters you've selected for display. These performance parameters are referred to as *counters*. When you install additional roles, role services, and features on a system, Performance Monitor might be updated with a set of counters for tracking performance of the related components. You can update counters when you install additional services and applications as well.

Performance Monitor, shown in Figure 12-2, creates a graph depicting the counters you're tracking. The update interval for this graph is configurable but is set to one second by default. Tracking information is most valuable when you record performance information in a log file so that it can be played back. When you create alerts, you can notify yourself or others any time specific performance criteria are met.

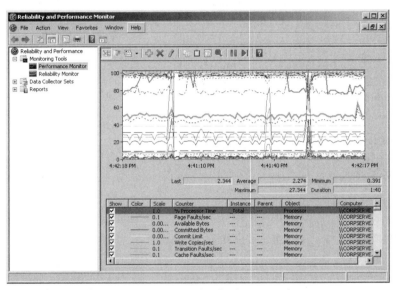

Figure 12-2 Performance Monitor graphically depicts performance.

Reliability Monitor, shown in Figure 12-3, tracks changes to the server and compares them to changes in system stability. In this way, you can see a graphical representation of the relationship between changes in the system configuration and changes in system stability. By recording software installation, software removal, application failure, hardware failure, and Windows failure events, as well as key events regarding the configuration of the server, you can see a time line of changes in both the server and its reliability and then use this information to pinpoint changes that are causing problems with stability. For example, if you see a sudden drop in stability, you can click a data point and then expand the related data set, such as Application Failure or Hardware Failure, to find the specific event that caused the drop in stability.

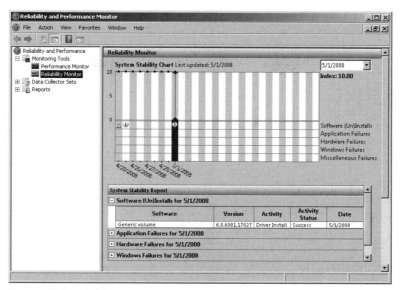

Figure 12-3 Reliability Monitor graphically depicts overall reliability.

Comprehensive Performance Monitoring

Reliability And Performance Monitor is a tool designed to track and display performance information in real time. It gathers information on any performance parameters you've configured for monitoring and presents it using a graphical display.

Using Performance Monitor

When you start the Reliability And Performance Monitor console, you can access Performance Monitor by expanding the Monitoring Tools node and then selecting Performance Monitor. When you are working with Performance Monitor, the right pane graphs any performance items you've configured for monitoring, as shown previously in Figure 12-2. Each performance item you want to monitor is defined by the following three components:

- **Performance objects** Represent any system component that has a set of measurable properties. A performance object can be a physical part of the operating system, such as the memory, the processor, or the paging file; a logical component, such as a logical disk or print queue; or a software element, such as a process or a thread.

- **Performance object instances** Represent single occurrences of performance objects. If a particular object has multiple instances, such as when a computer has multiple processors, you can use an object instance to track a specific occurrence of that object. You could also elect to track all instances of an object, such as whether you want to monitor all processors on a system.

- **Performance counters** Represent measurable properties of performance objects. For example, with a processor, you can measure the percentage of processor utilization using the % Processor Time counter.

In a standard installation of Windows Server 2008, many performance objects are available for monitoring. As you add services, applications, and components, additional performance objects can become available. For example, when you install the Domain Name System (DNS), the DNS object becomes available for monitoring on that computer.

The most common performance objects you'll want to monitor are summarized in Table 12-1. Like all performance objects, each performance object listed here has a set of counters that can be tracked.

Table 12-1 Commonly Tracked Performance Objects

Performance Object	Description
Cache	Monitors the file system cache, which is an area of physical memory that indicates application I/O activity.
Database ==> Instances	Monitors performance for instances of the embedded database management system used by Windows Server 2008.
DFS Replicated Folders	Monitors conflicts, deletions, replication, and other performance factors related to DFS replication folders.
DFS Replication Connections	Monitors the data sent and received and other performance statistics for DFS replication connections.
DHCPv6 Server	Monitors DHCPv6 message broadcasts and other types of DHCPv6 activities.
DirectoryServices	Monitors performance statistics related to Active Directory Domain Services.
DNS	Monitors DNS message traffic and other types of DNS activities.
IPv4	Monitors IPv4 communications and related activities.
IPv6	Monitors IPv6 communications and related activities.
LogicalDisk	Monitors the logical volumes on a computer.
Memory	Monitors memory performance for system cache (including pooled, paged memory and pooled, nonpaged memory), physical memory, and virtual memory.
Network Interface	Monitors the network adapters configured on the computer.
Objects	Monitors the number of events, mutexes, processes, sections, semaphores, and threads on the computer.
Paging File	Monitors page file current and peak usage.
PhysicalDisk	Monitors hard disk read/write activity as well as data transfers, hard faults, and soft faults.

Performance Object	Description
Print Queue	Monitors print jobs, spooling, and print queue activity.
Process	Monitors all processes running on a computer.
Processor	Monitors processor idle time, idle states, usage, deferred procedure calls, and interrupts.
Server	Monitors current server activity and important server usage statistics, including logon errors, access errors, and sessions.
Server Work Queues	Monitors server threading and client requests.
System	Monitors system-level counters, including processes, threads, context switching of threads, file system control operations, system calls, and system uptime.
TCPv4	Monitors TCPv4 communications and related activities.
TCPv6	Monitors TCPv6 communications and related activities.
Thread	Monitors all running threads and allows you to examine usage statistics for individual threads by process ID.
UDPv4	Monitors UDPv4 communications and related activities.
UDPv6	Monitors UDPv6 communications and related activities.

Selecting Performance Objects and Counters to Monitor

The most commonly tracked performance objects are Memory, PhysicalDisk, and Processor. When you first open Performance Monitor, Performance Monitor is configured to graph only the % Processor Time counter. Many other performance counters are available for tracking. To track additional counters, you use the Add Counters dialog box, as shown in Figure 12-4. After you select the Performance Monitor node in Reliability And Performance, you display this dialog box by pressing Ctrl+I or clicking the Add Counters button on the toolbar.

After you've displayed the Add Counters dialog box, you can select objects and counters to track by completing these steps:

1. In the Select Counters From Computer box, enter the Universal Naming Convention (UNC) name of the server you want to work with, such as \\CorpServer62, or choose <Local Computer> to work with the local computer. You'll need to be at least a member of the Performance Monitor Users group in the domain or the local computer to perform remote monitoring.

2. Adding counters to track is easy. Select the type of object you want to work with, such as Memory. When you select an object entry by clicking it, all related counters are selected. If you expand an object entry, you can see all the related counters and can then select individual counters by clicking them. Use Ctrl+click or Shift+click to select multiple counters.

Chapter 12

3. When you select an object or any of its counters, you will in most cases see the related instances. Choose _Total to work with a summary view of all counter instances. Choose All Instances to select all counter instances for monitoring. Or select one or more individual counter instances to monitor.

4. When you've selected an object or a group of counters for an object as well as the object instances, click Add to add the counters to the graph. Repeat steps 2 and 3 to add other performance parameters. You can then repeat this process, as necessary, to add counters for other performance objects. Click OK when you're finished adding counters.

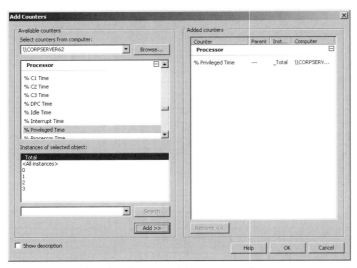

Figure 12-4 Select the objects and the counters that you want to track.

As you've seen, it's easy to add counters to track. What isn't so easy is determining which counters you should track. While you are working with the Add Counters dialog box, you can get a detailed explanation of a counter by selecting a counter and then selecting the Show Description check box. If you add too many counters or track the wrong counters, don't worry. In the Performance Monitor view, you can delete counters later by selecting their entries in the lower portion of the details pane and then clicking Delete on the toolbar or pressing the Delete key on your keyboard. You can also delete all counters being tracked and start over with a clean graph by selecting an entry in the lower portion of the details pane, pressing Ctrl+A, and then pressing the Delete key.

Performance Monitor displays each counter that you are tracking in a different color and line thickness. You can use the legend in the lower portion of the details pane to help you determine which counter is being graphed where. If you are unsure, click a line in the graph to select the corresponding counter in the legend list. To highlight a specific counter so that it is easy to pick out in the graph, select the counter in the legend list, and then press Ctrl+H.

Choosing Views and Controlling the Display

Performance Monitor can present counter statistics in several different ways. By default, it graphs the statistics. A graph is useful when you are tracking a limited number of counters because you can view historical data for each counter that you are working with. By default, Performance Monitor samples the counters once every second and updates the graph over a 100-second duration. This means at any given time there can be up to 100 seconds worth of data on the graph. If you change the sample interval and duration, you can get more information into the chart. For example, if you set the sample interval to once every 10 seconds and the duration to 1,000 seconds, you can get up to 1,000 seconds (or about 17 minutes) worth of data on the graph.

You can set the sample interval by using the General tab of the Performance Monitor Properties dialog box, as shown in Figure 12-5. To display this dialog box, right-click the Performance Monitor node and select Properties. Then set the sample interval and duration using the Sample Every and Duration text boxes.

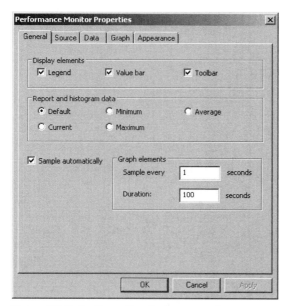

Figure 12-5 Configure the display properties.

The check boxes in the Display Elements panel on the General tab of the Performance Monitor Properties dialog box control the availability of the Legend, Value Bar, and Toolbar. The legend is displayed at the bottom of the details pane, and it shows the color and line style that are used for each counter. The value bar is displayed between the graph and the legend. It shows values related to the counter you've selected in the graph or in the legend. The toolbar is displayed above the graph and provides the basic toolbar functions for working with Performance Monitor. You might find that it is much

Chapter 12

easier to use the shortcut keys than to click the toolbar buttons. The toolbar buttons and their shortcut keys are as follows:

- **View Current Activity** Ctrl+T; switches the view so that current activity being logged is displayed.

- **View Log Data** Ctrl+L; switches the view so that data from a performance log can be replayed.

- **Change Graph Type** Ctrl+G; switches the view to toggle between bar graph, report list, and graph format.

- **Add** Ctrl+I; displays the Add Counter dialog box, which lets you add counters to track.

- **Delete** Delete key; removes the counter so that it is no longer tracked.

- **Highlight** Ctrl+H; highlights the counter using a white line so that it is easier to see. Highlighting works best with graphs. If you want to turn the Highlight function off, press Ctrl+H again.

- **Copy Properties** Ctrl+C; creates a copy of the counter list along with the individual configuration of each counter and puts it on the Clipboard. The information is formatted as an Extensible Markup Language (XML) file. If you open a text editor, you could paste in this information and save it for later use.

- **Paste Counter List** Ctrl+V; pastes a copied counter list into Performance Monitor so that it is used as the current counter set. If you saved a counter list to a file, you simply open the file, copy the contents of the file to the Clipboard, and then press Ctrl+V in Performance Monitor to use that counter list.

> **Save the Counter List or Use It on Different Computers**
>
> You can use the Copy and Paste commands to track the same set of counters quickly and easily at a later date or to use the set on other computers. Press Ctrl+C to copy the counter list and save it to a file. Then you or someone else could access the counter list when you want to use the same setup again. You could also paste the counter list into an e-mail message so that it could be sent to someone who wants to use the same counter list.

- **Properties** Ctrl+Q; displays the Properties dialog box for a selected item.

- **Freeze Display** Ctrl+F; freezes the display so that Performance Monitor no longer updates the performance information. Press Ctrl+F a second time to resume sampling.

- **Update Data** Ctrl+U; updates the display by one sampling interval. When you freeze the display, Performance Monitor still gathers performance information; it just doesn't update the display using the new information. If you want to update the display while it is frozen, use this option.

- **Help** F1; displays the Performance Monitor Help information.

The Histogram Bar and Report views deserve a bit of additional discussion. In the Histogram Bar view, Performance Monitor represents the performance information by using a bar graph with the last sampling value for each counter displayed on an individual bar within the graph. The sizes of the bars within the graph are adjusted automatically based on the number of performance counters being tracked and can be adjusted to accommodate hundreds of counters. That is, in fact, the biggest advantage of the histogram—it allows you to track a lot of counters more easily. In the following screen, approximately 100 counters are being tracked, and it is easy to pick out which counter is which.

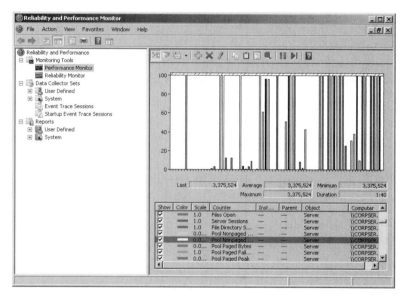

In the Report view, as shown in the following screen, Performance Monitor represents the performance information by using a report list format. In this view, objects and their counters are listed in alphabetical order. The performance information is displayed numerically rather than graphed. If you are trying to determine specific performance values for many different counters, this is the best view to use because the actual values are always shown.

Chapter 12

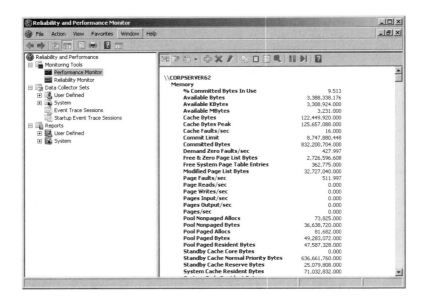

Monitoring Performance Remotely

Monitoring performance on the computer for which you are trying to establish a baseline can skew the results. The reason for this is that Performance Monitor uses resources when it is running, particularly when you are graphing performance information, taking frequent samples, or tracking many performance counters. To remove the resource burden (or at least most of it), you should consider monitoring performance remotely. Here, you use one computer to monitor the performance of another computer. Although this does generate some extra network traffic, you'll get more accurate results for the monitored computer because you're not using its resources for monitoring.

> **Note**
>
> By default, only administrators can monitor performance remotely. You'll need to be at least a member of the Performance Monitor Users group in the domain or the local computer to perform remote monitoring. When you use performance logging, you'll need to be at least a member of the Performance Log Users group in the domain or the local computer to work with performance logs on remote computers.

To begin remote monitoring, select the Performance Monitor node in the Reliability And Performance Monitor console. To start with a new counter set and clear out any existing counters, select a counter entry in the lower portion of the details pane, press Ctrl+A, and press the Delete key. Press Ctrl+I to display the Add Counters dialog box. In the Add Counters dialog box, type the UNC name or Internet Protocol (IP) address of the computer you want to monitor remotely in the Select Counters From Computer text box. A UNC computer name or IP address begins with two backslashes (\\). So, for instance, you could type **\\CorpServer03** or **\\192.168.1.56**.

Configure Remote Monitoring

You can use any computer running Microsoft Windows 2000 or later to perform remote monitoring, and that computer can monitor any computer running Windows 2000 or later. The only exceptions are for non-business editions of Windows. The computer you are using for monitoring can even monitor multiple computers. Don't, however, use a Remote Desktop Connection to connect to the computer you want to monitor and then start monitoring. Even though you are viewing from a different computer, the monitoring is still being performed on the computer to which you are connected.

After you type the UNC computer name or IP address, press Tab or click the Performance Object list. When you do this, Performance Monitor will attempt to connect to the remote computer and retrieve a list of available performance objects to monitor. You can then choose performance objects and counters to track just as you would for a local computer.

TROUBLESHOOTING

Try the IP address if you can't connect

Performance Monitor should be able to find any computer in any trusted domain of your organization's forest. Sometimes, however, it isn't able to do this and returns an error. If this happens, ensure that you entered the correct computer name. If you did and you still get an error, try entering the UNC path with the computer's IP address. Using an IP address saves Performance Monitor from having to perform a DNS lookup to resolve the computer's name to its IP address.

Compare Performance of Multiple Systems

The Legend area shows the associated UNC computer name or IP address for each performance counter you are tracking. If you want to see how performance compares on different computers, use your monitoring computer to track the same performance counters on these computers. You can then make direct comparisons of how these computers perform relative to each other.

Resolving Performance Bottlenecks

Generally, a bottleneck is any condition that keeps a computer from performing at its best. Bottlenecks can also apply to situations in which one resource is preventing another resource from performing optimally. For example, if a system doesn't have enough physical memory, it doesn't matter whether it has a fast processor or a slow processor. The system will still perform poorly because it doesn't have enough physical memory available and must rely heavily on the paging file, reading and writing to disk frequently.

Memory is usually the main bottleneck on both workstations and servers. It is the resource you should examine first to try to determine why a system isn't performing as expected. But memory isn't the only bottleneck. The processor, disk subsystem, and the networking components are also sources of potential performance bottlenecks.

Resolving Memory Bottlenecks

Windows applications use a lot of memory. If you install a server with the minimum amount of memory required, it isn't going to perform at its optimal level. The server cannot perform at its optimal level when you install the recommended amount of memory either. The reason for this is that a server's memory requirements depend on many factors, including the services, components, and applications that are installed on the server as well as the server's configuration.

Computers use both physical and virtual memory. Physical memory is represented by the amount of random access memory (RAM) installed. Virtual memory is memory written to a paging file on disk. Reading from and writing to the paging file involves the disk subsystem, and it is much slower than accessing physical memory. Because of this, you don't want a system to have to use the paging file too frequently.

Before you set out to monitor memory usage, you should check to ensure that the computer has the recommended amount of memory for the operating system and the applications it is running. After you've done this, you can determine how the system is using memory and check for problems. Look closely at the amount of memory available and the amount of virtual memory being used. If the server has very little available memory, you might need to add memory to the system. In general, you want the available memory to be no less than 5 percent of the total physical memory on the server. If the server has a high ratio of virtual memory being used to total physical memory on the system, you might need to add physical memory as well.

Look at the way the system is using the paged pool and nonpaged pool memory. The *paged pool* is an area of system memory for objects that can be written to disk when they aren't used. The *nonpaged pool* is an area of system memory for objects that can't be written to disk. If the size of the paged pool is large relative to the total amount of physical memory on the system, you might need to add memory to the system. If the size of the nonpaged pool is large relative to the total amount of virtual memory allocated to the server, you might want to increase the virtual memory size.

Look at the way the system is using the paging file. A page fault occurs when a process requests a page in memory and the system can't find it at the requested location. If the requested page is elsewhere in memory, the fault is called a *soft page fault*. If the requested page must be retrieved from the paging file on disk, the fault is called a *hard page fault*. Most processors can handle large numbers of soft faults. Hard faults, however, can cause significant delays. If there are a high number of hard page faults, you might need to increase the amount of memory or reduce the size of the system cache.

Counters you can use to check for memory bottlenecks include the following:

- **Memory\Available Bytes** Records the number of bytes of physical memory available to processes running on the server. When there is less than 5 percent of memory free, the system is low on memory and performance can suffer. For example, the server might page excessively to disk to try to keep up with resource demands. Memory is critically short if there is 128 megabytes (MB) or less of memory free, and in this case, the system might page excessively to disk and also try to borrow memory from running processes to keep up with resource demands. If the system is very low on memory, it could also point to a possible memory leak.

- **Memory\Committed Bytes** Records the number of bytes of committed virtual memory. This represents memory that has been paged to disk and is in use. If a server is using too much virtual memory relative to the total physical memory on the system, you might need to add physical memory.

- **Memory\Commit Limit** Shows the total physical and virtual memory available. As the number of committed bytes grows, the paging file is allowed to grow up to its maximum size, which can be determined by subtracting the total physical memory on the system from the commit limit. If you set the initial paging file size too small, the system will repeatedly extend the paging file and this requires system resources. It is better to set the initial page size as appropriate for typical usage or simply use a fixed paging file size. For a fixed paging file, set the size to at least two times the size of RAM.

- **Memory\Page Faults/Sec** Records the average number of page faults per second. It includes both hard and soft page faults. Soft faults result in memory lookups. Hard faults require access to disk.

- **Memory\Pages/Sec** Records the number of memory pages that are read from disk or written to disk to resolve hard page faults. It is the sum of Memory\Pages Input/Sec and Memory\Pages Output/Sec.

- **Memory\Pages Input/Sec** Records the rate at which pages are read from disk to resolve hard page faults. Hard page faults occur when a requested page isn't in memory and the computer has to go to disk to get it. Too many hard faults can cause significant delays and hurt performance.

- **Memory\Pages Output/Sec** Records the rate at which pages are written to disk to free up space in physical memory. If the server has to free up memory too often, this is an indicator that there isn't enough physical memory (RAM) on the system.

- **Memory\Pool Paged Bytes** Represents the size in bytes of the paged pool. The paged pool is an area of system memory for objects that can be written to disk when they aren't used. If the size of the paged pool is large relative to the total amount of physical memory on the system, you might need to add memory to the system. If this value slowly increases in size over time, a kernel mode process might have a memory leak.

- **Memory\Pool Nonpaged Bytes** Represents the size in bytes of the nonpaged pool. The nonpaged pool is an area of system memory for objects that can't be written to disk. If the size of the nonpaged pool is large relative to the total amount of virtual memory allocated to the server, you might want to increase the virtual memory size. If this value slowly increases in size over time, a kernel mode process might have a memory leak.

- **Paging File\% Usage** Records the percentage of the paging file currently in use. If this value approaches 100 percent for all instances, you should consider either increasing the virtual memory size or adding physical memory to the system. This will ensure that the server has additional memory if it needs it, such as when the server load grows.

- **Paging File\% Usage Peak** Records the peak size of the paging file as a percentage of the total paging file size available. A high value can mean that the paging file isn't large enough to handle increased load conditions.

- **Physical Disk\% Disk Time** Records the percentage of time that the selected disk spent servicing read and write requests. Keep track of this value for the physical disks that have paging files. If you see this value increasing over several monitoring periods, you should more closely monitor paging file usage and you might consider adding physical memory to the system.

- **Physical Disk\Avg Disk Queue Length** Records the average number of read and write requests that were waiting for the selected disk during the sample interval. Keep track of this value for the physical disks that have paging files. If you see this value increasing over time and the Memory\Page Reads/Sec is also increasing, the system is having to perform a lot of paging file reads.

- **Physical Disk\Avg Disk Sec/Transfer** Records the length in seconds of the average disk transfer. Track this value for the physical disks that have paging files in conjunction with Memory\Pages/Sec. Memory\Pages/Sec tracks the number of reads and writes for the paging file. If you multiply the Physical Disk\Avg Disk Sec/Transfer by the Memory\Pages/Sec value, you have an excellent indicator of how much of the disk access time is being used by paging. Use the result to help you decide whether to move the paging files to faster disks or add physical memory to the system.

Resolving Processor Bottlenecks

After you've eliminated memory as a potential bottleneck, you should examine the system's processor usage to determine whether there are any potential bottlenecks. Processor bottlenecks can occur if a process's threads need more processing time than is available. This in turn causes the processor queue to grow because threads have to wait to get processing time. As a result, the system response suffers and the system appears sluggish or nonresponsive.

Excess interrupts are another common reason for processor bottlenecks. Each time drivers or disk subsystem components, such as hard disk drives or network components, generate an interrupt, the processor has to stop what it is doing to handle the request because requests from hardware take priority. However, poorly designed drivers and components can generate false interrupts, which tie up the processor for no reason. System boards or components that are failing can generate false interrupts as well.

Watch Out for Bad Device Drivers and System Components

Generally, you'll see more interrupt problems with beta or nonsigned drivers than with signed drivers. A poorly designed driver could by itself generate several thousand interrupts per second, and a processor can get overloaded quickly under those conditions.

TROUBLESHOOTING

Rule out processor affinity as an issue on multiprocessor systems

On multiprocessor systems, you might need to rule out processor affinity as a cause of a processor bottleneck. By using processor affinity, you can set a program or process to use a specific processor to improve its performance. Assigning processor affinity can, however, block access to the processor for other programs and processes.

If a system's processors are the performance bottleneck, adding memory, drives, or network connections won't overcome the problem. Instead, you might need to upgrade the processors to faster clock speeds or add processors to increase the server's upper capacity. You could also move processor-intensive applications, such as Microsoft Exchange Server, to another server.

Counters you can use to check for processor bottlenecks include the following:

- **System\Processor Queue Length** Records the number of threads waiting to be executed. These threads are queued in an area shared by all processors on the system. If this counter has a sustained value of 10 or more threads, you might need to upgrade the processors to faster clock speeds or add processors to increase the server's upper capacity.

- **Processor\% Processor Time** Records the percentage of time the selected processor is executing a non-idle thread. You should track this counter separately for all processor instances on the server. If the % Processor Time values for all instances are high (above 75 percent) while the network interface and disk input/output (I/O) throughput rates are relatively low, you might need to upgrade the processors to faster clock speeds or add processors to increase the server's upper capacity.

- **Processor\% User Time** Records the percentage of time the selected processor is executing a non-idle thread in user mode. *User mode* is a processing mode for applications and user-level subsystems. A high value for all processor instances might indicate that you need to upgrade the processors to faster clock speeds or add processors to increase the server's upper capacity.

- **Processor\% Privileged Time** Records the percentage of time the selected processor is executing a non-idle thread in privileged mode. *Privileged mode* is a processing mode for operating system components and services, allowing direct access to hardware and memory. A high value for all processor instances might indicate that you need to upgrade the processors to faster clock speeds or add processors to increase the server's upper capacity.

- **Processor\Interrupts/Sec** Records the average rate, in incidents per second, that the processor received and serviced hardware interrupts. Compare this value to your baselines. If this value changes substantially (I mean by thousands of interrupts) without a corresponding increase in activity, the system might have a hardware problem. To resolve this problem, you must identify the device or component that is causing the problem. Start with devices that have drivers you've updated recently.

Resolving Disk I/O Bottlenecks

With the high-speed disks available today, a system's hard disks are rarely the primary reason for a bottleneck. It is more likely that a system is having to do a lot of disk reads and writes because there isn't enough physical memory available and the system has to page to disk. Because reading from and writing to disk is much slower than reading and writing memory, excessive paging can degrade the server's overall performance. To reduce the amount of disk activity, you want the system to manage memory as efficiently as possible and page to disk only when necessary.

That said, you can do several things with a system's hard disks to improve performance. If the system has faster drives than the ones used for the paging file, you might consider moving the paging file to those disks. If the system has one or more drives that are doing most of the work and other drives that are mostly idle, you might be able to improve performance by balancing the load across the drives more efficiently.

To help you better gauge disk I/O activity, use the following counters:

- **PhysicalDisk\% Disk Time** Records the percentage of time the physical disk is busy. Track this value for all hard disk drives on the system in conjunction with Processor\% Processor Time and Network Interface Connection\Bytes Total/Sec. If the % Disk Time value is high and the processor and network connection values aren't high, the system's hard disk drives might be creating a bottleneck. You might be able to improve performance by balancing the load across the drives more efficiently or by adding drives and configuring the system so that they are used.

> **Note**
> Redundant array of independent disks (RAID) devices can cause the PhysicalDisk\% Disk Time value to exceed 100 percent. For this reason, don't rely on PhysicalDisk\% Disk Time for RAID devices. Instead, use PhysicalDisk\Current Disk Queue Length.

- **PhysicalDisk\Current Disk Queue Length** Records the number of system requests that are waiting for disk access. A high value indicates that the disk waits are impacting system performance. In general, you want there to be very few waiting requests.

> **Note**
> Physical disk queue lengths are relative to the number of physical disks on the system and proportional to the length of the queue minus the number of drives. For example, if a system has two drives and there are 6 waiting requests, that can be considered a proportionally large number of queued requests; but if a system has eight drives and there are 10 waiting requests, that is considered a proportionally small number of queued requests.

- **PhysicalDisk\Avg. Disk Write Queue Length** Records the number of write requests that are waiting to be processed.

- **PhysicalDisk\Avg. Disk Read Queue Length** Records the number of read requests that are waiting to be processed.

- **PhysicalDisk\Disk Writes/Sec** Records the number of disk writes per second. It is an indicator of how much disk I/O activity there is. By tracking the number of writes per second and the size of the write queue, you can determine how write

Chapter 12

operations are impacting disk performance. If lots of write operations are queuing and you are using RAID 5, it could be an indicator that you would get better performance by using RAID 1. Remember that by using RAID 5 you typically get better read performance than with RAID 1. So, there's a trade-off to be made by using either RAID configuration.

- **PhysicalDisk\Disk Reads/Sec** Records the number of disk reads per second. It is an indicator of how much disk I/O activity there is. By tracking the number of reads per second and the size of the read queue, you can determine how read operations are impacting disk performance. If lots of read operations are queuing and you are using RAID 1, it could be an indicator that you would get better performance by using RAID 5. Remember that by using RAID 1 you typically get better write performance than with RAID 5. So, as mentioned, there's a trade-off to be made by using either RAID configuration.

Resolving Network Bottlenecks

The network that connects your computers is critically important. Its responsiveness, or lack thereof, weighs heavily on the way users perceive the responsiveness of their computers and any computers to which they connect. It doesn't matter how fast their computers are or how fast your servers are. If there's a big delay (and big network delays are measured in tens of milliseconds) between when a request is made and the time it's received, users might think systems are slow or nonresponsive.

Unfortunately, in most cases, the delay (latency) users experience is beyond your control. It's a function of the type of connection the user has and the route the request takes to your server. The total capacity of your server to handle requests and the amount of bandwidth available to your servers are factors you can control, however. Network capacity is a function of the network cards and interfaces configured on the servers. Network bandwidth availability is a function of your organization's network infrastructure and how much traffic is on it when a request is made.

Counters you can use to check network activity and look for bottlenecks include the following:

- **Network Interface\Bytes Total/Sec** Records the rate at which bytes are sent and received over a network adapter. Track this value separately for each network adapter configured on the system. If the Bytes Total/Sec for a particular adapter is substantially slower than what you'd expect given the speed of the network and the speed of the network card, you might want to check the network card configuration. Check to see whether the link speed is set for half duplex or full duplex. In most cases, you'll want to use full duplex.

- **Network Interface\Current Bandwidth** Estimates the current bandwidth for the selected network adapter in bits per second. Track this value separately for each network adapter configured on the system. Most servers use 10/100 network cards or Gigabit Ethernet cards, which can be configured in many ways. Someone might have configured a card for 10 megabits per second (Mbps). If that is the case, the current bandwidth might be off by a factor of 10.

- **Network Interface\Bytes Received/Sec** Records the rate at which bytes are received over a network adapter. Track this value separately for each network adapter configured on the system.

- **Network Interface\Bytes Sent/Sec** Records the rate at which bytes are sent over a network adapter. Track this value separately for each network adapter configured on the system.

TROUBLESHOOTING

Compare network activity to disk time and processor time

Compare these values in conjunction with PhysicalDisk\% Disk Time and Processor\% Processor Time. If the disk time and processor time values are low but the network values are very high, a capacity problem might exist. Solve the problem by optimizing the network card settings or by adding an additional network card.

Performance Logging

Windows Server 2008 introduces data collector sets and reports. Data collector sets allow you to specify sets of performance objects and counters that you want to track. When you've created a data collector set, you can easily start or stop monitoring the performance objects and counters included in the set. In a way, this makes data collector sets similar to the performance logs used in earlier releases of Windows. However, data collector sets are much more sophisticated. You can:

- Use a single data set to generate multiple performance counter and trace logs.

- Assign access controls to manage who can access collected data.

- Create multiple run schedules and stop conditions for monitoring.

- Use data managers to control the size of collected data and reporting.

- Generate reports based on collected data.

In the Reliability And Performance Monitor console, you can review currently configured data collector sets and reports under the Data Collector Sets and Reports nodes, respectively. As shown in Figure 12-6, you'll find data sets and reports that are user-defined and system-defined. User-defined data sets are created by users for general monitoring and performance tuning. System-defined data sets are created by the operating system to aid in automated diagnostics.

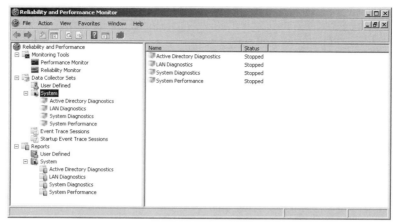

Figure 12-6 Review the available data collector sets and reports.

Creating and Managing Data Collector Sets

In Reliability And Performance Monitor, you can view the currently configured data collector sets by expanding the Data Collector Sets node and then expanding the User Defined and System nodes. When you select a data collector set in the left pane, you'll see a list of the related data collectors in the main pane listed by name and type.

Data collector set types include:

- **Configuration** The Configuration type is for data collectors that record changes to particular Registry paths.

- **Trace** The Trace type is for data collectors that record performance data whenever related events occur.

- **Performance Counter** The Performance Counter type is for data collectors that record data on selected counters when a predetermined interval has elapsed.

Windows Server 2008 uses event traces to track a wide variety of performance statistics. You can view running event traces by selecting Event Trace Sessions. You can then stop a data collector running a trace by right-clicking it and selecting Stop.

Some event traces are configured to start automatically with the operating system. These event traces are called startup event traces. You can view the enabled or disabled status of event traces configured to run automatically when you start the computer by selecting Startup Event Trace Sessions. You can start a trace by right-clicking a startup data collector and selecting Start As Event Trace Session. You can delete a startup data collector by right-clicking it and then selecting Delete.

You can save a data collector as a template that can be used as the basis of other data collectors by right-clicking the data collector and selecting Save Template. In the Save As dialog box, select a directory, type a name for the template, and then click Save. The data collector template is saved as an XML file that can be copied to other systems.

You can delete a user-defined data collector by right-clicking it and then selecting Delete. If a data collector is running, you'll need to stop collecting data first and then delete the collector. Deleting a collector deletes the related reports as well.

Collecting Performance Counter Data

Data collectors can be used to record performance data on the selected counters at a specific sample interval. For example, you could sample performance data for the CPU every 15 minutes. The default location for logging is %SystemRoot%\PerfLogs\Admin. Log files can grow in size very quickly. If you plan to log data for an extended period, be sure to place the log file on a drive with lots of free space. Remember, the more frequently you update the log file, the higher the drive space and CPU resource usage on the system.

To collect performance counter data, follow these steps:

1. In Reliability And Performance Monitor, under the Data Collector Sets node, right-click the User Defined node in the left pane, point to New, and then choose Data Collector Set.

2. In the Create New Data Collector Set wizard, shown in Figure 12-7, type a name for the data collector, such as **Memory Monitor** or **Physical Disk Monitor**. Afterward, select the Create Manually (Advanced) option and then click Next.

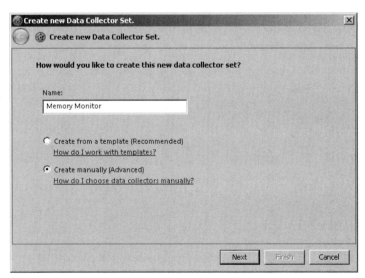

Figure 12-7 Specify the name of the collector set.

3. On the What Type Of Data Do You Want To Include page, the Create Data Logs option is selected by default. Select the Performance Counter check box and then click Next.

4. On the Which Performance Counters Would You Like To Log page, click Add. This displays the Add Counter dialog box, which you can use as previously discussed to select the performance counters to track. When you are finished selecting counters, click OK.

5. On the Which Performance Counters Would You Like To Log page, type in a sample interval and select a time unit in seconds, minutes, hours, days, or weeks. The sample interval specifies when new data is collected. For example, if you sample every 15 minutes, the data log is updated every 15 minutes. Click Next when you are ready to continue.

6. On the Where Would You Like The Data To Be Saved page, type the root path to use for logging collected data. Alternatively, click Browse and then use the Browse For Folder dialog box to select the logging directory. Click Next when you are ready to continue.

7. On the Create New Data Collector Set page, the Run As box lists <Default> as the user to indicate that the log will run under the privileges and permissions of the default system account. To run the log with the privileges and permissions of another user, click Change. Type the user name and password for the desired account, and then click OK. User names can be entered in DOMAIN\Username format, such as CPANDL\WilliamS for the WilliamS account in the CPANDL domain.

8. Select the Open Properties For This Data Collector Set option and then click Finish. This saves the data collector set, closes the wizard, and then opens the related Properties dialog box.

9. By default, logging is configured to start manually. To configure a logging schedule, click the Schedule tab and then click Add. You can now set the Active Range, Start Time, and run days for data collection. Figure 12-8 shows an example.

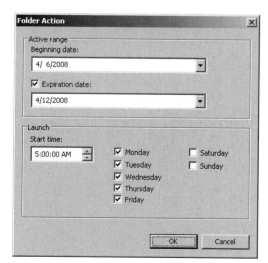

Figure 12-8 Set the run schedule for the collector set.

10. By default, logging stops only if you set an expiration date as part of the logging schedule. Using the options on the Stop Condition tab, you can configure the log file to stop manually after a specified period of time, such as seven days, or when the log file is full (if you've set a maximum size limit).

11. Click OK when you've finished setting the logging schedule and stop conditions. You can manage the data collector as explained in "Creating and Managing Data Collector Sets" on page 364. If you want Windows to run a scheduled task when data collection stops, configure the task on the Task tab in the Properties dialog box.

Collecting Performance Trace Data

You can use data collectors to record performance trace data whenever events related to their source providers occur. A source provider is an application or operating system service that has traceable events.

To collect performance trace data, follow these steps:

1. In Reliability And Performance Monitor, under the Data Collector Sets node, right-click the User Defined node in the left pane, point to New, and then choose Data Collector Set.

2. In the Create New Data Collector Set wizard, type a name for the data collector, such as **Disk IO Trace** or **Logon Trace**. Afterward, select the Create Manually (Advanced) option and then click Next.

3. On the What Type Of Data Do You Want To Include page, the Create Data Logs option is selected by default. Select the Event Trace Data check box and then click Next.

4. On the Which Event Trace Providers Would You Like To Enable page, click Add.

5. In the Event Trace Providers dialog box, shown in Figure 12-9, select an event trace provider to track, such as Active Directory Domain Services: Core, and then click OK.

6. On the Which Event Trace Providers Would You Like To Enable page, you can configure property values to track. By selecting individual properties in the Properties list and clicking Edit, you can track particular property values rather than all values for the provider. Repeat this process to select other event trace providers to track. Click Next when you are ready to continue.

7. Complete steps 6–11 from the previous procedure, "Collecting Performance Counter Data," on page 365.

Figure 12-9 Select a provider to trace.

Collecting Configuration Data

You can use data collectors to record changes in Registry configuration. To collect configuration data, follow these steps:

1. In Reliability And Performance Monitor, under the Data Collector Sets node, right-click the User Defined node in the left pane, point to New, and then choose Data Collector Set.

2. In the Create New Data Collector Set wizard, type a name for the data collector, such as **System Registry Info** or **Current User Registry Info**. Afterward, select the Create Manually (Advanced) option and then click Next.

3. On the What Type Of Data Do You Want To Include page, the Create Data Logs option is selected by default. Select the System Configuration Information check box and then click Next.

4. On the Which Registry Keys Would You Like To Record page, click Add. Type the Registry path to track. Repeat this process to add other Registry paths to track. Click Next when you are ready to continue.

5. Complete steps 6–11 from the earlier procedure, "Collecting Performance Counter Data," on page 365.

Viewing Data Collector Reports

When you're troubleshooting problems, you'll often want to log performance data over an extended period of time and then review the data to analyze the results. For each data collector that has been or is currently active, you'll find related data collector reports. As with data collector sets themselves, data collector reports are usually organized into two general categories: user-defined and system.

To view data collector reports in Reliability And Performance Monitor, expand the Reports node and then expand the individual report node for the data collector you want to analyze. Under the data collector's report node, you'll find individual reports for each logging session. A logging session begins when logging starts and ends when logging is stopped.

The most recent log is the one with the highest log number. To view a log and analyze its related data graphically, double-click it. Keep in mind that if a data collector is actively logging, you won't be able to view the most recent log. You can stop collecting data by right-clicking a data collector set and selecting Stop. Collected data is shown by default in a graph view from the start of data collection to the end of data collection. Only counters that you selected for logging will be available. If a report doesn't have a counter that you want to work with, you'll need to modify the data collector properties, restart the logging process, and then check the logs again.

You can modify the report details using the following techniques:

1. In Reliability And Performance Monitor, right-click the Performance Monitor node and then select Properties. In the Performance Monitor Properties dialog box, click the Source tab.

2. Specify data sources to analyze. Under Data Source, select Log Files and then click Add to open the Select Log File dialog box. You can now select an additional log file to analyze.

3. Specify the time window that you want to analyze. Click Time Range, and then drag the Total Range bar to specify the appropriate starting and ending times. Drag the left edge to the right to move up the start time. Drag the right edge to the left to move down the end time.

4. Click the Data tab. You can now select counters to view. Select a counter and then click Remove to remove it from the graph view. Click Add to display the Add Counters dialog box, which you can use to select the counters that you want to analyze.

5. Click OK. In the monitor pane, click the Change Graph Type button to select the type of graphing.

Configuring Performance Counter Alerts

You can configure alerts to notify you when certain events occur or when certain performance thresholds are reached. You can send these alerts as network messages and as events that are logged in the application event log. You can also configure alerts to start applications and performance logs.

To configure an alert, follow these steps:

1. In Reliability And Performance Monitor, under the Data Collector Sets node, right-click the User Defined node in the left pane, point to New, and then choose Data Collector Set.

Chapter 12

2. In the Create New Data Collector Set wizard, type a name for the data collector, such as **Memory Alert** or **Full Disk Alert**. Afterward, select the Create Manually (Advanced) option and then click Next.

3. On the What Type Of Data Do You Want To Include page, select the Performance Counter Alert option and then click Next.

4. On the Which Performance Counters Would You Like To Monitor page, click Add to display the Add Counters dialog box. This dialog box is identical to the Add Counters dialog box discussed previously. Use the Add Counters dialog box to add counters that trigger the alert. Click OK when you're finished.

5. In the Performance Counters panel, select the first counter and then use the Alert When text box to set the occasion when an alert for this counter is triggered. Alerts can be triggered when the counter is above or below a specific value. Select Above or Below, and then set the trigger value. The unit of measurement is whatever makes sense for the currently selected counter(s). For example, to alert if processor time is over 95 percent, you would select Over and then type **95**. Repeat this process to configure other counters you've selected.

6. Complete steps 7–11 from the earlier procedure, "Collecting Performance Counter Data," on page 365.

Monitoring Performance from the Command Line

Windows Server 2008 includes a command-line utility called Typeperf for writing performance data to the command line. You can use it to monitor the performance of both local and remote computers. The available parameters for Typeperf are summarized in Table 12-2.

Table 12-2 **Parameters for Typeperf**

Parameter	Description
-cf <*filename*>	Specifies a file containing a list of performance counters to monitor.
-config <*filename*>	Specifies the settings file containing command options.
-f <CSV|TSV|BIN|SQL>	Sets the output file format. The default is .csv for comma-separated values.
-o <*filename*>	Sets the path of an output file or SQL database.
-q [*object*]	Lists installed counters for the specified object.
-qx [*object*]	Lists installed counters with instances.
-s <*ComputerName*>	Sets the server to monitor if no server is specified in the counter path.
-sc <*samples*>	Sets the number of samples to collect.
-si <[[*hh:*]*mm:*]*ss*>	Sets the time between samples. The default is 1 second.
-y	Answers Yes to all questions without prompting.

Looks complicated, I know, but Typeperf is fairly easy to use after you get started. In fact, all you really need to provide to get basic monitoring information is the path to the performance counter you want to track. The performance counter path has the following syntax:

```
\\ComputerName\ObjectName\ObjectCounter
```

Here, the path starts with the UNC computer name or IP address of the local or remote computer you are working with and includes the object name and the object counter to use. If you wanted to track System\Processor Queue Length on CORPSVR02, you'd type:

```
typeperf "\\corpsvr02\System\Processor Queue Length"
```

> **Note**
> You might have noticed that I enclosed the counter path in double quotation marks. Although this is good form for all counter paths, it is required in this example because the counter path includes spaces.

You can also easily track all counters for an object by using an asterisk (*) as the counter name, such as in the following:

```
typeperf "\\corpsvr02\Memory\*"
```

Here, you track all counters for the Memory object.

A slight problem is introduced for objects that have multiple instances. For these objects, such as the Processor object, you must specify the object instance you want to work with. The syntax for this is as follows:

```
\\ComputerName\ObjectName(ObjectInstance)\ObjectCounter
```

Here, you follow the object name with the object instance in parentheses. To work with all instances of an object that has multiple instances, you use _Total as the instance name. To work with a specific instance of an object, use its instance identifier. For example, if you want to examine the Processor\% Processor Time counter, you must use either this to work with all processor instances:

```
typeperf "\\corpsvr02\Processor(_Total)\% Processor Time"
```

or this to work with a specific processor instance:

```
typeperf "\\corpsvr02\Processor(0)\% Processor Time"
```

In this case, that is the first processor on the system.

By default, Typeperf writes its output to the command line in a comma-delimited list. You can redirect the output to a file using the -o parameter and set the output format

Chapter 12

using the -f parameter. The output format indicators are CSV for a comma-delimited text file, TSV for a tab-delimited text file, BIN for a binary file, and SQL for a SQL binary file. Consider the following example:

```
typeperf "\\corpsvr02\Memory\*" -o perf.bin -f bin
```

Here, you track all counters for the Memory object and write the output to a binary file called Perf.bin in the current directory.

If you need help determining the available counters, type **typeperf -q** followed by the object name for which you want to view counters, such as in the following:

```
typeperf -q Memory
```

If an object has multiple instances, you can list the installed counters with instances by using the -qx parameter, such as in the following:

```
typeperf -qx PhysicalDisk
```

You can use this counter information as input to Typeperf as well. Add the -o parameter and write the output to a text file, such as in the following:

```
typeperf -qx PhysicalDisk -o perf.txt
```

Then edit the text file so that only the counters you want to track are included. You can then use the file to determine which performance counters are tracked by specifying the -cf parameter followed by the file path to this counter file. Consider the following example:

```
typeperf -cf perf.txt -o c:\perflogs\perf.bin -f bin
```

Here, Typeperf reads the list of counters to track from Perf.txt and then writes the performance data in binary format to a file in the C:\PerfLogs directory.

The one problem with Typeperf is that it will sample data once every second until you tell it to stop by pressing Ctrl+C. This is fine when you are working at the command line and monitoring the output. It doesn't work so well, however, if you have other things to do—and most administrators do. To control the sampling interval and set how long to sample, you can use the -si and -sc parameters, respectively. For example, if you wanted Typeperf to sample every 60 seconds and stop logging after 120 samples, you could type this:

```
typeperf -cf perf.txt -o C:\perf\logs\perf.bin -f bin -si 60 -sc 120
```

Analyzing Trace Logs at the Command Line

You can examine trace log data by using the Tracerpt command-line utility. Tracerpt processes trace logs and allows you to generate trace analysis reports and dump files for the events generated. The parameters for Tracerpt are summarized in Table 12-3.

Table 12-3 **Parameters for Tracerpt**

Parameter	Description
-o [*filename*]	Sets the text output file to which the parsed data should be written. The default is Dumpfile.xml.
-summary [*filename*]	Sets the name of the text file to which a summary report of the data should be written. The default is Summary.txt.
-report [*filename*]	Sets the name of the text file to which a detailed report of the data should be written. The default is Workload.xml.
-rt <*session_name* [*session_name* ...]>	Sets the real-time event trace session data source to use instead of a converted log file.
-config <*filename*>	Specifies a settings file containing command options.
-y	Answers Yes to all questions without prompting.
-of <CSV|EVTX|XML>	Sets the dump file format.
-f <XML|HTML>	Sets the report file format.
-export <*filename*>	Sets the name of the event schema export file. The default is schema.man.

The most basic way to use Tracerpt is to specify the name of the trace log to use. By default trace logs are written to C:\PerfLogs, so if a log in this directory was named SysP_000002.etl, you could analyze it by typing the following:

```
tracerpt C:\Perflogs\SysP_000002.etl
```

Here, four files are created in the current directory: The parsed output is written to Dumpfile.xml, a summary report is written to Summary.txt, a detailed report is written to Workload.xml, and a event schema report file is written to schema.man.

You could also specify the exact files to use for output as shown in the following example:

```
tracerpt C:\Perflogs\ SysP_000002.etl -o c:\sysp.csv
 -summary c:\sysp-summary.txt -report sysp-report-.txt
```

PART 3

Managing Windows Server 2008 Storage and File Systems

U nlike earlier releases of server operating systems for Windows, Windows Server 2008 doesn't boot from an initialization file. Instead, the operating system uses the Windows Boot Manager to initialize and start the operating system. The boot environment dramatically changes the way the operating system starts and is designed to resolve issues related to boot integrity, operating system integrity, and firmware abstraction. The boot environment is loaded prior to the operating system, making it a pre–operating system environment. This ensures that the boot environment can be used to validate the integrity of the startup process and the operating system itself before actually starting the operating system.

Boot from Hardware and Firmware

At first glance, startup and shutdown seem to be the most basic features of an operating system, but as you get a better understanding of how computers work, you quickly see that there's nothing simple or basic about startup, shutdown, or related processes and procedures. In fact, anyone who's worked with computers probably has had a problem with startup or shutdown at one time or another. Problems with startup and shutdown are compounded in Windows Vista and Windows Server 2008 because of their extended frameworks for advanced configuration and power management in firmware and hardware.

> **Note**
>
> Many administrators install Windows Server 2008 on desktop class systems without giving careful consideration to how this could affect the operation of the computer. When you install Windows Server 2008 on a desktop class system, it is critically important for you to understand how computers designed for Windows Vista handle advanced configuration and power management in hardware and firmware. This will enable you to modify the hardware and firmware settings so that they work with Windows Server 2008. Never install Windows Server 2008 on a desktop class system without first checking its hardware and firmware configuration settings for boot and power.

Hardware and Firmware Power States

Before the boot environment is loaded, computers start up from hardware and firmware. Windows Vista does things a bit differently from Windows Server 2008 when it comes to power state management features. In Windows Vista, turning off a computer and shutting down a computer are separate tasks. By default, when you turn off a computer running Windows Vista, the computer enters standby mode. When entering standby mode, the operating system automatically saves all work, turns off the display, and enters a low power consumption mode with the computer's fans and hard disks stopped. The state of the computer is maintained in the computer's memory. When the computer wakes from standby mode, its state is exactly as it was when you turned off your computer.

You can turn off a computer running Windows Vista and enter standby mode by clicking the Start button and then clicking the power button. To wake the computer from the standby state you can press the power button on the computer's case or a key on the computer's keyboard. Moving the mouse also wakes the computer.

Mobile computers running Windows Vista can be turned off and turned on by closing or opening the lid. When you close the lid, the laptop enters the standby state. When you open the lid, the laptop wakes up from the standby state.

There are, however, a few gotchas with the power button and the standby state in Windows Vista. The way the power button works depends on the following:

- **System hardware** For the power button to work, the computer hardware must support the standby state. If the computer hardware doesn't support the standby state, the computer can't use the standby state and turning off the computer powers it down completely.

- **System state** For the power button to work, the system must be in a valid state. If the computer has installed updates that require a reboot or you've installed programs that require a reboot, the computer can't enter the standby state and turning off the computer powers it down completely.

- **System configuration** For the power button to work, sleep mode must be enabled. If you've reconfigured the power options on the computer and set the power button to the Shut Down action, the computer can't use the standby state and turning off the computer powers it down completely.

You can determine exactly how Windows Vista is configured by clicking Start and looking at the power button icon. An amber power button, depicting a shield with a line through the top of it, indicates that the computer will turn off and enter low-power sleep state. A red power button, depicting a shield with a line in the middle of it, indicates that the computer will shut down and completely power off.

Diagnosing Hardware and Firmware Startup Problems

When you are working with Windows Vista or Windows Server 2008 and trying to diagnose and resolve startup problems, it is important to remember that power state management capabilities are provided by the hardware but are enabled by the operating system. Because of this, to fully diagnose and resolve problem boot issues, you must look at the computer's hardware and software, including:

- Motherboard/chipset

- Firmware

- Operating system

To better understand the hardware aspects related to boot issues, let's dig in and take a look at Advanced Configuration and Power Interface (ACPI). A computer's motherboard/chipset, firmware, and operating system must support ACPI for the advanced power state features to work. There are many different types of motherboards/chipsets. Although older motherboards/chipsets might not be updatable, most of the newer ones have updatable firmware. Chipset firmware is separate from and different from the computer's underlying firmware interface.

Currently, the two prevalent firmware interfaces are:

- Basic input/output system (BIOS)

- Extensible Firmware Interface (EFI)

A computer's BIOS or EFI programming provides the hardware-level interface between hardware components and software. Like chipsets themselves, BIOS and EFI can be updated. ACPI-aware components track the power state of the computer. An ACPI-aware operating system can generate a request that the system be switched into a different ACPI mode. BIOS or EFI responds to enable the requested ACPI mode.

As shown in Table 13-1, there are a total of six different power states ranging from S0 (the system is completely powered ON and fully operational) to S5 (the system is completely powered OFF) and the states (S1, S2, S3, and S4) are referred to as sleep states, in which the system appears OFF because of low power consumption and retains enough of the hardware context to return to the working state without a system reboot.

Motherboards/chipsets support specific power states. For example, the Intel Server Board SE7505VB2 supports S0, S1, S4, and S5 states, but does not support the S2 and S3 states. In Windows operating systems, the sleep power transition refers to switching off the system to a sleep or a hibernate mode, and the wake power transition refers to switching on the system from a sleep or a hibernate mode. The sleep and hibernate modes allow users to switch off and switch on systems much faster than the regular shutdown and startup processes.

Thus, a computer is waking up when the computer is transitioning from the OFF state (S5) or any sleep state (S1–S4) to the ON state (S0) and the computer is going to sleep when the computer is transitioning from the ON state (S0) to the OFF state (S5) or sleep state (S1–S4). A computer cannot enter one sleep state directly from another, as it must enter the ON state before entering any other sleep state.

Table 13-1 **Power States for ACPI in Firmware and Hardware**

State	Type	Description
S0	ON state	The system is completely operational, fully powered, and completely retains the context (such as the volatile registers, memory caches, and RAM).
S1	Sleep state	The system consumes less power than the S0 state. All hardware and processor contexts are maintained.
S2	Sleep state	The system consumes less power than the S1 state. The processor loses power and processor context and contents of the cache are lost.
S3	Sleep state	The system consumes less power than the S2 state. Processor and hardware contexts, cache contents, and chipset context are lost. The system memory is retained.
S4	Hibernate state	The system consumes the least power compared to all other sleep states. The system is almost at an OFF state. The context data is written to the hard disk and there is no context retained. The system can restart from the context data stored on the disk.
S5	OFF state	The system is in a shutdown state and the system retains no context. The system requires a full reboot to start.

Resolving Hardware and Firmware Startup Problems

On most computers, you can enter the BIOS or EFI during boot by pressing F2 or another function key. When you are in firmware, you can go to the Power screen or a similar screen to manage ACPI and related settings.

Power settings you might see include:

- **After Power Failure or AC Recovery** Determines the mode of operation if a power loss occurs and for which you'll see settings like Stay off/Off, Last state/Last, Power on/On. Stay Off means the system will remain off after power is restored. Last state restores the system to the state it was in before power failed. Power On means the system will turn on after power is restored.

- **Wake On LAN From S5 or Auto Power On** Determines the action taken when the system power is off and a PCI Power Management wake event occurs. You'll see settings like Stay off or Power on.

- **ACPI Suspend State or Suspend Mode** Sets the suspend mode. Typically, you'll be able to set S1 State or S3 State as the suspend mode.

> **Note**
>
> I provide two standard labels for each setting because your computer hardware may not have these exact labels. The firmware variant you are working with determines the actual labels that are associated with boot, power, and other settings.

Because Intel and AMD also have other technologies to help reduce startup and resume times, you might also see power settings for:

- Enhanced Intel SpeedStep Technology (EIST), which can be either Disabled or Enabled

- Intel Quick Resume Technology Driver (QRTD), which can be either Disabled or Enabled

Enhanced Intel SpeedStep Technology (EIST or SpeedStep) allows the system to dynamically adjust processor voltage and core frequency, which can result in decreased average power consumption and decreased average heat production. When EIST or a similar technology is enabled and in use, you'll see two different processor speeds on the System page in Control Panel. The first speed listed is the specified speed of the processor. The second speed is the current operating speed, which should be less than the first speed. If Enhanced Intel SpeedStep Technology is off, then both processor speeds will be equal. Advanced Settings for Power Options under Processor Power Management can also affect how this technology works. Generally speaking, although you might want to use this technology with Windows Vista, you won't want to use this technology with Windows Server 2008.

Intel Quick Resume Technology Driver (QRTD) allows an Intel Viiv technology-based computer to behave like a consumer electronic device with instant on/off after an initial boot. Intel QRTD manages this behavior through the Quick Resume mode function of the Intel Viiv chipset. Pressing the power button on the computer or a remote control puts the computer in the Quick Sleep state, and you can switch the computer to the Quick Resume state by moving the mouse, pressing an on/off key on the keyboard (if available), or pressing the sleep button on the remote control. Quick Sleep mode is different from standard sleep mode. In Quick Sleep mode, the computer's video card stops sending data to the display, the sound is muted, and the monitor LED indicates a lowered power state on the monitor but the power continues to be supplied to vital components on the system, such as the processor, fans, and so on. As this technology was originally designed for Windows XP Media Center Edition, in many cases it does not work with Windows Vista and generally should not be used with Windows Server 2008. You might need to disable this feature in firmware to allow Windows Vista to properly sleep and resume.

After you look at the computer's power settings in firmware, you should also review the computer's boot settings in firmware. Typically, you'll be able to configure the following boot settings:

- **Boot Drive Order** Determines the boot order for fixed disks

- **Boot To Hard Disk Drive** Determines whether the computer can boot to fixed disks and can be set to Disabled or Enabled

- **Boot To Removable Devices** Determines whether the computer can boot to removable media and can be set to Disabled or Enabled

- **Boot To Network** Determines whether the computer can perform a network boot and can be set to Disabled or Enabled

- **USB Boot** Determines whether the computer can boot to USB flash devices and can be set to Disabled or Enabled

As with power settings, your computer might not have these exact labels, but the labels should be similar. You'll need to optimize these settings for the way you plan to use the computer. In most cases, with server hardware, you'll only want to enable Boot To Hard Disk Drive. The exception is for when you use BitLocker Drive Encryption. With Bit-Locker, you'll want to enable Boot To Removable Devices, USB Boot, or both to ensure that the computer can detect the USB flash drive with the encryption key during the boot process.

Boot Environment Essentials

Windows Server 2008 supports several different processor architectures and several different disk partitioning styles. Generally, computers with x86-based and x64-based processors use the master boot record (MBR) disk partitioning style and BIOS. Computers with x64-based processors use the GUID partition table (GPT) disk partitioning style and Extensible Firmware Interface (EFI).

BIOS and EFI currently are the two most prevalent firmware interfaces. With earlier releases of the server operating system for Windows, BIOS-based computers use Ntldr and Boot.ini to boot into the operating system. Ntldr handles the task of loading the operating system while Boot.ini contains the parameters that enable startup, including identity of the boot partitions. Through Boot.ini parameters, you can add options that control the way the operating system starts, the way computer components are used, and the way operating system features are used.

On the other hand, with earlier releases of the server operating system for Windows, EFI-based computers use Ia64ldr.efi, Diskpart.efi, and Nvrboot.efi to boot into the operating system. Ia64ldr.efi handles the task of loading the operating system while Disk-part.efi identifies the boot partitions. Through Nvrboot.efi, you set the parameters that enable startup.

Windows Server 2008 doesn't use these boot facilities. Instead, it uses a pre–operating system boot environment. Figure 13-1 provides a conceptual overview of how the boot environment fits into the overall computer architecture.

The boot environment is an extensible abstraction layer that allows the operating system to work with multiple types of firmware interfaces without requiring the operating system to be specifically written to work with these firmware interfaces. Within the boot environment, startup is controlled using the parameters in the Boot Configuration Data (BCD) store.

The BCD store is contained in a file called the BCD registry. The location of this registry depends on the computer's firmware:

- On BIOS-based operating systems, the BCD registry file is stored in the \Boot\Bcd directory of the active partition.
- On EFI-based operating systems, the BCD registry file is stored on the EFI system partition.

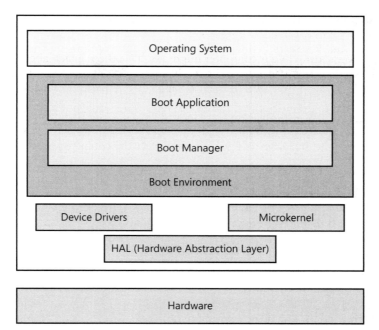

Figure 13-1 A conceptual view of how the boot environment works.

Entries in the BCD store identify the boot manager to use during startup and the specific boot applications available. The default boot manager is the Windows Boot Manager. Windows Boot Manager controls the boot experience and enables you to choose which boot application is run. Boot applications load a specific operating system or operating system version. For example, a Windows Boot Loader application loads Windows Server 2008. This allows you to boot BIOS-based and EFI-based computers in much the same way.

Managing Startup and Boot Configuration

As discussed in "Troubleshooting Startup and Shutdown" on page 1416, you can press F8 during startup of the operating system to access the Advanced Boot Options menu and then use this menu to select one of several advanced startup modes, including Safe Mode, Enable Boot Logging, and Disable Driver Signature Enforcement. Although these advanced modes temporarily modify the way the operating system starts to help you diagnose and resolve problems, they don't make permanent changes to the boot configuration or to the BCD store. Other tools you can use to modify the boot configuration and manage the BCD store include the Startup And Recovery dialog box, the System Configuration utility, and the BCD Editor. The sections that follow discuss how these tools are used.

Managing Startup and Recovery Options

The Startup And Recovery dialog box controls the basic options for the operating system during startup. You can use these options to set the default operating system, the time to display the list of available operating systems, and the time to display recovery options when needed. Whether you boot a computer to different operating systems or not, you'll want to optimize these settings to reduce the wait time during startup and in this way speed up the startup process.

You can access the Startup And Recovery dialog box by completing the following steps:

1. In Control Panel\System And Maintenance, click System to access the System window.

2. In the System window, click Advanced System Settings under Tasks in the left pane. This displays the System Properties dialog box.

3. On the Advanced tab of the System Properties dialog box, click Settings under Startup And Recovery. This displays the Startup And Recovery dialog box, as shown in Figure 13-2.

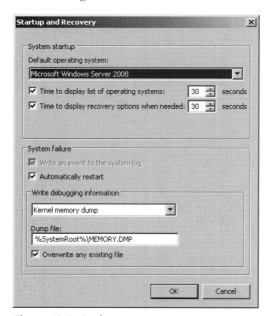

Figure 13-2 Configure system startup options.

4. On a computer with multiple operating systems, use the Default Operating System list to specify the operating system that you want to start by default.

5. Set the timeout interval for the operating system list by selecting the Time To Display List Of Operating Systems check box and specifying a timeout in seconds

in the field provided. To speed up the startup process, you might want to use a value of 5 seconds.

6.   Set the timeout interval for the recovery options list by selecting the Time To Display Recovery Options When Needed check box and specifying a timeout in seconds in the field provided. Again, to speed up the start up process, you might want to use a value of 5 seconds.

7.   Click OK to save your settings.

Managing System Boot Configuration

The System Configuration utility (Msconfig.exe) allows you to fine-tune the way a computer starts. Typically, you'll use this utility during troubleshooting and diagnostics. For example, as part of troubleshooting, you can configure the computer to use a diagnostic startup where only basic devices and services are loaded.

The System Configuration utility is available on the Administrative Tools menu. You can also start the System Configuration utility by clicking Start, typing **msconfig.exe** in the Search box, and pressing Enter. As shown in Figure 13-3, this utility has a series of tabs with options.

The General tab options allow you to configure the way startup works and are where you should start your troubleshooting and diagnostics. Using these options, you can choose to perform a normal startup, diagnostic startup, or selective startup. After you restart the computer and resolve any problems, access the System Configuration utility again, select Normal Startup on the General tab, and then click OK.

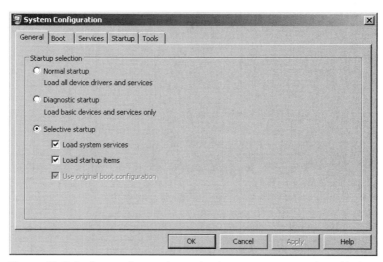

Figure 13-3 Perform a diagnostic or selective startup as part of troubleshooting.

The Boot tab options, shown in Figure 13-4, allow you to control the way the individual startup-related processes work. You can configure the computer to start in one of various Safe Boot modes and set additional options, such as No GUI Boot. If after troubleshooting you find that you want to keep these settings, you can select the Make All Boot Settings Permanent check box to save the settings to the boot configuration startup entry.

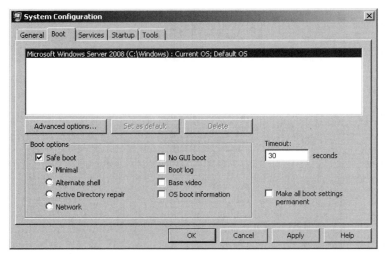

Figure 13-4 Fine-tune the boot options.

Clicking the Advanced Options button on the Boot tab displays the BOOT Advanced Options dialog box shown in Figure 13-5. In addition to being able to lock PCI, detect the correct HAL, and enable debugging, you can use the advanced options to:

- Specify the number of processors the operating system should use. You should use this option when you suspect there is a problem with additional processors you've installed in a server and you want to pinpoint which processors are possibly causing startup problems. Consider the following scenario: A server shipped with two processors and you installed two additional processors. Later, you find that you cannot start the server. You could eliminate the new processors as the potential cause by limiting the computer to two processors.

- Specify the maximum amount of memory the operating system should use. You should use this option when you suspect there is a problem with additional memory you've installed in a server. Consider the following scenario: A server shipped with 2 GB of RAM and you installed 2 additional GB of RAM. Later, you find that you cannot start the server. You could eliminate the new RAM as the potential cause by limiting the computer to 2048 MB of memory.

Figure 13-5 Set advanced boot options as necessary to help troubleshoot specific types of problems.

If you suspect services installed on a computer are causing startup problems, you can quickly determine this by choosing a diagnostic or selective startup on the General tab. After you've identified that services are indeed causing startup problems, you can temporarily disable services using the Services tab options and then reboot to see if the problem goes away. If the problem no longer appears, you might have pinpointed it. You can then permanently disable the service or check with the service vendor to see if an updated executable is available for the service. As shown in Figure 13-6, you disable a service by clearing the related check box on the Services tab.

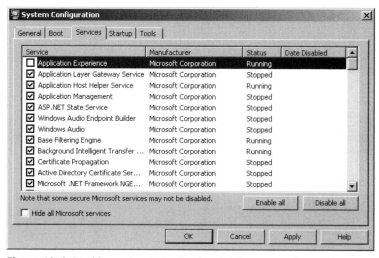

Figure 13-6 Disable services to try to pinpoint the source of a problem.

Similarly, if you suspect applications that run at startup are causing problems, you can quickly determine this using the options on the Startup tab. You disable a startup application by clearing the related check box on the Startup tab. If the problem no longer appears, you might have pinpointed the cause of it. You can then permanently disable the startup application or check with the software vendor to see if an updated version is available.

> **Note**
>
> If you are using the System Configuration utility for troubleshooting and diagnostics, you should later remove your selective startup options. After you restart the computer and resolve any problems, access the System Configuration utility again, restore the original settings, and then click OK.

Working with the BCD Editor

The BCD store contains multiple entries. On a BIOS-based computer, you'll see the following entries:

- One Windows Boot Manager entry. There is only one boot manager, so there is only one boot manager entry.

- One or more Windows Boot Loader application entries, with one for each Windows Server 2008 operating system, Windows Vista operating system, or later versions of Windows installed on the computer.

- One legacy operating system entry. The legacy entry is not for a boot application. This entry is used to initiate Ntldr and Boot.ini so that you can boot into Windows XP or an earlier release of Windows. If the computer has more than one Windows XP or earlier operating system, you'll be able to select the operating system to start after selecting the legacy operating system entry.

Windows Boot Manager is itself a boot loader application. There are other boot loader applications, including:

- Legacy OS Loader, identified as NTLDR

- Windows Vista or later operating system loader, identified as OSLOADER

- Windows Boot Sector Application, identified as BOOTSECTOR

- Firmware Boot Manager, identified as FWBOOTMGR

- Windows Resume Loader, identified as RESUME

You can directly view and manage the BCD store using the BCD Editor (BCDEdit.exe). The BCD Editor is a command-line utility. You can use the BCD Editor to view the entries in the BCD store by following these steps:

1. Click Start, click All Programs, and then click Accessories.

2. Right-click Command Prompt and then select Run As Administrator.

3. Type **bcdedit** at the command prompt.

Table 13-2 summarizes commands you can use when you are working with the BCD store. These commands allow you to:

- Create, import, export, and identify the entire BCD store.

- Create, delete, and copy individual entries in the BCD store.

- Set or delete entry option values in the BCD store.

- Control the boot sequence and the boot manager.

- Configure and control Emergency Management Services (EMS).

- Configure and control boot debugging as well as hypervisor debugging.

Table 13-2 Commands for the BCD Editor

Command	Description
/bootdebug	Enables or disables boot debugging for a boot application.
/bootems	Enables or disables Emergency Management Services for a boot application.
/bootsequence	Sets the one-time boot sequence for the boot manager.
/copy	Makes copies of entries in the store.
/create	Creates new entries in the store.
/createstore	Creates a new (empty) boot configuration data store.
/dbgsettings	Sets the global debugger parameters.
/debug	Enables or disables kernel debugging for an operating system entry.
/default	Sets the default entry that the boot manager will use.
/delete	Deletes entries from the store.
/deletevalue	Deletes entry options from the store.
/displayorder	Sets the order in which the boot manager displays the multiboot menu.
/ems	Enables or disables Emergency Management Services for an operating system entry.

Command	Description
/emssettings	Sets the global Emergency Management Services parameters.
/enum	Lists entries in the store.
/export	Exports the contents of the system store to a file. This file can be used later to restore the state of the system store.
/hypervisorsettings	Sets the hypervisor parameters.
/import	Restores the state of the system store using a backup file created with the /export command.
/set	Sets entry option values in the store.
/sysstore	Sets the system store device. Note that this only affects EFI systems.
/timeout	Sets the boot manager timeout value.
/toolsdisplayorder	Sets the order in which the boot manager displays the tools menu.
/v	Sets output to verbose mode.

Managing the Boot Configuration Data Store and Its Entries

The BCD Editor (BCDEdit.exe) is an advanced command-line tool for viewing and manipulating the configuration of the pre–operating system boot environment. Although I discuss tasks related to modifying the BCD data store in the sections that follow, you should attempt to modify the BCD store only if you are an experienced IT pro. As a safeguard, you should make a full backup of the computer prior to making any changes to the BCD store. Why? If you make a mistake, your computer might end up in a nonbootable state and you would then need to initiate recovery.

Viewing BCD Entries

Computers can have system and non-system BCD stores. The system BCD store contains the operating system boot entries and related boot settings. Whenever you work with the BCD Editor, you will be working with the system BCD store.

On a computer with only one operating system, the BCD entries for your computer will look similar to those in Listing 13-1. As the listing shows, the BCD store for this computer has two entries: one for the Windows Boot Manager and one for the Windows Boot Loader. Here, the Windows Boot Manager calls the boot loader and the boot loader uses Winload.exe to boot Windows Server 2008.

Listing 13-1 Entries in the BCD store on a single boot computer

```
Windows Boot Manager
--------------------
identifier              {bootmgr}
device                  partition=C:
description             Windows Boot Manager
locale                  en-US
inherit                 {globalsettings}
default                 {current}
displayorder            {current}
toolsdisplayorder       {memdiag}
timeout                 30

Windows Boot Loader
-------------------
identifier              {current}
device                  partition=C:
path                    \Windows\system32\winload.exe
description             Microsoft Windows Server 2008
locale                  en-US
inherit                 {bootloadersettings}
resumeobject            {6edc4bc2-e6d3-22bc-3234-3e33222d6dcf}
nx                      OptOut
```

BCD entries for Windows Boot Manager and Windows Boot Loader have similar properties. These properties include those summarized in Table 13-3.

Table 13-3 BCD Entry Properties

Property	Description
Description	Shows descriptive information to help identify the type of entry.
Device	Shows the physical device path. For a partition on a physical disk, you'll see an entry such as partition=C:.
FileDevice	Shows the path to a file device, such as partition=C:.
FilePath	Shows the file path to a necessary file, such as \hiberfil.sys.
Identifier	Shows a descriptor for the entry. This can be a boot loader application type, such as BOOTMGR or NTLDR. Or it can be a reference to the current OS entry or the GUID of a specific object.
Inherit	Shows the list of entries to be inherited.
Locale	Shows the computer's locale setting, such as en-US. The locale setting determines the UI language shown. In the \Boot folder, there are locale subfolders for each locale supported and each of these subfolders have language-specific UI details for the Windows Boot Manager (BootMgr.exe) and the Windows Memory Diagnostic utility (MemDiag.exe).
OSDevice	Shows the path to the operating system device, such as partition=C:.
Path	Shows the actual file path to the boot loader application, such as \Windows\System32\winresume.exe.

When you are working with the BCD store and the BCD Editor, you'll see references to well-known identifiers, summarized in Table 13-4, as well as globally unique identifiers (GUIDs). When a GUID is used, the GUID has the following format where each N represents a hexadecimal value:

```
{NNNNNNNN-NNNN-NNNN-NNNN-NNNNNNNNNNNN}
```

such as:

```
{6edc4bc2-e6d3-22bc-3234-3e33222d6dcf}
```

The dashes that separate the parts of the GUID must be entered in the positions shown.

Table 13-4 Well-Known Identifiers

Identifier	Description
{badmemory}	Contains the global RAM defect list that can be inherited by any boot application entry.
{bootloadersettings}	Contains the collection of global settings that should be inherited by all Windows Boot Loader application entries.
{bootmgr}	Indicates the Windows Boot Manager entry.
{current}	Represents a virtual identifier that corresponds to the operating system boot entry for the operating system that is currently running.
{dbgsettings}	Contains the global debugger settings that can be inherited by any boot application entry.
{default}	Represents a virtual identifier that corresponds to the boot manager default application entry.
{emssettings}	Contains the global Emergency Management Services settings that can be inherited by any boot application entry.
{fwbootmgr}	Indicates the firmware boot manager entry. This entry is used on EFI systems.
{globalsettings}	Contains the collection of global settings that should be inherited by all boot application entries.
{hypervisorsettings}	Contains the hypervisor settings that can be inherited by any OS loader entry.
{legacy}	Indicates the Windows Legacy OS Loader (Ntldr) that can be used to start operating systems earlier than Windows Vista.
{memdiag}	Indicates the memory diagnostic application entry.
{ntldr}	Indicates the Windows Legacy OS Loader (Ntldr) that can be used to start operating systems earlier than Windows Vista.
{ramdiskoptions}	Contains the additional options required by the boot manager for RAM disk devices.
{resumeloadersettings}	Contains the collection of global settings that should be inherited by all Windows resume from hibernation application entries.

When a computer has additional Windows Vista, Windows Server 2008, or later operating systems installed, the BCD store for has additional entries for each additional operating system. For example, the BCD store might have one entry for the Windows Boot Manager and one Windows Boot Loader for each operating system.

When a computer has a legacy operating system installed, the BCD store has three entries: one for the Windows Boot Manager, one for the Windows Legacy OS Loader, and one for the Windows Boot Loader. Generally, the entry for the Windows Legacy OS Loader will look similar to Listing 13-2.

Listing 13-2 Sample Legacy OS Loader entry

```
Windows Legacy OS Loader
------------------------
identifier:             {ntldr}
device:                 partition=C:
path:                   \ntldr
description:            Earlier version of Windows
```

Although the Windows Boot Manager, Windows Legacy OS Loader, and Windows Boot Loader are the primary types of entries that control startup, the BCD also stores information about boot settings and boot utilities. The Windows Boot Loader entry can have parameters that track the status of boot settings, such as whether No Execute (NX) policy is set for Opt In or Opt Out. The Windows Boot Loader entry also can provide information about available boot utilities, such as the Windows Memory Diagnostic utility.

To view the actual value of the GUIDs needed to manipulate entries in the BCD store, type **bcdedit /v** at an elevated command prompt.

Creating and Identifying the BCD Store

Using the BCD Editor, you can create a new, non-system BCD store by using the following command:

```
bcdedit /createstore StorePath
```

where *StorePath* is the actual folder path to the location where you want to create the non-system store, such as:

```
bcdedit /createstore c:\non-sys\bcd
```

On an EFI system, you can temporarily set the system store device using the /sysstore command. Use the following syntax:

```
bcdedit /sysstore StoreDevice
```

where *StoreDevice* is the actual system store device identifier, such as:

```
bcdedit /sysstore c:
```

> **Note**
>
> The device must be a system partition. Note that this setting does not persist across reboots and is used only in cases where the system store device is ambiguous.

Importing and Exporting the BCD Store

The BCD Editor provides separate commands for importing and exporting the BCD store. You can use the /export command to export a copy of the system BCD store's contents to a specified folder. Use the following command syntax:

```
bcdedit /export StorePath
```

where *StorePath* is the actual folder path to which you want to export a copy of the system store, such as:

```
bcdedit /export c:\backup\bcd
```

To restore an exported copy of the system store, you can use the /import command. Use the following command syntax:

```
bcdedit /import ImportPath
```

where *ImportPath* is the actual folder path from which you want to import a copy of the system store, such as:

```
bcdedit /import c:\backup\bcd
```

On an EFI system, you can add /clean to the import to specify that all existing firmware boot entries should be deleted. Here is an example:

```
bcdedit /import c:\backup\bcd /clean
```

Creating, Copying, and Deleting BCD Entries

The BCD Editor provides separate commands for creating, copying, and deleting entries in the BCD store. You can use the /create command to create identifier, application, and inherit entries in the BCD store.

As shown previously in Table 13-4, the BCD Editor recognizes many well-known identifiers, including {dbgsettings} used to create a debugger settings entry, {ntldr} used to create a Windows Legacy OS entry, and {ramdiskoptions} used to create a RAM disk additional options entry. To create identifier entries, you use the following syntax:

```
bcdedit /create Identifier /d "Description"
```

where *Identifier* is a well-known identifier for the entry you want to create, such as:

```
bcdedit /create {ntldr} /d "Earlier Windows OS Loader"
```

You can create entries for specific boot loader applications as well, including:

- **Bootsector** A real-mode boot sector application, used to set the boot sector for a real-mode application.

- **OSLoader** An operating system loader application, used to load a Windows Vista or Windows Server 2008 operating system.

- **Resume** A Windows Resume Loader application, used to resume the operating system from hibernation.

- **Startup** A real-mode application, used to identify a real-mode application.

Use the following command syntax:

```
bcdedit /create /application AppType /d "Description"
```

where *AppType* is one of the previously listed application types, such as:

```
bcdedit /create /application osloader /d "Windows Vista"
```

You can delete entries in the system store using the /delete command and the following syntax:

```
bcdedit /delete Identifier
```

If you are trying to delete a well-known identifier, you must use the /f command to force deletion, such as:

```
bcdedit /delete {ntldr} /f
```

By default, the /cleanup option is implied and this means the BCD Editor cleans up any other references to the entry being deleted. This ensures that the data store doesn't have invalid references to the identifier you removed. As entries are removed from the display order as well, this could result in a different default operating system being set. If you want to delete the entry and clean up all other references except the display order entry, you can use the /nocleanup command.

Setting BCD Entry Values

After you create an entry, you would then need to set additional entry option values as necessary. The basic syntax for setting values is:

```
bcdedit /set Identifier Option Value
```

where *Identifier* is the identifier of the entry to be modified, *Option* is the option you want to set, and *Value* is the option value, such as:

```
bcdedit /set {current} device partition=d:
```

To delete options and their values, use the /deletevalue command with the following syntax:

```
bcdedit /deletevalue Identifier Option
```

where *Identifier* is the identifier of the entry to be modified and *Option* is the option you want to delete, such as:

```
bcdedit /deletevalue {current} badmemorylist
```

> **Note**
> When you are working with options, Boolean values can be entered in several different ways. For true, you can use: 1, ON, YES, or TRUE. For false, you can use: 0, OFF, NO, or FALSE.

To view the BCD entries for all boot utilities and values for settings, type **bcdedit /enum all /v** at an elevated command prompt. This command enumerates all BCD entries regardless of their current state and lists them in verbose mode. The additional entries will look similar to those in Listing 13-3. Each additional entry has a specific purpose, and lists values that you can set, including the following:

Resume from Hibernate   The Resume from Hibernate entry shows the current configuration for the resume feature. The pre-operating system boot utility that controls resume is Winresume.exe, which in this example is stored in the C:\Windows\ System32 folder. The hibernation data, as specified in the Filepath parameter, is stored in the Hiberfil.sys file in the root folder on the OSDevice (C: in this example). Because the resume feature works differently if the computer has Physical Address Extension (PAE) and debugging enabled, these options are tracked by the Pae and Debugoptionenabled parameters.

Windows Memory Tester   The Windows Memory Tester entry shows the current configuration for the Windows Memory Diagnostic utility. The pre-operating system boot utility that controls memory diagnostics is Memtest.exe, which in this example is stored in the C:\Boot folder. Because the Windows Memory Diagnostic utility is designed to detect bad memory by default, the badmemoryaccess parameter is set to yes by default. You can turn this feature off by entering **bcdedit /set {memdiag} badmemoryaccess NO**. With memory diagnostics, you can configure the number of passes using Passcount and the test mix as BASIC or EXTENDED using Testmix. Here is an example: **bcdedit /set {memdiag} passcount 2**.

Windows Legacy OS Loader   The Windows Legacy OS Loader entry shows the current configuration for the loading of earlier versions of Windows. The Device parameter sets the default partition to use, such as C:, and the Path parameter sets the default path to the loader utility, such as Ntldr.

EMS Settings   The EMS Settings entry shows the configuration used when booting with Emergency Management Services. Individual Windows Boot Loader entries control whether EMS is enabled. If EMS is provided by the BIOS and you want to use the BIOS settings, you can enter **bcdedit /emssettings bios**. With EMS, you can set an EMS port and an EMS baud rate as well. Here is an example: **bcdedit /emssettings EMSPORT:2 EMSBAUDRATE:115200**. You can enable or disable EMS for a boot application using /bootems, and follow the identity of the boot application with the desired state, such as ON or OFF.

Debugger Settings The Debugger Settings entry shows the configuration used when booting with the debugger turned on. Individual Windows Boot Loader entries control whether the debugger is enabled. You can view the hypervisor debug settings by entering **bcdedit /debugsettings**. When debug booting is turned on, DebugType sets the type of debugger as SERIAL, 1394, or USB. With SERIAL debugging, DebugPort specifies the serial port being used as the debugger port and BaudRate specifies the baud rate to be used for debugging. With 1394 debugging, you can use Channel to set the debugging channel. With universal serial bus (USB) debugging, you can use TargetName to set the USB target name to be used for debugging. With any debug type, you can use the /Noumex flag to specify that user-mode exceptions should be ignored. Here are examples of setting the debugging mode: **bcdedit /dbgsettings SERIAL DEBUGPORT:1 BAUDRATE:115200, bcdedit /dbgsettings 1394 CHANNEL:23,** and **bcdedit /dbgsettings USB TARGETNAME:DEBUGGING.**

Hypervisor Settings The Hypervisor Settings entry shows the configuration used when working with the hypervisor with the debugger turned on. Individual Windows Boot Loader entries control whether the debugger is enabled. You can view the hypervisor debug settings by entering **bcdedit /hypervisorsettings**. When hypervisor debug booting is turned on, HypervisorDebugType sets the type of debugger, HypervisorDebugPort specifies the serial port being used as the debugger port, and HypervisorBaudRate specifies the baud rate to be used for debugging. These parameters work the same as with Debugger Settings. Here is an example: **bcdedit /hypervisorsettings SERIAL DEBUGPORT:1 BAUDRATE:115200**. You can also use FireWire for hypervisor debugging. When you do, you must set the debug channel, such as shown in this example: **bcdedit /hypervisorsettings 1394 CHANNEL:23**.

Listing 13-3 Additional entries in the BCD store on a single boot computer

```
Resume from Hibernate
---------------------
identifier            {8b78e490-02d0-11dd-af92-a72494804a8a}
device                partition=C:
path                  \Windows\system32\winresume.exe
description           Windows Resume Application
locale                en-US
inherit               {1afa9c49-16ab-4a5c-901b-212802da9460}
filedevice            partition=C:
filepath              \hiberfil.sys
pae                   Yes
debugoptionenabled    No

Windows Memory Tester
---------------------
identifier            {b2721d73-1db4-4c62-bf78-c548a880142d}
device                partition=C:
path                  \boot\memtest.exe
```

Chapter 13

```
description             Windows Memory Diagnostic
locale                  en-US
inherit                 {7ea2e1ac-2e61-4728-aaa3-896d9d0a9f0e}
badmemoryaccess         Yes
```

```
Windows Legacy OS Loader
------------------------
identifier              {466f5a88-0af2-4f76-9038-095b170dc21c}
device                  partition=C:
path                    \ntldr
description             Earlier Version of Windows
```

```
EMS Settings
------------
identifier              {0ce4991b-e6b3-4b16-b23c-5e0d9250e5d9}
bootems                 Yes
```

```
Debugger Settings
-----------------
identifier              {4636856e-540f-4170-a130-a84776f4c654}
debugtype               Serial
debugport               1
baudrate                115200
```

```
RAM Defects
-----------
identifier              {5189b25c-5558-4bf2-bca4-289b11bd29e2}
```

```
Global Settings
---------------
identifier              {7ea2e1ac-2e61-4728-aaa3-896d9d0a9f0e}
inherit                 {4636856e-540f-4170-a130-a84776f4c654}
                        {0ce4991b-e6b3-4b16-b23c-5e0d9250e5d9}
                        {5189b25c-5558-4bf2-bca4-289b11bd29e2}
```

```
Boot Loader Settings
--------------------
identifier              {6efb52bf-1766-41db-a6b3-0ee5eff72bd7}
inherit                 {7ea2e1ac-2e61-4728-aaa3-896d9d0a9f0e}
                        {7ff607e0-4395-11db-b0de-0800200c9a66}
```

```
Hypervisor Settings
-------------------
identifier              {7ff607e0-4395-11db-b0de-0800200c9a66}
hypervisordebugtype     Serial
hypervisordebugport     1
hypervisorbaudrate      115200
```

```
Resume Loader Settings
----------------------
identifier              {1afa9c49-16ab-4a5c-901b-212802da9460}
inherit                 {7ea2e1ac-2e61-4728-aaa3-896d9d0a9f0e}
```

Table 13-5 summarizes key options that apply to entries for boot applications (BOOTAPP). As Windows Boot Manager, Windows Memory Diagnostic, Windows OS Loader, and Windows Resume Loader are boot applications, these options apply to them as well.

Table 13-5 Key Options for Boot Application Entries

Option	Value Description
BadMemoryAccess	When true, allows an application to use the memory on the bad memory list. When false, applications are prevented from using memory on the bad memory list.
BadMemoryList	An integer list that defines the list of Page Frame Numbers of faulty memory in the system.
BaudRate	Sets an integer value that defines the baud rate for the serial debugger.
BootDebug	Sets a Boolean value that enables or disables the boot debugger.
BootEMS	Sets a Boolean value that enables or disables Emergency Management Services.
Channel	Sets an integer value that defines the channel for the 1394 debugger.
DebugAddress	Sets an integer value that defines the address of a serial port for the debugger.
DebugPort	Sets an integer value that defines the serial port number for the serial debugger.
DebugStart	Can be set to ACTIVE, AUTOENABLE, or DISABLE.
DebugType	Can be set to SERIAL, 1394, or USB.
EMSBaudRate	Defines the baud rate for Emergency Management Services.
EMSPort	Defines the serial port number for Emergency Management Services.
GraphicsModeDisabled	Sets a Boolean value that enables or disables graphics mode.
GraphicsResolution	Defines the graphics resolution, such as 1024 × 768 or 800 × 600.
Locale	Sets the locale of the boot application.
Noumex	When set to TRUE, user-mode exceptions are ignored. When set to FALSE, user-mode exceptions are not ignored.
NoVESA	Sets a Boolean value that enables or disables the use of Video Electronics Standards Association (VESA) display modes.
RelocatePhysical	Sets the physical address to which an automatically selected NUMA node's physical memory should be relocated.
TargetName	Defines the target name for the USB debugger as a string.
TruncateMemory	Sets a physical memory address at or above which all memory is disregarded.

Chapter 13

Table 13-6 summarizes key options that apply to entries for Windows OS Loader (OSLOADER) applications.

Table 13-6 Key Options for Windows OS Loader Applications

Option	Value Description
AdvancedOptions	Sets a Boolean value that enables or disables advanced options.
BootLog	Sets a Boolean value that enables or disables the boot initialization log.
BootStatusPolicy	Sets the boot status policy. Can be DisplayAllFailures, IgnoreAllFailures, IgnoreShutdownFailures, or IgnoreBootFailures.
ClusterModeAddressing	Sets the maximum number of processors to include in a single Advanced Programmable Interrupt Controller (APIC) cluster.
ConfigFlags	Sets processor-specific configuration flags.
DbgTransport	Sets the file name for a private debugger transport.
Debug	Sets a Boolean value that enables or disables kernel debugging.
DetectHal	Sets a Boolean value that enables or disables the hardware abstraction layer (HAL) and kernel detection.
DriverLoadFailurePolicy	Sets the driver load failure policy. Can be Fatal or UseErrorControl.
Ems	Sets a Boolean value that enables or disables kernel Emergency Management Services.
Hal	Sets the file name for a private HAL.
HalBreakPoint	Sets a Boolean value that enables or disables the special HAL breakpoint.
HypervisorLaunchType	Configures the hypervisor launch type. Can be Off or Auto.
HypervisorPath	Sets the path to a private hypervisor binary.
IncreaseUserVA	Sets an integer value that increases the amount of virtual address space that the user-mode processes can use.
Kernel	Sets the file name for a private kernel.
LastKnownGood	Sets a Boolean value that enables or disables boot to last known good configuration.
MaxProc	Sets a Boolean value that enables or disables the display of the maximum number of processors in the system.
Msi	Sets the MSI to use. Can be Default or ForceDisable.
NoCrashAutoReboot	Sets a Boolean value that enables or disables automatic restart on crash.

Option	Value Description
NoLowMem	Sets a Boolean value that enables or disables the use of low memory.
NumProc	Sets the number of processors to use on startup.
Nx	Controls No Execute protection. Can be OptIn, OptOut, AlwaysOn, or AlwaysOff.
OneCPU	Sets a Boolean value that forces only the boot CPU to be used.
OptionsEdit	Sets a Boolean value that enables or disables the options editor.
OSDevice	Defines the device that contains the system root.
Pae	Controls PAE. Can be Default, ForceEnable, or ForceDisable.
PerfMem	Sets the size (in megabytes) of the buffer to allocate for performance data logging.
QuietBoot	Sets a Boolean value that enables or disables the boot screen display.
RemoveMemory	Sets an integer value that removes memory from the total available memory that the operating system can use.
RestrictAPICCluster	Sets the largest APIC cluster number to be used by the system.
SafeBoot	Sets the computer to use a Safe Boot mode. Can be Minimal, Network, or DsRepair.
SafeBootAlternateShell	Sets a Boolean value that enables or disables the use of the alternate shell when booted into Safe mode.
Sos	Sets a Boolean value that enables or disables the display of additional boot information.
SystemRoot	Defines the path to the system root.
UseFirmwarePCISettings	Sets a Boolean value that enables or disables use of BIOS-configured Peripheral Component Interconnect (PCI) resources.
UsePhysicalDestination	Sets a Boolean value that forces the use of the physical APIC.
Vga	Sets a Boolean value that forces the use of the VGA display driver.
WinPE	Sets a Boolean value that enables or disables boot to Windows PE.

Chapter 13

Changing Data Execution Prevention and Physical Address Extension Options

Data Execution Prevention (DEP) is a memory protection technology. With DEP enabled, the computer's processor marks all memory locations in an application as non-executable unless the location explicitly contains executable code. If code is executed from a memory page marked as non-executable, the processor can raise an exception and prevent the code from executing. This behavior prevents malicious application code, such as virus code, from inserting itself into most areas of memory.

For computers with processors that support the non-execute (NX) page protection feature, you can configure the operating system to opt in to NX protection by setting the nx parameter to OptIn, or opt out of NX protection by setting the nx parameter to OptOut. Here is an example:

```
bcdedit /set {current} nx optout
```

When you configure NX protection to OptIn, DEP is turned on only for essential Windows programs and services. This is the default. When you configure NX protection to OptOut, all programs and services—not just standard Windows programs and services—use DEP. Programs that shouldn't use DEP must be specifically opted out. You can also configure NX protection to be always on or always off using AlwaysOn or AlwaysOff, such as:

```
bcdedit /set {current} nx alwayson
```

Processors that support and opt in to NX protection must be running in PAE mode. You can configure PAE by setting the pae parameter to Default, ForceEnable, or ForceDisable. When you set paeState to Default, the operating system will use the default configuration for PAE. When you set paeState to ForceEnable, the operating system will use PAE. When you set paeState to ForceDisable, the operating system will not use PAE. You can set DebugOptionEnabled to true or false. Here is an example:

```
bcdedit /set {current} pae default
```

Changing the Operating System Display Order

You can change the display order of boot managers associated with a particular Windows Vista, Windows Server 2008, or later operating system using the /Displayorder command. The syntax is:

```
bcdedit /displayorder id1 id2 … idn
```

where id1 is the operating system identifiers of the first operating system in the display order, id2 is the identifier of the second, and so on. Thus you could change the display order of the operating systems identified in these BCD entries:

```
Windows Boot Loader
-------------------
identifier              {14504de-e96b-11cd-a51b-89ace9305d5e}
```

```
Windows Boot Loader
-------------------
identifier              {8b78e48f-02d0-11dd-af92-a72494804a8a}
```

using the following command:

```
bcdedit /displayorder {14504de-e96b-11cd-a51b-89ace9305d5e}
{8b78e48f-02d0-11dd-af92-a72494804a8a}
```

You can set a particular operating system as the first entry using /Addfirst with /Displayorder, such as:

```
bcdedit /displayorder {8b78e48f-02d0-11dd-af92-a72494804a8a} /addfirst
```

You can set a particular operating system as the last entry using /Addlast with /Displayorder, such as:

```
bcdedit /displayorder {8b78e48f-02d0-11dd-af92-a72494804a8a} /addlast
```

Changing the Default Operating System Entry

You can change the default operating system entry using the /Default command. The syntax for this command is:

```
bcdedit /default id
```

where id is the operating system id in the boot loader entry. Thus you could set the operating system identified in this BCD entry as the default:

```
Windows Boot Loader
-------------------
identifier              {14504de-e96b-11cd-a51b-89ace9305d5e}
```

using the following command:

```
bcdedit /default {14504de-e96b-11cd-a51b-89ace9305d5e}
```

If you want to use a pre–Windows Server 2008 operating system as the default, you'd use the identifier for the Windows Legacy OS Loader. The related BCD entry looks like this:

```
Windows Legacy OS Loader
------------------------
identifier              {466f5a88-0af2-4f76-9038-095b170dc21c}
device                  partition=C:
path                    \ntldr
description             Earlier Microsoft Windows Operating System
```

Following this, you could set Ntldr as the default by entering:

```
bcdedit /default {466f5a88-0af2-4f76-9038-095b170dc21c}
```

Chapter 13

Changing the Default Timeout

You can change the timeout value associated with the default operating system using the /Timeout command. Set the /Timeout command to the desired wait time in seconds, such as:

```
bcdedit /timeout 30
```

To boot automatically to the default operating system, set the timeout to 0 seconds.

Changing the Boot Sequence Temporarily

Occasionally, you might want to boot to a particular operating system one time and then revert to the default boot order. To do this, you can use the /Bootsequence command. Follow the command with the identifier of the operating system to which you want to boot after restarting the computer, such as:

```
bcdedit /bootsequence {14504de-e96b-11cd-a51b-89ace9305d5e}
```

When you restart the computer, the computer will set the specified operating system as the default for that restart only. Then when you restart the computer again, the computer will use the original default boot order.

Storage Management

This chapter introduces Windows Server 2008 storage management. Data is stored throughout the enterprise on a variety of systems and storage devices, the most common of which are hard disk drives but also can include storage management devices and removable media devices. Managing and maintaining the myriad of systems and storage devices is the responsibility of administrators. If a storage device fails, runs out of space, or encounters other problems, serious negative consequences can result. Servers could crash, applications could stop working, and users could lose data, all of which affect the productivity of users and the organization's bottom line. You can help prevent such problems and losses by implementing sound storage management procedures that allow you to evaluate your current and future storage needs and also help you meet current and future performance, capacity, and availability requirements. You then must configure storage appropriately for the requirements you've defined.

Essential Storage Technologies

One of the few constants in Microsoft Windows operating system administration is that data storage needs are ever increasing. It seems that only a few years ago a 120-gigabyte (GB) hard disk was huge and something primarily reserved for Windows servers rather than Windows workstations. Now Windows workstations ship with 500-GB hard disks as standard equipment, and some even ship with striped drives that allow workstations to have a single 1-terabyte (TB) or larger volume that spans over several drives—and all of that data must be backed up and stored somewhere other than on the workstations to protect it. This has meant that back-end storage solutions have had to scale dramatically as well. Server solutions that were once used for enterprise-wide implementations are now being used increasingly at the departmental level, and the underlying architecture for the related storage solutions has had to change dramatically to keep up.

Using Internal and External Storage Devices

To help meet the increasing demand for data storage and changing requirements, servers are being deployed with a mix of internal and external storage. In internal storage configurations, drives are connected inside the server chassis to a local disk controller and are said to be directly attached. You'll sometimes see an internal storage device referred to as *direct-attached storage (DAS)*.

In external storage configurations, servers connect to external, separately managed collections of storage devices that are either network-attached or part of a storage area network. Although the terms *network-attached storage (NAS)* and *storage area network (SAN)* are sometimes used as if they are one and the same, the technologies differ in how servers communicate with the external drives.

NAS devices are connected through a regular Transmission Control Protocol/Internet Protocol (TCP/IP) network. All server-storage communications go across the organization's local area network (LAN), as shown in Figure 14-1. This means the available bandwidth on the network can be shared by clients, servers, and NAS devices. For best performance, the network should be running at 100 megabits per second (Mbps) or 1 gigabit per second (Gbps). Networks operating at slower speeds can experience a serious decrease in performance as clients, servers, and storage devices try to communicate using the limited bandwidth.

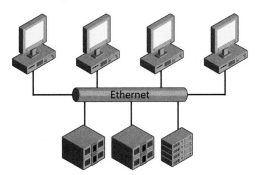

Figure 14-1 In NAS, server-storage communications are on the LAN.

A SAN is physically separate from the LAN and is independently managed. As shown in Figure 14-2, this isolates the server-to-storage communications so that traffic doesn't affect communications between clients and servers. Several SAN technologies are implemented, including Fibre Channel, a more traditional SAN technology that delivers high reliability and performance, and Internet SCSI (iSCSI), a newer SAN technology that delivers good reliability and performance at a lower cost than Fibre Channel. As the name implies, Internet SCSI uses TCP/IP networking technologies on the SAN, allowing servers to communicate with storage devices using the IP protocol. The SAN is still isolated from the organization's LAN.

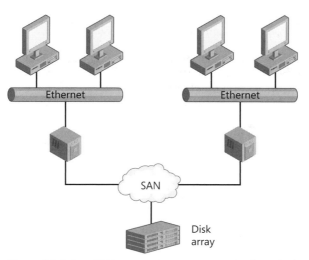

Figure 14-2 In a SAN, server-storage communications don't affect communications between clients and servers.

Improving Storage Management

Because of the increasing use of SANs, Windows Server 2008 includes many features for working with SANs and handling storage management in general. These features include the following:

- **Volume Shadow Copy Service (VSS)** VSS allows administrators to create point-in-time copies of volumes and individual files called *snapshots*. This makes it possible to back up these items while files are open and applications are running and to restore them to a specific point in time. VSS also makes it possible to create point-in-time copies of documents on shared folders. These copies are called *shadow copies*.

> **Note**
>
> Users can recover their own files when VSS is enabled. After you configure shadow copy, point-in-time backups of documents contained in the designated shared folders are created automatically, and users can quickly recover files that have been deleted or unintentionally altered as long as the Shadow Copy Client has been installed on their computer. For more information about VSS and the Shadow Copy Client, see Chapter 18, "Using Volume Shadow Copy."

- **Virtual Disk Service (VDS)** VDS makes it possible for storage devices from multiple vendors to interoperate. To do this, VDS provides application programming interfaces (APIs) that management tools and storage hardware can use, allowing for a unified interface for managing storage devices from multiple vendors and making it easier for administrators to manage a mixed-storage environment.

- **Volume automounting** Volume automounting makes it possible to better manage the way volumes are mounted. By using the Mountvol command, administrators can turn off volume automounting. By using volume mount points, administrators can mount volumes to empty NTFS folders, giving the volumes a drive path rather than a drive letter. This means it is easier to mount and unmount volumes, particularly with SANs.

- **Multipath I/O** Multipath I/O supports SAN connectivity by establishing multiple sessions or connections to storage devices. Using multipath I/O, you can configure as many as 32 separate physical paths to external storage devices that can be used simultaneously and load balanced if necessary. The purpose of having multiple paths is to have redundancy and possibly increased throughput. If you have multiple host bus adapters as well, you improve the chances of recovery from a path failure. However, if a path failure occurs, there might be a short period of time when the drives on the SAN aren't accessible.

- **Distributed File System (DFS)** DFS makes it possible to create a single directory tree that includes multiple file servers and their file shares. The DFS tree can contain more than 5,000 shared folders in a domain environment (or 50,000 shared folders on a stand-alone server), located on different servers, allowing users to find files or folders distributed across the enterprise easily. DFS directory trees can also be published in the Active Directory directory service so that they are easy to search.

> ### DFS Supports Multiple Roots and Closest-Site Selection
>
> Windows Server 2008 supports multiple DFS roots and closest-site selection. The capability to host multiple DFS roots allows you to consolidate and reduce the number of servers needed to maintain DFS. By using closest-site selection, DFS uses Active Directory site metrics to route a client to the closest available DFS server.

- **File Replication Service (FRS)** FRS makes it possible to synchronize data across the enterprise and is in fact the synchronization technology used by Active Directory. FRS works in conjunction with DFS to replicate data on file shares and automatically maintain synchronization of copies on multiple servers. FRS is capable of compressing replication traffic as well.

Windows Server 2008 has several command-line tools for managing local storage and storage replication services. These tools include the following:

- **DiskPart** Used to manage disks, partitions, and volumes. It is the command-line counterpart to the Disk Management tool and also includes features not found in the graphical user interface (GUI) tool, such as the capability to extend partitions on basic disks.

- **Dfscmd** Used to create DFS volumes by mapping DFS paths to server paths and manage replicas on DFS volumes.

- **Dfsdiag** Used to perform troubleshooting and diagnostics for DFS.

- **Dfsradmin** Used to manage and monitor DFS replication throughout the enterprise. You'll use this tool for troubleshooting and diagnosing problems as well. This tool replaces Health_Chk and the other tools it worked with.

- **Dfsrmig** Used to manually migrate the Sysvol from FRS replication to DFS replication.

> **Note**
>
> When a domain is running at Windows 2000 mixed, Windows 2000 native, or Windows Server 2003 functional level, domain controllers replicate the Sysvol using File Replication Service (FRS). When a domain is running at Windows Server 2008 functional level, domain controllers replicate the Sysvol using Distributed File System (DFS).

- **Dfsutil** Used to configure DFS, back up and restore DFS directory trees (namespaces), copy directory trees, and troubleshoot DFS.

- **Fsutil** Used to get detailed drive information and perform advanced file system maintenance. You can manage sparse files, reparse points, disk quotas, and other advanced features of NTFS.

- **Vssadmin** Used to view and manage the Volume Shadow Copy Service and its configuration.

Booting from SANs and Using SANs with Clusters

Windows Server 2008 supports booting from a SAN, having multiple clusters attached to the same SAN, and having a mix of clusters and stand-alone servers attached to the same SAN. To boot from a SAN, the external storage devices and the host bus adapters of each server must be configured appropriately to allow booting from the SAN.

When multiple servers must boot from the same external storage device, you must either configure the SAN in a switched environment or you must directly attach it from each host to one of the storage subsystem's Fibre Channel ports. A switched or direct-to-port environment allows the servers to be separate from each other, which is essential for booting from a SAN.

> **Fibre Channel-Arbitrated Loop Isn't Allowed**
>
> The use of a Fibre Channel-Arbitrated Loop (FC-AL) configuration is not supported because hubs typically don't allow the servers on the SAN to be isolated properly from each other—and the same is true when you have multiple clusters attached to the same SAN or a mix of clusters and stand-alone servers attached to the same SAN.

Each server on the SAN must have exclusive access to the logical disk from which it is booting, and no other server on the SAN should be able to detect or access that logical disk. For multiple-cluster installations, the SAN must be configured so that a set of cluster disks is accessible only by one cluster and is completely hidden from the rest of the clusters. By default, Windows Server 2008 will attach and mount every logical disk that it detects when the host bus adapter driver loads, and if multiple servers mount the same disk, the file system can be damaged.

TROUBLESHOOTING

Detecting SAN configuration problems

On an improperly configured SAN, multiple hosts are able to access the same logical disks. This isn't what you want to happen, but it does happen and you might be able to detect this configuration problem when you are working with the logical disks. Try using Windows Explorer from multiple hosts to access the logical disks on the SAN. If you try to access a logical disk and receive an "Access Denied," "Device Not Ready," or a similar error message, this can be an indicator that another server has access to the logical disk you are attempting to use. You might see another indicator of an improperly configured SAN when you add or configure logical disks. If you notice that multiple servers report that they've found new hardware when adding or configuring logical disks, there is a configuration problem with the SAN. If there is a configuration problem with clusters, you can see the following error events in the System logs:

- Warning event ID 11 with event source %HBADriverName%, "The driver detected a controller error on Device\ScsiPort*N*."

- Warning event ID 50 with event source Disk, "The system was attempting to transfer file data from buffers to \Device\HarddiskVolume*N*. The write operation failed, and only some of the data may have been written to the file."

- Warning event ID 51 with event source FTDISK, "An error was detected on device during a paging operation."

- Warning event ID 9 with event source %HBADriverName%, "Lost Delayed Write Data: The device, \Device\ScsiPort*N*, did not respond within the timeout period."

- Warning event ID 26 with event source Application Popup, "Windows—Delayed Write Failed: Windows was unable to save all the data for the file \Device\HarddiskVolume*N*\MFT$. The data has been lost. This error may be caused by a failure of your computer hardware or network connection. Please try to save this file elsewhere."

To prevent file system damage, the SAN must be configured in such a way that only one server can access a particular logical disk at a time. You can configure disks for exclusive access using a type of logical unit number (LUN) management such as LUN masking, LUN zoning, or a preferred combination of these techniques. With Windows Server 2008, you can use the Storage Manager For SANs console to manage Fibre Channel and iSCSI SANs that support the Virtual Disk Service (VDS) and have a configured VDS hardware provider. Before you can use this console, you must use the Add Features Wizard to add the Storage Manager For SANs feature to the server. After you add this feature, Storage Manager For SANs is available as an option on the Administrative Tools menu.

Configuring Multipath I/O

Hardware vendors typically supply a Device Specific Module (DSM) for SAN hardware and software for configuring multipath I/O. That said, the Multipath I/O feature now includes the Microsoft DSM and some basic configuration options. The Microsoft DSM supports the Active/Active controller model as well as the asymmetric logical unit access controller model. It also implements path selection policies failover, failback, and load balancing. Failover policies allow you to configure a secondary path that should be used if a preferred path fails. If you want the preferred path to be used automatically when it becomes operational again, you can configure a failback policy.

Several types of load balancing policies are available, including round-robin, dynamic least queue depth, and weighted path. With round-robin, you can configure the DSM to use all available I/O paths in a balanced, round-robin fashion. With dynamic least queue depth, you can configure the DSM to route I/O to the path with the least number of outstanding requests. With weighted path, you assign each path a weight to indicate its relative priority with regard to a particular application and the DSM selects the path with the least weight among the available paths.

Devices that support the Active/Active controller model are referred to as *Active/Active devices* and by default are configured to use round-robin. Generally, devices that support the asymmetric logical unit access (ALUA) controller model are compliant with the standard called SCSI Primary Commands-3 (SPC-3) or later and by default are configured to use failover.

You manage the multipath I/O configuration using the MPIO Properties dialog box or the Mpclaim command-line tool. After you install the Multipath I/O feature using the Add Features Wizard, both tools are available on the server. You open the MPIO Properties dialog box, shown in the following screen, by selecting MPIO on the Administrative Tools menu.

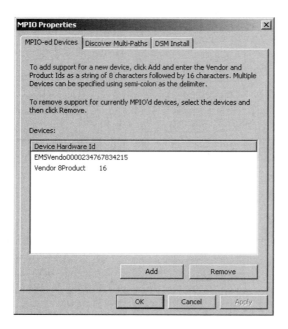

Adding Multipath Hardware Devices

When you open the MPIO Properties dialog box and select the Discover Multi-Paths tab, Windows checks for available multipath devices and lists them by their hardware ID. To also view iSCSI devices, select the Add Support For iSCSI Devices check box. Using the MPIO Properties dialog box, you can manually configure a device to use multipath I/O by following these steps:

1. Open the MPIO Properties dialog box. On the MPIO-ed Devices tab, you'll see a list of currently configured multipath devices. If the device you want to work with is not listed, click Add.

2. In the Add MPIO Support dialog box, type the vendor ID as an eight-character string followed by the product ID for the device as a 16-character string. Click OK.

3. You are prompted to restart the server to complete the operation. Click Yes to restart the server.

At an elevated command prompt, you can use Mpclaim to configure devices to use multipath IO as well. The basic syntax for installing a device follows:

```
mpclaim -r -i [-a | -c | -d DeviceId]
```

The -r parameter indicates that you want to restart the server to allow the device installation to be completed. Although you can suppress the restart using the -n parameter instead of -r, the device will not be installed and available for use until you restart the server. Use the -a parameter to configure multipath I/O support for all compatible devices. Use the -c parameter to configure multipath I/O support for all SPC-3 compliant devices. Use the -d parameter followed by a device's hardware ID to install a specific hardware device. The hardware ID of a device includes the vendor ID as an eight-character string followed by the product ID for the device as a 16-character string. In the following example, you install a device with EMSVendo0000234767834215 as the hardware ID:

```
mpclaim -r -i -d EMSVendo0000234767834215
```

Removing Multipath Hardware Devices

Using the MPIO Properties dialog box, you can uninstall MPIO for a device by following these steps:

1. Open the MPIO Properties dialog box. On the MPIO-ed Devices tab, you'll see a list of currently configured multipath devices.

2. Select the device that should no longer use multiple path I/O and then click Remove.

3. You are prompted to restart the server to complete the operation. Click Yes to restart the server.

At an elevated command prompt, you can use Mpclaim to uninstall multipath I/O for a device as well. The basic syntax for uninstalling a device follows:

```
mpclaim -r -u [-a | -c | -d DeviceId]
```

Except for the -u parameter for uninstalling a device, the other parameters are the same as when you are installing MPIO for a device. The following example uninstalls the previously installed device:

```
mpclaim -r -u -d EMSVendo0000234767834215
```

Meeting Performance, Capacity, and Availability Requirements

Whether you are working with internal or external disks, you should follow the same basic principles to help ensure that the chosen storage solutions meet your performance, capacity, and availability requirements. Storage performance is primarily a factor of the disk's access time (how long it takes to register a request and scan the disk), seek time (how long it takes to find the requested data), and transfer rate (how long it takes to read and write data). Storage capacity relates to how much information you can store on a volume or logical disk.

Although early NTFS implementations limited maximum volume size and file size limit to 32 GB, later implementations extended these limits. With Windows Server 2008, you can have a maximum NTFS volume size of 256 TB minus 64 KB when you are using 64-KB clusters, and 16 TB minus 4 KB when you are using 4-KB clusters. Windows Server 2008 has a maximum file size on an NTFS volume of up to 16 TB minus 64 KB. Further, Windows Server 2008 supports a maximum of 4,294,967,294 files on each volume, and a single server can manage hundreds of volumes (theoretically, around 2,000).

Storage availability relates to fault tolerance. As discussed in Chapter 39, "Preparing and Deploying Server Clusters," you ensure availability for essential applications and services by using cluster technologies. If a server has a problem or a particular application or service fails, you have a way to continue operations by failing over to another server. In addition to clusters, you can help ensure availability by saving redundant copies of data, keeping spare parts, and if possible making standby servers available. At the disk and data level, availability is enhanced by using redundant array of independent disks (RAID) technologies. RAID allows you to combine disks and to improve fault tolerance.

RAID can be implemented in software or in hardware. By using software RAID, the operating system maintains the disk sets at some cost to server performance. Windows Server 2008 supports RAID 0 (disk striping), RAID 1 (disk mirroring), and RAID 5 (disk striping with parity). Each of these software-implemented RAID levels requires processing power and memory resources to maintain. By using hardware RAID, you use separate hardware controllers (RAID controllers) to maintain the disk arrays. Although this requires the purchase of additional hardware, it takes the burden off the server and can improve performance. Why? In a hardware-implemented RAID system, processing power and memory aren't used to maintain the disk arrays. Instead, the hardware RAID controller handles all the necessary processing tasks. Some hardware RAID controllers have integrated disk caching as well, which can give a further boost to overall RAID performance.

The RAID levels available with a hardware implementation depend on the hardware controller and the vendor's implementation of RAID technologies. Some hardware RAID configurations include RAID 0 (disk striping), RAID 1 (disk mirroring), RAID 0+1 (disk striping with mirroring), RAID 5 (disk striping with parity), and RAID 5+1 (disk striping with parity plus mirroring).

> **Note**
>
> For more information about the advantages and disadvantages of various RAID levels, see Table 39-1, "Hardware RAID Configurations for Clusters," on page 1350.

Installing and Configuring File Services

File servers provide the central locations for storing and sharing files across the network. When many users require access to the same files and application data, you'll need to configure file servers throughout the organization. In earlier releases of the Windows Server operating system, all servers were installed with basic file services. With Windows Server 2008, you must specifically configure a server to be a file server by adding the File Services role and configuring this role to use the appropriate role services.

Optimizing the File Services Role

When you install the File Services role, you can install and configure several related role services as well. One of these related role services is Distributed File System (DFS), which provides tools and services for DFS Namespaces, and DFS Replication. DFS Replication is a newer and preferred replication technology. When a domain is running in Windows 2008 Domain functional level, domain controllers use DFS Replication to provide more robust and granular replication of the Sysvol directory. For DFS, there are two secondary role services:

- **DFS Namespaces** DFS Namespaces allow you to group shared folders located on different servers into one or more logically structured namespaces. Each namespace appears as a single shared folder with a series of subfolders. However, the underlying structure of the namespace can come from shared folders on multiple servers in different sites.

- **DFS Replication** DFS Replication allows you to synchronize folders on multiple servers across local or wide area network connections using a multimaster replication engine. The replication engine uses the Remote Differential Compression (RDC) protocol to synchronize only the portions of files that have changed since the last replication. You can use DFS Replication with DFS Namespaces or by itself.

Other role services available include: File Server Resource Manager (FSRM), Share and Storage Management, Services for Network File System (NFS), and Windows Search Service. FSRM installs a suite of tools that administrators can use to better manage data stored on servers. Using FSRM, administrators can:

- **Define file screening policies** File screening policies allow you to block unauthorized, potentially malicious types of content. You can configure active screening, which does not allow users to save unauthorized files, or passive screening, which allows users to save unauthorized files but monitors or warns about usage (or both).

- **Configure Resource Manager Disk Quotas** Using Resource Manager Disk Quotas, you can manage disk space usage by folder and by volume. You can configure quotas with a specific limit as a hard limit—meaning a limit can't be exceeded—or a soft limit, meaning a limit can be exceeded.

- **Generate storage reports** You can generate storage reports as part of disk quota and file screening management. Storage reports identify file usage by owner, type, and other parameters. They also help identify users and applications that violate screening policies.

Share and Storage Management installs the Share And Storage Management console and configures the server so that you can use this console. This console allows administrators to manage shared folders and allows users to access shared folders over the network. You can also use this console to configure logical unit numbers (LUNs) in a storage area network (SAN).

Chapter 14

Services for Network File System provides a file sharing solution for enterprises with mixed Windows and UNIX environments. When you install Services for Network File System (NFS), users can transfer files between Windows Server 2008 and UNIX operating systems using the NFS protocol.

Windows Search Service allows fast file searches of resources on the server from clients that are compatible with Windows Search Service. This feature is designed primarily for desktop and small office implementations. If you install Windows Search Service, you cannot also install the Indexing Service feature, which is provided for backward compatibility with existing Windows Server 2003 installations. Also provided for backward compatibility with Windows Server 2003 installations is the File Replication Service (FRS). FRS allows you to synchronize folders with file servers that use FRS instead of DFS for replication. It also allows synchronization with Windows 2000 implementations of DFS. If your organization has computers running FRS, you may need to install this role service to ensure compatibility with Windows Server 2008.

> **Note**
>
> When you install the File Services role, you might also want to install Multipath I/O, Storage Manager for SANs, and Windows Server Backup. Multipath I/O provides support for using multiple data paths between a file server and a storage device. Servers use multiple I/O paths for redundancy in case of failure of a path and to improve transfer performance. Storage Manager for SANs allows you to provision storage for storage area networks (SANs). Windows Server Backup is the new backup utility included with Windows Server 2008.

Configuring the File Services Role

You can add the File Services role to a server by following these steps:

1. In Server Manager, select the Roles node in the left pane and then click Add Roles. This starts the Add Roles Wizard. If the wizard displays the Before You Begin page, read the welcome text and then click Next.

> **Note**
>
> During the setup process, shared files are created on the server. If you encounter a problem that causes the setup process to fail, you will need to resume the setup process using the Add Role Services wizard. After you restart Server Manager, select the File Services node under Roles. In the main pane, scroll down and then click Add Role Services. You can continue with the installation, starting with step 3. If you were in the process of configuring domain-based DFS, you'll need to provide administrator credentials.

2. On the Select Server Roles page, select File Services and then click Next. Read the introductory page and then click Next again.

3. On the Select Role Services page, select the check boxes for one or more role services to install, as shown in Figure 14-3. To allow for interoperability with UNIX, be sure to add Services For Network File System. Click Next.

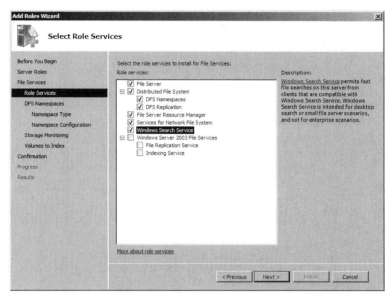

Figure 14-3 Select the appropriate role services for the file server.

4. A DFS namespace is a virtual view of shared folders located on different servers. If you are installing DFS Namespaces, you'll have three additional configuration pages:

○ On the Create A DFS Namespace page, set the root name for the first namespace or elect to create a namespace later. The namespace root name should be something that is easy for users to remember, such as CorpData. In a large enterprise, you might need to create separate namespaces for each major division.

○ On the Select Namespace Type page, specify whether you want to create a domain-based namespace or a stand-alone namespace. Domain-based namespaces can be replicated with multiple namespace servers to provide high availability but can have only up to 5,000 DFS folders. Stand-alone namespaces can have up to 50,000 DFS folders but are replicated only when you use failover server clusters and configure replication.

○ On the Configure Namespace page, you can add shared folders to the namespace as well as namespaces that are associated with a DFS folder. Click Add. In the Add Folder To Namespace dialog box, click Browse. In the Browse For Shared Folders dialog box, select the shared folder to add and then click OK. Next, type a name for the folder in the namespace. This name can be the same as the original folder name or a new name that will be associated with the original folder in the namespace. After you type a name, click OK to add the folder and complete the process.

> **Note**
>
> You do not have to configure DFS Namespaces at this time. After you've installed DFS Namespaces, DFS Replication, or both, you can use the DFS Management console to manage the related features. This console is installed and available on the Administrative Tools menu.

5. With File Server Resource Manager, you can monitor the amount of space used on disk volumes and create storage reports. If you are installing File Server Resource Manager, you'll have two additional configuration pages:

   ○ On the Configure Storage Usage Monitoring page, you can select disk volumes for monitoring. When you select a volume and then click Options, you can set the volume usage threshold and choose the reports to generate when the volume reaches the threshold value. By default, the usage threshold is 85 percent.

   ○ On the Set Report Options page, you can select a save location for usage reports. One usage report of each previously selected type is generated each time a volume reaches its threshold. Old reports are not automatically deleted. The default save location is %SystemDrive%\StorageReports. To change the default location, click Browse and then select the new save location in the Browse For Folder dialog box. You can also elect to receive reports by e-mail. To do this, you must specify the recipient e-mail addresses and the SMTP server to use.

> **Note**
>
> You do not have to configure monitoring and reporting at this time. After you've installed FSRM, you can use the File Server Resource Manager console to manage the related features. This console is installed and available on the Administrative Tools menu.

6. If you are installing Windows Search Service, you'll see an additional configuration page that allows you to select the volumes to index. Indexing a volume makes it possible for users to search a volume quickly. However, indexing entire volumes can affect service performance, especially if you index the system volume. Therefore, you might want to index only specific shared folders on volumes, which you'll be able to do later on a per-folder basis.

> **Note**
>
> You do not have to configure indexing at this time. After you've installed Windows Search Service, you can use the Indexing Options utility in Control Panel to manage the related features.

7. When you've completed all the optional pages, click Next. You'll see the Confirm Installation Options page. Click Install to begin the installation process. When Setup finishes installing the server with the features you've selected, you'll see the Installation Results page. Review the installation details to ensure that all phases of the installation completed successfully.

If the File Services role is installed already on a server and you want to install additional services for a file server, you can add role services to the server using a similar process. In Server Manager, expand the Roles node and then select the File Services node. In the main pane, the window is divided into several panels. Scroll down until you see the Role Services panel and then click Add Role Services. You can then follow the previous procedure starting with step 3 to add role services.

Configuring Storage

When you install disks, you must configure them for use by choosing a partition style and a storage type to use. After you configure drives, you prepare them to store data by partitioning them and creating file systems in the partitions. Partitions are sections of physical drives that function as if they are separate units. This allows you to configure multiple logical disk units even if a system has only one physical drive and to apportion disks appropriately to meet the needs of your organization.

Using the Disk Management Tools

When you want to manage storage, the primary tool you use is Disk Management, as shown in Figure 14-4. Disk Management is a snap-in included in Computer Management and Server Manager. It can be added to any custom MMC you create as well. As long as you are a member of the Administrators group, you can use Disk Management to configure drives and software RAID.

Chapter 14

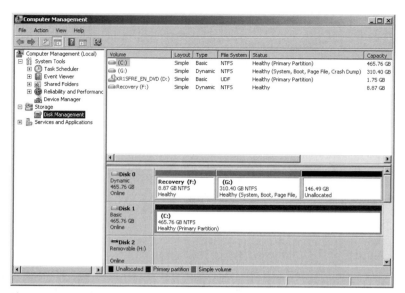

Figure 14-4 Disk Management is the primary tool for managing storage.

Disk Management makes it easy to work with any available internal and external drives on both local and remote systems. You can start Disk Management by clicking Start, pointing to All Programs, selecting Administrative Tools, and then Computer Management. You're automatically connected to the local computer on which you're running Computer Management. In Computer Management, expand Storage, and then select Disk Management. You can now manage the drives on the local system.

To use Disk Management to work with a remote system, right-click the Computer Management entry in the left pane, and select Connect To Another Computer on the shortcut menu. This displays the Select Computer dialog box (shown in the following screen). Type the domain name or IP address of the system whose drives you want to view, and then click OK.

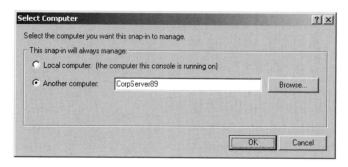

Disk Management has three views:

- **Disk List** Shows a list of physical disks on or attached to the selected system with details on type, capacity, unallocated space, and status. It is the only disk view that shows the device type, such as Small Computer System Interface (SCSI) or Integrated Device Electronics (IDE), and the partition style, such as master boot record (MBR) or GUID partition table (GPT).

- **Graphical View** Displays summary information for disks graphically according to disk capacity and the size of disk regions. By default, disk and disk region capacity are shown on a logarithmic scale, meaning the disks and disk regions are displayed proportionally.

> ### Change the Scaling Options to Get Different Disk Views
>
> You can also specify that you want all disks to be the same size regardless of capacity (which is useful if you have many disk regions on disks) or that you want to use a linear scale in which disk regions are sized relative to the largest disk (which is useful if you want to get perspective on capacity). To change the size settings for the Graphical View, click View, Settings, and then in the Settings dialog box, select the Scaling tab.

- **Volume List** Shows all volumes on the selected computer (including hard disk partitions and logical drives) with details on volume layout, type, file system, status, capacity, and free space. It also shows whether the volume has fault tolerance and the related disk usage overhead. The fault tolerance information is for software RAID only.

Volume List and Graphical View are the default views. In Figure 14-4, the Volume List view is in the upper-right corner, and the Graphical View is in the lower-right corner. To change the top view, select View, choose Top, and then select the view you want to use. To change the bottom view, select View, choose Bottom, and then select the view you want to use.

Disk Management's command-line counterpart is the DiskPart utility. You can use DiskPart to perform all Disk Management tasks. DiskPart is a text-mode command interpreter that you invoke so that you can manage disks, partitions, and volumes. As such, DiskPart has a separate command prompt and its own internal commands. Although earlier releases of DiskPart did not allow you to format partitions, logical drives, and volumes, the version that ships with Windows Server 2008 allows you to do this using the internal format command.

You invoke the DiskPart interpreter by typing **diskpart** at the command prompt. DiskPart is designed to work with physical hard disks installed on a computer, which can be internal, external, or a mix of both. Although it will list other types of disks, such as CD/DVD drives, removable media, and universal serial bus (USB)-connected flash random access memory (RAM) devices, and allow you to perform some minimal tasks, such as assigning a drive letter, these devices are not supported.

Chapter 14

After you invoke DiskPart, you can list available disks, partitions, and volumes by using the following list commands:

- **List Disk** Lists all internal and external hard disks on the computer
- **List Volume** Lists all volumes on the computer (including hard disk partitions and logical drives)
- **List Partition** Lists partitions, but only on the disk you've selected

Then you must give focus to the disk, partition, or volume you want to work with by selecting it. Giving a disk, partition, or volume focus ensures that any commands you type will act only on that disk, partition, or volume. To select a disk, type **select disk N**, where N is the number of the disk you want to work with. To select a volume, type **select volume N**, where N is the number of the volume you want to work with. To select a partition, first select its related disk by typing **select disk N**, and then select the partition you want to work with by typing **select partition N**.

If you use the list commands again after selecting a disk, partition, or volume, you'll see an asterisk (*) next to the item with focus. When you are finished working with Disk-Part, type **exit** at the DiskPart prompt to return to the standard command line.

Listing 14-1 shows a sample DiskPart session. As you can see, when you first invoke DiskPart, it shows the operating system and DiskPart version you are using as well as the name of the computer you are working with. When you list available disks, the output shows you the disk number, status, size, and free space. It also shows the disk partition style and type. If there's an asterisk in the Dyn column, the disk is a dynamic disk. Otherwise, it is a basic disk. If there's an asterisk in the Gpt column, the disk uses the GPT partition style. Otherwise, it is an MBR disk. You'll find more information on partition styles in "Using the MBR and GPT Partition Styles" on page 425.

Listing 14-1 Using DiskPart: an example

```
C:\> diskpart

    Microsoft DiskPart version 6.0.6001
    Copyright (C) 1999-2007 Microsoft Corporation.
    On computer: CORPSVR02

DISKPART> list disk

    Disk ###    Status        Size      Free     Dyn   Gpt
    --------    ----------    -------   ------    ---   ---
      Disk 0    Online        56 GB     0 B       *     *
      Disk 1    Online        29 GB     0 B
      Disk 2    Online        37 GB     9 GB

DISKPART> list volume

      Volume ###   Ltr   Label      Fs      Type      Size      Status   Info
      ----------   ---   --------   -----   -------   -------   ------   ------
      Volume 0     F                        DVD-ROM   0 B
      Volume 1     G     W2PFPP_EN  CDFS    CD-ROM    361 MB
```

```
         Volume 2    C    Apps     NTFS  Partition  56 GB   Healthy  System
         Volume 3    D    Data     NTFS  Partition  29 GB   Healthy
         Volume 4    N    Data2    NTFS  Partition  28 GB   Healthy
         Volume 5    S                   Partition  47 MB   Healthy

DISKPART> select disk 0

Disk 0 is now the selected disk.

DISKPART> list partition

  Partition ###   Type             Size      Offset
  -------------   ----------------  -------  -  -------
  Partition 1     Primary           56 GB      32 KB

DISKPART> select partition 1

Partition 1 is now the selected partition.

DISKPART> list partition

  Partition ###   Type             Size      Offset
  -------------   ----------------  -------  -  ------
* Partition 1     Primary           56 GB      32 KB

DISKPART> exit

Leaving DiskPart...

C:\>
```

Adding New Disks

Thanks to hot swapping and Plug and Play technologies—both supported by Windows Server 2008—the process of adding new disks has changed considerably from the days of Windows NT 4.0. If a computer supports hot swapping of disks, you can install new disks without having to shut down the computer. Simply insert the hard disk drives you want to use. If the computer doesn't support hot swapping, you will need to shut down the computer, insert the drives, and restart the computer.

Either way, after you insert the drives you want to use, log on and access Disk Management in the Computer Management tool. If the new drives have already been initialized, meaning they have disk signatures, they should be brought online automatically when you select Rescan Disks from the Action menu. If you are working with new drives that haven't been initialized, meaning they lack a disk signature, when you choose to initialize the new disk, Windows Server 2008 will start the Initialize Disk Wizard. This wizard will allow you to choose either the MBR or GPT partitioning style.

You can use Disk Management to initialize a new disk as well. In the Disk List view, the disk will be marked with a red down arrow icon, and the disk's status will be listed as Not Initialized. You can then right-click the disk's icon and select Initialize Disk.

When the Initialize Disk Wizard starts, follow these steps to configure the disks:

1. Click Next to get to the Select Disks To Initialize page. The disks you added are selected for initialization automatically, but if you don't want to initialize a particular disk, you can clear the related check box.

2. Select either the MBR or GPT partitioning style.

3. When the wizard finishes, the disk is ready for partitioning and formatting.

INSIDE OUT   Windows Server 2008 can use disk write caching

As discussed previously, storage performance is primarily a factor of a disk's access time (how long it takes to register a request and scan the disk), seek time (how long it takes to find the requested data), and transfer rate (how long it takes to read and write data). By enabling disk write caching, you could reduce the number of times the operating system accesses the disk by caching disk writes and then performing several writes at once. In this way, disk performance is primarily influenced by seek time and transfer rate.

The drawback of disk write caching is that in the event of a power or system failure the cached writes might not be written to disk, and this can result in data loss. Windows Server 2008 disables disk write caching by default, but you can enable it on a per-disk basis as long as write caching is supported by your hardware. Keep in mind that some server applications require disk write caching to be enabled or disabled, and if these applications use a particular set of disks, these disks must use the required setting for disk write caching.

To configure disk write caching, start Computer Management, expand the System Tools node, and select Device Manager. In the details pane, expand Disk Drives, right-click the disk drive you want to work with, and then select Properties. In the Device Properties dialog box, select the Policies tab. Select or clear Enable Write Caching On The Disk as appropriate, and click OK.

Using the MBR and GPT Partition Styles

The term *partition style* refers to the method that Windows Server 2008 uses to organize partitions on a disk. Two partition styles are available: MBR and GPT. Originally, only x86-based computers used the MBR partition style, and only Itanium-based computers running 64-bit versions of Windows used the GPT partition style. With Windows Server 2008, both 32-bit and 64-bit editions support both MBR and GPT. The GPT partition style will be recognized also in Windows Server 2003 as long as it has been upgraded to Service Pack 1 or later. This is true for both x86 and x64 platforms.

With 64-bit versions of Windows, the GPT partition style is preferred and it is the only partition style from which you can boot Itanium-based computers. The key difference between the MBR partition style and the GPT partition style has to do with how partition data is stored.

> **Note**
>
> For this discussion, I focus on the basic storage type and won't get into the details of the dynamic storage type. That's covered in the next section.

Working with MBR Disks

MBR uses a partition table that describes where the partitions are located on the disk. The first sector on a hard disk contains the MBR and a master boot code that's used to boot the system. The MBR resides outside of partitioned space.

> **Note**
>
> It's easy to confuse master boot record with boot sector. These are two different structures on the hard drive. The master boot record contains the disk signature and partition table and is the first sector of the hard drive. A boot sector contains the BIOS parameter block and marks the first sector of the file system.

MBR disks support a maximum volume size of up to 4 TB unless they're dynamic disks and use RAID. MBR disks have two special types of partitions associated with them. The first partition type, called a primary partition, is used with drive sections that you want to access directly for file storage. You make a primary partition accessible to users by creating a file system on it and assigning it a drive letter or mount point. The second partition type, called an extended partition, is used when you want to divide a section of a disk into one or more logical units called logical drives. Here, you create the extended partition first, then create the logical drives within it. You then create a file system on each logical drive and assign a drive letter or mount point.

Each MBR drive can have up to four primary partitions or three primary partitions and one extended partition. It is the extended partition that allows you to divide a drive into more than four parts.

> **Note**
>
> These rules apply to MBR disks that use the basic storage type. There's also a storage type called dynamic. I discuss basic and dynamic storage types in "Working with Basic and Dynamic Disks" on page 428.

Working with GPT Disks

GPT disks don't have a single MBR. With GPT disks, critical partition data is stored in the individual partitions, and there are redundant primary and backup partition tables. Further, checksum fields are maintained to allow for error correction and to improve partition structure integrity.

INSIDE OUT   GPT headers and error checking

GPT disks use a primary and backup partition array. Each partition array has a header that defines the range of logical block addresses on the disk that can be used by partition entries. The GPT header also defines its location on the disk, its globally unique identifier (GUID), and a 32-bit cyclic redundancy check (CRC32) checksum that is used to verify the integrity of the GPT header. The primary GPT header is created directly after the protected MBR on the disk. The backup GPT header is located in the last sector on the disk.

Firmware acts as the interface between a computer's hardware and its operating system. Although most *x*86-based computers use the basic input/ouput system (BIOS) as their firmware, Itanium-based computers and some newer computers use the Extensible Firmware Interface (EFI). Only systems that use EFI will be able to boot directly to a GPT disk. But all editions of Windows 2008 can use GPT disks for data.

A computer's firmware verifies the integrity of the GPT headers by using the CRC32 checksum. The checksum is a calculated value used to determine whether there are errors in a GPT header. If the primary GPT header is damaged, firmware checks the backup header. If the backup header's checksum is valid, the backup GPT header is used to restore the primary GPT header. The process of restoring the GPT header works much the same way if it is determined that the backup header is damaged—only in reverse. If both the primary and backup GPT headers are damaged, the Windows operating system won't be able to access the disk.

GPT disks support partitions of up to 18 exabytes (EB) in size and up to 128 partitions per disk. Itanium-based computers using GPT disks have two required partitions and one or more optional original equipment manufacturer (OEM) or data partitions. The required partitions are the EFI system partition (ESP) and the Microsoft Reserved (MSR) partition. Although the optional partitions that you see depend on the system configuration, the optional partition type you see the most is the primary partition. Primary partitions are used to store user data on GPT disks.

If you install the Windows Server 2008 64-bit edition on a new system with clean disks or an existing system with a clean disk, Setup will initialize the disk as a GPT disk (only for computers with EFI). Setup will offer to create the ESP and then will automatically create the MSR partition. The ESP is formatted automatically using a file allocation table (FAT). The ESP is required only on the first GPT disk, however. Additional GPT disks do not require an ESP. Further, a basic GPT disk might not contain primary partitions. For example, when you install a new disk and configure it as a GPT disk, the Windows operating system automatically creates the ESP and MSR partitions, but does not create primary partitions.

Although GPT offers a significant improvement over MBR, it does have limitations. You cannot use GPT with removable disks, disks that are direct-attached using USB or IEEE 1394 (FireWire) interfaces, or disks attached to shared storage devices on server clusters.

> **CAUTION**
>
> It is recommended that you don't use disk editing tools such as DiskProbe to make changes to GPT disks. Any change that you make using these tools renders the CRC32 checksums in the GPT headers invalid, and this can cause the disk to become inaccessible. To make changes to GPT disks, you should use only Disk Management or DiskPart. If you are working in the EFI firmware environment, you'll find there's a version of DiskPart available as well—DiskPart.efi.

Using and Converting MBR and GPT Disks

Tasks for using MBR and GPT disks are similar but not necessarily identical. On an x86-based computer, you can use MBR for booting or for data disks and GPT only for data disks. On an Itanium-based computer, you can have both GPT and MBR disks, but you must have at least one GPT disk that contains the ESP and a primary partition or simple volume that contains the operating system for booting.

Partitions and volumes on MBR and GPT disks can be formatted using FAT, FAT32, and NTFS. When you create partitions or volumes in Disk Management, you have the opportunity to format the disk and assign it a drive letter or mount point as part of the volume creation process. Although Disk Management lets you format the partitions and volumes on MBR disks using FAT, FAT32, and NTFS, you can format partitions and volumes on GPT disks using only NTFS. If you want to format GPT disks by using FAT or FAT32, you must use either the Format or DiskPart command at the command prompt. Further, keep in mind that you can use Windows Server Backup to back up only NTFS partitions. If your server has partitions using other formats and you want to back them up, you'll need to use a different backup utility.

You can change partition table styles from MBR to GPT or from GPT to MBR. Changing partition table styles is useful when you want to move disks between *x*86-based computers and Intel Architecture 64 (IA-64)-based computers or you receive new disks that are formatted for the wrong partition table style. You can convert partition table styles only on empty disks, however. This means the disks must either be new or newly formatted. You could, of course, empty a disk by removing its partitions or volumes.

You can use both Disk Management and DiskPart to change the partition table style. To use Disk Management to change the partition style of an empty disk, start Computer Management from the Administrative Tools menu or by typing **compmgmt.msc** at the command line, expand the Storage node, and then select Disk Management. All available disks are displayed. Right-click the disk to convert in the Graphical View, and then click Convert To GPT Disk or Convert To MBR Disk as appropriate.

To use DiskPart to change the partition style of an empty disk, invoke DiskPart by typing **diskpart**, and then selecting the disk you want to convert. For example, if you want to convert disk 3, type **select disk 3**. After you select the disk, you can convert it from MBR to GPT by typing **convert gpt**. To convert a disk from GPT to MBR, type **convert mbr**.

Using the Disk Storage Types

The term *storage type* refers to the method that Windows Server 2008 uses to structure disks and their contents. Windows Server 2008 offers three storage types: basic disk, dynamic disk, and removable disk. The storage type you use doesn't depend on the processor architecture—it does depend, however, on whether you are working with fixed or non-fixed disks. When you are working with fixed disks, you can use basic, dynamic, or both storage types on any edition of Windows Server 2008. When you are working with non-fixed disks, the disk has the removable storage type automatically.

Working with Basic and Dynamic Disks

Basic disks use the same disk structure as earlier versions of the Windows operating system. When using basic disks, you are limited to creating four primary partitions per disk, or three primary partitions and one extended partition. Within an extended partition, you can create one or more logical drives. For ease of reference, primary partitions and logical drives on basic disks are known as *basic volumes*. Dynamic disks were introduced in Windows 2000 as a way to improve disk support by requiring fewer restarts after disk configuration changes, improved support for combining disks, and enhanced fault tolerance using RAID configurations. All volumes on dynamic disks are known as *dynamic volumes*.

INSIDE OUT Disk issues when upgrading to Windows Server 2008

When you install Windows Server 2008 on a new system with unpartitioned disks, disks are initialized as basic disks. When you upgrade to Windows Server 2008, disks with partitions are initialized as basic disks. Windows 2000 had limited support for the fault-tolerant features found in Windows NT 4.0. In Windows 2000, you can use basic disks to maintain existing spanning, mirroring, and striping configurations and to delete these configurations. You cannot, however, create new combined or fault-tolerant drive sets using the basic disk type.

In Windows Server 2008, fault-tolerant sets that you created in Windows NT are not supported. Before upgrading to Windows Server 2008, it is recommended that you remove the fault-tolerant features. Start by backing up the data. If you have a mirror set, break the mirror set and then run Windows Server 2008 Setup. If you have a volume set, stripe set, or stripe set with parity, you must delete the set before you upgrade. As long as you have a working backup, you can upgrade the disks to dynamic after installation, re-create the fault-tolerant set, and then restore the data from backup.

Windows Server 2008 systems can use both basic and dynamic disks. You cannot, however, mix disk types when working with volume sets. All disks, regardless of whether they are basic or dynamic, have five special types of drive sections:

- **Active** The active partition or volume is the drive section for system cache and startup. Some devices with removable storage might be listed as having an active partition (though they don't actually have the active partition).

- **Boot** The boot partition or volume contains the operating system and its support files. The system and boot partition or volume can be the same.

- **Crash dump** The partition to which the computer attempts to write dump files in the event of a system crash. By default, dump files are written to the %SystemRoot% folder, but can be located on any desired partition or volume.

- **Page file** A partition containing a paging file used by the operating system. Because a computer can page memory to multiple disks, according to the way virtual memory is configured, a computer can have multiple page file partitions or volumes.

- **System** The system partition or volume contains the hardware-specific files needed to load the operating system. The system partition or volume can't be part of a striped or spanned volume.

The volume types are set when you install the operating system. On an x86-based computer, you can mark a partition as active to ensure that it is the one from which the computer starts. You can do this only for partitions on basic disks. You can't mark an existing dynamic volume as the active volume, but you can convert a basic disk containing the active partition to a dynamic disk. After the update is complete, the partition becomes a simple volume that's active.

TROUBLESHOOTING

Dynamic disks have limitations

You can't use dynamic disks on portable computers or with removable media. You can only configure disks for portable computers and removable media as basic disks with primary partitions. For computers that support booting multiple operating systems (multibooted), keep in mind that only Windows 2000 or later versions of the Windows operating system can use dynamic disks.

Using and Converting Basic and Dynamic Disks

Basic disks and dynamic disks are managed in different ways. For basic disks, you use primary and extended partitions. Extended partitions can contain logical drives. Dynamic disks allow you to combine disks to create spanned volumes, to mirror disks to create mirrored volumes, and to stripe disks using RAID 0 to create striped volumes. You can also create RAID-5 volumes for high reliability on dynamic disks.

You can change storage types from basic to dynamic and from dynamic to basic. When you convert a basic disk to a dynamic disk, existing partitions are changed to volumes of the appropriate type automatically and existing data is not lost. Converting a dynamic disk to a basic disk isn't so easy and can't be done without taking some drastic measures. You must delete the volumes on the dynamic disk before you can change the disk back to a basic disk. Deleting the volumes destroys all the information they contain, and the only way to get it back is to restore the data from backup.

You should consider a number of things when you want to change the storage type from basic to dynamic. To be converted successfully, an MBR disk must have 1 megabyte (MB) of free space at the end of the disk. This space is used for the dynamic disk database, which tracks volume information. Without this free space at the end of the disk, the conversion will fail. Because both Disk Management and DiskPart reserve this space automatically, primarily only if you've used third-party disk management utilities will you need to be concerned about whether this space is available. However, if the disk was partitioned using a much older version of the Windows operating system or a third-party utlity, this space might not be available either.

A GPT disk must have contiguous, recognized data partitions to be converted successfully. If the GPT disk contains partitions that the Windows operating system doesn't recognize, such as those created by another operating system, you won't be able to convert a basic disk to a dynamic disk. When you convert a GPT disk, the Windows operating system creates LDM Metadata and LDM Data partitions as discussed in "LDM Metadata and LDM Data Partitions" on page 451. GPT disks that are dynamic will store the dynamic disk database in the LDM partitions instead of out at the end of the drive like on an MBR disk

With either type of disk, you can't convert drives that use sector sizes larger than 512 bytes. If the disk has large sector sizes, you must reformat the disk before converting. You can't convert a disk if the system or boot partition uses software RAID. You must stop using the software RAID before you convert the disk.

Both Disk Management and DiskPart can be used to change the storage type.

Using Disk Management to Convert a Basic Disk to a Dynamic Disk   To use Disk Management to convert a basic disk to a dynamic disk, start Computer Management from the Administrative Tools menu or by typing **compmgmt.msc** at the command line, expand the Storage node, and then select Disk Management. In Disk Management, right-click a basic disk that you want to convert, either in Disk List view or in the left pane of Graphical View, and select Convert To Dynamic Disk.

In the Convert To Dynamic Disk dialog box (as shown in the following screen), select the disks you want to convert. If you're converting disks that will be used in a RAID volume, be sure to select all the basic disks in the set because they must be converted together. Click OK when you're ready to continue.

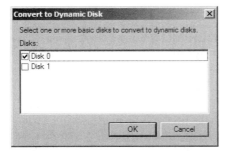

Next, the Disks To Convert dialog box shows the disks you're converting along with details of the disk contents. To see the drive letters and mount points that are associated with a disk, select the disk in the Disks list, and then click Details. If a disk cannot be converted for some reason, the Will Convert column will show No and the Disk Contents column will provide a reason, as shown in the following screen. You must correct whatever problem is noted before you can convert the disk.

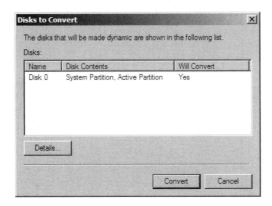

When you're ready to start the conversion, click Convert. Disk Management will then warn you that after you finish the conversion you won't be able to boot previous versions of the Windows operating system from volumes on the selected disks. Click Yes to continue. If a selected drive contains the boot partition, system partition, or a partition in use, you'll see another warning telling you that the computer will need to be rebooted to complete the conversion process.

Using DiskPart to Convert a Basic Disk to a Dynamic Disk   To use DiskPart to convert a basic disk to a dynamic disk, invoke DiskPart by typing **diskpart**, and then select the disk you want to convert. For example, if you want to convert disk 2, type **select disk 2**. After the disk is selected, you can convert it from basic to dynamic by typing **convert dynamic**.

Using Disk Management to Change a Dynamic Disk Back to a Basic Disk   To use Disk Management to change a dynamic disk back to a basic disk, you must first delete all dynamic volumes on the disk. Then right-click the disk, and select Convert To Basic Disk. This changes the dynamic disk to a basic disk, and you can then create new partitions and logical drives on the disk.

Using DiskPart to Convert a Dynamic Disk to a Basic Disk   To use DiskPart to convert a basic disk to a dynamic disk, invoke DiskPart by typing **diskpart**, and then select the disk you want to convert. For example, if you want to convert disk 2, type **select disk 2**. If there are any existing volumes on the disk, you must delete them. You can do this by typing **clean**. However, be sure to move any data the disk contains to another disk prior to deleting the disk volumes.

After you delete all the volumes on the disk, you can convert the disk from dynamic to basic by typing **convert basic**. This changes the dynamic disk to a basic disk, and you can then create new partitions and logical drives on the disk.

Converting FAT or FAT32 to NTFS

On both MBR and GPT disks, you can convert FAT or FAT32 partitions, logical drives, and volumes to NTFS by using the Convert command. This preserves the file and directory structure without the need to reformat. Before you use Convert, you should check to see whether the volume is being used as the active boot volume or is a system volume containing the operating system. If it is, Convert must have exclusive access to the volume before it can begin the conversion. Because exclusive access to boot or system volumes can be obtained only during startup, you will see a prompt asking if you want to schedule the drive to be converted the next time the system starts.

As part of preparation for conversion, you should check to see if there's enough free space to perform the conversion. You'll need a block of free space that's about 25 percent of the total space used by the volume. For example, if the volume stores 12 GB of data, you should have about 3 GB of free space. Convert checks for this free space before running, and if there isn't enough, it won't convert the volume.

CAUTION

Conversion is one-way only. You can convert only from FAT or FAT32 to NTFS. You can't convert from NTFS to FAT or NTFS to FAT32 without deleting the volume and re-creating it using FAT or FAT32.

You run Convert at the command line. Its syntax is as follows:

```
convert volume /FS:NTFS
```

where *volume* is the drive letter followed by a colon, drive path, or volume name. So, for instance, if you want to convert the E drive to NTFS, type **convert e: /fs:ntfs**. This starts Convert. As shown in the following example, Convert checks the current file system type and then prompts you to enter the volume label for the drive:

```
The type of the file system is FAT32.
Enter current volume label for drive E:
```

Provided you enter the correct volume label, Convert will continue as shown in the following example:

```
Volume CORPDATA created 4/10/2008 3:15 PM
Volume Serial Number is AA6A-D44A
Windows is verifying files and folders...
File and folder verification is complete.
Windows has checked the file system and found no problems.
   91,827,680 KB total disk space.
   91,827,672 KB are available.

   8,192 bytes in each allocation unit.
   11,478,460 total allocation units on disk.
   11,478,459 allocation units available on disk.

Determining disk space required for file system conversion...
Total disk space:           91927860 KB
Free space on volume:       91929680 KB
Space required for conversion:     12080460 KB
Converting file system
Conversion complete
```

Here, Convert examines the file and folder structure and then determines how much disk space is needed for the conversion. If there is enough free space, Convert performs the conversion. Otherwise, it exits with an error, stating there isn't enough free space to complete the conversion.

Several additional parameters are available as well, including /v, which tells Convert to display detailed information during the conversion, and /x, which tells Convert to force the partition or volume to dismount before the conversation if necessary. You can't dismount a boot or system drive—these drives can be converted only when the system is restarted.

On converted boot and system volumes, Convert applies default security the same as that applied during Windows setup. On other volumes, Convert sets security so the Users group has access but doesn't give access to the special group Everyone. If you don't want security to be set, you can use the /Nosecurity parameter. This parameter tells Convert to remove all security attributes and make all files and directories on the disk accessible to the group Everyone. In addition, you can use the /Cvtarea parameter to set the name of a contiguous file in the root directory to be a placeholder for NTFS system files.

Chapter 14

Working with Removable Disks

Removable is the standard disk type associated with removable storage devices. Working with removable disks is similar to working with fixed disks. Removable storage devices can be formatted with exFAT, FAT16, FAT32, or NTFS. Both Windows Vista with SP1 or later and Windows Server 2008 support exFAT with removable storage devices as well.

The exFAT file system is the next generation file system in the FAT (FAT12/16, FAT32) family. Although retaining the ease-of-use advantages of FAT32, exFAT overcomes FAT32's 4-GB file size limit and FAT32's 32-GB partition size limit on Windows systems. exFAT also supports allocation unit sizes of up to 32,768 KB. exFAT is designed so that it can be used with and easily moved between any compliant operating system or device.

> **Note**
>
> Both Windows Vista and Windows Server 2008 support hot-pluggable media that use NTFS volumes. This new feature allows you to format USB flash devices and other similar media with NTFS.

Removable disks support network file and folder sharing. You configure sharing on removable disks in the same way as you configure standard file sharing. You can assign share permissions, configure caching options for offline file use, and limit the number of simultaneous users. You can share an entire removable disk as well as individual folders stored on the removable disk. You can also create multiple share instances.

Where removable disks differ from standard NTFS sharing is that there isn't necessarily an underlying security architecture. With exFAT, FAT, or FAT32, folders and files stored do not have any security permissions or features other than the basic read-only or hidden attribute flags that you can set.

Managing MBR Disk Partitions on Basic Disks

A disk using the MBR partition style can have up to four primary partitions and up to one extended partition. This allows you to configure MBR disks in one of two ways: using one to four primary partitions or using one to three primary partitions and one extended partition. After you partition a disk, you format the partitions to assign drive letters or mount points.

INSIDE OUT   **Drive letter assignment is initiated during installation**

The drive letters that are available depend on how a system is configured. The initial drive letters used by a computer are assigned during installation of the operating system. Setup does this by scanning all fixed hard disks as they are enumerated.

For MBR disks, Setup assigns a drive letter to the first primary partition starting with C. Setup then scans floppy/Zip disks and assigns drive letters starting with A. Afterward, Setup scans CD/DVD-ROM drives and assigns the next available letter starting with D. Finally, Setup scans all fixed hard disks and assigns drive letters to all remaining primary partitions.

With GPT disks, Setup assigns drive letters to all primary partitions on the GPT disk starting with C. Setup then scans floppy/Zip drives and assigns the next available drive letter starting with A. Finally, Setup scans CD/DVD-ROM drives and assigns the next available letter starting with D.

Creating Partitions and Simple Volumes

Windows Server 2008 simplifies the Disk Management user interface by using one set of dialog boxes and wizards for both partitions and volumes. The first three volumes on a basic drive are created automatically as primary partitions. If you try to create a fourth volume on a basic drive, the remaining free space on the drive is converted automatically to an extended partition with a logical drive of the size you designate by using the new volume feature it created in the extended partition. Any subsequent volumes are created in the extended partitions and logical drives automatically.

In Disk Management, you create partitions, logical drives, and simple volumes by following these steps:

1. In Disk Management's Graphical View, right-click an unallocated or free area on the disk and then choose New Simple Volume. This starts the New Simple Volume Wizard. Read the Welcome page and then click Next.

2. Click Next to display the Specify Volume Size page, as shown in Figure 14-5. Then use the Simple Volume Size In MB field to specify how much of the available disk space you want to use for the volume. Keep the following in mind before you set the size and click Next:

    ○ You can size a primary partition to fill an entire disk, or you can size it as appropriate for the system you're configuring. Because of the availability of FAT32 and NTFS, you no longer must worry about the 4-GB volume size and 2-GB file size limits that applied to 16-bit FAT systems. This allows you to size partitions as you see fit.

○ You can size extended partitions to fill any available unallocated space on a disk. Because an extended partition can contain multiple logical drives, each with their own file system, consider carefully how you might want to size logical drives before creating the extended partition. Additionally, if a drive already has an extended partition or is removable, you won't be able to create an extended partition.

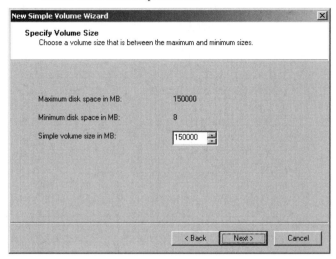

Figure 14-5 Size the partition appropriately.

3. If you are creating a primary partition, use the Assign Drive Letter Or Path page, as shown in Figure 14-6, to assign a drive letter or path. You can do one of the following:

○ Assign a drive letter by choosing Assign The Following Drive Letter and then selecting an available drive letter in the selection list provided. Generally, the drive letters E through Z are available for use (drive letters A and B are used with floppy/Zip drives, drive C is for the primary partition, and drive D is for the computer's CD/DVD-ROM drive).

○ Mount a path by choosing Mount In The Following Empty NTFS Folder and then typing the path to an existing folder. You can also click Browse to search for or create a folder.

○ Use Do Not Assign A Drive Letter Or Drive Path To if you want to create the partition without assigning a drive letter or path.

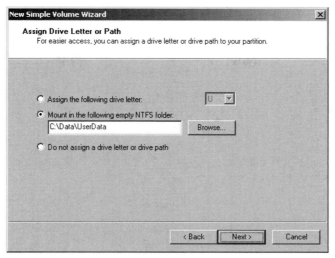

Figure 14-6 Specify how the partition should be used.

4. Using the Format Partition page, as shown in Figure 14-7, you can opt to not format the partition at this time or to select the formatting options to use. Formatting creates a file system in the new partition and permanently deletes any existing data. The formatting options are as follows:

  ○ File System sets the file system type as FAT, FAT32, or NTFS. FAT volumes can be up to 4 GB in size and have a maximum file size limit of 2 GB. FAT32 volumes can be up to 32 GB in size (a limitation of Windows Server 2008) and have a maximum file size of 4 GB. NTFS files and volumes can be up to 2 TB in size on MBR disks and up to 18 EB on GPT disks.

Choose the Partition Format with Care

If you don't know which file system to use, it is best in most cases to use NTFS. Only NTFS volumes can also use advanced file access permissions, compression, encryption, disk quotas, shadow copies, remote storage, and sparse files. There are exceptions, of course. If you want to be able to boot multiple operating systems, you might want to use FAT or FAT32. When a boot partition is formatted using FAT, you are able to boot to just about any operating system. When a boot partition is FAT32, you are able to boot to any version of the Windows operating system except Windows NT 4.0 and Windows 95 OSR1. Further, because FAT32 doesn't have the journaling overhead of NTFS, it is more efficient at handling large files that change frequently, and particularly files that have small incremental changes, such as log files. This means in some cases that FAT32 will read and write files faster than NTFS. However, if you use FAT32, you won't be able to use any of the advanced file system features of Windows Server 2008.

Chapter 14

○ Allocation Unit Size sets the cluster size for the file system. This is the basic unit in which disk space is allocated, and by default, it is based on the size of the volume.

Choosing an Allocation Unit Size

In most cases the default size is what is best but you can override this feature by setting a different value. If you use lots of small files, you might want to use a smaller cluster size, such as 512 or 1024 bytes. With these settings, small files use less disk space. Although sizes of up to 256 KB are allowed, you will not be able to use compression on NTFS if you use a size larger than 4 KB.

○ Volume Label sets a text label for the partition that is used as its volume name. If you must change a partition's volume label, you can do this from the command line by using the Label command or from Windows Explorer by right-clicking the volume, selecting Properties, and then typing a new label on the General tab.

○ Perform A Quick Format specifies that you want to format the partition without checking for errors. Although you can use this option to save you a few minutes, it's better to check for errors because this allows Disk Management to mark bad sectors on the disk and lock them out.

○ Enable File And Folder Compression turns on compression so that files and folders on this partition are compressed automatically. Compression is available only for NTFS. For more information about using compression, see "Using File-Based Compression" on page 521.

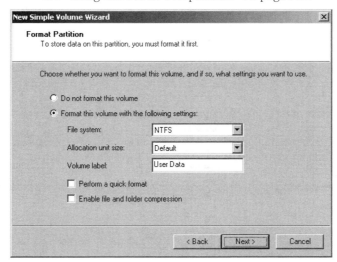

Figure 14-7 Format the partition now or opt to format the partition later.

5. Click Next. The final page shows you the options you've selected. If the options are correct, click Finish. The wizard then creates the partition and configures it.

Formatting a Partition, Logical Drive, or Volume

Before you can use a primary partition, logical drive, or volume, you must format it. Formatting creates the file structures necessary to work with files and folders. If you want to clean out a partition, logical drive, or volume and remove all existing data, you can use formatting to do this as well.

> **You Need Not Format If You Want to Convert to NTFS**
>
> Although you can use formatting to change the type of file system, you don't have to do this to change from FAT or FAT32 to NTFS. Instead, to convert to NTFS you can use the Convert command, which preserves any existing data. For more information about Convert, see "Converting FAT or FAT32 to NTFS" on page 432.

CAUTION

> A partition with unformatted space on a disk is listed with RAW as the file system type. A formatted partition is listed with its appropriate file system type, such as NTFS. If you reformat a formatted partition, you will destroy all data in the partition. A severely damaged file system might also show up as RAW. Don't reformat such a volume as you will lose any chance of recovering your data.

To format a primary partition, logical drive, or volume, follow these steps:

1. In Disk Management, right-click the primary partition, logical drive, or volume you want to format, and then choose Format. This displays the Format dialog box, as shown in Figure 14-8.

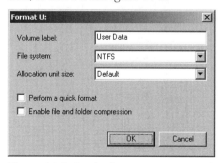

Figure 14-8 Set the formatting options, then click OK.

2. In the Volume Label box, type a descriptive label for the primary partition, logical drive, or volume. In most cases, you'll want to use a label that helps you and other administrators determine what type of data is stored in the partition or on the logical drive.

3. Select the file system type as FAT, FAT32, or NTFS. Keep in mind that only NTFS allows you to use the advanced file system features of Windows Server 2008, including advanced file access permissions, compression, encryption, disk quotas, shadow copies, remote storage, and sparse files.

4. Use the Allocation Unit Size field to specify the basic unit in which disk space should be allocated. In most cases the default size is what is best.

5. Select the Perform A Quick Format check box if you want to format the partition without checking for errors. Although this option can save you a few minutes, Disk Management won't mark bad sectors on the disk or lock them out, and this can lead to problems with data integrity later on.

6. If you want files and folders to be compressed automatically, select the Enable File And Folder Compression check box. Compression is available only for NTFS; you can learn more about compression in "Using File-Based Compression" on page 521.

7. Click OK to begin formatting using the specified options. When prompted to confirm, click OK again.

Configuring Drive Letters

Each primary partition, logical drive, or volume on a disk can have one drive letter and one or more drive paths associated with it. You can assign, change, or remove driver letters and mount points at any time without having to restart the computer. Windows Server 2008 also allows you to change the drive letter associated with CD/DVD-ROM drives. You cannot, however, change or remove the drive letter of a system volume, boot volume, or any volume that contains a paging file. Additionally, on GPT disks, you can assign drive letters only to primary partitions. You cannot assign driver letters to other types of partitions on GPT disks.

After you make a change, the new drive letter or mount point assignment is made automatically as long as the volume or partition is not in use. If the partition or volume is in use, Windows Server 2008 displays a warning. You must exit programs that are using the partition or volume and try again or allow Disk Management to force the change by clicking Yes when prompted.

To add, change, or remove a drive letter, right-click the primary partition, logical drive, or volume in Disk Management, and choose Change Drive Letter And Paths. This displays the dialog box shown in the following screen.

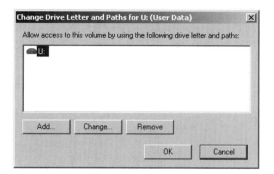

INSIDE OUT   Changing the drive letter of a system or boot volume

If you installed the operating system on a drive with an odd drive letter, such as F or H, it would seem that you are stuck with it, which might not be for the best if you really want the operating system to be on a different drive letter, such as C. Although Disk Management and DiskPart won't let you change the drive letter of a system volume, boot volume, or any volume that contains a paging file, there are workarounds. For volumes containing paging files, you must first move the paging file to a different volume, and then reboot the computer. You are then able to assign the volume a different drive letter—provided it isn't also a system or boot volume. To change the system or boot volume drive letter, you must edit the Registry using an account that is a member of the Administrators group. Don't do this without creating a full backup of the computer and its system state first.

Start Registry Editor by typing **regedit**, and then access the HKEY_LOCAL_MACHINE\SYSTEM\MountedDevices key. This key has value entries for each of the drive letters used on the computer. Find the value entry for the system or boot volume that you want to change. Right-click it, and choose Rename so that you can edit the name. Change the name of the value entry so that it points to the drive letter you want to use. If that drive letter is in use, you must rename two value entries. For example, if you want to rename D as C and C is already in use, you must rename C to an unused drive letter and then rename D as C. Make sure you edit the boot configuration data so the right disk is set for booting the operating system. Afterward, restart the computer.

Any current drive letter and mount points associated with the selected drive are displayed. You have the following options:

- **Add a drive letter** If the primary partition, logical drive, or volume doesn't yet have a drive letter assignment, you can add one by clicking Add. In the Add Drive Letter Or Path dialog box that appears, select the drive letter to use from the drop-down list, and then click OK.

- **Change an existing drive letter** If you want to change the drive letter, click Change, select the drive letter to use from the drop-down list, and then click OK. Confirm the action when prompted by clicking Yes.

- **Remove a drive letter** If you want to remove the drive letter, click Remove, and then confirm the action when prompted by clicking Yes.

> **Note**
> When you change or remove a drive letter, the volume or partition will no longer be accessible using the old drive letter, and this can cause programs using the volume to not work properly or can cause the partition to stop running.

Configuring Mount Points

Any volume or partition can be mounted to an empty NTFS folder as long as the folder is on a fixed disk drive rather than a removable media drive. A volume or partition mounted in such a way is called a *mount point*. Each volume or partition can have multiple mount points associated with it. For example, you could mount a volume to the root folder of the C drive as both C:\EngData and C:\DevData, giving the appearance that these are separate folders.

The real value of mount points, however, lies in how they allow you the capability to create the appearance of a single file system from multiple hard disk drives without having to use spanned volumes. Consider the following scenario: A department file server has four data drives—drive 1, drive 2, drive 3, and drive 4. Rather than mount the drives as D, E, F, and G, you decide it'd be easier for users to work with the drives if they were all mounted as folders of the system drive, C:\Data. You mount drive 1 to C:\Data\UserData, drive 2 to C:\Data\CorpData, drive 3 to C:\Data\Projects, and drive 4 to C:\Data\History. If you were then to share the C:\Data folder, users would be able to access all the drives using a single share.

> **Note**
> Wondering why I mounted the drives under C:\Data rather than C:\ as is recommended in some documentation? The primary reason I did this is to help safeguard system security. I didn't want users to have access to other directories, which includes the operating system directories, on the C drive.

To add or remove a mount point, right-click the volume or partition in Disk Management, and choose Change Drive Letter And Paths. This displays the Change Drive Letter And Paths dialog box (as shown in the following screen), which shows any current mount point and mount points associated with the selected drive.

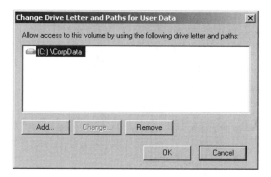

You now have the following options:

- **Add a mount point** Click Add, then in the Add Drive Letter Or Path dialog box, select Mount In The Following Empty NTFS Folder, as shown in the following screen. Type the path to an existing folder or click Browse to search for or create a folder. Click OK to mount the volume or partition.

- **Remove a mount point** If you want to remove a mount point, select the mount point, and then click Remove. When prompted to confirm the action, click Yes.

> Note
> You can't change a mount point assignment after making it. You can, however, simply remove the mount point you want to change and then add a new mount point so that the volume or partition is mounted as appropriate.

Extending Partitions

With Windows Server 2008, you can extend volumes on both basic and dynamic disks using either Disk Management or DiskPart. This is handy if you create a partition that's too small and you want to extend it so you have more space for programs and data. In extending a volume, you convert areas of unallocated space and add them to the existing volume. For spanned volumes on dynamic disks, the space can come from any available dynamic disk, not only those on which the volume was originally created.

Thus you can combine areas of free space on multiple dynamic disks and use those areas to increase the size of an existing volume.

Before you try to extend a volume, be aware of several limitations. First, you can extend simple and spanned volumes only if they are formatted and the file system is NTFS. You can't extend striped volumes. You can't extend volumes that aren't formatted or that are formatted with FAT or FAT32. You can extend NTFS volumes on basic disks but only by using DiskPart. If you try to use Disk Management to extend NTFS volumes on basic disks, Disk Management will display a warning that the Convert To Dynamic Disk Wizard will run first.

Using Disk Management, you can extend a simple or spanned volume by following these steps:

1. Open Disk Management. Right-click the volume that you want to extend and then select Extend Volume. This option is available only if the volume meets the previously discussed criteria and free space is available on one or more of the system's dynamic disks.

2. In the Extend Volume Wizard, read the introductory message and then click Next.

3. On the Select Disks page, shown in Figure 14-9, select the disk or disks from which you want to allocate free space. Any disks currently being used by the volume will automatically be selected. By default, all remaining free space on those disks will be selected for use.

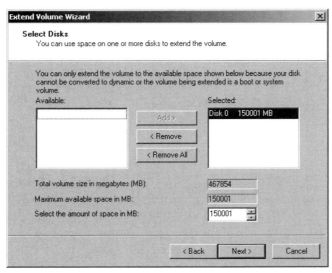

Figure 14-9 Specify the amount of space to add to the volume.

4. With dynamic disks, you can specify the additional space that you want to use on other disks. Select the disk and then click Add to add the disk to the Selected list box. In the Selected list box, select each disk that you want to use and in the Select The Amount Of Space In MB list box, specify the amount of unallocated space to use on the selected disk.

5. Click Next, confirm your options, and then click Finish.

By using DiskPart, you can extend partitions using the command line. To extend an NTFS-formatted partition, invoke DiskPart by typing **diskpart** at the command prompt. List the disks on the computer by typing **list disk**. After you check the free space of each disk, select the disk by typing **select disk N**, where *N* is the disk you want to work with. Next, list the partitions on the selected disk by typing **list partition**. Select the last partition in the list by typing **select partition N**, where *N* is the partition you want to work with.

Now that you've selected a partition, you can extend it. To extend the partition to the end of the disk, type **extend**. To extend the partition a set amount, type **extend size=N**, where *N* is the amount of space to add in megabytes. For example, if you want to add 1200 megabytes to the partition, type **extend size=1200**.

Listing 14-2 shows an actual DiskPart session in which a disk is extended. You can use this as an example to help you understand the process of extending disks. Here, disk 2 has 19 GB of free space, and its primary partition is extended so that it fills the disk.

Listing 14-2 Extending disks

```
C:\> diskpart

    Microsoft DiskPart version 5.2.3790
    Copyright (C) 1999-2001 Microsoft Corporation.
    On computer: CORPSVR02

    DISKPART> list disk

      Disk ###   Status     Size    Free   Dyn   Gpt
      --------   --------   -----   -----   ---   ---
      Disk 0     Online     56 GB   5 GB     *     *
      Disk 1     Online     29 GB   0 B
      Disk 2     Online     37 GB   19 GB

    DISKPART> select disk 2

    Disk 2 is now the selected disk.

    DISKPART> list partition

      Partition ###   Type      Size     Offset
      -------------   --------   -------   -------
      Partition 1     Primary    37 GB     32 KB

    DISKPART> select partition 1

    Partition 1 is now the selected partition.

    DISKPART> extend

    DiskPart successfully extended the partition.
```

```
DISKPART> exit

Leaving DiskPart...

C:\>
```

To extend a partition on a dynamic disk to free space on another disk, you use the syntax:

```
extend size=X disk=Y
```

where size=*X* sets the amount of space to use in megabytes and disk=*Y* sets the number of the disk from which to allocate the space. Following this, you could allocate 5000 MB of free space from disk 0 to the selected disk in the previous example (disk 2) using the following command:

```
extend size=5000 disk=0
```

Shrinking Partitions

With Windows Server 2008, you can shrink volumes on both basic and dynamic disks using either Disk Management or DiskPart. This is handy if you create a partition that's too large and you want to shrink it so you have more space for other partitions. In shrinking a volume, you convert areas of allocated but unused space to free space by removing them from an existing volume.

As with extending volumes, several limitations apply to shrinking volumes. First, you can shrink simple and spanned volumes only if they are formatted and the file system is NTFS. You can't shrink striped volumes. You can't shrink volumes that are formatted with FAT or FAT32. You can, however, shrink volumes that have not been formatted. If a volume is heavily fragmented, you may have to defragment the volume to free up additional space before shrinking.

Using Disk Management, you can shrink a simple or spanned volume by following these steps:

1. Open Disk Management. Right-click the volume that you want to shrink and then select Shrink Volume. This option is available only if the volume meets the previously discussed criteria.

2. In the field provided in the Shrink dialog box shown in Figure 14-10, enter the amount of space to shrink. The Shrink dialog box provides the following information:

   Total Size Before Shrink In MB Lists the total capacity of the volume in MB. This is the formatted size of the volume.

   Size Of Available Shrink Space In MB Lists the maximum amount by which the volume can be shrunk. This doesn't represent the total amount of free space on the volume; rather, it represents the amount of space that can be removed, not including any data reserved for the master file table, volume snapshots, page files, and temporary files.

Amount of Space To Shrink In MB Lists the total amount of space that will be removed from the volume. The initial value defaults to the maximum amount of space that can be removed from the volume. For optimal drive performance, you'll want to ensure that the drive has at least 10 percent of free space after the shrink operation.

Total Size After Shrink In MB Lists what the total capacity of the volume in MB will be after the shrink. This is the new formatted size of the volume.

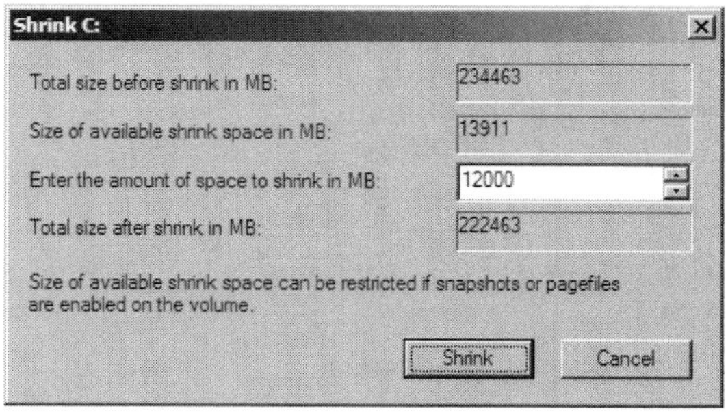

Figure 14-10 Specify the amount of space to shrink from the volume.

3. Click Shrink to shrink the volume.

By using DiskPart, you can shrink partitions using the command line. To shrink an NTFS-formatted partition, invoke DiskPart by typing **diskpart** at the command prompt. List the disks on the computer by typing **list disk**. After you check the free space of each disk, select the disk by typing **select disk N**, where N is the disk you want to work with. Next, list the partitions on the selected disk by typing **list partition**. Select the last partition in the list by typing **select partition N**, where N is the partition you want to work with.

Now that you've selected a partition, you can shrink it. To determine the maximum amount of space by which you can shrink the disk, type **shrink querymax**. To shrink the partition the maximum amount, type **shrink**. To shrink the partition a set amount, type **shrink desired=N**, where N is the amount of space to remove in megabytes. For example, if you want to remove 2000 megabytes from the partition, type **shrink desired=2000**.

Listing 14-3 shows an actual DiskPart session in which you shrink a disk. You can use this as an example to help you understand the process of shrinking disks. Here you determine that there are 4 GB of space available for shrinking on the selected partition and then shrink the partition by 3 GB.

Listing 14-3 Shrinking disks

```
C:\> diskpart

    Microsoft DiskPart version 5.2.3790
    Copyright (C) 1999-2001 Microsoft Corporation.
    On computer: CORPSVR02
```

```
DISKPART> list disk

  Disk ###   Status    Size    Free    Dyn    Gpt
  --------   --------  -----   -----   ---    ---
  Disk 0     Online    56 GB   5 GB     *      *
  Disk 1     Online    29 GB   0 B
  Disk 2     Online    37 GB   19 GB

DISKPART> select disk 2

Disk 2 is now the selected disk.

DISKPART> list partition

  Partition ###   Type        Size     Offset
  -------------   ---------   -------   -------
  Partition 1     Primary     37 GB     32 KB

DISKPART> select partition 1

Partition 1 is now the selected partition.

DISKPART> shrink querymax

The maximum number of reclaimable bytes is: 4 GB

DISKPART> shrink desired=3000

DiskPart successfully shrunk the partition by: 3000 MB

DISKPART> exit

Leaving DiskPart...

C:\>
```

Deleting a Partition, Logical Drive, or Volume

Deleting a partition, logical drive, or volume removes the associated file system and all associated data. When you delete a logical drive, the logical drive is removed from the associated extended partition and its space is marked as free. When you delete a partition or volume, the entire partition or volume is deleted and its space is marked as Unallocated. If you want to delete an extended partition that contains logical drives, however, you must delete the logical drives before trying to delete the extended partition.

In Disk Management, you can delete a partition, logical drive, or volume by right-clicking it and then choosing Delete Partition, Delete Logical Drive, or Delete Volume, as appropriate. When prompted to confirm the action, click Yes.

Managing GPT Disk Partitions on Basic Disks

GPT disks can have the following types of partitions:

- ESP
- MSR partition
- Primary partition
- Logical Disk Manager (LDM) Metadata partition
- LDM Data partition
- OEM or Unknown partition

Each of these partition types is used and managed in different ways.

ESP

An Itanium-based computer must have one GPT disk that contains an ESP. This partition is similar to the system volume on an *x86*-based computer in that it contains the files that are required to start the operating system. Windows Server 2008 creates the ESP during setup and formats it by using FAT. The partition is sized so that it is at least 100 MB in size or 1 percent of the disk up to a maximum size of 1000 MB.

The ESP is shown in Disk Management but isn't assigned a drive letter or mount point. All Disk Management commands associated with the ESP are disabled, however, and you cannot store data on it, assign a drive letter to it, or delete it by using Disk Management or DiskPart. The ESP has several directories that contain the operating system boot loader, such as Ia64ldr.efi, and other files that are necessary to start the operating system as well as utilities such as Diskpart.efi and Nvrboot.efi. Other directories are created as necessary by the operating system.

The only way to access these directories is to use the EFI firmware's Boot Manager or the MountVol command. If you access the ESP, don't make changes, additions, or deletions unless you've been specifically directed to by a Microsoft Knowledge Base article or other official documentation by an OEM vendor. Any changes you make could prevent the system from starting.

INSIDE OUT

You can create an ESP if necessary— but do so only if directed to

Although the ESP is normally created for you automatically when you install Windows Server 2008, there are some limited instances when you might be directed to create an ESP after installing an additional GPT disk on a server, such as when you want to use the new disk as a boot device rather than the existing boot device. You can create the necessary ESP by using DiskPart. Select the disk you want to work with, and then type the following command: **create partition efi size=N**, where N is at least 100 MB or 1 percent of the disk, up to a maximum size of 1000 MB. After you create the partition, follow the vendor-directed or Microsoft-directed guidelines for preparing the partition for use. Never create an ESP unless you are directed to do so, however. One instance in which you must create an ESP is when you want to establish and boot to mirrored GPT disks. Here, you must prepare the second disk of the mirror so that it can be booted, and you do this by creating the necessary ESP and MSR partition.

MSR Partitions

An Itanium-based computer must have an MSR partition on every GPT disk. The MSR partition contains additional space that might be needed by the operating system to store metadata. For example, when you convert a basic GPT disk to a dynamic GPT disk, the Windows operating system takes 1 MB of the MSR partition space and uses it to create the LDM Metadata partition, which is required for the conversion.

The MSR partition is not shown in Disk Management and does not receive a drive letter or mount point. The Windows operating system creates the MSR partition automatically. For the boot disk, it is created along with the ESP when you install the operating system. An MSR partition is also created automatically when a disk is converted from MBR to GPT and any time you access a GPT disk that doesn't already have an MSR partition in Disk Management or DiskPart.

If a GPT disk contains an ESP as the first partition on the disk, the MSR partition is usually the second partition on the disk. If a GPT disk does not contain an ESP, then the MSR partition is typically the first partition on the disk. However, if a disk already has a primary partition at the beginning of the disk, the MSR partition is placed at the end of the disk.

The MSR partition is sized according to the size of the associated disk. For disks up to 16 GB in size, it normally is 32 MB in size. For all other disks, it normally is 128 MB in size.

INSIDE OUT   **You can create an MSR partition if necessary—
but do so only if directed to**

The MSR partition is normally created for you automatically when you install Windows
Server 2008. It can also be created automatically when you access a secondary GPT
disk that doesn't already have an MSR partition in Disk Management or DiskPart. You
shouldn't attempt to create a Microsoft Reserved partition unless you are directed to by
vendor-specific or Microsoft-specific documentation. In this case, you can use DiskPart to
create the partition. Select the disk you want to work with, and then type the following
command: **create partition msr size=N**, where N is 32 for disks up to 16 GB in size and
128 for all other disks.

Primary Partitions

You create primary partitions on basic disks to store data. GPT disks support up to
128 partitions, which can be a mix of required and optional partitions. Every primary
partition you create appears in the GPT partition array. If you convert a basic disk that
contains primary partitions to a dynamic disk, the primary partitions become simple
volumes, and information about them is then stored in the dynamic disk database and
not in the GUID partition array.

To create a primary partition, complete the following steps:

1. In Disk Management Graphical View, right-click an area marked Unallocated on
    a basic disk, and then choose New Simple Volume. This starts the New Simple
    Volume Wizard. Click Next.

2. The partition is created as a primary partition automatically. Use the Assign Drive
    Letter Or Path page to assign a drive letter or path. You can also choose Do Not
    Assign A Drive Letter Or Drive Path if you want to create the partition without
    assigning a drive letter or path. Click Next.

3. Use the Format Partition page to set the formatting options. If you opt not to
    format the partition at this time, you can format the partition later as discussed in
    "Formatting a Partition, Logical Drive, or Volume" on page 439.

4. Click Next. The final page shows you the options you've selected. If the options
    are correct, click Finish. The wizard then creates the partition and configures it.

LDM Metadata and LDM Data Partitions

Windows Server 2008 creates LDM Metadata and LDM Data partitions when you convert a basic GPT disk to a dynamic GPT disk. The LDM Metadata partition is 1 MB in
size and is used to store the partitioning information needed for the conversion. The
LDM Data partition is the partition in which the actual dynamic volumes are created.

The LDM Data partition is used to represent sections of unallocated space on the converted disk as well as sections that had basic partitions that are now dynamic volumes. For example, if a disk had a primary boot partition that spanned the whole disk, the converted disk will have a single LDM Data partition. If a disk had a boot partition and other primary partitions, it will have two LDM Data partitions after the conversion: one for the boot volume, and one for all the rest of the partitions. Although the LDM Metadata and LDM Data partitions are not shown in Disk Management and do not receive drive letters or mount points, you are able to use this space by creating primary partitions as discussed in the previous section.

OEM or Unknown Partitions

GPT disks can have partitions that are specific to OEM implementations, and your vendor documentation should describe what they are used for. The Windows operating system displays these partitions in Disk Management as Healthy (Unknown Partition). You cannot, however, manipulate these partitions in Disk Management or DiskPart. Additionally, if an unknown partition lies between two known partitions on a GPT disk, you won't be able to convert the disk from the basic disk type to the dynamic disk type.

Managing Volumes on Dynamic Disks

Any disk using the MBR or GPT partition style can be configured as a dynamic disk. Unlike basic disks, which have basic volumes that can be created as primary partitions, extended partitions, and logical drives, dynamic disks have dynamic volumes that can be created as the following types:

- **Simple volumes** A simple volume is a volume that's on a single drive and has the same purpose as a primary partition. The space allocated for such a volume would be contiguous.

- **Spanned volumes** A spanned volume is a volume that spans multiple drives or can be on a single drive without needing to be contiguous.

- **Striped volumes** A striped volume is a volume that uses RAID 0 to combine multiple disks into a stripe set.

- **Mirrored volumes** A mirrored volume is a volume that uses RAID 1 to mirror a primary disk onto a secondary disk that is available for disaster recovery.

- **RAID-5 volumes** A RAID-5 volume is a volume that uses RAID 5 to create a fault-tolerant striped set on three or more disks.

Techniques for creating and managing these volume types are discussed in the sections that follow.

Creating a Simple or Spanned Volume

You create simple and spanned volumes in much the same way. The differences between these volume types are subtle:

- A simple volume uses free space from a single disk to create a volume. Windows is able to write to the selected disk until there is no more free space available within the volume.

- A spanned volume is used to combine the disk space on multiple disks to create the appearance of a single volume. Windows always writes to the first disk in the spanned set first and then when this disk fills, Windows writes to the second disk, and so on.

If you later need more space, you can extend a simple or spanned volume type by using Disk Management. Here, you select an area of free space on any available disk and add it to the volume. When you extend a simple volume onto other disks, it becomes a spanned volume. Any volume that you want to extend should be formatted using NTFS because only NTFS volumes can be extended.

Simple and spanned volumes aren't fault tolerant. If you create a volume that spans disks and one of those disks fails, you won't be able to access the volume. Any data on the volume will be lost. You must restore the data from backup after you replace the failed drive and re-create the volume.

To create a simple or spanned volume, complete the following steps:

1. In Disk Management Graphical View, right-click an area marked Unallocated on a dynamic disk, and then choose New Simple Volume or New Spanned Volume as appropriate. Read the Welcome page and then click Next.

2. If you select New Spanned Volume, you next see the Select Disks page shown in Figure 14-11. Use this page to select disks that should be part of the volume and to size the volume segments on the designated disks. Select one or more disks from the list of disks that are available and have unallocated space. Click Add to add the disk or disks to the Selected list box. Next, select each of the disks in turn, then specify the amount of space you want to use on the selected disk. Click Next when you are ready to continue.

> **Note**
>
> If you started with a dynamic disk, the wizard shows both basic and dynamic disks with available disk space. If you add space from a basic disk that is not a system or boot volume, the wizard will attempt to convert the disk to a dynamic disk before creating the volume set. Before clicking Yes to continue, make sure you really want to do this, as this can affect how the disk is used by the operating system.

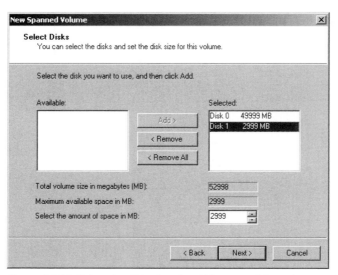

Figure 14-11 Select the disks that should be part of the volume, and then specify how much space to use on each disk.

3. Use the Assign Drive Letter Or Path page to assign a drive letter or path. You can also choose Do Not Assign A Drive Letter Or Drive Path if you want to create the partition without assigning a drive letter or path. Click Next.

4. Use the Format Volume page, as shown in Figure 14-12, to set the formatting options. Simple and spanned volumes can be formatted by using FAT, FAT32, or NTFS. If you think you might need to extend the volume at a later date, you might want to use NTFS because only volumes using NTFS can be extended. If you opt not to format the partition at this time you can format the partition later as discussed in "Formatting a Partition, Logical Drive, or Volume" on page 439.

5. Click Next. The final page shows you the options you've selected. If the options are correct, click Finish. The wizard then creates the volume and configures it.

Configuring RAID 0: Striping

RAID level 0 is disk striping. With disk striping, two or more volumes—each on a separate drive—are configured as a striped set. Unlike spanning, Windows breaks the data to be written into blocks called stripes and then writes the stripes sequentially to all disks in the set. So if there are three disks in the set, Windows writes part of the data to the first disk, part of the data to the second disk, and part of the data to the third disk—this process of alternating between the disks is called striping.

Although the boot and system volumes shouldn't be part of a striped set, you can place volumes for a striped set on up to 32 drives, but in most circumstances sets with 2 to 5 volumes offer the best performance improvements. When 3 to 32 drives are used, the major advantage of disk striping is speed. Data can be accessed on multiple disks using multiple drive heads, which improves performance considerably. When you try to use more than 32 drives, the performance improvement decreases significantly.

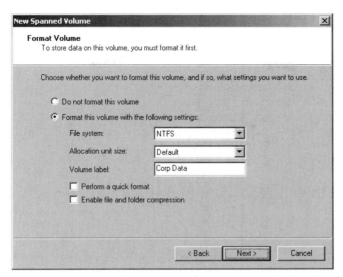

Figure 14-12 Format the volume preferably by using NTFS so that it can be expanded if necessary.

When you create striped sets, you'll want to use volumes that are approximately the same size. Disk Management bases the overall size of the striped set on the smallest volume size. Specifically, the maximum size of the striped set is a multiple of the smallest volume size. For example, if the smallest volume is 1 GB, the maximum size for a three-disk striped set is 3 GB.

You can maximize performance using disks that are on separate disk controllers. This allows the system to simultaneously access the drives. Keep in mind that this configuration offers no fault tolerance. If any hard disk drive in the striped set fails, the striped set can no longer be used, which essentially means that all data in the striped set is lost. You'll need to re-create the striped set and restore the data from backups. Data backup and recovery is discussed in Chapter 41, "Backup and Recovery."

You can create a striped set by following these steps:

1. In the Disk Management Graphical View, right-click an area marked Unallocated on a dynamic disk and then choose New Striped Volume. This starts the New Striped Volume Wizard. Read the Welcome page, and then click Next.

2. Create the volume as described previously in "Creating a Simple or Spanned Volume" on page 453. The key difference is that you need at least two dynamic disks to create a striped volume.

   After you create a striped volume, you can use the volume just like any other volume. You can't extend a striped set after it's created. Therefore, you should carefully consider the setup before you implement it.

Recovering a Failed Simple, Spanned, or Striped Disk

Simple disks are the easiest to troubleshoot and recover because there is only one disk involved. Spanned or striped disks, on the other hand, have multiple disks and the failure of any one disk makes the entire volume unusable. The drive status might show it is Missing, Failed, Online (Errors), Offline, or Unreadable.

The Missing (and sometimes Offline) status usually happens if drives have been disconnected or powered off. If the drives are part of an external storage device, check the storage device to ensure that it is connected properly and has power. Reconnecting the storage device or turning on the power should make it so the drives can be accessed. You then must start Disk Management and rescan the disks by selecting Rescan Disks from the Action menu. When Disk Management finishes, right-click the drive that was missing, and then choose Reactivate.

The Failed, Online (Errors), and Unreadable statuses indicate input/output (I/O) problems with the drive. As before, try rescanning the drive, and then try to reactivate the drive. If the drive doesn't come back to the Healthy state, you might need to replace it.

Moving Dynamic Disks

One of the advantages of dynamic disks over basic disks is that you can easily move them from one computer to another. For example, if after setting up a server, you decide that you don't really need its two additional hard disk drives, you could move them to another server where they could be better used. Before you move disks, you should access Disk Management on the server where the dynamic disks are currently installed and check their status. The status should be Healthy. If it isn't, you should fix any problems before moving the disks.

Moving System Disks Requires Additional Planning

Before you move a system disk from one computer to another, you must ensure that the computers have identically configured hard disk subsystems. If they don't, the Plug and Play ID on the system disk from the original computer won't match what the new computer is expecting. As a result, the new computer won't be able to load the right drivers and boot will fail.

You cannot move drives with BitLocker Drive Encryption using this technique. BitLocker Driver Encryption wraps drives in a protected seal so that any offline tampering is detected and results in the disk being unavailable until an administrator unlocks it. Before you can move a BitLocker encrypted drive, you must remove BitLocker Drive Encryption.

Next check to see whether any dynamic disks that you want to move are part of a spanned, extended, mirrored, striped, or RAID-5 set. If they are, you should make a note of which disks are part of which set and plan on moving all disks in a set together. If you are moving only part of a disk set, you should be aware of the consequences. For spanned, extended, or striped volumes, moving only part of the set will make the related volumes unusable on the current computer and on the computer to which you are planning to move the disks. If you plan to move only one disk of a mirrored volume, you should break the mirror before you move it. This ensures that you can keep using the disks on both computers. For RAID-5 volumes, you should move all of the disks in the set if possible. If you move only part of the RAID-5 set, you might find that you can't use the set on either computer.

To move the disks, start Computer Management and then in the left pane, select Device Manager. In the device list, expand Disk Drives. This shows a list of all the physical disk drives on the computer. Right-click each disk that you want to move, and then select Uninstall. If you are unsure which disks to uninstall, right-click each disk and select Properties. In the Properties dialog box, select the Volumes tab, and then choose Populate. This shows you the volumes on the selected disk. In Computer Management, select Disk Management. Right-click each disk that you want to move, and then select Remove Disk.

After you perform these procedures, you can move the dynamic disks. If the disks are hot swappable and this feature is supported on both computers, remove the disks from the original computer and then install them on the destination computer. Otherwise, turn off both computers, remove the drives from the original computer, and then install them on the destination computer. When you're finished, restart the computers. On the destination computer, access Disk Management, and then select Rescan Disks from the Action menu. When Disk Management finishes scanning the disks, right-click any disk marked Foreign, and click Import. You should now be able to access the disks and their volumes on the destination computer.

> **Note**
>
> When you move dynamic disks, the volumes on those disks should retain the drive letters they had on the previous computer. If a drive letter is already used on the destination computer, a volume receives the next available drive letter. If a dynamic volume previously did not have a drive letter, it does not receive a drive letter when moved to another computer. Additionally, if automounting is disabled, the volumes aren't automatically mounted and you must manually mount volumes and assign drive letters.

Configuring RAID 1: Disk Mirroring

For RAID 1, disk mirroring, you configure two volumes on two drives identically. Data is written to both drives. If one drive fails, there is no data loss because the other drive contains the data. After you repair or replace the failed drive, you can restore full mirroring so that the volume is once again fault tolerant.

By using disk mirroring, you gain the advantage of redundancy. Because disk mirroring doesn't write parity information, mirrored volumes can usually offer better write performance than disk striping with parity. The key drawback, however, is that disk mirroring has a 50 percent overhead, meaning it effectively cuts the amount of storage space in half. For example, to mirror a 60-GB drive, you need another 60-GB drive. That means you use 120 GB of space to store 60 GB of information.

As with disk striping, you'll often want the mirrored disks to be on separate disk controllers. This provides redundancy for the disk controllers. If one of the disk controllers fails, the disk on the other controller is still available. When you use two separate disk controllers to duplicate data, you're using a technique known as *disk duplexing* rather than disk mirroring–but why mince words?

You can create a mirrored set either by using two new disks or by adding a mirror to an existing volume. As with other RAID techniques, mirroring is transparent to users. Users see the mirrored set as a single volume that they can access and use like any other drive.

Creating a Mirrored Set Using Two New Disks

To create a mirrored set using two new disks, start Disk Management. In Graphical View, right-click an area marked Unallocated on a dynamic disk, and then choose New Mirrored Volume. This starts the New Mirrored Volume Wizard. Click Next. Create the volume as described in "Creating a Simple or Spanned Volume" on page 453. The key difference is that you must create two identically sized volumes and these volumes must be on separate dynamic drives. The volumes can be formatted as FAT, FAT32, or NTFS. You won't be able to continue past the Selected Disks page until you've selected the two disks that you want to work with.

When you click Finish, you'll return to the main Disk Management window, and Disk Management will create the mirrored set. During the creation of the mirror, you'll see a status of Resynching. This tells you that Disk Management is creating the mirror. When this process finishes, you'll have two identical volumes. Both volumes will show the same drive letter in Disk Management, but the separation of volumes is transparent to users. Users see the mirror set as a single volume. The volume status should be listed as Healthy. This is the normal status for volumes. If the status changes, you might need to repair or resync the mirrored set, as discussed in "Resolving Problems with Mirrored Sets" on page 464.

Adding a Mirror to an Existing Volume

You can also use an existing volume to create a mirrored set. For this to work, the volume you want to mirror must be a simple volume and you must have an area of unallocated space on a second dynamic drive of equal or larger space than the existing volume. When you add a mirror onto this unallocated space, Disk Management creates a volume that is the same size and file system type as the simple volume you are mirroring. It then copies the data from the simple volume to the new volume using a process called resynching.

To add a mirror to an existing volume, start Disk Management. In Graphical View, right-click the simple volume you want to mirror, and then select Add Mirror. This displays the Add Mirror dialog box. Use the Disks list to select a location for the mirror, and then click Add Mirror. Windows Server 2008 begins the mirror creation process, and you'll see a status of Resynching on both volumes.

When the resynching is complete, you have two identical copies of the original volume. Although both volumes show the same drive letter in Disk Management, the separation of volumes is transparent to users. Users see the mirror set as a single volume.

Mirroring Boot and System Volumes

Disk mirroring is often used to mirror boot and system volumes. Mirroring these volumes ensures that you'll be able to boot the server in case of a single drive failure.

Mirroring Boot and System Volumes on MBR Disks

When you want to mirror boot or system volumes on MBR disks, the process is fairly straightforward. You start with two disks, which I'll call Disk 0 and Disk 1, where Disk 0 has the system files and Disk 1 is a new disk. The system disk is typically a basic disk that must be upgraded to a dynamic disk before you can mirror it—mirroring is only possible on dynamic disks.

To begin, upgrade Disk 0 to a dynamic disk and then upgrade Disk 1 as discussed in "Using and Converting Basic and Dynamic Disks" on page 430. In Disk Management, right-click the boot or system volume that you want to mirror, and then select Add Mirror. This displays the Add Mirror dialog box. Select the disk onto which you want to add the mirror (Disk 1 in the example), and then click Add Mirror. Windows Server 2008 begins the mirror creation process, and you'll see a status of Resynching on both volumes. When the resynching is complete, the status should change to Healthy.

During the creation of the mirror, the operating system should add an entry to the system's Boot Manager that allows you to boot to the secondary mirror. Resolving a primary mirror failure is much easier with this entry in the Boot Manager file than without it because all you need to do is select the entry to boot to the secondary mirror. If you mirror the boot volume and a secondary mirror entry is not created for you, you could modify the boot entries in the Boot Manager to create one using the BCD Editor (bcdedit.exe).

If a system fails to boot to the primary system volume, restart the system and select the Boot Mirror - Secondary Plex option for the operating system you want to start. The system should start up normally. After you successfully boot the system to the secondary drive, you can schedule the maintenance necessary to rebuild the mirror if desired.

Mirroring Boot and System Volumes on GPT Disks

Mirroring boot and system volumes on GPT disks isn't the same as for MBR disks. Primarily, this is because GPT disks used to boot the operating system have an ESP and an MSR partition that must be created on the disk in a certain order. Thus, to mirror boot and system volumes on GPT disks, you must create the necessary partitions on the second disk of the mirrored set and tell the operating system that these partitions can be used for booting.

> **Note**
> As stated previously, not all computers are capable of booting to GPT disks. Only computers with EFI can boot to GPT disks.

To get started, you need two disks that use the GPT partition style and the basic storage type. One of the disks should already be designated as the boot volume. I'll refer to this volume as Disk 0. The other disk should be identical in size or larger than the boot volume. I'll refer to this volume as Disk 1. Disk 1 should be a clean disk, meaning it can't already have partitions on it; so, if necessary, copy any data on the disk to another disk or make a backup of the data and then delete any existing partitions. You can use Disk-Part to do this by completing the following steps:

1. At the command prompt, invoke DiskPart by typing **diskpart**. List the disks available on the system by typing **list disk**.

2. Select the disk you are going to use as the secondary boot disk. Following the example, this is Disk 1, so you would type **select disk 1**.

3. List the partitions on this disk by typing **list partition**.

4. If there are any existing partitions, select and delete each partition in turn. For example, if the disk had Partition 1, you'd type **select partition 1**, and then type **delete partition override**. The Override parameter ensures that you can delete nonuser partitions.

After you've made sure the second disk doesn't contain any partitions, list the available disks again by typing **list disk**, then select the disk you are going to use as the current boot disk. Following the example, this is Disk 0, so you would type **select disk 0**. List the partitions on this disk by typing **list partition**. The output you'll see will be similar to the following:

```
Partition ###   Type            Size        Offset
-------------   -------------------------   -------
Partition 1     System          316 MB      32 KB
Partition 2     Primary         9992 MB     312 MB
Partition 3     Reserved        32 MB       9 GB
```

The output shows you which partitions are being used as the ESP and MSR partitions. The ESP is listed with the partition type System. The MSR partition is listed with the partition type Reserved. Note the size of each partition. Here, System is 316 MB and Reserved is 32 MB.

You now must create the ESP and the MSR partition on the second disk by completing the following steps:

1. In DiskPart, select this disk to give it focus. Following the example, you'd type **select disk 1**.

2. Afterward, you would create the ESP first by typing **create partition efi size=N**, where *N* is the size previously noted, such as **size=316**.

> **Note**
> The target disk must still be basic at this point. If you already converted the disk to dynamic, then steps 2 and 3 will result in errors.

3. Create the MSR partition by typing **create partition msr size=N**, where *N* is the size previously noted, such as **size=32**.

4. If you type **list partition**, you should see that both partitions have been created and are sized appropriately, such as follows:

```
Partition ###    Type                    Size       Offset
-------------    --------------------    --------   -------
Partition 1      System                  316 MB     32 KB
Partition 2      Reserved                32 MB      316 MB
```

Next you must prepare the ESP for use by assigning it a drive letter, formatting it, and copying over the necessary startup files from the current boot volume. To do this, follow these steps:

1. In DiskPart, select the partition by typing **select partition 1**.

2. Assign a drive letter by typing **assign letter=X**, where *X* is the drive letter, such as **letter=H**.

3. Format the ESP as FAT. Following the example, you'd type **format /fs=fat quick**.

4. After formatting is complete, select the current boot volume. Following the example, you'd type **select disk 0**.

5. Type **select partition 1** to select the ESP on the current boot volume.

6. Assign this partition a drive letter by typing **assign letter=X**, where *X* is the drive letter to assign, such as **letter=I**.

7. Exit DiskPart by typing **exit**.

8. Use the Xcopy command to copy all the files from the ESP on the current boot volume to the ESP on the second disk. Following the example, you'd type **xcopy i:*.* h: /s /h**. The /s and /h parameters ensure that hidden system files are copied.

You now must convert both drives to the dynamic storage type. Start with the second disk and then convert the current boot disk. Follow these steps:

1. Invoke DiskPart by typing **diskpart**.

2. Select the disk you are going to use as the secondary boot disk. Following the example, this is Disk 1, so you would type **select disk 1**.

3. Convert the disk by typing **convert dynamic**.

4. Select the current boot disk. Following the example, this is Disk 0, so you would type **select disk 0**.

5. Convert the disk by typing **convert dynamic**.

6. Exit DiskPart by typing **exit**.

7. You must shut down and restart the computer to complete the conversion process for the current boot disk. In some cases, this process takes several reboots to complete.

Chapter 14

> **Note**
>
> You don't have to delete the drive letters assigned in the previous procedure. These drive letters will not be reassigned after the restart.

When the conversion process is complete, log on to the system, and then follow these steps to mirror the boot drive:

1. Invoke DiskPart by typing **diskpart**.

2. Select the current boot disk. Following the example, this is Disk 0, so you would type **select disk 0**.

3. Add the disk to use as the second drive to this volume to create the mirrored set. Following the example, you'd type **add disk=1**.

   DiskPart will then begin the mirror creation process by synchronizing the data on both volumes.

During the creation of the mirror, the operating system should add an entry to the system's Boot Manager that allows you to boot to the secondary mirror. Resolving a primary mirror failure is much easier with this entry in the Boot Manager file than without it because all you need to do is select the entry to boot to the secondary mirror. If you mirror the boot volume and a secondary mirror entry is not created for you, you could modify the boot entries in the Boot Manager to create one using the BCD Editor (bcdedit.exe).

If a system fails to boot to the primary system volume, restart the system and select the Boot Mirror - Secondary Plex option for the operating system you want to start. The system should start up normally. After you successfully boot the system to the secondary drive, you can schedule the maintenance necessary to rebuild the mirror if desired.

Now if you shut down the system and restart, you should be able to boot successfully to either the primary or secondary boot disk.

Configuring RAID 5: Disk Striping with Parity

RAID 5, disk striping with parity, offers fault tolerance with less overhead and better read performance than disk mirroring. To configure RAID 5, you use three or more volumes, each on a separate drive, as a striped set, similar to RAID 0. Unlike RAID 0, however, RAID 5 adds parity error checking to ensure that the failure of a single drive won't bring down the entire drive set. In the event of a single drive failure, the set continues to function with disk operations directed at the remaining disks in the set. The parity information can also be used to recover the data using a process called regeneration.

RAID 5 works like this: Each time the operating system writes to a RAID-5 volume, the data is written across all the disks in the set. Parity information for the data, used for error checking and correction, is written to disk as well, but always on a separate disk from the one used to write the data. For example, if you are using a three-volume

RAID-5 set and save a file, the individual data bytes of the file are written to each of the disks in the set. Parity information is written as well, but not to the same disk as one of the individual data bytes. Thus, a disk in the set could have a chunk of the data or the corresponding parity information, but not both, and this in turn means that the loss of one disk from the set doesn't cause the entire set to fail.

Like any type of RAID, RAID 5 has its drawbacks as well. First, if multiple drives in the set fail, the entire set will fail and you won't be able to regenerate the set from the parity information. Why? If multiple drives fail, there won't be enough parity information to use to recover the set. Second, having to generate and write parity information every time data is written to disk slows down the write process (and, in the case of software RAID, processing power). To compensate for the performance hit, hardware RAID controllers have their own processors that handle the necessary processing—and this is why hardware RAID is preferred over software RAID.

Okay, so RAID 5 gives you fault tolerance at some cost to performance. It does, however, have less overhead than RAID 1. By using RAID 1, you have a 50 percent overhead, which effectively cuts the amount of storage space in half. By using RAID 5, the overhead depends on the number of disks in the RAID set. With three disks, the overhead is about one-third. If you had three 60-GB drives using RAID 5, you'd use 180 GB of space to store about 120 GB of information. If you have additional disks, the overhead is reduced incrementally, but not significantly.

To create a RAID-5 set, start Disk Management. In Graphical View, right-click an area marked Unallocated on a dynamic disk, and then choose New RAID-5 Volume. This starts the New RAID-5 Volume Wizard. Click Next. Create the volume as described in "Creating a Simple or Spanned Volume" on page 453. The key difference is that you must select free space on three or more separate dynamic drives.

When you click Finish, you'll return to the main Disk Management window and Disk Management will create the RAID-5 set. During the creation of the mirror, you'll see a status of Resynching. This tells you that Disk Management is creating the RAID-5 set. When this process finishes, you'll have three or more identical volumes, all of which will show the same drive letter in Disk Management. Users, however, will see the RAID-5 set as a single volume. The volume status should be listed as Healthy. This is the normal status for volumes. If the status changes, you might need to repair or regenerate the RAID-5 set as discussed in "Resolving Problems with RAID-5 Sets" on page 463.

Breaking or Removing a Mirrored Set

Windows Server 2008 provides two ways to stop mirroring. You can break a mirrored set, creating two separate but identical volumes. Or you can remove a mirror, which deletes all the data on the removed mirror.

To break a mirrored set, follow these steps:

1. In Disk Management, right-click one of the volumes in the mirrored set, and then choose Break Mirrored Volume.

2. Confirm that you want to break the mirrored set by clicking Yes. If the volume is currently in use, you'll see another warning dialog box. Confirm that it's okay to continue by clicking Yes.

   Windows Server 2008 will then break the mirrored set, creating two independent volumes.

To remove a mirror, follow these steps:

1. In Disk Management, right-click one of the volumes in the mirrored set, and then choose Remove Mirror. This displays the Remove Mirror dialog box.

2. In the Remove Mirror dialog box, select the disk from which to remove the mirror. If the mirror contains a boot or system volume, you should remove the mirror from the secondary drive rather than the primary. For example, if Drive 0 and Drive 1 are mirrored, remove Drive 1 rather than Drive 0.

3. Confirm the action when prompted. All data on the removed mirror is deleted.

Resolving Problems with Mirrored Sets

Occasionally, data on mirrored volumes can get out of sync. Typically, this happens if one of the drives in the set goes offline or experiences temporary I/O problems and, as a result, data can be written only to the drive that's online. To reestablish mirroring, you must get both drives online and then resynchronize the mirror, but you should rebuild the set using disks with the same partition style—either MBR or GPT. The corrective action you take depends on the drive status.

> **Note**
>
> When mirroring boot volumes, Windows requires you to use the same partition style. With data volumes, you can mirror between GPT and MBR.

The Missing or Offline status usually happens if drives have been disconnected or powered off. If the drives are part of an external storage device, check the storage device to ensure that it is connected properly and has power. Reconnecting the storage device or turning on the power should make it so the drives can be accessed. You then must start Disk Management and rescan the missing drive by selecting Rescan Disks on the Action menu. When Disk Management finishes, right-click the drive, and choose Reactivate Volume. The drive status should change to Regenerating and then to Healthy. If the volume doesn't return to the Healthy status, right-click the volume, and then choose Resynchronize Mirror.

A status of Failed, Online (Errors), or Unreadable indicates I/O problems with the drive. As before, try rescanning the drive, and then try to reactivate the drive. The drive status should change to Regenerating and then to Healthy. If the volume doesn't return to the Healthy status, right-click the volume, and then choose Resynchronize Mirror.

If these actions don't work, you must remove the failed mirror, replace the bad drive, and then rebuild the mirror. To do this, follow these steps:

1. Right-click the failed volume, and then select Remove Mirror.

2. You now must mirror the volume on an Unallocated area of free space on a different disk. If you don't have free space, you must create space by shrinking a volume, deleting other volumes, or replacing the failed drive.

3. When you are ready to continue, right-click the remaining volume in the original mirror, and then select Add Mirror. This displays the Add Mirror dialog box.

4. Use the Disks list to select a location for the mirror, and then click Add Mirror. Windows Server 2008 begins the mirror creation process, and you'll see a status of Resynching on both volumes.

Repairing a Mirrored System Volume

When you mirror a system volume, an entry that allows you to boot to the secondary mirror is added to the system's boot configuration data. So, if a system fails to boot to the primary system volume, restart the system, and select the Boot Mirror - Secondary Plex option for the operating system you want to start. The system should start up normally. After you successfully boot the system to the secondary drive, you can schedule the maintenance necessary to rebuild the mirror if desired.

Rebuilding Mirrored System Volumes on MBR Disks

To rebuild the mirror, you must complete the following steps:

1. Shut down the system and replace the failed drive, and then restart the system using the secondary drive.

2. In Disk Management, right-click the remaining volume in the mirrored set, and choose Break Mirrored Volume. Click Yes at the prompts to confirm the action.

3. Next, right-click the volume again, and choose Add Mirror. Use the Add Mirror dialog box to select the second disk to use for the mirror, and then click Add Mirror.

If you want the primary mirror to be on the drive you added or replaced, perform these additional steps:

1. Use Disk Management to break the mirrored set again.

2. Make sure that the primary drive in the original mirror set has the drive letter that was previously assigned to the complete mirror. If it doesn't, assign the appropriate drive letter.

Chapter 14

3. Right-click the original system volume, select Add Mirror, and then re-create the mirror.

Rebuilding Mirrored System Volumes on GPT Disks

For GPT disks, rebuilding mirrored system volumes is a bit different. To rebuild the mirror, shut down the system and replace the failed drive, and then restart the system using the secondary drive. In Disk Management, right-click the remaining volume in the mirrored set, and choose Break Mirrored Volume. Click Yes at the prompts to confirm the action. After this, you can use the secondary boot disk as your primary boot disk and follow the procedures outlined in "Mirroring Boot and System Volumes on MBR Disks" on page 459 to reenable mirroring properly using the secondary disk as the primary.

Resolving Problems with RAID-5 Sets

Most problems with RAID-5 sets have to do with the intermittent or permanent failure of a drive. If one of the drives in the set goes offline or experiences temporary I/O problems, parity data cannot be properly written to the set and, as a result, the set's status will show as Failed Redundancy and the failed volume's status changes to Missing, Offline, or Online (Errors).

You must get all drives in the RAID-5 set online. If the status of the problem volume is Missing or Offline, make sure that the drive has power and is connected properly. You then must start Disk Management and rescan the missing drive by choosing Rescan Disks from the Action menu. When Disk Management finishes, right-click the drive, and choose Reactivate. The drive status should change to Regenerating and then to Healthy. If the volume doesn't return to the Healthy status, right-click the volume, and then click Regenerate Parity.

A status of Failed, Online (Errors), or Unreadable indicates I/O problems with the drive. As before, try rescanning the drive, and then try to reactivate the drive. The drive status should change to Regenerating and then to Healthy. If the volume doesn't return to the Healthy status, right-click the volume, and then click Regenerate Parity.

If one of the drives still won't come back online, you must repair the failed region of the RAID-5 set. Right-click the failed volume, and then select Remove Volume. You now must right-click an unallocated space on a separate dynamic disk with the same partition style—either MBR or GPT—and choose Repair Volume. This space must be at least as large as the region to repair, and it can't be on a drive that's already being used by the RAID-5 set. If you don't have enough space, the Repair Volume option is unavailable and you must free space by shrinking a volume, deleting other volumes, or replacing the failed drive.

TPM and BitLocker Drive Encryption

Many of the security features built into the Windows operating system are designed to protect a computer from attacks by individuals accessing the computer over the network or from the Internet. But what about when individuals have direct physical access to a computer? When someone has direct physical access to a computer, many of Windows security safeguards don't apply. For example, if someone can boot a computer—even if it is to another operating system they've installed—he or she could gain access to any data stored on the computer, perhaps even your organization's most sensitive data. To protect a computer from individuals who have direct access to a computer, Windows Vista and Windows Server 2008 include the Trusted Platform Module Services architecture and BitLocker Drive Encryption. Together these features help protect a computer from many types of attacks by individuals who have direct access to a computer.

Working with Trusted Platforms

Windows Vista and Windows Server 2008 include the Encrypting File System (EFS) for encrypting files and folders. Using EFS, users can protect sensitive data so that it can only be accessed using their public key certificate. Encryption certificates are stored as part of the data in a user's profile. As long as users have access to their profiles and the encryption keys they contain, they can access their encrypted files.

Although EFS offers excellent protection for your data, it doesn't safeguard the computer from attack by someone who has direct physical access. In a situation where a user loses a computer, a computer has been stolen, or the attacker is logging on to a computer, EFS might not protect the data because the attacker might be able to gain access to the computer before it boots. He could then access the computer from another operating system and change the computer's configuration. He might then be able to hack into a logon account on the original operating system so that he can log on as the user or configure the computer so that he can log on as a local administrator. Either way, the attacker could eventually gain full access to a computer and its data.

To seal a computer from physical attack and wrap it in an additional layer of protection, Windows Vista and Windows Server 2008 include the Trusted Platform Module (TPM) Services architecture. TPM Services protect a computer using a dedicated hardware component called a TPM. A TPM is a microchip that is usually installed on the motherboard of a computer where it communicates with the rest of the system using a hardware bus. Computers running Windows Vista or Windows Server 2008 can use a TPM to provide enhanced protection for data, to ensure early validation of the boot file's integrity, and to guarantee that a disk has not been tampered with while the operating system was offline.

A TPM has the ability to create cryptographic keys and encrypt them so that they can only be decrypted by the TPM. This process, referred to as wrapping or binding, protects the key from disclosure. A TPM has a master "wrapping" key called the Storage Root Key (SRK). The SRK is stored within the TPM itself to ensure that the private portion of the key is secure.

Computers that have TPM can create a key that has not only been wrapped but also sealed. The process of sealing the key ensures that the key is tied to specific platform measurements and can only be unwrapped when those platform measurements have the same values that they had when the key was created. This is what gives TPM-equipped computers increased resistance to attack.

Because TPM stores private portions of key pairs separately from memory controlled by the operating system, keys can be sealed to the TPM to provide absolute assurances about the state of a system and its trustworthiness. TPM keys are only unsealed when the integrity of the system is intact. Further, because the TPM uses its own internal firmware and logical circuits for processing instructions, it does not rely upon the operating system and is not subject to external software vulnerabilities.

The TPM can also be used to seal and unseal data that is generated outside of the TPM, and this is where the true power of the TPM lies. In Windows Vista and Windows Server 2008, the feature that accesses the TPM and uses it to seal a computer is called BitLocker Drive Encryption. Although BitLocker Drive Encryption can be used in both TPM or non-TPM configurations, the most secure method is to use TPM.

When you use BitLocker Drive Encryption and a TPM to seal the boot manager and boot files of a computer, the boot manager and boot files can be unsealed only if they are unchanged since they were last sealed. This means you can use the TPM to validate a computer's boot files in the pre–operating system environment. When you seal a hard disk using TPM, the hard disk can only be unsealed if the data on the disk is unchanged since it was last sealed. This guarantees that a disk has not been tampered with while the operating system was offline.

When you use BitLocker Drive Encryption and do not use a TPM to seal the boot manager and boot files of a computer, TPM cannot be used to validate a computer's boot files in the pre–operating system environment. This means there is no way to guarantee the integrity of the boot manager and boot files of a computer.

Managing TPM

A computer running Windows Server 2008 must be equipped with a compatible TPM and compatible firmware to take advantage of TPM. Both Windows Vista and Windows Server 2008 support TPM version 1.2 and require Trusted Computing Group (TCG)–compliant firmware. Firmware that is TCG-compliant is firmware that supports the Static Root of Trust Measurement as defined by the Trusted Computing Group. In some configurations of TPM and BitLocker Drive Encryption, you'll also need to make sure the firmware supports reading USB flash drives at startup.

Understanding TPM States and Tools

The TPM Services architecture in Windows Vista and Windows Server 2008 provides the basic features required to configure and deploy TPM-equipped computers. This architecture can be extended with a feature called BitLocker Drive Encryption, which is discussed in "Introducing BitLocker Drive Encryption" on page 477.

Before you can use TPM, you must turn on TPM in firmware and initialize the TPM for first use in software. As part of the initialization process, you'll set the owner password on the TPM. After TPM is enabled, you can manage the TPM configuration.

In some cases, computers that have TPM might ship with TPM turned on. However, in most cases, you'll find TPM is not turned on by default. You turn on TPM in firmware. With my servers, I needed to:

1. Start the computer. Press F2 during startup to access the firmware. In the firmware, I accessed the Advanced screen and then the Peripheral Configuration screen.

2. On the Peripheral Configuration screen, Trusted Platform Module was listed as an option. After scrolling down to highlight this option, I pressed Enter to display an options menu. On the options menu, I selected Enable and then pressed Enter.

3. To save the setting change and exit the firmware, I then pressed F10. When prompted to confirm that I wanted to exit, I pressed Y and the computer then rebooted.

Windows Vista and Windows Server 2008 provide several tools for working with TPM, including:

- **Trusted Platform Module Management** An MMC console for configuring and managing TPM. You can access this tool by clicking Start, typing **tpm.msc** in the Search box, and then pressing Enter.

- **Initialize The TPM Security Hardware** A wizard for creating the required TPM owner password. You can access this tool by clicking Start, typing **tpminit** in the Search box, and then pressing Enter.

When you are working with Trusted Platform Module Management, you'll be able to determine the exact state of the TPM. If you try to start Trusted Platform Module

Management without turning on TPM, you'll see an error like the one shown in the following screen:

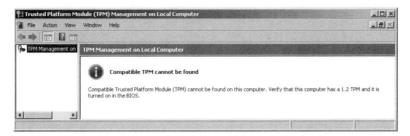

Similarly, if you try to run Initialize The TPM Security Hardware without turning on TPM, you'll see an error like the one shown in the following screen.

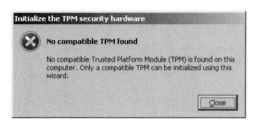

Only when you've turned on TPM in firmware will you be able to access and work with the TPM tools. When you are working with the Trusted Platform Module Management console, shown in Figure 15-1, you should note the TPM status and the TPM manufacturer information. The TPM status indicates the exact state of the TPM (see Table 15-1). The TPM manufacturer information shows that the TPM supports specification version 1.2. Support for TPM version 1.2 or later is required.

Table 15-1 TPM Status Indicators and Their Meanings

Status Indicator	Meaning
The TPM is on and ownership has not been taken	The TPM is turned on in firmware but hasn't been initialized yet.
The TPM is on and ownership has been taken	The TPM is turned on in firmware and has been initialized.
The TPM is off and ownership has not been taken	The TPM is turned off in software but hasn't been initialized yet.

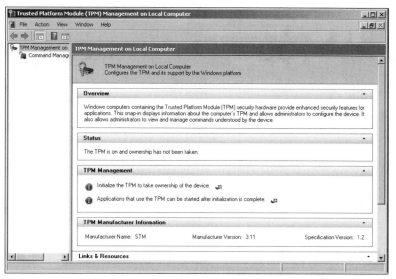

Figure 15-1 Use the Trusted Platform Module Management console to initialize and manage TPM.

Initializing a TPM for First Use

Initializing a TPM configures it for use on a computer. The initialization process involves turning on the TPM and then setting ownership of the TPM. By setting ownership of the TPM, you are assigning a password that helps ensure that only the authorized TPM owner can access and manage the TPM. The TPM password is required to turn off the TPM if you no longer want to use it and to clear the TPM if the computer is to be recycled. In an Active Directory domain, you can configure Group Policy to save TPM passwords.

To initialize the TPM and create the owner password, complete the following steps:

1. Start the Trusted Platform Module Management console. On the Action menu, choose Initialize TPM to start the Initialize The TPM Security Hardware wizard.

> Note
>
> If the Initialize The TPM Security Hardware wizard detects firmware that does not meet Windows requirements or no TPM is found, you will not be able to continue and should ensure that the TPM has been turned on in firmware. Otherwise, you'll see the Create The TPM Owner Password page.

2. On the Create The TPM Owner Password page, shown in Figure 15-2, click Automatically Create The Password (Recommended).

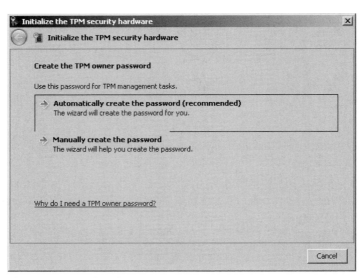

Figure 15-2 Initialize the TPM.

3. On the Save Your TPM Owner Password page, shown in Figure 15-3, note the 48-character TPM owner password. Click Save The Password.

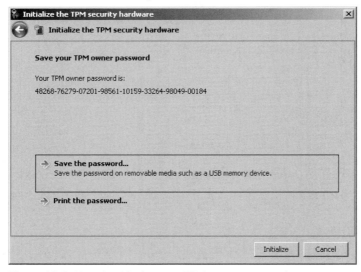

Figure 15-3 Note the 48-character TPM owner password.

4. In the Save As dialog box, shown in Figure 15-4, select a location to save the password backup file and then click Save. By default, the password backup file is saved as *ComputerName*.tpm. Ideally, you'll save the TPM ownership password to removable media, such as a USB flash drive.

Figure 15-4 Save the TPM owner password.

5. On the Save Your TPM Owner Password page, click Print The Password if you want to print a hard copy of the password. Be sure to save the printout containing the password in a secure location, such as a safe or locked file cabinet.

6. Click Initialize. The initialization process may take several minutes to complete. When initialization is complete, click Close. In the TPM Management console, the status should be listed as "The TPM is on and ownership has been taken," as shown in Figure 15-5.

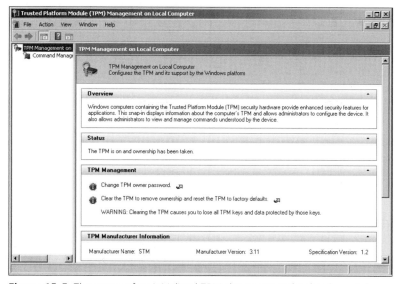

Figure 15-5 The status of an initialized TPM shows ownership has been taken.

Turning an Initialized TPM On or Off

Computers that have TPM might ship with TPM turned on. If you decide not to use TPM, you should turn off and clear the TPM. If you want to reconfigure or recycle a computer, you should also turn off and clear the TPM.

To turn off TPM, complete the following steps:

1. Start the Trusted Platform Module Management console. On the Action menu, choose Turn TPM Off. This starts the Manage The TPM Security Hardware wizard.

2. On the Turn Off The TPM Security Hardware page, shown in Figure 15-6, use one of the following methods for entering the current password and turning off the TPM:

    ○   If you have the removable media onto which you saved your TPM owner password, insert it and click I Have A Backup File With The TPM Owner Password. On the Select Backup File With The TPM Owner Password page, click Browse and then use the Open dialog box to locate the .tpm file saved on your removable media. Click Open, and then click Turn TPM Off.

    ○   If you do not have the removable media onto which you saved your password, click I Want To Type The TPM Owner Password. On the Type Your TPM Owner Password page, enter the TPM password (including dashes) and then click Turn TPM Off.

    ○   If you do not know your TPM owner password, click I Don't Have The TPM Owner Password, and then follow the instructions provided to turn off the TPM without entering the password. Because you are logged on locally to the computer, you will be able to turn off the TPM.

3. In the TPM Management console, the status should be listed as "The TPM is off and ownership has been taken." Do not discard the TPM owner password file or printout. You will need this information if you want to turn the TPM back on.

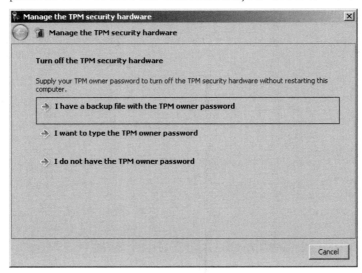

Figure 15-6 Click an option for turning off the TPM.

After you've used the previously listed procedure to turn off the TPM in software, you can turn on the TPM in software by following these steps:

1. Start the Trusted Platform Module Management console. On the Action menu, choose Turn TPM On. This starts the Manage The TPM Security Hardware wizard.

2. On the Turn On The TPM Security Hardware page, use one of the following methods for entering the current TPM password and turning on the TPM:

   ○ If you have the removable media onto which you saved your TPM owner password, insert it and click I Have A Backup File With The TPM Owner Password. On the Select Backup File With The TPM Owner Password page, click Browse and then use the Open dialog box to locate the .tpm file saved on your removable media. Click Open, and then click Turn TPM On.

   ○ If you do not have the removable media onto which you saved your password, click I Want To Type The TPM Owner Password. On the Type Your TPM Owner Password page, enter the TPM password (including dashes) and then click Turn TPM On.

   ○ If you do not know your TPM owner password, click I Don't Have The TPM Owner Password, and then follow the instructions provided to turn on the TPM without entering the password. Because you are logged on locally to the computer, you will be able to turn on the TPM.

3. In the TPM Management console, the status should be listed as "The TPM is on and ownership has been taken." Do not discard the TPM owner password file or printout. You will need this information if you want to manage the TPM.

Clearing the TPM

Clearing the TPM cancels the TPM ownership and finalizes the shutdown of the TPM. You should only clear the TPM when a TPM-equipped computer is to be recycled.

To clear the TPM, complete the following steps:

1. Start the Trusted Platform Module Management console. On the Action menu, choose Clear TPM. This starts the Manage The TPM Security Hardware wizard.

CAUTION

Clearing the TPM resets it to factory defaults and finalizes its shutdown. As a result, you will lose all created keys and data protected by those keys.

2. On the Clear The TPM Security Hardware page, select a method for entering the current password and clearing the TPM:

   ○ If you have the removable media onto which you saved your TPM owner password, insert it and click I Have A Backup File With The TPM Owner Password. On the Select Backup File With The TPM Owner Password page, click Browse and then use the Open dialog box to locate the .tpm file saved on your removable media. Click Open, and then click Clear TPM.

   ○ If you do not have the removable media onto which you saved your password, click I Want To Type The TPM Owner Password. On the Type Your

TPM Owner Password page, enter your password (including dashes) and then click Clear TPM.

○ If you do not know your TPM owner password, click I Don't Have The TPM Owner Password, and follow the instructions provided to clear the TPM without entering the password. Because you are logged on locally to the computer, you will be able to clear the TPM.

Changing the TPM Owner Password

You can change the TPM password at any time. To change the TPM owner password, complete the following steps:

1. Start the Trusted Platform Module Management console. On the Action menu, choose Change Owner Password. This starts the Manage The TPM Security Hardware wizard.

2. On the Change TPM Owner Password page, select a method for entering the current password:

   ○ If you have the removable media onto which you saved your TPM owner password, insert it and click I Have A Backup File With The TPM Owner Password. On the Select Backup File With The TPM Owner Password page, click Browse and then use the Open dialog box to locate the .tpm file saved on your removable media. Click Open, and then click Create New Password.

   ○ If you do not have the removable media onto which you saved your password, click I Want To Type The TPM Owner Password. On the Type Your TPM Owner Password page, enter your password (including dashes) and then click Create New Password.

3. On the Create The TPM Owner Password page, select Automatically Create The Password (Recommended) and then click Next.

4. On the Save Your TPM Owner Password page, note the 48-character TPM owner password. Click Save The Password. In the Save As dialog box, select a location to save the password backup file and then click Save. If you are saving the password backup file to the same location and name, click Yes when prompted to replace the existing file.

5. On the Save Your TPM Owner Password page, click Print The Password if you want to print a hard copy of the password. Be sure to save the printout containing the password in a secure location, such as a safe or locked file cabinet.

6. To complete the process, click Change Password.

Introducing BitLocker Drive Encryption

BitLocker Drive Encryption, a feature included in all editions of Windows Server 2008 and in the Ultimate and Enterprise editions of Windows Vista, is designed to protect the data on lost, stolen, or inappropriately decommissioned computers. Without Bit-Locker Drive Encryption, there are a variety of ways a user with direct physical access to a computer could gain full control and then access the computer's data whether that data was encrypted with EFS or not. For example, a user could use a boot disk to boot the computer and reset the administrator password. A user could also install and then boot to a different operating system, and then use this operating system to unlock the other installation.

BitLocker Drive Encryption prevents all access to a computer's drives except by authorized personnel by wrapping entire drives in tamper-proof encryption. If a user tries to access a BitLocker encrypted drive, the encryption prevents them from viewing or manipulating the data in any way. This dramatically reduces the risk of an unauthorized person gaining access to confidential data using offline attacks.

> **CAUTION**
>
> BitLocker Drive Encryption reduces disk throughput. Because of this, it should be used on an enterprise server only if the server is not in a physically secure location and requires additional protection.

BitLocker Drive Encryption can use a TPM to validate the integrity of a computer's boot manager and boot files at startup, and to guarantee that a computer's hard disk has not been tampered with while the operating system was offline. BitLocker Drive Encryption also stores measurements of core operating system files in the TPM.

Every time the computer is started, Windows validates the boot files, the operating system files, and any encrypted volumes to ensure that they have not been modified while the computer was offline. If the files have been modified, Windows alerts the user and refuses to release the key required to access Windows. The computer then goes into Recovery mode, prompting the user to provide a recovery key before allowing access to the boot volume. The Recovery mode is also used if a BitLocker encrypted disk drive is transferred to another system.

BitLocker Drive Encryption can be used in both TPM and non-TPM computers. If a computer has a TPM, BitLocker Drive Encryption uses the TPM to provide enhanced protection for your data and to ensure early boot file integrity. These features together help prevent unauthorized viewing and accessing of data by encrypting the entire Windows volume and by safeguarding the boot files from tampering. If a computer doesn't have a TPM or its TPM isn't compatible with Windows, BitLocker Drive Encryption can be used to encrypt entire volumes and in this way protect the volumes from tampering. This configuration, however, doesn't allow the added security of early boot file integrity validation.

On computers with a compatible TPM that is initialized, BitLocker Drive Encryption can use one of three TPM modes:

- **TPM-Only** In this mode, only TPM is used for validation. When the computer boots, TPM is used to validate the boot files, the operating system files, and any encrypted volumes. As the user doesn't need to provide an additional startup key, this mode is transparent to the user and the user logon experience is unchanged. However, if the TPM is missing or the integrity of files or volumes has changed, BitLocker will enter Recovery mode and require a recovery key or password to regain access to the boot volume.

- **TPM and PIN** In this mode, both TPM and a user-entered numeric key are used for validation. When the computer boots, TPM is used to validate the boot files, the operating system files, and any encrypted volumes. The user must enter a PIN when prompted to continue startup. If the user doesn't have the PIN or is unable to provide the correct PIN, BitLocker will enter Recovery mode instead of booting to the operating system. As before, BitLocker will also enter Recovery mode if the TPM is missing or the integrity of boot files or encrypted volumes has changed.

- **TPM and Startup Key** In this mode, both TPM and a startup key are used for validation. When the computer boots, TPM is used to validate the boot files, the operating system files, and any encrypted volumes. The user must have a USB flash drive with a startup key to log on to the computer. If the user doesn't have the startup key or is unable to provide the correct startup key, BitLocker will enter Recovery mode. As before, BitLocker will also enter Recovery mode if the TPM is missing or the integrity of boot files or encrypted volumes has changed.

On computers without a TPM or on computers that have incompatible TPMs, Bit-Locker Drive Encryption uses Startup Key Only mode. As the name implies, this mode requires a USB flash drive containing a startup key. The user inserts a USB flash drive in the computer before turning it on. The key stored on the flash drive unlocks the computer. If the user doesn't have the startup key or is unable to provide the correct startup key, BitLocker will enter Recovery mode. BitLocker will also enter Recovery mode if the integrity of encrypted volumes has changed.

Deploying BitLocker Drive Encryption

Deploying BitLocker Drive Encryption in an enterprise changes the way both administrators and users work with computers. A computer with BitLocker Drive Encryption requires user intervention to boot to the operating system—a user must either enter a PIN or insert a USB flash drive containing a startup key. Because of this, after you've deployed BitLocker Drive Encryption, you can no longer be assured that you can perform remote administration that requires a computer to be restarted without having physical access to the computer—someone will need to be available to type in the required PIN or insert the USB flash drive with the startup key.

Before you use BitLocker Drive Encryption, you should perform a thorough evaluation of your organization's computers. You will need to develop plans and procedures for:

- Evaluating the various BitLocker authentication methods and applying them as appropriate

- Determining whether computers support TPM and thus whether you must use TPM or non-TPM BitLocker configurations

- Storing, using, and periodically changing encryption keys, recovery passwords, and other validators used with BitLocker

You will need to develop new procedures for:

- Working with BitLocker encrypted drives

- Supporting BitLocker encrypted drives

- Recovering computers with BitLocker encrypted drives

These procedures will need to take into account the way BitLocker encryption works and the requirements to have PINs, startup keys, and recovery keys available whenever you work with BitLocker encrypted computers. After you've evaluated your organization's computers and developed basic plans and procedures, you'll need to develop a configuration plan for implementing BitLocker Drive Encryption.

> **Note**
>
> Two implementations of BitLocker Drive Encryption are available: the original BitLocker Drive Encryption as released with Windows Vista and the updated BitLocker Drive Encryption as released with Windows Server 2008. With the updated implementation, you can use BitLocker encryption on both system and data volumes. Because Windows Vista and Windows Server 2008 share the same core kernel and architecture, the updated BitLocker Drive Encryption should also become available in Windows Vista.

BitLocker Drive Encryption requires a specific disk configuration. On a computer with a compatible TPM, you must create or make available a BitLocker Drive Encryption partition on your hard drive and then initialize the TPM as discussed previously under "Initializing a TPM for First Use" on page 471. On a computer without a compatible TPM, you only need to create or make available a BitLocker Drive Encryption partition on your hard drive.

The way you create the BitLocker Drive Encryption partition depends on whether the computer has an operating system installed. If the computer doesn't have an operating system installed, follow the procedure discussed under "Creating the BitLocker Drive Encryption Partition for a Computer with No Operating System" on page 482. If the computer has an operating system installed, follow the procedure discussed under

Chapter 15

"Creating the BitLocker Drive Encryption Partition for a Computer with an Operating System" on page 482.

You can use Local Group Policy and Active Directory Group Policy to help you manage and maintain TPM and BitLocker configurations. TPM Services Group Policy settings are found in Computer Configuration\Administrative Templates\System\Trusted Platform Module Services and include:

- Turn On TPM Backup To Active Directory Domain Services

- Configure The List Of Blocked TPM Commands

- Ignore The Default List Of Blocked TPM Commands

- Ignore The Local List Of Blocked TPM Commands

BitLocker Group Policy settings are found in Computer Configuration\Administrative Templates\Windows Components\BitLocker Drive Encryption and include:

- Turn On BitLocker Backup To Active Directory Domain Services

- Control Panel Setup: Configure Recovery Folder

- Control Panel Setup: Configure Recovery Options

- Control Panel Setup: Enable Advanced Startup Options

- Configure Encryption Method

- Prevent Memory Overwrite On Restart

- Configure TPM Platform Validation Profile

BitLocker policy settings apply to both Windows Vista and Windows Server 2008. Unlike Active Directory Domain Services for Windows Server 2003, Active Directory Domain Services for Windows Server 2008 includes the TPM and BitLocker recovery extensions for Computer objects. For TPM, the extensions define a single property of the Computer object called ms-TPM-OwnerInformation. When the TPM is initialized or when the owner password is changed, the hash of the TPM ownership password can be stored as a value of the ms-TPM-OwnerInformation attribute on the related Computer object. For BitLocker, these extensions define Recovery objects as child objects of Computer objects and are used to store recovery passwords and associate them with specific BitLocker encrypted volumes.

INSIDE OUT   **Using TPM, BitLocker, and FIPS with AD DS**

To ensure that TPM and BitLocker recovery information is always available, you should configure Group Policy to require its backup. With Turn On TPM Backup To Active Directory Domain Services, enable the policy and then use the setting Require TPM Backup To AD DS. With Turn On BitLocker Backup To Active Directory Domain Services, enable the policy and then use the setting Require BitLocker Backup To AD DS.

For Federal Information Processing Standard (FIPS) compliance, you cannot create or save a BitLocker recovery password. So instead, you'll need to configure Windows to create recovery keys. The FIPS setting is located in the Security Policy Editor at Local Policies\ Security Options\System Cryptography: Use FIPS Compliant Algorithms For Encryption, Hashing, And Signing. To do this, enable the security option System Cryptography: Use FIPS Compliant Algorithms For Encryption, Hashing, And Signing in Local Group Policy or Active Directory Group Policy as appropriate. With this setting enabled, users can save a recovery key only to a USB flash drive. Users will not be able to save a recovery password to AD DS, local folders, or network folders, and also will not be to use the BitLocker Drive Encryption wizard or other method to create a recovery password. Because recovery passwords cannot be saved to AD DS when FIPS is enabled, Windows will display an error if AD DS backup is required by Group Policy.

Setting Up and Managing BitLocker Drive Encryption

With Windows Server 2008, you can configure and enable BitLocker Drive Encryption on both system volumes and data volumes. However, if you want to encrypt a server's data volumes you must first encrypt its system volume. When you use encrypted data volumes, the operating system mounts BitLocker data volumes as it would any other volume.

The encryption key for a protected data volume is created and stored independently from the system volume and all other protected data volumes. To allow the operating system to mount encrypted volumes, the key chain protecting the data volume is stored encrypted on the operating system volume. If the operating system enters Recovery mode, the data volumes are not unlocked until the operating system is out of Recovery mode.

Setting up BitLocker Drive Encryption is a multistep process that involves:

1. Partitioning a computer's hard disks appropriately and installing the operating system, if you are configuring a new computer.

2. Initializing and configuring a computer's TPM (if applicable).

3. Installing the BitLocker Drive Encryption feature (as necessary).

4. Checking firmware to ensure that the computer is set to first start from the disk containing the system partition and the Bitlocker partition, not the USB or CD/DVD drives.

5. Turning on and configuring BitLocker Drive Encryption.

After you've turned on and configured BitLocker encryption, there are several techniques you can use to maintain the environment and perform recovery.

Creating the BitLocker Drive Encryption Partition for a Computer with No Operating System

BitLocker Drive Encryption requires two NTFS drive partitions, one for the system volume and one for the operating system volume. The system volume partition must be at least 1.5 gigabytes (GB) and set as the active partition.

On new hardware, you create the BitLocker Drive Encryption partition on a computer with no operating system. To do this, you start the computer from the installation media and then create two partitions on the computer's primary disk:

- The first partition is the partition for BitLocker Drive Encryption. This partition holds the files required to start the operating system and is not encrypted.

- The second is the primary partition for the operating system and your data. This partition is encrypted when you turn on BitLocker.

You can partition a drive with no operating system for BitLocker Drive Encryption by following these steps:

1. Insert the Windows Installation disc for the hardware architecture and then boot from the installation disc by pressing a key when prompted. If the server does not allow you to boot from the installation disc, you might need to change firmware options to allow booting from a CD/DVD-ROM drive.

2. If Windows Setup doesn't start automatically, select Windows Setup (EMS Enabled) on the Windows Boot Manager menu to start Windows Setup.

3. On the Install Windows page, select the language, time, and keyboard layout options that you want to use. Click Next.

4. On the next Setup page, you have several options:

   ○ If a Repair Your Computer link is available in the lower-left corner of the Install Windows page, click this option to start the System Recovery Options wizard. On the System Recovery Options page, click Command Prompt to access the MIN-WINPC environment.

   ○ If a Repair Your Computer link is not available (such as when there is no current Windows Server 2008 or later operating system already installed), click Install Now. Proceed through the installation process until you get to the Where Do You Want To Install Windows page. At this point, press Shift+F10 to access a command prompt.

5. In the Command Prompt window, type **diskpart** and press Enter.

6. Select the hard disk to use by typing **select disk 0**.

7. Erase the existing partition table by typing **clean**. This destroys all data on the disk.

8. Create the BitLocker partition by typing **create partition primary size=1500**.

9. Designate the partition as S: by typing **assign letter=s**.

10. Make the partition the active partition by typing **active**.

11. Format the partition using NTFS as the file system by typing **format fs=ntfs**.

12. Create the operating system partition using the rest of the available disk space by typing **create partition primary**.

13. Designate the partition as C: by typing **assign letter=c**.

14. Format the partition using NTFS as the file system by typing **format fs=ntfs**.

15. Quit the DiskPart application by typing **exit**.

16. Quit the command prompt by typing **exit**.

17. Return to the main installation screen by clicking Close. Proceed with the installation process. Install Windows Server 2008 on drive C.

18. If the computer has a TPM, you will need to initialize it as discussed under "Initializing a TPM for First Use" on page 471. Although you are working with firmware, you should also ensure that the computer is set to first start from the disk containing the system partition and the Bitlocker partition, not the USB or CD/DVD drives.

Creating the BitLocker Drive Encryption Partition for a Computer with an Operating System

BitLocker Drive Encryption requires two NTFS drive partitions, one for the system volume and one for the operating system volume. The system volume partition must be at least 1.5 GB and set as the active partition.

On a computer running Windows Server 2008, Windows configures an available partition as the necessary BitLocker Drive Encryption partition during the BitLocker configuration process. As long as the server has at least two partitions on one or more disks, Windows will configure one partition as the boot partition and another partition as the active, system partition. The boot partition is the one containing the operating system files. The active, system partition is the one containing the boot manager and other files needed by BitLocker during startup. Because you will not be able to encrypt the active, system partition used by BitLocker, it is a recommended best practice that you size the first partition on the first available disk (typically disk 0) with BitLocker in mind.

Chapter 15

Specifically, this partition should be at least 1.5 GB in size and should not be used for other purposes, such as storing server data.

On a computer running Windows Vista Ultimate or Windows Vista Enterprise, you can, in most cases, create the required BitLocker Drive Encryption partition without having to reinstall the operating system. To do this, use the BitLocker Drive Preparation Tool (BdeHdCfg.exe), which you'll find in the %ProgramFiles%\BitLocker folder. If the tool is not available, you should be able to download it from the Microsoft Download Web site. See Microsoft Knowledge Base article 930063 for more information (*http://support.microsoft.com/kb/930063/en-us*).

The BitLocker Drive Preparation Tool automates the process of creating the BitLocker partition, moving the required files to this partition, and setting the partition as the active volume. There are many caveats to using this tool:

- The drive must be formatted as a basic disk with simple volumes. Although hardware RAID configurations can be implemented, no software spanning, mirroring, or other RAID configurations are supported.

- The partition must be a primary partition. Extended partitions and logical drives are not supported.

- The partition must be formatted as NTFS and the file system must not be compressed.

- The partition cluster size must be less than or equal to 4 KB in size.

You can perform four general operations with the BitLocker Drive Preparation Tool:

- **Query Disk** When you want to determine the current disk configuration, type **bdehdcfg -driveinfo** at the command prompt. The output shows the drive letter, total size, maximum free space, and partition type of the Windows Recovery Environment, operating system, and unallocated partitions.

- **Create Partition** When a disk has an area of unallocated space at least 1.5 GB in size, you can use this operation to automatically create the BitLocker partition, move the required files to this partition, and set the partition as the active volume. In the following example, you create a new S: partition in 1.5 GB of unallocated space:

```
bdehdcfg –target unallocated –newdriveletter s: –size 1500 –quiet –restart
```

- **Split Partition** When a disk has a large operating system partition that you want to split to create the required BitLocker partition, you can perform a split operation. For a split operation, at least 10 percent of the operating system partition must remain free after the partition is reduced by 1.5 GB to create the BitLocker partition. In the following example, you create a new S: partition by splitting the C: partition and using 1.5 GB of previously unallocated space on this partition:

```
bdehdcfg –target c: shrink –newdriveletter s: –size 1500 –quiet –restart
```

- **Merge Partition** When a disk has a separate partition (that is not being used as the operating system partition) you can merge the required boot files into the partition and set the partition as the active partition for BitLocker using a merge operation. For a merge operation, the partition must have a total capacity of at least 1.5 GB and at least 800 MB of free disk space. In the following example, you merge BitLocker required files and settings into the existing D: partition:

```
bdehdcfg -target d: merge -size 1500 -quiet -restart
```

If the computer has a TPM, you will need to initialize it as discussed under "Initializing a TPM for First Use" on page 471.

Configuring and Enabling BitLocker Drive Encryption

As discussed previously, BitLocker Drive Encryption can be used in a TPM or non-TPM configuration. Both configurations require some preliminary work before you can turn on and configure BitLocker Drive Encryption.

With Windows Vista Ultimate and Enterprise, BitLocker should be installed by default. With Windows Server 2008, you can install the BitLocker Drive Encryption feature using the Add Features Wizard. Alternatively, on a server, you can install BitLocker Drive Encryption by entering the following command at an elevated command prompt: **servermanagercmd -install bitlocker**. Either way, you will need to restart the computer to complete the installation process.

After you've installed BitLocker, you can determine the readiness status of a computer by accessing the BitLocker Drive Encryption console. Click Start, Control Panel, Security, and then BitLocker Drive Encryption. If the system isn't properly configured yet, you'll see a message similar to the one shown in the following screen.

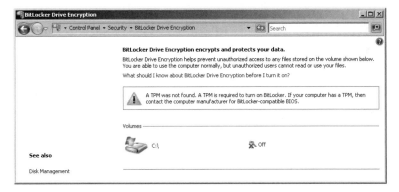

If you see this message on a computer with a compatible TPM, refer to "Understanding TPM States and Tools" on page 469 to learn more about TPM states and enabling TPM in firmware. If you see this message on a computer with an incompatible TPM or no TPM, you'll need to change the computer's Group Policy settings so that you can turn on BitLocker Drive Encryption without a TPM.

You can configure policy settings for BitLocker encryption in Local Group Policy or in Active Directory Group Policy. For local policy, you apply the desired settings to the computer's Local Group Policy object. For domain policy, you apply the desired settings to a Group Policy object processed by the computer. While you are working with domain policy, you can also specify requirements for computers with a TPM.

To configure the way BitLocker can be used with or without a TPM, follow these steps:

1. Open the appropriate Group Policy object for editing in the Group Policy Object Editor or the Group Policy Management Editor.

2. Double-click the setting Control Panel Setup: Enable Advanced Startup Options in the Computer Configuration\Administrative Templates\Windows Components\BitLocker Drive Encryption folder.

3. In the Control Panel Setup: Enable Advanced Startup Options Properties dialog box, shown in Figure 15-7, define the policy setting by selecting Enabled.

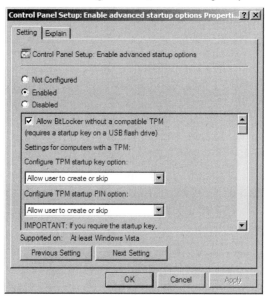

Figure 15-7 Choose an option for turning off the TPM.

4. If you want to allow BitLocker to be used without a compatible TPM, select the Allow BitLocker Without A Compatible TPM check box. This changes the policy setting so that you can use BitLocker encryption with a startup key on a computer without a TPM.

5. You can configure policy for computers with TPM in several ways. You can:

   ○ Allow users to create or skip creating a TPM startup key by setting the Configure TPM Startup Key Option list to Allow User To Create Or Skip.

   ○ Allow users to create or skip creating a TPM startup PIN by setting the Configure TPM Startup PIN Option list to Allow User To Create Or Skip.

   ○ Require a startup key with TPM while disallowing a startup PIN by setting the Configure TPM Startup Key Option list to Require Startup Key With TPM and the Configure TPM Startup PIN Option list to Disallow Startup PIN With TPM.

   ○ Require a startup PIN with TPM while disallowing a startup key by setting the Configure TPM Startup Key Option list to Disallow Startup Key With TPM and the Configure TPM Startup PIN Option list to Require Startup PIN With TPM.

> **Note**
>
> If you require a startup key, you must disallow a startup PIN. Similarly, if you require a startup PIN, you must disallow a startup key.

6. Click OK to save your settings. This policy is enforced the next time Group Policy is applied.

7. Close the Group Policy Object Editor. To force Group Policy to apply immediately to this computer, click Start, type **gpupdate.exe /force** in the Search box, and then press Enter.

Computers that have a startup key or a startup PIN also have a recovery password. The recovery password is required in the event that:

- Changes are made to the system startup information

- The encrypted drive must be moved to another computer

- The user is unable to provide the appropriate startup key or PIN

The recovery password should be managed and stored separately from the startup key or startup PIN. Although users are given the startup key or startup PIN, administrators should be the only ones with the recovery password. As the administrator, you will need the recovery password to unlock the encrypted data on the volume if BitLocker enters a locked state. The recovery password is unique to this particular BitLocker encryption. You cannot use it to recover encrypted data from any other BitLocker encrypted volume—even from other BitLocker encrypted volumes on the same computer. To increase security, you should store startup keys and recovery passwords apart from the computer.

When you install BitLocker Drive Encryption and configure policy (if necessary), the BitLocker Drive Encryption console becomes available in Control Panel. When you are configuring BitLocker encryption, the configuration options you have will depend on whether the computer has a TPM as well as how you've configured Group Policy.

To enable BitLocker encryption for use with a startup key, follow these steps:

1. Click Start, Control Panel, Security, and then double-click BitLocker Drive Encryption. As shown in the following screen, the Turn On BitLocker option will be listed under the operating system volume.

2. Click Turn On BitLocker. If you are warned about BitLocker degrading performance, as shown in the following screen, click Continue With BitLocker Drive Encryption.

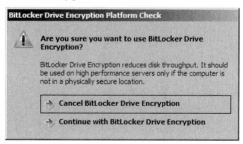

3. On the Set BitLocker Startup Preferences page, shown in the following screen, click the Require Startup USB Key At Every Startup option as you want to require a user to insert a startup key to boot to the operating system.

4. Insert a USB flash drive in the computer (if it is not already there).

5. On the Save Your Startup Key page, choose the location of your USB flash drive, and then click Save.

6. Next, you need to save the recovery password. As you should not store the recovery password and the startup key on the same media, remove the USB flash drive and insert a second USB flash drive.

> **Note**
>
> The startup key is different from the recovery password. If you create a startup key, this key will then be required to start the computer. The recovery password is required to unlock the computer if BitLocker enters Recovery mode, such as would happen if Bit-Locker suspects the computer has been tampered with while offline.

7. On the Save The Recovery Password page, shown in the following screen, click Save The Password On A USB Drive.

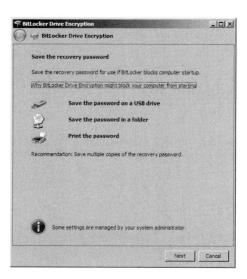

8. In the Save A Recovery Password To A USB Drive dialog box, choose the location of your USB flash drive, and then click Save. Do not remove the USB drive with the recovery password.

9. You can now optionally save the recovery password to a folder, print the recovery password, or both. For each option, click the option and follow the wizard steps to set the location for saving or printing the recovery password. When you are finished, click Next.

10. On the Encrypt The Volume page, shown in the following screen, confirm that the Run BitLocker System Check check box is selected, and then click Continue.

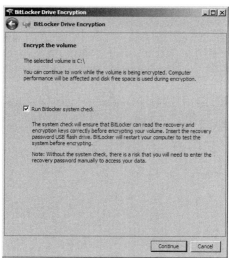

11. Confirm that you want to restart the computer by clicking Restart Now. The computer restarts and BitLocker ensures that the computer is BitLocker-compatible and ready for encryption. If the computer is not ready for encryption, you will see an error and will need to resolve the error status before you can complete this procedure. If the computer is ready for encryption, the Encryption In Progress status bar is displayed. You can monitor the ongoing completion status of the disk volume encryption by dragging your mouse cursor over the BitLocker Drive Encryption icon in the notification area at the bottom of your screen. By double-clicking this icon, you can open the Encrypting dialog box, shown in the following screen, and monitor the encryption process more closely. You also have the option to pause the encryption process. Volume encryption takes approximately one minute per gigabyte to complete.

By completing this procedure, you have encrypted the operating system volume and created a recovery password unique to that volume. The next time you turn your computer on, the USB flash drive with the startup key must be plugged into a USB port on the computer. If you do not have the USB flash drive containing your startup key, then to access the data you will need to use Recovery mode and supply the recovery password.

To enable BitLocker encryption for use with a startup PIN, follow these steps:

1. Click Start, Control Panel, Security, and then double-click BitLocker Drive Encryption. The Turn On BitLocker option will be listed under the operating system volume.

2. Click Turn On BitLocker. If you are warned about BitLocker degrading performance, click Continue With BitLocker Drive Encryption.

3. On the Set BitLocker Startup Preferences page, select the Require PIN At Every Startup option as you want to require a user to enter a PIN to boot to the operating system.

4. On the Type Your Startup PIN page, enter the desired PIN. The PIN can be any number you choose from 4 to 20 digits in length. The PIN is stored on the computer.

5. Insert a USB flash drive on which you want to save the recovery password and then click Next.

     Continue with steps 7 to 11 starting on page 489.

When the encryption process completes, you have encrypted the entire volume and created a recovery password unique to this volume. If you created a PIN or startup key, you will be required to use the PIN or startup key to start the computer. Otherwise, you will see no change to the computer unless the TPM changes or cannot be accessed, or if someone tries to modify the disk while the operating system is offline. In this case, the computer will enter Recovery mode and you will need to enter the recovery key to unlock the computer.

Determining Whether a Computer Has BitLocker Encrypted Volumes

You can determine whether a computer has BitLocker encrypted volumes using Disk Management. In Disk Management any such encrypted volume is listed as being Bit-Locker Encrypted, as shown in Figure 15-8.

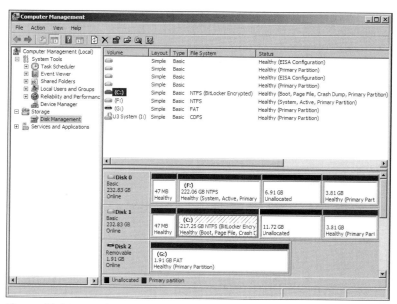

Figure 15-8 Use Disk Management to check for BitLocker encrypted volumes.

Managing BitLocker Passwords and PINs

After you create a startup key or PIN and a recovery password for a computer, you can create duplicates of the startup key, startup PIN, or recovery password at any time as might be necessary for backup or replacement purposes. To do this, follow these steps:

1. Click Start, Control Panel, Security, and then double-click BitLocker Drive Encryption.

2. Click Manage BitLocker Keys. This starts the BitLocker Drive Encryption wizard and displays the Select Keys To Manage page, as shown in Figure 15-9.

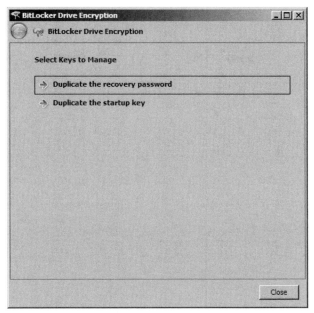

Figure 15-9 Manage the BitLocker keys to create duplicates for backup or replacement purposes.

3. If you want to duplicate the recovery password, click Duplicate The Recovery Password. You will then be able to save the recovery password to a USB drive or a folder. You will also be able to print the recovery password. When you are finished, click Next and then click Close.

4. If you want to duplicate the startup key, insert a USB flash drive and then click Duplicate The Startup Key. Select the USB drive and then click Save. When you are finished, click Close.

Encrypting Server Data Volumes

After you encrypt a server's system volume, you can use BitLocker to encrypt data volumes as well. A data volume that you want to BitLocker encrypt cannot also be configured as the active, system volume.

To turn on BitLocker Drive Encryption for server data volumes, type the following at an elevated command prompt: **manage-bde -on** *DriveDesignator* **-rp -rk** *USBDesignator* where *DriveDesignator* is the designator for the drive to encrypt, such as D:, and *USB-Designator* is the designator for a USB flash drive you've inserted and on which you want to store the recovery password, such as L:. In the following example, you encrypt the D drive, generate a recovery password, and store this recovery password on the USB flash drive designated as the L drive:

```
manage-bde -on D: -rp -rk L:
```

Write down the recovery password and the recovery key file name that are displayed on the console. The data volume will have to be unlocked after each reboot using either the recovery password or the recovery key stored in the recovery password file. To specify a recovery password, type the following at an elevated command prompt:

```
manage-bde -unlock DriveDesignator -rp RecoveryPassword
```

where *DriveDesignator* is the designator for the encrypted drive, such as D:, and *RecoveryPassword* is the 48-character recovery password with a dash separating each 6-character grouping, such as:

```
manage-bde -unlock d: -rp 646888-201663-710926-716432-480799-714714-043043
```

To specify a recovery password file, type the following at an elevated command prompt:

```
manage-bde -unlock DriveDesignator -rk USBDesignator\RecoveryPasswordFileName
```

where *DriveDesignator* is the designator for the drive to encrypt, such as the D drive, *USBDesignator* is the designator for a USB flash drive on which you stored the recovery password, such as the L drive, and *RecoveryPasswordFileName* is the name of the recovery password file.

You can enable automatic unlocking of a data volume by typing the following at an elevated command prompt:

```
manage-bde -autounlock -enable DriveDesignator
```

where *DriveDesignator* is the designator for the drive to automatically unlock, such as D:. This command generates a recovery key and stores it on the operating system volume. The operating system volume must be fully encrypted before this command is issued. After automatic unlocking is enabled, the data volume is automatically unlocked on each reboot.

Recovering Data Protected by BitLocker Drive Encryption

If you've configured BitLocker Drive Encryption and the computer enters Recovery mode, you will need to unlock the computer. To unlock the computer using a recovery password stored on a USB flash drive, follow these steps:

1. Turn on the computer. If the computer is locked, the computer opens the BitLocker Drive Encryption Recovery console.

2. When you are prompted, insert the USB flash drive that contains the recovery password and then press Enter.

3. The computer will unlock and reboot automatically. You will not need to enter the recovery key manually.

If you saved the recovery password file in a folder on another computer or on removable media, you can use another computer to open and validate the recovery password file. To locate the correct file, find Password ID on the recovery console display on the locked computer, and write down this number. The file containing the recovery password uses this Password ID as the file name. Open the file and locate the recovery password in the file.

To unlock the computer by typing the recovery password, follow these steps:

1. Turn on the computer. If the computer is locked, the computer opens the BitLocker Drive Encryption Recovery console.

2. Type the recovery password and press Enter.

   The computer will unlock and reboot automatically.

A computer can become locked if a user tried to enter the recovery key but was unsuccessful. In the recovery console, you can press Esc twice to exit the recovery prompt and turn off the computer. A computer might also become locked if an error related to TPM occurs or boot data is modified. In this case, the computer halts very early in the boot process, before the operating system starts. At this point, the locked computer cannot accept standard keyboard numbers, so you must use the function keys to enter the recovery password. Here, the function keys F1–F9 represent the digits 1 through 9, and the F10 function key represents 0.

Disabling or Turning Off BitLocker Drive Encryption

When you need to make changes to TPM or other changes to the system, you might first need to temporarily turn off BitLocker encryption on the system volume. You cannot temporarily turn off BitLocker encryption on data volumes; you can only decrypt data volumes.

To temporarily turn off BitLocker encryption on the system volume, follow these steps:

1. Click Start, Control Panel, Security, and then double-click BitLocker Drive Encryption.

2. Under the system volume, click Turn Off BitLocker Drive Encryption.

3. In the What Level Of Decryption Do You Want dialog box, click Disable BitLocker Drive Encryption. By completing this procedure, you have temporarily disabled BitLocker on the operating system volume.

To turn off BitLocker Drive Encryption and decrypt a volume, follow these steps:

1. Click Start, Control Panel, Security, and then double-click BitLocker Drive Encryption.

2. Under the appropriate volume, click Turn Off BitLocker Drive Encryption. Note that you must decrypt all data volumes before you decrypt the operating system volume.

3. In the What Level Of Decryption Do You Want dialog box, click Decrypt The Volume. By completing this procedure, you have decrypted the volume.

Chapter 15

Chapter 14 discussed storage management, which primarily focuses on storage technologies and techniques for configuring storage. As discussed in that chapter, disks can be apportioned in many ways but ultimately must be formatted with a particular file system. The file system provides the environment for working with files and folders. Windows Server 2008 provides the file allocation table (FAT) and NTFS file system (NTFS) as the basic file system types. These file systems and their various extensions are discussed in this chapter.

Understanding Disk and File System Structure

The basic unit of storage is a disk. Regardless of the partition style or disk type, Windows Server 2008 reads data from disks and writes data to disks using the disk input/output (I/O) subsystem. The I/O subsystem understands the physical and logical structures of disks, which allows it to perform read and write operations. The basic physical structure of a disk includes:

- Platters
- Cylinders
- Tracks
- Clusters
- Sectors

Each disk has one or more platters. Platters are the physical media from which data is read and to which data is written. The disk head travels in a circular path over the platter. This circular path is called a track. Tracks are magnetically encoded when you format a disk. Tracks that reside in the same location on each platter form a cylinder. For example, if a disk has four platters, Cylinder 1 consists of Track 1 from all four platters.

Tracks are divided into sectors. Sectors represent a subsection within a track and are made up of individual bytes. The number of sectors in a track depends on the disk type and the location of the track on the platter. Tracks closer to the outside of the platter can have more sectors than tracks near the center of the platter.

When you format a disk with a file system, the file system structures the disk using clusters, which are logical groupings of sectors. Both FAT and NTFS use a fixed sector size of 512 bytes but allow the cluster size to be variable. For example, the cluster size might be 4096 bytes, and if there are 512 bytes per sector, each cluster is made up of eight sectors. Table 16-1 provides a summary of the default cluster sizes for FAT, FAT32, exFAT, and NTFS. You have the option of specifying the cluster size when you create a file system on a disk, or you can accept the default cluster size setting. Either way, the cluster sizes available depend on the type of file system you are using.

> **Four Different FAT File Systems**
>
> There are actually four FAT file systems used by Windows platforms: FAT12, FAT16, FAT32, and exFAT. The difference between FAT12, FAT16, and FAT32 is the number of bits used for entries in their file allocation tables, namely 12, 16, or 32 bits. From a user's perspective, the main difference in these file systems is the theoretical maximum volume size, which is 16 MB for a FAT12 volume, 4 GB for FAT16, and 2 TB for FAT32. When the term *FAT* is used without an appended number, however, it always refers to FAT16. Extended FAT or exFAT is a new version of FAT for removable media that is available with Windows Vista Service Pack 1 or later and Windows Server 2008.

Table 16-1 Default Cluster Sizes for FAT16, FAT32, exFAT, and NTFS

Volume Size	Cluster Size			
	FAT16	FAT32	exFAT	NTFS
7 MB to 16 MB	512 bytes	Not supported	Not supported	512 bytes
17 MB to 32 MB	512 bytes	Not supported	Not supported	512 bytes
33 MB to 64 MB	1 KB	1 KB	4 KB	512 bytes
65 MB to 128 MB	2 KB	1 KB	4 KB	512 bytes
129 MB to 256 MB	4 KB	2 KB	4 KB	512 bytes
257 MB to 512 MB	8 KB	4 KB	32 KB	512 bytes
513 MB to 1024 MB	16 KB	4 KB	32 KB	1 KB
1025 MB to 2 GB	32 KB	4 KB	32 KB	2 KB
2 GB to 4 GB	64 KB	4 KB	32 KB	4 KB
4 GB to 8 GB	Not supported	4 KB	32 KB	4 KB
8 GB to 16 GB	Not supported	8 KB	32 KB	4 KB
16 GB to 32 GB	Not supported	16 KB	32 KB	4 KB
32 GB to 2 TB	Not supported	*	*	4 KB

The important thing to know about clusters is that they are the smallest unit in which disk space is allocated. Each cluster can hold one file at most. So, if you create a 1 kilobyte (KB) file and the cluster size is 4 KB, there will be 3 KB of empty space in the cluster that isn't available to other files. That's just the way it is. If a single cluster isn't big enough to hold an entire file, then the remaining file data will go into the next available cluster and the next until the file is completely stored. For FAT, for example, the first cluster used by the file has a pointer to the second cluster, and the second cluster has a pointer to the next, and so on until you get to the final cluster used by the file, which has an end-of-file (EOF) marker.

Although the disk I/O subsystem manages the physical structure of disks, Windows Server 2008 manages the logical disk structure at the file system level. The logical structure of a disk relates to the basic or dynamic volumes you create on a disk and the file systems with which those volumes are formatted. You can format both basic volumes and dynamic volumes using FAT or NTFS. As discussed in the next section, each file system type has a different structure, and there are advantages and disadvantages of each as well.

Using FAT

FAT volumes use an allocation table to store information about disk space allocation. FAT can be used with both fixed disks and removable media. For both fixed disks and removable media, FAT is available in 16-bit and 32-bit versions, which are referred to as FAT16 and FAT32. For removable media, you can also use exFAT. The advantage of using exFAT with removable media instead of FAT is that exFAT can be used with any operating system or device that supports this file system type.

> **Note**
>
> In the discussion that follows, I will focus on FAT16 and FAT32. As an administrator, you'll mostly work with FAT16 and FAT32.

File Allocation Table Structure

Disks formatted using FAT are organized as shown in Figure 16-1. They have a boot sector that stores information about the disk type, starting and ending sectors, the active partition, and a bootstrap program that executes at startup and boots the operating system. This is followed by a reserve area that can be one or more sectors in length.

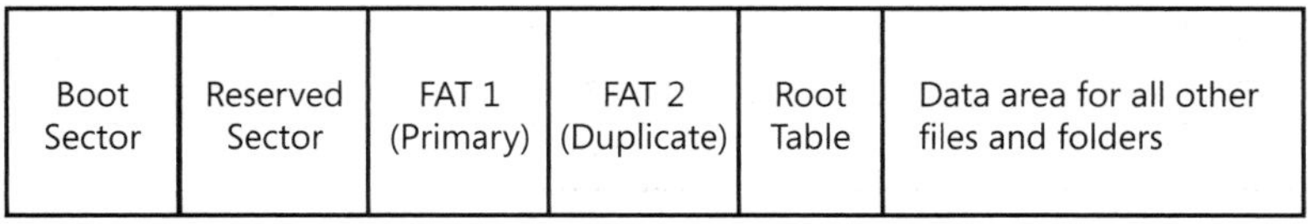

Boot Sector	Reserved Sector	FAT 1 (Primary)	FAT 2 (Duplicate)	Root Table	Data area for all other files and folders

Figure 16-1 An overview of FAT16 volume structure.

Chapter 16

The reserve area is followed by the primary file allocation table, which provides a reference table for the clusters on the volume. Each reference in the table relates to a specific cluster and defines the cluster's status as follows:

- Available (unused)
- In use (meaning it is being used by a file)
- Bad (meaning it is marked as bad and won't be written to)
- Reserved (meaning it is reserved for the operating system)

If a cluster is in use, the cluster entry identifies the number of the next cluster in the file or that it is the last cluster of a file, in which case the end of the file has been reached.

FAT volumes also have the following features:

- Duplicate file allocation table, which provides a backup of the primary file allocation table and can be used to restore the file system if the primary file allocation table gets corrupted
- Root directory table, which defines the starting cluster of each file in the file system
- Data area, which stores the actual data for user files and folders

When an application attempts to read a file, the operating system looks up the starting cluster of the file in the root directory table and then uses the file allocation table to find and read all the clusters in the file.

FAT Features

Although FAT supports basic file and folder operations, its features are rather limited. By using FAT, you have the following capabilities:

- You can use Windows file sharing but have limited control over remote access to files and folders.
- You can use long file names, meaning file and folder names containing up to 255 characters.
- You can use FAT with floppy disks and removable disks.
- You can use Unicode characters in file and folder names.
- You can use upper- and lowercase letters in file and folder names.

However, FAT has the following disadvantages:

- You can't control local access to files and folders using Windows file and folder access permissions.
- You can't use any advanced file system features of NTFS, including compression, encryption, disk quotas, and remote storage.

In addition, although FAT16 supports small cluster sizes, FAT32 does not. Table 16-2 provides a summary of FAT16, FAT32, and exFAT.

Table 16-2 Comparison of FAT16, FAT32, and exFAT Features

Feature	FAT16	FAT32	exFAT
File allocation table size	16-bit	32-bit	32-bit
Minimum volume size	See following Inside Out tip	33 MB	33 MB
Maximum volume size	4 GB; best at 2 GB or less	2 TB; limited in Windows Server 2008 to 32 GB	2 TB; limited in Windows Server 2008 to 32 GB
Maximum file size	2 GB	4 GB	Same as volume size
Supports small cluster size	Yes	No	No
Supports NTFS features	No	No	No
Use on fixed disks	Yes	Yes	No
Use on removable disks	Yes	Yes	Yes
Supports network file and folder sharing	No	No	Yes
Supports customized disk and folder views	No	No	Yes

> **Note**
>
> Although Windows Server 2008 can read to or write from FAT32 volumes as large as 2 TB, the operating system can only format FAT32 volumes up to 32 GB in size.

INSIDE OUT   FAT on very small media

It is important to note that FAT volumes are structured differently depending on volume size. When you format a volume that is less than 32,680 sectors (16 megabytes [MB]), the format program uses 12 bits for FAT12. This means less space is reserved for each entry in the table and more space is made available for data. This technique is meant to be used with very small media, such as floppy disks.

In FAT, disk sectors are 512 bytes. By default Windows Server 2008 sets the size of clusters and the number of sectors per cluster based on the size of the volume. Disk geometry also is a factor in determining cluster size because the number of clusters on the volume must fit into the number of bits used by the file system. The actual amount of data you can store on a single FAT volume is a factor of the maximum cluster size and the maximum number of clusters you can use per volume. This can be written out as a formula:

ClusterSize × MaximumNumberOfClusters = MaximumVolumeSize

FAT16 supports a maximum of 65,526 clusters and a maximum cluster size of 64 KB. This is where the limitation of 4 gigabytes (GB) for volume size comes from. With disks less than 32 MB but more than 16 MB in size, the cluster size is 512 bytes and there is one sector per cluster. This changes as the volume size increases up to the largest cluster size of 64 KB with 128 sectors per cluster on 2-GB to 4-GB volumes.

FAT32 volumes using 512-byte sectors can be up to 2 terabytes (TB) in size and can use clusters of up to 64 KB. To control the maximum number of clusters allowed, the Windows operating system reserves the upper 4 bits, however, limiting FAT32 to a maximum 28 bits worth of clusters. With a maximum recommended cluster size of 32 KB (instead of the maximum allowable 64 KB), this means a FAT32 volume on the Windows operating system can be up to 32 GB in size. Because the smallest cluster size allowed for FAT32 volumes is 512 bytes, the smallest FAT32 volume you can create is 33 MB.

FAT32 Volumes of Any Size Can Be Mounted

Windows Server 2008 does support mounting FAT32 volumes of up to the theoretical limit of 2 TB. This allows you to mount volumes larger than 32 GB that were created on other operating systems or by using third-party utilities.

INSIDE OUT Getting volume format and feature information

A quick way to check the file system type and available features of a volume is to type **fsutil fsinfo volumeinfo *DriveDesignator*** at the command prompt, where DriveDesignator is the drive letter of the volume followed by a colon, such as C:. For a FAT or FAT32 volume, you'll see output similar to the following:

```
Volume Name : LogData
Volume Serial Number : 0x70692a2e
Max Component Length : 255
File System Name : FAT32
Preserves Case of filenames
Supports Unicode in filenames
```

Using NTFS

NTFS is an extensible and recoverable file system that offers many advantages over FAT and FAT32. Because it is extensible, the file system can be extended over time with various revisions. As you'll learn shortly, the version of NTFS that ships with Windows Server 2008 has been extended with new features but is designated as having the same internal version as the revision of the NTFS version that shipped with Microsoft Windows Server 2003. Because it is recoverable, volumes formatted with NTFS can be reconstructed if they contain structure errors. Typically, restructuring NTFS volumes is a task performed at startup.

NTFS Structures

NTFS volumes have a very different structure and feature set than FAT volumes. The first area of the volume is the boot sector, which is located at sector 0 on the volume. The boot sector stores information about the disk layout, and a bootstrap program executes at startup and boots the operating system. A backup boot sector is placed at the end of the volume for redundancy and fault tolerance.

Instead of a file allocation table, NTFS uses a relational database to store information about files. This database is called the master file table (MFT). The MFT stores a file record of each file and folder on the volume, pertinent volume information, and details on the MFT itself. The first 16 records in the MFT store NTFS metadata as summarized in Table 16-3.

The MFT mirror stores a partial duplicate of the MFT that can be used to recover the MFT. If any of the records in the primary mirror become corrupted or are otherwise unreadable and there's a duplicate record in the MFT mirror, NTFS uses the data in the MFT mirror and if possible uses this data to recover the records in the primary MFT. It is also important to note that the NTFS version that ships with Windows Server 2003 and Windows Server 2008 (NTFS 5.1) has a slightly different metadata mapping than the version that originally shipped with Windows 2000 (NTFS 5). In the current version, the $LogFile and $Bitmap metadata files are located on a different position on disk than they were in Windows 2000. This gives a performance advantage of five to eight percent to disks that are formatted under Windows Server 2008 and comes close to approximating the performance of FAT.

The rest of the records in the MFT store file and folder information. Each of these regular entries includes the file or folder name, security descriptor, and other attributes, including file data or pointers to file data. The MFT record size is set when a volume is formatted and can be 1024 bytes, 2048 bytes, or 4096 bytes, depending on the volume size. If a file is very small, all of its contents might be able to fit in the data field of its record in the MFT. When all of a file's attributes, including its data, can be stored in the MFT record, the attributes are called *resident attributes*. Figure 16-2 shows an example of a small file with resident attributes.

Table 16-3 **NTFS Metadata**

MFT Record	Record Type	File Name	Description
0	MFT	$Mft	Stores the base file record of each file and folder on the volume. As the number of files and folders grows, additional records are used as necessary.
1	MFT mirror	$MftMirr	Stores a partial duplicate of the MFT used for failure recovery. Also referred to as MFT2.
2	Log file	$LogFile	Stores a persistent history of all changes made to files on the volume, which can be used to recover files.
3	Volume	$Volume	Stores volume attributes, including the volume serial number, version, and number of sectors.
4	Attribute definitions	$AttrDef	Stores a table of attribute names, numbers, and descriptions.
5	Root file name index	$	Stores the details on the volume's root directory.
6	Cluster bitmap	$Bitmap	Stores a table that details the clusters in use.
7	Boot sector	$Boot	Stores the bootstrap program on bootable volumes. Also includes the locations of the MFT and MFT mirror.
8	Bad cluster file	$BadClus	Stores a table mapping bad clusters.
9	Security file	$Secure	Stores the unique security descriptor for all files and folders on the volume.
10	Upcase table	$Upcase	Stores a table used to convert lowercase to matching uppercase Unicode characters.
11	NTFS extension file	$Extend	Stores information on enabled file system extensions.
12–15	To be determined	To be determined	Reserved records for future use.

If a file is larger than a single record, it has what are called *nonresident attributes*. Here, the file has a base record in the MFT that details where to find the file data. NTFS creates additional areas called runs on the disk to store the additional file data. The size of data runs is dependent on the cluster size of the volume. If the cluster size is 2 KB or less, data runs are 2 KB. If the cluster size is over 2 KB, data runs are 4 KB.

Record		Record Type
0		MFT
1		MFT mirror
2		Log file
3		Volume
4		Attribute definitions
5		Root file name index
6		Cluster bitmap
7		Boot sector
8		Bad cluster file
9		Security file
10		Upcase table
11		NTFS extension file
12–15		Reserved
16		Users' files/folders

	Standard Information	File Name	Security Descriptor	Data
Record for Small File				

Figure 16-2 A graphical depiction of the MFT and its records.

As Figure 16-3 shows, clusters belonging to the file are referenced in the MFT using virtual cluster numbers (VCNs). VCNs are numbered sequentially starting with VCN 0. The Data field in the file's MFT record maps the VCNs to a starting logical cluster number (LCN) on the disk and details the number of clusters to read for that VCN. When these mappings use up all the available space in a record, additional MFT records are created to store the additional mappings.

In addition to the MFT, NTFS reserves a contiguous range of space past the end of the MFT called the MFT zone. By default the MFT zone is approximately 12.5 percent of the total volume space. The MFT zone is used to allow the MFT to grow without becoming fragmented. Typically, the MFT zone shrinks as the MFT grows.

Chapter 16

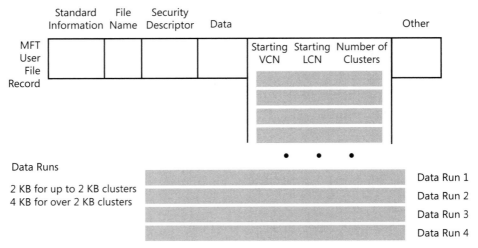

Figure 16-3 A graphical depiction of a user file record with data runs.

The MFT zone is not used to store user data unless the remainder of the volume becomes full. Fragmentation can and still does occur, however. On volumes with lots of small files, the MFT zone can get used up by the MFT, and as additional files are added, the MFT has to grow into unreserved areas of the volume. On volumes with but a few large files, the unreserved space on a volume can get used up before the MFT, and in this case, the files start using the MFT zone space.

INSIDE OUT   The MFT zone can be optimized

By default, the MFT is optimized for environments that have a mix of large and small files. This setting works well if the average file size is 8 KB or larger. It doesn't work so well if a volume has many very small files, such as when the average size of files is less than 2 KB or between 2 KB and 7 KB. Here, you might want to configure the volume so that it has a larger MFT zone than normal to help prevent the MFT from becoming fragmented. The MFT zone size is set in eighths of the disk.

You can determine the current MFT zone setting by typing the following command at the command prompt: **fsutil behavior query mftzone**. If this command returns "mft-zone=0," the MFT zone is using the default setting. The default setting, 0, specifies that the MFT zone should use one-eighth (12.5 percent) of the total volume space. This is the same as a setting of 1. You can also use a setting of 2, 3, or 4 to set the MFT zone to use two-eighths (25 percent), three-eighths (37.5 percent), or four-eighths (50 percent) of the total volume space.

You can configure the MFT zone by typing the command **fsutil behavior set mftzone** *Value*, where *Value* is the relative size setting to use, such as 2.

NTFS Features

Several versions of NTFS are available. NTFS 4 shipped with Microsoft Windows NT 4.0. NTFS 5 was first implemented in Windows 2000 and made available to Windows NT 4.0 through Service Pack 4. If you created NTFS volumes in Windows NT 4.0 and upgraded to Windows 2000 or Windows Server 2008, the volumes aren't upgraded automatically to NTFS 5. You must choose to upgrade the volumes during installation of the operating system or when you install the Active Directory directory service.

You have the following capabilities when you use NTFS 4:

- You can use advanced file and folder access permissions.
- You can use file sharing and full-control remote access to files and folders.
- You can use long file names, meaning file and folder names can contain up to 255 characters.
- You can use Unicode characters in file and folder names.
- You can use uppercase and lowercase letters in file and folder names.
- You can't use NTFS with floppy disks but can use NTFS with removable disks.

By using NTFS 5, you have all the features of NTFS 4 plus additional features:

- You can use Encrypting File System (EFS).
- You can use sparse files, disk quotas, and object identifiers.
- You can use reparse points, remote storage, and shadow copies.
- You can use data streams and change journals.

> **Note**
>
> For NTFS, you typically refer to major version numbers rather than the major version and the revision number. Technically, however, Shadow Copy is a feature of NTFS 5.1 or later. NTFS 5.1 is the version of NTFS that was first included in Windows XP (and is available with Windows 2000 Server Service Pack 4 or later). With NTFS 5.1 you gain some additional enhancements, primarily the ability to use shadow copies.

Table 16-4 provides a comparison of key features of NTFS 4 and NTFS 5.

Table 16-4 **Comparison of NTFS 4 and NTFS 5 Features**

Feature	NTFS 4	NTFS 5
Maximum volume size	32 GB	2 TB on basic master boot record (MBR) disks; 256 TB on dynamic MBR disks; 18 exabytes (EB) on GUID partition table (GPT) disks. See "Configuring Storage" on page 419 for details on MBR and GPT disks.
Maximum file size	32 GB	Only limited by volume size
Supports object identifiers	No	Yes
Supports advanced file access permissions	Yes	Yes
Supports disk quotas	No	Yes
Supports remote storage	No	Yes
Supports sparse files	No	Yes
Supports file-based compression	Yes	Yes
Supports EFS	No	Yes
Supports reparse points	No	Yes
Use on floppy disks	No	No
Use on removable disks	Yes	Yes

With NTFS, disk sectors are 512 bytes. Windows Server 2008 automatically sets the size of clusters and the number of sectors per cluster based on the size of the volume. Cluster sizes range from 512 bytes to 4 KB. As with FAT, NTFS has the following characteristics:

- Disk geometry also is a factor in determining cluster size because the number of clusters on the volume must fit into the number of bits used by the file system.

- The actual amount of data you can store on a single NTFS volume is a factor of the maximum cluster size and the maximum number of clusters you can use per volume.

Thus, although volumes have a specific maximum size, the cluster size used on a volume can be a limiting factor. For example, a dynamic volume with a 4-KB cluster size can have dynamic volumes up to 16 TB, which is different from the maximum allowed dynamic volume size on NTFS.

Analyzing NTFS Structure

If you want to examine the structure of a volume formatted using NFTS, you can use the FSUtil FSinfo command to do this. Type **fsutil fsinfo ntfsinfo** *DriveDesignator* at the command prompt, where *DriveDesignator* is the drive letter of the volume followed by a colon. For example, if you want to obtain information on the C drive, you'd type

```
fsutil fsinfo ntfsinfo c:
```

The output would be similar to the following:

```
NTFS Volume Serial Number :   0x2c64a9b264a97f68
Version :                     3.1
Number Sectors :              0x0000000006fcf9c2
Total Clusters :              0x0000000000df9f38
Free Clusters  :              0x0000000000c8a5e5
Total Reserved :              0x0000000000000030
Bytes Per Sector  :           512
Bytes Per Cluster :           4096
Bytes Per FileRecord Segment    :     1024
Clusters Per FileRecord Segment :     0
Mft Valid Data Length :       0x00000000049d9000
Mft Start Lcn  :              0x00000000000c0000
Mft2 Start Lcn :              0x00000000006fcf9c
Mft Zone Start :              0x00000000002801e0
Mft Zone End   :              0x0000000000283c00
```

As Table 16-5 shows, FSUtil FSinfo provides detailed information on NTFS volume structure, including space usage and configuration.

Table 16-5 Details from FSUtil FSinfo

Field	Description
NTFS Volume Serial Number	The unique serial number of the selected NTFS volume.
Version	The internal NTFS version. Here, 3.1 refers to NTFS 5.1.
Number Sectors	The total number of sectors on the volume in hexadecimal.
Total Clusters	The total number of clusters on the volume in hexadecimal.
Free Clusters	The number of unused clusters on the volume in hexadecimal.
Total Reserved	The total number of clusters reserved for NTFS metadata.
Bytes Per Sector	The number of bytes per sector.
Bytes Per Cluster	The number of bytes per cluster.
Bytes Per FileRecord Segment	The size of MFT file records.
Clusters Per FileRecord Segment	The number of clusters per file record segment, which is valid only if the file record size is as large as or larger than the volume cluster size.
Mft Valid Data Length	The current size of the MFT.
Mft Start Lcn	The location of the first LCN on the disk used by the MFT.
Mft2 Start Lcn	The location of the first LCN on the disk used by the MFT mirror.
Mft Zone Start	The cluster number that marks the start of the region on the disk reserved by the MFT.
Mft Zone End	The cluster number that marks the end of the region on the disk reserved by the MFT.

Using FSUtil, you can also obtain detailed statistics on NTFS metadata and user file usage since a system was started. To view this information, type **fsutil fsinfo statistics** *DriveDesignator* at the command prompt, where *DriveDesignator* is the drive letter of the volume followed by a colon. For example, if you want to obtain information on the C drive, you'd type

```
fsutil fsinfo statistics c:
```

The output is shown in two sections. The first section of the statistics details user file and disk activity as well as the overall usage of NTFS metadata. As shown in this example, the output shows the number of reads and writes as well as the number of bytes read or written:

```
File System Type :     NTFS
UserFileReads :        13270
UserFileReadBytes :    361323008
UserDiskReads :        13265
UserFileWrites :       1968
UserFileWriteBytes :   51138008
UserDiskWrites :       2049
MetaDataReads :        4294
MetaDataReadBytes :    17588224
MetaDataDiskReads :    4904
MetaDataWrites :       1218
MetaDataWriteBytes :   19656704
MetaDataDiskWrites :   1751
```

The second section of the statistics details usage of individual NTFS metadata files. As shown in this example, the output details the number of reads and writes as well as the number of bytes read or written for each NTFS metadata file:

```
MftReads :             2027
MftReadBytes :         8302592
MftWrites :            1015
MftWriteBytes :        4591616
Mft2Writes :           0
Mft2WriteBytes :       0
RootIndexReads :       0
RootIndexReadBytes :   0
RootIndexWrites :      0
RootIndexWriteBytes :  0
BitmapReads :          1738
BitmapReadBytes :      7118848
BitmapWrites :         91
BitmapWriteBytes :     13205504
MftBitmapReads :       4
MftBitmapReadBytes :   16384
MftBitmapWrites :      32
MftBitmapWriteBytes :  135168
UserIndexReads :       966
UserIndexReadBytes :   3956736
UserIndexWrites :      510
```

```
UserIndexWriteBytes :    2191360
LogFileReads :           7
LogFileReadBytes :       28672
LogFileWrites :          3244
LogFileWriteBytes :      36012032
LogFileFull :            0
```

Advanced NTFS Features

NTFS has many advanced features that administrators should know about and understand. These features include the following:

- Hard links
- Data streams
- Change journals
- Object identifiers
- Reparse points
- Sparse files
- Transactions

Each of these features is discussed in the sections that follow.

Hard Links

Every file created on a volume has a hard link. The hard link is the directory entry for the file and it is what allows the operating system to find files within folders. On NTFS volumes, files can have multiple hard links. This allows a single file to appear in the same directory with multiple names or to appear in multiple directories with the same name or different names. As with file copies, applications can open a file using any of the hard links you've created and modify the file. If you use another hard link to open the file in another application, the application can detect the changes.

Wondering why you'd want to use hard links? Hard links are useful when you want the same file to appear in several locations. For example, you might want a document to appear in a folder of a network share that is available to all users but have an application that requires the document to be in another directory so that it can be read and processed on a daily basis. Rather than moving the file to the application directory and giving every user in the company access to this protected directory, you decide to create a hard link to the document so that it can be accessed separately by both users and the application.

Regardless of how many hard links a file has, however, the related directory entries all point to the single file that exists in one location on the volume—and this is how hard links differ from copies. With a copy of a file, the file data exists in multiple locations.

With a hard link, the file appears in multiple locations but exists in only one location. Thus, if you modify a file using one of its hard links and save, and then someone opens the file using a different hard link, the changes are shown.

> **Note**
>
> Hard links have advantages and disadvantages. Hard links are not meant for environments where multiple users can modify a file simultaneously. If Sandra opens a file using one hard link and is working on the file at the same time Bob is working on the file, there can be problems if they both try to save changes. Although this is a disadvantage of hard links, the really big advantage of hard links shouldn't be overlooked: If a file has multiple hard links, the file will not be deleted from the volume until all hard links are deleted. This means that if someone were to accidentally delete a file that had multiple hard links, the file wouldn't actually be deleted. Instead, only the affected hard link would be deleted and any other hard links and the file itself would remain.

Because there is only one physical copy of a file with multiple hard links, the hard links do not have separate security descriptors. Only the source file has security descriptors. Thus, if you were to change the access permissions of a file using any of its hard links, you would actually change the security of the source file and all hard links that point to this file would have these security settings.

You can create hard links by using the FSUtil Hardlink command. Use the following syntax:

```
fsutil hardlink create NewFilePath CurrentFilePath
```

where *NewFilePath* is the file path for the hard link you want to create and *CurrentFilePath* is the name of the existing file to which you are linking. For example, if the file ChangeLog.doc is found in the file path C:\CorpDocs and you want to create a new hard link to this file with the file path C:\UserData\Logs\CurrentLog.doc, you would type

```
fsutil hardlink create C:\UserData\Logs\CurrentLog.doc C:\CorpDocs\ChangeLog.doc
```

Hard links can be created only on NTFS volumes, and you cannot create a hard link on one volume that refers to another volume. Following this, you couldn't create a hard link to the D drive for a file created on the C drive.

Data Streams

Every file created on a volume has a data stream associated with it. A data stream is a sequence of bytes that contains the contents of the file. The main data stream for a file is unnamed and is visible to all file systems. On NTFS volumes, files can also have named data streams associated with them. Named data streams contain additional information about a file, such as custom properties or summary details. This allows you to associate additional information with a file but still be able to manage the file as a single unit.

After you create a named data stream and associate it with a file, any applications that know how to work with named data streams can access the streams by their names and read the additional details. Many applications support named data streams, including Microsoft Office, Adobe Acrobat, and other productivity applications. This is how you can set summary properties for a Microsoft Word document, such as Title, Subject, and Author, and save that information with the file.

In fact, if you right-click any file on an NTFS volume, select Properties, and then click the Details tab, you can see information that is associated with the file using a data stream as shown in Figure 16-4.

Figure 16-4 Information entered on the Details tab is saved to a named data stream.

Generally speaking, the named data streams associated with a file are used to set the names of its property tabs and to populate the fields of those tabs. This is how some document types can have other tabs associated with them and how the Windows operating system can store a thumbnail image within an NTFS file containing an image.

The most important thing to know about streams is that they aren't supported on FAT. If you move or copy a file containing named streams to a FAT volume, you might see the warning prompt labeled "Confirm Stream Loss" telling you the file has additional information associated with it and asking you to confirm that it's okay that the file is saved without this information. If you click Yes, only the contents of the file are copied or moved to the FAT volume—and not the contents of the associated data streams. If you click No, the copy or save operation is canceled.

In a file's Properties dialog box, on the Details tab, you also have the option of removing properties and personal information associated with a file. You do this by clicking the Remove Properties And Personal Information link and then selecting a Remove Properties method. Windows accomplishes this task by removing the values from the related data streams associated with the file.

Change Journals

In Windows Server 2008, an NTFS volume can use an update sequence number (USN) change journal. A change journal provides a complete log of all changes made to the volume. It records additions, deletions, and modifications regardless of who made them or how the additions, deletions, and modifications occurred. As with system logs, the change log is persistent, so it isn't reset if you shut down and restart the operating system. The operating system writes records to the NTFS change log when an NTFS checkpoint occurs. The checkpoint tells the operating system to write changes that would allow NTFS to recover from failure to a particular point in time.

The change journal is enabled when you install certain services, including File Replication Service (FRS), Indexing Service, and Distributed File System Service. Domain controllers and any other computer in the domain that uses these services rely heavily on the change journal. The change journal allows these services to be very efficient at determining when files, folders, and other NTFS objects have been modified. Rather than checking time stamps and registering for file notifications, these services perform direct lookups in the change journal to determine all the modifications made to a set of files. Not only is this faster, it uses system resources more efficiently as well.

You can gather summary statistics about the change journal by typing **fsutil usn queryjournal** *DriveDesignator* at the command prompt, where *DriveDesignator* is the drive letter of the volume followed by a colon. For example, if you want to obtain change journal statistics on the C drive, you'd type

```
fsutil usn queryjournal c:
```

The output is similar to the following:

```
Usn Journal ID    : 0x01c2ed7bd1b73670
First Usn         : 0x000000001b700000
Next Usn          : 0x00000000237ceb40
Lowest Valid Usn  : 0x0000000000000000
Max Usn           : 0x00000ffffff0000
Maximum Size      : 0x0000000008000000
Allocation Delta  : 0x0000000000100000
```

The details show the following information:

- **Usn Journal ID** The unique identifier of the change journal.

- **First Usn** The first USN in the change journal.

- **Next Usn** The next USN that can be written to the change journal.

- **Lowest Valid Usn** The lowest valid USN that can be written to the change journal.

- **Max Usn** The highest USN that can be assigned.

- **Maximum Size** The maximum size in bytes that the change journal can use. If the change journal exceeds this value, older entries are overwritten.

- **Allocation Delta** The size in bytes of memory allocation that is added to the end and removed from the beginning of the change journal when it becomes full.

Individual records written to the change journal look like this:

```
File Ref#        : 0x18e90000000018e9
ParentFile Ref# : 0x17c00000000017c0
Usn              : 0x0000000000000000
SecurityId       : 0x00000119
Reason           : 0x00000000
Name (024)       : ocmanage.dll
```

The most important information here is the name of the affected file and the security identifier of the object that made the change. You can get the most recent change journal entry for a file by typing **fsutil usn readdata** *FilePath*, where *FilePath* is the name of the file for which you want to retrieve change information. For example, if you want to obtain the most recent change journal information on a file with the path C:\Domain-Computers.txt, you'd type

```
fsutil usn readdata c:\domaincomputers.txt
```

The output is similar to the following:

```
Major Version    : 0x2
Minor Version    : 0x0
FileRef#         : 0x000800000001c306
Parent FileRef#  : 0x0005000000000005
Usn              : 0x00000000237cf7f0
Time Stamp       : 0x0000000000000000
Reason           : 0x0
Source Info      : 0x0
Security Id      : 0x45e
File Attributes  : 0x20
File Name Length : 0x26
File Name Offset : 0x3c
FileName         : domaincomputers.txt
```

This data shows the file's reference number in the root file index and that of its parent. It also shows the current USN associated with the file and the file attributes flag. The File Name Length element shows the total length in characters of the file's long and short file names together. This particular file has a file name length of 38 (0 × 26). That's because the file name has more than eight characters followed by a dot and a three-letter extension. This means the file is represented by NTFS using long and short file names. The long file name is domaincomputers.txt. This is followed by an offset pointer that indicates where the short file name, domain~1.txt, can be looked up, which is where the total file name length of 38 characters comes from.

> **Note**
>
> You can examine a file's short file name by typing **dir /x** *FilePath* at the command prompt, where *FilePath* is the path to the file you want to examine, such as: **dir /x c:\ domaincomputers.txt**.

Object Identifiers

Another feature of NTFS is the ability to use object identifiers. Object identifiers are 16 bytes in length and are unique on a per-volume basis. Any file that has an object identifier also has the following:

- Birth volume identifier (BirthVolumeID), which is the object identifier for the volume in which the file was originally created

- Birth object identifier (BirthObjectID), which is the object identifier assigned to the file when it was created

- Domain identifier (DomainID), which is the object identifier for the domain in which the file was created

These values are also 16 bytes in length. If a file is moved within a volume or moved to a new volume, it is assigned a new object identifier, but information about the original object identifier assigned when the object was created can be retained using the birth object identifier.

Object identifiers are used by several system services to uniquely identify files and the volumes with which they are associated. For example, FRS uses object identifiers to locate files for replication. The Distributed Link Tracking (DLT) Client service uses object identifiers to track linked files that are moved within an NTFS volume, to another NTFS volume on the same computer, or to an NTFS volume on another computer.

Any file used by FRS or the DLT Client service has an object identifier field set containing values for the object ID, birth volume ID, birth object ID, and domain ID. The actual field set looks like this:

```
Object ID :       52eac013e3d34445334345453533ab3d
BirthVolume ID : a23bc3243a5a3452d32424332c32343d
BirthObject ID : 52eac013e3d34445334345453533ab3d
Domain ID :       00000000000000000000000000000000
```

Here, the file has a specific object ID, birth volume ID, and birth object ID. The domain ID isn't assigned, however, because this is not currently used. You can tell that the file is used by the DLT Client service because the birth volume ID and birth object ID have been assigned and these identifiers are used only by this service. Because the birth volume ID and birth object ID remain the same even if a file is moved, the DLT Client service uses these identifiers to find files no matter where they have been moved.

In contrast, FRS uses only the object ID, so the object identifier field set for a file used by FRS looks like this:

```
Object ID :       52eac013e3d34445334345453533ab3d
BirthVolume ID : 00000000000000000000000000000000
BirthObject ID : 00000000000000000000000000000000
Domain ID :       00000000000000000000000000000000
```

If you are trying to determine whether a file is used by FRS or the DLT Client service, you could use the FSUtil ObjectID command to see if the file has an object identifier field set. Type **fsutil objectid query** *FilePath* at the command prompt, where *FilePath* is the path to the file or folder you want to examine. If the file has an object identifier field set, it is displayed. If a file doesn't have an object identifier field set, an error message is displayed stating "The specified file has no object ID."

Reparse Points

On NTFS volumes, a file or folder can contain a reparse point. Reparse points are file system objects with special attribute tags that are used to extend the functionality in the I/O subsystem. When a program sets a reparse point, it stores an attribute tag as well as a data segment. The attribute tag identifies the purpose of the reparse point and details how the reparse point is to be used. The data segment provides any additional data needed during reparsing.

Reparse points are used for directory junction points and volume mount points. Directory junctions enable you to create a single local namespace using local folders, local volumes, and network shares. Mount points enable you to mount a local volume to an empty NTFS folder. Both directory junction points and volume mount points use reparse points to mark NTFS folders with surrogate names.

When a file or folder containing a reparse point used for a directory junction point or a volume mount point is read, the reparse point causes the pathname to be reparsed and a surrogate name to be substituted for the original name. For example, if you were to create a mount point with the file path C:\Data that is used to mount a hard disk drive, the reparse point is triggered whenever the file system opens C:\Data and points the file system to the volume you've mounted in that folder. The actual attribute tag and data for the reparse point would look similar to the following:

```
Reparse Tag Value :  0xa0000003
Tag value: Microsoft
Tag value: Name Surrogate
Tag value: Mount Point
Substitute Name offset:   0
Substitute Name length:   98
Print Name offset:  100
Print Name Length:  0
Substitute Name:  \??\Volume{3796c3c1-5106-11d7-911c-806d6172696f}\

Reparse Data Length: 0x0000006e
Reparse Data:
0000: 00 00 62 00 64 00 00 00  5c 00 3f 00 3f 00 5c 00  ..b.d...\.?.?.\.
0010: 56 00 6f 00 6c 00 75 00  6d 00 65 00 7b 00 33 00  V.o.l.u.m.e.{.3.
0020: 37 00 39 00 36 00 63 00  33 00 63 00 31 00 2d 00  7.9.6.c.3.c.1.-.
0030: 35 00 31 00 30 00 36 00  2d 00 31 00 31 00 64 00  5.1.0.6.-.1.1.d.
0040: 37 00 2d 00 39 00 31 00  31 00 63 00 2d 00 38 00  7.-.9.1.1.c.-.8.
0050: 30 00 36 00 64 00 36 00  31 00 37 00 32 00 36 00  0.6.d.6.1.7.2.6.
0060: 39 00 36 00 66 00 7d 00  5c 00 00 00 00 00        9.6.f.}.\.....
```

The reparse attribute tag is defined by the first series of values, which identifies the reparse point as a Microsoft Name Surrogate Mount Point and specifies the surrogate name to be substituted for the original name. The reparse data follows the attribute tag values and in this case provides the fully expressed surrogate name.

Examine Reparse Points

Using the FSUtil ReparsePoint command, you can examine reparse information associated with a file or folder. Type **fsutil reparsepoint query *FilePath*** at the command prompt, where *FilePath* is the path to the file or folder you want to examine.

Reparse points are also used by file system filter drivers to mark files so they are used with that driver. When NTFS opens a file associated with a file system filter driver, it locates the driver and uses the filter to process the file as directed by the reparse information. Reparse points are used in this way to implement Remote Storage.

Sparse Files

Often scientific or other data collected through sampling is stored in large files that are primarily empty except for sparsely populated sections that contain the actual data. For example, a broad-spectrum signal recorded digitally from space might have only several minutes of audio for each hour of actual recording. In this case, a multiple-gigabyte audio file such as the one depicted in Figure 16-5 might have only a few gigabytes of meaningful information. Because there are large sections of empty space and limited areas of meaningful data, the file is said to be sparsely populated and can also be referred to as a *sparse file*.

Stored normally, the file would use 20 GB of space on the volume. If you mark the file as sparse, however, NTFS allocates space only for actual data and marks empty space as nonallocated. In other words, any meaningful or nonzero data is marked as allocated and written to disk, and any data composed of zeros is marked as nonallocated and is not explicitly written to disk. In this example, this means the file uses only 5 GB of space, which is marked as allocated, and has nonallocated space of 15 GB.

For nonallocated space, NTFS records only information about how much nonallocated space there is, and when you try to read data in this space, it returns zeros. This allows NTFS to store the file in the smallest amount of disk space possible while still being able to reconstruct the file's allocated and nonallocated space.

In theory, all this works great, but it is up to the actual program working with the sparse file to determine which data is meaningful and which isn't. Programs do this by explicitly specifying the data for which space should be allocated. In Windows Server 2008, several services use sparse files. One of these is the Indexing Service, which stores its catalogs as sparse files.

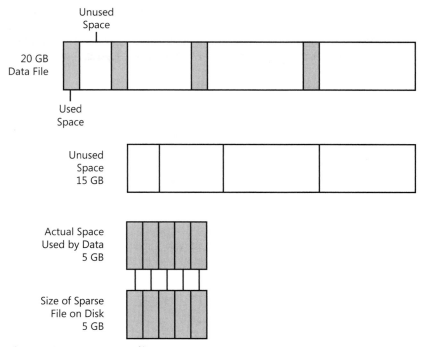

Figure 16-5 Using sparse files.

Using the FSUtil Sparse command, you can easily determine whether a file has the sparse attribute set. Type **fsutil sparse queryflag** *FilePath* at the command prompt, where *FilePath* is the path to the file you want to examine, such as

```
fsutil sparse queryflag c:\data\catalog.wci\00010002.ci
```

If the file has the sparse attribute, this command returns

```
This file is set as sparse
```

You can examine sparse files to determine where the byte ranges that contain meaningful (nonzero) data are located by using FSUtil Sparse as well. Type **fsutil sparse queryrange** *FilePath* at the command prompt, where *FilePath* is the path to the file you want to examine, such as

```
fsutil sparse queryrange c:\data\catalog.wci\00010002.ci
```

The output is the byte ranges of meaningful data within the file, such as

```
sparse range [0] [28672]
```

In this particular case, the output specifies that there's meaningful data at the start of the file to byte 28672. You can mark files as sparse as well. Type **fsutil sparse setflag** *FilePath* at the command prompt, where *FilePath* is the path to the file you want to mark as sparse.

Chapter 16

Transactional NTFS

Windows Server 2008 supports transactional NTFS and Self-Healing NTFS. Transactional NTFS allows file operations on an NTFS volume to be performed transactionally. This means programs can use a transaction to group together sets of file and Registry operations so that all of them succeed or none of them succeed. While a transaction is active, changes are not visible outside of the transaction. Changes are committed and written fully to disk only when a transaction is completed successfully. If a transaction fails or is incomplete, the program rolls back the transactional work to restore the file system to the state it was in prior to the transaction.

Transactions that span multiple volumes are coordinated by the Kernel Transaction Manager (KTM). The KTM supports independent recovery of volumes if a transaction fails. The local resource manager for a volume maintains a separate transaction log and is responsible for maintaining threads for transactions separate from threads that perform the file work.

Using the FSUtil Transaction command, you can easily determine transactional information. You can list currently running transactions by typing **fsutil transaction list** at the command prompt. You can display transactional information for a specific file by typing **fsutil transaction fileinfo** *FilePath* at the command prompt, where *FilePath* is the path to the file you want to examine, such as

```
fsutil transaction fileinfo c:\journal\ls-dts.mdb
```

Traditionally, you have had to use the Check Disk tool to fix errors and inconsistencies in NTFS volumes on a disk. Because this process can disrupt the availability of Windows systems, Windows Server 2008 uses Self-Healing NTFS to protect file systems without having to use separate maintenance tools to fix problems. Because much of the self-healing process is enabled and performed automatically, you might need to manually perform volume maintenance only when you are notified by the operating system that a problem cannot be corrected automatically. If such an error occurs, Windows Server 2008 will notify you about the problem and provide possible solutions.

Self-Healing NTFS has many advantages over Check Disk, including the following:

- Check Disk must have exclusive access to volumes, which means system and boot volumes can be checked only when the operating system starts up. On the other hand, with Self-Healing NTFS, the file system is always available and does not need to be corrected offline (in most cases).

- Self-Healing NTFS attempts to preserve as much data as possible if corruption occurs and reduces failed file system mounting that previously could occur if a volume was known to have errors or inconsistencies. During restart, Self-Healing NTFS repairs the volume immediately so that it can be mounted.

- Self-Healing NTFS reports changes made to the volume during repair through existing Chkdsk.exe mechanisms, directory notifications, and update sequence number (USN) journal entries. This feature also allows authorized users and administrators to monitor repair operations through Verification, Waiting For Repair Completion, and Progress Status messages.

- Self-Healing NTFS can recover a volume if the boot sector is readable but does not identify an NTFS volume. In this case, you must run an offline tool that repairs the boot sector and then allow Self-Healing NTFS to initiate recovery.

Although Self-Healing NTFS is a terrific enhancement, at times you might want to (or might have to) manually check the integrity of a disk. In these cases, you can use Check Disk (Chkdsk.exe) to check for and, optionally, repair problems found on FAT, FAT32, and NTFS volumes.

Using File-Based Compression

File-based compression allows you to reduce the number of bits and bytes in files so that they use less space on a disk. The Windows operating system supports two types of compression: NTFS compression, which is a built-in feature of NTFS, and compressed (zipped) folders, which is an additional feature of Windows available on both FAT and NTFS volumes.

NTFS Compression

Windows allows you to enable compression when you format a volume using NTFS. When a drive is compressed, all files and folders stored on the drive are automatically compressed when they are created. This compression is transparent to users, who can open and work with compressed files and folders just as they do with regular files and folders. Behind the scenes, Windows decompresses the file or folder when it is opened and compresses it again when it is closed. Although this can decrease a computer's performance, it saves space on the disk because compressed files and folders use less space.

You can turn on compression after formatting volumes as well, or if desired turn on compression only for specific files and folders. After you compress a folder, any new files added or copied to the folder are compressed automatically and they remain compressed even if you later move them to an uncompressed folder on an NTFS volume.

Moving uncompressed files to compressed folders affects their compression attribute as well. If you move an uncompressed file from a different drive to a compressed drive or folder, the file is compressed. However, if you move an uncompressed file to a compressed folder on the same NTFS drive, the file isn't compressed. Finally, if you move a compressed file to a FAT16 or FAT32 volume, the file is uncompressed because FAT16 and FAT32 volumes do not support compression.

To compress or uncompress a drive, follow these steps:

1. Right-click the drive that you want to compress or uncompress in Windows Explorer or in the Disk Management Volume List view, and then select Properties. This displays the disk's Properties dialog box, as shown in Figure 16-6.

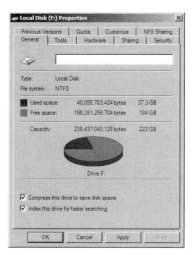

Figure 16-6 You can compress entire volumes or perform selective compression for specific files and folders.

2.   Select or clear the Compress This Drive To Save Disk Space check box as appropriate. When you click OK, the Confirm Attribute Changes dialog box shown in Figure 16-7 is displayed.

Figure 16-7 Choose a compression option.

3.   If you want to apply changes only to the root folder of the disk, select Apply Changes To *X* Only. Otherwise, accept the default, which will compress the entire contents of the disk. Click OK.

CAUTION

> Although Windows Server 2008 will let you compress system volumes, this is not recommended because the operating system will need to decompress and compress system files each time they are opened, which can seriously impact server performance. Additionally, you can't use compression and encryption together. You can use one feature or the other, but not both.

You can selectively compress and uncompress files and folders as well. The advantage here is that this affects only a part of a disk, such as a folder and its subfolders, rather than the entire disk. To compress or uncompress a file or folder, follow these steps:

1. In Windows Explorer, right-click the file or folder that you want to compress or uncompress, and then select Properties.

2. On the General tab of the related Properties dialog box, click Advanced. This displays the Advanced Attributes dialog box shown in Figure 16-8. Select or clear the Compress Contents To Save Disk Space check box as appropriate. Click OK twice.

Figure 16-8 Use the Advanced Attributes dialog box to compress the file or folder.

3. If you are changing the compression attributes of a folder with subfolders, the Confirm Attribute Changes dialog box is displayed. If you want to apply the changes only to the files in the folder and not files in subfolders of the folder, select Apply Changes To X Only. Otherwise, accept the default, which will apply the changes to the folder, its subfolders, and files. Click OK.

Windows Server 2008 also provides command-line utilities for compressing and uncompressing your data. The compression utility is called Compact (Compact.exe). The decompression utility is called Expand (Expand.exe).

You can use Compact to quickly determine whether files in a directory are compressed. At the command line, change to the directory you want to examine and enter **compact** without any additional parameters. If you want to check the directory and all subdirectories, enter **compact /s**. The output will list the compression status and compression ratio on every file and the final summary details will tell you exactly how many files and directories were examined and found to be compressed, such as:

```
Of 15435 files within 822 directories
0 are compressed and 15435 are not compressed.
2,411,539,448 total bytes of data are stored in 2,411,539,448 bytes.
The compression ratio is 1.0 to 1.
```

Chapter 16

Compressed (Zipped) Folders

Compressed (zipped) folders are another option for compressing files and folders. When you compress data using this technique, you use Zip compression technology to reduce the number of bits and bytes in files and folders so that they use less space on a disk. Compressed (zipped) folders are identified with a zipper on the folder icon and are saved with the .zip file extension.

> **Note**
>
> At the time of this writing, compressed (zipped) folders were not available on 64-bit editions of Windows Server 2008. Further, if you install a Zip utility, the compressed folder icon for this utility might be used and some of the built-in compressed (zipped) folder features can change.

Compressed (zipped) folders have several advantages over NTFS compression. Because Zip technology is an extension of the operating system rather than the file system, compressed (zipped) folders can be used on both FAT and NTFS volumes. Zipped folders can be password protected to safeguard their contents and can be sent by e-mail. They can also be transferred using File Transfer Protocol (FTP), Hypertext Transfer Protocol (HTTP), or other protocols. An added benefit of zipped folders is that some programs can be run directly from compressed folders without having to be decompressed. You can also open files directly from zipped folders.

You can create a zipped folder by selecting a file, folder, or a group of files and folders in Windows Explorer, right-clicking, pointing to Send To, and clicking Compressed (Zipped) Folder. The zipped folder is named automatically by using the file name of the last item selected and adding the .zip extension. If you double-click a zipped folder in Windows Explorer, you can access and work with its contents. As shown in Figure 16-9, the zipped folder's contents are listed according to file name, type, and date. The file information also shows the packed file size, the original file size, and the compression ratio. Double-clicking a program in a zipped folder runs it (as long as it doesn't require access to other files). Double-clicking a file in a zipped folder opens it for viewing or editing.

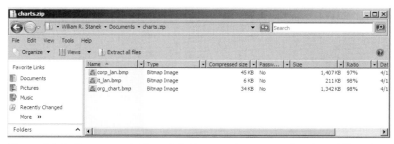

Figure 16-9 Compressed (zipped) folders can be accessed and used like other folders.

While you're working with a zipped folder, you can perform tasks similar to those you can with regular folders. You can do the following:

- Add other files, programs, or folders to the zipped folder by dragging them to it.

- Copy a file in the zipped folder and paste it into a different folder.

- Remove a file from the zipped folder using the Cut command so that you can paste it into a different folder.

- Delete a file or folder by selecting it and clicking Delete.

You also have the option to perform additional tasks, which are unique to zipped folders. You can choose File, Extract All to start the Extraction Wizard, which can be used to extract all the files in the zipped folder and copy them to a new location. You can click File, Add A Password to add a password to the zipped folder to control access to it.

Managing Disk Quotas

Even with the large disk drives available today, you'll often find that hard disk space is at a premium, and this is where disk quotas come in handy. Disk quotas are a built-in feature of NTFS that help you manage and limit disk space usage.

How Quota Management Works

Using disk quotas, you can monitor and control the amount of disk space people who access the network can use. Without quota management it is hard to monitor the amount of space being used by individual users and even harder to control the total amount of space they can use. I refer to monitoring and controlling separately because there's a very important difference between monitoring disk space usage and controlling it—and the disk quota system allows you to perform these tasks separately or together. You can, in fact, do the following:

- Configure the disk quota system to monitor disk space usage only, allowing administrators to check disk space usage manually

- Configure the disk quota system to monitor disk space usage and generate warnings when users exceed predefined usage levels

- Configure the disk quota system to monitor disk space usage, generate warnings when users exceed predefined usage levels, and enforce the limits by denying disk space to users who exceed the quota limit

Your organization's culture will probably play a major role in the disk quota technique you use. In some organizations the culture is such that it is acceptable to monitor space usage and periodically notify users that they are over recommended limits, but it wouldn't be well received if administrators enforced controls that limited disk space usage to specific amounts. In other organizations, especially larger organizations where there might be hundreds or thousands of employees on the network, it can make sense

Chapter 16

to have some controls in place and users might be more understanding of specific controls. Controls at some point become a matter of necessity to help ensure that the administrative staff can keep up with the disk space needs of the organization.

Disk quotas are configured on a per-volume basis. When you enable disk quotas, all users who store data on a volume will be affected by the quota. You can set exceptions for individual users as well that either set new limits or remove the limits altogether. As users create files and folders on a volume, an ownership flag is applied that says that this particular user owns the file or folder. Thus, if a user creates a file or folder on a volume that user is the owner of, the file or folder and the space used counts toward the user's quota limit. However, because each volume is managed separately, there is no way to set a specific limit for all volumes on a server or across the enterprise.

> **Note**
>
> For NTFS compressed files and sparse files, the space usage reported can reflect total space of files rather than the actual space the files use. This happens because the quota system reads the total space used by the file rather than its reduced file size.

Ownership of files and folders can change in several scenarios. If a user creates a copy of a file owned by someone else, the copy is owned by that user. This occurs because a file is created when the copy is made. File and folder ownership can also change when files are restored from backup. This can happen if you restore the files to a volume other than the one the files were created on and copy the files over to the original volume. Here, during the copy operation, the administrator becomes the owner of the files. A workaround for this is to restore files and folders to a different location on the same volume and then move the files and folders rather than copying them. When you move files and folders from one location to another on the same volume, the original ownership information is retained.

Administrators can be assigned as the owners of files in other ways as well, such as when they install the operating system or application software. To ensure that administrators can always install programs, restore data, and perform other administrative tasks, members of the Administrators group don't have a quota limit as a general rule. This is true even when you enforce disk quotas for all users. In fact, for the Administrators group, the only type of quota you can set is a warning level that warns administrators when they've used more than a set amount of space on a volume. When you think about it, this makes a lot of sense—you don't want to get into a situation where administrators can't recover the system because of space limitations.

That said, you can apply quotas to individual users—even those who are members of the Administrators group. You do this by creating a separate quota entry for each user. The only account that cannot be restricted in this way is the built-in Administrator account. If you try to set a limit on the Administrator account, the limit is not applied.

Finally, it is important to note that all space used on a volume counts toward the disk quota—even space used in the Recycle Bin. Thus, if a user who is over the limit deletes files to get under the limit, the disk quota might still give warnings or if quotas are enforced, the user still might not be able to write files to the volume. To resolve this issue, the user would need to delete files and then empty the Recycle Bin.

Configuring Disk Quotas

By default, disk quotas are disabled. If you want to use disk quotas, you must enable quota management for each volume on which you want to use disk quotas. You can enable disk quotas on any NTFS volume that has a drive letter or a mount point. Before you configure disk quotas, think carefully about the limit and warning level. Set values that make the most sense given the number of users who store data on the volume and the size of the volume. For optimal performance of the volume, you won't want to get in a situation where all or nearly all of the disk space is allocated. For optimal user happiness, you want to ensure that the warning and limit levels are adequate so the average user can store the necessary data to perform job duties. Quota limits and warning levels aren't one size fits all either. Engineers and graphic designers can have very different space needs than a typical user. In the best situations you'll have configured network shares so that different groups of users have access to different volumes, and these volumes should be sized to meet the typical requirements of a particular group.

In some organizations, I've seen administrators set very low quota limits and warning levels on data shares. The idea behind this was that the administrators wanted users to save most of their data on their workstations and only put files that needed to be shared on the data shares. I would discourage this for two reasons. Low quota limits and warning levels frustrate users—you don't want frustrated users; you want happy users. Second, you should be encouraging users to store more of their important files on central file servers, not less. Central file servers should be a part of regular enterprise-wide backup routines because corporate servers and backing up data safeguards it from loss. In addition, with the Volume Shadow Copy service, shadow copies of files on shared folders can be created automatically, allowing users to perform point-in-time file recovery without needing help from administrators.

To enable disk quotas on an NTFS volume, follow these steps:

1. In Computer Management, expand Storage, and then select Disk Management. In the details pane, right-click the volume on which you want to enable quotas, and then select Properties.

2. Click the Quota tab, and then select the Enable Quota Management check box as shown in Figure 16-10.

Chapter 16

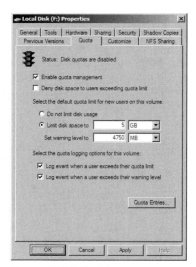

Figure 16-10 Enable quota management on the volume, and then configure the disk quota settings.

3. Define a default disk quota limit for all users by selecting Limit Disk Space To and then using the fields provided to set a limit in KB, MB, GB, TB, PB, or EB. Afterward, use the Set Warning Level To field to set the default warning limit. In most cases, you'll want the disk quota warning limit to be 90 to 95 percent of the disk quota limit. This should give good separation between when warnings occur and when the limit is reached.

4. To prevent users from going over the disk quota limit, select the Deny Disk Space To Users Exceeding Quota Limit check box. This sets a physical limitation for users that will prevent them from writing to the volume after the limit is reached.

5. NTFS sends warnings to users when they reach a warning level or limit. To ensure that you have a record of these warnings, you can configure quota logging options. Select the Log Event check boxes as appropriate.

6. Click OK. If the quota system isn't currently enabled, you'll see a prompt asking you to enable the quota system. Click OK to allow Windows Server 2008 to rescan the volume and update the disk usage statistics. Keep in mind that actions might be taken against users who exceed the current limit or warning levels, which can include preventing additional writing to the volume, notifying users the next time they try to access the volume that they've exceeded a warning level or have reached a limit, and logging applicable events in the application log.

Customizing Quota Entries for Individual Users

After you enable disk quotas, the configuration is set for and applies to all users who store data on the volume. The only exception, as noted previously, is for members of the Administrators group. The default disk quotas don't apply to these users. If you want to set a specific quota limit or warning level for an administrator, you can do this by creating a custom quota entry for that particular user account. You can also create custom quota entries for users who have special needs, requirements, or limitations.

To view and work with quota entries, access Disk Management, right-click the volume on which you enabled quotas, and then select Properties. In the Properties dialog box for the disk, click the Quota tab, and then click Quota Entries. You'll then see a list of quota entries for everyone who has ever stored data on the volume, as shown in Figure 16-11. The entries show the following information:

- **Status** The status of the disk entries. Normal status is OK. If a user has reached a warning level, the status is Warning. If a user is at or above the quota limit, the status is Above Limit.

- **Name** The display name of the user account.

- **Logon Name** The logon name and domain (if applicable).

- **Amount Used** The amount of disk space used by the user.

- **Quota Limit** The quota limit set for the user.

- **Warning Level** The warning level set for the user.

- **Percent Used** The percentage of disk space used toward the limit.

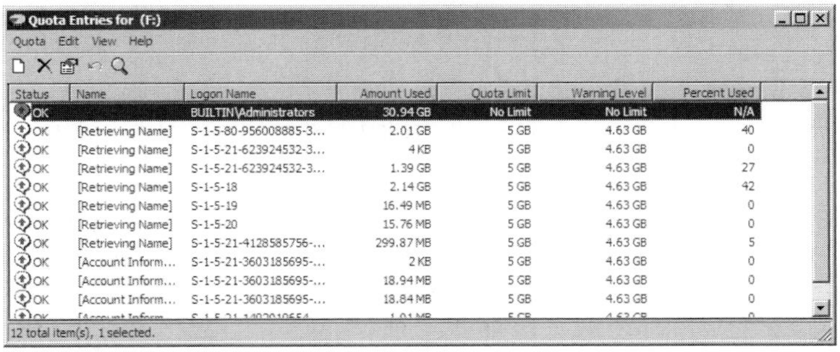

Figure 16-11 Any existing quota entries are shown.

Quota entries get on the list in one of two ways: either automatically if a user has ever stored data on the volume or by an administrator creating a custom entry for a user. You can customize any of these entries—even the ones automatically created—by double-clicking them, which displays the Quota Settings For dialog box shown in Figure 16-12, and selecting the appropriate options either to remove the disk quota limits or set new ones.

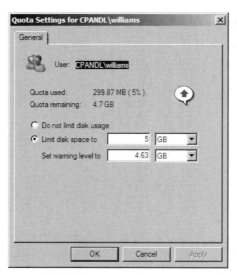

Figure 16-12 You can customize quota entries for individual users as necessary.

> **Note**
>
> You can't create quota entries for groups. The only group entry that is allowed is the one for the Administrators account, which is created automatically.

If a user doesn't have an entry in the Quota Entries For dialog box, it means that user has not yet saved files to the volume. You can still create a custom entry for the user if you want. To do this, choose Quota, New Quota Entry. This displays the Select Users dialog box shown in Figure 16-13. Use this dialog box to help you find the user account you want to work with. Type the name of the user account or part of the name, and click Check Names. If multiple names match the value you entered, you'll see a list of names and will be able to choose the one you want to use. Otherwise, the name will be filled in for you, and you can click OK to display the Add New Quota Entry dialog box, which has the same options as the Quota Settings For dialog box shown in Figure 16-12.

> **Use Locations to Access User Accounts from Other Domains**
>
> By default, the Select Users dialog box is set to work with users from your logon domain. If you want to add a user account from another domain, click Locations to display the Locations dialog box. Then either select the entire directory or the specific domain in which the account is located, and click OK.

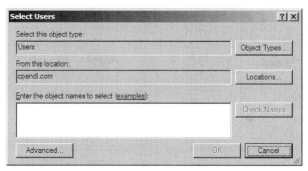

Figure 16-13 Type the name of the user account or part of the name, and click Check Names.

In the Quota Entries dialog box, there are a couple of tricks you can use to add or manage multiple quota entries at once. If you want to add identical quota entries for multiple users, you can do this by choosing Quota, New Quota Entry. This displays the Select Users dialog box. Click Advanced to display the advanced Select Users dialog box, as shown in Figure 16-14.

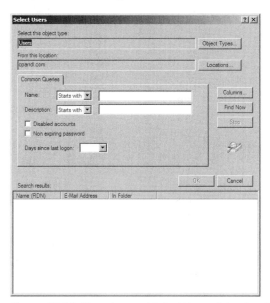

Figure 16-14 The advanced Select Users dialog box has additional options.

You can now search for users by name and description or by clicking Find Now without entering any search criteria to display a list of available users from the current location. You can select any of the users listed. Select multiple user accounts by holding down the Ctrl key and clicking each account you want to select or by holding down the Shift key, selecting the first account name, and then clicking the last account name to choose a range of accounts. Click OK twice, and then use the Add New Quota Entry dialog box to configure the quota options for all the selected users.

To manage multiple quota entries simultaneously, access the Quota Entries dialog box, then select the entries by holding down the Ctrl key and clicking each entry you want to select or by holding down the Shift key, selecting the first entry, and then clicking the last entry to choose a range of entries. Afterward, right-click one of the selected entries, and then choose Properties. You'll then be able to configure quota options for all the selected entries at once.

Managing Disk Quotas After Configuration

Users are notified that they have reached a warning level or quota limit when they access the volume on which you've configured disk quotas. As an administrator, you'll want to check for quota violations periodically, and there are several ways you can do this. One way is to access Disk Management, right-click the volume that you want to check on, and then select Properties. In the Properties dialog box for the disk, click the Quota tab, and then click the Quota Entries button. You can then check the current disk usage of users and see whether there are any quota violations. You can also copy selected entries to the Clipboard by pressing Ctrl+C and then pasting them into other applications, such as Microsoft Excel, using Ctrl+V to help you create reports or lists of disk space usage.

You can check quota entries from the command line as well. Type **fsutil quota query** *DriveDesignator* at the command prompt, where *DriveDesignator* is the drive letter of the volume followed by a colon, such as D:. If disk quotas are enabled on the volume, you'll then get a summary of the disk quota settings on the volume, as follows:

```
FileSystemControlFlags  =  0x00000031
   Quotas are tracked and enforced on this volume
   Logging enabled for quota limits and threshold
   The quota values are up to date

Default Quota Threshold  =  0x0000000038400000
Default Quota Limit      =  0x0000000040000000

SID Name         =   CPANDL\edwardh (User)
Change time      =   Saturday, April 12, 2008
Quota Used       =   528164252
Quota Threshold  =   943718400
Quota Limit      =   1073741824

SID Name         =   CPANDL\mollyp (User)
Change time      =   Monday, April 14, 2008
Quota Used       =   627384965
Quota Threshold  =   943718400
Quota Limit      =   1073741824
```

In this example, disk quotas are tracked and enforced on the volume, logging is enabled for both quota limits, and the warning levels and the disk quota values are current. In addition, the default warning limit (listed as the quota threshold) is set to 900 MB (0 × 038400000 bytes) and the default quota limit is set to 1 GB (0 × 040000000 bytes).

The disk quota summary is followed by the individual disk quota entries for each user who has stored data on the volume or has a custom entry regardless of whether the user has ever written data to the volume. The entries show the following information:

- **SID Name** The logon name and domain of user accounts or the name of a built-in or well-known group that has a quota entry.

- **Change Time** The last time the quota entry was changed or updated.

- **Quota Used** The amount of space used in bytes.

- **Quota Threshold** The current warning level set for the user in bytes.

- **Quota Limit** The current quota limit set for the user in bytes.

When you configure disk quotas, you also have the option of logging two types of events in the system logs: one for when a user exceeds the quota limit and another for when a user exceeds the warning level. By default, quota violations are written to the system log once an hour, so if you checked the logs periodically, you could see events related to any users who have disk quota violations. It's much easier to check for quota violations from the command line, however. Simply type **fsutil quota violations** at the command prompt, and the FSUtil Quota command will check the system and application event logs for quota violations.

> **Note**
>
> Wondering why FSUtil Quota Violations checks the system and application logs? Well, in some cases, quota violations for programs running under user accounts are logged in the application log rather than the system log. So, to ensure all quota violations are checked for, FSUtil Quota Violations checks both logs.

Chapter 16

If there are no quota violations found, the output is similar to the following:

```
Searching in System Event Log...
Searching in Application Event Log...
No quota violations detected
```

If there are quota violations, the output shows the event information related to each violation. In the following example, a user reached the warning level (listed as the quota threshold):

```
Searching in System Event Log...
**** A user hit their quota threshold ! ****
   Event ID : 0x40040024
   EventType : Information
   Event Category : 2
   Source : Ntfs
   User: CPANDL\harryt (User)
   Data: D:
Searching in Application Event Log...
```

As you can see, the output shows you the event ID, type, category, and source. It also shows the user who violated the disk quota settings and the volume on which the violation occurred.

INSIDE OUT **You can change the notification interval for quota violations**

As mentioned previously, quota violations are written to the event logs once an hour by default. You can check or change this behavior using the FSUtil Behavior command. Keep in mind, however, that any changes you make apply to all volumes on the system that use disk quotas. To check the notification interval, type **fsutil behavior query quotanotify**. If the notification interval has been set by you or another administrator, the notification interval is shown in seconds. To set the notification interval, type **fsutil behavior set quotanotify** *Interval*, where *Interval* is the notification interval you want to set expressed as the number of seconds. For example, if you want to receive less-frequent notifications, you might want to set the notification interval to 7200 seconds (2 hours), and you would do this by typing **fsutil behavior set quotanotify 7200**.

Exporting and Importing Quota Entries

If you want to use the same quotas on more than one NTFS volume, you can do this by exporting the quota entries from one volume and importing them on another volume. When you import quota entries, if there isn't a quota entry for the user already, a quota entry will be created. If a user already has a quota entry on the volume, you'll be asked if you want to overwrite it.

To export and import quota entries, access Disk Management, right-click the volume from which you want to export quota settings, and then select Properties. In the Properties dialog box for the disk, click the Quota tab, and then click the Quota Entries button. You'll then see the Quota Entries dialog box. Select Export from the Quota menu. This displays the Export Quota Settings dialog box.

Use the Save In selection list to choose the save location for the file containing the quota settings, and then set a name for the file using the File Name field. Afterward, click Save.

Next, access the Quota Entries dialog box for the drive on which you want to import settings. Select Import on the Quota menu. Then, in the Import Quota Settings dialog box, select the quota settings file that you saved previously. Click Open.

If prompted about whether you want to overwrite an existing entry, click Yes to replace an existing entry or click No to keep the existing entry. Select Do This For All Quota Entries prior to clicking Yes or No to use the same option for all existing entries.

Maintaining File System Integrity

As part of routine maintenance, you should periodically check disks for errors. The primary tool to do this is Check Disk, which is implemented in both a graphical and a command-line version.

How File System Errors Occur

File data is stored in clusters, and the Windows operating system uses a file table to determine where a file begins and on which clusters it is stored. With FAT, the file table used is called the root directory table. It defines the starting cluster of each file in the file system. This cluster has a pointer to the second cluster, and the second cluster has a pointer to the next, and so on until you get to the final cluster used by the file, which has an EOF marker. With NTFS, an MFT is used. If a file's data can't fit within a single record in this table, clusters belonging to the file are referenced using VCNs that map to starting LCNs on the disk. If a file's pointer or mapping is lost, you might not be able to access the file. Errors can also occur for pointers or mappings that relate to the file tables themselves and to the pointers or mappings for folders.

FAT tries to prevent disk integrity problems by maintaining a duplicate file allocation table that can be used to recover the primary file allocation table if it becomes corrupted. Beyond this, however, FAT doesn't do much else to ensure disk integrity. NTFS, on the other hand, has several mechanisms for preventing and correcting disk integrity problems automatically. NTFS stores a partial duplicate of the MFT, which can be used for failure recovery. NTFS also stores a persistent history of all changes made to files on the volume in a log file, and the log file can be used to recover NTFS metadata files, regular data files, and folders. What these file structure recovery mechanisms all have in common is that they are automatic and you as an administrator don't need to do anything to ensure that these disk housekeeping tasks are performed. These mechanisms aren't perfect, however, and errors can occur.

The most common errors relate to the following areas:

- Internal errors in a file's structure
- Free space being marked as allocated
- Allocated space being marked as free
- Partially or improperly written security descriptors
- Unreadable disk sectors not marked as bad

Fixing File System Errors by Using Check Disk

Using Check Disk, you can check for and correct any of the common disk errors discussed previously. Check Disk works on FAT, FAT32, and NTFS volumes and primarily looks for inconsistencies in the file system and its related metadata. It locates errors by comparing the volume bitmap to the disk sectors assigned to files. For files, Check Disk looks at structural integrity, but won't check for or attempt to repair corrupted data within files that appear to be structurally intact.

Check Disk has two modes in which it can be run. It can analyze a disk, checking for errors, but not repairing them. Or it can analyze a disk and attempt to repair any errors found. New for Windows Server 2008 is that Check Disk has been optimized so that it runs faster than previous versions.

You can run the graphical version of Check Disk by using either Windows Explorer or Disk Management. Right-click the volume, and choose Properties. On the Tools tab of the Properties dialog box, click Check Now to display the Check Disk dialog box, as shown in Figure 16-15. If you want to analyze the disk but not repair errors, click Start without selecting either of the available options. If you want to check for errors and repair them, select the Automatically Fix File System Errors check box, and click Start. You can also check for and repair bad sectors by selecting the Scan For And Attempt Recovery Of Bad Sectors check box.

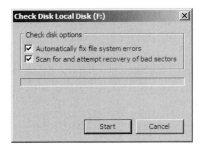

Figure 16-15 Check the disk for errors and repair them or perform analysis only.

To fix errors, Check Disk needs exclusive access to the volume. If Check Disk can't get exclusive access to files (because they have open file handles), Check Disk will prompt you, as shown in Figure 16-16. If you click Schedule Disk Check, Check Disk will analyze and repair the disk the next time the system is started.

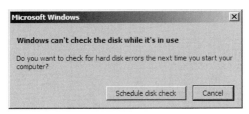

Figure 16-16 Check Disk needs exclusive access to some Windows files to fix errors.

INSIDE OUT   **Marking disks for checking on startup**

Check Disk can't get exclusive access to a volume if it has open file handles. As a result, you must either use the command-line version and dismount the volume or schedule Check Disk to run the next time the system is started. When you schedule Check Disk to run, the operating system marks the disk as dirty, which means it needs to be checked and repaired. You can mark a disk as dirty using the FSUtil Dirty command. Type **fsutil dirty set** followed by the drive designator, such as **fsutil dirty set c:**. If you want to determine if Check Disk is set to run the next time the system is started, you can use the FSUtil Dirty command to do this as well. Type **fsutil dirty query** followed by the drive designator, such as **fsutil dirty query c:**.

Check Disk can also be run at the command line using ChkDsk (Chkdsk.exe). The key advantage of using the command-line version is that you get a detailed report of the analysis and repair operations as detailed in "Analyzing FAT Volumes by Using ChkDsk" on the next page and "Analyzing NTFS Volumes by Using ChkDsk" on page 539.

You can run ChkDsk in analysis mode at the command line by typing **chkdsk** followed by the drive designator. For example, if you want to analyze the C drive, you'd type **chkdsk c:**. To have ChkDsk analyze and repair volumes, you add the /F parameter, such as **chkdsk c: /f**. If you want to check for bad sectors and try to repair them as well, use the /R parameter (which implies /F as well, meaning ChkDsk will perform a full analysis and repair and then check and repair bad sectors).

The complete syntax for ChkDsk is as follows:

```
chkdsk [volume[[path]filename]] [/f] [/v] [/r] [/x] [/i] [/c] [/l:size] [/b]
```

Note

The command-line version of Check Disk also needs exclusive access to some Windows files to fix errors. For nonsystem volumes, you will be given the opportunity to dismount the volume so that ChkDsk can run. You can also force dismount of a nonsystem volume by using the /X parameter. For system volumes, you will be prompted to schedule the analysis and repair for the next restart of the operating system.

Table 16-6 summarizes the options and parameters available and their uses.

Chapter 16

Table 16-6 **Command-Line Parameters for ChkDsk**

Option/Parameter	Description
Volume	Sets the volume to work with.
Filename	On FAT/FAT32, specifies files to check for fragmentation.
/F	Tells ChkDsk to analyze the disk and fix any errors noted.
/B	Tells ChkDsk to reevaluate any clusters marked as bad on the volume. (/R is implied when you use this parameter.)
/C	On NTFS only, tells ChkDsk to not check for cycles within the folder structure. A cycle is a very rarely occurring type of error in which a directory contains a pointer to itself, causing an infinite loop.
/I	On NTFS only, tells ChkDsk to perform a minimum check of indexes.
/L[:*Size*]	On NTFS only, changes the transaction log file size. The default size is 4096 KB, which is sufficient most of the time.
/R	Tells ChkDsk to analyze the disk and fix any errors noted and also to check for bad sectors. Any bad sectors found are marked as bad. (/F is implied when you use this parameter.)
/V	On FAT/FAT32, lists the full path of every file on the volume. On NTFS, displays cleanup messages related to fixing file system errors or other discrepancies.
/X	Forces the volume to dismount if necessary. All open file handles to the volume would then be invalid. (/F is implied when you use this parameter.)

Analyzing FAT Volumes by Using ChkDsk

When you run ChkDsk, you can get an analysis report. For FAT volumes, a disk analysis report looks like this:

```
The type of the file system is FAT.
Volume DATA3 created 2/19/2008 5:58 PM
Volume Serial Number is 7D11-2345
Windows is verifying files and folders...
File and folder verification is complete.
Windows has checked the file system and found no problems.

 209,489,920 bytes total disk space.
      24,576 bytes in 6 hidden files.
      12,288 bytes in 3 folders.
 200,679,936 bytes in 279 files.
   8,773,120 bytes available on disk.

       4,096 bytes in each allocation unit.
      51,145 total allocation units on disk.
       1,970 allocation units available on disk.
```

Here, ChkDsk examines each record in the file allocation table for consistency. It lists all the file and folder records in use and determines the starting cluster for each using the root directory table. It checks each file and notes any discrepancies in the output. Any clusters that were marked as in use by files or folders but that weren't actually in use are noted and during repair the clusters can be marked as available. Other discrepancies noted in the output can be fixed during repair as well.

Analyzing NTFS Volumes by Using ChkDsk

Disk analysis for NTFS volumes is performed in three stages, and ChkDsk reports its progress during each stage as shown in this sample report:

```
The type of the file system is NTFS.

WARNING!  F parameter not specified.
Running CHKDSK in read-only mode.

CHKDSK is verifying files (stage 1 of 3)...
  215184 file records processed.
File verification completed.
  849 large file records processed.
  0 bad file records processed.
  0 EA records processed.
  79 reparse records processed.
CHKDSK is verifying indexes (stage 2 of 3)...
  249098 index entries processed.
Index verification completed.
  0 unindexed files processed.
CHKDSK is verifying security descriptors (stage 3 of 3)...
  215184 security descriptors processed.
Security descriptor verification completed.
  16958 data files processed.
CHKDSK is verifying Usn Journal...
  176965056 USN bytes processed.
Usn Journal verification completed.
Windows has checked the file system and found no problems.

 232848672 KB total disk space.
  41306680 KB in 123087 files.
     54008 KB in 16959 indexes.
         0 KB in bad sectors.
    464520 KB in use by the system.
     65536 KB occupied by the log file.
 191023464 KB available on disk.

      4096 bytes in each allocation unit.
  58212168 total allocation units on disk.
  47755866 allocation units available on disk.
```

During the first stage of analysis, ChkDsk verifies file structures. This means ChkDsk examines each file's record in the MFT for consistency. It lists all the file records in use and determines which clusters the file records are stored in and then compares this with the volume's cluster bitmap stored in the $Bitmap metadata file. Any discrepancies are noted in the ChkDsk output. For example, any clusters that were marked as in use by files but that weren't actually in use are noted, and during repair the clusters can be marked as available.

During the second stage of analysis, ChkDsk verifies directory structure by examining directory indexes, starting with the volume's root directory index, which is stored in the $Metadata file. ChkDsk examines index records, making sure that each index record corresponds to an actual directory on the disk and that each file that is supposed to be in a directory is in the directory. It also checks to see whether there are files that have an MFT record but that don't actually exist in any directory, and during repair these lost files can be recovered.

During the third stage of the analysis, ChkDsk verifies the consistency of security descriptors for each file and directory object on the volume using the $Secure metadata file. It does this by validating that the security descriptors work. It doesn't actually check to see if the users or groups assigned in the security descriptors exist.

Repairing Volumes and Marking Bad Sectors by Using ChkDsk

If problems are found, ChkDsk will repair them only if you've used the /F parameter. Alternatively, you can use the /X or /R parameter as well, and each implies the /F parameter. If you use the /R parameter, ChkDsk will perform an additional step in the analysis and repair that involves checking each sector on the disk to make sure it can be read from and written to correctly. If it finds a bad sector, ChkDsk will mark it so data won't be written to that sector. If the sector was part of a cluster that was being used, ChkDsk will move the good data in that cluster to a new cluster.

The data in the bad sector can be recovered only if there's redundant data from which to copy it. The bad sector won't be used again, so at least it won't cause problems in the future. Checking each sector on a disk is a time-intensive process—and one that you won't perform often. More typically, you'll use ChkDsk /F to check for and repair common errors.

> **Note**
> You can force ChkDsk to reevaluate clusters it has marked as bad using the /B parameter. This parameter implies the /R parameter. Here, ChkDsk will again attempt to determine whether it can read from and write to the cluster correctly. If the cluster can be read from and written to correctly, ChkDsk marks the cluster as good so it can be used by the disk subsystem.

Defragmenting Disks

As files are created, modified, and moved, fragmentation can occur both within the volume's allocation table and on the volume itself. This happens because files are written to clusters on disk as they are used. The file system uses the first clusters available when writing new data, so as you modify files, different parts of files can end up in different areas of the disk. If you delete a file, an area of the disk is made available, but it might not be big enough to store the next file that is created and as a result, part of a new file might get written to this newly freed area and part of it might get written somewhere else on the disk.

Although the file system doesn't care if the file data is on contiguous clusters or spread out across the disk, the fact that data is in different areas of the disk can slow down read/write operations. This means it will take longer than usual to open and save files. It also makes it more difficult to recover files in case of serious disk error. Windows Server 2008 provides a tool for defragmenting volumes called the Disk Defragmenter. Unlike Check Disk, which cannot check and repair the operating system volume while it is in use, Disk Defragmenter can, in most cases, perform online defragmentation of any volume, including the operating system volume.

Configuring Automated Defragmentation

To reduce fragmentation, Windows Server 2008 can manually or automatically defragment disks periodically using Disk Defragmenter. The more frequently data is updated on drives, the more often you should run this tool. Windows Vista with SP1 or later and Windows Server 2008 automatically perform cyclic pickup defragmentation. With this feature, when a scheduled defragmentation pass is stopped and rerun, the computer automatically picks up the next unfinished volume in line to be defragmented.

When you enable automatic defragmentation, Windows Server 2008 runs Disk Defragmenter automatically at 1:00 A.M. every Wednesday. As long as the computer is on at the scheduled run time, automatic defragmentation will occur. You can configure and manage automated defragmentation by following these steps:

1. In Computer Management, select the Storage node and then the Disk Management node. Right-click a drive and then select Properties.

2. On the Tools tab, click Defragment Now. This displays the Disk Defragmenter dialog box, shown in Figure 16-17.

Chapter 16

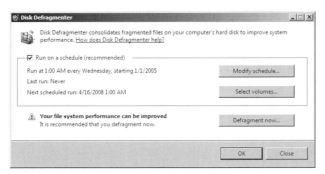

Figure 16-17 Configure defragmentation.

3. Enable automated defragmentation by selecting the Run On A Schedule check box. The default or last set run schedule is shown.

4. If you want to modify the run schedule, click Modify Schedule. In the Modify Schedule dialog box, shown in Figure 16-18, choose Daily, Weekly, or Monthly as the run schedule. If you choose a weekly or monthly run schedule, you'll need to select the run day of the week or month from the What Day selection list. Finally, the What Time selection list lets you set the time of the day that automated defragmentation should occur. Then click OK to complete setting the desired schedule.

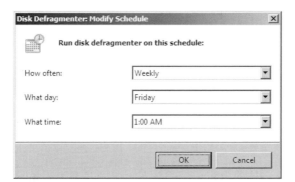

Figure 16-18 Set a run schedule.

5. If you want to manage which disks are defragmented, click Select Volumes. In the Advanced Options dialog box, shown in Figure 16-19, select the check boxes for disks that should be defragmented automatically and clear the check boxes for disks that should not be defragmented automatically. Click OK.

6. Click OK twice to save your settings and close all open dialog boxes.

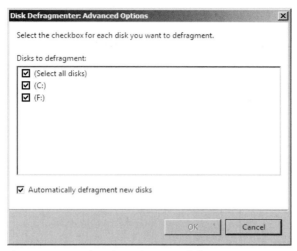

Figure 16-19 Select the volumes to defragment.

Fixing Fragmentation by Using Disk Defragmenter

Using Disk Defragmenter, you can check for and correct volume fragmentation problems on FAT, FAT32, and NTFS volumes. The areas checked for fragmentation include the volume, files, folders, the page file if one exists on the volume, and the MFT. Being able to check the MFT is a new feature for Windows Server 2008. Another new feature is the ability to defragment volumes with cluster sizes greater than 4 KB.

You can run the graphical version of Disk Defragmenter using either Windows Explorer or Computer Management. In Windows Explorer, right-click the volume, and choose Properties. On the Tools tab of the Properties dialog box, click Defragment Now to display the Disk Defragmenter dialog box. In Computer Management, select the Storage node and then the Disk Management node. Right-click a drive and then select Properties. On the Tools tab, click Defragment Now. This also displays the Disk Defragmenter dialog box.

When you open the Disk Defragmenter dialog box, Windows automatically analyzes the computer's volumes and determines whether defragmentation needs to be performed. If Windows reports that volumes need to be defragmented, you can defragment them by clicking Defragment Now. Then when prompted, select the disks to defragment and click OK.

If a disk is marked to be checked the next time the operating system is started, you won't be able to analyze it. Instead, you will be told that Check Disk is scheduled to run on the volume, and you must run it before you can defragment the disk. If the disk is possibly corrupt and has been marked as such, you won't be able to defragment it either. In this case, you will be told that you should run Check Disk. Otherwise, Disk Defragmenter will begin defragmenting the selected disks.

Chapter 16

> **Note**
>
> Disk Defragmenter needs at least 15 percent free space to defragment a disk completely. Disk Defragmenter uses this space as a sorting area for file fragments. If a volume has less than 15 percent free space, Disk Defragmenter will only partially defragment it. By default, Disk Defragmenter performs partial defragmentation by attempting to consolidate only fragments smaller than 64 megabytes.

Disk Defragmenter can also be run at the command line using Defrag (Defrag.exe). You can run Disk Defragmenter in analysis mode at the command line by typing **defrag -a** followed by the drive designator. For example, if you want to analyze the fragmentation of the D drive, you'd type **defrag -a d:**. To analyze and then defragment a volume if defragmentation is necessary, type **defrag** followed by the drive designator, such as **defrag d:**. No parameters are necessary.

Defrag has several syntaxes. The syntax for analyzing volumes without defragmentation is:

```
defrag volume -a [-v]
```

The -V parameter is used to display detailed output. The syntax for analysis and defragmentation of a specific volume is:

```
defrag volume [{-r | -w}] [-f] [-v]
```

With the -r parameter, Defrag performs a partial defragmentation, attempting to consolidate only fragments smaller than 64 MB. With the -w parameter, Defrag performs a full defragmentation, attempting to consolidate fragments of all sizes. The -F parameter is used to force defragmentation even if there is low free space on the volume.

The syntax for analysis and defragmentation of all volumes on the computer is:

```
defrag -c [{-r | -w}] [-f] [-v]
```

Table 16-7 summarizes the options and parameters available and their uses.

Table 16-7 Command-Line Parameters for Defrag

Option/Parameter	Description
Volume	Sets the volume to work with.
-A	Performs an analysis of only the specified volume.
-C	Used instead of a drive letter, telling Defrag to defragment all disks.
-F	Forces defragmentation of a volume even if it is low on free space.
-R	Performs a partial defragmentation, consolidating only fragments smaller than 64 MB. This is the default mode.
-V	Sets verbose mode for detailed output during analysis, defragmentation or both.
-W	Performs a full defragmentation, consolidating all fragments.

Understanding the Fragmentation Analysis

You can perform fragmentation analysis at the command line using the -a and -v parameters. The command-line report shows the summary of fragmentation. The summary looks like this:

```
Defragmentation report for volume F:

        Volume size                     = 222 GB
        Cluster size                    = 4 KB
        Used space                      = 185 GB
        Free space                      = 37 GB
        Percent free space              = 17 %

File fragmentation
        Percent file fragmentation      = 33 %
        Total movable files             = 140,025
        Average file size               = 368 KB
        Total fragmented files          = 2,321
        Total excess fragments          = 56,366
        Average fragments per file      = 1.45
        Total unmovable files           = 12

Free space fragmentation
        Free space                      = 37 GB
        Total free space extent         = 64,362
        Average free space per extent   = 3 MB
        Largest free space extent       = 1.19 GB

Folder fragmentation
        Total folders                   = 16,948
        Fragmented folders              = 90
        Excess folder fragments         = 717

Master File Table (MFT) fragmentation
        Total MFT size                  = 210 MB
        MFT record count                = 254,902
        Percent MFT in use              = 98
        Total MFT fragments             = 253

    Note: On NTFS volumes, file fragments larger than 64MB are not
included in the fragmentation statistics
```

The summary of the volume's configuration and space usage reports on the following areas:

- **File Fragmentation** Gives an overview of file-level fragmentation showing the percentage of used space that is fragmented, the total number of files on the volume that are movable, the average size of those files, how many files are fragmented, the total number of excess fragments, the average number of fragments per file, and the total number of unmovable files. Ideally, you want the percent fragmentation to be 10 percent or less and the number of fragments per file to be as close to 1.00 as possible.

- **Free Space Fragmentation** Gives on overview of fragmentation on a volume's unused space showing how much free space is available on the volume, the number of extents on which free space is located, the average free space per extent, and the largest free space extent.

- **Folder Fragmentation** Gives an overview of folder-level fragmentation showing the total number of folders on the volume and how many folders are fragmented.

- **Master File Table (MFT) Fragmentation** For NTFS volumes only, gives an overview of fragmentation in the MFT, showing the current size of the MFT, the number of records it contains, the percentage of the MFT in use, and the total number of fragments in the MFT. In this example, the MFT has some fragmentation. But the real concern is that it is at 98 percent of its maximum size. Because of this, the MFT could become more fragmented over time—there is still 17 percent free space on the volume, and if it needs to grow it will grow into the free space.

If you run Defrag again without the -A parameter, the Disk Defragmenter will set about cleaning up the drive to give optimal space usage. This won't clear up all fragmentation, but it will help so that disk space is used more efficiently—and on a moderately fragmented volume like the one shown, you should see some performance improvements after defragmentation as well.

File Sharing and Security

Sharing files means that you allow users to access those files from across the network. The most basic way to share files is to create a shared folder and make it accessible to users through a mapped network drive. In most cases, you don't want everyone with access to the network to be able to read, modify, or delete the shared files. So, when you share files, the access permissions on the shared folder and the local NTFS permissions are very important in helping to grant access as appropriate and to restrict access to files when necessary. File sharing and file security go hand in hand. You don't want to share files indiscriminately, and to help safeguard important data you can configure auditing. Auditing allows you to track who accessed files and what they did.

File Sharing Essentials

File sharing is one of the most fundamental features of a file server, and file servers running Windows Server 2008 have many file sharing features. The basic component that makes file sharing possible is the Server service, which is responsible for sharing file and printer resources over the network.

Understanding File-Sharing Models

Windows Server 2008 supports two file-sharing models: standard file sharing and public file sharing. Standard file sharing allows remote users to access network resources, such as files, folders, and drives. When you share a folder or a drive, you make all its files and subfolders available to a specified set of users. Standard file sharing also is referred to as *in-place file sharing* because you don't need to move files from their current location.

You can enable standard file sharing only on disks formatted with NTFS. Two sets of permissions determine precisely who has access to shared files: NTFS permissions and share permissions. Together, these permissions let you control who has access to shared files and the level of access assigned. You do not need to move the files you are sharing.

With public file sharing, you share files from a computer's %SystemDrive%\Users\ Public folder simply by copying or moving files to the folder. Public files are available to anyone who logs on to a computer locally regardless of whether he or she has a standard user account or an administrator user account on the computer. You can also grant network access to the Public folder. If you do this, however, there are no access restrictions. The public folder and its contents are open to everyone who can access the computer over the local network.

When you copy or move files to the Public folder, access permissions are changed to match those of the Public folder. Some additional permissions are added as well. When a computer is part of a workgroup, you can add password protection to the Public folder. Separate password protection isn't needed in a domain. In a domain, only domain users can access Public folder data.

You can change the default Public folder sharing configuration in two key ways:

- Allow users with network access to view and open public files but restrict them from changing, creating, or deleting public files. When you configure this option, the implicit group Everyone is granted Read & Execute and Read permissions to public files, and Read & Execute, List Folder Contents, and Read permissions on public folders.

- Allow users with network access to view and manage public files. This allows network users to open, change, create, and delete public files. When you configure this option, the implicit group Everyone is granted Full Control permissions to public files and public folders.

Windows Server 2008 can use either or both sharing models at any time. However, standard file sharing offers more security and better protection than public file sharing, and increasing security is essential to protecting your organization's data.

You can configure the basic file-sharing settings for a server using Network And Sharing Center. Separate options are provided for file sharing, public folder sharing, and printer sharing, and the status of each sharing option is listed as On or Off, as shown in the following screen.

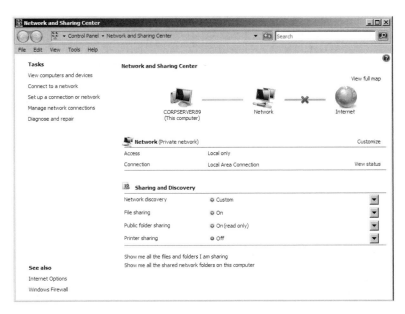

You can manage a computer's sharing configuration in Network And Sharing Center. To access this console, click Start and then click Network. On the Network Explorer toolbar, click Network And Sharing Center.

Standard file sharing controls network access to shared resources. To configure standard file sharing, expand the File Sharing panel by clicking the related Expand button. You then have the options shown in the following screen. As appropriate, select either Turn On File Sharing to enable file sharing or Turn Off File Sharing to disable file sharing, and then click Apply.

Public folder sharing controls access to a computer's Public folder. To configure Public folder sharing, expand the Public Folder Sharing panel by clicking the related Expand button. You then have the options shown in the following screen. Choose one of the following options and then click Apply:

- **Turn On Sharing So Anyone With Network Access Can Open Files** Enables Public folder sharing by granting the Read permission to the Public folder and all public data to anyone who can access the computer over the network. Windows Firewall settings might prevent external access.

- **Turn On Sharing So Anyone With Network Access Can Open, Change, And Create Files** Enables Public folder sharing by granting Co-Owner access to the Public folder and all public data to anyone who can access the computer over the network. Windows Firewall settings might prevent external access.

- **Turn Off Sharing** Disables Public folder sharing, preventing local network access to the Public folder. Anyone who logs on locally to your computer can still access the Public folder and its files.

Printer sharing controls access to printers that are attached to the computer. To configure printer sharing, expand the Printer Sharing panel by clicking the related Expand button. You then have the options shown in the following screen. As appropriate, select either Turn On Printer Sharing to enable printer sharing or Turn Off Printer Sharing to disable printer sharing, and then click Apply.

In a workgroup setting, password-protected sharing allows you to restrict access so that only people with a user account and password on your computer can access shared resources. To configure password-protected sharing, expand the Password Protected Sharing panel by clicking the related Expand button. As appropriate, select either Turn On Password Protected Sharing to enable password-protected sharing or Turn Off Password Protected Sharing to disable password-protected sharing, and then click Apply.

Using and Finding Shares

You share file resources over the network by creating a shared folder that users can map to as a network drive. For example, if the D:\Data directory on a computer is used to store user data, you might want to share this drive as UserData. This would allow users to map to it using a drive letter on their machines, such as X. After the drive is mapped, users can access it in Windows Explorer or by using other tools just like they would a local drive on their computer.

All shared folders have a share name and a folder path. The share name is the name of the shared folder. The folder path is the complete path to the folder on the server.

In the previous example, the share name is UserData and the associated folder path is D:\Data. After you share a folder, it is available to users automatically. All they have to know to map to the shared folder is the name of the server on which the folder is located and the share name.

In the Computer window, you map network drives by selecting Map Network Drive from the Tools menu or by clicking Map Network Drive on the toolbar. This displays the Map Network Drive wizard shown in Figure 17-1. You use the Drive field to select a free drive letter to use and the Folder field to enter the path to the network share. You use the Universal Naming Convention (UNC) path to the share. For example, to access a server called CORPSVR02 and a shared folder called CorpData, you would type **\\CorpSvr02\CorpData**. If you don't know the name of the share, you can click Browse to search for available shares. By default, Windows automatically reconnects mapped network drives at logon. Clear the Reconnect At Logon check box if you only want to map the network drive for the current user session.

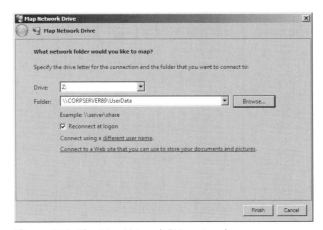

Figure 17-1 The Map Network Drive wizard.

When Network Discovery is enabled, users can browse the network using Network Explorer to find shares that have been made available, as shown in Figure 17-2. Here, you click Start and then click Network to open Network Explorer. You now see a list of computers on the network for which Network Discovery is enabled. When you double-click a computer entry, any publicly shared resources on that computer are listed and can be connected to simply by double-clicking the associated folder.

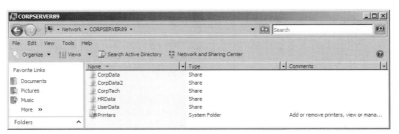

Figure 17-2 Network Explorer shows shares published in Active Directory on a per-server basis.

To make it easier for users to find shared folders, you can also publish information about shares in Active Directory. When you publish shared resources, users can use Network Explorer to find them, and administrators can find them using Active Directory Users And Computers. The procedures are similar regardless of which tool you are using. An example of how you can find shared folders follows:

1. In Network Explorer, click Search Active Directory on the toolbar. Or in Active Directory Users And Computers, right-click the domain name in the left pane, and click Find.

2. As shown in Figure 17-3, in the Find List, choose Shared Folders.

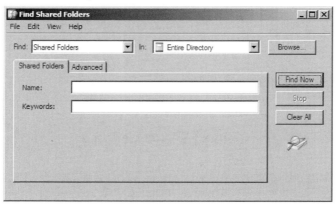

Figure 17-3 Using the Find Shared Folders dialog box to find shared resources, such as folders and printers.

3. In the Name field, type the name of the folder you want to find, and then click Find Now.

4. In the Search Results, you'll see a list of shared folders that match your search criteria, as shown in Figure 17-4. Right-click any of the shared folders to display a shortcut menu. You will then be able to open the shared folder, map a network drive to the folder, and access the share's properties.

Use Wildcards to Match Partial Names

If you know part of the folder name, you can use the asterisk (*) to match partial names. For example, if you know that the folder name ends with the word "data," you could type ***data** to search for all folders that end with the word "data."

Figure 17-4 Right-click the shared folder you want to work with to display its shortcut menu.

Hiding and Controlling Share Access

Because there are times when you don't want everyone to see or know about a share, Windows Server 2008 also allows you to create hidden shares. Hidden shares are shares that are made available to users but that are not listed in the normal file share lists or published in Active Directory. You can create hidden shares by adding the dollar sign ($) to the end of the share name. For example, if you want to share E:\Data-Dumps but don't want it to be displayed in the normal file share lists, you could name it Backup$ rather than Backup.

Hiding a share doesn't control access to the share, however. Access to shares is controlled using permissions. Two permissions sets apply to shared folders: share permissions and local file and folder permissions. Share permissions set the maximum allowable actions available within a shared folder. File and folder permissions assigned to the share's contents further constrain the actions users can perform. For example, share permissions can allow a user to access a folder, but file and folder permissions might not allow a user to view or modify files.

By default, when you create a share, everyone with access to the network has Read access to the share's contents. This is an important security change from previous versions of Windows in which the default permission was to give everyone Full Control over a share's contents.

Special and Administrative Shares

In Windows Server 2008, you'll find that several shares are created automatically. These shares are referred to as *special shares* or default shares. Most special shares are hidden because they are created for administrative purposes. Thus, they are also referred to as *administrative shares*.

Chapter 17

The special shares that are available on a system depend on its configuration. This means a domain controller might have more special shares than a member server. Or that a server that handles network faxing might have shares that other systems don't.

C$, D$, E$, and Other Drive Shares

All drives, including CD/DVD-ROM drives, have a special share to the root of the drive. These shares are known as C$, D$, E$, and so on, and are created to allow administrators to connect to a drive's root folder and perform administrative tasks. For example, if you map to C$, you are connecting to C:\ and have full access to this drive.

On workstations and servers, members of the Administrators or Backup Operators group can access drive shares. On domain controllers, members of the Server Operators group can also access drive shares.

> **Note**
> Windows allows you to delete drive shares. However, the next time you restart the computer or the Server service, the drive shares will be re-created.

ADMIN$

The ADMIN$ share is an administrative share for accessing the %SystemRoot% folder in which the operating system files reside. It is meant to be used for remote administration. For administrators working remotely with systems, it is a handy shortcut for directly accessing the operating system folder. Thus, rather than having to connect to C$ or D$ and then look for the operating system folder, which could be named Windows, Winnt, or just about anything else, you can connect directly to the right folder every time.

On workstations and servers, members of the Administrators or Backup Operators group can access the ADMIN$ share. On domain controllers, members of the Server Operators group can also access the ADMIN$ share.

FAX$

The FAX$ share is used to support network faxes. By default, the special group Everyone has Read permissions on these shared folders. This means that anyone with access to the network can access this folder.

IPC$

The IPC$ share is an administrative share used to support named pipes. Named pipes are used for interprocess (or process-to-process) communications. Because named pipes can be redirected over the network to connect local and remote systems, they also enable remote administration and are what allow you to manage resources remotely.

NETLOGON

The NETLOGON share is used by domain controllers. It supports the Netlogon service and is used by this service during processing of logon requests. After users log on, Windows accesses their user profiles and, if applicable, any related logon scripts. Logon scripts contain actions that should be run automatically when users log on to help set up the work environment, perform housekeeping tasks, or complete any other task that must be routinely performed every time users log on.

PRINT$

The PRINT$ share supports printer sharing by providing access to print drivers. Any time you share a printer, the system puts the print drivers in this share so that other computers can access them as needed.

PUBLIC

The PUBLIC share supports public folder sharing and is used to store public data. Access permissions on the Public folder determine which users and groups have access to publicly shared files as well as what level of access those users and groups have. When you copy or move files to the Public folder, access permissions are changed to match those of the Public folder. Some additional permissions are added as well.

SYSVOL

The SYSVOL share is used to support Active Directory. Domain controllers have this share and use it to store Active Directory data, including policies and scripts.

Accessing Shares for Administration

As Figure 17-5 shows, administrators can view information about existing shares on a computer, including the special shares, by using Computer Management. In Computer Management, expand System Tools, Shared Folders, and then select Shares.

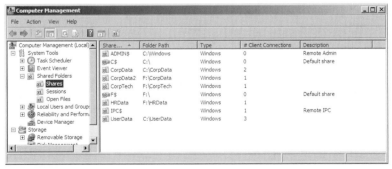

Figure 17-5 Use Computer Management to access shared folders.

If you want to work with shares on a remote computer, right-click the Computer Management node in the left pane and select Connect To Another Computer. This displays the Select Computer dialog box. Select Another Computer, and then type the computer name or Internet Protocol (IP) address of the computer you want to use. If you don't know the computer name or IP address, click Browse to search for the computer you want to work with.

Creating and Publishing Shared Folders

To create shares on a server running Windows Server 2008, you must be a member of the Administrators or Server Operators group. You can create shares using Windows Explorer, Computer Management, or Net Share from the command line.

- Windows Explorer works well when you want to share folders on the computer to which you are logged on.

- Using Computer Management, you can share the folders on the local computer and on any computer to which you can connect.

- Using Net Share, you can create shares from the command line or in scripts. Type **net share** /? at the command prompt for details on using this command.

As an administrator, Computer Management is the tool you'll use the most for creating and managing shares. After you create a share, you might want to publish it in Active Directory so it is easier to find.

Creating Shares by Using Windows Explorer

By using Windows Explorer, you can share folders on the computer to which you are logged on. In Windows Explorer, right-click the folder you want to share, and then select Properties. In the folder's Properties dialog box, click the Sharing tab to view the current sharing configuration (if any), as shown in Figure 17-6.

Click Share to display the File Sharing dialog box, as shown in Figure 17-7. Click the selection button (the down arrow) to the right of the text entry field provided and then select Find.

In the Select Users Or Groups dialog box, shown in Figure 17-8, check the value of the From This Location field. In workgroups, computers will always show only local accounts and groups. In domains, this field is changeable and set initially to the default (logon) domain of the currently logged on user. If this isn't the location you want to use for selecting user and group accounts to work with, click Locations to see a list of locations you can search, including the current domain, trusted domains, and other resources that you can access.

Figure 17-6 View the current sharing configuration.

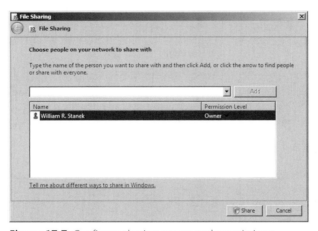

Figure 17-7 Configure sharing access and permissions.

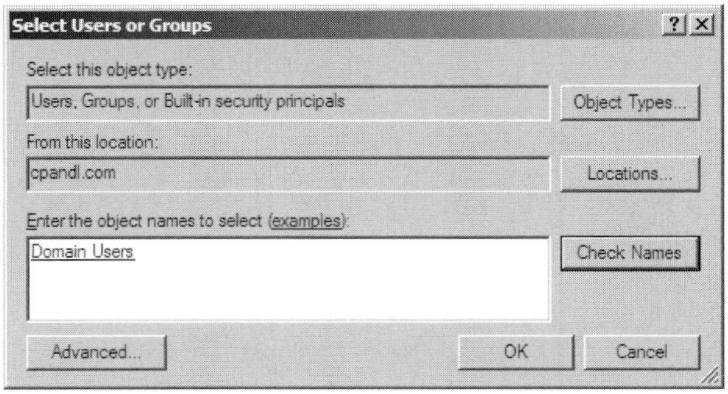

Figure 17-8 Choose users with which to share the folder.

In the Enter The Object Names To Select field, type the name of a user or a group account previously defined in the selected or default domain. Be sure to reference the user account name rather than a user's full name. When entering multiple names, separate them with semicolons.

Click Check Names. If a single match is found for each of your entries, the dialog box is automatically updated as appropriate and the entry is underlined. Otherwise, you'll see an additional dialog box. When no matches are found, you've either entered an incorrect name part or you're working with an incorrect location. Modify the name in the Name Not Found dialog box and try again, or click Locations to select a new location. When multiple matches are found, select the name(s) you want to use in the Multiple Names Found dialog box, and then click OK.

When you click OK, the users and groups are added to the Name list. You can then configure permissions for each user and group added by clicking an account name to display the Permission Level options and then choosing the appropriate permission level. The options for permission levels are Reader, Contributor, and Co-Owner.

Finally, click Share to create the share. After Windows creates the share and makes it available for use, note the share name. This is the name by which the shared resource can be accessed. If you want to e-mail a link to the shared resource to someone, click E-Mail. If you want to copy a link to the shared resource to the Windows Clipboard, click Copy. Click Done when you are finished.

The share is immediately available for use. In Windows Explorer, you'll see that the folder icon now includes a grouped user icon to indicate it is a share. If you click the Share button on the Sharing tab when sharing is already configured, you'll see a different view of the File Sharing dialog box. This view enables you to:

- **Change sharing permissions** Clicking Change Sharing Permissions displays the original view of the File Sharing dialog box. You can grant access to additional users and groups as discussed previously. To remove access for a user or group, select the user or group in the Name list and then select Remove. When you are finished making changes, click Share to reconfigure the sharing options and then click Done.

- **Stop sharing** Clicking Stop Sharing removes the share configuration. After Windows removes sharing, click Done to close the File Sharing dialog box.

If you click the Advanced Sharing button on the Sharing tab, you'll see the Advanced Sharing dialog box, as shown in Figure 17-9. Click Add to share the folder again using a different name and a different set of access permissions.

When you create multiple shares for the same folder, the Share Name box of the Sharing tab becomes a selection list that allows you to select a share to work with and configure. After you've selected a share to work with, the options on the Sharing tab apply to that share only. You'll also have a Remove option, which you can use to remove the additional share.

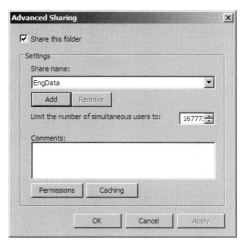

Figure 17-9 You can configure different shares of the same folder with different names and permissions as well.

Click Permissions to view and set the share permissions as discussed in "Managing Share Permissions" on page 563. Share permissions provide the top-level access controls to the share. By default, only users you specify have access to the share. This is an important security change for Windows Server 2008 that is designed to help ensure that permissions aren't given to users unless you grant them.

> **Note**
>
> After you set share permissions, you might want to configure the share for offline use. By default, the share is configured so that only files and programs that users specify are available for offline use. If you want to prohibit the offline use of files or programs in the share or specify that all files and programs in the share are available for offline use, click Caching, and then select the appropriate options in the Offline Settings dialog box.

Creating Shares by Using Computer Management

By using Computer Management, you can share the folders of any computer to which you can connect on the network. This is handy for when you are sitting at your desk and don't want to have to log on locally to share a server's folders. After you start Computer Management, you can connect to the computer you want to work with by right-clicking Computer Management in the console tree and then selecting Connect To Another Computer. Use the Select Computer dialog box to choose the computer you want to work with. When you are finished, expand System Tools, Shared Folders, and then select Shares to display the current shares on the system you are working with.

You can then create a shared folder by right-clicking Shares and then selecting New Share. This starts the Create A Shared Folder Wizard. Click Next to display the Folder Path page as shown in Figure 17-10. In the Folder Path field, type the full path to the folder you want to share. If you don't know the full path, click Browse, and then use the Browse For Folder dialog box to find the folder you want to share. The Browse For Folder dialog box will also let you create a new folder that you can then share. Click Next when you are ready to continue.

> **Note**
> At an elevated command prompt, you can start the Create A Shared Folder Wizard by entering **shrpubw**.

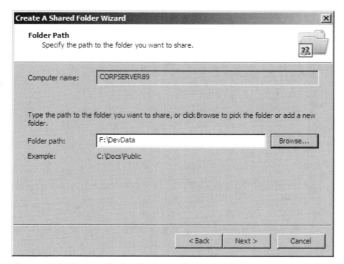

Figure 17-10 Specify the folder path or click Browse to search for a folder to use.

In the Share Name field, type a name for the share, as shown in Figure 17-11. This is the name of the folder to which users will connect, and it must be unique on the computer you are working with. Share names can be up to 80 characters in length and can contain spaces. If you want to provide support for MS-DOS clients, you should limit the share name to eight characters with a three-letter extension. If you want to hide the share from users (which means that they won't be able to see the shared resource when they try to browse to it in Windows Explorer or at the command line), type $ as the last character of the share name. Keep in mind that you can hide shares only from normal users. If users have Administrator privileges, they would be able to get a list of the shares.

Optionally, type a description of the share in the Description field. The description is displayed as comments when you view shares in Network Explorer and other Windows dialog boxes.

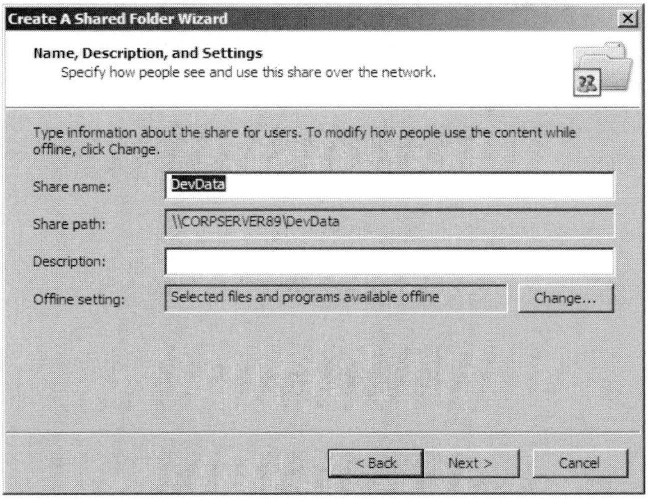

Figure 17-11 Set the share name and description.

When you are ready to continue, click Next to display the Shared Folder Permissions page shown in Figure 17-12. The available options are as follows:

- **All Users Have Read-Only Access** This is the default option. When you create shared folders in Windows Explorer, this permission is set automatically to give users the right to view files and read data but to restrict them from creating, modifying, or deleting files and folders.

Note

Granting Read access instead of Full Control by default is an important security change for Windows Server 2008. It is designed to help ensure that permissions aren't given to users unless you specifically grant them. Although it is a start on better controls, it isn't perfect because this permission is assigned to the special group Everyone, which means anyone with access to the network—even Guests—have Read access to the share.

- **Administrators Have Full Access; Other Users Have Read-Only Access** This option gives administrators full access to the share. This allows administrators to create, modify, and delete files and folders. On NTFS it also gives administrators the right to change permissions and to take ownership of files and folders. Other users can only view files and read data. They can't create, modify, or delete files and folders.

- **Administrators Have Full Access; Other Users Have No Access** This option gives administrators full access to the share but prevents other users from accessing the share.

- **Customize Permissions** This option allows you to configure access for specific users and groups, which is usually the best technique to use. Setting share permissions is discussed fully in "Managing Share Permissions" on the next page.

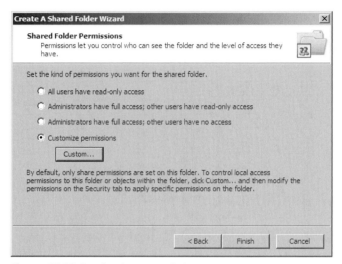

Figure 17-12 Set the share permissions.

After you set up permissions on the share, click Finish. The wizard displays a status report, which should state "Sharing Was Successful," as shown in Figure 17-13. Click Finish.

Figure 17-13 Shows a summary of the share that you created.

Publishing Shares in Active Directory

Sometimes, you'll also want to publish shares in Active Directory to make them easier to find. The quickest way to do this is to use Computer Management. After you start Computer Management and connect to the computer you want to work with, expand System Tools, Shared Folders, and then select Shares to display the current shares on the system you are working with.

You can then publish a shared folder by right-clicking the share in the details pane and then selecting Properties. In the share's Properties dialog box, click the Publish tab as shown in Figure 17-14. Finally, select the Publish This Share In Active Directory check box, and then click OK.

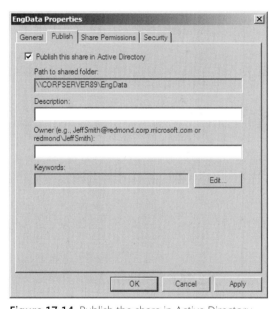

Figure 17-14 Publish the share in Active Directory.

Managing Share Permissions

As discussed previously, Windows Server 2008 has two levels of permissions for shared folders: share permissions and file and folder permissions. Share permissions are applied any time you access a file or folder over the network. These top-level permissions set the maximum allowable actions available within a shared folder. Although share permissions can get you in the door when you work remotely, the file and folder permissions can further constrain access and the allowable actions.

When accessing files locally, only the file and folder permissions are applied. However, when accessing files remotely, first the share permissions are applied and then the file and folder permissions. In the case of file allocation table (FAT) volumes, the share permissions are the only permissions, and if a user has local access to the folder, the user can perform any action.

Understanding Share Permissions

With shared folders, you use share permissions to set the maximum allowed access level. Share permissions are applied only when you access a folder remotely, and they can be used to grant access directly to users or implicitly through the groups to which users belong.

The share permissions available are as follows:

- **Full Control** By granting this permission, users have Read and Change permissions, as well as the additional capabilities to change file and folder permissions and take ownership of files and folders.

- **Change** By granting this permission, users have Read permissions and the additional capability to create files and subfolders, modify files, change attributes on files and subfolders, and delete files and subfolders.

- **Read** By granting this permission, you allow users to view file and subfolder names, access the subfolders of the share, read file data and attributes, and run program files.

If you have Read permissions on a share, the most you can do is perform read operations. If you have Change permissions on a share, the most you can do is perform read operations and change operations. If you have Full Control, you have full access. However, in any case, file and folder permissions can further constrain access.

Permissions assigned to groups work like this: If a user is a member of a group that is granted share permissions, the user also has those permissions. If a user is a member of multiple groups, the permissions are cumulative. This means that if one group of which the user is a member has Read access and another has additional access, the user has additional access as well.

INSIDE OUT   Changes might be needed to enhance security

When you create a shared folder, default access permissions are assigned. Watch out, though, because the default in most cases is to give Read access to the special group Everyone, which means that even Guests have access to shares. This doesn't mean Guests can read files, however, because this is determined by the base-level file and folder permissions. In most cases, it is more prudent to lock down access and only grant permissions to those users that truly need access to a shared folder. If you really want to grant wide access to a shared folder, you might want to use the Domain Users group to do this rather than the Everyone group. In this case, you would remove the Everyone group and add the Domain Users group. By using Domain Users, you require users to have a logon account to access the shared folder, which excludes Guests.

To override this behavior, you must specifically deny an access permission. Denying permission is the trump card—it takes precedence and overrides permissions that have been granted. When you want to single out a user or group and not let it have a permission, configure the share permissions to specifically deny that permission to the user or group. For example, if a user is a member of a group that has been granted Full Control over a share, but the user should have only Change permissions, configure the share to deny Full Control to that user.

Configuring Share Permissions

The easiest way to configure share permissions is to use Computer Management. After you start Computer Management, connect to the computer you want to work with by right-clicking Computer Management in the console tree and then selecting Connect To Another Computer. Then use the Select Computer dialog box to choose the computer you want to work with. When you are finished, expand System Tools, Shared Folders, and then select Shares to display the current shares on the system you are working with.

To view or manage the permissions of a share, right-click the share and then select Properties. In the share Properties dialog box, click the Share Permissions tab, as shown in Figure 17-15. You can now view the users and groups that have access to the share and the type of access they have.

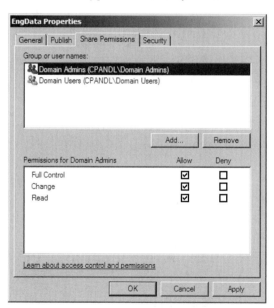

Figure 17-15 View or set share permissions.

In this example, members of the Domain Admins group have Full Control over the share and members of the Domain Users group have Change access. The group Everyone was removed to enhance security as discussed in "Changes Might Be Needed to Enhance Security" on the facing page.

You can grant or deny permission to access a share by following these steps:

1. In Computer Management, right-click the share and then select Properties. In the share Properties dialog box, click the Share Permissions tab.

2. On the Share Permissions tab, click Add. This opens the Select Users, Computers, Or Groups dialog box, as shown in Figure 17-16.

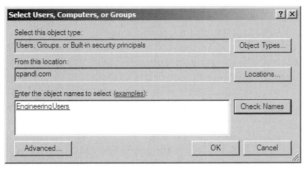

Figure 17-16 Specify the users or groups to add.

3. The Locations button allows you to access account names from other domains. Click Locations to see a list of the current domains, trusted domains, and other resources that you can access. Because of the transitive trusts in Windows Server 2008, you can usually access all the domains in the domain tree or forest.

4. Type the name of a user or group account in the selected or default domain, and then click Check Names. The options available depend on the number of matches found, as follows:

   ○ When a single match is found, the dialog box is automatically updated as appropriate and the entry is underlined.

   ○ When no matches are found, you've either entered an incorrect name part or you're working with an incorrect location. Modify the name and try again, or click Locations to select a new location.

   ○ If multiple matches are found, select the name(s) you want to use, and then click OK.

5. To add additional users or groups, type a semicolon (;), and then repeat this process.

6. When you click OK, the users and groups are added to the Name list for the share.

7. Configure access permissions for each user and group added by selecting an account name and then allowing or denying access permissions. If a user or group should be granted access permissions, select the check box for the permission in the Allow column. If a user or group should be denied access permissions, select the check box for the permission in the Deny column.

8. When you're finished, click OK.

Managing File and Folder Permissions

You can think of file and folder permissions as the base-level permissions—the permissions that are applied no matter what. For NTFS volumes, you use file and folder permissions and ownership to further constrain actions within the share as well as share permissions. For FAT volumes, share permissions provide the only access controls. The reason for this is that FAT volumes have no file and folder permission capabilities.

File and folder permissions are much more complex than share permissions, and to really understand how they can be used and applied, you must understand ownership and inheritance as well as the permissions that are available.

INSIDE OUT   Changes to basic file and folder attributes are sometimes necessary

As administrators, we often forget about the basic file and folder attributes that can be assigned. However, basic file and folder attributes can affect access, so let's look at these attributes first and then at the file and folder permissions you can apply to NTFS volumes. All files and folders have basic attributes regardless of whether you are working with FAT or NTFS. These attributes can be examined in Windows Explorer by right-clicking the file or folder icon and then selecting Properties. Folder and file attributes include Hidden and Read-Only. Hidden determines whether the file is displayed in file listings. You can override this by telling Windows Explorer to display hidden files. On NTFS, the Read-Only attribute for folders is initially shown as unavailable. Here, this means the attribute is in a mixed state regardless of the current state of files in the folder. If you override the mixed state by selecting the Read-Only check box for a folder, all files in the folder will be read-only. If you override the mixed state and clear the Read-Only check box for a folder, all files in the folder will be writable.

File and Folder Ownership

Before working with file and folder permissions, you should understand the concept of ownership as it applies to files and folders. In Windows Server 2008, the file or folder owner isn't necessarily the file or folder's creator. Instead, the file or folder owner is the person who has direct control over the file or folder. File or folder owners can grant access permissions and give other users permission to take ownership of a file or folder.

The way ownership is assigned initially depends on where the file or folder is being created. By default, the user who created the file or folder is listed as the current owner. Ownership can be taken or transferred in several ways. Any administrator can take ownership. Any user or group with the Take Ownership permission can take ownership. Any user who has the right to Restore Files And Directories, such as a member of the Backup Operators group, can take ownership as well. Any current owner can transfer ownership to another user as well.

Taking Ownership of a File or Folder

You can take ownership using a file or folder's Properties dialog box. Right-click the file or folder, and then select Properties. On the Security tab of the Properties dialog box, display the Advanced Security Settings dialog box by clicking Advanced. Next, on the Owner tab, click Edit to display an editable version of the Owner tab, as shown in Figure 17-17. In the Change Owner To list box, select the new owner. If you're taking ownership of a folder, you can take ownership of all subfolders and files within the folder by selecting the Replace Owner On Subcontainers And Objects check box. Click OK twice when you are finished.

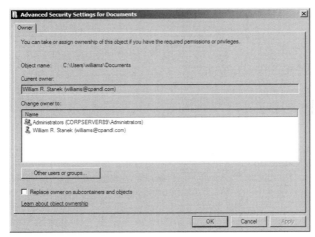

Figure 17-17 Taking ownership is done by using the Owner tab.

Transferring Ownership

If you are an administrator or a current owner of a file or folder, you can transfer ownership to another user by using a file or folder's Properties dialog box. In Windows Explorer, right-click the file or folder, and then select Properties. On the Security tab of the Properties dialog box, display the Advanced Security Settings dialog box by clicking the Advanced button. Next, on the Owner tab, click Edit to display an editable version of the Owner tab, as shown in Figure 17-17.

Click Other Users Or Groups to display the Select User, Computer, Or Group dialog box. Type the name of a user or group, and click Check Names. If multiple names match the value you entered, you'll see a list of names and will be able to choose the one you want to use. Otherwise, the name will be filled in for you, and you can click OK to close the Select User, Computer, Or Group dialog box. Under Change Owner To on the Owner tab of the Advanced Security Settings dialog box, the user you added is listed and selected. When you click OK, ownership is transferred to this user.

Permission Inheritance for Files and Folders

By default, when you add a folder or file to an existing folder, the folder or file inherits the permissions of the existing folder. For example, if the Domain Users group has access to a folder and you add a file to this folder, members of the Domain Users group will be able to access the file. Inherited permissions are automatically assigned when files and folders are created.

When you assign new permissions to a folder, the permissions propagate down and are inherited by all subfolders and files in the folder and supplement or replace existing permissions. If you add permissions on a folder to allow a new group to access a folder, these permissions are applied to all subfolders and files in the folder, meaning the additional group is granted access. On the other hand, if you were to change the permissions on the folder so that, for instance, only members of the Engineering group could access the folder, these permissions would be applied to all subfolders and files in the folder, meaning only members of the Engineering group would have access to the folder, its subfolders, and its files.

Inheritance is automatic. If you do not want the permissions of subfolders and files within folders to supplement or replace existing permissions, you must override inheritance starting with the top-level folder from which the permissions are inherited. A top-level folder is referred to as a *parent folder*. Files and folders below the parent folder are referred to as *child files and folders*. This is identical to the parent/child structure of objects in Active Directory.

Changing Shaded Permissions and Stopping Inheritance

If a permission you want to change is shaded, the file or folder is inheriting the permission from a parent folder. To change the permission, you must do one of the following:

- Access the parent folder and make the desired changes. These changes will then be inherited by child folders and files.

- Select the opposite permission to override the inherited permission if possible. In most cases, Deny overrides Allow, so if you explicitly deny permission to a user or group for a child folder or file, this permission should be denied to that user or group of users.

- Stop inheriting permissions from the parent folder and then copy or remove existing permissions as appropriate.

To stop inheriting permissions from a parent folder, right-click the file or folder in Windows Explorer and then select Properties. On the Security tab of the Properties dialog box, click Advanced to display the Advanced Security Settings dialog box. On the Permissions tab, click Edit to display an editable version of the Permissions tab, as shown in Figure 17-18.

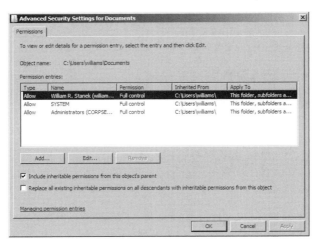

Figure 17-18 Change inheritance as necessary.

Clear the Include Inheritable Permissions From This Object's Parent check box. As shown in Figure 17-19, you now have the opportunity to copy over the permissions that were previously applied or remove the inherited permissions and apply only the permissions that you explicitly set on the folder or file. Click Copy or Remove as appropriate.

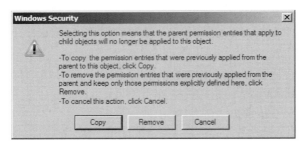

Figure 17-19 Copy over or remove the inherited permissions.

Resetting and Replacing Permissions

Another way to manage permissions is to reset the permissions of subfolders and files within a folder, replacing their permissions with the current permissions assigned to the folder you are working with. In this way, subfolders and files get all inheritable permissions from the parent folder and all other explicitly defined permissions on the individual subfolders and files are removed.

To reset permissions for subfolders and files of a folder, right-click the file or folder in Windows Explorer, and then select Properties. On the Security tab of the Properties dialog box, click Advanced to display the Advanced Security Settings dialog box. On the Permissions tab, click Edit to display an editable version of the Permissions tab.

Select Replace All Existing Inheritable Permissions..., and then click OK. As shown in Figure 17-20, you will see a prompt explaining that this action will remove all explicitly defined permissions and enable propagation of inheritable permissions. Click Yes.

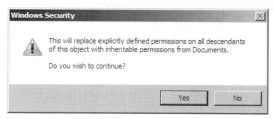

Figure 17-20 Confirm that you want to replace the existing permissions on subfolders and files.

Configuring File and Folder Permissions

On NTFS volumes, you can assign access permissions to files and folders. These permissions grant or deny access to users and groups.

Basic Permissions

In Windows Explorer you can view basic permissions by right-clicking the file or folder you want to work with, selecting Properties on the shortcut menu, and then in the Properties dialog box selecting the Security tab, as shown in Figure 17-21. The Group Or User Names list shows groups and users with assigned permissions. If you select a group or user in this list, the applicable permissions are shown in the Permissions For list. If permissions are unavailable, it means the permissions are inherited from a parent folder as discussed previously.

Figure 17-21 The Security tab shows the basic permissions assigned to each user or group.

The basic permissions you can assign to folders and files are shown in Table 17-1 and Table 17-2. These permissions are made up of multiple special permissions.

Table 17-1 Basic Folder Permissions

Permission	Description
Full Control	This permission permits reading, writing, changing, and deleting files and subfolders. If a user has Full Control over a folder, she can delete files in the folder regardless of the permission on the files.
Modify	This permission permits reading and writing to files and subfolders; allows deletion of the folder.
List Folder Contents	This permission permits viewing and listing files and subfolders as well as executing files; inherited by folders only.
Read & Execute	This permission permits viewing and listing files and subfolders as well as executing files; inherited by files and folders.
Write	This permission permits adding files and subfolders.
Read	This permission permits viewing and listing files and subfolders.

Table 17-2 Basic File Permissions

Permission	Description
Full Control	This permission permits reading, writing, changing, and deleting the file.
Modify	This permission permits reading and writing of the file; allows deletion of the file.
Read & Execute	This permission permits viewing and accessing the file's contents as well as executing the file.
Write	This permission permits writing to a file. Giving a user permission to write to a file but not to delete it doesn't prevent the user from deleting the file's contents.
Read	This permission permits viewing or accessing the file's contents. Read is the only permission needed to run scripts. Read access is required to access a shortcut and its target.

You can set basic permissions for files and folders by following these steps:

1. In Windows Explorer, right-click the file or folder you want to work with, and select Properties. In the Properties dialog box, select the Security tab, shown previously in Figure 17-21.

2. Click Edit to display an editable version of the Security tab. Users or groups that already have access to the file or folder are listed in the Name list box. You can change permissions for these users and groups by selecting the user or group you want to change and then using the Permissions list box to grant or deny access permissions.

3. To set access permissions for additional users, computers, or groups, click Add. This displays the Select Users, Computers, Or Groups dialog box.

4. The Locations button allows you to access account names from other domains. Click Locations to see a list of the current domain, trusted domains, and other resources that you can access. Because of the transitive trusts in Windows Server 2008, you can usually access all the domains in the domain tree or forest.

5. Type the name of a user or group account in the selected or default domain, and then click Check Names. The options available depend on the number of matches found as follows:

   ○ When a single match is found, the dialog box is automatically updated as appropriate and the entry is underlined.

   ○ When no matches are found, you've either entered an incorrect name part or you're working with an incorrect location. Modify the name and try again, or click Locations to select a new location.

   ○ If multiple matches are found, select the name(s) you want to use, and then click OK.

6. To add additional users or groups, type a semicolon (;), and then repeat this process.

7. When you click OK, the users and groups are added to the Name list for the file or folder. Configure access permissions for each user and group added by selecting an account name and then allowing or denying access permissions. If a user or group should be granted access permissions, select the check box for the permission in the Allow column. If a user or group should be denied access permissions, select the check box for the permission in the Deny column.

8. When you're finished, click OK.

Special Permissions

In Windows Explorer you can view special permissions by right-clicking the file or folder you want to work with and selecting Properties on the shortcut menu. In the Properties dialog box, select the Security tab, and then click Advanced to display the Advanced Security Settings dialog box, as shown in Figure 17-22.

The special permissions available are as follows:

- **Traverse Folder/Execute File** Traverse Folder lets you directly access a folder even if you don't have explicit access to read the data it contains. Execute File lets you run an executable file.

- **List Folder/Read Data** List Folder lets you view file and folder names. Read Data lets you view the contents of a file.

- **Read Attributes** Lets you read the basic attributes of a file or folder. These attributes include Read-Only, Hidden, System, and Archive.

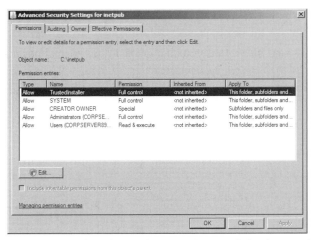

Figure 17-22 The Advanced Security Settings dialog box can be used to access the special permissions assigned to each user or group.

- **Read Extended Attributes** Lets you view the extended attributes (named data streams) associated with a file. As discussed in Chapter 16, "Managing Windows Server 2008 File Systems," these include Summary fields, such as Title, Subject, and Author, as well as other types of data.

- **Create Files/Write Data** Create Files lets you put new files in a folder. Write Data allows you to overwrite existing data in a file (but not add new data to an existing file because this is covered by Append Data).

- **Create Folders/Append Data** Create Folders lets you create subfolders within folders. Append Data allows you to add data to the end of an existing file (but not to overwrite existing data because this is covered by Write Data).

- **Write Attributes** Lets you change the basic attributes of a file or folder. These attributes include Read-Only, Hidden, System, and Archive.

- **Write Extended Attributes** Lets you change the extended attributes (named data streams) associated with a file. As discussed in Chapter 16, these include Summary fields, such as Title, Subject, and Author, as well as other types of data.

- **Delete Subfolders And Files** Lets you delete the contents of a folder. If you have this permission, you can delete the subfolders and files in a folder even if you don't specifically have Delete permission on the subfolder or file.

- **Delete** Lets you delete a file or folder. If a folder isn't empty and you don't have Delete permission for one of its files or subfolders, you won't be able to delete it. You can do this only if you have the Delete Subfolders And Files permission.

- **Read Permissions** Lets you read all basic and special permissions assigned to a file or folder.

- **Change Permissions** Lets you change basic and special permissions assigned to a file or folder.

- **Take Ownership** Lets you take ownership of a file or folder. By default, administrators can always take ownership of a file or folder and can also grant this permission to others.

Tables 17-3 and 17-4 show how special permissions are combined to make the basic permissions for files and folders. Because special permissions are combined to make the basic permissions, they are also referred to as *atomic permissions*.

Table 17-3 Special Permissions for Folders

Special Permissions	Full Control	Modify	Read & Execute	List Folder Contents	Read	Write
Traverse Folder/ Execute File	X	X	X	X		
List Folder/Read Data	X	X	X	X	X	
Read Attributes	X	X	X	X	X	
Read Extended Attributes	X	X	X	X	X	
Create Files/Write Data	X	X				X
Create Folders/ Append Data	X	X				X
Write Attributes	X	X				X
Write Extended Attributes	X	X				X
Delete Subfolders And Files	X					
Delete	X	X				
Read Permissions	X	X	X	X	X	X
Change Permissions	X					
Take Ownership	X					

Chapter 17

Table 17-4 **Special Permissions for Files**

Special Permissions	Full Control	Modify	Read & Execute	Read	Write
Traverse Folder/ Execute File	X	X	X		
List Folder/Read Data	X	X	X	X	
Read Attributes	X	X	X	X	
Read Extended Attributes	X	X	X	X	
Create Files/Write Data	X	X			X
Create Folders/ Append Data	X	X			X
Write Attributes	X	X			X
Write Extended Attributes	X	X			X
Delete Subfolders And Files	X				
Delete	X	X			
Read Permissions	X	X	X	X	X
Change Permissions	X				
Take Ownership	X				

You can set special permissions for files and folders in Windows Explorer. Right-click the file or folder you want to work with and then select Properties. In the Properties dialog box, click the Security tab, and then click Advanced. This displays the Advanced Security Settings dialog box with the Permissions tab selected. Click Edit to display an editable version of the Permissions tab. You now have the following options:

- **Add** Adds a user or group. Click Add to display the Select User, Computer, Or Group dialog box. Type the name of a user or group, and click Check Names. If multiple names match the value you entered, you'll see a list of names and will be able to choose the one you want to use. Otherwise, the name will be filled in for you. When you click OK, the Permission Entry For dialog box shown in Figure 17-23 is displayed.

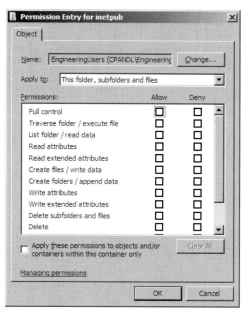

Figure 17-23 Use the Permission Entry For dialog box to set special permissions.

- **Edit** Edits an existing user or group entry. Select the user or group whose permissions you want to modify, and then click Edit. The Permission Entry For dialog box shown in Figure 17-23 is displayed.

- **Remove** Removes an existing user or group entry. Select the user or group whose permissions you want to remove, and then click Remove.

If you are adding or editing entries for users or groups, you use the Permission Entry For dialog box to grant or deny special permissions. Select Allow or Deny for each permission as appropriate. When finished, use the Apply Onto options shown in Table 17-5 to determine how and where these permissions are applied. If you want to prevent subfolders and files from inheriting these permissions, select Apply These Permissions To Objects And/Or Containers Within This Container Only. When you do this, all the related entries in Table 17-5 are No. This means the settings no longer apply onto subsequent subfolders or to files in subsequent subfolders.

Table 17-5 Special Permissions Apply Onto Options

Apply Onto	Applies to Current Folder	Applies to Subfolders in the Current Folder	Applies to File in the Current Folder	Applies to Subsequent Subfolders	Applies to Files in Subsequent Subfolders
This folder only	Yes	No	No	No	No
This folder, subfolders, and files	Yes	Yes	Yes	Yes	Yes
This folder and subfolders	Yes	Yes	No	Yes	No
This folder and files	Yes	No	Yes	No	Yes
Subfolders and files only	No	Yes	Yes	Yes	Yes
Subfolders only	No	Yes	No	Yes	No
Files only	No	No	Yes	No	Yes

> **Note**
>
> When Apply These Permissions To Objects And/Or Containers Within This Container Only is selected, all the values under Applies To Subsequent Subfolders and Applies To Files In Subsequent Subfolders are No. The settings no longer apply onto subsequent subfolders or to files in subsequent subfolders.

Determining Effective Permissions

Navigating the complex maze of permissions can be daunting even for the best administrators. Sometimes it won't be clear how a particular permission set will be applied to a particular user or group. If you ever want to know exactly how the current permissions will be applied to a particular user or group, you can use a handy tool called Effective Permissions.

Effective Permissions applies only to file and folder permissions—not share permissions—and is an option of the Advanced Security Settings dialog box. To get to it from Windows Explorer, right-click the file or folder you want to work with and select Properties. In the Properties dialog box, select the Security tab, and then click Advanced. To see how permissions will be applied to a user or group, click the Effective Permissions tab, click Select, type the name of the user or group, and then click OK. The Effective Permissions for the selected user or group are displayed as shown in Figure 17-24.

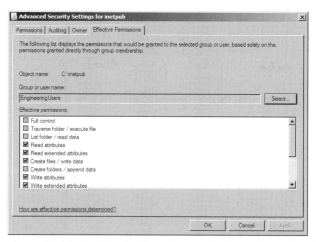

Figure 17-24 Use Effective Permissions to help you determine how permissions will be applied to a specific user or group.

Effective Permissions does have the following limitations:

- You need the proper access permissions to view the effective permissions of a user or group. That goes without saying, pretty much. But it is important to point out.

- You cannot determine permissions for global or universal security groups that are nested in domain local groups. For example, by default Users has access to most folders, and one of its members is Domain Users, which is a global security group. If you try to determine the effective permissions for Domain Users, no permissions are displayed.

- You cannot determine the effective permissions for implicit groups or special identities, such as Everyone, Interactive, Domain Controllers, Local Service, or Network Service.

Managing File Shares After Configuration

Configuring shares can be a time-consuming process especially if you are trying to troubleshoot why a particular user doesn't have access or set up a new server with the same file shares as a server you are decommissioning. Fortunately, there are some techniques you can use to help you better manage file shares and the way they are implemented.

Net Share is a handy command-line tool for helping you track file share and print share permissions. You can use it to display a list of shares and who has access. If you redirect the output of Net Share, you can save the share configuration and access information to a file, and this file can become a log that helps you track share changes over time.

Chapter 17

To view a list of configured shares, type **net share** at the command prompt. The output of Net Share shows you the name of each share on the server, the location of the actual folder being shared, and any descriptions you've added. Here is an example:

```
Share name    Resource                      Remark

-------------------------------------------------------------
ADMIN$        C:\Windows                    Remote Admin
C$            C:\                           Default share
F$            F:\                           Default share
IPC$                                        Remote IPC
CorpData      C:\CorpData
CorpTech      F:\CorpTech
DevData       F:\DevData
EngData       C:\EngData
HRData        F:\HRData
Public        C:\Users\Public
UserData      C:\UserData
The command completed successfully.
```

The list of shares shown includes the file shares CorpData, CorpTech, EngData, Public, and others, and administrative shares created and managed by Windows, including ADMIN$, IPC$, and any drive shares.

If you want to redirect the output to a file, you can do this by typing **net share > File-Name.txt**, where *FileName.txt* is the name of the file to create and to which you want to write, such as

```
net share > C:\logs\fileshares.txt
```

If you follow the Net Share command with the name of a configured share, you'll see the complete configuration details for the share as shown in the following example:

```
Share name      EngData
Path            C:\EngData
Remark
Maximum users   No limit
Users
Caching         Manual caching of documents
Permission      CPANDL\Domain Admins, FULL
                CPANDL\Domain Users, READ
                CPANDL\EngineeringUsers, READ

The command completed successfully.
```

You can append the share configuration details to the previously created log file by using the append symbol (>>) instead of the standard redirect symbol (>), as shown in the following example:

```
net share corpdata >> C:\logs\fileshares.txt
```

Listing 17-1 shows the source of a command-line script that you could use to create a configuration log for the key shares on the computer. Although the path in the example is set to c:\logs\fileshares.txt, you can set any log path you want.

Listing 17-1 A sample share logging script

```
net share > C:\logs\fileshares.txt
net share c$ >> C:\logs\fileshares.txt
net share f$ >> C:\logs\fileshares.txt
net share corpdata >> C:\logs\fileshares.txt
net share corptech >> C:\logs\fileshares.txt
net share devdata >> C:\logs\fileshares.txt
net share engdata >> C:\logs\fileshares.txt
net share hrdata >> C:\logs\fileshares.txt
net share public >> C:\logs\fileshares.txt
net share userdata >> C:\logs\fileshares.txt
```

Auditing File and Folder Access

Access permissions will only help protect data; they won't tell you who deleted important data or who was trying to access files and folders inappropriately. To track who accessed files and folders and what they did, you must configure auditing for file and folder access. Every comprehensive security strategy should include auditing.

To track file and folder access, you must:

- Enable auditing

- Specify which files and folders to audit

- Monitor the security logs

Enabling Auditing for Files and Folders

You configure auditing policies by using Group Policy or local security policy. Group Policy is used when you want to set auditing policies for an entire site, domain, or organizational unit, and is used as discussed in Part 5 of this book, "Managing Active Directory and Security." Local security policy settings apply to an individual workstation or server and can be overridden by Group Policy.

To enable auditing of files and folders for a specific computer, start the Local Security Policy tool by clicking Start, All Programs, Administrative Tools, and Local Security Policy. Expand Local Policies, and then select Audit Policy, as shown in Figure 17-25.

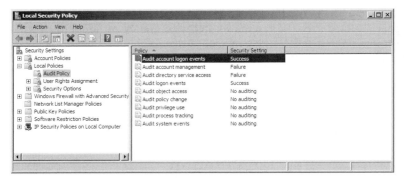

Figure 17-25 Access the local auditing policy settings.

Next, double-click Audit Object Access. This displays the Audit Object Access Properties dialog box shown in Figure 17-26. Under Audit These Attempts, select the Success check box to log successful access attempts, the Failure check box to log failed access attempts, or both check boxes, and then click OK. This enables auditing but it doesn't specify which files and folders should be audited.

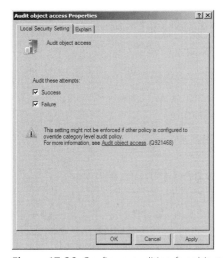

Figure 17-26 Configure auditing for object access.

Specifying Files and Folders to Audit

After you have enabled Audit Object Access, you can set the level of auditing for individual folders and files. This allows you to control whether and how folder and file usage is tracked. Keep in mind that auditing is available only on NTFS volumes. In addition, everything discussed about inheritance applies to files and folders as well—and this is a good thing. This allows you, for example, to audit access to every file or folder on a volume simply by specifying that you want to audit the root folder of the volume.

You specify files and folders to audit using Windows Explorer. In Windows Explorer, right-click the file or folder to be audited, and then, from the shortcut menu, select Properties. In the Properties dialog box, click the Security tab, and then click Advanced. In the Advanced Security Settings dialog box, click Edit on the Auditing tab. You can now view and manage auditing settings using the options shown in Figure 17-27.

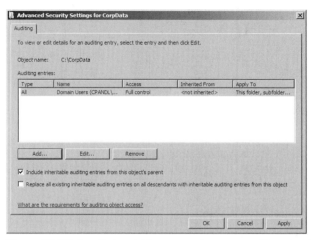

Figure 17-27 Specify to which users and groups auditing should apply.

You have the same two inheritance options discussed earlier in the chapter:

- If you want to inherit auditing settings from a parent object, ensure that the Include Inheritable Permissions From This Object's Parent check box is selected.

- If you want child objects of the current object to inherit the settings you are setting on the current folder, select the Replace All Existing Inheritable Auditing Entries check box.

Now use the Auditing Entries list box to select the users, groups, or computers whose actions you want to audit. To add specific accounts, click Add, and then use the Select User, Computer, Or Group dialog box to select an account name to add. If you want to audit actions for all users, use the special group Everyone. Otherwise, select the specific user groups or users, or both, that you want to audit. When you click OK, you'll see the Auditing Entry For dialog box, as shown in Figure 17-28.

Chapter 17

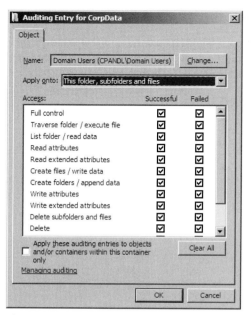

Figure 17-28 Determine the actions to audit for the designated user, group, or computer.

The Apply Onto drop-down list box allows you to specify which actions should be audited. Select the Successful or Failed check boxes, or both, for the events you want to audit. The events you can audit are the same as the special permissions listed in Tables 17-3 and 17-4, except you can't audit the synchronizing of offline files and folders. Click OK when you're finished. Repeat this process to audit other users, groups, or computers.

> **Note**
>
> Often you'll want to track only failed actions. This way, you know if someone was trying to perform an action and failed. Keep in mind a failed attempt doesn't always mean someone is trying to break into a file or folder. A user simply might have double-clicked a folder or file to which he or she didn't have access. In addition, some types of actions can cause multiple failed attempts to be logged even when the user performed the action only once. Regardless, as an administrator, you should always check multiple failed attempts because of the possibility that someone is attempting to breach your system's defenses.

Monitoring the Security Logs

Any time files and folders that you've configured for auditing are accessed, the action is written to the system's Security log, where it's stored for your review. The Security log is accessible from Event Viewer. Successful actions can cause successful events, such as successful file reads, to be recorded. Failed actions can cause failed events, such as failed file deletions, to be recorded.

Using Volume Shadow Copy

Volume Shadow Copy Service is a feature of Windows Server 2008. It offers two important features:

- **Shadow copying of files in shared folders** Allows you to configure volumes so that shadow copies of files in shared folders are created automatically at specific intervals during the day. This allows you to go back and look at earlier versions of files stored in shared folders. You can use these earlier versions to recover deleted, incorrectly modified, or overwritten files. You can also compare versions of files to see what changes were made over time. Up to 64 versions of files are maintained.

- **Shadow copying of open or locked files for backups** Allows you to use backup programs, such as Windows Backup, to back up files that are open or locked. This means you can back up when applications are using the files and do not have to worry about backups failing because files are in use. Backup programs must implement the Volume Shadow Copy Service (VSS) application programming interface (API).

Both features are independent of each other. You do not need to enable shadow copying of a volume to be able to back up open or locked files on a volume. This chapter primarily focuses on shadow copying of files in shared folders. Chapter 41, "Backup and Recovery," examines backups.

Shadow Copy Essentials

Shadow copying of files in shared folders is a feature administrators can use to create backup copies of files on designated volumes automatically. You can think of these backup copies as point-in-time snapshots that can be used to recover previous versions of files. Normally, when a user deletes a file from a shared folder, it is immediately deleted and doesn't go to the local Recycle Bin. This means the only way to recover it is from backup. The reason for this is that when you delete files over the network, the files are permanently deleted on the remote server and never make it to the Recycle Bin. This changes with shadow copying. If a user deletes a file from a network share, she can go back to a previous version and recover it—and she can do this without needing assistance from an administrator.

Using Shadow Copies of Shared Folders

Shadow copies of shared folders are designed to help recover files that were accidentally deleted, corrupted, or inappropriately edited. After you configure shadow copies on a server, the server creates and maintains previous versions of all files and folders created on the volumes you've specified. It does this by creating snapshots of shared folders at predetermined intervals and storing these images in shadow copy storage in such a way that users and administrators can easily access the data to recover previous versions of files and folders. Windows Server 2008 includes a feature enhancement that allows you to revert an entire volume to a previous shadow copy state.

Ideally, after you implement shadow copies throughout the organization and show users how to use the feature, users will be able to recover files and folders without needing assistance. This allows users to manage their own files, resolve problems, and fix mistakes. It also saves time and money because previous versions can be recovered quickly and easily and resources that would have been used to recover files and perform related tasks can be used elsewhere.

When planning to deploy shadow copies in your organization, look at the shared folders that are in use. When you identify the ones that would benefit from this feature, note the volumes on which those shares are located. Those are the volumes for which you will need to configure shadow copying. You might also want to consider changing the way users' personal data is stored. Windows Server 2008 enables you to centrally manage user data folders through file shares, and then if you configure shadow copies on these file shares, users will have access to previous versions of all their data files and folders. The folders you can centrally manage are the following:

- Application Data
- Desktop
- Start Menu
- Documents
- Pictures
- Music
- Videos
- Favorites
- Contacts
- Downloads
- Links
- Searches
- Saved Games

You configure central management of these folders through Group Policy. When you do this, you want to redirect the root path for these folders to a file share.

How Shadow Copies Works

Shadow Copies for Shared Folders is made possible through the Shadow Copy API. The shadow copy driver (Volsnap.sys) and the Volume Shadow Copy Service executable (Vssvc.exe) are key components used by this API. When you enable shadow copies on a server, the server is configured to be a client-accessible shadow copy service provider. The default provider is the Microsoft Software Shadow Copy Provider, and it is responsible for providing the necessary interface between clients that want to access shadow copies and clients that write shadow copies or information pertaining to shadow copies, called Volume Shadow Copy service writers.

A number of shadow copy service writers are installed by default and other writers can be installed when you install other programs, such as third-party backup software. The default writers installed depend on the system configuration and include the following:

- **BITS Writer** Shadow copies writer used to make backups of files in use by the Background Intelligent Transfer Service (BITS).

- **COM+ REGDB Writer** Shadow copies writer used by COM+ and the Windows internal database so that in-use files can be backed up.

- **Distributed File System (DFS) Service Writer** Shadow copies writer used by DFS so that in-use files can be backed up, primarily on domain controllers.

- **DHCP Jet Writer** Shadow copies writer used to make backups of files in use by the Dynamic Host Configuration Protocol (DHCP).

- **File Replication Service (FRS) Writer** Shadow copies writer used by FRS so that in-use files can be backed up, primarily on domain controllers.

- **IIS Config Writer** Shadow copies writer used to make backups of Microsoft Internet Information Services (IIS) configuration files.

- **MSSearch Service Writer** Shadow copies writer used to make backups of files in use by the Microsoft Search Service.

- **NT Directory Service (NTDS) Writer** Shadow copies writer used to make backups of files in use by NTDS.

- **Registry Writer** Shadow copies writer used by other writers to make Registry changes.

- **System Writer** The standard shadow copies writer used by the operating system.

- **Windows Management Instrumentation (WMI) Writer** Standard WMI writer for shadow copies.

- **WINS Jet Writer** Shadow copies writer used to make backups of files in use by the Windows Internet Naming Service (WINS).

Chapter 18

> **Note**
>
> You can list available shadow copy providers by typing **vssadmin list providers** at the command line. To list shadow copy writers, type **vssadmin list writers**.

To create copies of previous versions of files, Shadow Copies for Shared Folders uses a differential copy procedure. With this technique, only copies of files that have changed since the last copy are marked for copying. During the copy procedure, Shadow Copies for Shared Folders creates the previous version data in one of two ways:

- If the application used to change a file stored details of the changes, Shadow Copies for Shared Folders performs a block-level copy of any changes that have been made to files since the last save. Thus, only changes are copied, not the entire file.

- If the application used to change a file rewrote the entire file to disk, Shadow Copies for Shared Folders saves the entire file as it exists at that point in time.

If you're wondering exactly how this works, I was, too, at first. Then I started experimenting. An example of an application that can save changes or full copies is Microsoft Word. If you enable Fast Saves in Word, only changes to a file are written to disk. If you clear the Allow Fast Saves check box, Word writes a complete copy of the file when you save it.

As mentioned previously, Shadow Copies for Shared Folders runs at predefined intervals. These predefined intervals are set as the run schedule when you configure shadow copying of a volume. As with other processes that have a run schedule, a scheduled task is created that is used to trigger shadow copying at the specified times. Because of this, Shadow Copies for Shared Folders is dependent on the Task Scheduler service. If this service is stopped or improperly configured, shadow copying will not work.

Implementing Shadow Copies for Shared Folders

Implementing Shadow Copies for Shared Folders isn't something you should do haphazardly. You should take the time to plan out the implementation. Key issues that you should consider include the following:

- **Copy volumes** For which volumes should shadow copying be configured?

- **Disk space** How much disk space will be needed for shadow copying, and is there enough available space on existing volumes?

- **Shadow storage** Where should the shadow copies be stored and on which volumes?

- **Run schedule** How often should shadow copies be made?

Start your planning by considering for which volumes you want to configure shadow copies. After you configure this feature, shadow copies will be created of files in the shared folders on these volumes. To implement shadow copying of files of shared folders, you enable shadow copying of the volume in which the shared folders are located. The initial shadow copy requires at least 300 megabytes (MB) of free space to create, regardless of how much data is stored in the volume's shared folders. The disk space used by Shadow Copies for Shared Folders is referred to as *shadow storage*. Shadow Copies uses this space to store previous versions of files and as a work area when it is taking snapshots. Because of this, the actual amount of space used for shadow storage is different from the amount of space allocated for shadow storage.

The amount of disk space available shouldn't be overlooked. The Shadow Copy service will save up to 64 versions of each file in shared folders and, by default, will configure its maximum space usage as up to 10 percent of the volume. After you set this value, the maximum size is fixed unless you change it. The service won't, however, reexamine free space later to determine if this maximum value should be changed. If a volume runs out of space, shadow copying will fail and errors will be generated in the event logs.

When you plan out your shadow copies implementation, you should think carefully about where shadow storage will be located. Shadow storage can be created on the volumes for which you are creating shadow copies or on different volumes. If you have busy file servers or you must scale this feature to serve many users or an increasing number of users, it might be best to use a separate volume on a separate drive for shadow storage.

> ### Use the Command-Line Tools to Examine Shadow Storage
>
> You can determine how much space is allocated to and used by shadow storage by using the **vssadmin list shadowstorage** command. Working with this command is discussed in "Configuring Shadow Copies at the Command Line" on page 598.

Shadow copying is a resource-intensive process. By default, when you configure shadow copying on a volume, copies are made at two scheduled intervals during the day: once in the morning at 7:00 A.M. and once at midday at 12:00 P.M. The morning copy allows you to save the work from the previous day and is meant to occur before users come in to work in the morning. The midday copy allows you to save work up to that point in the day and is meant to occur when users are taking a break for lunch. In this way, a user would lose at most, a half day's work and the resource impact caused by creating shadow copies is minimized.

When you configure the shadow copy schedule for your organization, you should take these same issues into consideration. Start by determining the best times of the day to create shadow copies. Ideally, this is when the server's resources are being used the least. Then determine how much potential data loss is acceptable given the resources, the type of data stored, and the available disk space.

Plan Shadow Copies Around Backups

When planning the run schedule for shadow copies, be sure to take into account the backup schedule for the related volumes. If you schedule shadow copies during backup, the shadow copy service writers will experience timeout errors and any shadow copies that should have been created at that time will be lost. If you suspect a scheduling conflict, you can use the **vssadmin list writers** command to check the last error status of the shadow copy writers.

You can change the default shadow copy times, add new scheduled run times, and schedule recurring tasks that create copies at specific time intervals during the day. However, it is recommended that you avoid creating shadow copies more frequently than once per hour. When configuring run schedules, keep in mind how much work is saved and how long users will have to retrieve versions of files. If you save changes twice a day during weekdays, the maximum of 64 shadow copies means that users have about 32 working days during which they could retrieve the oldest version of a file before it is automatically deleted.

After you configure shadow copying, you must install a client on computers throughout the organization. Two clients are available: the Previous Versions Client and the Shadow Copy Client. The installation of these clients is discussed in "Using Shadow Copies on Clients" on page 603.

With either client, users can access the Previous Versions tab by right-clicking a shared file or folder, selecting Properties, and then clicking the Previous Versions tab. Users will then be able to view a version of a file, save a version of a file to a new location, or restore a previous version of a file. The clients can be distributed through Group Policy or Microsoft System Center.

Managing Shadow Copies in Computer Management

Shadow copies are configured on a per-volume basis. Each volume on a server that has shared folders must be configured separately for shadow copying.

TROUBLESHOOTING

Be careful when defragmenting

If you defragment a volume while shadow copies are enabled, the oldest shadow copies can be lost. Shadow copy loss can occur because the shadow copy provider uses a copy-on-write approach that uses a 16-kilobyte (KB) block level. If the volume's cluster size is smaller than 16 KB, the shadow copy provider cannot distinguish disk defragmentation I/O and normal write I/O operations and, as a result, can create an extra shadow copy. If there are already 64 copies of a file, the oldest file is then deleted, which is how the oldest shadow copy gets deleted accidentally. To prevent this, it is recommended that cluster size of volumes that use shadow copies be set to 16 KB or larger.

> **Defragment Volumes Before Enabling Shadow Copies**
>
> Shadow copies can become corrupted on volumes that are heavily fragmented. It is recommended that you defragment volumes before enabling shadow copies.

Configuring Shadow Copies in Computer Management

You can use Computer Management to configure shadow copying by following these steps:

1. Start Computer Management, expand Storage, and select Disk Management. Right-click a volume in the Disk Management Volume List view or Graphical View, and select Properties.

2. In the Properties dialog box, click the Shadow Copies tab, as shown in Figure 18-1.

> **Note**
>
> At an elevated command prompt, you can type **vssuirun** to open the Properties dialog box to the Shadow Copies tab directly.

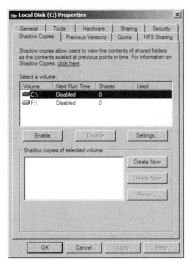

Figure 18-1 Enable shadow copies on a per-volume basis.

Chapter 18

3. Select the volume for which you want to configure shadow copies, and then click Settings. This displays the Settings dialog box shown in Figure 18-2.

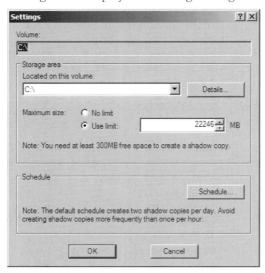

Figure 18-2 Set storage limits for shadow copies.

Configure Mount Points Separately

There's a limitation for volumes that have mount points. With a mount point, a volume is attached to an empty folder on an NTFS volume and made to appear as part of that volume. If you enable shadow copies on a volume with mounted drives, the mounted drives are not included and users will not be able to access previous versions of files on the mounted volume. The workaround is to share the mounted volume and enable shadow copies for this share. Users then must access the share path to the mounted volume to view previous versions. For example, if you have a folder named F:\Eng\Data, and the Data folder is a mount point for G, you enable shadow copies on both drives F and G. You share F:\Eng as \\CorpSvr01\Eng, and you share F:\Eng\Data as \\CorpSvr01\Data. In this example, users can access previous versions of \\CorpSvr01\Eng and \\CorpSvr01\Data, but not \\CorpSvr01\Eng\Data.

4. Use the Located On This Volume selection list to specify where the shadow copies should be created. Shadow copies can be created on the volume you are configuring or any other volume available on the computer.

5. Click Details to see the free space and total available disk space on the selected volume, and then click OK.

6. Use the Maximum Size options to set the maximum size that shadow copies for this volume can use.

7. Click Schedule to display the dialog box shown in Figure 18-3. Two run schedules are set automatically. Use the selection list to view these schedules. If you don't want to use a scheduled run time, select it, and then click Delete. To add a run schedule, configure the run times using the Schedule Task, Start Time, and Schedule Task Weekly options, then click New. When you are finished configuring run times, click OK twice to return to the volume's Properties dialog box.

Check Cluster Configuration to Ensure That Scheduling Can Work After Failover

To ensure that the VolumeShadowCopy task runs after failover on a clustered file server, the %SystemRoot% should be the same on the cluster to which the service is failed over. If it isn't in the same location and failover occurs, the VolumeShadowCopy task might not run. For example, if the %SystemRoot% on node 1 is C:\Windows and the %SystemRoot% on node 2 is C:\Winnt, the task might not run when the service fails over from node 1 to node 2. This is because the task runs in the %SystemRoot%\System32 folder and the Start In property setting for the task changes the environment variable to the actual folder location rather than using the environment variable once the task is set. See Chapter 39, "Preparing and Deploying Server Clusters," for more information about clustering.

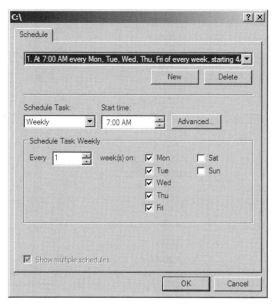

Figure 18-3 Set the schedule for when shadow copies are made.

8. Select the volume on which you want to enable shadow copies and click Enable. When prompted, click Yes to confirm the action. Windows will then create a snapshot of the volume.

9. Configure any additional volumes for shadow copying by repeating steps 3 through 8. Click OK when you are finished.

TROUBLESHOOTING

Shadow copy relies on the Task Scheduler

The schedule you set for shadow copies is set as a scheduled task on the server. Scheduled tasks are run by the Task Scheduler service and can be viewed in the Scheduled Tasks folder as discussed in Chapter 4, "Managing Windows Server 2008." The Task Scheduler service must be running and properly configured for shadow copying to work correctly. In addition, you should not modify ShadowCopyVolume tasks using the Scheduled Tasks folder. Instead, only configure the run schedule using a volume's Properties dialog box.

Maintaining Shadow Copies After Configuration

After you configure shadow copying, snapshots are made according to the schedule you've set. Keep the following in mind:

- Individual snapshots taken of a volume can be deleted. Start Computer Management, expand Storage, and select Disk Management. Right-click a volume in the Disk Management Volume List view or Graphical View, and select Properties. In the Properties dialog box, select the Shadow Copies tab. Click the volume you want to work with. Its snapshots are listed in the Shadow Copies Of Selected Volume list. To delete a specific snapshot, select it in the list and then click Delete Now.

- If you ever want to make a snapshot manually, you can do this by clicking Create Now on the Shadow Copies tab.

- You can change the settings and run schedule at a later date as well. Access the Shadow Copies tab, select the volume you want to change, and then click Settings. Make the necessary changes, and then click OK.

CAUTION !

Changing the maximum allowed size can cause existing shadow copies to disappear. This could happen if you set the maximum allowed size smaller than the amount of space currently in use.

- To delete a shadow copy of a volume, select the shadow copy in the bottom panel of the Shadow Copies tab, and then click Delete Now. When prompted to confirm the action, click Yes.

- To disable Shadow Copies for a volume, select the volume in the top panel of the Shadow Copies tab, and then click Disable. When prompted to confirm the action, click Yes.

CAUTION

Disabling shadow copies deletes all previously saved snapshot images. Because of this, disable snapshots only when you are sure previously saved snapshot images are no longer needed.

Disable Shadow Copies Before Removing the Associated Volume

If you want to remove a volume on which shadow copies have been enabled, you should first disable shadow copies or delete all scheduled tasks that create the shadow copies for the volume. This will ensure that error events aren't written to the system logs when the Scheduled Task service can't create the snapshot images.

Reverting an Entire Volume

Windows Server 2008 features a shadow copy enhancement that allows you to revert an entire volume to the state it was in when a particular shadow copy was created. This comes with a couple of caveats: The volume you want to revert must not contain operating system files or reside on a cluster shared disk.

You can revert an entire volume to a previous state by following these steps:

1. At an elevated command prompt, type **vssuirun** to open the Shadow Copies Properties dialog box. Alternatively, start Computer Management, expand Storage, and select Disk Management. Right-click a volume in the Disk Management Volume List view or Graphical View, and select Properties. In the Properties dialog box, click the Shadow Copies tab.

2. On the Shadow Copies tab, select the volume you want to work with in the Select A Volume list.

3. As shown in Figure 18-4, individual shadow copies of the currently selected volume are listed in the Shadow Copies Of Selected Volume panel by date and time. Select the shadow copy with the date and time stamp to which you want to revert and then click Revert.

4.   To confirm this action, select the Check Here If You Want To Revert This Volume
check box and then click Revert Now. Click OK to close the Shadow Copies
dialog box.

Figure 18-4 Select the shadow copy to which you want to revert.

Configuring Shadow Copies at the Command Line

The command-line tool for configuring shadow copies is VSSAdmin. Using VSSAdmin,
you can configure shadow copying of volumes on the computer you're logged on to
locally or remotely through Remote Desktop. As with Computer Management, each
volume on a server that has shared folders must be configured separately for shadow
copying.

Enabling Shadow Copying from the Command Line

To enable shadow copying of a volume, you use the Add ShadowStorage command. The
syntax is as follows:

```
vssadmin add shadowstorage /for=ForVolumeSpec / on=OnVolumeSpec
```

Here, /for=*ForVolumeSpec* is used to specify the local volume for which you are configuring or managing shadow copies and /on=*OnVolumeSpec* is used to specify the volume on
which the shadow copy data will be stored.

Consider the following example:

```
vssadmin add shadowstorage /for=c: /on=d:
```

Here, you are configuring the C volume to use shadow copies, and the shadow copy
data is stored on D. Both values can be set to the same volume as well, such as

```
vssadmin add shadowstorage /for=e: /on=e:
```

Here, you are configuring the E volume to use shadow copies, and the shadow copy data is stored on that same volume.

With VSSAdmin, shadow copying is configured by default so that there is no maximum size limit for shadow storage. To set a specific limit, you can use the /MaxSize parameter. This parameter expects to be passed a numeric value with a suffix of KB, MB, GB, TB, PB, or EB to indicate whether the value is set in kilobytes, megabytes, gigabytes, terabytes, petabytes, or exabytes. This parameter must be set to 100 MB or greater. Consider the following example:

```
vssadmin add shadowstorage /for=c: /on=d: /maxsize=2GB
```

Here, you are configuring the C volume to use shadow copies, and the shadow copy data is stored on D. The maximum size allowed for the shadow storage is 2 GB.

The most common errors that occur when you are configuring shadow copies from the command line relate to improper syntax. If you enter the wrong syntax, VSSAdmin shows the error message "Error: Invalid command" and will display the command syntax. If shadow copying is already configured for a volume, the error message states "Error: The specified shadow copy storage association already exists."

After you configure shadow storage, you can use the Resize Shadow command to resize the shadow storage. The command accepts the same parameters as the Add command and must be entered using the same storage association. Thus, if shadow storage for C is on D, you can resize shadow storage using the following command:

```
vssadmin resize shadowstorage /for=c: /on=d: /maxsize=5GB
```

Create Manual Snapshots from the Command Line

When you enable shadow copying, snapshots of shared folders are created automatically according to the default run schedule. If you ever want to make a snapshot manually, you can do this using the Create Shadow command. Type **vssadmin create shadow /for=***ForVolumeSpec*, where *ForVolumeSpec* is the local volume for which you are creating the snapshot. Consider the following example:

```
vssadmin create shadow /for=e:
```

Here, you create a snapshot of shared folders on the E volume.

Set the AutoRetry Interval to Retry Creation Automatically

Occasionally, the Shadow Copy service is busy, typically because it is creating a snapshot of this or another volume. Here, you can try again in a few minutes, or, by using the /AutoRetry parameter, you can specifically set the length of time during which Create Shadow should continue to try to create the snapshot. For example, if you want to retry automatically for 15 minutes, you'd use /AutoRetry=15.

Chapter 18

Viewing Shadow Copy Information

VSSAdmin provides several utility commands for viewing shadow copy information. The most useful are List Shadows and List ShadowStorage.

List Shadows lists the existing shadow copies on a volume. By default, all shadow copies on all volumes are displayed. The command accepts /for=*ForVolumeSpec* to list only the information for a particular volume and /shadow=*ShadowId* to list only the information for a particular shadow copy. However, it is much easier just to type **vssadmin list shadows** and go through the information to find what you are looking for.

The output from List Shadows shows summary information for each snapshot created according to its shadow copy identifier, such as:

```
Contents of shadow copy set ID: {ff70e4e6-4117-446a-8ffe-1708632664ff}
   Contained 1 shadow copies at creation time: 4/13/2008 7:03:55 AM
      Shadow Copy ID: {5ba0f3d3-afa8-4e4e-a00e-64a44e11bf81}
         Original Volume: (C:)\\?\Volume{3796c3c0-5106-11d7-911c-806d6172696f}\
            Shadow Copy Volume: \\?\GLOBALROOT\Device\HarddiskVolumeShadowCopy3
            Originating Machine: corpsvr02.cpandl.com
            Service Machine: corpsvr02.cpandl.com
            Provider: 'Microsoft Software Shadow Copy provider 1.0'
            Type: ClientAccessible
      Attributes: Persistent, Client-accessible, No auto release, No writers,
 Differential

Contents of shadow copy set ID: {6cb7fba8-afbb-415f-b47a-6800b332af9a}
   Contained 1 shadow copies at creation time: 4/14/2008 7:34:09 AM
      Shadow Copy ID: {3f44a086-2034-4c6b-bf3f-3489a5e98bd8}
         Original Volume: (C:)\\?\Volume{3796c3c0-5106-11d7-911c-806d6172696f}\
            Shadow Copy Volume: \\?\GLOBALROOT\Device\HarddiskVolumeShadowCopy4
            Originating Machine: corpsvr02.cpandl.com
            Service Machine: corpsvr02.cpandl.com
            Provider: 'Microsoft Software Shadow Copy provider 1.0'
            Type: ClientAccessible
            Attributes: Persistent, Client-accessible, No auto release, No writers,
 Differential

Contents of shadow copy set ID: {25f354e1-003a-4e54-8ba6-2f09bc499ef4}
   Contained 1 shadow copies at creation time: 4/15/2008 8:08:37 AM
      Shadow Copy ID: {f3899e11-613a-4a7d-95de-cb264d1dbb7b}
         Original Volume: (C:)\\?\Volume{3796c3c0-5106-11d7-911c-806d6172696f}\
            Shadow Copy Volume: \\?\GLOBALROOT\Device\HarddiskVolumeShadowCopy5
            Originating Machine: corpsvr02.cpandl.com
            Service Machine: corpsvr02.cpandl.com
            Provider: 'Microsoft Software Shadow Copy provider 1.0'
            Type: ClientAccessible
      Attributes: Persistent, Client-accessible, No auto release, No writers,
 Differential
```

Here, there is a data set for each snapshot that has been created. The most important information is the following:

- **Shadow Copy ID** The unique identifier for the snapshot image. This identifier can be copied and used to delete a particular snapshot if desired.

- **Original Volume** The volume for which shadow copies are configured.

- **Originating Machine** The name of the computer you are working with.

List ShadowStorage displays all shadow copy storage associations on the system. The command accepts /for=*ForVolumeSpec* and /on=*OnVolumeSpec* parameters to limit the output. But again, it is much easier just to type **vssadmin list shadowstorage** and go through the information to find what you are looking for. Here is an example of the output from this command:

```
Shadow Copy Storage association
   For volume: (C:)\\?\Volume{3796c3c0-5106-11d7-911c-806d6172696f}\
   Shadow Copy Storage volume:
   (C:)\\?\Volume{3796c3c0-5106-11d7-911c-806d6172696f}\
   Used Shadow Copy Storage space: 64.063 MB
   Allocated Shadow Copy Storage space: 952.578 MB
   Maximum Shadow Copy Storage space: 22.206 GB
```

Here, the output shows you the following information:

- **For Volume** The volume for which shadow copies are configured.

- **Shadow Copy Storage Volume** The volume on which shadow copy data is stored.

- **Used Shadow Copy Storage Space** The actual amount of disk space used on the storage volume.

- **Allocated Shadow Copy Storage Space** The amount of disk space allocated on the storage volume for shadow copies.

- **Maximum Shadow Copy Storage Space** The maximum size allowed for shadow copies on the storage volume.

Deleting Snapshot Images from the Command Line

If you want to delete individual snapshots on a volume, you can use the Delete Shadows command to do this. You can delete the oldest snapshot on the specified volume by typing **vssadmin delete shadows /for=***ForVolumeSpec* **/oldest**, where /for=*ForVolumeSpec* specifies the local volume for which the snapshot is used. For example, if you configured shadow copying on the C volume and want to delete the oldest snapshot on this volume, you'd enter the command:

```
vssadmin delete shadows /for=c: /oldest
```

When prompted to confirm that you really want to delete the snapshot, press Y. VSSAdmin should then report "Successfully deleted 1 shadow copies."

Chapter 18

To delete a snapshot by its shadow identifier, use the /Shadow=*ShadowID* parameter instead of the /For=*ForVolumeSpec* and /Oldest parameters. Here, *ShadowID* is the globally unique identifier for the snapshot image, including the brackets {}. For example, if you want to delete the snapshot image with the ID {f3899e11-613a-4a7d-95de-cb264d1dbb7b}, you'd use the following command:

```
vssadmin delete shadows /shadow={f3899e11-613a-4a7d-95de-cb264d1dbb7b}
```

Again, when prompted to confirm that you really want to delete the snapshot, press Y. VSSAdmin doesn't actually check to see if the snapshot exists until you confirm that you want to delete the snapshot. In this case, if the shadow copy ID is invalid or the snapshot has already been deleted, VSSAdmin reports a "not found" error, such as:

```
Error: Shadow Copy ID: {f3899e11-613a-4a7d-95de-cb264d1dbb7b} not found.
```

Delete Shadows also lets you delete all snapshots on all volumes configured for shadow copy on the computer. To do this, type **delete shadows /all**. When prompted to confirm that you really want to delete all snapshots, press Y. VSSAdmin should then report "Successfully deleted *N* shadow copies." Deleting all the shadow copies doesn't disable shadow copy on the volumes, however. To do this, you must use the Delete Shadow-Storage command.

Disabling Shadow Copies from the Command Line

To disable shadow copying on a volume, you can use the Delete ShadowStorage command. However, unlike the graphical user interface (GUI), you cannot disable shadow copying until all previously saved snapshot images on the affected volume are deleted. Because of this, you must first delete all the snapshots on the volume and then disable shadow copying. Type the command **vssadmin delete shadowstorage /for=*ForVolumeSpec***, where /for=*ForVolumeSpec* is used to specify the local volume for which you are disabling shadow copying. For example, if you want to disable shadow copying of the C volume, you'd use the command:

```
vssadmin delete shadowstorage /for=c:
```

As long as the shadow storage isn't in use, you will be able to delete and VSSAdmin will report "Successfully deleted the shadow copy storage association(s)."

Reverting Volumes from the Command Line

If you want to revert an entire volume to an earlier snapshot, you can use the Revert Shadow command to do this. You revert to a snapshot using its shadow identifier. Use the /Shadow=*ShadowID* parameter where *ShadowID* is the globally unique identifier for the snapshot image, including the brackets {}. For example, if you want to revert to the snapshot image with the ID {f3899e11-613a-4a7d-95de-cb264d1dbb7b}, which is associated with the C volume, you'd use the following command:

```
vssadmin revert shadow /shadow={f3899e11-613a-4a7d-95de-cb264d1dbb7b}
```

If the shadow copy ID is invalid, VSSAdmin reports a "not found" error, such as:

```
Error: Shadow Copy ID: {f3899e11-613a-4a7d-95de-cb264d1dbb7b} not found.
```

Otherwise, VSSAdmin prompts you to confirm that you really want to revert to this snapshot. If you do, press Y. After VSSAdmin has started the revert operation, you cannot cancel it. Keep in mind that VSSAdmin will be unable to revert the volume if there are any open file handles. In this case, you can force VSSAdmin to revert the volume using the /ForceDismount parameter. However, forcing dismount invalidates open handles and as a result, any unsaved data in open files may be lost.

You can check on the status of revert operations by typing:

```
vssadmin query reverts
```

Using Shadow Copies on Clients

Previous Versions is the client feature that you use to access shadow copies of shared folders. Windows Vista and Windows Server 2008 include the Previous Versions Client.

You can access shadow copies in several different ways. On Windows Server 2008, you can access previous versions of an entire shared folder using the following technique:

1. Click Start and then select Computer. Network drives that are mapped to a client's computer are listed in the Computer window under Network Location.

2. In the Computer window under Network Location, right-click the network drive for which you want to access previous file versions and then select Restore Previous Versions.

3. This opens the Properties dialog box for the network drive with the Previous Versions tab selected, as shown in Figure 18-5.

On business editions of Windows Vista with the Previous Versions Client, you can access previous versions of an entire shared folder using the following technique:

1. Click Start and then select Computer. In the Computer window under Network Location, right-click the network drive for which you want to access previous file versions, select Properties, and then click the Previous Versions tab.

2. This also opens the Properties dialog box for the network drive with the Previous Versions tab selected, as shown in Figure 18-5.

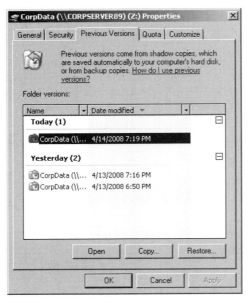

Figure 18-5 The Previous Versions tab is available for network drives that are mapped to shared folders using shadow copies.

Although you can view and work with an entire shared folder, more typically, you'll want to work with a subfolder within the shared folder and you can do this using the following technique:

1. In the Computer window under Network Location, double-click the network drive to display its contents.

2. Navigate through the network drive's contents until you see the folder you want to work with. Right-click the folder for which you want to access previous file versions, select Properties, and then click the Previous Versions tab.

3. This also opens the Properties dialog box for the selected folder with the Previous Versions tab selected, as shown in Figure 18-6.

> Note
>
> If you are logged on locally to the server and want to examine previous versions, simply right-click the shared folder or subfolder within the shared folder, and select Restore Previous Versions. This opens the Properties dialog box to the Previous Versions tab.

Chapter 18

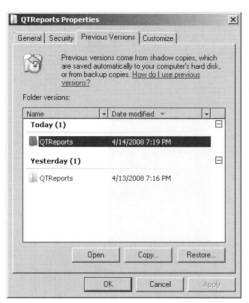

Figure 18-6 You can access previous versions of specific folders within a shared folder as well.

Access the Full Path for Mount Points

If a volume is a mount point, you must access the full mount point path to see its previous versions. For example, if you have a folder F:\Eng\Data, and the Data folder is a mount point for G, you enable shadow copies on both volumes F and G. You share F:\Eng as \\CorpSvr01\Eng, and you share F:\Eng\Data as \\CorpSvr01\Data. In this example, users can access previous versions of \\CorpSvr01\Eng and \\CorpSvr01\Data, but not \\CorpSvr01\Eng\Data.

After you access the Previous Versions tab, select the folder version that you want to work with. Each folder has a date and time stamp. Then click the button corresponding to the action you want to perform:

- **Open** Clicking Open opens the shadow copy in Windows Explorer. You can then work with the files it contains much like a normal folder. You won't, however, be able to delete files from this folder or save files to this folder—you can, of course, copy files to other locations.

- **Copy** Clicking Copy displays the Copy Items dialog box, which lets you copy the snapshot image of the folder to the location you specify.

- **Restore** Clicking Restore rolls back the shared folder to its state as of the snapshot image you selected. Because this could result in losing any changes subsequent to the date and time of the snapshot image, you are prompted to confirm the action. Click Restore to proceed with the restore.

Chapter 18

Using Remote Desktop for Administration

Remote support is an important part of administration. Using Remote Desktop for Administration, you can manage remote servers and workstations. Remote Desktop for Administration is a feature of Windows Server 2008 Terminal Services. You can use it to connect to and manage remote systems as if you were logged on locally. Because all the application processing is performed on the remote system, only the data from devices such as the display, keyboard, and mouse are transmitted over the network. You can use Remote Desktop for Administration to manage computers running Windows 2000 and later Windows operating systems.

Remote Desktop for Administration Essentials

Using Remote Desktop for Administration, you can use a local area network (LAN), wide area network (WAN), or Internet connection to manage computers remotely with the Windows graphical interface. Remote Desktop for Administration is part of Terminal Services. Microsoft has separated Terminal Services into two operating modes:

- Remote Desktop for Administration mode
- Terminal Server mode

You enable Remote Desktop for Administration using the System utility in Control Panel. You set up a Terminal Server by installing and configuring the appropriate role services for the Terminal Services role.

To be operational, the Remote Desktop for Administration and Terminal Server modes both depend on the Terminal Services service being installed and run on the server. By default, the Terminal Services service is installed and configured to run automatically. Both features use the same client, Remote Desktop Connection (RDC), for connecting to remote systems. Administrators can also use the Remote Desktops snap-in for the Microsoft Management Console (MMC).

> **Note**
>
> Remote Desktop for Administration isn't designed for application serving. Most productivity applications such as Microsoft Office Word, Outlook, and Excel require specific environment settings that are not available through this feature. If you want to work with these types of applications (rather than server applications), you should install and use the Terminal Services role.

No Terminal Server Client Access License (TS CAL) is required to use Remote Desktop for Administration. Windows Server 2008 allows two active administration sessions. This change from previous configurations allows:

- One administrator to be logged on locally and another administrator to be logged on remotely.

- Or two administrators to be logged on remotely.

Most remote sessions run in admin mode. The reason for this is that the admin session provides full functionality for administration. Standard Terminal Services connections are created as virtual sessions.

Why is this important? Using admin mode, you can interact with the server just as if you were sitting at the keyboard. This means all notification area messages directed to the console are visible remotely. For security, only two sessions are allowed. If a third administrator tries to log on, the administrator will be prompted to end an existing session so that he or she can log on.

Although it is recommended that administrators use admin sessions, you can use virtual sessions—hey, that's what they're there for. When working with a virtual session, you can perform most administration tasks, and your key limitation is in your ability to interact with the console session itself. This means users logged on using a virtual session do not see console messages or notifications, cannot install some programs, and cannot perform tasks that require console access.

You'll want to formalize a general policy on how Remote Desktop for Administration should be used in the organization. You don't want multiple administrators trying to perform administration tasks on a system because this could cause serious problems. For example, if two administrators are both working with Disk Management, this could cause serious problems with the volumes on the remote system. Because of this, you'll want to coordinate administration tasks with other administrators.

Configuring Remote Desktop for Administration

The two components of Remote Desktop for Administration you will need to support and configure are Terminal Services for the server portion and the Remote Desktop Connection (RDC) for the client portion. An alternative to using RDC is the Remote Desktops snap-in, which lets you connect to and manage multiple remote desktops.

Enabling Remote Desktop for Administration on Servers

Enabling the Remote Desktop for Administration mode on all servers on your network is recommended, especially for servers in remote sites that have no local administrators. To enable the Remote Desktop on the server, access Control Panel, click System And Maintenance, and then click System. On the System page, click Remote Settings in the left pane. This opens the System Properties dialog box to the Remote tab, as shown in Figure 19-1.

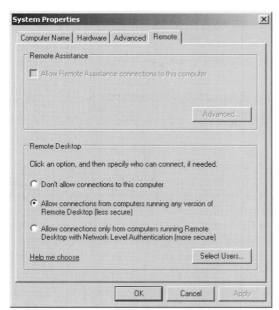

Figure 19-1 Enabling Remote Desktop.

You have two configuration options for enabling Remote Desktop:

- You can select Allow Connections From Computers Running Any Version Of Remote Desktop (Less Secure) to allow connections from any version of Windows

- Or you can select Allow Connections Only From Computers Running Remote Desktop With Network Level Authentication (More Secure) to allow connections only from Windows Vista or Windows Server 2008 (and computers with secure network authentication).

Keep the following details about using Remote Desktop for Administration in mind:

- All remote connections must be established using accounts that have passwords. If a local account on the system doesn't have a password, you can't use the account to connect to the system remotely.

- If the computer is running Windows Firewall, the operating system automatically creates an exception that allows Remote Desktop Protocol (RDP) connections to be established. The default port used is TCP port 3389. The Registry value HKEY_LOCAL_MACHINE\System\CurrentControlSet\Control\TerminalServer\Win-Stations\RDP-Tcp\PortNumber controls the actual setting.

- If you are running a different firewall on the computer, you must open a port on the firewall to allow incoming Remote Desktop Protocol (RDP) connections to be established. Again, the default port used is TCP port 3389.

INSIDE OUT   Authentication certificate validation

Prior to establishing an RDP connection, your computer will validate the remote computer's identify by default. If the remote computer's authentication certificate is invalid or has expired, you will not be allowed to connect and will see a warning prompt stating the following: "The authentication certificate received from the remote computer has expired or is not valid." As a date/time disparity between the two computers can make it appear that the authentication certificate is invalid, you should check the current date and time on both computers. If you don't want your computer to authenticate the remote computer's identity, you can disable this feature by setting the Server Authentication option to Connect And Don't Warn Me. To set the Server Authentication option, click Options to display the additional configuration tabs, click the Advanced tab, and then use the selection list in the Server Authentication panel to set the option as desired.

Permitting and Restricting Remote Logon

By default, all members of the Administrators group can log on remotely. The Remote Desktop Users group has been added to Windows Server 2008 Active Directory to ease managing Terminal Services users. Members of this group are allowed to log on remotely.

If you want to add a member to this group, access Control Panel, click System And Maintenance, and then click System. On the System page, click Remote Settings in the left pane. This opens the System Properties dialog box to the Remote tab. On the Remote tab, click Select Users. As shown in Figure 19-2, any current members of the Remote Desktop Users group are listed in the Remote Desktop Users dialog box. To add users or groups to the list, click Add. This opens the Select Users Or Groups dialog box.

Figure 19-2 Configuring Remote Desktop Users.

In the Select Users Or Groups dialog box, type the name of a user in the selected or default domain, and then click Check Names. If multiple matches are found, select the name(s) you want to use, and then click OK. If no matches are found, you've either entered an incorrect name part or you're working with an incorrect location. Modify the name and try again, or click Locations to select a new location. To add additional users or groups, type a semicolon (;), and then repeat this process. When you click OK, the users and groups are added to the list in the Remote Desktop Users dialog box.

In Group Policy, members of the Administrators and Remote Desktop Users groups have the user right Allow Log On Through Terminal Services by default. If you've modified Group Policy, you might need to double-check to ensure that this user right is still granted to these groups. Typically, you will want to do this through local policy on a per-machine basis. You can also do this through site, domain, and organizational policy. Access the appropriate Group Policy object and select Computer Configuration, Windows Settings, Security Settings, Local Policies, and User Rights Assignments. Double-click Allow Log On Through Terminal Services to see a list of users and groups currently granted this right.

INSIDE OUT   Restrict remote logon through Group Policy

If you want to restrict users or groups from remotely administering a server, access the appropriate Group Policy object and expand Computer Configuration\Windows Settings\ Security Settings\Local Policies\User Rights Assignments. Double-click Deny Log On Through Terminal Services. In the policy Properties dialog box, select Define These Policy Settings, and then click Add User Or Group. In the Add User Or Group dialog box, click Browse. This displays the Select Users, Computers, Or Groups dialog box. Type the name of the user or group for which you want to deny logon through Terminal Services, and then click OK. You can also change the default permissions for groups in the Terminal Services Configuration tool. For instance, you could remove Administrators from having Full Control of the Terminal Services objects.

Configuring Remote Desktop for Administration Through Group Policy

Remote Desktop for Administration is part of Terminal Services, and you can use Group Policy to configure Terminal Services. Microsoft recommends using Group Policy as the first choice when you are when configuring Terminal Services for use with Remote Desktop for Administration. The precedence hierarchy for Terminal Services configuration is as follows:

- Computer-level Group Policy

- User-level Group Policy

- Local computer policy using the Terminal Services Configuration tool

- User policy on the Local User and Group level

- Local client settings

You can configure local policy on individual computers or on an organizational unit (OU) in a domain. You can use Group Policy to configure Terminal Services settings per connection, per user, per computer, or for groups of computers in an OU of a domain. The Group Policy settings for Terminal Services are modified using the Group Policy Object Editor and are located in Computer Configuration\Administrative Templates\ Windows Components\Terminal Services and in User Configuration\Administrative Templates\Windows Components\Terminal Services.

> **Create a Separate OU for Terminal Services**
>
> Typically, Remote Desktop for Administration is used throughout an organization but Terminal Services servers are isolated to a particular group of servers operating in a separate OU. So, if you plan to use Terminal Services servers as well in the organization, you should consider creating a separate OU for the Terminal Services servers. In this way, you can manage Terminal Services servers separately from Remote Desktop for Administration.

Supporting Remote Desktop Connection Clients

The Remote Desktop Connection (RDC) client is the Terminal Services client. It uses the Microsoft Remote Desktop Protocol (RDP) version 6.0 or later. Clients can use the Remote Desktop Connection client to connect to a remote server or workstation that has been set up to be administered remotely.

Remote Desktop Connection Client

Windows Vista, Windows Server 2008, Windows Server 2003 SP1, and Windows XP SP2 all include version 6.0 of the Remote Desktop Connection client. As later service packs are released, these service packs might include updated versions of the RDC client. The features you should be aware of when supporting RDC are the following:

- Custom display resolutions allow high-color and full-screen viewing. Resolutions of 1680 × 1920, 1920 × 1200, and higher are now supported. To set the resolution from a command prompt or the Search box, add the /w and /h options, such as **mstsc /w:1920 /h:1200**. In an RDP file, you can set the screen size using desktopwidth and desktopheight, such as **desktopwidth:i:1920** or **desktopheight:i:1200**.

- Monitor spanning settings allow you to display remote sessions across multiple monitors. All monitors must be horizontally aligned and use the same resolution. The maximum resolution across all monitors cannot exceed 4096 × 2048. To enable monitor spanning from a command prompt or the Search box, add the /span option, such as **mstsc /span**. In an RDP file, you can enable spanning by entering: **Span:i:1**.

- By default, data sent between the client and the server is encrypted at the maximum key strength supported by the client. If you configure RDP on your Terminal Services server to require high encryption, a client can make a connection only if it supports 128-bit or higher encryption.

- If a connection is interrupted or lost while you are performing a task, the client software will attempt to reconnect to the session and in the interim, processing continues on the server so that any running processes can be finished without interruption. If for some reason you are unable to log on remotely after you are disconnected, your logon session can be accessed by logging on locally.

Enhanced experience settings include font smoothing and display data prioritization. Font smoothing ensures that computer fonts appear clear and smooth (provided that the desktop has ClearType enabled). Display data prioritization gives priority to display, keyboard, and mouse data over other types of data, such as printing or file transfers. The default bandwidth ratio is 70:30. This means that display and input data will be allocated 70 percent of the bandwidth, and all other traffic, such as file transfers or print jobs, will be allocated 30 percent of the bandwidth.

You can adjust the data prioritization settings by making changes to the Registry of the Terminal Services server. Change the value of the following entries under the HKEY_LOCAL_MACHINE\SYSTEM\CurrentControlSet\Services\TermDD subkey:

- FlowControlDisable
- FlowControlDisplayBandwidth
- FlowControlChannelBandwidth
- FlowControlChargePostCompression

When working with flow control keep the following in mind:

- If these entries do not appear, you can create them. To do this, right-click TermDD, point to New, and then click DWORD (32-Bit) Value.

- You can disable display data prioritization completely by setting the value of FlowControlDisable to 1. If you do this, all requests are handled on a first-in-first-out basis and other Registry settings are ignored.

- You can set the relative bandwidth priority for display and input data by setting the FlowControlDisplayBandwidth value. The default value is 70. The maximum allowed value is 255.

- You can set the relative bandwidth priority for other data, such as file transfers or print jobs, by setting the FlowControlChannelBandwidth value. The default value is 30. The maximum allowed value is 255.

- The bandwidth ratio for display data prioritization is based on the values you set. For example, if you set FlowControlDisplayBandwidth to 200 and FlowControlChannelBandwidth to 50, the ratio is 200:50 (or 4:1), so display and input data will be allocated 80 percent of the bandwidth.

- The FlowControlChargePostCompression value determines whether the bandwidth allocation is based on pre-compression or post-compression data size. The default value is 0, which means that the calculation will be made on the size of the data before it is compressed. In most cases, this is the value you'll want to use. This setting ensures that the client doesn't have to wait or perform compression calculations prior to sending data.

- If you make any changes to the Registry values, you need to restart the Terminal Services server for the changes to take effect.

Resource redirection allows audio, mapped drives, ports, printers, and certain keyboard combinations to be handled by the client computer. If an application generates audio feedback, such as an error notification, this can be redirected to the client. Key combinations that perform application functions are passed to the remote server except for Ctrl+Alt+Delete, which is handled by the client computer. In addition, local devices such as drives, printers, and serial ports are also available. Because both local and network drives are available on the client, users can easily access local drives and transfer files between the client and the server.

Plug and Play device redirection extends the resource redirection features to allow locally connected and supported Plug and Play devices to be installed on and used with a remote computer. You can now redirect media players that support Media Transfer Protocol (MTP) and digital cameras that support Picture Transfer Protocol (PTP). Plug and Play notifications will appear in the taskbar on the remote computer. When you start a remote session for the first time after connecting a supported device locally, you should see the device get installed automatically on the remote computer. After the redirected device is installed on the remote computer, the device is available for use in your session with the remote computer. For example, if you are redirecting a Windows Portable Device (WPD) such as a digital camera, you can access the device directly from a remote application.

You can control Plug and Play device redirection on the Client Settings tab in the Terminal Services Configuration tool (tsconfig.msc). Use the Supported Plug And Play Devices options. You can also control Plug and Play device redirection by using either of the following Group Policy settings:

- Computer Configuration\Administrative Templates\Windows Components\Terminal Services\Terminal Server\Device and Resource Redirection\Do Not Allow Supported Plug And Play Device Redirection policy setting

- Computer Configuration\Administrative Templates\System\Device Installation\ Device Installation Restrictions policy setting

Running the Remote Desktop Connection Client

As discussed previously, you now can open two administrator sessions on computers that run Windows Server 2008 without needing a TS CAL. Previously, Windows 2000 Terminal Services required a license for each client. The use of an admin or console session greatly enhances your capabilities as an administrator to successfully execute programs, applications, and processes that will not run in a virtual session.

There are several ways to start the Remote Desktop Connection client:

- **Run in admin mode** Admin mode is used by administrators to enable full interaction with the console of the remote system. To run the client in admin mode, you must do the following, as appropriate for your client: enter either **mstsc /admin** or **mstsc /console** at the command prompt or in the Run dialog box.

- **Run in virtual session mode** Virtual session mode is used by administrators as well as users to start a virtual session on a remote system. To run the client in virtual session mode, you can do either of the following:

  - Enter **mstsc** at the command prompt or in the Run dialog box.
  - Click Start and select All Programs, Accessories, Remote Desktop Connection.

> **Note**
>
> Earlier releases of the RDP client used console mode for administrators and virtual session mode for users. To clarify the distinction between the modes and accommodate changes to RDP that allow two simultaneous administrator sessions, the current versions of the RDP client use admin mode for administrators and virtual session mode for users. The RDP client as shipped originally with Windows Vista accepts the /console option but not the /admin option. The RDP client as shipped originally with Windows Server 2008 accepts either the /console or the /admin option. The updated client releases support only the /admin option.

After the client is started, enter the name or Internet Protocol (IP) address of the computer to which you want to connect, as shown in Figure 19-3. If you don't know the name of the computer, use the drop-down list provided to choose an available computer, or select Browse For More in the drop-down list to display a list of domains and computers in those domains.

Figure 19-3 Specifying the remote computer with which to establish a connection.

By default, Windows uses your current user name and domain to log on to the remote computer. If you want to use different account information, click Options, and then enter your user name in the field provided (see Figure 19-4) To set the domain, you can enter your user name in the DOMAIN\USERNAME format, such as ADATUM\ WILLIAMS. Select the Allow Me To Save Credentials check box to enable automatic logon if desired.

Note

Even if you select the Allow Me To Save Credentials check box, you might be prompted to enter your credentials during the logon process depending on your network's policies and the configuration of the Terminal Services server.

Figure 19-4 RDC options.

There are six tabs you can use to change the client settings:

- **General** You might want to use these options to save keystrokes by adding logon information. Rather than typing in your settings each time, you can save the connection settings and load them when you want to make a connection.

  To save the current connection settings, click Save As, and then use the Save As dialog box to save the .rdp file for the connection.

  To load previously saved connection settings, click Open, and then use the Open dialog box to find and open the previously saved connection settings.

- **Display** The default settings for RDC are full-screen and high-color. You can modify these settings here.

  Use the Remote Desktop Size option to set the screen size. The size options available depend on the display size on the local computer.

Use the Colors option to choose the preferred color depth. The default is 32-bit highest quality color, but settings on the remote computer might override this setting.

- **Local Resources** You can modify the way the resource and device redirection work, including audio redirection, keystroke combination redirection, and local device and resource redirection.

  By default, remote computer sound is redirected to the local computer. Using the Remote Computer Sound option, you can change the default setting by selecting Do Not Play or Leave At Remote Computer.

  By default, when you are working in full-screen mode, key combinations such as Alt+Tab and Ctrl+Esc are redirected to the remote system, and Ctrl+Alt+Delete is handled locally. Using Apply Windows Key Combinations, you change this behavior so key combinations are sent to the local computer or the remote computer only. However, if you send key combinations to the remote computer only, you could get in a situation where you cannot log on locally.

  By default, local printers are connected automatically when users are logged on to the remote computer. This makes it easy to print to your currently configured printers when you are working with a remote system.

  By default, anything you copy to the remote computer's Clipboard is copied to the local computer's Clipboard. This makes it easy to copy from a remote source and paste into a local source.

  Click More in the Local Devices And Resources panel to see additional options. By default, the additional options ensure that Smart Cards connected to a remote computer are available for use in your remote session. You can also connect serial ports, local disk drives, and supported Plug and Play devices to make them available for use. Drives and supported devices can be selected by name or you can simply select the Drives and Supported Plug And Play Devices options to make all drives and devices available for use. Selecting Drives allows you to easily transfer files between the local and remote computer. Selecting Supported Plug And Play Devices allows you to work with supported devices, including media players and digital cameras.

- **Programs** You can configure the execution of programs when a session starts from this tab. Select the Start The Following Program On Connection check box, and then set the program path or file name and the start folder for the program.

- **Experience** You can select the connection speed and other network performance settings. For optimal performance, choose the connection speed you are using, such as Modem (56 Kbps) or LAN (10 Mbps or higher), and allow only bitmap caching.

  Other options you can allow include Desktop Background, Font Smoothing, Desktop Composition, Show Contents Of Window While Dragging, Menu And Window Animation, and Themes. If you select these additional check boxes, you cause additional processing on the remote system and additional network traffic, which can slow down performance. Desktop Composition creates an enhanced desktop, providing that you've installed the Desktop Experience feature on the Terminal Services servers and clients that are using Windows Vista. Font Smoothing allows the client to pass through ClearType fonts, providing ClearType is enabled (which is the default setting).

By default, Reconnect If Connection Is Dropped is selected. If the session is interrupted, the RDC will try to reconnect it automatically. Getting disconnected from a connection doesn't stop processing. The session will go into a disconnected state and continue executing whatever processes the sessions was running.

● **Advanced** You can select these options to control the use of server authentication and the Terminal Server Gateway feature. By default, the RDP client is configured to warn you if the authentication protocol fails and automatically detect TS Gateway settings.

When you click Connect, you are connected to the remote system. Enter your account password if prompted, and then click OK. If the connection is successful, you'll see the Remote Desktop window on the selected computer, as shown in Figure 19-5, and you'll be able to work with resources on the computer. In the case of a failed connection, check the information you provided and then try to connect again.

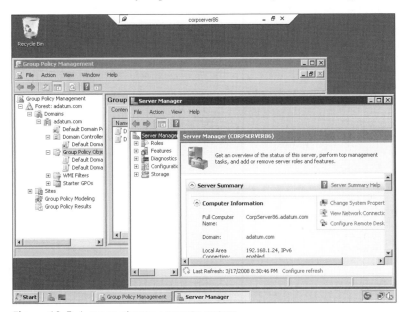

Figure 19-5 A connection to a remote system.

When you are working in full-screen mode, a connection bar is displayed at the top of the screen. On the left side of the connection bar is a push pin. If you click the push pin, it unpins the connection bar so that the bar disappears when you move the mouse away. To make the bar appear again, you would then need to point the mouse to the top part of the screen. On the right side of the connection bar are several other buttons. The first button switches you to the local desktop. The second button switches between full-screen mode and tile display mode. The third button disconnects the remote session.

Disconnecting from a session does not end a session. The session continues to run on the server, which uses resources and may prevent other users from connecting because only one console session and two virtual sessions are allowed. The proper way to end a session is to log off the remote computer just as you would a local computer. In the Remote Desktop Connection window, click Start, and then click the Shutdown Options button. On the shortcut menu, click Logoff.

> **CAUTION**
>
> Don't try to log off the remote session by pressing Ctrl+Alt+Delete and clicking Logoff. Doing this will log you off the console session on your local client but still leave the remote session running on the terminal server.

Running Remote Desktops

Remote Desktops allows you to connect to a number of computers running Remote Desktop for Administration and to switch between them within one window. To start Remote Desktops, click Start, All Programs, Administrative Tools, Terminal Services, Remote Desktops, or type **tsmmc.msc** at the command prompt.

You can then establish connections to the remote systems you want to work with. Right-click the Remote Desktops node in the console root, and then select Add New Connection. In the Add New Connection dialog box, enter the name or IP address of the computer to which you want to connect, as shown in Figure 19-6. Click Browse to display a list of domains and available computers in those domains. The Connection Name field is filled in automatically for you based on the server name or IP address you entered.

The Connect With /Admin Option check box controls whether you are connected to an admin session or a virtual session. By default, this check box is selected, meaning admin mode is used. Clear this check box to establish a virtual session with the remote computer. In the Logon Information area, type the user name that you want to use for logon. To set the domain, you can enter your user name in DOMAIN\USERNAME format, such as ADATUM\WILLIAMS. Select the Allow Me To Save Credentials check box to enable automatic logon if desired. When you are finished setting connection options, click OK.

An entry is added below Remote Desktops for the computer. Clicking this entry automatically connects to the remote system. Each configured connection can be selected and switched between without you having to log off each time. Following this, you could switch to a different remote system simply by clicking its entry in the left pane. To disconnect from a remote system, right-click the related entry in the left pane, and select Disconnect.

Figure 19-6 Connecting to a remote system in Remote Desktops.

Disconnecting from a session does not end a session. The session will go into a disconnected state and continue executing whatever processes the session was running. The proper way to end a session is to log off the remote computer just as you would a local computer. In the right pane of the Remote Desktops window, click Start, and then click the Shutdown Options button. On the shortcut menu, click Logoff.

When you connect to a remote system in Remote Desktops, the screen on the remote system fills the right pane, as shown in Figure 19-7. Before you make a connection, you should maximize the Remote Desktops window. If you don't do this, you'll end up with a small screen that cannot be resized.

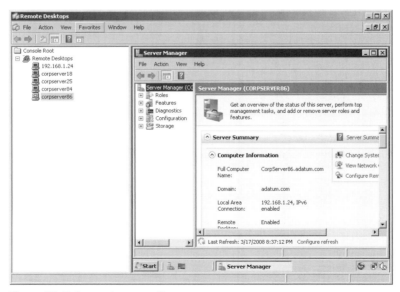

Figure 19-7 A remote connection.

To change this behavior or configure additional options, right-click the related entry in the left pane of Remote Desktops, and select Properties. In the Properties dialog box, shown in Figure 19-8, you can change the connection options using the following tabs:

- **General** You can set the connection options as discussed previously. You can also use this to change the connection mode and the credentials associated with the logon.

- **Screen Options** You can choose a desktop size or custom size to use for the connection. The screen size options available depend on the size of the display on your local computer. In most cases, you'll want to use the default option Expand To Fill MMC Result Pane.

- **Other** You can configure the execution of programs when a session starts, manage authentication security, and enable redirection of local drives when logged on to the remote computer. Drive redirection makes it easier to transfer files to and from the remote computer.

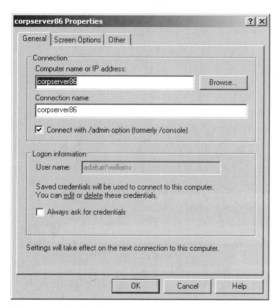

Figure 19-8 Modify connection options.

When you are finished configuring the connections you want to use for administration, you should save the Remote Desktops configuration. This ensures that the connections remain available if you exit the console. To save the options, press Ctrl+S or click File, Save.

Tracking Who's Logged On

When you deploy Terminal Services, you can use the Terminal Services Manager to view and manage logon sessions. With Remote Desktop for Administration, you can use this as well, but you typically don't need all the additional options and details. A more basic way to keep track of who is logged on to a server is to use the QUSER command. Type **quser** to see who is logged on to the system on which you are running the command prompt, or type **quser /server:***ServerName* to see who is logged on to a remote server. Consider the following example:

```
USERNAME      SESSIONNAME      ID    STATE     IDLE TIME   LOGON TIME
tedg          rdp-tcp#1        1     Active    .           3/16/2008 1:12 PM

Wrstanek      console          2     Active    1:34        3/16/2008 1:33 PM
```

Here, there are two active sessions:

- TEDG is logged on to an active RDP session. The session ID is 1, meaning it is Session 1.

- WRSTANEK is logged on locally to the console. The session ID is 2, meaning it is Session 2.

You can also use Task Manager to view user sessions. Press Ctrl+Alt+Delete, and then click Start Task Manager. In the Task Manager dialog box, click the Users tab, as shown in Figure 19-9. Similar details are shown as with the command line. The one useful addition is the name of the client machine from which the connection was established.

Figure 19-9 View and manage remote sessions from Task Manager.

You can also use Task Manager to manage remote user sessions:

- To disconnect a user session, select the user entry, click Disconnect, and then click Disconnect User when prompted to confirm the action.

- To log off a user, select the user entry, click Logoff, and then click Log Off User when prompted to confirm the action.

The difference between disconnecting a session and logging off a session is important. When you disconnect a session, the session goes into a disconnected state and continues executing current processes. If you log off a user, you end that user's session, closing any applications the user was running and ending any foreground processes the person was running as well. A foreground process is a process being run by an active application as opposed to a background or batch process being run independently from the user session.

PART 4

Managing Windows Server 2008 Networking and Print Services

TCP/IP is a protocol suite consisting of Transmission Control Protocol (TCP) and Internet Protocol (IP). TCP is a connection-oriented protocol designed for reliable end-to-end communications. IP is an internetworking protocol that is used to route packets of data called datagrams over a network. An IP datagram consists of an IP header and an IP payload. The IP header contains information about routing the datagram, including source and destination IP addresses. The IP payload contains the actual data being sent over the network.

TCP/IP is the backbone for Microsoft Windows networks. It is required for internetwork communications and for accessing the Internet. Before you can implement TCP/IP networking, you should understand IP addressing conventions, subnetting options, and name resolution techniques—all of which are covered in this chapter.

Navigating Networking in Windows Server 2008

The networking features in Windows Server 2008 are different from those in earlier releases of Windows. Windows Server 2008 has a new suite of networking tools, including:

- **Network Explorer** Provides a central console for browsing computers and devices on the network

- **Network And Sharing Center** Provides a central console for viewing and managing a computer's networking and sharing configuration

- **Network Map** Provides a visual map of the network that depicts how computers and devices are connected

- **Network Diagnostics** Provides automated diagnostics to help diagnose and resolve networking problems

Before discussing how these networking tools are used, we must first look at the Windows Server 2008 features on which these tools rely, including:

- **Network Discovery** A feature of Windows Server 2008 that controls the ability to see other computers and devices

- **Network Awareness** A feature of Windows Server 2008 that reports changes in network connectivity and configuration

The network discovery settings of the computer you are working with determine the computers and devices you can browse or view in Windows Server 2008 networking tools. Discovery settings work in conjunction with a computer's Windows Firewall to either block or allow the following:

- Discovery of network computers and devices

- Discovery of your computer by others

Network discovery settings are meant to provide the appropriate level of security for each of the various categories of networks to which a computer can connect. Three categories of networks are defined:

- **Domain Network** Intended as a designation for a network in which computers are connected to the corporate domain to which they are joined. By default, discovery is allowed on a domain network, which reduces restrictions and permits computers on the domain network to discover other computers and devices on that network.

- **Private Network** Intended as a designation for a network in which computers are configured as members of a workgroup and are not connected directly to the public Internet. By default, discovery is allowed on a private network, which reduces restrictions and permits computers on the private network to discover other computers and devices on that network.

- **Public Network** Intended as a designation for a network in a public place, such as a coffee shop or airport, rather than for an internal network. By default, discovery is blocked on a public network, which enhances security by preventing computers on the public network from discovering other computers and devices on that network.

Because a computer saves settings separately for each category of network, different block and allow settings can be used for each network category. When you connect to a network for the first time, you'll see a dialog box that allows you to specify the network category as either private or public. If you select private and the computer determines that it is connected to the corporate domain to which it is joined, the network category is set as Domain Network.

Based on the network category, Windows Server 2008 automatically configures settings that turn discovery either on or off. The On (Enabled) state means:

- The computer can discover other computers and devices on the network.

- Other computers on the network can discover the computer.

The Off (Disabled) state means:

- The computer cannot discover other computers and devices on the network.

- Other computers on the network cannot discover the computer.

Network Explorer, shown in Figure 20-1, displays a list of discovered computers and devices on the network. You can access Network Explorer by clicking Start and then clicking Network. The computers and devices listed in Network Explorer depend on the network discovery settings of the computer. If discovery is blocked, you'll see a note about this. When you click the warning message and then select Turn On Network Discovery, you enable network discovery. This opens the appropriate Windows Firewall ports so that network discovery is allowed. If no other changes have been made with regard to network discovery, the computer will be in the discovery-only state. You will need to manually configure the sharing of printers, files, and media, as discussed in Chapter 17, "File Sharing and Security."

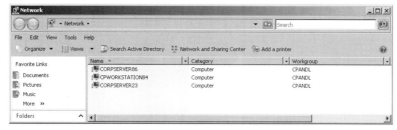

Figure 20-1 Use Network Explorer to browse network resources.

Network And Sharing Center, shown in Figure 20-2, provides the current network status, as well as an overview of the current network configuration. You can access Network And Sharing Center by clicking Start, clicking Network, and then clicking Network And Sharing Center on the toolbar in Network Explorer.

Network And Sharing Center has three main areas:

- **Summary network map** Provides a graphical depiction of the network configuration and connections. A normal status is indicated by a line connecting the various network segments. Any problems with the network configuration or connections are depicted with warning icons. A yellow warning icon indicates a possible configuration issue. A red X indicates a lack of a connection for a particular network segment. Clicking View Full Map opens Network Map, which displays an expanded network view.

- **Network details** Lists the current network by name and provides an overview of the network. The value in parentheses following the network name shows the category of the current network as Domain Network, Private Network, or Public Network. The Access field specifies whether and how the computer is connected to its current network as Local Only, Local And Internet, or Internet Only. The Connection field shows the name of the local area connection being used to connect to the current network. If you click Customize, you can change the network name, network category (for a private or public network only), and network icon.

Chapter 20

If you click View Status, you can view the connection status in the Local Area Connection Status dialog box.

- **Sharing and discovery** Provides the options for configuring the computer's sharing and discovery settings and lists the current state of each option. To manage an option, expand the option's view panel by clicking the Expand button (showing a down arrow), click the desired setting, and then click Apply. To turn on or turn off Network Discovery, you expand Network Discovery, select Turn On Network Discovery or Turn Off Network Discovery as appropriate, and then click Apply.

From Network And Sharing Center, you can attempt to diagnose a warning status. To do this, click the warning icon to start Windows Network Diagnostics. Windows Network Diagnostics will then attempt to identify the network problem and provide a possible solution.

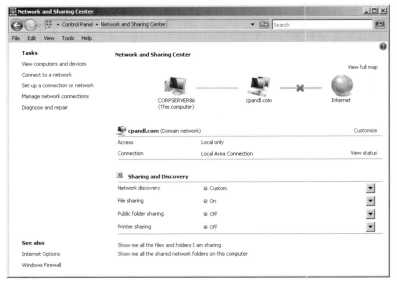

Figure 20-2 View and manage network settings with Network And Sharing Center.

Note

In Network And Sharing Center, you can run diagnostics manually at any time by selecting Diagnose And Repair under Tasks.

Using TCP/IP

The TCP and IP protocols make it possible for computers to communicate across various networks and the Internet using network adapters, including network interface cards, USB-attachable network adapters, PC Card network adapters, or built-in adapters on the motherboard. Windows Server 2008 has a dual IP layer architecture in which both Internet Protocol version 4 (IPv4) and Internet Protocol version 6 (IPv6) are implemented and share common Transport and Frame layers.

IPv4 and IPv6 are used in very different ways. IPv4 has 32-bit addresses and is the primary version of IP used on most networks, including the Internet. IPv6 has 128-bit addresses and is the next generation version of IP.

When networking hardware is detected during installation of the operating system, both IPv4 and IPv6 are enabled by default in Windows Server 2008 and Windows Vista and you don't need to install a separate component to enable support for IPv6. The modified IP architecture is referred to as the Next Generation TCP/IP stack. Table 20-1 summarizes the key TCP/IP enhancements implemented in the Next Generation TCP/IP stack. Table 20-2 summarizes the key TCP/IP enhancements that are specific to IPv6.

Table 20-1 Key TCP/IP Enhancements in the Next Generation TCP/IP Stack

Feature Supported	Description
Automatic Black Hole Router Detection	Prevents TCP connections from terminating due to intermediate routers silently discarding large TCP segments, retransmissions, or error messages.
Automatic Dead Gateway Retry	Ensures that an unreachable gateway is checked periodically to determine whether it has become available.
Compound TCP	Optimizes TCP transfers for the sending host by increasing the amount of data sent in a connection while ensuring that other TCP connections are not impacted.
Extended Selective Acknowledgments	Extends the way Selective Acknowledgments (SACKs) are used, enabling a receiver to indicate up to four noncontiguous blocks of received data and to acknowledge duplicate packets. This helps the receiver determine when it has retransmitted a segment unnecessarily and adjust its behavior to prevent future retransmissions.
Modified Fast Recovery Algorithm	Provides faster throughput by altering the way that a sender can increase the sending rate if multiple segments in a window of data are lost and the sender receives an acknowledgment stating only part of the data has been successfully received.
Neighbor Unreachability Detection for IPv4	Determines when neighboring nodes and routers are no longer reachable and reports the condition.
Network Diagnostics Framework	Provides an extensible framework that helps users recover from and troubleshoot problems with network connections.

Chapter 20

Feature Supported	Description
Receive Window Auto Tuning	Optimizes TCP transfers for the host receiving data by automatically managing the size of the memory buffer (the receive windows) to use for storing incoming data based on the current network conditions.
Routing Compartments	Prevents unwanted forwarding of traffic between interfaces by associating an interface or a set of interfaces with a logon session that has its own routing tables.
SACK-Based Loss Recovery	Makes it possible to use SACK information to perform loss recovery when duplicate acknowledgments have been received and to more quickly recover when multiple segments are not received at the destination.
Spurious Retransmission Timeout Detection	Provides correction for sudden, temporary increases in retransmission timeouts and prevents unnecessary retransmission of segments.
TCP Extended Statistics	Helps determine whether a performance bottleneck for a connection is the sending application, the receiving application, or the network.
Windows Filtering Platform	Provides application programming interfaces (APIs) for extending the TCP/IP filtering architecture so that it can support additional features.

Table 20-2 **Key TCP/IP Enhancements for IPv6**

Feature Supported	Description
DHCPv6-capable DHCP client	Extends the DHCP client to support IPv6 and allows stateful address autoconfiguration with a DHCPv6 server.
IP Security	Allows use of Internet Key Exchange (IKE) and data encryption for IPv6.
IPv6 over Point-to-Point Protocol (PPPv6)	Allows native IPv6 traffic to be sent over PPP-based connections, which in turn allows remote access clients to connect with an IPv6-based Internet service provider (ISP) through dial-up or PPP over Ethernet (PPPoE)-based connections.
Link-Local Multicast Name Resolution (LLMNR)	Allows IPv6 hosts on a single subnet without a DNS server to resolve each other's names.
Multicast Listener Discovery version 2 (MLDv2)	Provides support for source-specific multicast traffic and is equivalent to Internet Group Management Protocol version 3 (IGMPv3) for IPv4.
Random Interface IDs	Prevents address scanning of IPv6 addresses based on the known company IDs of network adapter manufacturers. By default, Windows Vista generates random interface IDs for nontemporary autoconfigured IPv6 addresses, including public and link-local addresses.
Symmetric Network Address Translators	Maps the internal (private) address and port number to different external (public) addresses and ports, depending on the external destination address.

Understanding IPv4 Addressing

The most important thing IPv4 gives us is the IPv4 address. It is the existence of IPv4 addresses that allows information to be routed from point A to point B over a network. An IPv4 address is a 32-bit logical address that has two components: a network address and a node address. Typically, IPv4 addresses are divided into four 8-bit values called octets and written as four separate decimal values delimited by a period (referred to as a dot). The binary values are converted to decimal equivalents by adding the numbers represented by the bit positions that are set to 1. The general way to write this value is in the form *w.x.y.z*, where each letter represents one of the four octets.

IPv4 addresses can be used in three ways:

- **Unicast** Unicast IPv4 addresses are assigned to individual network interfaces that are attached to an IPv4 network and are used in one-to-one communications.

- **Multicast** Multicast IPv4 addresses are addresses for which one or multiple IPv4 nodes can listen on the same or different network segments and are used in one-to-many communications.

- **Broadcast** Broadcast IPv4 addresses are designed to be used by every IPv4 node on a particular network segment and are used for one-to-everyone communications.

Each of these IPv4 addressing techniques is discussed in the sections that follow.

Unicast IPv4 Addresses

Unicast IPv4 addresses are the ones you'll work with the most. These are the IPv4 addresses that are assigned to individual network interfaces. In fact, each network interface that uses TCP/IPv4 must have a unique unicast IPv4 address. A unicast IPv4 address consists of two components:

- **A network ID** The network ID or address identifies a specific logical network and must be unique within its boundaries. Typically, IPv4 routers set the boundaries for a logical network, and this boundary is the same as the physical network defined by the routers. All nodes that are on the same logical network must share the same network ID. If they don't, routing or delivery problems occur.

- **A host ID** The host ID or address identifies a specific node on a network, such as a router interface or server. As with a network ID, it must be unique within a particular network segment.

Address classes are used to create subdivisions of the IPv4 address space. With unicast IPv4 addresses, the classes A, B, and C can be applied. Each describes a different way of dividing a subset of the 32-bit IPv4 address space into network addresses and host addresses.

Chapter 20

> **Note**
>
> Classes D and E are defined as well. Class D addresses are used for multicast, as discussed in the next section of this chapter. Class E addresses are reserved for experimental use. Class D addresses begin with a number between 224 and 239 for the first octet. Class E addresses begin with a number between 240 and 247 for the first octet. Although Windows Server 2008 supports the use of Class D addresses, it does not support Class E addresses.

Class A Networks

Class A networks are designed for when you need a large number of hosts but only a few network segments and have addresses that begin with a number between 1 and 127 for the first octet. As shown in Figure 20-3, the first octet (the first 8 bits of the address) defines the network ID, and the last three octets (the last 24 bits of the address) define the host ID. As you'll learn shortly, the Class A address 127 has a special meaning and isn't available for your use. This means that there are 126 possible Class A networks and each network can have 16,277,214 nodes. For example, a Class A network with the network address 100 contains all IPv4 addresses from 100.0.0.0 to 100.255.255.255.

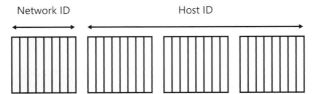

Figure 20-3 IPv4 addressing on Class A networks.

Class B Networks

Class B networks are designed for when you need a moderate number of networks and hosts and have addresses that begin with a number between 128 and 191 for the first octet. As shown in Figure 20-4, the first two octets (the first 16 bits of the address) define the network ID, and the last two octets (the last 16 bits of the address) define the host ID. This means that there are 16,384 Class B networks and each network can have 65,534 nodes.

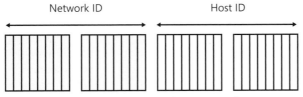

Figure 20-4 IPv4 addressing on Class B networks.

Class C Networks

Class C networks are designed for when you need a large number of networks and relatively few hosts and have addresses that begin with a number between 192 and 223 for the first octet. As shown in Figure 20-5, the first three octets (the first 24 bits of the address) define the network ID, and the last octet (the last 8 bits of the address) defines the host ID. This means that there are 2,097,152 Class C networks and each network can have 254 nodes.

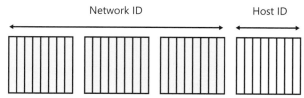

Figure 20-5 IPv4 addressing on Class C networks.

Loopback, Public, and Private Addresses

When using any of the IPv4 address classifications, there are certain rules that must be followed. The network ID cannot begin with 127 as the first octet. All IPv4 addresses that begin with 127 are reserved as loopback addresses. Any packets sent to an IPv4 address beginning with 127 are handled as if they've already been routed and reached their destination, which is the local network interface. This means any packets addressed to an IPv4 address of 127.0.0.0 to 127.255.255.255 are addressed to and received by the local network interface.

In addition, some addresses in the ranges are defined as public and others as private. Public IPv4 addresses are assigned by Internet service providers (ISPs). ISPs obtain allocations of IPv4 addresses from a local Internet registry (LIR) or national Internet registry (NIR) or from their appropriate regional Internet registry (RIR). Private addresses are addresses reserved for organizations to use on internal networks. Because they are nonroutable, meaning they are not reachable on the Internet, they do not affect the public Internet and do not have to be assigned by an addressing authority.

The private IPv4 addresses defined are as follows:

- **Class A private IPv4 addresses** 10.0.0.0 through 10.255.255.255
- **Class B private IPv4 addresses** 172.16.0.0 through 172.31.255.255
- **Class C private IPv4 addresses** 192.168.0.0 through 192.168.255.255

Because you shouldn't connect hosts on an organization's private network directly to the Internet, you should indirectly connect them using the Network Address Translation (NAT) protocol or a gateway program such as a proxy. When NAT is configured on the organization's network, a device, such as a router, is responsible for translating private addresses to public addresses, allowing nodes on the internal network to communicate with the nodes on the public Internet. When proxies are configured on the organization's network, the proxy acts as the go-between. It receives requests from nodes on the internal network and sends the requests to the public Internet. When the response is returned, the proxy sends the response to the node that made the original request. In both cases, the device providing NAT or proxy services has a private IP address on its internal network interface and a public address on its Internet interface.

Multicast IPv4 Addresses

Multicast IPv4 addresses are used only as destination IPv4 addresses and allow multiple nodes to listen for packets sent by a single originating node. In this way, a single packet can be delivered to and received by many hosts. Here's how it works: A sending node addresses a packet using a multicast IPv4 address. If the packet is addressed to the sending node's network, nodes on the network that are listening for multicast traffic receive and process the packet. If the packet is addressed to another network, a router on the sending node's network forwards the packet as it would any other packet. When it is received on the destination network, any nodes on the network that are listening for multicast traffic receive and process the packet.

The nodes listening for multicast packets on a particular IPv4 address are referred to as the host group. Members of the host group can be located anywhere—as long as the organization's routers know where members of the host group are located so that the routers can forward packets as appropriate.

One address class is reserved for multicast: Class D. Class D addresses begin with a number between 224 and 239 for the first octet.

Multicast IPv4 addresses in the range of 224.0.0.0 through 224.0.0.255 are reserved for local subnet traffic. For example, the address 224.0.0.1 is an all-hosts multicast address and is designed for multicasting to all hosts on a subnet. The address 224.0.0.2 is an all-routers multicast address and is designed for multicasting to all routers on a subnet. Other addresses in this range are used as specified by the Internet Assigned Numbers Authority (IANA). For details, see the IANA Web site at *http://www.iana.org/assignments/multicast-addresses*.

Broadcast IPv4 Addresses

Broadcast IPv4 addresses are used only as destination IPv4 addresses and allow a single node to direct packets to every node on the local network segment. When a sending node addresses a packet using a broadcast address, every node on that network segment receives and processes the packet.

To understand how broadcasts are used, you must understand the difference between classful networks and nonclassful networks. A *classful network* is a network that follows the class rules as defined, meaning a Class A, B, or C network is configured with network addresses and host addresses as described previously. A *nonclassful network* is a network that doesn't strictly follow the class rules. Nonclassful networks might have subnets that don't follow the normal rules for network and host IDs. You'll learn more about subnets in "Using Subnets and Subnet Masks" on page 639.

> **Note**
>
> A nonclassful network can also be referred to as a classless network. However, classless interdomain routing (CIDR) and all it implies are specifically spelled out in Request for Comments (RFCs), such as RFC 1812. RFC 1812 provides rules that supersede those of some previous RFCs, such as RFC 950, which prohibited the use of all-zeros subnets.

All nodes listen for and process broadcasts. Because IPv4 routers usually do not forward broadcast packets, broadcasts are generally limited by router boundaries. The broadcast address is obtained by setting all the network or host bits in the IPv4 address to 1 as appropriate for the broadcast type. Three types of broadcasts are used:

- **Network broadcasts** Network broadcasts are used to send packets to all nodes on a classful network. For network broadcasts, the host ID bits are set to 1. For a nonclassful network, there is no network broadcast address, only a subnet broadcast address.

- **Subnet broadcasts** Subnet broadcasts are used to send packets to all nodes on nonclassful networks. For subnet broadcasts, the host ID bits are set to 1. For a classful network, there is no subnet broadcast address, only a network broadcast address.

- **Limited broadcasts** Limited broadcasts are used to send packets to all nodes when the network ID is unknown. For a limited broadcast, all network ID and host ID bits are set to 1.

> **DHCP Uses Limited Broadcasts**
>
> Limited broadcasts are sent by nodes that have their IPv4 address automatically configured as is the case with Dynamic Host Configuration Protocol (DHCP). With DHCP, clients use a limited broadcast to advertise that they need to obtain an IPv4 address. A DHCP server on the network acknowledges the request by assigning the node an IPv4 address, which the client then uses for normal network communications.

> **Note**
>
> Previously, a fourth type of broadcast was available called an all-subnets-directed broadcast. This broadcast type was used to send packets to all nodes on all the subnets of a nonclassful network. Because of the changes specified in RFC 1812, all-subnets-directed broadcasts have been deprecated, meaning they are no longer to be supported.

Chapter 20

Special IPv4 Addressing Rules

As you've seen, certain IPv4 addresses and address ranges have special uses:

- The addresses 127.0.0.0 through 127.255.255.255 are reserved for local loopback.

- The addresses 10.0.0.0 through 10.255.255.255, 172.16.0.0 through 172.31.255.255, and 192.168.0.0 through 192.168.255.255 are designated as private and as such are nonroutable.

- On classful networks, the Class A addresses *w*.255.255.255, Class B addresses *w.x*.255.255, and Class C addresses *w.x.y*.255 are reserved for broadcasts.

- On nonclassful networks, the broadcast address is the last IPv4 address in the range of IPv4 addresses for the associated subnet.

> **Note**
>
> Certain IPv4 addresses are also reserved for other purposes as well. For example, the IPv4 addresses 169.254.0.1 to 169.254.255.254 are used for Automatic Private IPv4 Addressing (APIPv4A) as discussed in "Configuring TCP Networking" on page 660.

On classful networks, all the bits in the network ID cannot be set to 0 because this expression is reserved to indicate a host on a local network. Similarly, on a classful network all the bits in the host ID cannot be set to 0 because this is reserved to indicate the IPv4 network number.

Table 20-3 lists the ranges of network numbers based on address classes. You cannot assign the network number to a network interface. The network number is common for all network interfaces attached to the same logical network. On a nonclassful network, the network number is the first IPv4 address in the range of IPv4 addresses for the associated subnet—as specified in RFC 1812.

Table 20-3 **Network IDs for Classful Networks**

Address Class	First Network Number	Last Network Number
Class A	1.0.0.0	126.0.0.0
Class B	128.0.0.0	191.255.0.0
Class C	192.0.0.0	223.255.255.0

When you apply all the rules for IPv4 addresses, you find that many IPv4 addresses cannot be used by hosts on a network. This means the first available host ID and last available host ID are different from the range of available IPv4 addresses. Table 20-4 shows how these rules apply to classful networks. On a nonclassful network, the same rules apply—you lose the first and last available host IDs from the range of available IPv4 addresses.

Table 20-4 **Available Host IDs on Classful Networks**

Address Class	First Host ID	Last Host ID
Class A	*w*.0.0.1	*w*.255.255.254
Class B	*w*.*x*.0.1	*w*.*x*.255.254
Class C	*w*.*x*.*y*.1	*w*.*x*.*y*.254

INSIDE OUT   **Routers, gateways, and bridges connect networks**

A router is needed for hosts on a network to communicate with hosts on other networks. It is standard convention for the network router to be assigned the first available host ID. On Windows systems, you identify the address for the router as the gateway IPv4 address for the network. Although the terms "gateways" and "routers" are often used interchangeably, the two are technically different. A *router* is a device that sends packets between network segments. A *gateway* is a device that performs the necessary translation so that communication between networks with different architectures is possible. When working with networks, you might also hear the term "bridge." A *bridge* is a device that directs traffic between two network segments using physical machine addresses (Media Access Control, or MAC, addresses). Routers, gateways, and bridges can be implemented in hardware as separate devices or in software so that a system on the network can handle the role as a network router, gateway, or bridge as necessary.

Using Subnets and Subnet Masks

Anyone who works with computers should learn about subnetting and what it means. A *subnet* is a portion of a network that operates as a separate network. Logically, it exists separately from other networks even if hosts on those other networks share the same network ID. Typically, such networks are also physically separated by a router. This ensures that the subnet is isolated and doesn't affect other subnets.

Subnetting is designed to make more efficient use of the IPv4 address space. Thus, rather than having networks with hundreds, thousands, or millions of nodes, you have a subnet that is sized appropriately for the number of nodes that you use. This is important, especially for the crowded public IPv4 address space where it doesn't make sense to assign the complete IPv4 address range for a network to an individual organization. Thus, instead of getting a complete network address for the public Internet, your organization is more likely to get a block of consecutive IPv4 addresses to use.

Subnet Masks

You use a 32-bit value known as a subnet mask to configure nodes in a subnet to communicate only with other nodes on the same subnet. The mask works by blocking areas outside the subnet so that they aren't visible from within the subnet. Because it is a 32-bit value, subnet masks can be expressed as an address for which each 8-bit value (octet) is written as four separate decimal values delimited by a period (dot). As with IPv4 addresses, the basic form is *w.x.y.z*.

The subnet mask identifies which bits of the IPv4 address belong to the network ID and which bits belong to the host ID. Nodes can see only the portions of the IPv4 address space that aren't masked by a bit with a value of 1. If a bit is set to 1, it corresponds to a bit in the network ID. If a bit is set to 0, it corresponds to a bit in the host ID.

Because a subnet mask must be configured for each IPv4 address, nodes on both classful and nonclassful networks have subnet masks. On a classful network, all the bits in the network ID portion of the IPv4 address are set to 1 and can be presented in dotted decimal form as shown in Table 20-5.

Table 20-5 Standard Subnet Masks for Classful Networks

Address Class	Bits for Subnet Mask	Subnet Mask
Class A	11111111 00000000 00000000 00000000	255.0.0.0
Class B	11111111 11111111 00000000 00000000	255.255.0.0
Class C	11111111 11111111 11111111 00000000	255.255.255.0

INSIDE OUT   Blocks of IPv4 addresses on the public Internet

For internal networks that use private IPv4 addresses, you'll often be able to use the standard subnet masks. This isn't true, however, when you need public IPv4 addresses. Most of the time, you'll be assigned a small block of public IPv4 addresses to work with. For example, you might be assigned a block of eight (six usable) addresses. In this case, you must create a subnet that uses the subnet mask to isolate your nodes as appropriate for the number of nodes you've been assigned. I say there are six usable addresses out of eight because the lowest address is reserved as the network number and the highest address is reserved as the broadcast address for the network. This is always the case, as any good Cisco Certified Network Associate (CCNA) will tell you.

Network Prefix Notation

With subnetting, an IPv4 address alone doesn't help you understand how the address can be used. To be sure, you must know the number of bits in the network ID. As discussed, the subnet mask provides one way to determine which bits in the IPv4 address belong to the network ID and which bits belong to the host ID. If you have a block of IPv4 addresses, writing out each IPv4 address and the subnet mask is rather tedious. A shorthand way to do this is to use network prefix notation, which is also referred to as the classless interdomain routing (CIDR) notation.

In network prefix notation, the network ID is seen as the prefix of an IPv4 address, and the host ID as the suffix. To write a block of IPv4 addresses and specify which bits are used for the network ID, you write the network number followed by a forward slash and the number of bits in the network ID, as in

```
NetworkNumber/# of bits in the network ID
```

The slash and the number of bits in the network ID are referred to as the network prefix. Following this, you could rewrite Table 20-5 as shown in Table 20-6.

Table 20-6 Standard Network Prefixes for Classful Networks

Address Class	Bits for Subnet Mask	Network Prefix
Class A	11111111 00000000 00000000 00000000	/8
Class B	11111111 11111111 00000000 00000000	/16
Class C	11111111 11111111 11111111 00000000	/24

You now have two ways of detailing which bits are used for the network ID and which bits are used for the host ID. With the network number 192.168.1.0, you could use either of the following to specify that the first 24 bits identify the network ID:

- 192.168.1.0, 255.255.255.0

- 192.168.1.0/24

With either entry, you know that the first 24 bits identify the network ID and the last 8 bits identify the host ID. This in turn means the usable IPv4 addresses are 192.168.1.1 through 192.168.1.254.

Subnetting

When you use subnetting, nodes no longer follow the class rules for determining which bits in the IPv4 address are used for the network ID and which bits are used for the host ID. Instead, you set the 32 bits of the IPv4 address as appropriate to be either network ID bits or host ID bits based on the number of subnets you need and then number nodes for each subnet. There is an inverse relationship between the number of subnets and the number of nodes per subnet that can be supported. As the number of subnets goes up by a factor of 2, the number of hosts per subnet goes down by a factor of 2.

Because Class A, B, and C networks have a different number of host ID bits to start with, borrowing bits from the host ID yields different numbers of subnets and hosts. The technique is the same, however. Each bit represented as a 1 in the subnet mask corresponds to a bit that belongs to the network ID. This means the value of each bit can be represented as shown in Figure 20-6.

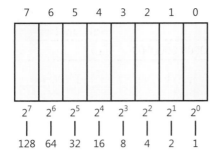

Figure 20-6 Represents the value of each bit when it is set to 1.

You start with the high-order bits and work your way to the low-order bits. When you borrow 1 bit of the host ID, you raise the number of possible subnets by a factor of 2 and reduce the number of possible hosts by a factor of 2.

Subnetting Class A Networks

The network entry mask for a standard Class A network can be defined as follows:

Address Class	Bits for Subnet Mask	Network Prefix	Decimal
Class A	11111111 00000000 00000000 00000000	/8	255.0.0.0

If you want to divide a Class A network into two separate subnets, you can borrow the high-order bit from the host ID in the second octet and add this bit to the network ID. Because the value of this bit taken from the host ID is 128, the corresponding subnet mask is 255.128.0.0. Thus, the network entry for the subnetted Class A network can be defined as follows:

Address Class	Bits for Subnet Mask	Network Prefix	Decimal
Class A	11111111 10000000 00000000 00000000	/9	255.128.0.0

> **Note**
> Each time you borrow a bit from the host ID, the network prefix bits go up by 1.

If you take an additional bit from the host ID bits, you allow the Class A network to be divided into up to four subnets. The value of this bit taken from the host ID is 64. When you add this value to the value of the previous bit taken from the host ID, the sum is 192 (128 + 64) and the corresponding subnet mask is 255.192.0.0. This means the network entry for a subnetted Class A network that can be divided into up to four subnets can be defined as follows:

Address Class	Bits for Subnet Mask	Network Prefix	Decimal
Class A	11111111 11000000 00000000 00000000	/10	255.192.0.0

Table 20-7 shows how Class A networks can be subnetted and how this affects the number of possible subnets and hosts per subnet.

Table 20-7 Subnetting Class A Networks

Maximum Subnets	Bits for Subnet Mask	Network Prefix	Decimal	Maximum Nodes
1	11111111 00000000 00000000 00000000	/8	255.0.0.0	16,777,214
2	11111111 10000000 00000000 00000000	/9	255.128.0.0	8,388,606
4	11111111 11000000 00000000 00000000	/10	255.192.0.0	4,194,302
8	11111111 11100000 00000000 00000000	/11	255.224.0.0	2,097,150
16	11111111 11110000 00000000 00000000	/12	255.240.0.0	1,048,574
32	11111111 11111000 00000000 00000000	/13	255.248.0.0	524,286
64	11111111 11111100 00000000 00000000	/14	255.252.0.0	262,142
128	11111111 11111110 00000000 00000000	/15	255.254.0.0	131,070
256	11111111 11111111 00000000 00000000	/16	255.255.0.0	65,534
512	11111111 11111111 10000000 00000000	/17	255.255.128.0	32,766
1,024	11111111 11111111 11000000 00000000	/18	255.255.192.0	16,382
2,048	11111111 11111111 11100000 00000000	/19	255.255.224.0	8,190
4,096	11111111 11111111 11110000 00000000	/20	255.255.240.0	4,094
8,192	11111111 11111111 11111000 00000000	/21	255.255.248.0	2,046
16,384	11111111 11111111 11111100 00000000	/22	255.255.252.0	1,022
32,768	11111111 11111111 11111110 00000000	/23	255.255.254.0	510
65,536	11111111 11111111 11111111 00000000	/24	255.255.255.0	254

Chapter 20

Maximum Subnets	Bits for Subnet Mask	Network Prefix	Decimal	Maximum Nodes
131,072	11111111 11111111 11111111 10000000	/25	255.255.255.128	126
262,144	11111111 11111111 11111111 11000000	/26	255.255.255.192	62
524,288	11111111 11111111 11111111 11100000	/27	255.255.255.224	30
1,048,576	11111111 11111111 11111111 11110000	/28	255.255.255.240	14
2,097,152	11111111 11111111 11111111 11111000	/29	255.255.255.248	6
4,194,304	11111111 11111111 11111111 11111100	/30	255.255.255.252	2

Subnetting Class B Networks

The network entry mask for a standard Class B network can be defined as follows:

Address Class	Bits for Subnet Mask	Network Prefix	Decimal
Class B	11111111 11111111 00000000 00000000	/16	255.255.0.0

A standard Class B network can have up to 65,534 hosts. If you want to divide a Class B network into two separate subnets, you can borrow the high-order bit from the host ID in the third octet and add this bit to the network ID. Because the value of this bit taken from the host ID is 128, the corresponding subnet mask is 255.255.128.0. Thus, the network entry for the subnetted Class B network can be defined as follows:

Address Class	Bits for Subnet Mask	Network Prefix	Decimal
Class B	11111111 11111111 10000000 00000000	/17	255.255.128.0

If you take an additional bit from the host ID bits, you allow the Class B network to be divided into up to four subnets. The value of this bit taken from the host ID is 64. When you add this value to the value of the previous bit taken from the host ID, the sum is 192 (128 + 64) and the corresponding subnet mask is 255.255.192.0. This means the network entry for a subnetted Class B network that can be divided into up to four subnets can be defined as follows:

Address Class	Bits for Subnet Mask	Network Prefix	Decimal
Class B	11111111 11111111 11000000 00000000	/18	255.255.192.0

Table 20-8 shows how Class B networks can be subnetted and how this affects the number of possible subnets and hosts per subnet.

Table 20-8 **Subnetting Class B Networks**

Maximum Subnets	Bits for Subnet Mask	Network Prefix	Decimal	Maximum Nodes
1	11111111 11111111 00000000 00000000	/16	255.255.0.0	65,534
2	11111111 11111111 10000000 00000000	/17	255.255.128.0	32,766
4	11111111 11111111 11000000 00000000	/18	255.255.192.0	16,382
8	11111111 11111111 11100000 00000000	/19	255.255.224.0	8,190
16	11111111 11111111 11110000 00000000	/20	255.255.240.0	4,094
32	11111111 11111111 11111000 00000000	/21	255.255.248.0	2,046
64	11111111 11111111 11111100 00000000	/22	255.255.252.0	1,022
128	11111111 11111111 11111110 00000000	/23	255.255.254.0	510
256	11111111 11111111 11111111 00000000	/24	255.255.255.0	254
512	11111111 11111111 11111111 10000000	/25	255.255.255.128	126
1,024	11111111 11111111 11111111 11000000	/26	255.255.255.192	62
2,048	11111111 11111111 11111111 11100000	/27	255.255.255.224	30
4,096	11111111 11111111 11111111 11110000	/28	255.255.255.240	14
8,192	11111111 11111111 11111111 11111000	/29	255.255.255.248	6
16,384	11111111 11111111 11111111 11111100	/30	255.255.255.252	2

Subnetting Class C Networks

The network entry mask for a standard Class C network can be defined as follows:

Address Class	Bits for Subnet Mask	Network Prefix	Decimal
Class C	11111111 11111111 11111111 00000000	/24	255.255.255.0

Chapter 20

A standard Class C network can have up to 254 hosts. If you want to divide a Class C network into two separate subnets, you can borrow the high-order bit from the host ID in the fourth octet and add this bit to the network ID. Because the value of this bit taken from the host ID is 128, the corresponding subnet mask is 255.255.255.128. Thus, the network entry for the subnetted Class C network can be defined as follows:

Address Class	Bits for Subnet Mask	Network Prefix	Decimal
Class C	11111111 11111111 11111111 10000000	/25	255.255.255.128

If you take an additional bit from the host ID bits, you allow the Class C network to be divided into up to four subnets. The value of this bit taken from the host ID is 64. When you add this value to the value of the previous bit taken from the host ID, the sum is 192 (128 + 64) and the corresponding subnet mask is 255.255.255.192. This means the network entry for a subnetted Class C network that can be divided into up to four subnets can be defined as follows:

Address Class	Bits for Subnet Mask	Network Prefix	Decimal
Class C	11111111 11111111 11111111 11000000	/26	255.255.255.192

Table 20-9 shows how Class C networks can be subnetted and how this affects the number of possible subnets and hosts per subnet.

Table 20-9 **Subnetting Class C Networks**

Maximum Subnets	Bits for Subnet Mask	Network Prefix	Decimal	Maximum Nodes
1	11111111 11111111 11111111 00000000	/24	255.255.255.0	254
2	11111111 11111111 11111111 10000000	/25	255.255.255.128	126
4	11111111 11111111 11111111 11000000	/26	255.255.255.192	62
8	11111111 11111111 11111111 11100000	/27	255.255.255.224	30
16	11111111 11111111 11111111 11110000	/28	255.255.255.240	14
32	11111111 11111111 11111111 11111000	/29	255.255.255.248	6
64	11111111 11111111 11111111 11111100	/30	255.255.255.252	2

Understanding IP Data Packets

With IPv4, computers send data in discrete packets of information with a header and a payload. IPv4 headers are variable in size, between 20 and 60 bytes, in 4-byte increments. Each bit range is broken into different sections and each section corresponds to the range of a related field in a packet. Header bit ranges consist of 0–3, 4–7, 8–15, 16–18, and 19–31. These correspond to the values 0, 32, 64, 96, 128, 160, and 160/152+ for data.

For examples of the ranges and their use, refer to Table 20-10. The IP payload is of variable size as well, ranging from 8 bytes to 65,515 bytes. Although most people will never use this information on a regular basis, it is very useful for understanding how to troubleshoot network problems.

Table 20-10 IPv4 Packets

+	Bits 0–3	4–7	8–15	16–18	19–31
0	Version	Header length	Type of service	Total length	
32	Identification			Flags	Fragment offset
64	Time to Live (TTL)		Protocol	Header checksum	
96	Source address information				
128	Destination address information				
160	Optional information				
160/152+	Data transmitted				

Getting and Using IPv4 Addresses

As discussed previously, there are two categories of IPv4 addresses:

- **Public** Public addresses are assigned by Network Solutions (formerly this was InterNIC) and can be purchased as well from IANA. Most organizations don't need to purchase their IPv4 addresses directly, however. Instead, they get the IPv4 addresses they need from their Internet service provider (ISP).

- **Private** Private addresses are reserved for Class A, B, and C networks and can be used without specific assignment. Most organizations follow the private addressing scheme as determined by their information technology (IT) department, and in which case, they would request IPv4 addresses from the IT department.

Chapter 20

> **Note**
>
> Technically, if your organization doesn't plan to connect to the Internet, you can use any IPv4 address. However, I still recommend using private IPv4 addresses in this case and taking the time to plan out the IPv4 address space carefully. If you do this and you later must connect the organization to the Internet, you won't have to change the IPv4 address of every node on the network. Instead, you'll only need to reconfigure the network's Internet-facing nodes, such as a proxy server or NAT router, to connect your organization to the Internet.

If you are planning out your organization's network infrastructure, you must determine how you want to structure the network. In many cases, you'll want to isolate the internal systems from the public Internet and place them on their own private network. An example of this is shown in Figure 20-7.

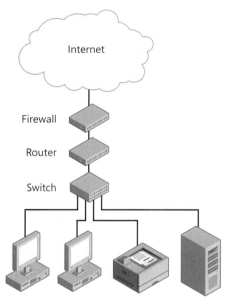

Figure 20-7 Overview diagram for connecting a private network to the Internet.

In this example, hosts on the internal network connect to a switch. The switch in turn connects to a router, which performs the necessary internal to external IPv4 address translation using NAT. The NAT router is in turn connected to a firewall, and the firewall connects to the Internet. If the internal network ID is 192.168.1.0/24, the internal IPv4 addresses would range from 192.168.1.1 to 192.168.1.254 and all hosts would use the network mask 255.255.255.0. After this occurs, the hosts might include the following:

- A router with IPv4 address 192.168.1.1 on the interface facing the internal network

- A manageable switch with IPv4 address 192.168.1.2

- Computers with IPv4 addresses 192.168.1.20 to 192.168.149

- Servers with IPv4 addresses 192.168.1.150 to 192.168.199

- A network printer with the IPv4 address 192.168.1.200

Follow an IPv4 Addressing Plan

Notice how the IPv4 addresses are assigned. I generally recommend reserving blocks of IPv4 addresses for the various types of hosts you'll have on a network. On an internal network with the ID 192.168.1.0/24 you might designate that IPv4 addresses 192.168.1.1 to 192.168.1.19 are reserved for network hardware, IPv4 addresses 192.168.1.20 to 192.168.1.149 are reserved for workstations, IPv4 addresses 192.168.1.150 to 192.168.1.199 are reserved for servers, and IPv4 addresses above 192.168.1.200 are reserved for other types of network hardware, such as printers.

You can then determine the number of public IPv4 addresses you need by assessing the number of public Internet-facing nodes you need. In this example, the NAT router needs a public IPv4 address as does the external firewall. To be able to send and receive e-mail, you'll need an IPv4 address for the organization's e-mail server. To set up a public Web site, you'll need an IPv4 address for the organization's Web server.

That's a total of four IPv4 addresses (six, including the network ID address and the broadcast address). In this case, your ISP might assign you a /29 subnet, giving you a total of six usable addresses. If you think you might need more than this, you could ask for a /28 subnet. However, keep in mind that you might have to pay a per–IPv4 address leasing fee.

Understanding IPv6

As with IPv4, the most important thing IPv6 gives us is the IPv6 address. Although IPv4 allows for more than four billion networked devices, the world is running out of available IPv4 addresses. To resolve this problem, IPv6 uses 128-bit addresses and this allows for 340,282,237,000,000,000,000,000,000,000,000,000,000 addresses—give or take a few hundred million quadrillion addresses. Or put another way, IPv6 makes available enough IP addresses so that every person on 100 billion worlds of 100 billion people could have 34 quadrillion IP addresses (and there would still be 2.8236×10^{33} IP addresses left over).

> **Note**
>
> Okay, so 128 bits might seem like overkill. However, the abundance of IPv6 addresses makes it possible to allocate addresses in large blocks. Not only does this help simplify administration, it avoids fragmentation of the address space, which in turn leads to smaller routing tables. One reason for selecting 128 bits for the address length is the increasing prevalence of 64-bit processors over 32-bit processors. 64-bit processors can efficiently work with 128-bit addresses. As we look to the future, the next logical step is 128-bit computing and 128-bit addresses will already be in place by that time. A key advantage of IPv6's larger address space is that it makes scanning certain IP blocks for vulnerabilities significantly more difficult than in IPv4, which makes IPv6 more resistant to malicious attacks by hackers looking for vulnerable computers.

Keeping track of so many IPv6 addresses using the numbering scheme used with IPv4 is impractical and this is why IPv6 uses hexadecimal numbers rather than decimal numbers to define the address space. This means that instead of allowing only the numbers 0 through 9 for each position in the IP address, IPv6 allows the values 0 through 9 and A through F, with A representing 10, B representing 11, and so on, up to F representing 15. Therefore, the values 0 through 15 can be represented using the values 0 through F.

IPv6's 128-bit addresses are divided into eight 16-bit blocks delimited by colons. Each 16-bit block is expressed in hexadecimal form. With standard unicast IPv6 addresses, the first 64 bits represent the network ID and the last 64 bits represent the network interface. An example of an IPv6 address follows:

```
FE80:0:0:02BC:00FF:BECB:FE4F:961D
```

Because many IPv6 address blocks are set to 0, a contiguous set of 0 blocks can be expressed as ::, a notation referred to as the double-colon notation. Using double-colon notation, the two 0 blocks in the previous address are compressed as follows:

```
FE80::02BC:00FF:BECB:FE4F:961D
```

Three or more 0 blocks would be compressed in the same way. For example, FFE8:0:0:0:0:0:0:1 becomes FFE8::1. However, more than one double-colon abbreviation in an address is invalid as it would make the notation ambiguous. Additionally, leading zeros in a group can be omitted. Thus FE80::02BC:00FF:BECB:FE4F:961D may be shortened to FE80::2BC:FF:BECB:FE4F:961D. Following this, the addresses below are all valid and equivalent:

- FE80:0000:0000:02BC:00FF:BECB:FE4F:961D

- FE80:0:0:02BC:00FF:BECB:FE4F:961D

- FE80::02BC:00FF:BECB:FE4F:961D

- FE80::2BC:FF:BECB:FE4F:961D

Finally, you can write a sequence of 4 bytes at the end of an IPv6 address in decimal, using dots as separators. You can use this notation with IPv4 compatibility addresses, such as FE80::192.168.10.52.

As with IPv4 addresses, there are different types of IPv6 addresses. As Table 20-11 shows, the type of an IPv6 address is identified by the high-order bits of the address. Link-local unicast IPv6 addresses are the equivalent of IPv4 private addresses because they are not globally reachable on the Internet. Global unicast IPv6 addresses are the equivalent of IPv4 public addresses because they are globally reachable on the Internet and must be assigned by an IP address authority.

Table 20-11 **IPv6 Address Types**

Address Type	Binary Prefix	IPv6 Notation	Description
Unspecified	00000000	::/128	The IPv6 address 0:0:0:0:0:0:0:0 is an unspecified address, and is only to be used in software.
Loopback	0000000001	::1/128	The IPv6 address 0:0:0:0:0:0:0:1 is used for local loopback. If an application sends packets to this address, the IPv6 stack will loop these packets back to the same host (corresponding to 127.0.0.1 in IPv4).
Multicast	1111111100	FF00::/8	IPv6 addresses beginning with FF00 are used for multicast transmissions (both link-local and across routers). There are no address ranges reserved for broadcast in IPv6—the same effect can be achieved by multicasting to the all-hosts group with a hop count of one.
Link-local unicast	1111111010	FE80::/10	IPv6 addresses beginning with FE80 are used for link-local unicast transmissions and valid only in the local physical link (similar to the Autoconfiguration IP address 169.254.x.x in IPv4).
Global unicast	All other addresses		All other IP addresses are used for global unicast transmissions and are valid on the public Internet.

IPv6 doesn't use subnet masks to identify which bits belong to the network ID and which bits belong to the host ID. Instead, each IPv6 address is assigned a subnet prefix length that specifies how the bits in the network ID are used. The subnet prefix length is represented in decimal form. Therefore, if 48 bits in the network ID are used, the subnet prefix length is written as shown in the following example:

FE01:1234:5678::/48	FE01:1234:5678:: through address FE01:1234:5678::FFFF:FFFF:FFFF:FFFF

As with IPv4, IPv6 packets are composed of two parts: a header and a payload. Unlike IPv4, IPv6 allows for sending jumbograms. A *jumbogram* is an IP datagram containing a payload larger than 64 KB. IPv4 does not support this type of transmission, and it has a 64 KB payload limit.

Jumbograms greatly increase the throughput of high-performance networks. The first 40 octets of an IPv6 packet contain the header, composed of the source and destination addresses, including an IPv4 version where necessary, traffic class section, flow label (for packet priority information), payload length, next header addressing section, and hop limit. The payload section consists of the actual data sent during transmission. The payload section can contain either 64 KB of information, as with IPv4 packets, or a jumbogram for true IPv6 networking architectures.

Another major difference between IPv4 and IPv6 is that IP Security (IPSec) is implemented within the IPv6 protocol. IPSec lies within the IP network layer, and encrypts and authenticates as an integrated part of the protocol by default. This eliminates additional overhead in encoding and decoding packets using separate IPSec functionality.

Understanding Name Resolution

Although IP addressing works well for computer-to-computer communications, it doesn't work so well when you and I want to access resources. Could you imagine having to remember the IP address of every computer that you work with? That would be difficult, and it would make working with computers on networks a chore. This is why computers are assigned names. Names are easier to remember than numbers—at least for most people.

When a computer has a name, you can type that name rather than its IP address to access it. This name resolution doesn't happen automatically. In the background, a computer process translates the computer name you type into an IP address that computers can understand. Windows Vista and Windows Server 2008 natively support three name-resolution systems:

- Domain Name System (DNS)
- Windows Internet Naming Service (WINS)
- Link-Local Multicast Name Resolution (LLMNR)

The sections that follow examine these services.

Domain Name System

DNS provides a distributed database that enables computer names to be resolved to their corresponding IP addresses. When working with DNS, it is important to understand what is meant by the terms "host name," "domain name," "fully qualified domain name," and "name resolution."

Host Names

A *host name* identifies an individual host in DNS. Ordinarily, you might call this a computer name. The difference, however, is that there is an actual record in the DNS database called a *host record* that corresponds to the computer name and details how the computer name is used on the network. Host names can be assigned by administrators and other members of the organization.

Domain Names

A *domain name* identifies a network in DNS. Domain names follow a specific naming scheme that is organized in a tree-like structure. Periods (dots) are used to separate the name components or levels within the domain name.

The first level of the tree is where you'll find the top-level domains. *Top-level domains* describe the kinds of networks that are within their domain. For example, the .edu top-level domain is for educational domains, the .gov top-level domain is for U.S. government domains, and .com is for commercial domains. As you can see, these top-level domains are organized by category. There are also top-level domains organized geographically, such as .ca for Canada and .uk for United Kingdom.

The second level of the tree is where you'll find parent domains. *Parent domains* are the primary domain names of organizations. For example, City Power & Light's domain name is cpandl.com. The domain name cpandl.com identifies a specific network in the .com domain. No parent domain can be used on the public Internet without being reserved and registered. Name registrars, such as Network Solutions, charge a fee for this service.

Additional levels of the tree belong to individual hosts or subsequent levels in the organization's domain structure. These subsequent levels are referred to as *child domains*. For example, City Power & Light might have Tech, Support, and Sales child domains, which are named tech.cpandl.com, support.cpandl.com, and sales.cpandl.com, respectively.

Connect the Network to the Internet

If your organization's network must be connected to the Internet, you should obtain a public domain name from a name registrar or use a similar service as provided by an ISP. Because many domain names have already been taken, you should have several previously agreed upon alternative names in mind when you go to register. After you obtain a domain name, you must configure DNS hosting for that domain. You do this by specifying the addresses of two or more DNS servers that will handle DNS services for this domain. Typically, these DNS servers belong to your ISP.

Fully Qualified Domain Name (FQDN)

All hosts on a TCP/IP network have what is called a fully qualified domain name (FQDN). The FQDN combines the host name and the domain name and serves to uniquely identify the host. For a host named CPL05 in the cpandl.com domain, the FQDN would be cpl05.cpandl.com. For a host named CORPSVR17 in the tech.cpandl.com domain, the FQDN would be corpsvr17.tech.cpandl.com.

Name Resolution

Name resolution is the process by which host names are resolved to IP addresses and vice versa. When a TCP/IP application wants to communicate with another host on a network, it needs the IP address of that host. Typically, the application knows only the name of the host it is looking for, so it has to resolve that name to an IP address.

To do this, the application first looks in its local DNS cache of names that it has previously looked up. If the name is in this cache, the IP address is found without having to look elsewhere and the application can connect to the remote host. If the name isn't in the cache, the application must ask the network's DNS server or servers to help resolve the name. These servers perform a similar lookup. If the name is in their database or cache, the IP address for the name is returned. Otherwise, the DNS server has to request this information from another DNS server.

That's the way it works—the simplified version at least. Most of the time, a TCP/IP application has the host name and needs to find the corresponding IP address. Occasionally, a TCP/IP application will have an IP address and needs the corresponding host name. To do this, the application must perform a reverse lookup, so instead of requesting an IP address, the application requests a host name using the IP address.

The application first looks in its local cache of information that has been previously looked up. If the IP address is in this cache, the name is found without having to look elsewhere and the application can perform whichever tasks are necessary. If the IP address isn't in the cache, the application must ask the network's DNS server or servers to help resolve the IP address. These servers perform a similar lookup. If the IP address is in their reverse lookup database or cache, the name for the IP address is returned. Otherwise, the DNS server has to request this information from another DNS server.

Windows Internet Naming Service (WINS)

WINS is a name resolution service that resolves computer names to IP addresses. Using WINS, the computer name COMPUTER84, for example, could be resolved to an IP address that enables computers on a Microsoft network to find one another and transfer information. WINS is needed to support pre–Windows 2000 systems and older applications that use Network Basic Input/Output System (NetBIOS) over TCP/IP, such as the NET command-line utilities. If you don't have pre–Windows 2000 systems or applications on the network, you don't need to use WINS.

WINS works best in client-server environments where WINS clients send queries to WINS servers for name resolution and WINS servers resolve the query and respond. To transmit WINS queries and other information, computers use NetBIOS. NetBIOS is an interface developed to allow applications to perform basic network operations, such as sending data, connecting to remote hosts, and accessing network resources.

NetBIOS computer names can be up to 15 characters long. They must be unique on the network and can be looked up on a server called a WINS server. WINS supports both forward lookups (NetBIOS computer name to IP address) and reverse lookups (IP address to NetBIOS computer name).

NetBIOS applications rely on WINS or the local LMHOSTS file to resolve computer names to IP addresses. On pre–Windows 2000 networks, WINS is the primary name resolution service available. On Windows 2000 and later networks, DNS is the primary name resolution service and WINS has a different function. This function is to allow pre–Windows 2000 systems to browse lists of resources on the network and to allow Windows 2000 and later systems to locate NetBIOS resources.

To enable WINS name resolution on a network, you need to configure WINS clients and servers. When you configure WINS clients, you tell the clients the IP addresses of WINS servers on the network. Using the IP address, clients can communicate with WINS servers anywhere on the network, even if the servers are on different subnets. WINS clients can also communicate using a broadcast method in which clients broadcast messages to other computers on the local network segment requesting their IP addresses. Because messages are broadcast, the WINS server isn't used. Any non-WINS clients that support this type of message broadcasting can also use this method to resolve computer names to IP addresses.

Your organization must set up WINS only if you are using Windows 95, Windows 98, Windows NT, or applications that rely on NetBIOS over TCP/IP. If you are currently using WINS, you can eliminate the need for this service by moving workstations and servers to Windows 2000 or a later version of Windows.

Link-Local Multicast Name Resolution (LLMNR)

LLMNR fills a need for peer-to-peer name-resolution services for devices with IPv4, IPv6, or both addresses, allowing IPv4 and IPv6 devices on a single subnet without a WINS or DNS server to resolve each other's names—a service that neither WINS nor DNS can fully provide. Although WINS can provide both client-server and peer-to-peer name-resolution services for IPv4, it does not support IPv6 addresses. DNS, on the other hand, supports IPv4 and IPv6 addresses, but it depends on designated servers to provide name-resolution services.

Both Windows Vista and Windows Server 2008 support LLMNR. LLMNR is designed for both IPv4 and IPv6 clients when other name-resolution systems are not available, such as on a small office or ad hoc network. LLMNR can also be used on corporate networks where DNS services are not available.

LLMNR is designed to complement DNS by enabling name resolution in scenarios in which conventional DNS name resolution is not possible. Although LLMNR can replace the need for WINS in cases where NetBIOS is not required, LLMNR is not a substitute for DNS because it operates only on the local subnet. As LLMNR traffic is prevented from propagating across routers, it cannot accidentally flood the network.

As with WINS, you use LLMNR to resolve a host name, such as COMPUTER84, to an IP address. By default, LLMNR is enabled on all computers running Windows Vista and Windows Server 2008, and these computers use LLMNR only when all attempts to look up a host name through DNS fail. As a result, name resolution works like this for Windows Vista and Windows Server 2008:

1. A host computer looks up the name in its internal name cache. If the name is not found in the cache, the host sends a query to its configured primary DNS server. If the host computer does not receive a response or receives an error, it tries each configured alternate DNS server in turn. If the host has no configured DNS servers or fails to connect to a DNS server without errors, name resolution fails over to LLMNR.

2. The host computer sends a multicast query over User Datagram Protocol (UDP) requesting the IP address for the name being looked up. This query is restricted to the local subnet (also referred to as the local link).

3. Each computer on the local link that supports LLMNR and is configured to respond to incoming queries receives the query and compares the name to its own host name. If the host name is not a match, the computer discards the query. If the host name is a match, the computer transmits a unicast message containing its IP address to the originating host.

You can also use LLMNR for reverse mapping. With a reverse mapping, a computer sends a unicast query to a specific IP address, requesting the host name of the target computer. An LLMNR-enabled computer that receives the request sends a unicast reply containing its host name to the originating host.

LLMNR-enabled computers are required to ensure that their names are unique on the local subnet. In most cases, a computer checks for uniqueness when it starts, when it resumes from a suspended state, and when you change its network interface settings. If a computer has not yet determined that its name is unique, it must indicate this condition when responding to a name query.

By default, LLMNR is automatically enabled on computers running Windows Vista and Windows Server 2008. You can disable LLMNR through Registry settings. To disable LLMNR for all network interfaces, create and set the following DWORD value to 0 (zero): HKLM/SYSTEM/CurrentControlSet/Services/Dnscache/Parameters/EnableMulticast. To disable LLMNR for a specific network interface, create and set the following DWORD value to 0 (zero): HKLM/SYSTEM/CurrentControlSet/Services/Tcpip/Parameters/Interfaces/*AdapterGUID*/EnableMulticast, where *AdapterGUID* is the globally unique identifier (GUID) of the network interface adapter for which you want to disable LLMNR.

You can reenable LLMNR at any time by setting these DWORD values to 1. You also can manage LLMNR through Group Policy.

Managing TCP/IP Networking

As an administrator, you enable networked computers to communicate by using the basic networking protocols built into Windows Server 2008. The key protocol you'll use is Transmission Control Protocol/Internet Protocol (TCP/IP). TCP/IP is actually a collection of protocols and services used for communicating over a network. It's the primary protocol used for internetwork communications. Compared to configuring other networking protocols, configuring TCP/IP communications is fairly complicated, but TCP/IP is the most versatile protocol available.

> **Note**
>
> Group Policy settings can affect your ability to install and manage TCP/IP networking. The key policies you'll want to examine are in User Configuration\Administrative Templates\Network\Network Connections and Computer Configuration\Administrative Templates\System\Group Policy. Group Policy is discussed in Chapter 36, "Managing Group Policy."

Installing TCP/IP Networking

If you want to install networking on a computer, you must install TCP/IP networking and a network adapter. Windows Server 2008 uses TCP/IP as the default wide area network (WAN) protocol. Normally, networking is installed during Windows Server 2008 setup. You can also install TCP/IP networking through local area connection properties. Although name resolution can be performed using DNS, WINS, or LLMNR, the preferred technique on Windows Server 2008 domains is DNS.

Preparing for Installation of TCP/IP Networking

Before you can configure TCP/IP networking on individual computers, you need the following information:

- **Domain name** The name of the domain in which the computer will be located. This can be a parent or a child domain.

- **IP address type, value, or both** The IP address information to assign to the computer, which can include both IPv4 and IPv6 addressing details.

- **Subnet mask** The subnet mask for the IPv4 network to which the computer is attached.

- **Subnet prefix length** The subnet prefix length for the IPv6 network to which the computer is attached.

- **Default gateway address** The address of the router or routers that will function as the computer's gateway.

- **DNS server address** The address of the DNS server or servers that provide DNS name resolution services on the network.

- **WINS server address** The address of the WINS server or servers that provide WINS name resolution services on the network.

If you are unsure of any of this information, you should ask the IT staff. In many cases, even if you are an administrator, there is a specific person you must ask for the IP address setup that should be used. Typically, this is your organization's network administrator and it is that person's job to maintain the spreadsheet or database that shows how IP addresses are assigned within the organization.

If no one in your organization has this role yet, this role should be assigned to someone or jointly managed to ensure that IP addresses are assigned following a specific plan. The plan should detail the following information:

- The address ranges that are reserved for network equipment and hardware and which individual IP addresses in this range are currently in use

- The address ranges that are reserved for DHCP and as such cannot be assigned using a static IP address

- The address ranges that are for static IP addresses and which individual IP addresses in this range are currently in use

Installing Network Adapters

Network adapters are hardware devices that are used to communicate on networks. You can install and configure network adapters by following these steps:

1. Configure the network adapter following the manufacturer's instructions. For example, you might need to use the software provided by the manufacturer to modify the Interrupt setting or the Port setting of the adapter.

2. If installing an internal network interface card, shut down the computer, unplug it, and install the adapter card in the appropriate slot on the computer. When you're finished, plug the computer in and start it.

3. Windows Server 2008 should detect the new adapter during startup. If you have a separate driver disc for the adapter, insert it now. Otherwise, you might be prompted to insert a driver disc.

4. If Windows Server 2008 doesn't detect the adapter automatically, follow the installation instructions in Chapter 8, "Managing and Troubleshooting Hardware."

5. If networking services aren't installed on the system, install them as described in the next section.

Installing Networking Services (TCP/IP)

If you're installing TCP/IP after installing Windows Server 2008, log on to the computer using an account with Administrator privileges and then follow these steps:

1. Click Start and then click Network. In Network Explorer, click Network And Sharing Center on the toolbar.

2. In Network And Sharing Center, click Manage Network Connections.

3. In Network Connections, right-click the connection you want to work with and then select Properties.

4. This displays the Local Area Connection Properties dialog box, shown in Figure 21-1.

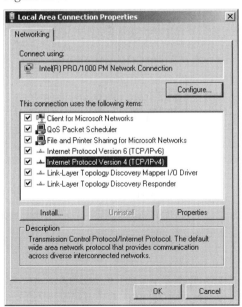

Figure 21-1 Install and configure TCP/IP in the Local Area Connection Properties dialog box.

Chapter 21

5. If Internet Protocol Version 6 (TCP/IPv6), Internet Protocol Version 4 (TCP/IPv4), or both aren't shown in the list of installed components, you'll need to install them. Click Install. Select Protocol, and then click Add. In the Select Network Protocol dialog box, select the protocol to install and then click OK. If you are installing both TCP/IPv6 and TCP/IPv4, repeat this procedure for each protocol.

6. In the Local Area Connection Properties dialog box, make sure that the following are selected as appropriate: Internet Protocol Version 6 (TCP/IPv6), Internet Protocol Version 4 (TCP/IPv4), or both. Then click OK.

7. As necessary, follow the instructions in the next section for configuring local area connections for the computer.

Configuring TCP/IP Networking

A local area connection is created automatically if a computer has a network adapter and is connected to a network. If a computer has multiple network adapters and is connected to a network, you'll have one local area connection for each adapter. If no network connection is available, you should connect the computer to the network or create a different type of connection, as explained in "Managing Network Connections" on page 671.

Computers use IP addresses to communicate over TCP/IP. Windows Server 2008 provides the following ways to configure IP addressing:

Manually IP addresses that are assigned manually are called static IP addresses. Static IP addresses are fixed and don't change unless you change them. You'll usually assign static IP addresses to Windows servers, and when you do this, you'll need to configure additional information to help the server navigate the network.

Dynamically A DHCP server (if one is installed on the network) assigns dynamic IP addresses at startup, and the addresses might change over time. Dynamic IP addressing is the default configuration.

Alternatively (IPv4 only) When a computer is configured to use DHCPv4 and no DHCPv4 server is available, Windows Server 2008 assigns an alternate private IP address automatically. By default, the alternate IPv4 address is in the range from 169.254.0.1 to 169.254.255.254 with a subnet mask of 255.255.0.0. You can also specify a user-configured alternate IPv4 address, which is particularly useful for laptop users.

> Note
>
> Unless an IP address is specifically reserved, DHCP servers assign IP addresses for a specific period of time, known as an *IP address lease*. If this lease expires and cannot be renewed, then the client assigns itself an automatic private IP address.

> **Note**
>
> To perform most TCP/IP configuration tasks, you must be a member of the Administrators group.

Configuring Static IP Addresses

When you assign a static IP address, you need to tell the computer the IP address you want to use, the subnet mask for this IP address, and, if necessary, the default gateway to use for internetwork communications. An IP address is a numeric identifier for a computer. IP addressing schemes vary according to how your network is configured, but they're normally assigned based on a particular network segment.

IPv6 addresses and IPv4 addresses are very different. With IPv6, the first 64 bits represent the network ID and the remaining 64 bits represent the network interface. With IPv4, a variable number of the initial bits represent the network ID and the rest of the bits represent the host ID. For example, if you're working with IPv4 and a computer on the network segment 192.168.10.0 with a subnet mask of 255.255.255.0, the first 24 bits represent the network ID and the address range you have available for computer hosts is from 192.168.10.1 to 192.168.10.254. In this range, the address 192.168.10.255 is reserved for network broadcasts.

If you're on a private network that is indirectly connected to the Internet, you should use private IPv6 addresses. Link-local unicast addresses are private IPv6 addresses. All link-local unicast addresses begin with FE80.

If you're on a private network that is indirectly connected to the Internet, you should use private IPv4 addresses. Table 21-1 summarizes private network IPv4 addresses.

Table 21-1 Private IPv4 Network Addressing

Private Network ID	Subnet Mask	Network Address Range
10.0.0.0	255.0.0.0	10.0.0.0–10.255.255.255
172.16.0.0	255.240.0.0	172.16.0.0–172.31.255.255
192.168.0.0	255.255.0.0	192.168.0.0–192.168.255.255

All other IPv4 network addresses are public and must be leased or purchased. If the network is connected directly to the Internet and you've obtained a range of IPv4 addresses from your Internet service provider, you can use the IPv4 addresses you've been assigned.

Using the PING Command to Check an Address

Before you assign a static IP address, you should make sure that the address isn't already in use or reserved for use with DHCP. With the PING command, you can check to see whether an address is in use. Open a command prompt and type **ping**, followed by the IP address you want to check.

To test the IPv4 address 10.0.10.12, you would use the following command:

```
ping 10.0.10.12
```

To test the IPv6 address FEC0::02BC:FF:BECB:FE4F:961D, you would use the following command:

```
ping FEC0::02BC:FF:BECB:FE4F:961D
```

If you receive a successful reply from the PING test, the IP address is in use and you should try another one. If no current host on the network uses this IP address, the PING command output should be similar to the following:

```
Pinging 192.168.1.100 with 32 bytes of data:

Request timed out.
Request timed out.
Request timed out.
Request timed out.

Ping statistics for 192.168.1.100:
Packets: Sent = 4, Received = 0, Lost = 4 (100% loss)
```

You can then use the IP address.

> **Note**
>
> Pinging an IP address will work as long as all the hosts are active and reachable on the network at the time you ping the address. However, a firewall could be blocking your PING request. More important is to plan the assignment of static addresses to machines on your network carefully.

Configuring a Static IPv4 or IPv6 Address

One local area network (LAN) connection is available for each network adapter installed. These connections are created automatically. To configure static IP addresses for a particular connection, follow these steps:

1. Click Start and then click Network. In Network Explorer, click Network And Sharing Center on the toolbar.

2. In Network And Sharing Center, click Manage Network Connections. In Network Connections, right-click the connection you want to work with and then select Properties.

3. Double-click Internet Protocol Version 6 (TCP/IPv6) or Internet Protocol Version 4 (TCP/IPv4) as appropriate for the type of IP address you are configuring.

4. For an IPv6 address, do the following:
    - Select Use The Following IPv6 Address and then type the IPv6 address in the IPv6 Address text box. The IPv6 address you assign to the computer must not be used anywhere else on the network.
    - Press the Tab key. The Subnet Prefix Length field ensures that the computer communicates over the network properly. Windows Server 2008 should insert a default value for the subnet prefix into the Subnet Prefix Length text box. If the network doesn't use variable-length subnetting, the default value should suffice. If your network does use variable-length subnets, you'll need to change this value as appropriate for your network.

5. For an IPv4 address, do the following:
    - Select Use The Following IP Address and then type the IPv4 address in the IP Address text box. The IPv4 address you assign to the computer must not be used anywhere else on the network.
    - Press the Tab key. The Subnet Mask field ensures that the computer communicates over the network properly. Windows Server 2008 should insert a default value for the subnet prefix into the Subnet Mask text box. If the network doesn't use variable-length subnetting, the default value should suffice. If your network does use variable-length subnets, you'll need to change this value as appropriate for your network.

6. If the computer needs to access other TCP/IP networks, the Internet, or other subnets, you must specify a default gateway. Type the IP address of the network's default router in the Default Gateway text box.

7. DNS is needed for domain name resolution. Select Use The Following DNS Server Addresses and then type a preferred address and an alternate DNS server address in the text boxes provided.

8. When you're finished, click OK three times to save your changes. Repeat this process for other network adapters and IP protocols you want to configure.

9. With IPv4 addressing, configure WINS as necessary, following the technique outlined in "Configuring WINS Resolution" on page 669.

Configuring Dynamic IP Addresses and Alternate IP Addressing

Many organizations use DHCP servers to dynamically assign IPv4 and IPv6 addresses. To receive an IPv4 or IPv6 address, client computers use a limited broadcast to advertise that they need to obtain an IP address. DHCP servers on the network acknowledge the request by offering the client an IP address. The client acknowledges the first offer it receives, and the DHCP server in turn tells the client that it has succeeded in leasing the IP address for a specified amount of time.

The message from the DHCP server can, and typically does, include the IP addresses of the default gateway, the preferred and alternate DNS servers, and the preferred and

Chapter 21

alternate WINS servers. This means these settings wouldn't need to be manually configured on the client computer.

> ### DHCP Is Primarily for Clients
>
> Dynamic IP addresses aren't for all hosts on the network, however. Typically, you'll want to assign dynamic IP addresses to workstations and, in some instances, member servers that perform noncritical roles on the network. But if you use dynamic IP addressing for member servers, these servers should have reservations for their IP addresses. For any server that has a critical network role or provides a key service, you'll definitely want to use static IP addresses. Finally, with domain controllers and DHCP servers, you must use static IP addresses, so don't try to assign dynamic IP addresses to these servers.

Although you can use static IP addresses with workstations, most workstations use dynamic addressing, alternative IP addressing, or both. You configure dynamic and alternative addressing by following these steps:

1. Click Start and then click Network. In Network Explorer, click Network And Sharing Center on the toolbar.

2. In Network And Sharing Center, click Manage Network Connections. In Network Connections, one LAN connection is shown for each network adapter installed. These connections are created automatically. If you don't see a LAN connection for an installed adapter, check the driver for the adapter. It might be installed incorrectly. Right-click the connection you want to work with and then select Properties.

3. Double-click Internet Protocol Version 6 (TCP/IPv6) or Internet Protocol Version 4 (TCP/IPv4) as appropriate for the type of IP address you are configuring.

4. Select Obtain An IPv6 Address Automatically or Obtain An IP Address Automatically as appropriate for the type of IP address you are configuring. If desired, select Obtain DNS Server Address Automatically. Or select Use The Following DNS Server Addresses and then type a preferred and alternate DNS server address in the text boxes provided.

5. When you use dynamic IPv4 addressing with desktop computers, you should configure an automatic alternative address. To use this configuration, on the Alternate Configuration tab, select Automatic Private IP Address. Click OK, click Close, and then skip the remaining steps.

6. When you use dynamic IPv4 addressing with mobile computers, you'll usually want to configure the alternative address manually. To use this configuration, on the Alternate Configuration tab, select User Configured and then type the IP address you want to use in the IP Address text box. The IP address that you assign to the computer should be a private IP address, as shown in Table 20-1 on page 631, and it must not be in use anywhere else when the settings are applied.

7. With dynamic IPv4 addressing, complete the alternate configuration by entering a subnet mask, default gateway, DNS, and WINS settings. When you're finished, click OK twice.

INSIDE OUT   Disabling APIPA

Whenever DHCP is used, APIPA is enabled by default. If you don't want a computer to use APIPA, you can either assign a static TCP/IP address or disable APIPA. For example, if your network uses routers or your network is connected to the Internet without a NAT or proxy server, you might not want to use APIPA. You can disable APIPA in the Registry.

On Windows 2000 or later, you can disable APIPA by creating the IPAutoconfiguration-Enabled as a DWORD value-entry under HKEY_LOCAL_MACHINE\SYSTEM\CurrentControlSet\Services\Tcpip\Parameters\Interfaces*AdapterGUID*, where *AdapterGUID* is the globally unique identifier (GUID) for the computer's network adapter. Set the value to 0×0.

If you create the IPAutoconfigurationEnabled as a DWORD value-entry, you can enable APIPA at any time by changing the value to 0×1.

For more information about disabling APIPA, see Microsoft Knowledge Base article 220874.

Configuring Multiple IP Addresses and Gateways

Using advanced TCP/IP settings, you can configure a single network interface on a computer to use multiple IP addresses and multiple gateways. This allows a computer to appear to be several computers and to access multiple logical subnets to route information or to provide internetworking services.

To provide fault tolerance in case of a router outage, you can choose to configure Windows Server 2008 computers so that they use multiple default gateways. When you assign multiple gateways, Windows Server 2008 uses the gateway metric to determine which gateway is used and at what time. The gateway metric indicates the routing cost of using a gateway. The gateway with the lowest routing cost, or metric, is used first. If the computer can't communicate with this gateway, Windows Server 2008 tries to use the gateway with the next lowest metric.

The best way to configure multiple gateways depends on the configuration of your network. If your organization's computers use DHCP, you'll probably want to configure the additional gateways through settings on the DHCP server. If computers use static IP addresses or you want to set gateways specifically, assign them by following these steps:

1. Click Start and then click Network. In Network Explorer, click Network And Sharing Center on the toolbar.

2. In Network And Sharing Center, click Manage Network Connections. In Network Connections, right-click the connection you want to work with and then select Properties.

3. Double-click Internet Protocol Version 6 (TCP/IPv6) or Internet Protocol Version 4 (TCP/IPv4) as appropriate for the type of IP address you are configuring.

4. Click Advanced to open the Advanced TCP/IP Settings dialog box. Figure 21-2 shows advanced settings for IPv4. The dialog box for IPv6 is similar.

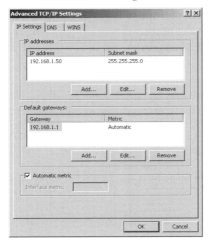

Figure 21-2 Configure multiple IP addresses and gateways in the Advanced TCP/IP Settings dialog box.

5. To add an IP address, click Add below IP Addresses to display the TCP/IP Address dialog box. After you type the IP address in the IP Address field, enter the subnet mask in the Subnet Mask field for IPv4 addresses or the subnet prefix length in the Subnet Prefix Length field for IPv6 addresses. Click Add to return to the Advanced TCP/IP Settings dialog box. Repeat this step for each IP address you want to add.

6. The Default Gateways panel shows the current gateways that have been manually configured (if any). To add a default gateway, click Add below Default Gateways to display the TCP/IP Gateway Address dialog box. Type the gateway address in the Gateway field. By default, Windows Server 2008 automatically assigns a metric to the gateway, which determines in which order the gateway is used. To assign the metric manually, clear the Automatic Metric check box, and then enter a metric in the field provided. Click Add, and then repeat this step for each gateway you want to add.

7. Click OK three times to close the open dialog boxes.

Configuring DNS Resolution

DNS is a host name resolution service that you can use to determine the IP address of a computer from its host name. This lets users work with host names, such as *http://www.msn.com* or *http://www.microsoft.com*, rather than an IP address, such as 192.168.5.102 or 192.168.12.68. DNS is the primary name service for Windows Server 2008 and the Internet.

As with gateways, the best way to configure DNS depends on the configuration of your network. If computers use DHCP, you'll probably want to configure DNS through settings on the DHCP server. If computers use static IP addresses or you want to configure DNS specifically for an individual user or system, you'll want to configure DNS manually.

Basic DNS Settings

You can configure basic DNS settings by following these steps:

1. Click Start and then click Network. In Network Explorer, click Network And Sharing Center on the toolbar.

2. In Network And Sharing Center, click Manage Network Connections. In Network Connections, right-click the connection you want to work with and then select Properties.

3. Double-click Internet Protocol Version 6 (TCP/IPv6) or Internet Protocol Version 4 (TCP/IPv4) as appropriate for the type of IP address you are configuring.

4. If the computer is using DHCP and you want DHCP to specify the DNS server address, select Obtain DNS Server Address Automatically. Otherwise, select Use The Following DNS Server Addresses and then type primary and alternate DNS server addresses in the text boxes provided.

5. Click OK three times to save your changes.

Advanced DNS Settings

You configure advanced DNS settings on the DNS tab of the Advanced TCP/IP Settings dialog box, shown in Figure 21-3. You use the fields of the DNS tab as follows:

DNS Server Addresses, In Order Of Use Use this area to specify the IP address of each DNS server that is used for domain name resolution. Click Add if you want to add a server IP address to the list. Click Remove to remove a selected server address from the list. Click Edit to edit the selected entry. You can specify multiple servers for DNS resolution. Their priority is determined by the order. If the first server isn't available to respond to a host name resolution request, the next DNS server in the list is accessed, and so on. To change the position of a server in the list box, select it and then click the up or down arrow button.

Append Primary And Connection Specific DNS Suffixes Normally, this option is selected by default. Select this option to resolve unqualified computer names in the primary domain. For example, if the computer name Gandolf is used and the parent domain is microsoft.com, the computer name would resolve to gandolf.microsoft.com. If the fully qualified computer name doesn't exist in the parent domain, the query fails. The parent domain used is the one set in the System Properties dialog box, on the Computer Name tab. (Click System And Maintenance\System in Control Panel, then click Change Settings and view the Computer Name tab to check the settings.)

Append Parent Suffixes Of The Primary DNS Suffix This option is selected by default. Select this check box to resolve unqualified computer names using the parent/ child domain hierarchy. If a query fails in the immediate parent domain, the suffix for the parent of the parent domain is used to try to resolve the query. This process continues until the top of the DNS domain hierarchy is reached. For example, if the computer name Gandolf is used in the dev.microsoft.com domain, DNS would attempt to resolve the computer name to gandolf.dev.microsoft.com. If this didn't work, DNS would attempt to resolve the computer name to gandolf.microsoft.com.

Append These DNS Suffixes (In Order) Select this option to set specific DNS suffixes to use rather than resolving through the parent domain. Click Add if you want to add a domain suffix to the list. Click Remove to remove a selected domain suffix from the list. Click Edit to edit the selected entry. You can specify multiple domain suffixes, which are used in order. If the first suffix doesn't resolve properly, DNS attempts to use the next suffix in the list. If this fails, the next suffix is used, and so on. To change the order of the domain suffixes, select the suffix and then click the up or down arrow button to change its position.

DNS Suffix For This Connection This option sets a specific DNS suffix for the connection that overrides DNS names already configured for use on this connection. You'll usually set the DNS domain name through the System Properties dialog box, on the Computer Name tab.

Register This Connection's Addresses In DNS Select this check box if you want all IP addresses for this connection to be registered in DNS under the computer's fully qualified domain name. This option is selected by default.

> **Note**
>
> Dynamic DNS updates are used in conjunction with DHCP to enable a client to update its A (Host Address) record if its IP address changes, and to enable the DHCP server to update the PTR (Pointer) record for the client on the DNS server. You can also configure DHCP servers to update both the A and PTR records on the client's behalf. Dynamic DNS updates are supported only by BIND 5.1 or higher DNS servers as well as server editions of Microsoft Windows.

Use This Connection's DNS Suffix In DNS Registration Select this check box if you want all IP addresses for this connection to be registered in DNS under the parent domain.

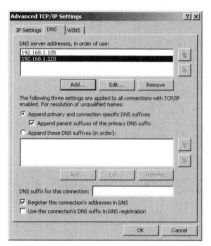

Figure 21-3 Configure advanced DNS settings on the DNS tab of the Advanced TCP/IP Settings dialog box.

Configuring WINS Resolution

You use WINS to resolve network basic input/output system (NetBIOS) computer names to IPv4 addresses. You can use WINS to help computers on a network determine the address of other computers on the network. If a WINS server is installed on the network, you can use the server to resolve computer names. Although WINS is supported on all versions of Windows, Windows Server 2008 primarily uses WINS for backward compatibility.

You can also configure Windows Server 2008 computers to use the local file LMHOSTS to resolve NetBIOS computer names. However, LMHOSTS is consulted only if normal name resolution methods fail. In a properly configured network, these files are rarely used. Thus, the preferred method of NetBIOS computer name resolution is WINS in conjunction with a WINS server.

As with gateways and DNS, the best way to configure WINS depends on the configuration of your network. If computers use DHCP, you'll probably want to configure WINS through settings on the DHCP server. If computers use static IPv4 addresses or you want to configure WINS specifically for an individual user or system, you'll want to configure WINS manually.

You can manually configure WINS by following these steps:

1. Access the Advanced TCP/IP Settings dialog box for IPv4 and click the WINS tab as shown in Figure 21-4. In the WINS Addresses, In Order Of Use panel, you can specify the IPv4 addresses of each WINS server that is used for NetBIOS name resolution. Click Add if you want to add a server IPv4 address to the list. Click Remove to remove a selected server from the list. Click Edit to edit the selected entry.

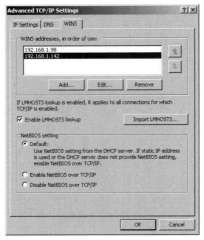

Figure 21-4 Configure WINS resolution for NetBIOS computer names on the WINS tab of the Advanced TCP/IP Settings dialog box.

2. You can specify multiple servers, which are used in order, for WINS resolution. If the first server isn't available to respond to a NetBIOS name resolution request, the next WINS server on the list is accessed, and so on. To change the position of a server in the list box, select it and then click the up or down arrow button.

3. To enable LMHOSTS lookups, select the Enable LMHOSTS Lookup check box. If you want the computer to use an existing LMHOSTS file defined somewhere on the network, retrieve this file by clicking Import LMHOSTS. You generally will use LMHOSTS only when other name resolution methods fail.

4. WINS name resolution requires NetBIOS over TCP/IP services. Select one of the following options to configure WINS name resolution using NetBIOS:

  ○ If you use DHCP and dynamic addressing, you can get the NetBIOS setting from the DHCP server. Select Default: Use NetBIOS Setting From The DHCP Server.

  ○ If you use a static IP address or the DHCP server does not provide NetBIOS settings, select Enable NetBIOS Over TCP/IP.

  ○ If WINS and NetBIOS are not used on the network, select Disable NetBIOS Over TCP/IP. This eliminates the NetBIOS broadcasts that would otherwise be sent by the computer.

5. Click OK three times. As necessary, repeat this process for other network adapters.

> **Note**
>
> LMHOSTS files are maintained locally on a computer-by-computer basis, which can eventually make them unreliable. Rather than relying on LMHOSTS, ensure that your DNS and WINS servers are configured properly and are accessible to the network for centralized administration of name resolution services.

Managing Network Connections

Local area connections make it possible for computers to access resources on the network and the Internet. One local area connection is created automatically for each network adapter installed on a computer. This section examines techniques you can use to manage these connections.

Checking the Status, Speed, and Activity for Local Area Connections

To check the status of a local area connection, follow these steps:

1. Click Start and then click Network. In Network Explorer, click Network And Sharing Center on the toolbar.

2. In Network And Sharing Center, click Manage Network Connections. In Network Connections, right-click the connection you want to work with and then click Status.

3. This displays the Local Area Connection Status dialog box. If the connection is disabled or the media is unplugged, you won't be able to access this dialog box. Enable the connection or connect the network cable to resolve the problem and then try to display the status dialog box again.

The General tab of this dialog box, shown in Figure 21-5, provides useful information regarding the following:

- **IPv4 Connectivity** The current IPv4 connection state and type. You'll typically see the status as Local when connected to an internal network or Not Connected when not connected to a network.

- **IPv6 Connectivity** The current IPv6 connection state and type. You'll typically see the status as Local when connected to an internal network or Not Connected when not connected to a network.

- **Media State** The state of the media. Because the status dialog box is available only when the connection is enabled, you'll typically see this as Enabled.

- **Duration** The amount of time the connection has been established. If the duration is fairly short, the user either recently connected to the network or the connection was recently reset.

- **Speed** The speed of the connection. This should read 10.0 megabits per second (Mbps) for 10-Mbps connections, 100.0 Mbps for 100-Mbps connections, and 1 gigabit per second (Gbps) for 1-gigabit connections. An incorrect setting can affect the computer's performance.

- **Bytes** The number of bytes sent and the number received by the connection. As the computer sends or receives packets, you'll see the computer icons light up to indicate the flow of traffic.

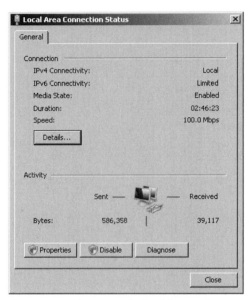

Figure 21-5 The General tab of the Local Area Connection Status dialog box provides access to summary information regarding connections, properties, and support.

Viewing Network Configuration Information

In Windows Server 2008, you can view the current configuration for network adapters in several ways. To view configuration settings using the Local Area Connection Status dialog box, follow these steps:

1. Click Start and then click Network. In Network Explorer, click Network And Sharing Center on the toolbar.

2. In Network And Sharing Center, click Manage Network Connections. In Network Connections, right-click the connection you want to work with and then click Status. This displays the Local Area Connection Status dialog box. If the connection is disabled or the media is unplugged, you won't be able to access this

dialog box. Enable the connection or connect the network cable to resolve the problem and then try to display the status dialog box again.

3. Click Details to view detailed information about the IP address configuration, including:

- ○ **Physical Address** The machine or Media Access Control (MAC) address of the network adapter. This address is unique for each network adapter.

- ○ **IPv4 IP Address** The IPv4 address assigned for IPv4 networking.

- ○ **IPv4 Subnet Mask** The subnet mask used for IPv4 networking.

- ○ **IPv4 Default Gateways** The IPv4 address of the default gateways used for IPv4 networking.

- ○ **IPv4 DNS Servers** IP addresses for DNS servers used with IPv4 networking.

- ○ **IPv4 WINS Servers** IP addresses for WINS servers used with IPv4 networking.

- ○ **IPv4 DHCP Server** The IP address of the DHCPv4 server from which the current lease was obtained (DHCPv4 only).

- ○ **Lease Obtained** A date and time stamp for when the DHCPv4 lease was obtained (DHCPv4 only).

- ○ **Lease Expires** A date and time stamp for when the DHCPv4 lease expires (DHCPv4 only).

You can also use the IPCONFIG command to view advanced configuration settings. To do so, follow these steps:

1. Click Start and type **cmd** in the Search field.

2. Press Enter.

3. At the command line, type **ipconfig /all** to see detailed configuration information for all network adapters configured on the computer.

> Note
>
> The command prompt is started in standard user mode. This is not an elevated command prompt.

Enabling and Disabling Local Area Connections

Local area connections are created and connected automatically. If you want to disable a connection so that it cannot be used, follow these steps:

1. Click Start and then click Network. In Network Explorer, click Network And Sharing Center on the toolbar.

2. In Network And Sharing Center, click Manage Network Connections. In Network Connections, right-click the connection and select Disable to deactivate the connection and disable it.

3. If you want to enable the connection later, right-click the connection in Network Connections and select Enable.

If you want to disconnect from a network or start another connection, follow these steps:

1. Click Start and then click Network. In Network Explorer, click Network And Sharing Center on the toolbar.

2. In Network And Sharing Center, click Manage Network Connections. In Network Connections, right-click the connection and select Disconnect. Typically, only remote access connections have a Disconnect option.

3. If you want to activate the connection later, right-click the connection in Network Connections and select Connect.

Renaming Local Area Connections

Windows Server 2008 initially assigns default names for local area connections. In Network Connections, you can rename the connections at any time by right-clicking the connection, selecting Rename, and then typing a new connection name. If a computer has multiple local area connections, proper naming can help you and others better understand the uses of a particular connection.

Troubleshooting and Testing Network Settings

Windows Server 2008 includes many tools for troubleshooting and testing TCP/IP connectivity. This section looks at automated diagnostics, basic tests that you should perform whenever you install or modify a computer's network settings, and techniques for resolving difficult networking problems involving DHCP and DNS. The final section shows you how to perform detailed network diagnostics testing.

Diagnosing and Resolving Local Area Connection Problems

Occasionally network cables can get unplugged or the network adapter might experience a problem that temporarily prevents it from working. After you plug the cable back in or solve the adapter problem, the connection should automatically reconnect. To diagnose local area connection problems, follow these steps:

1. Click Start and then click Network. In Network Explorer, click Network And Sharing Center on the toolbar.

2. In Network And Sharing Center, click Manage Network Connections.

3. Right-click the connection you want to work with and select Diagnose.

Windows Network Diagnostics will then try to identify the problem. A list of possible solutions is provided for identifiable configuration problems. Some solutions provide automated fixes that you can execute by clicking the solution. Other solutions require manual fixes, such as might be required if you need to reset a network router or broadband modem. If your actions don't fix the problem, refer to other appropriate parts of this troubleshooting section.

Diagnosing and Resolving Internet Connection Problems

Because of the many interdependencies between services, protocols, and configuration settings, troubleshooting network problems can be difficult. Fortunately, Windows Server 2008 includes a powerful network diagnostics tool for pinpointing problems that relate to the following:

- General network connectivity problems

- Internet service settings for e-mail, newsgroups, and proxies

- Settings for modems, network clients, and network adapters

- DNS, DHCP, and WINS configuration

- Default gateways and IP addresses

To diagnose Internet connection problems, follow these steps:

1. Click Start and then click Network. In Network Explorer, click Network And Sharing Center on the toolbar.

2. Click Diagnose And Repair.

Windows Network Diagnostics will then try to identify the problem. If identifiable configuration problems exist, a list of possible solutions is provided. Some solutions provide automated fixes that you can execute by clicking the solution. Other solutions require manual fixes, such as might be required if you need to reset a network router or broadband modem. If your actions don't fix the problem, refer to other appropriate parts of this troubleshooting section.

Performing Basic Network Tests

Whenever you install a new computer or make configuration changes to the computer's network settings, you should test the configuration. The most basic TCP/IP test is to use the PING command to test the computer's connection to the network. PING is a command-line command. To use it, type **ping <*host*>** at the command prompt, where <*host*> is either the computer name or the IP address of the host computer you're trying to reach.

With Windows Server 2008, you can use the following methods to test the configuration using PING:

- **Try to ping IP addresses** If the computer is configured correctly and the host you're trying to reach is accessible to the network, PING should receive a reply, as long as pinging is allowed by the computer's firewall. If PING can't reach the host or is blocked by a firewall, PING times out.

- **On domains that use WINS, try to ping NetBIOS computer names** If NetBIOS computer names are resolved correctly by PING, the NetBIOS facilities, such as WINS, are correctly configured for the computer.

- **On domains that use DNS, try to ping DNS host names** If fully qualified DNS host names are resolved correctly by PING, DNS name resolution is configured properly.

You might also want to test network browsing for the computer. If the computer is a member of a Windows Server 2008 domain and computer browsing is enabled throughout the domain, log on to the computer and then use Windows Explorer or Network Explorer to browse other computers in the domain. Afterward, log on to a different computer in the domain and try to browse the computer you just configured. These tests tell you if the DNS resolution is being handled properly in the local environment. If you can't browse, check the configuration of the DNS services and protocols.

In some cases, discovering and sharing might be set to block discovery. You'll need to allow discovery to resolve this by following these steps:

1. Click Start and then click Network.

2. In Network Explorer, click Network And Sharing Center on the toolbar.

3. If Network Discovery is set to Off, expand the Sharing And Discovery panel using the Expand button, click Turn On Network Discovery, and then click Apply to turn on this feature.

Diagnosing and Resolving IP Addressing Problems

The current IP address settings of a computer can be obtained as discussed in "Viewing Network Configuration Information" on page 672. If a computer is having problems accessing network resources or communicating with other computers, an IP addressing problem might exist. Take a close look at the IP address currently assigned, as well as other IP address settings, and use the following tips to help in your troubleshooting:

- If the IPv4 address currently assigned to the computer is in the range 169.254.0.1 to 169.254.255.254, the computer is using Automatic Private IP Addressing (APIPA). An automatic private IP address is assigned to a computer when it is configured to use DHCP and its DHCP client cannot reach a DHCP server. When using APIPA, Windows Server 2008 will automatically periodically check for a DHCP server to become available. If a computer doesn't eventually obtain a dynamic IP address, the network connection usually has a problem. Check the network cable, and if necessary trace the cable back to the switch or hub into which it connects.

- If the IPv4 address and the subnet mask of the computer are currently set as 0.0.0.0, the network is either disconnected or someone attempted to use a static IP address that duplicated another IP address already in use on the network. In this case, you should access Network Connections and determine the state of the connection. If the connection is disabled or disconnected, this should be shown. Right-click the connection and select Enable or Diagnose as appropriate. If the connection is already enabled, you will need to modify the IP address settings for the connection.

- If the IP address is dynamically assigned, make sure that another computer on the network isn't using the same IP address. You can do this by disconnecting the network cable for the computer that you are working with and pinging the IP address in question. If you receive a response from the PING test, you know that another computer is using the IP address. This computer probably has an improper static IP address or a reservation that isn't set up properly.

- If the IP address appears to be set correctly, check the subnet mask, gateway, DNS, and WINS settings by comparing the network settings of the computer you are troubleshooting with those of a computer that is known to have a good network configuration. One of the biggest problem areas is the subnet mask. When subnetting is used, the subnet mask used in one area of the network might look very similar to that of another area of the network. For example, the subnet mask in one IPv4 area might be 255.255.255.240, and it might be 255.255.255.248 in another IPv4 area.

When you are using static IP addressing, you can check the current IPv4 or IPv6 settings by entering **ipconfig /all** at a command prompt. The display of the ipconfig /all command includes IPv4/IPv6 addresses, default routers, and DNS servers for all interfaces. You can also check IPv4 and IPv6 addressing separately. To check the IPv4 addressing configuration, enter **netsh interface ipv4 show addres**s. To check IPv6 addressing, enter **netsh interface ipv6 show address**. To use Netsh to show the configuration of a remote computer use the **-r** *RemoteComputerName* command line option. For example, to display the configuration of the remote computer named CORPSERVER26, you would enter **netsh -r corpserver26 interface ipv4 show address**.

To make changes to the configuration of IP interfaces, use the **netsh interface ipv4 set interface** and **netsh interface ipv6 set interface** commands. To add the IP addresses of DNS servers, use the **netsh interface ipv4 add dns** and **netsh interface ipv6 add dns** commands.

Chapter 21

Diagnosing and Resolving Routing Problems

As part of troubleshooting, you can verify the reachability of local and remote destinations. You can ping your default router by its IPv4 or IPv6 address. You can obtain the local IPv4 address of your default router by entering **netsh interface ipv4 show routes**. You can obtain the link-local IPv6 address of your default router by entering **netsh interface ipv6 show routes**. Pinging the default router tests whether you can reach local nodes and whether you can reach the default router, which forwards IP packets to remote nodes.

When you ping the default IPv6 router, you must specify the zone identifier (ID) for the interface on which you want the ICMPv6 Echo Request messages to be sent. The zone ID for the default router is listed when you enter the ipconfig /all command.

If you are able to ping your default router, ping a remote destination by its IPv4 or IPv6 address. If you are unable to ping a remote destination by its IP address, there might be a routing problem between your node and the destination node. Enter **tracert -d** *IPAddress* to trace the routing path to the remote destination You use the -d command-line option to speed up the response by preventing Tracert from performing a reverse DNS query on every near-side router interface in the routing path.

The inability to reach a local or remote destination might be due to incorrect or missing routes in the local IP routing table. To view the local IP routing table, enter the **netsh interface ipv4 show routes** or **netsh interface ipv6 show routes** command. Use the command output to verify that you have a route corresponding to your local subnet. The route with the lowest metric is used first. If you have multiple default routes with the same lowest metric, you might need to modify your IP router configuration so that the default route with the lowest metric uses the interface that connects to the correct network.

You can add a route to the IP routing table by using the **netsh interface ipv4 add route** or **netsh interface ipv6 add route** command. To modify an existing route, use the **netsh interface ipv4 set route** or the **netsh interface ipv6 set route** command. To remove an existing route, use the **netsh interface ipv4 delete route** or **netsh interface ipv6 delete route** command.

If you suspect a problem with router performance, use the **pathping -d** *IPAddress* command to trace the path to a destination and display information on packet losses for each router in the path. You use the -d command-line option to speed up the response by preventing Pathping from performing a reverse DNS query on every near-side router interface in the routing path.

INSIDE OUT   Checking IPSec policies and Windows Firewall

The problem with reaching a destination node might be due to the configuration of Internet Protocol Security (IPSec) or packet filtering. Check for IPSec policies that have been configured on the computer having the problem, on intermediate IPv6 routers, and on the destination computer. On computers running Windows XP or later, IPSec is configured using Windows Firewall With Advanced Security.

In many cases, packet filtering is configured to allow specific types of traffic and discard all others, or to discard specific types of traffic and accept all others. Because of this, you might be able to view Web pages on a Web server, but not ping the Web server by its host name or IP address.

Each network connection configured on a computer can be enabled or disabled in the Windows Firewall. When enabled, IPv4 and IPv6 drop incoming requests. During troublehshooting, you can disable the Windows Firewall for a specific IPv4 or IPv6 interface with the **netsh interface ipv4 set interface interface=NameOrIndex firewall=disabled** and **netsh interface ipv6 set interface interface=NameOrIndex firewall=disabled** commands. You can also completely turn off the Windows Firewall with the **netsh firewall set opmode disable** command. Don't forget to reenable the firewall when you are done troubleshooting.

Releasing and Renewing DHCP Settings

DHCP servers can assign many network configuration settings automatically, including IP addresses, default gateways, primary and secondary DNS servers, primary and secondary WINS servers, and more. When computers use dynamic addressing, they are assigned a lease on a specific IP address. This lease is good for a specific time period and must be renewed periodically. When the lease needs to be renewed, the computer contacts the DHCP server that provided the lease. If the server is available, the lease is renewed and a new lease period is granted. You can also renew leases manually as necessary on individual computers or by using the DHCP server itself.

Problems that prevent network communications can occur during the lease assignment and renewal process. If the server isn't available and cannot be reached before a lease expires, the IP address can become invalid. If this happens, the computer might use the alternate IP address configuration to set an alternate address, which in most cases has settings that are inappropriate and prevent proper communications. To resolve this problem, you'll need to release and then renew the DHCP lease.

Another type of problem occurs when users move around to various offices and subnets within the organization. While moving from location to location, their computers might obtain DHCP settings from the wrong server. When the users return to their offices, the computer might seem sluggish or perform incorrectly because of the settings assigned by the DHCP server at another location. If this happens, you'll need to release and then renew the DHCP lease.

You can use the graphical interface to release and renew DHCP leases by following these steps:

1. Click Start and then click Network. In Network Explorer, click Network And Sharing Center on the toolbar.

2. In Network And Sharing Center, click Manage Network Connections. In Network Connections, right-click the connection you want to work with and then select Diagnose.

3. After Windows Network Diagnostics tries to identify the problem, a list of possible solutions is provided. If the computer has one or more dynamically assigned IP addresses, one of the solutions should be Automatically Get New IP Settings.... Click this option.

You can also follow these steps to use the IPCONFIG command to renew and release settings:

1. Start an elevated command prompt.

2. To release the current settings for all network adapters, type **ipconfig /release** at the command line. Then renew the lease by typing **ipconfig /renew**.

3. To renew a DHCP lease for all network adapters, type **ipconfig /renew** at the command line.

4. You can check the updated settings by typing **ipconfig /all** at the command line.

> **Note**
>
> If a computer has multiple network adapters and you only want to work with one or a subset of the adapters, specify all or part of the connection name after the **ipconfig /renew** or **ipconfig /release** command. Use the asterisk as a wildcard to match any characters in a connection's name. For example, if you want to renew the lease for all connections with names starting with *Loc*, type the command **ipconfig /renew Loc***. If you want to release the settings for all connections containing the word *Network*, type the command **ipconfig /release *Network***.

Diagnosing and Resolving Name Resolution Issues

When you can reach a destination using an IP address but not reach a host using a host name, you might have a problem with host name resolution. Typically, name resolution issues have to do with improper configuration of the DNS client or problems with DNS registration. You can use the following tasks to troubleshoot problems with DNS name resolution:

- Verify DNS configuration

- Test DNS name resolution with the Ping tool
- Use the Nslookup tool to view DNS server responses
- Display and flush the DNS client resolver cache

On the computer having DNS name resolution problems, verify the following information:

- Host name
- The primary DNS suffix
- DNS suffix search list
- Connection-specific DNS suffixes
- DNS servers

You can obtain this information by entering **ipconfig /all** at a command prompt. To obtain information about which DNS names should be registered in DNS, enter **netsh interface ip show dns**.

Computers running Windows Vista and Windows Server 2008 support DNS traffic over IPv6. By default, IPv6 configures the well-known site-local addresses of DNS servers at FEC0:0:0:FFFF::1, FEC0:0:0:FFFF::2, and FEC0:0:0:FFFF::3. To add the IPv6 addresses of your DNS servers, use the properties of the Internet Protocol Version 6 (TCP/IPv6) component in Network Connections or **the netsh interface ipv6 add dns** command. To register the appropriate DNS names as IP address resource records with DNS dynamic update, use the **ipconfig /registerdns** command. Computers running Windows XP or Windows Server 2003 do not support DNS traffic over IPv6.

TCP/IP checks the DNS client resolver cache before sending DNS name queries. The DNS resolver cache maintains a history of DNS lookups that have been performed when a user accesses network resources using TCP/IP. This cache contains forward lookups, which provide host name to IP address resolution, and reverse lookups, which provide IP address to host name resolution. After a DNS entry is stored in the resolver cache for a particular DNS host, the local computer no longer has to query external servers for DNS information on that host. This enables the computer to resolve DNS requests locally, providing a quicker response.

How long entries are stored in the resolver cache depends on the Time to Live (TTL) value assigned to the record by the originating server. To view current records and see the remaining TTL value for each record, type **ipconfig /displaydns** in an elevated command prompt. These values are given as the number of seconds that a particular record can remain in the cache before it expires. These values are continually being counted down by the local computer. When the TTL value reaches zero, the record expires and is removed from the resolver cache.

Occasionally, you'll find that you need to clear out the resolver cache to remove old entries and enable computers to check for updated DNS entries before the normal expiration and purging process takes place. Typically, this happens because server IP addresses have changed and the current entries in the resolver cache point to the old addresses rather than the new ones. Sometimes the resolver cache itself can get out of sync, particularly when DHCP has been misconfigured.

> **Note**
> Skilled administrators know that several weeks in advance of the actual change, they should start to decrease the TTL values for DNS records that are going to be changed. Typically, this means reducing the TTL from a number of days (or weeks) to a number of hours, which allows for quicker propagation of the changes to computers that have cached the related DNS records. After the change is completed, administrators should restore the original TTL value to reduce renewal requests.

In most cases, you can resolve problems with the DNS resolver cache by either flushing the cache or reregistering DNS. When you flush the resolver cache, all DNS entries are cleared out of the cache and new entries are not created until the next time the computer performs a DNS lookup on a particular host or IP address. When you reregister DNS, Windows Server 2008 attempts to refresh all current DHCP leases and then performs a lookup on each DNS entry in the resolver cache. By looking up each host or IP address again, the entries are renewed and reregistered in the resolver cache. You'll generally want to flush the cache completely and allow the computer to perform lookups as needed. Reregister DNS only when you suspect problems with DHCP and the DNS resolver cache.

You can test DNS name resolution by pinging a destination using its host name or fully qualified domain name (FQDN). If an incorrect IP address is shown, you can flush the DNS resolver cache and use the Nslookup tool to determine the set of addresses returned in the DNS Name Query Response message.

You can use the IPCONFIG command to flush and reregister entries in the DNS resolver cache by following these steps:

1. Start an elevated command prompt.

2. To clear out the resolver cache, type **ipconfig /flushdns** at the command line.

3. To renew DHCP leases and reregister DNS entries, type **ipconfig /registerdns** at the command line.

4. When the tasks are complete, you can check your work by typing **ipconfig /displaydns** at the command line.

To start Nslookup, enter **Nslookup** at a command prompt. At the Nslookup > prompt, use the **set d2** command to get detail information about DNS response messages. Then, use Nslookup to look up the desired FQDN. Look for A and AAAA records in the detailed display of the DNS response messages.

With IPv6, the DNS client maintains a neighbor's cache of recently resolved link-layer addresses as well as a standard resolver cache. To display the current contents of the neighbor cache, enter **netsh interface ipv6 show neighbors**. To flush the neighbor's cache, enter **netsh interface ipv6 delete neighbors**.

For IPv6, the DNS client also maintains a destination cache. The destination cache stores next-hop IPv6 addresses for destinations. To display the current contents of the destination cache, enter **netsh interface ipv6 show destinationcache** command. To flush the destination cache, enter **netsh interface ipv6 delete destinationcache**.

Managing DHCP

Most Microsoft Windows networks should be configured to use Dynamic Host Configuration Protocol (DHCP). DHCP simplifies administration and makes it easier for users to get their computer on the organization's network. How does DHCP do this? DHCP is a protocol that allows client computers to start up and automatically receive an Internet Protocol (IP) address and other related Transmission Control Protocol/Internet Protocol (TCP/IP) settings such as the subnet mask, default gateway, Domain Name System (DNS) server addresses, and Windows Internet Naming Service (WINS) server addresses. With Windows Server 2008, DHCP servers can assign a dynamic IP version 4 (IPv4), IP version 6 (IPv6), or both addresses to any of the network interface cards (NICs) on a computer.

DHCP Essentials

DHCP is a standards-based protocol that was originally defined by the Internet Engineering Task Force (IETF) and based on the Bootstrap Protocol (BOOTP). It is defined in Requests for Comments (RFCs) 3396 and 3442 and has been implemented on a variety of operating systems including UNIX and Windows. Because DHCP is a client/server protocol, there is a server component and a client component necessary to implement the protocol on a network. To make it easier to deploy DHCP in the enterprise, all server editions of Windows Server 2008 include the DHCP Server service, which can be installed to support DHCP, and all current versions of the Windows operating system automatically install the DHCP Client service as part of TCP/IP.

A computer that uses dynamic IP addressing and configuration is called a DHCP client. When you boot a DHCP client, a 32-bit IPv4 address, a 128-bit IPv6 address, or both can be retrieved from a pool of IP addresses defined for the network's DHCP server. It's the job of the DHCP server to maintain a database about the IP addresses that are available and the related configuration information. When an IP address is given out to a client, the client is said to have a lease on the IP address. The term "lease" is used because the assignment generally is not permanent. The DHCP server sets the duration of the lease when the lease is granted and can also change it later as necessary, such as when the lease is renewed.

DHCP also provides a way to assign a lease on an address permanently. To do this, you can create a *reservation* by specifying the IP address to reserve and the unique identifier of the computer that will hold the IP address. The reservation thereafter ensures that the client computer with the specified device address always gets the designated IP address. With IPv4, you specify the necessary unique identifier using the Media Access Control (MAC) address of the network card. With IPv6, you specify the DHCP unique identifier for the DHCPv6 client and the identity association identifier (IAID) being used by the DHCPv6 client.

Note

MAC addresses are tied to the network interface card (NIC) of a computer. If you remove a NIC or install an additional NIC on a computer, the MAC address of the new or additional card will be different from the address of the original NIC.

Consider DHCP for Non-DHCP Member Servers

You'll find that configuring member servers to use DHCP and then assigning them a reservation is an easy way to ensure that member servers have a fixed IP address while maintaining the flexibility provided by DHCP. After the member servers are configured for DHCP, they get all of their TCP/IP options from DHCP, including their IP addresses. If you ever need to change their addressing, you can do this from within DHCP rather than on each member server—and changing IP addressing and other TCP/IP options in one location is much easier than having to do so in multiple locations. Keep in mind that some server applications or roles might require a static IP address in order to work properly.

Microsoft recommends that a single DHCP server service no more than 10,000 clients. You define a set of IP addresses that can be assigned to clients using a scope. A *scope* is a pool of IPv4 or IPv6 addresses and related configuration options. The IP addresses set in a scope are contiguous and are associated with a specific subnet mask or network prefix length. To define a subset of IP addresses within a scope that should not be used, you can specify an exclusion. An *exclusion* defines a range of IP addresses that you can exclude so that it isn't assigned to client computers.

Windows Server 2008 supports integration of DHCP with dynamic DNS. When configured, this ensures that the client's DNS record is updated when it receives a new IP address. To ensure that client names can be resolved to IP addresses, you should configure integration of DHCP and DNS.

DHCP can be integrated with the Routing and Remote Access Service (RRAS). When configured, dial-up networking or virtual private network (VPN) clients can log on to the network remotely and use DHCP to configure their IP address and TCP/IP options.

The server managing their connection to the network is called a remote access server, and it is the responsibility of this server to obtain blocks of IP addresses from a DHCP server for use by remote clients. If a DHCP server is not available when the remote access server requests IP addresses, the remote clients are configured with automatic private IP addressing (APIPA). APIPA works differently for IPv4 and IPv6.

DHCPv4 and Autoconfiguration

The availability of a DHCP server doesn't affect startup or logon (in most cases). DHCP clients can start and users can log on to the local machine even if a DHCP server isn't available. During startup, the DHCP client looks for a DHCP server. If a DHCP server is available, the client gets its configuration information from the server. If a DHCP server isn't available and the client's previous lease is still valid, the client pings the default gateway listed in the lease.

A successful ping tells the client that it's probably on the same network it was on when it was issued the lease, and the client will continue to use the lease as described previously. A failed ping tells the client that it might be on a different network. In this case the client uses IP autoconfiguration. The client also uses IP autoconfiguration if a DHCP server isn't available and the previous lease has expired.

IPv4 autoconfiguration works like this:

1. The client computer selects an IP address from the Microsoft-reserved class B subnet 169.254.0.0 and uses the subnet mask 255.255.0.0. Before using the IPv4 address, the client performs an Address Resolution Protocol (ARP) test to make sure that no other client is using this IPv4 address.

2. If the IPv4 address is in use, the client repeats step 1, testing up to 10 IPv4 addresses before reporting failure. When a client is disconnected from the network, the ARP test always succeeds. As a result, the client uses the first IPv4 address it selects.

3. If the IPv4 address is available, the client configures the NIC with this address. The client then attempts to contact a DHCP server, sending out a broadcast every five minutes to the network. When the client successfully contacts a server, the client obtains a lease and reconfigures the network interface.

DHCPv6 and Autoconfiguration

You can use DHCP to configure IPv6 addressing in two key ways: DHCPv6 stateful mode and DHCPv6 stateless mode. In DHCPv6 stateful mode, clients acquire their IPv6 address as well as their network configuration parameters through DHCPv6. In DHCPv6 stateless mode, clients use autoconfiguration to acquire their IP address and acquire their network configuration parameters through DHCPv6.

A computer that uses dynamic IPv6 addressing, configuration, or both is called a *DHCPv6 client*. Both Windows Vista and Windows Server 2008 include a DHCPv6 client. Like DHCPv4, the components of a DHCPv6 infrastructure consist of DHCPv6 clients that request configuration, DHCPv6 servers that provide configuration, and DHCPv6 relay agents that convey messages between clients and servers when clients are on subnets that do not have a DHCPv6 server.

Unlike DHCPv4, you must also configure your IPv6 routers to support DHCPv6. A DHCPv6 client performs autoconfiguration based on the M and O flags in the Router Advertisement message sent by a neighboring router. When the Managed Address Configuration or M flag is set to 1, the client uses a configuration protocol to obtain stateful addresses. When the Other Stateful Configuration or O flag is set to 1, the client uses a configuration protocol to obtain other configuration settings.

Windows Vista and Windows Server 2008 obtain dynamic IPv6 addresses using a process similar to that used for dynamic IPv4 addresses. Typically, IPv6 autoconfiguration for DHCPv6 clients in stateful mode works like this:

1. The client computer selects a link-local unicast IPv6 address. Before using the IPv6 address, the client performs an Address Resolution Protocol (ARP) test to make sure that no other client is using this IPv6 address.

2. If the IPv6 address is in use, the client repeats step 1. Note that when a client is disconnected from the network, the ARP test always succeeds. As a result, the client uses the first IPv6 address it selects.

3. If the IPv6 address is available, the client configures the NIC with this address. The client then attempts to contact a DHCP server, sending out a broadcast every five minutes to the network. When the client successfully contacts a server, the client obtains a lease and reconfigures the network interface.

This is not how IPv6 autoconfiguration works for DHCPv6 clients in stateless mode. In stateless mode, DHCPv6 clients configure both link-local addresses and additional non-link-local addresses by exchanging Router Solicitation and Router Advertisement messages with neighboring routers.

DHCP Security Considerations

DHCP is inherently insecure. Anyone with access to the network can perform malicious actions that could cause problems for other clients trying to obtain IP addresses. A user could take the following actions:

-   Initiate a denial of service (DoS) attack by requesting all available IP addresses or by using large numbers of IP addresses, either of which could make it impossible for other users to obtain IP addresses.

-   Initiate an attack on DNS by performing a large number of dynamic updates through DHCP.

-   Use the information provided by DHCP to set up rogue services on the network, such as using a non-Microsoft DHCP server to provide incorrect IP address information.

To reduce the risk of attacks, you should limit physical access to the network. Don't make it easy for unauthorized users to connect to the network. If you use wireless technologies, configure the network so that it doesn't broadcast the service set identifier (SSID) or use Wired Equivalent Privacy (WEP) encryption, which prohibits wireless users from obtaining a DHCP lease until they provide an appropriate encryption key using strong data encryption. Wi-Fi Protected Access (WPA) and Wi-Fi Protected Access Version 2 (WPA2) are the preferred strong data encryption techniques.

To reduce the risk of a rogue DHCP server, configure the Active Directory on the network and use it to determine which DHCP servers are authorized to provide services. By using Active Directory, any computer running Microsoft Windows 2000 or later must be authorized to provide DHCP services. After a server is authorized, it is available for clients to use. This, unfortunately, doesn't restrict the use of unauthorized Microsoft Windows NT or non-Microsoft servers running DHCP, but it is a start.

In addition, the DHCP Server service should not be placed on an Active Directory domain controller if this can be avoided. The reason for this is because this changes security related to service locator (SRV) records, which domain controllers are responsible for publishing. SRV records detail the location of domain controllers, Kerberos servers, and other servers, and the changes to the security of these records when you install DHCP means that the records could be altered by any client on the network.

The reason this happens is because DHCP servers must be able to update client records dynamically if a client's IP address changes. Because of this, they are made members of the DNSUpdateProxy group, and members of this group do not have any security applied to objects they create in the DNS database. If you can't avoid placing DHCP on a domain controller, it is recommended that you remove the DHCP server from the DNSUpdateProxy group. This should avoid the security problem outlined here, but will also prevent the DHCP server from dynamically updating client records in DNS when the client IP addresses change.

Planning DHCPv4 and DHCPv6 Implementations

Planning a new DHCP implementation or revamping your existing DHCP implementation requires a good understanding of how DHCP works. You need to know the following information:

- How DHCP messages are sent and received
- How DHCP relay agents are used
- How multiple servers should be configured

These processes are essentially the same whether you are working with IPv4 or IPv6.

DHCPv4 Messages and Relay Agents

When a DHCP client is started, it uses network broadcasts to obtain or renew a lease from a DHCP server. These broadcasts are in the form of DHCP messages. A client obtains its initial lease as shown in Figure 22-1. Here, the client broadcasts a DHCP Discover message. All DHCP servers on the network respond to the broadcast with a DHCP Offer message, which offers the client an IP lease. The client accepts the first offer received by sending a DHCP Request message back to the server. The server accepts the request by sending the client a DHCP Acknowledgment message.

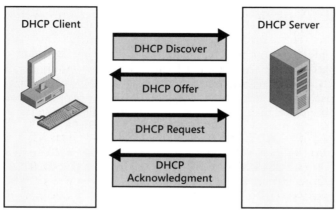

Figure 22-1 Obtaining an initial lease.

DHCP clients must renew their leases periodically, either at each restart or when 50 percent of the lease time has passed. If the renewal process fails, the client tries to renew the lease again when 87.5 percent of the lease time has passed. Renewing the lease involves the client sending the DHCP server a DHCP Request and the server accepting the request by sending a DHCP Acknowledgment. This streamlined communication process is shown in Figure 22-2.

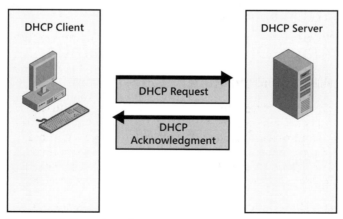

Figure 22-2 Renewing a lease.

If a DHCP client is unable to reach a DHCP server at startup or to renew its lease, it pings the default gateway that was previously assigned. If the default gateway responds, the client assumes it is on the subnet from which the lease was originally obtained and continues to use the lease. If the default gateway doesn't respond, the client assumes it has been moved to a new subnet and that there is no DHCP server on this subnet. It then autoconfigures itself. The client will continue to check for a DHCP server when it is autoconfigured. By default, it does this by sending a DHCP Discover message every five minutes. If the client gets a DHCP Offer back from a DHCP server, it sends a DHCP Request to the server. When it gets back a DHCP Acknowledgment, it abandons its auto-configuration and uses the address and other configuration settings sent by the DHCP server.

Typically, the messages sent by DHCP clients and servers are limited by the logical boundaries of the network. As a result, DHCP client broadcasts aren't routed and stay on only the originating network. In this configuration, you need at least one DHCP server per subnet.

To reduce the number of DHCP servers needed for your organization, you can configure a DHCP relay agent on any subnet that has no DHCP server. This relay agent is a router or a computer on the network that is configured to listen for DHCP broadcasts from clients on the local subnet and forward them as appropriate to a DHCP server on a different subnet. A router that supports BOOTP can be configured as a relay agent. You can also configure Windows Server 2008 computers on the network to act as DHCP relay agents.

Relay Agents Are Best for LANs

Relay agents work best in local area network (LAN) environments where subnets are all in the same geographic location. In a wide area network (WAN) environment where you are forwarding broadcasts across links, you might not want to use relay agents. If a WAN link goes down, clients won't be able to obtain or renew leases, and this could cause the clients to autoconfigure themselves.

DHCPv6 Messages and Relay Agents

The way a DHCPv6 client attempts DHCPv6-based configuration depends on the values of the M and O flags in received Router Advertisement messages. If there are multiple advertising routers for a given subnet, they should be configured to advertise the same stateless address prefixes and values of the M and O flags. IPv6 clients running Windows XP or Windows Server 2003 do not include a DHCPv6 client and therefore ignore the values of the M and O flags in received router advertisements.

You can configure an IPv6 router that is running Windows Vista or Windows Server 2008 to set the M flag to 1 in router advertisements with the **netsh interface ipv6 set interface** *InterfaceName* **managedaddress=enabled** command. Similarly, you can set the O flag to 1 in router advertisements with the **netsh interface ipv6 set interface** *InterfaceName* **otherstateful=enabled** command.

When you are working with the M and O flags, keep the following in mind:

- If both the M and O flags are set to 0, the network is considered not to have DHCPv6 infrastructure. Clients use router advertisements for non-link-local addresses and manual configuration to configure other settings.

- If both the M and O flags are set to 1, DHCPv6 is used for both IP addressing and other configuration settings. This combination is known as *DHCPv6 stateful mode*, in which DHCPv6 is assigning stateful addresses to IPv6 clients.

- If the M flag is set to 0 and the O flag is set to 1, DHCPv6 is used only to assign other configuration settings. Neighboring routers are configured to advertise non-link-local address prefixes from which IPv6 clients derive stateless addresses. This combination is known as *DHCPv6 stateless mode*.

- If the M flag is set to 1 and the O flag is set to 0, DHCPv6 is used for IP address configuration but not for other settings. Because IPv6 clients typically need to be configured with other settings, such as the IPv6 addresses of DNS servers, this combination typically is not used.

As with DHCPv4, DHCPv6 uses User Datagram Protocol (UDP) messages. DHCPv6 clients listen for DHCP messages on UDP port 546. DHCPv6 servers and relay agents listen for DHCPv6 messages on UDP port 547. The structure for DHCPv6 messages is much simpler than for DHCPv4, which had its origins in the BOOTP protocol to support diskless workstations.

DHCPv6 messages start with a 1-byte Msg-Type field that indicates the type of DHCPv6 message. This is followed by a 3-byte Transaction-ID field that is determined by a client and used to group the messages of a DHCPv6 message exchange together. Following the Transaction-ID field, DHCPv6 options are used to indicate client and server identification, addresses, and other configuration settings. Three fields are associated with each DHCPv6 option:

- A 2-byte Option-Code field indicates a specific option.

- A 2-byte Option-Len field indicates the length of the Option-Data field in bytes.

- An Option-Data field contains the data for the option.

Messages exchanged between relay agents and servers use a different message structure to transfer additional information. A 1-byte Hop-Count field indicates the number of relay agents that have received the message. A receiving relay agent can discard the message if it exceeds a configured maximum hop count. A 16-byte Link-Address field contains a non-link-local address that is assigned to an interface connected to the subnet on which the client is located. Based on the Link-Address field, the server can determine the correct address scope from which to assign an address. A 16-byte Peer-Address field contains the IPv6 address of the client that originally sent the message or the previous relay agent that relayed the message. Following the Peer-Address field are DHCPv6 options. A key option is the Relay Message option. This option provides an encapsulation of the messages being exchanged between the client and the server.

IPv6 does not have broadcast addresses. Because of this, the use of the limited broadcast address for some DHCPv4 messages has been replaced with the use of the All_DHCP_Relay_Agents_and_Servers address of FF02::1:2 for DHCPv6. A DHCPv6 client attempting to discover the location of the DHCPv6 server on the network sends a Solicit message from its link-local address to FF02::1:2. If there is a DHCPv6 server on the client's subnet, it receives the Solicit message and sends an appropriate reply. If the client and server are on different subnets, a DHCPv6 relay agent on the client's subnet receiving the Solicit message will forward it to a DHCPv6 server.

DHCP Availability and Fault Tolerance for IPv4 and IPv6

As part of planning, you must consider how many DHCP servers should be made available on the network. In most cases, you'll want to configure at least two DHCP servers. If they are configured properly, having multiple DHCP servers increases reliability and allows for fault tolerance.

In a large enterprise, a server cluster can be your primary technique for ensuring DHCP availability and providing for fault tolerance. Here, if a DHCP server fails, the DHCP Server service can be failed over to another server in the cluster, allowing for seamless transition of DHCP services.

Although you can configure the DHCP Server service for failover on a cluster, much simpler and less expensive fault-tolerance implementations are available, and these implementations work with large networks as well as small and medium networks. The implementations include the following:

- 50/50 failover approach
- 80/20 failover approach
- 100/100 failover approach

50/50 Failover

By configuring the 50/50 failover approach, you use two DHCP servers to make an equal amount of IP addresses available to clients for leasing. Here, each DHCP server is configured with an identical scope range but with different exclusions within that range. The first server gets the first half of the scope's IP address range and excludes the second half. The second server gets the second half of the scope's IP address range and excludes the first half.

To see how this would be implemented, consider the following example. The organization has two DHCP servers configured as follows:

- Server A's primary scope is configured to use the IPv4 address range 192.168.10.1 to 192.168.10.254 and has an exclusion range of 192.168.10.125 to 192.168.10.254.

- Server B's primary scope is configured to use the IPv4 address range 192.168.10.1 to 192.168.10.254 and has an exclusion range of 192.168.10.1 to 192.168.10.124.

Here, 254 IP addresses are available, which could be used to service 200 or more clients. When a client starts up on the network, both DHCP servers respond. The client accepts the first IP address offered, which could be on either Server A or Server B and which is often the server that is closest to the client. Because both servers are configured to use the same IP address range, both servers can service clients on that subnet. If one of the servers fails, a client using an IP address in the excluded range of the remaining server would be allowed to obtain a new lease. Why? The DHCP server is on the same subnet and its scope is configured for IP addresses in this range. It sees the exclusion and knows that IP addresses in this range cannot be assigned, but it can assign the client an IP address from the nonexcluded range. Thus, you achieve basic fault tolerance and availability.

Although this approach is designed to provide some redundancy and fault tolerance, it is possible that one of the servers would assign more IP addresses than the other. This could lead to a situation in which one of the servers doesn't have any available IP addresses, and if it is the other server that fails, no IP addresses would be available to clients seeking new leases and they would be configured to use automatic private IP addressing.

80/20 Failover

By configuring the 80/20 failover approach, you use two DHCP servers to make a disproportionate amount of IP addresses available to clients for leasing. Here, you have a primary DHCP server that is configured with 80 percent of the available IP addresses and a backup DHCP server that is configured with 20 percent of the available IP addresses. This situation is ideal when the DHCP servers are separated from each other, such as when the primary DHCP server is on the primary subnet and the backup DHCP server is on a smaller remote subnet.

To see how this would be implemented, consider the following example. The organization has two DHCP servers, as follows:

- Server A's primary scope is configured to use the IPv4 address range 192.168.10.1 to 192.168.10.254 and has an exclusion range of 192.168.10.203 to 192.168.10.254.

- Server B's primary scope is configured to use the IPv4 address range 192.168.10.1 to 192.168.10.254 and has an exclusion range of 192.168.10.1 to 192.168.10.202.

Here, 254 IP addresses are again available, which could be used to service 200 or more clients—the bulk of which are located on the primary subnet. You are using the remote DHCP server on a smaller subnet as a backup. If the primary server were to go down, the backup could respond to client requests and handle their leases. When the primary came back online, it would handle the majority of client leases because it is located on the primary subnet closer to the bulk of the client computers. Again, you achieve basic fault tolerance and availability.

Although this approach is designed to provide some redundancy and fault tolerance, it is possible that the primary would be offline too long and the backup DHCP server would run out of available IP addresses. If this were to happen, no IP addresses would be available to clients seeking new leases, and they would be configured to use APIPA.

100/100 Failover

By configuring the 100/100 failover approach, you make twice as many IP addresses available as are needed. Thus, if you must provide DHCP services for 200 clients, you make at least 400 IP addresses available to those clients. As with 50/50 failover, each DHCP server is configured with an identical scope range but with different exclusions within that range. The first server gets the first half of the scope's IP address range and excludes the second half. The second server gets the second half of the scope's IP address range and excludes the first half.

To make twice as many IP addresses available as are needed, you must think carefully about the IP address class you use and would most likely want to use a Class A or Class B network. With this in mind, the organization's two DHCP servers might be configured as follows:

- Server A's primary scope is configured to use the IPv4 address range 10.0.1.1 to 10.0.10.254 and has an exclusion range of 10.0.6.1 to 10.0.10.254. You also must block the potential broadcast addresses in the nonexcluded range, so you also exclude 10.0.1.255, 10.0.2.255, 10.0.3.255, 10.0.4.255, and 10.0.5.255.

- Server B's primary scope is configured to use the IPv4 address range 10.0.1.1 to 10.0.10.254 and has an exclusion range of 10.0.1.1 to 10.0.5.254. You also must block the potential broadcast addresses in the nonexcluded range, so you also exclude 10.0.6.255, 10.0.7.255, 10.0.8.255, 10.0.9.255, and 10.0.10.255.

Here, over 2,500 IP addresses are available, which is more than two times what is needed to service the network's 1,000 clients. When a client starts up on the network, both DHCP servers respond. The client accepts the first IP address offered, which could be on either Server A or Server B and which is often the server that is closest to the client. Because both servers are configured to use the same IP address range, both servers can service clients on that subnet. If one of the servers fails, a client using an IP address in the excluded range of the remaining server would be allowed to obtain a new lease.

Because more than two times as many IP addresses are available, every client on the network can obtain a lease even if one of the DHCP servers goes offline. Not only does this approach offer availability and fault tolerance, it gives you flexibility. You are able to take one of the DHCP servers offline and perform maintenance or upgrades without worrying about running out of available IP addresses.

Chapter 22

Setting Up DHCP Servers

The approach you use to set up DHCP servers depends on many factors, including the number of clients on the network, the network configuration, and the Windows domain implementation you are using. From a physical server perspective, the DHCP Server service doesn't use a lot of system resources and can run on just about any system configured with Windows Server 2008. The DHCP Server service is in fact often installed as an additional service on an existing infrastructure server or on an older server that isn't robust enough to offer other types of services. Either approach is fine as long as you remember the security precaution discussed previously about not installing DHCP on a domain controller if possible. Personally, however, I prefer to install the DHCP Server service on hardware that I know and trust. Rather than installing it on an older system that might fail, I install it on either a workstation-class system running Windows Server 2008 or an existing infrastructure server that can handle the additional load.

Speaking of server load, a single DHCP server can handle about 10,000 clients and about 1,000 scopes. This is, of course, if the system is a dedicated DHCP server with adequate processing power and memory. Because DHCP is so important for client startup and network access, I don't trust the service to a single server, and you shouldn't either. In most cases, you'll want to have at least two DHCP servers on the network. If you have multiple subnets, you might want two DHCP servers per subnet. However, configuring routers to forward DHCP broadcasts or having DHCP relay agents reduces the need for additional servers.

Many organizations have standby DHCP servers available as well. A standby DHCP server is a server that has the DHCP Server service fully configured but has its scopes deactivated. Then, if a primary DHCP server fails and can't be recovered immediately, the scopes can be activated to service clients on the network as necessary.

After you select the server hardware, you should plan out the IP address ranges and exclusions you want to use. "Planning DHCPv4 and DHCPv6 Implementations" on page 689 should have given you some good ideas on how to configure IP address ranges and exclusions for availability and fault tolerance. At the implementation stage, don't forget about IP addresses that might have been or will be assigned to computers using static IP addresses. You should either specifically exclude these IP address ranges or simply not include them in the scopes you configure.

The way you set up DHCP services depends on whether the network in which the DHCP server will be placed is using Active Directory domains or workgroups. With Active Directory domains, you set up DHCP services by completing the following steps:

1. Installing the DHCP Server service

2. Authorizing the DHCP server in Active Directory

3. Configuring the DHCP server with the appropriate scopes, exclusions, reservations, and options

4. Activating the DHCP server's scopes

With workgroups, you don't need to authorize the DHCP server in Active Directory. This means the steps for setting up DHCP services look like this:

1. Installing the DHCP Server service

2. Configuring the DHCP server with the appropriate scopes, exclusions, reservations, and options

3. Activating the DHCP server's scopes

The sections that follow examine the related procedures in detail.

Installing the DHCP Server Service

You install the DHCP Server service as a server role. To install the DHCP Server service using the Add Roles Wizard, follow these steps:

1. DHCP servers should be assigned a static IPv4 and IPv6 address on each subnet they will service and to which they are connected. Ensure that the server has static IPv4 and IPv6 addresses.

2. In Server Manager, select the Roles node in the left pane and then click Add Roles. This starts the Add Roles Wizard. If the wizard displays the Before You Begin page, read the welcome message and then click Next.

3. On the Select Server Roles page, select DHCP Server and then click Next twice.

4. On the Select Network Bindings page, you'll see a list of the network connections that have a static IPv4 address. As necessary, select the network connections that the server will use for servicing DHCPv4 clients and then click Next.

5. On the Specify IPv4 DNS Server Settings page, shown in Figure 22-3, enter the default DNS settings that the server will give to DHCPv4 clients for automatic DNS configuration.

6. In the Parent Domain text box, enter the DNS name of the parent domain, such as cpandl.com. In the Preferred DNS Server IPv4 Address and Alternate DNS Server IPv4 Address text boxes, enter the IPv4 address of the preferred and alternate DNS servers, respectively. Click each Validate button in turn to ensure you entered the right DNS address. Click Next to continue.

7. On the Specify IPv4 WINS Server Settings page, use the options provided to specify whether applications on the network require Windows Internet Naming Service (WINS). If WINS is required, you'll need to enter the IP address of the preferred and alternate WINS servers in the Preferred WINS Server IPv4 Address and Alternate WINS Server IPv4 Address text boxes, respectively. Click Next to continue.

8. On the Add Or Edit Scopes page, you can use the options provided to create the initial scopes for the DHCP server. If you want to create a scope for the DHCP server, click Add and then follow the steps outlined in "Creating and Configuring Scopes" on page 701. Otherwise, click Next and create the necessary DHCP scope(s) later.

Chapter 22

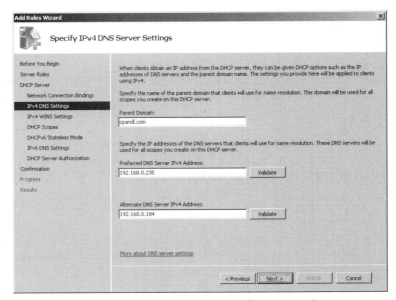

Figure 22-3 Configure the default DNS settings for DHCPv4 clients.

9. On the Configure DHCPv6 Stateless Mode page, shown in Figure 22-4, use the options provided to specify whether DHCPv6 stateless mode should be enabled or disabled. If you want DHCPv6 clients to obtain their IPv6 address and configuration settings from DHCPv6, disable stateless mode. Otherwise, enable stateless mode so clients only obtain configuration settings through DHCPv6. Click Next to continue.

10. If you enable stateless mode, configure the IPv6 DNS settings on the Specify IPv6 DNS Server Settings page and then click Next. You'll need to enter the parent domain to use as well as the preferred and alternate DNS servers to use for IPv6.

11. On the Authorize DHCP Server page, you can specify the credentials to use to authorize the DHCP server in Active Directory by doing one of the following:

   ○ Your current user name is shown in the User Name text box. If you have administrator privileges in the domain of which the DHCP server is a member and want to use your current credentials, click Next to attempt to authorize the server using these credentials.

   ○ If you want to use alternate credentials or if you were unable to authorize the server using your current credentials, select Use Alternate Credentials and then click Specify. In the Windows Security dialog box, enter the user name and password for the authorized account and then click OK. Click Next to continue.

   ○ If you want to authorize the DHCP server later, select the Skip Authorization... option and then click Next. However, keep in mind that only authorized DHCP servers can provide dynamic IP addresses to clients.

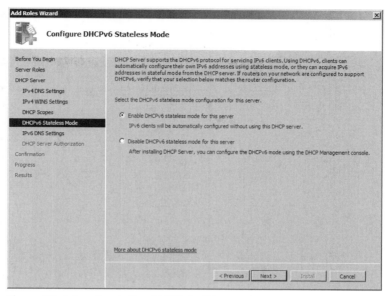

Figure 22-4 Specify whether DHCPv6 will be used.

12. Click Install. The wizard installs DHCP and begins configuring the server. To use the server, you must authorize the server in the domain as described in "Authorizing DHCP Servers in Active Directory" on page 701. You must create and activate any DHCP scopes that the server will use, as discussed in "Creating and Configuring Scopes" on page 701.

After you install the DHCP Server service, the DHCP console is available on the Administrative Tools menu. Start the console by clicking Start, Administrative Tools, DHCP. Then select the DHCP server you are working with to see its status. If you haven't yet created a scope, the details pane will appear, as shown in Figure 22-5. This tells you to create a scope so that the clients can get IP addresses dynamically assigned by this server.

You don't have to complete the rest of the configuration at the server. You can remotely manage and configure DHCP. Simply start the DHCP console on your workstation, right-click the DHCP node in the left pane, and select Add Server. In the Add Server dialog box, select This Server, type the name or IP address of the DHCP server, and then click OK.

Chapter 22

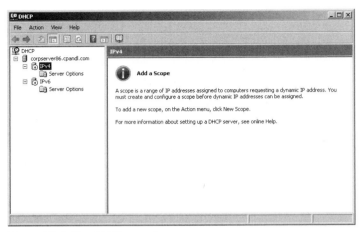

Figure 22-5 The DHCP console.

The command-line counterpart to the DHCP console is the **Netsh DHCP** command. From the command prompt on a computer running Windows Server 2008 you can use Netsh DHCP to perform all the tasks available in the DHCP console as well as to perform some additional tasks that can't be performed in the DHCP console. To start Netsh DHCP and access a particular DHCP server, follow these steps:

1. Start a command prompt, and then type **netsh** to start Netsh. The command prompt changes to netsh>.

2. Access the DHCP context within Netsh by typing **dhcp**. The command prompt changes to netsh dhcp>.

3. Type **server** followed by the Universal Naming Convention (UNC) name or IP address of the DHCP server, such as **\\corpsvr02** or **\\192.168.1.50**. If the DHCP server is in a different domain from your logon domain, you should type the fully qualified domain name (FQDN) of the server, such as **\\corpsvr02.cpandl.com**.

4. The command prompt changes to netsh dhcp server>. You can now work with the selected server. If you later want to work with a different server, you can do this without having to start over. Simply type **server** followed by the UNC name or IP address of that server.

> **Note**
>
> Technically, you don't need to type **** when you specify an IP address. You must, however, type **** when you specify a server's name or FQDN. Because of this discrepancy, you might want to use \\ all the time so that you remember that it is needed.

Authorizing DHCP Servers in Active Directory

Before you can use a DHCP server in an Active Directory domain, you must authorize the server in Active Directory. In the DHCP console, any unauthorized DHCP server to which you connect will have an icon showing a red down arrow. Authorized DHCP servers have an icon showing a green up arrow.

With Windows Server 2008, new DHCP servers are authorized automatically as part of the initial configuration process. In the DHCP console, you can authorize a DHCP server by right-clicking the server entry in the console tree and selecting Authorize. To remove the authorization later, right-click the server entry in the console tree and select Unauthorize.

In Netsh, you can authorize a server by typing the following command:

```
netsh dhcp server ServerID initiate auth
```

where *ServerID* is the UNC name or IP address of the DHCP server on which you want to create the scope, such as \\CORPSVR03 or \\192.168.1.1. Keep in mind that if you are already at the netsh dhcp server prompt, you only need to type **initiate auth**.

> **Note**
>
> If you install DHCP on a server acting as a domain controller, the DHCP server is automatically authorized and you cannot remove the authorization. Also note that if you install DHCP in a workgroup, you don't need to authorize the server for it to work. However, if you later install Active Directory, DHCP servers will detect this automatically and will stop running until they are authorized.

Creating and Configuring Scopes

After you install the DHCP Server service, the next thing you must do is create the scopes that will provide the range of IP addresses and TCP/IP options for clients. With IPv4, the DHCP Server service supports three types of scopes:

- **Normal scope** A normal scope is used to assign IPv4 address pools for Class A, B, and C networks. Normal scopes have an IP address range assignment that includes the subnet mask and can also have exclusions and reservations as well as TCP/IP options that are specific to the scope. When you create normal scopes, each scope must be in its own subnet. This means if you add a normal scope, it must be on a different subnet than any of the existing scopes configured on the server.

- **Multicast scope** A multicast scope is used to assign IP address pools for IPv4 Class D networks. Multicast scopes are created in the same way as normal scopes except that they do not have an associated subnet mask, reservations, or related TCP/IP options. This means there is no specific subnet association for multicast scopes. Instead of a subnet mask, you assign the scope a Time to Live (TTL) value that specifies the maximum number of routers the messages sent to computers over multicast can go through. The default TTL is 32. Additionally, because multicast IP addresses are used for destination addresses only, they have longer lease duration than unicast IP addresses, typically, from 30 to 60 days.

- **Superscope** A superscope is a container for IPv4 scopes. If you configure multiple scopes on a server and want to be able to activate or deactivate them as a unit or view the usage statistics for all the scopes at once, you can use a superscope to do this. Create the superscope and then add to it the scopes you want to manage as a group.

Before you create a normal scope, you should plan out the IP address range you want to use as well as any necessary exclusions and reservations. You must know the IP address of the default gateway and any DNS or WINS servers that should be used. You must also configure DHCPv4 and DHCPv6 relays to relay DHCPv4 and DHCPv6 broadcast requests between network segments.

> **Note**
>
> You can configure relay agents with the Routing and Remote Access Service (RRAS) and the DHCP Relay Agent Service. You can configure some routers as relay agents as well.

Creating Normal Scopes for IPv4 Addresses

In the DHCP console, you can create a normal scope for IPv4 addresses by expanding the node for the server you want to work with, and selecting and then right-clicking IPv4. From the shortcut menu, select New Scope.

In the New Scope Wizard, click Next to display the Scope Name page, as shown in Figure 22-6. Type a descriptive name for the scope and a description that will be used as a comment.

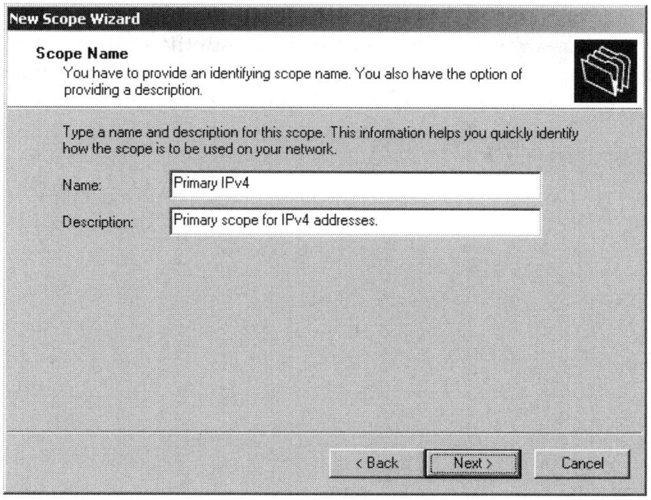

Figure 22-6 Set the scope name and description.

Click Next to display the IP Address Range page, as shown in Figure 22-7. Enter the start and end IP addresses to use for the scope in the Start IP Address and End IP Address boxes. Be sure to specify the first and last usable IP address only, which means you shouldn't include the *x.x.x*.0 and *x.x.x*.255 addresses. When you enter an IP address range, the bit length and subnet mask are filled in automatically for you. Change the default values if you use subnets.

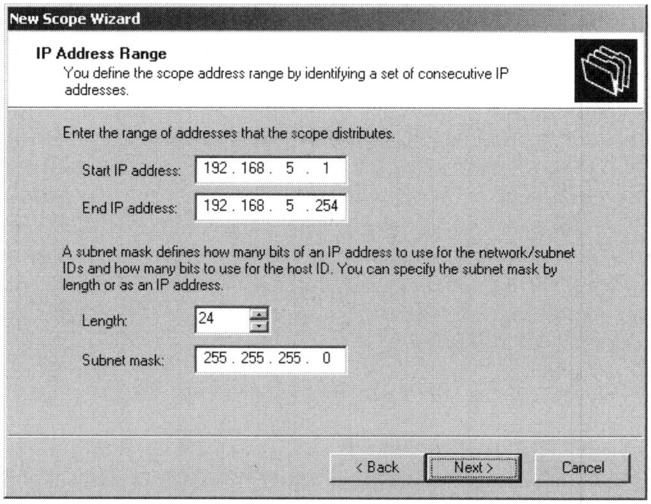

Figure 22-7 Set the IP address range and subnet information.

Click Next. If the IP address range you entered is on multiple subnets, you'll see a Create Superscope page as shown in Figure 22-8 instead of the Add Exclusions page. This page gives you the opportunity to create a superscope that contains separate scopes for each subnet. Click Yes to continue to the Lease Duration page.

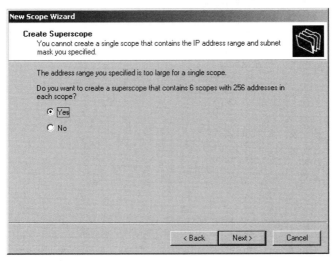

Figure 22-8 The New Scope Wizard knows when you cross subnet boundaries and will let you create a superscope with multiple scopes automatically.

INSIDE OUT   Multiple subnets on the same physical network

If you're wondering how it would work to have multiple subnets on the same network segment, it should work just fine and it generally won't matter to which subnet a client connects as long as you've set up DHCP to give clients the appropriate TCP/IP options. The physical network provides the boundaries for these subnets unless you've configured routers or DHCP relay agents to forward DHCP broadcasts. Incidentally, if you want to be sure that clients use a specific subnet, there is a way to do that using reservations. However, you wouldn't want to create reservations for a lot of clients. Instead, you might want to create a user- or vendor-defined class and allow clients to connect to any subnet to get their class-specific TCP/IP options.

If all the IP addresses you entered are on the same subnet, you'll have the opportunity to specify an exclusion range, as shown in Figure 22-9. Use the Start IP Address and End IP Address boxes to define IP address ranges that are to be excluded from the scope, such as servers that have static IP addresses assigned to them. After you enter the Start IP Address and End IP Address for the exclusion range, click Add. You can then add additional exclusion ranges as necessary.

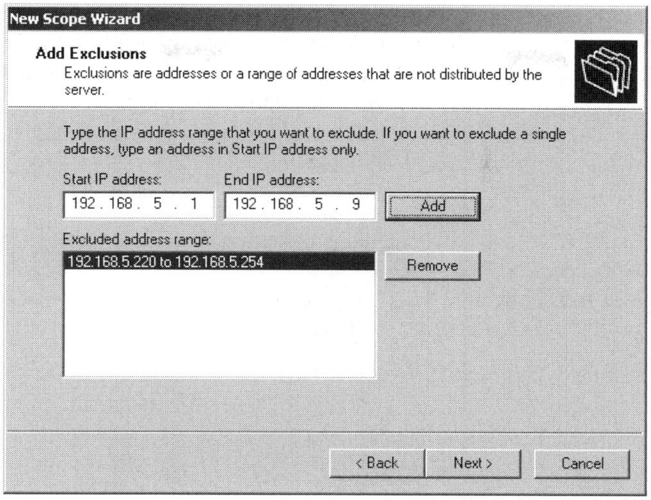

Figure 22-9 Set exclusion ranges.

Click Next to display the Lease Duration page, as shown in Figure 22-10. Specify the duration of leases for the scope. The default lease duration is 8 days, but don't accept the default without first giving some thought to how leases will be used. A lease duration that's too long or too short can reduce the effectiveness of DHCP. If a lease is too long, you could run out of IP addresses because the DHCP server is holding IP addresses for computers that are no longer on the network, such as when there are a lot of mobile users who connect and disconnect their portable computers. If a lease is too short, this could generate a lot of unnecessary broadcast traffic on the network as clients attempt to renew leases.

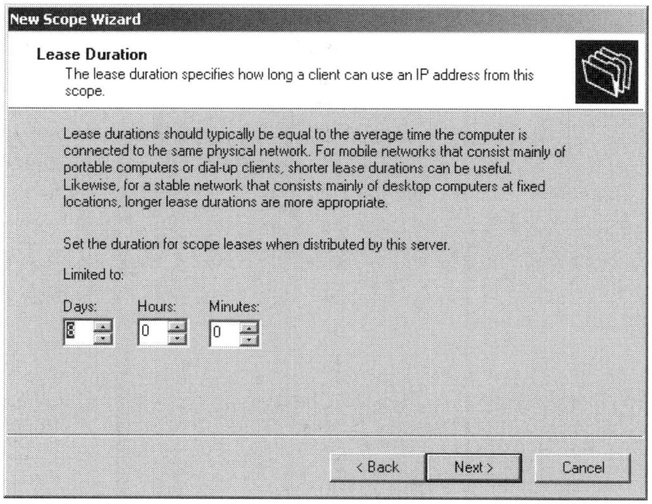

Figure 22-10 Set the lease duration.

By default, clients try to renew a lease when 50 percent of the lease time has passed and then again when 87.5 percent of the lease time has passed if the first attempt fails. With this in mind, you generally want to find a balance in the lease time that serves the type of clients on the subnet. If there are only fixed desktops and servers, you could use a longer lease duration of 14 to 21 days. If there are only mobile users with portable computers, you could shorten the lease duration to 2 to 3 days. If there's a mix of fixed systems and mobile systems, a lease duration of 5 to 7 days might be more appropriate.

Click Next to display the Configure DHCP Options page. If you want to set TCP/IP options now, select Yes, and then click Next to continue to the Router (Default Gateway) page, as shown in Figure 22-11. If you don't want to set TCP/IP options now, select No, click Next, and then click Finish to create the scope and exit the wizard.

On the Router (Default Gateway) page, in the IP Address box enter the IP address of the primary default gateway, and then click Add. You can repeat this process to specify other default gateways. Keep in mind that clients try to use gateways in the order they are listed, and you can use the Up and Down buttons to change the order of the gateways, as necessary.

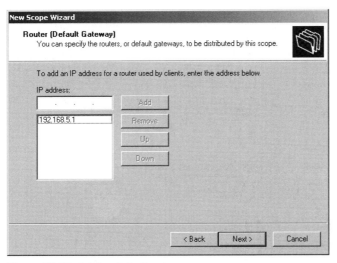

Figure 22-11 Set the default gateways.

Click Next to display the Domain Name And DNS Servers page, as shown in Figure 22-12. In the Parent Domain box, type the name of the parent domain to use for DNS resolution of computer names that aren't fully qualified. In the IP Address box, type the IP address of the primary DNS server, and then click Add. You can repeat this process to specify the IP addresses of additional DNS servers. As with gateways, the order of the entries determines which DNS server is used first, and you can change the order as necessary using the Up and Down buttons.

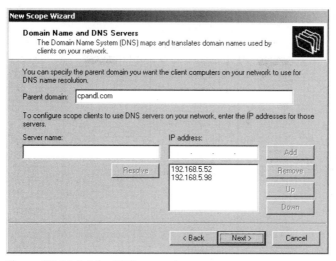

Figure 22-12 Set the DNS servers to use.

Click Next to display the WINS Servers page, as shown in Figure 22-13. In the IP Address box, type the IP address of the primary WINS server, and then click Add. You can repeat this process to specify additional WINS servers. As with gateways, the order of the entries determines which WINS server is used first, and you can change the order as necessary using the Up and Down buttons.

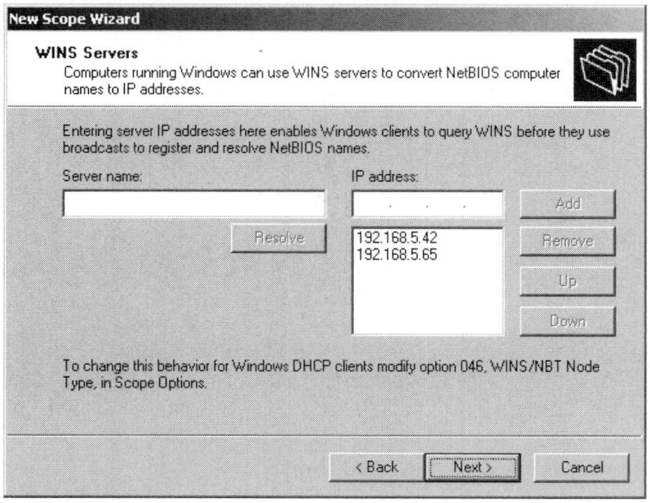

Figure 22-13 Set the WINS servers to use.

Click Next to display the Activate Scope page. If you want to activate the scope, select Yes, I Want To Activate This Scope Now. Otherwise, select No, I Will Activate This Scope Later. Click Next, and then click Finish to create the scope and exit the wizard.

Chapter 22

Creating Normal Scopes for IPv6 Addresses

Normal scopes, multicast scopes, and superscopes are all available with IPv4 addresses. With IPv6 addresses, only normal scopes are available. Your IPv6 scopes will use either link-local unicast addresses beginning with FE80 or multicast IPv6 addresses beginning with FF00.

You create normal scopes for IPv6 addresses using the New Scope Wizard. When you are configuring DHCP for IPv6 addresses, you must enter the network ID and a preference value. Typically, the first 64-bits of an IPv6 address identify the network and a 64-bit value is what the New Scope Wizard expects you to enter. The preference value sets the priority of the scope relative to other scopes. The scope with the lowest preference value will be used first. The scope with the second lowest preference will be used second, and so on.

In the DHCP console, you create a normal scope for IPv6 addresses by expanding the node for the server you want to work with, and selecting and then right-clicking IPv6. From the shortcut menu, select New Scope.

In the New Scope Wizard, click Next to display the Scope Name page. Type a name and description for the scope that will be used as a comment. Click Next to display the Scope Prefix page, shown in Figure 22-14. Enter the 64-bit network prefix and then set a preference value. Click Next.

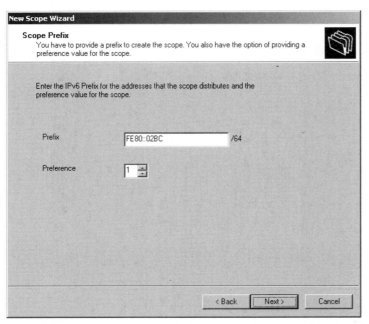

Figure 22-14 In the New Scope Wizard, enter the network prefix and preference value.

On the Add Exclusions page, shown in Figure 22-15, use the Start IPv6 Address and End IPv6 Address fields to define IPv6 address ranges that are to be excluded from the scope. You can exclude address as follows:

- To define an exclusion range, type a start address and an end address in the exclusion range's Start IPv6 Address and End IPv6 Address fields, respectively, and then click Add.

- To exclude a single IPv6 address, use that address as the start IPv6 address and then click Add.

- To track which address ranges are excluded, use the Excluded Address Range list box.

- To delete an exclusion range, select the range in the Excluded Address Range list box and click Remove.

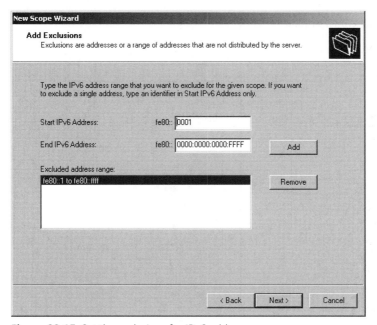

Figure 22-15 Set the exclusions for IPv6 addresses

Click Next to display the Scope Lease page, shown in Figure 22-16. Dynamic IPv6 addresses can be temporary or nontemporary. A nontemporary address is similar to a reservation. Specify the duration of leases for temporary and nontemporary addresses using the Day(s), Hour(s), and Minutes fields under Preferred Lifetime and Valid Life-time. The preferred lifetime is the preferred amount of time the lease should be valid. The valid lifetime is the maximum amount of time the lease is valid. Click Next.

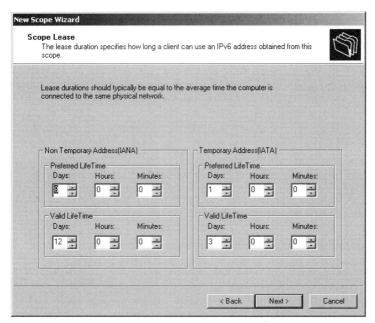

Figure 22-16 Specify the duration of temporary and nontemporary leases.

> **Note**
>
> Take a few minutes to plan the lease lifetime you want to use. A lease lifetime that's set too long can reduce the effectiveness of DHCP and might eventually cause you to run out of available IP addresses, especially on networks with mobile users or other types of computers that aren't fixed members of the network. A good lease lifetime for temporary leases is from one to three days. A good lease duration for nontemporary leases is from 8 to 30 days.

If you want to activate the scope, select Yes under Activate Scope Now and then click Finish. Otherwise, select No under Activate Scope Now and then click Finish.

Creating Normal Scopes Using Netsh

Using Netsh, you can create an IPv4 scope by typing the following command at an elevated command prompt:

```
netsh dhcp server ServerID add scope NetworkID SubnetMask ScopeName
```

where the following is true:

- *ServerID* is the UNC name or IP address of the DHCP server on which you want to create the scope, such as \\CORPSVR03 or \\192.168.1.1.

- *NetworkID* is the network ID of the scope, such as 192.168.1.0.

- *SubnetMask* is the subnet mask of the scope, such as 255.255.255.0.

- *ScopeName* is the name of the scope, such as Primary IPv4.

Using Netsh, you can create an IPv6 scope by typing the following command:

```
netsh dhcp server ServerID add scope NetworkPrefix PrefValue ScopeName
```

where the following is true:

- *ServerID* is the UNC name or IP address of the DHCP server on which you want to create the scope, such as \\CORPSVR03 or \\192.168.1.1.

- *NetworkPrefix* is the network prefix of the scope, such as FE80:0:0:0.

- *PrefValue* is the preference value of the scope, such as 1.

- *ScopeName* is the name of the scope, such as Primary IPv6.

After you create the scope, you must use separate commands to set the scope's IP address, exclusions, reservations/lease-permanence, and options. You can add an IP range to the scope using the **add iprange** command for the NETSH DHCP SERVER SCOPE context. Type the following:

```
netsh dhcp server ServerID scope NetworkID add iprange StartIP EndIP
```

where

- *ServerID* is the UNC name or IP address of the DHCP server on which you want to create the scope, such as \\CORPSVR03 or \\192.168.1.1.

- *NetworkID* is the network ID of the scope, such as 192.168.1.0.

- *StartIP* is the first IP address in the range, such as 192.168.1.1.

- *EndIP* is the last IP address in the range, such as 192.168.1.254.

Other commands available when you are working with the NETSH DHCP SERVER SCOPE context include the following:

- **add excluderange** *StartIP EndIP*—adds a range of excluded IP addresses to the scope.

- **delete iprange** *StartIP EndIP*—deletes an IP address range from the scope.

- **delete excluderange** *StartIP EndIP*—deletes an exclusion range from the scope.

- **show iprange**—shows currently configured IP address ranges for the scope.

- **show excluderange**—shows currently configured exclusion ranges for the scope.

- **show clients**—lists clients using the scope.

- **show state**—shows the state of the scope as active or inactive.

Chapter 22

Using Exclusions

To exclude IPv4 or IPv6 addresses from a scope, you can define an exclusion range. In the DHCP console, any existing exclusions for a scope can be displayed by expanding the scope and selecting Address Pool, as shown in Figure 22-17. To list exclusions at the command line, type the following:

```
netsh dhcp server ServerID scope NetworkID show excluderange
```

where *ServerID* is the UNC name or IP address of the DHCP server on which you want to create the scope, such as \\CORPSVR03 or \\192.168.1.1, and *NetworkID* is the network ID of the scope, such as 192.168.1.0.

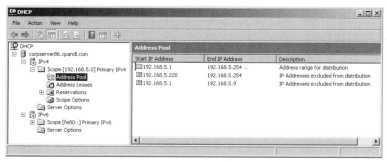

Figure 22-17 Exclusions are listed under the Address Pool node.

In the DHCP console, you can define an exclusion range by right-clicking Address Pool within the scope you want to work with and choosing New Exclusion Range. In the Add Exclusion dialog box, enter a start address and an end address for the exclusion range, as shown in Figure 22-18, and then click Add. Keep in mind that the range excluded must be a subset of the scope's range and must not currently be in use by DHCP clients.

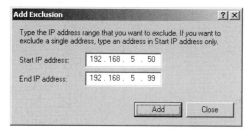

Figure 22-18 Set the exclusion range.

Using Netsh, you can add an exclusion range in much the same way. Type the following:

```
netsh dhcp server ServerID scope NetworkID add excluderange StartIP EndIP
```

where the following is true:

- *ServerID* is the UNC name or IP address of the DHCP server on which you want to create the scope, such as \\CORPSVR03 or \\192.168.1.1.

- *NetworkID* is the network ID of the scope, such as 192.168.1.0.

- *StartIP* is the first IP address in the exclusion range, such as 192.168.1.200.

- *EndIP* is the last IP address in the exclusion range, such as 192.168.1.219.

Using Reservations

Reservations provide a way to assign a permanent lease on an IPv4 address to a client. In this way, the client has a fixed IP address, but you retain flexibility in that you could change the IPv4 address at any time if necessary through DHCP rather than having to do so on the client. In the DHCP console, any existing reservations for a scope can be displayed by expanding the scope and selecting Reservations. As shown in Figure 22-19, existing reservations are shown according to the reservation name and IP address reserved. You can right-click a reservation and select Properties to see the associated MAC address. To list reservations by IPv4 address and MAC address at the command line, type the following:

```
netsh dhcp server ServerID scope NetworkID show reservedip
```

where *ServerID* is the UNC name or IP address of the DHCP server on which you want to create the scope, such as \\CORPSVR03 or \\192.168.1.1, and *NetworkID* is the network ID of the scope, such as 192.168.1.0.

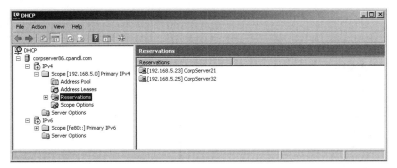

Figure 22-19 Current reservations are listed by reservation name and IP address.

To create a reservation, you need to know the MAC or device unique identifier (DUID) address of the computer that will hold the IP address. MAC and DUID addresses are specific to an individual network interface configured on the client. You can view the MAC address of an interface by typing **ipconfig /all** at the command prompt. The output will list the MAC address as the Physical Address of the network interface, as it does under Physical Address in the following example.

```
Windows IP Configuration
Host Name . . . . . . . . . . . . : corpserver84
Primary Dns Suffix . . . . . . . :
Node Type . . . . . . . . . . . : Hybrid
IP Routing Enabled. . . . . . . . : No
WINS Proxy Enabled. . . . . . . . : No
DNS Suffix Search List. . . . . . : cpandl.com.

Ethernet adapter Local Area Connection:
Connection-specific DNS Suffix . : cpandl.com.
Description . . . . . . . . . . . : Intel(R) PRO/1000 PM Network Connection
Physical Address. . . . . . . . . : 23-24-AE-67-B4-E8
DHCP Enabled. . . . . . . . . . . : Yes
Autoconfiguration Enabled . . . . : Yes
IPv4 Address. . . . . . . . . . . : 192.168.15.124(Preferred)
Subnet Mask . . . . . . . . . . . : 255.255.255.0
Lease Obtained. . . . . . . . . . : Sunday, June 15, 2008 9:41:46 AM
Lease Expires . . . . . . . . . . : Sunday, June 22, 2008 2:02:44 PM
Default Gateway . . . . . . . . . : 192.168.15.1
DHCP Server . . . . . . . . . . . : 192.168.15.1
DNS Servers . . . . . . . . . . . : 192.168.15.1
NetBIOS over Tcpip. . . . . . . . : Enabled

Tunnel adapter Local Area Connection* 6:
Connection-specific DNS Suffix . :
Description . . . . . . . . . . . : Teredo Tunneling Pseudo-Interface
Physical Address. . . . . . . . . : 23-24-AE-67-B4-E8
DHCP Enabled. . . . . . . . . . . : No
Autoconfiguration Enabled . . . . : Yes
IPv6 Address. . . . . . . . . . . : fe80::fd1b:2778:f7e1:67d2%10(Preferred)
Link-local IPv6 Address . . . . . : fe80::2beb:f99:fe57:f87b%10(Preferred)
Default Gateway . . . . . . . . . : ::
NetBIOS over Tcpip. . . . . . . . : Disabled
```

> **Note**
> You create IPv6 reservations in much the same way as you create IPv4 reservations. When you create the reservation, you enter the DUID and the IAID for the DHCPv6 client instead of a MAC address.

In the DHCP console, you can reserve a DHCPv4 address for a client as follows:

1. After you expand the scope you want to work with, right-click the Reservations folder and choose New Reservation. This opens the New Reservation dialog box, as shown in Figure 22-20.

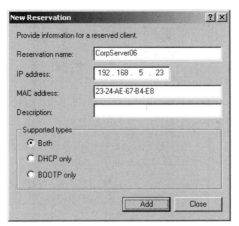

Figure 22-20 Create a reservation for an IP address using the MAC address of the client.

2. In the Reservation Name box, type a descriptive name for the reservation. This doesn't have to be the name of the computer to which the reservation belongs, but that does help simplify administration.

3. In the IP Address box, enter the IP address you want to reserve for the client. This IP address must be valid for the currently selected scope.

4. In the MAC Address text box, type the MAC address as previously obtained using the **ipconfig /all** command.

5. If desired, enter an optional comment in the Description box.

6. By default, the reservation is configured to accept both DHCP and BOOTP clients. Change the default only if you want to exclude a particular type of client. DHCP clients include computers running the standard version of the DHCP client as with most Windows operating systems. BOOTP clients are clients running other operating systems and could also include devices such as printers that can use dynamic IP addressing.

7. Click Add to create the address reservation.

In Netsh, you can create a reservation by typing the following command:

```
netsh dhcp server ServerID scope NetworkID add reservedip ReservedIP MacAddress
Name Comment
```

where the following is true:

- *ServerID* is the UNC name or IP address of the DHCP server on which you want to create the scope, such as \\CORPSVR03 or \\192.168.1.1.

- *NetworkID* is the network ID of the scope, such as 192.168.1.0.

- *ReservedIP* is the IP address you are reserving, such as 192.168.1.20.

- *MacAddress* is the MAC address of the client (excluding the dashes), such as 2324AE67B4E8.

- *Name* is the descriptive name of the reservation.

- *Comment* is the optional comment describing the reservation.

When you assign reservations, keep in mind that a client with an existing lease won't automatically use the reservation. If a client has a current lease, you must force the client to release that lease and then request a new one. If a client has an existing address and you want to force it to start using DHCP, you must force the client to stop using its current IP address and request a new IP address from DHCP.

To force a client to release an existing lease or drop its current IP address, log on to the client, and type **ipconfig /release** at the command prompt. Next, if the client isn't already configured to use DHCP, you must configure the client to use DHCP as discussed in "Configuring Dynamic IP Addresses and Alternate IP Addressing" on page 663.

To get a client to request a new IP address from DHCP, log on to the client, and type **ipconfig /renew** at the command prompt.

Activating Scopes

Scopes are available only when they are activated. If you want to make a scope available to clients, you must right-click it in the DHCP console and then select Activate. Activating a scope won't make clients switch to that scope. If you want to force clients to switch to a different scope or to use a different DHCP server, you can terminate the client leases in the DHCP console and then deactivate the scope the clients are currently using.

To terminate a lease, you expand the scope you want to work with in the DHCP console and then select Address Leases. You will then see a list of current leases and can terminate a lease by right-clicking it and selecting Delete. The next time the client goes to renew its lease, the DHCP server will tell the client the lease is no longer valid and that a new one must be obtained.

To prevent clients from reusing the original scope, you can deactivate that scope by right-clicking it in the DHCP console and then selecting Deactivate.

You can perform these same actions using Netsh. To terminate a lease, type the following command:

```
netsh dhcp server ServerID scope NetworkID delete lease IPAddress
```

where the following is true:

- *ServerID* is the UNC name or IP address of the DHCP server on which you want to create the scope, such as \\CORPSVR03 or \\192.168.1.1.

- *NetworkID* is the network ID of the scope, such as 192.168.1.0.

- *IPAddress* is the IP address for the lease you want to remove, such as 192.168.1.8.

To activate or deactivate a scope, type the following:

```
netsh dhcp server ServerID scope NetworkID state StateVal
```

where the following is true:

- *ServerID* is the UNC name or IP address of the DHCP server on which you want to create the scope, such as \\CORPSVR03 or \\192.168.1.1.

- *NetworkID* is the network ID of the scope, such as 192.168.1.0.

- *StateVal* is set to 0 to deactivate the scope and 1 to activate it. If you are using a switched network where multiple logical networks are hosted on a single physical network, use 2 to deactivate the scope and 3 to activate the scope.

Configuring TCP/IP Options

The messages clients and servers broadcast to each other allow you to set TCP/IP options that clients can obtain by default when they obtain a lease or can request if they need additional information. It is important to note, however, that the types of information you can add to DHCP messages is limited in several ways:

- DHCP messages are transmitted using User Datagram Protocol (UDP), and the entire DHCP message must fit into the UDP datagram. On Ethernet with 1500-byte datagrams, this leaves 1236 bytes for the body of the message (which contains the TCP/IP options).

- BOOTP messages have a fixed size of 300 bytes as set by the original BOOTP standard. Any clients using BOOTP are likely to have their TCP/IP options truncated.

- Although there are many options that you can set, clients understand only certain TCP/IP options. Thus, the set of options available to you is dependent upon the client's implementation of DHCP.

With that in mind, let's look at the levels at which options can be assigned and the options that Windows clients understand.

Levels of Options and Their Uses

Each individual TCP/IP option such as a default gateway is configured separately. There are different scope options for IPv4 and IPv6. DHCP administrators can manage options at five levels within the DHCP server configuration:

- **Predefined options** Allow DHCP administrators to specify the way in which options are used and to create new option types for use on a server. In the DHCP console, you can view and set predefined options by right-clicking the IPv4 or IPv6 node in the console tree and selecting Set Predefined Options.

- **Server options** Allow DHCP administrators to configure options that are assigned to all scopes created on the DHCP server. Think of server options as global options that would be assigned to all clients. Server options can be overridden by scope, class, and client-assigned options. In the DHCP console, you can view and set server options by expanding the entry for the server you want to work with, right-clicking Server Options, and then choosing Configure Options.

- **Scope options** Allow DHCP administrators to configure options that are assigned to all clients that use a particular scope. Scope options are assigned only to normal scopes and can be overridden by class and client-assigned options. In the DHCP console, you can view and set scope options by expanding the scope you want to work with, right-clicking Scope Options, and then choosing Configure Options.

- **Class options** Allow DHCP administrators to configure options that are assigned to all clients of a particular class. Client classes can be user-defined or vendor-defined. Two classes included with the DHCP Server service are Windows 98, which is used to assign specific options to clients running Windows 98, and Windows 2000, which is used to assign specific options to clients running Windows 2000 or later. Class options can be overridden by client-assigned options. You define new user and vendor classes by right-clicking the IPv4 or IPv6 entry and selecting either Define User Classes or Define Vendor Classes as appropriate. When defined, class options can be configured on the Advanced tab of the Server Options, Scope Options, and Reservation Options dialog boxes.

- **Reservation options** Allow administrators to set options for an individual client that uses a reservation. Also referred to as client-specific options. After you create a reservation for a client, you can configure reservation options by expanding the scope, expanding Reservations, right-clicking the reservation, and selecting Configure Options. Only TCP/IP options manually configured on a client can override client-assigned options.

Options Used by Windows Clients

RFC 3442 defines many TCP/IP options that you can set in DHCP messages. Although you can set all of these options on a DHCP server, the set of options available is dependent upon the client's implementation of DHCP.

Table 22-1 shows the options that can be configured by administrators and used by Windows computers running the DHCP Client service. Each option has an associated option code, which is used to identify it in a DHCP message, and a data entry, which contains the value setting of the option. These options are requested by clients to set their TCP/IP configuration.

Table 22-1 **Standard TCP/IP Options That Administrators Can Configure**

Option Name	Option Code	Description
Router	003	Sets a list of IP addresses for the default gateways that should be used by the client. IP addresses are listed in order of preference.
DNS Servers	006	Sets a list of IP addresses for the DNS servers that should be used by the client. IP addresses are listed in order of preference.
DNS Domain Name	015	Sets the DNS domain name that clients should use when resolving host names using DNS.
WINS/NBNS Servers	044	Sets a list of IP addresses for the WINS servers that should be used by the client. IP addresses are listed in order of preference.
WINS/NBT Node Type	046	Sets the method to use when resolving NetBIOS names. The acceptable values are: 0x1 for B-node (broadcast), 0x2 for P-node (peer-to-peer), 0x4 for M-node (mixed), and 0x8 for H-node (hybrid). See "NetBIOS Node Types" on page 824.
NetBIOS Scope ID	047	Sets the NetBIOS scope for the client.

Using User-Specific and Vendor-Specific TCP/IP Options

DHCP uses classes to determine which options are sent to clients. The user classes let you assign TCP/IP options according to the type of user the client represents on the network. The default user classes include the following:

- **Default User Class** An all-inclusive class that includes clients that don't fit into the other user classes, such as computers running Windows NT 4.0. Any computer running a version of the Windows operating system earlier than Windows 2000 is in this class.

- **Default BOOTP Class** Any computer running Windows 2000 or later has this user class if it is connected to the local network directly. This means Windows 2000, Windows XP, and Windows Server 2008 computers connected with a wired network interface have this class.

- **Default Routing And Remote Access Class** Any computer that connects to the network using RRAS has this class. Any settings applied to this class are used by dial-in and VPN users, which allows you to set different TCP/IP options for these users.

- **Default Network Access Protection Class** Any computer that connects to the network and is subject to Network Access Protection (NAP) policy has this class. Any settings applied to this class are used by restricted access clients, which allows you to set different TCP/IP options for these users.

Clients can be a member of multiple user classes, and you can view the user class memberships for each network interface by typing **ipconfig /showclassid *** at the command prompt. (The asterisk tells the command that you want to see all the network interfaces.) The output you'll see on a computer running Windows 2000 or later will be similar to the following:

```
Windows IP Configuration
DHCP Classes for Adapter "Local Area Connection":

    DHCP ClassID Name           :      Default Routing and Remote Access Class
    DHCP ClassID Description     :      User class for remote access clients

    DHCP ClassID Name           :      Default BOOTP Class
    DHCP ClassID Description     :      User class for BOOTP Clients
```

Here, the client is a member of the Default Routing And Remote Access Class and the Default BOOTP Class. The client doesn't, however, get its options from both classes. Rather, the class from which the client gets its options depends on its connection state. If the client is connected directly to the network, it uses the Default BOOTP Class. If the client is connected by Routing and Remote Access, it uses the Default Routing And Remote Access Class.

Vendor classes work a bit differently because they define the set of options available to and used by the various user classes. The default vendor class, DHCP Standard Options, is used to set the standard TCP/IP options, and the various user classes all have access to these options so that they can be implemented in a user-specific way. Additional vendor classes beyond the default define extensions or additional options that can be implemented in a user-specific way. This means that the vendor class defines the options and makes them available, while the user class settings determine which of these additional options (if any) are used by clients.

The default vendor classes that provide additional (add-on) options are as follows:

- **Microsoft Options**   Add-on options available to any client running any version of Windows

- **Microsoft Windows 98 Options**   Add-on options available to any client running Windows 98 or later

- **Microsoft Windows 2000 Options**   Add-on options available to any client running Windows 2000 or later

When it comes to these classes, a client applies the options from the most specific add-on vendor class. Thus, a Windows 98 client would apply the Microsoft Windows 98 Options vendor class, and a Windows 2000 or later client would apply the Microsoft Windows 2000 Options vendor class. Again, these options are in addition to the standard options provided through the DHCP Standard Options vendor class and can be implemented in a manner specific to a user class. This means you can have one set of add-on options for directly connected clients (Default BOOTP Class) and one set for remotely connected clients (Default Routing And Remote Access Class).

The add-on options that can be set for a client running Windows 2000 or later are listed in Table 22-2.

Table 22-2 Additional TCP/IP Options That Administrators Can Configure

Option Name	Option Code	Description
Microsoft Disable NetBIOS Option	001	Disables NetBIOS if selected as an option with a value of 0x1.
Microsoft Release DHCP Lease On Shutdown Option	002	Specifies that a client should release its DHCP lease on shutdown if selected as an option with a value of 0x1.
Microsoft Default Router Metric Base	003	Specifies that the default router metric base should be used if selected as an option with a value of 0x1.

Settings Options for All Clients

On the DHCP server, you can set TCP/IP options at several levels. You can set options for the following components:

- **All scopes on a server** In the DHCP console, expand the entry for the server and IP protocol you want to work with, right-click Server Options, and then choose Configure Options.

- **A specific scope** In the DHCP console, expand the scope you want to work with, right-click Scope Options, and then choose Configure Options.

- **A single reserved IP address** In the DHCP console, expand the scope, expand Reservations, right-click the reservation you want to work with, and select Configure Options.

Regardless of the level at which you are setting TCP/IP options, the dialog box displayed has the exact same set of choices as that shown in Figure 22-21. You can now select each standard TCP/IP option you want to use in turn, such as Router, DNS Servers, DNS Domain Name, WINS/NBNS Servers, and WINS/NBT Node Type, and configure the appropriate values. Click OK when you are finished.

Chapter 22

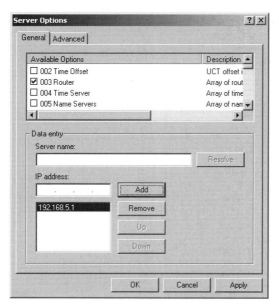

Figure 22-21 Set class-specific options using the General tab.

Settings Options for RRAS and NAP Clients

On the DHCP server, you can set TCP/IP options for RRAS and NAP clients at several levels. You can set options for the following components:

- **All scopes on a server** In the DHCP console, expand the entry for the server and IP protocol you want to work with, right-click Server Options, and then choose Configure Options.

- **A specific scope** In the DHCP console, expand the scope you want to work with, right-click Scope Options, and then choose Configure Options.

- **A single reserved IP address** In the DHCP console, expand the scope, expand Reservations, right-click the reservation you want to work with, and select Configure Options.

Regardless of the level at which you are setting TCP/IP options, the dialog box displayed has the exact same set of choices. You can now complete the following steps:

1. Click the Advanced tab, as shown in Figure 22-22. From the Vendor Class drop-down list, select DHCP Standard Options. As appropriate, from the User Class drop-down list, choose either Default Routing And Remote Access Class or Default Network Access Protection Class.

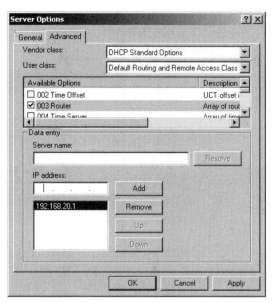

Figure 22-22 Set the DHCP Standard Options.

2. Select the check box for each standard TCP/IP option you want to use in turn, such as Router, DNS Servers, DNS Domain Name, WINS/NBNS Servers, and WINS/NBT Node Type, and configure the appropriate values.

3. Select each add-on TCP/IP option you want to use in turn, such as Microsoft Disable NetBIOS Option and Microsoft Release DHCP Lease On Shutdown Option, and accept the default value (0x1) to turn on the option.

4. Click OK.

Setting Add-On Options for Directly Connected Clients

You can set add-on options for directly connected clients that are different from those of remote access clients. Access the TCP/IP Options dialog box at the appropriate level, and then click the Advanced tab. For Windows 2000 or later clients, select Microsoft Windows 2000 Options as the vendor class and Default BOOTP Class as the user class, as shown in Figure 22-23. Now select each add-on TCP/IP option you want to use in turn, such as Microsoft Disable NetBIOS Option and Microsoft Release DHCP Lease On Shutdown Option, and accept the default value (0x1) to turn on the option. Then click OK when you are finished.

Chapter 22

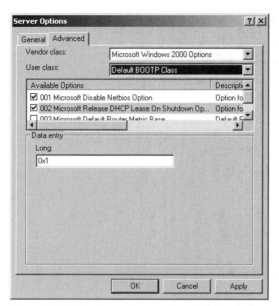

Figure 22-23 Set the add-on options for directly connected clients.

Defining Classes to Get Different Option Sets

If you want a group of DHCP clients to use a set of options different than other comput-ers, you can use classes to do this. It is a two-part process. First, create your own user-defined class on each DHCP server to which the clients might connect. Then configure the network interfaces on the clients to use the new class.

Creating the Class

In the DHCP console, you can define the new user class by right-clicking the IP protocol you want to work with and selecting Define User Classes. In the DHCP User Classes dialog box, shown in Figure 22-24, the existing classes are listed, except for the Default User Class because it is the base user class.

Click Add to display the New Class dialog box shown in Figure 22-25. In the Display Name box, type the name of the class you are defining. The name is arbitrary and should be short but descriptive enough so that you know what that class is used for by seeing its name. You can also type a description in the Description box. Afterward, click in the empty area below the word ASCII. In this space, type the class identifier, which is used by DHCP to identify the class. The class identifier cannot have spaces. Click OK to close the New Class dialog box, and then click Close to return to the DHCP console.

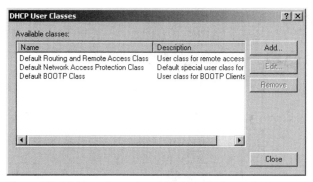

Figure 22-24 User classes in addition to the base class.

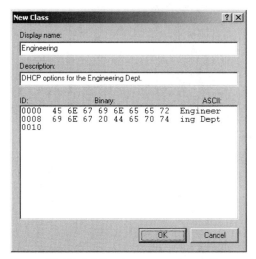

Figure 22-25 Set the class name, description, and class ID.

Next, you must configure the TCP/IP options that should be used by this class. In the DHCP console, expand the entry for the server you want to work with, right-click Server Options, and then choose Configure Options. In the Server Options dialog box, click the Advanced tab. Select DHCP Standard Options as the vendor class and the class you created as the user class.

Select each standard TCP/IP option you want to use in turn, such as Router, DNS Servers, DNS Domain Name, WINS/NBNS Servers, and WINS/NBT Node Type, and configure the appropriate values. If you want to set Windows options, select Microsoft Windows 2000 Options as the vendor class. Don't change the user class. Then select each add-on TCP/IP option you want to use in turn, such as Microsoft Disable Net-BIOS Option and Microsoft Release DHCP Lease On Shutdown Option, and accept the default value (0x1) to turn on the option. Click OK to complete the configuration of the new class.

Chapter 22

Configuring Clients to Use the Class

Now you must configure the network interfaces on the clients to use the new class. Assuming "Local Area Connection" is the name of the network interface on the client, you would type the following command to do this:

```
ipconfig /setclassid "Local Area Connection" ClassID
```

where *ClassID* is the ID of the user class to use. For example, if the class ID is Engineering, you would type

```
ipconfig /setclassid "Local Area Connection" Engineering
```

In these examples, I use "Local Area Connection" as the network interface name because that is the default connection created by Windows. If a client has multiple network interfaces or a user has changed the name of the default network interface, you must use the name of the appropriate interface. You can get a list of all network interfaces on a client by typing **ipconfig /all** at the command prompt.

After you set the class ID, type **ipconfig /renew** at the command prompt. This tells the client to renew the lease and because the client has a new class ID it also forces the client to request new TCP/IP options. The output should be similar to the following:

```
Windows IP Configuration
Ethernet adapter Local Area Connection:

    Connection-specific DNS Suffix    :
    IP Address                        :    192.168.1.22
    Subnet Mask                       :    255.255.255.0
    Default Gateway                   :    192.168.1.1
    DHCP Class ID                     :    Engineering
```

That's it. Because the class ID is persistent, you need to set it only once. So, if the client is restarted, the class ID will remain. To remove the class ID and use the defaults again, type the following command:

```
ipconfig /setclassid "Local Area Connection"
```

TROUBLESHOOTING

Class ID problems

Sometimes the network interface won't report that it has the new class ID. If this happens, try releasing the DHCP lease first by typing **ipconfig /release** and then obtaining a new lease by typing **ipconfig /renew**.

Advanced DHCP Configuration and Maintenance

When you install the DHCP Server service, many advanced features are configured for you automatically, including audit logging, network bindings, integration with DNS, integration with NAP, and DHCP database backups. All of these features can be fine-tuned to optimize performance, and many of these features, such as auditing, logging, and backups, should be periodically monitored.

Configuring DHCP Audit Logging

Auditing logging is enabled by default for the DHCP Server service and is used to track DHCP processes and requests in log files. Although you can enable and configure logging separately for IPv4 and IPv6, by default, the two protocols use the same log files. The DHCP logs are stored in the %SystemRoot%\System32\Dhcp folder by default. In this folder you'll find a different log file for each day of the week. For example, the log file for Monday is named DhcpSrvLog-Mon.log. When you start the DHCP Server service or a new day arrives, a header message is written to the log file. As shown in Listing 22-1, the header provides a summary of DHCP events and their meanings. The header is followed by the actual events logged by the DHCP Server service. The event IDs and descriptions are entered because different versions of the DHCP Server service can have different events.

Listing 22-1 DHCP Server Log File

```
Microsoft DHCP Service Activity Log
Event ID  Meaning
00        The log was started.
01        The log was stopped.
02        The log was temporarily paused due to low disk space.
10        A new IP address was leased to a client.
11        A lease was renewed by a client.
12        A lease was released by a client.
13        An IP address was found to be in use on the network.
14        A lease request could not be satisfied because the scope's
          address pool was exhausted.
15        A lease was denied.
16        A lease was deleted.
17        A lease was expired.
24        IP address cleanup operation has began.
25        IP address cleanup statistics.
30        DNS update request to the named DNS server
31        DNS update failed
32        DNS update successful
50+       Codes above 50 are used for Rogue Server Detection information.

ID,Date,Time,Description,IP Address,Host Name,MAC Address
00,04/27/09,11:30:26,Started,,,,
55,04/27/09,11:30:27,Authorized(servicing),,cpandl.com,,
10,04/27/09,11:56:03,Assign,192.168.1.1,corpserver03.cpandl.com,2324AE67B4E8,
```

```
12,04/27/09,11:56:32,Release,192.168.1.1,corpserver03.cpandl.com,2324AE67B4E8,
10,04/27/09,12:01:45,Assign,192.168.1.20,corpserver03.cpandl.com,2324AE67B4E8,
15,04/27/09,12:03:41,NACK,192.168.0.100,,2324AE67B4E8,
11,04/27/09,12:03:42,Renew,192.168.1.20,becka.,2324AE67B4E8,
24,04/27/09,12:30:30,Database Cleanup Begin,,,,
25,04/27/09,12:30:30,0 leases expired and 0 leases deleted,,,,
25,04/27/09,12:30:30,0 leases expired and 0 leases deleted,,,,
24,04/27/09,13:30:35,Database Cleanup Begin,,,,
25,04/27/09,13:30:35,0 leases expired and 0 leases deleted,,,,
25,04/27/09,13:30:35,0 leases expired and 0 leases deleted,,,,
01,04/27/09,14:10:23,Stopped,,,,
00,04/27/09,14:10:37,Started,,,,
55,04/27/09,14:10:37,Authorized(servicing),,cpandl.com,,
01,04/27t/09,20:15:50,Stopped,,,,
```

The events in the audit logs can help you troubleshoot problems with a DHCP server. As you examine Listing 22-1, the first event entry with ID 00 tells you the DHCP Server service was started. The second event entry with ID 55 tells you the DHCP server is authorized to service the cpandl.com domain. Every hour that the service is running, it also performs cleanup operations. Database cleanup is used to check for expired leases and leases that no longer apply.

The audit logs also serve as a record of all DHCP connection requests by clients on the network. Events related to lease assignment, renewal, and release are recorded according to the IP address assigned, the client's FQDN, and the client's MAC address.

Declined leases are listed with the event ID 13 and the description of the event is DECLINE. A DHCP client can decline a lease if it detects that the IP address is already in use. The primary reason this happens is that a system somewhere on the network is using a static IP address in the DHCP range or has leased it from another DHCP server during a network glitch. When the server receives the decline, it marks the address as bad in the DHCP database. See "Enabling Conflict Detection on DHCP Servers" on page 734 for details on how IP address conflicts can be avoided.

Denied leases are listed with the event ID 15 and the description of the event is NACK. DHCP can deny a lease to a client that is requesting an address that cannot be provided. This could happen if an administrator terminated the lease or if the client moved to a different subnet where the original IP address held is no longer valid. When a client receives a NACK, the client releases the denied IP address and requests a new one.

As discussed previously, audit logging is enabled by default. If you want to check or change the logging setting, you can do this in the DHCP console. Expand the node for the server you want to work with, right-click IPv4 or IPv6 as appropriate for the type of binding you want to work with, and then select Properties. This displays the dialog box shown in Figure 22-26.

On the General tab, select or clear the Enable DHCP Audit Logging check box as necessary. Afterward, select the Advanced tab. The Audit Log File Path box shows the current folder location for log files. Enter a new folder location or click Browse to find a new location. Click OK. If you change the audit log location, Windows Server 2008 will need to restart the DHCP Server service. When prompted to confirm that this is OK, click Yes.

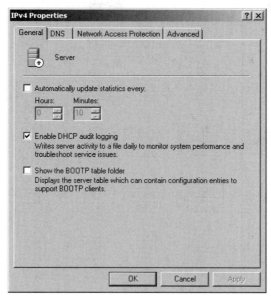

Figure 22-26 Audit logging is enabled by default.

Binding the DHCP Server Service to a Network Interface

The DHCP Server service should bind automatically to the first NIC on the server. This means that the DHCP Server service should use the IP address and TCP/IP configuration of this network interface to communicate with clients. In some instances, the DHCP Server service might not bind to any available network interface or it might bind to a network interface that you don't want it to use. To resolve this problem, you must bind the DHCP Server service to a specific network interface by following these steps:

1. In the DHCP console, expand the node for the server you want to work with, right-click IPv4 or IPv6 as appropriate for the type of binding you want to work with, and then select Properties.

2. On the Advanced tab of the IPv4 or IPv6 Properties dialog box, click Bindings to display the Bindings dialog box. This dialog box displays a list of available network connections for the DHCP server.

3. If you want the DHCP Server service to use a connection to service clients, select the option for the connection. If you don't want the service to use a connection, clear the related option.

4. Click OK twice when you are finished.

Chapter 22

Integrating DHCP and DNS

Using the DNS Dynamic Update protocol, DHCP clients running Windows 2000 or later can automatically update their forward (A) and reverse lookup (PTR) records in DNS or request that the DHCP server do this for them. Clients running versions of the Windows operating system earlier than Windows 2000 can't dynamically update any of their records, so DHCP must do this for them. In either case, when the DHCP server is required to update DNS records, this requires integration between DHCP and DNS.

In the default configuration of DHCP, a DHCP server will update DNS records for clients only if requested but will not update records for clients running versions of the Windows operating system earlier than Windows 2000. You can modify this behavior globally for each DHCP server or on a per scope basis.

To change the global DNS integration settings, start the DHCP console, expand the node for the server you want to work with, right-click IPv4, and then select Properties. Click the DNS tab, as shown in Figure 22-27, and then select the Dynamically Update DNS A And PTR Records For DHCP Clients That Do Not Request Updates check box. Don't change the other settings. These settings are configured by default, and you don't need to modify the configuration in most cases.

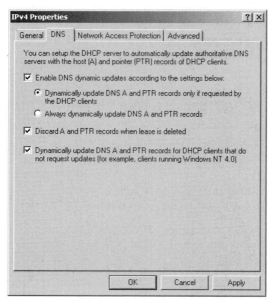

Figure 22-27 DHCP and DNS integration.

To change scope-specific settings, expand the node for the server you want to work with and then expand IPv4. Right-click the scope you want to work with and then select Properties. Click the DNS tab. The options available are the same as those shown in Figure 22-27. Because these settings are configured by default, you usually don't need to modify the configuration.

Integrating DHCP and NAP

Network Access Protection (NAP) is designed to protect the network from clients that do not have the appropriate security measures in place. The easiest way to enable NAP with DHCP is to set up the DHCP server as a Network Policy Server. To do this, you'll need to install the Network Policy console, configure a compliant policy for NAP and DHCP integration on the server, and then enable NAP for DHCP. This process enables NAP for network computers that use DHCP; it does not fully configure NAP for use.

You can create an NAP and DHCP integration policy by completing the following steps:

1. On the server that you want to act as the Network Policy Server, install the Network Policy console as an additional remote server administration tool using the Add Features Wizard.

2. In the Network Policy console, select the NPS (Local) node in the console tree and then click Configure NAP in the main pane. This starts the Configure NAP wizard.

3. In the Network Connection Method list, choose Dynamic Host Configuration Protocol (DHCP) as the connection method that you want to deploy on your network for NAP-capable clients. As shown in Figure 22-28, the policy name is set to NAP DHCP by default. Click Next.

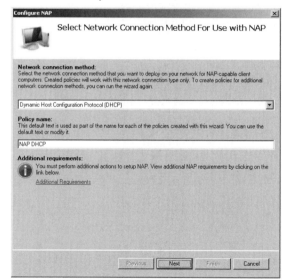

Figure 22-28 Configure Network Access Protection policy for the local DHCP server.

4. On the Specify NAP Enforcement Servers Running DHCP Server page, you need to identify all remote DHCP servers on your network by doing the following and then click Next:

    o   Click Add. In the Add RADIUS Client dialog box, type a friendly name for the remote server in the Friendly Name text box. Then type the DNS name or IP address of the remote DHCP server in the Address text box. Click Verify to ensure that the address is valid.

     ○ In the Shared Secret panel, select Generate and then click Generate to create a long shared secret keyphrase. You'll need to enter this keyphrase in the NAP DHCP policy on all remote DHCP servers. Be sure to write down this keyphrase. Alternatively, copy the keyphrase to Notepad and then save it in a file stored in a secure location. Click OK.

5. On the Specify DHCP Scopes page, you can identify the DHCP scopes to which this policy should apply. If you do not specify any scopes, the policy applies to all NAP-enabled scopes on the selected DHCP servers. Click Next twice to skip the Configure Groups page.

6. On the Specify A NAP Remediation Server Group And URL page, select a Remediation Server or click New Group to define a remediation group and specify servers to handle remediation. Remediation servers store software updates for NAP clients that need them. In the text box provided, type a URL to a Web page that provides users with instructions on how to bring their computers into compliance with NAP health policy. Ensure that all DHCP clients can access this URL. Click Next.

7. On the Define NAP Health Policy page, use the options provided to determine how NAP health policy works. In most cases, the default settings work fine. With the default settings, NAP ineligible clients are denied access to the network; NAP-capable clients are checked for compliance and automatically remediated, which allows them to get needed software updates that you've made available. Click Next and then click Finish.

You can modify NAP settings globally for each DHCP server or on a per-scope basis. To view or change the global NAP settings, complete the following steps:

1. In the DHCP console, expand the node for the server you want to work with, right-click IPv4, and then select Properties.

2. On the Network Access Protection tab, shown in Figure 22-29, click Enable On All Scopes or Disable On All Scopes to enable or disable NAP for all scopes on the server.

> **Note**
>
> When the local DHCP server is also a Network Policy Server, the Network Policy Server should always be reachable. If you haven't configured the server as a Network Policy Server or the DHCP server is unable to contact the designated Network Policy Server, you'll see an error stating this on the Network Access Protection tab.

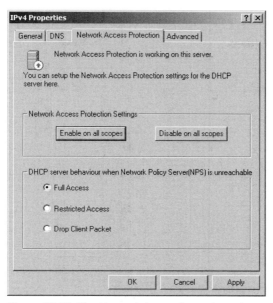

Figure 22-29 The Network Access Protection tab controls the protection óptions for DHCP.

3. Choose one of the following options to specify how the DHCP server behaves if the Network Policy Server is unreachable, and then click OK to save your settings:

- ○ **Full Access** Gives DHCP clients full (unrestricted) access to the network. This means clients can perform any permitted actions.
- ○ **Restricted Access** Gives DHCP clients restricted access to the network. This means clients can work with resources only on the server to which they are connected.
- ○ **Drop Client Packet** Blocks client requests and prevents the clients from accessing the network. This means clients have no access to resources on the network.

You can view and change the NAP settings for individual scopes by completing the following steps:

1. In the DHCP console, expand the node for the server you want to work with and then expand IPv4.

2. Right-click the scope you want to work with and then select Properties.

3. On the Network Access Protection tab, click Enable For This Scope or Disable For This Scope to enable or disable NAP for this scope.

4. If you're enabling NAP and want to use an NAP profile other than the default, click Use Custom Profile and then type the name of the profile, such as Alternate NAP DHCP.

5. Click OK to save your settings.

Chapter 22

Enabling Conflict Detection on DHCP Servers

No two computers on the network can have the same unicast IP address. If a computer is assigned the same unicast IP address as another, one or both of the computers might become disconnected from the network. To prevent this from happening, DHCP has built-in conflict detection that enables clients to check the IP address they've been assigned by pinging the address on the network. If a client detects that an IP address it has been assigned is in use, it sends the DHCP server a Decline message telling the server that it is declining the lease because the IP address is in use. When this happens, the server marks the IP address as bad in the DHCP database, and then the client requests a new lease. This process works fairly well but requires additional time because the client is responsible for checking the IP address, declining a lease, and requesting a new one.

To speed up the process, you can configure DHCP servers to check for conflicts before assigning an IP address to a client. When conflict detection is enabled, the process works in much the same way as before, except the server checks the IP address to see if it is in use and, if so, marks it as bad without interaction with the client. You can configure conflict detection on a DHCP server by specifying the number of conflict detection attempts that the DHCP server will make before it leases an IP address to a client. The DHCP server checks IP addresses by sending a ping request over the network.

You can configure conflict detection in the DHCP console by expanding the node for the server you want to work with, right-clicking IPv4, and then selecting Properties. On the Advanced tab, set Conflict Detection Attempts to a value other than zero. At the command line, type the following command:

```
netsh dhcp server ServerID set detectconflictretry Attempts
```

where *ServerID* is the name or IP address of the DHCP server and *Attempts* is the number of conflict detection attempts the server should use. You can confirm the setting by typing the following:

```
netsh dhcp server ServerID show detectconflictretry
```

Saving and Restoring the DHCP Configuration

After you finish configuring a DHCP server, you should save the configuration settings so that you can easily restore the server to a known state or use the same settings on another server. To do this, type the following command at the command prompt:

```
netsh dhcp server dump ServerID > SaveFile
```

where *ServerID* is the name or IP address of the DHCP server and *SaveFile* is the name of the file in which you want to store the configuration settings. When you are logged on locally, you can omit the server name or IP address, as shown in the following example:

```
netsh dhcp server dump > dhcpconfig.dmp
```

If you examine the file Netsh creates, you'll find that it is a Netsh configuration script. To restore the configuration, run the script by typing the following command:

```
netsh exec SaveFile
```

where *SaveFile* is the name of the file in which you stored the configuration settings. Here is an example:

```
netsh exec dhcpconfig.dmp
```

> ### Copy to a New DHCP Server
>
> You can run the script on a different DHCP server to configure it the same as the original DHCP server whose configuration you saved. Copy the configuration script to a folder on the destination computer, and then run it. The DHCP server will be configured like the original server.

Managing and Maintaining the DHCP Database

Information about leases and reservations used by clients is stored in database files on the DHCP server. Like any other data set, the DHCP database has properties that you can set and techniques you can use to maintain it.

Setting DHCP Database Properties

In the default configuration, these files are stored in the %SystemRoot%\System32\ Dhcp folder, and automatically created backups of the files are stored in %System-Root%\System32\Dhcp\Backup. The DHCP Server service performs two routine actions to maintain the database:

- Database cleanup during which the DHCP Server service checks for expired leases and leases that no longer apply

- Database backup during which the DHCP Server service backs up the database files

By default, both maintenance tasks are performed every 60 minutes, and you can confirm this as well as the current DHCP folders being used by typing the following command at the command prompt:

```
netsh dhcp server ServerID show dbproperties
```

where *ServerID* is the name or IP address of the DHCP server, such as

```
netsh dhcp server 192.168.1.50 show dbproperties
```

Chapter 22

The output of this command shows you the current database properties for the DHCP server:

```
Server Database Properties:

    DatabaseName            =    dhcp.mdb
    DatabasePath            =    C:\WINDOWS\System32\dhcp
    DatabaseBackupPath      =    C:\WINDOWS\System32\dhcp\backup
    DatabaseBackupInterval  =    60 mins.
    DatabaseLoggingFlag     =    1
    DatabaseRestoreFlag     =    0
    DatabaseCleanupInterval =    60 mins.
```

Note the DatabaseLoggingFlag and DatabaseRestoreFlag properties. DatabaseLogging-Flag tracks whether audit logging is enabled. If the flag is set to 0, audit logging is disabled. If the flag is set to 1, audit logging is enabled. DatabaseRestoreFlag is a special flag that tracks whether the DHCP Server service should restore the DHCP database from backup the next time it starts. If the flag is set to 0, the main database is used. If the flag is set to 1, the DHCP Server service restores the database from backup, overwriting the existing database.

You can use the following commands to set these properties:

- **Netsh dhcp server** *ServerID* **set databasename** *NewFileName*–Sets the new file name for the database, such as Dhcp1.mdb.

- **Netsh dhcp server** *ServerID* **set databasepath** *NewPath*–Sets the new path for the database files, such as C:\Dhcp\Dbfiles.

- **Netsh dhcp server** *ServerID* **set databasebackupinterval** *NewIntervalMinutes*–Sets the database backup interval in minutes, such as 120.

- **Netsh dhcp server** *ServerID* **set databasebackuppathname** *NewPath*–Sets the new path for the database backup files, such as C:\Dhcp\Dbbackup.

- **Netsh dhcp server** *ServerID* **set databaseloggingflag** *FlagValue*–Enables or disables audit logging. Set to 0 to disable or 1 to enable.

- **Netsh dhcp server** *ServerID* **set databaserestoreflag** *FlagValue*–Forces DHCP to restore the database from backup when it is started. Set to 1 to restore.

- **Netsh dhcp server** *ServerID* **set databasecleanupinterval** *NewIntervalMinutes*–Sets the database backup interval in minutes, such as 120.

> **Note**
> If you change the database name or folder locations, you must stop the DHCP server and then start it again for the changes to take effect. To do this, type **net stop "dhcp server"** to stop the server and then type **net start "dhcp server"** to start the server again.

Backing Up and Restoring the Database

The DHCP database is backed up automatically. You can manually back it up as well at any time. In the DHCP console, right-click the server you want to back up, and then choose Backup. In the Browse For Folder dialog box, select the backup folder, and then click OK.

If a server crash corrupts the database, you might need to restore and then reconcile the database. Start by restoring a good copy of the contents of the backup folder from tape or other archive source. Afterward, start the DHCP console, right-click the server you want to restore, and then choose Restore. In the Browse For Folder dialog box, select the folder that contains the backup you want to restore, and then click OK. During restoration of the database, the DHCP Server service is stopped and then started automatically.

INSIDE OUT   **Moving the DHCP database to a new server**

You can use the backup and restore procedure to move the DHCP database to a new server. For example, before upgrading a DHCP server or decommissioning it, you could configure a new DHCP server and move the current DHCP database from the old server to the new server. Start by installing the DHCP Server service on the destination server and then restart the server. When the server restarts, log on, and at the command prompt type **net stop "dhcp server"** to stop the DHCP Server service. Remove the contents of the %SystemRoot%\System32\Dhcp folder on this server.

Afterward, log on to the original (source) server, and at the command prompt type **net stop "dhcp server"** to stop the DHCP Server service. In the Services node of Computer Management, disable the DHCP Server service so that it can no longer be started, then copy the entire contents of the %SystemRoot%\System32\Dhcp folder to the %SystemRoot%\System32\Dhcp folder on the destination server. After all the necessary files are on the destination server, type **net start "dhcp server"** to start the DHCP Server service on the destination server, which completes the migration.

Setting Up DHCP Relay Agents

In an ideal configuration, you'll have multiple DHCP servers on each subnet. However, because this isn't always possible, you can configure your routers to forward DHCP broadcasts or configure a computer on the network to act as a relay agent. Any computer running Windows Server 2008 can act as a relay agent. Doing so requires that Routing and Remote Access be configured and enabled on the computer first, and then you can configure the computer as a relay agent using the Routing And Remote Access console.

Chapter 22

Configuring and Enabling Routing and Remote Access

In Windows Server 2008, Routing and Remote Access Services are installed as a role service for the Network Policy and Access Services role. On a server with no other policy and access role services configured, you can install this role service by completing the following steps:

1. In Server Manager, select the Roles node in the left pane and then click Add Roles. This starts the Add Roles Wizard. If the wizard displays the Before You Begin page, read the welcome message and then click Next.

2. On the Select Server Roles page, select Network Policy And Access Services and then click Next twice.

3. As shown in Figure 22-30, select the Routing And Remote Access Services role service to install. To enable RRAS, you must install Remote Access Service and Routing. Click Next.

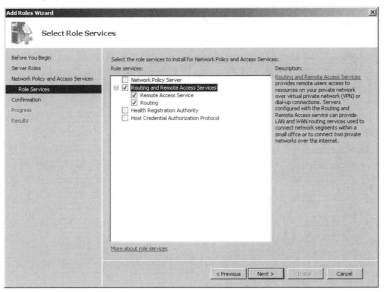

Figure 22-30 Select the role services to install.

4. Follow the prompts to complete other wizard pages as necessary. On the Confirm Installation Services page, click Install. The wizard installs the selected role services.

To start the Routing And Remote Access console, click Start, Administrative Tools, Routing And Remote Access. If the computer you want to use as the relay agent isn't listed as an available server, right-click the Routing And Remote Access node in the left pane, and select Add Server. In the Add Server dialog box, select The Following Computer, type the name or IP address of the computer, and then click OK.

If the computer isn't already configured for Routing and Remote Access, right-click the computer node in the left pane, and then select Configure And Enable Routing And Remote Access. This starts the Routing And Remote Access Server Setup Wizard. Click Next. Choose Custom Configuration, as shown in Figure 22-31, and then click Next again. On the Custom Configuration page, select LAN Routing. Click Next, and then click Finish.

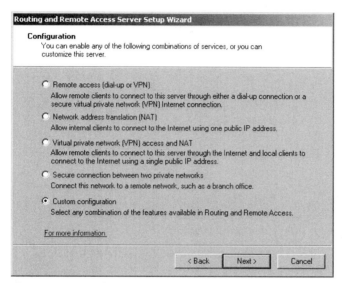

Figure 22-31 Configure and enable Routing and Remote Access.

The wizard will then create a default Network Policy Server connection request policy on your organization's Network Access Policy server. You will need to review this policy in the Network Policy console to ensure that it is configured properly and does not conflict with existing policies. Click OK. Finally, when prompted to start the Routing and Remote Access Service, click Start Service.

Adding and Configuring the DHCP Relay Agent

You can configure DHCP relay agents for IPv4 and IPv6. To configure a relay agent for IPv4 follow these steps:

1. In the Routing And Remote Access console, expand the node for the computer you just configured, and then expand IPv4.

2. Right-click the General node, and then choose New Routing Protocol.

3. In the New Routing Protocol dialog box, select DHCP Relay Agent, and then click OK. This adds an entry under IPv4 labeled DHCP Relay Agent.

4. In the Routing And Remote Access console, right-click the DHCP Relay Agent entry, and choose New Interface.

Chapter 22

5. The New Interface For DHCP Relay Agent dialog box is displayed, as shown in Figure 22-32, showing the currently configured network interfaces on the computer. Select the network interface that is connected to the same network as the DHCP clients whose DHCP broadcasts need forwarding, and then click OK.

Figure 22-32 Select the network interface on the same network as the DHCP clients.

6, The DHCP Relay Properties dialog box is displayed automatically, as shown in Figure 22-33. After you set the following relay options, click OK:

  o **Relay DHCP Packets** When selected, this option ensures that DHCP packets are relayed.

  o **Hop-Count Threshold** Determines the maximum number of relay agents a DHCP request can pass through. The default is 4. The maximum is 16.

  o **Boot Threshold (Seconds)** Determines the number of seconds the relay agent waits before forwarding DHCP packets. The delay is designed so that local DHCP servers will be the first to respond if they are available. The default delay is 4 seconds.

7. In the Routing And Remote Access console, right-click the DHCP Relay Agent entry, and choose Properties. This displays the DHCP Relay Agent Properties dialog box.

8. Type the IP address of the DHCP server to which DHCP packets should be forwarded, and then click Add. Click OK. The computer is then configured as a DHCPv4 relay agent.

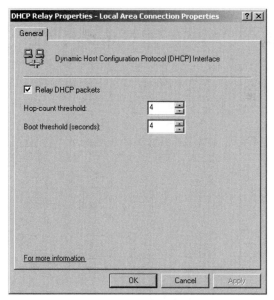

Figure 22-33 Set the relay options.

To configure a relay agent for IPv6 follow these steps:

1. In the Routing And Remote Access console, expand the node for the computer you just configured, and then expand IPv6.

2. Right-click the General node, and then choose New Routing Protocol.

3. In the New Routing Protocol dialog box, select DHCPv6 Relay Agent, and then click OK. This adds an entry under IPv6 labeled DHCPv6 Relay Agent.

4. In the Routing And Remote Access console, right-click the DHCPv6 Relay Agent entry, and choose New Interface.

5. The New Interface For DHCPv6 Relay Agent dialog box is displayed. Select the network interface that is connected to the same network as the DHCPv6 clients whose DHCPv6 broadcasts need forwarding, and then click OK.

6. The DHCP Relay Properties dialog box is displayed automatically. After you set the following relay options, click OK:

    ○ **Relay DHCP Packets** When selected, this option ensures that DHCPv6 packets are relayed.

    ○ **Hop-Count Threshold** Determines the maximum number of relay agents a DHCPv6 request can pass through. The default is 4. The maximum is 16.

    ○ **Elapsed-Time Threshold (Centi-Seconds)** Determines the number of seconds the relay agent waits before forwarding DHCPv6 packets. The delay is designed so that local DHCPv6 servers will be the first to respond if they are available. The default delay is 32 seconds (3200 centi-seconds).

Chapter 22

7. In the Routing And Remote Access console, right-click the DHCP Relay Agent entry, and choose Properties. This displays the DHCP Relay Agent Properties dialog box.

8. On the Servers tab, type the IPv6 address of the DHCPv6 server to which DHCPv6 packets should be forwarded, and then click Add. Click OK. The computer is then configured as a DHCPv6 relay agent.

Architecting DNS Infrastructure

The Domain Name System (DNS) is an Internet Engineering Task Force (IETF) standard name service. Its basic design is described in Requests for Comments (RFCs) 1034 and 1035, and it has been implemented on many operating systems including UNIX and Microsoft Windows. All versions of Windows automatically install a DNS client as part of Transmission Control Protocol/Internet Protocol (TCP/IP). To get the server component, you must install the DNS Server service. All editions of Windows Server 2008 include the DNS Server service. Because DNS is the name resolution service for Active Directory, DNS is installed automatically if you install Active Directory on a network.

DNS Essentials

Like Dynamic Host Configuration Protocol (DHCP), DNS is a client/server protocol. This means there is a client component and a server component necessary to successfully implement DNS. Because of the client/server model, any computer seeking DNS information is referred to as a *DNS client*, and the computer that provides the information to the client is referred to as a *DNS server*. It's the job of a DNS server to store a database containing DNS information, to respond to DNS queries from clients, and to replicate DNS information to other DNS servers as necessary.

DNS provides for several types of queries, including forward lookup queries and reverse lookup queries. Forward lookup queries allow a client to resolve a host name to an Internet Protocol (IP) address. A DNS client makes a forward lookup using a name query message that asks the DNS server for the host address record of a specific host. The response to this query is sent as a name query response message. If there's a host address record for the specified host, the name server returns this. If the host name is an alias, the name server returns the record for the alias (CNAME) as well as the host address record to which the alias points.

Reverse lookup queries allow a client to resolve an IP address to a host name, as Figure 23-1 shows. The DNS Server service supports IPv4 and IPv6 for reverse lookups.

Reverse lookups are primarily used by computers to find out who is contacting them so that they can communicate directly using an IP address rather than a host name. This can speed up communications in some cases because name queries aren't necessary. A DNS client makes a reverse lookup using a reverse name query message. The response to the query is sent as a reverse name query response message. This message contains the reverse address record (PTR) for the specified host.

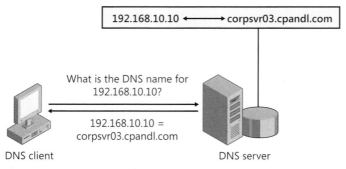

Figure 23-1 A reverse lookup query.

DNS also provides a way to cache DNS information to reduce the number of queries that are required. So, instead of having to send a query to a name server each time the host wants to resolve a particular name, the DNS client checks its local cache for the information first. DNS information in the cache is held for a set amount of time, referred to as the Time to Live (TTL) value of a record. When a record exists in cache and its TTL has not expired, it is used to answer subsequent queries. Not only does this reduce traffic on the network, it also speeds up the name resolution process. A record's TTL is set in the query response from a name server.

Planning DNS Implementations

Planning a new DNS implementation or revamping your existing DNS implementation requires good planning. You need a solid understanding of how DNS works, and the areas you should know about include the following:

- How DNS namespaces are assigned and used
- How DNS name resolution works and can be modified
- What resource records are available and how are they used
- How DNS zones and zone transfers can be used
- How internal and external servers can be used
- How DNS is integrated with other technologies

Public and Private Namespaces

The DNS domain namespace is a hierarchical tree in which each node and leaf in the tree represents a named domain. Each level of the domain namespace tree is separated by a period (called a "dot"). As discussed in "Understanding Name Resolution" on page 652, the first level of the tree is where you'll find the top-level domains, and these top-level domains form the base of the DNS namespace. The second level of the tree is for second-level or parent domains, and subsequent levels of the tree are for subdomains. For example, cpandl.com is the parent domain of the child domains sales.cpandl.com and tech.cpandl.com.

> **Note**
>
> Although the actual root of the DNS namespace is represented by "." and doesn't have a name, each level in the tree has a name, which is referred to as its label. The fully qualified domain name (FQDN) of a node in the DNS namespace is the list of all the labels in the path from the node to the root of the namespace. For example, the FQDN for the host named CORPSVR02 in the cpandl.com domain is corpsvr02.cpandl.com.

To divide public and private namespaces, the top-level domains are established and maintained by select organizations. The top authority, Internet Corporation for Assigned Names and Numbers (ICANN), is responsible for defining and delegating control over the top-level domains to individual organizations. Top-level domains are organized functionally and geographically. Table 23-1 lists the functions of key generic top-level domains; the list can be extended to include other generic top-level domains (see *http://www.iana.org/gtld/gtld.htm* for the most current list). The geographically organized top-level domains are identified by two-level country codes. These country codes are based on the International Organization for Standardization (ISO) country name and are used primarily by organizations outside the United States.

Table 23-1 Top-Level Domain Names for the Internet

Domain	Purpose
.aero	For aerospace firms, including airlines
.biz	For businesses, extends the .com area
.com	For commercial organizations
.coop	For business cooperatives
.edu	For educational institutions
.gov	For U.S. government agencies
.info	For information sources
.int	For organizations established by international treaties
.mil	For U.S. military departments and agencies
.museum	For museums
.name	For use by individuals
.net	For use by network providers
.org	For use by organizations, such as those that are nongovernmental or nonprofit
.pro	For professional groups such as doctors and lawyers

Chapter 23

> **Note**
>
> The United Kingdom is the exception to the ISO naming rule. Although the ISO country code for the United Kingdom is GB (Great Britain), its two-letter designator is UK.

After ICANN delegates control over a top-level domain, it is the responsibility of the designated organization to maintain the domain and handle registrations. After an organization registers a domain name with one of these authorities, the organization controls the domain and can create subdomains within this domain without having to make a formal request. For example, if you register the domain cpandl.com, you can create the subdomains seattle.cpandl.com, portland.cpandl.com, and sf.cpandl.com without having to ask the registration authority for permission.

Private namespaces aren't controlled by ICANN. You can create your own private namespace for use within your company. For example, you could use .local for your top-level domain. This keeps your internal network separate from the public Internet. You would then need to rely on Network Address Translation (NAT) or proxy servers to access the public Internet.

Name Resolution Using DNS

In DNS, name resolution is made possible using a distributed database. The resource records in this database detail host name and IP address information relating to domains. It is the job of DNS name servers to store the DNS database and respond to queries from clients about the information the database contains. A portion of the DNS namespace that is controlled by a DNS name server or a group of name servers is referred to as a *zone*.

Zones establish the boundaries within which a particular name server can resolve requests. On clients, it is the job of DNS resolvers to contact name servers and per-form queries about resource records. Thus, the three main components of DNS are as follows:

- Resource records stored in a distributed database
- DNS name servers that are responsible for maintaining specific zones
- DNS resolvers running on clients

These key components are used to perform DNS operations, which can consist of query operations, query replies, and DNS update operations. A basic query and reply work as shown in Figure 23-2. Here, a DNS client wants information from a DNS name server, so it sends a DNS query. The DNS server to which the query is sent checks its local data-base and forwards the request to an authoritative server. The authoritative server sends back a response to the local DNS server, and that response is forwarded to the client.

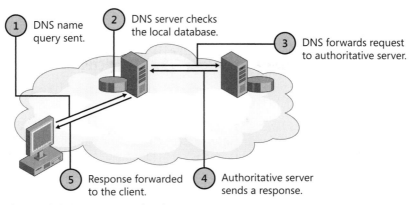

Figure 23-2 DNS query and reply.

As Figure 23-3 shows, things get a bit more complicated when a client requests the name of an external resource, such as a Web site. If you were on an internal domain and requested a resource on the public Internet, such as the IP address for the www.cpandl.com server, the DNS client on your computer queries the local name server as specified in its TCP/IP configuration. The local name server forwards the request to the root server for the external resource domain. This domain contacts the name server for the related top-level domain, which in turn contacts the name server for the cpandl.com domain. This authoritative server sends a response, which is forwarded to the client, who can then access the external resource.

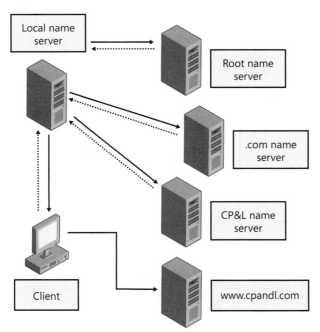

Figure 23-3 Name resolution using the DNS tree.

As you can see, in a normal DNS configuration, if your DNS name server can't resolve a request, it simply forwards the request to another name server for resolution. This allows your organization's name servers to get internal DNS information and external DNS information on the public Internet. However, what if the domain you were trying to reach was a resource in another one of your own internal domains. In this case, you wouldn't want requests to be forwarded to a public DNS name server for resolution. The public DNS server would have no idea how to resolve the request.

There are several ways to resolve this problem and one of these ways is to use conditional forwarding. By using conditional forwarding, you can tell your DNS name servers that if you see a request for domain XYZ, don't forward it to the public DNS name servers for resolution. Instead, forward the request directly to the XYZ name server—which is the authoritative name server for the domain being looked up. This name server will then be able to reply to the query and the DNS lookup will be resolved. For more information on resolving name resolution problems and conditional forwarding, see "Secondary Zones, Stub Zones, and Conditional Forwarding" on page 755.

DNS Resource Records

Resource records are used to store domain information. DNS name servers contain resource records for those portions of the DNS namespace for which they are authoritative. It is the job of administrators who maintain an authoritative DNS name server to maintain the resource records and ensure that they are accurate. DNS name servers can also cache resource records for those areas for which they can answer queries sent by hosts. This means DNS name servers can cache resource records relating to any part of the domain tree.

Although many types of resource records are defined and supported by DNS servers, only a few record types are actually used on a Windows Server 2008 network. So, with that in mind, Table 23-2 provides an overview of the resource records that you'll use.

Table 23-2 **Common Resource Records Used on Windows Server 2008 Networks**

Record Type	Common Name	Description
A	Host address	Contains the name of a host and its Internet Protocol version 4 (IPv4) address. Any computer that has multiple network interfaces or IP addresses should have multiple address records.
AAAA	IPv6 host address	Contains the name of a host and its Internet Protocol version 6 (IPv6) address.
CNAME	Canonical name	Creates an alias for a host name. This allows a host to be referred to by multiple names in DNS. The most common use is when a host provides a common service, such as World Wide Web (WWW) or File Transfer Protocol (FTP), and you want it to have a friendly name rather than a complex name. For example, you might want www.cpandl.com to be an alias for the host dc06.cpandl.com.

Record Type	Common Name	Description
MX	Mail exchanger	Indicates a mail exchange server for the domain, which allows mail to be delivered to the correct mail servers in the domain. For example, if an MX record is set for the domain cpandl.com, all mail sent to *username*@cpandl.com will be directed to the server specified in the MX record.
NS	Name server	Provides a list of authoritative servers for a domain, which allows DNS lookups within various zones. Each primary and secondary name server in a domain should be declared through this record.
PTR	Pointer	Enables reverse lookups by creating a pointer that maps an IP address to a host name.
SOA	Start of authority	Indicates the authoritative name server for a particular zone. The authoritative server is the best source of DNS information for a zone. Because each zone must have an SOA record, the record is created automatically when you add a zone. The SOA record also contains information about how resource records in the zone should be used and cached. This includes refresh, retry, and expiration intervals as well as the maximum time that a record is considered valid.
SRV	Service location	Makes it possible to find a server providing a specific service. Active Directory uses SRV records to locate domain controllers, global catalog servers, Lightweight Directory Access Protocol (LDAP) servers, and Kerberos servers. SRV records are created automatically. For example, Active Directory creates an SRV record when you set a domain controller as a global catalog. LDAP servers can add an SRV to indicate they are available to handle LDAP requests in a particular zone. SRV records are created in the forest root zone as discussed in "Using DNS with Active Directory" on page 767.

DNS Zones and Zone Transfers

DNS name servers that have complete information for a part of the DNS namespace are said to be authoritative. As mentioned earlier, a portion of the namespace over which an authoritative name server has control is referred to as a zone. Zones establish the boundaries within which a particular name server can resolve requests and are the main replication units in DNS. Zones can contain resource records for one or more related DNS domains.

Windows Server 2008 supports four types of zones:

- **Standard primary** Stores a writable master copy of a zone as a text file. All changes to a zone are made in the primary zone. The information in as well as changes to a primary zone can be replicated to secondary zones.

Chapter 23

- **Standard secondary** Stores a read-only copy of a zone as a text file. It is used to provide redundancy and load balancing for a primary zone. The information in and changes to a primary zone are replicated to a secondary zone using zone transfers.

- **Active Directory–integrated** Integrates zone information in Active Directory Domain Services and uses Active Directory Domain Services to replicate zone information. This is a proprietary zone type that is only possible when you deploy Active Directory Domain Services on the network. Active Directory–integrated zones were first introduced in Microsoft Windows 2000 and are new for previous Microsoft Windows NT users. Windows Server 2008 can selectively replicate DNS information.

> **Active Directory–Integrated Zones Are Only on Domain Controllers**
>
> Designating a zone as Active Directory–integrated means that only domain controllers can be primary name servers for the zone. These domain controllers can accept dynamic updates, and Active Directory security is used automatically to restrict dynamic updates to domain members. Any DNS servers in the zone that aren't domain controllers can act only as secondary name servers. These secondary name servers cannot accept dynamic updates.

- **Stub** Stores a partial zone that can be used to identify the authoritative DNS servers for a zone. A stub zone has no information about the hosts in a zone. Instead, it has information only about the authoritative name servers in a zone so queries can be forwarded directly to those name servers.

Each of these four DNS zone types can be created for forward or reverse lookups. A forward lookup zone is used to resolve DNS names into IP addresses and provide information about available network services. A reverse lookup zone is used to resolve IP addresses to DNS names.

Zones That Aren't Integrated with Active Directory

With standard zones that aren't integrated with Active Directory, a master copy of the zone is stored in a primary zone on a single DNS server, called a *primary DNS server.* This server's SOA record indicates that it is the primary zone for the related domain. Secondary zones are used to improve performance and provide redundancy. A server storing a copy of a secondary zone is referred to as a *secondary DNS server.*

A primary DNS server automatically replicates a copy of the primary zone to any designated secondary servers. The transfer of zone information is handled by a zone replication process and is referred to as a *zone transfer.* Although the initial zone transfer after configuring a new secondary server represents a full transfer of the zone information, subsequent transfers are made incrementally as changes occur. Here's how it works: When changes are made to a primary zone, the changes are made first to the primary zone and then transferred to the secondary zone on the secondary servers. Because only changes are transferred, rather than a complete copy of the zone, the amount of traffic required to keep a secondary zone current is significantly reduced.

You can implement DNS zones in many ways. One way to do this is to mimic your organization's domain structure. Figure 23-4 shows an example of how zones and zone transfers could be configured for child domains of a parent domain. Here, you have separate zones that handle name services for the cpandl.com, tech.cpandl.com, and sales.cpandl.com domains. Zone transfers are configured so that copies of the primary zone on cpandl.com are transferred to the name servers for the tech.cpandl.com and sales.cpandl.com domains. The reason for this is that users in these zones routinely work with servers in the cpandl.com zone. This makes lookups faster and reduces the amount of DNS traffic as well.

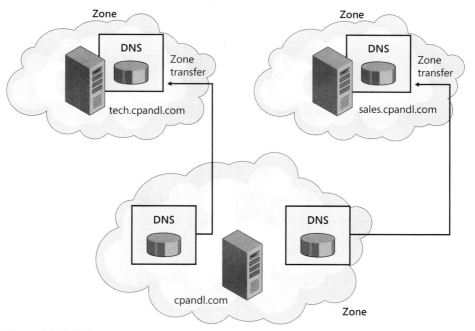

Figure 23-4 DNS zones on separate servers.

Although you can configure DNS services in this way, your organization's domain structure is separate from its zone configuration. If you create subdomains of a parent domain, they can either be part of the same zone or belong to another zone and these zones can be on separate DNS servers or the same DNS servers.

The example in Figure 23-5 shows a wide area network (WAN) configuration. The branch offices in Seattle and New York are separate from the company headquarters, and key zones are organized geographically. At company headquarters there's an additional zone running on the same DNS name server as the zone for the cpandl.com domain. This zone handles services.cpandl.com, tech.cpandl.com, and sales.cpandl.com.

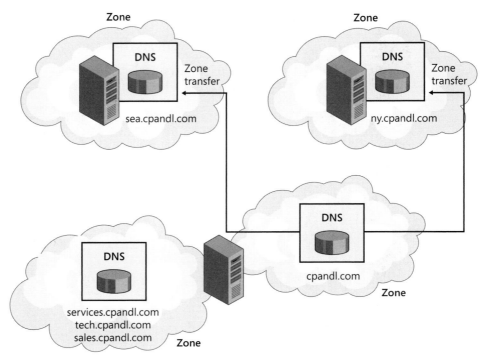

Figure 23-5 Zones can be separate from domain structure.

Zones That Are Integrated with Active Directory

Using Active Directory–integrated zones, you can store DNS zone information within Active Directory. This gives you several advantages. Any primary zone or stub zone integrated with Active Directory is automatically replicated to other domain controllers using Active Directory replication. Because Active Directory can compress replication data between sites, you can more efficiently replicate DNS information, and this is especially important over slow WAN links.

Figure 23-6 shows an example of Active Directory–integrated zones and replication. Here, zone information for cpandl.com, seattle.cpandl.com, portland.cpandl.com, and sf.cpandl.com has been integrated with Active Directory. This allows any DNS changes made at branch offices or at company headquarters to be replicated throughout the organization to all the available name servers. Because the decision to integrate zones with Active Directory isn't an all-or-nothing approach, there are also standard primary and secondary zones, and standard DNS zone transfers are used to maintain these zones.

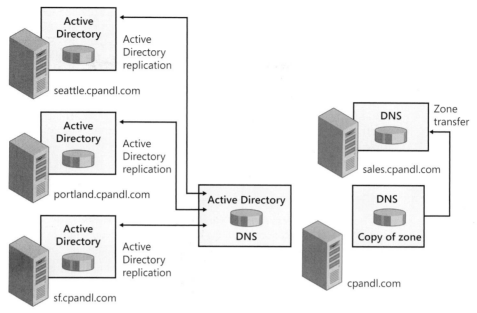

Figure 23-6 Active Directory–integrated zones.

INSIDE OUT   Multimaster replication for DNS changes

By using Active Directory integration, copies of zone information are maintained on all domain controllers that are also configured as DNS servers. This is different from standard DNS zones. When you use standard zones, there's a single authoritative DNS server for a zone, and it maintains a master copy of the zone. All updates to the primary zone must be made on the primary server. With Active Directory–integrated zones, each domain controller configured as a DNS server in a domain is an authoritative server for that domain. This means clients can make updates to DNS records on any of these servers and the changes will be automatically replicated.

Active Directory–integrated zones have changed substantially since they were first implemented. In Windows 2000, DNS information is stored in the same context as other Active Directory information. This means updates to DNS records are automatically replicated to all domain controllers in the domain regardless of whether those domain controllers are also DNS name servers. In an organization with many domain controllers but only a few DNS name servers, this means there is a lot of unnecessary traffic on the network. Additional planning is also required to ensure that all domain controllers are able to resolve the forest-side locator records stored in the _msdcs sub-domain in the forest root domain.

In Windows Server 2008, default application partitions are used to ensure that DNS information is replicated only to domain controllers that are also configured as DNS servers. Here's how it works: For every domain in an Active Directory forest, a separate application partition is created and used to store all records in each Active Directory–integrated zone configured for that domain. Because the application partition context is outside that of other Active Directory information, DNS information is no longer replicated with other Active Directory information. There's also a default application partition that stores DNS information and replicates that information to all DNS servers in an Active Directory forest. This simplifies DNS replication for organizations with multiple domains.

> **Note**
>
> Only domain controllers running Windows Server 2003, Windows Server 2008, or later can use default application partitions to replicate DNS information in this way. Because of this, you can take advantage of this feature when the domain controllers in all the domains of your forest are running Windows Server 2003 or later.

Another benefit of Active Directory integration is the ability to perform conditional forwarding. By using conditional forwarding, you can eliminate the split-brain syndrome when internal requests get incorrectly forwarded to external DNS servers. Finally, with dynamic updates using DHCP, clients gain the ability to use secure dynamic updates. Secure dynamic updates ensure that only those clients that created a record can subsequently update the record. You'll find more on secure dynamic updates in "Security Considerations" on page 757.

When you are working with earlier releases of DNS Server service for Windows Server, restarting a DNS server could take an hour or more in very large organizations with extremely large Active Directory Domain Services–integrated zones. The reason for this was that the zone data was loaded in the foreground while the server was starting the DNS Server service. To ensure that DNS servers can be responsive after a restart, the DNS Server service for Windows Server 2008 has been enhanced to load zone data from Active Directory Domain Services in the background while it restarts. This ensures that the DNS server is responsive and can handle requests for data from other zones.

DNS servers running Windows Server 2008 perform the following tasks at startup:

- Enumerate all zones to be loaded.

- Load root hints from files or Active Directory Domain Services storage.

- Load all zones that are stored in files rather than in Active Directory Domain Services.

- Begin responding to queries and Remote Procedure Calls (RPCs).

- Create one or more threads to load the zones that are stored in Active Directory Domain Services.

Because separate threads load zone data, the DNS server is able to respond to queries while zone loading is in progress. If a DNS client performs a query for a host in a zone that has already been loaded, the DNS server responds appropriately. If the query is for a host that has not yet been loaded into memory, the DNS server reads the host's data from Active Directory Domain Services and updates its record list accordingly.

Secondary Zones, Stub Zones, and Conditional Forwarding

Secondary zones, stub zones, and conditional forwarding can all be used to resolve name resolution problems—chiefly the split-brain scenario in which internal DNS servers blindly forward any requests that they can't resolve to external servers. Rather than blindly forwarding requests, you can configure internal servers so that they know about certain DNS domains. This ensures that name resolution works for domains that aren't known on the public Internet and can also be used to speed up name resolution for known domains, which makes users much happier than if name resolution fails or they have to wait all the time for name requests to be resolved.

By using a secondary zone, you create a complete copy of a zone on a DNS server that can be used to resolve DNS queries without having to go to the authoritative name server for that domain. Not only can this be used for subdomains of a parent domain that exists in different zones, but for different parent domains as well. For example, on the name servers for cpandl.com you could create secondary zones for a partner company, such as The Phone Company whose domain is thephone-company.com. In this way, DNS clients in the cpandl.com domain can perform fast lookups for hosts in thephone-company.com domain.

The downside is that you must replicate DNS information between the domains. If this replication takes place over the public Internet, the administrators at The Phone Company would need to configure firewalls on their network to allow this and make other security changes as well, which might not be acceptable. Because you are maintaining a full copy of the zone, any change generates replication traffic.

With a stub zone, you create a partial copy of a zone that has information about only the authoritative name servers in a zone. As Figure 23-7 shows, this allows a DNS server to forward queries directly to a name server for a particular domain and bypass the normal name server hierarchy. This speeds up the lookup because you don't have to go through multiple name servers to find the authoritative name server for a domain.

Stub zones work like this: When you set up a stub zone for a domain, only the resource records needed to identify the authoritative name servers for the related domain are transferred to the name server. These records include the SOA and NS records as well as the related A records for these servers (referred to as *glue records*). These records can be maintained in one of two ways. If you use Active Directory integration, the normal Active Directory replication process can be used to maintain the stub zone. If you use a standard stub zone, standard zone transfers are used to maintain the stub zone. Both techniques require access to the domain specified in the stub zone, which can be a security issue. Replication traffic isn't an issue, however, because you are maintaining a very small amount of data.

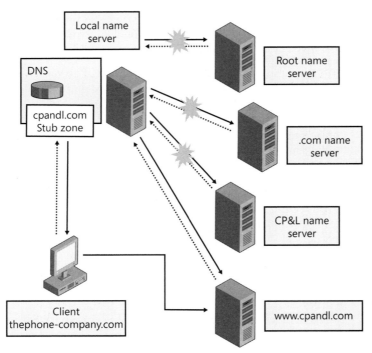

Figure 23-7 Using stub zones for lookups.

Conditional forwarding is very similar to stub zones except that you don't need to transfer any information from the domain to which you want to forward requests. Instead, you configure name servers in domain A so that they know the IP address of the authoritative name servers in domain B, allowing these name servers to be used as forwarders. There's no access requirement, so you don't need permission to do this, and there's no bandwidth requirement, so you don't need to worry about extra replication traffic.

By using conditional forwarding, there are some trade-offs to be made, however. If the authoritative name servers change, the IP addresses aren't updated automatically as they are with stub zones or secondary zones. This means you would have to reconfigure name servers manually in domain A with the new IP addresses of the authoritative name servers in domain B. When you configure conditional forwarders on a name server, the name server has to check the forwarders list each time it resolves a name. As the list grows, it requires more and more time to work through the list of potential forwarders.

Integration with Other Technologies

The DNS client built into computers running Windows Vista and Windows Server 2008 supports DNS traffic over IPv4 and IPv6. By default, IPv6 configures the well-known site-local addresses of DNS servers at FEC0:0:0:FFFF::1, FEC0:0:0:FFFF::2, and

FEC0:0:0:FFFF::3. To add the IPv6 addresses of your DNS servers, use the properties of the Internet Protocol Version 6 (TCP/IPv6) component in Network Connections or the **netsh interface ipv6 set dns** command.

When the network uses DHCP, you should configure DHCP to work with DNS. DHCP clients can register IPv4 and IPv6 addresses. To ensure proper integration of DHCP and DNS, you need to set the appropriate DHCP scope options. For IPv4, you should set the 006 DNS Servers and 015 DNS Domain Name scope options. For IPv6, you should set the 00023 DNS Recursive Name Server IPV6 Address and 00024 Domain Search List scope options.

DNS client computers running Windows Vista or Windows Server 2008 can use link-local multicast name resolution (LLMNR) to resolve names on a local network segment when a DNS server is not available. They also periodically search for a domain controller in the domain to which they belong and can be configured to locate the nearest domain controller instead of searching randomly. This functionality helps avoid performance problems that might occur should a DNS client create an association with a distant domain controller located on a slow link rather than a local domain controller because of a network or server failure. Previously, this association continued until the client was forced to seek a new domain controller, such as when the client computer was disconnected from the network for a long period of time. By periodically renewing its association with a domain controller, a DNS client can reduce the probability that it will be associated with an inappropriate domain controller.

Security Considerations

DNS security is an important issue, and this discussion focuses on three areas:

- DNS queries from clients
- DNS dynamic updates
- External DNS name resolution

DNS Queries and Security

A client that makes a query trusts that an authoritative DNS name server gives it the right information. In most environments, this works fine. Users or administrators specify the initial DNS name servers to which DNS queries should be forwarded in a computer's TCP/IP configuration. In some environments where security is a major concern, administrators might be worried about DNS clients getting invalid information from DNS name servers. Here, administrators might want to look at the DNS Security (DNSSEC) protocol. DNSSEC is especially useful for companies that have many branch locations, and DNS information is transferred over the public Internet using zone transfers.

> **Note**
>
> Windows Server 2008 provides basic support for DNSSEC, which enables a DNS name server running Windows Server 2008 to act as a secondary for a DNS Berkeley Internet Name Domain (BIND) server using DNSSEC. Additionally, the standard DNS Client for Windows computers doesn't validate any DNSSEC data that is returned to it.

> **Configure DNSSEC Support**
>
> In Windows Server 2008, you can configure DNSSEC support for a DNS server using the DNSCMD command. To enable DNSSEC support, type **dnscmd *ServerName* /config /enablednssec 1**, where *ServerName* is the name or IP address of the DNS server you want to configure, such as NS2 or 192.168.18.17. To disable DNSSEC support, type **dnscmd *ServerName* /config /enablednssec 0**.

DNSSEC provides authentication of DNS information. Using DNSSEC, you can digitally sign zone files so that they can be authenticated. These digital signatures can be sent to DNS clients as resource records from DNS servers hosting signed zones. The client can then verify that the DNS information sent from the DNS server is authentic.

DNSSEC digital signatures are encrypted using private key encryption on a per-zone basis. In private key encryption, there is a public key and a private key. A zone's public key is used to validate a digital signature. Like the digital signature itself, the public key is stored in a signed zone in the form of a resource record. A zone's private key is not stored in the zone; it is private and used only by the name server to sign the related zone or parts of the zone. The records used with DNSSEC are summarized in Table 23-3.

Table 23-3   DNSSEC Resource Records

Record Type	Common Name	Description
KEY	Public Key	Contains the public key that is related to a DNS domain name. The public key can be for a zone, host or other entity. KEY records are authenticated by SIG records.
NXT	Next	Indicates the next record in a digitally signed zone and states which records exist in a zone. It can be used to validate that a particular record doesn't exist in the zone. For example, if there's a record for corpsvr07.cpandl.com and the Next record points to corpsvr09.cpandl.com, there isn't a record for corpsvr08.cpandl.com, so that server doesn't exist in the zone.
SIG	Signature	Contains the digital signature for a zone or part of a zone and is used to authenticate a resource record set of a particular type.

DNS Dynamic Updates and Security

Windows Server 2008 fully supports DNS dynamic updates. Dynamic updates are defined in RFC 2136 and are used in conjunction with DHCP to allow a client to update its A record if its IP address changes and allow the DHCP server to update the PTR record for the client on the DNS server. DHCP servers can also be configured to update both the A and PTR records on the client's behalf. Dynamic DNS is also supported for IPv6 AAAA records, which allows for dynamic updating of host addresses on systems that use IPv6 and DHCP.

If dynamic updates are enabled, the DNS name server trusts the client to update its own DNS record and trusts the DHCP server to make updates on behalf of the client. There are two types of dynamic updates:

- **Secure dynamic updates** Using secure dynamic updates allows you to put security mechanisms in place to ensure that only a client that created a record can update a record.

- **Nonsecure dynamic updates** By using nonsecure dynamic updates, there is no way to ensure that only a client that created a record can update a record.

Secure dynamic updates are the default setting for Active Directory–integrated zones. By using secure updates, only clients capable of using secure dynamic updates can update their records. This means clients running Windows 2000 or later can update their own records, but clients running earlier versions of the Windows operating system cannot. DHCP servers can be configured to make updates on behalf of these clients. For more information on this, see "Integrating DHCP and DNS" on page 730.

With standard zones, the default setting is to allow both secure and nonsecure dynamic updates. The reason standard zones are configured for both secure and nonsecure dynamic updates is that this allows clients running Windows 2000 or later as well as earlier versions of Windows to update records dynamically. Although it seems to imply that security is involved, it is, in fact, not. Here, allowing secure updates simply means that the dynamic update process won't break when a secure update is made. DNS doesn't validate updates and this means dynamic updates are accepted from any client. This creates a significant security vulnerability because updates can be accepted from untrusted sources.

CAUTION

If you install DHCP on a domain controller, the DHCP server is made a member of the DNSUpdateProxy group. Because members of this group do not have security set on records they create, any records the DHCP server creates will have no security. This means they could be updated by any client.

Chapter 23

INSIDE OUT

Hidden "gotchas" with secure updates

There are hidden "gotchas" when you use secure dynamic updates that people don't often think about. When a DHCP server creates a record on a DNS server, the DHCP server becomes the owner of the record. If a DHCP server is replaced or its scopes are migrated to another computer, then the server no longer exists and no one else can update the records it created. Thus, any records that the server owns become outdated (stale) and nonupdateable (orphaned).

In addition, if you upgrade a client from a version of Windows earlier than Windows 2000 to Windows 2000 or later, the client's DNS records can become stale and orphaned as well. This happens because DHCP servers update the DNS records for pre–Windows 2000 clients but do not do so for clients using Windows 2000 or later.

The best solution for these hidden "gotchas" is to change ownership of records manually as appropriate after upgrades.

External DNS Name Resolution and Security

Typically, as part of a standard DNS configuration, you'll configure DNS servers on your internal network to forward queries that they can't resolve to DNS servers outside the organization. Normally, these servers are the name servers for the Internet service provider (ISP) that provides your organization's Internet connection. In this configuration, you know that internal servers forward to designated external servers. However, if those servers don't respond, the internal servers typically will forward requests directly to the root name servers, and this is where security problems can be introduced.

By default, DNS servers include a list of root servers that can be used for name resolution to the top-level domains. This list is maintained in what is called a *root hints file*. If this file is not updated regularly, your organization's internal name servers could point to invalid root servers, and this leaves a hole in your security that could be exploited. To prevent this, periodically update the root hints file.

On a DNS server that doesn't use Active Directory, the root hints are read from the %SystemRoot%\System32\DNS\Cache.dns file. You can obtain an update for this file from *ftp://ftp.rs.internic.net/domain/named.cache*. To determine whether an update is needed, compare the version information in your current root hints file with that of the published version. Within the root hints file, you'll find a section of comments like this:

```
;   This file holds the information on root name servers needed to
    ;       initialize cache of Internet domain name servers
    ;       (e.g. reference this file in the "cache  .  <file>"
    ;       configuration file of BIND domain name servers).
    ;
    ;       This file is made available by InterNIC
    ;       under anonymous FTP as
    ;           file                        /domain/named.root
    ;           on server                   FTP.INTERNIC.NET
```

```
;
;            last update:                  Feb 21, 2008
;            related version of root zone:  2008022105
```

Here, the version information is in the last two lines of the comments. If you changed the root hints file, you must stop and then start the DNS Server service so that the root hints file is reloaded. In the DNS console, you can do this by right-clicking the server entry, pointing to All Tasks, and selecting Restart.

On a DNS server that uses Active Directory Domain Services–integrated zones, the root hints are read from Active Directory and the Registry at startup. You can view and modify the root hints in the DNS console. To do this, right-click the DNS server entry and then select Properties. In the Properties dialog box, click the Root Hints tab. You can then manage each of the individual root hint entries using Add, Edit, or Remove as necessary. To update the entire root hints using a known good DNS server, click Copy From Server, type the IP address of the DNS server, and then click OK. If you suspect the root hints file is corrupted, see Microsoft Knowledge Base article 249868 for details on reloading the file into Active Directory using the %SystemRoot%\System32\DNS\Cache.dns file.

INSIDE OUT   Consider whether external root servers should be used

In some instances, you might not want to use a root hints file, or you might want to bypass using root servers. Here are two scenarios to consider:

- If your organization isn't connected to the Internet, your name servers don't need pointers to the public root servers. Instead, you should remove the entries in the Cache.dns file and replace them with NS and A records for the DNS server authoritative for the root domain at your site. For example, if you use a private top-level domain, such as .local, you must set up a root name server for the .local domain, and the Cache.dns file should point to these root name servers. You must then restart the DNS Server service so that the root hints file is reloaded. In the DNS console, you can do this by right-clicking the server entry, pointing to All Tasks, and selecting Restart.

- Making a connection to the root name servers exposes your internal name servers. The internal name server must connect through your organization's firewall to the root name server. While this connection is open and your name server is waiting for a response, there is a potential vulnerability that could be exploited. Here, someone could have set up a fake name server that is waiting for such connections and then could use this server to perform malicious activity on your DNS servers. To prevent this, you can configure forwarding to specific external name servers and tell your name servers not to use the root name servers. You do this by configuring the Do Not Use Recursion For This Domain option when you set up forwarding.

For more information, see "Configuring Forwarders and Conditional Forwarding" on page 786.

Chapter 23

Architecting a DNS Design

After you complete your initial planning, you should consider an overall design architecture. There are two primary DNS designs used:

- Split-brain design
- Separate-name design

Split-Brain Design: Same Internal and External Names

Most DNS implementations are architected to use a split-brain design. What this means is that your organization uses the same domain name internally as it does externally, and DNS is designed so that the name services for your organization's internal network are separate from that used for the organization's external network. Put another way, an organization's private network should be private and separate from its presence on the public Internet, so your internal name servers should be separate from your external name servers. You don't want a situation in which you have one set of name servers and they are used for both users within the organization and users outside the organization. That's a security no-no that could open your internal network to attack.

The concern with this design—and this is why it is called split-brain—is that if your internal network uses the same domain namespace as that of your public Internet presence, you can get in a situation in which users within the organization can't look up information related to the organization's public Internet presence and users outside the organization can't look up information for the organization's private network.

From an internal user perspective, it is a bad thing that users can't access the organization's public Internet resources. There's an easy fix, however. You simply create records on the authoritative name server for the internal network that specifies the IP address for the organization's public Internet resources. For example, to allow users on the internal cpandl.com domain to access www.cpandl.com on the public Internet, you create a host record on the internal DNS server for www in the cpandl.com domain that specifies its IP address.

From a security perspective, it is a good thing that outside users can't look up information for the organization's private network—you don't want them to be able to do this. If you have business partners at other locations that need access to the internal network, you should set up a secure link between your organizations or make other arrangements, such as using an extranet.

To implement split-brain design, you should do the following:

- **Complete your planning** Complete your planning and decide how many DNS servers you are going to use on the internal network. Decide on the host names and IP addresses these servers will use. In most cases, you'll need only two DNS servers for a domain. It is a standard convention to set the host names of DNS servers as Primary and Secondary if there are two servers and as NS01, NS02, and so on if there are more than two servers. You can use this naming convention or adopt a different one.

- **Install and configure the DNS Server service** Install the DNS Server service on each of the designated DNS servers. If you are using Active Directory, DNS is already implemented on some servers because it is required. With Active Directory Domain Services–integrated zones, every DNS server in a domain that is also configured as a domain controller is a primary name server–and any DNS server not configured as a domain controller can be only a secondary in that zone. With standard primary and secondary zones, you can have only one primary server for a zone–and every other DNS server in that zone must be a secondary.

- **Create records on internal name servers for your public resources** For each of the organization's public Internet resources to which internal users need access, you must create records on the internal name servers. This allows the internal users to access and work with these resources. This includes the organization's WWW, FTP, and mail servers.

- **Configure forwarding to your ISP's name servers** The ISP that provides your connection to the Internet should provide you with the host names and IP addresses of name servers to which internal users can forward DNS queries. Configure your internal name servers so that they forward to your ISP's name servers DNS queries that they cannot resolve. As necessary, configure secondary zones, stub zones, or conditional forwarding to any domains for which you desire direct lookups.

- **Configure internal systems to use your internal DNS servers** Every workstation and server on your internal network should be configured with the IP address of your primary and secondary DNS name servers. If you have more than two name servers, set the name servers that should be used as appropriate. Normally, you'll point a system to only one or two internal name servers. Don't point internal systems to external name servers–you don't want internal systems trying to resolve requests on these name servers.

- **Configure external name servers for internal resources as necessary** Consider whether you need to create resource records on your ISP's external name servers for servers on your internal network that need to be resolvable from the Internet, such as by mobile users. If you do, provide the necessary information to your ISP to set up these resource records.

Separate-Name Design: Different Internal and External Names

Another approach to DNS design is to use separate-name design in which your internal network uses different domain names than that of your organization's public Internet presence. This creates actual physical separation of your organization's internal and external namespaces by placing them in different parent domains. For example, your organization could use cohovineyard.com for its internal network and cohowinery.com

Chapter 23

for its external network. Now you have a situation in which completely different namespaces are used to create separation.

As with split-brain design, you have different internal name servers and different external name servers. Unlike split-brain design, internal users should be able to look up information related to the organization's public Internet presence, and you won't need to create additional records to do this. Here, it is only a matter of ensuring that the internal name servers forward to external name servers, which can perform the necessary lookups.

If you use different names than are in the public domain hierarchy, you should register all the internal and external domain names you use. In the previous example, you would register cohovineyard.com and cohowinery.com. This ensures that someone else can't register one of the domain names you use internally, which could mess up name resolution in some instances. You wouldn't need to register a domain name, such as cohowinery.local, however, because .local is not a public top-level domain.

To implement separate-name design, you should do the following:

- **Complete your planning** Complete your planning and decide how many DNS servers you are going to use on the internal network. Decide on the host names and IP addresses these servers will use. In most case, you'll need only two DNS servers for a domain. It is a standard convention to set the host names of DNS servers as Primary and Secondary if there are two servers and as NS01, NS02, and so on if there are more than two servers. You can use this naming convention or adopt a different one.

- **Install and configure the DNS Server service** Install the DNS Server service on each of the designated DNS servers. If you are using Active Directory, DNS is already implemented on some servers because it is required. With Active Directory Domain Services–integrated zones, every DNS server in a domain that is also configured as a domain controller is a primary name server—and any DNS server not configured as a domain controller can be only a secondary in that zone. With standard primary and secondary zones, you can have only one primary server for a zone—and every other DNS server in that zone must be a secondary.

- **Configure forwarding to your ISP's name servers** The ISP that provides your connection to the Internet should provide you with the host names and IP addresses of name servers to which internal users can forward DNS queries. Configure your internal name servers so that they forward DNS queries that they cannot resolve to your ISP's name servers. As necessary, configure secondary zones, stub zones, or conditional forwarding to any domains for which you desire direct lookups.

- **Configure internal systems to use your internal DNS servers** Every workstation and server on your internal network should be configured with the IP address of your primary and secondary DNS name servers. If you have more than two name servers, set the name servers that should be used as appropriate. Normally, you'll point a system to only one or two internal name servers. Don't point internal systems to external name servers—you don't want internal systems trying to resolve requests on these name servers.

- **Configure external name servers for internal resources as necessary** Consider whether you need to create resource records on your ISP's external name servers for servers on your internal network that need to be resolvable from the Internet, such as by mobile users. If you do, provide the necessary information to your ISP to set up these resource records.

Name services are essential for communications for Transmission Control Protocol/ Internet Protocol (TCP/IP) networking. Windows Server 2008 uses the Domain Name System (DNS) as its primary method of name resolution. DNS enables computers to register and resolve DNS domain names. DNS defines the rules under which computers are named and how names are resolved to IP addresses. Windows Server 2008 also supports Windows Internet Naming Service (WINS), which is covered in detail in Chapter 25, "Implementing and Maintaining WINS." WINS provides a similar service for NetBIOS names as DNS provides for DNS domain names. WINS maps NetBIOS names to IP addresses for hosts running NetBIOS over TCP/IP.

Installing the DNS Server Service

The way you install the DNS Server service depends on whether you plan to use DNS with the Active Directory or without Active Directory. After you make that decision, you can install DNS as necessary.

Using DNS with Active Directory

On a domain with Active Directory, DNS is required to install the first domain controller in a domain. Active Directory doesn't necessarily require Windows DNS, however. Active Directory is designed to work with any DNS server that supports dynamic updates and Service Location (SRV) records. This means Active Directory can work with any DNS server running Berkeley Internet Name Domain (BIND) version 8.1.2 or later. If you have DNS servers that use BIND version 8.1.2 or later, you can use those servers. If you don't already have BIND servers, you probably won't want to set these up because there are many benefits to using the Microsoft DNS Server service.

When you install the DNS Server service as part of the Active Directory installation process, you can use Active Directory–integrated zones and take advantage of the many replication and security benefits of Active Directory. Here, any server configured as a domain controller with DNS and using Active Directory–integrated zones is an Active Directory primary name server.

Here's how installation of DNS on the first domain controller in a domain works:

1. You use the Domain Controller Promotion tool (Dcpromo.exe) to install the first domain controller. During the installation process, you are prompted to specify the Active Directory domain name, as shown in the following screen. This sets the DNS name for the domain as well.

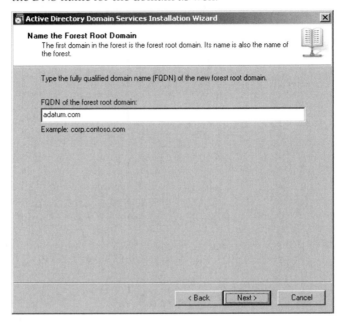

> **Note**
>
> For more information about promoting domain controllers, see "Installing Active Directory Domain Services" on page 1112.

2. When the Active Directory installation process begins, the Active Directory Domain Services Installation Wizard will check the current DNS configuration. If no authoritative DNS servers are available for the domain, the wizard selects DNS Server as an additional installation option, as shown in the following screen:

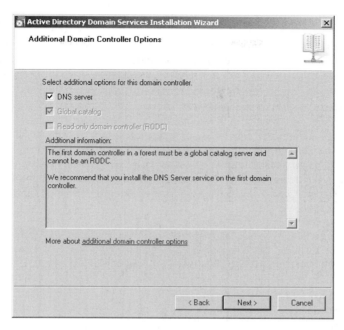

3. In most cases, you'll want to install DNS. If you install DNS, the Active Directory
    Domain Services Installation Wizard will install and then configure DNS. As
    the next screen shows, this means a forward lookup zone will be created for the
    domain. The forward lookup zone will have the Start of Authority (SOA), Name
    Server (NS), and host Address (A) records for the server you are working with.
    This designates it as the authoritative name server for the domain. If desired, you
    can also create reverse lookup zones to allow for IP address to host name lookups.
    DNS servers support IPv4 and IPv6 for reverse lookups.

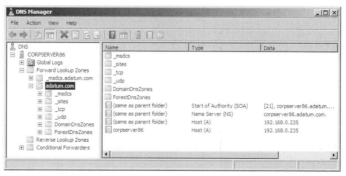

4. For the first DNS server in a forest, the Active Directory Domain Services
    Installation Wizard creates the forest-side locator records and stores them in the
    _msdcs subdomain. Windows Server 2008 creates this as a separate zone, which
    is referred to as the *forest root zone*.

INSIDE OUT **Forest root zones**

The forest root zone is an important part of Active Directory. It is in this zone that Active Directory creates SRV resource records used when clients are looking for a particular resource such as global catalog servers, Lightweight Directory Access Protocol (LDAP) servers, and Kerberos servers. The _msdcs subdomain is created as its own zone to improve performance with remote sites. With Windows 2000, remote sites have to replicate the entire DNS database to access forest root records, which means increased replication and bandwidth usage. As a separate zone, only the zone will be replicated to the DNS servers in remote sites as long as Active Directory application partitions are used. In Windows Server 2008, you can enable application partitions for use with DNS as discussed in "Configuring Default Application Directory Partitions and Replication Scope" on page 804.

On subsequent domain controllers, you must specifically install the DNS Server service. You do this using the Add Roles Wizard as detailed in "DNS Setup" on the next page.

In an Active Directory domain, secondary and stub zones can also be useful, as discussed in "DNS Zones and Zone Transfers" on page 749. In fact, in certain situations you might have to use a secondary or stub zone for name resolution to work properly. Consider the case when you have multiple trees in a forest, each in their own namespace. For instance, City Power & Light and The Phone Company are both part of one company and use the domains cpandl.com and thephone-company.com, respectively. If the namespaces for these domains are set up as separate trees of the same forest, your organization would have two namespaces. In the cpandl.com domain, you might want users to be able to access resources in thephone-company.com domain and vice versa. To do this, you would configure DNS as shown in Figure 24-1.

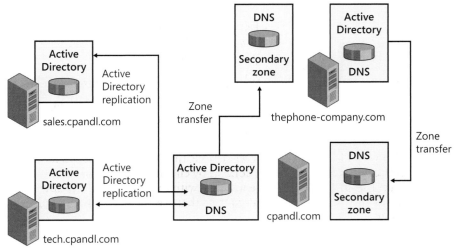

Figure 24-1 Using secondary zones with Active Directory.

The implementation steps for this example are as follows:

1. Set up a secondary or stub zone for thephone-company.com on the authoritative name server for cpandl.com.

2. Set up a secondary or stub zone for cpandl.com on the authoritative name server for thephone-company.com.

3. Configure zone transfers between cpandl.com and thephone-company.com.

4. Configure zone transfers between thephone-company.com and cpandl.com.

Using DNS Without Active Directory

On a domain without Active Directory, DNS servers act as standard primary or standard secondary name servers. You must install the DNS Server service on each primary or secondary server. You do this using the Add Roles Wizard as detailed in the next section.

On primary name servers, you configure primary zones for forward lookups and as necessary for reverse lookups. The forward lookup zone will have SOA, NS, and A records for the server you are working with. This designates it as the authoritative name server for the domain. You can also create reverse lookup zones to allow for IP address to host name lookups.

On secondary name servers, you configure secondary zones to store copies of the records on the primary name server. You can create secondary zones for the forward lookup zones as well as the reverse lookup zones configured on the primary.

Stub zones and forwarders are also options for these DNS servers.

DNS Setup

You can install the DNS Server service by completing the following steps:

1. In Server Manager, select the Roles node in the left pane and then click Add Roles. This starts the Add Roles Wizard. If the wizard displays the Before You Begin page, read the welcome message and then click Next.

2. On the Select Server Roles page, select DNS Server and then click Next twice.

3. Click Install. The wizard installs DNS Server. From now on, the DNS Server service should start automatically each time you reboot the server. If it doesn't start, you'll need to start it manually.

After you install the DNS Server service, the DNS console is available on the Administrative Tools menu. Start the console by clicking Start, Administrative Tools, DNS. Then select the DNS server you are working with to see its status as shown in Figure 24-2. This is telling you to create a scope so that the clients can get IP addresses dynamically assigned by this server.

Chapter 24

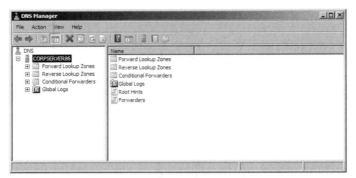

Figure 24-2 The DNS console.

You don't have to complete the rest of the configuration at the server. You can remotely manage and configure DNS. Simply start the DNS console on your computer, right-click the DNS node in the left pane, and select Connect To DNS Server. In the Connect To DNS Server dialog box, select The Following Computer, type the name or IP address of the DNS server, and then click OK. In the DNS console, host addresses are displayed as IPv4 or IPv6 addresses as appropriate.

The command-line counterpart to the DNS console is Dnscmd. The Dnscmd command-line tool accepts addresses in IPv4 and IPv6 format. From the command prompt on a computer running Windows Server 2008, you can use Dnscmd to perform most of the tasks available in the DNS console as well as to perform many troubleshooting tasks that are specific to Dnscmd. Unlike Netsh, Dnscmd doesn't offer internal command prompts. You can specify only the server you want to work with followed by the command and the command-line options to use for that command. Thus, the syntax is as follows:

```
dnscmd ServerName Command CommandOptions
```

where

- *ServerName* is the name or IP address of the DNS server you want to work with, such as CORPSVR03 or 192.168.10.15.

- *Command* is the command to use.

- *CommandOptions* are the options for the command.

> **Note**
>
> If you are working on the server you want to configure, you don't have to type the server name or IP address.

After you set up a DNS server, the setup process should configure the server's TCP/IP settings so that the server attempts to resolve its own DNS queries. Setup does this by setting the server's primary DNS server address to its own address for both IPv4 and IPv6. You can confirm this by entering **ipconfig /all** at a command prompt. In the output of the command, you should see that the DNS servers are set as:

- ::1

- 127.0.0.1

::1 is the local loopback address for IPv6 and 127.0.0.1 is the local loopback address for IPv4. If necessary, you can modify the DNS server entries as discussed in Chapter 21, "Managing TCP/IP Networking." For Preferred DNS Server, type the computer's own IP address. Set an alternate DNS server as necessary.

You can also set the preferred DNS server IP address from the command line. Type the following command:

```
netsh interface ip set dns ConnectionName static ServerIPAddress
```

where *ConnectionName* is the name of the local area connection and *ServerIPAddress* is the IP address of the server.

Consider the following example:

```
netsh interface ip set dns "Local Area Connection" static 192.168.1.100
```

Here, you set the preferred DNS server address for the network connection named Local Area Connection to 192.168.1.100. The Static option says that you want to use the local setting for DNS rather than the Dynamic Host Configuration Protocol (DHCP) setting when applicable.

You can confirm the new setting by typing **ipconfig /all** at the command prompt and checking for the DNS server entry. The server should have the same setting for the IP address and primary DNS server.

Configuring DNS Using the Wizard

From the DNS console, you can start the Configure A DNS Server Wizard and use it to help you set up a DNS server. This wizard is useful for helping you configure small networks that work with Internet service providers (ISPs) and large networks that use forwarding.

Chapter 24

INSIDE OUT   **Are reverse lookups needed?**

For small networks, the Configure A DNS Server Wizard creates only a forward lookup zone. For large networks, the Configure A DNS Server Wizard creates a forward lookup zone and a reverse lookup zone. This might get you to thinking whether reverse lookup zones are needed on your network. Computers use reverse lookups to find out who is contacting them. Often this is so that they can display a host name to users rather than an IP address. So, although a reverse lookup zone isn't created by the Configure A DNS Server Wizard for small networks, you might still want to create one. If so, follow the procedure discussed in "Creating Reverse Lookup Zones" on page 785.

Configuring a Small Network Using the Configure A DNS Server Wizard

For a small network, you can use the wizard to set up your forward lookup zone and query forwarding to your ISP or other DNS servers. You can also choose to configure this zone as a primary or secondary zone. You use the primary zone option if your organization maintains its own zone. You use the secondary zone if your ISP maintains your zone. This gives you a read-only copy of the zone that can be used by internal clients. Because small networks don't normally need reverse lookup zones, these are not created. You can, of course, create these zones later if needed.

To configure a small network using the Configure A DNS Server Wizard, follow these steps:

1. Right-click the server entry in the DNS console, select Configure A Server, and then when the wizard starts, click Next.

Note

If the server you want to work with isn't shown, right-click the DNS node in the left pane, and select Connect To DNS Server. In the Connect To DNS Server dialog box, select The Following Computer, type the name or IP address of the DNS server, and then click OK.

2. Choose Create A Forward Lookup Zone (Recommended For Small Networks), as shown in Figure 24-3, and then click Next.

Note

If Active Directory is installed on the network, this zone will be automatically integrated with Active Directory. To avoid this, you can choose the second option, Create Forward And Reverse Lookup Zones (Recommended For Large Networks), and then proceed as discussed in "Configuring a Large Network Using the Configure A DNS Server Wizard" on page 778. When the wizard gets to the reverse lookup zone configuration part, you can skip this if you don't want to create a reverse lookup zone.

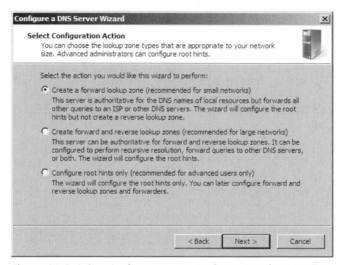

Figure 24-3 Select the first option to configure DNS for a small network.

3. As shown in Figure 24-4, you can now choose whether the DNS server or your ISP maintains the zone and then click Next. Keep the following in mind:

○ If the DNS server maintains the zone, the wizard configures a primary zone that you control. This allows you to create and manage the DNS records for the organization.

○ If your ISP maintains the zone, the wizard configures a secondary zone that will get its information from your ISP. This means the staff at the ISP will need to create and manage the DNS records for the organization—and you will need to pay them to do so.

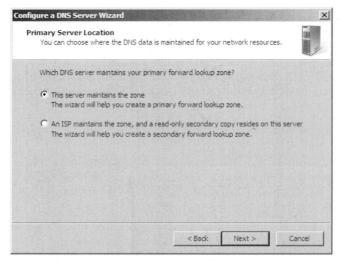

Figure 24-4 Specify whether the zone will be maintained on the server or by your ISP.

4. On the Zone Name page, type the full DNS name for the zone. The zone name should help determine how the zone fits into the DNS domain hierarchy. For example, if you're creating the primary server for the cpandl.com domain, you should type **cpandl.com** as the zone name. Click Next.

5. If your ISP maintains the zone, you see the Master DNS Servers page, as shown in Figure 24-5. Type the IP address of the primary DNS server that's maintaining the zone for you, and then press Enter. Repeat this step to specify additional name servers at your ISP. The wizard will automatically validate the IP address or addresses you've entered. Zone transfers will be configured to copy the zone information from these DNS servers.

6. If you choose to maintain the zone, you see the Dynamic Update page, as shown in Figure 24-6. Choose how you want to configure dynamic updates, and then click Next. You can use one of these options:

   ○ *Allow Only Secure Dynamic Updates*–This option is available only on domain controllers and when Active Directory is deployed. It provides for the best security possible by restricting which clients can perform dynamic updates.

   ○ *Allow Both Nonsecure And Secure Dynamic Updates*–This option allows any client to update resource records in DNS. Although it allows both secure and nonsecure updates, it doesn't validate updates, which means dynamic updates are accepted from any client.

   ○ *Do Not Allow Dynamic Updates*–This option disables dynamic updates in DNS. You should use this option only when the zone isn't integrated with Active Directory.

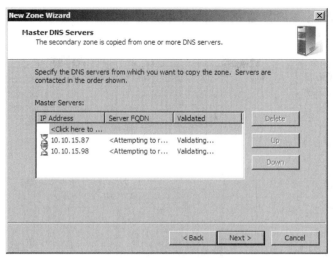

Figure 24-5 Specify the primary name server and other name servers at the ISP.

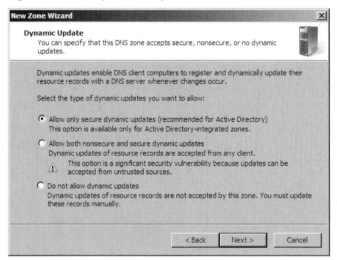

Figure 24-6 Set the dynamic updates options.

7. The Forwarders page allows you to configure forwarding of DNS queries. If you want internal DNS servers to forward queries that they can't resolve to another server, type the IP address for that server. You can optionally include the IP address for a second forwarder as well. If you don't want to use forwarders, select No, It Should Not Forward Queries.

> **Note**
>
> Selecting the No, It Should Not Forward Queries option won't prevent internal name servers from forwarding queries altogether. A root hints file will still be created, which lists the root name servers on the public Internet. Thus, if you don't designate forwarders, such as the primary and secondary name servers of your ISP, the internal name servers will still forward queries. To prevent this, you must modify the root hints file as discussed in "Security Considerations" on page 757.

8. When you click Next, the wizard will search for and retrieve the current root hints. Click Finish to complete the configuration and exit the wizard. If there is a problem configuring the root hints, you will need to configure the root hints manually or copy them from another server.

Configuring a Large Network Using the Configure A DNS Server Wizard

For a large network, you can use the wizard to set up your forward and reverse lookup zones and to set up forwarding with or without recursion. With recursion, queries for external resources are first forwarded to your designated servers, but if those servers are unavailable, the DNS server forwards queries to the root name servers. Without recursion, queries for external resources are only forwarded to your designated servers. The DNS Server service can send queries to IPv4, IPv4 and IPv6, and IPv6-only servers.

To configure a large network using the Configure A DNS Server Wizard, follow these steps:

1. Right-click the server entry in the DNS console, and select Configure A Server. When the wizard starts, click Next.

> **Note**
>
> If the server you want to work with isn't shown, right-click the DNS node in the left pane, and select Connect To DNS Server. In the Connect To DNS Server dialog box, select The Following Computer, type the name or IP address of the DNS server, and then click OK.

2. Choose Create Forward And Reverse Lookup Zones (Recommended For Large Networks), as shown in Figure 24-7, and then click Next.

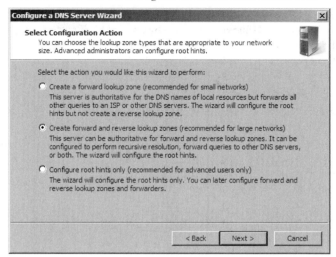

Figure 24-7 Select the second option to configure DNS for a large network.

3. To create a forward lookup zone, accept the default option on the Forward Lookup Zone page, and then click Next. Otherwise, click No, and skip to step 10.

4. As Figure 24-8 shows, you can now select the zone type. Choose one of the following options, and then click Next:

- *Primary Zone*–Use this option to create a primary zone and designate this server to be authoritative for the zone. Ensure that the Store The Zone In Active Directory check box is selected if you want to integrate DNS with Active Directory. Otherwise, clear this check box so that a standard primary zone is created.

- *Secondary Zone*–Use this option to create a secondary zone. This means the server will have a read-only copy of the zone and must use zone transfers to get updates.

- *Stub Zone*–Use this option to create a stub zone. This creates only the necessary glue records for the zone. Optionally, specify that this zone should be integrated with Active Directory. This means the zone will be stored in Active Directory and be updated using Active Directory replication.

Chapter 24

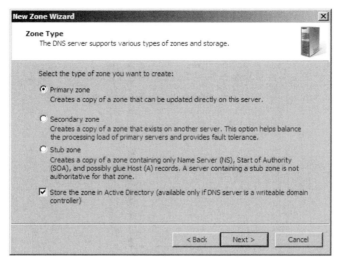

Figure 24-8 Select the zone type.

5. If you created an Active Directory–integrated zone, specify the replication scope, and then click Next. As Figure 24-9 shows, you have the following options:

○ *To All DNS Servers In This Forest*–Enables replication of the zone information to all domains in the Active Directory forest. Each DNS server in the forest will receive a copy of the zone information and get updates through replication.

○ *To All DNS Servers In This Domain*–Enables replication of the zone information in the current domain. Each DNS server in the domain will receive a copy of the zone information and get updates through replication.

○ *To All Domain Controllers In This Domain*–Replicates zone information to all domain controllers in the Active Directory domain. As with a Windows 2000 domain, all domain controllers will get a copy of the zone information and get updates through replication regardless of whether they are also running the DNS Server service.

○ *To All Domain Controllers Specified In The Scope Of This Directory Partition*–If you've configured application partitions other than the default partitions, you can limit the scope of replication to a designated application partition. Any domain controllers configured with the application partition will get a copy of the zone information and get updates through replication regardless of whether they are also running the DNS Server service.

6. On the Zone Name page, type the full DNS name for the zone. The zone name should help determine how the zone fits into the DNS domain hierarchy. For example, if you're creating the primary server for the cpandl.com domain, you should type **cpandl.com** as the zone name. Click Next.

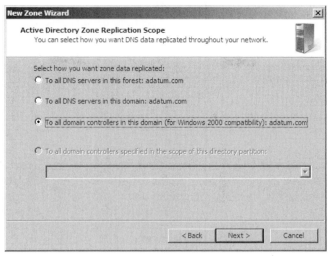

Figure 24-9 Select the replication scope if you are using Active Directory integration.

7. If you're creating a standard primary zone, you see the Zone File page. This page allows you to create a new zone file or use an existing zone file. In most cases, you'll simply accept the default name and allow the wizard to create the file for you in the %SystemRoot%\System32\Dns folder. If you are migrating from a BIND DNS server or have a preexisting zone file, you can select Use This Existing File, and then type the name of the file that you've copied to the %SystemRoot%\System32\Dns folder. Click Next when you are ready to continue.

8. If you're creating a secondary zone, you see the Master DNS Servers page. Type the IP address of the primary DNS server that's maintaining the zone, and then click Add. Repeat this step to specify additional name servers. Zone transfers will be configured to copy the zone information from these DNS servers.

9. On the Dynamic Update page, choose how you want to configure dynamic updates and then click Next. You can use one of the following options:

   ○ *Allow Only Secure Dynamic Updates*–This option is available only on domain controllers and when Active Directory is deployed. It provides for the best security possible by restricting which clients can perform dynamic updates.

   ○ *Allow Both Nonsecure And Secure Dynamic Updates*–This option allows any client to update resource records in DNS. Although it allows both secure and nonsecure updates, it doesn't validate updates, which means dynamic updates are accepted from any client.

   ○ *Do Not Allow Dynamic Updates*–This option disables dynamic updates in DNS. You should use this option only when the zone isn't integrated with Active Directory.

10. To create a reverse lookup zone, accept the default option on the Reverse Lookup Zone page, and then click Next. Otherwise, click No, and skip to step 16.

Chapter 24

11. On the Zone Type page, you can select the zone type. The options available are the same as when creating a forward lookup zone. Click Next after making a selection.

12. If you created an Active Directory–integrated zone, specify the replication scope, and then click Next.

13. Specify whether you are creating an IPv4 reverse lookup zone or an IPv6 reverse lookup zone and then click Next. Do one of the following:

    ○ If you are configuring a reverse lookup zone for IPv4, type the network ID for the reverse lookup zone as shown in Figure 24-10 and then click Next. The values you enter set the default name for the reverse lookup zone. If you have multiple subnets on the same network, such as 192.168.1, 192.168.2, and 192.168.3, you should enter only the network portion for the zone name, such as 192.168 rather than the complete network ID. The DNS Server service will then fill in the necessary subnet zones as you use IP addresses on a particular subnet.

    ○ If you are configuring a reverse lookup zone for IPv6, type the network prefix for the reverse lookup zone and then click Next. The values you enter are used to automatically generate the related zone names. Depending on the prefix you enter, up to eight zones may be created.

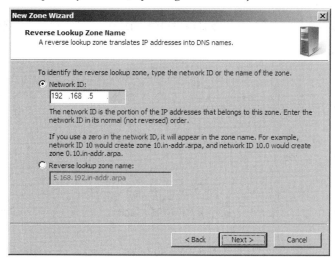

Figure 24-10 Set the network ID for the reverse lookup zone.

14. If you're creating a standard secondary zone, you see the Zone File page. This page allows you to create a new zone file or use an existing zone file.

15. On the Dynamic Update page, choose how you want to configure dynamic updates, and then click Next.

16. The Forwarders page allows you to configure forwarding of DNS queries. If you want internal DNS servers to forward queries that they can't resolve to another

server, type the IP address of that server. You can optionally include the IP address for a second forwarder as well. If you don't want to use forwarders, select No, It Should Not Forward Queries.

> **Note**
>
> Selecting the No, It Should Not Forward Queries option won't prevent internal name servers from forwarding queries altogether. A root hints file will still be created, which lists the root name servers on the public Internet. Thus, if you don't designate forwarders, such as the primary and secondary name servers of your ISP, the internal name servers will still forward queries. To prevent this, you must modify the root hints file as discussed in "Security Considerations" on page 757.

17. When you click Next, the wizard will search for and retrieve the current root hints. Click Finish to complete the configuration and exit the wizard. If there is a problem configuring the root hints, you will need to configure the root hints manually or copy them from another server.

Configuring DNS Zones, Subdomains, Forwarders, and Zone Transfers

Windows Server 2008 supports primary, secondary, Active Directory–integrated, and stub zones, each of which can be created to support either forward lookups or reverse lookups. Forward lookup queries allow a client to resolve a host name to an IP address. Reverse lookups allow a client to resolve an IP address to a host name. At times you might also need to configure subdomains, forwarders, and zone transfers. All of these topics are discussed in this section.

Creating Forward Lookup Zones

To create the initial forward lookup zone or additional forward lookup zones on a server, follow these steps:

1. In the DNS console, expand the node for the server you want to work with. Right-click the Forward Lookup Zones entry, and then choose New Zone. Afterward, in the New Zone Wizard, click Next.

2. Select the zone type. Choose one of the following options, and then click Next:

   ○ *Primary Zone*–Use this option to create a primary zone and designate this server to be authoritative for the zone. Ensure that the Store The Zone In Active Directory check box is selected if you want to integrate DNS with Active Directory. Otherwise, clear this check box so that a standard primary zone is created.

  ○ *Secondary Zone*–Use this option to create a secondary zone. This means the server will have a read-only copy of the zone and will need to use zone transfers to get updates.

  ○ *Stub Zone*–Use this option to create a stub zone. This creates only the necessary glue records for the zone. Optionally, specify that this zone should be integrated with Active Directory. This means the zone will be stored in Active Directory and be updated using Active Directory replication.

3. If you created an Active Directory–integrated zone, specify the replication scope, and then click Next. You have the following options:

  ○ *To All DNS Servers In This Forest*–Enables replication of the zone information to all domains in the Active Directory forest. Each DNS server in the forest will receive a copy of the zone information and get updates through replication.

  ○ *To All DNS Servers In This Domain*–Enables replication of the zone information in the current domain. Each DNS server in the domain will receive a copy of the zone information and get updates through replication.

  ○ *To All Domain Controllers In This Domain*–Replicates zone information to all domain controllers in the Active Directory domain. As with a Windows 2000 domain, all domain controllers will get a copy of the zone information and get updates through replication regardless of whether they are also running the DNS Server service.

  ○ *To All Domain Controllers Specified In The Scope Of This Directory Partition*–If you've configured application partitions, you can limit the scope of replication to a designated application partition. Any domain controllers configured with the application partition will get a copy of the zone information and get updates through replication regardless of whether they are also running the DNS Server service.

4. On the Zone Name page, type the full DNS name for the zone. The zone name should help determine how the zone fits into the DNS domain hierarchy. For example, if you're creating the primary server for the cpandl.com domain, you should type **cpandl.com** as the zone name. Click Next.

5. If you're creating a standard primary zone, you see the Zone File page. This page allows you to create a new zone file or use an existing zone file. In most cases, you'll simply accept the default name and allow the wizard to create the file for you in the %SystemRoot%\System32\Dns folder. If you are migrating from a BIND DNS server or have a preexisting zone file, you can select Use This Existing File and then type the name of the file that you've copied to the %SystemRoot%\System32\Dns folder. Click Next when you are ready to continue.

6. If you're creating a secondary zone, you see the Master DNS Servers page. Type the IP address of the primary DNS server that's maintaining the zone, and then click Add. Repeat this step to specify additional name servers. Zone transfers will be configured to copy the zone information from these DNS servers.

7. On the Dynamic Update page, choose how you want to configure dynamic updates, and then click Next. You can use one of these options:

   ○ *Allow Only Secure Dynamic Updates*–This option is available only on domain controllers and when Active Directory is deployed. It provides for the best security possible by restricting which clients can perform dynamic updates.

   ○ *Allow Both Nonsecure And Secure Dynamic Updates*–This option allows any client to update resource records in DNS. Although it allows both secure and nonsecure updates, it doesn't validate updates, which means dynamic updates are accepted from any client.

   ○ *Do Not Allow Dynamic Updates*–This option disables dynamic updates in DNS. You should use this option only when the zone isn't integrated with Active Directory.

8. Click Next and then click Finish to complete the configuration and exit the wizard.

Creating Reverse Lookup Zones

To create the initial reverse lookup zone or additional reverse lookup zones on a server, follow these steps:

1. In the DNS console, expand the node for the server you want to work with. Right-click the Reverse Lookup Zones entry, and choose New Zone. Afterward, in the New Zone Wizard, click Next.

2. On the Zone Type page, you can select the zone type. The options available are the same as for forward lookup zones. Click Next after making a selection.

3. If you created an Active Directory–integrated zone, specify the replication scope, and then click Next.

4. Specify whether you are creating an IPv4 reverse lookup zone or an IPv6 reverse lookup zone and then click Next. Do one of the following:

   ○ If you are configuring a reverse lookup zone for IPv4, type the network ID for the reverse lookup zone and then click Next. The values you enter set the default name for the reverse lookup zone. If you have multiple subnets on the same network, such as 192.168.1, 192.168.2, and 192.168.3, you should enter only the network portion for the zone name, such as 192.168 rather than the complete network ID. The DNS Server service will then fill in the necessary subnet zones as you use IP addresses on a particular subnet.

   ○ If you are configuring a reverse lookup zone for IPv6, type the network prefix for the reverse lookup zone and then click Next. The values you enter are used to automatically generate the related zone names. Depending on the prefix you enter, up to eight zones may be created.

5. If you're creating a standard secondary zone, you see the Zone File page. This page allows you to create a new zone file or use an existing zone file.

6. On the Dynamic Update page, choose how you want to configure dynamic updates, and then click Next.

7. Click Next and then click Finish to complete the configuration and exit the wizard.

Configuring Forwarders and Conditional Forwarding

In a normal configuration, if a DNS name server can't resolve a request, it forwards the request for resolution. A server to which DNS queries are forwarded is referred to as a *forwarder*. You can specifically designate forwarders that should be used by your internal DNS servers. For example, if you designate your ISP's primary and secondary name servers as forwarders, queries that your internal name servers can't resolve will be forwarded to these servers. Forwarding can still take place, however, even if you don't specifically designate forwarders. The reason for this is that the root hints file specifies the root name servers for the public Internet and these servers can be used as forwarders.

Any time forwarders are not specified or available, requests can be forwarded to the root name servers. The root name servers then forward the requests to the appropriate top-level domain name server, which forwards them to the next-level domain server, and so on. This process is referred to as *recursion*, and, as you can see, this involves a number of forwarding actions. DNS servers can send recursive queries to IPv4, IPv4 and IPv6, and IPv6-only servers.

Another forwarding option is to configure what is called a *conditional forwarder*. When using conditional forwarding, you can tell your DNS name servers that if they see a request for domain XYZ, they should not forward it to the public DNS name servers for resolution. Instead, the name servers should forward the request directly to the authoritative name server for the XYZ domain.

You can configure forwarding options by following these steps:

1. In the DNS console, right-click the server you want to work with, and select Properties. In the Properties dialog box, click the Forwarders tab, as shown in Figure 24-11.

2. To allow forwarding to root name servers when configured forwarders are not available, select the Use Root Hints If No Forwarders Are Available check box.

3. Display the Edit Forwarders dialog box by clicking Edit. To forward queries that internal servers can't resolve to another server, type the IP address or DNS name for the other server, and then press Enter. Repeat this process to add other forwarders. You can organize the forwarders in priority order by selecting each in turn and clicking the Up or Down buttons as appropriate.

4. Use the Number Of Seconds Before Forward Queries Time Out box to set the query timeout in seconds. By default, a DNS server will continue to attempt to contact and use a listed forwarder for 3 seconds. When the timeout expires, the server moves to the next forwarder in the list and does the same. When there are no additional forwarders, the server uses the root hints to locate a root server to which the query can be forwarded.

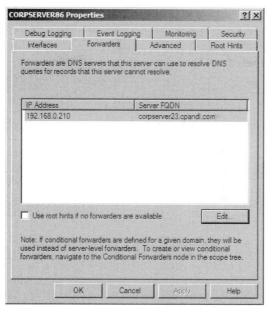

Figure 24-11 The Forwarders tab.

5. Click OK to close the Edit Forwarders dialog box.

6. In the Properties dialog box, click the Advanced tab. Ensure that the Disable Recursion check box is cleared and then click OK to close the Properties dialog box.

If you have multiple internal domains, you might want to consider configuring conditional forwarding, which allows you to direct requests for specific domains to specific DNS servers for resolution. Conditional forwarding is useful if your organization has multiple internal domains and you need to resolve requests between these domains. To configure conditional forwarding, follow these steps:

1. In the DNS console, select and then right-click the Conditional Forwarders folder for the server you want to work with. Select New Conditional Forwarder on the shortcut menu.

2. In the New Conditional Forwarder dialog box, enter the name of the domain to which queries should be forwarded, such as **adatum.com**.

3. Click in the IP Address list, type the IP address of an authoritative DNS server in the specified domain, and then press Enter. Repeat this process to specify additional IP addresses.

4. If you're integrating DNS with Active Directory, select the Store This Conditional Forwarder In Active Directory check box and then choose a replication strategy:

   ○ *All DNS Servers In This Forest*—Choose this strategy if you want the widest replication strategy. Remember, the Active Directory forest includes all domain trees that share the directory data with the current domain.

○   *All DNS Servers In This Domain*—Choose this strategy if you want to replicate forwarder information within the current domain and child domains of the current domain.

○   *All Domain Controllers In This Domain*—Choose this strategy if you want to replicate forwarder information to all domain controllers within the current domain and child domains of the current domain. Although this strategy gives wider replication for forwarder information within the domain, not every domain controller is a DNS server as well (and you don't need to configure every domain controller as a DNS server either).

5.   Set the Number Of Seconds Before Forward Queries Time Out option. This value controls how long the server tries to query the forwarder if it gets no response. When the Number Of Seconds Before Forward Queries Time Out interval passes, the server tries the next authoritative server in the list. The default is 5 seconds. Click OK.

6.   Repeat this procedure to configure conditional forwarding for other domains.

You can disable recursion and forwarders using the DNS console. In the DNS console, right-click the server you want to work with, and select Properties. In the Properties dialog box, click the Advanced tab. Disable recursion and forwarders by selecting the Disable Recursion check box and clicking OK.

Configuring Subdomains and Delegating Authority

Your organization's domain structure is separate from its zone configuration. If you create subdomains of a parent domain, you can add these subdomains to the parent domain's zone or create separate zones for the subdomains. When you create separate zones, you must tell DNS about the other servers that have authority over a particular subdomain. You do this by telling the primary name server for the parent domain that you've delegated authority for a subdomain.

When you add subdomains of a parent domain to the same zone as the parent domain, you have a single large namespace hosted by primary servers. This gives you a single unit to manage, which is good when you want centralized control over DNS in the domain. The disadvantage is that as the number of subdomains in the zone grows, there's more and more to manage, and at some point, the DNS server can become over-burdened, especially if dynamic updates are allowed and there are hundreds or thousands of host records.

When you create a separate zone for a subdomain, you have an additional unit of management that can be placed on the same DNS server or on a different DNS server. This means that you can delegate control over the zone to someone else, which would allow branch offices or other departments within the organization to manage their own DNS services. If the zone is on another DNS server, you shift the load associated with that zone to another server. The disadvantage is that you lose centralized control over DNS.

> **Note**
>
> It isn't possible to combine domains from different branches of the namespace and place them in a single zone. As a result, domains that are part of the same Active Directory forest but on different trees must be in separate zones. Thus, you would need separate zones for cohowinery.com and cohovineyards.com.

To create subdomains in separate zones on the same server as the parent domain, complete the following steps:

1. Create the necessary forward and reverse lookup zones for the subdomains as described earlier in this chapter in "Creating Forward Lookup Zones" on page 783 and "Creating Reverse Lookup Zones" on page 785.

2. You don't need to delegate authority because these subdomains are on the primary name server for the parent domain. This server automatically has control over the zones.

To create subdomains in separate zones and on separate servers, complete the following steps:

1. Install a DNS server in each subdomain, and then create the necessary forward and reverse lookup zones for the subdomains as described earlier in "Creating Forward Lookup Zones" on page 783 and "Creating Reverse Lookup Zones" on page 785.

2. On the primary DNS server for the parent domain, you must delegate authority to each subdomain. In the DNS console, expand the node for the server on which the parent domain is located, and then expand the related Forward Lookup Zones folder.

3. Right-click the parent domain entry, and then select New Delegation. This starts the New Delegation Wizard. Click Next.

4. As shown in Figure 24-12, type the name of the subdomain, such as **ny**. Check the fully qualified domain name (FQDN) to ensure that it is correct, and then click Next.

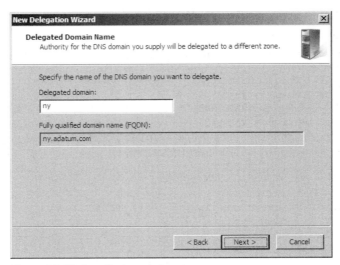

Figure 24-12 Specify the subdomain name.

5. On the Name Servers page, click Add. As shown in Figure 24-13, the New Name Server Record dialog box is displayed.

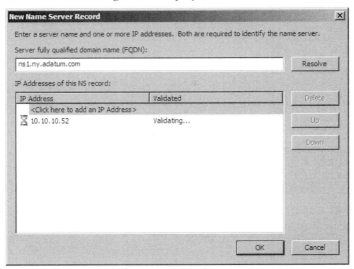

Figure 24-13 Specify the server name and IP address.

6. In the Server Fully Qualified Domain Name (FQDN) box, type the fully qualified host name of a DNS server for the subdomain, such as **ns1.ny.cpandl.com**, and then click Resolve. The wizard then validates name server and fills in its IP address. You can add additional IP addresses for the name server by clicking in the IP Address list, typing the IP address, and pressing Enter.

> **Note**
>
> You must specify the server name and at least one IP address. The order of the entries determines which IP address is used first. You can change the order as necessary using the Up and Down buttons.

7. Click OK to close the New Name Server Record dialog box. Repeat steps 5 and 6 to specify other authoritative DNS servers for the subdomain.

8. Click Next, and then click Finish.

Configuring Zone Transfers

Zone transfers are used to send a read-only copy of zone information to secondary DNS servers, which can be located in the same domain or in other domains. Windows Server 2008 supports three zone transfer methods:

- Standard zone transfers, in which a secondary server requests a full copy of a zone from a primary server.

- Incremental zone transfers, in which a secondary server requests only the changes that it needs to synchronize its copy of the zone information with the primary server's copy.

- Active Directory zone transfers, in which changes to zones are replicated to all domain controllers in the domain (or a subset if application partitions are configured) using Active Directory replication.

Active Directory zone transfers are automatically used and configured when you use Active Directory–integrated zones. If you have secondary name servers, these name servers can't automatically request standard or incremental zone transfers. To allow this, you must first enable zone transfers on the primary name server. Zone transfers are disabled by default to enhance DNS server security. Speaking of security, although you can allow zone transfers to any DNS server, this opens the server to possible attack. It is better to designate specific name servers that are permitted to request zone transfers.

INSIDE OUT   Incremental zone transfers

To manage incremental zone transfers, DNS servers track changes that have been made to a zone between each increment of a zone's serial number. Secondary servers use the zone's serial number to determine whether changes have been made to the zone. If the serial number matches what the secondary server has for the zone, no changes have been made and an incremental transfer isn't necessary. If the serial number doesn't match, the secondary server's copy of the zone isn't current and the secondary server then requests only the changes that have occurred since the last time the secondary zone was updated.

Zone transfers can be enabled for domains and subdomains in forward lookup zones and subnets in reverse lookup zones. You enable zone transfers on primary name servers. If a server is a secondary name server, it is already configured to perform zone transfers with the primary name server in the zone.

Using the DNS console, you can enable zone transfers on a primary name server and restrict the secondary name servers that can request zone transfers. In the DNS console, expand the node for the primary name server, and then expand the related Forward Lookup Zones or Reverse Lookup Zones folder as appropriate. Right-click the domain or subnet you want to configure, and then choose Properties. In the Properties dialog box, click the Zone Transfers tab, as shown in Figure 24-14.

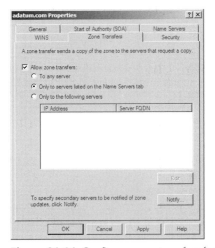

Figure 24-14 Configure zone transfers for a domain or subnet.

Select the Allow Zone Transfers check box. You have three zone transfer options:

- **To Any Server** Select To Any Server to allow any DNS server to request zone transfers.

- **Only To Servers Listed On The Name Servers Tab** Select Only To Servers Listed On The Name Servers Tab to restrict transfers to name servers listed on the Name Servers tab, and then click the Name Servers tab. Then complete these steps:

    1. The Name Servers list shows the DNS servers currently configured to be authoritative for the zone and includes DNS servers that host secondary zones. If a secondary server isn't listed and you want to authorize the server to request zone transfers, click Add. This displays the New Name Server Record dialog box.

    2. In the Server Fully Qualified Domain Name (FQDN) field, type the fully qualified host name of a secondary server for the domain, and then click Resolve. The wizard then validates name server and fills in its IP address. You can add additional IP addresses for the name server by clicking in the IP Address list, typing the IP address, and pressing Enter.

3. Click OK to close the New Name Server Record dialog box. Repeat this process to specify other secondary DNS servers for the domain or subnet.

- **Only The Following Servers** Select Only The Following Servers to restrict transfers to a list of approved servers. Then complete these steps:

    1. Click Edit to display the Allow Zone Transfers dialog box.

    2. Type the IP address of a secondary server that should receive zone transfers, and then press Enter.

    3. Repeat this process to specify other secondary DNS servers for the domain or subnet.

    4. Click OK to close the Allow Zone Transfers dialog box.

When you are finished, click OK to close the Properties dialog box.

Configuring Secondary Notification

When changes are made to a zone on the primary server, secondary servers can be automatically notified of the changes. This allows the secondary servers to request zone transfers. You can configure automatic notification of secondary servers using the DNS console.

In the DNS console, expand the node for the primary name server, and then expand the related Forward Lookup Zones or Reverse Lookup Zones folder as appropriate. Right-click the domain or subnet you want to configure, and then choose Properties. In the Properties dialog box, click the Zone Transfers tab. Click Notify in the lower-right corner of the Zone Transfers tab. This displays the Notify dialog box, as shown in Figure 24-15.

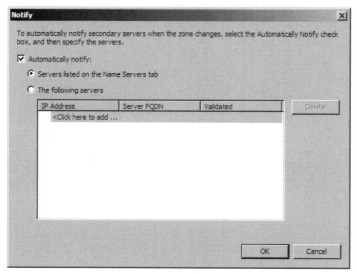

Figure 24-15 Configure secondary notification.

Select the Automatically Notify check box. You have two notification options:

- **Servers Listed On The Name Servers Tab**   Select Servers Listed On The Name Servers Tab to notify only the name servers listed on the Name Servers tab.

- **The Following Servers**   Select The Following Servers to specify the name servers that should be notified. Then complete these steps:

    1. Type the IP address of a secondary server that should receive notification, and then press Enter.

    2. Repeat this process to notify other secondary DNS servers for the domain or subnet.

    3. When you are finished, click OK twice.

Adding Resource Records

When you create a zone in Windows Server 2008, several records are created automatically.

- For a forward lookup zone, these records include an SOA record, an NS record, and an A record. The SOA record contains information about how resource records in the zone should be used and cached. The NS record contains the name of the authoritative name server, which is the server on which the zone was configured. The A record is the host address record for the name server.

- For a reverse lookup zone, these records include an SOA record, an NS record, and a PTR record. The SOA record contains information about how resource records in the zone should be used and cached. The NS record contains the name of the authoritative name server, which is the server on which the zone was configured. The PTR record is the pointer record for the name server that allows reverse lookups on the server's IP address.

- When you use Active Directory, SRV records are automatically created as well for domain controllers, global catalog servers, and PDC emulators.

- When you allow dynamic updates, A, AAAA, and PTR records for clients are automatically created for any computer using DHCP.

Any other records that you need must be created manually. The technique you use to create additional records depends on the type of record.

> **Create and Change Records on Primary Servers**
>
> When you create records or make changes to records, you should do so on a primary server. For Active Directory–integrated zones, this means any domain controller running the DNS Server service. For standard zones, this means the primary name server only. After you make changes to standard zones, right-click the server entry in the DNS console and select Update Server Data Files. This increments the serial number for zones as necessary to ensure that secondary name servers know changes have been made. You do not need to do this for Active Directory–integrated zones because Active Directory replicates changes automatically.

Host Address (A and AAAA) and Pointer (PTR) Records

Host Address (A) records contain the name of a host and its IPv4 address and host Address (AAAA) records contain the name of a host and its IPv6 address. Any computer that has multiple network interfaces or IP addresses should have multiple address records. Pointer (PTR) records enable reverse lookups by creating a pointer that maps an IP address to a host name.

You do not need to create A, AAAA, and PTR records for hosts that use dynamic DNS. These records are created automatically. For hosts that don't use dynamic DNS, you can create a new host entry with A and PTR records by completing the following steps:

1. In the DNS console, expand the node for the primary name server, and then expand the related Forward Lookup Zones folder. Right-click the domain to which you want to add the records, and then choose New Host (A Or AAAA). This displays the dialog box shown in Figure 24-16.

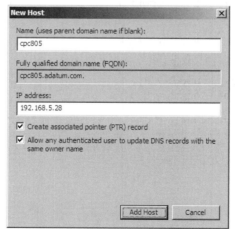

Figure 24-16 Create a host record.

2. Type the host name, such as **corpsrvl7**, and then type the IP address, such as **192.168.15.22**.

3. If a reverse lookup zone has been created for the domain and you want to create a PTR record for this host, select the Create Associated Pointer (PTR) Record check box.

> **Note**
> If you are working with an Active Directory–integrated zone, you have the option of allowing any authenticated client with the designated host name to update the record. To enable this, select Allow Any Authenticated User To Update DNS Records With The Same Owner Name. This is a nonsecure dynamic update where only the client host name is checked.

4. Click Add Host. Repeat this process as necessary to add other hosts.

5. Click Done when you're finished.

If you opt not to create a PTR record when you create an A record, you can create the PTR later as necessary. In the DNS console, expand the node for the primary name server, and then expand the related Reverse Lookup Zones folder. Right-click the sub-net to which you want to add the record, and then choose New Pointer (PTR). This displays the dialog box shown in Figure 24-17. Type the host ID part of the IP address, such as **49**, and then type the host name, such as **corpsvr05**. Click OK.

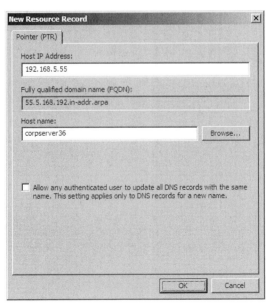

Figure 24-17 Create a PTR record.

INSIDE OUT   Using round robin for load balancing

If a host name has multiple A records associated with it, the DNS Server service will use round robin for load balancing. With round robin, the DNS server cycles between the A records so that queries are routed proportionally to the various IP addresses that are configured. Here's how round robin works: Say that your organization's Web server gets a ton of hits—so much that the single Web server you've set up can't handle the load anymore.

To spread the workload, you configure three machines, one with the IP address 192.168.12.18, one with the IP address 192.168.12.19, and one with the IP address 192.168.12.20. On the DNS server, you configure a separate A record for each IP address, but use the same host name: www.cpandl.com. This tells the DNS server to use round robin to balance the incoming requests proportionally. As requests come in, DNS will respond in a fixed circular fashion with an IP address. For a series of requests, the first user might be directed to 192.168.12.18, the next user to 192.168.12.19, and the next user to 192.168.12.20. The next time around the order will be the same so the fourth user is directed to 192.168.12.18, the next user to 192.168.12.19, and the next user to 192.168.12.20. As you can see, with three servers, each server will get approximately one-third of the incoming requests and hopefully about one-third of the workload as well.

Round robin isn't meant to be a replacement for clustering technologies, but it is an easy and fast way to get basic load balancing. Support for round robin is enabled by default. If you have to disable round robin, type **dnscmd *ServerName* /config /roundrobin 0**. To enable round robin again later, type **dnscmd *ServerName* /config /roundrobin 1**. In both cases, *ServerName* is the name or IP address of the DNS server you want to configure.

Canonical Name (CNAME) Records

Canonical Name (CNAME) records create aliases for host names. This allows a host to be referred to by multiple names in DNS. The most common use is when a host provides a common service, such as World Wide Web (WWW) or File Transfer Protocol (FTP) service, and you want it to have a friendly name rather than a complex name. For example, you might want www.cpandl.com to be an alias for the host dc06.cpandl.com.

To create an alias for a host name in the DNS console, expand the node for the primary name server, and then expand the related Forward Lookup Zones folder. Right-click the domain to which you want to add the record, and then choose New Alias (CNAME). This displays the dialog box shown in Figure 24-18. Type the alias for the host name, such as **www**, and then type the FQDN for the host, such as **corpsvr17.cpandl.com**. Click OK.

Chapter 24

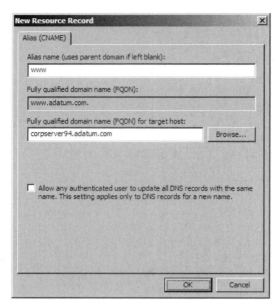

Figure 24-18 Create a new alias.

Mail Exchanger (MX) Records

Mail Exchanger (MX) records designate a mail exchange server for the domain, which allows mail to be delivered to the correct mail servers in the domain. For example, if an MX record is set for the domain cpandl.com, all mail sent to *Username*@cpandl.com will be directed to the server specified in the MX record.

You can create an MX record by completing the following steps:

1. In the DNS console, expand the node for the primary name server, and then expand the related Forward Lookup Zones folder. Right-click the domain to which you want to add the record, and then choose New Mail Exchanger (MX). This displays the dialog box shown in Figure 24-19.

2. Consider leaving the Host Or Child Domain box blank. A blank entry specifies that the mail exchanger name is the same as the parent domain name, which is typically what is desired.

3. Type the FQDN of the mail exchange server in the Fully Qualified Domain Name (FQDN) Of Mail Server box, such as **exchange.cpandl.com**. This is the name used to route mail for delivery.

4. Specify the priority of the mail server relative to other mail servers in the domain. The mail server with the lowest priority is the mail server that is tried first when mail must be routed to a mail server in the domain.

5. Click OK.

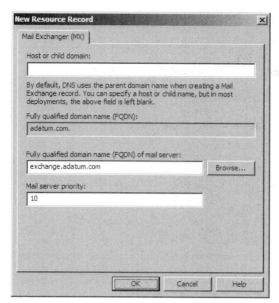

Figure 24-19 Create an MX record.

Name Server (NS) Records

Name Server (NS) records provide a list of authoritative servers for a domain, which allows DNS lookups within various zones. Each primary and secondary name server in a domain should be declared through these records. These records are created automatically when Active Directory–integrated zones are used. For standard zones, you can create an NS record by doing the following:

1. In the DNS console, expand the node for the primary name server, and then expand the related Forward Lookup Zones or Reverse Lookup Zones folder as appropriate.

2. Right-click the domain of the subnet for which you want to create name servers, and then select Properties. In the Properties dialog box click the Name Servers tab, as shown in Figure 24-20.

3. The Name Servers list shows the DNS servers currently configured to be authoritative for the zone and includes DNS servers that host secondary zones. If a name server isn't listed and you want to add it, click Add. This displays the New Name Server Record dialog box.

4. In the Server Fully Qualified Domain Name (FQDN) field, type the fully qualified host name of a secondary server for the domain, and click Resolve. If the IP address of the name server is filled in for you, click Add, and then add other IP addresses for this name server as necessary.

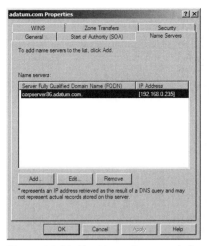

Figure 24-20 The Name Servers tab lists current name servers for the domain or subnet.

5. Click OK to close the New Name Server Record dialog box. Repeat this process to specify other name servers for the domain.

Start of Authority (SOA) Records

Start of Authority (SOA) records indicate the authoritative name server for a particular zone. The authoritative server is the best source of DNS information for a zone. Because each zone must have an SOA record, the record is created automatically when you add a zone. The SOA record also contains information about how resource records in the zone should be used and cached. This includes refresh, retry, and expiration intervals as well as the maximum time that a record is considered valid.

To view the SOA record for a zone in the DNS console, expand the node for the primary name server, and then expand the related Forward Lookup Zones or Reverse Lookup Zones folder as appropriate. Right-click the domain or subnet whose SOA record you want to view, and then select Properties. In the Properties dialog box click the Start Of Authority (SOA) tab, as shown in Figure 24-21.

The key field here is the Serial Number field. When you make changes manually to records in standard zones, you must update the serial number in the related zone or zones to show that changes have been made. Rather than updating the serial number manually for each individual zone, you can have the DNS server do this automatically for all zones as applicable. In the DNS console, right-click the server entry, and then choose Update Server Data Files. As discussed previously, you do not need to do this with Active Directory–integrated zones as changes are replicated automatically.

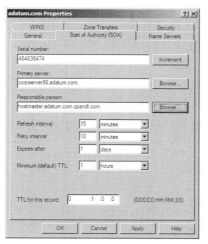

Figure 24-21 The Start Of Authority (SOA) tab for a domain or subnet.

Service Location (SRV) Records

Service Location (SRV) records make it possible to find a server providing a specific service. Active Directory uses SRV records to locate domain controllers, global catalog servers, LDAP servers, and Kerberos servers. SRV records are created automatically. For example, Active Directory creates an SRV record when you promote a domain controller. LDAP servers can add an SRV record to indicate they are available to handle LDAP requests in a particular zone.

In the forest root zone, SOA, NS, CNAME, and SRV records are created. The SOA record contains information about the forest root zone. The NS records indicate the primary DNS servers for the forest root zone. The CNAME records are used to designate aliases that allow Active Directory to use the globally unique identifier (GUID) of a domain to find the forest root name servers for that domain. The SRV records used to locate Active Directory resources are organized by function as follows:

- **DC** Contains SRV records for domain controllers. These records are organized according to the Active Directory site in which domain controllers are located.

- **Domains** Contains SRV records for domain controllers by domain. Folders for each domain in the forest are organized by the domain's GUID.

- **GC** Contains SRV records for global catalog servers in the forest. These records are primarily organized according to the Active Directory site in which domain controllers are located.

- **PDC** Contains SRV records for PDC emulators in the forest.

In the forward lookup zone for a domain, you'll find similar SRV records used to locate Active Directory resources. These records are organized by the following criteria:

- Active Directory site

- The Internet protocol used by the resource; either TCP or UDP

- Zone, either DomainDnsZones or ForestDnsZones

As Figure 24-22 shows, each record entry identifies a server that provides a particular service according to the following:

- **Domain** The DNS domain in which the record is stored.

- **Service** The service being made available. LDAP is for directory services on a domain controller. Kerberos indicates a Kerberos server that enables Kerberos authentication. GC indicates a global catalog server. KPasswd indicates Kerberos password service.

- **Protocol** The protocol the service uses, either TCP or User Datagram Protocol (UDP).

- **Priority** The priority or level of preference given to the server providing the service. The highest priority is 0. If multiple servers have the same priority, clients can use the weight to load balance between available servers.

- **Weight** The relative weight given to the server for load balancing when multiple servers have the same priority level.

- **Port Number** The TCP/IP port used by the server to provide the service.

- **Host Offering This Service** The FQDN of the host providing the service.

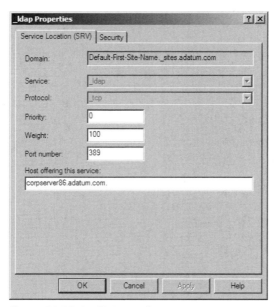

Figure 24-22 An SRV record.

Deploying Global Names

The GlobalNames zone is a specially named forward lookup zone that is available when all the DNS servers for your zones are running Windows Server 2008. Deploying a GlobalNames zone creates static, global records with single label names without relying on WINS. This allows users to access hosts using single-label names rather than fully qualified domain names (FQDNs).

You'll want to use the GlobalNames zone when name resolution depends on DNS, such as when your organization is no longer using WINS and you are planning to deploy only IPv6. When you are using global names, an authoritative DNS server will try to resolve queries in the following order:

1. Using local zone data

2. Using the GlobalNames zone

3. Using DNS suffixes

4. Using WINS

The GlobalNames zone should be created as an Active Directory–integrated zone. As dynamic updates cannot be used to register updates in the GlobalNames zone, you should configure single-label name resolution only for your primary servers. An authoritative DNS server will first check the GlobalNames zone before checking the local zone data. If you want DNS clients in another forest to use the GlobalNames zone for resolving names, you'll need to add a Service Location (SRV) resource record with the service name _globalnames._msdcs to that forest's forest-wide DNS partition. The record must specify the FQDN of the DNS server that hosts the GlobalNames zone.

You can deploy a GlobalNames zone by completing the following steps:

1. In the DNS console, right-click the Forward Lookup Zones node and then select New Zone. In the New Zone Wizard, click Next twice to accept the defaults to create a primary zone integrated with Active Directory Domain Services.

2. On the Active Directory Zone Replication Scope page, choose to replicate the zone throughout the forest and then click Next.

3. On the Zone Name page, enter **GlobalNames** as the zone name. Click Next twice and then click Finish.

4. On every authoritative DNS server in the forest now and in the future, you'll need to type the following at an elevated command prompt:

   ```
   dnscmd ServerName /enableglobalnamessupport 1
   ```

   where *ServerName* is the name of the DNS server that hosts the GlobalNames zone. To specify the local computer, use a period (.) instead of the server name, such as:

   ```
   dnscmd . /enableglobalnamessupport 1
   ```

Chapter 24

5. For each server that you want users to be able to access using a single-label name, add an alias (CNAME) record to the GlobalNames zone. In the DNS console, right-click the GlobalZones node, select New Alias (CNAME), and then use the dialog box provided to create the new resource record.

Maintaining and Monitoring DNS

When using DNS, you can perform many routine tasks to maintain and monitor domain name resolution services. Key tasks you might need to perform include the following:

- Configuring default application directory partitions and replication scope
- Setting aging and scavenging
- Configuring logging and checking event logs

Configuring Default Application Directory Partitions and Replication Scope

When the domain controllers running DNS in all the domains of your forest are using Windows Server 2008, you can create default application directory partitions for DNS. This reduces DNS replication traffic because DNS changes are replicated only to domain controllers also configured as DNS servers. There are two ways to configure default application directory partitions:

- **Forest-wide** Creates a single application directory partition that stores DNS zone data and replicates that data to all DNS servers in the forest. The default partition name is ForestDnsZones.*DnsForestName*, where *DnsForestName* is the domain name of the forest.

- **Domain-wide** Creates a single application directory partition that stores DNS zone data and replicates that data to all DNS servers in a designated domain. The default partition name is DomainDnsZones.*DnsDomainName*, where *DnsDomainName* is the domain name of the domain.

Check the DNS Configuration Fast

A fast way to check for the default application partitions and other DNS server configuration settings is to use Dnscmd. At a command prompt, type **dnscmd *ServerName* /info**, where *ServerName* is the name or IP address of a DNS server, such as CORPSVR03 or 192.168.10.15.

By default, the DNS Server service will try to create the default application directory partitions when you install it. You can verify this by connecting to the primary DNS server in the forest root domain and looking for subdomains of the forest root domain named DomainDnsZones and ForestDnsZones. Figure 24-23 shows an example in which these partitions have been created.

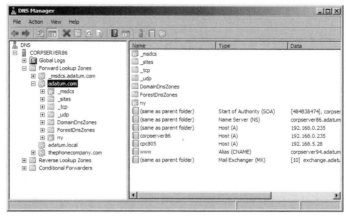

Figure 24-23 The default application partitions.

If the DNS Server service is unable to create these partitions, you will need to create the partitions manually. To do so, you must use an account that is a member of the Enterprise Admins group. If the default application partitions are currently available, the option to create them should not be available in the DNS console.

If the default application partitions have not yet been created, you can create them in the DNS console by following these steps:

1. In the DNS console, connect to the DNS server handling the zone for the parent domain of your forest root, such as cpandl.com rather than tech.cpandl.com.

2. Right-click the server entry, and select Create Default Application Directory Partitions. The DNS dialog box is displayed, as shown in Figure 24-24.

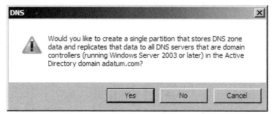

Figure 24-24 Creating the default domain partition.

3. The first prompt asks: Would You Like To Create A Single Partition That Stores DNS Zone Data And Replicates That Data To All DNS Servers That Are Domain Controllers In The Active Directory Domain *DomainName*? Click Yes if you want to create the DomainDnsZones.*DnsDomainName* default partition.

4. As Figure 24-25 shows, the next prompt states: Would You Like To Create A Single Partition That Stores DNS Zone Data And Replicates That Data To All DNS Servers In The Active Directory Forest *ForestName*. Click Yes if you want to create the ForestDnsZones.*DnsForestName* default partition.

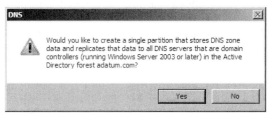

Figure 24-25 Creating the default forest partition.

When you create Active Directory–integrated zones, you have the option of setting the replication scope. Four replication scopes are available:

- To All DNS Servers In The Active Directory Forest

- To All DNS Servers In The Active Directory Domain

- To All Domain Controllers In The Active Directory Domain

- To All Domain Controllers Specified In The Scope Of This Directory Partition

To check or change the replication scope for a zone in the DNS console, right-click the related domain or subnet entry, and select Properties. In the Properties dialog box, the current replication scope is listed to the right of the Replication entry. If you click the related Change button, you can change the replication scope using the dialog box shown in Figure 24-26.

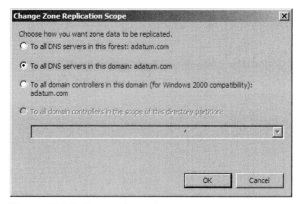

Figure 24-26 Change the replication scope as necessary.

Setting Aging and Scavenging

By default, the DNS Server service doesn't clean out old records. In some ways this is a good thing, because you don't want records you created manually to be deleted. However, for records created automatically through dynamic DNS, you might want to clear out old records periodically. Why? Consider the case of systems that register with DNS and then are removed from the network. Records for these systems will not be cleared automatically, which mean the DNS database might contain records for systems that are no longer in use.

DNS can help you clear out old records by using aging and scavenging. These rules determine how long a record created through a dynamic DNS update is valid, and if a record isn't reregistered within the allotted time, it can be cleared out. Aging and scavenging rules are set at two levels:

- **Zone** Zone aging/scavenging properties apply to an individual zone on a DNS server. To set zone-level options, right-click a zone entry, and select Properties. In the Properties dialog box, click Aging on the General tab. After you enable and configure aging/scavenging, click OK.

- **Server** Server aging/scavenging properties apply to all zones on a DNS server. To set server-level options in the DNS console, right-click a server entry, and select Set Aging/Scavenging For All Zones. After you enable and configure aging/scavenging, click OK. You'll see a prompt telling you these settings will be applied to new Active Directory–integrated zones created on the server. To apply these settings to existing zones, select Apply These Settings To The Existing Active Directory–Integrated Zones before you click OK.

In either case, the dialog box you see is similar to the one shown in Figure 24-27. To enable aging/scavenging, select the Scavenge Stale Resource Records check box, and then set these intervals:

- **No-Refresh Interval** Sets a period of time during which a DNS client cannot reregister its DNS records. When aging/scavenging is enabled, the default interval is 7 days. This means that if a DNS client attempts to reregister its record within 7 days of creating it, the DNS server will ignore the request. Generally, this is what is wanted because each time a record is reregistered this is seen as a change that must be replicated. The No-Refresh Interval doesn't affect clients whose IP address has changed and who therefore need to reregister their DNS records. The reason for this is that the previous records are actually deleted and new records are then created.

- **Refresh Interval** Sets the extent of the refresh window. Records can be scavenged only when they are older than the combined extent of the No-Refresh Interval and the Refresh Interval. When aging/scavenging is enabled, the default No-Refresh Interval is 7 days and the default Refresh Interval is 7 days. This means their combined extent is 14 days, and the DNS server cannot scavenge records until they are older than 14 days.

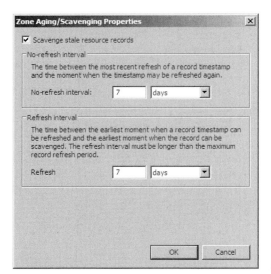

Figure 24-27 Set scavenging/aging options.

Scavenge Stale Records Manually

In addition to configuring automatic aging/scavenging, you can manually scavenge for stale (old) records. To do this in the DNS console, right-click a server entry, and select Scavenge Stale Resource Records. When prompted to confirm the action, click Yes. You can start scavenging at the command prompt by typing **dnscmd** *ServerName* **/startscavenging**, where *ServerName* is the name or IP address of the DNS server to work with, such as NS1 or 10.10.1.52.

Configuring Logging and Checking DNS Server Logs

By default the DNS Server service is configured to record all types of events (error, warning, and informational events) in the DNS Server log. You change this behavior in the DNS console; right-click a server entry, and then select Properties. In the Properties dialog box, click the Event Logging tab. Select the appropriate logging option so that no events, errors only, or errors and warnings are logged, and then click OK.

Using the DNS console, you can view only DNS-related events that have been logged in the system log by expanding the Global Logs node in the left pane and selecting DNS events. As Figure 24-28 shows, you'll then see the current DNS events for the server. The primary events you will want to examine are error and warning events.

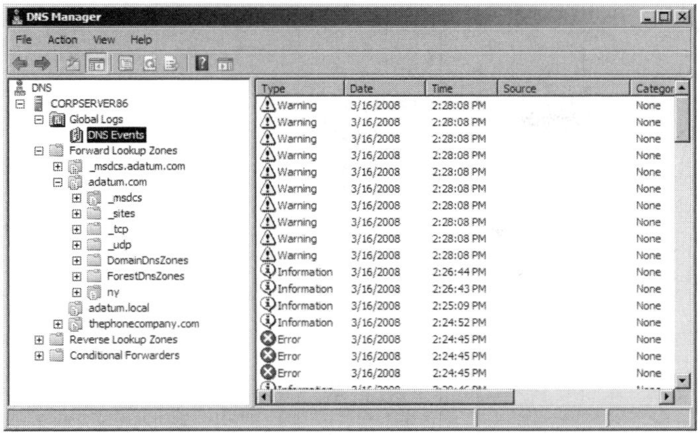

Figure 24-28 Check the event logs for warnings and errors.

Troubleshooting the DNS Client Service

Frequently, when you are trying to troubleshoot DNS problems, you will want to start on the client that is experiencing the problem. If you don't find a problem on the client, then try troubleshooting the DNS Server service.

Try Reregistering the Client

If the problem has to do with a client not showing up in DNS, force the client to reregister itself in DNS by typing **ipconfig /registerdns**. This works only for dynamic updates. For clients with fixed IP addressing, you must create or update the client's A and PTR records.

> **Note**
>
> Although Windows NT 4.0 computers have an IPConfig command, most of the features discussed here are available only on computers running Windows 2000 or later. In addition, on Windows 95, the related command is WinIPCfg, and for Windows 98 the IPConfig command has a slightly different syntax.

Check the Client's TCP/IP Configuration

If the problem has to do with the client making lookups, start by checking the DNS servers configured for the client to use.

Checking IPv4

You can display IPv4 information by typing **netsh interface ipv4 show dnsserver**. The output will show you the DNS servers for the client. If the DNS servers are configured through DHCPv4, the output will look similar to the following:

```
Configuration for interface "Local Area Connection"
    DNS servers configured through DHCP:  192.168.20.21
    Register with which suffix:           Primary only
```

If the DNS servers are configured locally, the output will look similar to the following:

```
Configuration for interface "Local Area Connection"
    Statically Configured DNS Servers:   192.168.20.11
    Register with which suffix:          Primary only
```

If you see a problem with the client's DNS configuration, you can change a locally assigned DNS server IP address by typing the following command:

```
netsh interface ipv4 set dns ConnectionName static ServerIPAddress
```

where *ConnectionName* is the name of the local area connection and *ServerIPAddress* is the IP address of the server, such as

```
netsh interface ipv4 set dns "Local Area Connection" static 192.168.0.1
```

If you see a problem with a DHCP-assigned DNS server IP address, try renewing the client's IP address lease by typing **ipconfig /renew**.

Checking IPv6

You can display IPv4 information by typing **netsh interface ipv6 show dnsserver**. The output will show you the DNS servers for the client. If the DNS servers are configured through DHCPv6, the output will look similar to the following:

```
Configuration for interface "Local Area Connection"
    DNS servers configured through DHCP: fec0:0:0:ffff::1%1
                                         fec0:0:0:ffff::2%1
                                         fec0:0:0:ffff::3%1
    Register with which suffix:          Primary only
```

If the DNS servers are configured locally, the output will look similar to the following:

```
Configuration for interface "Local Area Connection"
    Statically Configured DNS Servers: fec0:0:0:ffff::1%1
                                       fec0:0:0:ffff::2%1
                                       fec0:0:0:ffff::3%1
    Register with which suffix:        Primary only
```

If you see a problem with the client's DNS configuration, you can change a locally assigned DNS server IP address by typing the following command:

```
netsh interface ipv6 set dns ConnectionName static ServerIPAddress
```

where *ConnectionName* is the name of the local area connection and *ServerIPAddress* is the IP address of the server, such as

```
netsh interface ipv6 set dns "Local Area Connection" static fe80::fdc2:3222:ab7e:23b1
```

If you see a problem with a DHCP-assigned DNS server IP address, try renewing the client's IP address lease by typing **ipconfig /renew**.

Check the Client's Resolver Cache

If you don't see a problem with the client's DNS configuration, you will want to check the client's DNS resolver cache. All systems running Windows 2000 or later have a built-in DNS resolver cache that caches resource records from query responses that the DNS Client service receives. When performing lookups, the DNS client first looks in the cache. Records remain in the cache until one of the following events occurs:

- Their Time to Live (TTL) expires.

- The system or the DNS Client service is restarted.

- The cache is flushed.

You can display the records in a cache by typing **ipconfig /displaydns** at the command prompt. Records in the cache look like this:

```
Windows IP Configuration

    1.0.0.127.in-addr.arpa
    ----------------------------------------
    Record Name.......... : 1.0.0.127.in-addr.arpa.
    Record Type.......... : 12
    Time To Live......... : 573686
    Data Length.......... : 4
    Section.............. : Answer
    PTR Record........... : localhost


    www.williamstanek.com
    ----------------------------------------
    Record Name.......... : www.williamstanek.com
    Record Type.......... : 5
    Time To Live......... : 12599
    Data Length.......... : 4
    Section.............. : Answer
    CNAME Record ........ : williamstanek.com
```

If you suspect a client has stale records in its cache, you can force it to flush the cache. To do so, type **ipconfig /flushdns** at the command prompt.

Chapter 24

Perform Lookups for Troubleshooting

Another useful command to use when troubleshooting DNS is NSLookup. You can use NSLookup to query the default DNS server of a client and check to see the actual records it is using. To perform a basic lookup simply follow NSLookup with the FQDN of the host to look up. Consider the following example:

```
nslookup www.microsoft.com
```

The response shows the information that the default DNS server has on that host, such as

```
C:\Documents and Settings\WS>nslookup www.microsoft.com
DNS request timed out.
    timeout was 2 seconds.
Non-authoritative answer:
Name:   www2.microsoft.akadns.net
Addresses:  207.46.244.188, 207.46.156.252, 207.46.144.222, 207.46.245.92
            207.46.134.221, 207.46.245.156, 207.46.249.252, 207.46.156.220
Aliases:  www.microsoft.com, www.microsoft.akadns.net
```

If you want to look up a particular type of record, follow these steps:

1. Type **nslookup** at the command prompt. The prompt changes to >.

2. Type **set query=***RecordType*, where *RecordType* is the type of record, such as **set query=mx**, **set query=soa**, or **set query=ns**.

3. Type the FQDN for the domain in which you want to search, such as **microsoft.com**.

The output shows you matching records in the specified domain, such as

```
microsoft.com MX preference = 10, mail exchanger = mailb.microsoft.com

microsoft.com nameserver = dns1.cp.msft.net
microsoft.com nameserver = dns1.dc.msft.net
mailb.microsoft.com internet address = 131.107.3.122
mailb.microsoft.com internet address = 131.107.3.123
```

Troubleshooting the DNS Server Service

If you suspect the DNS problem is on the server itself, you can begin troubleshooting on the server. There are, of course, many troubleshooting techniques. This section covers the key ones you'll want to use.

Check the Server's TCP/IP Configuration

When you are troubleshooting DNS on a DNS server, start with the server's TCP/IP configuration. After you verify or modify the TCP/IP configuration as necessary, you can continue to troubleshoot. Like DNS clients, DNS servers have a resolver cache. The cache on servers is for query responses to lookups the server has performed either on behalf of clients or for its own name resolution purposes.

Check the Server's Cache

If the problem with DNS is that you think the server has stale records, you can check the DNS Server cache (as opposed to DNS Client cache) by using the following command:

```
dnscmd ServerName /zoneprint .
```

where *ServerName* is the name or IP address of the DNS server and "." indicates that you want to examine the server cache. This cache list includes the root name servers being used by the server.

If necessary, you can force a server to clear out its cache. To do so, in the DNS console, right-click the server entry and select Clear Cache. You can clear the cache at the command prompt by typing the following:

```
dnscmd ServerName /clearcache
```

where *ServerName* is the name or IP address of the DNS server whose cache you want to clear.

Check Replication to Other Name Servers

Active Directory replication of changes to DNS zones is automatic. By default, Active Directory checks for changes to zones every 180 seconds. This interval is called the *directory service polling interval*. For advanced configuration needs, you can set the directory service polling interval using Dnscmd. Type **dnscmd** *ServerName* **/config /dspollinginterval** *Interval*, where *ServerName* is the name or IP address of the DNS server you want to configure and *Interval* is the polling interval in seconds.

If the problem has to do with failure to replicate changes to secondary servers, start by ensuring that zone transfers are enabled as discussed in "Configuring Zone Transfers" on page 791. If zone transfers are properly configured, try updating the serial number on the zone records on the primary server. In the DNS console, right-click the server entry in the DNS console, and select Update Server Data Files. This increments the serial number for zones as necessary, which should trigger zone transfers if they are necessary.

Examine the Configuration of the DNS Server

Frequently, DNS problems have to do with a DNS server's configuration. Rather than trying to navigate multiple tabs and dialog boxes to find the configuration details, you can use Dnscmd to help you out. You can view a DNS server's configuration by typing **dnscmd** *ServerName* **/info** at the command prompt, where *ServerName* is the name or

IP address of the DNS server you want to check, such as Primary or 10.10.1.52. The output looks like this:

```
Query result:
Server info
    server name = corpsvr86.cpandl.com
    version = 177100006 (6.0 build 7001)
    DS container = cn=MicrosoftDNS,cn=System,DC=cpandl,DC=com
    forest name = cpandl.com
    domain name = cpandl.com
    builtin domain partition = ForestDnsZones.cpandl.com
    builtin forest partition = DomainDnsZones.cpandl.com
    last scavenge cycle = not since restart (0)
Configuration:
    dwLogLevel = 00000000
    dwDebugLevel = 00000000
    dwRpcProtocol = FFFFFFFF
    dwNameCheckFlag = 00000002
    cAddressAnswerLimit = 0
    dwRecursionRetry = 3
    dwRecursionTimeout = 8
    dwDsPollingInterval = 180
Configuration Flags:
    fBootMethod = 3
    fAdminConfigured = 1
    fAllowUpdate = 1
    fDsAvailable = 1
    fAutoReverseZones = 1
    fAutoCacheUpdate = 0
    fSlave = 0
    fNoRecursion = 0
    fRoundRobin = 1
    fStrictFileParsing = 0
    fBindSecondaries = 1
    fWriteAuthorityNs = 0
    fLocalNetPriority = 1
Aging Configuration:
    ScavengingInterval = 0
    DefaultAgingState = 0
    DefaultRefreshInterval = 168
    DefaultNoRefreshInterval = 168
ServerAddresses:
  Ptr = 00120968
  MaxCount = 3
  AddrCount = 1
    Addr[0] => 192.168.1.50
  ListenAddresses:
    NULL IP Array.
  Forwarders:
    NULL IP Array.
    forward timeout = 3
    slave = 0
```

Table 24-1 summarizes section by section the output from Dnscmd /Info. Using Dnscmd /Config, you can configure most of these options. The actual subcommand to use is indicated in parentheses in the first column, and examples of acceptable values are indicated in the final column. For example, if you wanted to set the fBindSecondaries configuration setting to allow maximum compression and efficiency (assuming you are using Windows 2000 or later DNS servers or BIND 4.9.4 or later), you would type **dnscmd *ServerName* /config /bindsecondaries 0**, where *ServerName* is the name or IP address of the DNS server you want to configure. This overrides the default setting to support other DNS servers.

Table 24-1 DNS Server Configuration Parameters

Section/Entry (Command)	Description	Example/Accepted Values
Server Info		
Server name	The FQDN of the DNS server.	Corpsvr86.cpandl.com
Version	The operating system version and build. Version 6.0 is Windows Server 2008.	177100006 (6.0 build 7001)
DS container	The directory services container for a DNS server that uses Active Directory–integrated zones.	cn=MicrosoftDNS, cn=System, DC=cpandl,DC=com
Forest name	The name of the Active Directory forest in which the server is located.	cpandl.com
Domain name	The name of the Active Directory domain in which the server is located.	cpandl.com
Builtin domain partition	The default application partition for the domain.	ForestDnsZones.cpandl.com
Builtin forest partition	The default application partition for the forest.	DomainDnsZones.cpandl.com
Last scavenge cycle	The last time records were aged/scavenged.	not since restart (0)
Configuration		
dwLogLevel (/loglevel)	Indicates whether debug logging is enabled. A value other than zeros means it is enabled.	0x0; default, no logging.
dwDebugLevel	The debug logging level, not used. dwLogLevel is used instead.	00000000

Section/Entry (Command)	Description	Example/Accepted Values
dwRpcProtocol (/rpcprotocol)	The RPC protocol used.	0x0; disables remote procedure call (RPC) for DNS. 0x1; default, uses TCP/IP. 0x2; uses named pipes. 0x4; uses LPC.
dwNameCheckFlag (/namecheckflag)	The name-checking flag. By default, DNS names can be in multibyte Unicode format as indicated by the example entry.	0; Strict RFC (ANSI). 1; Non RFC (ANSI). 2; Multibyte (UTF8). 3; All Names.
cAddressAnswerLimit (/addressanswerlimit)	The maximum number of records the server can send in response to a query.	0; default with no maximum. [5–28]; sets a maximum.
dwRecursionRetry (/recursionretry)	The number of seconds the server waits before trying to contact a remote server again.	3
dwRecursionTimeout (/recursiontimeout)	The number of seconds the server waits before stopping contact attempts.	8
dwDsPollingInterval (/dspollinginterval)	How often in seconds Active Directory polls for changes in Active Directory–integrated zones.	180
Configuration Flags		
fBootMethod (/bootmethod)	The source from which the server gets its configuration information.	1; loads from BIND file. 2; loads from Registry. 3; loads from Active Directory and the Registry.
fAdminConfigured	Indicates whether the settings are administrator-configured.	1; default for yes.
fAllowUpdate	Indicates whether dynamic updates are allowed.	1; default dynamic updates are allowed. 0; dynamic updates not allowed.
fDsAvailable	Indicates whether Active Directory directory services are available.	1; Active Directory is available. 0; Active Directory isn't available.
fAutoReverseZones (/disableautoreversezone)	Indicates whether automatic creation of reverse lookup zones is enabled.	1; default enabled. 0; disabled.

Section/Entry (Command)	Description	Example/Accepted Values
fAutoCacheUpdate (/secureresponses)	Indicates how server caching works.	0; default, saves all responses to name queries to cache. 1; saves only records in same DNS subtree to cache.
fSlave (/isslave)	Determines how the DNS server responds when forwarded queries receive no response.	0; default, recursion is enabled. If the forwarder does not respond, the server attempts to resolve the query itself using recursion. 1; recursion is disabled. If the forwarder does not respond, the server terminates the search and sends a failure message to the resolver.
fNoRecursion (/norecursion)	Indicates whether the server performs recursive name resolution.	0; default, DNS server performs if requested. 1; DNS server doesn't perform recursion.
fRoundRobin (/roundrobin)	Indicates whether server allows round robin load balancing when there are multiple A records for hosts.	1; default, automatically load balances using round robin for any hosts with multiple A records. 0; disables round robin.
fStrictFileParsing (/strictfileparsing)	Indicates server behavior when it encounters bad records.	0; default, continues to load, logs error. 1; stops loading DNS file and logs error.
fBindSecondaries (/bindsecondaries)	Indicates the zone transfer format for secondaries. By default, DNS server is configured for compatibility with other DNS server types.	1; default, for pre-BIND 4.9.4 compatibility. 0; enables compression and multiple transfers on Windows secondaries and others with BIND 4.9.4 or later.
fWriteAuthorityNs (/writeauthorityns)	Indicates whether the server writes NS records in the authority section of a response.	0; default, writes for referrals only. 1; writes for all successful authoritative responses.
fLocalNetPriority (/localnetpriority)	Determines the order in which host records are returned when there are multiple host records for the same name.	1; returns records with similar IP addresses first. 0; returns records in the order in which they are in DNS.

Section/Entry (Command)	Description	Example/Accepted Values
Aging Configuration		
ScavengingInterval (/scavenginginterval)	Indicates the number of hours between scavenging intervals.	0x0; scavenging is disabled.
DefaultAgingState (/defaultagingstate)	Indicates whether scavenging is enabled by default in new zones.	0; default, scavenging is disabled. 1; scavenging is enabled.
DefaultRefreshInterval (/defaultrefreshinterval)	Indicates the default refresh interval in hours.	168 (set in hexadecimal)
DefaultNoRefreshInterval (/defaultnorefreshinterval)	Indicates the default no-refresh interval in hours.	168 (set in hexadecimal)
ServerAddresses		
Addr Count	The number of IP addresses configured on the server and the IP address used.	1 Addr[0] => 192.168.1.50
ListenAddresses		
Addr Count	The number and value of IP addresses configured for listening for requests from clients. NULL IP Array when there are no specific IP addresses that are designated for listening for requests from clients.	1 Addr[0] => 192.168.1.50
Forwarders		
Addr Count	The number and value of IP addresses of servers configured as forwarders. NULL IP Array when there are no forwarders.	1 Addr[0] => 192.168.12.8
Forward timeout (/forwardingtimeout)	Timeout for queries to forwarders in seconds.	3
Slave	Indicates whether recursion is enabled.	0; recursion is enabled 1; recursion is disabled

Another useful command for troubleshooting a DNS server is Dnscmd /Statistics. This command shows you the following information:

- DNS server time statistics, including server start time, seconds since start, and stats of last cleared date and time

- Details on queries and responses, including total queries received, total responses sent; the number of UDP queries received and sent, UDP responses received and sent; and the number of TCP queries received and sent, TCP responses received and sent

- Details on queries by record, including the exact number of each type of record sent

- Details on failures and where they occurred, including recursion failures, retry limits reached, and partial answers received

- Details on the total number of dynamic updates, the status for each update type; later breakdowns on number and status of secure updates, the number of updates that were forwarded, and the types of records updated

- Details on the amount of memory used by DNS, including total amount of memory used, standard allocations, and allocations from standard to the heap

Save the Stats to a File

Write the output of Dnscmd /Statistics to a file so that you don't overflow the history buffer in the command prompt. This also allows you to go through the stats at your leisure. Type **dnscmd *ServerName* /statistics > *FileName***, where *ServerName* is the name or IP address of the DNS server and *FileName* is the name of the file to use, such as **dnscmd corpsvr02 /statistics > dns-stats.txt**.

Examine Zones and Zone Records

Dnscmd provides several useful commands for helping you pinpoint problems with records. To get started, list the available zones by typing **dnscmd *ServerName* /enum-zones**, where *ServerName* is the name or IP address of the DNS server you want to check. The output shows a list of the zones that are configured as follows:

```
Enumerated zone list:

  Zone count = 4

Zone name                  Type       Storage      Properties

.                          Cache      File
_msdcs.cpandl.com          Primary    AD-Forest    Secure
1.168.192.in-addr.arpa     Primary    AD-Legacy    Secure Rev
cpandl.com                 Primary    AD-Domain    Secure Aging
```

The zone names you can work with are listed in the first column. The other values tell you the type of zone and the way it is configured as summarized in Table 24-2.

Table 24-2 **Zone Entries and Their Meanings**

Column/Entry	Description
Type	
Cache	A cache zone (server cache).
Primary	A primary zone.
Secondary	A secondary zone.
Stub	A stub zone.
Storage	
AD-Forest	Active Directory–integrated with forest-wide replication scope.
AD-Legacy	Active Directory–integrated with legacy replication scope to all domain controllers in the domain.
AD-Domain	Active Directory–integrated with domain-wide replication scope.
File	Indicates the zone data is stored in a file.
Properties	
Secure	Zone allows secure dynamic updates only and is a forward lookup zone.
Secure Rev	Zone allows secure dynamic updates only and is a reverse lookup zone.
Secure Aging	Zone allows secure dynamic updates only and is configured for scavenging/aging.
Aging	Zone is configured for scavenging/aging but isn't configured for dynamic updates.
Update	Zone is a forward lookup zone configured to allow both secure and nonsecure dynamic updates.
Update Rev	Zone is a reverse lookup zone configured to allow both secure and nonsecure dynamic updates.
Down	Secondary or stub zone hasn't received a zone transfer since startup.

After you examine the settings for zones on the server, you can print out the zone records of a suspect zone by typing **dnscmd** *ServerName* **/zoneprint** *ZoneName* at the command prompt, where *ServerName* is the name or IP address of the DNS server and *ZoneName* is the name of the zone as reported previously.

Consider the following example:

```
dnscmd corpsvr02 /zoneprint cpandl.com
```

Here, you want to examine the cpandl.com zone records on the CORPSVR02 server. The output from this command shows the records in this zone and their settings. Here is a partial listing:

```
;
;  Zone:     cpandl.com
;  Server:   corpsvr02.cpandl.com
;  Time:     Wed Mar 10 18:38:14 2008 UTC
;
@ [Aging:3534235] 600 A 192.168.1.50
    [Aging:3534235] 3600 NS  corpsvr02.cpandl.com.
    3600 SOA    corpsvr02.cpandl.com. hostmaster. 383 900 600 86 400 3600
    3600 MX     10 exchange.cpandl.com._msdcs 3600 NS
corpsvr01.cpandl.com._gc._tcp.Default-First-Site-Name._sites
    [Aging:35265] 600 SRV 0 100 3268
corpsvr02.cpandl.com._kerberos._tcp.Default-First-Site-Name._sites
    [Aging:35235] 600 SRV  0 100 88
corpsvr02.cpandl.com._ldap._tcp.Default-First-Site-Name._sites
    [Aging:35335] 600 SRV  0 100 389
corpsvr02.cpandl.com._gc._tcp [Aging:3534265] 600 SRV     0 100 3268
corpsvr02.cpandl.com._kerberos._tcp [Aging:3534235] 600 SRV    0 100 88
corpsvr02.cpandl.com._kpasswd._tcp [Aging:3534235] 600 SRV    0 100 464
corpsvr02.cpandl.com.corpsvr02 [Aging:3534281] 3600 A     192.168.1.50
corpsvr17 3600 A        192.168.15.22
DomainDnsZones [Aging:3534265] 600 A    192.168.1.50
_ldap._tcp.Default-First-Site-Name._sites.DomainDnsZones
    [Aging:35365] 600 SRV    0 100 389
corpsvr02.cpandl.com._ldap._tcp.DomainDnsZones [Aging:3534265] 600 SRV  0 100 389
corpsvr02.cpandl.com.ForestDnsZones [Aging:3534265] 600 A    192.168.1.50
_ldap._tcp.Default-First-Site-Name._sites.ForestDnsZones
    [Aging:35365] 600 SRV    0 100 389
corpsvr02.cpandl.com._ldap._tcp.ForestDnsZones [Aging:35365] 600 SRV  0 100 389
corpsvr02.cpandl.com.ny 3600 NS
ns1.ny.cpandl.com.ns1.ny 3600 A        10.10.10.52
www 3600 CNAME        corpsvr17.cpandl.com.
```

As you can see from the listing, Dnscmd /Zoneprint shows all the records, even the ones created by Active Directory. This is particularly useful because it means you don't have to try to navigate the many subfolders in which these SRV records are stored.

Implementing and Maintaining WINS

Windows Internet Naming Service (WINS) enables computers to register and resolve NetBIOS names on IPv4 networks. WINS is not used with IPv6 networks. WINS is maintained primarily for backward support and compatibility with legacy applications and early versions of Microsoft Windows, including Windows 95, Windows 98, and Windows NT, that used WINS for computer name resolution; or for networks running Windows 2000 or Windows Server 2003 that don't have Active Directory deployed and thus don't require DNS. On most large networks, WINS is needed to support legacy applications and computers running Windows 95, Windows 98, and Windows NT.

If you are setting up a new network, you probably don't need WINS. On an existing network running all Windows 2000, Windows XP, and Windows Server 2008 systems, only the Domain Name System (DNS) is needed because these computers rely exclusively on DNS for name resolution if Active Directory is deployed. Because WINS is not required, WINS support could be removed from the network. Doing so, however, would mean that legacy applications and services that rely on NetBIOS, such as the computer Browser service, would no longer function.

WINS Essentials

Like DNS, WINS is a client/server protocol. All Windows servers have a WINS service that can be installed to provide WINS services on the network. All Windows computers have a WINS client that is installed automatically. The Workstation and Server services on computers are used to specify resources that are available, such as file shares. These resources have NetBIOS names as well.

NetBIOS Namespace and Scope

WINS architecture is very different from DNS. Unlike DNS, WINS has a flat namespace and doesn't use a hierarchy or tree. Each computer or resource on a Windows network has a NetBIOS name, which can be up to 15 characters long. This name must be unique on the network—no other computer or resource can have the same name. Although there are no extensions to this name per se that indicate a domain, a NetBIOS scope can be set in Dynamic Host Configuration Protocol (DHCP).

The NetBIOS scope is a hidden 16th character (suffix) for the NetBIOS name. It is used to limit the scope of communications for WINS clients. Only WINS clients with the same NetBIOS scope can communicate with each other. See "Configuring TCP/IP Options" on page 717 for details on setting the NetBIOS scope for computers that use DHCP.

NetBIOS Node Types

The way WINS works on a network is determined by the node type set for a client. The node type defines how name services work. WINS clients can be one of four node types:

- **B-Node (Broadcast Node)** Broadcast messages are used to register and resolve names. Computers that need to resolve a name broadcast a message to every host on the local network, requesting the IP address for a computer name. Best for small networks.

- **P-Node (Peer-to-Peer Node)** WINS servers are used to register and resolve computer names to Internet Protocol (IP) addresses. Computers that need to resolve a name send a query message to the server and the server responds. Best if you want to eliminate broadcasts. In some cases, however, resources might not be seen as available if the WINS server isn't updated by the computer providing the resources.

- **M-Node (Mixed Node)** A combination of B-Node and P-Node. WINS clients first try to use broadcasts for name resolution. If this fails, the clients then try using a WINS server. Still means a lot of broadcast traffic.

- **H-Node (Hybrid Node)** A combination of B-Node and P-Node. WINS clients first try to use a WINS server for name resolution. If this fails, the clients then try broadcasts for name resolution. Best for most networks that use WINS servers because it reduces broadcast traffic.

Small Networks Might Not Need a WINS Server

On a small network without subnets and a limited number of computers, WINS clients can rely on broadcasts for name resolution. In this case, it isn't necessary to set up a WINS server.

WINS Name Registration and Cache

WINS maintains a database of name to IP address mappings automatically. Whenever a computer or resource becomes available, it registers itself with the WINS server to tell the server the name and IP address it is using. As long as no other computer or resource on the network is using that name, the WINS server accepts the request and registers the computer or resource in its database.

Name registration isn't permanent. Each name that is registered has a lease period associated with it, which is called its Time to Live (TTL). A WINS client must reregister its name before the lease expires and attempts to do so when 50 percent of the lease period has elapsed or when it is restarted. If a WINS client doesn't reregister its name, the lease expires and is marked for deletion from the WINS database. During normal shutdown, a WINS client will send a message to the WINS server requesting release of the registration. The WINS server then marks the record for deletion. Whenever records are marked for deletion, they are said to be *tombstoned*.

As with DNS clients, WINS clients maintain a cache of NetBIOS names that have been looked up. The WINS cache, however, is designed to hold only names looked up recently. By default, names are cached for up to 10 minutes and the cache is limited to 16 names. You can view entries in the NetBIOS cache by typing **nbtstat -c** at the command prompt.

WINS Implementation Details

On most networks that use WINS, you'll want to configure at least two WINS servers for name resolution. When there are multiple WINS servers, you can configure replication of database entries between the servers. Replication allows for fault tolerance and load balancing by ensuring that entries in one server's database are replicated to its replication partners. These replication partners can then handle renewal and release requests from clients as if they held the primary registration in the first place.

WINS supports:

- **Persistent connections** In a standard configuration, replication partners establish and release connections each time they replicate WINS database changes. With persistent connections, replication partners can be configured to maintain a persistent connection. This reduces the overhead associated with opening and closing connections and speeds up the replication process.

- **Automatic replication partners** Using automatic replication partners, WINS can automatically configure itself for replication with other WINS servers. To do this, WINS sends periodic multicast messages to announce its availability. These messages are addressed to the WINS multicast group address (224.0.1.24), and any other WINS servers on the network that are listening for datagrams sent on this group address can receive and process the automatic replication request. After replication is set up with multicast partners, the partners use standard replication with either persistent or nonpersistent connections.

- **Manual tombstoning** Manual tombstoning allows administrators to mark records for deletion. A record marked for deletion is said to be tombstoned. This state is then replicated to a WINS server's replication partners, which prevents the record from being re-created on a replication partner and then being replicated back to the original server on which it was marked for deletion.

- **Record export** The record export feature allows administrators to export the entries in the WINS database to a file that can be used for tracking or reporting on which clients are using WINS.

Setting Up WINS Servers

To make a computer running Windows Server 2008 into a WINS server, you must install the WINS service. This service doesn't require a dedicated server and uses limited resources in most cases. This means you could install the WINS service on a DNS server, DHCP server, or domain controller. The only key requirement is that the WINS service can be installed only on a computer with a static IPv4 address. Although you can install WINS on a server with multiple IPv4 address or multiple network interfaces, this isn't recommended because the server might not be able to replicate properly with its replication partners. In most cases, you won't want to configure a domain controller as a WINS server.

You can install the WINS service by following these steps:

1. In Server Manager, select the Features node in the left pane and then click Add Features. This starts the Add Features Wizard.

2. On the Select Features page, select WINS Server and then click Next.

3. Click Install. When the wizard finishes installing the WINS service, click Close.

After you install the WINS service, the WINS console is available on the Administrative Tools menu. Start the console by clicking Start, Administrative Tools, WINS. Then, select the WINS server you are working with to see its entries, as shown in Figure 25-1.

Figure 25-1 The WINS console.

The only key postinstallation task for the WINS service is to configure replication partners. However, you should check the Transmission Control Protocol/Internet Protocol (TCP/IP) configuration of the WINS server. It should have only itself listed as the WINS server to use and shouldn't have a secondary WINS server. This prevents the WINS client on the server from registering itself with a different WINS database, which can cause problems.

To set the server's primary WINS server address to its own IP address and clear out any secondaries from the list, click Start and then click Network. In Network Explorer, click Network And Sharing Center on the toolbar. In Network And Sharing Center, click Manage Network Connections. In Network Connections, right-click the connection you want to work with and then select Properties. In the Properties dialog box, open the Internet Protocol (TCP/IP) Properties dialog box by double-clicking Internet Protocol Version 4 (TCP/IPv4). Click Advanced to display the Advanced TCP/IP Settings dialog box, and then click the WINS tab. Set the WINS server's IP address as the WINS server to use and remove any additional WINS server addresses. When you're finished, click OK twice and then click Close.

You can remotely manage and configure WINS. Simply start the WINS console, right-click the WINS node in the left pane, and select Add Server. In the Add Server dialog box, select WINS Server, type the name or IP address of the WINS server, and then click OK.

The command-line counterpart to the WINS console is Netsh WINS. From the command prompt on a computer running Windows Server 2008, you can use Netsh WINS to perform all the tasks available in the WINS console as well as to perform some additional tasks that can't be performed in the WINS console. To start Netsh WINS and access a particular WINS server, follow these steps:

1. Start a command prompt, and then type **netsh** to start Netsh. The command prompt changes to netsh>.

2. Access the WINS context within Netsh by typing **wins**. The command prompt changes to netsh wins>.

3. Type **server** followed by the Universal Naming Convention (UNC) name or IP address of the WINS server, such as **\\wins2** or **\\10.10.15.2**. If the WINS server is in a different domain from your logon domain, you should type the fully qualified domain name (FQDN) of the server, such as **\\wins2.cpandl.com**.

4. The command prompt changes to netsh wins server>. You can now work with the selected server. If you later want to work with a different server, you can do this without having to start over. Simply type **server** followed by the UNC name or IP address of that server.

> **Note**
>
> Technically, you don't need to type the double backslashes (\\) when you specify an IP address. You must, however, type **** when you specify a server's name or FQDN. Because of this discrepancy, you might want to use \\ all the time so that you won't leave it out by accident when you need it.

TROUBLESHOOTING

Resolving WINS replication errors

Most WINS replication errors involve incorrectly configured WINS servers. If you see replication errors in the event logs, check the TCP/IP configuration of your WINS servers. Every WINS server in the organization should be configured as its own primary WINS server, and you should delete any secondary WINS server addresses. This ensures that WINS servers register their NetBIOS names only in their own WINS databases. If you don't configure WINS in this way, WINS servers might register their names with other WINS servers. This can result in different WINS servers owning the NetBIOS names that a particular WINS server registers and, ultimately, to problems with WINS itself. For more information on this issue, see Microsoft Knowledge Base article 321208 (*http://support.microsoft.com/default.aspx?scid=kb;en-us;321208*).

Configuring Replication Partners

When you have two or more WINS servers on a network, you should configure replication between them. When servers replicate database entries with each other, they are said to be *replication partners*.

Replication Essentials

There are two replication roles for WINS servers:

- **Push partner** A push partner is a replication partner that notifies other WINS servers that updates are available.

- **Pull partner** A pull partner is a replication partner that requests updates.

By default, all WINS servers have replication enabled and replication partners are configured to use both push and pull replication. After a replication partner notifies a partner that there are changes using push replication, the partner can request the changes using pull replication. This pulls the changes down to its WINS database. In addition, all replication is done using persistent connections by default to increase efficiency.

Because replication is automatically enabled and configured, all you have to do to start replication is tell each WINS server about the other WINS servers that are available. On a small network, you can do this using the automatic replication partners feature. Because this can cause a lot of broadcast traffic on medium or large networks that contain many clients and servers, you'll probably want to designate specific replication partners to reduce broadcast traffic.

Configuring Automatic Replication Partners

To configure automatic replication partners, follow these steps:

1. Start the WINS console. Right-click the WINS node in the left pane, and select Add Server. In the Add Server dialog box, select WINS Server, type the name or IP address of the WINS server, and then click OK.

2. Expand the server entry, right-click the Replication Partners entry in the left pane, and then select Properties. In the Replication Partners Properties dialog box, click the Advanced tab, as shown in Figure 25-2.

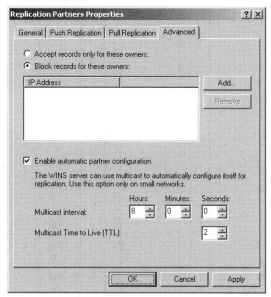

Figure 25-2 Enable automatic replication.

3. Select the Enable Automatic Partner Configuration check box.

4. Use the Multicast Interval options to set the interval between multicast broadcasts to the WINS server group address. These broadcasts are used to tell other WINS servers about the availability of the server you are configuring. The default interval is 0 minutes, which disables WINS broadcasts.

Registrations Remain Until Restart

After a server is discovered and added as a partner through multicasting, the server remains as a configured partner until you restart the WINS service or until you restart the server. When WINS is shut down properly, part of the shutdown process is to send messages to current replication partners and remove its registration.

5. Use the Multicast Time To Live (TTL) combo box to specify how many links multicast broadcasts can go through before being discarded. The default is 2, which would allow the broadcasts to be relayed through two routers.

6. Click OK.

Multicast Through Routers Is Possible

The Multicast TTL is used to allow the discovery broadcasts to be routed between subnets. This means you could use automatic replication partners on networks with subnets. However, routing isn't automatic just because a datagram has a TTL. You must configure the routers on each subnet to forward multicast traffic received from the WINS multicast group address (224.0.1.24).

Using Designated Replication Partners

To designate specific replication partners, start the WINS console. Right-click the WINS node in the left pane, and select Add Server. In the Add Server dialog box, select WINS Server, type the name or IP address of the WINS server, and then click OK.

Right-click the Replication Partners entry in the left pane, and select New Replication Partners. In the New Replication Partner dialog box, type the name or IP address of the WINS server that should be used as a replication partner, and then click OK. The replication partner is added and listed as available in the WINS console. As shown in Figure 25-3, replication partners are listed by server name, IP address, and replication type.

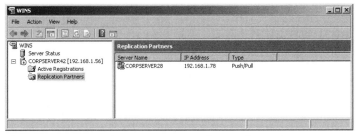

Figure 25-3 View replication partners in the WINS console.

By default, the replication partner is configured to use both push and pull replication as well as persistent connections. After you configure a replication partner, the configuration is permanent. If you restart a server, you do not need to reconfigure replication partners.

To view or change the replication settings for a replication partner, start the WINS console. Expand the server entry for the server you want to work with, and then select the Replication Partners entry in the left pane. Double-click the replication partner in the details pane. This displays the replication partner's Properties dialog box. Click the Advanced tab, as shown in Figure 25-4.

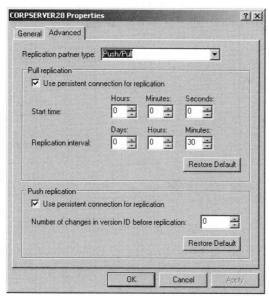

Figure 25-4 Configure replication partner settings.

The configuration options are used as follows:

- Replication Partner Type—Sets the replication type as push, pull, or push/pull.

- Pull Replication

  ○ *Use Persistent Connection For Replication*—Configures pull replication so a persistent connection is used. This reduces the time spent opening and closing connections and improves performance.

  ○ *Start Time*—Sets the hour of the day when replication should begin using a 24-hour clock.

  ○ *Replication Interval*—Sets the frequency of replication. The default is every 30 minutes.

- Push Replication

  ○ *Use Persistent Connection For Replication*—Configures push replication so a persistent connection is used. This reduces the time spent opening and closing connections and improves performance.

  ○ *Number Of Changes In Version ID Before Replication*—Can be used to limit replication by allowing replication to occur only when a set number of changes have occurred in the local WINS database.

> **Note**
>
> By default Number Of Changes In Version ID Before Replication is set to 0, which allows replication at the designated interval whenever there are changes. If you set a specific value, that many changes must occur before replication takes place.

Configuring and Maintaining WINS

WINS is fairly easy to configure and maintain after you set it up and replication partners are configured. The key configuration and maintenance tasks are related to the following issues:

- Configuring burst handling as the network grows
- Checking server status and configuration
- Checking active registrations and scavenging records if necessary
- Maintaining the WINS database

Configuring Burst Handling

If you configured the WINS server on a network with more than 100 clients, you should enable burst handling of registrations. As your network grows, you should change the burst-handling sessions as appropriate for the number of clients on the network. To configure burst handling of registration and name refresh requests, start the WINS console. Right-click the server entry in the WINS console, and then select Properties. In the Properties dialog box, click the Advanced tab, as shown in Figure 25-5.

Select the Enable Burst Handling check box, and then select a burst-handling setting. The settings available are the following:

- Low for handling up to 300 registration and name refresh requests
- Medium for handling up to 500 registration and name refresh requests
- High for handling up to 1,000 registration and name refresh requests

Set a Custom Threshold for Burst Handling

You can also set a custom threshold value for burst handling. To do this, select Custom and then enter a threshold value between 50 and 5,000. For example, if you set the threshold to 5,000, up to 5,000 requests could be queued at once. Keep in mind that you would do this only if your network environment needs this setting. If you set the value to 5,000 but only need a queue that allows up to 100 name registration requests, you would waste a lot of server resources maintaining a very large queue that you don't need.

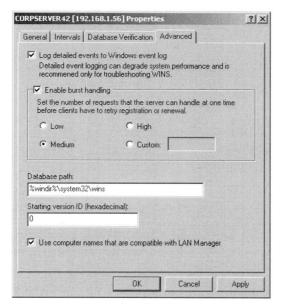

Figure 25-5 Set burst handling for medium and large networks.

Checking Server Status and Configuration

Using the WINS console, you can do the following:

- View the status of all WINS servers on the network by clicking the Server Status entry in the left pane. The status of the servers is then displayed in the right pane.

- View the current replication partners for a server by expanding the server entry and selecting Replication Partners in the left pane. The replication partners for that server are displayed in the right pane.

- View server statistics for startup, replication, queries, releases, registrations, and replication partners by right-clicking the server entry in the left pane and selecting Display Server Statistics.

Using Netsh WINS, you can view server statistics by typing the command

```
netsh wins server ServerName show statistics
```

where *ServerName* is the name or IP address of the WINS server you want to work with, such as \\WINS02 or 10.10.12.15. An example of the statistics follows:

```
***You have Read and Write access to the server corpsvr02.cpandl.com***

    WINS Started                            : 3/10/2008 at 14:46:1
    Last initialization                     : 3/12/2008 at 02:14:12
    Last planned scavenging                 : 3/19/2008 at 12:30:25
    Last admin triggered scavenging         : 3/10/2008 at 16:52:24
    Last replicas tombstones scavenging     : 3/21/2008 at 09:12:26
    Last replicas verification scavenging   : 3/23/2008 at 12:38:9
    Last planned replication                : 3/10/2008 at 16:20:39
    Last admin triggered replication        : 3/27/2008 at 08:27:30
    Last reset of counter                   : 4/01/2008 at 18:23:45

Counter Information :
        No of U and G Registration requests = (250 222)
        No of Successful/Failed Queries = (812/67)
        No of U and G Refreshes = (213 144)
        No of Successful/Failed Releases = (68/12)
        No of U. and G. Conflicts = (12 10)

~~~~~~~~~~~~~~~~~~~~~~~~~~~~~~~~~~~~~~~~~~~~~~~~~~~~~~~~~~~~~~~~~~~~~~~~~~~~~~~~
WINS Partner IP Address     -No. of Replication      -No. of Comm Failure
~~~~~~~~~~~~~~~~~~~~~~~~~~~~~~~~~~~~~~~~~~~~~~~~~~~~~~~~~~~~~~~~~~~~~~~~~~~~~~~~
    192.168.15.18           -    153                 -    2
```

These statistics are useful for troubleshooting registration and replication problems. Scavenging and replication are automatic once configured. Problems to look for include the following:

- **Replication** If there are problems with replication, you should see a high number of communication failures relative to the number of replications. Check the links over which replication is occurring to see if there are intermittent failures or times when links aren't available.

- **Name resolution** If WINS clients are having problems with name resolution, you'll see a high number of failed queries. You might need to scavenge the database for old records more frequently. Check the server statistics for the renew interval, extinction interval, extinction timeout, and verification interval or the Intervals tab in the server's Properties dialog box.

- **Registration release** If WINS clients aren't releasing registrations properly, you'll see a high number of failed releases. Clients might not be getting shut down properly.

You can view the configuration details for a WINS server by typing the command

```
netsh wins server ServerName show info
```

where *ServerName* is the name or IP address of the WINS server. The output looks like this:

```
WINS Database backup parameter
~~~~~~~~~~~~~~~~~~~~~~~~~~~~~~~~~~~~~~~~~~~~~~~~~~~~~~~~~~~~~~~
Backup Dir                        :
Backup on Shutdown                : Disabled


Name Record Settings(day:hour:minute)
~~~~~~~~~~~~~~~~~~~~~~~~~~~~~~~~~~~~~~~~~~~~~~~~~~~~~~~~~~~~~~~
Refresh Interval                  : 006:00:00
Extinction(Tombstone) Interval    : 004:00:00
Extinction(Tombstone) TimeOut     : 006:00:00
Verification Interval             : 024:00:00


Database consistency checking parameters :
~~~~~~~~~~~~~~~~~~~~~~~~~~~~~~~~~~~~~~~~~~~~~~~~~~~~~~~~~~~~~~~
Periodic Checking                 : Disabled


WINS Logging Parameters:
~~~~~~~~~~~~~~~~~~~~~~~~~~~~~~~~~~~~~~~~~~~~~~~~~~~~~~~~~~~~~~~

Log Database changes to JET log files  : Enabled
Log details events to System Event Log : Enabled


Burst Handling Parameters :
~~~~~~~~~~~~~~~~~~~~~~~~~~~~~~~~~~~~~~~~~~~~~~~~~~~~~~~~~~~~~~~

Burst Handling State              : Enabled
Burst handling queue size         : 500
```

Checking Active Registrations and Scavenging Records

Using the WINS console, you can view the active registrations in the WINS database by expanding the server entry, right-clicking Active Registrations, and choosing Display Records. In the Display Records dialog box, click Find Now without making any selections to see all the available records or use the filter options to specify the types of records you want to view, and then click Find Now. To tombstone a record manually, right-click it, and then select Delete. This deletes it from the current server, and this deletion is then replicated to other WINS servers; that is, the record will be replicated marked as Tombstoned.

Netsh provides many ways to examine records in the WINS database. Because this is something you won't use that frequently, the easiest way to do it is to list all available records and write the information to a file that you can search. To do this, type the command

```
netsh wins server ServerName show database Servers={}
```

where *ServerName* is the name or IP address of the WINS server. The output shows you the registration entries in the database as follows:

```
~~~~~~~~~~~~~~~~~~~~~~~~~~~~~~~~~~~~~~~~~~~~~~~~~~~~~~~~~~~~~~~~~~~~~~~~~~~~~~
     NAME  -T-S-VERSION  -G-  IPADDRESS  -  EXPIRATION DATE
~~~~~~~~~~~~~~~~~~~~~~~~~~~~~~~~~~~~~~~~~~~~~~~~~~~~~~~~~~~~~~~~~~~~~~~~~~~~~~
Retrieving database from the Wins server 192.168.1.50
CPANDL    [1Bh]-D-A- 2  -U- 192.168.1.50  -3/25/2008 2:46:01 PM
CORPSVR02 [00h]-D-A- 7  -U- 192.168.1.50  -3/25/2008 2:46:01 PM
CORPSVR02 [20h]-D-A- 6  -U- 192.168.1.50  -3/25/2008 2:46:01 PM
CPANDL    [00h]-D-A- 4  -N- 192.168.1.50  -3/25/2008 2:46:01 PM
CPANDL    [1Ch]-D-A- 3  -I- 192.168.1.50  -3/25/2008 2:46:01 PM
CPANDL    [1Eh]-D-A- 1  -N- 192.168.1.50  -3/25/2008 2:46:01 PM
```

WINS automatically scavenges the database to mark old records for deletion. To see when this is done, check the server statistics for the renew interval, extinction interval, extinction timeout, and verification interval on the Intervals tab in the server's Properties dialog box.

You can initiate scavenging (referred to as an admin-triggered scavenging in the server statistics) by right-clicking the server entry in the WINS console and selecting Scavenge Database. To initiate scavenging at the command prompt, type **netsh wins server** *ServerName* **init scavenge**, where *ServerName* is the name or IP address of the WINS server.

After scavenging, the renew interval, extinction interval, extinction timeout, and verification interval are used to mark each record as follows:

- If the renew interval has not expired, the record remains marked as Active.

- If the renew interval has expired, the record is marked as Released.

- If the extinction interval has expired, the record is marked as Tombstoned.

If the record was tombstoned, it is deleted from the database. If the record is active and was replicated from another server but the verification interval has expired, the record is revalidated.

Maintaining the WINS Database

The WINS database, like any database, should be maintained. You should routinely perform the following maintenance operations:

- Verify the database consistency

- Compact the database

- Back up the database

Verifying the WINS Database Consistency

WINS can be configured to verify the database consistency automatically. This operation checks and verifies the registered names. To configure automatic database consistency checks, follow these steps:

1. Start the WINS console. Right-click the WINS node in the left pane, and select Add Server. In the Add Server dialog box, select WINS Server, type the name or IP address of the WINS server, and then click OK.

2. Right-click the server entry in the WINS console, and select Properties. In the Properties dialog box, click the Database Verification tab, as shown in Figure 25-6.

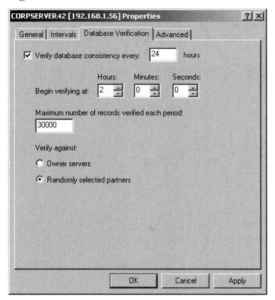

Figure 25-6 Set automatic verification of the WINS database.

3. Select the Verify Database Consistency Every check box, and then set a check interval. Typically, you'll want to perform this operation no more frequently than once every 24 hours.

4. Use the Begin Verifying At section to set the time at which verification checks are started. This time is on a 24-hour clock and the default time is 2 hours, 0 minutes, and 0 seconds, meaning 2:00 A.M. If you wanted verification checks to begin at 2:00 P.M. instead, you would set the time to 14 hours, 0 minutes, and 0 seconds.

5. Set other options as necessary, and then click OK.

Compacting the WINS Database

The WINS database should be compacted periodically, at least once a month or once every other month, depending on how often computers are added to or removed from your network. In addition to reducing the size of the database by squeezing out unneeded space that has been allocated and is no longer needed, compacting the database can improve performance and make the database more reliable.

At the command prompt, you can compact the WINS database by following these steps:

1. Change to the WINS directory by typing **cd %SystemRoot%\System32\Wins**.

2. Stop the WINS service by typing **net stop wins**.

3. Compact the WINS database by typing **jetpack wins.mdb winstemp.mdb**.

4. Start the WINS service by typing **net start wins**.

Backing Up the WINS Database

By default, the WINS database is not backed up—but it should be. You can perform manual or automatic backups. To back up the WINS database manually, follow these steps:

1. Start the WINS console. Right-click the server entry, and then select Back Up Database.

2. In the Browse For Folder dialog box, select the folder where the WINS server should store the database backup files, and then click OK.

3. The WINS server will then write the backup files to a subfolder of the designated folder called Wins_bak. When it finishes, click OK.

To configure automatic backups of the WINS database, follow these steps:

1. Start the WINS console. Right-click the server entry, and then select Properties.

2. In the Properties dialog box, click Browse on the General tab.

3. Use the Browse For Folder dialog box to select the folder where the WINS server should store the database backup files, and then click OK. The WINS server will write backup files to a subfolder of the designated folder called Wins_bak.

4. Select Back Up Database During Shutdown.

5. Click OK. Now whenever you shut down the server or the WINS service on the server, the WINS service will back up the database to the designated folder.

Restoring the WINS Database

If something happens to the WINS database, you can use the backup files to recover it to the state it was in prior to the problem. To restore the WINS database from backup, follow these steps:

1. Start the WINS console. Right-click the server entry, point to All Tasks, and then select Stop. This stops the WINS service.

2. Right-click the server entry again, and select Restore Database.

3. In the Browse For Folder dialog box, select the parent folder of the Wins_bak folder created during backup (not the Wins_bak folder itself), and click OK.

4. The WINS server will then restore the database from backup. When it finishes, click OK.

5. The WINS service will be restarted automatically.

Enabling WINS Lookups Through DNS

You can enable WINS lookups through DNS. This integration of WINS and DNS provides for an additional opportunity to resolve an IP address to a host name when normal DNS lookups fail. Typically, this might be necessary for clients that can't register their IP addresses in DNS using dynamic updates.

You enable WINS name resolution on a zone-by-zone basis from within the DNS console. Follow these steps:

1. In the DNS console, right-click the zone you want to work with, and then select Properties.

2. In the Properties dialog box, click the WINS or WINS-R tab as appropriate for the type of zone. The WINS tab is used with forward lookup zones and the WINS-R tab is used with reverse lookup zones.

3. Select Use WINS Forward Lookup or Use WINS Reverse Lookup as appropriate.

4. If you're not using DNS servers running on Windows 2000 or later as secondary servers, select Do Not Replicate This Record. This ensures that the WINS record that is created during this configuration won't be replicated to servers that don't support this feature.

5. Type the IP address of a WINS server you want to use for name resolution, and click Add. Repeat this step for other WINS servers that should be used.

6. Click OK.

CHAPTER 26

Deploying Print Services

Print services have changed substantially over the years and the changes for Windows Server 2008 offer many new features and improvements. The techniques you need to master to successfully deploy print services are what this chapter is about. You'll find detailed discussions on print services architecture, print server selection and optimization, printer hardware selection and optimization, printer connection deployment, and more.

Understanding Windows Server 2008 Print Services

In a perfect world, the printers used by an organization would be selected after careful planning. You'd select the best printer for the job based on the expected use of the printer and the features required. The reality is that in many organizations printers are purchased separately by departments and individuals without much thought given to how the printer will be used. Someone sees that a printer is needed and one is purchased. The result is that many organizations have a hodgepodge of printers. Some printers are high-volume and others are low-volume, low-cost. The high-volume printers are designed to handle heavy, daily loads from multiple users, and the low-volume, low-cost printers are designed to handle printing for small groups or individuals. If you are responsible for printers in your department or the organization as a whole, you might want to look at ways to consolidate or standardize so the hodgepodge of printers spread around the department or throughout the organization is easier to manage and maintain.

All printers regardless of type have one thing in common: A device is needed to manage the communication between the printer and the client computers that want to print to the printers. This device is called a *print server*. In most cases, a print server is a computer running the Windows operating system. When a Windows computer acts as a print server, it provides many services. It provides clients with the drivers they need for printing. It stores documents that are spooled for printing and maintains the associated print queue. It provides for security and auditing of printer access.

From a process perspective, it helps to understand how printing works so that you can better manage and better troubleshoot printing problems. The way printing works depends on the data type of the print driver being used. There are two main data types for print drivers:

- **Enhanced metafile format (EMF)** EMF uses the Printer Control Language (PCL) page description language. EMF documents are sent to the print server with minimal processing and are then further processed on the print server.

- **RAW** RAW is most commonly used with the PostScript page description language. RAW documents are fully processed on clients before being sent to a print server and aren't modified by the print server.

When you print a document, many processes are involved. Figure 26-1 shows the standard EMF printing process.

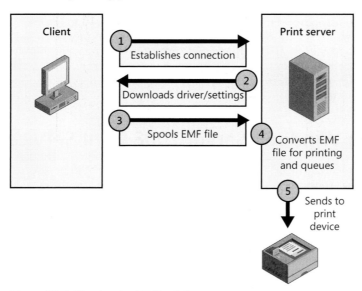

Figure 26-1 The standard EMF printing process.

Here, the client establishes a connection to the print server. If it needs a print driver or if there is a new driver available, it downloads the driver and the associated settings. The client first uses the print driver to partially render the document into EMF and then spools the EMF file to the print server. The print server converts the EMF file to final form and then queues the file to the printer queue (printer). When the document reaches the top of the print queue it is sent to the physical print device.

Figure 26-2 shows the standard RAW printing process. Here, the client establishes a connection to the print server. If it needs a print driver or if there is a new driver available, it downloads the driver and the associated settings. The client then fully processes the file for printing and spools the RAW file to the print server. The print server queues the file to the logical print device (printer). When the document reaches the top of the print queue it is sent to the physical print device.

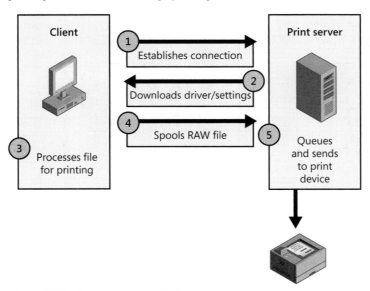

Figure 26-2 The standard RAW printing process.

Okay, so that's the version at 10,000 feet—the fine details are much more complicated, as Figure 26-3 shows. The model can be applied to the mechanics of the initial printing of a document on a client to the handling on the print server to the actual printing on the print device.

Chapter 26

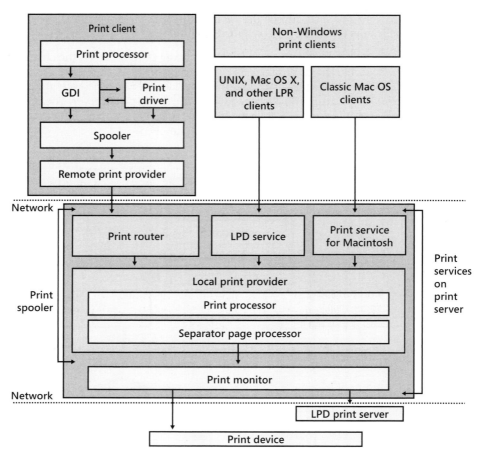

Figure 26-3 A representation of printing from the client to the server to the print device.

Print drivers are stored in the %SystemRoot%\System32\Spool\Drivers folder on the print server. Assuming that a client already has the current print drivers, the printing process works like this:

1. On a client running Microsoft Windows 2000 or later, the application you're printing from calls the Graphics Device Interface (GDI), which uses the print driver to determine how to format the document for the selected print device. The GDI is responsible for any necessary preprocessing (converting into EMF or RAW format) of the document, which, depending on the print driver type and configuration settings, might or might not be necessary. When it's finished with the document, the GDI passes the document to the local print spooler (Winspool.drv).

2. The local print spooler makes a Remote Procedure Call (RPC) connection to the Print Spooler service (Spoolsv.exe) on the print server. The Print Spooler service calls the print router (Spoolss.dll). The print router makes an RPC connection to

the remote print provider (Win32spl.dll) on the client. The remote print provider then connects directly to the Print Spooler service on the print server and sends the document.

3. The local print provider on the print server saves the document in the print queue as a print job. By default, all print jobs for all printers on a print server are stored in the %SystemRoot%\System32\Spool\Printers folder. The primary spool file has an .spl extension and the control information needed to print the spool file is stored in an .shd file.

4. The local print provider is responsible for any necessary postprocessing of the document, which, depending on the print driver type and configuration settings, might or might not be necessary. The local print provider uses the print processor to do any necessary processing or conversion and the separator page processor to insert any separator pages if necessary. The local print provider processes the document when it reaches the top of the print queue and before it sends the print job to the print monitor.

5. The print monitor sends the print job to the physical print device, where it is actually printed. The way spooling works depends on the print queue configuration and the printer buffer. If possible, the entire document is transferred to the print device. Otherwise, the print monitor sends the print job gradually as the print buffer allows.

Like the Registry, printing is one of those areas of the Windows operating system that is obfuscated by varying use of terminology. From a user perspective, a printer is the device that prints out their documents. From a technical perspective, a logical print device or printer is a software component used for printing. Because it is where documents are queued before printing, it is also referred to as a print queue. When you add or install a printer on a Windows system, you are installing the software—the logical print device—as opposed to the physical print device itself.

Windows Server 2008 has built-in support for both 32-bit and 64-bit print drivers. Support for 64-bit print drivers is important because systems running 64-bit editions of Windows need 64-bit drivers. As with previous versions of Windows, print drivers are installed automatically on clients when they first try to print to a new printer device on a print server.

Windows uses two types of print drivers. Print drivers that operate in kernel mode are Type 2 drivers. With a kernel-mode driver, an error with a print driver can cause the server to crash. This happens because the driver is running in the operating system kernel process. Print drivers that operate in user mode are Type 3 drivers. User-mode drivers operate in a process separate from the operating system kernel process and this means that an error in a user-mode driver affects only its related process. In Windows Server 2008, print drivers operate in user mode and kernel-mode drivers are supported only for backward compatibility.

INSIDE OUT   **Automatic restart of services is for errors only**

An error in a user-mode driver typically means the Print Spooler process hangs up and has to be restarted. Because Windows Server 2008 is configured by default to restart the Print Spooler process automatically within 1 minute if it stops with an error or hangs up, no administrator action is required.

When a service is configured to restart automatically, the restart is performed only when an error occurs. Two general types of errors can occur: either the service will hang up and stop responding or the service will stop running and exit with an error code. In these cases, automatic restart can usually recover the service and get the service to resume normal operations. If you stop a service manually, automatic restart does not take place.

In Windows Server 2008, the Microsoft Universal Printer Driver (Unidrv) provides core printing functions that print driver manufacturers can use. These functions are implemented in the two primary print engines:

- **Unidrv.dll** Provides the core printing functions for PCL print devices. Uses EMF-formatted files.

- **PScript5.dll** Provides core printing functions for PostScript print devices. Uses RAW-formatted files.

The availability of these print engines gives printer manufacturers several options for developing print drivers. They can create a mini driver that implements only the unique functionality of a particular print device and rely on the appropriate print engine for print services, or they can make their own custom driver that uses its own print engine.

INSIDE OUT   **Automatic print driver distribution on clusters**

On clusters, any print driver that you install on a virtual cluster is automatically distributed from the cluster spooler resource to all nodes of the cluster. This is an important feature that simplifies installation and management of print clusters. Administrators must install drivers only once rather than once in each node in the cluster. Additionally, Terminal Services and print services can coexist. This important change allows Terminal Services and print services to be installed on the same nodes in a cluster.

Planning for Printer Deployments and Consolidation

Print servers and printers are the key components needed for printing. You can size and optimize both print servers and printers in many ways.

> **Optimize and Monitor After Installation as Well**
>
> After sizing and optimization, you should consider optimizing the way printing is handled using print queues. To better support deployed print services, you can periodically monitor performance, check for and install print driver upgrades, and prepare for print server failure.

Sizing Print Server Hardware and Optimizing Configuration

The maximum load and performance level of a print server depends on its configuration. You can configure print servers in many ways, and as a print server's workload changes over time, so should its configuration. As the workload of the print server scales, so does the amount of processing and memory required to handle print services. Any computer, including a desktop-class system, can act as a print server. However, although Windows Vista systems are limited to 10 active connections, Windows Server 2008 systems are not limited in this way.

You should consider the print server's central processing unit (CPU) speed, total random access memory (RAM), and network card speed. When PCL printers and EMF print drivers are used, most of the document processing is performed on the server and the server will need a fairly fast processor and sufficient RAM to process documents. When PostScript printers and RAW print drivers are used, most of the document processing is performed on clients before documents are transferred to the server and the server's processor speed and memory are less important. In many cases, a print server will provide services for multiple printers so there's a good chance that some of the printers will be PCL and some of the printers will be PostScript. In this case, the processing power and total RAM of the print server are again important.

Complex print jobs, such as those containing high-resolution graphics, can use additional resources on the print server. They require more memory to process and more processing power. The number of clients connecting to a print server can also affect resource requirements:

- Most print clients running Windows 2000 or later establish RPC connections to print servers. With RPC, a connection between a client and server remains open as long as there is one or more open handles. Typically, applications open handles to a print server when a user prints but don't close those open handles until the user shuts down or exits the application. If a user accesses the printer folder or views the printer queue on the print server, this opens handles to the print server because the folders or queues are open as well. As a result, there can be many open handles to a print server using resources even when a print server isn't busy.

- Most non-Windows clients establish Server Message Block (SMB) connections to print servers. If the Line Printer Daemon (LPD) service is configured, SMB clients running UNIX, Mac OS X, or other operating systems can use the Line Printer Remote (LPR) service to communicate with the LDP service on the print server. Because these clients maintain their own printer spools, the print server acts as the gateway between the client and the printer. These clients use very little resources on the server, but have very few options.

> **Note**
>
> Microsoft Windows 95, Windows 98, and Windows Millennium Edition (Windows Me) clients use SMB connections as well. These clients do not, however, use the LPR or LPD service. They render files using the GDI and spool RAW-formatted files to the print server. This means they perform their own processing of printed documents.

Print servers must have sufficient disk space to handle print jobs. The amount of disk space required depends on the size of print jobs and the number of print jobs that are queued for printing at any one time. It also depends on the print server configuration because in some cases a print server can be configured to save documents after they have been spooled for faster reprinting. By default, print jobs are spooled to files on the print server's system drive (%SystemRoot%\System32\Spool\PRINTERS), but this is completely configurable, as discussed in "Configuring Print Spool, Logging, and Notification Settings" on page 889.

Print servers perform a substantial amount of disk input/output (I/O) operations. To ensure optimal performance, you should consider moving the spool folder to a separate drive or array of drives that isn't used for other purposes. A separate drive should help to ensure that disk space isn't a constraint on the number of jobs the print server can handle and that the disk I/O operations related to the spooler are separate from that of other disk I/O operations.

> **Note**
>
> Paging and spooling are both disk I/O–intensive operations. If possible, use a separate disk that uses a separate Small Computer System Interface (SCSI) controller rather than the disk and controller used for the server's paging file.

The network interfaces on a print server are also important, but often overlooked. The print server needs sufficient connectivity to communicate with both clients and printers. Network cards should operate at 100 megabits per second (Mbps) or higher when possible.

Sizing Printer Hardware and Optimizing Configuration

Many types of printers are available including ink-jet and laser. Both types have advantages and disadvantages.

Ink-jet printers typically have lower up-front costs but higher costs later because they often require more maintenance and use consumables (ink cartridges) quicker. A typical ink-jet printer will print several hundred pages before you have to replace its ink cartridges. Higher-capacity cartridges are available for some business-class models. As part of periodic maintenance, you must perform nozzle checks to check for clogged nozzles and then clean the print heads if they are clogged. You might also need to align the print heads periodically.

Laser printers typically have higher up-front costs and moderate incremental costs because these printers typically require less maintenance and use consumables (toner cartridges and drum/fuser kits) less frequently. A typical laser printer will print thousands of pages before you have to replace toner cartridges and tens of thousands of pages or more before you have to replace the drum, fuser, or transfer components. Higher-capacity toner cartridges are also available for most business-class models. Replacing the toner cartridges and the drum, fuser, and transfer components are the key maintenance tasks.

> ## Use Laser Printers for High-Volume Printing
>
> In most cases, laser printers have a lower per-sheet print cost than ink-jet printers. This is true for black-and-white as well as color printing. Because of the lower cost, longer life cycle of consumables, and less frequent preventative maintenance schedule, laser printers typically are better suited to high-volume printing.

Most business-class printers can be expanded. The options available depend on the printer model and can include the following:

- **RAM expansion modules** The amount of RAM on a printer determines how much information it can buffer. At a minimum, a printer should be sized so that the average document being printed can be buffered in RAM in its entirety. As the workload of the printer increases, the RAM should allow for buffering of multiple documents simultaneously, which allows for faster and more efficient printing.

> ## Consider the Type of Document Being Printed
>
> Most word-processing documents are relatively small—several hundred pages of text use only a few hundred kilobytes. When you add in graphics, such as with presentations or Portable Document Format (PDF) files, even files with few pages can use several megabytes of disk space. Digital art, computer-aided design (CAD), and other types of files with high-resolution graphics can use hundreds of megabytes.

- **Paper or envelope trays** Add-on paper or envelope trays can improve performance substantially—more than you'd think. If a group within the organization routinely prints with different paper sizes or prints transparencies or envelopes, you should consider getting an add-on tray to accommodate the additional paper size or type. Otherwise, every time someone prints to the alternate paper size or type, the printer can stop and wait for the user to insert the appropriate type of paper. On a busy printer, this can lead to big delays in printing, frustrated users, and major problems.

- **Duplexers** Duplexers allow for printing on both sides of a sheet of paper. If a printer has a duplexer, Windows Server 2008 will use that feature automatically to reduce the amount of paper used by the printer. This doesn't necessarily save time, but it does mean the printer's tray will have to be refilled less frequently. Users can of course change the default settings and elect not to duplex.

- **Internal hard disks** An internal hard disk shifts much of the printing burden from the print server to the printer itself. A printer with an internal hard disk is able to store many documents internally and queue them for printing directly. Because the documents are stored on the printer, printing is more efficient and can be quicker than if the printer had to wait for documents to be transferred over the network.

Many groups of users have specific needs, so if you are purchasing a printer for a particular group, be sure to ask their needs, which might include the need for the following:

- **Photo printing** Usually an option for ink-jet printers rather than laser printers

- **Large-format printing** The capability to print documents larger than 11 by 17 inches

Both ink-jet and laser printers are available in direct-attached and network-attached models. Direct-attached printers (more commonly known as *local printers*) connect directly to a print server by a parallel, universal serial bus (USB), or FireWire (IEEE 1394) interface. For faster transmission speeds and easier configuration, consider printers with USB 2 or FireWire interfaces and stay away from those with slower parallel interfaces. USB and FireWire interfaces are also fully Plug and Play–compliant.

Network-attached printers have a network card and connect to the network like other devices with network cards. A printer with a built-in network interface gives you flexibility in where you place the printer relative to the print server. Unlike a local printer, which must be placed in close proximity to the print server, you can place a network-attached printer just about anywhere with a network connection. If you have a choice, choose a network-attached printer over a local printer.

INSIDE OUT   **The ins and outs of color printing**

The price of color printers and the per-sheet cost of printing in color have both dropped substantially over the years. This makes color printing more affordable than ever and that has led many organizations to increase their use of color printers. If your organization is considering the use of color printers, you should look closely at the type of ink or toner cartridges used by the printer.

Most business-class color printers have separate cartridges for each basic color—cyan, magenta, and yellow—and black. Some high-end printers have additional cartridges for producing true-to-life colors, and these printers are often referred to by the number of ink/toner cartridges, such as a six-color printer. Look closely at the capacity options for cartridges. Some printers can use both standard-capacity and high-capacity cartridges, but not always for both color and black ink. For example, you might be able to use high-capacity black ink cartridges that can print up to 4,500 pages, but only standard-capacity color cartridges that can print up to 1,500 pages.

If a group or individual needs a printer for photo printing, it is important to consider whether special photo ink/toner cartridges are available. For example, some Hewlett-Packard (HP) DeskJet models have the option to use a photo ink cartridge. This special cartridge prints digital photos with richer colors that are more true to life. Also, don't assume a color laser printer will be able to print on specialty photo paper because this might or might not be the case. See "Configuring Color Profiles" on page 906 for details on how Integrated Color Management (ICM) is used in Windows Server 2008.

Chapter 26

Whether you are working with an ink-jet or a laser printer, you should determine the number of pages printed per minute and the recommended monthly print volume or duty cycle. Most color printers print in monochrome slightly faster than they print in color. In a small office, you may be able to use a printer that prints 20 to 25 pages a minute, but in a workgroup setting, you may find that you need a printer that prints 45 to 50 pages a minute.

When you find a printer that prints at a suitable rate, look at the printer's monthly duty cycle. The monthly duty cycle is a gauge of how robust the printer is and how many pages a printer can print each month. For example, a printer with a monthly duty cycle of 35,000 pages could handle printing a maximum of 35,000 pages each month (though this probably is not recommended on a sustained basis, and if users really print that many pages each month, you'll probably find that the printer is unable to keep up with its workload or that it has frequent problems requiring maintenance).

INSIDE OUT   Printer duty cycles and consumables

A printer's monthly duty cycle may be completely different from its recommended monthly print volume. Typically, a printer's monthly duty cycle is the maximum number of pages per month that a printer can handle at the ideal best, while the recommended monthly print volume (which may be substantially less) is what the printer really can handle for optimal performance. Thus, just because a printer is listed as having a huge monthly duty cycle, it doesn't mean that users can print that number of pages each month. As an example, the HP 4350n printer has a monthly duty cycle of 250,000 pages but its recommended monthly print volume is 5000 to 20,000 pages—a substantial difference. Also consider the case of the printer's consumables: its standard black print cartridge can print up to 10,000 pages and its high-capacity print cartridge can print up to 20,000 pages. Based on this capacity, if users *really* print 250,000 pages a month, you would need to change the standard black print cartridge almost every day.

Most laser printers require periodic replacement of drum, fuser, and transfer components. These components are the laser printer's dirty little secret. Most printer manufacturers do no list drum, fuser, or transfer component life cycles along with product information. In fact, in a search of printer manufacturer Web sites at the time I was writing this book, I found that most manufacturers list toner cartridges as replacement parts on the printer pages but only list drum, fuser, and transfer components separately. I had to search separately for "drum," "fuser," and "transfer kit" to find the necessary replacement kits. With some high-end printers, the necessary replacement kits might not even be available for direct purchase, requiring your organization to have a service contract or obtain the kit from a third-party source.

One of the reasons it is so hard to find information about these components is that they can be expensive. Consider, for example, the HP 9500 printer series. These high-speed, high-capacity laser printers designed for large offices have a transfer kit, a fuser kit, and four separate drum kits—one each of black, cyan, yellow, and magenta. Based on 5% average coverage per printed page, the fuser kit yields 100,000 pages and costs $280, the black drum yields 40,000 pages and costs around $298, each of the color drums yield 20,000 pages and cost around $464, and the transfer kit yields 200,000 pages and costs about $380. This means that if users print 120,000 monochrome pages and 120,000 color pages each year, your total costs in drum, fuser, and transfer components alone would be around $8800. As your toner cartridge cost would be about another $2300 per year, the total annual cost of all printer consumables would be about $11,100.

Setting Up Print Servers

Windows Server 2008 allows you to set up local printers as well as network-attached printers. You can share either type of printer on the network so that it is available to other computers and users. The computer sharing the printer is called a *print server*, regardless of whether it is actually running a server version of the Windows operating system.

As discussed previously, you can configure more than one logical print device (printer) for a physical print device. The key reason to do this is when you want to use different options, such as when you want to create a priority or scheduled print queue. If you configure multiple printers, you must use a different local name and share name each time. Other than that, you can choose the exact same initial settings each time and modify them as desired.

Installing a Print Server

You configure a server as a print server by adding the Print Services role. Follow these steps to install and configure this role:

1. In Server Manager, select the Roles node in the left pane and then click Add Roles. This starts the Add Roles Wizard. If the wizard displays the Before You Begin page, read the welcome text and then click Next.

2. On the Select Server Roles page, select Print Services and then click Next twice.

3. On the Select Role Services page, select one or more of the following role services (see Figure 26-4) and then click Next:

   ○ **Print Server** Configures the server as a print server and installs the Print Management console. You can use the Print Management console to manage multiple printers and print servers, to migrate printers to and from other print servers, and to manage print jobs.

   ○ **Line Printer Daemon (LPD) Service** Installs and starts the TCP/IP Print Server (LPDSVC) service, which allows UNIX-based or other computers that are using the Line Printer Remote (LPR) service to print to shared printers on this server. The wizard also creates an inbound TCP exception on port 515 in the Windows Firewall with Advanced Security.

   ○ **Internet Printing** Creates a Web site where authorized users can manage print jobs on the server. It also lets users who have Internet Printing Client installed connect and print to the shared printers on the server using the Internet Printing Protocol (IPP). The default Internet address for Internet Printing is *http://ServerName/Printers*, where *ServerName* is a placeholder for the actual internal or external server name, such as *http://PrintServer24/Printers* or *http://www.adatum.com/Printers*.

> **Note**
>
> When you install Internet Printing, you must also install Web Server (IIS) and Windows Process Activation Service. You'll be prompted to automatically add the required role services. If you click Yes to continue and install these role services, you'll have the opportunity to add other role services for Web Server (IIS).

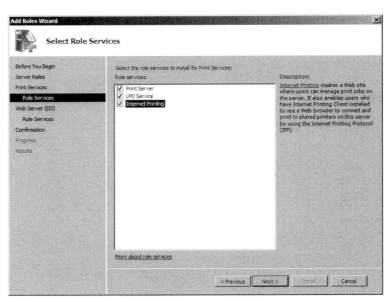

Figure 26-4 Select the role services to install for the printer.

4. When you've completed all the optional pages, click Next. You'll see the Confirm Installation Options page. Click Install to begin the installation process. When Setup finishes installing the server with the features you've selected, you'll see the Installation Results page. Review the installation details to ensure that all phases of the installation completed successfully.

5. Printer sharing controls access to printers that are attached to the computer. With Windows Server 2008, printer sharing is disabled by default. To change the printer sharing settings, click Start and then click Network. On the Network Explorer toolbar, click Network And Sharing Center. Expand the Printer Sharing panel by clicking the related Expand button. Select Turn On Printer Sharing to enable printer sharing and then click Apply.

When you configure a computer running Windows Server 2008 as a print server, you'll find several new management tools. The new management tools include the Print Management console and the Printbrm.exe command-line tool. You'll find the Print Management console on the Administrative Tools menu. Printbrm.exe is in the %SystemRoot%\System32\Spool\Tools folder.

You'll also find a set of scripts for managing print services from the command line. These scripts are stored in the %SystemRoot%\System32\Printing_Admin_Scripts folder and include:

- **PrnCnfg** A script for managing printer configuration settings, including printer name, printer properties, and printer sharing

- **PrnDrvr** A script for listing and managing print drivers

- **PrnJobs** A script for viewing and managing print jobs in a print queue

- **PrnMngr** A script for installing printers and managing printers configured on a computer

- **PrnPort** A script for creating and managing Transmission Control Protocol/Internet Protocol (TCP/IP) ports for printers

- **PrntQctl** A script for managing print queues

- **Pubprn** A script for printer publishing in Active Directory

Installing Network Printers Automatically

Print Management can automatically detect all network printers located on the same subnet as the computer on which the console is running. After detection, Print Management can automatically install the appropriate print drivers, set up print queues, and share the printers. To automatically install network printers and configure a print server, follow these steps:

1. Start Print Management by clicking Start, clicking Administrative Tools, and then selecting Print Management.

2. In Print Management, expand the Print Servers node by double-clicking it and then right-click the entry for the local or remote server you want to work with.

3. Select Add Printer. This starts the Network Printer Installation Wizard.

4. On the Print Installation page, select Search The Network For Printers and then click Next.

5. The wizard will then search the local subnet for network printers. If printers are found, you'll see a list of printers by name, IP address, and status. Select a printer to install and then click Next.

6. If there are multiple possible drivers for a detected printer, you'll be prompted to select the driver to use. Click Close.

Adding Local Printers

Typically, a local printer is a desktop version for use by an individual or a small group. Most desktop printers allow you to connect to them using either a parallel, USB, or FireWire interface. All of these techniques require a cable to connect from the computer to the printer. You might also have the option of using wireless infrared (IrDA or Bluetooth), which doesn't require a cable. Windows Server 2008 supports all of these options.

To set up a local printer, you'll need to use an account that is a member of the Administrators or Print Operators group. To get started, connect the print device to the server.

If Windows Server 2008 automatically detects the print device, follow these steps to configure the printer:

1. If Windows Server 2008 automatically detects the print device, Windows begins installing the device and the necessary drivers. If the necessary drivers aren't found, you might need to insert the printer's driver disc into the CD-ROM drive.

2. When Windows finishes the installation process, you can configure the printer. In Print Management, expand the Print Servers node and the node for the server you want to work with. When you select the Printers node for the server you are configuring, you'll see a list of available printers in the main pane. Right-click the printer you want to configure and then click Manage Sharing. This displays the printer's Properties dialog box with the Sharing tab selected, as shown in Figure 26-5.

Figure 26-5 Configure the printer in the Properties dialog box.

3. When you select the Share This Printer check box, Windows Server 2008 sets the default share name to the name of the printer. If desired, you can type a different name for the printer share in the Share Name field.

> **Note**
> Windows 2000 and later share names can be up to 256 characters and can include spaces. In a large organization you'll want the share name to be logical and helpful in locating the printer. For example, you might want to give the printer that points to a color laser printer on the second floor of building 3506 a name such as Building 3506 Color Laser 2nd Floor.

INSIDE OUT
Choosing an interface type

With any available printer interface option, your key concern shouldn't be having to spend additional money on a cable—spend the money if you have to—it should be on getting the best performance. Consider the following:

- A standard parallel printer interface (IEEE 1284–compliant) has a maximum transmission speed of 250 kilobits per second (Kbps).

- A high-speed parallel printer interface (ECP/EPP-compliant) has a maximum transmission speed of 3–5 Mbps.

- A wireless interface that is IrDA-compliant has a maximum transmission speed of around 4 Mbps; a wireless interface that is Bluetooth-compliant has a speed of 2–3 Mbps.

- A USB interface has a maximum transmission speed of 12 Mbps for USB 1 and 480 Mbps for USB 2.

- A FireWire interface has a transmission speed of up to 400 Mbps for FireWire 400 (IEEE 1394a) and up to 800 Mbps for FireWire 800 (IEEE 1394b).

Given these transmission speeds and that USB and FireWire are Plug and Play–compliant, they should be the preferred interfaces to use when you have a choice. With USB 2 and FireWire 800, it is important to note that you get only the speed benefit if both the computer interface and the printer interface are USB 2-compliant or FireWire 800–compliant.

4. When you share a printer, Windows Server 2008 automatically makes drivers available so that users can download them when they first connect to the printer. Typically, only Type 3 *x*86 drivers are available by default. To make additional drivers available, click Additional Drivers. In the Additional Drivers dialog box, select operating systems that can download the print driver. As necessary, insert the Windows Server 2008 CD, the print driver disc, or both, for the selected operating systems. The Windows Server 2008 CD has drivers for most Windows operating systems. Click OK twice.

If Windows Server 2008 doesn't detect the print device automatically, you must install the print device by following these steps:

1. In Print Management, expand the Print Servers node and the node for the server you want to work with.

2. Right-click the server's Printers node and then select Add Printer. This starts the Network Printer Installation Wizard.

3. On the Printer Installation page, shown in Figure 26-6, select Add A New Printer Using An Existing Port and then choose the appropriate LPT, COM, or USB port. You can also print to a file. If you do, Windows Server 2008 prompts users for a file name each time they print. Click Next.

4. On the Printer Driver page, choose one of the following options:

○ If Windows detected the printer type on the selected port and found a compatible driver automatically, it lists a print driver according to the printer manufacturer and model, and the Use The Printer Driver That The Wizard Selected option is selected by default. To accept this setting, simply click Next.

○ If a compatible driver is not available and you want to choose an existing driver installed on the computer, choose the Use An Existing Driver On The Computer option. After you choose the appropriate driver from the selection list, click Next.

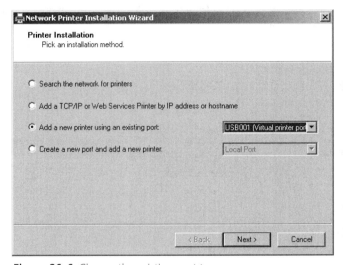

Figure 26-6 Choose the existing port to use.

5. If a compatible driver is not available and you want to install a new driver, select Install A New Driver and then click Next. You must now specify the print device manufacturer and model, and then click Next. This allows Windows Server 2008 to assign a print driver to the print device. After you choose a print device manufacturer, choose a printer model.

> **Use a Driver Disc**
>
> If the print device manufacturer and model you're using aren't displayed in the list, click Have Disk to install a new driver. If a driver for the specific printer model you're using isn't available, you can usually select a generic driver or a driver for a similar print device.

6. As shown in Figure 26-7, assign a name to the printer. This is the name you'll see in Print Management. Then specify whether the printer is available to remote users. To create a printer accessible to remote users, select the Share This Printer check box and enter a name for the shared resource. If you like, you can enter a location description and comment. This information can help users find a printer and determine its capabilities. Click Next when you are ready to continue.

Choose Names That Have the Widest Compatibility

Although you can use just about any share name for a printer, you should keep the printer name as short as possible. For maximum compatibility, it is recommended that the printer name be no more than 31 characters and not contain spaces. This will make the printer easier to work with from the command line and in applications that have printer name limitations.

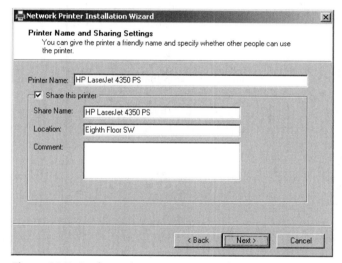

Figure 26-7 Configure the printer name and sharing settings.

7. The final page lets you review the settings. Click Next when you're ready to complete the installation. After Windows installs the print driver and configures the printer, you'll see a status page. Ensure that the driver and printer installation succeeded before continuing. If there were errors, you'll need to correct any problems and repeat this process. To test the printer, select Print Test Page and then click Finish. To install another printer, select Add Another Printer and then click Finish.

When the Network Printer Installation Wizard finishes installing the new printer, the Printers folder will have an additional icon with the name set the way you specified. You can change the printer properties and check printer status at any time. For more information, see "Managing Printer Properties" on page 890.

> **Note**
>
> All printers configured for sharing on Windows Server 2008 systems are automatically listed in Active Directory. Printers can be removed from the directory as necessary, however.

Adding Network-Attached Printers

Network-attached printers are printers that have their own network cards. Typically, a network-attached printer is a workgroup-class printer for use by groups of users. Most network-attached printers use the RAW protocol or the LPR protocol to communicate over a standard TCP/IP port. This includes network-attached printers that use TCP/IP as well as those that use network devices such as Hewlett-Packard JetDirect or Intel NetPort.

INSIDE OUT   Printing to UNIX print servers

In some cases, users might want to print to a UNIX print server. To do this, you must install the LPR Port Monitor feature on the users' computers.

On Windows Vista, you can install the LPR Port Monitor feature using the Windows Features dialog box. Click Start, click Control Panel, and then click Programs. On the Programs page, click Turn Windows Features On Or Off under Programs And Features. In the Windows Features dialog box, expand the Print Services node by double-clicking it, select the LPR Port Monitor check box, and then click OK.

On Windows Server 2008, you can install the LPR Port Monitor feature using the Add Features Wizard. In Server Manager, select the Features node in the left pane and then click Add Features. This starts the Add Features Wizard. On the Select Features page, select LPR Port Monitor and then click Next. Click Install. When the wizard finishes installing the feature, click Close.

You can set up a network-attached printer using an account that is a member of the Administrators or Print Operators group. Follow these steps:

1. Make sure the printer is connected to the network and turned on. One way to do this is to ping the printer's IP address. As a final check of the printer, you might want to print its configuration or check its network settings to ensure that it has the appropriate IP address and subnet mask.

2. In Print Management, expand the Print Servers node and the node for the server you want to work with. Start the Network Printer Installation Wizard by right-clicking the server's Printers node and then selecting Add Printer.

3. On the Printer Installation page, shown in Figure 26-8, select Add A TCP/IP Or Web Services Printer By IP Address Or Hostname and then click Next.

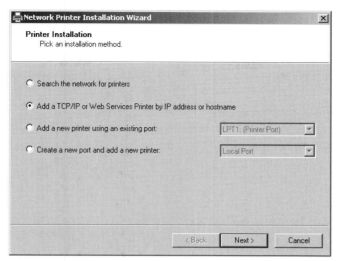

Figure 26-8 Configure the printer by IP address or host name.

4. On the Printer Address page, shown in Figure 26-9, choose one of the following options in the Type Of Device List:

   ○ **Autodetect** Choose this option if you are unsure of the printer device type. Windows Server 2008 will then try to detect the type of device automatically.

   ○ **TCP/IP Device** Choose this option if you are sure the printer is a TCP/IP device.

   ○ **Web Services Printer** Choose this option if you are sure the printer is an Internet print device.

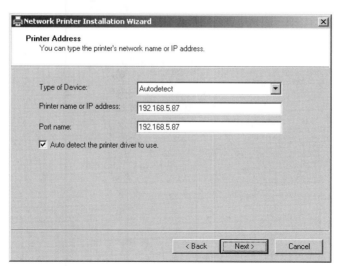

Figure 26-9 Enter the printer's address information.

5. Enter the host name or IP address for the printer in the Printer Name Or IP Address text box, such as 192.168.5.87. With the Printer Name Or IP Address option, the wizard will set the port name to the same value. Because this port name must be unique on the print server, you can't have two printers with the same port name on a print server. If you're configuring multiple printers on the print server, be sure to write down the port to printer mapping.

6. When you click Next, the wizard will look for the printer on the network. If the wizard is unable to find the print device or needs additional information, select the printer device type using the Standard list, as shown in Figure 26-10.

> **Note**
>
> If the wizard is unable to find the print device on the network, make sure that you entered the printer name or IP address correctly. If you have, make sure the device is on, that it is properly configured, and that the network is set up correctly. If the wizard still can't detect the printer, select the device type and continue with the installation. Keep in mind that you might need to change the standard TCP/IP port monitor settings before you can use the printer. You can do this by selecting Custom and clicking Settings, or you can perform the necessary changes later. Both techniques are discussed in "Changing Standard TCP/IP Port Monitor Settings" on the next page.

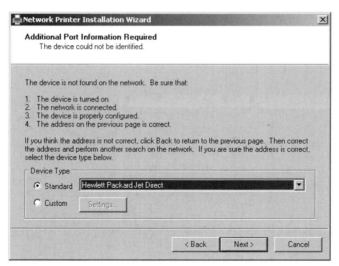

Figure 26-10 Select the printer device type.

7. On the Printer Driver page, choose one of the following options:

- ⚬ If Windows detected the printer type on the selected port and a compatible driver was found automatically, a print driver is listed according to the printer manufacturer and model, and the Use The Printer Driver That The

Wizard Selected option is selected by default. To accept this setting, simply click Next.

○ If a compatible driver is not available and you want to choose an existing driver installed on the computer, select the Use An Existing Driver option. After you use the selection list to choose the appropriate driver, click Next.

○ If a compatible driver is not available and you want to install a new driver, select Install A New Driver and then click Next. Specify the print device manufacturer and model, and then click Next. This allows Windows Server 2008 to assign a print driver to the print device. After you choose a print device manufacturer, choose a printer model. If the print device manufacturer and model you're using aren't displayed in the list, click Have Disk to install a new driver. For example, if you have an HP LaserJet 4350 PS printer, you'd choose HP as the manufacturer and HP LaserJet 4350 PS as the printer.

8. On the Printer Name And Sharing Settings page, assign a name to the printer. This is the name you'll see in Print Management.

9. Specify whether the printer is available to remote users. To create a printer accessible to remote users, select the Share Name check box and enter a name for the shared resource. In a large organization you'll want the share name to be logical and helpful in locating the printer.

10. If you like, you can enter a location description and comment. This information can help users find a printer and determine its capabilities.

11. Click Next to continue. The final page lets you review the settings. When you're ready to complete the installation, click Next.

12. After Windows installs the print driver and configures the printer, you'll see a status page. Ensure that the driver and printer installation succeeded before continuing. If there were errors, you'll need to correct any problems and repeat this process. To test the printer, select Print Test Page and then click Finish. To install another printer, select Add Another Printer and then click Finish.

When the Network Printer Installation Wizard finishes installing the new printer, the Printers folder will have an additional icon with the name set the way you specified. You can change the printer properties and check printer status at any time. For more information, see "Managing Printer Properties" on page 890.

Changing Standard TCP/IP Port Monitor Settings

The standard TCP/IP port monitor settings determine how a print server connects to a network-attached printer. As discussed previously, most network-attached printers use the RAW protocol or the LPR protocol to communicate over a standard TCP/IP port. If the Network Printer Installation Wizard had problems detecting a network-attached printer, the chances are good the printer was set up to use the RAW protocol and port 9100. In most cases, this is what you want as most current printers use the RAW protocol over TCP port 9100, including laser printers from HP, Minolta, Epson, and other printer manufacturers.

Chapter 26

To view or change a printer's standard TCP/IP port monitor settings, follow these steps:

1. In Print Management, right-click the printer, and select Properties. In the printer's Properties dialog box, click the Ports tab. The port used by the printer is selected and highlighted by default. Click Configure Port.

2. In the Configure Standard TCP/IP Port Monitor dialog box, shown in Figure 26-11, select the protocol that the printer uses, either RAW or LPR, as follows:

   ○ When you select RAW, the Raw Settings panel is available and you can set a port number. Because the default port number used by most RAW printers is 9100, this value is filled in for you. Change the default setting only if the printer documentation instructs you to do so.

   ○ When you select LPR, the LPR Settings panel is available. Set the queue name to be used by the port. If you are unsure, use the queue name the printer documentation instructs you to use, such as crownnet.

> **Note**
>
> With LPR, you also have the option to enable LPR Byte Counting. When you select this check box, the print server counts the bytes in a document before sending it to the printer, and the byte count can be used by the printer to verify that a complete document has been received. However, this option slows down printing and uses processor resources on the print server.

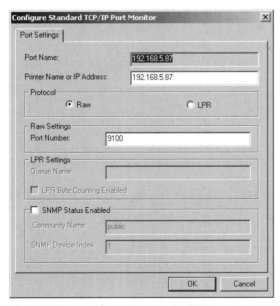

Figure 26-11 Configure the standard TCP/IP port monitor for the printer.

3. Click OK when you are finished configuring the TCP/IP port monitor settings.

Connecting Users to Shared Printers

After you configure and share a printer, users on client computers can connect to it. The technique is similar for all versions of Windows.

Accessing Shared Printers on Windows 2000 or Later

Computers running Windows 2000 or later can install print drivers automatically. All you need to do is connect the client computer to the shared printer.

For Windows Vista, users can connect to the shared printer by following these steps:

1. Click Start and then click Control Panel. In Control Panel, click the Printer link under the Hardware And Sound heading. This opens the Printers window.

2. Open a second window by clicking Start and then clicking Network.

3. In the Network window, double-click the computer sharing the printer.

4. In the Network window, click the printer and then drag it to the Printers window.

> **Note**
>
> On the print server, you must ensure that printer sharing is turned on in Network And Sharing Center and that the printer is shared. You must also ensure that Network Discovery is turned on for the domain network.

For Windows 2000 or Windows XP, users can use any of the following techniques to connect to a shared printer:

- **UNC Path** Click Start, and then click Run. In the Run dialog box, shown in the following screen, type the Universal Naming Convention (UNC) path to the printer share, and click OK. That's it. The syntax for UNC paths to printer shares is *ServerName**PrintShareName*, where *ServerName* is the name or IP address of the print server and *PrintShareName* is the name of the printer share, such as **\\CorpSvr02\EngMain**.

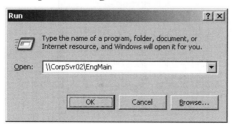

Chapter 26

- **My Network Places** In Windows Explorer, expand Control Panel so that the Printers And Faxes entry is visible, and then navigate My Network Places to the print server, as shown in the following screen. With the print server selected in the left pane under My Network Places, select the printer and drag it to the Printers And Faxes folder.

- **Add Printer Wizard** In the Printers And Faxes folder, select or double-click Add Printer to start the Add Printer Wizard. Afterward, as shown in the following screen, select A Network Printer, Or A Printer Attached To Another Computer, and then click Next.

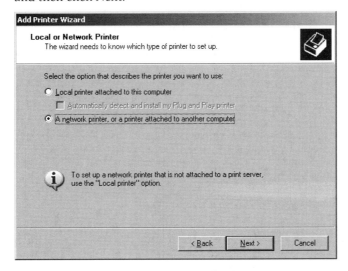

In the Specify A Printer dialog box, choose a method for finding the network printer as follows:

- Choose Find A Printer In The Directory if you want to search Active Directory for the printer.

- Choose Connect To This Printer, and type the printer name or browse the network for shared printers just as you'd browse in My Network Places.

- Choose Connect To A Printer On The Internet if you want to enter the Uniform Resource Locator (URL) of an Internet printer.

When the printer is selected, click OK. Select whether the printer is the default used by Windows applications by selecting Yes or No and then clicking Next. Click Finish to complete the operation.

Connecting to Shared Printers Using the Command Line and Scripts

With any Windows operating system, you can connect users to shared printers using the command line and scripts. In a logon script that uses batch scripting or at the command line, you can use the Net Use command to connect to a network printer. Consider the following example:

```
net use \\corpsvr02\engmain /persistent:yes
```

Here, you use the Net Use command to add a persistent connection to the EngMain printer on CORPSVR02. That's all there is to it.

You could also use Microsoft VBScript in a logon script to set a printer connection. With VBScript, you must initialize the variables and objects you plan to use and then call the AddWindowsPrinterConnection method of the Network object to add the printer connection. If desired, you can also use the SetDefaultPrinter method of the Network object to set the printer as the default for the user. After you are done using variables and objects, it is good form to free the memory they use by setting them to vbEmpty. Consider the following example:

```
Option Explicit
Dim wNetwork, printerPath
Set wNetwork = WScript.CreateObject("WScript.Network")
printerPath = "\\corpsvr02\engmain"

wNetwork.AddWindowsPrinterConnection printerPath
wNetwork.SetDefaultPrinter printerPath

Set wNetwork = vbEmpty
Set printerPath = vbEmpty
```

Here, you use the AddWindowsPrinterConnection method to add a connection to the EngMain printer on CORPSVR02. You then use the SetDefaultPrinter method to set the printer as the default for the user.

Deploying Printer Connections

As you've seen, it is fairly easy to connect to shared printers. That said, however, you can make the process even easier by deploying printer connections to computers or users via the Group Policy objects (GPOs) that Windows applies. When choosing whether to deploy printer connections to computers or users, keep the following in mind:

- Deploy to groups of computers when you want all users of the computers to access the printers. For per-computer connections, Windows adds or removes printer connections when the computer starts.

- Deploy to groups of users when you want users to be able to access the printers from any computer they log on to. For per-user connections, Windows adds or removes printer connections when the user logs on.

To deploy printer connections to computers running Windows Vista or later, you must follow these steps:

1. In Print Management, expand the Print Servers node and the node for the server you want to work with.

2. Select the server's Printers node. In the main pane, right-click the printer you want to deploy and then select Deploy With Group Policy. This displays the Deploy With Group Policy dialog box, shown in Figure 26-12.

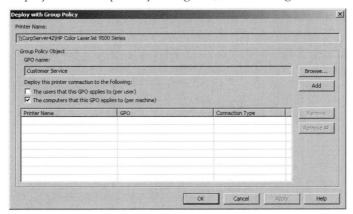

Figure 26-12 Choose the GPO you want to work with.

3. Click Browse. In the Browse For Group Policy Object dialog box, select the GPO to use and then click OK.

4. Do one or both of the following and then click Add to create a print connection entry:

- ○ To deploy the printer connection on a per-user basis, select the The Users That This GPO Applies To (Per User) check box under Deploy This Printer Connection To The Following.

- ○ To deploy the printer connection on a per-computer basis, select the The Computers That This GPO Applies To (Per Machine) check box under Deploy This Printer Connection To The Following.

5. Repeat steps 3 and 4 to deploy the printer connection to other GPOs.

6. Click OK to save the GPO changes.

To deploy printer connections to computers running versions of Windows earlier than Windows Vista, you must follow these steps:

1. In the Group Policy Management Console (GPMC), right-click the GPO for the site, domain, or organizational unit you want to work with and then select Edit. This opens the policy editor for the GPO.

2. In the Group Policy Management Editor, do one of the following:

- ○ To deploy the printer connections on a per-computer basis, double-click the Windows Settings folder in the Computer Configuration node. Then click Scripts.

- ○ To deploy the printer connections on a per-user basis, double-click the Windows Settings folder in the User Configuration node. Then click Scripts.

3. Using Windows Explorer, copy PushPrinterConnections.exe from the %SystemRoot%\System32 folder to the Computer\Scripts\Startup, User\Scripts\ Logon, or the User\Scripts\Logoff folder for the related policy. Policies are stored in the %SystemRoot%\Sysvol\Domain\Policies folder on domain controllers.

4. In the Group Policy Management Editor, right-click Startup or Logon and then select Properties.

5. In the Startup Or Logon Properties dialog box, click Show Files. If you copied the executable to the correct location in the Policies folder, you should see the executable.

6. In the Startup Or Logon Properties dialog box, click Add. This displays the Add A Script dialog box.

7. In the Script Name text box, type **PushPrinterConnections.exe** and then click OK.

Configuring Point and Print Restrictions

In Group Policy, the Point And Print Restrictions setting controls several important aspects of printer security. For Windows XP Professional and later versions of Windows, the setting controls the servers to which a client computer can connect for point and print. For Windows Vista and later, the setting controls security warnings and elevation prompts when users point and print as well as when drivers for printer connections need to be configured. Table 26-1 summarizes how this policy setting is used.

Table 26-1 Point and Print Restrictions

When the Policy Setting Is...	The Policy Works As Follows
Enabled	Windows XP and Windows Server 2003 clients can only point and print to an explicitly named list of servers in the forest. Windows Vista and later clients can point and print to any server. You can configure Windows Vista and later clients to show or hide warning and elevation prompts when users point and print and when a driver for an existing printer connection needs to be updated.
Not Configured	Windows XP and later clients can point and print to any server in the forest. Windows Vista and later clients also will not show a warning and elevation prompt when users point and print or when a driver for an existing printer connection needs to be updated.
Disabled	Windows XP and later clients can point and print to any server. Windows Vista and later clients also will not show a warning and elevation prompt when users point and print or when a driver for an existing printer connection needs to be updated.

By default, Windows Vista and Windows Server 2008 allow a user who is not a member of the local Administrators group to install only trustworthy print drivers, such as those provided by Windows or in digitally signed print driver packages. When you enable the Point And Print Restrictions setting, you also allow users who are not members of the local Administrators group to install printer connections deployed using Group Policy that include additional or updated print drivers that are not in the form of digitally signed print driver packages. If you do not enable this setting, users might need to provide the credentials of a user account that belongs to the local Administrators group.

You can enable and configure the Point And Print Restrictions setting in Group Policy by following these steps:

1. In the Group Policy Management Console (GPMC), right-click the GPO for the site, domain, or organizational unit you want to work with and then select Edit. This opens the policy editor for the GPO.

2. In the Group Policy Management Editor, expand User Configuration\
   Administrative Templates\Control Panel and then select the Printers node.

3. In the main pane, double-click Point And Print Restrictions. In the Point And
   Print Restrictions Properties dialog box, shown in Figure 26-13, select Enabled.

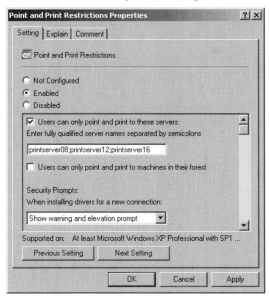

Figure 26-13 Configure point and print restrictions.

4. When you enable pointing and printing restrictions, you can configure policy
   so that users can only point and print to a named list of servers. To enforce this
   restriction, select the related check box and enter a list of fully qualified server
   names separated by semicolons. To remove this restriction, clear the Users Can
   Only Point And Print To These Servers check box.

5. When you enable pointing and printing restrictions, you can configure policy
   so that users can only point and print to servers in their forest. To enforce this
   restriction, select the related check box. To remove this restriction, clear the Users
   Can Only Point And Print To Machines In Their Forest check box.

6. When you install drivers for a new connection, Windows Vista and later clients
   can show or not show a warning or elevation prompt. Use the related selection list
   to choose the desired option.

7. When you update drivers for an existing connection, Windows Vista and later
   clients can show or not show a warning or elevation prompt. Use the related
   selection list to choose the desired option. Click OK to save your policy settings.

Managing Printers Throughout the Organization

Print Management should be your tool of choice for working with printers and print servers. After you install Print Services, Print Management is available as a stand-alone console on the Administrative Tools menu. You can also add Print Management as a snap-in to any custom console you've created. Using Print Management, you can install, view, and manage all of the printers and Windows print servers in your organization.

Managing Your Printers

Print Management allows you to manage local print servers. You can manage and monitor other print servers in the organization by adding them to the console, provided these print servers are running Windows 2000 or later. If the printer provides a Web-based management interface, Print Management can display additional information about the printer's status, its physical properties, and its configuration, and sometimes allows remote administration.

To manage a remote print server, you must be a member of the local Administrators group on the print server or a member of the Administrators group in the domain of which the print server is a member. When you select a print server's Printers node, as shown in Figure 26-14, the main pane lists the associated printer queues by printer name, queue status, number of jobs in the queue, and server name. If you right-click Printers and then select Show Extended View, you can turn on the Extended view. Extended view makes it easy to track the status of both printers and print jobs by displaying detailed information about the print job. Additionally, if the printer has a Web page, Extended view displays a Printer Web Page tab that lets you directly access the printer's Web page.

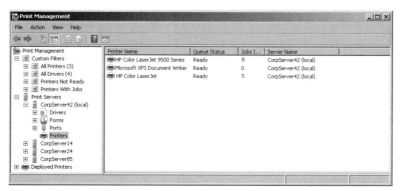

Figure 26-14 Use Print Management to manage your print servers and printers.

To add print servers to Print Management, follow these steps:

1. In Print Management, right-click the Print Servers node in the left pane and then select Add/Remove Servers.

2. In the Add/Remove Servers dialog box, shown in Figure 26-15, you'll see a list of the print servers you've previously added. Do one of the following and then click Add The Local Server:

    ○ In the Add Servers list box, type or paste the names of the print servers you want to add, using commas to separate computer names.

    ○ Click Browse to display the Select Print Servers dialog box. Click the print server you want to use and then click Select Server.

3. Repeat the previous step as necessary and then click OK.

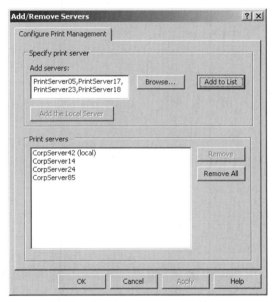

Figure 26-15 Add print servers to Print Management so that you can manage and monitor them.

To remove print servers from Print Management, follow these steps:

1. In Print Management, right-click the Print Servers node in the left pane and then select Add/Remove Servers.

2. In the Add/Remove Servers dialog box, you'll see a list of the print servers that are being monitored. Under Print Servers, select one or more servers, and then click Remove.

Migrating Printers and Print Queues

You can use the Printer Migration Wizard to move printers and their print queues from one print server to another. This is an efficient way to consolidate multiple print servers or replace an older print server.

When you move printers, the server on which the printers are currently located is the source server, and the server to which you want to move the printers is the destination server. With this in mind, you can move printers to a new print server by following these steps:

1. In Print Management, right-click the source server and then click Export Printers To A File. This starts the Printer Migration Wizard.

2. On the initial page, shown in Figure 26-16, note the printer-related objects that will be exported and then click Next.

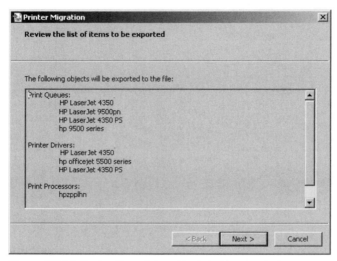

Figure 26-16 Review the printer objects to be exported.

3. On the Select The File Location page, click Browse. In the dialog box provided, select a save location for the printer migration file. After you type a name for the file, click Open.

4. Printer migration files are saved with the .printerExport extension. Click Next to save the printer settings to this file.

5. After the wizard completes the export process, click Open Event Viewer to review the events generated during the export process. If an error occurred during processing, you can use the event entries to determine what happened and possible actions to take to resolve the problem. When you are finished, exit the Event Viewer.

6. On the Exporting page, click Finish to exit the Printer Migration Wizard.

7. In Print Management, right-click the destination server and then click Import Printers From A File. This launches the Printer Migration Wizard.

8. On the Select The File Location page, click Browse. In the dialog box provided, select the printer migration file you created previously, as shown in Figure 26-17, and then click Open.

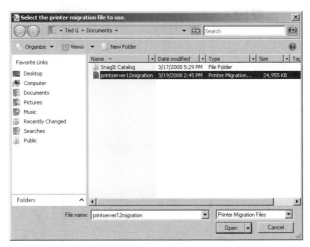

Figure 26-17 Select the printer migration file.

9. Click Next. Note the objects that will be imported and then click Next. On the Select Import Options page, shown in Figure 26-18, choose one of the following options in the Import Mode selection list:

- **Keep Existing Printers; Import Copies** When you choose this option and existing printer queues have the same names as those you are importing, the wizard will create copies to ensure that the original printer queues and the imported printer queues are both available.

- **Overwrite Existing Printers** When you choose this option and existing printer queues have the same names as those you are importing, the wizard will overwrite the existing printer queues with the information from the printer queues you are importing.

10. On the Select Import Options page, choose one of the following options in the List In The Directory list:

- **List Printers That Were Previously Listed** Choose this option to ensure that only printers that were previously listed are listed in Active Directory.

- **List All Printers** Choose this option to ensure that all printers are listed in Active Directory.

- **Don't List Any Printers** Choose this option to ensure that no printers are listed in Active Directory.

Chapter 26

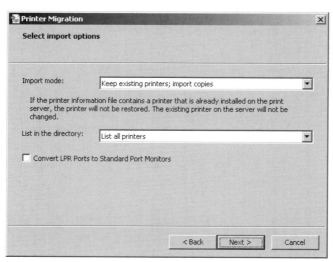

Figure 26-18 Choose the import options for the migration.

11. Click Next to begin the import process. After the wizard completes the import process, click Open Event Viewer to review the events generated during the import process. If an error occurred during processing, you can use the event entries to determine what happened and possible actions to take to resolve the problem. When you are finished, exit the Event Viewer.

12. On the Importing page, click Finish to exit the Printer Migration Wizard.

Monitoring Printers and Printer Queues Automatically

You can use print filters to display only the printers, printer queues, and print drivers that meet specific criteria. Through automated notification, you can also use printer filters to automate monitoring of printers.

In Print Management, you can view existing filters by expanding the Custom Filters node. If you expand the Custom Filters node and then select a filter, the main pane will show all printers or print drivers that match the filter criteria. Print Management includes the following default print filters:

- **All Printers** Lists all printers associated with print servers that have been added to the console

- **All Drivers** Lists all print drivers associated with print servers that have been added to the console

- **Printers Not Ready** Lists all printers that are not in a Ready state, such as those with errors

- **Printers With Jobs** Lists all printers associated with print servers that have active or pending print jobs

You can create a new custom filter by follow these steps:

1. In Print Management, right-click the Custom Filters node and then select Add New Printer Filter. This starts the New Printer Filter Wizard.

2. On the Printer Filter Name And Description page, enter a filter name and description. If you'd like the number of matching items to be displayed after the filter name, select the Display The Total Number Of Printers... check box. Click Next.

3. On the Define A Printer Filter page, define the filter by specifying Field, Condition, and Value to match in the first row. If you want to further narrow the possible matches, define additional criteria as necessary in the second, third, and subsequent rows. Click Next when you are ready to continue.

> **Note**
>
> When you use filters for monitoring and notification, you'll use the Queue Status field most. This allows you to receive notification when a printer has a specific status. You can match the following status values: Busy, Deleting, Door Open, Error, Initializing, IO Active, Manual Feed Required, No Toner/Ink, Not Available, Offline, Out Of Memory, Out Of Paper, Output Bin Full, Page Punt, Paper Jam, Paper Problem, Paused, Printing, Processing, Ready, Toner/Ink Low, User Intervention Required, Waiting, and Warming Up.

> **Note**
>
> When you are matching conditions, you can match when an exact condition exists or does not exist. For example, if you want to be notified only of conditions that need attention, you can look for Queue Status conditions that are not exactly the following: Deleting, Initializing, Printing, Processing, Warming Up, and Ready.

4. On the Set Notifications page, you can specify whether to send an e-mail, run a script, or both when the specified criteria are met. Click Finish to complete the configuration.

You can modify an existing custom filter by follow these steps:

1. In Print Management, expand the Custom Filters node. Select and then right-click the filter you want to work with. On the shortcut menu, select Properties.

Chapter 26

2. In the filter's Properties dialog box, use the options provided to manage the filter settings. This dialog box has the following three tabs:

   ○ **General** Shows the name and description of the print filter. Enter a new name and description as necessary.

   ○ **Filter Criteria** Shows the filter criteria. Enter new filter criteria as necessary.

   ○ **Notification** Shows the e-mail and script options. Enter new e-mail and script options as necessary.

Managing and Maintaining Print Services

When you point to Print in an application and click, the document is supposed to print on a printer somewhere. Most users don't care to know how or why printing works; they only care that it works. In that respect, printing is like networking services—something most people take for granted until it doesn't work the way they expect it to or it stops working altogether. The problem with this way of thinking is that next to file and networking services, print services are the most used feature of the Windows operating system. It takes a lot of behind-the-scenes work to ensure that printing is as easy as point and click.

Managing Printer Permissions

By default, everyone with access to the network can print to a shared printer. This means any user with a domain account or any user logged on as a guest can print to any available printer. Because this isn't always what is wanted, you might want to consider whether you need to restrict access to a printer. Restricting access to printers ensures that only those users with appropriate permissions can use a printer.

With specialty printers, such as those used for color or large-format printing, you'll find that restricting access to specific groups or individuals makes the most sense. But you might also want to restrict access to other types of printers as well. For example, you might not want everyone with network access to be able to print. Instead, you might want only users with valid domain accounts to be able to print. While you are configuring printer security, you might also want to configure printer auditing to track who is using printers and what they are doing.

Understanding Printer Permissions

Printer permissions set the maximum allowed access level for a printer. These permissions are applied whenever someone tries to print, whether the person is connected locally or remotely, and include both special and standard permissions.

Special permissions are assigned individually and include the following:

- **Read Permissions** Allows users to view permissions

- **Change Permissions** Allows users to change permissions

- **Take Ownership** Allows users to take ownership of a printer, its print jobs, or both

The standard printer permissions available are the following:

- **Print** With this permission, users can connect to a printer and submit documents for printing. They can also manage their own print jobs. If a user or group has Print permission, it also has the special permission called Read Permissions for any documents it prints.

- **Manage Printers** With this permission, users have complete control over a printer and can set printer permissions. This means they can share printers, change permissions, assign ownership, pause and restart printing, and change printer properties. If a user or group has the Manage Printers permission, it also has the special permissions called Read Permissions, Change Permissions, and Take Ownership for any documents on the printer.

- **Manage Documents** With this permission, users can manage individual print jobs. This allows them to pause, restart, resume, or cancel documents. It also allows them to change the order of documents in the queue. It doesn't, however, allow them to print, because this permission is assigned separately. If a user or group has Manage Documents permission, it also has the special permissions called Read Permissions, Change Permissions, and Take Ownership for the printer.

By default, the permissions on printers are assigned as shown in Table 27-1.

Table 27-1 **Default Printer Permissions**

Group	Print	Manage Documents	Manage Printers
Creator Owner		Yes	
Everyone	Yes		
Administrators	Yes	Yes	Yes
Power Users	Yes	Yes	Yes
Print Operators	Yes	Yes	Yes
Server Operators	Yes	Yes	Yes

As you examine printer permissions, keep in mind that if a user is a member of a group that is granted printer permissions, the user also has those permissions and the permissions are cumulative. This means that if one group of which the user is a member has Print permission and another has Manage Printers permission, the user has both permissions. To override this behavior, you must specifically deny a permission.

TROUBLESHOOTING

Check permissions on the spool folder

By default, the spool folder is located on the system drive. The default permissions give Full Control to Administrators, Print Operators, Server Operators, and the SYSTEM user. System is the account under which the Print Spooler service runs, and this account needs Full Control to be able to create and manage spool files. Administrators, Print Operators, and Server Operators are given full control so that they can spool documents and clear out the spool folder if necessary. Creator Owner has special permissions that grant Full Control so that anyone that prints a document can manage it. Authenticated Users are given Read & Execute permissions so that an authenticated user can access the spool folder and create files and folders. If these permissions get changed, print spooling might fail.

Configuring Printer Permissions

To view or manage the permissions of a printer, right-click the printer in Print Management, and then select Properties. In the Properties dialog box, select the Security tab, shown in Figure 27-1. You can now view the users and groups that have printer permissions and the type of permissions they have.

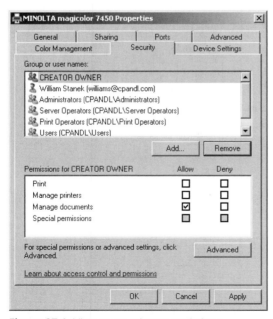

Figure 27-1 View or set printer permissions.

To grant or deny printer permissions, follow these steps:

1. In Print Management, expand the Print Servers node and the node for the server you want to work with.

2. Select the server's Printers node. In the main pane, right-click the printer you want to work with and then select Properties.

3. In the printer Properties dialog box, click the Security tab. On the Security tab, click Add. This opens the Select Users, Computers, Or Groups dialog box, as shown in Figure 27-2.

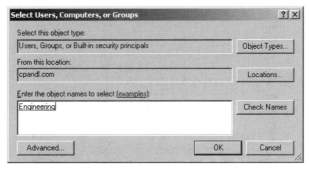

Figure 27-2 Specify the users or groups to add.

4. The default location is the current domain. Click Locations to see a list of the available domains and other resources that you can access. Because of the transitive trusts in Windows Server 2008, you can usually access all the domains in the domain tree or forest.

5. Type the name of a user or group account in the selected or default domain, and then click Check Names. The options available depend on the number of matches found as follows:

    ○ When a single match is found, the dialog box is automatically updated as appropriate and the entry is underlined.

    ○ When no matches are found, you've either entered an incorrect name part or you're working with an incorrect location. Modify the name and try again, or click Locations to select a new location.

    ○ If multiple matches are found, select the name(s) you want to use, and then click OK.

6. To add additional users or groups, type a semicolon (;), and then repeat this process.

7. When you click OK, the users and groups are added to the Group Or User Names list for the printer.

8. Configure access permissions for each user and group added by selecting an account name and then allowing or denying access permissions. If a user or group should be granted access permissions, select the check box for the permission in the Allow column. If a user or group should be denied access permissions, select the check box for the permission in the Deny column.

> **Note**
>
> If you give a group a permission, such as Print, the related special permission, Read Permissions, is also granted. For this reason, you usually need not configure special permissions for printers.

9. When you're finished, click OK.

Assigning Printer Ownership

The owner of a printer has permission to manage its documents. By default, the SYSTEM user is listed as the current owner of a printer and the printer's actual creator is listed as a person who can take ownership. Ownership can be taken or transferred in several ways. Any administrator can take ownership. Any user or group with the Take Ownership permission can take ownership. You can take ownership using the printer's Properties dialog box. Right-click the printer, and then select Properties. On the Security tab of the Properties dialog box, display the Advanced Security Settings dialog box by clicking Advanced. Next, click the Owner tab, as shown in Figure 27-3.

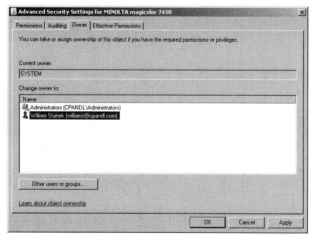

Figure 27-3 Assigning printer ownership.

If you are an administrator or a current owner of a file or folder, you can grant permission to take ownership of the printer. Click Other Users Or Groups to display the Select User, Computer, Or Group dialog box. Type the name of a user or group, and click Check Names. If multiple names match the value you entered, you'll see a list of names and will be able to choose the one you want to use. Otherwise, the name will be filled in for you, and you can click OK.

Chapter 27

Auditing Printer Access

Auditing printer access can help you track who is accessing printers and what they are doing. You configure auditing policies on a per-printer basis. In Print Management, right-click the printer to be audited, and then select Properties. In the Properties dialog box, click the Security tab, and then click Advanced. In the Advanced Security Settings dialog box, click the Auditing tab, shown in Figure 27-4.

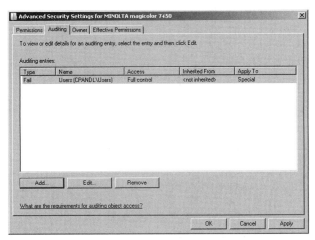

Figure 27-4 Specify to which users and groups auditing should apply.

Now use the Auditing Entries list box to select the users, groups, or computers whose actions you want to audit. To add specific accounts, click Add, and then use the Select User, Computer, Or Group dialog box to select an account name to add. If you want to audit actions for all users, use the special group Everyone. Otherwise, select the specific user groups or users, or both, that you want to audit. When you click OK, you'll see the Auditing Entry For *Printer Name* dialog box, shown in Figure 27-5.

The Apply Onto drop-down list box allows you to specify whether the actions should be audited for:

- This Printer Only
- Documents Only
- This Printer And Documents

After you make a selection, under Access, select the Successful or Failed check boxes, or both, for each of the events you want to audit. The events you can audit are the same as the printer permissions discussed previously. Click OK when you're finished. Repeat this process to audit other users, groups, or computers. Any time printers for which you've configured auditing are accessed, the action is written to the system's security log, where it's stored for your review. The security log is accessible from Event Viewer.

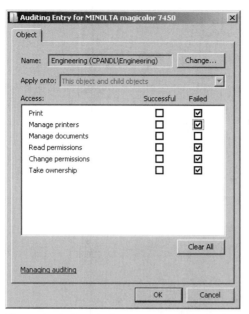

Figure 27-5 Specify the actions to audit for the designated user, group, or computer.

Managing Print Server Properties

Print server properties control the global settings for all printers on a server. You can access print server properties from Print Management. In Print Management, when you select a server node, you'll see additional nodes for Drivers, Forms, Ports, and Printers. By selecting these nodes, you can determine the drivers, forms, ports, and printers that are configured on the print server. By right-clicking the print server and then selecting Properties, you can configure settings for all printers, including the following:

- Forms

- Ports

- Drivers

- Advanced settings

Viewing and Creating Printer Forms

Forms are used by print servers to define the standard sizes for paper, envelopes, and transparencies. Print servers have many predefined forms from which you can choose, but you can also define your own forms.

To view the current settings for a printer form, right-click the print server in Print Management and then select Properties. Then click the Forms tab, as shown in Figure 27-6.

Use the Forms On list to select the form you want to view. The form settings are shown in the Form Description (Measurements) area.

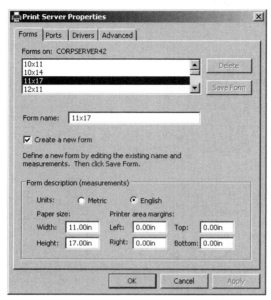

Figure 27-6 View and configure forms for paper, envelopes, and transparencies.

To create a new form, follow these steps:

1. Access the Forms tab of the Print Server Properties dialog box. Use the Forms On list box to select the existing form on which you want to base the new form.

2. Select the Create A New Form check box, and then enter a new name for the form in the Form Name field.

3. Use the fields in the Form Description (Measurements) area to set the paper size and margins. When you are finished, click the Save Form button to save the form.

Although you can't change or delete the default forms, you can delete forms users have created. In Print Management, select the Forms node for the server, right-click the form, and then select Delete.

Viewing and Configuring Printer Ports

Ports are used to define the interfaces and TCP/IP addresses to which the print server can connect. Using the Print Server Properties dialog box, you can view and manage all the ports configured for use on the print server. This gives you one location for viewing, adding, deleting, and configuring ports.

To work with ports, right-click the print server in Print Management and then select Properties. Then click the Ports tab, as shown in Figure 27-7. If you want to view or change a port's settings, select it in the Ports On This Server list and then click Configure Port. For details on configuring TCP/IP ports, see "Changing Standard TCP/IP Port Monitor Settings" on page 863.

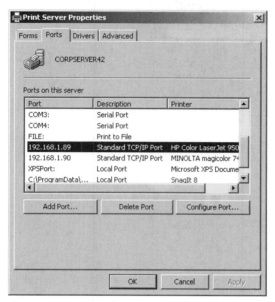

Figure 27-7 View and configure printer ports.

Viewing and Configuring Print Drivers

As discussed in "Installing and Updating Print Drivers on Clients" on page 894, printer clients download print drivers the first time they access a printer and any time the print drivers have been updated. After you've configured each printer so that clients can download drivers, you can manage the installed print drivers through the Print Server Properties dialog box. As with ports, the key here is convenience. Not only can you view all the print drivers that are available but you can add and remove drivers as well.

To work with drivers, right-click the print server in Print Management and then select Properties. Then click the Drivers tab. As shown in Figure 27-8, drivers are listed by

- **Name** Typically, this is the manufacturer and model number of the printer
- **Processor** The chip architecture for the listed driver
- **Type** The driver type as either a Type 2 or Type 3 driver

Chapter 27

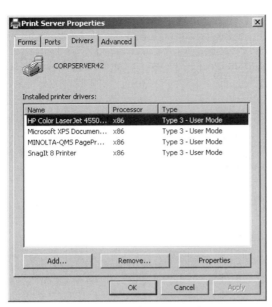

Figure 27-8 View and configure print drivers.

You can now do the following:

- **View driver properties and file associations** If you select a driver and click Properties, you'll see detailed information on the driver, which includes all the files associated with the driver. This includes all related help, configuration, data, driver settings, and dependent files.

- **Add or update an existing print driver** If you want to add or update an existing print driver, click Add to start the Add Printer Driver Wizard, and then follow these steps:

    1. In the Add Printer Driver Wizard, click Next. On the Processor And Operating System Selection page, choose all the Windows clients that will be connecting to this printer from the network. To install additional print drivers for clients, you need access to the installation files for the appropriate driver version either on the network or on a CD.

    2. On the Printer Driver Selection page, choose the manufacturer and model of the printer for which you are adding support. If the print device manufacturer and model you're using aren't displayed in the list or you have a newer driver from the manufacturer, click Have Disk to install a new driver. In either case, make sure the driver you use is digitally signed. This is indicated after you select a manufacturer and model and means that the driver is certified for use by Microsoft.

    3. When you click Next, Windows will install any available drivers and then prompt you to provide additional drivers as necessary. Click Finish when you are done.

- **Remove print drivers** If you want to remove a driver, select it, and then click Remove. You are prompted to remove the driver only or the driver and the driver package. If you want to be able to use the driver again in the future, select Remove Driver Only and then click OK. Otherwise, click Remove Driver And Driver Package and then click OK.

Configuring Print Spool, Logging, and Notification Settings

Using the Advanced tab of the Print Server Properties dialog box, you can configure properties related to spooling. Not only can you change the location of the spool folder but you can also control event logging and notification actions related to the Print Spooler service.

To configure the print spool, logging, and notification settings, right-click the print server and then select Properties. Then click the Advanced tab. As shown in Figure 27-9, you can configure the following options:

- **Spool Folder** Shows the current location of the print spool folder. To change the spool folder location, type a new folder path, click Apply, and then when prompted, click Yes.

Spooling Changes Immediately

The changes to the spool folder will occur immediately. This means the Print Spooler service will look to this folder for documents to print and any previously spooled documents in the old spool folder will not print. Because of this, you should allow all current documents to print before changing the spool folder location.

CAUTION

The security on the selected folder will not be changed and this could affect spooling of files to the selected folder. For best results, you should set security permissions on the new folder so they are the same as the original spool folder. See the Troubleshooting sidebar "Check permissions on the spool folder" on page 881.

- **Log Spooler Error Events** Writes error events related to the Print Spooler service to the event logs.

- **Log Spooler Warning Events** Writes warning events related to the Print Spooler service to the event logs.

- **Log Spooler Information Events** Writes information events related to the Print Spooler service to the event logs.

Chapter 27

- **Beep On Errors Of Remote Documents** Windows 2000 and Windows XP clients display a warning balloon in the notification area when a document has failed to print. This warning is displayed for 10 seconds or until clicked. Don't use this if you have earlier client versions, because they will actually get alerts.

- **Show Informational Notifications For Local Printers** Displays the status of all jobs sent to this print server on the computer of the user that submitted the print job.

- **Show Informational Notifications For Network Printers** Displays the status of print jobs sent by users on this computer to print services on other print servers.

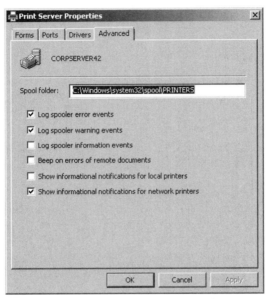

Figure 27-9 Configure the print spool, logging, and notification.

Managing Printer Properties

Printer properties control the settings for an individual printer. You can access a printer's properties in Print Management. In Print Management, right-click the printer and select Properties.

> **Note**
>
> The specific properties displayed depend to some extent on the make and model of the printer you are working with. Because of this, some of the settings described on the following pages won't necessarily apply to all printers.

Setting General Properties, Printing Preferences, and Document Defaults

To help users find printers and ensure that they don't have to waste time trying to configure default settings such as paper size and paper tray to use, you should take a close look at the general properties, printing preferences, and document defaults assigned to a printer after you install it. Although this will take you a few minutes to go through, it will save users much more time, especially when you consider that this is something that every user in the organization would otherwise have to do.

As Figure 27-10 shows, the general settings are accessed from the General tab of the printer's Properties dialog box.

Figure 27-10 Configure general settings.

In Print Management, right-click the printer, and then select Properties. On the General tab, you can view or change the following options:

- **Local printer name** The name of the printer on the print server

- **Location** The location description of the printer

- **Comment** An additional comment about the printer

To make sure the printer is ready for use, you should next go through the printing preferences and device settings to configure the settings that will be used by default on the printer. Click Printing Preferences in the lower portion of the General tab. Check the settings on the following tabs:

- **Layout** Controls the paper orientation and page order for printing
- **Paper/Quality** Controls the paper source (tray), the media (paper type), and the printing preference for black and white or color

In the Printing Preferences dialog box, click OK. Then in the printer's Properties dialog box, click the Device Settings tab, as shown in Figure 27-11. Check the following device settings and change them as necessary and applicable to your printer:

- **Form To Tray Assignment** Form To Tray Assignment options ensure that the printer paper trays are configured for the proper paper types. Selecting a tray entry highlights it and displays a selection list that you can use to set the paper type for the tray.

- **Job Timeout** Job Timeout optimizes the print job wait times. Job Timeout specifies the maximum amount of time the printer allows for a job to get from the computer to the printer. If this time is exceeded, the printer will stop trying to print the document. The default value is 0, which means the printer will continue trying to print a document indefinitely. To change this value, select Job Timeout, and then type a new timeout.

- **Wait Timeout** Wait Timeout optimizes in-process printing wait times. Wait Timeout specifies how long the printer waits for additional information from the print server If this time elapses, the printer stops trying to print the document and prints an error message. Typically, the default wait timeout is 300 seconds. Although this is sufficient for most types of print jobs, a print server that is under a heavy load or processing very complex documents might exceed this. If you notice that the printer unexpectedly stops printing photos, CAD drawings, digital art, or other types of complex documents, try increasing the wait timeout to resolve this problem. To change this value, select Wait Timeout, then type a new timeout.

- **Installed Memory/Installable Options** Installed Memory (sometimes known as Installable Options) tells the computer about the amount of memory installed on the printer. Although you should never use a value less than the default setting for the printer, you can use this option to tell the print server about additional RAM that you installed on the printer. This ensures that the computer knows the extra RAM is available. To change this value, select Installed Memory, then choose the appropriate value in the selection list.

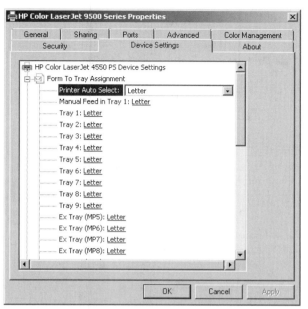

Figure 27-11 Configure Form To Tray Assignment and other device settings.

Setting Overlays and Watermarks for Documents

In secure environments, it might be necessary to set a watermark in the background of every page that is printed. A watermark is a word or phrase, such as DRAFT, CON-FIDENTIAL, or TOP SECRET, that is printed lightly in the background of every page using a very large font size—typically 72-point Courier. If your printer supports this feature, you can print the watermark in the background of every page or only the first page of a document.

To clear or set a default watermark for all printed documents, follow these steps:

1. In Print Management, right-click the printer, and select Properties. On the General tab, click Printing Preferences. Then in the Printing Preferences dialog box, browse the available tabs until you see Watermarks options. Typically this tab is labeled Overlays or Effects, but it depends on the printer.

2. To clear a default watermark, select None as the watermark type. Afterward, click OK and skip the remaining steps.

3. To set a default watermark, select a watermark type. You can in some cases select an existing type, such as CONFIDENTIAL, COPY, DRAFT, FINAL, ORIGINAL, or PROOF.

Chapter 27

4. To create a new watermark, click Add or Edit, then use the Watermark Details dialog box to set the watermark name, text, and options. The watermark text sets the word or phrase that will be printed lightly in the background. When you are finished creating the watermark, click OK.

5. To set the watermark on the first page only, select First Page Only.

6. Click OK to save your settings.

Installing and Updating Print Drivers on Clients

When a print server runs Windows Server 2008, print drivers can be installed and updated automatically on clients as discussed in "Understanding Windows Server 2008 Print Services" on page 841. A client downloads print drivers the first time it accesses a printer and any time the print drivers have been updated.

By default, printers installed on a Windows Server 2008 network support Windows 2000 or later with user-mode drivers. Drivers for several processor architectures can be made available to clients for automatic download, including:

- **Itanium-based drivers** Used on 64-bit Windows systems with the Intel Itanium processor architecture

- **x86 user-mode drivers** Used on Windows 2000 and later systems running 32-bit processors for Intel x86-based architectures

- **x64 user-mode drivers** Used on Windows 2000 and later systems running 64-bit processors

You confirm and configure print driver availability on a per-printer basis by following these steps:

1. In Print Management, right-click the printer you want to work with, and then select Properties.

2. In the Properties dialog box, click the Sharing tab, and then click Additional Drivers. This displays the Additional Drivers dialog box, as shown in Figure 27-12.

3. Select the check box for any client drivers you want to install, and then click OK.

4. To install additional print drivers for clients, you need access to the installation files for the appropriate driver version either on the network or on a CD.

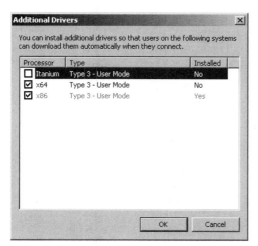

Figure 27-12 Select the additional operating systems that should be supported.

After you've installed the print drivers for clients, clients will download them when they first connect to the printer you've configured on the print server.

Configuring Printer Sharing and Publishing

When you set up a printer, you are given the chance to share it. If you share a printer, it is published in Active Directory automatically. Published printers can be searched for by users in a variety of ways, including when a user is attempting to connect to a network printer using the Add Printer Wizard. You can check or change the printer sharing and publishing options using the Sharing tab of the printer's Properties dialog box. In Print Management, right-click the printer, and then select Properties.

On the Sharing tab, you have the following options, as shown in Figure 27-13:

- **Share This Printer** Selecting this check box shares the printer so that it is accessible to users as discussed in "Connecting Users to Shared Printers" on page 865.

- **Render Print Jobs On Client Computers** Shifts the print job processing to the client computer rather than the print server. Use this option to reduce the workload on the print server.

- **List In The Directory** For a shared printer, selecting this check box lists the printer in Active Directory, and clearing the check box removes the listing from Active Directory.

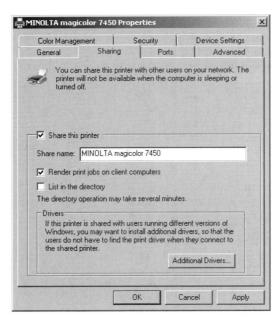

Figure 27-13 Configure sharing settings.

Optimizing Printing Through Queues and Pooling

A printer queue is a logical print device. You can have one logical print device associated with a printer, or you can have multiple logical print devices associated with a printer. It is the latter option that gives you more flexibility and can help improve printing in general, especially if you create different logical print devices for different purposes and educate users how they should be used. With multiple logical print devices, you can use print queue priority and scheduling settings to control how and when a logical print device is used.

Configuring Queue Priority and Scheduling

Queue priority lets you prioritize printing based on the type of document being printed. Queue scheduling lets you schedule when documents in a queue can be printed—it doesn't restrict spooling to the queue, only printing from the queue. Print queue priority and scheduling settings can be used separately or together. Consider the following scenarios:

- **A printer has a normal queue and a priority queue** You configure the normal queue so that it can be used for all routine print jobs. You configure the priority queue so that it is used for all urgent print jobs. Because the priority queue has a higher priority than the normal queue, any documents printed to the priority queue are printed before and preempt documents in the normal queue. To ensure that the priority queue isn't abused, you might want to restrict access to those groups or individuals that actually have priority printing needs on a printer.

- **A printer has a normal queue and a scheduled bulk queue** You configure the normal queue so that it can be used any time for all routine print jobs. You configure the bulk print queue so that it is used for large documents and only after hours or during nonpeak hours. Any document spooled to the normal queue can be printed immediately. Any document spooled to the bulk queue is printed only within the scheduled availability hours, which keeps large documents from tying up the printer and causing a lengthy backup for other documents during peak usage times. If you set the priority of the bulk queue to be lower than that of the normal queue, the normal queue will always have priority.

To set the printer availability schedule and priority, follow these steps:

1. In Print Management, right-click the printer, and then select Properties. Then click the Advanced tab, as shown in Figure 27-14.

Figure 27-14 Use the Advanced tab to set the printer availability schedule and priority.

2. Printers are either always available or available only during the hours specified. Select Always Available to make the printer available at all times, or select Available From to set specific hours of operation.

3. Use the Priority box to set the default priority for the print queue. The priority range goes from 1, which is the lowest priority, to 99, which is the highest priority. Print jobs always print in order of priority, and jobs with higher priority print before jobs with lower priority. The priority you use is assigned to all print jobs spooled to this printer.

4. If you are configuring a priority queue, select the Security tab, and configure permissions to allow only those users and groups that you want to print at this priority. Remove or deny print permissions for users and groups that should

have a different priority level. These users will use the normal priority queue that you've configured for the printer. If you haven't configured one yet, do so now.

5. When you are finished, click OK. Repeat this process for all other logical print devices you configured for this printer.

Configuring Printer Pooling

Using a technique called printer pooling, you can associate a single logical print device with multiple physical print devices. In this configuration, you have one print queue but multiple printers, and the print server sends jobs to the first available physical printer. To take advantage of printer spooling, the printers must use the same print driver. Typically, this means they must be from the same manufacturer and have the same model. They must also have the same amount of memory installed.

Figure 27-15 shows an example of printer pooling. As the figure shows, the advantage of printer pooling is that users see a single print queue but multiple printers are available to handle their print jobs. Behind the scenes, administrators are free to add or remove physical printers without affecting the users' configuration.

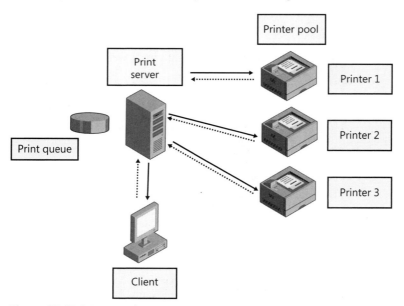

Figure 27-15 Printer pooling.

Printer pooling is useful in several scenarios:

- **Print-capacity scaling** To scale print capacity, you can place two, three, four, or more identical printers side by side and then use printer pooling to effectively double, triple, quadruple, or more your printing capacity. In this arrangement, users have one queue for printing to these printers, and the only changes you must make are on the print server. On the print server, you enable printer pooling so that the first available printer prints a document.

- **Printer maintenance and replacement** Printer pooling can facilitate printer maintenance and replacement as well. If you must maintain or repair a printer that is part of a printer pool, you can take it offline whenever necessary without impacting print operations. Users will still be able to print to the print queue and the additional printers in the pool will handle printing for their documents.

> **Cluster the Print Server**
>
> Printer pooling provides high availability and fault tolerance for the printers themselves. It doesn't provide high availability or fault tolerance for the print server. If a group of users requires high performance and high reliability, you can set up a print cluster as discussed in "Managing Failover Clusters and Their Resources" on page 1361. Setting up a print cluster provides additional capacity and fault tolerance should one of the print servers stop responding.

You can configure printer pooling by following these steps:

1. Printer pooling is managed using a single logical print device and multiple ports. This means you must add a printer so that it uses a particular port and then add one additional port for each additional physical print device you want to pool.

2. After you set up the printer and configure additional ports, access the printer's Properties dialog box. In Print Management, right-click the printer, and select Properties. Then click the Ports tab, as shown in Figure 27-16.

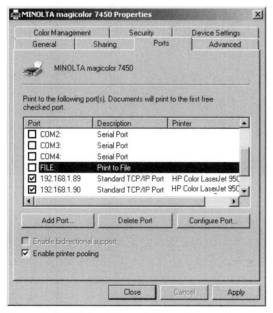

Figure 27-16 Select the ports to use for pooling.

3. Select the Enable Printer Pooling check box, and then select the check boxes for all the ports to which printers in the pool are attached. These ports can be local ports as well as network ports. As long as the physical print devices to which they connect are all identical, meaning they are from the same manufacturer, have the same model, and have the same amount of memory installed, you should be able to pool the printers.

4. When you are finished configuring printer pooling, click OK.

> **Put Pooled Printers Next to Each Other and Consider Using Separator Pages**
>
> Printer pooling works best when the pooled printers are all in the same location. You might want to put the printers back to back or side by side. It also helps if you use separator pages. Separator pages help to keep print jobs organized and make it easier for users to identify which printouts are theirs.

Configuring Print Spooling

The way print spooling is configured on a printer affects how clients perceive printing performance and the actual printing options. You can configure printers to start printing immediately after a print job is received or to wait until the last page is spooled. If a print server's drives are full or can't be written to, you can change printer spooling settings so clients can print directly. Although this can slow printing down on a busy printer, it allows clients to continue printing. Other spooling options allow you to keep printed documents for faster reprinting and to hold mismatched documents so that jobs using alternate types of paper or envelopes don't cause the printer to stop and wait.

To configure print spooling options, access the printer's Properties dialog box. In Print Management, right-click the printer, and select Properties. Then click the Advanced tab. You can now use the following options to configure print spooling:

- **Spool Print Documents So Program Finishes Printing Faster** Spools print jobs to the print server, allowing clients to finish faster so they can perform other tasks.

- **Start Printing After Last Page Is Spooled** Ensures that the entire document is spooled to the print server and available to the printer when printing begins. This option gives more control over the print job. If printing is canceled or not completed, the job won't be printed. If a higher-priority job becomes available, it will print first.

- **Start Printing Immediately** Reduces the time it takes to print by allowing the printing to begin immediately when the print device isn't already in use. This option is preferred if you want print jobs to complete faster and if you want to ensure that the client finishes printing faster.

- **Print Directly To The Printer** Turns off spooling completely and documents are sent directly to the printer. This option can seriously degrade print performance. Use this option only if there is a problem writing to the spool folder and you want to ensure that printing can continue.

- **Hold Mismatched Documents** Holds documents that don't match the setup for the print device without affecting other documents in the print queue. This speeds up the overall printing throughput by keeping the printer from waiting for alternate paper and envelope types. For example, if a user prints a transparency, rather than stopping printing and waiting for the user to insert a transparency sheet, the printer holds the document and continues printing.

- **Print Spooled Documents First** Allows jobs that have completed spooling to print before jobs in the process of spooling without regard to priority. The document with the highest priority that is already spooled will print even if a higher-priority document is in the process of spooling. This speeds up the overall printing throughput by keeping the printer from waiting for documents that are in the process of spooling.

- **Keep Printed Documents** Keeps a copy of documents in the print queue in case users need to print the same document again. When selected, if a user reprints a document that's already in the queue, the document can be taken directly from the queue rather than having to be transferred and spooled again. In most cases, you'll want to consider selecting this check box only when users print specialty types of documents that can take a long time to transfer and spool. Selecting this check box substantially increases the amount of disk space required for spooling.

- **Enable Advanced Printing Features** Enables advanced printing features for metafile (EMF) spooling, including Page Order, Booklet Printing, and Pages Per Sheet. Typically, this check box is selected because metafile spooling is desired.

Viewing the Print Processor and Default Data Type

Every printer has a print processor. The default print processor for Windows systems is Winprint. Other print processors can be installed when you set up a printer. The print processor and the default data type for the processor determine how much processing the printer performs. As discussed previously, the RAW data type is processed on the client and minimally processed on the print server. The EMF data type is sent to the print server for processing.

Generally speaking, you do not need to change either the print processor or the default data type. However, if you want to determine the print processor and default data type used by a printer, you can access the printer's Properties dialog box, click the Advanced tab, and then click Print Processor. This displays the Print Processor dialog box. As shown in Figure 27-17, the current Print Processor and Default Data Type are selected and highlighted by default.

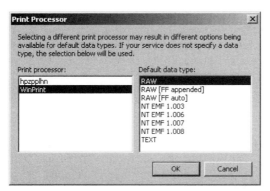

Figure 27-17 The current Print Processor and Default Data Type are selected.

Configuring Separator Pages

On a busy printer or when you use printer pooling, you might need some help keeping print jobs organized so that users can easily find their print jobs among other print jobs. This is where separator pages come in handy. Separator pages are used at the beginning of each print job to help identify the related document and who printed it.

Using Separator Pages

By default, printers don't use separator pages. If you want to use separator pages, you must configure them on a per-printer (logical print device) basis. Windows Server 2008 includes four default separator pages. These default separator pages are stored in the %SystemRoot%\System32 folder and are defined using standard American Standard Code for Information Interchange (ASCII) text. This means you can view and edit them using any standard text editor, including Notepad.

The default separator pages include the following types:

- **Pcl.sep** Sets the print device to PCL mode and prints a separator page before each document. The separator page shows the print job ID, date, and time. The Pcl.sep file uses the PCL page definition language and has the following contents:

  ```
  \
  \H1B\L%-12345X@PJL ENTER LANGUAGE=PCL
  \H1B\L&l1T\0
  \M\B\S\N\U
  \U\LJob : \I
  \U\LDate: \D
  \U\LTime: \T
  \E
  ```

- **Pscript.sep** Sets a dual-language printer to PostScript mode but doesn't print a separator page. The Pscript.sep file uses the PostScript page definition language and has the following contents:

  ```
  \
  \H1B\L%-12345X@PJL ENTER LANGUAGE=POSTSCRIPT\0
  ```

- **Sysprint.sep** Sets the print device to PostScript mode and prints a separator page before each document. The separator page has banner text to help easily identify who printed the document and when. The Sysprint.sep file uses the PostScript page definition language. The key definition assignments are the following:

```
@L/name (@N@L) def
@L/jobid(@I@L) def
@L/date (@D@L) def
@L/time (@T@L) def
```

- **Sysprtj.sep** Sets the print device to PostScript mode and prints a separator page before each document. The Sysprtj.sep file uses the PostScript page definition language and is essentially an alternate version of the Sysprint.sep file that uses a different version of the banner text.

You can install other separator pages in the %SystemRoot%\System32 folder as well. Some printers install their own separator pages. Typically, they do this because they can't use any of the standard separator pages. For example, Minolta QMS MagiColor Laser printers install their own separator page. The default name of this separator page is Msep01_b.sep. The contents of this file are as follows:

```
\
\M\B\S\N\U
\U\LJob : \I
\U\LDate: \D
\U\LTime: \T
\E
```

Here, the user name is printing in banner text and then job ID, date, and time are printed in standard text. It is important to know what the definitions look like in a separator page because you can customize all separator pages. The way you do this is to modify existing definitions or add definitions.

Setting a Separator Page

To use one of the default separator pages, access the printer's Properties dialog box, click the Advanced tab, and then click Separator Page. In the Separator Page dialog box, shown in Figure 27-18, click Browse. This opens a Find dialog box in the %SystemRoot%\System32 folder so you can easily choose available separator pages. Select a separator page that uses the same page description language as the printer, and then click Open. Afterward, in the Separator Page dialog box, click OK.

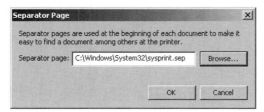

Figure 27-18 Select a separator page.

Chapter 27

> ### Test the Separator Page
>
> After you select a separator page, you should print a test document to ensure that printing works as expected. To do this, click Print Test Page on the General tab of the printer's Properties dialog box. If there's any printing error, you've chosen an incompatible separator page and will need to try a different one.

Customizing Separator Pages

You can customize separator pages for your organization. Although PCL, PostScript, and other types of separator pages use a different syntax, they all use the same variables. These variables are summarized in Table 27-2.

Table 27-2 Separator Page Variables

Variable	Usage
B	Turns on banner printing of text for which each character is block printed using pound signs (#) until you exit banner printing with the U variable.
D	Prints the date the document was printed using the default date format.
E	Inserts a page break. Typically used at the end of the separator page so that the document starts printing on a new sheet of paper.
F*filepath*	Prints the contents of the specified text file to the separator page. The specified file must contain only text and the formatting of the text is not retained.
H*nn*	Sets a printer-specific code, which is used to control printer functions. Refer to the printer manual for control codes that might be available.
I	Prints the job ID. The job ID is set when a document is spooled to the printer.
L*text*	Prints the literal text following the variable until the next escape code or variable is reached.
L%	Marks the start of comment text that isn't printed. The next escape code or variable marks the end of the comment.
M	Turns on emphasis (bold) print. Switch off with S.
N	Prints the logon name of the user who submitted the print job.
N	Skips *n* lines, where *n* is a number from 0 to 9.
S	Switches off emphasis (bold).
T	Prints the time the document was printed using the default time format.
U	Turns off banner text printing.
W*nn*	Sets the line character width. Any lines with more characters than the specified width are truncated. The default width is 80 characters.

Knowing the available variables and their meanings, you can now examine the separator page listings shown previously to see exactly what they are doing.

Now that we know what the variables mean, let's take another look at Pcl.sep:

1. The first line sets the escape code for the separator page:

```
\
```

2. On the second and third lines, the separator page uses control codes to set the page description language to PCL:

```
\H1B\L%-12345X@PJL ENTER LANGUAGE=PCL
\H1B\L&l1T\0
```

3. On the fourth line, the separator page switches to bold banner text mode and then prints the name of the logon user:

```
\M\B\S\N\U
```

> **Note**
>
> The order of these elements must be as follows: Enable Emphasis (M), Enable Banner Text (B), Stop Emphasis (S), Print Name (N), Stop Banner Text (U). If you don't follow this order, the emphasis, banner text format, or both may be enabled for the entire separator page.

4. On lines 5 through 8, the separator page prints literal text followed by a value—either the job ID, date, or time:

```
\U\LJob : \I
\U\LDate: \D
\U\LTime: \T
```

5. On the last line, the separator page inserts a page break:

```
\E
```

The PostScript separator pages are a bit more difficult to follow but have similar definitions. With PostScript, @ typically is used as an escape character to mark the start of variables instead of \. However, the first line of the separator page specifies the escape code that will be used.

With both PCL and PostScript, you have two options for customizing separator pages: you can either try to edit the existing separator pages or create your own. Before you edit an existing separator page, you should make a backup copy and work with the copy instead of the original file. If you elect to make your own separator page, you can do so using Notepad.

When you start from scratch, you can use either \ and @ as escape codes or $. Set the escape code on the first line of the document and stick with the escape code you start with. With that in mind, if you want to print out the user name, date, and time in bold banner text, you would create a separator page with the following contents:

```
$
$M$B$S$S$N$U
$M$B$S$S$D$U
$M$B$S$S$T$U
$E
```

You would then save the file to the %SystemRoot%\System32 folder and name it with the .sep extension, such as Working.sep. To use the custom separator page, set it as the one to use as discussed previously.

Configuring Color Profiles

With more and more color printers being used, it has become increasingly important to ensure that color printers accurately reproduce colors. Windows Server 2008 supports Integrated Color Management (ICM). ICM uses color profiles to ensure that colors are printed consistently. A color profile is a file that describes the color characteristics of a particular device.

Display devices and print devices have separate profiles. Typical displays can't show the same set of colors that a color printer can reproduce. The reason for this is that displays and printers use completely different processes to produce color. To help reduce the disparity between what is displayed and what is printed, you can use color management techniques and this is where color profiles become important.

By default, Windows includes only a few color profiles. When you install a color printer or graphics software on a computer, additional color profiles typically are installed. All color profiles are stored in the %SystemRoot%\System32\Spool\Drivers\Color folder. In most cases, color profiles installed with a printer are set as the defaults to use.

To view or configure color profiles, follow these steps:

1. In Print Management, right-click the printer, and select Properties. On the Color Management tab, click Color Management.

> **Create a Separate Printer for Experimenting**
>
> Before you change the default color profiles, you might want to create a separate printer (logical print device). This way you can experiment with the printer's color settings without affecting other users.

2. Click the All Profiles tab to view a summary of all color profiles that are currently available. To add a profile, click Add and then use the Install Profile dialog box to browse for and select the profile you want to use. To remove a profile, select the profile, click Remove, and then click Yes when prompted to confirm.

3. To associate a color profile with a device, click the Devices tab. In the Device list, select the device you want to configure and then select Use My Settings For This Device. Under Profiles Associated With This Device, you'll see a list of profiles associated with the device (if any) and the current default (if any). Click Add to add an additional profile association for the selected device. To make a selected profile the default profile, click Set As Default Profile.

4. Click Close.

> **Copy Needed Color Profiles to the Print Server**
>
> Color profiles available to users, such as graphic designers using Adobe PhotoShop, are installed with the software. These profiles will exist on the user's desktop but not on the print server. To make the profiles available for use, you can copy available profiles from a user's desktop to the print server.

Managing Print Jobs

To manage a printer and its print jobs, you can use Print Management's Extended view. To display the Extended view, right-click the Printers node and then select Show Extended View. Now when you select a printer, the lower portion of the main window will display the related print queue. Alternatively, you can access a separate management window for the printer. In Print Management, simply right-click the printer you want to work with and select Open Printer Queue.

Pausing, Starting, and Canceling All Printing

Occasionally, you might find that you must temporarily pause printing so that you can replace a toner cartridge, clear a paper jam, or perform some other maintenance procedure. To do this, right-click the printer in Print Management, and then select Pause Printing. You can resume printing later by right-clicking the printer and then selecting Resume Printing.

If you need to clear all documents out of the print queue, you can do this as well. Right-click the printer in Print Management, and then select Cancel All Jobs. When prompted to confirm the action, click Yes.

Viewing Print Jobs

Every document in the process of printing is shown in the Extended view or in the printer queue window. Documents are listed by the following information:

- **Document Name** The full name of the document

- **Job Status** The print status of the document

- **Owner** The user that printed the document

- **Pages** The number of pages in the document

- **Size** The file size of the document

- **Submitted** The date and time the document was spooled to the printer

- **Port** The ports used for printing

Managing a Print Job and Its Properties

When you select a document in the Extended view or the printer queue window, you can manage it. To stop the document from printing or to pause printing if it is currently being printed, right-click the document, and then select Pause. You can enable or resume printing later by right-clicking the document and selecting Resume. If you need to clear a document out of the print queue, right-click the document, and then select Cancel. When prompted to confirm the action, click Yes.

You can change a document's properties by right-clicking the document and selecting Properties. This opens the document's Properties dialog box, as shown in Figure 27-19. To change a document's properties when it is in the process of printing, you should pause the print job first.

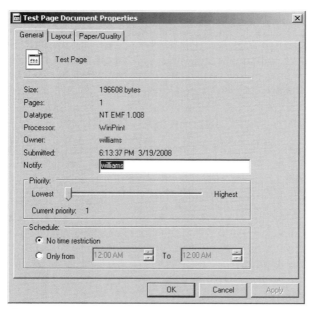

Figure 27-19 You can change the properties of documents in the print queue.

Typically, you might want to edit a document's properties to set its priority. For example, if someone printed a very long document and you want to ensure that other documents print before it, you could lower the long document's priority. Similarly, if there's an important document that you want to be printed ahead of other documents, you can raise the document's priority.

TROUBLESHOOTING

Clear out stuck documents

The Print Spooler service is configured to restart automatically if there's a problem. Sometimes it won't completely freeze or it will hang up in such a way that it can't be restarted automatically. You can tell this because the print queue will have error documents that you can't clear manually. In this case, restart the Print Spooler service manually. On the Administrative Tools menu, select Services. In the Services console, select and then right-click Print Spooler. On the shortcut menu, select Start or Restart as appropriate.

Printer Maintenance and Troubleshooting

Regular printer maintenance is an important part of printer administration. In addition to checking the print queue periodically for stuck documents and clearing them out as discussed in "Managing Print Jobs" on page 907, you should check to see how the print server is performing. As part of routine maintenance, you should also prepare for print server failure by periodically backing up the print server configuration. Finally, when things go wrong, you must perform troubleshooting.

Monitoring Print Server Performance

Monitoring print server performance can help you track usage statistics and determine whether a print server is performing as expected. It can also help you determine whether changes or upgrades are needed and plan for future needs. You monitor print server performance using the performance objects available in System Monitor. You access System Monitor from within the Performance Monitor console. Click Start, Programs or All Programs, Administrative Tools, Performance or type **perfmon** at the command line.

Get started by following the techniques discussed in Chapter 12, "Comprehensive Performance Analysis and Logging," for establishing performance baselines and detecting performance bottlenecks. These topics are discussed in "Establishing Performance Baselines" on page 344 and "Resolving Performance Bottlenecks" on page 356, respectively. After you've done this, zero in on the server's print spooling and queuing performance using the SpoolSv instance of the Process object and the Print Queue object as detailed in the following steps:

1. On a server you want to use for remote monitoring, start Reliability And Performance Monitor, and then select Performance Monitor in the left pane.

2. Click the Change Graph Type button and then select View Report.

3. Select and then delete the default counters by pressing the Delete key.

Chapter 27

4. Press Ctrl+I to display the Add Counters dialog box. In the Add Counters dialog box, type the UNC name or IP address of the print server you want to monitor remotely in the Select Counters From Computer box. An UNC computer name or IP address begins with \\. So, for instance, you could enter **PrintServer02** or **192.168.12.15**.

5. After you type the UNC computer name or IP address, press Tab or click the performance object list. When you do this, Performance Monitor will attempt to connect to the remote computer and retrieve a list of available performance objects to monitor.

6. Choose Process, and then in the Instances Of Selected Object list, choose Spoolsv, as shown in Figure 27-20.

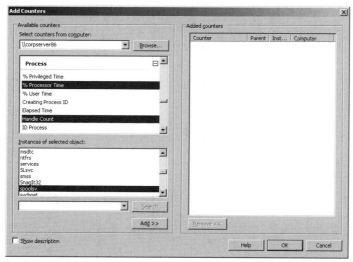

Figure 27-20 Monitor the Process object's Spoolsv instance.

7. Choose the following counters in the counters list box:

○ *% Processor Time*–Shows the percentage of elapsed time of all process threads used by the Print Spooler service. A dedicated print server that is very busy will have a relatively high amount of processor time.

○ *Handle Count*–Shows the total number of handles open by the Print Spooler process. This is important to track because each open handle uses resources, and open handles can be from clients that aren't actively printing.

○ *Virtual Bytes/Virtual Bytes Peak*–Shows the current/peak size in bytes of the virtual address space used by the Print Spooler process.

○ *Page File Bytes*–Shows the current amount in bytes of the virtual memory that the Print Spooler process has reserved in the paging file.

○ *Pool Paged Bytes*–Shows the current size in bytes of the paged pool used by the Print Spooler process. Memory in the paged pool can be written to disk when it is not in use.

○ *Pool Nonpaged Bytes*–Shows the current size in bytes of the nonpaged pool used by the Print Spooler process. Memory in the nonpaged pool cannot be written to disk and must remain in physical memory.

○ *Working Set/Working Set Peak*–Shows the current/peak size in bytes of the set of memory pages (working set) used by the Print Spooler process.

8. Click Add to add the selected counters to the chart.

9. In the performance object list, expand the Print Queue object, and then choose All Instances to track all print queues on the server.

10. Choose the following counters in the counters list box:

○ *Bytes Printed/Sec*–Shows the number of bytes printed per second and is a relative indicator of how busy a printer is.

○ *Jobs*–Shows the current number of print jobs in a print queue.

○ *Jobs Spooling/Max Jobs Spooling*–Shows the current/peak number of print jobs being spooled to the print queue. These are incoming print jobs.

○ *Job Errors*–Shows the total number of job errors in a print queue since the last restart. Job errors can occur if there are problems transferring print jobs to the printer. A relatively high number of job errors can indicate networking problems or problems with network cards.

○ *References/Max References*–Shows the current/peak number of handles open to a print queue. This is important to track because each open handle uses resources, and open handles can be from clients that aren't actively printing.

○ *Not Ready Errors*–Shows the total number of printer not ready errors in a print queue since the last restart. These errors occur if the printer is waiting or not ready for printing.

○ *Out Of Paper Errors*–Shows the total number of out of paper errors in a print queue since the last restart. If a printer is frequently running out of paper, paper might not be getting refilled properly or you might need an additional paper tray.

○ *Total Jobs Printed*–Shows the total number of jobs printed in a print queue since the last restart. This is a relative indicator of how busy a printer is.

○ *Total Pages Printed*–Shows the total number of pages printed in a print queue since the last restart. This is a relative indicator of how busy a printer is.

Chapter 27

> **Note**
>
> Total Pages Printed doesn't show pages printed by Windows 95, Windows 98, Windows Me, and non-Windows clients. These clients use SMB.

11. Click Add to add the selected counters to the chart, and then click OK.

You can now monitor the print server to determine activity levels and how many system resources are being used for printing.

Preparing for Print Server Failure

As part of your print services optimization and maintenance process, you should consider how you are going to handle printer and print server failure. Several techniques have been discussed previously for increasing availability and fault tolerance. These techniques include print queue pooling and print clusters as discussed in "Optimizing Printing Through Queues and Pooling" on page 896. Because these options aren't practical for all environments, you should have other backup plans ready.

Start by considering how you would handle printer failure. If you have an identical printer available as a spare, you can configure this printer to take the place of the failed printer. As long as the printer uses the same print drivers, users can access it from the same print queue. If you have other printers available, you could instruct users how to access one of these printers or, ideally, already have a second printer added for use on their computers as a backup in case the primary printer fails. Trust me; you'll have happier users if you do this.

Next, consider how you would handle print server failure, which could mean that several printers are inaccessible. It's often a good idea to have a secondary print server available if a primary print server fails. You could then switch users from the primary print server to the secondary print server. Assuming the print server is already configured to provide print services for the printers originally serviced by the primary, you could simply tell users how to access the print queues on the secondary print server.

A more complete disaster recovery plan for a print server would be similar to the following:

1. As part of periodic backups, back up the printer configuration on the print server using the Export Printers To A File option in Print Management. This creates a .printerExport file that you can store on a network share that is itself regularly backed up to tape.

2. In the event that the primary print server failed, you would disconnect the primary server from the network. Then use the Import Printers To A File option to restore the .printerExport file containing the printer configuration on the secondary server.

3. You would then change the secondary print server's IP address and computer name to match that of the original print server. Users would then be able to access printers and resume printing.

Solving Printing Problems

Windows Server 2008 has improvements that reduce the amount of printing problems you'll encounter. The biggest change is the automatic restart of spooling if the Print Spooler service hangs up due to errors, which takes a lot of guesswork out of trouble-shooting. However, if the Print Spooler has a critical problem, such as when the volume on which the spool folder is located runs out of space, the Print Spooler can stop running.

Printer Troubleshooting Essentials

When you are troubleshooting printing problems, as with troubleshooting any problems, first try to figure out where the problem is and then try to fix it. As with most problems, you'll usually want to start with the client experiencing the printing problem before you start troubleshooting on the print server. Of course, the printer might also have a problem and the network might be a culprit as well. So, this gives you four key areas to examine:

- **Client/application software** The client or the application software on the client might be improperly configured. This could include problems with print drivers, permissions, and print settings.

- **Printer hardware** The printer might have a problem. This could include being out of paper, out of toner, or having a paper jam.

- **Print server** The print server might have a problem. This could include the spool folder running out of space, permissions set for a printer or the spool folder, print drivers used by the server, and device status.

- **Network connectivity** The network might have a problem, or the network card on the client, server, or printer might be misconfigured or bad.

TROUBLESHOOTING

Running out of space may indicate a deeper problem

Occasionally, the .spl and .shd files won't get cleared out of the spool folder. This can happen if print spooling is not functioning as it should. To correct this problem, manually clear out the print spooler folder and then restart the Print Spooler service. And if Windows won't allow you to delete the files, stop the Print Spooler service first, delete the files, and restart the service.

Start by trying to figure out which area has a problem. If the user is asking you directly for help, make sure the user is connected to the right printer and knows which print device is associated with the printer he or she is using. Try printing to the printer from your machine. You can print a test page from the printer's Properties dialog box by clicking Print Test Page on the General tab. If you can print a test page, printing is working and the problem might have to do with permissions or the user's system or configuration. Try printing from someone else's computer. If this succeeds, the problem might be with this particular user's system or configuration. If this fails, try printing from the print server. If this fails, the problem might be with the printer configuration or with the network.

While you are printing test pages, be sure to keep track of the printer status. Most current printers have a mini Hypertext Transfer Protocol (HTTP) server and an online status page that you can check simply by typing the printer's IP address in your Web browser. If you can't check current status that way, right-click the Printers node in Print Management and then select Show Extended View. In the main pane, select the printer. You can then view the printer's current jobs by selecting the Jobs tab in the lower portion of the main pane. Select the Printer Web Page tab to download the printer's Web page and view the current status of the printer (as shown in Figure 27-21).

Figure 27-21 Check the status of the remote printer.

You can then right-click the printer entry and select Open Printer Queue to access its management window. If there's a document with an error status at the top of the print queue, remove it, which should restore printing, and then see "Configuring Print Spooling" on page 900 to see how you can try to prevent that type of error from happening again. If all documents have a printing error or if each time you clear a bad document out of the queue, the status changes to Error-Printing, there might be a problem with the network or the printer itself. If the title bar shows the printer is paused, click Printer, and then select Pause Printing to resume printing.

Note

If you can't check the status of the printer online, don't spend more than five minutes on a printer problem without walking over to the printer and checking its status. Most printers with an error status will have a blinking yellow light and the display will state the problem. Also, you might want to check the event logs on the print server for error or warning events.

Hopefully, after performing these procedures, you'll have isolated the problem to a particular area or have a better understanding of where the problem might exist. With that said, let's delve into specific scenarios and troubleshooting options.

INSIDE OUT   Solve the printing problem with a clear plan

Few things frustrate users more than when printing goes awry. One of the most important things you can do is to communicate with the user or users having the problem, but don't do this too many times. Don't forget that your account might have permissions and privileges other user accounts don't, so you might want to have a default user account for troubleshooting. In this case, you would log on to your computer or a spare computer at your desk and try printing. Try to solve the problem without taking over a user's machine for troubleshooting. If you must access a user's machine, do this when you are fairly sure the problem is specific to a user or a group of users. If the problem cannot be resolved within a reasonable amount of time or you know it's going to be a long time, such as when the print server has stopped working, you should consider implementing your recovery plan as discussed in "Preparing for Print Server Failure" on page 912.

Chapter 27

Comprehensive Printer Troubleshooting

When someone states there is a printing problem, you should try to determine who is affected by the problem. Try printing from your machine and other machines. Try printing from the print server. Hopefully, after taking these steps you'll know whether the problem affects:

- Everyone, meaning no one can print. In these circumstances, the problem likely has to do with the printer itself or the network. Perform the following actions:
  - Check the printer status either by walking over to the printer or by using a browser to check the printer's status page. (Try typing the printer's IP address in your Web browser.) Afterward, check the event logs on the print server. Look for error or warning events that might indicate a problem.

○ Check the print queue (logical print device). Look to see if the printer is paused or if there are documents with a status of Error-Printing. Clear out these documents by right-clicking them and selecting Cancel.

○ Print or check the configuration of the printer. Someone might have set it to use Dynamic Host Configuration Protocol (DHCP) and might not have made a reservation for it. In this case, if the printer was shut down and then restarted, it might have a different IP address. The printer port would then point to the wrong IP address. Check the printer's subnet mask as well.

○ Check the network. See if you can ping the printer's IP address from your system and from other systems. At the command line, type **ping** *PrinterIP*, where *PrinterIP* is the IP address of the printer. If you can't ping the printer's IP address from any system, the printer might be turned off or its network cable might be disconnected. The printer might also have a bad network card. The problem could also be in the switch into which the printer is plugged or with routing to the printer.

○ Determine when the last time the printer worked and if the printer configuration has been changed. If the printer never worked, it might not have been configured correctly in the first place. If the printer configuration was changed, change the configuration back to the previous settings if possible. If you suspect a problem with the print driver, try reinstalling it or installing a new driver as discussed in "Viewing and Configuring Print Drivers" on page 887.

○ Check the free space on the volume on which the spool folder is located. If the volume is low on space or out of space, the print server won't be able to create spool files and, therefore, documents won't print. Also check the permissions on the spool folder. If the permissions are set incorrectly, the spooling won't work. See "Configuring Print Spool, Logging, and Notification Settings" on page 889 and the Troubleshooting sidebar "Check permissions on the spool folder" on page 881.

○ Check the print processor and separator page settings to ensure that they are correct. If an incorrect print processor is set, the printer might print garbled pages or might not print at all. Try using the RAW data type or the EMF data type to see if this clears up the problem. If the separator page is set incorrectly, the printer might print out the contents of the separator page or it might not print at all. See "Viewing the Print Processor and Default Data Type" on page 901 and "Configuring Separator Pages" on page 902.

○ Check the Print Spooler service. It is configured for automatic restart, but if restart fails twice within a minute, the Print Spooler service won't try to start again. Also, if the print queue has error documents and you can't clear them out, it is usually the fault of the Print Spooler service. In this case, restart the service manually. In the Administrative Tools folder, select Services, and then select Print Spooler in the right pane. Right-click Print Spooler, and select Start or Restart as appropriate.

- Some people, meaning only some users can't print and some can. If some people can't print, the problem likely has to do with the permissions, application software, or the network. Perform the following actions:

  ○ Check the network using a computer in the same subnet as the people having the problem. See if you can ping the printer's IP address. At the command line, type **ping** *PrinterIP*, where *PrinterIP* is the IP address of the printer. If you can't ping the printer's IP address from any system on the subnet, a switch or routing between the user's computer and the printer might be bad or disconnected. This happens a lot if local switches/hubs are under people's desks.

  ○ Check the printer permissions and the permissions on the spool folder to see if the groups of which the users are members have appropriate access. If the permissions are set incorrectly, the spooling won't work. See "Configuring Print Spool, Logging, and Notification Settings" on page 889 and the Troubleshooting sidebar "Check permissions on the spool folder" on page 881.

  ○ Check the print processor. Windows 95, Windows 98, and Windows Me clients can print only if the print processor uses the RAW data type. See "Viewing the Print Processor and Default Data Type" on page 901.

  ○ Check the application being used for printing. The application might be incorrectly configured or the default printer might not be what users think it is.

  ○ Check the error message generated when printing. If the client gets an error stating it must install a print driver when connecting to a printer, this means the correct drivers are installed on the server but aren't available to the client. Additionally, Windows 95, Windows 98, and Windows Me clients do not automatically check for updated drivers and must be updated manually. See "Installing and Updating Print Drivers on Clients" on page 894.

- One person, meaning only one user can't print. If only one person can't print, the problem likely has to do with application software, the user's computer, or permissions. Start with the user's computer and perform the following actions:

  ○ Check the application being used for printing. The application might be incorrectly configured, or the default printer might not be what the user thinks it is.

  ○ Check the user's computer. The Print Spooler service must be running for the user to print. The computer must have sufficient temporary space to generate the initial spool file. The computer must have other essential services configured. The list goes on. Essentially, it is better if you restart the computer if you suspect the problem has to do with that computer specifically.

  ○ Check to make sure the user's computer can connect over the network to other resources. Try pinging the router or the printer in question.

○ Check the error message generated when printing. If the client gets an error stating it must install a print driver when connecting to a printer, this means the correct drivers are installed on the server but aren't available to the client. See "Installing and Updating Print Drivers on Clients" on page 894. If the client gets an "Access Denied" error, this is a permissions issue.

○ Check the printer permissions and the permissions on the spool folder to see if the user or groups of which the user is a member have appropriate access. If the permissions are set incorrectly, the spooling won't work. See "Configuring Print Spool, Logging, and Notification Settings" on page 889 and the Troubleshooting sidebar "Check permissions on the spool folder" on page 881.

Resolving Garbled or Incorrect Printing

If the printer prints garbled or incorrect pages, this can be a sign that the printer is incorrectly configured. You should check the print driver and the print processor settings. You might want to reinstall the print driver as discussed in "Viewing and Configuring Print Drivers" on page 887. You might want to change the print processor data type to RAW or EMF to see if this clears up the problem. See "Viewing the Print Processor and Default Data Type" on page 901.

To resolve this problem, check the following:

● Ensure that the complete document is transferred to the printer before printing starts by selecting the Start Printing After Last Page Is Spooled option. See "Configuring Print Spooling" on page 900.

● Try using the RAW data type or the EMF data type to see if this clears up the problem. See "Viewing the Print Processor and Default Data Type" on page 901.

● Try removing any separator page that is used, because this might be setting the printer page description language incorrectly. See "Configuring Separator Pages" on page 902.

● Try clearing the Enable Advanced Printing Features check box on the Advanced tab. This disables metafile spooling. Windows 95, Windows 98, and Windows Me clients use SMB connections and spool RAW-formatted files to the print server. See "Configuring Print Spooling" on page 900.

Deploying Terminal Services

Terminal Services lets users run Microsoft Windows–based applications on a remote server. When users run an application on a terminal server, the execution and processing take place on the server, and only the data from devices such as the display, keyboard, and mouse are transmitted over the network. A client logged on to a terminal server and running applications remotely is said to be using a *virtual session*. Although there may be dozens or hundreds of users simultaneously logged on to a terminal server, users see only their own virtual sessions.

Using Terminal Services

You can use Terminal Services to rapidly deploy and centrally manage Windows-based applications. One advantage of this method is that you can be sure that all users are running the same version of an application and that they can do so from any computer. Another advantage is that organizations with older computers running earlier versions of Windows can get more mileage out of their computers by having users run applications on terminal servers instead of locally on their desktops. Terminal Services involves these key elements:

- Terminal Services clients

- Terminal Services servers

- Terminal Services licensing

Terminal Services Clients

Within the organization, the primary client used to establish connections to a terminal server is the Remote Desktop Connection (RDC) client. This client comes installed on the Microsoft Windows XP, Windows Vista, Windows Server 2003, and Windows Server 2008 operating systems and is available for installation on other versions of Windows as well. For details on the use and features of this client, see "Supporting Remote Desktop Connection Clients" on page 613.

By sending only the data required for I/O devices to and from the server, Terminal Services significantly reduces the amount of data transferred between a client and a server. This reduces the amount of network bandwidth used, allowing Terminal Services to operate in low-bandwidth environments. In addition, users are able to optimize performance based on the speed of their connection. On a 28.8 Kbps modem, a user has only the essential features to ensure the best overall performance possible. As a user goes from a 28.8 Kbps modem connection to a LAN connection at 10 Mbps or higher, Windows features are automatically added to enhance the user experience. Administrators can also configure Terminal Services to restrict the additional features. For example, if hundreds of users are using a terminal server, you might need to restrict enhancements to ensure the overall performance of the server. If you don't do this and the terminal server is overworked, it might fail.

For access to remote applications from the Internet or the enterprise intranet, Microsoft provides several new options for Windows Server 2008:

- Terminal Services Remote Application (RemoteApp) is a program that a user accesses remotely through Terminal Services and appears as if it is running on the user's local computer. Thus, instead of being presented to the user on the desktop of the remote terminal server, a RemoteApp runs in its own resizable window and has its own entry on the taskbar. Although each RemoteApp appears to be separate on the desktop, multiple RemoteApps running on the same desktop share the same Terminal Services session.

- Terminal Services Gateway (TS Gateway) enables authorized users to connect to network resources from any Internet-connected device that can run the Remote Desktop Connection client. TS Gateway uses the Remote Desktop Protocol (RDP) over HTTPS to establish secure, encrypted connections between remote users and network resources. Network resources available through TS gateways include terminal servers as well as computers with Remote Desktop enabled. Because TS gateways operate over HTTPS, they can be used to easily traverse firewalls and NATs.

- TS Web Access, which provides access to terminal servers through a Web browser. The default TS Web Access Web page includes a customizable frame and Web part. This page provides clickable links to the available programs designated as Remote Applications (RemoteApps). When you install TS Web Access, Windows installs Internet Information Services (IIS) 7.0 as well and uses IIS 7.0 to provide access to your RemoteApps.

These options allow you to deploy Terminal Services in many additional ways and to improve the overall experience for end users. However, TS Gateway and TS Web Access can greatly increase the overall complexity of a Terminal Services implementation. Because of these additional complexities, you might want to consider having separate Terminal Services installations, as follows:

- One or more installations that'll be used internally only with standard options, such as the RDC client and RemoteApps. For ease of reference throughout this chapter, I will refer to servers with this type of installation as standard terminal servers when I need to differentiate between the two types of installations.

- One or more installations that'll be used for Internet-based or intranet-based access with TS Gateway and TS Web Access. For ease of reference throughout this chapter, I will refer to servers with this type of installation as Web access or gateway terminal servers when I need to differentiate between the two types of installations.

In this way, you ensure that there are separate environments with separate requirements and separate procedures.

Terminal Services Servers

It's very easy to set up a standard terminal server. What isn't so easy is getting the infrastructure right before you do so and maintaining the installation after it's in place. Before you install Terminal Services, it is essential to plan the environment and to deploy Terminal Services before you install applications on the terminal server. After you deploy Terminal Services, you will configure the environment, install applications, and make those applications available to remote users.

The features for the Remote Desktop Connection client were discussed in "Supporting Remote Desktop Connection Clients" on page 613. For Windows Server 2008, there are many standard features and enhancements as well. The administration tools for Terminal Services include the following:

- **Terminal Services Manager** Terminal Services Manager, shown in the following screen, is the primary tool for managing terminal servers and client connections. Unlike previous versions, the current version doesn't automatically enumerate all the terminal servers that are available. Instead, it gives direct access to a local server if it is running Terminal Services and allows you to selectively enumerate servers and add servers to a list of favorites for easier management. In a large installation with many terminal servers, this makes Terminal Services Manager more responsive.

> **Note**
>
> It is important to note that certain features of Terminal Services Manager work only when you run the tool from a client. For example, if you run Terminal Services Manager on a terminal server, you won't be able to use the Remote Control and Connect features.

Chapter 28

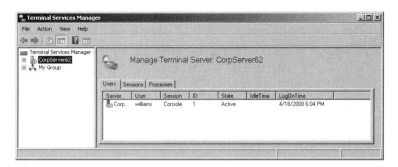

- **TS Licensing Manager** TS Licensing Manager, shown in the following screen, is used to install licenses and activate a Terminal Services license server. The enhanced interface makes it easier to install licenses and to activate or deactivate license servers.

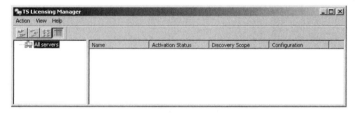

- **Terminal Services Configuration** Terminal Services Configuration, shown in the following screen, is used to manage terminal server connections as well as global and default server settings. Terminal server connections and the Remote Desktop Protocol (RDP) are what allow users to establish remote connections to a terminal server. Server settings also enable you to easily set terminal server policy. A key policy is the single session policy, which, when activated, limits a user to a single session, whether the session is active or not.

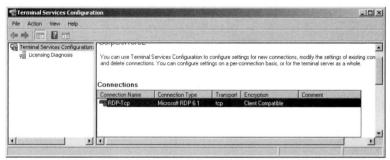

- **TS RemoteApp Manager** TS RemoteApp Manager, shown in the following screen, configures RemoteApps as well as deployment settings that apply to RemoteApps. After you've configure a terminal server, you can copy the list of RemoteApp programs and deployment settings from that server to another using export and import tasks.

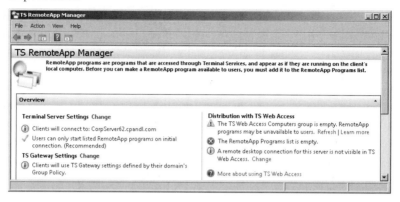

- **TS Gateway Manager** TS Gateway Manager, shown in the following screen, is used to configure authorization policies that control access to network resources according to group membership. You use Terminal Services connection authorization policies (TS CAPs) to specify who can connect to a TS Gateway server, and Terminal Services resource authorization policies (TS RAPs) to specify the internal network resources to which users can connect through a TS Gateway server.

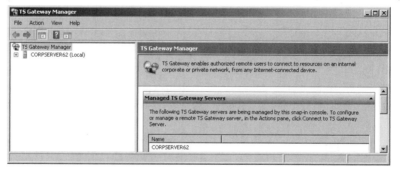

- **TS Web Access Administration** TS Web Access Administration, shown in the following screen, provides access to the IIS server hosting the Web applications required for Web access to Terminal Services, including a primary TS application and two RPC proxy applications. Similar to what a user sees, you can view the list of available RemoteApp programs or connect to remote desktops to which you have access.

Chapter 28

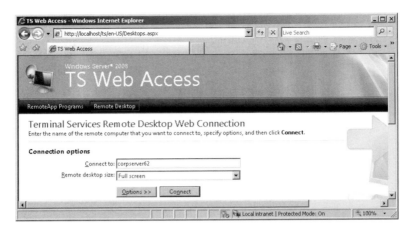

You can access the Terminal Services administration tools on the Administrative Tools\ Terminal Services menu. To access a tool, click Start, All Programs, Administrative Tools, Terminal Services, and then select the desired tool, such as Terminal Services Manager.

Terminal Services has important changes for security as well. For internal access, you have the option of adding users and groups to the Remote Desktop Users group. This is a standard group for which you can configure membership in Active Directory Users And Computers. By adding the Domain Users group to the Remote Desktop Users group, you allow all authenticated users to use Terminal Services. If instead you were to add the special group Everyone, anyone with access to the network could use Terminal Services.

For Internet-based or intranet-based access, you can specify TS Gateway user groups that can access Terminal Services using RDP over HTTPS. No standard groups are created for you, so you should consider what groups you might need as part of your deployment plans and then create these groups in Active Directory Users And Computers. For example, you might want to create a group called External TS Users. To grant Internet-based or intranet-based access, you would then add specific groups or users as members of this group. To enhance security you typically would not want to make the Domain Users or Everyone groups members of your special external access group or groups.

Terminal Services supports 128-bit encryption as well as encryption compliant with the Federal Information Processing Standard (FIPS). Using 128-bit encryption ensures a high level of encryption, which provides powerful protection of the data sent between a Terminal Services client and a server. FIPS encryption is added to provide compliance with FIPS 140-1 and FIPS 140-2, which are standards for Security Requirements for Cryptographic Modules, a necessity for some organizations.

Terminal Services printing has been enhanced in Windows Server 2008 with the addition of the Terminal Services Easy Print driver and a Group Policy setting that enables you to redirect only the default client printer. The Terminal Services Easy Print driver allows users to reliably print from a RemoteApp program or from a terminal server desktop session to the correct printer configured for use on their client computers. It also enables users to have a much more consistent printing experience between local and remote sessions.

The Redirect Only The Default Client Printer setting in Group Policy allows you to specify whether the default client printer is the only printer that is redirected in Terminal Services sessions, which helps to limit the number of printers that the spooler must enumerate, therefore improving terminal server scalability.

> **Note**
>
> To use the Terminal Services Easy Print driver, clients must be running Remote Desktop Connection (RDC) client version 6.1 or later and have Microsoft .NET Framework 3.0 Service Pack 1 (SP1) installed. Note also that the terminal server fallback printer driver is not included with Windows Server 2008. Although the Specify Terminal Server Fallback Printer Driver Behavior setting still exists in Group Policy, it cannot be used with terminal servers running Windows Server 2008.

Terminal Services Licensing

A Terminal Services license server is required to set up Terminal Services (see Figure 28-1). The license server, responsible for issuing licenses and tracking their usage, maintains a pool of all available licenses. The assigned licenses are also tracked so that they can be validated. Terminal Services requires that you get official licenses from Microsoft and activate them through the Microsoft Clearinghouse.

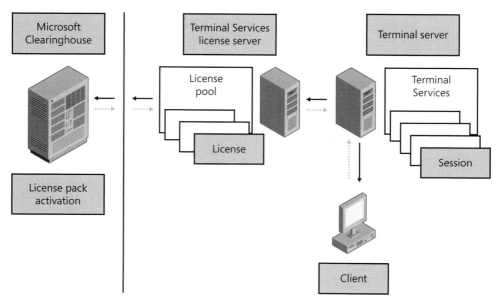

Figure 28-1 Terminal Services implementation with a license server.

The first time a client connects to a terminal server, the terminal server checks for a license. If the client has a license, the terminal server validates it and allows the client to connect. If the client doesn't have a license, the terminal server locates a license server (using a network broadcast in workgroups or through Active Directory in domains) and requests a new license. If that license server doesn't have a license to offer, the client is not allowed to connect.

> **Note**
>
> For the first 120 days after deployment, clients can be granted a temporary license if an activated license server is not available. After this grace period, Terminal Services will stop serving unlicensed clients.

Provided that the server has a license, it will give the license to the terminal server, which in turn issues it to the client. Client access licenses provided by Terminal Services are issued per device or per user, so the way licensing works depends on the licensing configuration—which can be mixed and matched as necessary. With per-device licensing, the license is valid only for a particular computer and will be validated in the future to the globally unique identifier (GUID) of the machine on which the client is running. With per-user licensing, the license is valid only for that user and will be validated in the future to the GUID of the user's account.

> **Note**
>
> Terminal Services client access licenses are issued per device or per user only. They are not available in per-server mode because Windows sessions are not allowed in per-server mode.

An issued license is valid for a period of 52 to 89 days; the interval is assigned randomly. When the client later disconnects or logs off the terminal server, the license is not returned to the pool. The expiration date serves to return unused licenses to the license pool. Each time a client connects to a terminal server, the expiration date of its license is checked. If the current date is within seven days of the expiration date, the license server renews the license for another 52 to 89 days. If a client doesn't log back on to the terminal server before its license expires, the license is returned to the license pool, which makes it available to other clients.

TS Licensing for Windows Server 2008 now includes the ability to track the issuance of TS Per User CALs in TS Licensing Manager. If the terminal server is in Per User licensing mode, the user connecting to it must have a TS Per User CAL. If the user does not have the required TS Per User CAL, the terminal server will contact the license server to get the CAL for the user. After the license server issues a TS Per User CAL to the user, you can track the issuance of the CAL in TS Licensing Manager.

You can reassign a client access license from one device to another device or from one user to another user. However, there are some limitations. The license must be either permanently reassigned away from its existing owner (device or user), or it must be temporarily reassigned to a loaner device while a permanent device is out of service, or to a temporary worker while a regular employee is absent.

INSIDE OUT   Terminal Services licensing changes

Anyone who wants to use Terminal Services must have a client access license. This remains true whether a user connects to the terminal server using Remote Desktop Protocol (RDP), RDP over HTTPS, or another vendor's protocol. You can purchase client access licenses using the licensing programs discussed in "Selecting a Software Licensing Program" on page 63. This means that small companies can purchase licenses in packs of 5, 20, or more, while bigger companies can purchase licenses under programs such as the Microsoft Open License.

When you purchase licenses in packs, you'll receive a product activation code that can be used one time to activate the number of licenses purchased. When you use Open License or other programs, you purchase a set number of licenses. With Open License, you are then issued an Open License Authorization and a set of license numbers that you can use to activate licenses. Under Select and Enterprise licensing agreements, you provide your Enrollment Agreement Number to activate licenses.

In the past, the requirement for a Terminal Services client access license was waived if the device accessing the terminal server was running the same or later version of an equivalent desktop operating system. For example, a client running Windows XP Professional could access a Windows 2000 terminal server without needing a Terminal Services client access license. With the release of Windows Server 2003 and Windows Server 2008, all clients are required to have a Terminal Services client access license.

Designing the Terminal Services Infrastructure

Terminal Services can be deployed in single-server and multi-server environments. The first thing to plan is Terminal Services capacity. Capacity planning can help you determine the actual number of users that a specific Terminal Services configuration can support.

Capacity Planning for Terminal Services

It is important to note that Windows Server 2008 has significant scalability advantages over its predecessors. Primarily this is because the Windows Server 2008 kernel provides better use of the 32-bit virtual address space. Because a terminal server must allocate virtual resources for all users who are logged on, whether they are active or in a disconnected state, the improved memory handling in Windows Server 2008 gives it significant advantages over Windows 2000 Server and some advantage over Windows

Server 2003. In addition, Windows Server 2008 is more effective at using faster processors and system buses. This again gives Windows Server 2008 significant advantages over Windows 2000 Server and some advantage over Windows Server 2003.

Because remote serving of applications is both processor-intensive and memory-intensive, the most significant limits on the number of users a server can support are imposed by a server's processing power and available RAM. Network bandwidth and disk performance can also be factors, but typically, a server's capacity to handle requests will be exhausted well before the network bandwidth and disk drive subsystems have reached maximum utilization.

Planning should start by looking at not only the number of users you need to support but also the following factors:

- The type of users you need to support

- The applications users will be running

- The way users work

These latter characteristics play a significant role in the actual usage of a server. Users can be divided into three general types as follows:

- **Data entry worker** Data entry workers provide data input. They typically perform data entry, transcription, order entry, or clerical work. Data entry workers typically have low impact on a server on a per-user basis. This means a server used primarily by data entry workers could scale to a larger number of users than a server used by other types of workers.

- **Knowledge worker** Knowledge workers perform day-to-day tasks using business applications. Rather than providing strictly data input, knowledge workers create documents, spreadsheets, presentations, and reports. Knowledge workers typically have moderate impact on a server on a per-user basis. This means a server being used primarily by knowledge workers would not scale as well as a server being used by data entry workers.

- **Productivity worker** Productivity workers are the high-performance workers in the business environment. Their daily tasks include specialized applications for graphic design, CAD, 3D animation, and applications that perform complex calculations or require a high amount of processing. Productivity workers typically have high impact on a server on a per-user basis. This means a server being used primarily by productivity workers would scale to a lower number of users than a server used by the other types of workers.

The impact of these types of users can best be illustrated graphically. Consider the scenario in Figure 28-2. The chart shows the number of different types of users that can be supported on three different server configurations.

- Server A is a four-processor system with high-end processors and 4 GB RAM.

- Server B is a two-processor system with high-end processors and 4 GB RAM.

- Server C is a one-processor system with a high-end processor and 4 GB RAM.

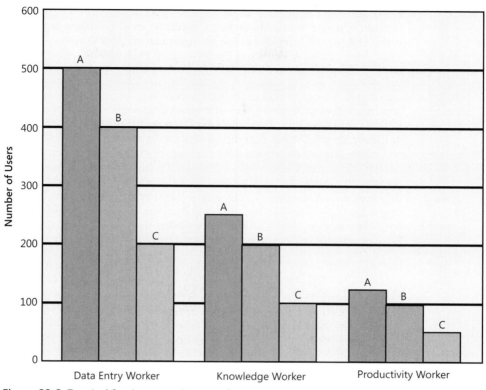

Figure 28-2 Terminal Services capacity example.

As you can see from the example, each server can handle a large number of data entry workers relative to other types of workers. Because CPU power and RAM are so important, the servers are given fast processors and a lot of RAM. These results are based on using Intel Xeon processors operating at 3.2 gigahertz (GHz) and using a 2 megabyte (MB) L2 cache with an 800 megahertz (MHz) front side bus.

Although the example takes into account the types of users and the types of applications being used, it doesn't take into account the way users work. The way users work can also have a significant impact on Terminal Services. You should also consider these factors:

- Users' typing speed
- Users' work habits
- Experience settings on the client

Believe it or not, typing speed can affect performance. Many users who type very quickly will make more updates and require more processing than a group of users who type slowly. You don't want to tell users to type more slowly, but you do want to take their typing skills into account.

Chapter 28

Users with poor work habits can have a significant impact on performance. Consider the case of a user who exits applications rather than switching among them: The user starts Microsoft Outlook to check his mail, exits Outlook, starts Microsoft Word to type a document, exits Word, starts Outlook again to check his e-mail, exits Outlook, and so on—and does this all day long. Starting and exiting applications requires more processing and resources than simply switching among applications as you use them.

The experience settings on the client can have a significant impact on performance as well. If users have optimized their experience settings for LAN connections of 10 Mbps or higher, they will have desktop backgrounds, themes, menu and window animation, and other extras that require a lot more processing on the server. The only experience setting that actually improves performance is bitmap caching, which ensures that caching is used as much as possible to reduce the amount of data that has to be passed to the client. Client display settings also affect server performance. The default display setting is for High Color (16 bit). An additional option is available for True Color (24 bit). As 24-bit color requires a lot more processing than 16-bit color, this setting should only be used only by those who need high-end color resolution, such as graphic designers.

Having covered factors that can affect performance, let's take a closer look at how to plan for capacity. Start by determining the average number of Terminal Services users. Remember that both active users and those with inactive or disconnected sessions use system resources. Then consider the types and average numbers of applications users will be running. Run those applications and use the techniques discussed in Chapter 11, "Performance Monitoring and Tuning," and Chapter 12, "Comprehensive Performance Analysis and Logging," to determine how much physical and virtual memory each application uses on average. This should give you a good baseline for capacity planning.

If a server will have 100 users, who each run four applications on average, and those applications collectively use 10 MB of physical memory and 24 MB of virtual memory on average, you know the system will need a minimum of 1 gigabyte (GB) of RAM for good performance. That's the baseline. You typically want to have 50 percent capacity above the baseline usage to ensure that the server can handle peak usage loads and can support additional users if necessary. Therefore, in this scenario you'd want to have a minimum of 1.5 GB of RAM above what the operating system and configured roles, role services, and features require.

Processing power is as important as RAM. A server's processors need to be able to keep up with the processing workload. As you scale up, you need to be able to add processors to handle the additional processing load of additional users. If you are monitoring server performance, pay particular attention to the Copy Read Hits % performance counter of the Cache performance object. This counter tracks the percentage of cache copy read requests that did not require a disk read to provide access to the page in cache. For best performance, you want this counter to be at 95 percent or above (optimally at 99 percent). If the counter is below 95 percent, the server is reading from the page file on disk frequently and this can affect performance. You can resolve this problem by adding RAM to the system.

Also consider network bandwidth and disk configuration in capacity planning. A network running at 100 megabits per second (Mbps) can handle hundreds of Terminal Services users. A network running at 1,000 Mbps (Gigabit Ethernet) can handle thousands of Terminal Services users. Consider existing traffic on the network before Terminal Services is deployed as a limiting factor. For capacity planning, you can test the average amount of bandwidth a client uses when working with a terminal server by monitoring the Bytes Total/Sec counter of the Network Interface performance object. If a client uses 1,250 bytes per second on average, this is 10,000 bits per second. In theory, a network running at 100 Mbps could handle 10,000 of these clients. Reduce this by 50 percent to shift from the theoretical to what is probably possible, and then subtract current bandwidth usage to come up with a working number.

Disk subsystem performance can also have a substantial impact on overall performance, especially on a server that makes moderate to heavy use of the paging file. Because the number and frequency of standard read/write operations for files affects the design of the disk subsystem, these operations will also affect overall performance. Ideally, the disk subsystem on a terminal server will be configured with hardware RAID and multiple RAID controllers rather than software RAID. When multiple SCSI/RAID controllers are used, disks should be configured to distribute the load. When you install applications that will be used with Terminal Services, you can help spread the load by installing and configuring applications to use different disk sets on different SCSI/RAID controllers.

Planning Organizational Structure for Terminal Services

When you are deploying Terminal Services, your planning should include deciding where in the organizational structure your terminal servers should be located. As discussed in Chapter 19, "Using Remote Desktop for Administration," servers running in Terminal Server mode should be clearly separated from servers running in Remote Desktop for Administration mode. This ensures that administrators and support personnel can use Remote Desktop for Administration throughout the organization and that selected users can make use of terminal servers.

The best way to achieve separation of these services is to deploy terminal servers in a separate organizational unit (OU), which I will call the Terminal Services OU. You can then implement policies and restrictions for Terminal Services separately from those for the rest of the organization. To start, you should place the computer accounts for your terminal servers in the Terminal Services OU. When you do this, you can apply system-wide restrictions to terminal servers and enforce these restrictions using a computer-based policy. These restrictions then replace or are added to the restrictions a Terminal Services user usually has when logging on to the domain.

If you need to provide additional restrictions for Terminal Services users, you can do so on a per-user basis by placing the user account in the Terminal Services OU and defining user-based policy restrictions. In this way, the restrictions are enforced wherever the user logs on to the domain.

Deploying TS Gateway and TS Web Access requires considerable additional planning. To ensure secure connectivity, you'll need:

- A terminal server
- An IIS server
- A Network Policy Server
- A Routing and Remote Access server

Although one physical server could act as all these servers in a small installation, the configuration required to make it all work is fairly extensive. You must:

- Create an authentication certificate for the server using either a certificate authority or a self-signed certificate
- Define authorization policies that control connections and resource access on terminal servers
- Configure network policy and access services that control connections from remote locations
- Configure IIS to provide the necessary Web hosting services for Terminal Services

Not only must you develop plans to configure these servers, but you must also develop maintenance plans that include regular monitoring and periodic optimization of the environment.

Deploying Single-Server Environments

Deploying Terminal Services in a single-server environment is much easier than deploying Terminal Services in a multi-server environment. In a single-server deployment, a group of clients always connects to the same server, so that although your organization might have three terminal servers, Group A always uses Server 1, Group B always uses Server 2, and Group C always uses Server 3, as shown in Figure 28-3.

A single-server configuration is the easiest to set up, as you need to perform only the following steps:

1. Install the operating system on your designated server and configure the server so it is optimized as appropriate for its intended use.

2. Install the required Terminal Services roles using the Add Roles Wizard to make Terminal Services available to clients.

3. Install applications to be used by clients using the Install Application On Terminal Server tool under Programs in Control Panel, which ensures that the applications are set up using Install mode for Terminal Services rather than Execute mode.

4. Install a Terminal Services license server and configure licenses for use.

5. Install terminal clients and configure them to use the Remote Desktop Connection client or RDC over HTTP. Alternately, configure applications to run as RemoteApps.

Steps 2 through 4 are discussed in detail in this chapter. Chapter 19 discussed Remote Desktop Connection client setup and support.

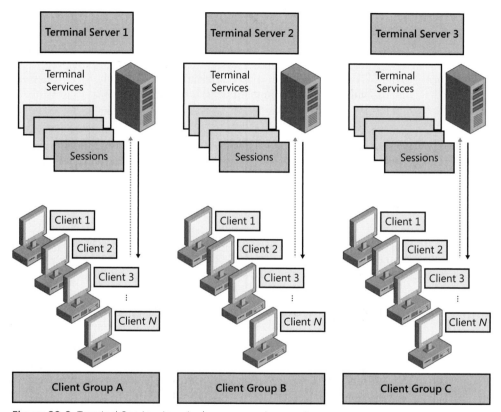

Figure 28-3 Terminal Services in a single-server environment.

Deploying Multi-Server Environments

Deploying Terminal Services in a multi-server environment requires a lot of planning and an advanced setup. In a multi-server environment, you use load balancing to create a farm of terminal servers whose incoming connections are distributed across multiple servers. Clients see the load-balanced terminal server farm as a single server. The farm has a single virtual IP address, and client requests are directed to this virtual IP address, allowing for seamless use of multiple servers.

Multi-server Terminal Services environments can be implemented using load balancing. A variety of techniques is possible, including using TS Session Broker Load Balancing with DNS round robin, TS Session Broker Load Balancing with routing tokens,

Microsoft Network Load Balancing, and hardware load balancers. A client that connects to a load-balanced terminal server is said to be in a virtual session. If that session is disconnected, processing continues in a disconnected state and the client can be configured to automatically try to reconnect the session. In a load-balanced farm, you always want a client to connect to the server it was originally working with. This enables users to continue where they left off without loss of data and without having to restart their applications, open documents, and so on.

For multi-server Terminal Services environments, session information is managed using a TS Session Broker server (see Figure 28-4). A TS Session Broker server is a server that uses the Terminal Services Session Broker (TS Session Broker) role service to maintain a TS Session Broker database, which contains a record for each session. The record includes the user name under which the session was established, the session ID, and the server to which the session is connected in the load-balanced farm. TS Session Broker servers are a new feature for Windows Server 2008.

Whenever a client tries to establish a Terminal Services connection and the user is authenticated, the session database is queried to see if a session record for that user exists. In this way, a user who was disconnected from a session can reconnect to the original session on the correct server. Without session management, the user might be connected to a different server and have to start a new session.

The TS Session Broker server can be a separate server running the TS Session Broker service as shown in Figure 28-4, or it can be one of the servers in the load-balanced farm running the TS Session Broker service. The advantage to using a separate server is that the overhead of maintaining sessions doesn't eat up resources that would otherwise be available to provide network resources to users.

To use a TS Session Broker, all servers in the farm must be running Windows Server 2008 Enterprise or Windows Server 2008 Datacenter. A multi-server environment is more complex to set up than a single-server environment. To configure Terminal Services in a multi-server environment, you must follow these steps:

1. Install the operating system on your designated server and configure the server so it is optimized as appropriate for its intended use.

2. Install the required Terminal Services roles using the Add Roles Wizard to make Terminal Services available to clients.

3. Install applications to be used by clients using the Install Application On Terminal Server tool under Programs in Control Panel, which ensures that the applications are set up using Install mode for Terminal Services rather than Execute mode.

4. Install and configure the TS Session Broker role service on a separate TS Session Broker server or on one of the member servers in the load-balanced farm. This installs and starts the Terminal Services Session Broker service and creates a local Session Directory Computers group.

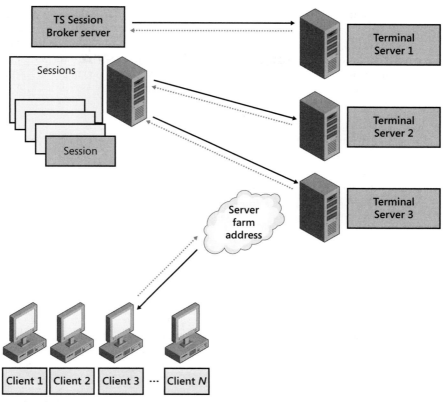

Figure 28-4 A multi-server Terminal Services deployment.

5. Add each terminal server in the farm to the local Session Directory Computers group on the TS Session Broker server.

6. Configure a terminal server to join a farm in TS Session Broker and to participate in TS Session Broker Load Balancing (or your desired load balancing technique).

7. Install a Terminal Services license server and configure licenses for use.

8. Install terminal clients and configure them to use the Remote Desktop Connection client or RDC over HTTP. Alternatively, configure applications to run as RemoteApps.

Steps 2 through 7 are discussed in detail in this chapter. Chapter 39, "Preparing and Deploying Server Clusters," discussed Microsoft Network Load Balancing setup and support. Chapter 19 discussed Remote Desktop Connection client setup and support.

Chapter 28

Setting Up Terminal Services

The tasks required to set up Terminal Services in single-server and multi-server environments are discussed in the sections that follow. As you read these sections, remember that if you want to use a multi-server environment with the TS Session Broker service, all the servers involved must be running Windows Server 2008 Enterprise or later.

Installing a Terminal Server

You can install a terminal server by following these steps:

1. In Server Manager, select the Roles node in the left pane and then click Add Roles. This starts the Add Roles Wizard. If the wizard displays the Before You Begin page, read the welcome text and then click Next.

2. On the Select Server Roles page, select the Terminal Services check box and then click Next. Read the introductory page and then click Next again.

3. On the Select Role Services page, select the check box for one or more role services to install, as shown in Figure 28-5.

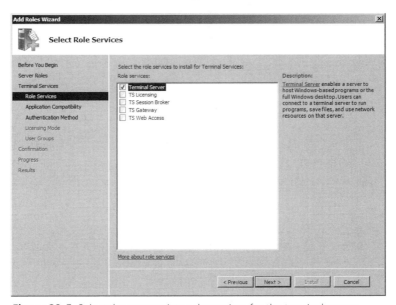

Figure 28-5 Select the appropriate role services for the terminal server.

4. Click Next to display the Uninstall And Reinstall Applications For Compatibility page. This page tells you the basic rules for using applications with Terminal

Services. Essentially, any already installed applications that you want to use with Terminal Services should be uninstalled and then reinstalled to ensure proper operations. After you read the information, click Next again.

5. On the next page of the wizard, as shown in Figure 28-6, you can select the default authentication method for the terminal server and then click Next. If you want to ensure that strict security measures are in place, select Require Network Level Authentication to ensure that only computers running Windows Vista or later or another operating system with Network Level Authentication can connect to the terminal server. Otherwise, select Do Not Require Network Level Authentication.

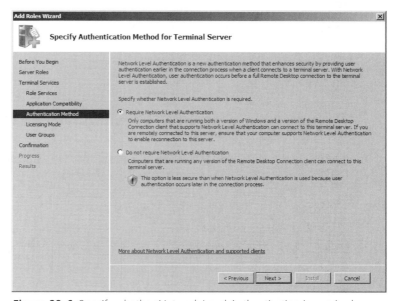

Figure 28-6 Specify whether Network Level Authentication is required.

6. On the Specify Licensing Mode page, shown in Figure 28-7, choose a licensing mode. If you want to use the 120 day grace period and configure licensing later, select Configure Later. Otherwise, set the default licensing mode as either Per Device or Per User and then click Next. With per device, a TS Per Device CAL must be available for each device that connects to the terminal server. With per user, a TS Per User CAL must be available for each user who connects to the terminal server.

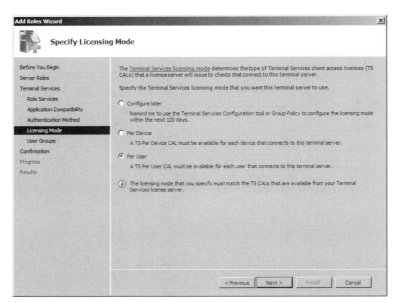

Figure 28-7 Set a default licensing mode.

7. On the Select User Groups Allowed Access To This Terminal Server, you can click Add to specify users and groups that will be added to the local Remote Desktop Users group on the server. Membership in local Remote Desktop Users allows users to connect to the terminal server.

8. Click Next and then click Install. Internet Explorer Enhanced Security Configuration will be turned off during configuration of the terminal server.

9. When Windows finishes installing Terminal Services, click Close. When prompted to restart the server, click Yes to allow the installation process to be completed.

10. After the server restarts, the installation will continue. When this process is completed and you log on to the terminal server, Windows starts the Resume Configuration wizard and shows the Installation Results page. Note any warnings and informational messages provided. On a terminal server with a 70% or greater load, you'll want to install the Windows System Resource Manager feature and use it to manage the way system memory and processors are used. To enable Windows Vista desktop features for TS clients, add the Desktop Experience feature.

INSIDE OUT   **Verify the remote connection settings**

When you install the Terminal Server role service, remote connections are enabled by default. To verify remote connection settings, access Control Panel, click System And Maintenance, and then click System. On the System page, click Remote Settings in the left pane. This opens the System Properties dialog box to the Remote tab.

Remote Desktop should be configured to allow connections. Select Allow Connections From Computers Running Any Version Of Remote Desktop (Less Secure) to allow connections from any version of Windows. Or select Allow Connections Only From Computers Running Remote Desktop With Network Level Authentication (More Secure) to allow connections only from Windows Vista or Windows Server 2008 (and computers with secure network authentication).

To add the users and groups that need to connect to the terminal server by using Remote Desktop, click Select Users, and then click Add. Users and groups that you add become members of the Remote Desktop Users group. Members of the local Administrators group can connect even if they are not listed.

Installing Applications for Clients to Use

After you install Terminal Services, there are decisions to make about the applications that you want to make available to users. Not all applications work well in multi-user environments. Some applications simply shouldn't be used; others can be used with some modifications or using a compatibility script. Regardless, all applications must be installed so that they are made available to users correctly.

Choosing Applications for Terminal Services Users

The best applications to run on a terminal server are those that can run multiple instances and perform well in a multi-user environment. The characteristics of applications that perform well in a multi-user environment include the following:

- Storing global data separately from local data

- Storing user data by user rather than by machine

- Identifying users by user name rather than by computer name

Although Terminal Services can be used to run Win16, MS-DOS, and Win32 applications, Terminal Services works best with Win32 applications. With Win16 and MS-DOS applications, Windows Server 2008 creates a virtual MS-DOS machine and runs the 16-bit or MS-DOS application within that context. Because 16-bit and MS-DOS applications are run in a different context, there is additional overhead and the applications won't perform as well as Win32 applications.

Chapter 28

If possible, you should limit the use of MS-DOS applications altogether as they are designed for single-user and non-multitasking environments and can cause serious performance problems. In addition, you should avoid using applications with known memory bugs or leaks; running multiple instances of such programs only multiplies the problem.

Application Licensing for Terminal Services Users

Unlike client access licensing, application licensing for Terminal Services users is pretty straightforward. Essentially, the licensing that is set for the product in a single-user environment is used in the Terminal Services environment. With Microsoft Office, for example, licensing is per seat, so every computer that runs Office needs a license whether one user or several use the computer. Thus, a client computer connecting to a terminal server and using Office needs a license per seat. If the client computer already has a license for Office, another license is not needed.

Installing Applications for Terminal Services Users

Terminal Services has two operating modes:

- **Execute mode** Execute mode is used for working with clients. When a client connects to a terminal server, the client and server use Execute mode.

- **Install mode** Install mode is used to install applications on a terminal server. When you install an application, you use this mode to ensure that the application is configured for use with multiple users.

You really don't have to do anything complicated to ensure that you install applications in Install mode: Merely install the application using the Install Application On Terminal Server tool under Programs in Control Panel rather than using the application's normal setup program, as follows:

1. In Control Panel, select Programs and then click Install Application On Terminal Server. This starts the Install Program From Floppy Disk Or CD-ROM wizard.

2. Insert the first installation floppy disk or CD-ROM and then click Next.

3. The wizard will then look for a Setup program on all available removable media, starting with the computer's floppy disk (if applicable).

4. If the wizard finds the appropriate Setup program, click Next to begin installation. Otherwise, click Browse to find the appropriate Setup program, and then click Next to begin the installation.

5. Install the application as you normally would. When the installation has ended, click Finish.

When you install an application on a terminal server using this technique, Windows changes to Install mode before installing the application and then changes back to Execute mode when the installation is completed. Any configuration information that an application writes under HKCU or HKLM is written to HKLM\Software\Microsoft\ Windows NT\Current Version\Terminal Server\Install as well. Any later changes to an application's configuration that affect HKCU or HKLM are also written to HKLM\Software\Microsoft\Windows NT\Current Version\Terminal Server\Install.

Any time a client using Terminal Services runs an application and that application attempts to read HKCU or HKLM, Terminal Services uses HKLM\Software\Microsoft\Windows NT\Current Version\Terminal Server\Install instead and copies the necessary information to the appropriate location under HKCU. User-specific .ini files or DLLs are copied to the user's home directory. If a user doesn't have a designated home directory, the .ini files or DLLs are copied to the user's profile. All of this works to ensure that the core settings for an application are machine specific and that users can customize applications to meet their needs.

In addition to using the Install Application On Terminal Server tool to install applications in Install mode, you can explicitly put a session in Install mode using the Change User command. Change User accepts three parameters:

- **/Query** Displays the current mode as either "Application EXECUTE mode is enabled" or "Application INSTALL mode is enabled"

- **/Execute** Changes Terminal Services to Execute mode

- **/Install** Changes Terminal Services to Install mode

If you want to install an application using its setup program, you can do this by typing **change user /install** at an elevated command prompt and then running the setup program. Any changes you make to the application in Install mode will apply to all users who use the application for the first time.

When you use Change User, you may also want to use Change Logon. The Change Logon command is used to enable or disable user logon to the terminal server. It can also be used to query the logon state. Change Logon accepts three parameters:

- **/Query** Displays the current logon status as either "Session logins are currently ENABLED" or "Session logins are currently DISABLED"

- **/Enable** Enables user logon

- **/Disable** Disables user logon

Note

A related but less frequently used command is Change Port. This command is used to map COM ports for MS-DOS compatibility. Type **change port /?** to learn more about this command.

Chapter 28

After you install an application, you will probably need to optimize its configuration for a multi-user environment. Two techniques can be used: application compatibility scripts, discussed in the following section, "Using Application Compatibility Scripts;" and hand-tuning, as discussed in "Modifying Applications After Installation," below.

Using Application Compatibility Scripts

Some applications need a compatibility script to work properly in a multi-user environment. For these applications, you can develop an application compatibility script or use the techniques discussed next in "Modifying Applications After Installation." Several application compatibility scripts are provided with Windows Server 2008, including:

- **RootDrv.cmd** Sets a drive letter to be mapped to each user's home directory when you run the ChkRoot.cmd script.

- **SetPaths.cmd** Extracts user paths into environment variables, allowing the scripts to run without hardcoded system paths and independently of system language.

These scripts are located in the %SystemRoot%\Application Compatibility Scripts folder. After you edit an application compatibility script, you run the script to customize the application's setup so that it works with Terminal Services. This can involve setting up the command environment, making changes to the Registry, and configuring file and folder paths for multi-user use. The scripts are written as batch programs and can be edited if you do not want to accept the default values.

Modifying Applications After Installation

After installation, you'll often need to manipulate an application to get it to work well in a multi-user environment. Here are some techniques you can use:

- **Configure application settings in Install mode** You should make changes to application settings in Install mode. This ensures that the configuration settings are available to all users.

- **Set user file paths to drive letters** Many applications have settings for file paths that need to be set on a per-user basis. In this case, you can enter a drive letter, and then map the drive letter to a network share as appropriate for each user. For example, you could set the file path to X: and then map X: to the user's home directory. Every user has a separate Terminal Services profile, which you can use for mapping home folders.

- **Configure Registry settings under HKLM\Software\Microsoft\Windows NT\Current Version\Terminal Server\Compatibility\Applications** Only a limited set of application settings can be changed through the Registry. If you need to tune an application's Registry settings, you must do this in Install mode and make changes only to keys and values under HKLM\Software\Microsoft\Windows NT\Current Version\Terminal Server\Compatibility\Applications. This means you would type **change user /install** and then start the Registry Editor.

Some applications don't work well in multi-user environments. If an application performs poorly or hogs system resources, you might need to fine-tune its configuration in the Registry. Each application configured on a terminal server should have a separate subkey under HKLM\Software\Microsoft\Windows NT\Current Version\Terminal Server\Compatibility\Applications. The name of the application subkey is the same as the name of the application's executable without the .exe extension.

Table 28-1 shows the values you can use under an application's subkey to modify the behavior of the application. All these values must be set as the REG_DWORD type. Create or edit the values as discussed in Chapter 9, "Managing the Registry." Any changes you make are applied the next time the application is started.

Table 28-1 Performance-Tuning Registry Values for 16-Bit and 32-Bit Windows Applications

Value Entry	Description	Default Value
FirstCountMsgQPeeks-SleepBadApp	Sets the number of times the application must query the message queue before Terminal Services decides that it is a bad application. The lower this value, the more often the application will be deemed to be bad and the more quickly the application will be suspended so that it uses less CPU time.	0xF (15 decimal)
MsgQBadAppSleep-TimeInMillisec	Sets the number of milliseconds the application is suspended when Terminal Services has decided that it is a bad application. The higher this value is set, the longer the application will be suspended. If this value is zero, polling detection is disabled.	0
NthCountMsgQPeeks-SleepBadApp	Sets the number of times the application must query the message queue before it is suspended again. The lower this value, the more often the application will be deemed to be bad and the more quickly the application will be suspended so that it uses less CPU time.	0x5 (5 decimal)
Flags	Describes the type of Windows application. Valid values are: 0x4 for Win16 applications; 0x8 for Win32 applications; 0xC for either Win16 or Win32 applications	0x8 (Win32 only)

Chapter 28

> **Note**
>
> The hyphens inserted in the names in the Value Entry column are not part of the actual name.

Enabling and Joining the Terminal Services Session Broker Service

When you are using a load-balanced terminal server farm, you need to configure a TS Session Broker server and configure Terminal Services to join the TS Session Broker. As discussed previously, the TS Session Broker server can be a member of the load-balanced farm or it can be a separate server. If you use a separate TS Session Broker server, it probably doesn't need to be a high-end server. The session management work-load on the TS Session Broker server typically is very light, but depends on the number of clients connecting to Terminal Services. Regardless of configuration, the TS Session Broker server and all terminal servers in the load-balanced farm must be running Windows Server 2008 Enterprise or later.

To set up the TS Session Broker server, you need to ensure that the Terminal Services Session Broker service is configured for automatic startup. This service should be installed automatically and enabled when you install the TS Session Broker server. Next, you need to tell the TS Session Broker server about the computers that can con-nect to the service. The Terminal Services Session Broker service will not accept any connections from servers that it doesn't know are authorized. To tell the service which servers are authorized, add the computer account for each server in the load-balanced farm to a local computer group called Session Directory Computers. This group is cre-ated automatically when you install the TS Session Broker role service.

With TS Session Broker load balancing, you can configure:

- **Load balancing by relative weighting** With load balancing by relative weighting, the TS Session Broker is responsible for load-balancing. Although maintaining the load-balancing state for each server in the farm requires additional system resources (primarily memory and processing time), the TS Session Broker can load balance using relative weighting, giving you more options.

- **Load balancing using round robin DNS** With load balancing using round robin, the TS Session Broker shifts much of the load-balancing burden to DNS and maintains very little information about the load-balancing state, reducing the load on the TS Session Broker. Although shifting processing to the DNS client/server environment reduces the burden on the server, the configuration isn't as flexible as relative weighting and you ultimately have fewer options.

With relative weighting, you assign each terminal server in the farm a weight. The weight determines the relative percentage of sessions that the TS Session Broker will direct to the server. Here are some examples:

- A server assigned a weight of 25 will receive one-fourth the number of sessions as compared to a server with a weight of 100.

- A server assigned a weight of 50 will receive one-half the number of sessions as compared to a server with a weight of 100.

- A server assigned a weight of 75 will receive three-fourths the number of sessions as compared to a server with a weight of 100.

- A server assigned a weight of 100 will receive the same approximate number of sessions as compared to a server with a weight of 100.

With round robin DNS, the TS Session Broker directs new session requests to terminal servers in the farm in round robin fashion. As an example, in a four-server farm, the first request is directed to Server 1, the second to Server 2, the third to Server 3, the fourth to Server 4, the fifth to Server 1, and so on. If you want to use DNS round robin, you'll need to configure DNS specifically for this and turn on the advanced setting Enable Round Robin in DNS.

To complete the process, you need to configure each server in the farm so that it knows the farm name, TS Session Broker server name or IP address, and the load-balancing technique to use. These settings enable Terminal Services to use load balancing and the Terminal Services Session Broker service. To make these changes, you can use the Terminal Services Configuration tool or Group Policy.

Enable and Start the Terminal Services Session Broker Service

Follow these steps to check the Terminal Services Session Broker service:

1. Start Computer Management by clicking Start, All Programs, Administrative Tools, and then Computer Management. To work with a remote system, right-click the Computer Management entry in the left pane and select Connect To Another Computer on the shortcut menu. This displays the Connect To Another Computer dialog box. Type the domain name or IP address of the system for which you want to manage the Terminal Services Session Broker service, and then click OK.

2. In Computer Management, expand Services And Applications, and then select Services. In the right pane, double-click Terminal Services Session Broker. This displays a Properties dialog box.

3. On the General tab, ensure that Automatic is set as the Startup Type as shown in Figure 28-8, and that the Service Status is listed as Started. Make changes as necessary and then click OK.

Chapter 28

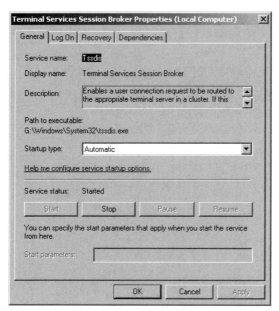

Figure 28-8 Configure the Terminal Services Session Broker service startup.

Authorize Terminal Servers to Use the Terminal Services Session Broker Service

When the Terminal Services Session Broker service is started, the service looks for a computer group named Session Directory Computers. If this group doesn't exist, the service creates it. You need to add the computer account for each server in the load-balanced farm to the Session Directory Computers group.

In an Active Directory domain, you add the computer account for each server by following these steps:

1. Start Computer Management by clicking Start, All Programs, Administrative Tools, Computer Management. To work with a remote system, right-click the Computer Management entry in the left pane, and then select Connect To Another Computer on the shortcut menu. This displays the Connect To Another Computer dialog box. Type the domain name or IP address of a server in the load-balanced farm, and then click OK.

2. In Computer Management, expand Local Users And Groups under System Tools, and then select Groups. In the main pane, double-click Session Directory Computers. This displays a Properties dialog box.

3. Click Add. This displays the Select Users, Contacts, Computers, Or Groups dialog box.

4. Click Object Types to display the Object Types dialog box as shown in Figure 28-9. In the Object Types dialog box, select the Computers check box, and then click OK.

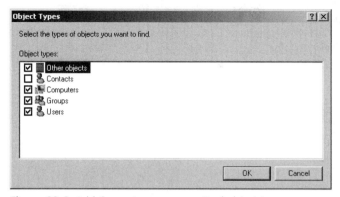

Figure 28-9 Add Computers as a permitted object type.

5. In the Select Users, Contacts, Computers, Or Groups dialog box, you can now type and validate the names of computer accounts, as shown in Figure 28-10. Type a computer account name, and then click Check Names. If multiple matches are found, select the name or names you want to use, and then click OK. If no matches are found, either you've entered an incorrect name part or you're working with an incorrect location. Modify the name and try again or click Locations to select a new location. To add additional computer accounts, type a semicolon (;), and then repeat this process.

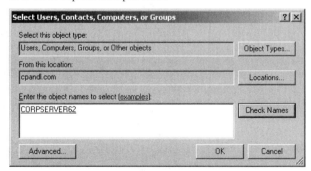

Figure 28-10 Select the computer accounts that should be members of the group.

6. When you click OK, the computer accounts are added to the list in the Session Directory Computers Properties dialog box. Click OK again to close the Properties dialog box.

In a workgroup, you add the computer account for each server by following these steps:

1. Start Computer Management by clicking Start, All Programs, Administrative Tools, Computer Management. To work with a remote system, right-click the Computer Management entry in the left pane, and then select Connect To

Another Computer on the shortcut menu. This displays the Connect To Another Computer dialog box. Type the domain name or IP address of a server in the load-balanced farm, and then click OK.

2. In Computer Management, expand Services And Applications, and then select Services. In the right pane, double-click Terminal Services Session Broker. This displays a Properties dialog box.

3. Click Add, and then use the Select Users dialog box to add each of the computer accounts in turn.

4. Click OK when you are finished.

Configure Each Server to Join the TS Session Broker

Now that you've set up the TS Session Broker server and authorized servers to use it, you need to tell the terminal servers in the farm about the load-balancing and TS Session Broker configuration. You do this using the Terminal Services Configuration tool to set the TS Session Broker properties. These properties tell clients about the load-balanced farm and the TS Session Broker server.

On each server in the load-balanced farm, complete these steps:

1. Start the Terminal Services Configuration tool by clicking Start, All Programs, Administrative Tools, Terminal Services, and then Terminal Services Configuration, or by typing **tsconfig.msc** at the command prompt.

> **Note**
> Configuring each individual server as shown in this technique is time-consuming. To save time when you are using TS Session Broker Load Balancing and your terminal servers are in a separate OU, you can configure the required settings using the TS Session Broker Farm Name policy setting under Computer Configuration\Administrative Templates\ Windows Components\Terminal Services\Terminal Server\TS Session Broker. The setup is the same as discussed in this procedure. Keep in mind that Group Policy will need to be refreshed before the settings are applied, which you can accomplish by typing **gpupdate /target:computer** at an elevated command prompt.

2. In the Terminal Services Configuration tool, select Terminal Services Configuration in the left pane, and then, in the main pane, double-click Member Of Farm In TS Session Broker. This displays a Properties dialog box with the TS Session Broker tab selected (see Figure 28-11).

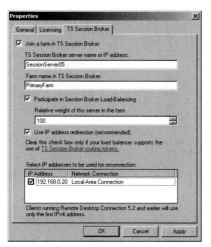

Figure 28-11 Join the farm in the TS Session Broker.

3. Select the Join A Farm In TS Session Broker check box.

4. In the TS Session Broker Server Name Or IP Address box, type the name or IP address of the TS Session Broker server. This is the server on which you installed the TS Session Broker role service.

5. In the Farm Name In TS Session Broker box, type a name for the farm or accept the default value. You must use the same farm name for all servers that are part of the same load-balanced terminal server farm. This name must be unique and it should be the same name with which you register the farm in DNS.

> **Note**
>
> The terminal server farm name in DNS represents the virtual name to which clients will connect. If you type an existing farm name, the server joins the existing farm. If you type a new name, a new farm is created in the TS Session Broker and the server joins this farm.

6. If the server will use TS Session Broker load balancing with relative weighting, select the Participate In Session Broker Load-Balancing check box and then assign a relative weight to the server in the farm. The default weight is 100. The weight determines the relative percentage of sessions that the TS Session Broker will direct to the server. For example, a server assigned a weight of 25 will receive one-fourth of the number of sessions as compared to a server with a weight of 100.

Chapter 28

7. Do one of the following to configure how redirection works:

   ○ Select the Use IP Address Redirection (Recommended) check box, as per the default, to use IP address redirection. IP address redirection is where a client queries the TS Session Broker and is redirected to their existing session by using the IP address of the server where their session exists. This method is recommended only when clients can connect directly by IP address to terminal servers in the farm. You must use IP address redirection if you use TS Session Broker Load Balancing with DNS round robin, Microsoft Network Load Balancing, or hardware load balancers that don't support TS Session Broker routing tokens.

   ○ Clear the Use IP Address Redirection (Recommended) check box to use token redirection mode. With token redirection, the IP address of the terminal server is not sent to the client. Instead, the IP address is embedded in a token that the client can use to reconnect to the TS Session Broker, which in turn redirects the client to their existing session on the correct terminal server in the farm.

8. In the Select IP Addresses To Be Used For Reconnection box, select the check box next to each IP address you want to use. Keep in mind the following:

   ○ With token redirection, only one IP address can be used for redirection. This IP address must also be configured on the load balancer for the terminal server.

   ○ Clients running the RDC 5.2 or earlier client will use only the first IPv4 address.

9. Click OK.

> **Note**
> Some third-party load-balancing solutions act as routers as well as load balancers. For these devices, you must clear the IP Address Redirection check box to allow the load balancer to use router token redirection. If you clear this check box, you will be able to set only one IP address to which client computers should connect.

Configure Round Robin DNS

To use round robin DNS instead of relative weighting for load balancing, configure each server to join the TS Session Broker as discussed in the previous procedure. However, in step 6, clear the Participate In Session Broker Load-Balancing check box. Afterward, create a Host record for each terminal server in the farm using the following technique:

1. In the DNS console, expand the server entry, expand Forward Lookup Zones, and then expand the domain name.

2. Right-click the appropriate zone and then click New Host (A Or AAAA).

3. In the Name box, type the terminal server farm name. The farm name is the virtual name that clients will use to connect to the terminal server farm. Do not use the name of an existing server.

4. In the IP Address box, type the IP address of a terminal server in the farm and then click Add Host.

By default, DNS round robin is enabled when using Microsoft DNS with Windows Server 2008. To check the status of DNS round robin, follow these steps:

1. In the DNS console, right-click the server entry and then select Properties.

2. In the Properties dialog box, select the Advanced tab.

3. The Enable Round Robin check box should be selected. If it isn't, select it and then click OK.

Setting Up a Terminal Services License Server

Licensing is required to use Terminal Services, which means you must do the following:

1. Install a Terminal Services license server.

2. Activate the license server.

3. Configure licenses for use.

Considerations for Installing a Terminal Services License Server

A Terminal Services license server is a server running the Terminal Server Licensing service. Although you can use any server in the organization, the license server should be well connected in the domain. The Terminal Services license server will need network access to the organization's terminal servers and to the Internet for the following reasons:

- The internal network connection is required to issue and validate client licenses.

- The connection to the Internet is needed to connect to the Microsoft Clearinghouse server for activation of the license server and any licenses you've purchased.

Note

The connection to the Microsoft Clearinghouse uses HTTP ports 80 and 443 for the connection. If you've set up a proxy or Network Address Translation (NAT) server and enabled Web browsing in the organization, the license server shouldn't have a problem connecting to the Internet over these ports. If, however, you do not allow Web browsing or you restrict Web browsing, you will need to activate the license server and its licenses over the telephone.

You can configure the Terminal Services license server for enterprise-wide use or for use in a specific domain or workgroup.

- If you choose enterprise-wide use, you need only one license server regardless of how many single-server or multi-server Terminal Services environments you've implemented in the organization.

- If you choose domain or workgroup use, you need one license server for each domain or workgroup that uses Terminal Services.

Think carefully about your approach, as it determines how licenses are issued and made available to Terminal Services clients. If you want all client access licenses to be available to all clients, you might want to use the enterprise-wide configuration. If you want to organize licensing by department or functional groups, you might want to use a domain or workgroup approach to restrict users' access to licenses per domain or per workgroup. When making infrastructure design decisions, keep the following in mind:

- In a single-server Terminal Services environment, the terminal server and the Terminal Services license server can be the same system.

- In a multi-server Terminal Services environment, you probably don't want one of the terminal servers to be a license server as well. If you have a separate TS Session Broker server, however, you might want to make this server the Terminal Services license server as well.

Prior to activation of a license server, you have a 120-day grace period during which you can perform unlimited testing and client connections. Use this time to ensure that your Terminal Services environment is as you want it to be. After you activate the license server, you will need to configure actual licenses for use, and those licenses will work only on the license server for which you've activated them. The activation code necessary for the license server is the product ID.

Installing a Terminal Services License Server

The way you configure a server to be a Terminal Services license server depends on the server's current configuration:

- On a server that doesn't have any Terminal Services role services installed, you can configure the server as a license server using the Add Roles Wizard. In Server Manager, select the Roles node in the left pane and then click Add Roles. If the Add Roles Wizard displays the Before You Begin page, read the welcome text and then click Next. On the Select Server Roles page, select the Terminal Services check box and then click Next. Read the introductory page and then click Next again. On the Select Role Services page, select the TS Licensing check box and then click Next.

- On a server that already has Terminal Services role services installed, you can configure the server as a license server using the Add Role Services wizard. In Server Manager, expand the Roles node in the left pane and then select Terminal

Services. Scroll down in the main pane and then click Add Role Services. On the Select Role Services page, select the TS Licensing check box and then click Next.

As shown in Figure 28-12, you can specify the role of the license server. When the terminal server is part of a workgroup, the This Workgroup option is available and selected by default. When the terminal server is part of a domain, the This Domain option is available and selected by default. In a domain, you also have the option of selecting The Forest to configure the license server for enterprise-wide use. By default, the license server database is installed in the %SystemRoot%\System32\LServer folder. You can accept this setting or click Browse to specify a new location. When you are ready to continue, click Next, and then click Install to begin the installation. When the installation process is finished, click Close.

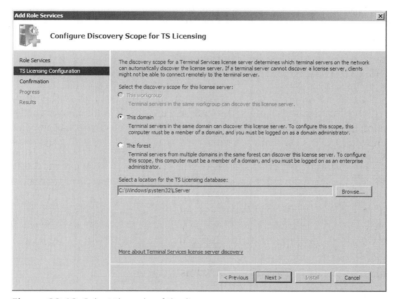

Figure 28-12 Select the role of the license server.

Consider the License Database Location

Every time a client attempts to connect to a terminal server, a lookup is made to the license server database. If the client has an existing license, the terminal server to which the client is connected queries the license server about the client's license and the license server performs a lookup to validate it. If the client doesn't have an existing license, the terminal server to which the client is connected queries the availability of licenses and the license server performs a lookup to determine if licenses are available. If a license is available, it is issued to the client. For optimal performance in a large network with many hundreds or thousands of clients, you might want to consider putting the license database on a separate physical disk from that used by the operating system.

Activating the License Server and Configuring Licenses for Use

After you install the Terminal Services Licensing service, you can activate the license server and configure licenses for use with the TS Licensing Manager. To start the TS Licensing Manager, click Start, All Programs, Administrative Tools, Terminal Services, and then TS Licensing Manager, or type **licmgr.exe** at the command prompt.

When you first start the TS Licensing Manager, it will search for license servers on the network and then list the ones it has found, as shown in Figure 28-13. Here, a license server is present but not yet activated (as indicated by the red circle with a white X on its icon).

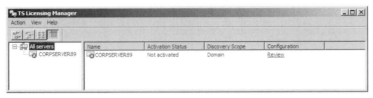

Figure 28-13 Available license servers are listed in the TS Licensing Manager.

You use the Terminal Server License Server Activation Wizard to activate the license server, and the Terminal Server CAL Installation Wizard to configure licenses for use. (The acronym CAL stands for client access license.) When you activate a server, both wizards can be run in turn if desired.

To activate the license server and configure licenses for use, follow these steps:

1. Right-click the server entry in the TS Licensing Manager, and then select Activate Server. This starts the Activate Server Wizard.

2. Click Next. On the Connection Method page, select the connection method to use for activation, as shown in Figure 28-14.

Figure 28-14 Select a connection method.

3. The default technique used for license server and license activation is an Automatic Connection to the Microsoft Clearinghouse. You can also use specify Web Browser or Telephone if you want to get an activation code manually. Keep the following in mind:

○ *With the Automatic Connection method*–When you click Next, the wizard attempts to connect over the Internet to the Microsoft Clearinghouse, as shown in the following screen. If you choose this method, you will need to identify yourself and your organization to obtain an authorization code, which is automatically sent to the server.

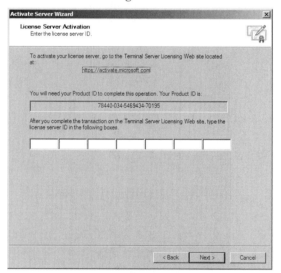

○ *With the Web Browser method*–When you click Next, the wizard tells you that you need to go to the Terminal Server Licensing Web site (*https://activate.microsoft.com*) and provide your product ID, as shown in the following screen. You will then get a license server ID to use.

○ *With the Telephone method*–When you click Next, the wizard prompts you to select your country or region. After you select your country or region and click Next, you will see a telephone number specific to your region or country to call, and you will be given your product ID to provide during the call, as shown in the following screen. You will then get a license server ID to use.

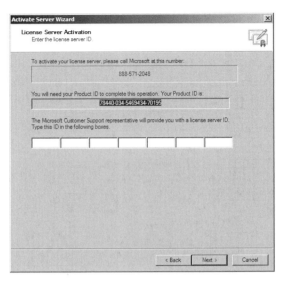

4. When you finish this process, you'll see the Completing The Terminal Server License Server Activation Wizard page as shown in Figure 28-15. On this page, the Start Terminal Server Client Licensing Wizard check box is automatically selected so that if you click Next from here, the wizard starts.

Figure 28-15 Finishing the activation and starting the client licensing wizard.

5. The Terminal Server Client Licensing Wizard uses the previously selected connection method to activate client licenses. You will need to click Next twice and then enter a license code from your retail product packaging. Select

Enterprise Agreement or Open License Contract. As before, the way this works depends on the connection method.

To install licenses separately or at a later date, right-click the server entry in the TS Licensing Manager, and then select Install Licenses. This starts the Terminal Server Client Licensing Wizard, which you can use to configure licenses for use.

The Terminal Server License Server Activation Wizard and the Terminal Server CAL Installation Wizard store information about the connection method and your contact information. If you want to use a different connection method or change contact information, you need to edit the default properties for the license server. To do this, right-click the server entry in the TS Licensing Manager and select Properties. You can then make changes as necessary using the Licensing Wizard Properties dialog box shown in Figure 28-16.

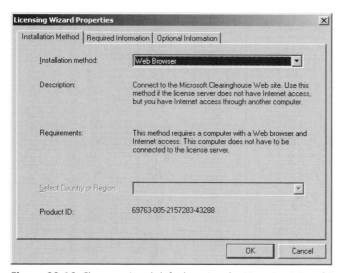

Figure 28-16 Change wizard defaults using the Licensing Wizard Properties dialog box.

Using the Terminal Services Configuration Tool

The Terminal Services Configuration tool is found in the Administrative Tools program group on the Start menu. Click Start, All Programs, Administrative Tools, Terminal Services, and then Terminal Service Configuration, or else type **tsconfig.msc** at a command prompt. As shown in Figure 28-17, you can configure connections and server settings using the Terminal Services Configuration tool. Each terminal server must be configured separately.

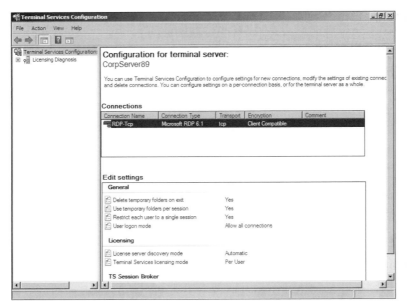

Figure 28-17 Editing settings with the Terminal Services Configuration tool.

Configuring Global Connection Settings

With Terminal Services and Remote Desktop for Administration, data transmission between the server and the client uses Remote Desktop Protocol (RDP), which is encapsulated and encrypted within TCP. RDP version 6.1 is the default version of the protocol used with Windows Server 2008. In the Terminal Services Configuration tool, you can configure the settings for RDP. RDP settings are used to set global defaults and to override the local and default settings used by clients.

To modify the RDP settings, select Terminal Services Configuration in the left pane and then in the details pane double-click on RDP-Tcp. This displays the RDP-Tcp Properties dialog box as shown in Figure 28-18. If any of these settings are unavailable, they have probably been configured using Group Policy.

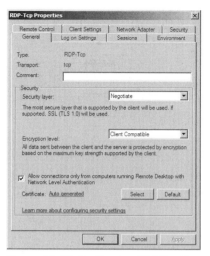

Figure 28-18 Configuring RDP-Tcp Properties and settings.

The RDP-Tcp Properties dialog box has the following tabs:

- **General** Sets the encryption level for the server. Use Client Compatible if you are using a mixed environment that might include computers running Windows 2000. You can also require High (128-bit) or FIPS-compliant encryption. You can improve security by enabling Allow Connections Only From Computers Running Remote Desktop With Network Level Authentication. Windows Vista and later versions of Windows have Network Level Authentication.

- **Logon Settings** Configures specific logons to use. In most cases, however, you'll want to use the default setting Use Client-Provided Logon Information. If you want clients always to be prompted for a password regardless of their client settings, choose Always Prompt For Password.

- **Sessions** Configures session reconnection and timeout. Any settings used here override the user settings. You can configure whether and when Terminal Services ends disconnected sessions, limits active sessions, or limits idle sessions.

- **Environment** Sets an initial program to run. This setting overrides client settings for Remote Desktop clients.

- **Remote Control** Determines whether remote control of user sessions is enabled, and sets remote control options. Remote control can allow an administrator to view a user's Terminal Services sessions, interact with a user's Terminal Services sessions, or both. These remote control options set the global defaults used by all users.

- **Client Settings** Determines how the client screen resolution and redirection features are managed. By default, the connection settings from the Remote Desktop clients are used, and clients are limited to a maximum color depth of 16 bits. Additionally, audio mapping is disabled by default.

Chapter 28

- **Network Adapter** Determines the network adapters on the server to which Terminals Services connections can be made. The All Network Adapters option is selected by default.

- **Security** Lets you view or modify security permissions for the server. Rather than configuring permissions per server, it is much easier to add users to the Remote Desktop Users group if they should have access to Terminal Services. It should be noted that this group has limited permissions. By default, members of the Remote Desktop Users group have User Access and Guest Access permission. This means users can log on to a session on the server, query information about a session, connect to other users' sessions, and connect to another session.

Configuring Server Settings

As shown in Figure 28-19, the Edit Settings panel contains options for all connections on a terminal server.

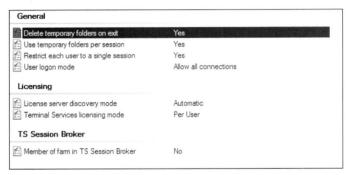

Figure 28-19 Configure general server settings for all connections.

The settings available depend on the Terminal Services configuration and include the following:

- **Delete Temporary Folders On Exit** Determines whether temporary folders created by clients are deleted automatically when a user logs off. By default, this setting is enabled, so temporary folders are deleted when a user logs off the terminal server. To change this setting, double-click it, clear or select the Delete Temporary Folders On Exit check box as appropriate, and then click OK.

- **Use Temporary Folders Per Session** Determines whether temporary folders are used on a per-session basis. By default, this setting is enabled, so each session has its own set of temporary folders. To change this setting, double-click it, clear or set the Use Temporary Folders Per Session check box as appropriate, and then click OK.

- **Restrict Each User To A Single Session** Determines whether users are limited to a single session on the terminal server. By default, this is enabled to conserve resources on the terminal server. To change this setting, double-click it, clear or set the Restrict Each User To A Single Session check box as appropriate, and then click OK.

- **User Logon Mode** Determines whether users are allowed to reconnect to the terminal server and whether the server accepts new logons for user reconnections. By default, terminal servers allow all connections. You can also allow reconnections but prevent new logons. To change this setting, double-click it, select the desired user logon mode, and then click OK.

- **License Server Discovery Mode** Determines whether the terminal server tries to automatically discover license servers. By default, terminal servers automatically try to detect the available license servers. To specify the license servers to use rather than using automatic detection, double-click this setting and then select Use The Specified License Servers. In the box provided, type the name or IP address of the license servers to use, separating each name or IP address with a comma, and then click OK to save your settings.

- **Terminal Services Licensing Mode** Determines whether the licensing mode for clients is set Per Device or Per User. To change this setting, double-click it, select Per Device or Per User as appropriate, and then click OK.

- **Member Of Farm In TS Session Broker** Determines whether the server uses a TS Session Broker, and sets the TS Session Broker properties. To change this setting, double-click it and then configure it as discussed in "Configure Each Server to Join the TS Session Broker" on page 948. Click OK.

Configuring Terminal Services Security

Terminal Services permissions set the maximum allowed permissions for a Terminal Services connection. These permissions are applied whenever a client connects to a terminal server. The basic permissions for Terminal Services are the following:

- **Full Control** Users have full control over their own sessions as well as the sessions of other users. In addition to setting user access permissions, they can set information, take control of or view other user sessions, disconnect sessions, or establish virtual channels.

- **User Access** Users have limited control over their own sessions. This means users can log on to a session on the server, query information about a session, or connect to another session.

- **Guest Access** Users can log on to a terminal server. They do not have other permissions.

If users have a basic permission, they also have special permissions built into the basic permission, as shown in Table 28-2. Note that the Logon permission implicitly gives users the right to log off their own session and the Connect permission implicitly gives users the right to disconnect their own session.

Table 28-2 Special Permissions for Terminal Services

Special Permission	Description	Included In
Query Information	Allows a user to gather information about users connected to the terminal server, processes running on the server, and so on.	Full Control, User Access
Set Information	Allows a user to configure connection properties.	Full Control
Remote Control	Allows a user to view or remotely control another user's session.	Full Control
Logon	Allows a user to log on to a session on the server.	Full Control, User Access, Guest Access
Logoff	Allows a user to log off another user from a session. This is different from being able to log off your own session.	Full Control
Message	Allows a user to send a message to another user's session.	Full Control
Connect	Allows a user to connect to another session.	Full Control
Disconnect	Allows a user to disconnect another user from a session.	Full Control
Virtual Channels	Allows a user to use virtual channels.	Full Control

With Windows Server 2008, you must use the Remote Desktop Users group to control access to Terminal Services. In addition, to have default security permission, this group is given default user rights, which allow members of the group to log on to a terminal server.

To view or manage the permissions of a terminal server, in the Terminal Services Configuration tool select Terminal Services Configuration in the left pane, and then in the details pane double-click on RDP-Tcp. In the Properties dialog box, select the Security tab. As shown in Figure 28-20, you can now view the users and groups that have Terminal Services permissions and their permissions.

You can grant or deny Terminal Services permissions. In the Terminal Services Configuration tool, select Terminal Services Configuration in the left pane and then in the details pane double-click on RDP-Tcp. In the Properties dialog box, select the Security tab.

On the Security tab, configure access permissions for each user and group added by selecting an account name, and then allowing or denying access permissions. To grant a user or group access permissions, select the check box for the permission in the Allow column. To deny a user or group access permissions, select the check box for the permission in the Deny column.

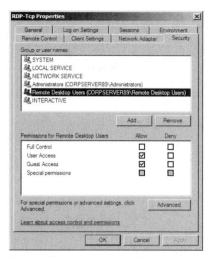

Figure 28-20 View or set Terminal Services permissions.

You can set special permissions for Terminal Services using the Terminal Services Configuration tool as well. In the Properties dialog box, select the Security tab, and then click Advanced. This displays the dialog box shown in Figure 28-21.

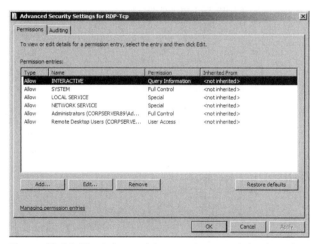

Figure 28-21 The Advanced Security Settings dialog box shows the special permissions assigned to each user or group.

You now have the following options:

- **Add** Adds a user or group. Click Add to display the Select User, Computer, Or Group dialog box. Type the name of a user or group and click Check Names. If multiple names match the value you entered, you'll see a list of names and will be able to choose the one you want to use. Otherwise, the name will be filled in for you. When you click OK, the Permission Entry For dialog box shown in Figure 28-22 appears.

- **Edit** Edits an existing user or group entry. Select the user or group whose permissions you want to modify, and then click Edit. The Permission Entry For dialog box appears.

- **Remove** Removes an existing user or group entry. Select the user or group whose permissions you want to remove, and then click Remove.

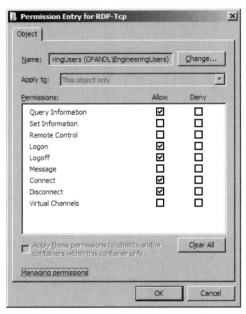

Figure 28-22 Use the Permission Entry For dialog box to set special permissions.

If you are adding or editing entries for users or groups, you use the Permission Entry For dialog box to grant or deny special permissions. Select Allow or Deny for each permission as appropriate.

Auditing Terminal Services Access

Auditing Terminal Services access can help you track who is accessing Terminal Services and what they are doing. You configure auditing policies per server using the Terminal Services Configuration tool. In the Terminal Services Configuration tool, select Terminal Services Configuration in the left pane and then in the details pane double-click on RDP-Tcp. In the Properties dialog box, select the Security tab and then click Advanced. In the Advanced Security Settings dialog box, select the Auditing tab, as shown in Figure 28-23.

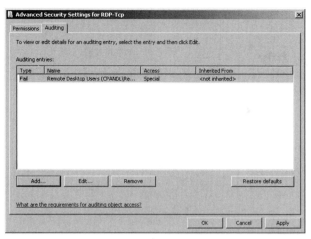

Figure 28-23 Specify to which users and groups auditing should apply.

Use the Auditing Entries list to select the users, groups, or computers whose actions you want to audit. To add specific accounts, click Add, and then use the Select User, Computer, Or Group dialog box to select an account name to add. If you want to audit actions for all Terminal Services users, use the Remote Desktop Users group. Otherwise, select the specific user groups or users, or both, that you want to audit. When you click OK, you'll see the Auditing Entry For dialog box, shown in Figure 28-24.

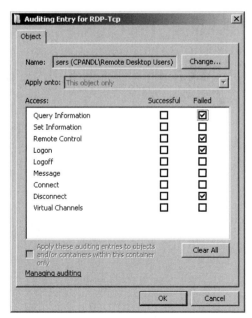

Figure 28-24 Specify the actions to audit for the designated user, group, or computer.

Chapter 28

After you make a selection, under Access, select the Successful or Failed check boxes, or both, for each event you want to audit. The events you can audit are the same as those for which you control Terminal Services permissions, as discussed previously. Click OK when you're finished. Repeat this process to audit other users, groups, or computers. Any time permissions that you've configured for auditing are used, the action is written to the system's security log, where it's stored for your review. The security log is accessible from Event Viewer.

Configuring RemoteApps

As discussed previously, a RemoteApp is a program that a user accesses remotely through Terminal Services and appears as if it is running on the user's local computer. When you install the Terminal Server role service, the RemoteApps feature and its related components are installed as well, including TS RemoteApp Manager.

Making Programs Available as RemoteApps

You use TS RemoteApp Manager to make applications available to users as Remote-Apps. Only applications that you've previously configured for use with Terminal Services can be made into RemoteApps.

To make an application available as a RemoteApp and add it to the RemoteApp Programs list, follow these steps:

1. Start the TS RemoteApp Manager tool by clicking Start, All Programs, Administrative Tools, Terminal Services, and then TS RemoteApp Manager, or by typing **remoteprograms.msc** at the command prompt.

2. In the Actions pane or on the Action menu, click Add RemoteApp Programs. This starts the RemoteApp Wizard. Click Next.

3. On the Choose Programs To Add To The RemoteApp Programs List page, shown in Figure 28-25, select the check box next to each program that you want to add to the list of RemoteApp programs.

> **Note**
> You can select multiple programs. In Figure 28-25, I previously installed Microsoft Office 2007 as a terminal server application, making all the Office applications available as remote applications. Other listed programs are the programs that are found on the All Users Start menu on the terminal server. If a program that you want to add to the RemoteApp Programs list is not in the list, click Browse, and then specify the location of the program's .exe file.

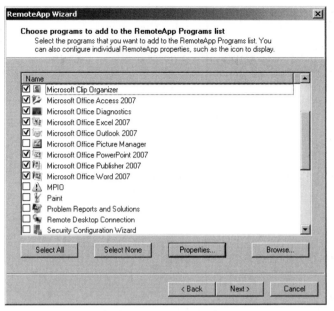

Figure 28-25 Specify the programs to configure as RemoteApps.

4. To configure the properties for a RemoteApp, select the application name and then click Properties. Then using the following options in the RemoteApp Properties dialog box, shown in Figure 28-26, you can configure the way the application can be used:

- **RemoteApp Program Name** Sets the program name that will be displayed to users. To change the name, type a new name in the RemoteApp Program Name box.

- **Location** Sets the path of the program executable file. To change the path, type the new path in the Location box, or click Browse to locate the .exe file. Although you can use system environment variables in the path, you cannot use per-user environment variables.

- **Alias** Sets a unique identifier for the program that defaults to the program's file name without the file extension. In most cases, you will not need to change this name.

- **RemoteApp Program Is Available Through TS Web Access** Determines whether the program is available through TS Web Access as per the default setting. To disable TS Web Access of the RemoteApp, clear the check box.

- **Command-Line Arguments** Determines whether command-line arguments are allowed, not allowed, or whether to always use the same command-line arguments.

- **Change Icon** Sets the program icon that will be associated with the application.

Chapter 28

When you are finished configuring program properties, click OK, and then click Next.

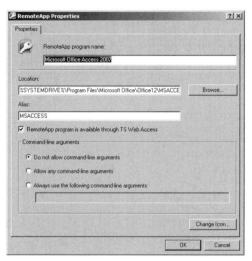

Figure 28-26 Optionally, set configuration properties for individual programs.

5. On the Review Settings page, review the settings, and then click Finish. The programs that you selected should appear in the RemoteApp Programs list in the lower portion of the TS RemoteApp Manager main window, as shown in Figure 28-27.

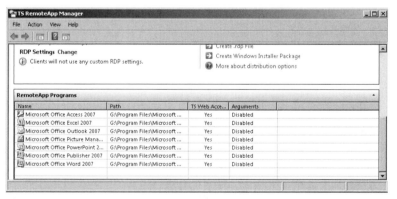

Figure 28-27 Review the list of available RemoteApps.

Deploying RemoteApps

RemoteApps appear as if they are running on the end user's local computer. Instead of being presented to the user on the desktop of the remote terminal server, RemoteApps run in their own resizable window and have their own entry on the taskbar. If a user is running more than one RemoteApp on the same terminal server, the RemoteApps will share the same Terminal Services session.

Users can access RemoteApps in several ways. They can:

- Access a link to the program on a Web site by using TS Web Access.

- Double-click a program icon on their desktop or Start menu that has been created and distributed by an administrator with a Windows Installer (.msi) package.

- Double-click a file where the file name extension is associated with a RemoteApp program. This can be configured by an administrator with a Windows Installer package.

- Double-click a Remote Desktop Protocol (.rdp) file that has been created and distributed by their administrator.

As a Terminal Services administrator, you'll need to configure related options to make these access techniques possible.

Accessing RemoteApps Using TS Web Access

With TS Web Access, you provide users with the Web address of the IIS server configured with TS Web Access and then they see a list of available RemoteApps that they can click to start, as shown in Figure 28-28. The default TS Web Access link is http://*ServerID*/ts/, where *ServerID* is the host name or IP address of the IIS server running TS Web Access. When a user accesses this link, he must sign in to the server by providing his user credentials. Afterward, he is forwarded to the default page for RemoteApp Programs automatically.

> **Note**
>
> The TS Web Access application running on the IIS server uses JScript, which might be a restricted feature in the Web browser. You can resolve this by changing the browser settings to allow JScript to run or by adding the Web site as a trusted site.

Figure 28-28 Users access RemoteApps on the IIS server running TS Web Access.

Chapter 28

When a user clicks the link for a RemoteApp, the RemoteApp Starting dialog box is displayed as shown in the following screen:

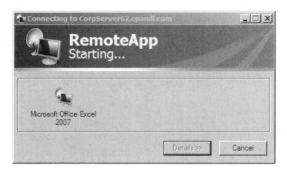

The user next sees a warning prompt with details about the remote connection being established as shown in the following screen:

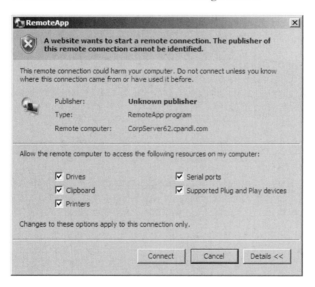

The preconfigured resources for the connection are available by default. The user can change these options as necessary (but cannot include resources restricted in Terminal Services). Clicking Connect runs the application. The user can then interact with the program that is running on the terminal server as if it were running locally.

Creating an .RDP File

You can use the RemoteApp Wizard to create a Remote Desktop Protocol (.rdp) file for any application in the RemoteApp Programs list. To do this, follow these steps:

1. Open TS RemoteApp Manager, right-click the program in the RemoteApp Programs list, and then choose Create .RDP File. Alternatively, to create an .rdp file for multiple programs, press and hold the Ctrl key when you select each program name, then right-click and choose Create .RDP File.

2. When the wizard starts, click Next. On the Specify Package Settings page, shown in the following screen, enter the location to save the .rdp file or click Browse to specify a new location to save the .rdp file. In the Terminal Server Settings area, as shown in the following screen, click Change to modify the terminal server or farm name, the Remote Desktop Protocol (RDP) port number, and the Require Server Authentication setting. Click OK when you are finished.

3. In the TS Gateway Settings area, click Change to specify TS Gateway settings. Click OK when you are finished.

4. To digitally sign the .rdp file, in the Certificate Settings area, click Change. Select the certificate that you want to use, and then click OK.

5. When you are finished, click Next. On the Review Settings page, click Finish. When the wizard is finished, the folder where the .rdp file was saved opens in a new window, allowing you to confirm that the .rdp file was created. This is the file you must distribute to users to access the RemoteApps.

Creating a Windows Installer Package

You can use the RemoteApp Wizard to create a Windows Installer package for any application in the RemoteApp Programs list. To do this, follow these steps:

1. Open TS RemoteApp Manager, right-click the program in the RemoteApp Programs list, and then select Create Windows Installer Package. Alternatively, to create a Windows Installer package for multiple programs, press and hold the Ctrl key when you select each program name, then right-click and select Create Windows Installer Package. Note that a separate Windows Installer package is created for each program.

CAUTION

Don't install Windows Installer packages that were created with this setting enabled on the terminal server itself. If you do, clients that use the Windows Installer packages might not be able to start the associated RemoteApp programs.

2. When the wizard starts, click Next. On the Specify Package Settings page, enter the location to save the installer package. Alternatively, click Browse to select a new location to save the installer package. In the Terminal Server Settings area, click Change to modify the terminal server or farm name, the Remote Desktop Protocol (RDP) port number, and the Require Server Authentication setting. Click OK when you are finished.

3. In the TS Gateway Settings area, click Change to specify TS Gateway settings. Click OK when you are finished.

4. To digitally sign the installer package, in the Certificate Settings area, click Change. Select the certificate that you want to use, and then click OK.

5. Click Next to continue. On the Configure Distribution Package page, shown in the following screen, specify where the shortcut icon for the program will appear on client computers. Shortcut icons can appear on the user's desktop, a named submenu of the Start menu, or both. The default submenu is Remote Programs.

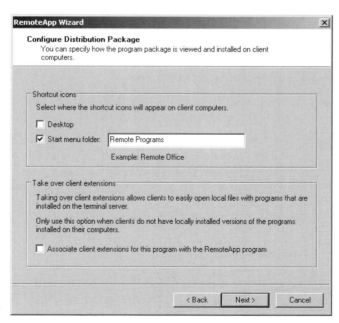

6. In the Take Over Client Extensions area, configure whether to associate the file name extensions on the client computer with the RemoteApp program or programs. If you do this, all file name extensions that are handled by the program or programs on the terminal server will also be associated on the client computer with the RemoteApp program or programs. Also, users are not prompted whether the terminal server should take over file extensions for the program or programs.

7. Click Next to continue. On the Review Settings page, review the settings and then click Finish. When the wizard is finished, the folder where the Windows Installer package was saved opens in a new window, allowing you to confirm that the Windows Installer (.msi) packages were created. You must distribute these packages to users so they can access the RemoteApps.

Configuring Deployment Settings for All RemoteApps

Deployment settings control how users connect to Terminal Services to access Remote-Apps. You can configure deployment settings using TS RemoteApp Manager and additional settings through Group Policy. Additional Group Policy settings are located in both the Computer Configuration and the User Configuration node under Administrative Templates\Windows Components\Terminal Services\Remote Desktop Connection Client.

To configure deployment settings for all RemoteApps, follow these steps:

1. Start TS RemoteApp Manager. In the Actions pane or on the Action menu, click Terminal Server Settings.

2. On the Terminal Server tab, shown in Figure 28-29, under Connection Settings, accept or modify the server or farm name, the Remote Desktop Protocol (RDP) port number, and server authentication settings.

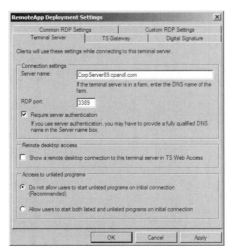

Figure 28-29 Configure general deployment settings for the terminal server.

Chapter 28

3. To provide a link to a full terminal server desktop session through TS Web Access, under Remote Desktop Access, select the Show A Remote Desktop Connection To This Terminal Server In TS Web Access check box.

4. Under Access To Unlisted Programs, choose either of the following:

- ○ **Do Not Allow Users To Start Unlisted Programs On Initial Connection (Recommended)** Use this setting to help protect against malicious users, or a user unintentionally starting a program from an .rdp file on initial connection. This setting does not prevent users from starting unlisted programs remotely after they connect to the terminal server by using a RemoteApp program.

- ○ **Allow Users To Start Both Listed And Unlisted Programs On Initial Connection** Use this setting to allow users to start any program remotely from an .rdp file on initial connection, not just those programs in the RemoteApp Programs list.

5. On the TS Gateway tab, shown in Figure 28-30, configure the desired TS Gateway behavior. You can configure whether to automatically detect the TS Gateway server settings, to use the TS Gateway server settings that you specify, or to not use a TS Gateway server. If you select Automatically Detect TS Gateway Server Settings, the client tries to use Group Policy settings to determine the behavior of client connections to TS Gateway.

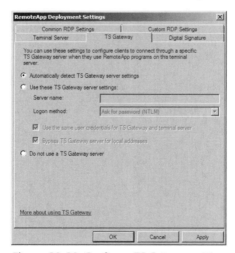

Figure 28-30 Configure TS Gateway settings.

6. The options on the Common RDP Settings tab control the preconfigured resources available when using RemoteApps. Under Devices And Resources, configure which devices and resources on the client computer you want to make available in the remote session. Under User Experience, choose whether to enable font smoothing and the desired color depth.

7. To configure additional RDP settings, such as audio redirection, click the Custom RDP Settings tab. Type the desired settings into the Custom RDP Settings box. Or, alternatively, copy the desired settings from an existing .rdp file and then paste them into the Custom RDP Settings box.

8. When you are finished, click Apply to save your deployment settings.

Modifying or Removing a RemoteApp Program

After you have added programs to the RemoteApp Programs list, you can easily modify the properties of a RemoteApp or delete a RemoteApp from the list. To change the properties of a RemoteApp, open TS RemoteApp Manager, right-click the program in the RemoteApp Programs list, and then choose Properties. You can then use the Properties dialog box to configure the desired settings.

To delete a program in the RemoteApp Programs list, open TS RemoteApp Manager, right-click the program in the RemoteApp Programs list, and then choose Remove. When prompted, click Yes to confirm the deletion. When you delete a program in the RemoteApp Programs list, any .rdp files or Windows Installer packages that you created for the RemoteApp are not deleted.

Using Terminal Services Manager

You can use Terminal Services Manager, shown in Figure 28-31, to inspect data about terminal servers in trusted domains. You can examine users, connections, sessions, or processes, as well as execute certain administrative commands against the remote terminal servers. Start Terminal Services Manager from the Administrative Tools menu or by typing **tsadmin.exe** at the command prompt.

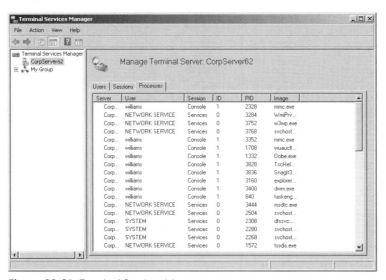

Figure 28-31 Terminal Services Manager.

Connecting to Terminal Servers

Unlike previous versions of Terminal Services Manager, the current version does not automatically enumerate all the terminal servers that are available. By right-clicking the Terminal Services Manager node in the console tree, you can perform the following actions:

- **Connect To Computer** Connect to a terminal server by name or IP address.

- **Refresh** Refresh the information related to the current servers you are working with.

- **Import From TS Session Broker** Allows you to import the farm and server names from a TS Session Broker that you specify. You must manually refresh the list to ensure that it is current.

- **New Group** Allows you to create a new group for tracking a group of related terminal servers.

After a server is listed, you can right-click its entry to perform one of these actions:

- **Add To Group** Adds the server to a specific group so it's more easily managed.

- **Remove From Group** Removes the server from a group.

- **Refresh** Refreshes information about that specific server only.

With groups, you can right-click the group entry to perform one of these actions:

- **Add Computer** Connects to a terminal server by name or IP address and adds it to the group.

- **Empty Group** Removes all terminal servers from the group but doesn't disconnect from the servers.

- **Disconnect All** Disconnects from all terminal servers in the group.

- **Refresh** Refreshes information about all servers in the group.

Getting Terminal Services Information

In the Terminal Services Manager console, terminal servers are organized by group or individual servers. When you select a group entry, the details pane on the right will display information about the related users, sessions, and processes for all servers in the group. After you expand a group entry, you can select a terminal server, and the details pane on the right will display information about the related users, sessions, and processes only for the selected server.

- When you select the Users tab in the right pane, you can view and manage user sessions. Each user with a current session is shown regardless of whether the session is active or inactive. See the following section, "Managing User Sessions in Terminal Services Manager," for more information.

- When you select the Sessions tab in the right pane, you can view and manage user and listener sessions. If users are permitted multiple sessions, this lets you see the individual sessions separately from the users who started them.

- When you select the Processes tab in the right pane, you can view and manage all running process on the server. If you right-click a process, you can select End Process to stop the process.

Managing User Sessions in Terminal Services Manager

Whenever you select a user entry or session in Terminal Services Manager, you can right-click the related entry to perform one of the following actions:

- **Connect** Allows you to connect to a user's session if you have the appropriate permissions. After you choose Connect, you are prompted to enter the user's password if the user running the session is different from your current user account. Note that the Connect option is available only if Terminal Services Manager is running on a remote machine and not locally on the terminal server.

- **Disconnect** Disconnects an active session. When a session is disconnected, all the processes in that session continue to run in a disconnected state. This means that no information is transmitted to the remote client. To disconnect multiple sessions, simply select all the sessions you want to disconnect, and then choose Disconnect from the Action menu.

- **Log Off** Logs the user off and ends any processes the user is currently running. You can use this option to free resources being used by a session. However, this can result in the loss of data if the user hasn't saved her work. This option is available only when you select the server entry in the left pane and the Users tab in the right pane.

- **Remote Control** Allows you to view or interact with a user's session. When you select Remote Control, you are prompted to set the shortcut key that can be used to log off the remote control session. The default shortcut key is Ctrl+Asterisk (*). By default, when you take remote control of a session, the user is notified and prompted to give permission. You won't be able to continue until the user clicks Yes to accept the request. If you don't want users to be prompted, you can change this behavior using the Remote Control tab in the RDP-Tcp Properties dialog box. Note that the Remote Control option is available only if Terminal Services Manager is running on a remote machine and not locally on the terminal server.

  It is important to note that remote control can be enabled or disabled globally through the Terminal Services Configuration tool and per user in each user's Properties dialog box.

- **Reset** Resets a user session that is frozen or unresponsive. When you reset a session, you terminate the session and free up all resources being used by the session. Unlike logging a user off, this action does not use the normal logoff processes. This means that not only could users lose data, but any changes they've made to their profiles or settings could also be lost. Use Reset only when a session cannot be logged off.

- **Send Message** Sends a console message to the user. To send the same console message to several users, simply select all the users to whom you want to send a message, and then choose Send Message from the Action menu.

- **Status** Displays the status of the user session.

Managing Terminal Services from the Command Line

In addition to the tools in Terminal Services Manager, there are quite a few command-line tools for working with Terminal Services. These commands can be divided into two categories:

- Gathering information

- Controlling user sessions

Gathering Terminal Services Information

Several commands are available for gathering Terminal Services information at an elevated command prompt including the following:

- Query Process [* | *ProcessId* | *UserName* | *SessionName* | /ID:*SessionId* | *ProgramName*] [/Server:*ServerName*]—Displays information about processes being run in Terminal Services sessions on the server.

- Query Session [*SessionName* | *UserName* | *SessionId*] [/Server:*ServerName*]—Displays information about Terminal Services sessions. You can also add /mode, /flow, /connect, and /counter options to get additional information about current line settings, flow control settings, connect settings, and counters, respectively.

- Query Termserver [*ServerName*] [/Domain:*domain*] [/Address]—Displays the available application terminal servers on the network. The /Address parameter adds network and node addresses to the output. Add the /continue option to remove the pause between screens of information.

- Query User [*UserName* | *SessionName* | *SessionId*] [/Server:*ServerName*]—Displays information about users logged on to the system.

These commands accept many common parameters, including the following:

- *ProcessId*—The ID of the process on the terminal server that you want to examine

- *ServerName*—The name of the remote terminal server you want to work with

- *SessionId*—The ID of the session on the terminal server that you want to examine

- *SessionName*—The name of the session on the terminal server that you want to examine

- *UserName*—The name of the user whose sessions or processes you want to examine

These commands are very helpful when you are looking for Terminal Services informa-tion and you do not have to use parameters to obtain information. If you type **query process** at the command line, you get a list of all processes being run in Terminal Ser-vices sessions on the local terminal server, for example:

```
USERNAME      SESSIONNAME    ID    PID      IMAGE
>wrstanek     console        0     3204     explorer.exe
>wrstanek     console        0     3372     mshta.exe
>wrstanek     console        0     3656     licmgr.exe
```

If you type **query session** at the command line, you get a list of all sessions on the local terminal server, for example:

```
SESSIONNAME    USERNAME     ID    STATE      TYPE      DEVICE
>console       wrstanek     0     Active     wdcon
```

If you type **query user** at the command prompt, you get a list of all users who have ses-sions on the local server, for example:

```
USERNAME      SESSIONNAME    ID    STATE      IDLE TIME    LOGON TIME
>wrstanek     console        0     Active     .            4/18/2008 11:15 AM
tomc          rdp-tcp#4      1     Active     1            4/18/2008 12:03 PM
```

If you type **query termserver** at the command prompt, you get a list of all known termi-nal servers in the enterprise:

```
Known Terminal servers
----------------------
TSSVR02
TSSVR03
TSSVR04
```

Query Is a Server Command in Windows Server 2008

The Query command is available in Windows Server 2008 but not from a desktop com-puter. If you are using Windows Vista as your desktop system, however, you can resolve this dilemma by copying the Query.exe command from a server to your desktop. Type **where query.exe** at the command line on the server to locate the command, and then copy the command to your desktop.

Managing User Sessions from the Command Line

When you want to manage user sessions from the command line, you can use these commands:

- Shadow [*SessionName* | *SessionId*] [/Server:*ServerName*] [/v]—Allows you to take remote control of a user's session

- TSCon [*SessionName* | *SessionId*] [/Password:*password*] [/v]–Allows you to connect to a user's session if you know that user's password

- TSDisCon [*SessionName* | *SessionId*] [/Server:*ServerName*] [/v]–Allows you to disconnect a user's session

- Reset Session [*SessionName* | *SessionId*] [/Server:*ServerName*] [/v]–Allows you to reset a user's session

- Logoff [*SessionName* | *SessionId*] [/Server:*ServerName*] [/v]–Allows you to log off a user's session

As you can see, all these commands accept similar parameters. These parameters include the following:

- *SessionName*–The name of the session on the terminal server that you want to work with

- *SessionId*–The ID of the session on the terminal server that you want to work with

- *ServerName*–The name of the remote terminal server you want to work with

These commands also allow you to set verbose output using the /V parameter.

Using these commands is fairly straightforward. For example, if you want to disconnect a user session with the session ID 2 on the remote server TS06, you'd type the command **tsdiscon 2 /server:ts06**.

If you are logged on locally to the terminal server, it's even easier, as all you have to type is **tsdiscon 2**.

Other Useful Terminal Services Commands

There are a few other useful commands for working with Terminal Services, including the following:

- Msg [*UserName* | *SessionName* | *@filename* | *SessionId* | ***] [/Server:*ServerName*] [*Message*]–Use Msg to send a console message to users by user name, session name, and session ID. Use the asterisk wildcard (*) to send the same message to all sessions on a designated server. Use *@filename* to specify a file containing a list of user names, session names, or both. Add /W to wait for acknowledgment and /Time:*numSecondsToWait* to set the time delay to wait for acknowledgment of the message.

- TSKill *ProcessId* | *ProcessName* [/Server:*ServerName*] [/ID:*SessionId* | /a] [/v]–Use TSKill to end a process using the process ID or process name. A process can be shut down for a particular session ID using /ID:*SessionID* or for all sessions running the process by using the option /a.

Configuring Terminal Services Per-User Settings

When you install Terminal Services, the properties pages of users are updated to include two additional tabs: Remote Control and Terminal Services Profile. The settings on these tabs can be used to configure per-user settings for Terminal Services.

Getting Remote Control of a User's Session

Being able to get remote control of a user's session is helpful for troubleshooting. Rather than guess what a user is trying to do when working with an application, you can view the user's session and see the mistakes yourself. If allowed, you can also take over a user's session and manipulate the session from your desktop while still allowing the user to view the session from the desktop. By watching the task being performed correctly, the user should be better able to perform the task independently next time.

By default, remote control is enabled and administrators are allowed to interact with user sessions. However, this occurs only if the user gives permission for an administrator to do so. Although global remote control settings for all users are set with the Terminal Services Configuration tool, you can change the settings for individual users as necessary. To do this, follow these steps:

1. Click Start, All Programs, Administrative Tools, and then Active Directory Users And Computers. In Active Directory Users And Computers, expand the organizational unit or container in which the user's account was created, and then double-click the account to display its Properties dialog box.

2. As shown in Figure 28-32, select the Remote Control tab. If you want to configure the account so that it cannot be controlled remotely, clear the Enable Remote Control check box. Otherwise, select the Enable Remote Control check box and configure the way in which remote control works, as follows:

   ○ If you want to ensure that permission is required to view or interact with a user's account, select the Require User's Permission check box.

   ○ If you want to be able to remotely control a user's account without explicit permission, clear the Require User's Permission check box.

3. Afterward, set the level of control allowed as follows:

   ○ If you want only to be able to view the account, select View The User's Session.

   ○ If you want to be able to view and take control of the account, select Interact With The Session.

4. Click OK.

Chapter 28

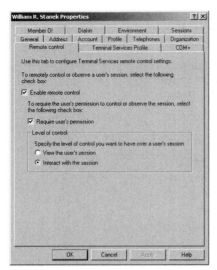

Figure 28-32 Enable and configure remote control of an individual user's account.

Setting Up the Terminal Services Profile for Users

All user accounts have a separate Terminal Services profile and home directory, which is used when the users log on to a terminal server. To configure these optional settings, follow these steps:

1. Click Start, All Programs, Administrative Tools, and then Active Directory Users And Computers. In Active Directory Users And Computers, expand the organizational unit or container in which the user's account was created, and then double-click the account to display its Properties dialog box.

2. As shown in Figure 28-33, select the Terminal Services Profile tab. Using this tab, you can set the following fields:

    ○   *Profile Path*–The path to the user's Terminal Services profile. Terminal Services profiles provide the environment settings for users when they connect to a terminal server. Each time a user logs on to a terminal server, that user's profile determines desktop and Control Panel settings, the availability of menu options and applications, and so on. Typically, you set the profile path to a network share and use the %UserName% environment variable to set a user-specific profile path.

    ○   *Terminal Services Home Folder*–The directory in which the user should store files when connected to Terminal Services. Assign a specific directory for the user's files as a local path on the user's system or a connected network drive. If the directory is available to the network, the user can access the directory regardless of which computer is used to connect to Terminal Services.

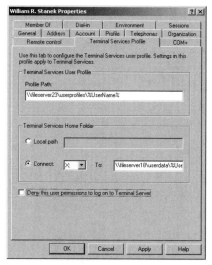

Figure 28-33 Configure the Terminal Services profile for a user as necessary to help customize an individual environment.

3. The Deny This User Permission To Log On To Terminal Server option controls whether a user can log on to a terminal server. If you select this check box, a user who tries to connect to Terminal Services will get an error message stating that the logon privilege has been disabled.

4. Click OK.

PART 5

Managing Active Directory and Security

Active Directory Architecture

Active Directory is an extensible directory service that enables you to manage network resources efficiently. A directory service does this by storing detailed information about each network resource, which makes it easier to provide basic lookup and authentication. Being able to store large amounts of information is a key objective of a directory service, but the information must be also organized so that it is easily searched and retrieved.

Active Directory provides for authenticated search and retrieval of information by dividing the physical and logical structure of the directory into separate layers. Understanding the physical structure of Active Directory is important for understanding how a directory service works. Understanding the logical structure of Active Directory is important for implementing and managing a directory service.

Active Directory Physical Architecture

Active Directory's physical layer controls the following features:

- How directory information is accessed

- How directory information is stored on the hard disk of a server

Active Directory Physical Architecture: A Top-Level View

From a physical or machine perspective, Active Directory is part of the security subsystem (see Figure 29-1). The security subsystem runs in user mode. User-mode applications do not have direct access to the operating system or hardware. This means that requests from user-mode applications have to pass through the executive services layer and must be validated before being executed.

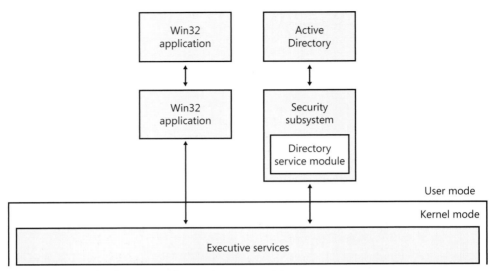

Figure 29-1 Top-level overview of Active Directory architecture.

> **Note**
> Being part of the security subsystem makes Active Directory an integrated part of the access control and authentication mechanism built into Windows Server 2008. Access control and authentication protect the resources in the directory.

Each resource in Active Directory is represented as an object. Anyone who tries to gain access to an object must be granted permission. Lists of permissions that describe who or what can access an object are referred to as access control lists (ACLs). Each object in the directory has an associated ACL.

You can restrict permissions across a broader scope by using Group Policy. The security infrastructure of Active Directory uses policy to enforce security models on several objects that are grouped logically. Trust relationships between groups of objects can also be set up to allow for an even broader scope for security controls between trusted groups of objects that need to interact. From a top-level perspective, that's how Active Directory works, but to really understand Active Directory, you need to delve into the security subsystem.

Active Directory Within the Local Security Authority

Within the security subsystem, Active Directory is a subcomponent of the Local Security Authority (LSA). As shown in Figure 29-2, the LSA consists of many components that provide the security features of Windows Server 2008 and ensure that access control and authentication function as they should. Not only does the LSA manage local security policy, it also performs the following functions:

- Generates security identifiers

- Provides the interactive process for logon

- Manages auditing

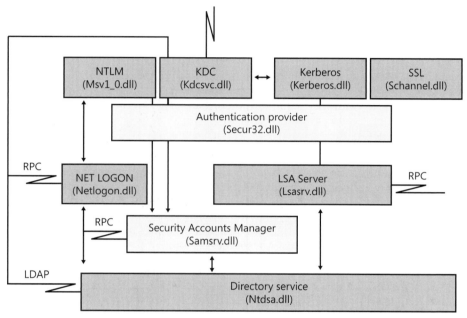

Figure 29-2 Windows Server 2008 security subsystem using Active Directory.

When you work through the security subsystem as it is used with Active Directory, you'll find the three following key areas:

- Authentication mechanisms
  - NTLM (Msv1_0.dll) used for Windows NT LAN Manager (NTLM) authentication
  - Kerberos (Kerberos.dll) and Key Distribution Center (Kdcsvc.dll) used for Kerberos V5 authentication
  - SSL (Schannel.dll) used for Secure Sockets Layer (SSL) authentication
  - Authentication provider (Secur32.dll) used to manage authentication

- Logon/access control mechanisms
  - NET LOGON (Netlogon.dll) used for interactive logon via NTLM. For NTLM authentication, NET LOGON passes logon credentials to the directory service module and returns the security identifiers for objects to clients making requests.

- LSA Server (Lsasrv.dll) used to enforce security policies for Kerberos and SSL. For Kerberos and SSL authentication, LSA Server passes logon credentials to the directory service module and returns the security identifiers for objects to clients making requests.

- Security Accounts Manager (Samsrv.dll) used to enforce security policies for NTLM.

- Directory service component

  - Directory service (Ntdsa.dll) used to provide directory services for Windows Server 2008. This is the actual module that allows you to perform authenticated searches and retrieval of information.

As you can see, users are authenticated before they can work with the directory service component. Authentication is handled by passing a user's security credentials to a domain controller. After they are authenticated on the network, users can work with resources and perform actions according to the permissions and rights they have been granted in the directory. At least, this is how the Windows Server 2008 security subsystem works with Active Directory.

When you are on a network that doesn't use Active Directory or when you log on locally to a machine other than a domain controller, the security subsystem works as shown in Figure 29-3. Here, the directory service is not used. Instead, authentication and access control are handled through the Security Accounts Manager (SAM). This is, in fact, the model used for authentication and access control in Microsoft Windows NT 4. In this model, information about resources is stored in the SAM, which itself is stored in the Registry.

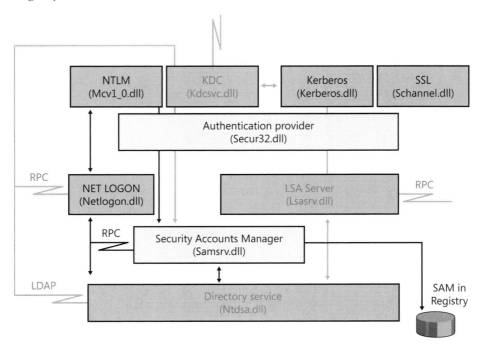

Figure 29-3 Windows Server 2008 security subsystem without Active Directory.

Directory Service Architecture

As you've seen, incoming requests are passed through the security subsystem to the directory service component. The directory service component is designed to accept requests from many different kinds of clients. As shown in Figure 29-4, these clients use specific protocols to interact with Active Directory.

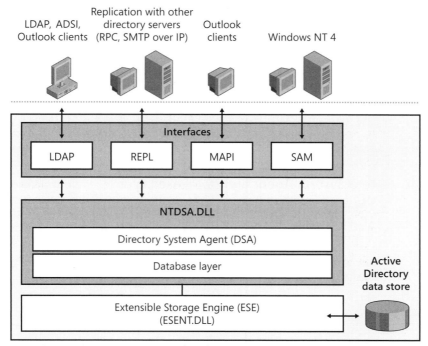

Figure 29-4 The directory service architecture.

Protocols and Client Interfaces

The primary protocol for Active Directory access is Lightweight Directory Access Protocol (LDAP). LDAP is an industry-standard protocol for directory access that runs over TCP/IP. Active Directory supports LDAP versions 2 and 3. Clients can use LDAP to query and manage directory information, depending on the level of permissions they have been granted, by establishing a TCP connection to a domain controller running the directory service. The default TCP port used by LDAP clients is 389 for standard communications and 636 for SSL.

Active Directory supports intersite and intrasite replication through the REPL interface, which uses either Remote Procedure Calls (RPCs) or Simple Mail Transport Protocol over Internet Protocol (SMTP over IP), depending on how replication is configured. Each domain controller is responsible for replicating changes to the directory to other domain controllers, using a multimaster approach. Unlike Windows NT 4, which used a single primary domain controller and one or more backup domain controllers, the multimaster approach used in Active Directory allows updates to be made to the directory, via any domain controller, and then replicated to other domain controllers. For Windows Server 2008, the algorithms used for replication have been improved to reduce the performance impact on domain controllers and improve the overall replication performance.

For older messaging clients, Active Directory supports the Messaging Application Programming Interface (MAPI). MAPI allows messaging clients to access Active Directory (which is used by Microsoft Exchange for storing information), primarily for address book lookups. Messaging clients use Remote Procedure Calls (RPCs) to establish connection with the directory service. UDP port 135 and TCP port 135 are used by the RPC Endpoint Mapper. Current messaging clients use LDAP instead of RPC.

For clients running Windows NT 4, Active Directory supports the Security Accounts Manager (SAM) interface, which also uses RPCs. This allows Windows NT 4 clients to access the Active Directory data store the same way they would access the SAM database. The SAM interface is also used during replication with Windows NT 4 backup domain controllers.

Directory System Agent and Database Layer

Clients and other servers use the LDAP, REPL, MAPI, and SAM interfaces to communicate with the directory service component (Ntdsa.dll) on a domain controller. From an abstract perspective, the directory service component consists of the following:

- Directory System Agent (DSA), which provides the interfaces through which clients and other servers connect

- Database Layer, which provides an Application Programming Interface (API) for working with the Active Directory data store

From a physical perspective, the DSA is really the directory service component, and the database layer resides within it. The reason for separating the two is that the database layer performs a vital abstraction. Without this abstraction, the physical database on the disk would not be protected from the applications the DSA interacts with. Furthermore, the object-based hierarchy used by Active Directory would not be possible. Why? Because the data store is in a single data file using a flat (record-based) structure, while the database layer is used to represent the flat file records as objects within a hierarchy of containers. Like a folder that can contain files as well as other folders, a container is simply a type of object that can contain other objects as well as other containers.

Each object in the data store has a name relative to the container in which it is stored. This name is aptly called the object's relative distinguished name (RDN). An object's full name, also referred to as an object's distinguished name (DN), describes the series of logical containers, from the highest to the lowest, of which the object is a part.

To make sure every object stored in Active Directory is truly unique, each object also has a globally unique identifier (GUID), which is generated when the object is created. Unlike an object's RDN or DN, which can be changed by renaming an object or moving it to another container, the GUID can never be changed. It is assigned to an object by the DSA and it never changes.

The DSA is responsible for ensuring that the type of information associated with an object adheres to a specific set of rules. This set of rules is referred to as the *schema*. The schema is stored in the directory and contains the definitions of all object classes and describes their attributes. In Active Directory, the schema is the set of rules that determine the kind of data that can be stored in the database, the type of information that can be associated with a particular object, the naming conventions for objects, and so on.

INSIDE OUT   The schema saves space and helps validate attributes

The schema serves to separate an object's definition from its actual values. Thanks to the schema, Active Directory doesn't have to write information about all of an object's possible attributes when it creates the object. When you create an object, only the defined attributes are stored in the object's record. This saves a lot of space in the database. Furthermore, as the schema not only specifies the valid attributes but also the valid values for those attributes, Active Directory uses the schema both to validate the attributes that have been set on an object and to keep track of what other possible attributes are available.

The DSA is also responsible for enforcing security limitations. It does this by reading the security identifiers (SIDs) on a client's access token and comparing it with that of the SID for an object. If a client has appropriate access permissions, it is granted access to an object. If a client doesn't have appropriate access permissions, it is denied access.

Finally, the DSA is used to initiate replication. Replication is the essential functionality that ensures that the information stored on domain controllers is accurate and consistent with changes that have been made. Without proper replication, the data on servers would become stale and outdated.

Extensible Storage Engine

The Extensible Storage Engine (ESE) is used by Active Directory to retrieve information from and write information to the data store. The ESE uses indexed and sequential storage with transactional processing, as follows:

- **Indexed storage** Indexing the data store allows the ESE to access data quickly without having to search the entire database. In this way, the ESE can rapidly retrieve, write, and update data.

- **Sequential storage** Sequentially storing data means that the ESE writes data as a stream of bits and bytes. This allows data to be read from and written to specific locations.

- **Transactional processing** Transactional processing ensures that changes to the database are applied as discrete operations that can be rolled back if necessary.

Chapter 29

Any data that is modified in a transaction is copied to a temporary database file. This gives two views of the data that is being changed: one view for the process changing the data and one view of the original data that is available to other processes until the transaction is finalized. A transaction remains open as long as changes are being processed. If an error occurs during processing, the transaction can be rolled back to return the object being modified to its original state. If Active Directory finishes processing changes without errors occurring, the transaction can be committed.

As with most databases that use transactional processing, Active Directory maintains a transaction log. A record of the transaction is written first to an in-memory copy of an object, then to the transaction log, and finally to the database. The in-memory copy of an object is stored in the version store. The version store is an area of physical memory (RAM) used for processing changes. If a domain controller has 400 megabytes (MB) of RAM or more, the version store is 100 MB. If a domain controller has less than 400 MB of RAM, the version store is 25 percent of the physical RAM.

The transaction log serves as a record of all changes that have yet to be committed to the database file. The transaction is written first to the transaction log to ensure that even if the database shuts down immediately afterward, the change is not lost and can take effect. To ensure this, Active Directory uses a checkpoint file to track the point up to which transactions in the log file have been committed to the database file. After a transaction is committed to the database file, it can be cleared out of the transaction log.

The actual update of the database is written from the in-memory copy of the object in the version store and not from the transaction log. This reduces the number of disk I/O operations and helps ensure that updates can keep pace with changes. When many updates are made, however, the version store can reach a point where it is overwhelmed. This happens when the version store reaches 90 percent of its maximum size. When this happens, the ESE temporarily stops processing cleanup operations that are used to return space after an object is modified or deleted from the database.

Because changes need to be replicated from one domain controller to another, an object that is deleted from the database isn't fully removed. Instead, most of the object's attributes are removed and the object's Deleted attribute is set to TRUE to indicate that it has been deleted. The object is then moved to a hidden Deleted Objects container where its deletion can be replicated to other domain controllers. In this state, the object is said to be *tombstoned*. To allow the tombstoned state to be replicated to all domain controllers, and thus removed from all copies of the database, an attribute called tombstoneLifetime is also set on the object. The tombstoneLifetime attribute specifies how long the tombstoned object should remain in the Deleted Objects container. The default lifetime is 180 days.

The ESE uses a garbage-collection process to clear out tombstoned objects after the tombstone lifetime has expired and performs automatic online defragmentation of the database after garbage collection. The interval at which garbage collection occurs is a factor of the value set for the garbageCollPeriod attribute and the tombstone lifetime. By default, garbage collection occurs every 12 hours. When there are more than 5,000 tombstoned objects to be garbage-collected, the ESE removes the first 5,000 tombstoned objects, and then uses the CPU availability to determine if garbage collection can continue. If no other process is waiting for the CPU, garbage collection continues for up to the next 5,000 tombstoned objects whose tombstone lifetime has expired and the CPU availability is again checked to determine if garbage collection can continue. This process continues until all the tombstoned objects whose tombstone lifetime has expired are deleted or another process needs access to the CPU.

Data Store Architecture

After you have examined the operating system components that support Active Directory, the next step is to see how directory data is stored on a domain controller's hard disks. As Figure 29-5 shows, the data store has a primary data file and several other types of related files, including working files and transaction logs.

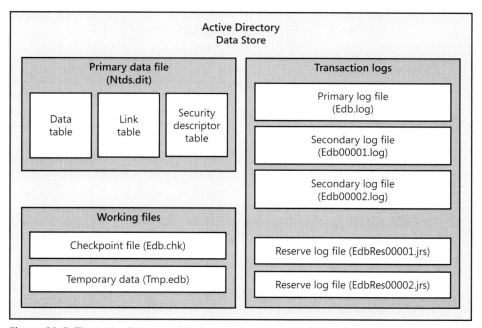

Figure 29-5 The Active Directory data store.

These files are used as follows:

- **Primary data file (Ntds.dit)** Physical database file that holds the contents of the Active Directory data store

- **Checkpoint file (Edb.chk)** Checkpoint file that tracks the point up to which the transactions in the log file have been committed to the database file

- **Temporary data (Tmp.edb)** Temporary workspace for processing transactions

- **Primary log file (Edb.log)** Primary log file that contains a record of all changes that have yet to be committed to the database file

- **Secondary log files (Edb00001.log, Edb00002.log, …)** Additional logs files that are used as needed

- **Reserve log files (EdbRes00001.jrs, EdbRes00002.jrs, …)** Files that are used to reserve space for additional log files if the primary log file becomes full

The primary data file contains three indexed tables:

- **Active Directory data table** The data table contains a record for each object in the data store, which can include object containers, the objects themselves, and any other type of data that is stored in Active Directory.

- **Active Directory link table** The link table is used to represent linked attributes. A linked attribute is an attribute that refers to other objects in Active Directory. For example, if an object contains other objects (that is, it is a container), attribute links are used to point to the objects in the container.

- **Active Directory security descriptor table** The security descriptor table contains the inherited security descriptors for each object in the data store. Windows Server 2008 uses this table so that inherited security descriptors no longer have to be duplicated on each object. Instead, inherited security descriptors are stored in this table and linked to the appropriate objects. This makes Active Directory authentication and control mechanisms much more efficient than they were in Microsoft Windows 2000.

Think of the data table as having rows and columns; the intersection of a row and a column is a field. The table's rows correspond to individual instances of an object. The table's columns correspond to attributes defined in the schema. The table's fields are populated only if an attribute contains a value. Fields can be a fixed or a variable length. If you create an object and define only 10 attributes, only these 10 attributes will contain values. Although some of those values might be fixed length, other might be variable length.

Records in the data table are stored in data pages that have a fixed size of 8 kilobytes (KB, or 8,192 bytes). Each data page has a page header, data rows, and free space that can contain row offsets. The page header uses the first 96 bytes of each page, leaving 8,096 bytes for data and row offsets. Row offsets indicate the logical order of rows on a page, which means that offset 0 refers to the first row in the index, offset 1 refers to the second row, and so on. If a row contains long, variable-length data, the data may not be stored with the rest of the data for that row. Instead, Active Directory can store an 8-byte pointer to the actual data, which is stored in a collection of 8-KB pages that aren't necessarily written contiguously. In this way, an object and all its attribute values can be much larger than 8 KB.

The primary log file has a fixed size of 10 MB. When this log fills up, Active Directory creates additional (secondary) log files as necessary. The secondary log files are also limited to a fixed size of 10 MB. Active Directory uses the reserve log files to reserve space on disk for log files that may need to be created. As several reserve files are already created, this speeds up the transactional logging process when additional logs are needed.

By default, the primary data file, working files, and transaction logs are all stored in the same location. On a domain controller's system volume, you'll find these files in the %SystemRoot%\NTDS folder. Although these are the only files used for the data store, there are other files used by Active Directory. For example, policy files and other files, such as startup and shutdown scripts used by the DSA, are stored in the %System-Root%\Sysvol folder.

> **Note**
>
> A distribution copy of Ntds.dit is also placed in the %SystemRoot%\System32 folder. This is used to create a domain controller when you install Active Directory on a server running Windows Server 2008. If the file doesn't exist, the Active Directory Installation Wizard will need the installation CD to promote a member server to be a domain controller.

INSIDE OUT   The log files have attributes you can examine

When you stop Active Directory Domain Services, you can use the Extensible Storage Engine Utility (esentutl.exe) to examine log file properties. At an elevated command prompt, enter **esentutl.exe -ml** *LogName* where *LogName* is the name of the log file to examine, such as edb.log, to obtain detailed information on the log file, including base name, creation time, format version, log sector sizes, and logging parameters. While Active Directory Domain Services is offline, you can also use esentutl.exe to perform defragmentation, integrity checks, copy, repair, and recovery operations. To learn more about this utility, enter **esentutl.exe** at an elevated command prompt. Following the prompts, you can then enter the letter corresponding to the operation you want to learn more about. For example, enter **esentutl.exe** and then press the D key to learn the defragmentation options.

Active Directory Logical Architecture

The logical layer of Active Directory determines how you see the information contained in the data store and also controls access to that information. The logical layer does this by defining the namespaces and naming schemes used to access resources stored in the directory. This provides a consistent way to access directory-stored information regardless of type. For example, you can obtain information about a printer resource stored in the directory in much the same way that you can obtain information about a user resource.

To better understand Active Directory's logical architecture, you need to understand the following topics:

- Active Directory objects
- Active Directory domains, trees, and forests
- Active Directory trusts
- Active Directory namespaces and partitions
- Active Directory data distribution

Active Directory Objects

Because so many different types of resources can be stored in the directory, a standard storage mechanism was needed and Microsoft developers decided to use the LDAP model for organizing data. In this model, each resource that you want to represent in the directory is created as an object with attributes that define information you want to store about the resource. For example, the user object in Active Directory has attributes for a user's first name, middle initial, last name, and logon name.

An object that holds other objects is referred to as a *container object* or simply a *container*. The data store itself is a container that contains other containers and objects. An object that can't contain other objects is a *leaf object*. Each object created within the directory is of a particular type or class. The object classes are defined in schema and include the following types:

- User
- Group
- Computer
- Printer
- Organizational unit

When you create an object in the directory, you must comply with the schema rules for that object class. Not only do the schema rules dictate the available attributes for an object class, they also dictate which attributes are mandatory and which attributes are optional. When you create an object, mandatory attributes must be defined. For example, you can't create a user object without specifying the user's full name and logon name. The reason is that these attributes are mandatory.

Some rules for attributes are defined in policy as well. For example, the default security policy for Windows Server 2008 specifies that a user account must have a password and the password must meet certain complexity requirements. If you try to create a user account without a password or with a password that doesn't meet these complexity requirements, the account creation will fail because of the security policy.

The schema can be extended or changed as well. This allows administrators to define new object classes, to add attributes to existing objects, and to change the way attributes are used. However, you need special access permissions and privileges to work directly with the schema.

Active Directory Domains, Trees, and Forests

Within the directory, objects are organized using a hierarchical tree structure called a *directory tree*. The structure of the hierarchy is derived from the schema and is used to define the parent-child relationships of objects stored in the directory.

A logical grouping of objects that allows central management of those objects is called a *domain*. In the directory tree, a domain is itself represented as an object. It is in fact the parent object of all the objects it contains. Unlike Windows NT 4.0, which limited the number of objects you could store in a domain, an Active Directory domain can contain millions of objects. Because of this, you probably do not need to create separate user and resource domains as was done commonly with Windows NT 4.0. Instead, you can create a single domain that contains all the resources you want to manage centrally. In Figure 29-6, a domain object is represented by a large triangle and the objects it contains are as shown.

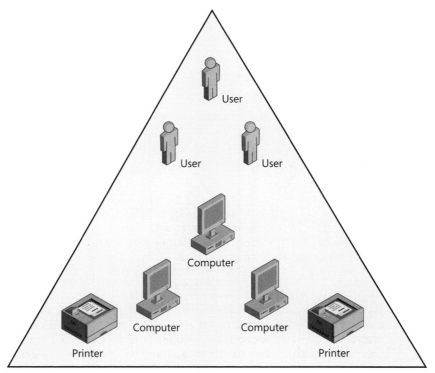

Figure 29-6 An Active Directory domain.

Domains are only one of several building blocks for implementing Active Directory structures. Other building blocks include the following:

- Active Directory trees, which are logical groupings of domains

- Active Directory forests, which are logical groupings of domain trees

As described above, a directory tree is used to represent a hierarchy of objects, showing the parent-child relationships between those objects. Thus, when we're talking about a domain tree, we're looking at the relationship between parent and child domains. The domain at the top of the domain tree is referred to as the *root domain (think of this as an upside-down tree)*. More specifically, the root domain is the first domain created in a new tree within Active Directory. When talking about forests and domains, there is an important distinction made between the first domain created in a new forest—a forest root domain—and the first domain created in each additional tree within a forest—a root domain.

In the example shown in Figure 29-7, cohovineyard.com is the root domain in an Active Directory forest with a single tree, that is, it is the forest root domain. As such, cohovineyard.com is the parent of the sales.cohovineyard.com domain and the mf.cohovineyard.com domain. The mf.cohovineyard.com domain itself has a related subdomain: bottling.mf.cohovineyard.com. This makes mf.cohovineyard.com the parent of the child domain bottling.mf.cohovineyard.com.

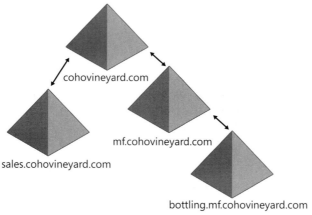

Figure 29-7 An Active Directory forest with a single tree.

The most important thing to note about this and all domain trees is that the namespace is contiguous. Here, all the domains are part of the cohovineyard.com namespace. If a domain is a part of a different namespace, it can be added as part of a new tree in the forest. In the example shown in Figure 29-8, a second tree is added to the forest. The root domain of the second tree is cohowinery.com, and this domain has cs.cohowinery.com as a child domain. The forest root domain does not change; cohovineyard.com remains the forest root domain.

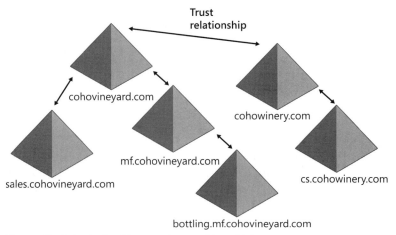

Figure 29-8 An Active Directory forest with multiple trees.

You create a forest root domain by installing Active Directory on a stand-alone server and establishing the server as the first domain controller in a new forest. To add an additional tree to an existing forest, you install Active Directory on a stand-alone server and configure the server as a member of the forest, but with a domain name that is not part of the current namespace being used. You make the new domain part of the same forest to allow associations called trusts to be made between domains that belong to different namespaces.

Active Directory Trusts

In Active Directory, two-way transitive trusts are established automatically between domains that are members of the same forest. Trusts join parent and child domains in the same domain tree and join the roots of domain trees. Because trusts are transitive, this means that if domain A trusts domain B and domain B trusts domain C, domain A trusts domain C as well. As all trusts in Active Directory are two-way and transitive, by default every domain in a forest implicitly trusts every other domain. It also means that resources in any domain are available to users in every domain in the forest. For example, with the trust relationships in place, a user in the sales.cohovineyard.com domain could access a printer or other resources in the cohovineyard.com domain or even the cs.cohowinery.com domain.

However, the creation of a trust doesn't imply any specific permission. Instead, it implies only the ability to grant permissions. No privileges are automatically implied or inherited by the establishment of a trust relationship. The trust doesn't grant or deny any permission. It only exists to allow administrators to be able to grant permissions.

There are several key terms used to describe trusts, including the following:

- **Trusting domain** A domain that establishes a trust is referred to as a trusting domain. Trusting domains allow access by users from another domain (the trusted domain).

- **Trusted domain** A domain that trusts another domain is referred to as a trusted domain. Users in trusted domains have access to another domain (the trusting domain).

To make it easier for administrators to grant access throughout a forest, Active Directory allows you to designate two types of administrators:

- **Enterprise administrators** Enterprise administrators, which are the designated administrators of the enterprise. Enterprise administrators can manage and grant access to resources in any domain in the Active Directory forest.

- **Domain administrators** Domain administrators, which are the designated administrators of a particular domain. Domain administrators in a trusting domain can access user accounts in a trusted domain and set permissions that grant access to resources in the trusting domain.

Going back to the example, an enterprise administrator in this forest could grant access to resources in any domain in the forest. If Jim, in the sales.cohovineyard.com domain, needed access to a printer in the cs.cohowinery.com domain, an enterprise administrator could grant this access. As cs.cohowinery.com is the trusting domain and sales.cohovineyard.com is the trusted domain in this example, a domain administrator in the cs.cohowinery.com could grant permission to use the printer as well. A domain administrator for sales.cohovineyard.com could not grant such permissions, however, as the printer resource exists in a domain other than the one the administrator controls.

To continue working with Figure 29-8, take a look at the arrows that designate the trust relationships. For a user in the sales.cohovineyard.com domain to access a printer in the cs.cohowinery.com domain, the request must pass through the following series of trust relationships:

1. The trust between sales.cohovineyard.com and cohovineyard.com

2. The trust between cohovineyard.com and cohowinery.com

3. The trust between cohowinery.com and cs.cohowinery.com

The *trust path* defines the path that an authentication request must take between the two domains. Here, a domain controller in the user's local domain (sales.cohovineyard.com) would pass the request to a domain controller in the cohovineyard.com domain. This domain controller would in turn pass the request to a domain controller in the cohowinery.com domain. Finally, the request would be passed to a domain controller in the cs.cohowinery.com domain, which would ultimately grant or deny access.

In all, the user's request has to pass through four domain controllers—one for each domain between the user and the resource. Because the domain structure is separate from your network's physical structure, the printer could actually be located right beside the user's desk and the user would still have to go through this process. If you expand this scenario to include all the users in the sales.cohovineyard.com domain, you could potentially have many hundreds of users whose requests have to go through a similar process to access resources in the cs.cohowinery.com domain.

Omitting the fact that the domain design in this scenario is very poor—because if many users are working with resources, those resources are ideally in their own domain or a domain closer in the tree—one solution for this problem would be to establish a shortcut trust between the user's domain and the resource's domain. With a shortcut trust, you could specify that cs.cohowinery.com explicitly trusts sales.cohovineyard.com. Now when a user in the sales.cohovineyard.com requests a resource in the cs.cohowinery.com domain, the local domain controller knows about cs.cohowinery.com and can directly submit the request for authentication. This means that the sales.cohovineyard.com domain controller sends the request directly to a cs.cohowinery.com domain controller.

Shortcut trusts are meant to help make more efficient use of resources on a busy network. On a network with a lot of activity, the explicit trust can reduce the overhead on servers and on the network as a whole. Shortcut trusts shouldn't be implemented without careful planning. They should only be used when resources in one domain will be accessed by users in another domain on a regular basis. They don't need to be used between two domains that have a parent-child relationship, because a default trust already exists explicitly between a parent and a child domain.

With Active Directory, you can also make use of external trusts that work the same they did in Windows NT 4. External trusts are manually configured and are always nontransitive. One of the primary reasons for establishing an external trust is to create a trust between an Active Directory domain and a legacy Windows NT domain. In this way, existing Windows NT domains continue to be available to users while you are implementing Active Directory. For example, you could upgrade your company's main domain from Windows NT 4 to Windows Server 2008, and then create external trusts between any other Windows NT domains. You should create these external trusts as two-way trusts to ensure that users can access resources as their permissions allow.

Active Directory Namespaces and Partitions

Any data stored in the Active Directory database is represented logically as an object. Every object in the directory has a relative distinguished name (RDN). That is, every object has a name relative to the parent container in which it is stored. The relative name is the name of the object itself and is also referred to as an object's *common name*. This relative name is stored as an attribute of the object and must be unique for the container in which it is located. Following this, no two objects in a container can have the same common name, but two objects in different containers could have the same name.

In addition to an RDN, objects also have a distinguished name (DN). An object's DN describes the object's place in the directory tree and is logically the series of containers from the highest to the lowest of which the object is a part. It is called a distinguished name because it serves to distinguish like-named objects and as such must be unique in the directory. No two objects in the directory will have the same distinguished name.

Every object in the directory has a parent, except the root of the directory tree, which is referred to as the rootDSE. The rootDSE represents the top of the logical namespace for a directory. It has no name *per se*. Although there is only one rootDSE, the information stored in the rootDSE specifically relates to the domain controller on which the directory is stored. In a domain with multiple domain controllers, the rootDSE will have a slightly different representation on each domain controller. The representation relates to the capability and configuration of the domain controller in question. In this way, Active Directory clients can determine the capabilities and configuration of a particular domain controller.

Below the rootDSE, every directory tree has a root domain. The root domain is the first domain created in an Active Directory forest and is also referred to as the forest root domain. After it is established, the forest root domain never changes, even if you add new trees to the forest. The LDAP distinguished name of the forest root domain is: DC=*ForestRootDomainName* where DC is an LDAP identifier for a domain component and *ForestRootDomainName* is the actual name of the forest root domain. Each level within the domain tree is broken out as a separate domain component. For example, if the forest root domain is cohovineyard.com, the domain's distinguished name is DC=cohovineyard,DC=com.

When Active Directory is installed on the first domain controller in a new forest, three containers are created below the rootDSE:

- Forest Root Domain container, which is the container for the objects in the forest root domain

- Configuration container, which is the container for the default configuration and all policy information

- Schema container, which is the container for all objects, classes, attributes, and syntaxes

From a logical perspective, these containers are organized as shown in Figure 29-9. The LDAP identifier for an object's common name is CN. The DN for the Configuration container is CN=configuration,DC=*ForestRootDomainName* and the DN for the Schema container is CN=schema,CN=configuration,DC=*ForestRootDomainName*. In the cohovineyard.com domain, the DNs for the Configuration and Schema containers are CN=configuration,DC=cohovineyard,DC=com and CN=schema,CN=configuration,DC= cohovineyard,DC=com, respectively. As you can see, the distinguished name allows you to walk the directory tree from the relative name of the object you are working with to the forest root.

As shown in the figure, the forest root domain and the Configuration and Schema containers exist within their own individual partitions. Active Directory uses partitions to logically apportion the directory so that each domain controller does not have to store a complete copy of the entire directory. To do this, object names are used to group objects into logical categories so that the objects can be managed and replicated as appropriate. The largest logical category is a directory partition. All directory partitions are created as instances of the domainDNS object class.

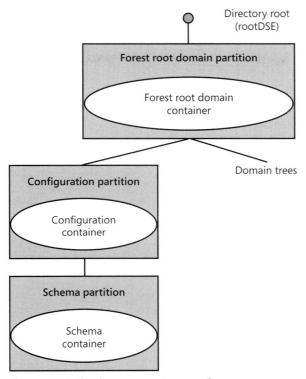

Figure 29-9 The directory tree in a new forest.

As far as Active Directory is concerned, a domain is a container of objects that is logi-cally partitioned from other container objects. When you create a new domain in Active Directory, you create a new container object in the directory tree, and that container is in turn contained by a domain directory partition for the purposes of management and replication.

Active Directory Data Distribution

Active Directory uses partitions to help distribute three general types of data:

- Domain-wide data, which is data replicated to every domain controller in a domain

- Forest-wide data, which is data replicated to every domain controller in a forest

- Application data, which is data replicated to an arbitrary set of domain controllers

Every domain controller stores at least one domain directory partition as well as two forest-wide data partitions: the schema partition and the configuration partition. Data in a domain directory partition is replicated to every domain controller in the domain as a writable replica.

Forest-wide data partitions are replicated to every domain controller in the forest. The configuration partition is replicated as a writable replica. The schema partition is replicated as a read-only replica and the only writable replica is stored on a domain controller that is designated as having the schema operations master role. Other operations master roles are defined as well.

Active Directory can replicate application-specific data that is stored in an application partition such as the default application partitions used with zones in Domain Name System (DNS) that are integrated with Active Directory. Application partition data is replicated on a forest-wide, domain-wide, or other basis to domain controllers that have a particular application partition. If a domain controller doesn't have an application partition, it doesn't receive a replica of the application partition.

> **Note**
>
> Application partitions can be created on domain controllers running only Windows Server 2003 and later. Domain controllers running Windows 2000 or earlier versions of Windows do not recognize application partitions.

In addition to full replicas that are distributed for domains, Active Directory distributes partial replicas of every domain in the forest to special domain controllers designated as global catalog servers. The partial replicas stored on global catalog servers contain information on every object in the forest and are used to facilitate searches and queries for objects in the forest. Because only a subset of an object's attributes is stored, the amount of data replicated to and maintained by a global catalog server is significantly smaller than the total size of all object data stored in all the domains in the forest.

Every domain must have at least one global catalog server. By default, the first domain controller installed in a domain is set as that domain's global catalog server. You can change the global catalog server, and you can designate additional servers as global catalog servers as necessary.

Designing and Managing the Domain Environment

As you learned in the previous chapter, the physical structure of Active Directory is tightly integrated with the security architecture of the Microsoft Windows operating system. At a high level, Active Directory provides interfaces to which clients can connect, and the directory physically exists on disk in a database file called Ntds.dit. When you install Active Directory on a computer, the computer becomes a domain controller. When you implement Active Directory, you can have as many domain controllers as are needed to support the directory service needs of the organization.

Before you implement or modify the Active Directory domain environment, you need to consider the limitations and architecture requirements for the following processes:

- Replication

- Search and global catalogs

- Compatibility and functional levels

- Authentication and trusts

- Delegated authentication

- Operations masters

Remember that planning for Active Directory is an ongoing process that you should think about whether you are planning to deploy Active Directory for the first time or have already deployed Active Directory in your organization. Why? Because every time you consider making changes to your organizational structure or network infrastructure, you should consider how this affects Active Directory and plan accordingly.

In planning for Active Directory, few things are outside the scope of the design. When you initially deploy Active Directory, you need to develop an Active Directory design and implementation plan that involves every level of your organization and your network infrastructure. After you deploy Active Directory, any time you plan to change your organizational structure or network infrastructure, you should determine the impact on Active Directory. You then need to plan for and implement any changes to Active Directory that are required.

Design Considerations for Active Directory Replication

Because Active Directory uses a multimaster replication model, there are no primary or backup domain controllers. Every domain controller deployed in the organization is autonomous, with its own copy of the directory. When you need to make changes to standard directory data, you can do so on any domain controller and you can rely on Active Directory's built-in replication engine to replicate the changes to other domain controllers in the organization as appropriate.

As shown in Figure 30-1, the actual mechanics of replication depend on the level and role of a domain controller in the organization. To help manage replication, Active Directory uses partitions in the following ways:

- Forest-wide data is replicated to every domain controller in the forest and includes the configuration and schema partitions for the forest. A domain controller designated as the schema master maintains the only writable copy of the schema data. Every writable domain controller maintains a writable copy of the configuration data.

- Domain-wide data is replicated to every domain controller in a domain and includes only the data for a particular domain. Every writable domain controller in a domain has a writable copy of the data for that domain.

> **Note**
>
> Domain controllers designated as DNS servers also replicate directory partitions for DNS. Every domain controller that is designated as a DNS server has a copy of the ForestDNSZones and DomainDNSZones partitions. Windows Server 2008 and later versions of Windows Server support two different types of domain controllers: writable domain controllers and read-only domain controllers. Writable domain controllers are the standard type of domain controller introduced with Windows 2000 and used with Windows Server 2003 and Windows Server 2008. Writable domain controllers are the only type of domain controller with writable directory partitions. Read-only domain controllers, on the other hand, only have read-only directory partitions. To help make the architecture and design discussions easier to follow, I discuss architecture and design considerations for read-only domain controllers separately and you'll find a complete discussion in Chapter 34, "Deploying Read-Only Domain Controllers."

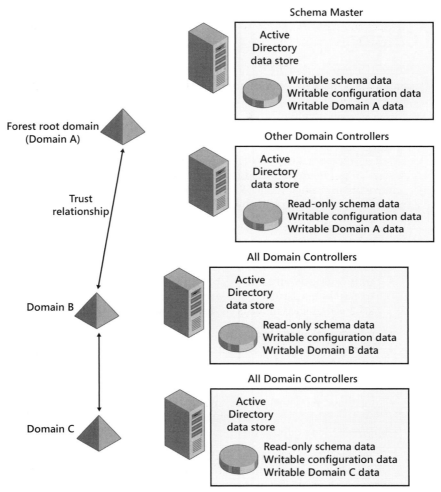

Figure 30-1 Replication of data in the Active Directory data store.

Design Considerations for Active Directory Search and Global Catalogs

Active Directory uses the Lightweight Directory Access Protocol (LDAP) model to query and manage directory information. Objects in the directory can be located using an LDAP query.

Searching the Tree

Every object has a name relative to its location in the directory and a distinguished name that points to its exact location in relation to the root of the directory tree. The relative distinguished name (RDN) is the actual name of the object. The distinguished name (DN) is the complete object name as seen by Active Directory.

When you work your way down the tree, you add a naming component for each successive level. In Figure 30-2, the relative names of several objects are shown on the left and the distinguished names of those objects are shown on the right.

- **cohovineyards.com** The cohovineyards.com domain object is near the top of the tree. In Active Directory, its relative distinguished name is DC=cohovineyards and its distinguished name is DC=cohovineyards,DC=com.

- **mf.cohovineyards.com** The mf.cohovineyards.com domain object is at the next level of the tree. In Active Directory, its relative name is DC=mf and its distinguished name includes the path to the previous level as well as its relative name. This means that the DN is DC=mf,DC=cohovineyards,DC=com.

- **bottling.mf.cohovineyards.com** The bottling.mf.cohovineyards.com domain object is below the mf.cohovineyards.com domain in the directory tree. In Active Directory, its relative distinguished name is DC=bottling and its distinguished name includes the path to all the previous levels as well as its relative name. This means the DN is DC=bottling,DC=mf,DC=cohovineyards,DC=com.

Being able to find objects in the directory efficiently regardless of their location in the directory tree is extremely important. If objects can't be easily located, users won't be able to find resources that are available and administrators won't be able to manage the available resources either. To make it easier to find resources, Active Directory uses special-purpose domain controllers that function as global catalog servers.

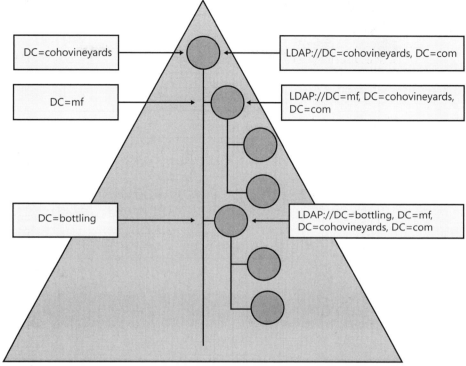

Figure 30-2 Active Directory uses the LDAP model to query and manage the directory.

Accessing the Global Catalog

A domain controller designated as a global catalog server contains an additional data store called the global catalog, as shown in Figure 30-3. The global catalog contains a partial, read-only replica of all the domains in the Active Directory forest. Although the catalog is a partial replica, it does contain a copy of every object in the directory, but only the base attributes of those objects. Queries to global catalog servers are made over TCP port 3268 for standard communications and TCP port 3269 for secure communications.

Global catalog data is replicated to global catalog servers using the normal Active Directory replication process. In an Active Directory forest with domains A, B, and C, this means that any domain controller designated as a global catalog server has a partial replica of all three domains. If a user in domain C searches for a resource located in domain A, the global catalog server in domain C can respond to the query using an attribute that has been replicated to the global catalog without needing to refer to another domain controller. Without a global catalog server, a domain controller in domain C would need to forward the query to a domain controller in domain A.

Chapter 30

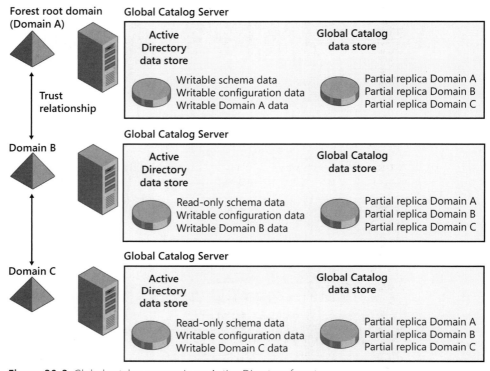

Figure 30-3 Global catalog servers in an Active Directory forest.

Designating Global Catalog Servers

The first domain controller installed in a domain is automatically designated as a global catalog server. You can designate additional domain controllers to be global catalog servers as well. To do this, you use the Active Directory Sites And Services tool to set the Global Catalog Server option for the domain controller you want to be a global catalog server.

Start Active Directory Sites And Services by clicking Start, Programs or All Programs, Administrative Tools, and Active Directory Sites And Services. Expand the site you want to work with, such as Default-First-Site-Name, expand the related Servers node, and then select the server you want to designate as a global catalog, as shown in the following screen:

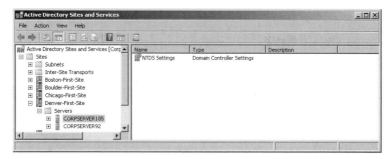

In the right pane, right-click NTDS Settings, and then select Properties. This displays the NTDS Settings Properties dialog box, as shown in the following screen:

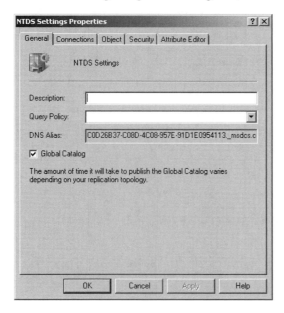

If you want the selected server to be a global catalog, select the Global Catalog check box. If you want the selected server to stop being a global catalog, clear the Global Catalog check box. When you designate a new global catalog server, the server will request a copy of the global catalog from an existing global catalog server in the domain. The amount of time it takes to replicate the global catalog depends on the size of the catalog and the network configuration.

> **Note**
>
> Exchange Server 2007 is tightly integrated with Active Directory. Exchange Server 2007 stores schema data, configuration data, domain data, and application data in the directory. It also uses Active Directory replication topology to determine how to route messages within the organization. To learn more about Exchange Server 2007 and Active Directory, please refer to the *Exchange Server 2007 Administrator's Pocket Consultant* (Microsoft Press, 2007).

Designating Replication Attributes

The contents of the global catalog are determined by the attributes that are replicated for each object class. Common object classes you'll work with include the following:

- **Computer** Represents a computer account in the domain or forest
- **Contact** Represents a contact in the domain or forest
- **Domain** Represents a domain
- **Group** Represents a group account in the domain or forest
- **InetOrgPerson** Represents a special type of user account, which typically has been migrated from another directory service
- **PrintQueue** Represents a logical printer (print queue) in the domain or forest
- **Server** Represents a server account in the domain or forest
- **Site** Represents an Active Directory site
- **Subnet** Represents an Active Directory subnet
- **User** Represents a user account in the domain or forest

Schema administrators can configure additional attributes to be replicated by global catalog servers. The primary reason for replicating additional attributes is to add attributes for which users routinely search. You shouldn't add attributes for which users search infrequently. You should rarely, if ever, remove attributes that are being replicated.

If you are a member of the Schema Admins group, you can manage the attributes that are replicated through the global catalog by using the Active Directory Schema snap-in for the Microsoft Management Console (MMC). When you start this snap-in, it makes a direct connection to the schema master for the forest.

The Active Directory Schema snap-in is not available by default. You must install this tool by registering its DLL. To do this, enter the following at an elevated command prompt:

```
regsvr32 schmmgmt.dll
```

After you install this tool, you can add the Active Directory Schema snap-in to a custom console by following these steps:

1. Open a blank MMC in Author mode. Click Start, type **mmc** in the Search box, and then press Enter.

2. In your MMC, choose Add/Remove Snap-In from the File menu in the main window. This displays the Add Or Remove Snap-Ins dialog box.

3. The Available Snap-Ins list shows all the snap-ins that are available. Select Active Directory Schema, and then click Add. The Active Directory Schema snap-in is added to the Selected Snap-Ins list.

4. Now close the Add Or Remove Snap-Ins dialog box by clicking OK and return to the console you are creating.

After you add the snap-in to a custom console, you can edit the schema for the object whose attribute you want to replicate in the global catalog. In Active Directory Schema, expand the Active Directory Schema node, and then select the Attributes node. A list of the attributes for all objects in the directory appears in the right pane as shown in the following screen:

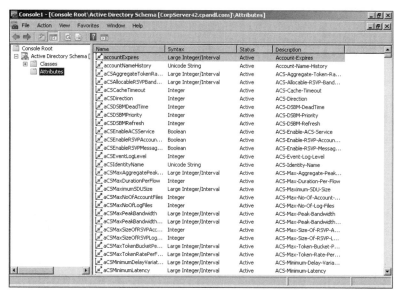

Double-click the attribute you want to replicate to the global catalog. In the attribute's Properties dialog box, mark the attribute to be replicated by selecting the Replicate This Attribute To The Global Catalog check box as shown in the following screen. If you want the attribute to be indexed in the database for faster search and retrieval, select the Index This Attribute check box. Although indexing an attribute allows it to be found more quickly, each index you create slightly increases the size of the Active Directory database.

Chapter 30

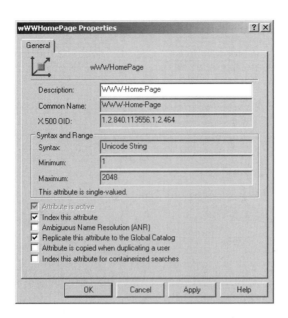

TROUBLESHOOTING

You cannot change an attribute even though you are a member of the Administrators group

As a member of the Administrators group, you can view Active Directory schema. To change schema, you must be a member of the Schema Admins group. The Active Directory Schema snap-in doesn't check to ensure that you are a member of the Schema Admins group until you try to change attribute settings. If you aren't a member of the group, it states that you have insufficient permissions.

Design Considerations for Compatibility

In Windows Server 2008, each forest and each domain within a forest can be assigned a functional level. The functional level for a forest is referred to as the *forest functional level*. The functional level for a domain within a forest is referred to as the *domain functional level*. Functional levels affect the inner workings of Active Directory and are used to enable features that are compatible with the installed server versions of the Windows operating system.

Understanding Domain Functional Level

When you set a functional level for a domain, the level of functionality applies only to that domain. This means that other domains in the forest can have a different functional level.

As shown in Table 30-1, there are several domain functional levels. Changing a functional level changes the operating systems that are supported for domain controllers. For example, in Windows 2000 native functional level, the domain can have domain controllers running Microsoft Windows 2000 Server, Microsoft Windows Server 2003, or Windows Server 2008.

> **Note**
>
> You cannot use the Windows 2000 mixed domain functional level with Windows Server 2008 domain controllers. If your domain is operating at this level and you want to install a domain controller running Windows Server 2008, you'll first need to raise the domain functional level to Windows 2000 native or higher. Although you can raise the domain functional level, you can never lower it. This means that if you raise the domain functional level to Windows Server 2008, you can configure only Windows Server 2008 domain controllers in the domain.

Table 30-1 **Domain Functional Levels**

Domain Functional Level	Supported Domain Controllers
Windows 2000 mixed	Windows Server 2003 Windows 2000 Server Windows NT 4.0 backup domain controller (BDC)
Windows 2000 native	Windows Server 2008 Windows Server 2003 Windows 2000 Server
Windows Server 2003	Windows Server 2008 Windows Server 2003
Windows Server 2008	Windows Server 2008

Domains operating in Windows 2000 native mode can use group nesting, group type conversion, universal groups, and migration of security principals. Domains operating in this mode aren't able to use easy domain controller renaming, update logon time stamps, or Kerberos key distribution center (KDC) key version numbers.

Domains in Windows Server 2003 mode can use many improved Active Directory features, including group nesting, group type conversion, universal groups, easy domain controller renaming, update logon time stamps, migration of security principals, and Kerberos KDC key version numbers. Applications can use constrained delegation to take advantage of the secure delegation of user credentials through the Kerberos authentication protocol. You can also redirect the Users and Computers containers to define a new well-known location for user and computer accounts.

Windows 2008 domain functional level adds the following features above those available with Windows Server 2003:

- Distributed File System Replication for Sysvol, which provides more robust and granular replication of Sysvol.

- Advanced Encryption Services (AES) support for the Kerberos protocol, allowing user accounts to use AES 128-bit or AES 256-bit encryption.

- Last interactive logon information, which displays the time of the last successful interactive logon for a user, the number of failed logon attempts since last logon, and the time of the last failed logon.

- Fine-grained password policies, which make it possible for password and account lockout policy to be specified for user and global security groups in a domain.

Understanding Forest Functional Level

Forest functional level is a bit simpler, as shown in Table 30-2. When you raise the forest functional level to Windows Server 2008, all domains using the Windows 2000 native domain functional level or higher are automatically raised to the Windows Server 2008 domain functional level. As with the domain functional level, after you raise the forest functional level, you cannot lower it.

Table 30-2 Forest Functional Levels

Forest Functional Level	Supported Domain Controllers
Windows 2000	Windows Server 2008 Windows Server 2003 Windows 2000 Server
Windows Server 2003	Windows Server 2008 Windows Server 2003
Windows Server 2008	Windows Server 2008

Forests operating in Windows 2000 mode can't use many Active Directory features, including extended two-way trusts between forests, domain rename, domain restructure using renaming, and global catalog replication enhancements.

Windows Server 2003 forest functional level adds the following features:

- Linked-value replication to improve the replication of changes to group memberships

- Extended two-way trusts between forests

- Domain rename and domain restructure using renaming

- More efficient generation of complex replication topologies by the KCC

With the original release of the operating system, Windows Server 2008 forest functional level does not add any specific features.

Raising the Domain or Forest Functional Level

You can raise the domain or forest functional level using Active Directory Domains And Trusts. To raise the domain functional level, follow these steps:

1. Click Start, choose Administrative Tools, and then select Active Directory Domains And Trusts.

2. In the console tree, right-click the domain you want to work with, and then select Raise Domain Functional Level. The current domain name and functional level appear in the Raise Domain Functional Level dialog box.

3. To change the domain functionality, select the new domain functional level using the selection list provided, and then click Raise.

CAUTION

You can't reverse this action. After you raise the functional level, there's no going back, so you should consider the implications carefully before you do this.

4. When you click OK, the new domain functional level is replicated to each domain controller in the domain. This operation can take some several minutes or longer in a large organization.

You can raise the forest level functionality by completing the following steps:

1. Click Start, choose Administrative Tools, and then select Active Directory Domains And Trusts.

2. Right-click the Active Directory Domains And Trusts node in the console tree, and then select Raise Forest Functional Level. The current forest name and functional level appear in the Raise Forest Functional Level dialog box.

3. To change the forest functionality, select the new forest functional level using the selection list provided, and then click Raise.

CAUTION

You can't reverse this action. After you raise the functional level, there's no going back, so you should consider the implications carefully before you do this.

4. When you click OK, the new forest functional level is replicated to each domain controller in each domain in the forest. This operation can take several minutes or longer in a large organization.

As a planning option, you can determine the steps you need to take to raise the forest functional level by clicking Save As in the Raise Forest Functional Level dialog box. When you click Save As, a Save As dialog box appears, allowing you to select a save location for a log file. The log file details show the following information:

- The forest root domain and the current forest functional level.

- The domains and the domain controllers in those domains that are running versions of Windows earlier than Windows Server 2008. These are the servers that need to be upgraded.

- The domain functional level of each domain for which the functional level must be raised. As long as the domain functional level of all domains is set to at least Windows 2000 native, you can raise the forest functional level—doing so raises the domain functional level in all the domains to Windows Server 2008 and sets the forest functional level to Windows Server 2008 as well.

Design Considerations for Active Directory Authentication and Trusts

Authentication and trusts are integral parts of Active Directory. Before you implement any Active Directory design or try to modify your existing Active Directory infrastructure, you should have a firm understanding of how both authentication and trusts work in an Active Directory environment.

Universal Groups and Authentication

When a user logs on to a domain, Active Directory looks up information about the groups of which the user is a member to generate a security token for the user. The security token is needed as part of the normal authentication process and is used whenever a user accesses resources on the network.

Understanding Security Tokens and Universal Group Membership Caching

To generate the security token, Active Directory checks the domain local and global group memberships for the user. All the supported domain functional levels in Windows Server 2008 support a special type of group called a *universal group*. Universal groups can contain user and group accounts from any domain in the forest. As global catalog servers are the only servers in a domain with forest-wide domain data, the global catalog is essential for logon in any domain operating at the Windows 2000 native functional level or higher.

Because of problems authenticating users when global catalog servers are not available, Windows Server 2003 introduced a technique for caching universal group membership. In a domain with domain controllers running either Windows Server 2003 or Windows Server 2008, universal group membership caching can be enabled. After you enable caching, the cache is where domain controllers store universal group membership information that they have previously looked up. Domain controllers can then use this cache for authentication the next time the user logs on to the domain. The cache is maintained indefinitely and updated periodically to ensure that it is current. By default, domain controllers check the consistency of the cache every eight hours.

Thanks to universal group membership caching, remote sites running Windows Server 2003, Windows Server 2008, or both domain controllers don't necessarily have to have global catalog servers configured as well. This gives you additional options when configuring the Active Directory forest. The assignment of security tokens is only part of the logon process. The logon process also includes authentication and the assignment of a user principal name (UPN) to the user.

INSIDE OUT   The user principal name (UPN) suffix can be changed

Every user account has a user principal name (UPN) which consists of the user logon name combined with the at symbol (@) and a UPN suffix. The names of the current domain and the root domain are set as the default UPN suffix. You can specify an alternate UPN suffix to use to simplify logon or provide additional logon security. This name is used only within the forest and does not have to be a valid DNS name. For example, if the UPN suffix for a domain is it.seattle.cpandl.local, you could use an alternate UPN suffix to simplify this to cpandl.local. This would allow the user Williams to log on using williams@cpandl.local rather than williams@it.seattle.cpandl.local.

You can add or remove UPN suffixes for an Active Directory forest and all domains within that forest by completing the following steps:

1. Start Active Directory Domains And Trusts from the Administrative Tools menu.

2. Right-click the Active Directory Domains And Trusts node and then click Properties.

3. To add a UPN suffix, type the alternate suffix in the box provided and then click Add.

4. To remove a UPN suffix, click the suffix to remove in the list provided and then click Remove.

5. Click OK.

Enabling Universal Group Membership Caching

In a domain with domain controllers running Windows Server 2003, Windows Server 2008, or both, you use the Active Directory Sites And Services tool to configure universal group membership caching. You enable caching on a per-site basis. Start

Active Directory Sites And Services by clicking Start, Programs or All Programs, Administrative Tools, and Active Directory Sites And Services. Expand and then select the site in which you want to enable universal group membership caching, as shown in the following screen:

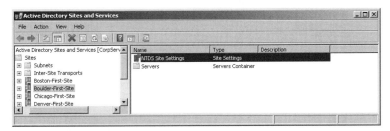

In the right pane, right-click NTDS Site Settings, and then select Properties. This displays the NTDS Site Settings Properties dialog box as shown in the following screen:

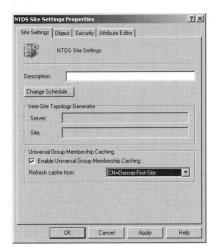

To enable universal group membership caching for the site, select the Enable Universal Group Membership Caching check box and continue as follows:

- If the directory has multiple sites, you can replicate existing universal group membership information from a specific site's cache by selecting the site in the Refresh Cache From list. With this option, universal group membership information doesn't need to be generated and then replicated; it is simply replicated from the other site's cache.

- If the directory has only one site or you'd rather get the information from a global catalog server in the nearest site, accept the default setting <Default>. With this option, universal group membership information is generated and then replicated.

When you are finished configuring universal group membership caching, click OK.

NTLM and Kerberos Authentication

Windows NT 4.0 uses a form of authentication known as NT LAN Manager (NTLM). With NTLM, an encrypted challenge/response is used to authenticate a user without sending the user's password over the network. The system requesting authentication must perform a calculation that proves it has access to the secured NTLM credentials. It does this by sending a one-way hash of the user's password that can be verified.

NTLM authentication has interactive and non-interactive authentication processes. Interactive NTLM authentication over a network typically involves a client system from which a user is requesting authentication, and a domain controller on which the user's password is stored. As the user accesses other resources on the network, non-interactive authentication may take place as well to permit an already logged-on user to access network resources. Typically, non-interactive authentication involves a client, a server, and a domain controller that manages the authentication.

To see how NTLM authentication works, consider the situation that occurs when a user tries to access a resource on the network and she is prompted for her user name and password. Assuming the resource is on a server that is not also a domain controller, the authentication process would be similar to the following:

1. When prompted, the user provides a domain name, user name, and password. The client computer generates a cryptographic hash of the user's password, discards the actual password, then sends the user name to the server as unencrypted text.

2. The server generates a 16-byte random number, called a *challenge*, and sends it to the client.

3. The client encrypts the challenge with the hash of the user's password and returns the result, called a *response*, to the server. The server then sends the domain controller the user name, the challenge sent to the client, and the response from the client.

4. The domain controller uses the user name to retrieve the hash of the user's password from the Security Account Manager (SAM) database. The domain controller uses this password hash to encrypt the challenge then compares the encrypted challenge it computed to the response computed by the client. If they are identical, the authentication is successful.

Starting with Windows 2000, Active Directory uses Kerberos as the default authentication protocol, and NTLM authentication is maintained only for backward compatibility with older clients. Whenever a client running Windows 2000 or later tries to authenticate with Active Directory, the client tries to use Kerberos. Kerberos has a number of advantages over NTLM authentication, including the use of mutual authentication. Mutual authentication in Kerberos allows for two-way authentication, so that not only can a server authenticate a client, but a client can also authenticate a server. Thus, mutual authentication ensures that not only is an authorized client trying to access the network, but also that an authorized server is the one responding to the client request.

Kerberos uses the following three main components:

- A client that needs access to resources
- A server that manages access to resources and ensures that only authenticated users can gain access to resources
- A Key Distribution Center (KDC) that acts as a central clearinghouse

Establishing the Initial Authentication

All domain controllers run the Kerberos Key Distribution Center service to act as KDCs. With Kerberos authentication, a user password is never sent over the network. Instead, Kerberos authentication uses a shared secret authentication model. In most cases, the client and the server use the user's password as the shared secret. With this technique, authentication works as shown in Figure 30-4.

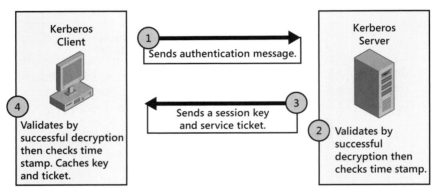

Figure 30-4 The Kerberos authentication process.

The details of the initial authentication of a user in the domain are as follows:

1. When a user logs on to the network, the client sends the KDC server a message containing the user name, domain name, and a request for access to the network. In the message is a packet of information that has been encrypted using the shared secret information (the user's password), which includes a time stamp.

2. When the KDC server receives the message, the server reads the user name, and then checks the directory database for its copy of the shared secret information (the user's password). The KDC server then decrypts the secret part of the message and checks the message time stamp. As long as the message time stamp is within five minutes of the current time on the server, the server can then authenticate the user. If the decryption fails or the message time stamp is more than five minutes off the current time, the authentication fails. Five minutes is the default value; the allowable time difference can be configured through domain security policy, using the Kerberos policy Maximum Tolerance For Computer Clock Synchronization.

3. After the user is authenticated, the KDC server sends the client a message that is encrypted with the shared secret information (the user's password). The message includes a session key that the client will use when communicating with the KDC server from now on and a session ticket that grants the user access to the domain controller. The ticket is encrypted with the KDC server's key, which makes it valid only for that domain controller.

4. When the client receives the message, the client decrypts the message and checks the message time stamp. As long as the message time stamp is within five minutes of the current time on the server, the client can then authenticate the server and assume that the server is valid. The client then caches the session key so it can be used for all future connections with the KDC server. The session key is valid until it expires or the user logs off. The session ticket is cached as well, but it isn't decrypted.

Accessing Resources After Authentication

After initial authentication, the user is granted access to the domain. The only resource to which the user has been granted access is the domain controller. When the user wants to access another resource on the network, the client must request access through the KDC. An overview of the process for authenticating access to network resources is shown in Figure 30-5.

The details of an access request for a network resource are as follows:

1. When a user tries to access a resource on the network, the client sends the KDC server a session ticket request. The message contains the user's name, the session ticket the client was previously granted, the name of the network resource the client is trying to access, and a time stamp that is encrypted with the session key.

2. When the KDC server receives the message, the server decrypts the session ticket using its key. Afterward, it extracts the original session key from the session ticket and uses it to decrypt the time stamp, which is then validated. The validation process is designed to ensure that the client is using the correct session key and that the time stamp is valid.

3. If all is acceptable, the KDC server sends a session ticket to the client. The session ticket includes two copies of a session key that the client will use to access the requested resource. The first copy of the session key is encrypted using the client's session key. The second copy of the session key contains the user's access information and is encrypted with the resource's secret key known only by the KDC server and the network resource.

4. The client caches the session ticket, and then sends the session ticket to the network resource to gain access. This request also contains an encrypted time stamp.

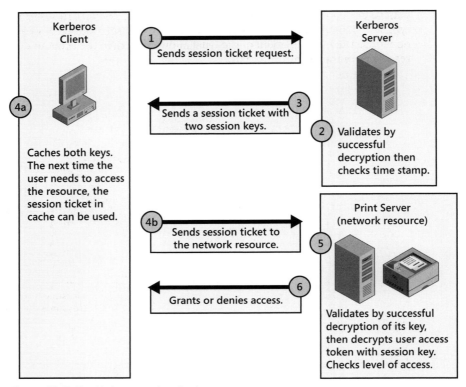

Figure 30-5 The Kerberos authentication process.

5. The network resource decrypts the second session key in the session ticket, using the secret key it shares with the KDC server. If this is successful, the network resource has validated that the session ticket came from a trusted KDC. It then decrypts the user's access information, using the session key, and checks the user's access permissions. The time stamp sent from the client is also decrypted and validated by the network resource.

6. If the authentication and authorization are successful (meaning that the client has the appropriate access permissions), the user is granted the type of access to the network resource that the particular permissions allow. The next time the user needs to access the resource, the session ticket in cache is used, as long as it hasn't expired. Using a cached session ticket allows the client to send a request directly to the network resource. If the ticket has expired, however, the client must start over and get a new ticket.

Authentication and Trusts Across Domain Boundaries

Active Directory uses Kerberos security for server-to-server authentication and the establishment of trusts, while allowing older clients and servers on the network to use NTLM if necessary. Figure 30-6 shows a one-way trust in which one domain is the trusted domain and the other domain is the trusting domain. In Windows NT 4.0, you typically implemented one-way trusts when you had separate account and resource domains. The establishment of the trust allowed users in the account domain to access resources in the resource domain.

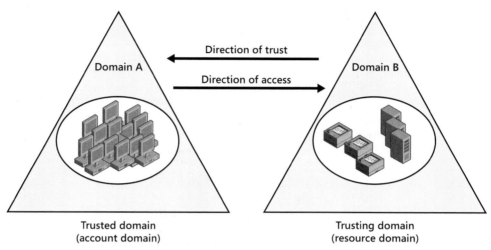

Figure 30-6 One-way trust with a trusted domain and a trusting domain.

Two-Way Transitive Trusts

With Active Directory, trusts are automatically configured between all the domains in a forest and are implemented as two-way, transitive trusts. As a result, if the domains shown in Figure 30-6 were Windows domains, users in domain A can automatically access resources in domain B and users in domain B can automatically access resources in domain A. Because the trusts are automatically established between all domains in the forest, no setup is involved and there are many more design options for implementing Active Directory domains.

> **Note**
>
> The physical limitation on the number of objects that necessitated having separate account and resource domains in Windows NT 4.0 no longer applies. Active Directory domains can have millions of objects, a fact that changes the fundamental reason for creating additional domains.

As trusts join parent and child domains in the same domain tree and join the roots of domain trees, the structure of trusts in a forest can be referred to as a *trust tree*. When a user tries to access a resource in another domain, the trust tree is used, and the user's request has to pass through one domain controller for each domain between the user

Chapter 30

and the resource. This type of authentication takes place across domain boundaries. Authentication across domain boundaries also applies when a user with an account in one domain visits another domain in the forest and tries to log on to the network from that domain.

Consider the example shown in Figure 30-7. If a user from domain G visits domain K and tries to log on to the network, the user's computer must be able to connect to a domain controller in domain K. Here, the user's computer sends the initial logon request to the domain K domain controller. When the domain controller receives the logon request, it determines that the user is located in domain G. The domain controller refers the request to a domain controller in the next domain in its trust tree, which in this case is domain J. A domain controller in domain J refers the request to domain I. A domain controller in domain I refers the request to domain H. This process continues through domains A, E, and F until the request finally gets to domain G.

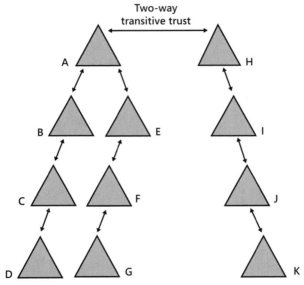

Figure 30-7 A forest with many domains.

Shortcut Trusts

This rather lengthy referral process could be avoided if you established an explicit trust between domain G and domain K as shown in Figure 30-8. Technically, explicit trusts are one-way transitive trusts, but you can establish a two-way explicit trust by creating two one-way trusts. Thus unlike standard trusts within the trust tree, which are inherently two-way and transitive, explicit trusts can be made to be two-way if desired. As they can be used to establish authentication shortcuts between domains, they are also referred to as *shortcut trusts*. In this example, it was decided to create two one-way trusts: one from domain G to domain K and one from domain K to domain G. With these shortcut trusts in place, users in domain G could visit domain K and be rapidly authenticated and users in domain K could visit domain G and be rapidly authenticated.

If you examine the figure closely, you'll see that several other shortcut trusts were add to the forest as well. Shortcut trusts have been established between B and E and between E and I. Establishing the shortcut trusts in both directions allows for easy access to resources and rapid authentication in several combinations, such as the following:

- Using the B to E shortcut trust, users in domain B can rapidly access resources in domain E.

- Using the B to E and E to I shortcut trusts, users in domain B can also rapidly access resources in domain I.

- Using the B to E shortcut trust, users in domain B can visit domain E and be rapidly authenticated.

- Using the B to E and E to I shortcut trusts, users in domain B can visit domain I and be rapidly authenticated.

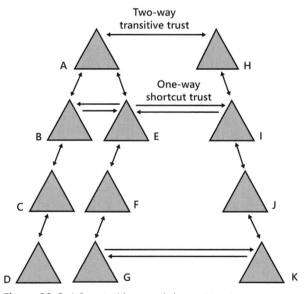

Figure 30-8 A forest with several shortcut trusts.

The trusts work similarly for users in domain E. Users in domain E have direct access to both domain B and domain I. Imagine that domain B is sales.cohovineyard.com, domain E is mf.cohovineyard.com, and domain I is cs.cohowinery.com, and you may be able to better picture how the shortcut trusts allow users to cut across trees in the Active Directory forest. Hopefully, you can also imagine how much planning should go into deciding your domain structure, especially when it comes to access to resources and authentication.

Authentication and Trusts Across Forest Boundaries

You can establish authentication and trusts across forest boundaries as well. As discussed in Chapter 29, "Active Directory Architecture," while you are upgrading your network to implement Active Directory, you can establish external trusts to Windows NT domains to ensure that Windows NT domains continue to be available to users.

One-way external trusts, such as the one depicted in Figure 30-9, are nontransitive. This means that if, as in the example, a trust is established between domain H and domain L only, a user in any domain in forest 1 could access a resource in domain L but not in any other domain in forest 2. The reason for this limitation is that the trust doesn't continue past domain L and it does not matter that a two-way transitive trust does exist between domain L and domain M or that a two-way trust also exists between domain L and domain O.

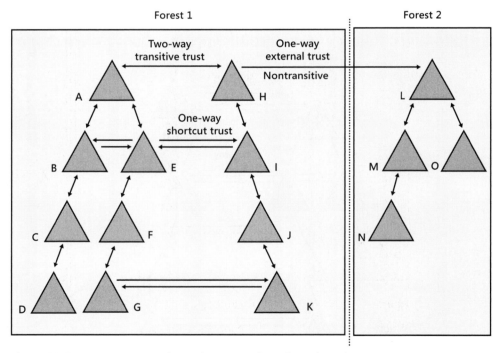

Figure 30-9 A one-way external trust that crosses forest boundaries but is nontransitive.

Like Windows Server 2003, Windows Server 2008 supports cross-forest transitive trusts also referred to simply as *forest trusts*. With this type of trust, you can establish a one-way or two-way transitive trust between forests to share resources and to authenticate users. With a two-way trust, as shown Figure 30-10, you enable cross-forest authentication and cross-forest authorization. Before you can use cross-forest trusts, all domain controllers in all domains of both forests must be upgraded to Windows Server 2003 or higher, and the forest must be running at the Windows Server 2003 or higher functional level.

As discussed in "NTLM and Kerberos Authentication" on page 1023, Kerberos is the default authentication protocol, but NTLM can also be used. This allows current clients and servers as well as older clients and servers to be authenticated. After you establish a two-way cross-forest trust, users get all the benefits of Active Directory regardless of where they sign on to the network. With cross-forest authentication, you ensure secure access to resources when the user account is in one forest and the computer account is in another forest, and when the user in one forest needs access to network resources in another trusted forest. As part of cross-forest authorization, administrators can select users and global groups from trusted forests for inclusion in local groups. This ensures the integrity of the forest security boundary while allowing trust between forests.

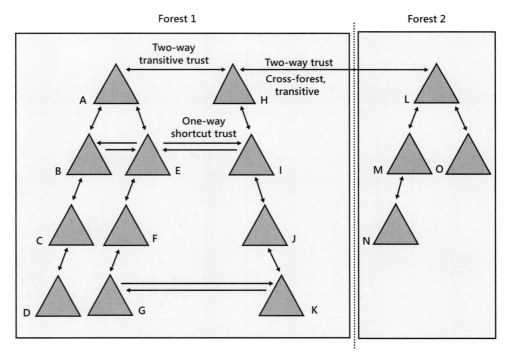

Figure 30-10 A two-way transitive trust between forests.

When you connect two or more forests using cross-forest trusts, the implementation is referred to as a *federated forest design*. The federated forest design is most useful when you need to join two separate Active Directory structures, for example, when two companies merge, when one company acquires another, or when an organization has a major restructuring. Consider the case in which two companies merge, and, rather than migrate their separate Active Directory structures into a single directory tree, the staff decides to link the two forests using cross-forest trusts. As long as the trusts are two-way, users in forest 1 can access resources in forest 2 and users in forest 2 can access resources in forest 1.

Having separate forests with cross-forest trusts between them is also useful when you want a division or group within the organization to have more autonomy but still have a link to the other divisions or groups. By placing the division or group in a separate forest, you ensure strict security and give that division or group ownership of the Active Directory structure. If users in the forest needed access to resources in another forest, you could establish a one-way cross-forest trust between the forests. This would allow users in the secured forest to gain access to resources in the second forest, but would not allow users in the second forest to gain access to the secure forest.

Organizations that contain groups or divisions with high security requirements could use this approach. For example, consider Figure 30-11.

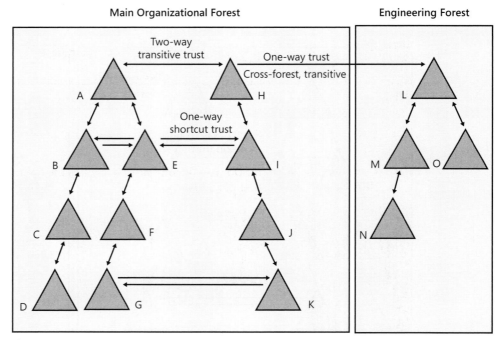

Figure 30-11 A one-way transitive trust between forests.

In this situation, the users in the organization's Engineering department need access to resources in other departments, but for security reasons they should be isolated from the rest of the organization. Here the organization has implemented two forests: a main organizational forest and a separate Engineering forest. Using a one-way cross-forest trust from the main forest to the Engineering department forest, the organization allows Engineering users to access other resources, but ensures that the Engineering department is secure and isolated.

Examining Domain and Forest Trusts

You can examine existing trusts using Active Directory Domains And Trusts. Click Start, choose Programs or All Programs as appropriate, choose Administrative Tools, and then select Active Directory Domains And Trusts. As shown in the following screen, you see a list of available domains:

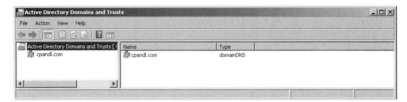

To examine the existing trusts for a domain, right-click the domain entry, and then select Properties. Then, in the domain's Properties dialog box, click the Trusts tab as shown in the following screen. The Trust tab is organized into two panels:

- **Domains Trusted By This Domain (Outgoing Trusts)** Lists the domains that this domain trusts (the trusted domains).

- **Domains That Trust This Domain (Incoming Trusts)** Lists the domains that trust this domain (the trusting domains).

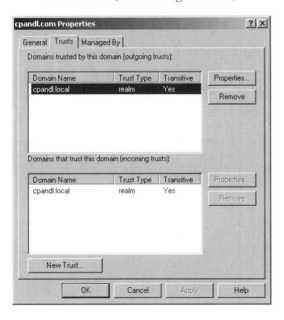

To view the details of a particular trust, select it, and then click Properties. The following screen shows the trust's Properties dialog box:

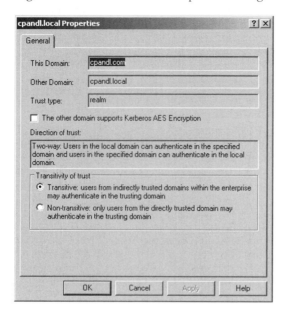

The Properties dialog box contains the following information:

- **This Domain** The domain you are working with.

- **Other Domain** The domain with which the trust is established.

- **Trust Type** The type of trust. By default, two-way transitive trusts are created automatically when a new domain is added to a new domain tree within the forest or a subdomain of a root domain. There are two default trust types: Tree Root and Parent And Child. When a new domain tree is added to the forest, the default trust that is established automatically is a tree-root trust. When a new domain is a subdomain of a root domain, the default trust that is established automatically is a parent and child trust. Other trust types that may appear include the following:

    - External, which is a one-way or two-way nontransitive trust used to provide access to resources in a Windows NT 4.0 domain or to a domain in a separate forest that is not joined by a forest trust

    - Forest, which is a one-way or two-way transitive trust used to share resources between forests

    - Realm, which is a transitive or nontransitive trust that can be established as one way or two way between a non-Windows Kerberos realm and a Windows Server 2008 domain

    - Shortcut, which is a one-way or two-way transitive trust used to speed up authentication and resource access between domain trees

- **Direction Of Trust** The direction of the trust. All default trusts are established as two-way trusts. This means that users in the domain you are working with can authenticate in the other domain and users from the other domain can authenticate in the domain you are working with.

- **Transitivity Of Trust** The transitivity of the trust. All default trusts are transitive, which means that users from indirectly trusted domains can authenticate in the other domain.

Establishing External, Shortcut, Realm, and Cross-Forest Trusts

All trusts, regardless of type, are established in the same way. For all trusts there are two sides: an incoming trust and an outgoing trust. To configure both sides of the trust, keep the following in mind:

- For domain trusts, you need to use two accounts: one that is a member of the Domain Admins group in the first domain and one that is a member of the Domain Admins group in the second domain. If you don't have appropriate accounts in both domains, you can establish one side of the trust and allow another administrator in the other domain to establish the other side of the trust.

- For forest trusts, you will need to use two accounts: one that is a member of the Enterprise Admins group in the first forest and one that is a member of the Enterprise Admins group in the second forest. If you don't have appropriate accounts in both forests, you can establish one side of the two-way trust and allow another administrator in the other forest to establish the other side of the trust.

- For realm trusts, you will need to establish the trust separately for the Windows domain and for the Kerberos realm. If you don't have appropriate administrative access to both the Windows domain and the Kerberos realm, you can establish one side of the trust and allow another administrator to establish the other side of the trust.

To establish a trust, follow these steps:

1. Click Start, choose Programs or All Programs as appropriate, choose Administrative Tools, and then select Active Directory Domains And Trusts.

2. Right-click the domain for which you want to establish a one-way incoming, one-way outgoing, or two-way trust and then choose Properties. For a cross-forest trust, this must be the forest root domain in one of the participating forests.

3. In the domain Properties dialog box, click the Trusts tab, and then click the New Trust button. This starts the New Trust Wizard. Click Next to skip the welcome page.

4. On the Trust Name page, specify the domain name of the other domain, as shown in Figure 30-12. For a cross-forest trust, this must be the name of the forest root domain in the other forest.

Chapter 30

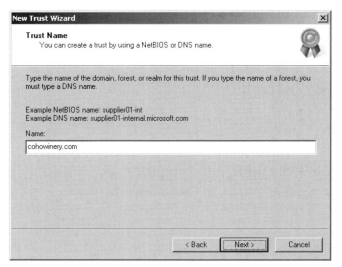

Figure 30-12 Specify the name of the other domain.

5. When you click Next, the wizard tries to establish a connection to the other domain. The options on the next page depend on whether you are connecting to a Windows domain, a Windows forest, or a non-Windows forest.

○ If the domain is determined to be a Windows forest, you have the option of creating an external trust that is nontransitive or a forest trust that is transitive. Choose either External Trust or Forest Trust, and then click Next.

○ If the domain is determined to be a Windows domain, it is assumed that you are creating a shortcut trust, and the wizard goes directly to the Direction Of Trust page.

○ If the domain is determined to be a non-Windows domain, you have the option of creating a realm trust with a Kerberos version 5 realm. Select Realm Trust, and then, on the Transitivity Of Trust page, select either Nontransitive or Transitive, and then click Next.

6. On the Direction Of Trust page, shown in Figure 30-13, choose the direction of trust and then click Next. The following options are available:

○ Two-Way—Users in the domain initially selected and in the designated domain can access resources in either domain or realm.

○ One-Way: Incoming—Users in the domain initially selected will be able to access resources in the designated domain. Users in the designated domain will not be able to access resources in the domain initially selected.

○ One-Way: Outgoing—Users in the designated domain will be able to access resources in the domain initially selected. Users in the domain initially selected will not be able to access resources in the designated domain.

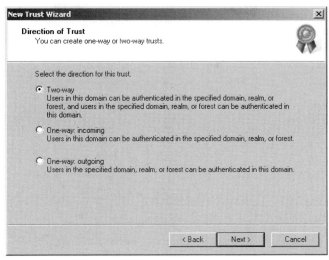

Figure 30-13 Choose the direction of trust.

7. For shortcut or forest trusts, the next page you see is the Sides Of Trust page. To begin using a trust, you must create both sides of the trust. You have the option of setting the sides of the trust for This Domain Only or for Both This Domain And The Specified Domain.

○ If you are creating only one side of the trust, select This Domain Only, and then click Next.

○ If you are setting both sides of the trust or the administrator from the other domain is at your desk, select Both This Domain And The Specified Domain, and then click Next. When prompted, type, or let the other administrator type, the name and password of an appropriate account in the other domain or forest, and then click OK.

8. On the Trust Password page, shown in Figure 30-14, type and then confirm the initial password you want to use for the trust. The password is arbitrary but must follow the strong security rules, meaning that it must have at least eight characters, contain a combination of uppercase and lowercase characters, and contain either numerals or special characters.

Chapter 30

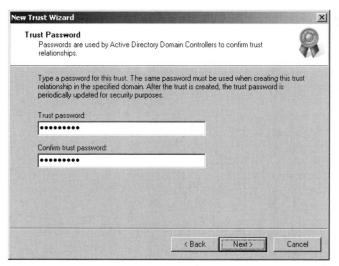

Figure 30-14 Set the initial password for the trust.

You may need the password

The trust password you use must be the same for both the domain initially selected and the specified domain, so be sure to securely store the password so that you can use it when configuring the other side of the trust. After you create the trust, Active Directory periodically updates the password, using an automatic password reset. This helps safeguard the integrity of the trust.

9. For domain or realm trusts, click Next twice to begin the trust creation process.

10. For forest trusts, you can set the outgoing trust authentication level as either Domain-Wide Authentication or Selective Authentication. With domain-wide authentication, users in the trusted domain can be authenticated to use all the resources in the trusting domain (and any trusted domains). This means that authentication is automatic for all users. With Selective Authentication, only the users or groups to which you explicitly grant permission can access resources in the trusting domain. This means that authentication is not automatic and you will need to grant individual access to each server that you want to make available to users in the trusting domain. Click Next twice.

11. After the trust is created, you are given the opportunity to verify the trust.

Verifying and Troubleshooting Trusts

By default, Windows validates all incoming trusts automatically. If the credentials used to establish the trust are no longer valid, the trust fails verification. If you want to revalidate a trust by providing new credentials or to specify that incoming trusts should not be validated, follow these steps:

1. Click Start, choose Programs or All Programs as appropriate, choose Administrative Tools, and then select Active Directory Domains And Trusts.

2. Right-click the trusted domain for which you want to verify the incoming trust, and then select Properties.

3. In the domain's Properties dialog box, click the Trusts tab, and then click Validate and select one of the following options:

   ○ If you want to stop validation of the incoming trust, select No, Do Not Validate The Incoming Trust.

   ○ If you want to revalidate the incoming trust, select Yes, Validate The Incoming Trust, and then type the user account and password for an administrator account in the other (trusting) domain.

4. Click OK. For a two-way trust, repeat this procedure for the other (trusting) domain.

You may want to revalidate trusts or specify that incoming trusts should not be validated for the following reasons:

● If clients are unable to access resources in a domain outside the forest, the external trust between the domains may have failed. In this case, you should verify the trust for the trusted domain. Note that a primary domain controller (PDC) emulator must be available to reset and verify the external trust.

● If clients cannot connect to a domain controller running Windows 2000, check the service pack level on the domain controller. The Windows 2000 domain controller should be running Service Pack 3 or later. If it isn't, upgrade it.

● If clients or servers get trust errors within an Active Directory forest, there could be several causes. The time on the clients or servers trying to authenticate may be more than five minutes off, which is the default maximum time difference allowed for Kerberos authentication. In this case, synchronize the time on the clients and servers. The problem could also be that the domain controller may be down or the trust relationship could be broken. For the latter case, you can run NETDOM to verify or reset the trust.

● If clients are experiencing trust errors connecting to a Windows NT 4.0 domain, the automatic password reset for the trust may not have reached the PDC emulator. You can run NETDOM to verify or reset the trust. If this doesn't resolve the problem, see Knowledge Base article 317178 for more information.

- After upgrading a Windows NT 4.0 domain that has existing trusts with one or more Active Directory domains, you need to delete and re-create all the previously existing trusts. These trusts are not automatically upgraded from Windows NT 4.0 trusts. If this doesn't resolve the problem, see Knowledge Base article 275221 for more information.

Delegating Authentication

The delegation of authentication is often a requirement when a network service is distributed across several servers, such as when the organization uses Web-based application services with front-end and back-end servers. In this environment, a client connects to the front-end servers and the user's credentials may need to be passed to back-end servers to ensure that the user only gets access to information to which she has been granted access.

Delegated Authentication Essentials

In Windows 2000, this functionality is provided using Kerberos authentication, either using proxy tickets or using forwarded tickets:

- With proxy tickets, the client sends a session ticket request to a domain controller acting as a KDC, asking for access to the back-end server. The KDC grants the session ticket request and sends the client a session ticket with a PROXIABLE flag set. The client can then send this ticket to the front-end server, and the front-end server in turn uses this ticket to access information on the back-end server. In this configuration, the client needs to know the name of the back-end server, which in some cases is problematic, particularly if you need to maintain strict security for the back-end databases and don't want their integrity to be compromised.

- With forwarding tickets, the client sends an initial authorization request to the KDC, requesting a session ticket that the front-end server will be able to use to access the back-end servers. The KDC grants the session ticket request, and sends it to the client. The client can then send the ticket to the front-end server, which then uses the session ticket to make a network resource request on behalf of the client. The front-end server then gets a session ticket to access the back-end server using the client's credentials.

> **Note**
> In the Windows 2000 model, the front-end server is not constrained in terms of the network resources it can request on the client's behalf. That means the front-end server could try to access any network resource using the client's credentials.

Although both techniques are effective, the requirement to use Kerberos in Windows 2000 limits the types of clients that can be used. In this scenario, only clients running Windows 2000 or later can be used. With Windows Server 2003 and Windows Server 2008, you can use both NTLM and Kerberos for authentication, which allows older clients to be used, as well as clients running Windows 2000 or later. In addition, with Windows Server 2003 and Windows Server 2008, you can use constrained delegation. Constrained delegation allows you to configure accounts so that they are delegated only for specific purposes. This kind of delegation is based on service principal names. Thus, unlike Windows 2000, in which the front-end server can access any network service on the client's behalf, with Windows Server 2003 and Windows Server 2008, a front-end server can only access network resources for which delegation has been granted.

Configuring Delegated Authentication

To use delegated authentication, the user account, as well as the service or computer account acting on the user's behalf, must be configured to support delegated authentication.

Configuring the Delegated User Account

For the user account, you must ensure that the account option Account Is Sensitive And Cannot Be Delegated is not selected, which by default it isn't. If you want to check this option, use Active Directory Users And Computers, as shown in the following screen. Double-click the user's account entry in Active Directory Users And Computers, and then click the Account tab. You'll find the Account Is Sensitive And Cannot Be Delegated check box under Account Options. Scroll through the list until you find it.

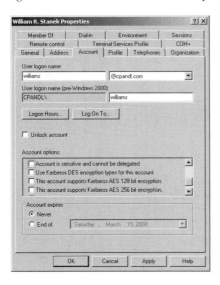

Configuring the Delegated Service or Computer Account

For the service acting on the user's behalf, you must first determine if the service is running under a normal user account or under a special identity, such as LocalSystem. If the service runs under a normal user account, check the account in Active Directory Users And Computers and ensure that the Account Is Sensitive And Cannot Be Delegated check box is not selected. If the service runs under a special identity, you need to configure delegation for the computer account of the front-end server.

When the domain is operating in Windows 2000 native functional level, you have limited options for configuring a computer for delegation. In Active Directory Users And Computers, double-click the computer account. On the General tab, select the Trust Computer For Delegation check box to allow delegation. This option sets the Windows 2000 level of authentication, which allows the service to make requests for any network resources on the client's behalf.

In Active Directory Users And Computers, double-click the computer account to display its Properties dialog box, and then click the Delegation tab, as shown in the following screen:

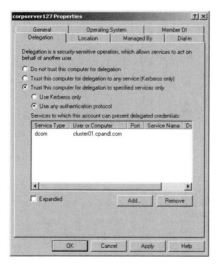

When the domain is operating in Windows Server 2003 or higher functional level, you have the following options for configuring a computer for delegation:

- **Do Not Trust This Computer For Delegation** Select this option if you don't want the computer to be trusted for delegation.

- **Trust This Computer For Delegation To Any Service (Kerberos Only)** Select this option to use the Windows 2000 level of authentication, which allows the service to make requests for any network resources on the client's behalf.

- **Trust This Computer For Delegation To Specified Services Only** Select this option to use the Windows Server 2008 level of authentication, which allows the service to make requests only for specified services. You can then specify whether the client must authenticate using Kerberos only or can use any authentication protocol.

When you are using the Windows Server 2008 level of authentication, you must next specify the services to which the front-end server can present a client's delegated credentials. To do this, you need to know the name of the computers running the services and the types of services you are authorizing. Click Add to display the Add Services dialog box and then click Users Or Computers to display the Select Users Or Computers dialog box.

In the Select Users Or Computers dialog box, type the name of the computer providing the service, such as CORPSVR02, and then click Check Names. If multiple matches are found, select the name or names you want to use, and then click OK. If no matches are found, you've either entered an incorrect name or you're working with an incorrect location. Modify the name and try again or click Locations to select a new location. To add additional computers, type a semicolon (;), and then repeat this process. When you click OK, the Add Services dialog box is updated with a list of available services on the selected computer or computers, as shown in the following screen:

Use the Add Services dialog box to select the services for which you are authorizing delegated authentication. You can use Shift+click or Ctrl+click to select multiple services. After you've selected the appropriate services, click OK. The selected services are added to the Services To Which This Account Can Present Delegated Credentials list. Click OK to close the computer's Properties dialog box and save the delegation changes.

Chapter 30

Design Considerations for Active Directory Operations Masters

Active Directory's multimaster replication model creates a distributed environment that allows any domain controller to be used for authentication and allows you to make changes to standard directory information without regard to which domain controller you use. The approach works well for most Active Directory operations—but not all. Some Active Directory operations can only be performed by a single authoritative domain controller called an *operations master.*

Operations Master Roles

A designated operations master has a flexible single-master operations (FSMO) role. The five designated roles are

- Schema master

- Domain naming master

- Relative ID (RID) master

- PDC emulator

- Infrastructure master

As depicted in Figure 30-15, two of the roles, schema master and domain naming master, are assigned on a per-forest basis. This means that there is only one schema master and only one domain naming master in a forest. The other three roles, RID master, infrastructure master, and PDC emulator, are assigned on a per-domain basis. For each domain in the forest, there is only one of these operations master roles.

When you install Active Directory and create the first domain controller in a new forest, all five roles are assigned to that domain controller. As you add domains, the first domain controller you install in a domain is automatically designated the RID master, infrastructure master, and PDC emulator for that domain.

As part of domain design, you should consider how many domain controllers you need per domain, and whether you need to transfer operations master roles after you install new domain controllers. In all cases, you'll want to have at least two domain controllers in each domain in the forest. The reasons for transferring the operations master roles depend on several factors. First, you might want to transfer an operations master role to improve performance, as you might do when a server has too heavy a workload and you need to distribute some of the load. Second, you might need to transfer an operations master role if you plan to take the server with that role offline for maintenance or if the server fails.

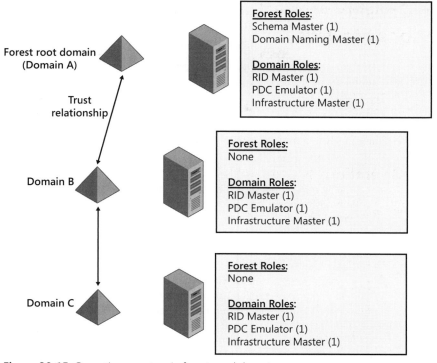

Figure 30-15 Operations masters in forests and domains.

You can determine the current operations masters for your logon domain by typing the following at a command prompt:

```
netdom query fsmo
```

As shown here, the output lists each role owner by its fully qualified domain name:

```
Schema master            CorpServer26.cpandl.com
Domain naming master     CorpServer26.cpandl.com
PDC                      CorpServer32.tech.cpandl.com
RID pool manager         CorpServer32.tech.cpandl.com
Infrastructure master    CorpServer41.tech.cpandl.com
```

From the output in this example, you can also determine that the forest root domain is cpandl.com and the current logon domain is tech.cpandl.com. If you want to determine the operations masters for a specific domain, use the following command:

```
netdom query fsmo /d:DomainName
```

where *DomainName* is the name of the domain, such as eng.cpandl.com.

Operations master roles can be changed in two ways:

- If the current operations master is online, you can perform a role transfer, gracefully shifting the role from one domain controller to another.

- If the current operations master has failed and will not be coming back online, you can seize the role and forcibly transfer it to another domain controller.

INSIDE OUT   Recommended placement of operations master roles

Microsoft recommends the following configuration:

- Ideally, you should place the forest-wide roles, schema master and domain naming master, on the same domain controller. There is very little overhead associated with these roles, so placement on the same server adds very little load overall. However, it is important to safeguard this server, because these are critical roles in the forest. In addition, the server acting as the domain naming master should also be a global catalog server.

- Ideally, you should place the relative ID master and PDC emulator roles on the same domain controller. The reason for this is that the PDC emulator uses more relative IDs than most other domain controllers. If the relative ID master and PDC emulator roles aren't on the same domain controller, the domain controllers on which they are placed should be in the same Active Directory site, and the domain controllers should have a reliable connection between them.

- Ideally, you should not place the infrastructure master on a domain controller that is also a global catalog server. The reason for this is a bit complicated, and there are some important exceptions to note.

  The infrastructure master is responsible for updating cross-domain group membership and determines whether its information is current or out of date by checking a global catalog and then replicating changes to other domain controllers as necessary. If the infrastructure master and the global catalog are on the same server, the infrastructure master doesn't see that changes have been made and thus doesn't replicate them.

  The exceptions are for a single-domain forest or a multi-domain forest where all domain controllers are global catalog servers. In the case of a single-domain forest, there are no cross-group references to update, so it doesn't matter where the infrastructure master is located. In the case of a multi-domain forest where all domain controllers are global catalog servers, all the domain controllers know about all the objects in the forest already, so the infrastructure master doesn't really have to make updates.

Using, Locating, and Transferring the Schema Master Role

The schema master is the only domain controller in the forest with a writable copy of the schema container. This means that it is the only domain controller in the forest on which you can make changes to the schema. You make changes to the schema using the Active Directory Schema snap-in. When you start the Active Directory Schema snap-in, it makes a direct connection to the schema master, allowing you to view the schema for the directory. To make changes to the schema, however, you must use an account that is a member of the Schema Admins group.

By default, the schema master is the first domain controller installed in the forest root domain. You can transfer this role using the Active Directory Schema snap-in or the NTDSUTIL command-line utility.

To locate the schema master, open the Active Directory Schema snap-in in a custom console. Right-click the Active Directory Schema node, and then select Operations Master. The Change Schema Master dialog box, shown in the following screen, shows the current schema master:

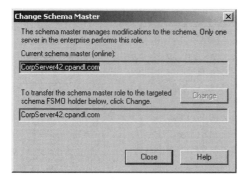

To transfer the schema master role to another server, follow these steps:

1. Open the Active Directory Schema snap-in in a custom console. Right-click the Active Directory Schema node, and then select Change Active Directory Domain Controller.

2. In the Change Directory Server dialog box, type the fully qualified domain name of the domain controller to which you want to transfer the schema master role, and then click OK.

3. Right-click the Active Directory Schema node, and then select Operations Master. In the Change Schema Master dialog box, click Change, and then click Close.

Using, Locating, and Transferring the Domain Naming Master Role

The domain naming master is responsible for adding or removing domains from the forest. Any time you create a domain, a Remote Procedure Call (RPC) connection is made to the domain naming master, which assigns the domain a globally unique identifier (GUID). Any time you remove a domain, an RPC connection is made to the domain naming master and the previously assigned GUID reference is removed. If you cannot connect to the domain naming master when you are trying to add or remove a domain, you will not be able to create or remove the domain.

To locate the domain naming master, start Active Directory Domains And Trusts. Right-click the Active Directory Domains And Trusts node, and then select Operations Master. The Operations Master dialog box, shown in the following screen, shows the current domain naming master:

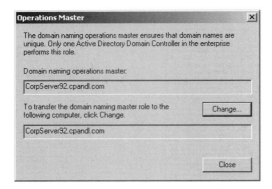

To transfer the domain naming master role to another server, follow these steps:

1. Start Active Directory Domains And Trusts. Right-click the Active Directory Domains And Trusts node, and then select Change Active Directory Domain Controller.

2. In the Change Directory Server dialog box, type the forest root domain name in the Look In This Domain field, and then press Tab. Select an available domain controller to which you want to transfer the role, and then click OK.

3. Right-click the Active Directory Domains And Trusts node, and then select Operations Master. In the Operations Master dialog box, click Change, and then click Close.

Using, Locating, and Transferring the Relative ID Master Role

The relative ID (RID) master controls the creation of new security principals such as users, groups, and computers throughout its related domain. Every domain controller in a domain is issued a block of relative IDs by the RID master. These relative IDs are used to build the security IDs that uniquely identify security principals in the domain.

The actual security ID generated by a domain controller consists of a domain identifier, which is the same for every object in a domain, and a unique relative ID that differentiates the object from any other objects in the domain.

The block of relative IDs issued to a domain controller is called a RID pool. Typically, blocks of relative IDs are issued in lots of 10,000. When the RID pool on a domain controller is nearly exhausted, the domain controller requests a new block of 10,000 RIDs. It is the job of the RID master to issue blocks of RIDs and it does so as long as it is up and running. If a domain controller cannot connect to the RID master and for any reason runs outs of RIDs, no new objects can be created on the domain controller and object creation will fail. To resolve this problem, the RID master must be made available or the RID master role must be transferred to another server.

To locate the RID master, start Active Directory Users And Computers. Right-click the domain you want to work with, and then select Operations Masters. The Operations Masters dialog box, shown in the following screen, shows the current RID master on the RID tab:

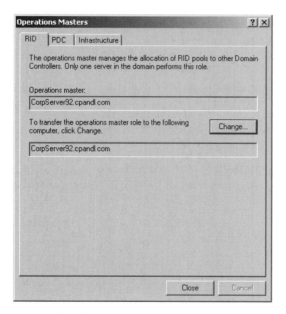

To transfer the RID master role to another server, follow these steps:

1. Start Active Directory Users And Computers. Right-click the Active Directory Users And Computers node, and then select Change Domain. In the Change Domain dialog box, type the DNS name of the domain, and then click OK.

2. Right-click the domain node, and then select Change Domain Controller. In the Change Directory Server dialog box, select an available domain controller to which you want to transfer the role, and then click OK.

   3. Right-click the domain node again, and then select Operations Masters. In the Operations Masters dialog box, the RID tab is selected by default. Click Change, and then click Close.

Using, Locating, and Transferring the PDC Emulator Role

In a domain using the Windows 2000 native or higher functional level, the Windows Server 2008 domain controller with the PDC emulator role is responsible for processing password changes. When a user changes a password, the change is first sent to the PDC emulator, which in turn replicates the change to all the other domain controllers in the domain.

All domain controllers in a domain know which server has the PDC emulator role. If a user tries to log on to the network but provides an incorrect password, the domain controller checks the PDC emulator to see that it has a recent password change for this account. If so, the domain controller retries the logon authentication on the PDC emulator. This approach is designed to ensure that if a user has recently changed a password he is not denied logon with the new password.

To locate the PDC emulator, start Active Directory Users And Computers. Right-click the domain you want to work with, and then select Operations Masters. The Operations Masters dialog box shows the current PDC emulator on the PDC tab.

To transfer the PDC emulator role to another server, follow these steps:

   1. Start Active Directory Users And Computers. Right-click the Active Directory Users And Computers node, and then select Change Domain. In the Change Domain dialog box, type the DNS name of the domain, and then click OK.

   2. Right-click the domain node, and then select Change Domain Controller. In the Change Directory Server dialog box, select an available domain controller to which you want to transfer the role, and then click OK.

   3. Right-click the domain node again, and then select Operations Masters. In the Operations Masters dialog box, select the PDC tab. Click Change, and then click Close.

Using, Locating, and Transferring the Infrastructure Master Role

The infrastructure master is responsible for updating cross-domain group-to-user references. This means that the infrastructure master is responsible for ensuring that changes to the common name of a user account are correctly reflected in the group membership information for groups in other domains in the forest. The infrastructure master does this by comparing its directory data to that of a global catalog. If the data is outdated, it updates the data and replicates the changes to other domain controllers in the domain. If for some reason the infrastructure master is unavailable, group-to-user name references will not be updated, and cross-domain group membership may not accurately reflect the actual names of user objects.

To locate the infrastructure master, start Active Directory Users And Computers. Right-click the domain you want to work with, and then select Operations Masters. The Operations Masters dialog box shows the current infrastructure master on the Infrastructure tab.

To transfer the infrastructure master role to another server, follow these steps:

1. Start Active Directory Users And Computers. Right-click the Active Directory Users And Computers node, and then select Change Domain. In the Change Domain dialog box, type the DNS name of the domain, and then click OK.

2. Right-click the domain node, and then select Change Domain Controller. In the Change Directory Server dialog box, select an available domain controller to which you want to transfer the role, and then click OK.

3. Right-click the domain node again, and then select Operations Masters. In the Operations Masters dialog box, select the Infrastructure tab. Click Change, and then click Close.

Seizing Operations Master Roles

When an operations master fails and is not coming back online, you need to seize the role to forcibly transfer it to another domain controller. Seizing a role is a drastic step that you should perform only when the previous role owner will never be available again. Don't seize an operations master role when you can transfer it gracefully using the normal transfer procedure. Only seize a role as a last resort.

Before you seize a role and forcibly transfer it, you should determine how up to date the domain controller that will take over the role is with respect to the previous role owner. Active Directory tracks replication changes using Update Sequence Numbers (USNs). Because of replication latency, domain controllers might not all be up to date. If you compare a domain controller's USN to that of other servers in the domain, you can determine whether the domain controller is the most up to date with respect to changes from the previous role owner. If the domain controller is up to date, you can transfer the role safely. If the domain controller isn't up to date, you can wait for replication to occur and then transfer the role to the domain controller.

Windows Server 2008 includes Repadmin for working with Active Directory replication. To display the highest sequence number for a specified naming context on each replication partner of a designated domain controller, type the following at a command prompt:

```
repadmin /showutdvec DomainControllerName NamingContext
```

where *DomainControllerName* is the fully qualified domain name of the domain controller and *NamingContext* is the distinguished name of the domain in which the server is located, such as:

```
repadmin /showutdvec corpserver52 dc=cpandl,dc=com
```

Chapter 30

The output shows the highest USN on replication partners for the domain partition:

```
Main-Site\corpserver31    @ USN    678321 @ Time 2008-03-15 12:42:32
Main-Site\corpserver26    @ USN    681525 @ Time 2008-03-15 12:42:35
```

In this example, if CorpServer31 was the previous role owner and the domain controller you are examining has an equal or larger USN for CorpServer31, the domain controller is up to date. However, if CorpServer31 was the previous role owner and the domain controller you are examining has a lower USN for CorpServer31, the domain controller is not up to date and you should wait for replication to occur before seizing the role. You could also use Repadmin /Syncall to force the domain controller that is the most up to date with respect to the previous role owner to replicate with all of its replication partners.

To seize an operations master role, follow these steps:

1. Open a command prompt on the console of the server you want to assign as the new operations master locally or via Remote Desktop.

2. List current operations masters by typing **netdom query fsmo**.

3. Enter **ntdsutil**. At the ntdsutil prompt, enter **roles**.

4. At the fsmo maintenance prompt, type **connections**.

5. At the server connections prompt, type **connect to server** followed by the fully qualified domain name of the domain controller to which you want to assign the operations master role.

6. After you've established a connection to the domain controller, type **quit** to exit the server connections prompt.

7. At the fsmo maintenance prompt, type one of the following:
   - seize pdc
   - seize rid master
   - seize infrastructure master
   - seize schema master
   - seize domain naming master

8. At the fsmo maintenance prompt, type **quit**.

9. At the ntdsutil prompt, type **quit**.

After seizing operations master role, you may need to remove the related data from Active Directory.

Whether you are implementing a new Active Directory environment or updating your existing environment, there's a lot to think about when it comes to design. Every Active Directory design is built from the same basic building blocks. These basic building blocks include the following:

- **Domains** A domain is a logical grouping of objects that allows central management and control over replication of those objects. Every organization has at least one domain, which is implemented when Active Directory is installed on the first domain controller.

- **Domain trees** A domain tree is a single domain in a unique namespace or a group of domains that share the same namespace. The domain at the top of a domain tree is referred to as the *root domain*. Two-way transitive trusts join parent and child domains in the same domain tree.

- **Forests** A forest is a single domain tree or a group of domain trees that are grouped together to share resources. The first domain created in a new forest is referred to as the forest root domain. Domain trees in a forest have two-way transitive trusts between their root domains.

Many organizations have only one domain and although I'll discuss reasons why you might want to have additional domains, domain trees, and forests in this chapter, you might also want to add structure to a domain. The building block you use to add structure to a domain is the organizational unit (OU), which I'll discuss in depth in this chapter.

Creating an Active Directory Implementation or Update Plan

Creating or modifying an existing domain and forest plan is the single most important design decision you make when implementing Active Directory. As such, this isn't a decision you should make alone. When you design Active Directory for an organization of any size, you should get the organization's management involved in the high-level design process.

Involvement doesn't mean letting other groups decide on all aspects of the design. There are many complex components that all have to fit together, and the actual implementation of Active Directory should be the responsibility of the IT group. Involvement means getting feedback from and working with the business managers of other groups to ensure that the high-level design meets their business requirements.

In addition, you almost certainly need to get approval of the high-level design goals with regard to security, access, usability, and manageability. Plan for this as you are developing the initial implementation plan. Your plan should start with the highest-level objects and work toward the lowest-level objects. This means that you must do the following:

1. Develop a forest plan.

2. Develop a domain plan that supports the forest plan.

3. Develop an organizational unit plan that supports the domain and forest plan.

The sections that follow discuss how to develop the necessary plans. After you have completed the planning and the plans are approved, you can implement the plan.

As part of your Active Directory planning, you should keep in mind the planning strategies discussed in Chapter 2, "Planning for Windows Server 2008." This means your plan should meet or exceed your organization's service level agreements (SLAs) and include the necessary hardware and network plans to make sure your implementation or upgrade is a success. For remote locations, such as branch offices, you should also determine whether Read-Only Domain Controllers (RODCs) are appropriate. RODCs are discussed in Chapter 34, "Deploying Read-Only Domain Controllers."

Developing a Forest Plan

Forest planning involves developing a plan for the namespace and administration needs of the organization as a whole. As part of this planning, you should decide who are the owners of the forest or forests you intend to implement. From an administration standpoint, the owners of a forest are the users who are the members of the Schema Admins and Enterprise Admins groups of the forest as well as users who are members of the Domains Admins group in the root domain of the forest. Although these users have direct control over the forest structure, they typically don't make the final decisions when it comes to implementing forest-wide changes. Typically, the final authority for making forest-wide changes is an IT or business manager who is requesting changes based on a specific business need or requirement and acting after coordinating with business managers from other groups as necessary.

Forest Namespace

The top structure in any Active Directory implementation is the forest root domain. The forest root domain is established when you install Active Directory on the first domain controller in a new forest. Any time you add a new domain that is part of a different namespace to an existing forest, you establish a root domain for a new tree. The name given to a root domain—either the forest root domain itself or the root domain of a new tree in a forest—acts as the base name for all domains later created in that tree. As you add subsequent domains, the domains are added below an established root domain. This makes the domains child domains of a root domain (see Figure 31-1).

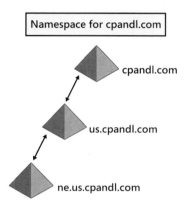

Figure 31-1 A hierarchy of domains.

Regardless of whether your forest uses a single namespace or multiple namespaces, additional domains in the same forest have the following characteristics:

- **Share a common schema** All domain controllers in the forest have the same schema and a single schema master is designated for the forest.

- **Share a common configuration directory partition** All domain controllers share the same configuration container, and it stores the default configuration and policy information.

- **Share a common trust configuration** All domains in the forest are configured to trust all the other domains in the forest, and the trust is two-way and transitive.

- **Share a common global catalog** All domains in the forest have the same global catalog, and it stores a partial replica of all objects in the forest.

- **Share common forest-wide administrators** All domains in the forest have the same top-level administrators: Enterprise Admins and Schema Admins, who have the following roles.

  - Enterprise Admins are the only administrators with forest-level privileges, which let them add or remove domains. The Enterprise Admins group is also a member of the local Administrators group of each domain, so, by default, these users can manage any domain in the forest.

  - Schema Admins are the only administrators who have the right to modify the schema.

Single vs. Multiple Forests

Part of creating a forest plan is deciding how many forests you need or whether you need additional forests. This isn't an easy decision or a decision that should be made lightly. With a single forest, you have a single top-level unit for sharing and managing resources. You can share information across all domains in the forest. However, this requires a great deal of trust and cooperation among all the groups in the organization.

With multiple forests you change the dynamic considerably. You no longer have a single top-level unit for sharing and managing resources. You have separate structures that are fully autonomous and isolated from one another. The forests do not share schema, configuration information, trusts, global catalogs, or forest-wide administrators. If desired, you can join the forests with a cross-forest trust.

Should you decide to implement a cross-forest trust between the forests, you can control whether a trust is one-way or two-way and the trust authentication level. Unlike inter-forest trusts, which are two-way and transitive by default, cross-forest trusts are either two-way or one-way. With a two-way trust, users in either forest have access to resources in the other forest. With a one-way trust, users in one forest have access to resources in the other forest but not vice versa.

The trust authentication level is set on outgoing trusts and is either domain-wide or selective. Domain-wide authentication is open and implies a certain level of trust as users in the trusted forest can be authenticated to use all of the resources in the trusting forest. Selective authentication is closed and more secure, because only the users or groups to which you explicitly grant permission can access resources in the trusting domain.

INSIDE OUT   Geographically separated sites

Geographically separated business units may want completely separate forests or domains. Although there may be business reasons for this, you should not make the decision based on perceived limitations in Active Directory. As long as a connection can be made between locations, there is no need for separate forests or domains. Active Directory sites provide the solution for connecting across limited-bandwidth links. With the automatic compression feature for site bridgehead servers, replication traffic is compressed 85 to 90 percent, meaning that it is 10 to 15 percent of its non-compressed size. This means that even low-bandwidth links can often be used effectively for replication. For more information on sites, see Chapter 32, "Configuring Active Directory Sites and Replication."

INSIDE OUT **Consider the size of the organization**

You should consider the size of the organization when deciding forest structure. However, the size of an organization alone is not a reason for deploying multiple forests. A forest can contain multiple domains. The domains can be deployed in multiple namespaces. Each domain is a separate unit of administration and each domain can have millions of objects.

Forest Administration

Most companies opt to deploy a single forest, and it is only through merger or acquisition that additional forests enter the picture. In part this is because there is no easy way to merge forests if you decide to do so later: You must migrate objects from one forest to the other, which can be a very long process. For this and other reasons, you should decide from the start how many forests are going to be implemented and you should justify the need for each additional forest. Sometimes additional forests are deployed because of organizational politics or the inability of business units to decide how to manage the top-level forest functions. At other times, additional forests are deployed to isolate business units or give complete control of the directory to a business unit.

The organization should consider the following factors before creating additional forests:

- Additional forests make it more difficult for users to collaborate and share information. For example, users have direct access to the global catalog and can search for resources easily only for their own forest. You must configure access to resources in other forests, and the users cannot directly search for available resources in other forests.

- Additional forests mean additional administrative overheard and duplication of infrastructure. Each forest has its own forest-level configuration and one or more additional domain-level configurations that need to be managed. The ability to share resources and synchronize information across forests must be specifically configured rather than implemented by using built-in trusts and synchronization.

Sometimes, however, you need the additional controls put in place with additional forests to give reasonable assurance that administrators from other domains in a forest do not make harmful changes to the directory, which are then replicated throughout the organization. All the domain controllers in a forest are tightly integrated. A change made on one domain controller is replicated to all other domain controllers. Replication is automatic, and there are no security checks other than the fact that the person making the change must have the appropriate permissions in the first place; that is, the person must be a member of the appropriate administrator group for the type of change being made. If such an administrator is acting maliciously in making changes, those changes will be replicated regardless of the effect on the organization.

That said, reasonable assurance can be addressed by putting strict administration rules and procedures in place. With strict rules and procedures, the organization has the following multiple levels of administrators:

- Top-level administrators with enterprise-wide privileges who are trusted with forest-wide administration. These administrators are members of the Enterprise Admins group.

- High-level administrators with domain-wide privileges who are trusted with domain-wide administration. These administrators are members of the Domain Admins, Administrators, Server Operators, or Backup Operators groups.

- Administrators who are delegated responsibilities for specific tasks, which might include being a member of the Server Operators, Backup Operators, or similar groups.

To give reasonable assurance, the organization also needs to physically secure domain controllers, set policies about how administrators use their accounts (such as running tasks as an administrator only when needed for administration), and configure auditing of all actions performed by both users and administrators.

Developing a Domain Plan

After you determine how many forests are needed based on the current namespace and administration needs of the organization as a whole, you next need to determine the domain structure that needs to be implemented. Whether your organization has an existing Active Directory structure or is implementing Active Directory for the first time, this means assessing the current environment and determining what changes are needed.

You need to thoroughly document the existing infrastructure and determine what—if anything—needs to be restructured, replaced, or upgraded. You also need to determine if it is even possible or practical to update the existing infrastructure as proposed. In some cases, you may find that the current design is not ideal for updating as proposed and you may need to revise your plans.

That's all acceptable, because design is usually an iterative process in which you go from the theoretical to the practical during successive revisions. Just remember that it is difficult to change the domain namespace as well as the number of forests and domains after you've started implementing the design. Other parts of a design, such as the OU and site structure, are easier to change after implementation.

> **Note**
>
> For tips and techniques on naming domains and establishing a naming hierarchy, see Chapter 23, "Architecting DNS Infrastructure." You'll also find detailed information on using DNS (Domain Name System) with Active Directory in Chapter 24, "Implementing and Managing DNS."

Domain Design Considerations

Domains allow you to logically group objects for central management and control over replication of those objects. You use domains to partition a forest into smaller components. As part of domain design, you should consider the following:

- **Replication** Domains set the replication boundary for the domain directory partition and for domain policy information stored in the Sysvol folder on every domain controller in the domain. Any changes made to the domain directory partition or domain policy information on one of the domain controllers is replicated automatically to the other domain controllers in the domain. Although other directory partitions, such as the schema and configuration, are replicated throughout a forest, the domain information is replicated only within a particular domain, and the more objects in the domain container, the more data that potentially needs to be replicated.

- **Resource access** The trusts between and among domains in a forest do not by themselves grant permission to access resources. A user must be specifically given permission to access a resource in another domain. By default, an administrator of a domain can manage only resources in that domain and cannot manage resources in another domain. This means that domain boundaries are also boundaries for resource access and administration.

- **Policy** The policies that apply to one domain are independent from those applied to other domains. This means that policies for user and computer configuration and security can be applied differently in different domains. Certain policies can be applied only at the domain level. These policies, referred to as *domain security policies*, include password policies, account lockout policies, and Kerberos policies, and are applied to all domain accounts.

- **Language** For organizations in which multiple languages are used, servers within a domain should all be configured with the same language. Although English is supported by all installations, any additional language should be the same on all servers within a domain. This is a consideration for administration purposes but not a requirement.

Single vs. Multiple Domains

With domain design, part of the decision involves the number of domains that are needed. You may need to implement additional domains or continue using a single domain. A single domain is the easiest to manage. It is also the ideal environment for users, because it is easier for users to locate resources in a single domain environment than in a multi-domain or multi-tree forest.

Beyond simplicity, there are several other reasons for implementing or keeping to a single domain design, such as the following:

- You do not need to create additional domains to limit administrative access, delegate control, or create a hierarchical structure. In Active Directory, you can use OUs for these purposes.

- You may want to make authentication and resource access easier to configure and less prone to problems. A single domain doesn't have to rely on trusts or the assignment of resource access in other domains.

- You may want to make domain structure easier to manage. A single domain only has one set of domain administrators and one set of domain policy. A single domain doesn't need duplicate domain-wide infrastructure for domain controllers.

- Your organization may frequently restructure its business units. It is easy to rename OUs, but very difficult to rename domains. It is easy to move accounts and resources between OUs, but much more difficult to move accounts and resources between domains.

With Active Directory, you can have millions of objects in a single domain, so the reason for using multiple domains should not be based solely on the number of objects—although the number of objects is certainly still a factor to consider from a manageability standpoint. That said, using multiple domains sometimes makes sense, particularly if your organization has multiple business locations. With multiple locations, domain changes need to be replicated to all domain controllers and geographic separation is often—but not always—a key factor in deciding to use multiple domains. Primarily, this is because there is less replication traffic between domains than within domains (relatively speaking), and if business locations are geographically separated, it makes sense to limit the replication traffic between locations if possible.

The need to limit replication traffic is a key reason for using multiple domains even within a single business location. For example, a large organization with groups of users spread out over several floors of a building or in multiple buildings in a campus setting may find that the connection speed between locations isn't adequate. In this case, using multiple domains may make sense, because it will limit the scope of updates that initiate replication of changes.

Restricting access to resources and the need to enforce different sets of security policies are also reasons for using multiple domains. Using multiple domains creates boundaries for resource access and administration. It also creates boundaries for security policy.

So, if you need to limit resource access or tighten security controls for both users and administrators, you will probably want to use multiple domains.

Like additional forests, multiple domains require additional administrative and infrastructure overhead. Each domain has its own domain-level configuration, which requires server hardware and administrators to manage that hardware. Because users may be accessing, authenticating, and accessing resources across trusts, there is more complexity and there are more points of failure.

Forest Root Domain Design Configurations

The forest root domain can be either a dedicated root or a non-dedicated root. A dedicated root, also referred to as an *empty root*, is used as a placeholder to start the directory. No user or group accounts are associated with it other than accounts created when the forest root is installed and accounts that are needed to manage the forest. Because no additional user or group accounts are associated with it, a dedicated root domain is not used to assign access to resources. A non-dedicated root is used as a normal part of the directory. It has user and group accounts associated with it and is used to assign access to resources.

For an organization that is going to use multiple domains anyway, using a dedicated root domain makes a lot of sense. The forest root domain contains the forest-wide administrator accounts (Enterprise Admins and Schema Admins) and the forest-wide operations masters (domain naming master and schema master). It must be available when users log on to domains other than their home domain and when users access resources in other domains.

A dedicated root domain is easier to manage than a root domain that contains accounts. It allows you to separate the root domain from the rest of the forest. The separation also helps safeguard the entire directory, which is important, as the forest root domain cannot be replaced. If the root domain is destroyed and cannot be recovered, you must re-create the entire forest.

Changing Domain Design

Ideally, after you implement a domain structure, the domain names never need to change. In the real world, however, things change. Organizations change their names, merge with other companies, are acquired, or restructure more often than we'd like. With Active Directory, you have several options for changing structure. If you find that you need to move a large number of objects from one domain to another, you can use the Active Directory Migration Tool (ADMT). You can rename domains as long as the forest is running at the Microsoft Windows Server 2003 or higher functional level. Changing the domain design after implementation is difficult, however, and involves using the Domain Rename utility (Rendom.exe). While the Domain Rename utility is now included with Windows, ADMT is only available as a separate download online at the Windows Server TechCenter Downloads area (*http://www.microsoft.com/downloads*).

You can rename domains in the following key ways:

- Rename domains to move them within a domain tree. For example, you could rename a child domain from eng.it.cohowinery.com to eng.cohowinery.com.

- Rename domains so that a new tree is created. For example, you could change the name of a child domain from vineyard.cohowinery.com to cohovineyard.com.

- Rename domains to move them to a new tree. For example, you could change the name of a child domain from it.cohowinery.com to it.cohovineyard.com.

- Rename domains to set new domain names without changing the parent-child structure. For example, if the company name changes from Coho Vineyard to Coho Winery, you could change the existing domain names to use coho-winery.com instead of cohovineyard.com.

You *cannot* use the Domain Rename utility to change which domain is the forest root domain. Although you *can* change the name of the forest root domain so that it is no longer the forest root logically, the domain remains the forest root domain physically in Active Directory. It still contains the forest-wide administrator accounts (Enterprise Admins and Schema Admins) and the forest-wide operations masters (domain naming master and schema master). This occurs because there is no way to change the forest root domain assignment within Active Directory after the forest root has been established.

You cannot use Domain Rename to make changes to a domain in which Microsoft Exchange 2000 or later is deployed. Exchange 2000 Server and Exchange Server 2003 do not have their own directory service functionality. They use Active Directory for this purpose.

As you might imagine, renaming a domain in a single-domain forest is the easiest renaming operation. As you increase the number of domains within a forest, you increase the complexity of the Domain Rename operation. Regardless of how many domains you are working with, you should always plan the project completely from start to finish and back up the entire domain infrastructure before trying to implement Domain Rename.

The reason for this planning and backup is that when you rename domains, even if you rename only one domain in a forest of many domains, you must make a change to every domain controller in the forest so that it recognizes the renamed domain. When you are finished, you must reboot each domain controller. If you don't perform the rename change on every domain controller, you must remove from service the domain controllers that did not get the updates. Furthermore, from the time you start the rename operation to the time you reboot domain controllers, the forest is out of service.

To complete the process after renaming a domain and updating domain controllers, you must reboot each workstation or member server in the renamed domain twice. Any computers running Windows NT 4.0 in the renamed domain must be unjoined from the domain and then rejoined to the domain. While you are working with domain controllers and other computers that don't use Dynamic Host Configuration Protocol (DHCP) in the renamed domain, you should rename the computer so the DNS name is correct and make other DNS name changes as appropriate.

Developing an Organizational Unit Plan

So far in this book, I've discussed domains, domain trees, and forests. These are the components of Active Directory that can help you scale the directory to meet the needs of any organization regardless of its size. Sometimes, however, what you want to do is not scale the directory but create hierarchical structures that represent parts of the organization or to limit or delegate administrative access for a part of the organization. This is where OUs come in handy.

Using Organizational Units (OUs)

An *organizational unit* (OU) is a logical administrative unit that is used to group objects within a domain. Within a domain, you can use OUs to delegate administrator privileges while limiting administrative access and to create a hierarchy that mirrors the business's structure or functions. So rather than having multiple domains to represent the structure of the organization or its business functions, you can create OUs within a domain to do this.

At its most basic level, an OU is a container for objects that can contain other OUs as well as the following objects:

- Computers
- Contacts
- Groups
- inetOrgPerson
- Printers
- Shared Folders
- Users

> **Note**
>
> OUs are used to contain objects within a domain. They cannot, however, contain objects from other domains.

> **Note**
>
> An inetOrgPerson object is used to represent user accounts that have been migrated from other directory services. Except for having a different object name, you manage inetOrgPerson objects the same way as user objects.

For administrative purposes, OUs can be used in two key ways. First, you can use OUs to delegate administrative rights. This allows you to give someone limited or full administrative control over only a part of a domain. For example, if you have a branch office, you could create an OU for all the accounts and resources at that office, and then delegate administration of that OU to the local administrator.

Second, you can use OUs to manage a group of objects as a single unit. Unlike domains, OUs are not a part of DNS structure. Within Active Directory, OUs are seen as container objects that are part of a domain. In the directory tree, they are referenced with the OU= identifier, such as OU=Sales for an OU named Sales. The distinguished name (DN) of an OU includes the path to its parent as well as its relative name. As you may recall, the DC= identifier is used to reference domain components. This means that the Sales OU in the cpandl.com domain has a DN of OU=Sales,DC=cpandl,DC=com.

Because OUs can contain other OUs, you can have multiple levels of OUs. For example, if you had a USA OU and a Europe OU within the Sales OU, the DNs of these OUs would be OU=USA,OU=Sales,DC=cpandl,DC=com and OU=Europe,OU=Sales, DC=cpandl,DC=com, respectively. When you nest OUs in this way, the nested OUs inherit the Group Policy settings of the top-level OUs by default, but you can override inheritance if you want to use unique Group Policy settings for a particular OU.

From a user perspective, OUs are fairly transparent. As OUs aren't a part of DNS structure, users don't have to reference OUs when they log on, during authentication, or for searches of Active Directory. This makes multiple OUs much easier to work with than multiple domains. Also, it is fairly easy to change the names and structures of OUs, which isn't the case with domains.

Using OUs for Delegation

Although you will want to centrally manage Active Directory structure, many other administrative tasks related to Active Directory can be delegated to specific groups or individuals. Delegating administrative rights allows a user to perform a set of assigned administrative tasks for a specific OU. The tasks allowed depend on the way you configure delegation and include allowing an individual to perform the following actions:

- Create, delete, and manage accounts
- Reset user passwords and force password changes at next logon
- Read all user information
- Create, delete, and manage groups
- Modify the membership of a group
- Manage Group Policy links
- Generate Resultant Set of Policy

One of the common reasons for delegating administrative rights is to allow an individual in a department or business unit to reset user passwords. When you delegate this right, you allow a trusted person to change someone's password should the need arise. As the right is delegated to a user within a particular OU, this right is limited to that specific OU. In many organizations, this type of right is granted to Help Desk staff to allow them to reset passwords while preventing the Help Desk staff from changing other account properties.

Using OUs for Group Policy

Group Policy allows you to specify a set of rules for computer and user configuration settings. These rules control the working environment for computers and users. Although I'll discuss Group Policy in depth in Chapter 35, "Managing Users, Groups, and Computers," the important thing to know about Group Policy is that you can use it to set default options, to limit options, and to prevent changing options in virtually every aspect of computer and user configuration.

Every domain you create has a default Group Policy rule set, referred to as the *Default Domain Policy*. Group Policy can also be applied to OUs, which makes OUs important in helping administrators manage groups of accounts and resources in a particular way. By default, OUs inherit the Group Policy settings of their parent object. For top-level OUs within a domain, this means that the Default Domain Policy is inherited by default. For lower-level OUs, this means that the OUs inherit the Group Policy of the OUs above them (and if the higher-level OUs inherit Group Policy from the domain, so do the lower-level OUs).

To manage Group Policy, you can use the Group Policy Management Console (GPMC). Group Policy is a very important part of Active Directory. Not only can you use it to manage the functionality available to users, you can also use it to enforce security, standardize desktop configuration, install software, specify scripts that should run when a computer starts or shuts down and when a user logs on or logs off, and so on.

Because Group Policy is so important in Active Directory, you should plan your OU structure with Group Policy in mind. You do this by grouping objects that require the same Group Policy settings. For example, if a group of users requires a specific environment configuration to use an application or if a group of users requires a standard set of mapped drives, you can configure this through Group Policy.

Creating an OU Design

OUs simplify administration by organizing accounts and resources in ways that best fit the organizational structure. When designing OU structure, you should plan the structure before you try to implement it. Often you'll find that you need multiple levels of OUs. This is fine. The levels of OUs will form a hierarchy, much like the hierarchy formed when you use multiple levels of domains. The key thing to understand about any OU design is that it is really for administrators. As such, the design needs to be meaningful for your organization's administrators—and ideally, it should help make administration easier.

Creating a good OU design isn't always as easy as it seems. It is a good idea to go through several possible scenarios on paper before trying to implement a design.

Through successive revisions on paper, you should be able to improve the design substantially. Common design models for OUs are discussed in the sections that follow.

OU Design: Division or Business Unit Model

With a division or business unit model, you use OUs to reflect the department structure within the organization. The advantage to this model is that users will know and understand it. The disadvantage to this model is that when the company restructures, you may need to redesign the OU structure.

In the example shown in Figure 31-2, OUs are organized by department within the company, and, to allow for separate controls for accounts and resources, the related objects are put in second-level OUs. If you want to have only one level of OUs, you could do this by putting all the objects in the top-level OU.

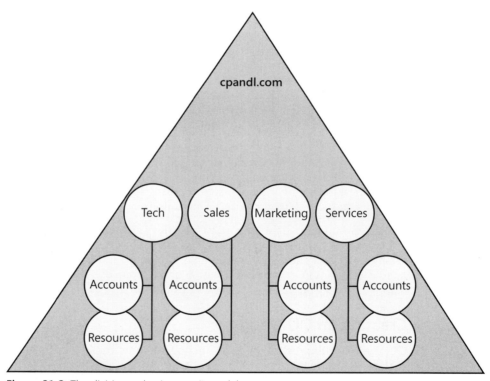

Figure 31-2 The division or business unit model.

OU Design: Geographic Model

With a geographic model, you use OUs to reflect geographic location. In this model, top-level OUs represent the largest geographic units, such as continents, and the lower-level OUs represent successively smaller geographic units, such as countries (see Figure 31-3).

There are several advantages to this model. A geographic structure is fairly stable. Many companies reorganize internally frequently, but only rarely change geographic structure. Additionally, when you use a geographic model, it is easy to determine where accounts and resources are physically located.

The disadvantages to this model have to do with its scope. For a global company, this design would put all accounts and resources in a single domain. As a result, changes made to Active Directory at any location would be replicated to every office location. Additionally, the OU structure doesn't relate to the business structure of the organization.

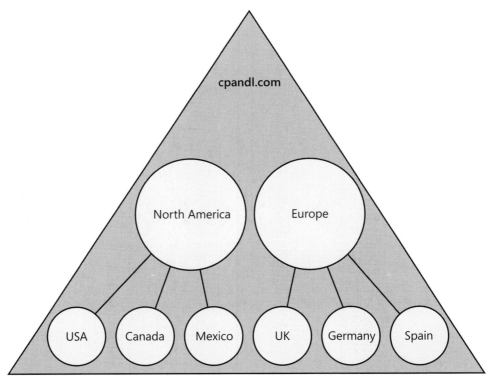

Figure 31-3 The geographic model.

OU Design: The Cost Center Model

With a cost center model, you use OUs to reflect cost centers. In this model, top-level OUs represent the major cost centers within the organization and the lower-level OUs represent geographic locations, projects, or business structures, as shown in Figure 31-4. In a company where budget is the top priority, the cost center model may be an effective way to reflect this priority. Cost centers could also be independent divisions or business units within the company that have their own management and cost controls.

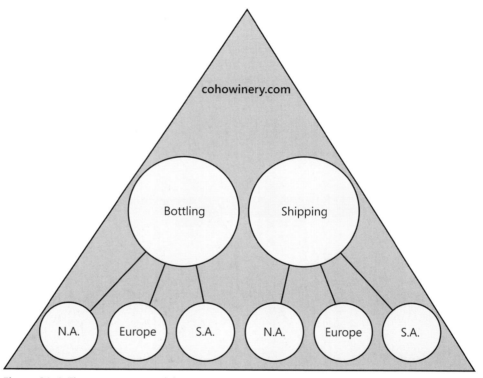

Figure 31-4 The cost center model.

The ability to represent costs and budgets in this way is a definite advantage but could also be a disadvantage. Cost center structure is not a structure well known to most administrators, and it may be confusing.

OU Design: The Administration Model

With an administration model, you use OUs to reflect the way resources and accounts are managed. As this model reflects the business structure of a company, it is very similar to the division or business unit model. The key difference is that the top-level OU is for administrators and second-level OUs are for business structure (see Figure 31-5). If successive levels are needed, they can be organized by resource type, geographic location, project type, or some combination of the three.

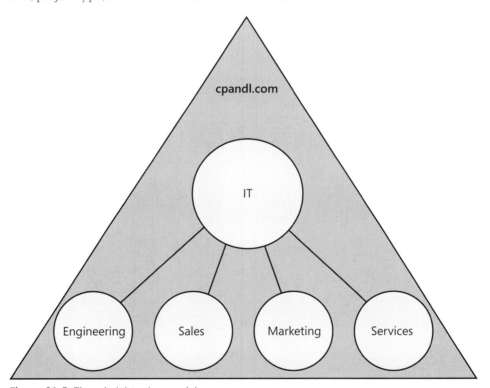

Figure 31-5 The administration model.

In a large company, you may use multiple implementations of this model for each division or business unit. In this case, the top-level administrative group would be for the division or business unit and the second-level OUs would be for groups within the division.

The advantage to this model is that it is designed around the way administrators work and represents the business structure of the company. The disadvantage to this model is that when the company or divisions within the company restructure, you may need to redesign the OU structure.

Configuring Active Directory Sites and Replication

As part of the design of Active Directory Domain Service, you should examine the network topology and determine if you need to manage network traffic between subnets or business locations. To manage network traffic related to Active Directory, you use sites, which can be used to reflect the physical topology of your network. Every Active Directory implementation has at least one site. An important part of understanding sites involves understanding Active Directory replication. Active Directory uses two replication models: one model for replication within sites and one model for replication between sites. You need a solid understanding of these replication models to plan your site structure.

Working with Active Directory Sites

A *site* is a group of Transmission Control Protocol/Internet Protocol (TCP/IP) subnets that are implemented to control directory replication traffic and isolate logon authentication traffic between physical network locations. Each subnet that is part of a site should be connected by reliable, high-speed links. Any business location connected over slow or unreliable links should be part of a separate site. Because of this, individual sites typically represent the sets of local area networks (LANs) within an organization, and the wide area network (WAN) links between business locations typically mark the boundaries of these sites. However, sites can be used in other ways as well.

Sites do not reflect the Active Directory namespace. Domain and site boundaries are separate. From a network topology perspective, a single site can contain multiple TCP/IP subnets as well. However, a single subnet can be in only one site. This means that the following conditions apply:

- A single site can contain resources from multiple domains.

- A single domain can have resources spread out among multiple sites.

- A single site can have multiple subnets.

As you design site structure, you have many options. Sites can contain a domain or a portion of a domain. A single site can have one subnet or multiple subnets. It is important to note that replication is handled differently between sites than it is within sites. Replication that occurs within a site is referred to as *intrasite replication*. Replication between sites is referred to as *intersite replication*. Each side of a site connection has one or more designated bridgehead servers.

Figure 32-1 shows an example of an organization that has one domain and two sites at the same physical location. Here, the organization has an East Campus site and a West Campus site. As you can see, the organization has multiple domain controllers at each site. The domain controllers in the East Campus site perform intrasite replication with each other, as do the domain controllers in the West Campus site. Designated servers in each site, referred to as site *bridgehead* servers, perform intersite replication with each other.

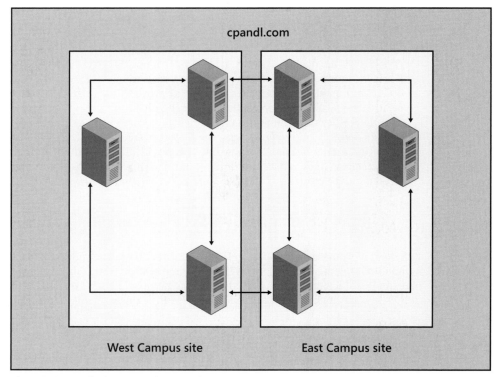

Figure 32-1 Multiple sites at the same location.

Figure 32-2 shows an example of an organization that has two different physical locations. Here, the organization has decided to use two domains and two sites. The Main site is for the cohowinery.com domain and the Seattle site is for the sea.cohowinery.com domain. Again, replication occurs both within and between the sites.

Single Site vs. Multiple Sites

One reason to create additional sites at the same physical location is to control replication traffic. Replication traffic between sites is automatically compressed, reducing the amount of traffic passed between sites by 85 to 90 percent of its original size. Because network clients try to log on to network resources within their local site first, this means that you can use sites to isolate logon traffic as well.

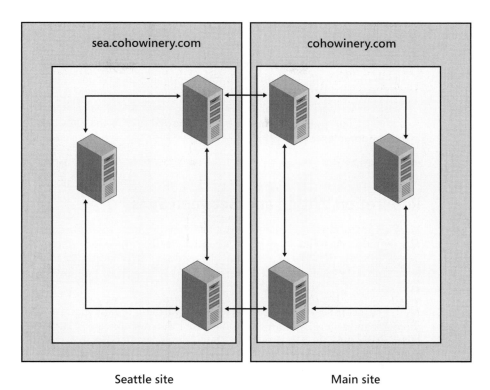

Figure 32-2 Multiple sites at different locations.

In most cases, you'll want to optimize sites for Active Directory replication control. Here, it is recommended that each site have at least one domain controller and one global catalog for client authentication. For name resolution and IP address assignment, it is also recommended that each site have at least one Domain Name System (DNS) server and one Dynamic Host Configuration Protocol (DHCP) server. Then, by creating multiple sites in the same physical location and establishing a domain controller, global catalog, and DNS and DHCP server within each site, you can closely control the logon process.

You can also design sites with other network resources in mind, including distributed file system (DFS) file shares, certificate authorities, and Microsoft Exchange servers. Generally speaking, you want to configure sites so that clients' network queries can be answered within the site. If every client query for a network resource has to be sent to a remote site, there could be substantial network traffic between sites, which could be a problem over slow WAN links. As part of your site design, you should also consider site-aware applications and services. These applications and services will use site boundaries to ensure that clients don't select resources across a WAN link when a local resource is available and preferable.

> **Note**
>
> Enterprises often have branch offices where each branch office is defined as a separate site to control traffic for high-bandwidth–consuming applications rather than Active Directory replication. Here, traffic for high-bandwidth–consuming applications, such as DFS or software control and change management (SCCM), is carefully managed but authentication and global catalog traffic is allowed to cross the WAN because it is less bandwidth-intensive.

Replication Within and Between Sites

Most organizations implementing Active Directory have multiple domain controllers. The domain controllers may be located in a single server room where they are all connected to a fast network or they may be spread out over multiple geographic locations, from which they are connected over a WAN that links the company's various office locations.

All domain controllers in the same forest—regardless of how many domain controllers there are and where domain controllers are located—replicate information with each other either directly or indirectly. Although more replication is performed within a domain than between domains, replication between domains occurs nonetheless. The same replication model is used in both cases.

When a change is made to a domain partition in Active Directory, the change is replicated to all domain controllers in the domain. If the change is made to an attribute of an object tracked by the global catalog, the change is replicated to all global catalog servers in all domains of the forest. Similarly, if you make a change to the forest-wide configuration or schema partitions, these changes are replicated to all domain controllers in all the domains of the forest.

Authentication within and between domains is also handled by domain controllers. If a user logs on to his or her home domain, the local domain controller authenticates the logon. If a user logs on to a domain other than the home domain, the logon request is forwarded through the trust tree to a domain controller in the user's home domain.

Active Directory's replication model is designed for consistency, but the consistency is loosely defined. By loosely defined, I mean that at any given moment the information on one domain controller can be different from the information on a different domain controller. This can happen when Windows Server 2008 has not yet replicated the changes on the first domain controller to the other domain controller. Over time, Windows Server 2008 replicates the changes made to Active Directory on one domain controller to all domain controllers as necessary.

When multiple sites are involved, the replication engine uses the Site model to store and then forward changes as necessary between sites. In this case, a domain controller in the site where the changes were originally made forwards the changes to a domain controller in another site. This domain controller in turn stores the changes, and then forwards the changes to all the domain controllers in the second site. In this way, the domain controller on which a change is made doesn't have to replicate directly with all the other domain controllers. It can instead rely on the store-and-forward technique to ensure that the changes are replicated as necessary.

Determining Site Boundaries

When trying to determine site boundaries, you should configure sites so that they reflect the physical structure of your network. Use connectivity between network segments to determine where you should locate site boundaries. Areas of the network that are connected with fast connections should all be part of the same site, unless you have specific requirements for controlling replication or the logon process. Areas of the network that are connected with limited bandwidth or unreliable links should be part of different sites.

As you examine each of the organization's business locations, determine whether placing domain controllers and other network resources at that location is necessary. If you elect not to place a domain controller at a remote location, you can make the location a part of a separate site. This has the following advantages:

- No Active Directory replication between the business locations
- No remote domain controllers to manage
- No additional site infrastructure to manage

There are also several disadvantages to this approach:

- All logon traffic must cross the link between the business locations.
- Users may experience slow logon and authentication to network resources.

In the end, the decision to establish a separate site may come down to the user experience and the available bandwidth. If you have fast connections between sites—which should be dedicated and redundant—you may not want to establish a separate site for the remote business location. If you have limited bandwidth between business locations and want to maintain the user experience, you may want to establish a separate site and place domain controllers and possibly other network resources at the site. This speeds up the logon and authentication process and allows you to better control the network traffic between sites.

Understanding Active Directory Replication

When you are planning site structure, it is important that you understand how replication works. As discussed previously, Active Directory uses two replication models, each of which is handled differently. The intrasite replication model is used for replication within sites and is optimized for high-bandwidth connections. The intersite replication model is used for replication between sites and is optimized for limited-bandwidth connections. Before I get into the specifics of replication and the replication models, let's look at the way replication has changed since Active Directory Domain Service was introduced with Microsoft Windows 2000.

Chapter 32

Replication Enhancements for Active Directory

The replication model used for Microsoft Windows Server 2003 and now Windows Server 2008 has changed in several important ways from the model in Windows 2000. In Windows 2000, the smallest unit of replication is an individual attribute. At first examination, this seems to be what is wanted; after all, you don't want to have to replicate an entire object if only an attribute of that object has changed. The problem with this approach is that some attributes are multivalued. That is, they have multiple values. An example is the membership attribute of a universal group. This attribute represents all the members of the universal group.

In Windows 2000, by adding or removing a single user from the group, you caused the entire group membership to be replicated. In large organizations, a significant amount of replication traffic was often generated because universal groups might have several thousand members. Windows Server 2003 and Windows Server 2008 resolve this problem by replicating only the attribute's updated value. With universal group membership, this means that only the users you've added or removed are updated, rather than the entire group membership.

As discussed in "Extensible Storage Engine" on page 993, Active Directory uses transactional processing. When there are many changes, Active Directory processes the changes in batches of 5,000 at a time. This means that Active Directory processes a single transaction or multiple transactions in sequence until it reaches 5,000 changes, then it stops and checks to see if other processes are waiting for the CPU. Because a transaction must complete before processing stops in this way, this places a practical limit on the number of changes that can be made in a single transaction—that number is 5,000.

In Windows 2000, because all the members of a group were processed any time a group's membership was changed, the limit on transactions also placed a practical limit on the number of members in a group. Again, this value is 5,000. The change in the way Windows Server 2003 and later versions of Windows Server replicate multivalued attributes also removes the limitation of 5,000 members for groups.

> **Note**
>
> When a forest is running at Windows Server 2003 or higher functional level, the members of the forest can take advantage of the previously discussed replication enhancements. For Windows Server 2003 or higher functional level, this means that all domain controllers in all domains within the forest must be running Windows Server 2003 or higher.

Other replication enhancements involve intersite replication. Windows Server 2003 and later versions of Windows Server introduce the ability to turn off compression for intersite replication and to enable notification for intersite replication. They also have an improved knowledge consistency checker (KCC), which allows Active Directory to support a greater number of sites. These changes affect intersite replication in the following key ways:

- In Windows 2000, Windows Server 2003, and Windows Server 2008, all intersite replication traffic is compressed by default. Although this significantly reduces the amount of traffic between sites, it increases the processing overhead required on the bridgehead servers to replicate traffic between sites. Therefore, if processor utilization on bridgehead servers is a concern, and you have adequate bandwidth connections between sites, you may want to disable compression, which Windows Server 2003 and Windows Server 2008 allow you to do.

- In Windows 2000, Windows Server 2003, and Windows Server 2008, replication between sites occurs at scheduled intervals according to the site link configuration. With Windows Server 2003 and Windows Server 2008, you can enable notification for intersite replication, which allows the bridgehead server in a site to notify the bridgehead server on the other side of a site link that changes have occurred. This allows the other bridgehead server to pull the changes across the site link and thereby get more frequent updates.

- In Windows 2000, the maximum number of sites you can have in a forest is greatly influenced by the knowledge consistency checker (KCC). As a result, the KCC has a practical limit of about 100 sites per forest. Because the KCC in Windows Server 2003 and Windows Server 2008 has been revised, the KCC itself is no longer the limiting factor. This means that you can have many hundreds of sites per forest.

> **Note**
>
> To turn off compression or enable notification, you need to edit the related site link or connection object. See "Configuring Replication Schedules for Site Links" on page 1293.

Replication Enhancements for the Active Directory System Volume

The Active Directory system volume (Sysvol) contains domain policy, as well as scripts used for log on, log off, shutdown, and startup, and other related files as well as files stored within Active Directory. The way domain controllers replicate the Sysvol depends on the domain functional level:

- When a domain is running at Windows 2000 native or Windows Server 2003 functional level, domain controllers replicate the Sysvol using File Replication Service (FRS).

- When a domain is running at Windows Server 2008 functional level, domain controllers replicate the Sysvol using distributed file system (DFS).

Chapter 32

FRS and DFS are replication services that use the Active Directory replication topology to replicate files and folders in the Sysvol shared folders on domain controllers. The way this works is that the replication service checks with the KCC to determine the replication topology that has been generated for Active Directory replication, and then uses this replication topology to replicate Sysvol files to all the domain controllers in a domain. Because DFS has been significantly enhanced, you'll want to use DFS instead of FRS whenever possible.

INSIDE OUT Why DFS instead of FRS?

When used with Active Directory, DFS has several advantages over FRS. DFS was enhanced for Windows Server 2003 Release 2. Not only did these enhancements make DFS easier to manage, they also introduced new replication and compression technologies. With Windows Server 2003 Release 2 and later, DFS Replication (DFS-R) and Remote Differential Compression (RDC) are used instead of Rsync version 2.6.2 to provide up to 300 percent faster replication and 200 to 300 percent faster compression. Operational overhead for managing content and replication also was reduced by 40 percent. Additionally, DFS-R supports automated recovery from database loss or corruption, replication scheduling, and bandwidth throttling. Together these features make DFS-R significantly more scalable than FRS.

RDC is the secret ingredient associated with enhanced DFS that allows for granular replication of changes when using Active Directory with Windows Server 2008—this is what's referred to when you read a vague statement that says DFS allows for granular replication of the Sysvol. RDC enables granular replication by accurately identifying changes within and across files and transmitting only those changes to achieve significant bandwidth savings. More specifically, RDC detects insertions, removals, or rearrangements of data in files, enabling DFS-R to replicate only the changed file blocks when files are updated. Changes within or across files are called file deltas.

In addition to calculating file deltas and transferring only the differences, RDC also can copy any similar file from any client or server to another using data that is common to both computers. This further reduces the amount of the data sent and the overall bandwidth requirements for file transfers. Local differencing techniques are used to transform the old version into a new version. The differences between two versions of the file are calculated on the source domain controller and then sent to the DFS client on the target domain controller.

The storage techniques and replication architectures for DFS and FRS are decidedly different. Figure 32-3 shows a conceptual view of how File Replication Service is used with Active Directory on a domain controller. The File Replication Service (Ntfrs.exe) stores FRS topology and schedule information in Active Directory and periodically polls Active Directory to retrieve updated information using Lightweight Directory Access Protocol (LDAP). Most administrator tools that work with FRS use LDAP as well. Internally, FRS makes direct calls to the file system using standard I/O. FRS uses the Remote Procedure Call (RPC) protocol when communicating with remote servers.

FRS stores various types of data in the NTFS file system, including transactions in the FRS Jet database (Ntfrs.jdb), events and error messages in the FRS Event log (NtFrs.evt), and debug logs stored in the debug log folder (%SystemRoot%\Debug). Esent.dll is a dynamic link library used by the Jet database to store transactions. Ntfrsres.dll is a dynamic-link library used by FRS to store events and error messages.

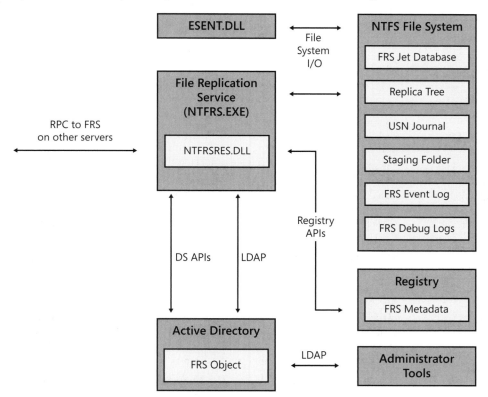

Figure 32-3 A conceptual view of how File Replication Service works.

The contents of the replica tree determine what FRS replicates. The replica tree for Active Directory is the Sysvol. The Sysvol contains domain, staging, staging areas, and sysvol folders. The USN journal is a persistent log of changes made to files on an NTFS volume. NTFS uses the USN journal to track information about added, deleted, and modified files. FRS in turn uses the USN journal to determine when changes are made to the contents of the replica tree. FRS then replicates changes according to the schedule in Active Directory. FRS stores configuration data in the Registry.

Figure 32-4 shows a conceptual view of how the Distributed File System (DFS) service is used with Active Directory on a domain controller. The DFS service (Dfssvc.exe) stores information about stand-alone namespaces in the Registry and information about domain-based namespaces in Active Directory.

INSIDE OUT The replica root

The actual replica root begins at the %SystemRoot%\Sysvol\domain folder, but the folder that is actually shared is the %SystemRoot%\Sysvol\sysvol folder. These folders appear to contain the same content because Sysvol uses junction points (also known as reparse points). A junction point is a physical location on a hard disk that points to data that is located elsewhere on the hard disk or on another storage device.

The Sysvol\domain folder contains policies and scripts in separate subfolders. The Sysvol\ Staging folder acts as a queue for changed files that need to be replicated. Within the Sysvol\Staging Areas folder, the *DomainName* folder is a junction point to the Sysvol\ staging\domain folder. Within the Sysvol\sysvol folder, the *DomainName* folder is a junction point to the Sysvol\domain folder.

After a user or the operating system changes a Sysvol file and the file is closed, FRS creates the file in the staging folder using the backup application programming interfaces (APIs) and replicates the file according to a schedule set in Active Directory. The same backup APIs are used to ensure that Volume Shadow Copy service-compatible backup programs, such as Windows Backup, can make point-in-time, consistent backups of the replica tree. Before such a program takes a shadow copy of a replica tree, the program instructs FRS to stop requesting new work items. After all currently active items are complete, FRS enters a pause state during which no new items can be processed.

The stand-alone DFS metadata contains information about the root, root target, links, link targets, and configuration settings defined for each stand-alone namespace. This metadata is maintained in the Registry of the root server at HKLM\SOFTWARE\Microsoft\Dfs\Roots\Standalone.

Domain-based root servers have a Registry entry for each root under HKLM\SOFTWARE\Microsoft\Dfs\Roots\Domain, but these entries do not contain the domain-based DFS metadata. When the DFS service starts on a domain controller using Active Directory with DFS, the service checks this path for Registry entries that correspond to domain-based roots. If these entries exist, the root server polls the PDC emulator master to obtain the DFS metadata for each domain-based namespace and stores the metadata in memory.

In the Active Directory data store, the DFS object stores the DFS metadata for a domain-based namespace. The DFS object is created in Active Directory when you install a domain at or raise a domain to the Windows Server 2008 domain functional level. Active Directory replicates the entire DFS object to all domain controllers in a domain.

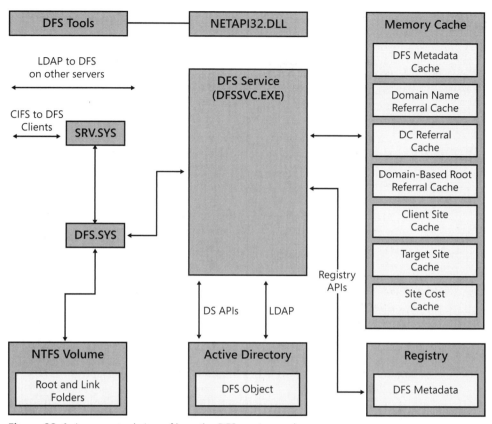

Figure 32-4 A conceptual view of how the DFS service works.

DFS uses a client-server architecture. A domain controller hosting a DFS name space has both the client and the server components, allowing the domain controller to perform local lookups in its own data store and remote lookup in data stores on other domain controllers. DFS uses the Common Internet File System (CIFS) for communication between DFS clients, root servers, and domain controllers. CIFS is an extension of the Server Message Block (SMB) file sharing protocol.

When a domain controller receives a CIFS request, the SMB Service server driver (Srv.sys) passes the request to the DFS driver (Dfs.sys) and this driver in turn directs the request to the DFS service. Dfs.sys also handles the processing of links when they are encountered during file system access.

When a client requests a referral for a domain-based namespace, the domain controller first checks its domain-based root referral cache for an existing referral. If the referral cache exists, the domain controller uses the cache to create the referral. If the referral cache does not exist, the domain controller locates the DFS object for that namespace and uses the metadata in the object to create the necessary referral. A referral contains a list of UNC paths that the client can use. DFS uses LDAP to retrieve metadata about the domain-based namespace from Active Directory and stores this information in its in-memory cache. Various types of in-memory cache are used:

- Domain Name Referral Cache contains the host names and fully qualified names of the local domain, all trusted domains in the forest, and domains in trusted forests.

- Domain Controller Referral Cache contains the host names and fully qualified names of the domain controllers for the list of domains it has cached.

- Domain-Based Root Referral Cache contains a list of root targets that host a given domain-based namespace.

- Client Site Cache stores information about the site in which a client is located (as determined using a DSAddressToSiteNames lookup).

- Target Site Cache stores information about the site in which a target UNC path is located (as determined using a DSAddressToSiteNames lookup)

- Site Cost Cache contains a mapping of sites to their associated cost information as defined in Active Directory.

After this information is cached, DFS can provide this to clients that are requesting information about DFS namespaces. The physical structures and caches on a domain controller vary according to the type of namespace the server hosts (domain-based or stand-alone). Each root and link in a namespace has a physical representation on an NTFS volume on each domain controller. The DFS root for Active Directory corresponds to the Sysvol shared folder. If a domain controller hosts additional namespaces, the domain controller will have additional roots and links.

Replication Architecture: An Overview

Active Directory replication is a multipart process that involves a source domain controller and a destination domain controller. From a high level, replication works much as shown in Figure 32-5.

The step-by-step procedure goes like this:

1. When a user or a system process makes a change to the directory, this change is implemented as an LDAP write to the appropriate directory partition.

2. The source domain controller begins by looking up the IP address of a replication partner. For the initial lookup or when the destination DNS record has expired, the source domain controller does this by querying the primary DNS server. Subsequent lookups can be done using the local resolver cache.

3. The source and destination domain controllers use Kerberos to mutually authenticate each other.

4. The source domain controller then sends a change notification to the destination domain controller using RPC over IP.

5. The destination domain controller sends a request for the changes using RPC over IP, including information that allows the source domain controller to determine if those changes are needed.

6. Using the information sent by the destination domain controller, the source domain controller determines what changes (if any) need to be sent to the destination domain controller, and then sends the required changes using RPC over IP.

7. The destination domain controller then uses the replication subsystem to write the changes to the directory database.

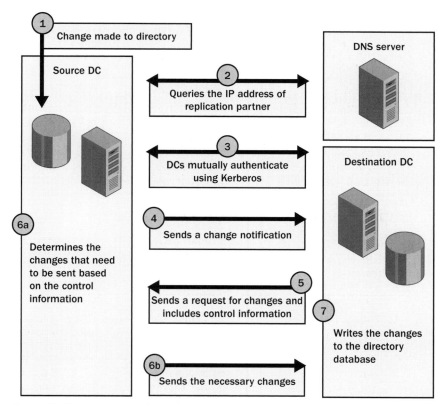

Figure 32-5 An overview of replication.

> **Note**
>
> For intersite replication, two transports are available: RPC over IP and SMTP. With this in mind, SMTP could also be used as an alternate transport. SMTP uses TCP port 25.

As you can see from this overview, Active Directory replication depends on the following key services:

- LDAP
- Domain Name System (DNS)
- Kerberos version 5 authentication
- Remote Procedure Call (RPC)

These Windows services must be functioning properly to allow directory updates to be replicated. Active Directory also uses either FRS or DFS to replicate files in the System Volume (Sysvol) shared folders on domain controllers. The User Datagram Protocol (UDP) and TCP ports used during replication are similar regardless of whether FRS or DFS is used. Table 32-1 summarizes the ports that are used.

Table 32-1 Ports Used During Active Directory Replication

Service/Component	Port	
	UDP	TCP
LDAP	389	389
LDAP Secure Sockets Layer (SSL)		686
Global catalog (LDAP)		3268
Kerberos version 5	88	88
DNS	53	53
RPC with FRS		Dynamic
RPC endpoint mapper with DFS		135
Server Message Block (SMB) over IP	445	445

INSIDE OUT

Intrasite replication essentials

Active Directory's multimaster replication model is designed to ensure that there is no single point of failure. In this model, every domain controller can access changes to the database, and can replicate those changes to all other domain controllers. When replication occurs within a domain, the replication follows a specific model that is very different from the replication model used for intersite replication.

With intrasite replication, the focus is on ensuring that changes are rapidly distributed. Intrasite replication traffic is not compressed, and replication is designed so that changes are replicated almost immediately after a change has been made. The main component in Active Directory responsible for the replication structure is the KCC. One of the main responsibilities of the KCC is to generate the replication topology—that is, the way replication is implemented.

As domain controllers are added to a site, the KCC configures a ring topology for intrasite replication with pull replication partners. Why use this model? For the following reasons:

- In a ring topology model, there are always at least two paths between connected network resources to provide redundancy. Creating a ring topology for Active Directory replication ensures that there are at least two paths that changes can follow from one domain controller to another.

- In a pull replication model, two servers are used. One is designated the push partner, the other the pull partner. It is the responsibility of the push partner to notify the pull partner that changes are available. The pull partner can then request the changes. Creating push and pull replication partners allows for rapid notification of changes and for updating after a request for changes has been made.

The KCC uses these models to create a replication ring. As domain controllers are added to a site, the size and configuration of this ring change. When there are at least three domain controllers in a site, each domain controller is configured with at least two incoming replication connections. As the number of domain controllers changes, the KCC updates the replication topology.

When a domain controller is updated, it waits approximately 15 seconds before initiating replication. This short wait is implemented in case additional changes are made. The domain controller on which the change is made notifies one of its partners, using an RPC, and specifies that changes are available. The partner can then pull the changes. After replication with this partner completes, the domain controller waits approximately 3 seconds, and then notifies its second partner of changes. The second partner can then pull the changes. Meanwhile, the first partner is notifying its partners of changes as appropriate. This process continues until all the domain controllers have been updated.

Chapter 32

INSIDE OUT Replicating urgent changes

The 15-second delay for replication applies to Windows Server 2003 and Windows Server 2008. For Windows 2000, the default delay is 300 seconds. In either case, however, the delay is overridden to allow immediate replication of priority changes. Priority (urgent) replication is triggered if you perform one of the following actions:

- Lock out an account, change the account lockout policy, or if an account is locked out automatically due to failed logon attempts
- Change the domain password policy
- Change the password on a domain controller computer account
- Change the relative ID master role owner
- Change a shared secret password used by the Local Security Authority (LSA) for Kerberos authentication

Urgent replication means that there is no delay to initiate replication. Note that all other changes to user and computer passwords are handled by the designated primary domain controller (PDC) emulator in a domain. When a user changes a normal user or computer password, the domain controller to which that user is connected immediately sends the change to the PDC emulator. This way, the PDC emulator always has the latest password for a user. This is why the PDC emulator is checked for a new password if a logon fails initially. After the new password is updated on the PDC emulator, the PDC emulator replicates the change using normal replication. The only exception is when a domain controller contacts the PDC emulator requesting a password for a user. In this case, the PDC emulator immediately replicates the current password to the requesting domain controller so that no additional requests are made for that password.

Figure 32-6 shows a ring topology that a KCC would construct if there were three domain controllers in a site.

As you can see from the figure, replication is set up as follows:

- DC1 has incoming replication connections from DC2 and DC3.
- DC2 has incoming replication connections from DC1 and DC3.
- DC3 has incoming replication connections from DC1 and DC2.

If you make changes to DC1, DC1 notifies DC2 of the changes. DC2 then pulls the changes. After replication completes, DC1 notifies DC3 of the changes. DC3 then pulls the changes. Because all domain controllers in the site have now been notified, no additional replication occurs. However, DC2 still notifies DC3 that changes are available. DC3 does not pull the changes, however, because it already has them.

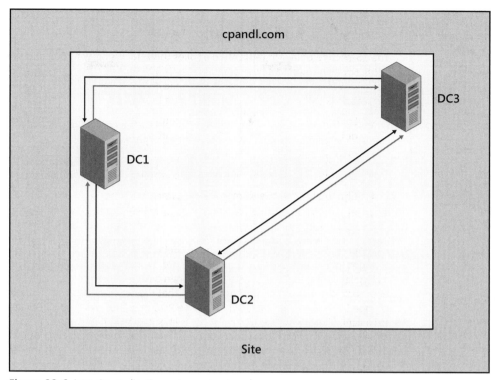

Figure 32-6 Intrasite replication using a ring topology.

Domain controllers track directory changes using Update Sequence Numbers (USNs). Any time a change is made to the directory, the domain controller assigns the change a USN. Each domain controller maintains its own local USNs and increments their values each time a change occurs. The domain controller also assigns the local USN to the object attribute that changed. Each object has a related attribute called uSNChanged. The uSNChanged attribute is stored with the object and identifies the highest USN that has been assigned to any of the object's attributes.

To see how this works, consider the following example. The local USN for DC1 is 125. An administrator connected to DC1 changes the password on a user's account. DC1 registers the change as local USN 126. The local USN value is written to the uSN-Changed attribute of the user object. If the administrator next edits a group account and changes its description, DC1 registers the change as local USN 127. The local USN value is written to the uSNChanged attribute of the Group object.

> **Note**
>
> With replication, there is sometimes a concern that replication changes from one domain controller may overwrite similar changes made to another domain controller. However, as object changes are tracked on a per-attribute basis, this rarely happens. It is very unlikely that two administrators would change the exact same attributes of an object at the exact same time. By tracking changes on a per-attribute basis, Active Directory effectively minimizes the possibility of any conflict. Should such a conflict occur, Active Directory resolves the conflict using a last-write-wins algorithm.

Each domain controller tracks not only its local USN but also the local USNs of other domain controllers in a table referred to as an *up-to-dateness vector*. During the replication process, a domain controller that is requesting changes includes its up-to-dateness vector. The receiving domain controller can then compare the USN values to those it has stored. If the current USN value for a particular domain controller is higher than the stored value, changes associated with that domain controller need to be replicated. If the current value for a particular domain controller is the same as the stored value, changes for that domain controller do not need to be replicated.

As only necessary changes are replicated, this process of comparing up-to-dateness vectors ensures that replication is very efficient and that changes propagate only when necessary. The up-to-dateness vectors are in fact the mechanism that enables domain controllers with redundant connections to know that they've already received the necessary updates.

INSIDE OUT Schema changes have priority

Several types of replication changes have priority. If you make changes to object attributes in the schema, these changes take precedence over most other changes. In this case, Active Directory blocks replication of normal changes and replicates the schema changes. Active Directory continues to replicate schema changes until the schema configuration is synchronized on all domain controllers in the forest. This ensures that schema changes are applied rapidly. Still, it's a good idea to make changes to the schema during off-hours, because schema changes need to propagate throughout the forest before other changes such as resetting passwords can be made to Active Directory.

The Windows Server 2008 schema adds indexed attributes to the schema directory partition. When you upgrade or install the first Windows Server 2008 domain controller, these changes replicate throughout the forest. Because of this, it is recommended that you plan your deployment carefully and use the Active Directory Preparation tool (adprep.exe) to perform updates to Active Directory to prepare a domain or forest for Windows Server 2008 installation. See Chapter 2, "Planning for Windows Server 2008," for more information.

Intersite Replication Essentials

Although intrasite replication focuses on speed, intersite replication focuses on efficiency. The primary goal of intersite replication is to transfer replication information between sites while making the most efficient use of the available resources. With efficiency as a goal, intersite replication traffic uses designated bridgehead servers and a default configuration that is scheduled rather than automatic, and compressed rather than uncompressed.

- With designated bridgehead servers, the Inter-Site Topology Generator (ISTG) limits the points of replication between sites. Instead of allowing all the domain controllers in one site to replicate with all the domain controllers in another site, the ISTG designates a limited number of domain controllers as bridgehead servers. These domain controllers are then the only ones used to replicate information between sites.

- With scheduled replication, you can set the valid times during which replication can occur and the replication frequency within this scheduled interval. By default, when you configure intersite replication, replication is scheduled to occur every 180 minutes 24 hours a day. When there's limited bandwidth between sites, you might want to change the default schedule to better accommodate the users who also use the link. For example, you might want to allow replication to occur every 180 minutes 24 hours a day on Saturday and Sunday, but during the week set the schedule to allow more bandwidth during the day. For example, you might set replication to occur every 60 minutes from 6 A.M. to 8 A.M. and from 7 P.M. to 3 A.M. Monday through Friday.

- With compression, replication traffic is compressed 85 to 90 percent, meaning that it is 10 to 15 percent of its uncompressed size. This means that even low-bandwidth links can often be used effectively for replication. Compression is triggered when the replication traffic is more than 32 kilobytes (KB) in size.

As discussed previously, there are two key ways to change intersite replication, as follows:

- Turn off automatic compression if you have sufficient bandwidth on a link and are more concerned about the processing power used for compression.

- Enable automatic notification of changes to allow domain controllers on either side of the link to indicate that changes are available. Automatic notification allows those changes to be requested rather than making domain controllers wait for the next replication interval.

Regardless of the site link configuration, replication traffic is sent through designated bridgehead servers rather than through multiple replication partners. When changes are made to the directory in one site, those changes replicate to the other site via the designated bridgehead servers. The bridgehead servers then initiate replication of the changes exactly as was discussed in "Intrasite Replication Essentials" on page 1085, except that the servers can use SMTP instead of RPC over IP if you use SMTP as a transport. Thus, intersite replication is really concerned with getting changes from one site to another across a site link.

Figure 32-7 shows an example of intersite replication using a single designated bridge-head server on each side of a site link. In this example, DC3 is the designated bridge-head server for Site 1 and DC4 is the designated bridgehead server for Site 2.

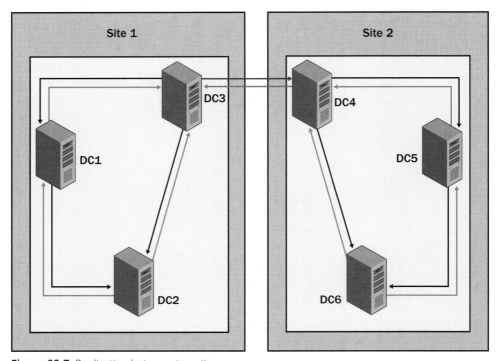

Figure 32-7 Replication between two sites.

As you can see from the figure, replication is set up as follows:

- DC1 has incoming replication connections from DC2 and DC3.

- DC2 has incoming replication connections from DC1 and DC3.

- DC3 has incoming replication connections from DC1 and DC2.

- DC4 has incoming replication connections from DC5 and DC6.

- DC5 has incoming replication connections from DC4 and DC6.

- DC6 has incoming replication connections from DC4 and DC5.

If changes are made to DC1 in Site 1, DC1 notifies DC2 of the changes. DC2 then pulls the changes. After replication completes, DC1 notifies DC3 of the changes. DC3 then pulls the changes. Because all domain controllers in the Site 1 have now been notified, no additional replication occurs within the site. However, DC2 still notifies DC3 that changes are available. DC3 does not pull the changes, however, because it already has them.

According to the site link configuration between Site 1 and Site 2, DC3 notifies DC4 that changes are available. DC4 then pulls the changes. Next DC4 notifies DC5 of the changes. DC5 then pulls the changes. After replication completes, DC4 notifies DC6 of the changes. DC6 then pulls the changes. Because all domain controllers in Site 2 have now been notified, no additional replication occurs. However, DC5 still notifies DC6 that changes are available. DC6 does not pull the changes, however, because it already has the changes.

So far, I've talked about designated bridgehead servers but haven't said how bridgehead servers are designated. That's because it is a rather involved process. When you set up a site, the knowledge consistency checker (KCC) on a domain controller that Active Directory has designated the Inter-Site Topology Generator (ISTG) is responsible for generating the intersite topology. Each site has only one ISTG and its job is to determine the best way to configure replication between sites.

The ISTG does this by identifying the bridgehead servers that are to be used. Replication between sites is always sent from a bridgehead server in one site to a bridgehead server in another site. This ensures that information is replicated only once between sites. As domain controllers are added and removed from sites, the ISTG regenerates the topology automatically.

The ISTG also creates the connection objects that are needed to connect bridgehead servers on either side of a site link. This is how Active Directory logically represents a site link. The ISTG continuously monitors connections and will create new connections when a domain controller acting as a designated bridgehead server is no longer available. In most cases, there will be more than one designated bridgehead server, and I'll discuss why in "Replication Rings and Directory Partitions" below.

> **Note**
> You can manually configure intersite replication in several ways. In addition to the techniques discussed previously for scheduling, notification, and compression, you can also configure site link costs, configure connection objects manually, and designate preferred bridgehead servers.

Replication Rings and Directory Partitions

The KCC is responsible for generating the intrasite replication topology, and the ISTG uses the KCC to generate the intersite replication topology. The KCC always configures the replication topology so that each domain controller in a site has at least two incoming connections if possible, as already discussed. The KCC also always configures intrasite replication so that each domain controller is no more than three hops from any other domain controller. This also means that *maximum replication latency*, the delay in replicating a change across an entire site, is approximately 45 seconds for normal replication.

When there are two domain controllers in a site, each domain controller is the replication partner of the other. When there are between three and seven domain controllers in the domain, each domain controller has two incoming connections and two replication partners. Figure 32-8 shows the replication topology for City Power & Light's Sacramento campus. Here the network is spread over two buildings that are connected with high-speed interconnects. Because the buildings are connected over redundant high-speed links, the organization uses a single site with three domain controllers in each building. The replication topology for the six domain controllers as shown ensures that no domain controller is more than three hops from any other domain controller.

When the number of domain controllers increases beyond seven, additional connection objects are added to ensure that no domain controller is more than three hops from any other domain controller in the replication topology. To see an example of this, consider Figure 32-9. Here, City Power & Light has built a third building that connects its original buildings to form a U-shaped office complex. The administrators have placed two new domain controllers in building 3. As a result of adding the additional domain controllers, some domain controllers now have three replication partners.

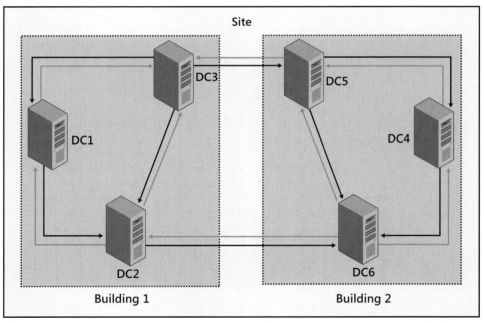

Figure 32-8 Campus replication with two buildings and three domain controllers in each building.

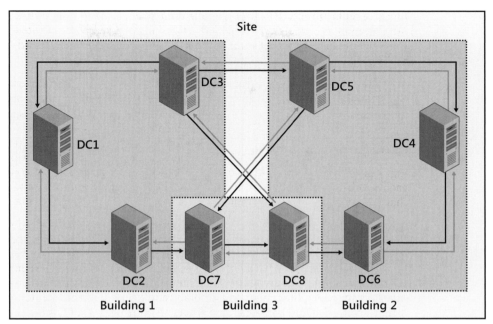

Figure 32-9 Campus replication with three buildings and eight domain controllers.

At this point, you may be wondering what role, if any, directory partitions play in replication topology. After all, from previous discussions, you know that Active Directory has multiple directory partitions and that those partitions are replicated in the following ways:

- Forest-wide basis for configuration and schema directory partitions

- Domain-wide basis for the domain directory partition

- Select basis for the global catalog partition or other application-specific partitions, which include special application partitions as well as the ForestDnsZones and DomainDnsZones application partitions used by DNS

In previous discussions, I didn't want to complicate things unnecessarily by adding a discussion of partition replication. From a logical perspective, partitions do play an important role in replication. Replication rings, the logical implementation of replication, are based on the types of directory partitions that are available. The KCC generates a replication ring for each kind of directory partition.

Table 32-2 details the replication partners for each kind of directory partition. Replication rings are implemented on a per-directory partition basis. There is one replication ring per directory partition type, and some rings include all the domain controllers in a forest, all the domain controllers in a domain, or only those domain controllers using application partitions.

Table 32-2 **Per-Directory Partition Replication Rings**

Directory Partition	Replication Partners
Configuration directory partition	All the domain controllers in the forest
Schema directory partition	All the domain controllers in the forest
Domain directory partition	All the domain controllers in a domain
Global catalog partition	All domain controllers in the forest that host global catalogs
Application directory partition	All the domain controllers using the application partition on either a forest-wide, domain-wide, or selective basis, depending on the configuration of the application partition
ForestDnsZones directory partition	All the domain controllers in the forest that host DNS
DomainDnsZones directory partition	All the domain controllers that host DNS for that domain

When replication rings are within a site, the KCC on each domain controller is responsible for generating the replication topology and keeping it consistent. When replication rings go across site boundaries, the ISTG is responsible for generating the replication topology and keeping it consistent. Because replication rings are merely a logical representation of replication, the actual implementation of replication rings is expressed in the replication topology by using connection objects. Regardless of whether you are talking about intrasite or intersite replication, there is one connection object for each incoming connection. The KCC and ISTG do not create additional connection objects for each replication ring. Instead, they reuse connection objects for as many replication rings as possible.

When you extend the reuse of connection objects to the way intersite replication is performed, this is how multiple bridgehead servers might be designated. Typically, each site also has a designated bridgehead server for replicating the domain, schema, and configuration directory partitions. Other types of directory partitions may be replicated between sites by domain controllers that host these partitions. For example, if two sites have multiple domain controllers and only a few have application partitions, a connection object may be created for the intersite replication of the application partition.

Figure 32-10 shows an example of how you might use multiple bridgehead servers. Here, the domain, schema, and configuration partitions replicate from Site 1 to Site 2 and vice versa using the connection objects between DC3 and DC5. A special application partition is replicated from Site 1 to Site 2 and vice versa using the connection objects between DC2 and DC6.

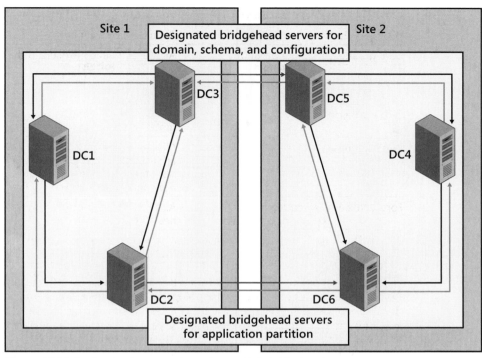

Figure 32-10 Replication between sites using multiple bridgehead servers.

The global catalog partition is a special exception. The global catalog is built from all the domain databases in a forest. Each designated global catalog server in a forest must get global catalog information from the domain controllers in all the domains of the forest. This means that a global catalog server must connect to a domain controller in every domain and there must be an associated connection object to do this. Because of this, global catalog servers are another reason for having more than one designated bridgehead server per site.

Figure 32-11 provides an example of how replication might work for a more complex environment that includes domain, configuration, and schema partitions as well as DNS and global catalog partitions. Here, the domain, schema, and configuration partitions replicate from Site 1 to Site 2 and vice versa using the connection objects between DC3 and DC5. The connection objects between DC1 and DC4 replicate the global catalog partition from Site 1 to Site 2 and vice versa. In addition, the connection objects between DC2 and DC6 replicate the DNS partitions from Site 1 to Site 2 and vice versa.

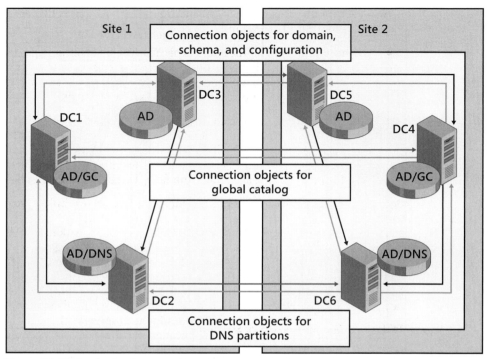

Figure 32-11 Replication in a complex environment.

Developing or Revising a Site Design

Site design depends on the networking infrastructure of your organization. As you set out to implement an initial site design, you must start by mapping your organization's existing network topology. Any time you plan to revise your network infrastructure, you must also plan the necessary revisions to your existing site design.

Mapping Network Infrastructure

Although site design is relatively independent from domain structure, the replication topology depends on how available domain controllers are and how they are configured. The KCC running on each domain controller monitors domain controller availability and configuration, and updates replication topology as changes occur. The ISTG performs similar monitoring to determine the best way to configure intersite replication. This means that as you implement or change the domain controller configuration, you may change the replication topology.

To develop a site design, you should start by mapping your existing network architecture. Be sure to include all the business locations in the organization that are part of the forest or forests for which you are developing a site plan. Document the subnets on each network segment and the connection speed on the links connecting each network segment. Keep the following in mind:

- You need to document the subnets because each site in the organization will have separate subnets. Although a single subnet can exist only in one site, a single site can have multiple subnets associated with it. After you create sites, you will create subnet-to-site associations by adding subnets to these sites.

- You need to document the connection speeds for links because the available bandwidth on a connection affects the way you configure site links. Each site link is assigned a link cost, which determines its priority order for replication. If there are several possible routes to a site, the route with the lowest link cost is used first. In the event that a primary link fails, a secondary link can be used.

Because site design and network infrastructure are so closely linked, you'll want to work closely with your organization's network administrators. If you wear both hats, start mapping the network architecture by listing each network location, the subnets at that location, and the links that connect the location. For an organization with its headquarters in Chicago and four regional offices in Seattle, New York, Los Angeles (LA), and Miami, this information might come together as shown in Table 32-3. Notice that I start with the hubs and work my way to the central office. This way, the multiple connections to the central office are all accounted for when I finally make this entry.

Table 32-3 Mapping Network Structure

Location	Subnets	Connections
Seattle	10.1.11.0/24, 10.1.12.0/24	256 kilobits per second (Kbps) Seattle–Chicago, 128 Kbps Seattle–LA
LA	10.1.21.0/24, 10.1.22.0/24	512 Kbps LA–Chicago, 128 Kbps LA–Seattle
New York	10.1.31.0/24, 10.1.32.0/24	512 Kbps New York–Chicago, 128 Kbps New York–Miami
Miami	10.1.41.0/24, 10.1.42.0/24	256 Kbps Miami–Chicago, 128 Kbps Miami–New York
Chicago	10.1.1.0/24, 10.1.2.0/24	256 Kbps Seattle–Chicago, 512 Kbps LA–Chicago, 512 Kbps New York–Chicago, 256 Kbps Miami– Chicago

I then use the table to create a diagram similar to the one shown in Figure 32-12, in which I depict each network and the connections between them. I've also noted the subnets at each location. Although it is also helpful to know the number of users and computers at each location, this information alone isn't enough to help you determine how links connecting sites are used. The only certain way to know that is to monitor the network traffic going over the various links.

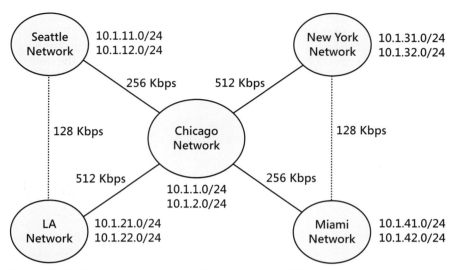

Figure 32-12 Network diagram for a wide area network (WAN).

Creating a Site Design

After you've mapped the network structure, you are ready to create a site design. Creating a site design involves the following steps:

1. Mapping the network structure to site structure

2. Designing each individual site

3. Designing the intersite replication topology

4. Considering the impact of site link bridging

5. Planning the placement of servers in sites

Each of these steps is examined in the sections that follow.

Mapping the Network Structure to Site Structure

To map the network structure to site structure, start by examining each network location and the speed of the connections between those locations. In general, if you want to make separate network locations part of the same site, the sites should have at least 512 Kbps of available bandwidth. If the sites are in separate geographic locations, I also recommend that the network locations have redundant links for fault tolerance.

These recommended speeds are for replication traffic only, not for other user traffic. Smaller organizations with fewer than 100 users at branch locations may be able to scale down to dedicated 128-Kbps or 256-Kbps links. Larger organizations with 250 or more users at branch locations may need to scale up.

Following the previous example, the Chicago-based company would probably be best served by having separate sites at each network location. With this in mind, the site-to-network mapping would be as shown in Figure 32-13. By creating the additional sites at the other network locations, you help control replication over the slow links, which can significantly improve the performance of Active Directory. More good news is that sites are relatively low maintenance once you configure them, so you get a significant benefit without a lot of additional administration overhead.

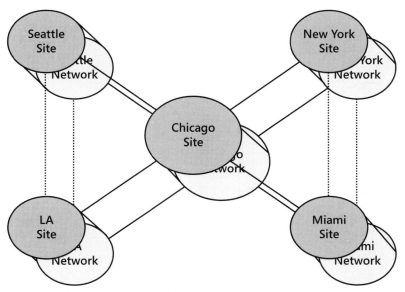

Figure 32-13 Initial site-to-network mapping.

Designing Each Individual Site

After you have determined how many sites you will have, you next need to consider the design of each site. A key part of the site design has to do with naming the sites and identifying the subnets that are associated with each site. Site names should reflect the physical location of the site. The default site created by Active Directory is Default-First-Site-Name, and most site names should follow a similar naming scheme. Continuing the example, you might use the following site names:

- Seattle-First-Site
- LA-First-Site
- NewYork-First-Site
- Miami-First-Site
- Chicago-First-Site

I've used dashes instead of spaces, following the style Active Directory uses for the default first site. I've named the sites *City*-First-Site rather than *City*-Site to allow for easy revision of the site architecture to include additional sites at each location. Now, if a location receives additional sites, the naming convention is very clear, and it is also very clear that if you have a Seattle-First-Site, Seattle-Second-Site, and Seattle-Third-Site, these are all different sites at the Seattle location.

To determine the subnets that you should associate with each site, use the network diagram developed in the previous section. It already has a list of the subnets. In your site documentation, simply note the IP subnet associations that are needed and update your site diagram to include the subnets.

Designing the Intersite Replication Topology

After you name the sites and determine subnet associations, you should design the intersite replication topology. You do this by planning the details of replication over each link designated in the initial site diagram. For each site link, plan the following components:

- Replication schedule
- Replication interval
- Link cost

Typically, you want replication to occur at least every 180 minutes, 24 hours a day, 7 days a week. This is the default replication schedule. If you have limited bandwidth, you may need to alter the schedule to allow user traffic to have priority during peak usage times. If bandwidth isn't a concern or if you have strong concerns about keeping branch locations up to date, you may want to increase the replication frequency. In all cases, if possible you should monitor any existing links to get a sense of the bandwidth utilization and the peak usage periods.

Calculating the link cost can be a bit complicated. When there are multiple links between locations, you need to think carefully about the appropriate cost of each link. Even if there is only one link between all your sites now, you should set an appropriate link cost now to ensure that if links are added between locations, all the links are used in the most efficient way possible.

Valid link costs range from 1, which assigns the highest possible preference to a link, to 99999, which assigns the lowest possible preference to a link. When you create a new link, the default link cost is set to 100. If you were to set all the links to this cost, all the links would have equal preference for replication. But would you really want replication to go over a 128-Kbps link when you have a 512-Kbps link to the same location? Probably not.

In most cases, the best way to set link cost is to assign a cost based on the available network bandwidth over a link. Table 32-4 provides an example of how this could be done.

Table 32-4 **Setting Link Cost Based on Available Bandwidth**

Available Bandwidth	Link Cost	Preference
100 megabits per second (Mbps) or greater	20	Very high
100 Mbps to 10 Mbps	40	Moderately high
10 Mbps to 1.544 Mbps	100	High
1.544 Mbps to 512 Kbps	200	Above normal
512 Kbps to 256 Kbps	400	Normal
256 Kbps to 128 Kbps	800	Below normal
128 Kbps to 56 Kbps	1600	Moderately low
56 Kbps or less	3200	Low

You can use the costs in the table to assign costs to each link you identified in your site diagram. After you do this, update your site diagram so that you can determine the route that is used for replication if all the links are working. As Figure 32-14 shows, your site diagram should now show the names of the sites, the associated subnets, and the cost of each link.

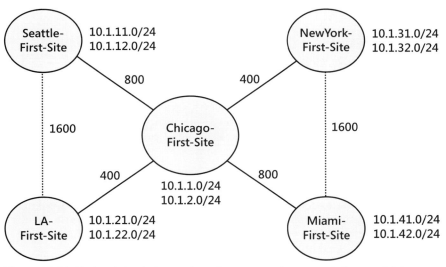

Figure 32-14 Updated site design to show site names, subnet associations, and link costs.

Considering the Impact of Site Link Bridging

By default, Active Directory automatically configures site link bridges, which makes links transitive between sites in much the same way that trusts are transitive between domains in a single forest. When a site is bridged, any two domain controllers can make a connection across any consecutive series of links. The site link bridge cost is the sum of all the costs of the links included in the bridge. Let's calculate the site link bridge costs using the links shown in Figure 32-14. Because of site link bridges, the domain controllers at the Chicago headquarters have two possible routes for replication to each of the branch office locations. The costs of these routes are summarized in Table 32-5.

Table 32-5 **Link and Bridge Costs**

Site/Link	Link/Bridge Cost
Seattle Site	
Chicago–Seattle	800
Chicago–LA–Seattle	2000
LA Site	
Chicago–LA	400
Chicago–Seattle–LA	2400
New York Site	
Chicago–New York	400
Chicago–Miami–New York	2400
Miami Site	
Chicago–Miami	800
Chicago–New York–Miami	2000

Knowing the costs of links and link bridges, you can calculate the effects of a network link failure. In this example, if the primary link between Chicago and Seattle went down, replication would occur over the Chicago-LA-Seattle site link bridge. It's relatively straightforward in this example, but if you were to introduce additional links between network locations, the scenarios become very complicated very quickly.

The network topology used in the previous example is referred to as a *hub-and-spoke* design. The headquarters in Chicago is the hub, and the rest of the offices are spokes. Automatic site link bridging works well with a hub-and-spoke design. It doesn't work so well when you have multiple hubs. Consider the example shown in Figure 32-15. In this example, Chicago is the main hub, but because Seattle and LA have a spoke, they are also considered hubs.

Site link bridging can have unintended consequences when you have multiple hubs and spokes on each hub. Here, when the bridgehead servers in the Chicago site replicate with other sites, they replicate with Seattle, New York, LA, and Miami bridgehead servers as before, but they also replicate with the Vancouver and San Diego bridgehead servers across the site bridge from Chicago-Seattle-Vancouver and from Chicago-LA-San Diego. This means that the same replication traffic could go over the Chicago-Seattle and Chicago-LA links twice. This can happen because of the rule of three hops for optimizing replication topology.

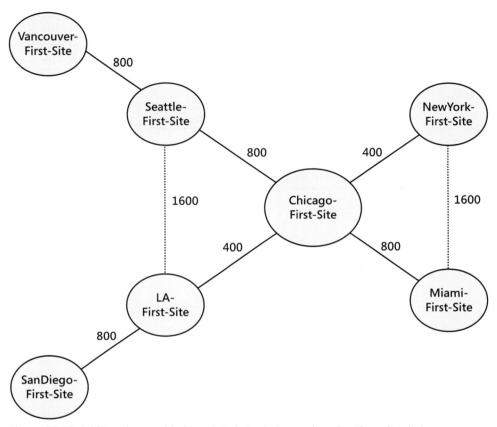

Figure 32-15 Additional sites added to original site design, making Seattle and LA hubs.

The repeat replication over the hub links becomes worse as you add additional spokes. Consider Figure 32-16. Here, the LA hub has connections to sites in Sacramento, San Diego, and San Francisco. As a result of site link bridging, the same replication traffic could go over the Chicago-LA links four times. This happens because of the rule of three hops for optimizing replication topology.

The solution to the problem of repeat replication traffic is to disable automatic site bridging. Unfortunately, the automatic bridging configuration is all or nothing. This means that if you disable automatic site link bridging and still want to bridge some site links, you must configure those bridges manually. You can enable, disable, and manually configure site link bridges as discussed in "Configuring Site Link Bridges" on page 1295.

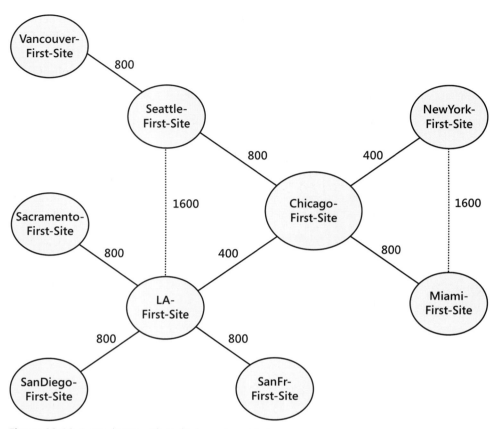

Figure 32-16 A site design with multiple spokes at hubs.

Planning the Placement of Servers in Sites

When you finish configuring site links, you should plan the placement of servers in the sites. Think about which types of domain controllers and how many of each will be located in a site. Answer the following questions:

- Will there be domain controllers? If so, how many?

- Will any of the domain controllers host a global catalog? If so, how many?

- Will any of the domain controllers host DNS? If so, how many?

- Will any of the domain controllers have an operations master role? If so, what roles and on which domain controllers?

Think about which Active Directory partitions will be replicated between the sites as a result of the domain controller placement, and about any additional partitions that may need to be replicated to a site. Answer the following questions:

- Will domain, configuration, and schema partitions be replicated to the site?

- Will a global catalog be replicated to the site?

- Will ForestDnsZones and DomainDnsZones partitions be replicated to the site?

- Will any special application partitions be replicated to the site? If so, what partitions, how are they used, and which domain controllers will host them?

By answering all these questions, you know what servers will be placed in each site as well as what information will be replicated between sites. Don't forget about dependent services for Active Directory. At a minimum, when optimizing for Active Directory replication control, each site should have at least one domain controller, a global catalog, and a DNS server. Obviously, there are other reasons for creating sites and it is possible to have sites without domain controllers, such as when you are optimizing for DFS, SCCM, or other high-bandwidth–consuming services and applications. That said, this configuration allows intrasite replication to occur without having to go across site links for dependent services. To improve the user experience, keep in mind the following facts:

- Global catalogs are needed for logon (unless universal group membership caching is enabled). If there is a local global catalog, logon can complete without a request having to go across a site link.

- DHCP servers are needed for dynamic IP addressing. If there is a local DHCP server, clients with dynamic IP addressing will be able to start up and get an IP address assignment without having to go across a site link.

- DNS servers are needed for forward and reverse lookups. If there is a local DNS server, clients will be able to perform DNS queries without having to go across a site link.

Chapter 32

Implementing Active Directory Domain Services

After you've completed planning, the process of implementing Active Directory Domain Services (AD DS) is similar whether you are installing Active Directory for the first time or extending your existing Active Directory infrastructure. In either case, you need to take the following steps:

1. Install the necessary domain controllers and assign any other needed roles to these servers.

2. Create the necessary organizational units (OUs) and delegate administrative control over these OUs as necessary.

3. Create any necessary user, group, and computer accounts as well as the resources that are required for use in a domain.

4. Use group policy and local security policy to set default settings for user and computer environments in any domains and OUs you've created.

5. Create the necessary sites and configure those sites for use and replication.

In this chapter, I examine the steps for installing domain controllers, creating OUs, and delegating administrative control. Chapter 35, "Managing Users, Groups, and Computers," discusses creating user, group, and computer accounts as well as related group policy. Chapter 36, "Managing Group Policy," discusses managing group policy and local security policy. Chapter 37, "Active Directory Site Administration," discusses creating sites and managing replication.

Preinstallation Considerations for Active Directory

Whenever you work with a server role as complex as Active Directory Domain Services, you should take time to carefully consider the physical implementation. As with the installation of Microsoft SQL Server, Microsoft Exchange Server, or Microsoft Internet Information Systems (IIS), you should evaluate hardware requirements, plan for the system's backup needs, and consider how the system will be used.

Hardware and Configuration Considerations for Domain Controllers

Every domain controller is essentially a database server with a complex replication system, and as such, when you select hardware for and configure domain controllers, you should use all the care and attention that you'd give to one of your mainstay database servers. The hardware you choose for the domain controllers should be as robust as the hardware for your database servers.

The following guidelines should be taken into consideration:

- **Processor** The CPU for a domain controller needs to be relatively fast. As soon as you install the second domain controller in a forest, a process called the *knowledge consistency checker (KCC)* begins running on every domain controller. The KCC is responsible for generating the replication topology and dynamically handling changes and failures within the replication topology. By default, the KCC on every domain controller recalculates the replication topology every 15 minutes. The more complex the replication topology, the more processing power it takes to perform, and, in many cases, even in small domain environments, the calculations performed by the KCC considerably increase CPU utilization. This is acceptable for short durations. However, if the domain controller doesn't have a fast enough CPU, generating the replication topology in a complex environment could take several minutes rather than several seconds, which could severely affect the performance of all other processes running on the server.

- **Multiprocessing** Some installations may benefit from having domain controllers with multiple CPUs. With multiple processors, you may see significant performance improvements. However, rather than having a single beefy domain controller, it is better to have multiple domain controllers placed appropriately.

- **Memory** Domain controllers may use more memory than other servers. In addition to running standard processes, domain controllers must run special processes, such as storage engine processes, knowledge consistency checking, replication, and garbage collection. Therefore, most domain controllers should have at least 2 gigabytes (GB) of RAM as a recommended starting point for full server installations and 1 GB of RAM for core server installations. Be sure to monitor memory usage and upgrade as necessary.

- **Disks** The data storage capacity you need depends entirely on the number of objects related to users, computers, groups, and resources that are stored in the Active Directory database. The initial installation of Active Directory requires a small amount of available space. By default, the database is stored in the Ntdis.dit database file on the system volume, as are related log files. When the database and log files are stored together, the storage volume should have free disk space of at least 20 percent of the combined size of the database and log files. When the database and log files are stored separately, each storage volume should have free disk space of at least 20 percent of either the database or the log files, as appropriate.

- **Data protection** Domain controllers should use fault-tolerant drives to protect against hardware failure of the system volume and any other volumes used by Active Directory. I recommend using a redundant array of independent disks (RAID), either RAID 1 or RAID 5. Hardware RAID is preferable to software RAID.

As part of the hardware configuration, you should consider where you will install the files used by Active Directory. Active Directory database and log files are stored by default in the %SystemRoot%\NTDS folder, although the Active Directory system volume (Sysvol), which is created as a shared folder, and contains policy, scripts, and other related files, is stored by default in the %SystemRoot%\Sysvol folder. These locations are completely configurable during installation; some consideration should be given to whether you want to accept the defaults or store the files elsewhere. You'll get much better scalability and performance if you put the database and log files on different volumes, each on a separate drive. The Active Directory Sysvol can remain in the default location in most cases.

> **Note**
>
> If you decide to move the Sysvol, you must move it to an NTFS volume. For security reasons, the database and log folders should be on NTFS volumes as well, but this isn't a requirement.

Active Directory is dependent on network connectivity and the Domain Name System (DNS). You should configure domain controllers to use static Internet Protocol (IP) addresses and have the appropriate primary and secondary DNS servers set in their Transmission Control Protocol/Internet Protocol (TCP/IP) configuration, as discussed in Chapter 21, "Managing TCP/IP Networking." If DNS isn't available on the network, you have the opportunity to make DNS available during the installation of Active Directory. Implement DNS as discussed in Chapter 23, "Architecting DNS Infrastructure," and Chapter 24, "Implementing and Managing DNS," and be sure to configure the DNS server to use itself for DNS resolution. If you previously deployed Microsoft DNS, as discussed in Chapters 23 and 24, the DNS environment should already be set to work with Active Directory.

If you are using a DNS server that does not use the Windows DNS, you can verify that the DNS server will work properly with Active Directory by using the Domain Controller Diagnostic Utility (Dcdiag.exe). This utility is included with Windows Server 2008. You can run Dcdiag and test the DNS configuration by typing the following command at the command prompt:

```
dcdiag /test:dcpromo /dnsdomain:DomainName /newforest
```

where *DomainName* is the name of the DNS domain in which the domain controller is located. Consider the following example:

```
dcdiag /test:dcpromo /dnsdomain:cpandl.com /newforest
```

Here, you run a test of the Active Directory Domain Services Installation Wizard (Dcpromo.exe) to see if the DNS domain cpandl.com is compatible for creating a new forest. Any errors in the output of the test would need to be examined closely and resolved.

Configuring Active Directory for Fast Recovery with Storage Area Networks

Domain controllers are backed up differently than other servers are. To back up Active Directory, you must back up the System State. On Windows Server 2008, there are approximately 50,000 System State files, which use approximately 4 GB of disk space in the default installation of an x86-based computer. These files must be backed up as a set and cannot be divided. To keep the System State intact when you place the volumes related to Active Directory on a storage area network (SAN), you must also place the operating system (system and boot volume) on the SAN. This means that you must then boot from the SAN.

Booting from a SAN and configuring Active Directory so that the related volumes are on a SAN enables several fast recovery scenarios—most of which make use of the Volume Shadow Copy service (VSS). For instance, a domain controller is using the C, D, and E volumes: C for the operating system and Sysvol, D for the Active Directory database, and E for the Active Directory logs. Using a third-party backup utility that makes use of the Volume Shadow Copy service, you might be able to use that backup software to create shadow copies of the System State on separate logical unit numbers (LUNs) on the SAN.

On the SAN, let's say that volumes C, D, and E correspond to LUNs 1, 2, and 3 and that the current shadow copy of those volumes is on LUNs 7, 8, and 9. If Active Directory were to fail at this point, you could recover by performing the following steps:

1. Use the DiskRAID utility to mask the failed LUNs (1, 2, and 3) so that they are no longer accessible.

> **Note**
>
> The DiskRaid utility is a command-line tool for configuring and managing RAID storage subsystems, such as those associated with network-attached storage (NAS) and storage area networks (SANs). When you install the Windows Server 2008 Resource Kit, this tool is available for use.

2. Use the DiskRAID utility to unmask the shadow-copied LUNs (7, 8, and 9) so they are usable.

3. You would then boot the domain controller to the BIOS, set the boot device to LUN 6, and then reboot.

4. You've now recovered Active Directory. When the domain controller starts, it will recover the Active Directory database and synchronize with the rest of the domain controllers in the organization through regular replication.

Connecting Clients to Active Directory

Network clients connect to Active Directory for logon and authentication and to perform Lightweight Directory Access Protocol (LDAP) lookups. In a standard configuration of Active Directory running on Windows Server 2008, communications between clients and servers are secure and use either Server Message Block (SMB) signing or secure channel encryption and signing. Secure communications are used by default because the default security policy for Windows Server 2008 has higher security settings than the security policies for previous versions of Windows.

Windows clients running versions earlier than Microsoft Windows 2000 do not natively support either of these secure communications methods. Therefore, these Windows clients cannot log on or authenticate in a Windows Server 2008 domain until you update them. To allow Microsoft Windows 95 and Microsoft Windows 98 clients to securely communicate with Active Directory, you need to install the Directory Services Client on these systems.

Windows clients running Windows 2000 or later do not need to have a separate client installed. These clients all natively support SMB signing, secure channel encryption and signing, or both.

Chapter 33

INSIDE OUT   Secure communications for domain controllers

One reason for configuring secure communications by default is to prevent certain types of security attacks. Secure communications specifically thwarts man-in-the-middle attacks, among others. In this attack, a third machine gets between the client and the server and pretends to be the other machine to each. This allows the man-in-the-middle machine to intercept and modify data that is transmitted between the client and the server. That said, if you must disable secure communications, you can do so. Remember that disabling the secure communications requirement won't allay the need to install an Active Directory client on Windows clients running versions earlier than Windows 2000—they'll still need a client.

To disable the secure communications requirement, follow these steps:

1. Open the related GPO for editing in the Group Policy Management Editor.

2. Expand Computer Configuration, Windows Settings, Security Settings, Local Policies, and then select Security Options.

3. Under Security Options, right-click Domain Member: Digitally Encrypt Or Sign Secure Channel Data (Always), and then select Properties.

4. In the Properties dialog box, select Disabled, and then click OK.

Installing Active Directory Domain Services

Any server running Windows Server 2008 can act as a domain controller. You configure a server as a domain controller by following a two-part process. You install the necessary binaries for Active Directory Domain Services (AD DS) and then configure the services using the Active Directory Domain Services Installation Wizard (Dcpromo.exe).

Active Directory Installation Options and Issues

You have several options for installing Active Directory binaries. You can:

- Use the Add Role feature in Server Manager to add the Active Directory Domain Services role to the server.

- Enter the following command at an elevated command prompt:
  servermanagercmd -install adds-domain-controller

- Start the Active Directory Domain Services Installation Wizard by entering **dcpromo** at a command prompt or by clicking Start, typing **dcpromo** in the Search box, and then pressing Enter.

All these installation techniques do the same thing: they prepare the server by installing the AD DS binaries. The AD DS binaries include the Windows components that enable servers to act as domain controllers as well as the related administration tools. The technique you use depends primarily on your personal preference. However, although any administrator can install the AD DS binaries, you may need additional administrator permissions to fully configure a domain controller. Additionally, when you are automating the installation process, you typically will want to install the binaries prior to running Dcpromo.

When you configure Active Directory using Dcpromo, you are given the option of setting the domain controller type as a domain controller either for a new domain or as an additional domain controller in an existing domain. If you make the domain controller part of a new domain, you can create a new domain in a new forest, a child domain in an existing domain tree, or a new domain tree in an existing forest. In fact, this is how you extend Active Directory structure from the first domain in a new forest to include additional domains and domain trees.

To configure Active Directory using Dcpromo, you must use an account with administrator privileges. The administrator privileges and installation requirements are as follows:

- **Creating a domain controller in a new forest** If you are creating a domain controller in a new forest, you should log on to the local machine using either the local Administrator account or an account that has administrator privileges on the local machine, and then start the installation. As you are creating the new forest, the server should have a static IP address. After you install DHCP servers in the new forest, you can assign the domain controller a dynamic IP address.

- **Creating a domain controller in a new domain or a domain tree** If you are creating a domain controller in a new domain or a new domain tree in an existing forest, you should log on to the local machine using either the local Administrator account or an account that has administrator privileges on the local machine, and then start the installation. You will also be required to provide the credentials for an account that is a member of the Enterprise Admins group in the forest of which the domain will be a part.

  As you are creating a new domain or domain tree, the server should have a static IP address. After you install DHCP servers in the new domain or domain tree, you can assign the domain controller a dynamic IP address.

- **Creating an additional domain controller in an existing domain** If you are creating an additional domain controller in an existing domain, you should consider whether you want to perform an installation from media rather than creating the domain controller from scratch. With either technique, you will need to log on to the local machine using either the local Administrator account or an account that has administrator privileges on the local machine, and then start the installation.

  You will also be required to provide the credentials for an account that is a member of the Domain Admins group in the domain of which the domain controller will be a part. It is not necessary for the server to be a member of the domain, as you will be given the opportunity to join the domain controller to the domain if necessary.

> **Note**
>
> Domain controllers that also act as DNS servers should not have dynamic IP addresses. The reason for this is that the IP address of a DNS server should be fixed to ensure reliable DNS operations.

As you are installing an additional domain controller, the server should already be a member of the domain and must have a valid IP address. The IP address can be a static IP address or a dynamic IP address assigned by a DHCP server.

Before starting an Active Directory installation, you should examine local accounts and check for encrypted files and folders. As domain controllers do not have local accounts or separate cryptographic keys, making a server a domain controller deletes all local accounts and all certificates and cryptographic keys from the server. Any encrypted data on the server, including data stored using the Encrypting File System (EFS), must be decrypted before installing Active Directory or it will be permanently inaccessible.

INSIDE OUT   Finding encrypted files

To search an entire volume for encrypted files, change directories to the root directory using the CD command, and then examine the entire contents of the directory by using the EFSInfo utility as follows:

```
efsinfo /s:DriveDesignator /i | find ": Encrypted"
```

where *DriveDesignator* is the drive designator of the volume to search, such as C:, as shown in the following example:

```
efsinfo /s:c: /i | find ": Encrypted"
```

Here, EFSInfo is used to search the root directory of C: and all its subdirectories and display the encryption status of all files and folders. As you care about only the encrypted file and folders, you pipe the output to the Find utility and search it for the string ": Encrypted", which is a text string that appears only in the output for encrypted files and folders. EFSInfo is available in the resource kits for Windows Server 2003 and Windows Server 2008.

Using the Active Directory Domain Services Installation Wizard

You can start the Active Directory Domain Services Installation Wizard by clicking Start, typing **dcpromo** in the Search box, and pressing Enter. Before the wizard starts, it checks to ensure the AD DS binaries are installed. After installing the AD DS binaries as necessary, the wizard displays an introductory page. The way you continue depends on whether you are creating an additional domain controller for an existing domain, creating a new domain in a new forest, or creating a new domain tree or domain in an existing forest.

Creating Additional Domain Controllers for an Existing Domain

To create an additional domain controller for an existing domain, follow these steps:

1. Start the Active Directory Domain Services Installation Wizard as discussed previously. If you haven't installed the AD DS binaries, the wizard installs them.

2. By default, the wizard uses Basic Installation mode. If you want to install from media as discussed in "Performing an Active Directory Installation from Media" on page 1126, select the Use Advanced Installation Mode check box before clicking Next to continue.

3. If the server doesn't have an appropriate IP address, you see the Configure TCP/IP page. This page display a warning about the invalid IP address or improper network configuration and you'll need to correct the issue before you can continue.

4. On the Choose A Deployment Configuration page, shown in Figure 33-1, select Existing Forest and then select Add A Domain Controller To An Existing Domain.

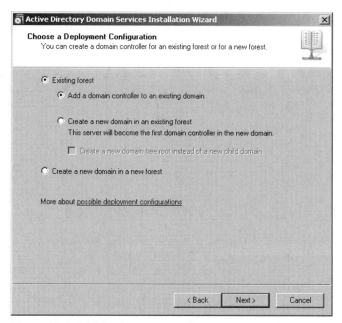

Figure 33-1 Add the domain controller to an existing domain.

5. When you click Next, you see the Network Credentials page, shown in Figure 33-2. In the field provided, type the full DNS name of any domain in the forest where you plan to install the domain controller. Preferably, this should be the name of the forest root domain, such as cpandl.com. If you are logged on to a domain in this forest and have the appropriate permissions, you can use your current logged on credentials to perform the installation. Otherwise, select Alternate Credentials, click Set, type the user name and password for an enterprise administrator account in the previously specified domain, and then click OK.

6. When you click Next, the wizard validates the domain name you provide and then lists all domains in the related forest. On the Select A Domain page shown in Figure 33-3, select the domain for the domain controller and then click Next.

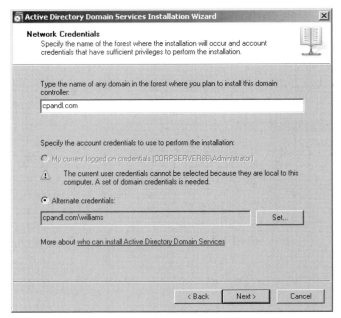

Figure 33-2 Specify a domain in the forest and network credentials.

Figure 33-3 Select the domain for the domain controller.

7. When you click Next, the wizard determines the available Active Directory sites. On the Select A Site page, select the site in which you want to locate the domain controller and then click Next.

8. When you click Next, the wizard examines the DNS configuration and attempts to determine whether any authoritative DNS servers are available. As shown in Figure 33-4, the number of authoritative DNS servers in the domain will be listed on the Additional Domain Controller Options page as shown in the figure. As permitted, select additional installation options for the domain controller and then click Next.

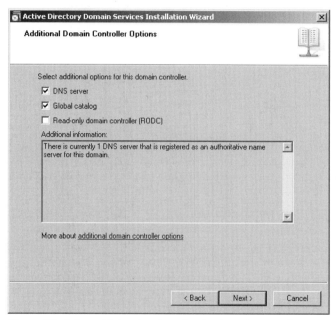

Figure 33-4 Set additional options for the domain controller.

9. If you are installing the DNS Server service as an additional option and the server doesn't have static IP addresses for both IPv4 and IPv6, you see a warning prompt regarding the server's dynamic IP address or addresses. Click Yes only if you plan to use the dynamic IP address or addresses despite the possibility that this could result in an unreliable DNS configuration. Click No if you plan to change the IP configuration before continuing.

Chapter 33

> **Note**
>
> During installation of the operating system, Windows Setup installs and configures IPv4 and IPv6 if it detects networking components. If you've configured a static IPv4 address but haven't configured a static IPv6 address, you also see this warning. You can ignore this warning if your network uses only IPv4 (but keep in mind that you may need to make changes to DNS records later if your organization starts using IPv6 addresses).

10. If you are installing the DNS Server service as an additional option, the wizard next attempts to register a delegation for the DNS server with an authoritative parent zone. If you are integrating with an existing DNS infrastructure, you should manually create a delegation to the DNS server and then click Yes to continue. Otherwise, you can ignore this warning and click Yes to continue.

> **Note**
>
> Before continuing, make sure you check for encrypted files and folders as discussed earlier in "Active Directory Installation Options and Issues" on page 1112. If you don't do this and there are encrypted files and folders present, you will no longer be able to decrypt them.

11. If you are performing an advanced installation and are adding a domain controller to an existing domain, you can specify whether to replicate the necessary Active Directory data from media or over the network, as shown in Figure 33-5. When you are installing from media, you must specify the folder location of the media before continuing.

12. If you are performing a basic installation or you choose to replicate data over the network, you'll see the Source Domain Controller page when you click Next. This page allows you to choose a replication partner for the installation. When you install a domain controller and do not use backup media, all directory data is replicated from the replication partner to the domain controller you are installing. As this can be a considerable amount of data, you typically want to ensure that both domain controllers are located in the same site or connected over reliable, high-speed networks.

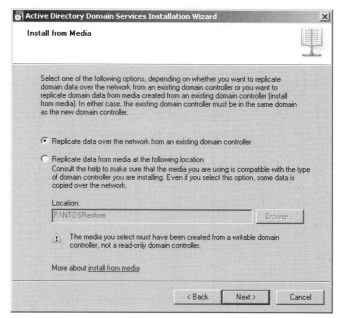

Figure 33-5 Specify whether to replicate over the network or from media.

13. On the Location For Database, Log Files, And SYSVOL page, shown in Figure 33-6, select a location to store the Active Directory database folder, log folder, and SYSVOL. Keep the following in mind when configuring these locations:

- ○ The default location for the database and log folders is a subfolder of %SystemRoot%\NTDS. As discussed in "Hardware and Configuration Considerations for Domain Controllers" on page 1108, you'll get better performance if these folders are on two separate volumes, each on a separate disk.

- ○ The default location for the SYSVOL folder is %SystemRoot%\Sysvol. In most cases, you'll want to accept the default as the replication services store their database in a subfolder of the %SystemRoot% folder anyway, so by keeping the folders on the same volume, you reduce the need to move files between drives.

> **Note**
>
> When the domain functional level is Windows 2000 Server or Windows Server 2003, the File Replication Service (FRS) is used to replicate the SYSVOL. FRS enables interoperability with Windows 2000 Server and Windows Server 2003 but does not support the latest replication enhancements. When the domain functional level is Windows Server 2008, the Distributed File System (DFS) service is used to replicate the SYSVOL and the latest replication enhancements are available, including replication of changes only within files, bandwidth throttling, and improved replication topology.

Chapter 33

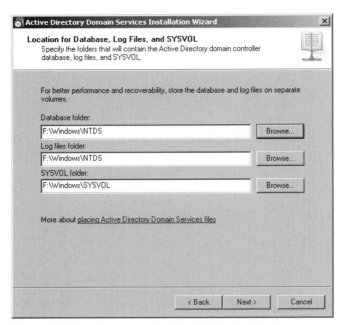

Figure 33-6 Set the storage locations for Active Directory data.

14. Click Next. Type and confirm the password that should be used when you want to start the computer in Directory Services Restore mode. Be sure to track this password carefully. This special password is used only in Restore mode and is different from the Administrator account password.

15. Click Next. Review the installation options. Optionally, click Export Settings to save these settings to an answer file that you can use to perform unattended installation of other domain controllers. When you click Next again, the wizard will use the options you've selected to install and configure Active Directory. This process can take several minutes. Keep the following in mind:

○ If you specified that the DNS Server service should be installed, the server will also be configured as a DNS server at this time.

○ If you are installing an additional domain controller in an existing domain, the domain controller will need to obtain updates of all the directory partitions from other domain controllers and will do this by initiating a full synchronization. The only way to avoid this is to make a media backup of Active Directory on an existing domain controller, start the Active Directory Domain Services Installation Wizard in Advanced mode, and then specify the backup media to use during installation of Active Directory.

16. When the wizard finishes configuring Active Directory, click Finish. You are then prompted to restart the computer. Click Restart Now to reboot.

After installing Active Directory, you should verify the installation by doing the following (in no particular order):

- Examine the log of the installation, which is stored in the Dcpromo.log file in the %SystemRoot%\Debug folder. As shown in the following screen, the log is very detailed and takes you through every step of the installation process, including the creation of directory partitions and the securing of the Registry for Active Directory.

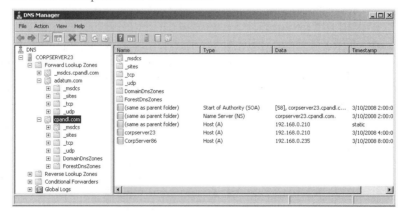

- Check for DNS updates in the DNS console shown in the following screen. If you added a domain controller to an existing domain, DNS is updated to add SRV records for the server. If you created a new domain, DNS is updated to include a forward lookup zone for the domain.

- Check for updates in Active Directory Users And Computers. For example, check to make sure the new domain controller is listed in the Domain Controllers OU, as shown in the following screen.

Chapter 33

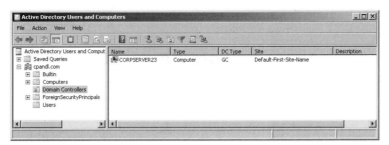

If you created a new domain, the following containers are created and populated as appropriate:

- ○ Builtin contains the built-in accounts for administration, including Administrators and Account Operators.

- ○ Computers contains computer accounts for the domain.

- ○ Domain Controllers contains the domain controller accounts and should have an account for the domain controller you installed.

- ○ ForeignSecurityPrinicipals is a container for security principals from other domain trees.

- ○ Users is the default container for user accounts in the domain.

Additionally, if you created a new domain, you also need to configure DNS so that name resolution works appropriately with any existing domains. To enable name resolution for computers within the new domain, you typically want to create secondary zones for all existing domains in the new domain and set up zone transfers. To enable name resolution into the new domain from existing domains, you typically want to create a secondary zone in existing domains for the new domain and set up zone transfers.

Creating New Domains in New Forests

To create a new domain in a new forest, follow these steps:

1. Start the Active Directory Domain Services Installation Wizard as discussed previously. If you haven't installed the AD DS binaries, the wizard installs them. Additionally, keep in mind that the currently logged on local administrator account will be created as a user account in the new domain with full administrator permissions. This means the account will be a member of the Users, Domain Users, and Domain Admins groups.

2. By default, the wizard uses Basic Installation mode. If you want to set the NetBIOS name of the domain, select Use Advanced Installation Mode before clicking Next to continue.

3. f the server doesn't have an appropriate IP address, you'll see the Configure TCP/IP page. This page displays a warning about the invalid IP address or improper network configuration and you'll need to correct the issue before you can continue.

4. On the Choose A Deployment Configuration page, select Create A New Domain In A New Forest as shown in Figure 33-7.

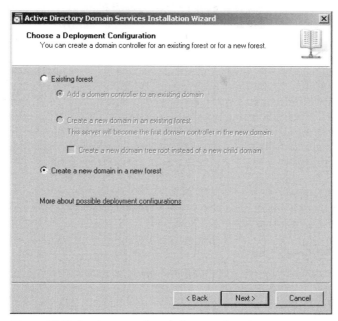

Figure 33-7 Create a new domain in a new forest.

5. Click Next to display the Name Of The Forest Root Domain page. Type the full DNS name for the new domain. Domain names are not case-sensitive and use the letters A to Z, the numerals 0 to 9, and the hyphen (-) character. Each component of the domain name must be separated by a dot (.) and cannot be longer than 63 characters.

6. When you click Next, the wizard will determine whether the name you've entered is already in use on your network. If the name is already in use, you will need to enter a different name or go back and make a different configuration selection.

7. After the wizard validates the domain name, it uses the name to generate a default NetBIOS name. If you are using Advanced Installation mode or the wizard has detected a conflict, you will be able to accept the wizard-generated name or type a new NetBIOS name of up to 15 characters and then click Next to continue.

8. On the Set Forest Functional Level page, choose the desired functional level for the new Active Directory forest. The forest functional level can be set to Windows 2000, Windows 2003 or Windows 2008. See "Domain Design Considerations" on page 1059 for a complete discussion on forest functional levels.

9. If you set the forest functional level to Windows 2008, the domain functional level is set automatically to Windows 2008 and you do not see the Set Domain Functional Level page. Otherwise, on the Set Domain Functional Level page, choose the desired functional level for the new domain. The domain functional level can be set to Windows 2000 native, Windows 2003, or Windows 2008. See "Domain Design Considerations" on page 1059 for a complete discussion on domain functional levels.

10. When you click Next, the wizard examines the network environment and attempts to register the domain and the domain controller in DNS. If the wizard detects that a DNS server is not available, DNS server will be selected as an additional option on the Additional Domain Controller Options page and the descriptive text also will recommend that you install the DNS Server service. Click Next to continue.

> **Note**
>
> If you choose to let the wizard install DNS, the DNS Server service will be installed and the domain controller will also act as a DNS server. A primary DNS zone will be created as an Active Directory–integrated zone with the same name as the new domain you are setting up. The wizard will also update the server's TCP/IP configuration so that its primary DNS server is set to itself.

11. If you are installing the DNS Server service as an additional option and the server doesn't have static IP addresses for both IPv4 and IPv6, you'll see a warning prompt regarding the server's dynamic IP address or addresses. Click Yes only if you plan to use the dynamic IP address or addresses despite the possibility that this could result in an unreliable DNS configuration. Click No if you plan to change the IP configuration before continuing.

> **Note**
>
> During installation of the operating system, Windows Setup installs and configures IPv4 and IPv6 if networking components are detected. If you've configured a static IPv4 address but haven't configured a static IPv6 address, you'll also see this warning. You can ignore this warning if your network only uses IPv4 (but keep in mind that you may need to make changes to DNS records later if your organization starts using IPv6 addresses).

12. If you are installing the DNS Server service as an additional option, the wizard next attempts to register a delegation for the DNS server with an authoritative parent zone. If you are integrating with an existing DNS infrastructure, you should manually create a delegation to the DNS server and then click Yes to continue. Otherwise, you can ignore this warning and click Yes to continue.

CAUTION !

Before continuing, make sure you check for encrypted files and folders as discussed in "Active Directory Installation Options and Issues" on page 1112. If you don't do this and there are encrypted files and folders present, you will no longer be able to decrypt them.

13. The rest of the installation proceeds as previously discussed. Continue with steps 13–16 and the post-installation checks discussed in the previous section, "Creating Additional Domain Controllers for an Existing Domain."

Creating a New Domain or Domain Tree Within an Existing Forest

To create a new domain or domain tree within an existing forest, follow these steps:

1. Start the Active Directory Domain Services Installation Wizard as discussed previously. If you haven't installed the AD DS binaries, the wizard installs them.

2. On the initial wizard page, select the Use Advanced Installation Mode check box before clicking Next to continue. If you don't use Advanced Installation mode, you can create new child domains in an existing forest but cannot create a new domain tree in an existing forest.

3. If the server doesn't have an appropriate IP address, you see the Configure TCP/IP page. This page displays a warning about the invalid IP address or improper network configuration and you'll need to correct the issue before you can continue.

4. On the Choose A Deployment Configuration page, you need to choose one of the following:

○ **Choose Existing Forest and then choose Create A New Domain In An Existing Forest** Choose this option to establish the first domain controller in a domain that is a child domain of an existing domain. By choosing this option, you are specifying that the necessary parent domain already exists. For example, you would choose this option if the parent domain cpandl. com had already been created and you wanted to create the tech.cpandl. com domain as a child of this domain.

When you click Next, you see the Network Credentials page. In the field provided, type the full DNS name of any domain in the forest where you plan to install the domain controller. Preferably, this should be the name of the forest root domain, such as cpandl.com. If you are logged on to a domain in this forest and have the appropriate permissions, you can use your current logged on credentials to perform the installation. Otherwise, select Alternate Credentials, click Set, type the user name and password for an enterprise administrator account in the previously specified domain, and then click OK.

Chapter 33

Click Next again to display the Name The New Domain page. In the field provided, type the full DNS name for the parent domain, such as cpandl.com, or click Browse to search for an existing domain to use. In the next field, type the single name component of the child domain, such as tech.

○ **Choose Existing Forest, choose Create A New Domain In An Existing Forest, and then choose Create A New Domain Tree Root Instead Of A New Child Domain** Choose this option to establish a new domain tree that is separate from any existing trees in the existing Active Directory forest. By choosing this option, you specify that there isn't an existing parent domain with which you want to associate the new domain. For example, you should choose this option if the cohowinery.com domain already exists and you want to establish the cohovineyard.com domain in a new tree in the existing forest.

When you click Next, you see the Network Credentials page. In the field provided, type the full DNS name of any domain in the forest where you plan to install the domain controller. Preferably, this should be the name of the forest root domain, such as cpandl.com. If you are logged on to a domain in this forest and have the appropriate permissions, you can use your current logged on credentials to perform the installation. Otherwise, select Alternate Credentials, click Set, type the user name and password for an enterprise administrator account in the previously specified domain, and then click OK.

Click Next again to display the Name The New Domain Tree Root page. Type the full DNS name for the new domain. The domain name you use should not be a subdomain of an existing parent domain in any tree of the forest.

5. The rest of the installation proceeds as previously discussed. Continue with steps 7–16 and the post-installation checks discussed in "Creating Additional Domain Controllers for an Existing Domain" on page 1114. Note that you do not have the option to install from media so the Install From Media page does not appear.

Performing an Active Directory Installation from Media

Whenever you install an additional domain controller in an existing domain, you should consider whether you want to perform an installation from media rather than creating the domain controller from scratch. Doing so allows the Active Directory Domain Services Installation Wizard to get the initial data for the Configuration, Schema, and Domain directory partitions and optionally the SYSVOL from backup media rather than performing a full synchronization over the network.

Not only does this reduce the amount of network traffic, which is especially important when installing domain controllers in remote sites that are connected by low-bandwidth WAN links, it can also greatly speed up the process of installing an additional domain controller and getting the directory partition data synchronized. This means that rather than having to replicate the full data across the network, the domain controller needs to get only the changes made since the backup media was made. This can mean that only several megabytes of replication traffic are generated rather than several gigabytes, and on a busy or low-bandwidth network this can be very important.

> **Note**
>
> Installing Active Directory from media is not designed to be used to restore failed domain controllers. To restore failed domain controllers, you should use System State restore as this ensures that all the data that needs to be restored is recovered as necessary, including Registry settings, Sysvol data, and Active Directory data.

In Windows Server 2008, you can create installation media by restoring a System State backup of another domain controller. This process works the same as it did for Windows Server 2003. Windows Server 2008 also gives you the option of performing an installation from media backup. A media backup is preferred to a System State backup as it only includes directory data. On the other hand, a System State backup of Windows Server 2008 includes over 50,000 files that require 4 GB of space, not including the directory data.

Regardless of which technique you want to use, there are a few guidelines that you should follow when installing Active Directory from backup media:

- Always try to use the most recent media backup of Active Directory as possible. This reduces the number of updates that must replicate to the domain controller, which in turn minimizes the post-installation replication traffic.

- Always use a backup of a domain controller in the same domain in which the new domain controller is being created, and always use a backup from another Windows Server 2008 domain controller.

- Always copy the backup to a local drive on the server for which you are installing Active Directory. You cannot use backup media from Universal Naming Convention (UNC) paths or mapped drives.

- Never use backup media that is older than the tombstone lifetime of the domain. The default value is 60 days. If you try to use backup media older than 60 days, the Active Directory installation fails. For more information on tombstone lifetime and why it is important, see "Extensible Storage Engine," on page 993.

With these guidelines in mind, you can create an additional domain controller from backup media by completing the following steps:

1. Open an elevated command prompt window. At the command prompt, type **ntdsutil**. This starts the Directory Services Management Tool.

2. At the ntdsutil prompt, type **activate instance ntds**. This sets Active Directory as the directory service instance to work with.

Chapter 33

3. Type **ifm** to access the install from media prompt and then type one of the following commands where *FolderPath* is the full path to the folder in which to store the Active Directory backup media files:

   ○ **Create Full *FolderPath*** Creates a full writable installation media backup of Active Directory. You can use the media to install a writable domain controller or a read-only domain controller.

   ○ **Create RODC *FolderPath*** Creates a read-only installation media backup of Active Directory. You can use the media to install a read-only domain controller. The backup media does not contain security credentials, such as passwords.

   ○ **Create Sysvol Full *FolderPath*** Creates a full writable installation media backup of Active Directory and the Sysvol. You can use the media to install a writable domain controller or a read-only domain controller. The Sysvol files include computer and user scripts as well as group policy settings.

   ○ **Create Sysvol RODC *FolderPath*** Creates a read-only installation media backup of Active Directory and the Sysvol. You can use the media to install a read-only domain controller.

4. Ntdsutil then creates snapshots of Active Directory partitions. When it is finished creating the snapshots, Ntdsutil mounts the snapshots as necessary and then defragments the media backup of the Active Directory database. The progress of the defragmentation is shown as a percent complete.

5. Next, Ntdsutil copies Registry data related to Active Directory. If you are creating backup media for the Sysvol, Ntdsutil also creates backups of all policy settings, scripts, and other data stored on the Sysvol. When it finishes this process, Ntsdsutil unmounts any snapshots it was working with. The backup process should complete successfully. If it doesn't, note and resolve any issues that prevented successful creation of the backup media, such as the target disk running out of space or insufficient permissions to copy to the folder path.

6. Type **quit** at the ifm prompt and type **quit** at the ntdsutil prompt.

7. Copy the backup media to a local drive on the server for which you are installing Active Directory.

8. On the server you want to make a domain controller, start the Active Directory Domain Services Installation Wizard in Advanced Installation mode. Follow all the same steps as you would if you were adding a domain controller to the domain without media. After you select additional domain controller installation options and get past any DNS prompts, you see the Install From Media page, shown previously in Figure 33-5. On the Install From Media page, select Replicate From Media Stored At The Following Location, and then type the location of the backup media files or click Browse to find them.

9. You can now complete the rest of the installation as discussed in "Creating Additional Domain Controllers for an Existing Domain" on page 1114. Continue with the rest of the steps and perform the post-installation checks as well.

You can create an additional domain controller using System State backup media by completing the following steps:

1. Create a System State backup on a domain controller in the domain using Windows Backup or by typing the following at an elevated command prompt:

   ```
   wbadmin start systemstatebackup -backupTarget:VolumeName
   ```

   where *VolumeName* is the storage location for the backup, such as F:.

2. Restore the System State backup to an alternate location using Windows Backup or by typing the following at an elevated command prompt:

   ```
   wbadmin start systemstaterecovery -backupTarget:VolumeName
   -recoveryTarget:OtherLocation
   ```

   where *VolumeName* is the storage location that contains the System State backup you want to recover, such as F: and *OtherLocation* is the alternate folder location in which the backup should be restored, such as F:\NTDSRestore.

3. Copy the backup media to a local drive on the server for which you are installing Active Directory.

4. On the server you want to make a domain controller, start the Active Directory Domain Services Installation Wizard in Advanced Installation mode. Follow all the same steps as you would if you were adding a domain controller to the domain without media. After you select additional domain controller installation options and get past any DNS prompts, you see the Install From Media page, shown previously in Figure 33-5. On the Install From Media page, select Replicate From Media Stored At The Following Location, and then type the location of the backup media files or click Browse to find them.

5. You can now complete the rest of the installation as discussed in "Creating Additional Domain Controllers for an Existing Domain" on page 1114. Continue with the rest of the steps and perform the post-installation checks as well.

Uninstalling Active Directory

You uninstall Active Directory using the same techniques as you used to install it. Simply click Start, type **dcpromo** in the Search box, and then press Enter to start the Active Directory Domain Services Installation Wizard. When you uninstall Active Directory, you demote the domain controller and make it a member server in the domain. If you remove Active Directory from the last domain controller in the domain, the computer becomes a stand-alone server in a workgroup. You must be a member of the Domain Admins group to remove an additional domain controller in a domain, and a member of the Enterprise Admins group to remove the last domain controller from a domain.

INSIDE OUT   Considerations for removing global catalogs

If you run the Active Directory Domain Services Installation Wizard on a domain controller that is also a global catalog server, you see the warning prompt shown in the following screen:

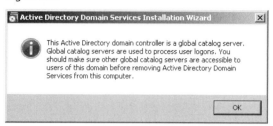

This prompt appears because you don't want to remove the last global catalog from the domain accidentally. If you remove the last global catalog from the domain, users won't be able to log on to the domain. A quick way to check to determine the global catalog servers in a domain is to type the following command at a command prompt:

```
dsquery server -domain DomainName | dsget server -isgc -dnsname
```

where *DomainName* is the name of the domain you want to examine. Consider the following example:

```
dsquery server -domain cpandl.com | dsget server -isgc -dnsname
```

Here, you are examining the cpandl.com domain to obtain a list of the global catalog servers according to their DNS names. The output is shown in two columns, for example:

```
dnsname                 isgc
corpsvr15.cpandl.com    no
corpsvr17.cpandl.com    yes
```

The first column is the DNS name of each domain controller in the domain. The second column is a flag that indicates whether the domain controller is also a global catalog. Thus, if the *isgc* value is set to *yes* for a domain controller, it is also a global catalog server.

When the wizard starts, click Next to display the Delete The Domain page, shown in Figure 33-8. If this is the last domain controller in the domain and you want to permanently remove the domain from the forest, select Delete The Domain Because This Server Is The Last Domain Controller In The Domain check box before you continue. After you remove the last domain controller in the domain, you can no longer access any application partition data, domain accounts, or encrypted data. Therefore, before you uninstall the last domain controller in a domain, you should examine domain accounts and look for encrypted files and folders.

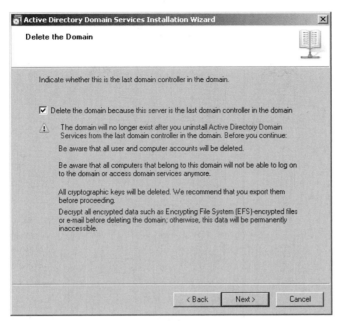

Figure 33-8 Removing Active Directory from a server.

> **Note**
>
> Because the deleted domain no longer exists, its accounts and cryptographic keys are no longer applicable, and this results in the deletion of all domain accounts and all certificates and cryptographic keys from the server. You must decrypt any encrypted data on the server, including data stored using the Encrypting File System (EFS), before removing Active Directory or the data will be permanently inaccessible.

When you click Next, you see the Network Credentials page. If you are logged on with an account that has appropriate permissions for uninstalling Active Directory, you can use your current logged on credentials. Otherwise, select Alternate Credentials, click Set, type the user name and password for an account with appropriate forest-wide permissions, and then click OK.

When you are ready to continue, click Next. The Active Directory Domain Services Installation Wizard then examines the Active Directory forest, checking the credentials you provided and attempting to contact a domain controller in the domain listed previously on the Network Credentials page. Afterward, the wizard checks DNS to see if any active delegations for the server need to be removed. If the wizard has trouble with DNS, ensure that the host (A) records that map the domain controllers to their IP addresses are correct.

Next, you are prompted to type and confirm the password for the local Administrator account on the server. This is necessary because domain controllers don't have local accounts but member or stand-alone servers do, so this account will be re-created as part of the Active Directory removal process. Click Next.

On the Summary page, review your selections. Optionally, click Export Settings to save these settings to an answer file that you can use to perform unattended demotion of other domain controllers. When you click Next again, the wizard uses the options you've selected to demote the domain controller. This process can take several minutes. Keep the following in mind:

- If there are updates to other domains in the forest that have not been replicated, the domain controller replicates these updates and then the wizard begins the demotion process.

- If the domain controller is also a DNS server, the DNS data in the ForestDnsZones and DomainDnsZones partitions are removed. If the domain controller is the last DNS server in the domain, this results in the last replica of the DNS information being removed from the domain. All associated DNS records are lost and may need to be re-created.

At this point, the actions the Active Directory Domain Services Installation Wizard performs depend on whether you are removing an additional domain controller or removing the last domain controller from a domain. If you are removing an additional domain controller from a domain, the wizard does the following:

- Removes Active Directory and all related services from the server and makes it a member server in the domain

- Changes the computer account type and moves the computer account from the Domain Controllers container in Active Directory to the Computers container

- Transfers any operations master roles from the server to another domain controller in the domain

- Updates DNS to remove the domain controller SRV records

- Creates a local Security Accounts Manager (SAM) account database and a local Administrator account

If you are removing the last domain controller from a domain, the wizard verifies that there are no child domains of the current domain before continuing. If child domains are found, removal of Active Directory fails with an error telling you that you cannot remove Active Directory. When the domain being removed is a child domain, the wizard notifies a domain controller in the parent domain that the child domain is being removed. For a parent domain in its own tree, a domain controller in the forest root domain is notified. Either way, the domain object is tombstoned, and this change is then replicated to other domain controllers. The domain object and any related trust objects are also removed from the forest. As part of removing Active Directory from the last domain controller in a domain, all domain accounts, all certificates, and all cryptographic keys are removed from the server. The wizard creates a local SAM account database and a local Administrator account. It then changes the computer account type to a stand-alone server and puts the server in a new workgroup.

Creating and Managing Organizational Units (OUs)

Organizational units (OUs) are logical administrative units that can help you limit the scope of a domain. They can contain many types of objects, including those for computers, contacts, groups, printers, or users. Because they can also contain other OUs, you can build a hierarchy of OUs within a domain. You can also use OUs to delegate administrator privileges on a limited basis.

Creating an OU

You can create OUs in Active Directory Users And Computers. As long as you use an account that is a member of the Administrators group, you'll be able to create OUs anywhere in the domain. The only exception is that you cannot create OUs within the default containers created by Active Directory.

> **Note**
>
> Note that you can create OUs within the Domain Controllers container. This is possible because this container is created as an OU. Creating OUs within Domain Controllers is useful if you want to organize domain controllers.

To create an OU, follow these steps:

1. Click Start, Administrative Tools, and Active Directory Users And Computers. This starts Active Directory Users And Computers.

2. By default, you are connected to your logon domain. If you want to create OUs in a different domain, right-click the Active Directory Users And Computers node in the console tree, and then select Change Domain. In the Change Domain dialog box, type the name of the domain to which you want to connect, and then click OK. Alternatively, in the Change Domain dialog box, you can click Browse to open the Browse For Domain dialog box so that you can find the domain to which you want to connect.

3. You can now create the OU. If you want to create a top-level OU (that is, an OU that has the domain container as its parent), right-click the domain node in the console tree, point to New, and then select Organizational Unit. If you want to create a lower-level OU, right-click the OU in which you want to create the new OU, point to New, and then select Organizational Unit.

4. In the New Object–Organizational Unit dialog box, type a name for the OU, as shown in Figure 33-9, and then click OK. Although the OU name can be any string of up to 256 characters, the best OU names are short and descriptive.

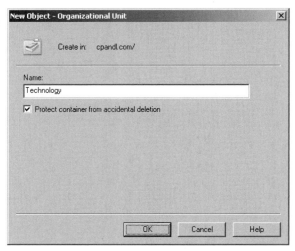

Figure 33-9 Specify the name of the OU to create.

INSIDE OUT   Understanding deletion protection for OUs

All OUs have deletion protection by default. Deletion protection is new in Windows Server 2008. When you create a new OU, the Protect Container From Accidental Deletion check box is selected automatically. This prevents any user or administrator in the domain from deleting the OU. To delete a protected OU, you must complete the following steps:

1. In Active Directory Users And Computers, you must enable the Advanced Features view by selecting Advanced Features on the View menu.

2. Right-click the OU and then select Properties.

3. On the Object tab of the Properties dialog box, clear the Protect Object From Accidental Deletion check box and then click OK.

4. In Active Directory Users And Computers, right-click the OU and then select Delete.

5. When prompted to confirm, click Yes.

Setting OU Properties

OUs have properties that you can set to add descriptive information. This helps other administrators know how the OU is used.

To set the properties of an OU, right-click the OU in Active Directory Users And Computers and then select Properties. This displays the OU's Properties dialog box, as shown in Figure 33-10.

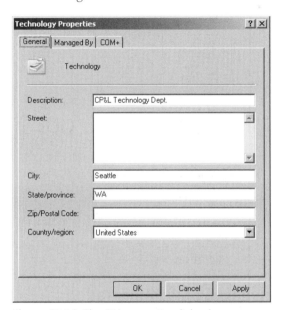

Figure 33-10 The OU properties dialog box.

In the OU Properties dialog box, you can do the following:

- On the General tab, you can enter descriptive information about the OU, including a text description and address information.

- On the Managed By tab, you can specify the user or contact responsible for managing the OU. This gives a helpful point of contact for questions regarding the OU.

When Advanced view is enabled, you have the following additional tabs and options:

- On the Object tab, you can determine the canonical name of the OU object and specify whether the OU should be protected from accidental deletion.

- On the COM+ tab, you can specify the COM+ partition of which the OU should be a member (if any).

- On the Attribute Editor tab, you can view and set attributes of the OU object.

Creating or Moving Accounts and Resources for Use with an OU

After you create an OU, you might want to place accounts and resources in it. In Active Directory Users And Computers you follow one of these procedures:

- You create accounts in the OU. To do so, right-click the OU, point to New, and then select the type of object to create, such as Computer, Group, or User.

- You move existing accounts or resources to an OU. To do so, select the account or resource in its existing container by clicking and holding the left mouse button. You can then drag the account or resource to the OU. When you release the mouse button, the account or resource is moved to the OU. Using Ctrl+click or Shift+click, you can select and move multiple accounts or resources as well.

Delegating Administration of Domains and OUs

When you create domains and OUs, you'll often want to be able to delegate control over them to specific individuals. This is useful if you want to give someone limited administrative privileges for a domain or OU. Before you delegate administration, you should carefully plan the permissions to grant. Ideally, you want to delegate the permissions that allow a user to perform necessary tasks, while preventing your delegate from performing tasks he or she should not. Often, figuring out the tasks that a user with limited administrative permissions should be able to perform requires talking to the department or office manager or the individual.

Understanding Delegation of Administration

You delegate control of Active Directory objects to grant users permission to manage users, groups, computers, OUs, or other objects stored in Active Directory. You can grant permissions in the following ways:

- **Grant full control over an OU** Useful when you have local administrators within departments or at branch offices and you want those individuals to be able to manage all objects in the OU. Among other things, this allows local administrators to create and manage accounts in the OU.

- **Grant full control over specific types of objects in an OU** Useful when you have local administrators who should only be able to manage specific types of objects in an OU. For example, you might want local administrators to be able to manage users and groups but not to be able to manage computer accounts.

- **Grant full control over specific types of objects in a domain** Useful when you want to allow an individual to be able only to manage specific types of objects in a domain. Rather than adding the user as a member of the Administrators group, you grant the user full control over specific objects. For example, you might allow the user to manage user and group accounts in the domain but not to perform other administrative tasks.

- **Grant rights to perform specific tasks** Useful when you want to allow an individual to perform a specific task. For example, you might want to allow a department manager to read information related to user accounts in Active Directory Users And Computers or you might want to allow help desk staff to be able to reset user passwords.

When you delegate permissions, it is important to remember how inheritance works in Active Directory. As you may recall from previous discussions of permissions, lower-level objects inherit permissions from top-level objects. In a domain, the top-level object is the domain object itself. This has the following results:

- Any user designated as an administrator for a domain automatically has full control over the domain.

- If you grant permissions at the domain level, the user has those permissions for all OUs in the domain as well.

- If you grant permissions in a top-level OU, the user has those permissions for all OUs that are created within the top-level OU.

Delegating Administration

To delegate administration of a domain or OU, follow these steps:

1. Start Active Directory Users And Computers. Click Start, Administrative Tools, and Active Directory Users And Computers.

2. Right-click the domain or OU for which you want to delegate administration, and then select Delegate Control. When the Delegation Of Control Wizard starts, click Next.

3. On the Users Or Groups page shown in Figure 33-11, click Add to display the Select Users, Computers, Or Groups dialog box.

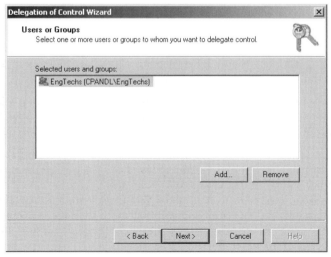

Figure 33-11 Select the users and groups for which you want to delegate control.

4. The default location is the current domain. Click Locations to see a list of the available domains and other resources that you can access. Because of the transitive trusts in Windows Server 2008, you can usually access all the domains in the domain tree or forest.

5. Type the name of a user or group account in the selected or default domain, and then click Check Names. The options available depend on the number of matches found as follows:

   ○ When a single match is found, the dialog box is automatically updated as appropriate and the entry is underlined.

   ○ When no matches are found, you've either entered an incorrect name part or you're working with an incorrect location. Modify the name and try again or click Locations to select a new location.

   ○ If multiple matches are found, select the name(s) you want to use, and then click OK.

6. To add additional users or groups, type a semicolon (;), and then repeat this process.

7. When you click OK, the users and groups are added to the Selected Users And Groups list in the Delegation Of Control Wizard. Click Next to continue.

8. On the Tasks To Delegate page, as shown in Figure 33-12, a list of common tasks is provided. If you want to delegate any of these common tasks, select the tasks. Afterward, click Next, and then click Finish. Skip the remaining steps.

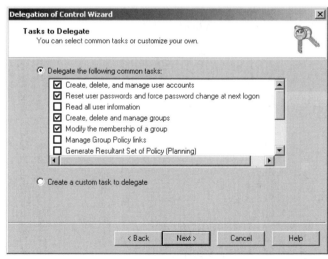

Figure 33-12 Select the tasks to delegate or choose to create a custom task.

9. If you want to create a custom task to delegate, choose Create A Custom Task To Delegate, and then click Next. On the Active Directory Object Type page, shown

in Figure 33-13, you can now choose to delegate management of all objects in the container or limit the delegation to specific types of objects.

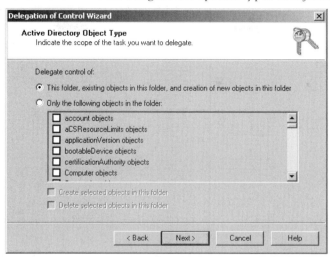

Figure 33-13 Select the tasks to delegate or choose to create a custom task.

10. On the Permissions page, shown in Figure 33-14, you can select the levels of permissions to delegate for the previously selected objects. You can choose to allow Full Control over the object or objects, or you can delegate very specific permissions.

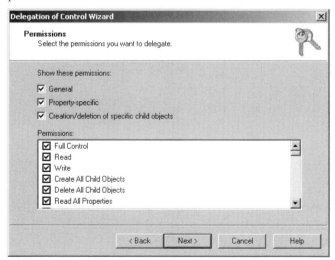

Figure 33-14 Specify the permissions to delegate for the previously selected objects.

11. Click Next, and then click Finish.

Chapter 33

Deploying Read-Only Domain Controllers

In the previous chapter, you learned about installing domain controllers using a standard read/writable installation. That chapter, however, did not discuss read-only domain controllers (RODCs) or detail the differences between read-only domain controllers and read/writable domain controllers (RWDCs), which is exactly what this chapter is about. After you've worked with RODCs and RWDCs for a time, you'll understand why it is important to consider them as separate and distinct from each other.

When working with RODCs, it is important to understand that they represent the tip of a paradigm shift. Although writable domain controllers are everywhere in today's enterprise, tomorrow's enterprise will use read/writable domain controllers only in the data center and on trusted networks, and will deploy only readable domain controllers everywhere else. The primary reason for this paradigm shift is that RODCs offer improved security and reduced risk as compared to their RWDC counterparts.

That said, it is also important to understand that the infrastructure and techniques related to RODCs are in the process of being defined and will change over time. For this reason, I discuss RODCs with a look to the future and also deviate from common terminology in my references to RODCs and RWDCs. My hope is that my several years of experience with RODCs and many years of experience with RWDCs will help you successfully deploy both in your organization and that when you do so, you'll do so by prefacing the installation plans with enough caveats to see you safely through the changes ahead.

Introducing Read-Only Domain Controllers

When the domain and forest are operating at the Windows Server 2003 functional level or higher and your PDC emulator for the domain is running Windows Server 2008 or higher, you have the option of deploying read-only domain controllers. A read-only domain controller (RODC) is an additional domain controller that hosts a read-only replica of a domain's Active Directory data store. RODCs are designed to be placed in locations that require fast and reliable authentication services but aren't necessarily secure. This makes RODCs ideally suited to the needs of branch offices where a domain controller's physical security cannot be guaranteed.

Only Windows Server 2008 and later releases of Windows Server can act as read-only domain controllers. Typically, you do not need to make any changes to client computers to allow them to use an RODC. Client computers running any of the following operating systems are supported for use with RODCs:

- Microsoft Windows 2000

- Microsoft Windows XP

- Microsoft Windows Server 2003

- Microsoft Windows Vista

- Member servers running Windows Server 2008

RODCs support the same features as RWDCs and can be used in both core server and full server installations. Except for passwords and designated, nonreplicated attributes, RODCs store the same objects and attributes as writable domain controllers. These objects and attributes are replicated to RODCs using unidirectional replication from a writable domain controller acting as a replication partner. Because no changes are written directly to RODCs, writable domain controllers acting as replication partners do not have to pull changes from RODCs. This reduces the workload of bridgehead servers in the hub site and the scope of your replication monitoring efforts. See Figure 34-1 for a top-level overview of how the replication of data works.

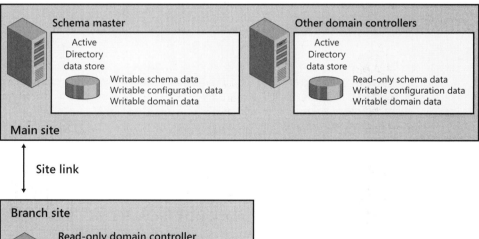

Figure 34-1 Replication of read-only Active Directory data.

Although Active Directory clients and applications can access the directory to read data, the clients are not able to write changes directly to an RODC. Instead, they are referred to a writable domain controller in a hub site.

INSIDE OUT **Test your applications before deploying RODCs**

Test all your applications that work with Active Directory before deploying RODCs. Most applications that work with Active Directory are read-intensive and do not require write access. Some applications, however, update information that is stored in Active Directory and expect this capability always to be available. If an application tries to use a serverless bind operation to write to an RODC, it is referred to a writable domain controller (DC) running Windows Server 2008. If the write operation succeeds, subsequent read operations might fail because the application will attempt to read from the RODC, which might not have received the updates through replication yet. To ensure proper operations, applications that require write access to the directory should be updated to use binding calls to writable domain controllers.

You can install the Domain Name System (DNS) Server service on an RODC. When you do this, the RODC receives a read-only replica of all application directory partitions that are used by DNS, including ForestDNSZones and DomainDNSZones (see Figure 34-2). Clients can query DNS on the RODC for name resolution as they would query any other DNS server. As with Active Directory data, the DNS server on an RODC does not support client updates directly.

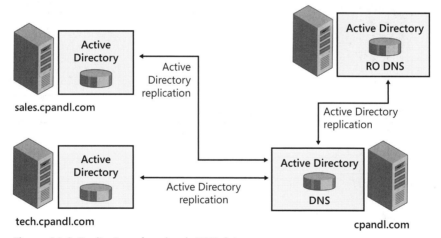

Figure 34-2 Replication of read-only DNS data.

The RODC does not register name server (NS) resource records for any Active Directory–integrated zone that it hosts. When a client attempts to update its DNS records on an RODC, the RODC returns a referral to another DNS server and the client can then attempt the update with this DNS server. In the background, the DNS server on the RODC will then attempt to pull the updated record from the DNS server that made the update. This replication request is only for the updated DNS record. The entire list of changed zone or domain data does not get replicated during this special replicate request.

Because RODCs by default do not store passwords or credentials other than for their own computer accounts and the Kerberos Target (krbtgt) accounts, RODCs pull user and computer credentials from a writable domain controller running Windows Server 2008 and clients can, in turn, authenticate against an RODC as shown in Figure 34-3. You must explicitly allow any other credentials to be cached on that RODC using Password Replication Policy. If allowed by a Password Replication Policy that is enforced on the writable domain controller, an RODC retrieves and then caches credentials as necessary until the credentials change. As only a subset of credentials is stored on an RODC, this limits the number of credentials that can possibly be compromised.

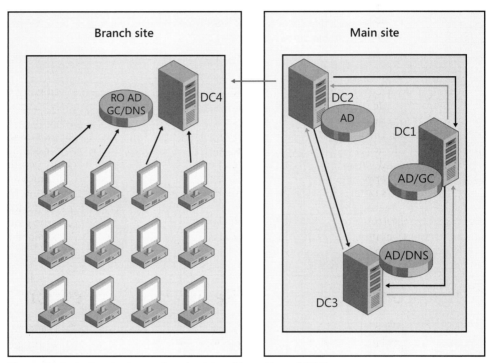

Figure 34-3 Authentication and credential caching with an RODC.

The RODC is advertised as the Key Distribution Center (KDC) for the branch office. After an account is successfully authenticated, the RODC attempts to contact and pull the user credentials or computer credentials from a writable domain controller that is running Windows Server 2008 in the hub site. The hub site can be any Active Directory site with writable domain controllers running Windows Server 2008.

The writable domain controller recognizes that the request is coming from an RODC because of the use of the special Kerberos Target account of the RODC. The Password Replication Policy that is enforced at the writable domain controller determines whether a user's credentials or a computer's credentials can be replicated to the RODC. If the Password Replication Policy allows it, the RODC pulls and then caches the credentials from the writable domain controller. After the credentials are cached on the

RODC, the RODC can directly service that user's or computer's logon requests until the credentials change. This limits the exposure of credentials in case an RODC is compromised.

> **Note**
>
> The RODC uses a different Kerberos Target account and password than the KDC on a writable domain controller uses when it signs or encrypts Ticket-Granting Target (TGT) requests. This provides cryptographic isolation between KDCs in different branches and prevents a compromised RODC from issuing service tickets to resources in other branches or in a hub site.

RODCs reduce the administration burden on the enterprise by allowing any domain user to be delegated as a local administrator without granting any other rights in the domain. This creates a clear separation between domain administrators and delegated administrator users at branch offices. An RODC cannot act as an operations master role holder. Although RODCs can pull information from domain controllers running Windows Server 2003, RODCs can only pull updates of the schema, configuration, and application partitions from a writable domain controller running Windows Server 2003 or later in the same domain; pull updates of the domain partition from a writable domain controller running Windows Server 2008 or later in the same domain; and pull a partial attribute set of the other domain partitions in the forest (the global catalog). Although RODCs can host a global catalog, they cannot act as bridgehead servers or hold operations master roles.

Design Considerations for Read-Only Replication

Before you can deploy any RODCs in a domain, the primary domain controller (PDC) emulator operations master role holder for the domain must be running Windows Server 2008 and you must ensure that there is a bidirectional communications path open between the RODC and the PDC emulator. As necessary to accommodate this requirement, you might need to modify router and firewall configurations.

RODCs are designed to be placed in sites that have no other domain controllers. Consider the example shown in Figure 34-4. Here, the organization has one domain and two sites at the same physical location. As the East Campus site is used for the organization's primary operations and is more secure from a physical perspective, the administrative staff decided to configure this site with the writable domain controllers and the operations masters for the domain. As the West Campus site is less secure from a physical perspective, the administrative staff decided to remove all other domain controllers and place only a read-only domain controller in this site.

> **Note**
>
> You cannot place more than one RODC from the same domain in the same site. How-
> ever, you can place an RODC in a site with RWDCs from the same or different domains
> or RODCs from different domains. Doing so has a number of constraints and requires
> additional planning.

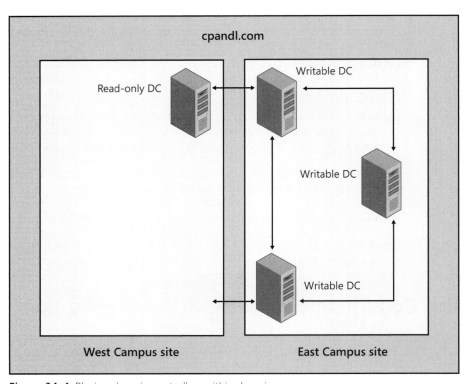

Figure 34-4 Placing domain controllers within domains.

RODCs perform inbound replication only by pulling data from a designated replication partner. RODCs cannot perform outbound replication and therefore cannot be a source domain controller for any other domain controller. An RODC can replicate data from a domain controller running Windows Server 2003 or Windows Server 2008. However, it can only replicate updates of the domain partition from a domain controller located in the same domain and that is running Windows Server 2008.

Table 34-1 lists the specific partitions that can be replicated and the permitted replication partners. Only an RODC also configured as a DNS server can obtain the application partitions containing DNS data. In contrast, writable domain controllers running Windows Server 2008 and domain controllers running Windows Server 2003 can perform inbound and outbound replication of all available partitions.

Table 34-1 Replicating Directory Partitions with RODCs

Directory Partition	Replication Partner
Schema	DC running Windows Server 2008 or Windows Server 2003
Configuration	DC running Windows Server 2008 or Windows Server 2003
Domain	DC running Windows Server 2008
Application	DC running Windows Server 2008 or Windows Server 2003
DNS	DC running Windows Server 2008 or Windows Server 2003 with Active Directory–integrated DNS zones
Global catalog	DC running Windows Server 2008 or Windows Server 2003

Generally speaking, you should place writable domain controllers in hub sites and read-only domain controllers in spoke sites. This configuration can relieve the inbound replication load on bridgehead servers because RODCs never replicate any changes. Consider the example shown in Figure 34-5. In this example, Main Site is the hub site and there are four branch office sites: Site A, Site B, Site C, and Site D. In this example, sites are connected in several different ways with redundant pathways. However, the site link with the lowest cost is always the link between the Main Site and a particular branch site.

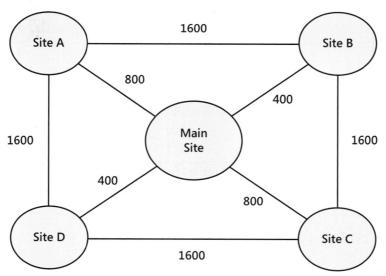

Figure 34-5 Placing domain controllers within sites.

In order to put an RODC in any branch site, a domain controller running Windows Server 2008 for the same domain should be placed in Main Site to replicate the domain partition to the RODC. Placing only a domain controller running Windows Server 2003 in Main Site would permit the RODC in the branch site to replicate the schema, configuration, and application directory partitions, but not the domain partition.

The replication schedule for site links can cause delays in receiving directory updates when replicating to other sites across a WAN. To improve replication performance, RODCs refer many types of write operations to a writable domain controller immediately and this can cause unscheduled network traffic over WAN links. Additionally, for these select operations, RODCs immediately attempt inbound replication of individual changes:

- Password changes made using the Security Accounts Manager (SAM) interface rather than the Lightweight Directory Access Protocol (LDAP).

- DNS updates where a client attempts to make a DNS update and is then referred to DNS server where the updates are registered.

Installing RODCs

RODCs can cache passwords for accounts that you've explicitly allowed in the Password Replication Policy. After an RODC has cached the password for a user, it remains in the Active Directory database until the user changes the password or the Password Replication Policy for the RODC changes such that the user's password should no longer be cached. Accounts that will not have credentials cached on the RODC can still use the RODC for domain logon. The RODC retrieves the credentials from its RWDC replication partner. The credentials, however, will not be cached for subsequent logons using the RODC.

Preparing for an RODC Installation

You can install an RODC only in an existing domain. Before you install RODCs in any domain, you must ensure that the following are true:

- The forest functional level is Windows Server 2003 or higher. This ensures that linked-value replication is available to help ensure replication consistency.

- The domain functional level is Windows Server 2003 or higher. This ensures that Kerberos constrained delegation is available so that security calls can be impersonated under the context of the caller.

- The domain in which you are deploying the RODC includes domain controllers running Windows Server 2003 and domain controllers running Windows Server 2008.

- The domain controller that holds the PDC emulator operations master role is running Windows Server 2008 and the RODC can communicate over a secure channel with the PDC emulator.

- At least one domain controller running Windows Server 2008 for the same domain must be located in the site closest to the site that includes the RODC. To ensure that the RODC can replicate all directory partitions, this domain controller must be a global catalog server.

- To run the DNS server on the RODC, another domain controller running Windows Server 2008 must be running in the domain and hosting the Active Directory–integrated DNS domain zone. An Active Directory–integrated DNS zone on an RODC is always a read-only copy of the zone file.

- You must run the **Adprep /rodcprep** command before installing any RODCs. This ensures that the RODC can replicate DNS partitions. This is not required for new forests with only domain controllers that run Windows Server 2008 or when you are not using Active Directory–integrated DNS in the existing forest.

> **Note**
>
> To use Adprep /rodcprep, log on to a domain controller using an account that is a member of the Enterprise Admins group. Next, copy the contents of the \Sources\Adprep folder on the Windows Server 2008 installation DVD to the schema master. Finally, at a command prompt, change directories to the \Adprep folder and then enter **adprep /rodcprep**.

When you install an RODC, I recommend that you use Advanced Installation mode. This allows you to:

- **Configure the Password Replication Policy** The Password Replication Policy controls whether user and computer passwords are replicated to the RODC. You can configure Denied Accounts for which passwords are never replicated and Allowed Accounts for which passwords are always replicated. See "Managing Password Replication Policy" on page 1158 for more information.

- **Delegate administrative permissions** By delegating administrative permissions, you allow a specified user or group to act as the local administrator of the RODC. Delegating permissions in this way grants the user or group no other administrative permissions in the domain. For ease of administration, you should create a new group for this purpose prior to deploying an RODC. See "Delegating Administrative Permissions" on page 1165 for more information.

- **Install from media** When you install from media, the RODC can get the required directory data from a local or shared folder rather than over the network. Performing an RODC installation from media reduces directory replication traffic over the network. You must create the media before installing the RODC as discussed in "Installing an RODC from Media" on page 1156.

Installing an RODC

To install an RODC in an existing domain, follow these steps:

1. Log on to the server that you want to configure as an RODC. In Server Manager, select the Roles node in the left pane and then click Add Roles. This starts the Add Roles Wizard. If the wizard displays the Before You Begin page, click Next.

2. On the Select Server Roles page, select Active Directory Domain Services. Click Next twice and then click Install. When the installation is complete, click Close.

3. Start the Active Directory Domain Services Installation Wizard by clicking Start, typing **dcpromo** in the Search box, and then pressing Enter.

4. By default, the wizard will use Basic Installation mode. Select Use Advanced Mode Installation before clicking Next to continue.

5. If the server doesn't have an appropriate IP address, you'll see the Configure TCP/IP page. This page displays a warning about the invalid IP address or improper network configuration and you'll need to correct the issue before you can continue.

6. On the Choose A Deployment Configuration page, shown in Figure 34-6, select Existing Forest and then select Add A Domain Controller To An Existing Domain.

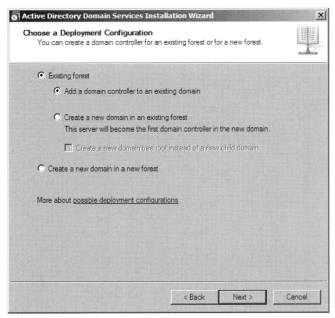

Figure 34-6 Add the domain controller to an existing domain.

7. When you click Next, you will see the Network Credentials page, shown in Figure 34-7. In the field provided, type the full DNS name of any domain in the forest where you plan to install the domain controller. Preferably, this should be the name of the forest root domain, such as cpandl.com. If you are logged on to a domain in this forest and have the appropriate permissions, you can use your current logged on credentials to perform the installation. Otherwise, select Alternate Credentials, click Set, type the user name and password for a domain administrator account in the previously specified domain, and then click OK.

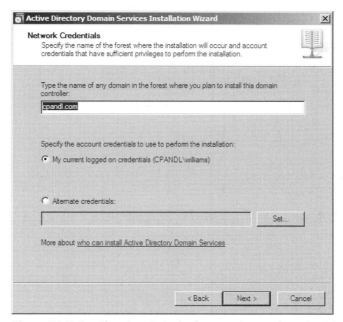

Figure 34-7 Specify a domain in the forest and network credentials.

8. When you click Next, the wizard will validate the domain name you provided and then list all domains in the related forest. On the Select A Domain page, select the domain for the domain controller and then click Next.

9. When you click Next, the wizard will determine the available Active Directory sites. On the Select A Site page, select the site in which the domain controller should be located and then click Next.

10. When you click Next, the wizard examines the DNS configuration and attempts to determine whether any authoritative DNS servers are available. As shown in Figure 34-8, select the Read-Only Domain Controller check box as an additional installation option for the domain controller. If you want the RODC to act as a read-only DNS server, select the DNS Server check box. If you want the RODC to act as a global catalog, select the Global Catalog check box. Click Next when you are ready to continue.

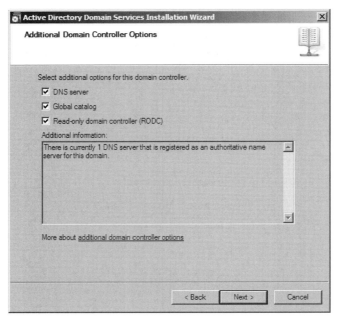

Figure 34-8 Configure the RODC.

11. If you are installing the DNS Server service as an additional option and the server doesn't have static IP addresses for both IPv4 and IPv6, you'll see a warning prompt regarding the server's dynamic IP address or addresses. Click Yes only if you plan to use the dynamic IP address or addresses despite the possibility that this could result in an unreliable DNS configuration. Click No if you plan to change the IP configuration before continuing.

> **Note**
>
> During installation of the operating system, Windows Setup installs and configures IPv4 and IPv6 if it detects networking components. If you've configured a static IPv4 address but haven't configured a static IPv6 address, you'll also see this warning. You can ignore this warning if your network uses only IPv4 (but keep in mind that you might need to make changes to DNS records later if your organization starts using IPv6 addresses).

12. You'll next be able to configure the Password Replication Policy for the RODC as shown in Figure 34-9. Add or remove any users, computers, or groups for which you want to allow or deny password replication. See "Allowing or Denying Accounts in Password Replication Policy" on page 1160 for more information. Click Next to continue.

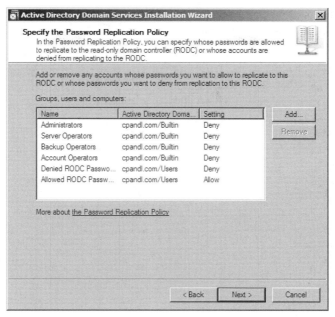

Figure 34-9 Configure the Password Replication Policy.

13. You'll next be able to configure delegation as shown in Figure 34-10. The delegated user or group will have local administrative permissions on the RODC. Click Set, use the Select User Or Group dialog box to specify a delegated user or group, and then click OK. Click Next to continue.

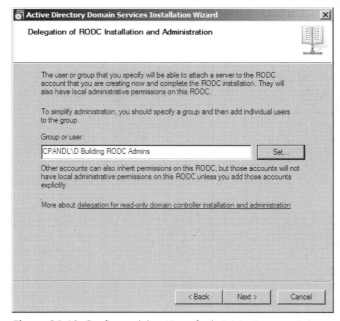

Figure 34-10 Configure delegation of administrative permissions.

Chapter 34

14. You'll next be able to configure the Install From Media options as shown in Figure 34-11. If you don't want to install from media, use the default selection to allow data to replicate over the network. If you want to install from media, select Replicate Data From Media At The Following Location and then type the folder path to use in the Location box. Alternatively, click Browse and then use the Browse For Folder dialog box to locate the folder to use. The media you specify must already be available. Click Next to continue.

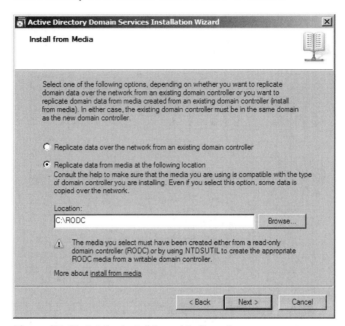

Figure 34-11 Set the Install From Media options.

15. On the Source Domain Controller page, you can let the wizard choose a replication partner for the installation of the RODC or select a desired replication partner for the installation. When you install a domain controller and do not use backup media, all directory data is replicated from the replication partner to the domain controller you are installing. As this can be a considerable amount of data, you typically want to ensure that both domain controllers are located in the same site or connected over reliable, high-speed networks. On the other hand, when you install from media, the RODC replicates only the changes or the missing data over the network from the replication partner. Click Next to continue.

16. On the Location For Database, Log Files, And SYSVOL page, shown in Figure 34-12, select a location to store the Active Directory database folder, log folder, and Sysvol. Keep the following in mind when configuring these locations:

○ The default location for the database and log folders is a subfolder of %SystemRoot%\NTDS. As discussed in "Hardware and Configuration Considerations for Domain Controllers" on page 1108, you'll get better performance if these folders are on two separate volumes, each on a separate disk.

○ The default location for the Syvol folder is %SystemRoot%\Sysvol. In most cases, you'll want to accept the default as the replication services store their database in a subfolder of the %SystemRoot% folder anyway, so by keeping the folders on the same volume, you reduce the need to move files between drives.

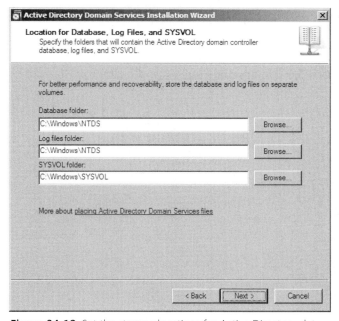

Figure 34-12 Set the storage locations for Active Directory data.

17. Click Next. Type and confirm the password that should be used when you want to start the computer in Directory Services Restore Mode. Be sure to track this password carefully. This special password is used only in Restore mode and is different from the Administrator account password.

18. Click Next. Review the installation options. Optionally, click Export Settings to save these settings to an answer file that you can use to perform unattended installations of other read-only domain controllers. When you click Next again, the wizard will use the options you've selected to install and configure Active Directory. This process can take several minutes. Keep the following in mind:

○ If you specified that the DNS Server service should be installed, the server will also be configured as a DNS server at this time.

○ If you are installing an additional domain controller in an existing domain, the domain controller will need to obtain updates of all the directory partitions from other domain controllers and will do this by initiating a full synchronization. The only way to avoid this is to make a media backup of

Active Directory on an existing domain controller, start the Active Directory Domain Services Installation Wizard in Advanced mode, and then specify the backup media to use during installation of Active Directory.

19. When the wizard finishes configuring Active Directory, click Finish. You are then prompted to restart the computer. Click Restart Now to reboot. You should then verify the installation using similar techniques as you'd use to verify the installation of a writable domain controller.

Installing an RODC from Media

You can create the necessary installation media by completing these steps:

1. Log on to a domain controller for the domain in which you are creating the RODC.

2. At an elevated command prompt, type **ntdsutil**.

3. At the ntdsutil prompt, type **activate instance ntds**.

4. At the ntdsutil prompt, type **ifm**.

5. You can now create a copy of the directory data with or without the Sysvol.

a. To create a copy of directory data without the Sysvol data, type **create RODC** *SaveFolder*, where *SaveFolder* is an empty folder into which you want to write the RODC data, such as C:\RODC. Ntdsutil will then perform a number of housekeeping tasks while creating the snapshot for the RODC media. The output while performing these tasks will look similar to the following:

```
Creating snapshot for RODC media...
Snapshot set {7aff6bd4-5f0e-42f2-8864-31d2fb2e82ed} generated
    successfully.
Snapshot {511aa261-fac4-4901-a447-a99c8a25f0fe} mounted
    as G:\$SNAP_200804222102_VOLUMEG$\
Initiating DEFRAGMENTATION mode...
    Source Database: G:\$SNAP_200804222102_VOLUMEG$\Windows\NTDS\ntds.dit
    Target Database: c:\rodc\Active Directory\ntds.dit

                Defragmentation  Status (% complete)

         0    10   20   30   40   50   60   70   80   90   100
         |----|----|----|----|----|----|----|----|----|----|
         ...................................................

Converting Full DC IFM media to Read-only DC IFM media...
Records scanned:      3467
Records scanned:        50
Read-only DC IFM media conversion completed successfully.
got 432441 buffers
```

```
                   Securing   Status (% complete)

        0    10   20   30   40   50   60   70   80   90   100
        |----|----|----|----|----|----|----|----|----|----|
        ..................................................
```

```
1536 pages seen
337 blank pages seen
0 unchanged pages seen
2 unused pages zeroed
1146 used pages seen
0 pages with unknown objid
63373 nodes seen
2 flag-deleted nodes zeroed
0 flag-deleted nodes not zeroed
0 version bits reset seen
0 orphaned LVs
Snapshot {511aa261-fac4-4901-a447-a99c8a25f0fe} unmounted.
IFM media created successfully in c:\rodc
```

b. To create a copy of directory data with the Sysvol data, type **create sysvol rodc** *SaveFolder*, where *SaveFolder* is a different, empty folder into which you want to write Sysvol data for the RODC, such as C:\SysvolSave. Ntdsutil will then perform a number of housekeeping tasks while creating the snapshot of the Sysvol. The output while performing these tasks will look similar to the following:

```
Creating snapshot for RODC media...
Snapshot set {f2a901f0-6f81-4926-8926-2b8e77673e00} generated
    successfully.
Snapshot {d2c435e5-a952-413d-83b3-0636dcb2e39c} mounted
    as G:\$SNAP_200804222115_VOLUMEG$\
Snapshot {d2c435e5-a952-413d-83b3-0636dcb2e39c} is already mounted.
Initiating DEFRAGMENTATION mode...
    Source Database: G:\$SNAP_200804222115_VOLUMEG$\Windows\NTDS\ntds.dit
    Target Database: c:\sysvolcopy\Active Directory\ntds.dit

                Defragmentation   Status (% complete)

        0    10   20   30   40   50   60   70   80   90   100
        |----|----|----|----|----|----|----|----|----|----|
        ..................................................

Converting Full DC IFM media to Read-only DC IFM media...
Records scanned:      3467
Records scanned:        50
Read-only DC IFM media conversion completed successfully.
got 428324 buffers

                   Securing   Status (% complete)

        0    10   20   30   40   50   60   70   80   90   100
        |----|----|----|----|----|----|----|----|----|----|
        ..................................................
```

```
1536 pages seen
337 blank pages seen
0 unchanged pages seen
2 unused pages zeroed
1146 used pages seen
0 pages with unknown objid
63373 nodes seen
2 flag-deleted nodes zeroed
0 flag-deleted nodes not zeroed
0 version bits reset seen
0 orphaned LVs
Copying SYSVOL...
Copying c:\sysvolcopy\SYSVOL
Copying c:\sysvolcopy\SYSVOL\cpandl.com
Copying c:\sysvolcopy\SYSVOL\cpandl.com\Policies
...
Copying c:\sysvolcopy\SYSVOL\cpandl.com\scripts
Snapshot {d2c435e5-a952-413d-83b3-0636dcb2e39c} unmounted.
IFM media created successfully in c:\sysvolcopy
```

6. Copy the save folder and its entire contents to a local folder on the RODC. The amount of data written to the save folder will vary depending on the number of objects and the properties those objects contain in the directory.

Because you've created installation media for an RODC, passwords are not included in the data. You can use this same technique to create installation media for writable domain controllers. In step 5, instead of typing **create rodc**, type **create full**. Instead of typing **create sysvol rodc**, type **create sysvol full**. That's it; it's that easy. However, a full copy of the directory data contains passwords and other critically important security data that requires additional safeguards.

Managing Password Replication Policy

When you deploy an RODC, you must configure the Password Replication Policy on the writable domain controller that will be its replication partner. The Password Replication Policy acts as an access control list (ACL) and determines whether an RODC should be permitted to cache a password for a particular user or computer. After the RODC receives an authenticated user or computer logon request, it refers to the Password Replication Policy to determine whether it should cache the password for the account.

Working with Password Replication Policy

You can configure Password Replication Policy in several ways. You can:

- Allow no accounts to be cached for the strictest control, such as when the physical security of the RODC cannot be guaranteed.

- Allow few accounts to be cached for strong control, such as when the physical security of the RODC is good but cannot be reasonably assured at all times.

- Allow many accounts to be cached for less strict control, such as when the physical security of the RODC can be reasonably assured at all times.

> **Note**
>
> The fewer account passwords replicated to RODCs, the less risk that security could be breached in case an RODC is compromised. The more account passwords replicated to RODCs, the greater the risk involved in case an RODC is compromised.

Password Replication Policy is managed on a per-computer basis. The computer object for an RODC is updated to include the following multi-valued directory attributes that contain security principals (users, computers, and groups):

- msDS-Reveal-OnDemandGroup, which defines the Allowed Accounts list
- msDS-NeverRevealGroup, which defines the Denied Accounts list
- msDS-RevealedUsers, which defines the Revealed Accounts list
- msDS-AuthenticatedToAccountList, which defines the Authenticated To list

The RODC uses these attributes together to determine whether an account password can be replicated and cached. The passwords for Denied Accounts are never replicated and cached. The passwords for Allowed Accounts can always be replicated and cached. Whether a password is cached or not doesn't depend on whether a user or computer has logged on to the domain via the RODC. At any time, an RODC can replicate the passwords for Allowed Accounts and administrators can also prepopulate passwords for Allowed Accounts using Active Directory Users And Computers.

During an advanced installation of an RODC, you can configure the initial Password Replication Policy settings. To support RODCs, Windows Server 2008 introduces four new built-in groups:

- **Enterprise Read-Only Domain Controllers** Every RODC in the Active Directory forest is a member of this group automatically. Membership in this group is required for proper operations.

- **Read-Only Domain Controllers** Every RODC in the Active Directory domain is a member of this group automatically. Membership in this group is required for proper operations.

- **Allowed RODC Password Replication Group** You can manage Allowed Accounts using the Allowed RODC Password Replication Group. Passwords for members of this group are always replicated to RODCs.

- **Denied RODC Password Replication Group** You can manage Denied Accounts using the Denied RODC Password Replication Group. Passwords for members of this group are never replicated to RODCs.

Chapter 34

By default, the Allowed RODC Password Replication Group has no members. Also by default, the Allowed RODC Password Replication Group is the only Allowed Account defined in Password Replication Policy.

By default, the Denied RODC Password Replication Group contains the following members:

- Cert Publishers
- Domain Admins
- Domain Controllers
- Enterprise Admins
- Group Policy Creator Owners
- Read-Only Domain Controllers
- Schema Admins
- The domain-wide krbtgt account

Also by default, the Denied Accounts list contains the following security principals, all of which are built-in groups:

- Account Operators
- Administrators
- Backup Operators
- Denied RODC Password Replication Group
- Server Operators

Allowing or Denying Accounts in Password Replication Policy

Each RODC has a separate Password Replication Policy. To manage the Password Replication Policy, you must be a member of the Domain Admins group. The easiest way to manage Password Replication Policy is to:

- Add accounts for which passwords should not be replicated to the Denied RODC Password Replication Group.
- Add accounts for which passwords should be replicated to the Allowed RODC Password Replication Group.

However, this would not meet security requirements if the desire were to limit cached passwords only to users and computers at the target location. Therefore, a better way to manage Password Replication Policy while limiting cached passwords is to edit Password Replication Policy settings directly. To edit the Password Replication Policy for an RODC, follow these steps:

1. In Active Directory Users And Computers, ensure that Active Directory Users And Computers points to a writable domain controller that is running Windows

Server 2008. Right-click the Active Directory Users And Computers node and then select Change Domain Controller. As shown in Figure 34-13, the domain controller to which you are connected should be a writable domain controller; that is, it should not list RODC under DC Type. If you are connected to an RODC, change to a writable domain controller. Click Cancel or OK as appropriate.

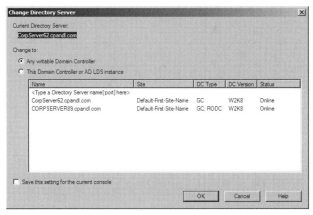

Figure 34-13 Make sure you are connected to a writable domain controller.

2. In Active Directory Users And Computers, expand the domain node and then select Domain Controllers.

3. In the details pane, right-click the RODC computer account and then choose Properties.

4. On the Password Replication Policy tab, shown in Figure 34-14, you'll see the current settings for Password Replication Policy on the RODC.

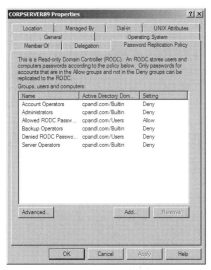

Figure 34-14 Review the current Password Replication Policy settings for the RODC.

Chapter 34

5. You can now:

   ○ Define an Allowed Account. Click Add, select Allow Passwords For The Account To Replicate To This RODC, and then click OK. In the Select Users, Contacts, Computers, Or Groups dialog box, type an account name and then click Check Names. If the account name is listed correctly, click OK to add it to the Password Replication Policy as an Allowed Account.

   ○ Define a Denied Account. Click Add, select Deny Passwords For The Account To Replicate To This RODC, and then click OK. In the Select Users, Contacts, Computers, Or Groups dialog box, type an account name and then click Check Names. If the account name is listed correctly, click OK to add it to the Password Replication Policy as a Denied Account.

   ○ Remove an account from Password Replication Policy. Select the account name in the Groups, Users And Computers list and then click Remove. When prompted to confirm, click Yes.

Viewing and Managing Credentials on an RODC

You can review cached credentials or prepopulate credentials using the Advanced Password Replication Policy dialog box. When you are prepopulating user accounts, you should also consider prepopulating the passwords of computer accounts that the users will be using.

To view and work with this dialog box, follow these steps:

1. In Active Directory Users And Computers, expand the domain node and then select Domain Controllers.

2. In the details pane, right-click the RODC computer account and then choose Properties.

3. On the Password Replication Policy tab, click Advanced to display the Advanced Password Replication Policy dialog box, shown in Figure 34-15.

4. You now have the following options:

   ○ Accounts for which passwords are stored on the RODC are displayed by default. To view accounts that have been authenticated to this RODC, select Accounts That Have Been Authenticated To This Read-Only Domain Controller in the Display Users And Computers list.

   ○ To prepopulate passwords for an account, click Prepopulate Passwords. In the Select Users Or Computers dialog box, type an account name, and then click Check Names. If the account name is listed correctly, click OK to add a request that its password be replicated to the RODC. When prompted to confirm, click Yes. The password is then prepopulated. Click OK.

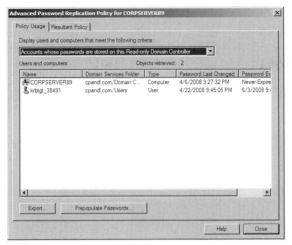

Figure 34-15 Review stored credentials.

Determining Whether an Account Is Allowed or Denied Access

To determine whether an account is allowed or restricted, you can use Resultant Set of Policy to examine all related group memberships and determine exactly what rules apply. Follow these steps:

1. In Active Directory Users And Computers, expand the domain node and then select Domain Controllers.

2. In the details pane, right-click the RODC computer account and then choose Properties.

3. On the Password Replication Policy tab, click Advanced to display the Advanced Password Replication Policy dialog box.

4. On the Resultant Policy tab, click Add.

5. In the Select Users Or Computers dialog box, type an account name, and then click Check Names. If the account name is listed correctly, click OK to display the resultant set of policy as shown in Figure 34-16.

Figure 34-16 Determine whether an account is allowed or denied access using Resultant Set of Policy.

Resetting Credentials

In the event that an RODC is compromised or stolen, you can reset the passwords for all accounts for which credentials were cached on the RODC by following these steps:

1. In Active Directory Users And Computers, ensure that Active Directory Users And Computers points to the writable domain controller that is running Windows Server 2008. Right-click the Active Directory Users And Computers node and then select Change Domain Controller. The domain controller to which you are connected should be a writable domain controller; that is, it should not list RODC under DC Type. If you are connected to an RODC, change to a writable domain controller. Click Cancel or OK as appropriate.

2. In Active Directory Users And Computers, expand the domain node and then select Domain Controllers.

3. In the details pane, right-click the RODC computer account and then choose Delete.

4. When prompted to confirm, click Yes.

5. When prompted again, specify that you want to reset all passwords for user accounts that were cached on this RODC.

6. Next, click Export to export the list of cached accounts to a file. The password for every user whose account is listed in this file has been reset.

Delegating Administrative Permissions

During configuration of an RODC, you have an opportunity to specify a user or group account that should be delegated administrative permissions. After the initial configuration, you can add or remove administrative permissions using Dsmgmt.

To grant administrative permissions to an additional user, follow these steps:

1. At an elevated command prompt, type **dsmgmt**.

2. At the dsmgmt prompt, type **local roles**.

3. At the local roles prompt, type **show roles administrators** to list current administrators. In the default configuration, no users or groups are listed.

4. At the local roles prompt, type **add** *Domain\User* **administrator** to grant administrative permissions where *Domain* is the domain in which the user account is located and *User* is the account name, such as CPANDL\williams.

5. Confirm the addition by typing **show roles administrators**.

6. Type **quit** twice to exit dsmgmt.

To remove administrative permissions, follow these steps:

1. At an elevated command prompt, type **dsmgmt**.

2. At the dsmgmt prompt, type **local roles**.

3. At the local roles prompt, type **show roles administrators** to list current administrators. In the default configuration, no users or groups are listed.

4. At the local roles prompt, type **remove** *Domain\User* **administrator** to remove administrative permissions for a specified user where *Domain* is the domain in which the user account is located and *User* is the account name, such as CPANDL\williams.

5. Confirm the removal by typing **show roles administrators**.

6. Type **quit** twice to exit dsmgmt.

Chapter 34

Managing Users, Groups, and Computers

As an administrator, managing users, groups, and computers will probably be a significant part of your duties and responsibilities. Managing users, groups, and computers encapsulates the important duties of a system administrator because of the way you must balance convenience, performance, fault tolerance, and security.

Managing Domain User Accounts

The next part of this chapter is dedicated to helping you plan, manage, and administer user accounts in a secure and efficient manner. Microsoft Windows operating systems have come a long way since the early days of Windows Server and you have many options for managing users in Windows Server 2008.

Types of Users

It is a good idea to have a solid grasp of fundamental concepts that underpin the managing of users. In the first part of the chapter, I will describe the types of users Microsoft Windows Server 2008 defines.

- **User** In Windows Server 2008, you can have local user accounts or domain user accounts. On a domain controller, local users and groups are disabled. In Active Directory, the domain user account contains user name, password, the groups of which the user is a member, and other descriptive information, such as address and phone numbers, as well as many other user descriptions and attributes, such as security and remote control configurations.

- **InetOrgPerson** InetOrgPerson is a type of user introduced in Windows Server 2003. InetOrgPerson has attributes based on Request for Comments (RFC) 2798, such as vehicle license number, department number, display name, employee number, JPEG photograph, and preferred language. Used by X.500 and Lightweight Directory Access Protocol (LDAP) directory services, the InetOrgPerson account is used when you migrate non-Microsoft LDAP directories to Active Directory. Derivative of the user class, the InetOrgPerson can be used as a security principal. The InetOrgPerson is compatible with X.500 and LDAP directory services.

- **Contact** Sometime you may want to create an account that will only be used as an e-mail account. This is when you would create a contact. It is not a security principal and does not have a security identifier (SID). There are neither passwords nor logon functionality available with a contact account. However, it can be a member of a distribution group.

- **Default user accounts** These are the built-in user accounts created when a Windows Server 2008 installation or stand-alone server is configured to be a domain controller and Active Directory is installed. It is a good idea to rename the Administrator account for security reasons. The default user accounts are found by opening Active Directory Users And Computers, then examining the contents of the Builtin and Users containers. They include the following accounts:

  - *Administrator* This is the account that has full control over the computer or domain. You should have a very strong password for this account. The Administrator is a member of these groups: Administrators, Domain Admins, Domain Users, and Group Policy Creator Owners. In a forest root domain, the Administrator is also a member of the Enterprise Admins and Schema Admins groups. The Administrator account can never be deleted. However, you can disable it or rename it. Either of these actions is a good practice to ensure a secure domain and network.

  - *Guest* The Guest account can be used by users who don't have an account in the domain. It is a member of the Guests domain local group and the Domain Guests global group. The Guest account is disabled by default when you make a stand-alone Windows Server 2008 server a domain controller.

Naming User Accounts

Think about the naming scheme you plan to use for user accounts. As the organization changes and grows, the original naming scheme may need to change but not the need for a naming scheme of some kind. Although account names for operating systems earlier than Windows 2000 are limited to 20 characters for a user name, Windows Server 2003 and Windows Server 2008 have a 256-character limitation for a user name.

Small organizations commonly use a person's first name and last name initial for their user account. In a larger organization, it may be a better idea to use their full name for their user account name. For example, in a small organization, John Smith could have a user name of JohnS. However, in a larger organization, John Smith should have a username of JohnSmith.

This becomes a problem when an organization has more than one John Smith who needs a user account. Full names are likely to be an issue; using middle name initials can solve it. However, administrators may implement a numbering system. For example: JSmith1, Jsmith2. Another naming system uses a dot-delimited scheme, such as John.W.Smith@cpandl.com. Regardless of the naming scheme you choose, the key is to be as consistent as possible and to allow for exceptions as needed. Keep in mind that although a user name can be 256 characters in length, a name of this length really isn't practical in most cases.

Configuring User Account Policies

Because domain controllers share the domain accounts database, user account policies must be consistent across all domain controllers. The way consistency is ensured is by having domain controllers obtain user account policies only from the domain container and only allowing one top-level account policy for domain accounts. The one top-level account policy allowed for domain accounts is determined by the highest precedence Group Policy object (GPO) linked to the domain container. This top-level account policy is then enforced by the domain controllers in the domain. Domain controllers always obtain the top-level account policy from the highest precedence GPO linked to the domain container. By default, this is the Default Domain Policy GPO.

When a domain is operating at the Windows Server 2008 functional level, two new object classes in the Active Directory schema allow you to fine-tune the way account policy is applied:

- Password Settings container
- Password Settings object

The default Password Settings container (PSC) is created under the System container in the domain, and it stores the Password Settings objects (PSOs) for the domain. Although you cannot rename, move, or delete the default PSC, you can add PSOs to this container that define the various sets of secondary account policy settings you want to use in your domain. You can then apply the desired secondary account policy settings to users, inetOrgPersons, and global security groups as discussed in "Creating Password Settings Objects and Applying Secondary Settings" on page 1173.

> ### Local Account Policy Is Used for Local Log On
>
> Local account policies can be different from the domain account policy, such as when you specifically define an account policy for local accounts in a computer's local GPO (LGPO). For example, if you configure an account policy for a computer's LGPO, when users log on to Active Directory they'll obtain their account policy from the Default Domain Policy instead of the LGPO. The only exception is when users log on locally to their machines instead of logging on to Active Directory; in that case any account policy applied to their machine's local GPO is applied and enforced.

As discussed in Chapter 36, "Managing Group Policy," account policies in a domain are configured through the policy editors accessible from the Group Policy Management Console (GPMC). When you are editing policy settings, you'll find account policies under Computer Configuration\Windows Settings\Security Settings\Account Policies. To change group policies, you must be a member of the Domain Admins group or Enterprise Admins group in Active Directory. Members of the Group Policy Creator Owners group can also modify group policy for the domain.

The account policies for a domain contain three subsets—Password Policy, Account Lockout Policy, and Kerberos Policy. Although secondary account policies include Password Policy and Account Lockout Policy, they do not include Kerberos Policy. Kerberos Policy can only be set at the domain level for the top-level account policy.

> ### Some Security Options Are Also Obtained from the Default Domain Policy GPO
>
> Two policies in Computer Configuration\Windows Settings\Security Settings\Local Policies\Security Options also behave like account policies. These policies are Network Access: Allow Anonymous SID/NAME Translation and Network Security: Force Logoff When Logon Hours Expire. For domain accounts, the settings for these policies are obtained only from the Default Domain Policy GPO. For local accounts, the settings for these policies can come from a local OU GPO if one is defined and applicable.

Enforcing Password Policy

Password policies for domain user accounts and local user accounts are very important in preventing unauthorized access. These settings should help enforce your organization's written computing policies. There are six settings for password policies that enable you to control how passwords are managed. When you are setting top-level account policy for the Default Domain Policy, these policies are located in Computer Configuration\Windows Settings\Security Settings\Account Policies\Password Policy (see Figure 35-1). When you are setting secondary account policy for a PSO, you configure these settings using similarly named object attributes.

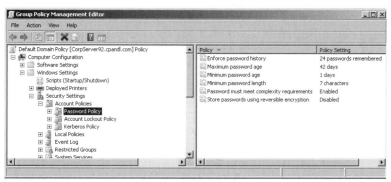

Figure 35-1 Managing Password Policy in the Default Domain Policy.

The settings are as follows:

- **Enforce Password History** When users change their passwords, this setting determines how many old passwords will be maintained and associated with each user. The maximum value is 24. If you enter zero (0), a password history is not kept. On a domain controller, the default is 24 passwords, on a stand-alone server, it is zero passwords.

- **Maximum Password Age** This determines when users are required to change their passwords. For example, if this is set to 90 days, on the 91st day the user will be required to change his or her password. The default on domain controllers is 42 days. The minimum number of days is 0, which effectively means that the password never changes. The maximum number of days is 999. In an environment where security is critical, you probably want to set the value low—in contrast, for environments where security is less stringent, you could set the password age high (rarely requiring users to change passwords).

- **Minimum Password Age** How long users must use passwords before they are allowed to change the password is determined by this setting. It must be more than zero days for the Enforce Password History Policy to be effective. In an environment where security is critical, you would probably set this to a shorter time, and to a longer time where security not as tight. This setting must be configured to be less than the Maximum Password Age policy. The maximum value is 998. If you enter zero (0), a password can be changed immediately. The default is 1 day on a domain controller and 0 days on stand-alone servers. This setting helps to deter password reuse by making a user keep a password for at least a certain amount of time

- **Minimum Password Length** This is the number of characters that sets the minimum requirement for the length of the password. Again, a more critically secure environment might require longer password lengths than one with reduced security requirements. The maximum value is 14. If you enter zero (0), a password is not required. As shown in Figure 35-2, the default length is seven characters on domain controllers. The default is zero characters on stand-alone servers.

- **Password Must Meet Complexity Requirements** Complexity requirements for passwords for the domain user accounts are set at a higher requirement than previously in Windows 2000. If this policy is defined, passwords can't contain the user account name, must contain at least six characters, and must consist of uppercase letters, lowercase letters, numerals, and special non-alphabetical characters, such as the percentage sign (%) and the asterisk (*). (Complexity requirements are enabled by default on domain controllers and disabled by default on stand-alone servers for Windows Server 2008.)

- **Store Passwords Using Reversible Encryption** This is basically an additional policy that allows for plain text encryption of passwords for applications that may need it. By default, it is disabled on Windows Server 2008. Enabling this policy is basically the same as storing passwords as plain text and is used when applications use protocols that need information about the user's password. Because this policy degrades the overall security of the domain, it should be used only when necessary.

Chapter 35

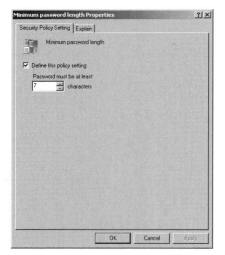

Figure 35-2 Configuring domain user Minimum Password Length in the Default Domain Policy.

Configuring Account Lockout Policy

The Account Lockout Policy is invoked after a local user or a domain user has been locked out of his or her account. These settings are designed to help protect user accounts from attacks that involve password guessing or other types of attacks where random passwords are repeatedly entered to try to gain access to an account. There are three settings for account lockout policies. They are the following:

- **Account Lockout Duration** If a user does become locked out, this setting determines how long the user will be locked out before the user account is unlocked. There is no default setting, because this setting is dependent on the Account Lockout Threshold setting. The range is from 0 through 99,999 minutes. The account will be locked out indefinitely when this is set to 0 and therefore will require an administrator to unlock it.

- **Account Lockout Threshold** This setting determines how many failed attempts at logon Windows Server 2008 permits before a user will be locked out of the account. The range is from 0 to 999. If this setting is 0, the account will never be locked out and the Account Lockout Duration security setting is disabled. The default setting is 0.

- **Reset Account Lockout Counter After** This setting is the number of minutes after a failure to log on before the logon counter is reset to zero. This must be less than or equal to the Account Lockout Duration setting if the Account Lockout Threshold policy is enabled. The valid range is from 1 to 99,999 minutes.

When you are setting top-level account policy for the Default Domain Policy, these policies are located in Computer Configuration\Windows Settings\Security Settings\ Account Policies\Account Lockout Policy. When you are setting secondary account policy for a PSO, you configure these settings using similarly named object attributes.

Setting Kerberos Policy

Kerberos is an authentication system designed for secure exchange of information as discussed in "NTLM and Kerberos Authentication" on page 1023. Windows Server 2008 has five settings for Kerberos Policy, which are applied only to domain user accounts. The policies can only be set for top-level account policy and are located in Computer Configuration\Windows Settings\Security Settings\Account Policies\Kerberos Policy. They are as follows:

- **Enforce User Logon Restrictions** If you want to validate every ticket session request against the user rights, keep the default setting enabled.

- **Maximum Lifetime For Service Ticket** The default is 600 minutes, but this setting must be greater than 10 minutes, and also must be less than or equal to what is configured for the Maximum Lifetime For User Ticket setting. The setting does not apply to sessions that have already been validated.

- **Maximum Lifetime For User Ticket** This is different from the Maximum Lifetime For Service Ticket setting. Maximum Lifetime For User Ticket sets the maximum amount of time that a ticket may be used before either a new one must be requested or the existing one is renewed, whereas the Maximum Lifetime For Service Ticket setting is used to access a particular service. The default is 10 hours.

- **Maximum Lifetime For User Ticket Renewal** This user account security policy object configures the maximum amount of time the ticket may be used. The default is seven days.

- **Maximum Tolerance For Computer Clock Synchronization** Sometimes workstations and servers have different local clock times. This setting allows you to configure a tolerance level (defaults to 5 minutes) for this possible difference so that Kerberos authentication does not fail.

> **Note**
>
> If you change the Minimum Password Length setting to less than seven characters (the default), you may not be able to create a new user or change a user's password. To work around this limitation, set the password length to seven or higher.

Creating Password Settings Objects and Applying Secondary Settings

When you want to fine-tune the way account policy is applied, you need to create a Password Settings group and add users, inetOrgPersons, and global security groups as members of the Password Settings group. A Password Settings group is simply a global security group that applies the desired secondary PSO rather than the default PSO.

Afterward, you have to create a Password Settings object with attributes that define the desired policy settings and then link this object to the Password Settings group.

Before you start, you should consider how you will organize your Password Settings groups. In most cases, you'll want to create Password Settings groups that closely resemble the OUs in your domain. To do this, you'll create Password Settings groups with the same names as your OUs and then add users, inetOrgPersons, and global security groups as members of these groups as appropriate to reflect the organizational structure of your OUs.

You can create the Password Settings group and define its members using Active Directory Users And Computers, as discussed in "Managing Groups" on page 1215. By default, only members of the Domain Admins and Schema Admins groups can create PSOs. You can create a PSO and set its attributes by completing these steps:

1. Start ADSI Edit by clicking Start, clicking Administrative Tools, and then clicking ADSI Edit.

2. Right-click the ADSI Edit node in the MMC and then select Connect To. This displays the Connection Settings dialog box as shown in the following screen:

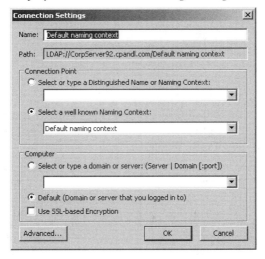

3. Choose Default Naming Context in the Select A Well Known Naming Context list and then click Advanced. This displays the Advanced dialog box.

4. Select the Specify Credentials check box. In the Credentials panel, type the user name and password of an account that is a member of Schema Admins.

5. Click OK to close both open dialog boxes.

6. In ADSI Edit, select and then expand the Default Naming Context node, and then select and expand the CN=System node.

7. In the left pane, select the CN=Password Settings Container entry. A list of any previously created Password Settings objects appears in the details pane.

8. Right-click the CN=Password Settings Container entry, point to New and then select Object. This starts the Create Object wizard as shown in the following screen:

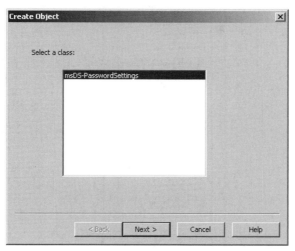

9. On the Select A Class page, choose msDS-PasswordSettings and then click Next. msDS-PasswordSettings is the internal directory name for PSOs.

10. In the Value text box, type the name of the Password Settings group and then click Next. If you are naming your Password Settings groups after your OUs, this should be the name of an OU in your domain.

11. In the Value text box, type the precedence order for the group and then click Next. When multiple Password Settings objects apply to a user, the precedence of the group determines which account policy settings are applied. A group with a precedence of 1 always has precedence over a group with a lower precedence.

12. Set the reversible encryption status for passwords as either false or true and then click Next. In most cases, you'll want to turn this feature off to ensure passwords are stored with strong encryption.

13. Set the password history length and then click Next. The maximum value is 24. If you enter zero (0), a password history is not kept.

14. Set the password complexity status for passwords as either false or true and then click Next. In most cases, you'll want to turn this feature on to ensure users enter complex passwords.

15. Set the minimum password length for user accounts and then click Next. The maximum value is 14. If you enter zero (0), a password is not required.

Chapter 35

16. Set the minimum password age and then click Next. The age must be set in duration format as DD:HH:MM:SS. The maximum value is 998:00:00:00 (998 days). If you enter zero (0), a password can be changed immediately.

17. Set the maximum password age and then click Next. The age must be set in duration format as DD:HH:MM:SS. The maximum value is 999:00:00:00 (999 days). If you enter zero (0), passwords never expire.

18. Specify how many failed attempts at logon before a user is locked out and then click Next. The maximum value is 999. If you enter zero (0), accounts will never be locked.

19. Specify the number of minutes after a logon failure before the logon counter is reset and then click Next. The counter time must be set in duration format as DD:HH:MM:SS. The maximum value is 69:10:39:00 (99,999 minutes). The valid range is from 1 to 99,999 minutes.

20. Specify how long a user will be locked out before the account is unlocked automatically and then click Next. The counter time must be set in duration format as DD:HH:MM:SS. The maximum value is 69:10:39:00 (99,999 minutes). The valid range is from 1 to 99,999 minutes.

21. Click Finish to create the object with the attributes you've defined. If you've made any mistakes in setting the attribute values, you'll see an error message regarding this and you can use the Back function to make changes to the previously specified values.

22. In ADSI Edit, right-click the PSO you just created and select Properties. In the Properties dialog box, scroll through the list of attributes until you see msDS-PSOAppliesTo. Select this attribute and then click Edit. This opens the Multi-Valued Distinguished Name With Security Principal Editor dialog box.

23. Click Add Windows Account. This displays the Select Users, Computers, Or Groups dialog box. Type the name of the Password Settings group you previously created using Active Directory Users And Computers and then click Check Names.

24. Click OK three times to close all open dialog boxes.

> **Note**
> You can link a PSO to other types of groups in addition to global security groups. However, when the resultant set of policy is determined for a user or group, only PSOs that are linked to global security groups, user objects, and inetOrgPerson objects are considered. PSOs that are linked to distribution groups or other types of security groups are ignored.

INSIDE OUT
Understanding PSO precedence

A user, inetOrgPerson, or global security group can have multiple PSOs linked to it. This can occur either because of membership in multiple groups that each have different PSOs applied to them or because multiple PSOs are applied directly to the object. However, only one PSO is applied as the effective policy and only the settings from that PSO affect the user, inetOrgPerson, or group. The settings from other PSOs do not apply and cannot be merged in any way.

Active Directory determines the applicable PSO according to the precedence value assigned to its msDS-PasswordSettingsPrecedence attribute. This attribute has an integer value of 1 or greater. A lower value for the precedence attribute indicates that the PSO has a higher priority than other PSOs. For example, suppose an object has three PSOs linked to it. One PSO has a precedence value of 5, one has a precedence of 8, and the other PSO has a precedence value of 12. In this case, the PSO that has the precedence value of 5 has the highest priority and is the one applied to the object.

If multiple PSOs are linked to a user or group, the PSO that is applied is determined as follows:

1. A PSO that is linked directly to the user object is applied. If more than one PSO is linked directly to the user object, the PSO with the lowest precedence value is applied.

2. If no PSO is linked directly to the user object, all PSOs that are applicable to the user based on the user's global group memberships are compared and the PSO with the lowest precedence value is applied.

3. If no PSO is linked directly or indirectly to the user object, the Default Domain Policy is applied.

Microsoft recommends that you assign each PSO in the domain a unique precedence value. However, you can create multiple PSOs with the precedence value. If multiple PSOs have the same precedence value, the PSO with the lowest GUID is applied. Typically, this means Active Directory will apply the PSO with the earliest creation date.

The user object has three attributes that override the settings that are present in the applicable PSO: Reversible Password Encryption Required, Password Not Required, and Password Does Not Expire. You can set these attributes in the userAccountControl attribute of the user object in Active Directory Users And Computers.

Understanding User Account Capabilities, Privileges, and Rights

All user accounts have specific capabilities, privileges, and rights. When you create a user account, you can grant the user specific capabilities by making the user a member of one or more groups. This gives the user the capabilities of these groups. You then assign additional capabilities by making a user a member of the appropriate groups or withdraw capabilities by removing a user from a group.

In Windows Server 2008, some capabilities of accounts are built in. The built-in capabilities of accounts are assigned to groups and include the group's automatic capabilities. Although built-in capabilities are predefined and unchangeable, they can be granted to users by making them members of the appropriate group or delegated by granting the capability specifically, for example, the ability to create, delete, and manage user accounts. This capability is assigned to administrators and account operators. Thus, if a user is a member of the Administrators group, the user can create, delete, and manage user accounts.

Other capabilities of accounts, such as permissions, privileges, and logon rights, can be assigned. The access permissions for accounts define the operations that can be performed on network resources. For example, permissions control whether a user can access a particular shared folder. You can assign access permissions to users, computers, and groups as discussed in Chapter 17, "File Sharing and Security." The privileges of an account grant permissions to perform specific tasks, such as the ability to change the system time. The logon rights of an account grant logon permissions, such as the ability to log on locally to a server.

An important part of an administrator's job is being able to determine and set permissions, privileges, and logon rights as necessary. Although you can't change a group's built-in capabilities, you can change a group's default privileges and logon rights. For example, you could revoke network access to a computer by removing a group's right to access the computer from the network. Table 35-1 provides an overview of the default privileges assigned to groups. Table 35-2 provides an overview of the default logon rights assigned to groups.

Table 35-1 Default Privileges Assigned to Groups

Privilege	Description	Groups Assigned by Default in Domains
Act As Part Of The Operating System	Allows a process to authenticate as any user. Processes that require this privilege must use the LocalSystem account, which already has this privilege.	None
Add Workstations To Domain	Allows users to add new computers to an existing domain.	Authenticated Users
Adjust Memory Quotas For A Process	Allows users to set the maximum amount of memory a process can use.	Administrators, Local Service, and Network Service
Back Up Files And Directories	Allows users to back up the system regardless of the permissions set on files and directories.	Administrators, Backup Operators, and Server Operators
Bypass Traverse Checking	Allows users to go through directory trees even if a user doesn't have permissions to access the directories being passed through. The privilege doesn't allow the user to list directory contents.	Administrators, Authenticated Users, Everyone, Local Service, and Network Service

Privilege	Description	Groups Assigned by Default in Domains
Change The System Time	Allows users to set the time for the computer's clock.	Administrators, Server Operators, and Local Service
Change The Time Zone	Allows users to set the time zone for the system clock.	Administrators, Server Operators, and Local Service
Create A Pagefile	Allows users to create and modify the paging file size for virtual memory.	Administrators
Create A Token Object	Allows processes to create token objects that can be used to gain access to local resources. Processes that require this privilege must use the LocalSystem account, which already has this privilege.	None
Create Global Objects	Allows a process to create global directory objects. Most components already have this privilege and it's not necessary to specifically assign it.	Administrators, Service, Local Service, and Network Service
Create Permanent Shared Objects	Allows processes to create directory objects in the Windows object manager. Most components already have this privilege and it's not necessary to specifically assign it.	None
Create Symbolic Link	Allows an application that a user is running to create symbolic links. Symbolic links make it appear as if a document or folder is in a specific location when it actually resides in another location. Use of symbolic links is restricted by default to enhance security.	Administrators
Debug Programs	Allows users to perform debugging.	Administrators
Enable User And Computer Accounts To Be Trusted For Delegation	Permits users and computers to change or apply the trusted account for delegation setting, provided they have write access to the object.	Administrators
Force Shutdown Of A Remote System	Allows users to shut down a computer from a remote location on the network.	Administrators and Server Operators
Generate Security Audits	Allows processes to make security log entries for auditing object access.	Local Service and Network Service
Increase A Process Working Set	Allows an application that a user is running to increase the memory that the related process working set uses. A process working set is the set of memory pages currently visible to a process in physical memory. Allowing for increases in memory pages reduces page faults and enhances performance.	Users

Privilege	Description	Groups Assigned by Default in Domains
Increase Scheduling Priority	Allows processes with write access to a process to increase the scheduling priority assigned to those processes.	Administrators
Load And Unload Device Drivers	Allows users to install and uninstall Plug and Play device drivers. This doesn't affect device drivers that aren't Plug and Play, which can only be installed by administrators.	Administrators and Printer Operators
Lock Pages In Memory	In Windows NT, allowed processes to keep data in physical memory, preventing the system from paging data to virtual memory on disk.	Not used in Windows 2000 or later
Manage Auditing And Security Log	Allows users to specify auditing options and access the security log. You must turn on auditing in the group policy first.	Administrators
Modify An Object Label	Allows a user process to modify the integrity label of objects, such as files, Registry keys, or processes owned by other users. This privilege can be used to lower the priority of other processes. Processes running under a user account can modify the label of any object the user owns without requiring this privilege.	None
Modify Firmware Environment Values	Allows users and processes to modify system environment variables (not user environment variables).	Administrators
Perform Volume Maintenance Tasks	Allows administration of removable storage, disk defragmenter, and disk management.	Administrators
Profile A Single Process	Allows users to monitor the performance of non-system processes.	Administrators on domain controllers; on member servers and workstations, Administrators and Users
Profile System Performance	Allows users to monitor the performance of system processes.	Administrators
Remove Computer From Docking Station	Allows undocking a laptop and removing from network.	Administrators and Users
Replace A Process Level Token	Allows processes to modify the default token for subprocesses.	Local Service and Network Service

Privilege	Description	Groups Assigned by Default in Domains
Restore Files And Directories	Allows restoring backed-up files and directories, regardless of the permissions set on files and directories.	Administrators, Backup Operators, and Server Operators
Shut Down The System	Allows shutting down the local computer.	Administrators, Backup Operators, Print Operators, and Server Operators
Synchronize Directory Service Data	Allows users to synchronize directory service data on domain controllers.	None
Take Ownership Of Files Or Other Objects	Allows users to take ownership of any Active Directory objects.	Administrators

Table 35-2 Default Logon Rights Assigned to Groups

Logon Right	Description	Groups Assigned by Default in Domains
Access Credential Manager As A Trusted Caller	Grants permission to establish a trusted connection to Credential Manager. Credentials, such as a user name and password or smart card, provide identification and proof of identification.	None
Access This Computer From The Network	Permits remote access to the computer.	Administrators, Authenticated Users, and Everyone
Allow Logon Locally	Grants permission to log on to the computer interactively at the console.	Administrators, Account Operators, Backup Operators, Print Operators, and Server Operators
Allow Logon Through Terminal Services	Allows access through Terminal Services; necessary for remote assistance and remote desktop.	None
Deny Access To This Computer From The Network	Denies remote access to the computer through network services.	None
Deny Logon As Batch Job	Denies the right to log on through a batch job or script.	None
Deny Logon As Service	Denies the right to log on as a service.	None

Chapter 35

Logon Right	Description	Groups Assigned by Default in Domains
Deny Logon Locally	Denies the right to log on to the computer's keyboard.	None
Deny Logon Through Terminal Services	Denies right to log on through Terminal Services.	None
Log On As A Batch Job	Grants permission to log on as a batch job or script.	Administrators, Backup Operators, and Performance Log Users
Log On As A Service	Grants permission to log on as a server. LocalSystem account has this right. Services that run under separate accounts should be assigned this right.	None

Assigning User Rights

The most efficient way to assign user rights is to make the user a member of a group that already has the right. In some cases, however, you might want a user to have a particular right but not have all the other rights of the group. One way to resolve this problem is to give the user the rights directly. Another way to resolve this is to create a special group for users that need the right. This is the approach used with the Remote Desktop Users group, which was created by Microsoft to grant Allow Logon Through Terminal Services to groups of users.

You assign user rights through the Local Policies node of Group Policy. Local policies can be set on a per-computer basis using a computer's local security policy or on a domain or OU basis through an existing group policy for the related domain or OU. When you do this, the local policies apply to all accounts in the domain or OU.

Assigning User Rights for a Domain or OU

You can assign user rights for a domain or OU by completing the following steps:

1. In the Group Policy Management Console, select the policy you want to work with, and then click Edit. Access the User Rights Assignment node by working your way down the console tree. Expand Computer Configuration, Windows Settings, Security Settings, Local Policies, and User Rights Assignment, as shown in Figure 35-3.

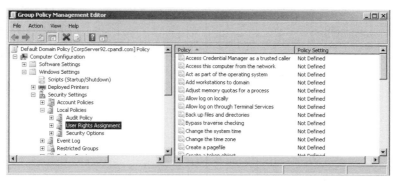

Figure 35-3 Configuring user rights in Group Policy.

2. To configure a user right, double-click a user right or right-click it and select Properties. This opens a Properties dialog box, as shown in Figure 35-4. If the policy isn't defined, select Define These Policy Settings. To apply the right to a user or group, click Add User Or Group. Then, in the Add User Or Group dialog box, click Browse. This opens the Select Users, Computers, Or Groups dialog box.

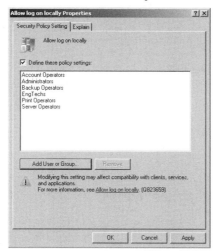

Figure 35-4 Define the user right, and then assign the right to users and groups.

3. Type the name of the user or group you want to use in the field provided, and then click Check Names. By default, the search is configured to find built-in security principals, groups, and user accounts. After you select the account names or groups to add, click OK. The Add User Or Group dialog box should now show the selected accounts. Click OK again.

4. The Properties dialog box is updated to reflect your selections. If you made a mistake, select a name and remove it by clicking Remove. When you're finished granting the right to users and groups, click OK.

Assigning User Rights on a Specific Computer

User rights can also be applied to a specific computer. However, remember that domain and OU policy take precedence over local policy. This means that any settings in these policies will override settings you make on a local computer.

You can apply user rights locally by completing the following steps:

1. Start Local Security Policy by clicking Start, Programs or All Programs, Administrative Tools, Local Security Policy. All computers, even domain controllers, have Local Security Policy. Settings available in the Local Security Policy console are a subset of the computer's local policy.

2. Under Security Settings, expand Local Policies and then select User Rights Assignment.

3. Double-click the user right you want to modify. The Properties dialog box shows current users and groups that have been given the user right.

4. You can apply the user right to additional users and groups by clicking Add User Or Group. This opens the Select Users, Computers, Or Groups dialog box, which you can use to add users and groups.

5. Click OK twice to close the open dialog boxes.

> **Note**
> If the options in the Properties dialog box are dimmed, it means the policy has been set at a higher level and can't be overridden locally.

Creating and Configuring Domain User Accounts

As a member of the Account Operators, Enterprise Admins, or Domain Admins group, you can use Active Directory Users And Computers to create user accounts. Follow these steps:

1. Click Start, Administrative Tools, and Active Directory Users And Computers. This starts Active Directory Users And Computers.

2. By default, you are connected to your logon domain. If you want to create OUs in a different domain, right-click the Active Directory Users And Computers node in the console tree, and then select Change Domain. In the Change Domain dialog box, type the name of the domain to which you want to connect, and then click OK. Alternatively, you can click Browse to find the domain to which you want to connect in the Browse For Domain dialog box.

3. You can now create the user account. Right-click the container in which you want to create the user, point to New, and then select User. This will start the New Object–User Wizard.

When you create a new user, you're prompted for the first name, initials, last name, full name, and logon name, as shown in Figure 35-5. The pre–Windows 2000 logon name then appears automatically. This logon name is used when a user logs on to Windows NT, Microsoft Windows 95, or Microsoft Windows 98.

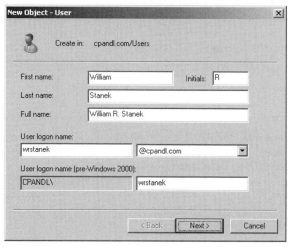

Figure 35-5 Creating a user account.

4. When you click Next, you can set the user's password and account options. The password must meet the complexity requirements set in the group policy. As shown in Figure 35-6, these options are as follows:

    ○ User Must Change Password At Next Logon

    ○ User Cannot Change Password

    ○ Password Never Expires

    ○ Account Is Disabled

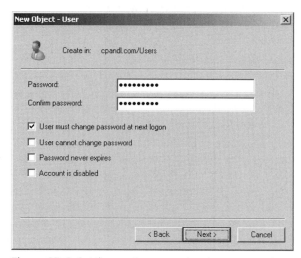

Figure 35-6 Set the user's password and account options.

INSIDE OUT Creating group accounts at the command line

At the command line, you can create a user account using DSADD USER. For users, the distinguished name (DN) for the account is used to set the account's full name. For example, you want to create a user account with the display name William Stanek in the Technology OU for the cpandl.com domain. When creating the user object using DSADD, you must specify the path as follows:

```
dsadd user "CN=William Stanek,OU=Technology,DC=cpandl,DC=com"
```

When you create an account in this way, the other properties of the account are set automatically and the account is disabled by default. To resolve this, you would need to create a password for the account and then enable the account.

Often, rather than have some properties set automatically, you'll want to define them with specific values. This gives you more control and allows you to create the account so that it is enabled for use. Use the following parameters:

```
-FN        to set the first name
-MI        to set the middle initials
-LN        to set the last name
-Display   to set the display name
-samid     to set the logon name
-pwd       to set the password
```

To see how these parameters are used, consider the following example:

```
dsadd user "CN=William Stanek,OU=Technology,DC=cpandl,DC=com" -fn
    William -mi R -ln stanek -Display "William Stanek" -samid williamstanek
    -pwd TradeWinds45!
```

For the full syntax and usage, type **dsadd user /?** at a command prompt. The directory services commands can also be used to manage user accounts. Use DSMOD USER to set properties, including passwords and group membership. Use DSMOVE USER to move users to a new container or OU. Use DSRM USER to remove user accounts. Tasks that you might want to perform from the command line include:

- Searching the entire domain for users with disabled accounts by typing **dsquery user -disabled**.

- Using **dsmod user UserDN** to set account flags -mustchpwd (yes | no), -canchpwd (yes | no), -pwdneverexpires (yes | no), -disabled (yes | no).

- Determining all users who have not changed their passwords in a specified number of days by typing **dsquery user -stalepwd NumDays** where NumDays is the number of days.

- Determining all users who have not logged on in a specified number of weeks by typing **dsquery user -inactive NumWeeks** where NumWeeks is the number of weeks.

- Determining all the groups of which a user is a member by typing **dsget user UserDN -memberof** and using the optional -expand parameter to determine all the inferred group memberships based on the group of which other groups are members.

5. Click Next, and then click Finish. If you use a password that doesn't meet the complexity requirements of group policy, you'll see an error and you'll have to click Back to change the user's password before you can continue.

Viewing and Setting User Account Properties

If you double-click a user account in Active Directory Users And Computers, a Properties dialog box appears, with tabs allowing you to configure the user's settings. Table 35-3 lists the tabs you see in the Properties dialog box.

Table 35-3 User Account Properties

Account Tab	Description
Account	Used to manage logon name, account options, logon times, and account lockout
Address	Used to manage geographical address information
Attribute Editor	Used to edit the attributes of the related user object
COM+	Used to select the user's COM+ partition set
Dial-In	Used to set the user's dial-in or virtual private network (VPN) access controls as well as callback, IP address, and routing options for dial-in or VPN
Environment	Used to manage the Terminal Services startup environment
General	Used to manage the account name, display name, e-mail address, telephone number, and Web page
Member Of	Used to add the user to or remove the user from selected groups
Object	Displays the canonical name of the user object with dates and Update Sequence Numbers
Organization	Used to manage the user's title and corporate information (department, manager, direct reports)
Profile	Used to manage the user profile configuration (profile path, logon script) and home folder
Published Certificates	Used to install or remove user's X.509 certificates
Remote Control	Used to manage remote control settings for Terminal Services
Security	Used to configure advanced permissions for users and groups that can access this user object in Active Directory
Sessions	Used to manage Terminal Services timeout and reconnection settings
Telephones	Used to manage home phone, pager, fax, IP phone, and cell phone numbers
Terminal Services Profile	Used to manage the user profile for Terminal Services

Chapter 35

> **Note**
>
> The number of tabs in a user's Properties dialog box will vary depending upon the software installed. For example, adding Exchange mail services will add multiple property sheets (tabs) to each user's Active Directory account. Also, to view the Published Certificates, Objects, or Security property sheets, you must be in Advanced view. To access Advanced view, select Advanced Features from the View menu in Active Directory Users And Computers.

Most of the time, as the administrator, you will use a number of the account settings regularly. The General tab has the name and e-mail for the user. The Account tab has the user name and lets you configure logon hours or logon settings. There is also an area on the Account tab that allows the account to be unlocked. This latter setting is a quick way to unlock an account when a user has forgotten a password or is locked out of the account for some other reason. The Profile tab lets you set a user profile, logon script, and home folder. The Member Of tab lets you add the user to various groups. The Security tab lets you set the way permissions for groups or users are configured and provides access to the Effective Permissions tool via the Advanced button.

Obtaining Effective Permissions

In Active Directory, user accounts are defined as objects—as are group and computer accounts. This means that user accounts have security descriptors that list the users and groups that are granted access. Security descriptors also define ownership of the object and specify the permissions that those users and groups have been assigned with respect to the object.

Individual entries in the security descriptor are referred to as access control entries (ACEs). Active Directory objects can inherit ACEs from their parent objects. This means that permissions for a parent object can be applied to a child object. For example, all members of the Account Operators group inherit permissions granted to this group.

Because of inheritance, sometimes it isn't clear whether a particular user, group, or computer has permission to work with another object in Active Directory. This is where the Effective Permissions tool comes in handy. The Effective Permissions tool allows you to examine the permissions that a user, group, or computer has with respect to another object. For example, if you wanted to determine what permissions, if any, a user who has received delegated control has over another user or group, you could use Effective Permissions to do this.

The Effective Permissions tool is available in Active Directory Users And Computers—but only if you are in the Advanced Features view. Select Advanced Features from the View menu if necessary, and then double-click the user, group, or computer for which you are trying to determine the effective permissions of another user or group. In the Properties dialog box, click the Advanced button on the Security tab to open the Advanced Security Settings dialog box, and then click the Effective Permissions tab. Next, click Select, type the name of the user or group for which you want to see the effective permissions with regard to the previously selected object, and then click OK.

The effective permissions for the selected user or group in relation to the previously selected object appear, as shown in Figure 35-7. The Effective Permissions box will have check marks showing which permissions are in effect. If there are no effective permissions, none of the permissions' check boxes will be selected.

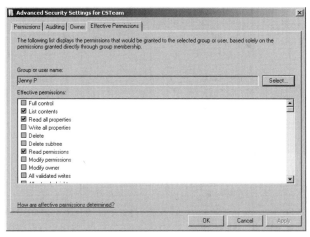

Figure 35-7 Obtaining effective permissions for a user, group, or computer.

Configuring Account Options

Every user account created in Active Directory has account options that control logon hours, the computers to which a user can log on, account expiration, and so on. To manage these settings for a user, double-click the user account in Active Directory Users And Computers, and then select the Account tab, as shown in Figure 35-8.

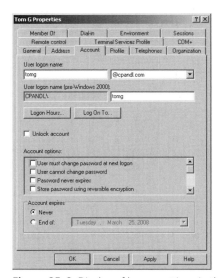

Figure 35-8 Display of logon settings in the user account Properties dialog box.

Chapter 35

Below the general account name fields, the available options are divided into three main areas. The first area that you can configure controls the Logon Hours and Log On To options.

- **Setting logon hours** Click Logon Hours to configure when a user can log on to the domain. By default, users can log on 24 hours a day, seven days a week. To deny a user a specific day or time, select the area that you want to restrict them from logging on, and then select the Logon Denied option, as shown in the following screen. For example, this option can be used to restrict shift workers to certain hours or to restrict working days to weekdays.

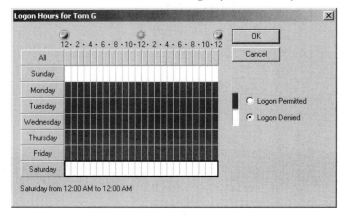

- **Configuring logon computer** When you click Log On To, you can restrict which computers a user can log on from. The default setting allows users to log on from all computers. To restrict which computers a user can log on from, click The Following Computers, as shown in the following screen. Type a host name or a fully qualified domain name in the Computer Name field, such as Workstation18 or Workstation.cpandl.com. Click Add. Repeat this procedure to set other logon computers.

> **Note**
>
> Earlier releases of Windows required the NetBIOS protocol to restrict which computers a user can log on from. In Windows Server 2008, this requirement has been phased out.

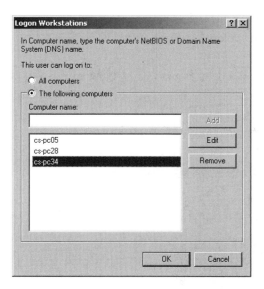

Below the Logon Hours and Log On To buttons is a check box called Unlock Account. If the user has locked herself or himself out by trying to log on with the wrong password too many times, you can unlock the account by clearing this check box. Next is the Account Options list, which includes a number of account options you can configure. These options include the following:

- **User Must Change Password At Next Logon** This is the default setting when a user is created. It requires the user to change the password the first time he or she logs on. This allows the user to be the only person with the knowledge of the password, though you as the administrator can change it.

- **User Cannot Change Password** This setting prevents the user from changing the password and gives the administrator more control over accounts like the Guest account. This is a good setting for service and application accounts.

- **Password Never Expires** This prevents passwords from ever expiring. It is a good idea to use this on service accounts. This is another good setting for an application or service account where a password is hard-coded into an application or service.

- **Store Password Using Reversible Encryption** Saves the user password as encrypted clear text. Select this check box if you have computers from Apple Computer, Inc., in your domain, because they store passwords as plain text.

- **Account Is Disabled** This prevents a user from logging on to his or her account. It enables network administrators to immediately disable an account for security reasons.

Chapter 35

- **Smart Card Is Required For Interactive Logon** To ensure higher security on a network, smart card technology can be implemented. Enabling the setting requires all users to use a smart card and reader to log on and to be authenticated. This domain setting also requires a personal identification number (PIN) configured on the smart card. This option also sets the Password Never Expires option to be enabled.

- **Account Is Trusted For Delegation** If a service is running under a user account rather than as a local system, you can set a user account to execute procedures on behalf of a different account on the network. By enabling this option, you can mimic a client to gain access to network resources on the local computer.

- **Account Is Sensitive And Cannot Be Delegated** Select this option if this account cannot be assigned for delegation by another account. This is the opposite of the preceding setting, and could be used in a high-security network environment.

- **Use Kerberos DES Encryption Types For This Account** Data Encryption Standard (DES) is used for many encryption protocols, including Microsoft Point-to-Point Encryption (MPPE) and Internet Protocol Security (IPSec) and supports up to 128-bit strong encryption. Enable this option if you want to use DES encryption.

- **This Account Supports Kerberos AES 128 Bit Encryption** Advanced Encryption Standard (AES) is more secure than DES and increasingly preferred over DES. Enable this option if you want to use AES 128-bit encryption with this account when applicable and available. Before selecting this option ensure the user will only log on to computers running Windows Vista or later or other computers that support AES 128-bit encryption.

- **This Account Supports Kerberos AES 256 Bit Encryption** Advanced Encryption Standard (AES) is more secure than DES and increasingly preferred over DES. Enable this option if you want to use AES 256-bit encryption with this account when applicable and available. Before selecting this option ensure the user will only log on to computers running U.S. domestic releases of Windows Vista or later or other computers that support AES 256-bit encryption.

- **Do Not Require Kerberos Preauthentication** You should enable this if the account uses a different implementation of the Kerberos protocol.

Finally, the Account Expires panel lets you set expiration options for the account. The default is Never, but you might need to configure this setting for some users. For example, temporary or contract users, summer help, or consultants may be working on your network for only a specified amount of time. If you know how long they need access to resources in your domain, you can use the Account Expires settings to automate the disabling of their account.

> **Disabling Accounts**
>
> In most network environments, administrators to whom managing users has been delegated will not be able to remove users immediately upon their leaving the company, creating a window of vulnerability. Yet, when accounts have scheduled end points, you can schedule them to be disabled on a specific date. So, it is a good idea to schedule accounts to be disabled if you are sure that the user will no longer be working. If the account is automatically disabled, but the user needs access, he or she will let you know. But, if the account is not disabled automatically, it can represent a big security problem. To handle this on an enterprise level, many businesses are reviewing (or implementing) provisioning applications to automate the process of taking away access to company resources when employees leave the company.

Configuring Profile Options

User accounts can also have profiles, logon scripts, and home directories associated with them. To configure these options, double-click a user account in Active Directory Users And Computers, and then click the Profile tab, as shown in the following screen:

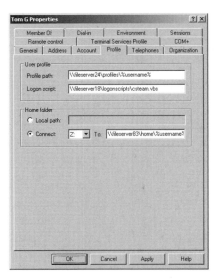

As the screen shows, you can set the following options on the Profile tab:

- **Profile Path** Profiles provide the environment settings for users. Each time a user logs on to a computer, that user's profile is used to determine desktop and Control Panel settings, the availability of menu options and applications, and so on. Setting the profile path and working with profiles is covered in "Managing User Profiles" on page 1195.

- **Logon Script** As the name implies, logon scripts are accessed when users log on to their accounts. Logon scripts set commands that should be executed each time a user logs on. One user or many users can use a single logon script, and, as the administrator, you control which users run which scripts. You can specify a logon script to use by typing the path to the logon script in the Logon Script field. Be sure to set the full path to the logon script, such as \\Corpdc05\LogonScripts\ eng.vbs.

> **Note**
>
> You shouldn't use scripts to set environment variables. Environment settings used by scripts aren't maintained for subsequent user processes. Also, you shouldn't use logon scripts to specify applications that should run at startup. You should set startup applications by placing the appropriate shortcuts in the user's Startup folder.

- **Home Folder** A home folder can be assigned to each user account. Users can store and retrieve their personal files in this directory. Many applications use the home folder as the default for File Open and Save As operations, helping users find their resources easily. Home directories can be located on a user's local hard drive or on a shared network drive. If you don't assign a home folder, Windows Server 2008 uses a default local home folder.

  To specify a home folder, do either of the following:

  - You specify a local home folder by clicking the Local Path option, and then typing the path to the home folder on the user's computer. Here's an example: C:\Home\%UserName%.

  - You specify a network home folder by selecting the Connect option in the Home Folder section, and then selecting a drive letter for the home folder. For consistency, you should use the same drive letter for all users. Also, be sure to select a drive letter that won't conflict with any currently configured physical or mapped drives. To avoid problems, you might want to use Z as the drive letter. After you select the drive letter, type the complete path to the home folder, using the Universal Naming Convention (UNC) notation, such as: \\Corpdc09\Home\%UserName%.

> **Note**
>
> %UserName% refers to the UserName environment variable. The Windows operating system has many environment variables, which are used to refer to user-specific and system-specific values. In this case, %UserName% is used to dynamically assign the user name as appropriate for the applicable user account.

Troubleshooting User Accounts

When a user logs on to the network using their domain user account, the account credentials are validated by a domain controller. By default, users can log on using their domain user accounts even if the network connection is down or there is no domain controller available to authenticate the user's logon. However, the user must have previously logged on to the computer and have valid, cached credentials. If the user has no cached credentials on the computer and the network connection is down or there is no domain controller available, the user will not be able to log on to the domain.

Each member computer in a domain can cache up to 10 credentials by default. Authentication can also fail if the system time on the member computer deviates from the logon domain controller's system time more than is allowed in the Kerberos Policy: Maximum Tolerance For Computer Clock Synchronization. The default tolerance is 5 minutes for member computers.

Users' accounts can be disabled by administrators or locked out due to Account Lockout Policy. When a user tries to log on using an account that is disabled or locked out, he sees a prompt that notifies him he cannot log on due to his account being disabled or locked out. The prompt also tells him to contact an administrator.

Active Directory Users And Computers shows disabled accounts with a red warning icon next to the account name. To enable a disabled account, right-click the account in Active Directory Users And Computers and then select Enable Account. You can search the entire domain for users with disabled accounts by typing **dsquery user -disabled** at a command prompt. To enable a disabled account from the command line, type **dsmod user UserDN -disabled no**.

When a user account has been locked out by the Account Lockout Policy, the account cannot be used for logging on until the lockout duration has elapsed or the account is reset by an administrator. If the account lockout duration is indefinite, the only way to unlock the account is to have an administrator reset it. In Active Directory Users And Computers, you can unlock an account by right-clicking the locked account and then selecting Properties. On the Account tab of the Properties dialog box, clear the Unlock Account check box.

Additionally, when account logon failure auditing is enabled, logon failure is recorded in the security log on the logon domain controller. Auditing policies for a site, domain, or OU GPO are stored under Computer Configuration\Windows Settings\Security Settings\Local Policies\Audit Policy.

Managing User Profiles

User profiles contain global user settings and configuration information and are stored for each user account created on a server or in a domain. A user profile allows a user to maintain his or her desktop environment so it is the same whenever they log on. The profile is created the first time a user logs on. Different profiles are created for local user accounts and domain user accounts.

Profile Essentials

The following three types of user profiles can be used:

- **Local** Local user profiles are the means for saving user settings and restoring them when the user logs on to the local machine.

- **Roaming** Roaming profiles allow user settings to move with a user from computer to computer by storing the information on domain controllers and then downloading it when the user logs on to the domain. For an administrator, roaming profiles allow you to roam from server to server and not have to reconfigure the desktop each time you log on. For instance, in your roaming profile, Windows Explorer can be configured through the Default Domain Policy to show file details regardless of where you log on or whether it was the first time you logged on to a particular computer.

- **Mandatory** Mandatory profiles are roaming profiles, originated by you and kept on a server, that are applied to users or groups, and that can be changed only by system administrators. For instance, a company may want all its sales clerks to have the same desktop settings at every workstation. This requires the creation of a preconfigured profile.

When a user has a local profile, all the user data is stored locally on that user's machine. When a user has a roaming profile, all the user data is stored in the profile itself and can be located on a network share. You can examine the contents of the profile folders using Windows Explorer. However, many of the folders are hidden from view by default. To configure Windows Explorer so that you can view the additional folders, choose Folder Options from the Tools menu, and then click the View tab. Under Advanced Settings, select Show Hidden Files And Folders and then click OK.

On Windows XP and Windows Server 2003, local user profiles are stored by default in the %SystemDrive%\Documents and Settings folder. On Windows Vista and Windows Server 2008, local user profiles are stored by default in the %SystemDrive%\Users\ %UserName% folder. Like Windows Server 2003, Windows Server 2008 saves roaming profiles to a server when a user logs off, even if an application has the Registry open. When a user logs on to a domain or that user's profile is in use on the network, the Delete and Copy To buttons on the Advanced tab of the System Properties dialog box are not available.

> **Note**
> You might need to delete a user profile that is in use. To delete a user profile while someone is using it, take ownership of it using Windows Explorer. Right-click the profile file (ntuser.dat), and then select Properties. Click the Advanced button on the Security tab. Then click the Owner tab in the Advanced Security dialog box to set ownership to your account. You can then delete the profile in Windows Explorer.

Policies for user profiles have their own node in Group Policy. They are located in Computer Configuration\Administrative Templates\System\User Profiles. These policies affect many aspects of how profiles are used. When working with the related policies, keep the following in mind:

- To add roaming user profiles to the Administrators security group, use the Add The Administrator Security Group To Roaming User Profiles policy. This allows an administrator full control over the folder containing the user's profile. Only computers running Microsoft Windows XP Professional or later are affected by this policy.

- To deny access to a user's roaming profile on a per-computer basis, use the Only Allow Local Users Profiles policy. This prevents a user from getting his or her roaming profile on a particular computer or in the domain. Only computers running Windows XP Professional or later are affected by this policy.

- You can prevent changes to a user's roaming profile on a local machine from being sent back to the server when the user logs off. To do this, enable the Prevent Roaming Profile Changes From Propagating To The Server policy. Users will receive their roaming profile when they log on, but if they change anything on their desktop, those changes will not be retained when they log off. Only computers running Windows XP Professional or later are affected by this policy.

- You can ensure profiles that haven't been used for a specified number of days are deleted automatically to free up disk space. To do this, enable the Delete User Profiles Older Than... policy and then specify how long a profile should go unused before it is deleted, such as 60 days. When a profile hasn't been used for the specified number of days, it is automatically deleted the next time you restart the computer.

- You can set the roaming profile to the same folder path for all users logging on to a computer. To do this, enable the Set Roaming Profile Path... policy and then specify the desired profile path. Be sure to use the %UserName% variable as part of the path; this will ensure each user has a unique profile path.

> **Note**
>
> The Group Policy Management Editor has an Extended tab in the details pane. By selecting any of the user group policies and clicking the Extended tab in the details pane (if necessary), the description explains what the policy will do in each configuration and indicates which operating system supports the policy.

Chapter 35

Implementing and Creating Preconfigured Profiles

Preconfigured user profiles are used to define default user configuration and environment settings. They make it easier for new users to get started in a new environment and can be used for local, roaming, or mandatory profiles. For instance, you could have one preconfigured user profile for each department in the organization. Any of these preconfigured profiles could be saved and then used as a local, roaming, or mandatory profile for new users.

Before creating a preconfigured user profile, you should be aware of these guidelines:

- Use NTFS file system volumes for user profiles that are on shares. This allows you to configure profiles with different file and share permissions. By doing this you can have multiple roaming user profiles for users or groups. It also allows for higher security than a file allocation table (FAT) or FAT32 volume does.

- Do not use Encrypted File System for shared profiles. Encryption is configured on a per-user basis and the user logging on won't have access to the profile.

- It is a good idea to use a test computer that has video and hardware components similar to the production computers.

For mandatory user profiles, the shares where the mandatory user profiles are stored should have permissions set to read-only. A mandatory profile must also be created before a user logs on to a computer for the first time and copied to the user's profile location.

To create a preconfigured user profile, follow these steps:

1. Log on to the test computer. (If you are creating multiple profiles, it is a good idea to create a separate account for each preconfigured profile to ensure that the configurations are correct.)

2. Install or configure all programs that meet the requirements of the department or group of users for which you are creating the profile. Arrange the desktop and the Start menu as desired. Configuring the applications and the user desktop will create a model desktop profile template.

3. Log off, and then log on again as a member of the Administrators group.

4. Click System And Maintenance\System in Control Panel. Under Tasks, click Advanced System Settings. This displays the System Properties dialog box with the Advanced tab selected. On the Advanced Tab, under User Profiles, click Settings. The User Profiles dialog box appears, as shown in Figure 35-9.

5. Select the user profile you just created, and then click Copy To. In the Copy To dialog box, type the path where you want to save a copy of the selected profile. Save a local profile to the %SystemDrive%\Documents and Settings\Default User folder. If you want a default profile for the domain, copy the preconfigured profile to a location on a network share. Then, when you set up a user's account, you can copy the saved profile to the path for the user's profile. For example, if the path

for the user's profile is \\CorpSvr17\Profiles\JennyP, you would enter this as the Copy Profile To path.

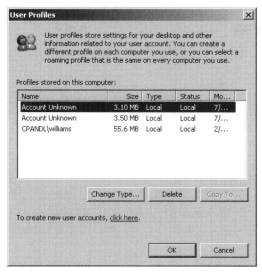

Figure 35-9 The User Profiles dialog box.

6. Set the profile permissions so that the profile can be used by other users. To do this, click Change under Permitted To Use, and then, in the Select User Or Group dialog box, type **Everyone** or the name of the specific user or group that should have access to the profile, and then click OK.

7. Click OK twice to close the open dialog boxes.

Configuring Local User Profiles

Local user profiles are created the first time a user logs on to a computer, unless there is a roaming or mandatory profile previously configured. For Windows Vista and Windows Server 2008, this means that the contents of the %SystemDrive%\Users\ Default folder are copied to the new user's profile folder. This creates the user's desktop and Start menu.

Chapter 35

Each new user has a unique path for the local user profile that includes the user's logon name as a subdirectory of the path. For Windows Vista and Windows Server 2008, the default location for profiles is %SystemDrive%\Users\%UserName%\Ntuser.dat, such as C:\Users\wrstanek\Ntuser.dat.

> **Note**
>
> In the user's main subdirectory for his or her profile, there is a file with a default name of Ntuser.ini. By default, this file contains the items that will be excluded from the copy process. For example, Microsoft Internet Explorer temporary files and history files, and individual application data are not copied as part of the user profile.

Configuring local user profiles is similar to configuring domain profiles. On the local machine, start Computer Management and access the Local Users And Groups node. Double-click a user's local account, and then select the Profile tab. Type the local path for the profile. Domain controllers do not have local accounts, so you cannot access Local Users And Groups on a domain controller.

Configuring Roaming User Profiles

Roaming user profiles are settings that follow a user from computer to computer. They are especially valuable for administrators or troubleshooters who may need to log on to many different workstations or servers and need to maintain desktop and common settings for security and convenience reasons. To manage roaming profiles, you must be a member of the Account Operators, Domain Admins, or Enterprise Admins group in Active Directory, or have been delegated the right to configure roaming user profiles. Use either Active Directory Users And Computers or Server Manager to configure roaming profiles.

If you are using Active Directory Users And Computers to configure roaming profiles, double-click the user's account to display the related Properties dialog box. Click the Profile tab. Type the unique path of the roaming user profile chosen for that user in the Profile Path field. The path can be a local path on the user's computer such as C:\Profiles\%UserName% or a path to a network share on a remote server.

If you choose to put the user profiles on a remote server, the path should be in the Uniform Naming Convention (UNC) form such as \\ServerName\ShareName\%UserName% where ServerName is the name of the server, ShareName is the name of the share created for storing roaming profiles, and %UserName% is an environment variable that allows the profile path to be unique for each user. For example, if you set the profile path to \\FileServer92\Profiles\%UserName%, as shown in Figure 35-10, and were configuring the account for Ed K, the profile path would be set as \\File-Server92\Profiles\EdK. The subfolder, EdK, is created automatically, and the roaming profile is then stored in the folder as Ntuser.dat.

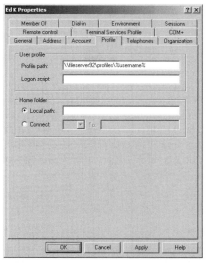

Figure 35-10 Set the profile path in the user's Properties dialog box.

CAUTION

When logged on to multiple computers using roaming profiles, changes to the profile settings and configuration may be lost if the order of logging off is incorrect. Imagine you are using a roaming profile and are logged on to two computers. You then change or install an application or program on the first computer. If you then log off that computer, any changes you made will be lost if you go to a second computer and log off without making the same changes. This is because your roaming profile on the second computer will be the one that is saved to the server and will not contain the changes made on the first computer. When using roaming profiles, the profile stored on the server is the one from the computer from which you logged off last.

Implementing Mandatory User Profiles

Mandatory user profiles are a type of roaming user profile. They can be used to maintain a higher security level and consistent environment for users. Although users can log on to different computers and get the same desktop settings, changes made to the desktop on the local computer will not be saved to the server where the mandatory user profiles are stored. Mandatory user profiles have the .man extension, for example, Ntuser.man.

To configure a mandatory user profile for a user, you set the user's profile path as previously discussed for roaming profiles. Then copy the profile that you want the user to have to the profile folder and change the name from Ntuser.dat to Ntuser.man. That's

Chapter 35

it—you rename the Ntuser.dat file to Ntuser.man using Windows Explorer, and it becomes a mandatory user profile.

> **Note**
>
> Because profiles contain hidden system files, they aren't automatically displayed in Windows Explorer. Choose Folder Options from the Tools menu, and then click the View tab. Under Advanced Settings, select Show Hidden Files And Folders, clear the Hide Protected Operating System Files check box, and then click OK. Note also that a mandatory profile must be available for a user to log on. If for some reason the user profile becomes unavailable, the user will not be able to log on. Because of this, you should check the security on the profile to ensure that the user can access it.

Switching Between a Local and a Roaming User Profile

Sometimes you may want to switch from a roaming to a local user profile or vice versa. This could be for personal preference, you may be troubleshooting, or you may have a slow network connection and the roaming profile takes too long to download to the local computer.

To switch between local and roaming profiles, complete these steps:

1. Click System And Maintenance\System in Control Panel. Under Tasks, click Advanced System Settings. This displays the System Properties dialog box with the Advanced tab selected.

2. On the Advanced Tab, under User Profiles, click Settings. The User Profiles dialog box appears.

3. After selecting the profile that is to be changed, click Change Type, and then select Roaming Profile or Local Profile as appropriate.

4. Click OK three times.

> **Note**
>
> You can change the profile type only if the profile was originally a roaming profile. If the change options aren't available, the user's profile was originally created as a local profile.

Managing User Data

It is important that users have access to the business data, software code, or accounting data on the network. They need access to the data to get their work done, and the organization needs to be operational 24 hours a day, seven days a week. Managing user data using folder redirection, group policy, offline files, and synchronization can help increase the network reliability and the availability of data. It can also reduce the time it takes to restore data in the event of hardware or software failures.

You want to make access to the data that each user and group requires invisible and seamless, and at the same time provide the most efficient process for restoring the data in case of a failure. Managing user data for fault tolerance and to reduce the amount of administrative load is accomplished using the IntelliMirror technology. This technology allows users to have their data available to them regardless of which operating system and computer they log on. Using a combination of folder redirection, offline files, group policy, and synchronization, user data can be made available efficiently and reliably.

Using Folder Redirection

One useful approach to managing user data is folder redirection. In this process, the administrator uses group policy to configure where on the network the user's data, for example the Documents folder, is saved. This data is synchronized between the network storage site and the local copies in the background. This allows the user to change machines or to work offline and always have the same data available.

Using Group Policy, the ways in which you can redirect folders depends on the operating system. For Windows Server 2003, Windows XP Professional, and earlier releases of Windows, the special folders you can centrally manage are Application Data, Start Menu, Desktop, My Documents, and My Pictures. For Windows Vista and Windows Server 2008, the special folders you can manage are AppData(Roaming), Desktop, Start Menu, Documents, Pictures, Music, Videos, Favorites, Contacts, Downloads, Links, Searches, and Saved Games.

Before configuring the policy, however, you must first create a share to hold the user data. Create the share on a file server and configure the share so that the special group Everyone has the List Contents, Read, and Write permissions to it. After you do this, you can configure Group Policy settings in order to implement folder redirection.

> **Note**
>
> Are you wondering what happens if the user's computer fails and folder redirection is in effect? Because the data is stored on the network server, if the user's local computer has a disk failure, the network-stored data will not be lost, This data can be accessed from a different machine or from the original machine after it is rebuilt.

Folder redirection for domain users can be set in the domain policy or at an OU level. In the GPMC, right-click the GPO for the site, domain, or organizational unit you want to work with and then select Edit. This opens the Group Policy Management Editor for the GPO. In the policy editor, expand the following nodes: User Configuration, Windows Settings, and then select Folder Redirection. As Figure 35-11 shows, the folders that can be redirected are listed separately. This allows you to configure redirection of each folder separately.

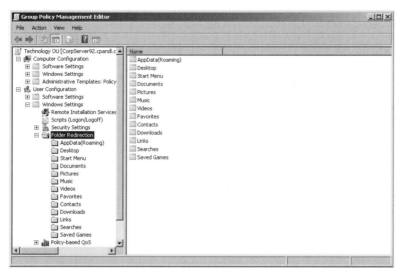

Figure 35-11 Select the folder you want to redirect.

In the Group Policy Management Editor, right-click the folder you want to redirect, and then select Properties. The default tab for the Properties dialog box is the Target tab. The Setting option of this tab provides three choices for configuring how folder redirection behaves. You can select from the following choices:

- **Not Configured** Use this setting to disable redirection of the selected folder.

- **Basic—Redirect Everyone's Folder To The Same Location** Use this setting to designate one location where all the related folders for users will be redirected. This would normally be a share on a server that is part of the daily backup schedule. The redirected folder data would then be available in the event of a disk crash. In most cases, the individual user folders will then be a subfolder of the designated folder. For example, if you wanted the Documents folders for all users to be redirected to \\CorpSvr15\UserData, this folder would contain subfolders for each domain user, and the user's Documents data would be stored in the appropriate subfolder.

- **Advanced—Specify Locations For Various User Groups** Use this setting if you want to set different user data locations for various groups. If you select this option, you can set an alternative target folder location for each group. Depending on the size of your network and domain, and its business model, this may be beneficial. You could, for example, set different folders for the Sales, Engineering, and Customer Service groups.

> **Note**
>
> Remember, the group policy you are working with applies only to user accounts that are in the container for which you are configuring Group Policy. So if you set a redirection policy for a user account that isn't defined in the domain or OU you are working with, the user's data will not be redirected.

If you choose Basic redirection, the Target tab is updated, as shown in Figure 35-12, and you have the following options:

- **Redirect To The User's Home Directory** This setting applies only to redirection of a user's Documents folder. If you have configured the user's home folder in their account properties, you can use this setting to redirect the Documents folder to the home folder. Use this setting only if the home folder has already been created.

- **Create A Folder For Each User Under The Root Path** This is a common setting. It appends the user's name to the file share created on a file server, allowing a folder to be created automatically under the file share root path for each user. The folder name is based on the %UserName% variable. This option is not available with redirection of the Start Menu folder.

- **Redirect To The Following Location** This setting allows you to specify a root path to a file share and folder location for each user. If you add %UserName% to the path, you can create individual folders for each user as in the previous option. If you do not include a user-specific environment variable, all the users are redirected to the same folder.

- **Redirect To The Local User Profile Location** This setting causes the default location of the user's profile to be used as the location for the user data. This is the default configuration if no redirection policies are enabled. If you use this option, the folders are not redirected to a network share and you essentially undo folder redirection. This option is not available with redirection of the Start Menu folder.

If you choose Advanced redirection, the Target tab is updated so that you can define different redirection settings for different groups of users. Click Add to display the Specify Group And Location dialog box shown in Figure 35-13.

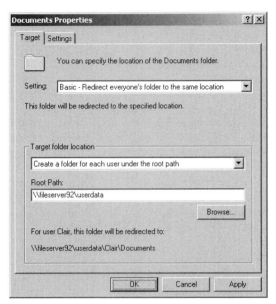

Figure 35-12 Configure basic folder redirection to redirect all the folders to the same location.

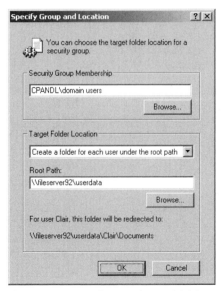

Figure 35-13 Configure advanced folder redirection to define different redirection settings for different groups.

In the Specify Group And Location dialog box, click Browse to display the Select Group dialog box. Type the name of a group account in the selected container, and then click Check Names. When a single match is found, the dialog box is automatically updated as appropriate and the entry is underlined. When you click OK, the group is added to the Security Group Membership list in the Specify Group And Location dialog box. You now have the same options for setting the Target Folder Location and the Root Path as you have with Basic redirection. When you are finished configuring these options, click OK. You can then repeat this process to configure the redirection of the selected folder for other groups.

Using Offline Files

Offline files offer another way to manage user data. Think about how many of your users travel with their computers and may not be able to have a network connection to needed data. Using offline files in conjunction with folder redirection and synchronization, you ensure that user data will be available and consistent. To use offline files with folder redirection, you simply enable offline files on the shares created for redirection. By default, when you create shares, only the files and programs that users specify will be available for offline use. You can change this configuration so that all files and programs that users open from a share are automatically available offline. Or you can configure the share so that files and programs will not be available offline.

Offline files work by storing client data and documents in the file system cache on the client computer, making the data and documents available if there is no network connection. Windows Vista and Windows Server 2008 provide two key enhancements to the way offline files are used:

- **Change-only syncing** Windows Vista allows for faster synchronization by syncing only the changed blocks of files. Thus, unlike Windows XP where the entire contents of a changed file are written back to the server during synchronization, with Windows Vista only the changed blocks are written back to the server during synchronization.

- **Unavailable file and folder ghosting** When partial contents of a folder are made available offline, Windows Vista and Windows Server 2008 create ghosted entries of other files and folders to preserve the online context. Because of this, when you are not connected to a remote location, you'll see ghost entries for online items as well as normal entries for offline items.

Configuring Offline Files on File Servers

The quickest way to configure offline files is to use Computer Management. After you start Computer Management and connect to the computer you want to work with, expand System Tools and Shared Folders, and then select Shares to display the current shares on the system you are working with.

You can then configure offline settings for a shared folder by right-clicking the share in the details pane, and then selecting Properties. In the share's Properties dialog box, click Offline Settings on the General tab to display the Offline Settings dialog box. As shown in Figure 35-14, there are three settings:

- **Only The Files And Programs That Users Specify Will Be Available Offline** This allows the user to decide which files will be available offline and is the default setting.

- **All Files And Programs That Users Open From The Share Will Be Automatically Available Offline** If a user opens a file from a share, this setting makes it automatically available offline. The subsetting, Optimized For Performance, allows programs and application data to be available offline as well. Selecting this check box will help network performance when applications are run over the network. Clear this check box if you are not going to use folder redirection or offline files for application data.

- **Files Or Programs From The Share Will Not Be Available Offline** This setting blocks users from storing files on the client computer for offline use.

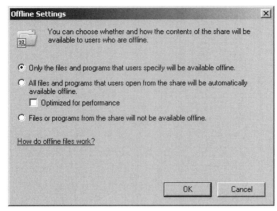

Figure 35-14 Configuring offline files settings on the server.

Configuring Offline Files on Clients

You can configure offline files for users on a Windows Vista computer by completing the following steps:

1. Map a network drive to a shared file or folder as discussed in "Using and Finding Shares" on page 550.

2. Click Start and then click Computer. This opens the Computer console. If you scroll down in the main pane, you should see a list of mapped network drives under the Network Location heading.

3. Create the offline file cache by doing one of the following:

   - To copy the entire contents of a shared folder to the user's computer and make it available for offline use, under Network Location, right-click the shared location and then select Always Available Offline.

   - To copy only a selected folder (and its contents) or a selected file to the user's computer and make it available offline, use the Computer console to locate the network file or folder, and then right-click the file or folder and select Always Available Offline.

> **Note**
>
> With Windows Vista, designating files and folders for offline use creates a local cache of the contents of the files and folders on the user's computer. It also either establishes a sync partnership between the local computer and the sharing computer or extends an existing sync partnership to incorporate the additional shared files and folders. Sync partnerships can be managed using Sync Center.

Configuring Offline Files in Group Policy

Group Policy can manage access and configuration of offline files more efficiently than the methods mentioned previously. You can use Offline Files to manage the most common user data, including the Documents, Start Menu, and Desktop folders. Offline Files policy objects are located in Computer Configuration\Administrative Templates\ Network\Offline Files, and in User Configuration\Administrative Templates\Network\ Offline Files.

When you use Group Policy to manage user data via Offline Files, be aware that precedence and dependencies are varied. For example: If you enable Prohibit User Configuration Of Offline Files in User Configuration, but enable it in Computer Configuration, offline files will be enabled, because the Computer Configuration setting has precedence over the User Configuration setting.

Managing File Synchronization

When you are managing files in a network using folder redirection or offline files, you need to make sure that the files on the network share remain synchronized with the files on the user's system. This allows you to ensure availability and that the latest version of the user's data is stored and available. Full synchronization provides the latest version, whereas Quick synchronization provides a complete version of the user data but not necessarily the most current version. By configuring the synchronization in Group Policy, you can ensure a full synchronization for either a logging on or logging off scenario.

There are four times for configuring Offline Files caching on a workstation:

- Logging on or off by the user
- Scheduled times
- During specific intervals of idleness on the computer
- When the user locks or unlocks Windows

You will need to configure synchronization of redirected or offline files by using the Sync Center. On Windows Vista, you run the Sync Center by clicking Start, All Programs, Accessories, Sync Center. When multiple sync partnerships have been established, you can sync all offline files and folders by clicking Sync All. When you want to sync the offline files and folders for a particular shared network folder, you can sync a specific network share by clicking the sync partnership that you want to work with, and then clicking Sync. You can create and manage scheduled synchronization by selecting the sync partnership you want to work with and then clicking Schedule.

Maintaining User Accounts

User accounts are fairly easy to maintain after they've been configured. Most of the maintenance tasks you need to perform involve user profiles and group membership, which are covered in separate sections of this chapter. Other than these areas, you might also need to perform the following tasks:

- Delete user accounts
- Disable, enable, or unlock user accounts
- Move user accounts
- Rename user accounts
- Reset a user's domain password
- Set logon scripts and home folders
- Create a local user account password backup

Each of these tasks is examined in the sections that follow.

Deleting User Accounts

Each user account created in the domain has a unique security identifier (SID) and that SID is never reused. If you delete an account, you cannot create an account with the same name and regain all the same permissions and settings of the previously deleted account. The SID for the new account will be different than the old one, and you will have to redefine all the necessary permissions and settings. Because of this, you should delete accounts only when you know they are not going to be used again. If you are unsure, disable the account rather than deleting it.

To delete an account, select the account in Active Directory Users And Computers and press Delete. When prompted to confirm the deletion, click Yes and the account is permanently deleted. Deleting a user account doesn't delete a user's on-disk data. It only deletes the user account from Active Directory. This means the user's profile and other personal data will still be available on disk until you manually delete them.

CAUTION !

> The permissions on users are internally characterized within Active Directory by unique SIDs that are allocated when the user is created. If you delete a user account and then re-create it, it will have a new SID and thus new permissions.

Disabling and Enabling User Accounts

If you need to deactivate a user account temporarily so that it cannot be used for logon or authentication, you can do this by disabling the account. Although disabling an account makes it unusable, you can later enable the account so that it can be used again. To disable an account, right-click the account in Active Directory Users And Computers, and then select Disable Account.

When prompted that the account has been disabled, click OK. A white circle with a down arrow is added to the account's icon to show that it is disabled. If you later need to enable the account, you can do so by right-clicking the account in Active Directory Users And Computers and then selecting Enable Account.

Moving User Accounts

When there is a reorganization or a user otherwise changes departments, you might need to move the user account to a new container in Active Directory Users And Computers. To move a user account, right-click the account, and then select Move. The Move dialog box appears, allowing you to select the container to which you want to move the user account. Alternatively, you can drag the user account into a new container. You can also select multiple users to move by using Windows keyboard shortcuts such as Ctrl then selecting multiple users, or using Shift and selecting the first and last user.

Renaming User Accounts

Active Directory tracks objects by their SIDs. This allows you to safely rename user, computer, and group accounts without worrying about having to change access permissions as well. That said, however, the process of renaming a user account is not as easy as renaming other types of accounts. The reason is that users have several name components that are all related to a user's last name, including a full name, display name, and user logon name. So when a person's last name changes as the result of a marriage, adoption, or divorce, you not only need to update the user's account name in Active Directory but the rest of the related name components as well. To simplify the process of renaming user accounts, Active Directory Users And Computers provides a dialog box (shown in the following screen) that you can use to rename a user's account and all the related name components.

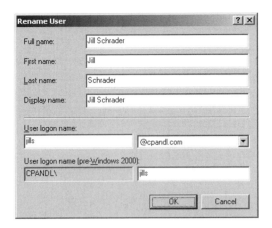

The process for renaming user accounts is as follows:

1. Find the user account that you want to rename in Active Directory Users And Computers.

2. Right-click the user account and then select Rename. Active Directory Users And Computers then highlights the account name for editing. Press the Backspace or Delete key to erase the existing name and then press Enter to open the Rename User dialog box.

3. Make the necessary changes to the user's name information and then click OK. If the user is logged on, you'll see a warning prompt telling you that the user should log off and then log back on using the new account logon name.

4. The account is renamed and the SID for access permissions remains the same. You may still need to modify other data for the user in the account's Properties dialog box, including the following:

    ○ *User Profile Path* As necessary change the Profile Path on the Profile tab, and then rename the corresponding directory on disk.

    ○ *Logon Script Name* If you use individual logon scripts for each user, change the Logon Script Name on the Profile tab, and then rename the logon script on disk.

    ○ *Home Folder* As necessary change the home folder path on the Profile tab, and then rename the corresponding directory on disk.

Resetting a User's Domain Password

One of the good things about using domain policy to require users to change their passwords is that the overall security of the network is improved by doing so. One of the downsides of frequent password changes is that users occasionally forget their password. If this happens, it is easy to fix by doing the following:

1. Find the user account whose password you want to reset in Active Directory Users And Computers.

2. Right-click the user account and then select Reset Password.

3. In the Reset Password dialog box shown in the following screen, type and then confirm the new password for the user.

4. If you want, select the User Must Change Password At Next Logon check box.

5. If the account status is listed as locked, select the Unlock The User's Account check box.

6. Click OK.

> **Note**
>
> The password change is immediately replicated to the PDC emulator as discussed in "Using, Locating, and Transferring the PDC Emulator Role" on page 1050. This makes the password available for the user to log on anywhere in the domain.

Unlocking User Accounts

Whenever users violate group policy, such as when they fail to change their passwords before they expire or exceed the limit for bad logon attempts, Active Directory locks their accounts. After an account is locked, the user can no longer log on. As accounts can also be locked because someone is trying to break into an account, you shouldn't automatically unlock accounts. Instead, either wait until the user asks you to unlock his or her account or go speak to the user when you notice his or her account has been locked.

You can unlock accounts by completing the following steps:

1. In Active Directory Users And Computers, right-click the locked account and then select Properties.

2. In the Properties dialog box, select the Account tab.

3. Select the Unlock Account check box and then click OK.

Creating a User Account Password Backup

Sometimes a user (or even an admin) will forget the local Administrator's or another user's account password. If you manually reset a user's account password, and the user has encrypted e-mail, files that have been encrypted or passwords they use for Internet accounts will be lost or not available with the new or reset password. With Windows Vista and Windows Server 2008 you can reset a user's password without losing that encrypted data. You can consider this as backing up a user password and you do this by creating a password reset disk.

You can make a reset disk for any computer running Windows Vista or Windows Server 2008, except for domain controllers. Reset disks can be for both local accounts and domain accounts. Be careful of the following when creating a reset disk:

- You are not allowed to create a reset disk and change your password from the Log On screen simultaneously.

- You do not have to create a new reset disk each time you change a user's password; you need to create the reset disk only once for an account.

- Users should create their own reset disks for each account they use.

Follow these steps to make a password reset disk:

1. Press Ctrl+Alt+Del, and then click the Change A Password option.

2. Click Create A Password Reset Disk to start the Forgotten Password Wizard.

3. In the Forgotten Password Wizard, read the introductory message and then click Next.

4. You can use a floppy disk or a USB flash key as your password key disk. To use a floppy disk, insert a blank, formatted disk into drive A and then select Floppy Disk Drive (A:) in the drive list. To use a USB flash key, select the device you want to use in the drive list. Click Next.

5. Type the password for the current account in the text box provided and then click Next.

6. After the wizard creates the password reset disk, remove the disk and then click Finish.

Store the floppy disk or USB flash key in a secure place, because now anyone can use it to gain access to the account. If a user is unable to log on because he or she has forgotten the password, you can use the password reset disk to create a new password and log on to the account using this password by following these steps:

1. On the Log On screen, click the arrow button without entering a password. The Reset Password option should be displayed. If the user has already entered the wrong password, the Reset Password option may already be displayed.

2. Click Reset Password. This starts the Reset Password Wizard.

3. In the Reset Password Wizard, read the introductory message and then click Next.

4. Insert the disk into drive A or the USB flash key containing the password recovery file and then click Next.

5. Follow the prompts to complete the password reset process.

INSIDE OUT **How the password reset disk works**

The reset disk process generates a public/private key pair. There are no passwords stored on the reset disk. The reset disk contains the private key and the public key encrypts the account password. When a user forgets the account password, the restore process uses the private key on the reset disk to decrypt the current password and create a new one that is encrypted with the same key. Data is not lost because the same encryption is used for any other encrypted data.

Managing Groups

Active Directory groups are objects that may hold users, contacts, computers, or other groups. When you want to manage users, computers, and other resources, such as files, directories, printers, network shares, and e-mail distribution lists, using groups can decrease administration time and improve network performance.

Understanding Groups

Types of groups and group scope are essential topics in planning and managing an efficient network. Planning an environment that uses Active Directory and groups is critical—failing to plan or taking shortcuts could negatively affect network traffic and create more administrative work in the long run. There are two types of groups and three group scopes.

Group management was enhanced for Windows Server 2003 and Windows Server 2008. Before Windows Server 2003, all changes to universal groups would be replicated to all global catalog servers across the enterprise. Thus, if you used universal groups on your network, and you had slow network connectivity between global cata-log servers, careful implementation of universal groups was crucial to preventing slow network throughput. To alleviate this possible bottleneck in network traffic, Microsoft has enhanced universal groups with caching of universal group membership and global catalog replication.

Caching universal groups is useful to enhance performance during log on. You con-figure caching of a universal group when Active Directory sites are widely scattered geographically or connected by a slow network and you want to minimize network traf-fic and increase logon efficiency and authentication. For instance, suppose you have a small remote office that has a slow wide area network (WAN) connection to the main office. Instead of the users having to connect to a domain controller in the main office, a domain controller can be configured in the remote office to cache the universal groups. This way you do not have to have the global catalog on the remote domain controller. When someone logs on in the remote office, the process uses cached logon credentials on the remote domain controller. By default, this cached data is refreshed every eight hours.

To improve dependability and performance, Microsoft has made some primary changes in replication and synchronization of Active Directory data. Within groups, all group membership data is no longer replicated between global catalog sites when group mem-bers are added, deleted, or changed. Rather, only the changed group member data is replicated. This helps reduce network traffic and also lowers the amount of required processing.

Before Windows Server 2008, all values associated with a multi-valued attribute were replicated. With a domain operating in Windows Server 2008 domain functional level, only the changed attribute is replicated.

Types of Groups

There are two types of groups used in Windows Server 2008: security groups and dis-tribution groups.

- Security groups are used to control access to resources. This is the kind of group you will probably use most often, and it may already be familiar. Security groups are listed in discretionary access control lists (DACLs). DACLs are part of an object's descriptor and are used to define permissions on objects and resources.

- Distribution groups are used for unsecured e-mail lists. Distribution lists do not use the functionality of the DACL permissions that security groups do. Distribu-tion groups are not security-enabled but can be used by e-mail servers such as Microsoft Exchange Server.

Understanding the Scopes of Groups

Windows Server 2008 uses three group scopes: domain local, global, and universal. Each of these groups has a different scope that determines the types of objects that can be included as members of a group and the permissions and rights those objects can be granted. In practice, you will almost always use security groups, because they include distribution group functionality and are the only types of groups that have DACLs.

Domain Local Groups

Consider using domain local groups first when you are giving groups or users access to local domain resources. For instance, if you have a domain named northwind.com and you want users or groups in that local domain to access a shared folder in the northwind.com local domain, you could create a domain local group called SalesPersons, insert in the SalesPersons group the users and global groups you want to give access to the shared folder, and then assign the SalesPersons group permissions on the resource.

Access policies for domain local groups are not stored in Active Directory. This means that they do not get replicated to the global catalog and thus queries performed on the global catalog will not return results from domain local groups. This is because domain local groups cannot be determined across domains.

Global Groups

Use global groups to give users or groups access to resources according to how they have been organized. For instance, users from the Marketing or Development departments could be put in separate global groups in order to simplify administration of their need to access resources like printers and network shares. Global groups can be nested in order to grant access to any domain in the forest.

Universal Groups

Universal groups have very few fundamental restrictions. Universal groups can be a tempting shortcut for administrators to use, because they can be used across domains in the forest. Memberships in universal groups can be drawn from any domain, and permissions can be set within any domain. However, using universal groups as your main method of grouping users, groups, and computers has a significant caveat.

Universal groups are stored in the global catalog, and whenever changes are made to a universal group, the changed properties must be replicated to other domain controllers configured as global catalog servers. The replication of individual property changes rather than entire objects is an improvement for Windows Server 2008 that should allow wider use of universal groups without causing network bottlenecks or slowed performance during authentication and global catalog changes.

Which Group Scope Should You Use?

There is a strategy in choosing when to use a group scope and which group scope to use. A common strategy is to organize user accounts into logical groups based on the permissions they need to access specific resources. In a business model, this often can be determined according to the department the user belongs to. For instance, the Development department of a software business may put all their developers in a Dev group, and then assign permissions to a network share to the Dev group. On the other hand, in a Windows Server 2008 environment it becomes more complex than this, because there are different scopes for groups. Furthermore, groups may contain not only users, but also computers and even other groups, and can be nested to any scale.

Some important constraints on group scope in Windows Server 2008 include the following:

- Universal groups are stored in the global catalog and replicated across the network. However, Windows Server 2008 has new features that allow caching of the global catalog and replication of only the changes in it.

- Global groups can be included in an object's security data structure only if that object is in the same domain as the global group. In Windows 2000 native functional level or higher, global groups can be nested in order to grant access to any domain in the forest.

- Domain local groups cannot be processed in other domains.

Group scope functionality and limitations include member inclusion and permissions. Table 35-4 lists how the three scopes function.

Table 35-4 How Group Scope Functions Using Windows Server 2003 and Higher Domain Functional Levels

Group	Member Inclusion	Permissions
Universal	You can include users, computer accounts, global groups, and universal groups from any domain.	Within any domain, universal groups can be added to other groups and granted permissions.
Global	You can put in a global group any user or computer account or other global groups from the same domain.	Global groups can be added to other global groups in any domain in the forest and assigned permissions.
Domain local	Same as universal groups, but you can also include domain local groups from the same domain.	Domain local groups can be added only to other domain local groups in the same domain and assigned permissions.

In native mode, Windows Server 2008 groups have nesting limitations that are dependent on the group scope. Limitations for nesting are listed in Table 35-5.

Table 35-5 Group Scope Nesting in Windows 2000 Native Functional Level

Group Type	Can Nest in Universal?	Can Nest in Global?	Can Nest in Domain Local?
Universal	No	Yes	Yes
Global	Yes	Yes (only in the same domain)	Yes
Domain local	No	No	No

Why Use Domain Local Groups?

Domain local groups are used when you want to give users, computers, or specific groups access to resources in a single local domain. In a domain local group, you can include other domain local groups with domain local scope, global groups, or universal groups. You can also include single accounts in the domain local group. However, including single user accounts can increase the amount of administration for you instead of reducing it, so unless management has specifically requested a special permission, this may not be the best route.

A common scenario for using domain local groups is to provide access to printers for members of a department (such as the Developers department).

In this scenario, you would use Active Directory Users And Computers:

1. Create a domain local group by right-clicking an OU, and then selecting New, Group.

2. Assign permissions to use the printer by adding the new domain local group to the printer by opening Control Panel, Printers And Faxes, then right-clicking Properties, selecting the Security tab, and finally adding the domain local group to the printer.

3. Create a global group.

4. Add the user accounts from the Development department to the global group

5. Add the global group to the domain local group you created at the beginning.

This way, if you ever add a new printer, all you have to do is add access to it in the domain local group, and the developers automatically get access because their global group is part of the domain local group.

If a new domain is added, all you have to do to give the people in the new domain access to the printer is add the new global groups from the new domain to the domain local group.

Why Use Global Groups?

An important aspect of global groups is they are not replicated outside their own domain. They are not part of the global catalog replication. Thus, you should use global group membership for objects that need high regular maintenance or modifications. These changes will not be replicated across your network and thus will not slow network traffic over slow links. Therefore, a main reason to use global groups is to organize users with similar needs within a domain to give them access to resources. For instance, you have two domains, one in the United States, the other in India. In each domain you have developers. Because your business model requires that neither group of developers needs access to the other's source code, you could create two global groups, USA\Dev and India\Dev, and give the global groups permissions to different source code shares.

Why Use Universal Groups?

Using universal groups extends this idea so that users in groups of different domains may be able to access resources without affecting network traffic because of global catalog replication. By creating a universal group and adding global groups to it, you can give users from different domains in the forest access to the same resource. For instance, in the preceding scenario, a third group could be created for the developers, called UniDev. This would be a universal group to which you would add both global groups, USA\Dev and India\Dev, and assign permissions to perhaps even a second network share of source code that both groups of users must access. This is a good strategy, because if you add new user accounts to the global groups, the changes are not replicated to the global catalog and little if no impact to network traffic is incurred. However, be careful about changing memberships to universal groups, because those changes are replicated across all links to other domain controllers configured with global catalogs.

Creating a Group

You may create groups in the Users container or in a new OU that you have created in the domain. To create a group, start Active Directory Users And Computers. Right-click the Users container or the OU in which you want to place the group, point to New, and then select Group. This displays the New Object–Group dialog box shown in Figure 35-15. Type a group name, and then select the Group Scope and Group Type. Click OK to create the group.

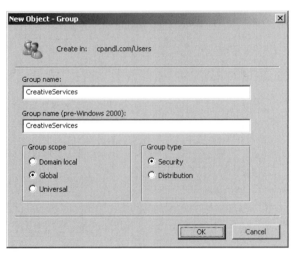

Figure 35-15 Creating a group.

Windows Server 2008 has three group scopes and two group types you can select from. This allows you to create six different combinations of groups. You must be a member of the Account Operators, Domain Admins, or Enterprise Admins group to create new groups.

> **Note**
>
> The built-in accounts for Active Directory in Windows Server 2008 are located in two places. The built-in domain local groups such as Administrators, Account Operators, and Backup Operators are located in the Builtin container. Built-in global groups such as Domain Admins and Enterprise Admins are located in the Users container.

INSIDE OUT

Creating group accounts at the command line

At the command line, you can create groups using DSADD. For groups, AD path strings describe the group's location in the directory from the group name to the actual containers in which it is stored. You specify whether the group is a security group using -secgrp yes or that a group is a distribution group using -secgrp no. You specify the scope of the group using -scope u for universal, -scope g for global, and -scope l for domain local.

For example, if you want to create a global security group called SeattleServices in the Services OU for the cpandl.com domain, the full path to this group object is CN=SeattleServices,OU=Services,DC=cpandl,DC=com. When creating the group object using DSADD, you must specify this path as follows:

```
dsadd group "CN=SeattleServices,OU=Services,DC=cpandl,DC=com" -secgrp yes -
scope g
```

For the full syntax and usage, type **dsadd group /?** at a command prompt. Although quotation marks aren't required in this example, I always use them to ensure that I don't forget them when they actually are needed, such as when name components contain spaces.

The directory services commands can also be used to perform many group management tasks. Using DSGET GROUP at a command prompt, you can:

- Determine whether a group is a security group by typing **dsget group *GroupDN* -secgrp**.

- Determine group scope by typing **dsget group *GroupDN* -scope**.

- Determine the members of a group by typing **dsget group *GroupDN* -members** where *GroupDN* is the distinguished name of the group.

- Determine the groups of which a group is a member by typing **dsget group *GroupDN* -memberof**. The -expand option can be added to display the recursively expanded list of groups of which a group is a member.

Using DSMOD GROUP at a command prompt, you can:

- Change group scope using **dsmod group *GroupDN* -scope u** for universal, **-scope g** for global, and **-scope l** for domain local.

- Add members by typing **dsmod group *GroupDN* -addmbr *MemberDN*** where *GroupDN* is the distinguished name of the group and *MemberDN* is the distinguished name of the account or group you want to add to the designated group.

- Remove members by typing **dsmod group *GroupDN* -rmmbr MemberDN**.

- Convert the group to a security group using **dsmod group *GroupDN* -secgrp yes** or to a distribution group using **dsmod group *GroupDN* -secgrp no**.

Chapter 35

Adding Members to Groups

The easiest way to add users to a group is to right-click the user in the details pane of Active Directory Users And Computers, and then select Add To A Group. The Select Groups dialog box appears and you can select the group of which the user is to become a member. You can also get to the same dialog box by right-clicking on the user name, selecting Properties, clicking the Member Of tab, and then clicking Add.

> **Note**
>
> To add multiple users to a group, select more than one user, using Shift+click or Ctrl+click, and follow the same steps.

If you want to add both users and groups as members of a group, you can do this by performing the following steps:

1. Double-click the group entry in Active Directory Users And Computers. This opens the group's Properties dialog box.

2. On the Members tab, click Add to add accounts to the group.

3. Use the Select Users, Contacts, Computers, Or Groups dialog box to choose users, computers, and groups that should be members of the currently selected group. Click OK.

4. Repeat steps 2 and 3 as necessary to add additional users, computers, and groups as members.

5. Click OK.

Deleting a Group

Deleting a group is as simple as right-clicking the group name within Active Directory Users And Computers, and then selecting Delete. You should be very careful when deleting groups because, though it does not delete the user accounts contained by the group, the permissions you may have assigned to the group are lost and cannot be recovered by merely re-creating the group with the same name.

> **CAUTION**
>
> The permissions on groups are internally characterized within Active Directory by unique SIDs that are allocated when the group is created. If you delete a group and then re-create it, it will have a new SID and thus new permissions.

Modifying Groups

There are a number of modifications, property changes, and management procedures you may want to apply to groups. You can change the scope, the members, and other groups contained in the group; move a group; delegate management of a group; and send mail to a group.

Finding a Group

When you have a substantial number of groups, you can use the Find function to locate the one you need to manage. Just right-click the domain or OU, and then select Find. In the Find Users, Contacts, And Groups dialog box, you can specify what type of object to find, change the starting point, or structure a search query from the available tabs. After the query has run, many administrative or management functions can be performed on the objects returned in the results window.

INSIDE OUT Saved queries in Active Directory

In Active Directory Users And Computers, you can reuse and save queries. This allows you to find groups quickly and repeatedly when you want to manage and modify them. You can locate the Saved Queries folder in the default position at the top of the Active Directory Users And Computers console tree (left pane). You cannot save queries using the Find menu when you right-click a group. You can only save them using the Saved Query procedure that is found in the uppermost part of the tree in Active Directory Users And Computers and creating a new query.

Managing the Properties of Groups

When you double-click a group name in Active Directory Users And Computers, the Group Properties dialog box appears. You can configure the following six areas or functions:

- **General** You change the description or group e-mail address here. In addition, you may be able to change the type of group or the scope of the group. When in Windows Server 2003 or higher domain functional level, there are limitations on changing group scope, as shown in Table 35-6.

- **Members** You can list, add, and remove group members.

- **Member Of** Lists the groups the current group is a member of. These can be domain local groups or universal groups from the local domain or universal groups from other domains in the current domain tree or forest.

- **Managed By** Add, clear, or modify the user account you want to make responsible for managing this group.

- **Object**   View the canonical name of the group object. This tab is visible only in Advanced view. To access Advanced view, select Advanced Features from the View menu in Active Directory Users And Computers.

- **Security**   Used to configure advanced permissions for users and groups that can access the group object in Active Directory. This tab is visible only in Advanced view.

Table 35-6 Group Scope Conversions in Windows Server 2003 or Higher Domain Functional Level

Scope of Group	Can Be Converted to Universal	Can Be Converted to Global	Can Be Converted to Domain Local
Universal	NA	Yes	Yes
Global	Yes	NA	No
Domain local	Yes	No	NA

Modifying Other Group Settings

You can modify other group settings using Active Directory Users And Computers. You can perform the following tasks:

- **Move a group**   To move a group, right-click it, and then select Move. The Move dialog box appears, allowing you to select the container to which you want to move the group. Alternatively, you can drag the group icon into a new container. You can also select multiple groups to move by using Windows keyboard shortcuts such as Ctrl, then selecting multiple groups, or using Shift and selecting the first and last group.

- **Rename a group**   Right-click the group name, and then select Rename. Type the new group name, and then press Enter. Multiple group selection is disabled for this function.

- **Send mail to a group**   Right-click the group name, and then select Send Mail. An error will occur if no e-mail address has been configured on the General tab of Group Properties. Otherwise, the default mail client will be used to open a new mail message addressed to the group, which you can complete and send.

> **Note**
> Moving or renaming groups can alter the effective permissions of users and groups in unpredictable ways. With this in mind, you might want to check the effective permissions for member users and groups to ensure that the permissions are as expected.

Managing Computer Accounts

Computer accounts are managed and configured using Active Directory Users And Computers. By default, computer accounts are stored in the Computers container and domain controller accounts are stored in the Domain Controllers container. Computer accounts can also be stored in other containers, such as the OUs you've created. Computers may be joined and removed from a domain using Computer Management or the System tool in Control Panel.

Creating a Computer Account in Active Directory

When you create a new computer account in your domain, you must be a member of the Account Operators, Domain Admins, or Enterprise Admins group in Active Directory. To create a new computer account, start Active Directory Users And Computers. Right-click the container in which you want to create the new computer account, point to New, and then select Computer. This starts the New Object–Computer Wizard shown in Figure 35-16.

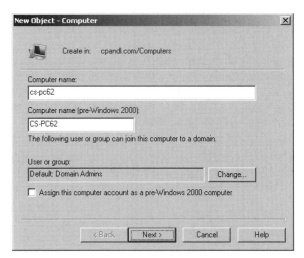

Figure 35-16 Creating a computer account.

Type a computer name. By default, only members of Domain Admins can join computers to the domain. To allow a different user or group to join the computer to the domain, click Change, and then use the Select User Or Group dialog box to select a user or group account that is authorized to join the computer to the domain. If Windows NT systems can use this account, select the Assign This Computer Account As A Pre–Windows 2000 Computer check box. Click Next twice, and then click Finish.

> **Note**
>
> Creating a computer account does not join the computer to the domain. It merely creates the account to simplify the process of joining a domain. You can, however, create a computer account when you join a computer to a domain.

INSIDE OUT Creating computer accounts at the command line

You can create computer accounts using DSADD as well. To do this, you'll need to know the Active Directory service path string you want to use. For example, suppose you want to create a computer account called CustServicePC27 in the Computers container for the cpandl.com domain. The full path to this computer object is CN=CustServicePC27, CN=Computers,DC=cpandl,DC=com. When creating the computer object using DSADD, you must specify this path as follows:

```
dsadd computer "CN=CustServicePC27,CN=Computers,DC=cpandl,DC=com"
```

Here, CN= is used to specify the common name of an object and DC= is used to specify a domain component. With Active Directory path strings, you will also see OU=, which is used to specify the name of an organizational unit object. For the full syntax and usage, type **dsadd computer /?** at a command prompt. Although quotation marks aren't required in this example, I always use them to ensure that I don't forget them when they actually are needed, such as when name components contain spaces.

The directory services commands can also be used to perform many computer management tasks. Use DSMOD COMPUTER to set properties, disable accounts, and reset accounts. Use DSMOVE COMPUTER to move computer accounts to a new container or OU. Use DSRM COMPUTER to remove the computer account.

Joining Computers to a Domain

When you join a computer to a domain, you must supply the credentials for creating a new computer account in Active Directory. The new computer will be placed in the default Computers container in Active Directory. Most of the time, there is a dialog box for joining a computer to the domain when you install or set up Windows 2000 or later for the first time. You must be a member of the Administrators group on the local computer to join it to the domain. Windows Server 2008 allows any authenticated user to join workstations to the domain—up to a total of 10—providing that you've already created the necessary computer accounts. To join a server to a domain, you must be a member of the Account Operators, Domain Admins, or Enterprise Admins group.

To join a server or workstation to a domain, follow these steps:

1. Click System And Maintenance\System in Control Panel. In the Computer Name, Domain, And Workgroup Settings section, click Change Settings. This displays the System Properties dialog box with the Computer Name tab selected.

2. On the Computer Name tab, click Change.

3. Select Domain and type the name of the domain to which the computer should join. Click OK.

4. When prompted, type the name and password of a domain account that has the permissions to create a computer account in Active Directory, or join the computer to the domain, or both. Click OK.

5. The computer is joined to the domain, and a new computer account is created as necessary. If the changes are successful, you'll see a confirmation dialog box.

TROUBLESHOOTING

The computer won't join the domain

If there are problems joining the computer to the domain, there may be an existing computer in the domain with the same name. In this case, you would change the computer name and then repeat this procedure. The computer must also have Transmission Control Protocol/Internet Protocol (TCP/IP) properly configured. If you suspect a problem with the TCP/IP configuration, ping the loopback address 127.0.0.1 to ensure TCP/IP is installed correctly and then check the configuration settings by typing **ipconfig /all** at the command prompt.

Moving a Computer Account

A corporation may have organizational changes requiring you to move a computer account. The computer account may be moved from one container to another. Plan and test moving the computer account to ensure that possible conflicts in permissions or rights don't occur. You can use the Effective Permissions tool in planning mode to simulate moving computer accounts and to determine if there could be conflicts.

To move a computer account, you can drag and drop the computer object from one container to another within the details pane of Active Directory Users And Computers. Alternatively, you can right-click the computer account name, select Move, and then select the container to which you want to move the account using the Move dialog box. You cannot move computer accounts for domain controllers across domains. You must first demote the domain controller, then move the computer account.

Chapter 35

Disabling a Computer Account

Security issues, such as malicious viral attacks or rogue user actions, may require you to temporarily disable a computer account. Perhaps a critical software bug has caused an individual computer to repeatedly try to receive authentication from a domain controller. You disable a computer account to prevent it from authenticating until you fix the problem.

You disable a computer account by right-clicking it in Active Directory Users And Computers and selecting Disable Account. This prevents the computer from logging on to the domain but does not remove the related account from Active Directory.

Deleting a Computer Account

When you delete a computer account using Active Directory Users And Computers, you cannot just re-create a new computer account with the same name and access. The SID of the original computer account will be different from that of the new account.

To remove a computer account, right-click the computer account in Active Directory Users And Computers, and then select Delete.

Managing a Computer Account

Managing a remote computer is a common task when troubleshooting server or workstation problems. You see and configure computer management settings such as shares, system settings, services and applications, and the event log of the remote computer. Care should be taken when changing settings or restarting services on remote machines.

Right-click the computer account name in Active Directory Users And Computers, and then select Manage to bring up Computer Management for that computer.

Resetting a Computer Account

Computer accounts, like user accounts, have passwords. Unlike user account passwords, computer account passwords are managed automatically. Sometimes, however, the password can get out of sync or there can be another issue that doesn't allow the computer account to be authenticated in the domain. If this happens, the computer account can no longer access resources in the domain and you should reset the computer account.

To reset a computer account, right-click the computer account name in Active Directory Users And Computers, and then select Reset Account. If you reset the computer account, the computer must be removed from the domain (by placing it in a workgroup or other domain) and then rejoined to the domain.

However, the Reset Account feature is not the best technique to use with member servers and domain controllers. With member servers and domain controllers, you should use NETDOM RESETPWD. You can reset the computer account password of a member server or domain controller by completing the following steps:

1. Log on locally to the computer. If you are resetting the password of a domain controller, you must stop the Kerberos Key Distribution Center service and set its startup type to Manual.

2. Open a command prompt. Type **netdom resetpwd /s:***ComputerName* **/ud:** *domain\user* **/pd:*** where *ComputerName* is the name of a domain controller in the computer account's logon domain, *domain\user* is the name of an administrator account with the authority to change the computer account password, and * tells NETDOM to prompt you for the account password before continuing.

3. When you enter your password, NETDOM will change the computer account password locally and on the domain controller. The domain controller will then distribute the password change to other domain controllers.

4. When NETDOM completes this task, restart the computer and verify that the password has been successfully reset. If you reset a domain controller's password, restart the Kerberos Key Distribution Center service and set its startup type to Automatic.

Configuring Properties of Computer Accounts

As with users and groups, there are many configuration tabs you can select when you are modifying a computer account. Right-click the computer name in Active Directory Users And Computers, and then select Properties. The following tabs are available:

- **Delegation** Allows you to configure delegation for the computer account as discussed in "Configuring the Delegated Service or Computer Account" on page 1112. This tab is available only when the domain is operating in Windows Server 2003 or higher functional level.

- **General** Shows the computer's name and role and allows you to set a description. You configure the computer for delegation by selecting the Trust This Computer For Delegation option.

- **Location** Allows you to set a location for the computer.

- **Managed By** Allows you to specify the person or group responsible for the computer.

- **Member Of** Allows you to configure the group membership for the computer.

- **Object** Displays the canonical name of the user object with dates and Update Sequence Numbers. This tab is visible only in Advanced view.

- **Operating System** Displays the operating system version and service pack used by the computer.

Chapter 35

- **Remote Install**   Allows you to set the unique identifier (globally unique identifier [GUID]/universal unique identifier [UUID]) and the remote installation server to use for a managed computer. This tab is available only for a managed computer.

- **Security**   Used to configure advanced permissions for users and groups that can access this computer object in Active Directory. This tab is visible only in Advanced view.

- **Dial-In**   Used to set the computer's dial-in or VPN access controls as well as call-back, IP address, and routing options for dial-in or VPN or both.

As you can see, much of the data for computer account properties is informational. The data you may need to change is probably on the Security tab, where you can add users or groups to the account and change permissions for users and groups that already exist or that you have added. You may also have to change the dial-in configuration as well as allow or deny dial-in access using the computer.

Troubleshooting Computer Accounts

As an administrator, you may see a variety of problems related to computer accounts. When you are joining a computer to a domain, you may experience problems due to incorrect network settings. The computer joining the domain must be able to communicate with the domain controller in the domain. You can resolve connectivity problems by configuring the computer's local area network connection settings appropriately for the domain to which you are connecting. Be sure to check the IP address, default gateway, and DNS server settings.

Another common problem is related to insufficient permissions The user joining the computer to the domain must have appropriate permissions in the domain. Be sure to use an account with appropriate permissions to join the domain.

After a computer is joined to a domain, you sometimes may see problems with the computer password or trust between the computer and the domain. Diagnosing a password/trust problem is fairly straightforward. If you try to access or browse resources in the domain and are prompted for a user name and password when you normally are not, you may have a password/trust issue with the computer account. For example, if you are trying to connect to a remote computer in Computer Management, and you are repeatedly prompted for a user name and password where you weren't previously, the computer account password should probably be reset.

You can verify a password/trust problem by checking the System event log. Look for an error with event ID 3210 generated by the NETLOGON service. The related error message should read as follows:

```
This computer could not authenticate with RESOURCENAME, a Windows domain controller
for domain DOMAINNAME, and therefore this computer might deny logon requests. This
inability to authenticate might be caused by another computer on the same network
using the same name or the password for this computer account is not recognized. If
this message appears again, contact your system administrator.
```

As part of the troubleshooting process, you should always check the status of the account in Active Directory Users And Computers. A disabled account has a white circle with a down arrow. A deleted account will no longer be listed, and you won't be able to search for and find it in the directory. If a user was trying to connect to a resource on a remote computer, the computer to which they are connecting should have a related error or warning event in the event logs.

If the related computer account is disabled or deleted, you will be denied access to remote resources when connecting to those resources from this computer. As an example, if you are trying to access FileServer75 from CustServicePC83 you will be denied access if the computer account is disabled or deleted. The system event log on the remote computer (FileServer75) should log related NETLOGON errors specifically related to the computer account, such as the following with event ID 5722:

```
The session setup from the computer CORPPC18 failed to authenticate. The name(s) of
the account(s) referenced in the security database is CORPPC18$. The following error
occurred: Access is denied.
```

With Kerberos authentication, a computer's system time can affect authentication. If a computer's system time deviates outside the permitted norms set in group policy, the computer will fail authentication.

If you are still experiencing problems, check the computer's group membership and the container in which it is located in Active Directory. Computer accounts, like user accounts, can be made members of specific groups and are placed in a specific container in Active Directory. The group membership of a computer determines many permissions with regard to security and resource access. Changing a computer's group membership can significantly affect security and resource access. The container in which a computer is placed determines how Group Policy is applied to the computer. Moving a computer to a different container or OU can significantly affect the way policy settings are applied.

G roup Policy is designed to simplify administration by allowing administrators to configure user and computer settings in Active Directory Domain Services and then have those policies automatically applied to computers and enforced for computer and user accounts throughout an organization. Not only does this provide central management of computers, it also helps to automate key administrative tasks. Using Group Policy, you can accomplish the following tasks:

- Configure security policies for account lockout, passwords, Kerberos, and auditing

- Redirect special folders such as a user's Documents folder to centrally managed network shares

- Lock down computer desktop configurations

- Define logon, logoff, shutdown, and startup scripts

- Automate the installation of application software

- Maintain Microsoft Internet Explorer and configure standard settings

Some of these features such as security policies and folder redirection have been discussed in previous chapters. Other features are discussed in this chapter. The focus of this chapter, however, is on the management of Group Policy, which is the most challenging aspect of implementing Group Policy in an organization.

> **Note**
>
> Group Policy settings for Windows Server 2008 have changed considerably. Under the Computer Configuration and User Configuration nodes, you find two new nodes: Policies and Preferences. Settings for general policies are listed under the Policies node. Settings for general preferences are listed under the Preferences node. When referencing settings under the Policies node, I'll use shortcut references, such as User Configuration\Administrative Templates\Windows Components rather than User Configuration\Policies\Administrative Templates: Policy Definitions\Windows Components. This shortcut reference tells you the policy setting being discussed is under User Configuration rather than Computer Configuration and can be found under Administrative Templates\Windows Components.

Understanding Group Policy

You can think of Group Policy as a set of rules that help you manage users and computers. Like any set of rules, Group Policy is effective only under certain conditions. You can use Group Policy to manage servers running Microsoft Windows 2000 Server and later as well as client workstations running Windows 2000 and later. You cannot use Group Policy to manage Windows NT, Windows 95, Windows 98, or Windows Me.

> **Note**
>
> Like Active Directory, Group Policy has gone through several revisions. As a result of these revisions, some policies work only with a version of the Windows operating system that is compatible with a particular revision. For example, some group policies are compatible with Windows 2000, Windows XP Professional, Windows Vista, Windows Server 2003 and Windows Server 2008, while others are compatible only with Windows XP Professional and Windows Server 2003 or with Windows Vista and Windows Server 2008. You can check compatibility when you are editing individual policy settings.

Local and Active Directory Group Policy

Two types of group policies are available. The first type is local group policy, which is stored locally on individual computers in the %SystemRoot%\System32\GroupPolicy folder and applies only to a particular computer. Every computer running Windows 2000 or later has one or more local group policies. For a computer in a workgroup, local group policy is the only group policy available. A computer in a domain also has a local group policy, but it is not the only group policy available, and this is where the second type of group policy, called Active Directory group policy (or more commonly just "group policy"), comes into the picture.

Active Directory group policy physical components called Group Policy Template (GPT) are stored in the Sysvol folder. This folder is used by Active Directory for replicating policies and is represented logically as an object called a Group Policy object (GPO). A GPO is simply a container for the policies you configure and their settings that can be linked to sites, domains, and organizational units (OUs) in your Active Directory structure. You can create multiple GPOs, and by linking those objects to different locations in your Active Directory structure, you can apply the related policy settings to the users and computers in those Active Directory containers.

When you create a domain, two Active Directory group policies are created:

- **Default Domain Controllers Policy GPO** A default GPO created for the Domain Controllers OU and applicable to all domain controllers in a domain as long as they are members of this OU.

- **Default Domain Policy GPO** A default GPO that is created for and linked to the domain within Active Directory.

You can create additional GPOs as necessary and link them to the sites, domains, and OUs you've created. Linking a GPO to Active Directory structure is how you apply Group Policy. For example, you could create a GPO called Technology Policy and then link it to the Technology OU. The policy then applies to that OU.

Group Policy Settings

Group Policy applies only to users and computers. Although groups can be used to specify to which users a particular policy applies, the actual policies are applied only to members of these groups. Group Policy settings are divided into two categories: Computer Configuration and User Configuration. Computer Configuration contains settings that apply to computers. User Configuration contains settings that apply to user accounts.

Figure 36-1 shows the Default Domain Policy for a computer. As you can see in the figure, both Computer Configuration–related and User Configuration–related settings are divided into three major classes, each of which contains several subclasses of settings:

- **Software Settings** Allow you to install software on computers and then maintain it by installing patches or upgrades. You can also uninstall software.

- **Windows Settings** Allow you to manage key Windows settings for both computers and users, including scripts and security. For users, you can also manage Remote Installation Services, folder redirection, and Internet Explorer maintenance.

- **Administrative Templates** Allow you to control Registry settings that configure the operating system, Windows components, and applications. Administrative Templates are implemented for specific operating system versions.

Chapter 36

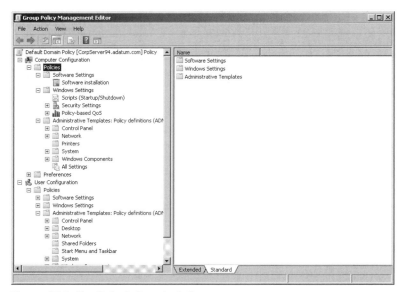

Figure 36-1 The Default Domain Policy.

Group Policy Architecture

Within the Windows operating system, the components of Group Policy have separate server and client implementations (see Figure 36-2). Each Group Policy client
has client-side extensions that are used to interpret and apply Group Policy settings.
The client-side extensions are implemented as dynamic-link libraries (DLLs) that are
installed with the operating system. The main DLL for processing Administrative Templates is Userenv.dll.

The Group Policy engine running on a client triggers the processing of policy when
one of two events occurs: either the system is started or a user logs on to the computer.
When a system is started and the network connection is initialized, computer policy
settings are applied.

Administrators and others delegated permissions in Group Policy can use the Group
Policy Management Editor to manage Group Policy. This snap-in for the Microsoft
Management Console (MMC) provides the three top-level classes (Software Settings,
Windows Settings, and Administrative Templates) that can be managed and makes use
of a number of extensions. These extensions provide the functionality that allows you
to configure various Group Policy settings. Some client-side extensions don't have specific implementations on the server because they are Registry-based and can be configured through Administrative Templates.

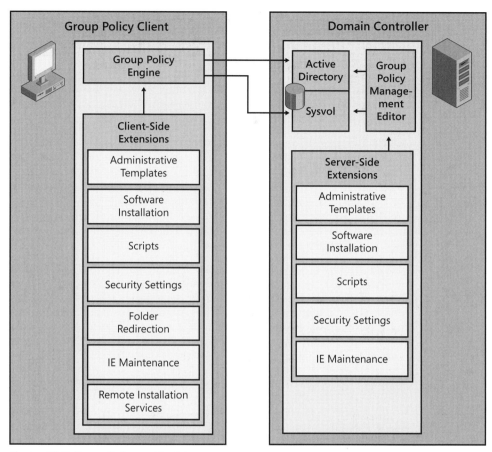

Figure 36-2 Group Policy architecture.

Although GPOs are represented logically in Active Directory and replicated through normal replication, most server-side Group Policy components are represented on the Sysvol as physical files. The default location for the Sysvol folder is %SystemRoot%\Sysvol with the subfolder %SystemRoot%\Sysvol\sysvol shared as Sysvol. Within the shared Sysvol folder, you'll find subfolders organized by domain and the globally unique identifier (GUID) of each GPO created in a particular domain.

Administrative Templates

Windows Vista and Windows Server 2008 introduce a new format for displaying the Registry-based policy settings in the Administrative Templates. Registry-based policy settings are now defined using a standards-based, XML file format, called ADMX. This new format replaces the ADM format previously used with Windows XP Professional and Windows Server 2003.

You can edit GPOs using ADMX files only on computers running Windows Vista and Windows Server 2008. The reason for this is that Windows Vista and Windows Server 2008 have new versions of the standard policy editors that have been updated to work with ADMX. That said, the policy editors automatically read and display Administrative Templates policy settings from both the ADMX and ADM files. This means any custom ADM files you've created will still be available. However, the policy editors will exclude ADM files that were included by default in earlier releases of Windows because the ADMX files supersede these files.

ADMX files are divided into language-neutral files ending with the .admx file extension and language-specific files ending with the .adml extension. The language-neutral files ensure that a GPO has identical core policies. The language-specific files allow policies to be viewed and edited in multiple languages. Because the language-neutral files store the core settings, policies can be edited in any language for which a computer is configured, thus allowing one user to view and edit policies in English and another to view and edit policies in Spanish, for example. The mechanism that determines the language used is the language pack installed on the computer.

Unlike ADM files, ADMX files are not stored in individual GPOs by default. Language-neutral ADMX files are installed on computers running Windows Vista and Windows Server 2008 in the %SystemRoot%\PolicyDefinitions folder. Language-specific ADMX files are installed on computers running Windows Vista and Windows Server 2008 in the %SystemRoot%\PolicyDefinitions\LanguageCulture folder. Each subfolder is named after the appropriate International Organization for Standardization (ISO) language/culture name, such as en-US for US English.

When you start a policy editor, it automatically reads in ADMX files from the policy definitions folders. Because of this, you can copy ADMX files that you want to use to the appropriate policy definitions folder to make them available when you are editing GPOs. If the policy editor is running when you copy the file or files, you must restart the policy editor to force it to read in the file or files.

Because of these changes, only the current state of a setting is stored in the GPO and the details related to the settings are stored in the ADMX files. This reduces the amount of storage space used as the number of GPOs increases and also reduces the amount of data being replicated throughout the enterprise. As long as you edit GPOs using Windows Vista or Windows Server 2008, new GPOs will contain neither ADM nor ADMX files inside the GPO.

Implementing Group Policy

As discussed previously, there are two types of Group Policy: local group policy and Active Directory group policy. Local group policy applies to a local machine only, and there is only one local GPO per local machine. Active Directory group policy, on the other hand, can be implemented separately for sites, domains, and OUs.

In an effort to streamline management of Group Policy, Microsoft removed management features from Active Directory–related tools and moved to a primary console called the

Group Policy Management Console (GPMC). The GPMC is a feature that you can add to any installation of Windows Server 2008 by using the Add Features Wizard. The GPMC is also included with Windows Vista and available as a download from the Microsoft Web site. After you add the GPMC to a server, it is available on the Administrative Tools menu.

When you want to edit a GPO in the GPMC, the GPMC opens the Group Policy Management Editor, which you use to manage the policy settings. Also available are the Group Policy Starter GPO Editor and Local Group Policy Object Editor. You'll use the Group Policy Starter GPO Editor to create and manage starter Group Policy objects, which are meant to provide a starting point for new policy objects that you'll use throughout your organization. When you create a new policy object, you can specify a starter GPO as the source or basis of the new object. You'll use the Local Group Policy Object Editor to create and manage policy objects for the local computer as opposed to those settings for an entire site, domain, or organizational unit.

When you use any of these tools to create a new GPO or modify an existing GPO in Active Directory (but not with local policy), the related changes are made on the domain controller acting as the PDC emulator if it is available. The reason the PDC emulator is used is so that there is a central point of contact for GPO creation and editing, and this in turn helps to ensure that only one administrator is granted access to edit a particular GPO at a time. This also simplifies replication of the changes because changes are always replicated from the same point of origin—the PDC emulator. However, if the PDC emulator cannot be reached or is otherwise unavailable when you try to work with GPOs, you are given the opportunity to choose to make changes on the domain controller to which you are currently connected or any available domain controller.

Working with Local Group Policy

Windows Vista and Windows Server 2008 support multiple Local Group Policy objects (LGPOs) on a single computer (as long as the computer is not a domain controller). Previously, computers had only one LGPO. Windows Vista and Windows Server 2008 allow you to:

- Have a top-level LGPO referred to simply as Local Group Policy. Local Group Policy is the only LGPO that allows both computer configuration and user configuration settings to be applied to all users of the computer.

- Assign a different LGPO to each general user type. There are two general user types: Administrators, which includes only the user accounts that are members of the local Administrators group, and Non-Administrators, which includes only the user accounts that are not members of the local Administrators group. Administrators and Non-Administrators Local Group Policy contain only user configuration settings.

- Assign a different LGPO to each local user. User-Specific Group Policy is applied to a specific user or group and contains only user configuration settings.

These multiple LGPOs act as policy layers and are processed by Windows in the following order:

1. Local Group Policy

2. Administrators and Non-Administrators Group Policy

3. User-Specific Local Group Policy

When computers are being used in a stand-alone configuration rather than a domain configuration, you might find that multiple LGPOs are useful because you no longer have to explicitly disable or remove settings that interfere with your ability to manage a computer before performing administrator tasks. Instead, you can implement one LGPO for administrators and another LGPO for non-administrators. In a domain configuration, however, you might not want to use multiple LGPOs. In domains, most computers and users already have multiple Group Policy objects applied to them—adding multiple Local Group Policy objects to this already varied mix can make managing Group Policy confusing. This is especially true when you consider that a setting in one LGPO can possibly conflict with a setting in another LGPO, which, in turn, could conflict with domain GPO settings.

Windows resolves conflicts in settings by overwriting any previous setting with the last read and most current setting (unless blocking or enforcing is enabled). Regardless, the final setting applied is the one that Windows uses. When Windows resolves conflicts, only the enabled or disabled state of settings matters. If a setting is set as Not Configured, this has no effect on the state of the setting from a previous policy application. You can simplify domain administration by disabling processing of all Local Group Policy objects on computers running Windows Vista and Windows Server 2008. You do this by enabling the Turn Off Local Group Policy Objects Processing policy setting in a domain Group Policy object. In Group Policy, this setting is located under Computer Configuration\Administrative Templates\System\Group Policy. When this setting is enabled, as shown in Figure 36-3, computers in the domain process only domain-based policy.

You can access the top-level Local Group Policy object in several ways. One way is to type the following command at a command prompt:

```
gpedit.msc /gpcomputer:"%computername%"
```

This command starts the Group Policy Object Editor in an MMC and tells the Group Policy Object Editor to target the local computer. Here, %ComputerName% is an environment variable that sets the name of the local computer and must be enclosed in double quotation marks as shown. To access Local Group Policy on a remote computer, type the following command at a command prompt:

```
gpedit.msc /gpcomputer: "RemoteComputer"
```

where *RemoteComputer* is the host name or fully qualified domain name (FQDN) of the remote computer, such as:

```
gpedit.msc /gpcomputer: "CorpServer08"
```

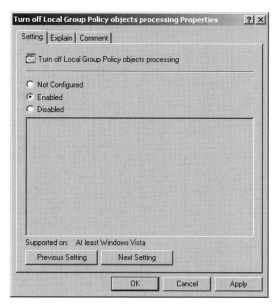

Figure 36-3 Simplify administration by configuring processing of only domain policy.

You can also manage the top-level local policy on a computer by following these steps:

1. Click Start, type **mmc** into the Search box, and then press Enter.

2. In the Microsoft Management Console, choose File and then choose Add/Remove Snap-In.

3. In the Add Or Remove Snap-Ins dialog box, select Group Policy Object Editor and then click Add.

4. If you want to work with local policy on the computer, click Finish because the local computer is the default object. Click OK.

5. If you want to work with local policy on another computer, click Browse. In the Browse For A Group Policy Object dialog box, on the Computers tab, select Another Computer and then click Browse again.

If you want to work with security settings only in the top-level Local Group Policy object, you can use the Local Security Policy console. Click Start, All Programs, Administrative Tools, and then select Local Security Policy.

In the Group Policy Object Editor and Local Security Policy console, you can configure security settings that apply to users and the local computer itself. Any policy changes you make are applied to that computer the next time Group Policy is refreshed. The settings you can manage locally depend on whether the computer is a member of a domain or a workgroup, and they include the following:

- Account policies for passwords, account lockout, and Kerberos

- Event logging options for configuring log size, access, and retention options for the application, system, and security logs

- Local policies for auditing, user rights assignment, and security options

- Security restriction settings for groups, system services, Registry keys, and the file system

- Security settings for wireless networking, public keys, and Internet Protocol Security (IPSec)

- Software restrictions that specify applications that aren't allowed to run on the computer

Figure 36-4 shows the Local Group Policy Editor. You configure Local Group Policy in the same way that you configure Active Directory–based Group Policy. To apply a policy, you enable it and then configure any additional or optional values as necessary. An enabled policy setting is turned on and active. If don't want a policy to apply, you must disable it. A disabled policy setting is turned off and inactive.

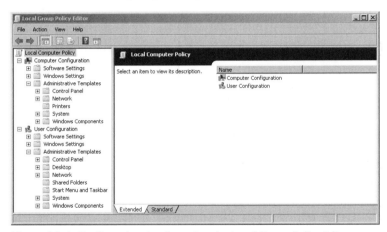

Figure 36-4 Configure local policy using the Local Group Policy Editor.

Working with the Group Policy Management Console

The Group Policy Management Console (GPMC) provides an integrated interface for working with GPOs. You must install the GPMC using the Add Features Wizard. Alternatively, you can install the GPMC by entering the following command at an elevated command prompt: **servermanagercmd –install gpmc**. When you install the GPMC, several related snap-ins and tools are installed as well. The sections that follow provide an overview of using the GPMC.

Using the Group Policy Management Console

You can run the Group Policy Management Console from the Administrative Tools menu. Click Start, Programs or All Programs, Administrative Tools, and Group Policy Management Console.

When you start the Group Policy Management Console, the tool connects to Active Directory running on the domain controller acting as the PDC emulator for your logon domain and obtains a list of all GPOs and OUs in that domain. It does this using Lightweight Directory Access Protocol (LDAP) to access the directory store and Server Message Block (SMB) protocol to access the Sysvol. The result, as shown in Figure 36-5, is that for each domain to which you are connected, you have all the related GPOs and OUs available to work with in one location.

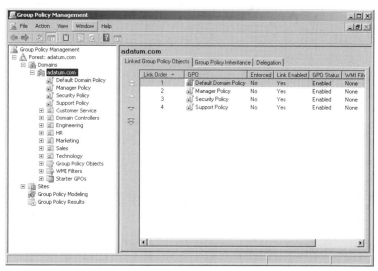

Figure 36-5 The Group Policy Management Console.

Accessing Forests, Domains, and Sites in the Group Policy Management Console

Working with forests, domains, and sites in the Group Policy Management Console is fairly straightforward, as follows:

- **Accessing forests** The forest root is listed for each forest to which you are connected. You can connect to additional forests by right-clicking the Group Policy Management node in the console tree and selecting Add Forest. In the Add Forest dialog box, shown in the following screen, type the name of a domain in the forest to which you want to connect, and then click OK. As long as there is an external trust to the domain, you can establish the connection and obtain forest information—even if you don't have a forest trust with the entire forest.

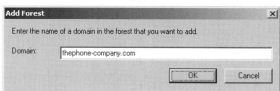

- **Accessing domains** You can view the domain to which you are connected in a forest by expanding the forest node and then expanding the related Domains node. By default, you are connected to your logon domain in the current forest. If you want to work with other domains in a particular forest, right-click the Domains node in the designated forest, and then select Show Domains. In the Show Domains dialog box, which has the same options as the Show Sites dialog box, select the options for the domains you want to work with and clear the options for the domains you don't want to work with. Then click OK.

- **Accessing sites** Because Group Policy is primarily configured for domains and OUs, sites are not shown by default in the GPMC. If you want to work with the sites in a particular forest, right-click the Sites node in the designated forest, and then select Show Sites. In the Show Sites dialog box, shown in the following screen, select the check boxes for the sites you want to work with and clear the check boxes for the sites you don't want to work with. Then click OK.

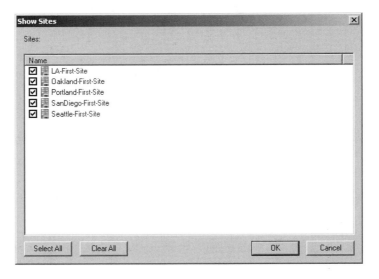

Creating and Linking a New GPO in the Group Policy Management Console

In the Group Policy Management Console, you can create and link a new GPO by completing the following steps:

1. Access the domain or OU you want to work with in the Group Policy Management Console. Do this by expanding the forest node and the related Domains node as necessary, with the following guidelines:

   - If you select a domain node, you see a list of the current GPOs and OUs in the domain.

   - If you select an OU node, you see a list of the current GPOs for the OU (if any).

2. Right-click the domain or OU node, and select Create A GPO In This Domain, And Link It Here.

3. In the New GPO dialog box, type a descriptive name for the GPO, such as Support Policy. If you want to use a starter GPO as the source for the initial settings, select the starter GPO to use from the Source Starter GPO drop-down list. Click OK.

> **Note**
>
> The Group Policy Management Console doesn't let you create and link a new GPO for sites. You can, however, use the Group Policy Management Console to link a site to an existing GPO. For more information, see "Linking to an Existing GPO in the Group Policy Management Console" on page 1246.

The new GPO is added to the current list of linked GPOs. If you select the domain or OU node, you can change the preference order of the GPO by selecting it on the Linked Group Policy Objects tab and then clicking the Move Link Up or Move Link Down buttons to change the preference order (see Figure 36-6).

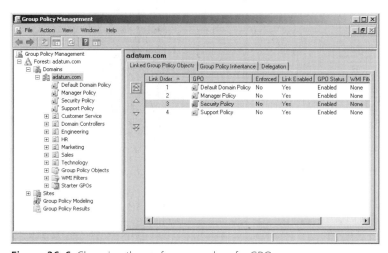

Figure 36-6 Changing the preference order of a GPO.

Editing an Existing GPO in the Group Policy Management Console

In the Group Policy Management Console, you can edit an existing GPO linked to the selected container by right-clicking it and then selecting Edit. This displays the Group Policy Object Editor. You can then make changes to Group Policy as necessary. The changes will be applied the next time Active Directory is refreshed, according to the inheritance and preference options used by Active Directory.

Linking to an Existing GPO in the Group Policy Management Console

Linking a GPO to a container applies the object to the container. In the Group Policy Management Console, you can link an existing GPO to a domain, OU, or site by completing the following steps:

1. Access the domain or OU you want to work with in the Group Policy Management Console. Do this by expanding the forest node and the related Domains node as necessary.

2. Right-click the domain, OU, or site node, and select Link An Existing GPO.

3. In the Select GPO dialog box, shown in Figure 36-7, select the GPO to use, and then click OK.

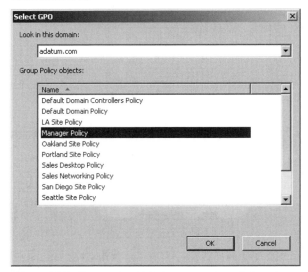

Figure 36-7 Choose the GPO that you want to link to the currently selected container.

4. The linked policy will be applied the next time Active Directory is refreshed, according to the inheritance and preference options used by Active Directory.

Working with Starter GPOs

Any time you create a new GPO in the Group Policy Management Console, you can base the new GPO on a starter GPO. Because the settings of the starter GPO are then imported into the new GPO, this allows you to use a starter GPO to define the base configuration settings for a new GPO. In the enterprise, you'll want to create different categories of starter GPOs based on the users and computers they will be used with, or based on the required security configurations.

To create a starter GPO, follow these steps:

1. In the Group Policy Management Console, expand the entry for the forest you want to work with, and then double-click the related Domains node to expand it.

2. Right-click the Starter GPOs node, and then select New. In the New Starter GPO dialog box, type a descriptive name for the new starter GPO, such as Standard User GPO. If desired, enter comments describing the GPO's purpose. Click OK.

3. Right-click the new GPO, and then choose Edit. In the Group Policy Object Editor, configure policy settings as necessary, and then close the Group Policy Object Editor.

Deleting an Existing GPO in the Group Policy Management Console

In the Group Policy Management Console, you use different techniques to remove GPO links and the GPOs themselves, as follows:

- If you want to remove a link to a GPO, you right-click the GPO in the container to which it is linked and then select Delete. When prompted to confirm that you want to remove the link, click OK.

- If you want to remove a GPO and all links to the object, expand the forest, the Domains node, and the Group Policy Objects node. Right-click the GPO, and then select Delete. When prompted to confirm that you want to remove the GPO and all links to it, click OK.

Working with the Default Group Policy Objects

When you create a domain, Windows creates the Default Domain Controllers Policy GPO and the Default Domain Policy GPO. These default GPOs are essential to the proper operation and processing of Group Policy. By default, in the precedence order of GPOs, the Default Domain Controllers Policy GPO is the highest-precedence GPO linked to the Domain Controllers OU and the Default Domain Policy GPO is the highest-precedence GPO linked to the domain.

Although the Default Domain Policy GPO is a complete policy set that includes settings for managing the many policy areas we've discussed previously, this GPO isn't meant for general management of Group Policy. You should edit the Default Domain Policy GPO only to manage the default settings for Account Policies (and three specific policies, which I'll specify in a moment).

The areas of Account Policy you manage through the Default Domain Policy GPO are as follows:

- Password Policy—Determines the default password policies for domain controllers, such as the password history and minimum password length settings.

- Account Lockout Policy—Determines the default account lockout policies for domain controllers, such as the account lockout duration and account lockout threshold.

- Kerberos Policy—Determines default Kerberos policies for domain controllers, such as the maximum tolerance for computer clock synchronization.

The Default Domain Policy GPO is the only GPO through which Account Policies should be set. To manage other areas of policy, you should create a new GPO and link it to the domain or an appropriate OU within the domain. This occurs because only the Account Policy settings for the GPO linked to the domain level with the highest precedence in Active Directory are applied, and, by default, this is the Default Domain Policy GPO.

A few additional policy settings should be managed through the GPO linked to the domain level and having highest precedence as well. These policies, located under Computer Configuration, Windows Settings, Security Settings, Local Policies, Security Options in Group Policy, are as follows:

- **Accounts: Rename Administrator Account** Configure this policy setting if you want to rename the Administrator account throughout the domain. This sets a new name for the built-in Administrator account so that it is better protected from malicious users. It is important to point out that this specifically affects the logon name of the account and not the display name. The display name will continue to be set to Administrator or whatever else you've set it to. Further, if you or another administrator changes the logon name for this account through Active Directory Users And Computers, the logon name will automatically change back to what is set in policy the next time Group Policy is refreshed.

- **Accounts: Rename Guest Account** Configure this policy setting if you want to rename the Guest account throughout the domain. This sets a new name for the built-in Guest account so that it is better protected from malicious users. It is important to point out that this specifically affects the logon name of the account and not the display name. The display name will continue to be set to Guest or whatever else you've set it to. Further, if you or another administrator changes the logon name for this account through Active Directory Users And Computers, the logon name will automatically change back to what is set in policy the next time Group Policy is refreshed.

- **Network Access: Allow Anonymous SID/Name Translation** Determines whether an anonymous user can request security identifier (SID) attributes for another user. This setting is disabled by default in most configurations. If this setting is enabled, a malicious user could use the well-known Administrators SID to obtain the real name of the built-in Administrator account, even if the account has been renamed.

- **Network Security: Force Logoff When Logon Hours Expire** Configure this policy setting if you want to force users to log off from the domain when logon hours expire. For example, if you have set the logon hours from 7 A.M. to 7 P.M. for the user, the user will be forced to log off at 8 P.M.

The Default Domain Controllers Policy GPO is designed to ensure that all domain controllers in a specified domain have the same security settings. This is important because all domain controllers in an Active Directory domain are equal and if there were different security settings on each domain controller, different domain controllers might behave differently and this would be bad, bad, bad. If one domain controller has a specific policy setting, this policy setting should be applied to all domain controllers to ensure consistent behavior across a domain.

Because all domain controllers are placed in the Domain Controllers OU by default, any security setting changes you make will apply to all domain controllers by default. You should use the Default Domain Controllers Policy GPO only to set user rights and audit policies. Audit Policy determines default auditing policies for domain controllers, such as logging event success, failure, or both. User Rights Assignment determines the default user rights assignment for domain controllers, such as the Log On As A Service and Allow Log On Locally rights.

> **CAUTION**
>
> If you move a domain controller out of the Domain Controllers OU, you could adversely affect domain management, which also could lead to inconsistent behavior during logon and authentication. To prevent problems, any time you move a domain controller out of the Domain Controllers OU you should carefully manage its security settings thereafter. As an example, whenever you make security changes to the Default Domain Controllers Policy GPO, you should ensure that those security changes are applied to domain controllers stored in OUs other than the Domain Controllers OU.

Managing Group Policy Through Delegation

In Active Directory, administrators are automatically granted permissions for performing different Group Policy management tasks. Other individuals can be granted such permissions through delegation. You delegate to allow a user who is not a member of Enterprise Admins or Domain Admins to perform any management tasks.

Managing GPO Creation Rights

In Active Directory, administrators have the ability to create GPOs in a domain, and anyone who has created a GPO in a domain has the right to manage that GPO. You can determine who can create GPOs in a domain by following these steps:

1. In the Group Policy Management Console, expand the entry for the forest you want to work with, expand the related Domains node, and then select the Group Policy Objects node.

2. As shown in Figure 36-8, the users and groups who can create GPOs in the selected domain are listed on the Delegation tab.

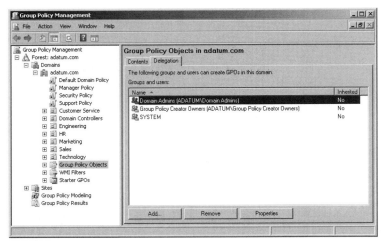

Figure 36-8 Determining creation rights for GPOs

You can delegate permission to create GPOs (and thus implicitly grant them the ability to manage the GPOs they've created). To grant GPO creation permission to a user or group, follow these steps:

1. In the Group Policy Management Console, expand the entry for the forest you want to work with, expand the related Domains node, and then select the Group Policy Objects node.

2. In the right pane, select the Delegation tab. The current GPO creation permissions for individual users and groups are listed. To grant the GPO creation permission to another user or group, click Add.

3. In the Select User, Computer, Or Group dialog box, select the user or group and then click OK.

4. The options on the Delegation tab are updated as appropriate. If you later want to remove the GPO creation permission, access the Delegation tab, select the user or group, and then click Remove.

Reviewing Group Policy Management Privileges

The Group Policy Management Console provides several ways to determine who can manage Group Policy. You can determine Group Policy permissions for a specific site, domain, or OU by following these steps:

1. In the Group Policy Management Console, expand the entry for the forest you want to work with, and then expand the related Domains or Sites node as appropriate.

2. When you select the domain, site, or OU you want to work with, the right pane is updated with several tabs. Select the Delegation tab as shown in Figure 36-9.

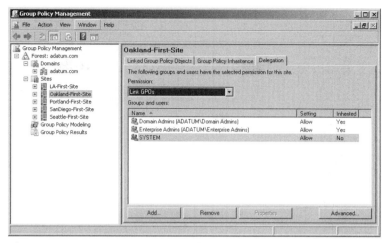

Figure 36-9 Determining permissions for a site, domain, or OU.

3. In the Permission list, select the permission you want to check. The options are:

   ○ **Link GPOs** The user or group can create and manage links to GPOs in the selected site, domain, or OU.

   ○ **Perform Group Policy Modeling Analyses** The user or group can determine the Resultant Set of Policy (RSoP) for the purposes of planning.

   ○ **Read Group Policy Results Data** The user or group can determine the RSoP that is currently being applied, for the purposes of verification or logging.

4. The individual users or groups with the selected permissions are listed under Groups And Users.

You can determine which users or groups have access to a particular GPO and what permissions have been granted to them by following these steps:

1. In the Group Policy Management Console, expand the entry for the forest you want to work with, expand the related Domains node, and then select the Group Policy Objects node.

2. When you select the GPO whose permissions you want to check, the right pane is updated with several tabs. Select the Delegation tab as shown in Figure 36-10.

3. The permissions for individual users and groups are listed. You'll see three general types of allowed permissions:

   ○ **Read** Enables the user or group to view the GPO and its settings.

   ○ **Edit Settings** Enables the user or group to view the GPO and its settings. The user or group can also change settings—but not delete the GPO or modify its security.

○ **Edit Settings, Delete, Modify Security** Enables the user or group to view the GPO and its settings. The user or group can also change settings, delete the GPO, and modify its security.

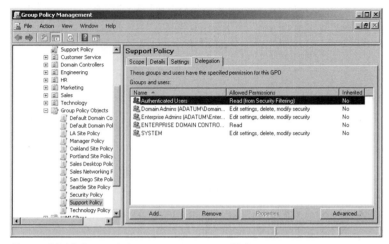

Figure 36-10 Determining permissions on a GPO.

Delegating Group Policy Management Privileges

You can allow a non-administrative user or a group (including users and groups from other domains) to work with a domain, site, or OU GPO by granting one of three specific permissions:

- **Read** Permits the user or group to view the GPO and its settings.

- **Edit Settings** Permits the user or group to view the GPO and its settings. The user or group can also change settings—but not delete the GPO or modify its security.

- **Edit Settings, Delete, Modify Security** Permits the user or group to view the GPO and its settings. The user or group can also change settings, delete the GPO, and modify its security.

You can grant these permissions to a user or group by following these steps:

1. In the Group Policy Management Console, expand the entry for the forest you want to work with, expand the related Domains node, and then expand the Group Policy Objects node.

2. Select the GPO you want to work with in the left pane. In the right pane, select the Delegation tab.

3. The current permissions for individual users and groups are listed. To grant permissions to another user or group, click Add.

4. In the Select User, Computer, Or Group dialog box, select the user or group and then click OK.

5. In the Add Group Or User dialog box, select the permission to grant: Read, Edit Settings, or Edit Settings, Delete, Modify Security. Click OK.

6. The options of the Delegation tab are updated to reflect the permissions granted. If you later want to remove this permission, access the Delegation tab, select the user or group, and then click Remove.

Delegating Privileges for Links and RSoP

You can allow a non-administrative user or a group (including users and groups from other domains) to manage GPO links and RSoP. The related permissions can be granted in any combination and are defined as follows:

- **Link GPOs** Permits the user or group to create and manage links to GPOs in the selected site, domain, or OU.

- **Perform Group Policy Modeling Analyses** Permits the user or group to determine RSoP for the purposes of planning.

- **Read Group Policy Results Data** Permits the user or group to determine RSoP that is currently being applied, for the purposes of verification or logging.

You can grant these permissions to a user or group by following these steps:

1. In the Group Policy Management Console, expand the entry for the forest you want to work with, and then expand the related Domains or Sites node as appropriate.

2. In the left pane, select the domain, site, or OU you want to work with. In the right pane, select the Delegation tab.

3. In the Permission list, select the permission you want to grant. The options are Link GPOs, Perform Group Policy Modeling Analyses, and Read Group Policy Results Data.

4. The current permissions for individual users and groups are listed. To grant the selected permission to another user or group, click Add.

5. In the Select User, Computer, Or Group dialog box, select the user or group and then click OK.

6. In the Add Group Or User dialog box, specify how the permission should be applied. To apply the permission to the current container and all child containers, select This Container And All Child Containers. To apply the permission only to the current container, select This Container Only. Click OK.

7. The options of the Delegation tab are updated to reflect the permissions granted. If you later want to remove this permission, access the Delegation tab, select the user or group, and then click Remove.

Managing Group Policy Inheritance and Processing

GPOs can be linked to sites, domains, and OUs in Active Directory. When you create and link a GPO to one of these containers in Active Directory, the GPO is applied to the user and computer objects in that container according to the inheritance and preference options used by Active Directory. Computer-related policies are processed during startup of the operating system. User-related policies are processed when a user logs on to a computer. After they are applied, Group Policy settings are automatically refreshed at a specific interval to ensure that they are current. Group Policy settings can also be refreshed manually.

Group Policy Inheritance

Active Directory uses inheritance to determine how Group Policy is applied. By default, Group Policy settings are inherited from top-level containers by lower-level containers. The order of inheritance goes from the site level to the domain level to the OU level. This means the Group Policy settings for a site are passed down to the domains within the site, and the settings for a domain are passed down to the OUs within that domain.

When multiple group policies are in place, the policies are applied in the following order:

- **Local group policies** Each computer running Windows 2000 or later has local group policy. The local policy is applied first.

- **Site group policies** Policies linked to sites are processed second. If there are multiple site policies, they are processed synchronously in the listed preference order.

- **Domain group policies** Policies linked to domains are processed third. If there are multiple domain policies, they are processed synchronously in the listed preference order.

- **OU group policies** Policies linked to top-level OUs are processed fourth. If there are multiple top-level OU policies, they are processed synchronously in the listed preference order.

- **Child OU group policies** Policies linked to child OUs are processed fifth. If there are multiple child OU policies, they are processed synchronously in the listed preference order. When there are multiple levels of child OUs, policies for higher-level OUs are applied first and policies for the lower-level OUs are applied next.

The order in which policies are applied determines which policy settings take effect if multiple policies modify the same settings. Most policies have three configuration options: Not Configured, Enabled, and Disabled. The default state of most policies is Not Configured, meaning the policy setting is not configured and does not apply. If a policy is set to Enabled, the policy is enforced and does apply to users and computers that are subject to the GPO. If a policy is set to Disabled, the policy is not enforced and does not apply to users and computers that are subject to the GPO.

To override a policy that is enabled in a higher-level container, you can specifically disable it in a lower-level policy. For example, if the user policy Prohibit Access To The Control Panel is enabled for a site, users in the site should not be able to access Control Panel. However, if domain policy specifically disables the user policy Prohibit Access To The Control Panel, users in the domain would be able to access Control Panel. On the other hand, if the domain policy was set to Not Configured, the policy setting would not be modified and would be inherited as normal from the higher-level container.

To override a policy that is disabled in a higher-level container, you can specifically enable it in a lower-level policy. For example, if the user policy Force Classic Control Panel Style is disabled for a domain, users in the domain would be able to choose whether they wanted to use Classic or Simple Control Panel. However, if the Engineering OU policy specifically enables the user policy Force Classic Control Panel Style, users in the Engineering OU would be able to use only the Classic Control Panel style. Again, if the OU policy was set to Not Configured instead, the policy setting would not be modified and would be inherited as normal from the higher-level container.

Changing Link Order and Precedence

The order of inheritance for Group Policy goes from the site level to the domain level, then to each nested OU level. When there are multiple policy objects linked to a particular level, the link order determines the order in which policy settings are applied. Linked policy objects are always applied in link ranking order. Lower-ranking policy objects are processed first and then higher-ranking policy objects are processed.

In Figure 36-11, these policies will be processed from the lowest link order to the highest. Here the Technology Policy (with link order 2) will be processed before the Manager Policy (with link order 1). Because Manager Policy settings are processed after Technology Policy settings, Manager Policy settings have precedence and take priority.

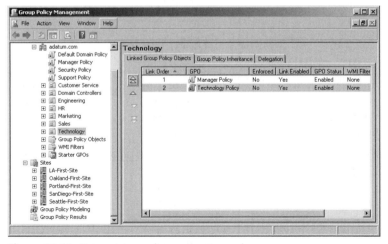

Figure 36-11 Determining policy processing order.

To view all inherited GPOs, click the Group Policy Inheritance tab as shown in Figure 36-12. The precedence order shows exactly how policy objects are being processed for a site, domain, or OU. As with link order, lower-ranking policy objects are processed first and then higher-ranking policy objects are processed. Here the Support Policy (with precedence 4) will be processed first, then Security Policy (with precedence 3), and so on. Because Default Domain Policy is processed last, any policy settings configured in this policy object are final and will override those of other policy objects (unless inheritance blocking or enforcing is used).

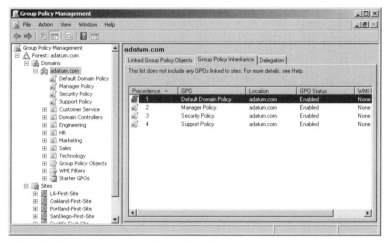

Figure 36-12 Determining order of inheritance.

When multiple policy objects are linked at a specific level, you can easily change the link order (and thus the precedence order) of policy objects linked at that level. Follow these steps:

1. In the Group Policy Management Console, select the container for the site, domain, or OU with which you want to work.

2. In the right pane, the Linked Group Policy Objects tab should be selected by default. Select the policy object with which you want to work.

3. Click the Move Link Up or Move Link Down buttons as appropriate to change the link order of the selected policy object.

4. When you are done changing the link order, confirm that policy objects are being processed in the expected order by checking the precedence order on the Group Policy Inheritance tab.

Overriding Inheritance

As you know, Group Policy settings are inherited from top-level containers by lower-level containers. If multiple policy objects modify the same settings, the order in which the policy objects are applied determines which policy settings take effect. Essentially, the order of inheritance goes from the site level to the domain level to the OU level. This means Group Policy settings for a site are passed down to the domains within the site, and the settings for a domain are passed down to the OUs within that domain.

You can override policy in two key ways:

- **Disable an enabled (and inherited) policy**—When a policy is enabled in a higher-level policy object, you can override inheritance by disabling the policy in a lower-level policy object. By disabling the policy in a lower-level policy you override the policy that is enabled in the higher-level container. For example, if the user policy Prohibit Use Of Internet Connection Sharing On Your DNS Domain is enabled for a site, users in the site should not be able to use Internet Connection Sharing. However, if domain policy specifically disables this user policy, users in the domain would be able to use Internet Connection Sharing. On the other hand, if the domain policy was set to Not Configured, the policy setting would not be modified and would be inherited as normal from the higher-level container.

- **Enable a disabled (and inherited) policy**—When a policy is disabled in a higher-level policy object, you can override inheritance by enabling the policy in a lower-level policy object. By enabling the policy in a lower-level policy you override the policy that is disabled in the higher-level container. For example, if the user policy Allow Shared Folders To Be Published is disabled for a domain, users in the domain would not be able to publish shared folders in Active Directory. However, if the Support Team OU policy specifically enables this user policy, users in the Support Team OU would be able to publish shared folders in Active Directory. Again, if the OU policy was set to Not Configured instead, the policy setting would not be modified and would be inherited as normal from the higher-level container.

Overriding inheritance is a basic technique for changing the way inheritance works. As long as a policy is not blocked or enforced, this technique will achieve the desired effect.

Blocking Inheritance

Sometimes you will want to block inheritance so that no policy settings from higher-level containers are applied to users and computers in a particular container. When inheritance is blocked, only configured policy settings from policy objects linked at that level are applied. This means all GPOs from all high-level containers are blocked (providing there is no policy enforcement).

Domain administrators can use inheritance blocking to block inherited policy settings from the site level. OU administrators can use inheritance blocking to block inherited policy settings from both the domain and the site levels. Here are some examples of inheritance blocking in action:

- You don't want a domain to inherit any site policies so you configure the domain to block inheritance from higher-level containers. Because inheritance is blocked, only the configured policy settings from policy objects linked to the domain are applied. Although blocking inheritance of site policy doesn't affect inheritance of the domain policy objects by OUs, it does mean that OUs in that domain will not inherit site policies either.

- You don't want an OU to inherit any site or domain policies so you configure the OU to block inheritance from higher-level containers. Because inheritance is blocked, only the configured policy settings from policy objects linked to the OU are applied. If the OU contains other OUs, inheritance blocking won't affect inheritance of policy objects linked to this OU, but the child OUs will not inherit site or domain policies.

Using the Group Policy Management Console, you can block inheritance by right-clicking the domain or OU that should not inherit settings from higher-level containers and selecting Block Inheritance. If Block Inheritance is already selected, selecting it again removes the setting. When you block inheritance in the Group Policy Management Console, a blue circle with an exclamation point is added to the container's node in the console tree. The notification icon provides a quick way to tell whether any domain or OU has the Block Inheritance setting enabled.

Enforcing Inheritance

To prevent administrators who have authority over a container from overriding or blocking the inherited Group Policy settings, you can enforce inheritance. When inheritance is enforced, all policy settings from higher-level policy objects are inherited and applied regardless of the policy settings in lower-level policy objects. Thus, enforcement of inheritance is used to supersede overriding and blocking of policy settings.

Forest administrators can use inheritance enforcement to ensure that policy settings from the site level are applied and to prevent overriding or blocking of policy settings by both domain and OU administrators. Domain administrators can use inheritance enforcement to ensure that policy settings from the domain level are applied and prevent overriding or blocking of policy settings by OU administrators. Here are some examples of inheritance enforcement in action:

- As a forest administrator, you want to ensure that domains inherit a particular site policy so you configure the site policy so that inheritance is enforced. Because inheritance is enforced, all policy settings from the site policy are applied regardless of whether domain administrators have tried to override or block policy settings from the site level. Enforcement of the site policy also affects inheritance for OUs in the affected domains. OUs in the affected domains will inherit the site policy regardless of whether overriding or blocking has been used.

- As a domain administrator, you want to ensure that OUs within the domain inherit a particular domain policy so you configure the domain policy so that inheritance is enforced. Because inheritance is enforced, all policy settings from the domain policy are applied regardless of whether OU administrators have tried to override or block policy settings from the domain level. Enforcement of the domain policy also affects inheritance for child OUs within the affected OUs.

Child OUs within the affected OUs will inherit the domain policy regardless of whether overriding or blocking has been used.

Using the Group Policy Management Console, you enforce policy inheritance by expanding the container to which the policy is linked, right-clicking the policy, and then selecting Enforced. If Enforced is already selected, selecting it again removes the enforcement. In the Group Policy Management Console, you can determine which policies are inherited and which policies are enforced in several ways:

- Select a policy object anywhere in the Group Policy Management Console and then view the related Scope tab in the right pane. If the policy is enforced, the Enforced column under Links will have a Yes entry. After you select a policy object, you can right-click a location entry on the Scope tab to display a shortcut menu. This shortcut menu allows you to manage linking and policy enforcement.

- Select a domain or OU container in the Group Policy Management Console and then view the related Group Policy Inheritance tab in the right pane. If the policy is enforced, you'll see an (Enforced) entry in the Precedence column.

Filtering Group Policy Application

By default, GPOs apply to all users and computers in the container to which the GPO is linked. The GPO applies to all users and computers in this way because of the security settings on the GPO, which specify that Authenticated Users have Read permission as well as Apply Group Policy permission. Thus, all users and computers with accounts in the domain are affected by the policy. Permissions are also assigned to administrators and the operating system. All members of the Enterprise Admins and Domain Admins groups as well as the LocalSystem account have permission to edit GPOs and manage their security.

You can modify which users and computers are affected by a particular GPO by changing the accounts for which the Apply Group Policy permission is set. In this way, you can selectively apply a GPO, which is known as filtering Group Policy. For example, say that you create a Technology OU with separate Group Policy objects for users and managers. You want the user GPO to apply to all users who are members of the TechUsers group and the manager GPO to apply to all users who are members of the TechMgrs group. To do this, you must configure the user policy so that the Read and Apply Group Policy permissions apply to the TechUsers group only, and configure the manager policy so that the Read and Apply Group Policy permissions apply to the TechMgrs group only.

Before you selectively apply a GPO, you must carefully consider the types of policies it sets. If the GPO sets computer policies, you must ensure that the computer accounts are included so that the computer reads the GPO and applies it at the startup of networking. If the GPO sets user policies, you must ensure that the groups in which the users are members or the individual user accounts are included so that the Group Policy engine reads the GPO and applies it when users log on.

Use the following guidelines to help you determine how permissions should be configured:

- **Group Policy should be applied to all members of a group** Add the group to the access control list (ACL) for the GPO. Set Read to Allow and set Apply Group Policy to Allow. The Group Policy object will then be applied to all members of the group except those who are members of another group to which Read or Apply Group Policy is set to Deny.

- **Group Policy should not be applied to members of a group** Add the group to the ACL for the GPO. Set Read to Deny and set Apply Group Policy to Deny. The Group Policy object will not be applied to any members of the group regardless of which other groups members belong to.

- **Membership in this group should not determine whether Group Policy is applied** Remove the group from the ACL for the GPO. Or clear both the Allow and Deny check boxes for the Read permission as well as the Apply Group Policy permission. After you do this, membership in the group will determine whether the GPO is applied.

You can selectively apply a GPO by completing the following steps:

1. In the Group Policy Management Console, select the policy in a container to which it is linked or in the Group Policy Objects node.

2. In the details pane, select the Delegation tab, and then click the Advanced button in the lower-right corner of the dialog box. This displays the policy's Security Settings dialog box, as shown in Figure 36-13.

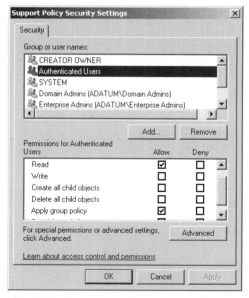

Figure 36-13 Accessing the security settings for a GPO.

3. You can then add or remove groups as necessary. After a group is added, you can select the Allow or Deny check boxes for the Read and Apply Group Policy permissions as necessary.

4. When you are finished configuring the ACL for the GPO, click OK until all open dialog boxes are closed.

Group Policy Processing

Group Policy settings are divided into two categories:

- **Computer Configuration settings** Policies that apply to computer accounts only
- **User Configuration settings** Policies that apply to user accounts only

Normally, Computer Configuration settings are applied during startup of the operating system and User Configuration settings are applied when a user logs on to a computer. The sequence of events is often important in troubleshooting system behavior. The events that take place during startup and logon are as follows:

1. When the client computer starts, networking is started as part of the normal system startup. The computer reads the Registry to determine the Active Directory site in which the computer is located. The computer then sends a query to its primary Domain Name System (DNS) server to determine the Internet Protocol (IP) addresses of domain controllers in the site.

2. When the DNS server replies to the query, the computer connects to a domain controller in the local site. The client computer and domain controller authenticate each other. The client computer then requests a list of all the GPOs that apply to the computer.

3. The domain controller sends a list of GPOs that apply to the computer. The computer processes and applies the GPOs, starting with the local policy and continuing as discussed in "Group Policy Inheritance" on page 1254. It is important to note that only the Computer Configuration settings are sent at this point.

4. After processing computer policies, the computer runs any startup scripts. Startup scripts are hidden from view by default, and if there are multiple startup scripts, the scripts run in sequential order by default. Each script must finish running before the next one can be started. The default timeout for scripts is 600 seconds. Both the synchronous processing of scripts and their timeout value can be modified using Group Policy.

5. When a user logs on to the computer and is validated, the computer loads the user profile, and then requests a list of all the GPOs that apply to the user.

6. The domain controller sends a list of GPOs that apply to the user. The computer processes and applies the GPOs, starting with the local policy and continuing

Chapter 36

as discussed in "Group Policy Inheritance" on page 1254. Although only the User Configuration settings are sent and applied at this point, it is important to note that any computer policy settings that overlap with user policy settings are overwritten by default. User policy settings have precedence by default.

7. After processing user policies, the computer runs any logon scripts. Logon scripts are hidden from view by default, and if there are multiple startup scripts, the scripts run asynchronously by default. Thus, unlike startup scripts for which each script must finish running before the next one can be started, logon scripts are all started and run simultaneously. The default timeout for scripts is 600 seconds.

8. The user interface as defined in the user's profile and governed by the policy settings that are in effect is displayed. If the user logs off the computer, any logoff scripts defined for the user are run. If the user shuts down the computer, logoff is part of the shutdown process, so the user is first logged off and any logoff scripts defined for the user are run. Then the computer runs any shutdown scripts defined for the computer.

INSIDE OUT   All Group Policy processing is handled as a refresh

Technically, all Group Policy processing is handled as a Group Policy refresh. Thus, processing during startup and logon is technically a refresh, which is handled as discussed in "Group Policy Refresh" on page 1268. The most important note about refresh is that if the client computer detects that it is using a slow network connection, only the Security Settings and Administrative Templates are processed. Although there is no way to turn off processing of these extensions, you can configure other extensions so that they are processed even across a slow network connection. For more information, see "Modifying Group Policy Refresh" on page 1269.

Modifying Group Policy Processing

You can modify Group Policy processing by disabling a policy in whole or in part. Disabling a policy is useful if you no longer need a policy but might need to use that policy again in the future. Disabling part of a policy is useful so that the policy applies only to either users or computers but not both.

In the Group Policy Management Console, you can enable and disable policies partially or entirely by completing the following steps:

1. In the Group Policy Management Console, select the container for the site, domain, or OU with which you want to work.

2. In the right pane, select the Details tab, and then use the GPO Status selection list to choose a status as one of the following:

   ○ Enabled—Allows processing of the policy object and all its settings.

   ○ All Settings Disabled—Disallows processing of the policy object and all its settings.

   ○ Computer Configuration Settings Disabled—Disables processing of Computer Configuration settings, which means only User Configuration settings are processed.

   ○ User Configuration Settings Disabled—Disables processing of User Configuration settings, which means only Computer Configuration settings are processed.

3. When prompted to confirm that you want to change the status of this GPO, click OK.

Modifying User Policy Preference Using Loopback Processing

When a user logs on, the client computer applies User Configuration settings. Because user policy settings have precedence by default, any computer policy settings that overlap with user policy settings are overwritten. However, for some computers, particularly special-use computers in classrooms, labs, or public places, you might want to restrict the computer to a specific configuration. In this case, you might not want less-restrictive user policy settings to be applied.

To change the default behavior that gives preference to user policy, you can enable the loopback processing policy. By enabling the loopback processing policy, you ensure that the Computer Configuration settings always apply. Loopback processing can be set in one of two ways, either with Replace or Merge. When you use the Replace option, user settings from the computer's GPOs are processed and the user settings in the user's GPOs are not processed. This means the user settings from the computer's GPOs replace the user settings normally applied to the user.

When you use the Merge option, user settings in the computer's GPOs are processed first, then user settings in the user's GPOs are processed, and then user settings in the computer's GPOs are processed again. This processing technique serves to combine the user settings in both the computer and user GPOs. If there are any conflicts, the user settings in the computer's GPOs have preference and overwrite the user settings in the user's GPOs.

To configure loopback processing, follow these steps:

1. Start the Group Policy Object Editor. In the Group Policy Management Console, right-click the Group Policy object you want to modify, and then select Edit.

2. Double-click the User Group Policy Loopback Processing Mode in the Computer Configuration\Administrative Templates\System\Group Policy folder.

Chapter 36

3. Define the policy by selecting Enabled, as shown in Figure 36-14, then use the Mode selection list to set the processing mode as either Replace or Merge.

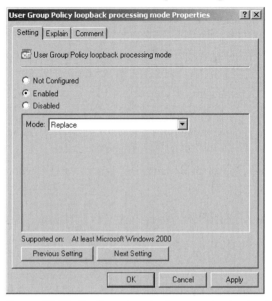

Figure 36-14 Configure loopback processing to give Computer Configuration settings preference.

4. Click OK. This policy is supported by all computers running Windows 2000 or later.

Using Scripts in Group Policy

In Windows Server 2008 you can configure computer startup and shutdown scripts as well as user logon and logoff scripts. You can write these scripts as command-shell batch scripts ending with the .bat or .cmd extension, or as scripts that use the Windows Script Host (WSH). WSH is a feature of Windows Server 2008 that lets you use scripts written in a scripting language, such as Microsoft JScript and Microsoft VBScript.

Configuring Computer Startup and Shutdown Scripts

You can assign computer startup and shutdown scripts as part of a Group Policy object. In this way, all computers in a site, domain, or OU run scripts automatically when they're started or shut down.

To configure a script that should be used during computer startup or shutdown, follow these steps:

1. For easy management, copy the scripts you want to use to the Machine\Scripts\ Startup or Machine\Scripts\Shutdown folder for the related policy. By default,

policies are stored in the %SystemRoot%\Sysvol\Domain\Policies folder on domain controllers.

2. Start the Group Policy Object Editor. In the Group Policy Management Console, right-click the Group Policy object you want to modify, and then select Edit.

3. In the Computer Configuration node, double-click the Windows Settings folder, and then select Scripts.

4. To work with startup scripts, right-click Startup, and then select Properties. Or right-click Shutdown, and then select Properties to work with shutdown scripts.

5. Click Show Files. If you copied the computer script to the correct location in the Policies folder, you should see the script.

6. Click Add to assign a script. This opens the Add A Script dialog box. In the Script Name field, type the name of the script you copied to the Machine\Scripts\ Startup or the Machine\Scripts\Shutdown folder for the related policy. Repeat this step to add other scripts.

7. During startup or shutdown, scripts are run in the order in which they're listed in the Properties dialog box. Use the Up or Down button to reposition scripts as necessary.

8. To delete a script, select the script in the Script For list, and then click Remove.

Configuring User Logon and Logoff Scripts

You can assign logon and logoff scripts as part of a Group Policy object. In this way, all users in a site, domain, or OU run scripts automatically when they log on or log off.

To configure a script that should be executed when a user logs on or logs off, complete the following steps:

1. For easy management, copy the scripts you want to use to the User\Scripts\ Logon or the User\Scripts\Logoff folder for the related policy. By default, policies are stored in the %SystemRoot%\Sysvol\Domain\Policies folder on domain controllers.

2. Start the Group Policy Object Editor. In the Group Policy Management Console, right-click the Group Policy object you want to modify, and then select Edit.

3. Double-click the Windows Settings folder in the User Configuration node, and then click Scripts.

4. To work with logon scripts, right-click Logon and then select Properties. Or right-click Logoff, and then select Properties to work with logoff scripts.

5. Click Show Files. If you copied the user script to the correct location in the Policies folder, you should see the script.

6. Click Add to assign a script. This opens the Add A Script dialog box. In the Script Name field, type the name of the script you copied to the User\Scripts\Logon or the User\Scripts\Logoff folder for the related policy. Repeat this step to add other scripts.

7. During logon or logoff, scripts are executed in the order in which they're listed in the Properties dialog box. Use the Up or Down button to reposition scripts as necessary.

8. To delete a script, select the script in the Script For list, and then click Remove.

Applying Group Policy Through Security Templates

Security templates take the guesswork out of configuring a computer's initial security. You use security templates to apply customized sets of Group Policy definitions that are security-related. These policy definitions generally affect the following components:

- Account policy settings that control security for passwords, account lockout, and Kerberos

- Local policy settings that control security for auditing, user rights assignment, and other security options

- Event log policy settings that control security for event logging

- Restricted group policies that control security for local group membership and administration

- System services policy settings that control the startup mode for local services

- File system policy settings that control security for the local file system

- Registry policy settings that control the values of security-related Registry keys

Working with Security Templates

Security templates are available in all Windows Server 2008 installations and can be imported into any GPO. The templates are stored in the %SystemRoot%\Security\Templates folder by default, and you can access them using the Security Templates snap-in. You can also use the snap-in to create new templates. The standard template for domain controllers is Dc Security, which contains the default security settings for a domain controller.

After you select the template that you want to use, you should go through each setting that the template will apply and evaluate how the setting will affect your environment. If a setting doesn't make sense, you should modify or delete it as appropriate.

You use the Security Templates snap-in only for viewing templates. You apply templates using the Security Configuration And Analysis snap-in. You can also use Security Configuration And Analysis to compare the settings in a template to the existing settings on a computer. The results of the analysis will highlight areas in which the current settings don't match those in the template. This is useful to determine whether security settings have changed over time.

You can access the security snap-ins by completing the following steps:

1. Click Start, type **mmc** into the Search box, and then press Enter.

2. In the Microsoft Management Console, choose File and then choose Add/Remove Snap-In.

3. In the Add Or Remove Snap-Ins dialog box, select Security Templates and then click Add.

4. Select Security Configuration And Analysis and then click Add. Click OK.

5. By default, the Security Templates snap-in looks for security templates in the %SystemDrive%\Users\%UserName%\Documents\Security\Templates folder. To add other search paths select New Template Search Path on the Action menu.

6. Select the template location to add from the Browse For Folder dialog box, such as %SystemRoot%\Security\Templates. Click OK.

You can create a new template by following these steps:

1. In the Security Templates snap-in, right-click the search path where the template should be created and then select New Template.

2. Type a name and description for the template in the text boxes provided.

3. Click OK to create the template. The template will have no settings configured, so you will need to modify the settings carefully before the template is ready for use.

Applying Security Templates

You use the Security Templates snap-in to view existing templates or to create new templates. After you've created a template or determined that you want to use an existing template, you can then configure and analyze the template by completing the following steps:

1. Access the Security Configuration And Analysis snap-in. Right-click the Security Configuration And Analysis node, and then select Open Database. This displays the Open Database dialog box.

2. Type a new database name in the File Name field, and then click Open. The Import Template dialog box is displayed next. Select the security template that you want to use, and then click Open.

3. Right-click the Security Configuration And Analysis node, and then choose Analyze Computer Now. When prompted to set the error log path, type a new path or click OK to use the default path.

Chapter 36

4. Wait for the snap-in to complete the analysis of the template. Afterward, review the findings and update the template as necessary. You can view the error log by right-clicking the Security Configuration And Analysis node and choosing View Log File.

5. When you're ready to apply the template, right-click the Security Configuration And Analysis node, and choose Configure Computer Now. When prompted to set the error log path, click OK. The default path should be fine.

6. View the configuration error log by right-clicking the Security Configuration And Analysis node and choosing View Log File. Note any problems and take action as necessary.

Maintaining and Troubleshooting Group Policy

Most Group Policy maintenance and troubleshooting tasks have to do with determining when policy is refreshed and applied and then changing the refresh options as appropriate to ensure that policy is applied as expected. Thus, maintaining and troubleshooting Group Policy requires a keen understanding of how Group Policy refresh works and how it can be changed to meet your needs. You also need tools for modeling and viewing the GPOs that would be or have been applied to users and computers. The Group Policy Management Console provides these tools through the Group Policy Modeling and Group Policy Results Wizards, which can be used instead of the running the Resultant Set Of Policy (RSoP) Wizard in logging mode or planning mode.

Group Policy Refresh

Computer policies are applied when a computer starts, and user policies are applied when a user logs on. After they are applied, Group Policy settings are automatically refreshed to ensure that they are current. The default refresh interval for domain controllers is every 5 minutes. For all other computers, the default refresh interval is every 90 minutes with up to a 30-minute variation to avoid overloading the domain controller with numerous client requests at the same time.

Change the Refresh Interval Through Group Policy

You can change the Group Policy refresh interval if desired. The related policies are stored in the Computer Configuration\Administrative Templates\System\Group Policy folder. To set the refresh interval for domain controllers, configure the Group Policy Refresh Interval For Domain Controllers policy. Select Enabled, set the refresh interval, and then click OK. To set the refresh interval for all other computers, configure the Group Policy Refresh Interval For Computers policy. Select Enabled, set the refresh interval and random offset, and then click OK.

During Group Policy refresh, the client contacts an available domain controller in its local site. If one or more of the GPOs defined in the domain have changed, the domain controller provides a list of all the GPOs that apply to the computer and to the user that is currently logged on, as appropriate. The domain controller does so regardless of whether the version numbers on all the listed GPOs have changed.

By default, the computer processes the GPOs only if the version number of at least one of the GPOs has changed. If any one of the related policies has changed, all of the policies have to be processed again. This is required because of inheritance and the interdependencies within policies. Security Settings are a noted exception to the processing rule. By default, Security Settings are refreshed every 16 hours (960 minutes) regardless of whether GPOs contain changes. Additionally, if the client computer detects that it is connecting over a slow network connection, it tells the domain controller this and only the Security Settings and Administrative Templates are transferred over the network, which means only the Security Settings and Administrative Templates are applied.

Modifying Group Policy Refresh

Group Policy refresh can be changed in several ways. First, client computers determine that they are using a slow network connection by pinging the domain controller to which they are connected with a zero-byte packet. If the response time from the domain controller is more than 10 milliseconds, the computer then pings the domain controller three times with a 2-kilobyte (KB) message packet to determine if it is on a slow network. The computer uses the average response time to determine the network speed. By default, if the connection speed is determined to be less than 500 kilobits per second (Kbps), the computer interprets that as having a slow network connection, in which case it notifies the domain controller of this. As a result, only the Security Settings and Administrative Templates in the applicable GPOs are sent by the domain controller.

You can configure slow link detection using the Group Policy Slow Link Detection policy, which is stored in the Computer Configuration\Administrative Templates\System\Group Policy folder. To configure this policy, follow these steps:

1. Start the Group Policy Object Editor. In the Group Policy Management Console, right-click the Group Policy object you want to modify, and then select Edit.

2. Double-click the Group Policy Slow Link Detection policy in the Computer Configuration\Administrative Templates\System\Group Policy folder.

3. Define the policy by selecting Enabled, as shown in Figure 36-15, and then use the Connection Speed combo box to specify the speed that should be used to determine whether a computer is on a slow link. For example, if you want connections less than 128 Kbps to be deemed "slow connections," you'd type **128**. If you want to disable slow link detection, you'd type **0** in the Connection Speed box.

Chapter 36

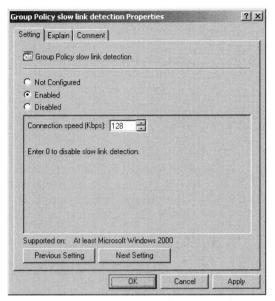

Figure 36-15 Configure slow link detection as necessary.

4. Click OK. This policy is supported by all computers running Windows 2000 or later.

If there is any area of Group Policy for which you want to configure refresh, you can do this in the Group Policy Object Editor. The related policies are stored in the Computer Configuration\Administrative Templates\System\Group Policy folder and include Applications Policy Processing, Data Sources Policy Processing, Devices Policy Processing, Disk Quota Policy Processing, Drive Maps Policy Processing, EFS Recovery Policy Processing, Environment Policy Processing, and several dozen other specific areas of policy processing.

> **Note**
>
> You use Registry Policy Processing to control the processing of all other Registry-based extensions.

To configure the refresh of an extension, follow these steps:

1. Start the Group Policy Object Editor. In the Group Policy Management Console, right-click the Group Policy object you want to modify, and then select Edit.

2. Double-click the policy in the Computer Configuration\Administrative Templates\System\Group Policy folder.

3. Define the policy by selecting Enabled, as shown in Figure 36-16. The options you have differ slightly depending on the policy selected and include the following:

   ○ Allow Processing Across A Slow Network Connection—Select this option to ensure that the extension settings are processed even on a slow network.

   ○ Do Not Apply During Periodic Background Processing—Select this option to override refresh when extension settings change after startup or logon.

   ○ Process Even If The Group Policy Objects Have Not Changed—Select this option to force the client computer to process the extension settings during refresh even if the settings haven't changed.

   ○ Background Priority—Determines when background processing occurs. If you select Idle, background processing of related policy occurs only when the computer is idle. Other processing options are for lowest activity levels, below normal activity levels, or normal activity levels.

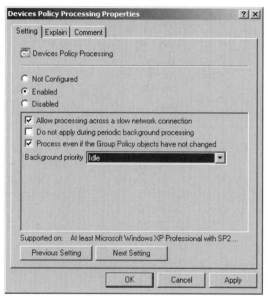

Figure 36-16 Change the way refresh works as necessary.

4. Click OK.

Viewing Applicable GPOs and Last Refresh

In the Group Policy Management Console, you can view all of the GPOs that apply to a computer as well as the user logged on to that computer. You can also view the last time the applicable GPOs were processed (refreshed). To do this, you run the Group Policy Results Wizard.

To start the Group Policy Results Wizard and view applicable GPOs and the last refresh, follow these steps:

1. Start the Group Policy Management Console. Right-click Group Policy Results, and then select Group Policy Results Wizard.

2. When the Group Policy Results Wizard starts, click Next. On the Computer Selection page shown in Figure 36-17, select This Computer to view information for the local computer. If you want to view information for a remote computer, select Another Computer and then click Browse. In the Select Computer dialog box, type the name of the computer, and then click Check Names. After the correct computer account is selected, click OK.

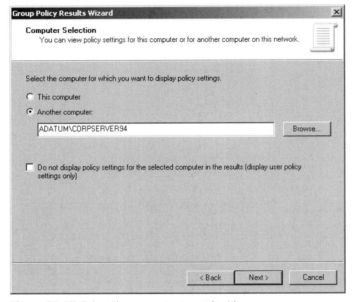

Figure 36-17 Select the computer to work with.

3. In the Group Policy Results Wizard, click Next. On the User Selection page, shown in Figure 36-18, select the user whose policy information you want to view. You can view policy information for any user who has logged on to the computer.

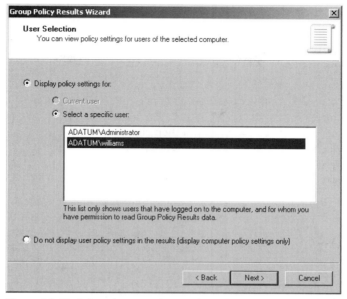

Figure 36-18 Select the user whose policy information you want to view.

4. Click Next twice, and then after the wizard gathers the policy information, click Finish. The wizard then generates a report, the results of which are displayed in the details pane as shown in Figure 36-19.

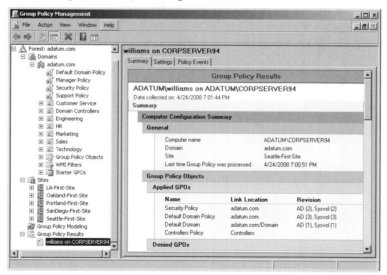

Figure 36-19 Use the report to view policy information.

5. On the report, click Show All to display all of the policy information that was gathered.

Computer and user policy information is listed separately. Computer policy information is listed under Computer Configuration Summary, as follows:

- To view the last time the computer policy was refreshed, look under Computer Configuration Summary, General for the Last Time Group Policy Was Processed entry.

- To view all applicable GPOs, look under Computer Configuration Summary, Group Policy Objects.

User policy information is listed under User Configuration Summary, as follows:

- To view the last time the user policy was refreshed, look under User Configuration Summary, General for the Last Time Group Policy Was Processed entry.

- To view all applicable GPOs, look under User Configuration Summary, Group Policy Objects.

The Applied GPOs entry shows all GPOs that have been applied. The Denied GPOs entry shows all GPOs that should have been applied but weren't processed for some reason, such as because they were empty or did not contain any computer policy settings. The GPO also might not have been processed because inheritance was blocked. If so, the Reason Denied is Blocked Scope of Management (SOM).

Modeling GPOs for Planning

In the Group Policy Management Console, you can test different scenarios for modifying Computer Configuration and User Configuration settings. For example, you can model the effect of a slow link or the use of loopback processing. You can also model the effect of moving a user or computer to another container in Active Directory or adding the user or computer to an additional security group. To do this, you run the Group Policy Modeling Wizard.

To start the Group Policy Modeling Wizard and test various scenarios, follow these steps:

1. Start the Group Policy Management Console. Right-click Group Policy Modeling, and then select Group Policy Modeling Wizard.

2. When the Group Policy Modeling Wizard starts, click Next. On the Domain Controller Selection page, as shown in Figure 36-20, under Show Domain Controllers In This Domain, select the domain for which you want to model results. Next, select either Any Available Domain Controller or This Domain Controller, and then choose a specific domain controller. Click Next.

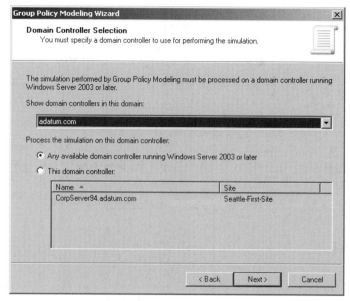

Figure 36-20 Select the domain controller to work with.

3. On the User And Computer Selection page, shown in Figure 36-21, select the modeling options for users and computers.

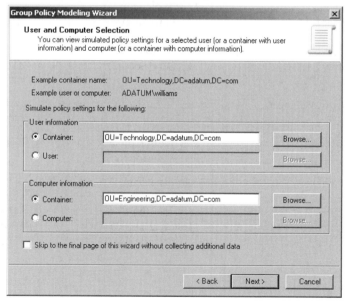

Figure 36-21 Select the modeling options for users and computers.

Typically, you'll want to model policy for a specific container using user and computer information. In this case, the following would apply:

- ○ Under User Information, select Container, and then click Browse to display the Choose User Container dialog box, which you can use to choose any of the available user containers in the selected domain.

- ○ Under Computer Information, select Container, and then click Browse to display the Choose Computer Container dialog box, which you can use to choose any of the available computer containers in the selected domain.

4. Click Next. On the Advanced Simulation Options page, as shown in Figure 36-22, select any advanced options for slow network connections, loopback processing, and sites as necessary, and then click Next.

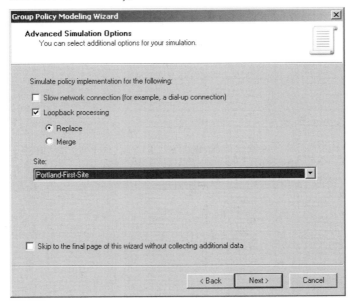

Figure 36-22 Select advanced options as necessary.

5. On the User Security Groups page, shown in Figure 36-23, you can simulate changes to security group membership to model the results on Group Policy. Any changes you make to group membership affect the previously selected user container. For example, if you want to see what would happen if a user in the designated user container is a member of the Domain Admins group, you could add this group to the Security Groups list. Click Next to continue.

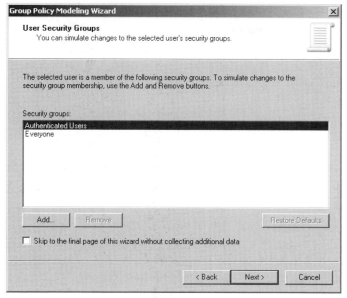

Figure 36-23 Simulate changes to security groups for users.

6. On the Computer Security Groups page, you can simulate changes to security group membership to model the results on Group Policy. Any changes you make to group membership affect the previously selected computer container. For example, if you want to see what would happen if a computer in the designated computer container is a member of the Domain Controllers group, you could add this group to the Security Groups list. Click Next to continue.

7. WMI filters can be linked to GPOs. By default, it is assumed that the selected users and computers meet all the WMI filter requirements, which is what you want in most cases for modeling, so click Next twice to skip past the WMI Filters For Users and WMI Filters For Computers pages.

8. To complete the modeling, click Next, and then click Finish. The wizard then generates a report, the results of which are displayed in the details pane.

9. The name of the modeling report is generated based on the containers you chose and highlighted for editing. Type a new name as required, and then press Tab. On the report, click Show All to display all of the policy information that was modeled. Figure 36-24 shows an example.

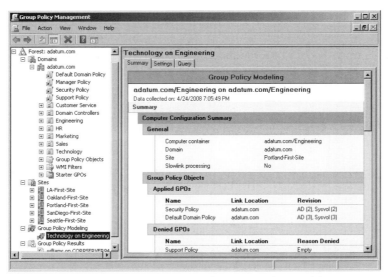

Figure 36-24 Use the report to examine the Group Policy model.

Refreshing Group Policy Manually

You can refresh Group Policy manually using the Gpupdate command-line utility. Gpupdate replaces the Secedit /refreshpolicy tool provided in Windows 2000. If you type **gpupdate** at a command prompt, both the Computer Configuration settings and the User Configuration settings in Group Policy are refreshed on the local computer.

You can also selectively refresh Group Policy. If you want to refresh only Computer Configuration settings, you type **gpupdate /target:computer** at the command prompt. If you want to refresh only User Configuration settings, you type **gpupdate /target:user** at the command prompt. By default, only policy settings that have changed are processed and applied. You can change this behavior using the /Force parameter. This parameter forces a refresh of all policy settings.

Gpupdate can also be used to log off a user or restart a computer after Group Policy is refreshed. This is useful because some Group Policy objects are applied only when a user logs on or when a computer starts up. To log off a user after a refresh, add the /Logoff parameter. To restart a computer after a refresh, add the /Boot parameter.

Backing Up GPOs

In the Group Policy Management Console, you can back up GPOs so that you can restore them at a later time to recover Group Policy to the state it was in when the backup was performed. The ability to back up and restore GPOs is one of the reasons why the Group Policy Management Console is more useful than the older Group Policy tools that come with Windows Server 2008. It is also important to add that you can back up and restore GPOs only when you have installed the Group Policy Management Console.

You can either back up an individual GPO in a domain or all GPOs in a domain by completing the following steps:

1. Start the Group Policy Management Console. Expand the forest, the Domains node, and the Group Policy Objects node.

2. If you want to back up all GPOs in the domain, right-click the Group Policy Objects node, and then select Back Up All.

3. If you want to back up a specific GPO in the domain, right-click the GPO, and then select Back Up.

4. In the Back Up Group Policy Object dialog box, shown in Figure 36-25, click Browse, and then use the Browse For Folder dialog box to set the location in which the GPO backup should be stored.

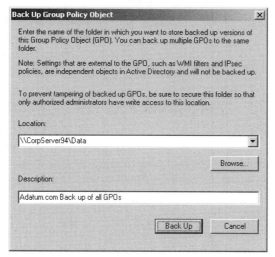

Figure 36-25 Set the backup location and description.

5. In the Description field, type a clear description of the contents of the backup.

6. Click Back Up to start the backup process. The Backup dialog box, shown in Figure 36-26, shows the progress and status of the backup. If a backup fails, check the permissions on the GPO and the folder to which you are writing the backup. You need Read permission on a GPO and Write permission on the backup folder to create a backup. By Default, members of the Domain Admins and Enterprise Admins groups should have these permissions.

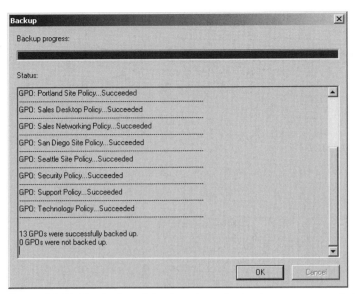

Figure 36-26 The Backup dialog box shows the backup progress and status.

Restoring GPOs

Using the Group Policy Management Console, you can restore a GPO to the state it was in when it was backed up. The Group Policy Management Console tracks the backup of each GPO separately, even if you back up all GPOs at once. Because version information is also tracked according to the backup time stamp and description, you can restore the last version of each GPO or a particular version of any GPO.

You can restore a GPO by completing the following steps:

1. Start the Group Policy Management Console. Expand the forest, the Domains node, and then the Group Policy Objects node.

2. If you want to restore all GPOs in the domain, right-click the Group Policy Objects node, and then select Manage Backups. This displays the Manage Backups dialog box (see Figure 36-27).

3. In the Backup Location field, type the folder path to the backup or click Browse to use the Browse For Folder dialog box to find the folder.

4. All GPO backups in the designated folder are listed under Backed Up GPOs. To show only the latest version of the GPOs according to the time stamp, select the Show Only The Latest Version Of Each GPO check box.

5. Select the GPO you want to restore. If you want to confirm its settings, click View Settings, and then verify that the settings are as expected using Internet Explorer. When you are ready to continue, click Restore. Confirm that you want to restore the selected GPO by clicking OK.

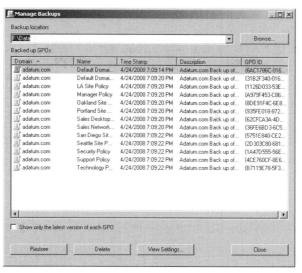

Figure 36-27 Use the Manage Backups dialog box to restore a GPO.

6. The Restore dialog box, shown in Figure 36-28, shows the progress and status of the restore. If a restore fails, check the permissions on the GPO and the folder from which you are reading the backup. To restore a GPO, you need Edit, Delete, and Modify permissions on the GPO and Read permission on the folder containing the GPO backup. By default, members of the Domain Admins and Enterprise Admins groups should have these permissions.

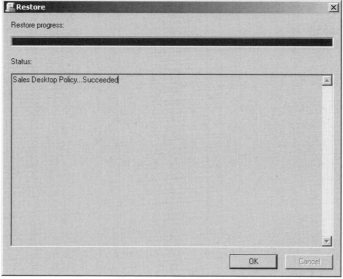

Figure 36-28 The Restore dialog box shows the restore progress and status.

7. Click OK, and then either restore additional GPOs as necessary or click Close.

Fixing Default Group Policy

The Default Domain Policy and Default Domain Controllers Policy GPOs are vital to the health of Active Directory in a domain. If for some reason these policies become corrupted, Group Policy will not function properly. To resolve this, you must run the Dcgpofix utility. This utility restores the default GPOs to their original, default state, meaning the state they are in when you first install Active Directory in a new domain. You must be a member of Domain Admins or Enterprise Admins to run Dcgpofix.

By default, when you run Dcgpofix, both the Default Domain Policy and Default Domain Controllers Policy GPOs are restored and you will lose any base changes made to these GPOs. The only exceptions are for the following extension settings: Remote Installation Services (RIS), Security Settings, and Encrypting File System (EFS). These extension settings are maintained separately and will not be lost. Non-default Security Settings are not maintained, however. All other extensions settings are restored to their default postinstallation state, and any changes you've made are lost.

To run Dcgpofix, log on to a domain controller in the domain in which you want to fix default Group Policy, and then type **dcgpofix** at the command prompt. Dcgpofix checks the Active Directory schema version number to ensure compatibility between the version of Dcgpofix you are using and the Active Directory schema configuration. If the versions are not compatible, Dcgpofix exits without fixing the default Group Policy. By specifying the /Ignoreschema parameter, you can enable Dcgpofix to work with different versions of Active Directory. However, default policy objects might not be restored to their original state. Because of this, you should always be sure to use the version of Dcgpofix that is installed with the current operating system.

You also have the option of fixing only the Default Domain Policy or the Default Domain Controllers Policy GPO. If you want to fix only the Default Domain Policy, type **dcgpofix /target:** *domain*. If you want to fix only the Default Domain Controllers Policy, type **dcgpofix /target: dc**.

Active Directory Site Administration

In this chapter, I discuss administration of sites, subnets, site links, and related components. Active Directory sites are used to control directory replication traffic and isolate logon authentication traffic between physical network locations. Every site has one or more subnets associated with it. Ideally, each subnet that is part of a site should be connected by reliable, high-speed links. Any physical location connected over slow or unreliable links should be part of a separate site, and these individual sites are linked to other sites using site links.

Managing Sites and Subnets

When you install the Active Directory directory service in a new forest, a new site called the Default-First-Site-Name is created. As you add additional domains and domain controllers to the forest, these domains and domain controllers are added to this site as they are installed unless you have configured other sites and associated subnets with those sites as necessary.

Administration of sites and subnets involves determining the sites and subnets you need and creating those sites and subnets. All sites have one or more subnets associated with them. It is in fact the subnet assignment that tells Active Directory where the site boundaries are established. As you create additional sites, you might also need to specify which domain controllers are a part of the sites. You do this by moving domain controllers to the site containers with which they should be associated. Thus, the most common administrative tasks for sites involve the following:

- Creating sites
- Creating subnets and associating them with sites
- Moving domain controllers between sites

Creating an Active Directory Site

As part of Active Directory design, discussed in Chapter 32, "Configuring Active Directory Sites and Replication," you must consider whether separate sites are needed. If your organization has multiple locations with limited bandwidth or unreliable connections between locations, you will typically want to create additional sites. In some cases you might also want to create additional sites to separate network segments even if they are connected with high-speed links; the reason for doing this is to control logon authentication traffic between the network segments.

To create an additional site, follow these steps:

1. Start Active Directory Sites And Services by clicking Start, Administrative Tools, and Active Directory Sites And Services.

> **Connect to the Forest You Want to Work With**
>
> Active Directory Sites And Services is used to view a single forest. If your organization has multiple forests, you might need to connect to another forest. To do this, right-click the Active Directory Sites And Services node in the console tree, and then select Change Forest. In the Change Forest dialog box, type the name of the root domain in the forest to which you want to connect, and then click OK.

2. Right-click the Sites container in the console tree, and select New Site. This displays the New Object–Site dialog box, as shown in Figure 37-1.

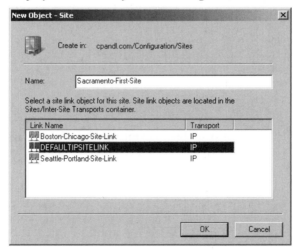

Figure 37-1 Use the New Object–Site dialog box to create a new site.

3. In the New Object–Site dialog box, type a descriptive name for the site. The site name serves as a point of reference for administrators and should clearly depict the purpose or physical location of the site.

4. Choose which site link will be used to connect this site to other sites. If the site link you want to use doesn't exist, that's okay—the site must exist before you can

create links to it. Select the default site link DEFAULTIPSITELINK for now, and change the site link settings after you've created the necessary site link or links.

5. When you are ready to continue, click OK. A prompt is displayed detailing the steps you must complete to finish the site configuration. Click OK again. As the prompt details, you should do the following:

   ○ lEnsure the links to this site are appropriate by creating the necessary site links. The catch in this is that both endpoints in a site link—the sites you want to link—must exist before you can create a site link.

   ○ Create subnets and associate them with the site. This tells Active Directory the network addresses that belong to a site.

Each site should have one or more domain controllers. Ideally, at least one of these domain controllers should also be a global catalog server. Because of this, you should install one or more domain controllers in the site or move existing domain controllers into the site.

Creating a Subnet and Associating It with a Site

You create subnets and associate them with sites to allow Active Directory to determine the network segments that belong to the site. Any computer with an Internet Protocol (IP) address on a network segment associated with a site is considered to be located in the site. A site can have one or more subnets associated with it. Each subnet, however, can be associated with only one site.

You can create a subnet and associate it with a site by completing the following steps:

1. Start Active Directory Sites And Services by clicking Start, Administrative Tools, and Active Directory Sites And Services.

2. Right-click the Subnets container in the console tree, and select New Subnet. This displays the New Object–Subnet dialog box, as shown in Figure 37-2.

3. In the Prefix field, type the address prefix for the subnet. As discussed in "Network Prefix Notation" on page 640, the address prefix for a network address consists of the network ID address followed by a forward slash followed by the number of bits in the network ID. Typically, the subnet address ends with a 0, such as 192.168.1.0, except when subnetting is used. For example, if the network address is 192.168.1.0 and the subnet mask is 255.255.255.0, you should enter the address prefix as 192.168.1.0/24.

4. Select the site with which the subnet should be associated, and then click OK. If you ever need to change the site association for the subnet, double-click the subnet in the Subnets folder and then, on the General tab, use the Site Selection list to change the site association.

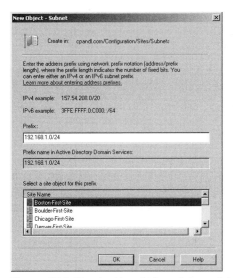

Figure 37-2 Use the New Object–Subnet dialog box to create a new subnet.

Associating Domain Controllers with a Site

After you associate subnets with a site, any domain controllers you install will automatically be located in the site where the IP address subnet matches the domain controller's IP address. Any future domain controllers installed before you established the site and associated subnets with it will not be moved to the site automatically. You must manually move existing domain controllers if necessary. In addition, if you associate a subnet with a different site, you might need to move domain controllers in that subnet to the new site.

Before you can move a domain controller from one site to another, you must determine in which site the domain controller is currently located. One way to do this would be to examine the Servers nodes for each site in Active Directory Sites And Services. You can also do this by typing the following command at a command prompt:

```
dsquery server -s DomainControllerName | dsget server -site
```

where *DomainControllerName* is the fully qualified domain name of the domain controller, such as:

```
dsquery server -s corpserver92.cpandl.com | dsget server -site
```

The output of this command is the name of the site in which the designated domain controller is located.

You can move a domain controller to a site by completing the following steps:

1. Start Active Directory Sites And Services by clicking Start, Administrative Tools, and Active Directory Sites And Services.

2. Domain controllers associated with a site are listed in the site's Servers node. To locate the domain controller that you want to move, expand the site node, and then expand the related Servers node.

3. Right-click the domain controller, and then select Move. This displays the Move Server dialog box.

4. In the Move Server dialog box, select the site that should contain the server, and then click OK.

Another way to move a domain controller from one site to another in Windows Server 2008 is to drag the domain controller from its current site to the new site. But don't move a domain controller to a site arbitrarily. Move a domain controller to a site only if it is on a subnet associated with the site.

Managing Site Links and Intersite Replication

Site links are used to connect two or more sites together for the purpose of replication. When you install Active Directory in a new forest, a new site link called the DEFAULTIPSITELINK is created. As you add additional sites to the forest, these sites are included in the default site link unless you have configured other site links. If all of the network connections between sites are the same speed and priority, the default configuration can work. In this case, the intersite replication configuration for all sites will have the same properties. If you were to change these properties, the changes would affect the replication topology for all sites. By creating additional site links, you can configure different replication properties when the network connections between sites have different speeds and priorities.

Creating additional site links helps the designated Inter-Site Topology Generator (ISTG) for a site to prioritize the site links and determine when a site link should be used. It doesn't, however, change the way intersite replication works. Replication traffic between sites is always sent from a bridgehead server in one site to a bridgehead server in another site. Although it is the job of the ISTG to generate the intersite replication topology and designate bridgehead servers, you can manually designate bridgehead servers as well. After you've established site links and designated bridgehead servers as necessary, you might want to change the way replication between sites is handled. For example, you might want to disable compression or enable notification so changes can be replicated more quickly between sites.

Following this, the most common administrative tasks related to site links involve the following:

- Creating site links
- Configuring site link bridges
- Determining the ISTG
- Configuring site bridgehead servers
- Setting site link replication options

Before looking at these administrative tasks, however, let's first look at the available replication transports.

Understanding IP and SMTP Replication Transports

When you create a site link, you will have to select a replication transport protocol. Two replication transports are available: IP and Simple Mail Transfer Protocol (SMTP). All replication connections within sites are synchronous and use RPC over IP. In this configuration, domain controllers establish an RPC over IP connection with a single replication partner at a time and replicate Active Directory changes. By default, the Remote Procedure Call (RPC) connection uses dynamic port mapping. During replication, a replication client establishes a connection to a server on the RPC endpoint mapper port 135 and determines which port is to be used for replication on the server. Any additional replication traffic is sent over the ports defined in Table 32-1 on page 1084. When RPC over IP is used for intersite replication, these same ports are used. If there are firewalls between the sites, the appropriate ports on the firewalls must be opened to allow replication to occur.

Because RPC over IP is synchronous, both replication partners must be available at the time the connection is established. This is important because of the transitive nature of site links. For example, if Site 1 has a link to Site 2, and Site 2 has a link to Site 3, there is an automatic bridge between Site 1 and Site 3 that allows Site 1 to replicate traffic directly to Site 3. Because of this, you must carefully configure site link schedules so that all potential RPC over IP replication partners are available as necessary—more on this in a moment.

Replication between sites can also be configured to use SMTP. By using SMTP as the transport, all replication traffic is converted to e-mail messages that are sent between the sites. Because SMTP replication is asynchronous, it can be a good choice when you do not have a permanent connection between sites or when you have unreliable connections between sites. It is also a good choice when you have to replicate between locations over the public Internet.

Before you use SMTP as the replication protocol, there are several important considerations. First, SMTP can be used only to replicate information between domain controllers in different domains because the domain directory partition cannot be replicated using SMTP—only the configuration, schema, and global catalog directory partitions can be replicated. Second, SMTP messages are digitally signed and encrypted to ensure that replication traffic is secure even if replication traffic is routed over the public Internet. All domain controllers that will use SMTP for replication require additional components to create, digitally sign, and then encrypt e-mail messages. Specifically, you must install the SMTP Server feature on each domain controller and you must install a Microsoft certificate authority (CA) in your organization. The certificates from the CA are used to digitally sign and encrypt the SMTP messages sent between the sites.

> ### Configure Replication Through Firewalls
>
> If you plan to use SMTP for replication, you must open port 25 on the firewall between sites. Port 25 is the default port used for SMTP. Although SMTP has definite security advantages over standard IP, you can encrypt RPC communications between domain controllers using IP Security (IPSec) and then open the appropriate ports on your firewalls for RPC over IP. Encrypting the RPC traffic between domain controllers would then be a viable alternative for replication over the public Internet when you have a dedicated connection between sites.

Creating a Site Link

After you create the sites that your organization needs, you can create site links between those sites to better manage intersite replication. Each site link must have at least two sites associated with it. These sites establish the endpoints or transit points for the link. For example, if you create a site link and add Portland-First-Site and LA-First-Site to the link, the Portland and LA sites are the endpoints for the link and the ISTG will use the link to create the connection objects that are required to replicate traffic between these sites.

Before you create a site link, you should determine the transport that you want to use as discussed in "Understanding IP and SMTP Replication Transports" on the previous page. You should also consider the following:

- **Link cost** The cost for a site link determines the relative priority of the link in relationship to other site links that might be available. If there are multiple possible routes to a site, the route with the lowest link cost is used first. In the event a primary link fails, a secondary link can be used. Typically, the link cost reflects the bandwidth available for a specific connection. It can also reflect the actual cost of sending traffic over a particular link if the organization has to pay a fee based on bandwidth usage.

- **Replication schedule** The replication schedule determines the times during the day that the site link is available for replication. By default, replication is allowed 24 hours a day. If you have a limited-bandwidth connection or you want user traffic to have priority at certain times of the day, you might want to configure a different availability schedule.

- **Replication interval** The replication interval determines the intervals at which the bridgehead servers in each site check to see if there are directory updates available. By default, the interval is set to 180 minutes. Following this, if the replication schedule is configured to allow replication from 7 P.M. to 7 A.M. each day, the bridgehead servers will check for updates at 7 P.M., 10 P.M., 1 A.M., 4 A.M., and 7 A.M. daily.

You can create a site link between two or more sites by completing the following steps:

1. Start Active Directory Sites And Services by clicking Start, Administrative Tools, and Active Directory Sites And Services. If your organization has multiple forests, you might need to connect to another forest. To do this, right-click the Active Directory Sites And Services node in the console tree, and then select Change Forest. In the Change Forest dialog box, type the name of the root domain in the forest to which you want to connect, and then click OK.

2. Expand the Sites container, and then expand the Inter-Site Transports container. Right-click the container for the transport protocol you want to use, either IP or SMTP, and select New Site Link. This displays the New Object–Site Link dialog box, as shown in Figure 37-3.

3. In the New Object–Site Link dialog box, type a descriptive name for the site link. The site name serves as a point of reference for administrators and should clearly depict the sites the link connects.

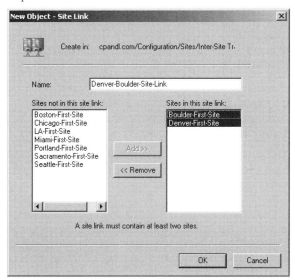

Figure 37-3 Create the site link.

4. In the Sites Not In This Site Link list, select a site that should be included in the link, and then click Add to add the site to the Sites In This Site Link list. Repeat this process for each site you want to add to the link. The link must include at least two sites.

5. Click OK to close the New Object–Site Link dialog box.

6. In Active Directory Sites And Services, the site link is added to the appropriate transport folder (IP or SMTP). Select the transport folder in the console tree, and then double-click the site link in the right pane. This displays the site link's Properties dialog box, as shown in Figure 37-4.

7. Use the Cost combo box to set the relative cost of the link. The default cost is 100. For pointers on determining what cost to use, see "Mapping Network Infrastructure" on page 1096 and "Designing the Intersite Replication Topology" on page 1100.

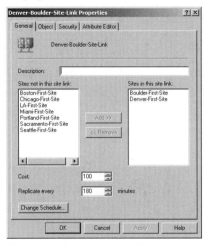

Figure 37-4 Set the site link properties.

8. Use the Replicate Every combo box to set the replication interval. The default interval is 180 minutes.

9. By default, the site link is available for replication 24 hours a day. To set a different schedule, click Change Schedule, and then use the Schedule For dialog box to set the desired replication schedule. When you are finished, click OK.

10. Click OK to close the site link's Properties dialog box.

INSIDE OUT

The transitive nature of site links

Site links are transitive and follow the three hops rules as discussed in "Replication Rings and Directory Partitions" on page 1091. This means that if Site 1 is linked to Site 2, Site 2 is linked to Site 3, and Site 3 is linked to Site 4, the domain controllers in Site 1 can replicate with Site 2, Site 3, and Site 4. Because of the transitive nature of site links, site link replication schedules and intervals for each site link are combined to determine the effective replication window and interval. To see the impact of combining replication schedules and intervals, consider the following examples:

- Site 1 to Site 2 link has a replication schedule of 7 P.M. to 7 A.M. and an interval of 60 minutes.

- Site 2 to Site 3 link has a replication schedule of 9 P.M. to 5 A.M. and an interval of 60 minutes.

- Site 3 to Site 4 link has a replication schedule of 1 P.M. to 3 A.M. and an interval of 180 minutes.

Because of the overlapping windows and intervals, replication between Site 1 and Site 2 could occur every 60 minutes from 7 P.M. to 7 A.M. Replication between Site 1 and Site 3 could occur every 60 minutes from 9 P.M. to 5 A.M. Replication between Site 1 and Site 4 could occur every 180 minutes from 9 P.M. to 3 A.M. This occurs because the replication availability window must overlap for replication to occur using transitive links.

If the site replication schedules do not overlap, replication is still possible between multiple sites. To see how replication would work if schedules do not overlap, consider the following example:

- Site 1 to Site 2 link has a replication schedule of 11 P.M. to 3 A.M. and an interval of 60 minutes.

- Site 2 to Site 3 link has a replication schedule of 6 P.M. to 9 P.M. and an interval of 60 minutes.

- Site 3 to Site 4 link has a replication schedule of 1 A.M. to 5 A.M. and an interval of 180 minutes.

Assuming there are no alternate links between the sites, replication between Site 1 and Site 2 could occur every 60 minutes from 11 P.M. to 3 A.M. Site 1 would not be able to replicate with Site 3 and Site 4, however. Instead, Site 2 would replicate changes to Site 3 every 60 minutes from 6 P.M. to 9 P.M. daily. Site 3 would in turn replicate changes to Site 4 every 180 minutes from 1 A.M. to 5 A.M. daily. In this configuration, there is significant replication latency (delay). Changes made at 5 P.M. in Site 1 would not be replicated to Site 2 until 11 P.M. The following day the changes would be replicated to Site 3 at 6 P.M., and then at 1 A.M. on the third day the changes would be replicated to Site 4.

Configuring Replication Schedules for Site Links

You can manage the replication schedule for site links in one of two ways: globally or individually. By default, IP site links use individual replication schedules and replicate within these schedules according to the replication interval. On the other hand, by default, SMTP site links ignore individual replication schedules and replicate only according to the replication interval. You can control whether global or individual schedules are used by following these steps:

1. Start Active Directory Sites And Services by clicking Start, Administrative Tools, and Active Directory Sites And Services.

2. Expand the Sites container, and then expand the Inter-Site Transports container. Right-click the container for the transport protocol you want to work with, either IP or SMTP, and then select Properties. This displays a Properties dialog box (see Figure 37-5).

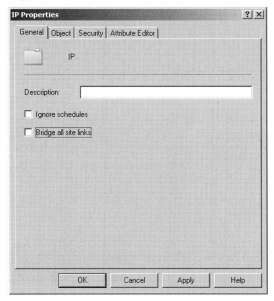

Figure 37-5 Configuring global replication.

3. You can now configure global replication for the selected transport. To ignore individual replication schedules on site links, select the Ignore Schedules check box. To use individual schedules, clear the Ignore Schedules check box. Click OK.

When you use individual schedules, you can manage the times when replication is permitted by setting a replication schedule for each site link. By default, replication is available 24 hours a day, 7 days a week. To better manage the traffic flow over intersite links, you may need to change the permitted replication times. For example, if you find that a particular link is too saturated at specific times of the day, you may want to limit replication to ensure users have more bandwidth for collaboration and communication.

When individual schedules are allowed, you can configure a site link's replication schedule by following these steps:

1. Start Active Directory Sites And Services by clicking Start, Administrative Tools, and Active Directory Sites And Services.

2. Expand the Sites container, expand the Inter-Site Transports container, and then select the container for the transport protocol you want to work with, either IP or SMTP.

3. In the details pane, right-click the site link you want to configure and then select Properties.

4. Click Change Schedule. You can now set the valid and invalid replication hours using the Schedule For *SiteLink* dialog box. In this dialog box each hour of the day or night is a field that you can turn on and off.

   ○ Hours that are allowed are filled in with a dark bar—you can think of these hours as being turned on.

   ○ Hours that are disallowed are blank—you can think of these hours as being turned off.

5. To change the setting for an hour, click it. Then select either Replication Not Available or Replication Available.

Scheduling features are listed in Table 37-1.

Table 37-1 Scheduling Features

Feature	Function
All	Allows you to select all the time periods
Day of week buttons	Allow you to select all the hours in a particular day
Hourly buttons	Allow you to select a particular hour for all the days of the week
Replication Available	Sets the allowed replication hours
Replication Not Available	Sets the disallowed replication hours

> **Note**
>
> When you set replication hours, you'll save yourself a lot of work in the long run if you consider peak usage times and use a moderately restricted time window. For example, you might be tempted to restrict replication from 8 A.M. to 6 P.M. every weekday on a limited-bandwidth link. However, such a wide restriction would not allow replication during the day. Instead, you might want to allow replication from 10 A.M. to 1 P.M. and from 6 P.M. to 6 A.M.

Configuring Site Link Bridges

Be default, all site links are transitive, which allows Active Directory to automatically configure site link bridges between sites. When a site is bridged, any two domain controllers can make a connection across any consecutive series of links as long as the site links are all using the same transport. The site link bridge cost is the sum of all the links included in the bridge.

A significant advantage of automatically created site link bridges is that fault tolerance is built in whenever there are multiple possible routes between sites. Another significant advantage is that Active Directory automatically manages the site link bridges and the ISTG monitors for changes and reconfigures the replication topology accordingly—and all without any administrator involvement required. Site link bridges are discussed in more detail in "Considering the Impact of Site Link Bridging" on page 1101.

You can enable or disable site link bridges on a per-transport basis. By default, both the IP and SMTP transports have site link bridging enabled. If you disable site link bridging, Active Directory will no longer manage site link bridges for the transport. You must then create and manage *all* site link bridges for that transport. Any sites you add to a site link bridge are considered to be transitive with each other. Site links that are not included in the site link bridge are not transitive.

To see how this would work, consider the previous example in which Site 1 is linked to Site 2, Site 2 is linked to Site 3, and Site 3 is linked to Site 4. If you disable site link bridging and then create a site link bridge that includes Site 1, Site 2, and Site 3, only those sites would have a transitive site link. Site 4 would be excluded. This would mean Site 1 could replicate changes to Site 2 and Site 1 could replicate changes to Site 3. Site 1 could not, however, replicate changes to Site 4. Only Site 3 would replicate changes to Site 4. This would occur because adjacent sites can always replicate changes with each other.

> **Note**
>
> One reason to create site link bridges manually is to reduce the processing overhead on the designated ISTGs in each site. When you disable transitive links, the ISTGs no longer have to create and manage the site link bridges, and this reduces the number of computations required to create the intersite replication topology.

To turn off transitive site links and manually configure site link bridges, follow these steps:

1. Start Active Directory Sites And Services by clicking Start, Administrative Tools, and Active Directory Sites And Services.

2. Expand the Sites container, and then expand the Inter-Site Transports container. Right-click the container for the transport protocol you want to work with, either

IP or SMTP, and then select Properties. This displays a Properties dialog box shown previously in Figure 37-5.

3. Clear the Bridge All Site Links check box, and then click OK. If you later want to enable transitive links and have Active Directory ignore the site link bridges you've created, you can select the Bridge All Site Links check box.

After you've disabled transitive links, you can manually create a site link bridge between two or more sites by completing the following steps:

1. In Active Directory Sites And Services, expand the Sites container, and then expand the Inter-Site Transports container. Right-click the container for the transport protocol you want to use, either IP or SMTP, and then select New Site Link Bridge. This displays the New Object–Site Link Bridge dialog box, as shown in Figure 37-6.

2. In the New Object–Site Link Bridge dialog box, type a descriptive name for the site link bridge. This name serves as a point of reference for administrators and should clearly depict all the site links that are a part of the bridge.

3. In the Site Links Not In This Site Link Bridge list, select a site link that should be included in the bridge and then click Add to add the site link to the Site Links In This Site Link Bridge list. Repeat this process for each site link you want to add to the bridge. The bridge must include at least two site links.

4. Click OK to close the New Object–Site Link Bridge dialog box.

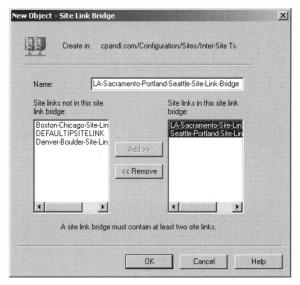

Figure 37-6 Create a site link bridge.

INSIDE OUT   **Intersite transport options**

In Active Directory Sites And Services, you can control the way site links work using the Bridge All Site Links and Ignore Schedules check boxes in the IP Properties and SMTP Properties dialog boxes, and as discussed previously in "Configuring Replication Schedules for Site Links" on page 1293 and "Configuring Site Link Bridges" on page 1295.

Selecting or clearing these check boxes modifies the flag values on the Options attribute, which you can view on the Attribute Editor tab in the related Properties dialog box. The Options attribute has two flags: IGNORE_SCHEDULES with an enabled value of 1 and BRIDGES_REQUIRED with an enabled value of 2.

BRIDGES_REQUIRED enables or disables transitive site links. When you disable transitive site links by clearing the Bridge All Site Links check box, you are setting the BRIDGES_REQUIRED flag on the Options attribute. When you enable transitive site links by selecting the Bridge All Site Links check box, you are clearing the BRIDGES_REQUIRED flag on the Options attribute.

IGNORE_SCHEDULES enables or disables the use of individual replication schedules for site links. When you override the replication schedule for individual site links by selecting the Ignore Schedules check box, you are setting the IGNORE_SCHEDULES flag on the Options attribute. When allow each site link to have a replication schedule by clearing the Ignore Schedules check box, you are clearing the IGNORE_SCHEDULES flag on the Options attribute.

Determining the ISTG

Each site has an ISTG that is responsible for generating the intersite replication topology. As your organization grows and you add domain controllers and sites, the load on the ISTG can grow substantially because each addition means the ISTG must perform additional calculations to determine and maintain the optimal topology. When it is calculating the replication topology, its processor typically will reach 100 percent utilization. As the topology becomes more and more complex, the process will stay at maximum utilization longer and longer.

Because there is the potential for the ISTG to get overloaded, you should monitor the designated ISTG in a site more closely than other domain controllers. At the command line you can determine the ISTG for a particular site by typing **repadmin /istg "site: SiteName"** where *SiteName* is the name of the site that you want to work with such as **repadmin /istg "site:Denver-First-Site"**. If you want to examine the site in which your computer is located, simply type **repadmin /istg**. You also can determine the ISTG by completing the following steps:

1. In Active Directory Sites And Services, expand the Sites container, and then select the site whose ISTG you want to locate in the console tree.

2. In the details pane, double-click NTDS Site Settings.

3. In the NTDS Site Settings Properties dialog box, the current ISTG is listed in the Inter-Site Topology Generator panel, as shown in Figure 37-7.

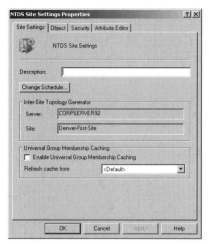

Figure 37-7 Locating the ISTG.

Configuring Site Bridgehead Servers

Replication between sites is performed by bridgehead servers in each site. A bridgehead server is a domain controller designated by the ISTG to perform intersite replication. Bridgehead servers are discussed in detail in "Intersite Replication Essentials" on page 1089 and "Replication Rings and Directory Partitions" on page 1091.

As with the ISTG role, operating as a bridgehead server can add a significant load to a domain controller. This load increases with the number and frequency of replication changes. Because of this, the designated bridgehead servers should also be closely monitored to make sure they don't become overloaded.

Determine Bridgehead Servers

You can list the bridgehead servers in a site by typing the following command at a command prompt: **repadmin /bridgeheads site:***SiteName* where *SiteName* is the name of the site, such as **repadmin /bridgeheads site:Seattle-First-Site**. If you omit the site:*SiteName* values, the details for the current site are returned.

In situations in which you have domain controllers that are already overloaded or not equipped to possibly handle the additional load of being a bridgehead server, you might want to control which domain controllers operate as bridgehead servers. You do this by designating preferred bridgehead servers in a site.

There are several important considerations for designating bridgehead servers. First, after you designate a preferred bridgehead server, the ISTG will use only the preferred bridgehead server for intersite replication. This means if the domain controller acting as the bridgehead server goes offline or is unable to replicate for any reason, intersite replication will stop until the server is again available for replication or you change the preferred bridgehead server configuration options. In the latter case, you would need to do one of the following:

- Remove the server as a preferred bridgehead server and then specify a different preferred bridgehead server

- Remove the server as a preferred bridgehead server and then allow the ISTG to select the bridgehead servers that should be used

Because you can designate multiple preferred bridgehead servers, you can prevent this situation simply by specifying more than one preferred bridgehead server. When there are multiple preferred bridgehead servers, the ISTG will choose one of the servers you've designated as the preferred bridgehead server. If this server fails, it would then choose another server from the list of preferred bridgehead servers.

An additional consideration to make when designating preferred bridgehead servers is that you must configure a bridgehead server for each partition that needs to be replicated. This means you must configure at least one domain controller with a replica of each directory partition as a bridgehead server. If you don't do this, replication of the partition will fail and the ISTG will log an event in the Directory Services event log detailing the failure. Consider the example shown in Figure 37-8.

Here, the Denver-Site and the NY-Site are part of the same domain, ThePhone-Company.com. Each site has a global catalog and a DNS server that is integrated with Active Directory. In this configuration, the bridgehead servers must replicate the following directory partitions: domain, configuration, schema, global catalog, and DNS (for the Domain Name System). If you designated DC3 and DC5 as the preferred bridgehead servers, only the domain, configuration, schema directory partitions would be replicated. This means replication for the global catalog and the DNS partition would fail and the ISTG would log an event in the Directory Services event log specifying the reason for the failure. On the other hand, if you designated DC1 and DC2 as the preferred bridgehead servers for the Denver-Site and DC4 and DC6 as the preferred bridgehead servers for the NY-Site, all the directory partitions would be replicated.

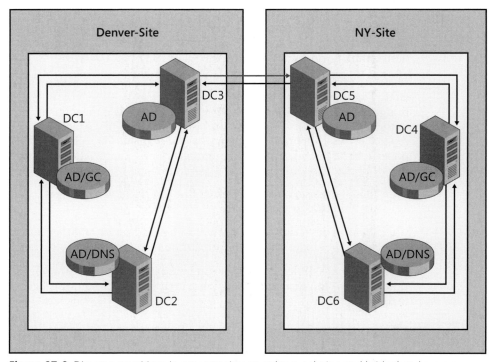

Figure 37-8 Directory partitions in separate sites must have a designated bridgehead server.

To configure a domain controller as a preferred bridgehead server, complete the following steps:

1. Start Active Directory Sites And Services by clicking Start, Administrative Tools, and Active Directory Sites And Services.

2. Domain controllers associated with a site are listed in the site's Servers node. To locate the domain controller that you want to work with, expand the site node, and then expand the related Servers node.

3. Right-click the server you want to designate as a preferred bridgehead, and then select Properties.

4. In the Properties dialog box, shown in Figure 37-9, you have the option of configuring the server as a preferred bridgehead server for either IP or SMTP. Select the appropriate transport in the Transports Available For Inter-Site Data Transfer list, and then click Add. If you later want the server to stop being a preferred bridgehead, select the transport in the This Server Is A Preferred Bridgehead Server For The Following Transports list, and then click Remove.

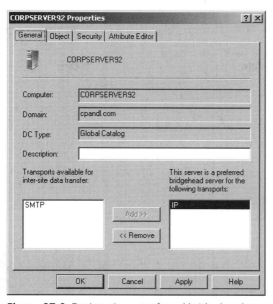

Figure 37-9 Designating a preferred bridgehead server.

5. Click OK.

Configuring Advanced Site Link Options

After you've configured sites and site links, you might want to or need to optimize the configuration options to better suit the needs of your organization. Using site link options, you can manage compression and notification during replication. You do this by editing the Options attribute on either the site link object or the connection object related to the site link you want to modify. Only members of the Enterprise Admins group can change these options.

You can configure a site link object's Options attribute by following these steps:

1. Start Active Directory Sites And Services by clicking Start, Administrative Tools, and Active Directory Sites And Services.

2. Expand the Sites container, and then expand the Inter-Site Transports container. Right-click the container for the transport protocol you want to work with, either IP or SMTP, and then select Properties.

3. In the Properties dialog box, click the Attribute Editor tab. Scroll through the list of attributes until you find the Options attribute. When you find this attribute, select it, and then click Edit.

4. In the Integer Attribute Editor dialog box, you can now do the following:

   ○ Type **1** to enable notification for intersite replication. This means the bridge-head servers on either side of the link will no longer use compression. Use this option only when you have sufficient bandwidth for a site connection and are concerned about high processor utilization on the affected bridgehead servers.

- Type **2** to enable two-way synchronization for intersite replication. This means bridgehead servers on either side of the link can synchronize changes at the same time. This allows simultaneous synchronization in two directions for faster updates. Only use this setting on links with sufficient bandwidth to handle two-way sync traffic.

- Type **4** to turn off compression for intersite replication. This means the bridgehead servers on either side of the link can notify each other that changes have occurred. This allows the bridgehead server receiving the notification to pull the changes across the site link and thereby get more frequent updates.

- Use combinations of the flag values to set multiple flags. For example, a value of 5 means compression will be turned off and notification for intersite replication will be enabled.

- Click Clear to reset the Options attribute to its default value of <not set>. When Options is not set, notification for intersite replication is disabled and compression is turned on.

5. Click OK twice.

Monitoring and Troubleshooting Replication

When you have problems with replication, you'll find that monitoring is an important part of your diagnostics and troubleshooting process. Several tools are available to help you, including the Replication Administrator (RepAdmin), which is a command-line utility.

Using the Replication Administrator

You run the Replication Administrator from the command line. Most command-line parameters accept a list of the domain controllers you want to work with called *DCList* and specified as follows:

- * is a wildcard that includes all domain controllers in the enterprise.

- *PartialName** is a partial server name that includes a wildcard to match the remainder of the server name.

- Site:*SiteName* includes only domain controllers in the named site.

- Gc: includes all global catalog servers in the enterprise.

Knowing this, there are many tasks you can perform using the Replication Administrator. These tasks are summarized in Table 37-2.

Table 37-2 **Key Replication Administrator Commands**

Command to Type	Description
repadmin /bridgeheads *DCList*] [*/verbose*]	Lists bridgehead servers.
repadmin /failcache *DCList*	Lists failed replication events that were detected by the knowledge consistency checker (KCC).
repadmin /istg *DCList* [*/verbose*]	Lists the name of the ISTG for a specified site.
repadmin /kcc *DCList* [*/async*]	Forces the KCC to recalculate the intrasite replication topology for a specified domain controller. By default, this recalculation occurs every 15 minutes. Use the /Async options to start the KCC and not wait for it to finish the calculation.
repadmin /latency *DCList* [*/verbose*]	Lists the amount of time between intersite replications using the ISTG Keep Alive time stamp.
repadmin /queue *DCList*	Lists tasks waiting in the replication queue.
repadmin /replsummary *DCList*	Displays a summary of the replication state.
repadmin /showcert *DCList*	Displays the server certificates loaded on the specified domain controllers.
repadmin /showconn *DCList*	Displays the connection objects for the specified domain controllers. Defaults to the local site.
repadmin /showctx *DCList*	Lists computers that have opened sessions with a specified domain controller.
repadmin/showoutcalls *DCList*	Lists calls that were made by the specified server to other servers but that have not yet been answered.
repadmin /showrepl *DCList*	Lists the replication partners for each directory partition on the specified domain controller.
repadmin /showtrust *DCList*	Lists all domains trusted by a specified domain.

Monitoring Replication

Using the Performance Monitor, you can perform in-depth monitoring and analysis of Active Directory. You open the Performance Monitor by clicking Start, All Programs, Administrative Tools, and then Reliability And Performance Monitor. You can track the performance of multiple domain controllers from a single, monitoring server using the Performance Monitor's remote monitoring capabilities.

DirectoryServices is the performance object you'll use for monitoring Active Directory. Several hundred performance counters are available for selection. Most counters have a prefix that reflects the aspect of Active Directory to which the counter relates. These prefixes include:

- **AB** AB counters relate to the Address Book in Active Directory.

- **ATQ** ATQ counters relate to the Asynchronous Thread Queue in Active Directory.

- **DRA** DRA counters relate to the Directory Replication Agent in Active Directory.

- **DS** DS counters relate to the Directory Service in Active Directory.

- **LDAP** LDAP counters relate to the Lightweight Directory Access Protocol in Active Directory.

- **SAM** SAM counters relate to the Security Accounts Manager in Active Directory.

Depending on the operations mode, either DFS or FRS is used for replication of the Sysvol. When the Distributed File System (DFS) Service is used to replicate the Sysvol files between domain controllers, you can monitor the DFS Service using the DFS Replicated Folders, DFS Replication Connections, and DFS Replication Service Volumes objects. When the File Replication Service (FRS) is used to replicate the Sysvol files between domain controllers, you can monitor the File Replication Service using the FileReplicaConn and FileReplicatSet monitoring objects. Each object has a number of counters that can be used to track the status and health of replication.

You can specify counters to monitor by following these steps:

1. In the Reliability And Performance Monitor console, expand the Monitoring Tools node and then select the Performance Monitor node.

2. Click the Add (+) button on the toolbar or press Ctrl+L. In the Add Counters dialog box, use the Select Counters From Computer list to select the computer to monitor.

3. Double-click the object you want to work with on the Available Counters list. Specify counters to track by selecting them in the Select Counters From Computer list and then clicking Add. You can learn more about counters by selecting the Show Description check box.

4. Click OK when you are finished adding counters.

You also can configure performance logging and performance alerting if desired:

- Events related to Active Directory are also logged in the event logs. Active Directory–related events, including NTDS replication events, are logged in the Directory Service log on the domain controller.

- Events related to DFS are recorded in the DFS Replication log on the domain controller. The primary source for events is DFSR, which is the DFS Service itself.

- Events related to the File Replication Service (FRS) are recorded in the File Replication Service log on the domain controller. The primary source for events is NtFrs, which is the File Replication Service itself.

Modifying Intersite Replication for Testing

Occasionally, when you are testing or troubleshooting intersite replication, you may need to temporarily modify the way intersite replication works. You can modify the way intersite replication works by editing the Options attribute on a bridgehead server's server object. Only members of the Enterprise Admins group can change these options.

You can configure a server object's Options attribute by following these steps:

1. Start Active Directory Sites And Services by clicking Start, Administrative Tools, and Active Directory Sites And Services.

2. Domain controllers associated with a site are listed in the site's Servers node. To locate the domain controller that you want to work with, expand the site node, and then expand the related Servers node.

3. Right-click the bridgehead server you want to work with, and then select Properties.

4. In the Properties dialog box, click the Attribute Editor tab. Scroll through the list of attributes until you find the Options attribute. When you find this attribute, select it, and then click Edit.

5. In the Integer Attribute Editor dialog box, you can now do the following:

   ○ Type **2** to disable inbound replication. This means the bridgehead server will no longer perform inbound replication. The server will still accept replication connections and will also perform outbound replication.

   ○ Type **4** to disable outbound replication. This means the bridgehead server will no longer perform outbound replication. The server will still accept replication connections and will also perform inbound replication.

   ○ Type **8** to prevent connections from forming replication partnerships. This means the bridgehead servers will not allow connections to be established for inbound or outbound replication. Existing connections will continue, but no new connections will be established.

   ○ Use combinations of the flag values to set multiple flags. For example, a value of 14 means inbound and outbound replication are disabled and that servers are prevented from forming replication partnerships.

   ○ Click Clear to reset the Options attribute and undo your changes. When Options is not set, notification for intersite replication is disabled and compression is turned on.

6. Click OK twice.

Chapter 37

Note

When the original value for the Options attribute is 1, the server hosts a global catalog and you must add 1 to all values you enter to ensure the server can continue to act as a global catalog. When you are finished testing, you can restore the original settings by entering a value of 1.

CAUTION

Setting these options changes the way the KCC works and also may disable the KCC's ability to automatically generate replication topology. Before you make any changes note the current value of the Options attribute. Typically, the attribute has a value of <not set> or 1. When the original value is <not set>, you can click Clear to reset the Options attribute and undo your changes. Failure to restore your changes after testing or troubleshooting can cause replication failure throughout the enterprise.

PART 6

Windows Server 2008 Disaster Planning and Recovery

Planning for High Availability

The enterprise depends on highly available, scalable, and manageable systems. High availability refers to the ability of the system to withstand hardware, application, or service outages while maintaining system availability. High scalability refers to the ability of the system to expand processor and memory capacity, as business needs demand. High manageability refers to the ability of the system to be managed locally and remotely and the ease with which components, services, and applications can be administered.

Planning for high availability is critical to the success of using Windows Server 2008 Enterprise and Windows Server 2008 Datacenter, and you need a solid understanding of the recommendations and operating principles for deploying and maintaining high-availability servers before you deploy servers running these editions. You should also understand the types of hardware, software, and support facilities needed for enterprise computing. These concepts are all covered in this chapter.

Planning for Software Needs

Software should be chosen for its ability to support the high-availability needs of the business system. Not all software is compatible with clustering or load balancing. Not all software must be compatible, either. Instead of making an arbitrary decision, you should let the uptime needs of the application determine the level of availability required.

An availability goal of 99 percent uptime is usual for most noncritical business systems. If an application must have 99 percent uptime, the application might not need to support clustering or load balancing. To achieve 99 percent uptime means that the application can have about 88 hours of downtime in an entire year, or 100 minutes of downtime a week.

To have 99.9 percent uptime is the availability goal for highly available business systems. If an application must have 99.9 percent uptime, the application must support clustering or load balancing. To achieve 99.9 percent uptime means that the application has less than 9 hours of downtime in an entire year, or, put another way, less than 10 minutes of downtime a week.

INSIDE OUT Clustering support alone isn't enough

Applications that support clustering are said to be cluster-aware. Microsoft SQL Server and Microsoft Exchange Server are examples of applications that are cluster-aware. Although both applications can be configured to provide high availability in the enterprise, they don't achieve high availability through cluster support alone. High-availability applications must support online backups and be tested for compatibility with Windows Server 2008. Support for online backups ensures that you don't have to take the application offline to back up critical data. Compatibility testing ensures that the software has been thoroughly evaluated for operation with Windows Server 2008.

To evaluate the real-world environment prior to deployment, you should perform integration testing on applications that will be used together. The purpose of integration testing is to ensure that disparate applications interact as expected and to uncover problem areas if they don't. During integration testing, testers should look at system performance and overall system utilization, as well as compatibility. Testing should be repeated prior to releasing system or application changes to a production environment.

You should standardize the software components needed to provide system services. The goal of standardization is to set guidelines for software components and technologies that will be used in the enterprise. Standardization accomplishes the following:

- Reduces the total cost of maintaining and updating software

- Reduces the amount of integration and compatibility testing needed for upgrades

- Improves recovery time because problems are easier to troubleshoot

- Reduces the amount of training needed for administration support

Software standardization isn't meant to limit the organization to a single specification. Over the life of the datacenter, new application versions, software components, and technologies will be introduced, and the organization can implement new standards and specifications as necessary. The key to success lies in ensuring that there is a standard process for deploying software updates and new technologies. The standard process must include the following:

- Software compatibility and integration testing

- Software support training for personnel

- Predeployment planning

- Step-by-step software deployment checklists

- Postdeployment monitoring and maintenance

The following checklist summarizes the recommendations for designing and planning software for high availability:

- Choose software that meets the availability needs of the solution or service.
- Choose software that supports online backups.
- Test software for compatibility with other applications.
- Test software integration with other applications.
- Repeat testing prior to releasing updates.
- Create and enforce software standards.
- Define a standard process for deploying software updates.

Planning for Hardware Needs

Sound hardware strategy helps increase system availability while reducing total cost of ownership and improving recovery times. Windows Server 2008 is designed and tested for use with high-performance hardware, applications, and services. To ensure that hardware components are compatible, choose only components that are listed in the Windows Server Catalog (*http://www.windowsservercatalog.com/*) or that are on the Hardware Compatibility List (HCL) (*http://winqual.microsoft.com/hcl/*).

> ### Note
> All components on the HCL undergo rigorous testing in the Microsoft Windows Hardware Quality Labs (WHQL). The initial testing is 14 days with a 7-day retest for firmware revision, service pack updates, and other minor revisions. After a component is certified through testing, hardware vendors must maintain the configuration through updates and resubmit for testing and certification. The program requirements and the tight coordination with vendors greatly improve the reliability and availability of Windows Server 2008.

You should standardize on a hardware platform and this platform should have standardized components. Standardization accomplishes the following:

- Reduces the amount of training needed for support
- Reduces the amount of testing needed for upgrades
- Requires fewer spare parts because subcomponents are the same
- Improves recovery time because problems are easier to troubleshoot

Standardization isn't meant to restrict the datacenter to a single type of server. In an *n*-tier environment, standardization typically means choosing a standard server configuration for the front-end servers, a standard server configuration for middle-tier business logic, and a standard server configuration for back-end data services. The reason for this is that Web servers, application servers, and database servers all have different resource needs. For example, although a Web server might need to run on a dual-processor system with limited hardware RAID control and 4 gigabytes (GB) of random access memory (RAM), a database server might need to run on an eight-way system with dual-channel RAID control and 64 GB of RAM.

Standardization isn't meant to limit the organization to a single hardware specification either. Over the life of the datacenter, new equipment will be introduced and old equipment likely will become unavailable. To keep up with the pace of change, new standards and specifications should be implemented when necessary. These standards and specifications, as with the previous standards and specifications, should be published and made available to you.

Redundancy and fault tolerance must be built into the hardware design at all levels to improve availability. You can improve hardware redundancy by using the following components:

- **Clusters** Clusters provide failover support for critical applications and services.

- **Standby systems** Standby systems provide backup systems in case of total failure of a primary system.

- **Spare parts** Spare parts ensure replacement parts are available in case of failure.

- **Fault-tolerant components** Fault-tolerant components improve the internal redundancy of the system.

Storage devices, network components, cooling fans, and power supplies all can be configured for fault tolerance. For storage devices, you should be sure to use multiple disk controllers, hot-swappable drives, and redundant drive arrays. For network components, you should look well beyond the network adapter and also consider whether fault tolerance is needed for routers, switches, firewalls, load balancers, and other network equipment.

A standard process for deploying hardware must be defined and distributed to all support personnel. The standard process must include the following:

- Hardware compatibility and integration testing

- Hardware support training for personnel

- Predeployment planning

- Step-by-step hardware deployment checklists

- Postdeployment monitoring and maintenance

The following checklist summarizes the recommendations for designing and planning hardware for high availability:

- Choose hardware that is listed on the HCL.

- Create and enforce hardware standards.

- Use redundant hardware whenever possible.

- Use fault-tolerant hardware whenever possible.

- Provide a secure physical environment for hardware.

- Define a standard process for deploying hardware.

If possible, add these recommendations to the preceding checklist:

- Use fully redundant internal networks from servers to border routers.

- Use direct peering to major tier-1 telecommunications carriers.

- Use redundant external connections for data and telephony.

- Use direct connection with high-speed lines.

Planning for Support Structures and Facilities

The physical structures and facilities supporting your server room are critically important. Without adequate support structures and facilities, you will have problems. The primary considerations for support structures and facilities have to do with the physical environment of the servers. These considerations also extend to the physical security of the server environment.

Just as hardware and software have availability requirements so should support structures and facilities. Factors that affect the physical environment are as follows:

- Temperature and humidity

- Dust and other contaminants

- Physical wiring

- Power supplies

- Natural disasters

- Physical security

Temperature and humidity should be carefully controlled at all times. Processors, memory, hard drives, and other pieces of physical equipment operate most efficiently when they are kept cool; between 65 and 70 degrees Fahrenheit is the ideal temperature in most situations. Equipment that overheats can malfunction or cease to operate altogether. Servers should have multiple redundant internal fans to ensure that these and other internal hardware devices are kept cool.

> **Note**
>
> You should pay particular attention to fast-running processors and hard drives. Typically, fast processors and hard drives can become overheated and need additional cooling fans—even if the surrounding environment is cool.

Humidity should be kept low to prevent condensation, but the environment shouldn't be dry. A dry climate can contribute to static electricity problems. Antistatic devices and static guards should be used in most environments.

Dust and other contaminants can cause hardware components to overheat or short out. Servers should be protected from these contaminants whenever possible. You should ensure that an air filtration system is in place in the server room or hosting facility that is used. The regular preventive maintenance cycle on the servers should include checking servers and their cabinets for dust and other contaminants. If dust is found, the servers and cabinets should be carefully cleaned.

Few things affect the physical environment more than wiring and cabling. All electrical wires and network cables should be tested and certified by qualified technicians. Electrical wiring should be configured to ensure that servers and other equipment have adequate power available for peak usage times. Ideally, multiple dedicated circuits are used to provide power.

Improperly installed network cables are the cause of most communications problems. Network cables should be tested to ensure their operation meets manufacturer specifications. Redundant cables should be installed to ensure availability of the network. All wiring and cabling should be labeled and well maintained. Whenever possible, use cable management systems and tie wraps to prevent physical damage to wiring.

Ensuring that servers and their components have power is also important. Servers should have hot-swappable, redundant power supplies. Being hot swappable ensures that the power supply can be replaced without having to turn off the server. Redundancy ensures that one power supply can malfunction and the other will still deliver power to the server. You should be aware that having multiple power supplies doesn't mean that a server or hardware component has redundancy. Some hardware components require multiple power supplies to operate. In this case, an additional (third or fourth) power supply is needed to provide redundancy.

The redundant power supplies should be plugged into separate power strips, and these power strips should be plugged into separate local uninterruptible power supply (UPS) units if other backup power sources aren't available. Some facilities have enterprise UPS units that provide power for an entire room or facility. If this is the case, redundant UPS systems should be installed. To protect against long-term outages, gas-powered or diesel-powered generators should be installed. Most hosting and colocation facilities have generators. But having a generator isn't enough; the generator must be rated to support the peak power needs of all installed equipment. If the generator cannot support the installed equipment, brownouts (temporary outages) will occur.

> ### Protect Equipment Against Earthquakes
>
> To protect against earthquakes, server racks should have seismic protection. Seismic protection should be extended to other components and to wiring. All cables should be securely attached at both ends and, whenever possible, should be latched to something other than the server, such as a server rack.

CAUTION

> A fire-suppression system should be installed to protect against fire. Dual gas-based systems are preferred, because the systems do not harm hardware when they go off. Water-based sprinkler systems, on the other hand, can destroy hardware.

In addition, access controls should be used to restrict physical access to the server room or facility. Use locks, key cards, access codes, or biometric scanners to ensure that only designated individuals can gain entry to the secure area. If possible, use surveillance cameras and maintain recorded tapes for at least a week. When the servers are deployed in a hosting or colocation facility, ensure that locked cages are used and that fencing extends from the floor to the ceiling.

The following checklist summarizes the recommendations for designing and planning structures and facilities:

- Maintain temperature at 65 to 70 degrees Fahrenheit.
- Maintain low humidity (but not dry).
- Install redundant internal cooling fans.
- Use an air filtration system.
- Check for dust and other contaminants periodically.
- Install hot-swappable, redundant power supplies.
- Test and certify wiring and cabling.
- Use wire management to protect cables from damage.
- Label hardware and cables.
- Install backup power sources, such as UPS and generators.
- Install seismic protection and bracing.
- Install dual gas-based fire-suppression systems.
- Restrict physical access by using locks, key cards, access codes, and so forth.

- Use surveillance cameras and maintain recorded tapes (if possible).

- Use locked cages, cabinets, and racks at offsite facilities.

- Use floor-to-ceiling fencing with cages at offsite facilities.

Planning for Day-to-Day Operations

Day-to-day operations and support procedures must be in place before deploying mission-critical systems. The most critical procedures for day-to-day operations involve the following activities:

- Monitoring and analysis

- Resources, training, and documentation

- Change control

- Problem escalation procedures

- Backup and recovery procedures

- Postmortem after recovery

- Auditing and intrusion detection

Monitoring is critical to the success of business system deployments. You must have the necessary equipment to monitor the status of the business system. Monitoring allows you to be proactive in system support rather than reactive. Monitoring should extend to the hardware, software, and network components but shouldn't interfere with normal systems operations—that is, the monitoring tools chosen should require limited system and network resources to operate.

> **Note**
>
> Keep in mind that too much data is just as bad as not collecting any data. The monitoring tools should gather only the data required for meaningful analysis.

Without careful analysis, the data collected from monitoring is useless. Procedures should be put in place to ensure that personnel know how to analyze the data they collect. The network infrastructure is a support area that is often overlooked. Be sure you allocate the appropriate resources for network monitoring.

INSIDE OUT   **Use monitoring to ensure availability**

A well-run and well-maintained network should have 99.99 percent availability. There should be less than 1 percent packet loss and packet turnaround of 80 milliseconds or less. To achieve this level of availability and performance the network must be monitored. Any time business systems extend to the Internet or to wide area networks (WANs), internal network monitoring must be supplemented with outside-in monitoring that checks the availability of the network and business systems.

Resources, training, and documentation are essential to ensuring that you can manage and maintain mission-critical systems. Many organizations cripple the operations team by staffing minimally. Minimally manned teams will have marginal response times and nominal effectiveness. The organization must take the following steps:

- Staff for success to be successful.

- Conduct training before deploying new technologies.

- Keep the training up-to-date with what's deployed.

- Document essential operations procedures.

Every change to hardware, software, and the network must be planned and executed deliberately. To do this, you must have established change control procedures and well-documented execution plans. Change control procedures should be designed to ensure that everyone knows what changes have been made. Execution plans should be designed to ensure that everyone knows the exact steps that were or should be performed to make a change.

Change logs are a key part of change control. Each piece of physical hardware deployed in the operational environment should have a change log. The change log should be stored in a text document or spreadsheet that is readily accessible to support personnel. The change log should show the following information:

- Who changed the hardware

- What change was made

- When the change was made

- Why the change was made

Establish and Follow Change Control Procedures

Change control procedures must take into account the need for both planned changes and emergency changes. All team members involved in a planned change should meet regularly and follow a specific implementation schedule. No one should make changes that aren't discussed with the entire implementation team.

You should have well-defined backup and recovery plans. The backup plan should specifically state the following information:

- When full, incremental, differential, and log backups are used
- How often and at what time backups are performed
- Whether the backups must be conducted online or offline
- The amount of data being backed up as well as how critical the data is
- The tools used to perform the backups
- The maximum time allowed for backup and restore
- How backup media is labeled, recorded, and rotated

Backups should be monitored daily to ensure that they are running correctly and that the media is good. Any problems with backups should be corrected immediately. Multiple media sets should be used for backups, and these media sets should be rotated on a specific schedule. With a four-set rotation, there is one set for daily, weekly, monthly, and quarterly backups. By rotating one media set offsite, support staff can help ensure that the organization is protected in case of a disaster.

The recovery plan should provide detailed step-by-step procedures for recovering the system under various conditions, such as procedures for recovering from hard disk drive failure or troubleshooting problems with connectivity to the back-end database. The recovery plan should also include system design and architecture documentation that details the configuration of physical hardware, application logic components, and back-end data. Along with this information, support staff should provide a media set containing all software, drivers, and operating system files needed to recover the system.

Note

One thing administrators often forget about is spare parts. Spare parts for key components, such as processors, drives, and memory, should also be maintained as part of the recovery plan.

You should practice restoring critical business systems using the recovery plan. Practice shouldn't be conducted on the production servers. Instead, the team should practice on test equipment with a configuration similar to the real production servers. Practicing once a quarter or semiannually is highly recommended.

You should have well-defined problem escalation procedures that document how to handle problems and emergency changes that might be needed. Many organizations use a three-tiered help desk structure for handling problems:

- Level 1 support staff forms the front line for handling basic problems. They typically have hands-on access to the hardware, software, and network components they manage. Their main job is to clarify and prioritize a problem. If the problem has occurred before and there is a documented resolution procedure, they can resolve the problem without escalation. If the problem is new or not recognized, they must understand how, when, and to whom to escalate it.

- Level 2 support staff includes more specialized personnel that can diagnose a particular type of problem and work with others to resolve a problem, such as system administrators and network engineers. They usually have remote access to the hardware, software, and network components they manage. This allows them to troubleshoot problems remotely and to send out technicians after they've pinpointed the problem.

- Level 3 support staff includes highly technical personnel who are subject matter experts, team leaders, or team supervisors. The level 3 team can include support personnel from vendors as well as representatives from the user community. Together, they form the emergency response or crisis resolution team that is responsible for resolving crisis situations and planning emergency changes.

All crisis situations and emergencies should be responded to decisively and resolved methodically. A single person on the emergency response team should be responsible for coordinating all changes and executing the recovery plan. This same person should be responsible for writing an after-action report that details the emergency response and resolution process used. The after-action report should analyze how the emergency was resolved and what the root cause of the problem was.

In addition, you should establish procedures for auditing system usage and detecting intrusion. In Windows Server 2008, auditing policies are used to track the successful or failed execution of the following activities:

- **Account logon events** Tracks events related to user logon and logoff

- **Account management** Tracks those tasks involved with handling user accounts, such as creating or deleting accounts and resetting passwords

- **Directory service access** Tracks access to the Active Directory Domain Service (AD DS)

- **Object access** Tracks system resource usage for files, directories, and objects

- **Policy change** Tracks changes to user rights, auditing, and trust relationships

Chapter 38

- **Privilege use** Tracks the use of user rights and privileges
- **Process tracking** Tracks system processes and resource usage
- **System events** Tracks system startup, shutdown, restart, and actions that affect system security or the security log

You should have an incident response plan that includes priority escalation of suspected intrusion to senior team members and provides step-by-step details on how to handle the intrusion. The incident response team should gather information from all network systems that might be affected. The information should include event logs, application logs, database logs, and any other pertinent files and data. The incident response team should take immediate action to lock out accounts, change passwords, and physically disconnect the system if necessary. All team members participating in the response should write a postmortem that details the following information:

- What date and time they were notified and what immediate actions they took
- Who they notified and what the response was from the notified individual
- What their assessment of the issue is and the actions necessary to resolve and prevent similar incidents

The team leader should write an executive summary of the incident and forward this to senior management.

The following checklist summarizes the recommendations for operational support of high-availability systems:

- Monitor hardware, software, and network components 24/7.
- Ensure that monitoring doesn't interfere with normal systems operations.
- Gather only the data required for meaningful analysis.
- Establish procedures that let personnel know what to look for in the data.
- Use outside-in monitoring any time systems are externally accessible.
- Provide adequate resources, training, and documentation.
- Establish change control procedures that include change logs.
- Establish execution plans that detail the change implementation.
- Create a solid backup plan that includes onsite and offsite tape rotation.
- Monitor backups and test backup media.
- Create a recovery plan for all critical systems.
- Test the recovery plan on a routine basis.
- Document how to handle problems and make emergency changes.

- Use a three-tier support structure to coordinate problem escalation.

- Form an emergency response or crisis resolution team.

- Write after-action reports that detail the process used.

- Establish procedures for auditing system usage and detecting intrusion.

- Create an intrusion response plan with priority escalation.

- Take immediate action to handle suspected or actual intrusion.

- Write postmortem reports detailing team reactions to the intrusion.

Planning for Deploying Highly Available Servers

You should always create a plan before deploying a business system. The plan should show everything that must be done before the system is transitioned into the production environment. After a system is in the production environment, the system is deemed operational and should be handled as outlined in "Planning for Day-to-Day Operations" on page 1316.

The deployment plan should include the following items:

- Checklists

- Contact lists

- Test plans

- Deployment schedules

Checklists are a key part of the deployment plan. The purpose of a checklist is to ensure that the entire deployment team understands the steps they need to perform. Checklists should list the tasks that must be performed and designate individuals to handle the tasks during each phase of the deployment—from planning to testing to installation. Prior to executing a checklist, the deployment team should meet to ensure that all items are covered and that the necessary interactions among team members are clearly understood. After deployment, the preliminary checklists should become a part of the system documentation and new checklists should be created any time the system is updated.

The deployment plan should include a contact list. The contact list should provide the name, role, telephone number, and e-mail address of all team members, vendors, and solution provider representatives. Alternative numbers for cell phones and pagers should be provided as well.

The deployment plan should include a test plan. An ideal test plan has several phases. In Phase I, the deployment team builds the business system and support structures in a test lab. Building the system means accomplishing the following tasks:

- Creating a test network on which to run the system

- Putting together the hardware and storage components
- Installing the operating system and application software
- Adjusting basic system settings to suit the test environment
- Configuring clustering or network load balancing as appropriate

The deployment team can conduct any necessary testing and troubleshooting in the isolated lab environment. The entire system should undergo burn-in testing to guard against faulty components. If a component is flawed, it usually fails in the first few days of operation. Testing doesn't stop with burn-in. Web and application servers should be stress tested. Database servers should be load tested. The results of the stress and load tests should be analyzed to ensure that the system meets the performance requirements and expectations of the customer. Adjustments to the configuration should be made to improve performance and optimize for the expected load.

In Phase II, the deployment team tests the business system and support equipment in the deployment location. They conduct similar tests as before but in the real-world environment. Again, the results of these tests should be analyzed to ensure that the system meets the performance requirements and expectations of the customer. Afterward, adjustments should be made to improve performance and optimize as necessary. The team can then deploy the business system.

After deployment, the team should perform limited, nonintrusive testing to ensure that the system is operating normally. After Phase III testing is completed, the team can use the operational plans for monitoring and maintenance.

The following checklist summarizes the recommendations for predeployment planning of mission-critical systems:

- Create a plan that covers the entire testing to operations cycle.
- Use checklists to ensure that the deployment team understands the procedures.
- Provide a contact list for the team, vendors, and solution providers.
- Conduct burn-in testing in the lab.
- Conduct stress and load testing in the lab.
- Use the test data to optimize and adjust the configuration.
- Provide follow-on testing in the deployment location.
- Follow a specific deployment schedule.
- Use operational plans once final tests are completed.

Preparing and Deploying Server Clusters

Clustering technologies allow servers to be connected into multiple-server units called *server clusters*. Each computer connected in a server cluster is referred to as a node. Nodes work together, acting as a single unit, to provide high availability for business applications and other critical resources, such as Microsoft Internet Information Services (IIS), Microsoft SQL Server, or Microsoft Exchange Server. Clustering allows administrators to manage the cluster nodes as a single system rather than as individual systems. Clustering allows users to access cluster resources as a single system as well. In most cases, the user doesn't even know the resources are clustered.

The main cluster technologies that Windows Server 2008 supports are:

- **Failover clustering** Failover clustering provides improved availability for applications and services that require high availability, scalability, and reliability. By using server clustering, organizations can make applications and data available on multiple servers linked together in a cluster configuration. The clustered servers (called nodes) are connected by physical cables and by software. If one of the nodes fails, another node begins to provide service. This process, known as failover, ensures that users experience a minimum of disruptions in service. Back-end applications and services, such as those provided by database servers, are ideal candidates for failover clustering.

- **Network Load Balancing** Network Load Balancing (NLB) provides failover support for Internet Protocol (IP)–based applications and services that require high scalability and availability. By using Network Load Balancing, organizations can build groups of clustered computers to support load balancing of Transmission Control Protocol (TCP), User Datagram Protocol (UDP), and Generic Routing Encapsulation (GRE) traffic requests. Front-end Web servers are ideal candidates for Network Load Balancing.

These cluster technologies are discussed in this chapter so that you can plan for and implement your organization's high-availability needs.

Introducing Server Clustering

A server cluster is a group of two or more servers functioning together to provide essential applications or services seamlessly to enterprise clients. The servers are physically connected together by a network and might share storage devices. Server clusters are designed to protect against application and service failure, which could be caused by application software or essential services becoming unavailable; system and hardware failure, which could be caused by problems with hardware components such as central processing units (CPUs), drives, memory, network adapters, and power supplies; and site failure, which could be caused by natural disaster, power outages, or connectivity outages.

You can use cluster technologies to increase overall availability while minimizing single points of failure and reducing costs by using industry-standard hardware and software. Each cluster technology has a specific purpose and is designed to meet different requirements. Network Load Balancing is designed to address bottlenecks caused by Web services. Failover clustering is designed to maintain data integrity and allow a node to provide service if another node fails.

The clustering technologies can be and often are combined to architect a comprehensive service offering. The most common scenario in which both solutions are combined is a commercial Web site where the site's Web servers use Network Load Balancing and back-end database servers use failover clustering.

Benefits and Limitations of Clustering

A server cluster provides high availability by making application software and data available on several servers linked together in a cluster configuration. If a server stops functioning, a failover process can automatically shift the workload of the failed server to another server in the cluster. The failover process is designed to ensure continuous availability for critical applications and data.

Although clusters can be designed to handle failure, they are not fault tolerant with regard to user data. The cluster by itself doesn't guard against loss of a user's work. Typically, the recovery of lost work is handled by the application software, meaning the application software must be designed to recover the user's work or it must be designed in such a way that the user session state can be maintained in the event of failure.

Clusters help to resolve the need for high availability, high reliability, and high scalability. *High availability* refers to the ability to provide user access to an application or a service a high percentage of scheduled times while attempting to reduce unscheduled outages. A cluster implementation is highly available if it meets the organization's scheduled uptime goals. Availability goals are achieved by reducing unplanned downtime and then working to improve total hours of operation for the related applications and services.

High reliability refers to the ability to reduce the frequency of system failure while attempting to provide fault tolerance in case of failure. A cluster implementation is highly reliable if it minimizes the number of single points of failure and reduces the risk that failure of a single component or system will result in the outage of all applications and services offered. Reliability goals are achieved by using redundant, fault-tolerant hardware components, application software, and systems.

High scalability refers to the ability to add resources and computers while attempting to improve performance. A cluster implementation is highly scalable if it can be scaled up and out. Individual systems can be scaled up by adding more resources such as CPUs, memory, and disks. The cluster implementation can be scaled out by adding more computers.

> ### Design for Availability
>
> A well-designed cluster implementation uses redundant systems and components so that the failure of an individual server doesn't affect the availability of the related applications and services. Although a well-designed solution can guard against application failure, system failure, and site failure, cluster technologies do have limitations.

Cluster technologies depend on compatible applications and services to operate properly. The software must respond appropriately when failure occurs. Cluster technology cannot protect against failures caused by viruses, software corruption, or human error. To protect against these types of problems, organizations need solid data protection and recovery plans.

Cluster Organization

Clusters are organized in loosely coupled groups often referred to as farms or packs. A *farm* is a group of servers that run similar services but don't typically share data. They are called a farm because they handle whatever requests are passed out to them using identical copies of data that are stored locally. Because they use identical copies of data rather than sharing data, members of a farm operate autonomously and are also referred to as *clones*.

A *pack* is a group of servers that operate together and share partitioned data. They are called a pack because they work together to manage and maintain services. Because members of a pack share access to partitioned data, they have unique operations modes and usually access the shared data on disk drives to which all members of the pack are connected.

In most cases, Web and application services are organized as farms, while back-end databases and critical support services are organized as packs. Web servers running IIS and using Network Load Balancing are an example of a farm. In a Web farm, identical data is replicated to all servers in the farm and each server can handle any request that comes to it by using local copies of data. For example, you might have a group of five Web servers using Network Load Balancing, each with its own local copy of the Web site data.

Chapter 39

Database servers running SQL Server and failover clustering with partitioned database views are an example of a pack. Here, members of the pack share access to the data and have a unique portion of data or logic that they handle rather than handling all data requests. For example, in a two-node SQL Server cluster, one database server might handle accounts that begin with the letters A through M and another database server might handle accounts that begin with the letters N through Z.

Servers that use clustering technologies are often organized using a three-tier structure. The tiers in the architecture are composed as follows:

- Tier 1 includes the Web servers, which are also called front-end Web servers. Front-end Web servers typically use Network Load Balancing.

- Tier 2 includes the application servers, which are often referred to as the middle-tier servers. Middle-tier servers typically use the Windows Communications Foundation (WCF) or other Web Services technologies to implement load balancing for application components that use COM+. Using a WCF-based load balancer, COM+ components can be load balanced over multiple nodes to enhance the availability and scalability of software applications.

- Tier 3 includes the database servers, file servers, and other critical support servers, which are often called back-end servers. Back-end servers typically use failover clustering.

As you set out to architect your cluster solution, you should try to organize servers according to the way they will be used and the applications they will be running. In most cases, Web servers, application servers, and database servers are all organized in different ways.

By using proper architecture, the servers in a particular tier can be scaled out or up as necessary to meet growing performance and throughput needs. When you are looking to scale out by adding servers to the cluster, the clustering technology and the server operating system used are both important:

- All editions of Windows Server 2008 support up to 32-node Network Load Balancing clusters.

- Windows Server Enterprise and Windows Server Datacenter support failover clustering, allowing up to 8-node clusters.

When looking to scale up by adding CPUs and random access memory (RAM), the edition of the server operating system used is extremely important. In terms of both processor and memory capacity, Windows Server Datacenter is much more expandable than either Windows Server Standard or Windows Server Enterprise.

As you look at scalability requirements, keep in mind the real business needs of the organization. The goal should be to select the right edition of the Windows operating system to meet current and future needs. The number of servers needed depends on the anticipated server load as well as the size and types of requests the servers will handle. Processors and memory should be sized appropriately for the applications and services the servers will be running as well as the number of simultaneous user connections.

Cluster Operating Modes

For Network Load Balancing, cluster nodes usually are identical copies of each other. Because of this, all members of the cluster can actively handle requests, and they can do so independently of each other. When members of a cluster share access to data, however, they have unique operating requirements, as is the case with failover clustering.

For failover clustering, nodes can be either active or passive. When a node is active, it is actively handling requests. When a node is passive, it is idle, on standby waiting for another node to fail. Multinode clusters can be configured by using different combinations of active and passive nodes.

When you are architecting multinode clusters, the decision as to whether nodes are configured as active or passive is extremely important. If an active node fails and there is a passive node available, applications and services running on the failed node can be transferred to the passive node. Because the passive node has no current workload, the server should be able to assume the workload of the other server without any problems (providing all servers have the same hardware configuration). If all servers in a cluster are active and a node fails, the applications and services running on the failed node can be transferred to another active node. Unlike a passive node, however, an active server already has a processing load and must be able to handle the additional processing load of the failed server. If the server isn't sized to handle multiple workloads, it can fail as well.

In a multinode configuration where there is one passive node for each active node, the servers could be configured so that under average workload they use about 50 percent of processor and memory resources. In the four-node configuration depicted in Figure 39-1, in which failover goes from one active node to a specific passive node, this could mean two active nodes (A1 and A2) and two passive nodes (P1 and P2) each with four processors and 4 GB of RAM. Here, node A1 fails over to node P1, and node A2 fails over to node P2 with the extra capacity used to handle peak workloads.

In a configuration in which there are more active nodes than passive nodes, the servers can be configured so that under average workload they use a proportional percentage of processor and memory resources. In the four-node configuration also depicted in Figure 39-1, in which nodes A, B, C, and D are configured as active and failover could go between nodes A and B or nodes C and D, this could mean configuring servers so that they use about 25 percent of processor and memory resources under an average workload. Here, node A could fail over to B (and vice versa) or node C could fail over to D (and vice versa). Because the servers must handle two workloads in case of a node failure, the processor and memory configuration would at least be doubled, so instead of using four processors and 4 GB of RAM, the servers would use eight processors and 8 GB of RAM.

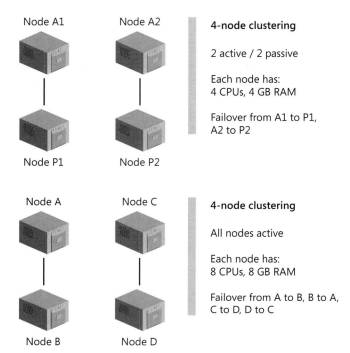

Node A1   Node A2   **4-node clustering**

2 active / 2 passive

Each node has:
4 CPUs, 4 GB RAM

Failover from A1 to P1,
A2 to P2

Node P1   Node P2

Node A   Node C   **4-node clustering**

All nodes active

Each node has:
8 CPUs, 8 GB RAM

Failover from A to B, B to A,
C to D, D to C

Node B   Node D

Figure 39-1 Clustering can be implemented in many ways; these are examples.

When failover clustering has multiple active nodes, data must be shared between applications running on the clustered servers. In many cases, this is handled by using a shared-nothing database configuration. In a shared-nothing database configuration, the application is partitioned to access private database sections. This means that a particular node is configured with a specific view into the database that allows it to handle specific types of requests, such as account names that start with the letters A through F, and that it is the only node that can update the related section of the database (which eliminates the possibility of corruption from simultaneous writes by multiple nodes). Both Exchange Server 2003 and SQL Server 2000 support multiple active nodes and shared-nothing database configurations.

As you consider the impact of operating modes in the cluster architecture, you should look carefully at the business requirements and the expected server loads. By using Network Load Balancing, all servers are active and the architecture is scaled out by adding more servers, which typically are configured identically to the existing Network Load Balancing nodes. By using failover clustering, nodes can be either active or passive, and the configuration of nodes depends on the operating mode (active or passive) as well as how failover is configured. A server that is designated to handle failover must be sized to handle the workload of the failed server as well as the current workload (if any). Additionally, both average and peak workloads must be considered. Servers need additional capacity to handle peak loads.

Multisite Options for Clusters

Some large organizations build disaster recovery and increased availability into their infrastructure using multiple physical sites. Multisite architecture can be designed in many ways. In most cases, the architecture has a primary site and one or more remote sites. Figure 39-2 shows an example of a primary site and a remote site for a large commercial Web site.

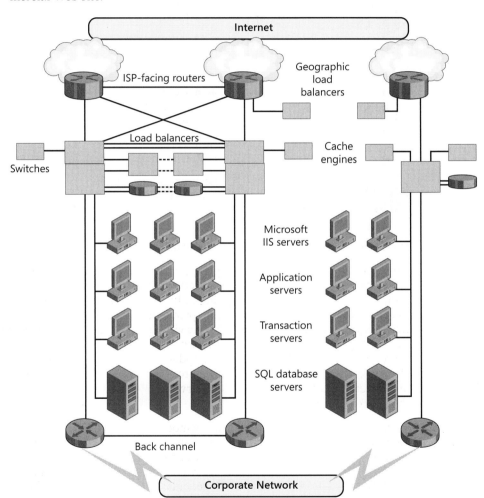

Figure 39-2 Enterprise architecture for a large commercial Web site that has multiple physical locations.

As shown in Figure 39-2, the architecture at the remote site mirrors that of the primary site. The level of integration for multiple sites and the level at which components are mirrored between sites depends on the business requirements. With a full implementation, the complete infrastructure of the primary site could be re-created at remote sites.

This allows for a remote site to operate independently or to handle the full load of the primary site if necessary. Here, the design should incorporate real-time replication and synchronization for databases and applications. Real-time replication ensures a consistent state for data and application services between sites. If real-time updates are not possible, databases and applications should be replicated and synchronized as rapidly as possible.

With a partial implementation, only essential components are installed at remote sites with the goal of handling overflow in peak periods, maintaining uptime on a limited basis in case the primary site fails, or providing limited services on an ad hoc basis. One technique is to replicate static content on Web sites and read-only data from databases. This would allow remote sites to handle requests for static content and other types of data that is infrequently changed. Users could browse sites and access account information, product catalogs, and other services. If they must access dynamic content or modify information (add, change, delete), the sites' geographical load balancers could redirect the users to the primary site.

Another partial implementation technique is to implement all layers of the infrastructure but with fewer redundancies in the architecture or to implement only core components, relying on the primary site to provide the full array of features. By using either technique, the design might need to incorporate near real-time replication and synchronization for databases and applications. This ensures a consistent state for data and application services.

A full or partial design could also use geographically dispersed clusters running failover clustering. Geographically dispersed clusters use virtual local area networks (VLANs) to connect storage area networks (SANs) over long distances. A VLAN connection with latency of 500 milliseconds or less ensures that cluster consistency can be maintained. If the VLAN latency is over 500 milliseconds, the cluster consistency cannot be easily maintained. Geographically dispersed clusters are also referred to as stretched clusters.

Windows Server 2008 supports a majority node set quorum resource. Majority node clustering changes the way the cluster quorum resource is used to allow cluster servers to maintain consistency in the event of node failure. In a standard cluster configuration, the quorum resource writes information on all cluster database changes to the recovery logs, ensuring that the cluster configuration and state data can be recovered. Here, the quorum resource resides on the shared disk drives and can be used to verify whether other nodes in the cluster are functioning.

In a majority node cluster configuration, the quorum resource is configured as a majority node set resource. This allows the quorum data, which includes cluster configuration changes and state information, to be stored on the system disk of each node in the cluster. Because the data is localized, the cluster can be maintained in a consistent state. As the name implies, the majority of nodes must be available for this cluster configuration to operate normally. Should the cluster state become inconsistent, you can force the quorum to get a consistent state. An algorithm also runs on the cluster nodes to help ensure the cluster state.

Using Network Load Balancing

Each server in a Network Load Balancing cluster is referred to as a *node*. Network Load Balancing nodes work together to provide availability for critical IP-based resources, which can include TCP, UDP, and GRE traffic requests.

Using Network Load Balancing Clusters

Network Load Balancing provides failover support for IP-based applications and services that require high scalability and availability. You can use Network Load Balancing to build groups of up to 32 clustered computers, starting with as few as 2 computers and incrementally scaling out as demand increases. Network Load Balancing is ideally suited to improving the availability of Web servers, media servers, terminal servers, and e-commerce sites. Load balancing these services ensures that there is no single point of failure and that there is no performance bottleneck.

Network Load Balancing uses virtual IP addresses, and client requests are directed to these virtual IP addresses, allowing for transparent failover and failback. When a load-balanced resource fails on one server, the remaining servers in the group take over the workload of the failed server. When the failed server comes back online, the server can automatically rejoin the cluster group, and Network Load Balancing starts to distribute the load to the server automatically. Failover takes less than 10 seconds in most cases.

Network Load Balancing doesn't use shared resources or clustered storage devices. Instead, each server runs a copy of the TCP/IP application or service that is being load balanced, such as a Web site running Internet Information Services (IIS). Local storage is used in most cases as well. As with failover clustering, users usually don't know that they're accessing a group of servers rather than a single server. The reason for this is that the Network Load Balancing cluster appears to be a single server. Clients connect to the cluster using a virtual IP address and, behind the scenes, this virtual address is mapped to a specific server based on availability.

Anyone familiar with load-balancing strategies might be inclined to think of Network Load Balancing as a form of round robin Domain Name System (DNS). In round robin DNS, incoming IP connections are passed to each participating server in a specific order. For example, an administrator defines a round robin group containing Server A, Server B, and Server C. The first incoming request is handled by Server A, the second by Server B, the third by Server C, and then the cycle is repeated in that order (A, B, C, A, B, C, . . .). Unfortunately, if one of the servers fails, there is no way to notify the group of the failure. As a result, the round robin strategy continues to send requests to the failed server. Windows Network Load Balancing doesn't have this problem.

To avoid sending requests to failed servers, Network Load Balancing sends heartbeats to participating servers. These heartbeats are similar to those used by the Cluster service. The purpose of the heartbeat is to track the condition of each participant in the group. If a server in the group fails to send heartbeat messages to other servers in the group for a specified interval, the server is assumed to have failed. The remaining servers in the group take over the workload of the failed server. While previous connections to the failed host are lost, the IP-based application or service continues to be available. In most cases, clients automatically retry the failed connections and experience only a few seconds delay in receiving a response. When the failed server becomes available again, Network Load Balancing automatically allows the server to rejoin the group and starts to distribute the load to the server.

Network Load Balancing Configuration

Although Network Load Balancing is normally used to distribute the workload for an application or service, it can also be used to direct a specific type of traffic to a particular server. For example, an administrator might want to load Hypertext Transfer Protocol (HTTP) and File Transfer Protocol (FTP) traffic to a group of servers but might want a single server to handle other types of traffic. In this latter case, Network Load Balancing allows traffic to flow to a designated server and reroutes traffic to another server only in case of failure.

Network Load Balancing runs as a network driver and requires no hardware changes to install and run. Its operations are transparent to the TCP/IP networking stack. Because Network Load Balancing is IP-based, IP networking must be installed on all load-balanced servers. At this time, Network Load Balancing supports Ethernet and Fiber Distributed Data Interface (FDDI) networks but doesn't support Asynchronous Transfer Mode (ATM). Future versions of Network Load Balancing might support this network architecture. There are four basic models for Network Load Balancing:

- **Single network adapter in unicast mode** This model is best for an environment in which ordinary network communication among cluster hosts is not required and in which there is limited dedicated traffic from outside the cluster subnet to specific cluster hosts.

- **Multiple network adapters in unicast mode** This model is best for an environment in which ordinary network communication among cluster hosts is necessary or desirable and in which there is moderate to heavy dedicated traffic from outside the cluster subnet to specific cluster hosts.

- **Single network adapter in multicast mode** This model is best for an environment in which ordinary network communication among cluster hosts is necessary or desirable but in which there is limited dedicated traffic from outside the cluster subnet to specific cluster hosts.

- **Multiple network adapters in multicast mode** This model is best for an environment in which ordinary network communication among cluster hosts is necessary and in which there is moderate to heavy dedicated traffic from outside the cluster subnet to specific cluster hosts.

Network Load Balancing uses unicast or multicast broadcasts to direct incoming traffic to all servers in the cluster. The Network Load Balancing driver on each host acts as a filter between the cluster adapter and the TCP/IP stack, allowing only traffic bound for the designated host to be received. For Windows Server 2008, the NLB network driver has been completely rewritten to use the NDIS 6.0 lightweight filter model. NDIS 6.0 features enhanced driver performance and scalability, a simplified driver model, and backward compatibility with earlier NDIS versions.

Network Load Balancing controls only the flow of TCP, UDP, and GRE traffic on specified ports. It doesn't control the flow of TCP, UDP, and GRE traffic on nonspecified ports, and it doesn't control the flow of other incoming IP traffic. All traffic that isn't controlled is passed through without modification to the IP stack. For Windows Server 2008, IP address handling has been extended to accommodate IP version 6 (IPv6) as well as multiple dedicated IP addresses for IPv4 and IPv6. This allows you to configure NLB clusters with one or more dedicated IPv4 and IPv6 addresses.

> **Note**
>
> Network Load Balancing can be used with Microsoft Internet Security and Acceleration (ISA) Server. For Windows Server 2008, both NLB and ISA have been extended for improved interoperability. With ISA Server, you can configure multiple dedicated IP addresses for each node in the NLB cluster when clients use both IPv4 and IPv6. ISA can also notify NLB about node overloads and SYN attacks. Synchronize (SYN) and acknowledge (ACK) are part of the TCP connection process. A SYN attack is a denial-of-service attack that exploits the retransmission and time-out behavior of the SYN-ACK process to create a large number of half-open connections that use up a computer's resources.

To provide high-performance throughput and responsiveness, Network Load Balancing normally uses two network adapters, as shown in Figure 39-3. The first network adapter, referred to as the cluster adapter, handles network traffic for the cluster, and the second adapter, referred to as the dedicated adapter, handles client-to-cluster network traffic and other traffic originating outside the cluster network.

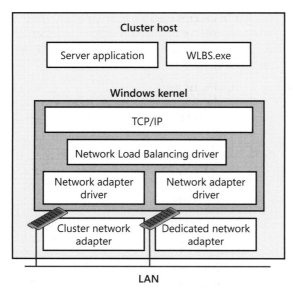

Figure 39-3 Network Load Balancing with two network adapters.

Chapter 39

Network Load Balancing can also work with a single network adapter. When it does so, there are limitations. With a single adapter in unicast mode, node-to-node communications are impossible, which means nodes within the cluster cannot communicate with each other. Servers can, however, communicate with servers outside the cluster subnet. By using a single adapter in multicast mode, node-to-node communications are possible as are communications with servers outside the cluster subnet. However, the configuration is not optimal for handling moderate to heavy traffic from outside the cluster subnet to specific cluster hosts. For handling node-to-node communications and moderate to heavy traffic, two adapters should be used.

Regardless of whether a single adapter or multiple adapters are used, all servers in the group operate in either unicast or multicast mode—not both. In unicast mode, the cluster's Media Access Control (MAC) address is assigned to the computer's network adapter and the network adapter's built-in MAC address is disabled. All participating servers use the cluster's MAC address, allowing incoming packets to be received by all servers in the group and passed to the Network Load Balancing driver for filtering. Filtering ensures that only packets intended for the server are received and all other packets are discarded. To avoid problems with Layer 2 switches, which expect to see unique source addresses, Network Load Balancing uniquely modifies the source MAC address for all outgoing packets. The modified address shows the server's cluster priority in one of the MAC address fields.

Because the built-in MAC address is used, the server group has some communication limitations when a single network adapter is configured. Although the cluster servers can communicate with other servers on the network and with servers outside the network, the cluster servers cannot communicate with each other. To resolve this problem, two network adapters are needed in unicast mode.

In multicast mode, the cluster's MAC address is assigned to the computer's network adapter and the network adapter's built-in MAC address is maintained so that both can be used. Because each server has a unique address, only one adapter is needed for network communications within the cluster group. Multicast offers some additional performance benefits for network communications as well. However, multicast traffic can flood all ports on upstream switches. To prevent this, a virtual LAN should be set up for the participating servers.

INSIDE OUT Using Network Load Balancing with routers

If Network Load Balancing clients are accessing a cluster through a router, be sure that the router is configured properly. For unicast clusters, the router should accept a dynamic Address Resolution Protocol (ARP) reply that maps the unicast IP address to its unicast MAC address. For multicast clusters, the router should accept an ARP reply that has a MAC address in the payload of the ARP structure. If the router isn't able to do this, you can also create a static ARP entry in the router to handle these requirements. Some routers will require a static ARP entry because they do not support the resolution of unicast IP addresses to multicast MAC addresses.

Network Load Balancing Port and Client Affinity Configurations

Several options can be used to optimize performance of a Network Load Balancing cluster. Each server in the cluster can be configured to handle a specific percentage of client requests, or the servers can handle client requests equally. The workload is distributed statistically and does not take into account CPU, memory, or drive usage. For IP-based traffic, the technique does work well, however. Most IP-based applications handle many clients, and each client typically has multiple requests that are short in duration.

Many Web-based applications seek to maintain the state of a user's session within the application. A session encompasses all the requests from a single visitor within a specified period of time. By maintaining the state of sessions, the application can ensure that the user can complete a set of actions, such as registering for an account or purchasing equipment. Network Load Balancing clusters use filtering to ensure that only packets intended for the server are received and all other packets are discarded. Port rules specify how the network traffic on a port is filtered. Three filtering modes are available:

- **Disabled** No filtering
- **Single Host** Direct traffic to a single host
- **Multiple Hosts** Distribute traffic among the Network Load Balancing servers

Port rules are used to configure Network Load Balancing on a per-port basis. For ease of management, port rules can be assigned to a range of ports as well. This is most useful for UDP traffic when many different ports can be used.

When multiple hosts in the cluster will handle network traffic for an associated port rule, you can configure client affinity to help maintain application sessions. Client affinity uses a combination of the source IP address and source and destination ports to direct multiple requests from a single client to the same server. Three client affinity settings can be used:

- **None** Specifies that Network Load Balancing doesn't need to direct multiple requests from the same client to the same server
- **Single** Specifies that Network Load Balancing should direct multiple requests from the same client IP address to the same server
- **Network** Specifies that Network Load Balancing should direct multiple requests from the same Class C address range to the same server

Network affinity is useful for clients that use multiple proxy servers to access the cluster.

Chapter 39

Planning Network Load Balancing Clusters

Many applications and services can work with Network Load Balancing, provided they use TCP/IP as their network protocol and use an identifiable set of TCP or UDP ports. Key services that fit these criteria include the following:

- FTP over TCP/IP, which normally uses TCP ports 20 and 21

- HTTP over TCP/IP, which normally uses TCP port 80

- HTTPS over TCP/IP, which normally uses TCP port 443

- IMAP4 over TCP/IP, which normally uses TCP ports 143 and 993 (SSL)

- POP3 over TCP/IP, which normally uses TCP ports 110 and 995 (SSL)

- SMTP over TCP/IP, which normally uses TCP port 25

Network Load Balancing can be used with virtual private network (VPN) servers, terminal servers, and streaming media servers as well. For Network Load Balancing, most of the capacity planning focuses on the cluster size. *Cluster size* refers to the number of servers in the cluster. Cluster size should be based on the number of servers necessary to meet anticipated demand.

Stress testing should be used in the lab to simulate anticipated user loads prior to deployment. Configure the tests to simulate an environment with increasing user requests. Total requests should simulate the maximum anticipated user count. The results of the stress tests will determine whether additional servers are needed. The servers should be able to meet demands of the stress testing with 70 percent or less server load with all servers running. During failure testing, the peak load shouldn't rise above 80 percent. If either of these thresholds is reached, the cluster size might need to be increased.

Servers that use Network Load Balancing can benefit from optimization as well. Servers should be optimized for their role, the types of applications they will run, and the anticipated local storage they will use. Although you might want to build redundancy into the local hard drives on Network Load Balancing servers, this adds to the expense of the server without significant availability gains in most instances. Because of this, Network Load Balancing servers often have drives that do not use redundant array of independent disks (RAID) and do not provide fault tolerance, the idea being that if a drive causes a server failure, other servers in the Network Load Balancing cluster can quickly take over the workload of the failed server.

If it seems odd not to use RAID, keep in mind that servers using Network Load Balancing are organized so they use identical copies of data on each server. Because many different servers have the same data, maintaining the data with RAID sets isn't as important as it is with failover clustering. A key point to consider when using Network Load Balancing, however, is data synchronization. The state of the data on each server must be maintained so that the clones are updated whenever changes are made. The need to synchronize data periodically is an overhead that must be considered when designing the server architecture.

> **Note**
>
> With IIS 7.0, the Shared Configuration feature greatly simplifies the process of sharing configuration across multiple Web servers. All you need to do is point the servers to a shared configuration location and then copy the desired configuration to this location. For complete details on configuring IIS 7.0, see Chapter 5 "Managing Global IIS Configuration," in the *Internet Information Services (IIS) 7.0 Administrator's Pocket Consultant* (Microsoft Press, 2008).

Managing Network Load Balancing Clusters

Network Load Balancing is a feature that you must install using the Add Features Wizard. Alternatively, you can install NLB by entering the following command at an elevated command prompt: **servermanagercmd -install nlb**. When you install NLB, two tools are installed as well: Network Load Balancing Manager (Nlbmgr.exe) and NLB Cluster Control Utility (Nlb.exe). Network Load Balancing Manager provides the graphical interface for managing, monitoring, and configuring Network Load Balancing clusters. Its command-line counterpart is Nlb.exe. Both tools use the NLB application programming interface (API) to manage Network Load Balancing.

Creating a New Network Load Balancing Cluster

You create Network Load Balancing clusters using Network Load Balancing Manager (see Figure 39-4). Start Network Load Balancing Manager from the Administrative Tools menu or by typing **nlbmgr** at the command prompt.

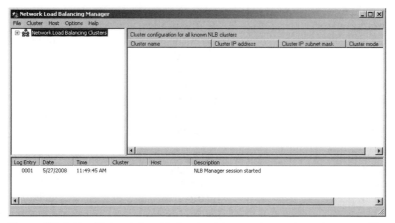

Figure 39-4 Use Network Load Balancing Manager to create and manage Network Load Balancing clusters.

Chapter 39

> **Note**
>
> To create an NLB cluster and configure NLB, you must use an account that is a member of the Administrators group on each host. If you are not using such an account, you will be prompted for credentials each time you try to work with NLB. You can avoid this prompt by specifying the default credentials to be used when connecting to NLB hosts. In Network Load Balancing Manager, click Credentials on the Options menu. In the NLB Manager Default Credentials dialog box, type the user name and password for the default account and then click OK.

After you've started Network Load Balancing Manager, you can create the new Network Load Balancing cluster by following these steps:

1. Right-click Network Load Balancing Clusters in the left pane, and then choose New Cluster. This displays the New Cluster: Connect wizard, as shown in Figure 39-5.

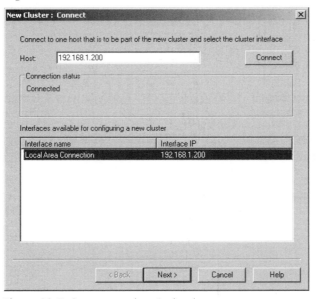

Figure 39-5 Connect to a host in the cluster.

2. Enter the domain name or IP address of the first host that will be a member of the cluster. Click Connect to connect to the server and display a list of available network interfaces. Select the network adapter that you want to use for Network Load Balancing, and then click Next. The IP address configured on this network adapter will be the dedicated IP address for this host and will be used for the public traffic of the cluster (as opposed to the private, node-to-node traffic).

3. Click Next to display the New Cluster: Host Parameters page, shown in Figure 39-6. Using the options in the Priority list, set the unique priority for this host in the cluster. The host priority is a unique host identifier that indicates the order in which traffic is routed among members of the cluster, and it ranges from 1 to 32. The host with ID 1 is the first to receive traffic, the host with ID 2 is the second, and so on. Additionally, the host with the lowest priority among cluster members handles all of the cluster's network traffic that is not covered by a specific port rule.

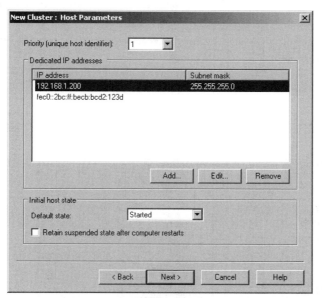

Figure 39-6 Use the New Cluster: Host Parameters page to specify the host priority and dedicated IP address.

4. The Dedicated IP Addresses list shows the dedicated IP address or addresses that will be used to connect to this specific server. Each NLB host can have multiple dedicated IPv4 and IPv6 addresses. Dedicated IP addresses for the host are used for private, node-to-node traffic (as opposed to the public traffic for the cluster). They must be fixed IP addresses and not DHCP addresses. You can add, edit, or remove IPv4 and IPv6 addresses using the Add, Edit, and Remove buttons provided.

5. Using the options in the Default State list, set the initial state of this host when the Windows operating system is started. In most cases with deployed systems, you want the default state to be set as Started as opposed to Suspended or Stopped. If you don't want the NLB host to be activated when you restart the server, select the Retain Suspended State After Computer Restarts check box.

6. Click Next to display the New Cluster: Cluster IP Addresses page, shown in Figure 39-7. The Cluster IP Addresses list shows the virtual IP address or addresses that will be used for the cluster. An NLB cluster can have multiple

virtual IPv4 and IPv6 addresses. You can add, edit, or remove IPv4 and IPv6 addresses using the buttons provided.

Note

The IP address you assign is used to address the cluster as a whole and should be the IP address that maps to the full Internet name of the cluster that you provide in the Full Internet Name field on the next wizard page. For clusters operating in unicast mode, the IPv4 address can be any Class A, B, or C IPv4 address, but typically is a private IPv4 address, such as 192.168.88.20. For clusters operating in multicast mode, the IPv4 address typically is a Class D IP address (224.0.0.0 to 239.255.255.255). Similarly, when you use IPv6 addresses, you typically assign a link-local or site-local IPv6 address as opposed to a global IPv6 address. With IPv6, you have the option of generating the IP addresses to use as well using the Add IP Address dialog box.

Note

Virtual IP addresses are used for addressing throughout the cluster. You must use these IP addresses for all hosts in the cluster, and it is fixed, so it cannot be a Dynamic Host Configuration Protocol (DHCP) address.

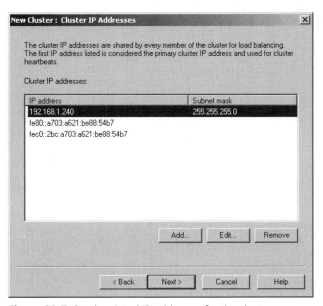

Figure 39-7 Set the virtual IP addresses for the cluster.

7. Click Next to display the New Cluster: Cluster Parameters page, shown in Figure 39-8. In the Full Internet Name field, type the fully qualified domain name for the cluster, such as cluster.cpandl.com. This is the domain name by which the cluster will be known.

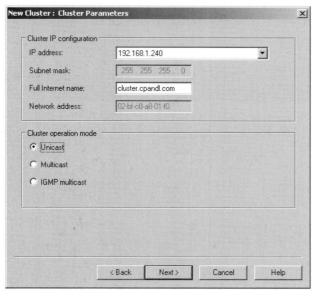

Figure 39-8 Set the domain name for the cluster and the cluster operations mode.

8. Next, set the Cluster Operation Mode as Unicast, Multicast, or IGMP Multicast. With IGMP Multicast, multicast IPv4 addresses are then restricted to the standard Class D address range (224.0.0.0 to 239.255.255.255).

Limit Switch Flooding

If the cluster hosts are directly connected to a hub and Internet Group Membership Protocol (IGMP) support is not enabled, incoming client traffic is automatically sent to all switch ports and can produce switch flooding. By enabling IGMP support for multicast clusters, you can limit switch flooding.

Note

Keep in mind that if you are working from a computer that has a single network adapter and that computer uses Network Load Balancing in unicast mode, you cannot use Network Load Balancing Manager on this computer to configure and manage other hosts. A computer with a single network adapter operating in unicast mode cannot communicate with other hosts in the cluster. You can, however, communicate with computers outside the cluster.

Chapter 39

9. Click Next. Using the New Cluster: Port Rules page, as shown in Figure 39-9, you can specify how the network traffic on a port is filtered. When you've configured multiple IP addresses for the cluster, you might want to configure filtering on a per–IP address basis. By default all TCP and UDP traffic directed to any cluster IP address that arrives on ports 0 to 65535 is balanced across all members of the cluster based on the load weight of each cluster member.

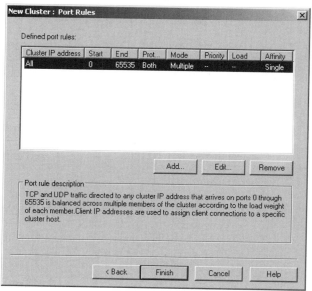

Figure 39-9 Use the New Cluster: Port Rules page to specify how network traffic on a port is filtered.

10. Click Finish to start the Network Load Balancing service and configure the cluster using the specific initial host. You can then add hosts into the cluster as appropriate. If you need to change the cluster parameters later, right-click the cluster in the left pane, and select Cluster Properties. You are then able to change the cluster IP addresses, cluster parameters, and port rules.

Adding Nodes to a Network Load Balancing Cluster

After you've created a cluster and added an initial host, at any time you can add other nodes to the cluster, up to a maximum of 32. Additional hosts automatically inherit the cluster port rules from the initial host. As mentioned previously, if you are working from a computer that has a single network adapter and that computer uses Network Load Balancing in unicast mode, you cannot use Network Load Balancing Manager on this computer to configure and manage other hosts.

To add a node to a Network Load Balancing cluster, follow these steps:

1. Start Network Load Balancing Manager from the Administrative Tools menu or by typing **nlbmgr** at the command prompt. If the cluster you want to work with

isn't shown in Network Load Balancing Manager, you can connect to it by right-clicking Network Load Balancing Clusters in the left pane and selecting Connect To Existing. On the Connect page, enter the domain name or IP address of any host in the cluster, and then click Connect. Select the cluster name to work with, and then click Finish.

2. In the left pane, right-click the cluster to which you want to add a node, and select Add Host To Cluster. Enter the domain name or IP address of the host to add to the cluster. Click Connect to connect to the server and display a list of available network interfaces. Select the network adapter that you want to use for Network Load Balancing. The IP address configured on this network adapter will be the dedicated IP address for this host and will be used for the public traffic of the cluster (as opposed to the private, node-to-node traffic).

3. Click Next to display the Host Parameters page. Set the unique priority for this host in the cluster and the dedicated IP address or addresses that will be used to connect to this specific server. Afterward, set the initial state of this host when the Windows operating system is started. In most cases with deployed systems, you want the default state to be set as Started.

4. Click Finish to add the host to the cluster. When the host is added to the cluster, the cluster status changes to Converged temporarily while Network Load Balancing updates the cluster configuration. If you must change the host parameters later, right-click the host in the left pane, and select Host Properties. You are then able to change the host priority, IP configuration, and initial state.

Removing Nodes from a Network Load Balancing Cluster

Network Load Balancing Manager provides several techniques for temporarily removing a node from a cluster, including the capability to suspend and resume load balancing on a per-node basis. If you no longer want a node to be a member of a Network Load Balancing cluster, you can remove it permanently from the cluster as well. To do this, start Network Load Balancing Manager from the Administrative Tools menu or by typing **nlbmgr** at the command prompt. Right-click the node in the left pane, and then select Delete Host. When prompted to confirm the action, click Yes.

> Note
>
> If the cluster you want to work with isn't shown in Network Load Balancing Manager, you can connect to it by right-clicking Network Load Balancing Clusters in the left pane and selecting Connect To Existing. On the Connect page, enter the domain name or IP address of any host in the cluster, and click Connect. Select the cluster name to work with, and then click Finish.

Configuring Event Logging for Network Load Balancing Clusters

Events related to Network Load Balancing are stored in the System logs and can be accessed in Event Viewer. You can also enable logging related to the use of Network Load Balancing Manager. These events show the operations being performed in Network Load Balancing Manager.

To enable Network Load Balancing Manager logging, select Log Settings on the Options menu, select the Enable Logging check box, and specify the full file path to the file you want to use for logging. Because this file contains sensitive information regarding the cluster, it should be stored in a secure folder accessible only to administrators.

Controlling Cluster and Host Traffic

Network Load Balancing Manager allows you to control operations on the cluster as a whole as well as for individual hosts within the cluster. You control cluster operations by right-clicking the cluster in the left pane of Network Load Balancing Manager, pointing to Control Hosts, and then selecting one of the following options:

- **Stop** Stops all Network Load Balancing cluster traffic. Cluster operations are immediately stopped, and all existing connections are immediately closed.

- **Drainstop** Disables all new traffic to the cluster but allows hosts to continue servicing active connections.

- **Suspend** Stops all Network Load Balancing cluster traffic and also suspends cluster-control commands, including remote control, except for resume and query. Cluster operations are immediately stopped, and all existing connections are immediately closed.

- **Resume** Reenables the use of cluster-control commands for the cluster, including remote control. This option doesn't restart cluster operations, however.

- **Start** Starts or restarts the handling of Network Load Balancing traffic for the cluster.

You can manage the Cluster service on a specific host by right-clicking the host, pointing to Control Host, and then selecting one of the following options:

- **Stop** Stops Network Load Balancing on the host, and all existing connections to the host are immediately closed.

- **Drainstop** Disables all new traffic to the host but allows the host to continue servicing any active connections.

- **Suspend** Stops all Network Load Balancing on the host and also suspends cluster-control commands, including remote control, except for resume and query.

- **Resume** Reenables the use of cluster-control commands for the host, including remote control. This option doesn't restart cluster operations, however.

- **Start** Starts or restarts the handling of Network Load Balancing traffic for the host.

Using Failover Clustering

Failover clustering is a feature that you must install using the Add Features Wizard. Alternatively, you can install failover clustering by entering the following command at an elevated command prompt: **servermanagercmd -install failover-clustering**. Failover clustering is implemented using the Microsoft Cluster service and is used to provide failover support for applications and services. A failover cluster can consist of up to eight nodes. Each node is attached to one or more cluster storage devices. Cluster storage devices, such as those configured on storage area networks (SANs) or using direct-attached storage (DAS), allow different servers to share the same data and thus, by reading this data, provide failover for resources.

Failover Cluster Configurations

Failover clusters can be set up using many different configurations. Servers can be either active or passive, and different servers can be configured to take over the failed resources of another server. Failover can take several minutes, depending on the configuration and the application being used, but is designed to be transparent to the user.

When a node is active, it makes its resources available. Clients access these resources through dedicated virtual servers. The Cluster service uses the concept of virtual servers to specify groups of resources that fail over together. Thus, when a server fails, the group of resources configured on that server for clustering fail over to another server. The server that handles the failover should be configured for the extra capacity needed to handle the additional workload. When the failed server comes back online, the Cluster service can be configured to allow failback to the original server or to allow the current server to continue to process requests.

Windows Server 2008 supports three basic types of failover clusters:

- Single-node clusters

- Single quorum device multinode clusters

- Majority node clusters

Figure 39-11 shows an example of a single-node cluster. A single-node cluster doesn't make use of failover but does provide easier administration for sharing resources and network storage. The main advantage of a single-node cluster is that the Cluster service monitors and automatically restarts applications and dependent resources that fail or freeze. A single-node cluster could work with file, print, or Web shares when the primary concern is to make it easy for users to access resources, but it isn't practical otherwise. Single-node clusters are also useful for test and development purposes, allowing you to develop cluster-aware applications and test them using limited hardware.

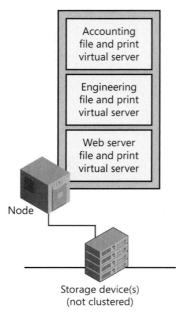

Figure 39-11 A single-node failover cluster.

To get the full benefit of clustering, administrators must implement a multinode cluster. The key multinode cluster models are active/passive and active/active. In an active/passive configuration, one or more nodes are actively processing user, application, and system requests, while one or more other nodes are idle. The nodes processing requests are referred to as *active*, or *primary*, nodes. The idle nodes are referred to as *standby*, or *passive*, nodes. The passive nodes are ready to be used when a failover occurs on a primary node. By contrast, in an active/active configuration all nodes actively process user, application, and system requests and there are no standby nodes. Then when an active node fails the other primary nodes temporarily take up the slack until the failed node can be restarted.

Figure 39-12 shows a multinode cluster with a single quorum device configuration. The nodes are configured so that every node is attached to one or more cluster storage devices that all nodes share and the cluster configuration data is stored on a single cluster storage device called the quorum device. Alternatively, the quorum device can be referred to as the witness device.

Another type of failover cluster is the majority node set. In a majority node cluster configuration, nodes don't have to be connected to shared storage devices. Each node can have its own storage device. The cluster configuration data is stored on multiple disks across the cluster. This allows each node to have a local quorum device.

Majority node clusters are often used with geographically separated servers. Primarily, this is because each node can have its own storage and its own copy of the cluster configuration data. Geographic separation isn't a requirement, however. The servers could just as easily be in the same location.

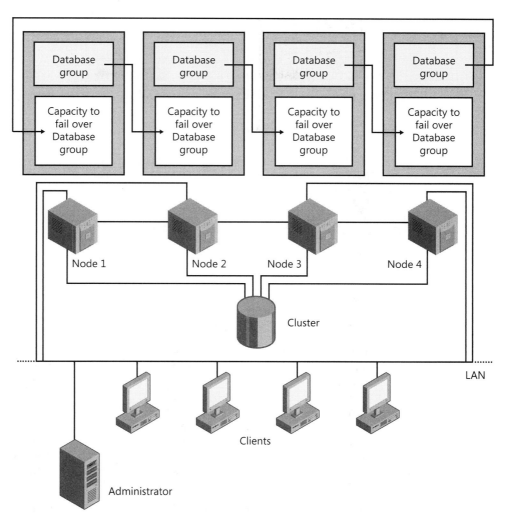

Figure 39-12 Failover cluster using shared storage.

Understanding Failover Cluster Resources

A high-availability resource is a unit of failover. Resources that are related or dependent on each other are associated through resource groupings. All resources grouped together must be from the same node. If any of the services in a high-availability resource fails, all the services fail over together according to the failover policy defined for the resource. When the cause of a failure is resolved, the resource fails back to its original location based on the failback policy of the resource.

> **Note**
>
> Only applications that need high availability should be part of a resource. Other applications can run on a cluster server but don't need to be a part of a resource.

Before adding an application as a high-availability resource, you must determine whether the application can work within the cluster environment. Applications that can work within the cluster environment and support cluster events are called cluster-aware. Cluster-aware applications can register with the Failover cluster to receive status and notification information. Applications and services that are cluster-aware include the following:

- Distributed File System (DFS) Namespace Server
- DHCP Server
- Exchange Server
- File Server
- Internet Storage Name Service (iSNS) Server
- Microsoft Distributed Transaction Coordinator (MS DTC)
- Microsoft Message Queuing (MSMQ)
- Print Server
- SQL Server
- Windows Internet Naming Service (WINS) Server

Generic applications and services can also be cluster-aware. Check with the software vendor to determine compatibility with the Cluster service.

Applications that do not support cluster events are called cluster-unaware. Some cluster-unaware applications can be configured as high-availability resources and can be failed over. The following provisions apply:

- IP-based protocols are used for cluster communications. The application must use an IP-based protocol for its network communications. Applications cannot use NetBIOS Extended User Interface (NetBEUI), Internetwork Packet Exchange (IPX), AppleTalk, or other protocols to communicate.

- Nodes in the cluster access application data through shared storage devices. If the application isn't able to store its data in a configurable location, the application data won't be available on failover.

- Client applications experience a temporary loss of network connectivity when failover occurs. If client applications cannot retry and recover from this, they will cease to function normally.

Applications that meet these criteria can be configured as high-availability resources.

Optimizing Hardware for Failover Clusters

After determining which applications and services need high availability and which don't, administrators should focus on selecting the right hardware to meet the needs of the business system. A cluster model should be chosen to adequately support resource failover and the availability needs of the system. Based on the model chosen, excess capacity should be added to ensure that resources are available in the event a resource fails and failover to a server substantially increases the workload.

The configuration of the hardware should be adjusted to maximize total throughput and optimize performance for the types of applications and services that will experience the greatest demand. Different servers have different optimization needs. A Web server with static HTML pages might need fast hard disk drives and additional RAM to cache files in memory but typically doesn't need high-end CPUs. A typical database server needs high-end CPUs, fast hard disk drives, and additional RAM.

Administrators should carefully optimize performance of each server in the cluster node. A key area where optimization can have huge benefits is with paging files. Key rules for paging files are as follows:

- Paging files should have a fixed size to prevent excess paging and shouldn't be located on the shared cluster storage device.

- Whenever more than 4 GB of RAM is installed, the paging file size should be set as per the hardware manufacturer's recommendation.

- If multiple local drives are available, consider placing the paging file on separate drives to improve performance.

With a clustered SQL Server configuration, you should consider using high-end CPUs, fast hard disk drives, and additional memory. Carefully review the baseline memory usage for SQL Server and standard services as well as the estimated number of simultaneous user connections and queries. Each user connection uses a small amount of memory. Each user query requires a larger amount of memory. Other SQL Server processes use memory as well.

Cluster storage devices should be optimized based on performance and availability needs. Table 39-1 provides an overview of common hardware RAID configurations for clusters. The table entries are organized listing the highest RAID level to the lowest.

Table 39-1 **Hardware RAID Configurations for Clusters**

RAID Level	RAID Type	RAID Description	Advantages and Disadvantages
5+1	Disk striping with parity + mirroring	Uses at least six volumes, each on a separate drive. Each volume is configured identically as a mirrored stripe set with parity error checking.	Provides very high level of fault tolerance but has a lot of overhead.
5	Disk striping with parity	Uses at least three volumes, each on a separate drive. Each volume is configured as a stripe set with parity error checking. In the case of failure, data can be recovered.	Provides fault tolerance with less overhead than mirroring. Better read performance than disk mirroring.
1	Disk mirroring	Uses two volumes on two drives. The drives are configured identically and data is written to both drives. If one drive fails, there is no data loss because the other drive contains the data. This approach does not include disk striping.	Provides redundancy with better write performance than disk striping with parity.
0+1	Disk striping with mirroring	Uses two or more volumes, each on a separate drive. The volumes are striped and mirrored. Data is written sequentially to drives that are identically configured.	Provides redundancy with good read and write performance.
0	Disk striping	Uses two or more volumes, each on a separate drive. Volumes are configured as a stripe set. Data is broken into blocks, called stripes, and then written sequentially to all drives in the stripe set.	Provides speed and performance without data protection.

Failover clusters have many specific hardware requirements as well. In order to implement failover clustering with Windows Server 2008, all hardware components must be compatible with Windows Server 2008. Hardware components certified as compatible with Windows Server 2008 have the Designed For Windows Server 2008 logo. To help validate a configuration prior to deploying failover clustering, the cluster administration tool includes a configuration validation feature that ensures all hardware and storage components are compatible with Windows Server 2008. The pre-deployment validation tests also ensure that the network configuration is suitable for a cluster.

You should use identical hardware in all clustered servers. Using identical hardware components makes the configuration easier to manage and can eliminate potential compatibility issues. In each clustered server, you need at least two network adapters that are dedicated to network communications. Storage devices can use serial attached SCSI, fibre channel, or Internet SCSI (iSCSI). If you are using iSCSI, each have either a network adapter or a host bus adapter dedicated to storage communications over the network.

Your storage devices should have multiple separate volumes (LUNs) configured at the hardware level. These volumes must be configured as basic disks and be formatted with NTFS. For the partition style of the disk, you can use either the master boot record (MBR) or GUID partition table (GPT). With SANs, the storage must support Persistent Reservations as specified in the SCSI Primary Commands-3 (SPC-3) standard and storage used with one set of cluster servers must be isolated from all other servers using LUN masking or zoning.

When planning failover clusters, you should keep in mind these additional requirements:

- Servers in the same cluster must all run the same hardware architecture version of the Windows Server 2008 operating system. For example, they should all use either the x64 or the Itanium version.

- Servers in the same cluster must all be members of the same Active Directory domain and must be using DNS for name resolution. DNS dynamic updates can be used. Because of changes in DNS for Windows Server 2008, WINS and NetBIOS names are no longer required for name resolution.

- Servers in the same cluster should be member servers, as a recommended best practice. If all servers are member servers, you will need additional servers to act as domain controllers.

Optimizing Networking for Failover Clusters

The network configuration of the cluster can also be optimized. Typically, nodes in a cluster are configured with both private and public network addresses. Private network addresses are used for node-to-node communications, and public network addresses are used for client-to-cluster communications. However, some clusters might not need public network addresses and instead can be configured to use two private networks. Here, the first private network is for node-to-node communications and the second private network is for communicating with other servers that are a part of the service offering.

Increasingly, clustered servers and storage devices are connected over SANs. SANs use high-performance interconnections between secure servers and storage devices to deliver higher bandwidth and lower latency than comparable traditional networks. Enterprise Edition and Datacenter Edition implement a feature called Winsock Direct that allows direct communication over a SAN using SAN providers.

SAN providers have user-mode access to hardware transports. When communicating directly at the hardware level, the individual transport endpoints can be mapped directly into the address space of application processes running in user mode. This allows applications to pass messaging requests directly to the SAN hardware interface, which eliminates unnecessary system calls and data copying.

SANs typically use two transfer modes. One mode is for small transfers, which primarily consist of transfer control information. For large transfers, SANs can use a bulk mode whereby data is transferred directly between the local system and the remote system by the SAN hardware interface without CPU involvement on the local or remote system. All bulk transfers are prearranged through an exchange of transfer-control messages.

In addition to improved communication modes, SANs have other benefits. They allow you to consolidate storage needs, using several highly reliable storage devices instead of many. They also allow you to share storage with non-Windows operating systems, allowing for heterogeneous operating environments.

Running Failover Clusters

For Windows Server 2008, Cluster Administrator is renamed Failover Cluster Management and given a simplified interface. Like its predecessor, Failover Cluster Management (Cluadmin.exe) provides the graphical interface for managing, monitoring, and configuring failover clusters. Its command-line counterpart is Cluster.exe. Both tools use the Cluster API to manage the Cluster service.

The Cluster Service and Cluster Objects

The Cluster service is responsible for all aspects of failover clustering and also maintains the cluster database. The Cluster service uses objects to control the physical and logical units within the cluster. Many types of cluster objects are defined, including those pertaining to the following components:

- Cluster networks
- Cluster interfaces
- Nodes
- Cluster resources
- Resource types

Cluster objects have properties that define their behavior within the cluster. The Cluster API contains the control codes and management functions needed to manage the object through the Cluster service. As shown in Figure 39-13, each node in a cluster runs an instance of the Cluster service (Clussvc.exe), the Cluster Network Driver (Clusnet.sys), and the Cluster Disk Driver (Clusdisk.sys). The Cluster Network Driver is responsible for the following activities:

- Providing reliable, guaranteed communication between nodes
- Monitoring network paths between nodes
- Routing cluster messages
- Detecting communication failure

Failover Cluster Management

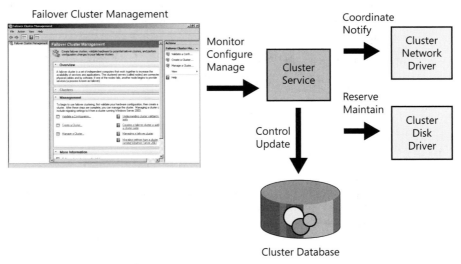

Figure 39-13 Overview of cluster administration.

Each node's Cluster Network Driver periodically exchanges messages called *heartbeats* with other active nodes. The heartbeat is a UDP packet that is sent between cluster nodes. If a node fails to respond to a heartbeat message, the Cluster Network Driver on the node that detects the failure notifies the Cluster service.

Each node's Cluster Disk Driver is responsible for maintaining exclusive ownership of shared disks. Only the node that owns the physical disk resource can access the disk. All other nodes cannot access the disk resource. The Cluster Disk Driver also is responsible for replacing reservations on disks for the local system.

The Cluster Heartbeat

The Cluster service transmits heartbeat messages on a dedicated network adapter, called the cluster adapter, to other computers in the failover cluster. The number of nodes in the failover cluster determines how these additional network adapters are connected. With a four-node cluster and standard Ethernet cabling, the dedicated network adapters are normally connected to a dedicated hub or switch. For redundancy, communications can be transmitted over multiple networks as well.

As the name implies, the heartbeat is used to track the condition of each node in the cluster. If the Cluster service doesn't receive a heartbeat from a server in the cluster within a specified time, the service assumes the server has failed and initiates failover. The Cluster service uses the concept of virtual servers to specify high-availability resources that fail over together. Failover occurs when a clustered resource fails on one server and another server takes over management of the resource. When the failed resource is restored, the original server is able to regain control of the resource and come back online. The process of returning to service is called *failback*.

The Cluster Database

The heartbeat isn't the only traffic transmitted between clusters. The clusters also exchange synchronization and management data. Most management information is stored in the cluster database. This database contains information on the configuration of the cluster and the resources it uses.

The cluster database contains information on all physical and logical elements in the cluster, referred to as cluster objects, as well as configuration data. The Cluster service maintains the database by using global updates and periodic check pointing. Global updates are used to replicate changes across all nodes. Any changes that the Cluster service fails to replicate to all nodes are logged to a recovery log. These changes are synchronized at a subsequent checkpoint.

The Cluster Quorum Resource

Every cluster has a resource that is responsible for maintaining the recovery logs. This resource is called the quorum resource. The quorum resource writes information on all cluster database changes to the recovery logs, ensuring that the cluster configuration and state data can be recovered. The importance of the quorum resource is evident in any failover situation. Consider the following scenario:

1. Nodes in a cluster are using the quorum resource and then node 1 fails. Nodes 2, 3, and 4 continue to operate. Node 2 takes over resources of the failed node.

2. Node 2 writes configuration changes to the recovery logs.

3. Node 2 fails before node 1 comes back online. Nodes 3 and 4 take over the resources of the failed nodes.

4. Shortly afterward, node 1 comes back online and must update its private copy of the cluster database with the changes made by node 2.

5. The Cluster service uses the quorum resource's recovery logs to synchronize changes and perform the configuration updates. Node 1 is then able to rejoin and regain control of its resources.

The full function of a cluster depends on the quorum and on the capacity of each node to support the services and applications that fail over to that node. When you configure clustering, the Cluster service automatically determines the appropriate quorum configuration for your cluster. The quorum configuration determines the number of failures that the cluster can sustain. If an additional failure occurs, the cluster must stop running.

To understand this, consider the following examples:

- A cluster that has four nodes no longer has a quorum majority after two nodes fail, and can no longer continue running.

- A cluster that has five nodes has a quorum majority after two nodes fail, but must also have enough capacity to handle the services and applications that failed over to it.

The Cluster Interface and Network States

The network adapter used to transfer cluster management and state data is referred to as the cluster adapter. Traffic between nodes in the cluster is transmitted over the cluster network, which is typically a private network used only by the cluster nodes. To determine failure, the Cluster service tracks the status of the cluster adapter interface and the cluster network.

The cluster adapter interface states are shown in Table 39-2. Administrators can use the CLUSTER NETINTERFACE command or Failover Cluster Management to check the interface state.

Table 39-2 Cluster Adapter Interface States

Network Interface State	Description
Up	The normal operation state. The interface is active and can communicate with all other interfaces on the network (except those that are Failed or Unavailable).
Unknown	The state cannot be determined at this time.
Unavailable	The interface is disabled for cluster use or the node associated with the network interface is down.
Unreachable	The node cannot communicate through the interface. The reason is unknown.
Failed	The node associated with the interface is active but cannot communicate through its interface. The Cluster service has isolated the error to the interface as determined by failure to receive heartbeats from the node and receipt of hardware failure notifications from an adapter that supports Network Driver Interface Specification (NDIS).

The network states are shown in Table 39-3. Administrators can use the CLUSTER NETWORK command or Failover Cluster Management to check network state.

Table 39-3 Cluster Network States

Network State	Description
Up	The normal operation state. The network is functioning normally.
Unknown	The state cannot be determined at this time.
Unavailable	The network is disabled for cluster use or all the nodes attached to the network are inactive.
Partitioned	The network has partially failed. Some active clusters cannot communicate with one another over the network.
Down	The network has failed. None of the active clusters can communicate with another using the network.

When a network interface enters the Failed state, the Cluster service triggers failover of all IP address resources that use the network interface. The Cluster service does not do this when a network interface is unreachable. When the interface is unreachable, the Cluster service cannot isolate the problem in a way that is sufficient to implement a recovery policy. Additionally, if the interface is in the Unavailable state, the Cluster service assumes the node is down.

The cluster network should normally be in the Up state. When in the Up state, the cluster network is working normally and all active nodes are communicating. If the network enters the Partitioned state, it means one or more of the nodes is having communication problems or has recently failed. The Down state indicates the cluster network has failed and isn't functioning. In the Down state, clusters cannot communicate with each other over this network.

Creating Failover Clusters

After you finish the cluster planning and set up the server hardware, you can create the cluster. You create the cluster using Failover Cluster Management, which can be started from the Administrative Tools menu or by typing **cluadmin** at the command prompt.

> **Note**
>
> If you are using a shared storage device, only one node in the cluster should have access to the cluster disk while you are creating the cluster. Otherwise, the cluster disk can become corrupted. To prevent this, either shut down all but the primary node or use another technique such as logical unit number (LUN) masking to keep the other nodes from accessing the cluster disk.

When you start Failover Cluster Management for the first time, you can select the following options as shown in Figure 39-14:

- **Validate A Configuration** Runs validation tests to determine whether the servers, attached storage, and network configuration are compatible with Windows Server 2008 and set up correctly to support failover.

- **Create A Cluster** Creates a cluster using the Create Cluster Wizard. Before you create a cluster, you should validate the configuration.

- **Manage A Cluster** Allows you to manage an existing cluster. In the Select A Cluster To Manage dialog box, connect to an existing cluster by typing the cluster name or IP address and then clicking OK. Alternatively, click Browse to browse the network and Active Directory for clusters.

The sections that follow detail how to create a new cluster and add nodes to it.

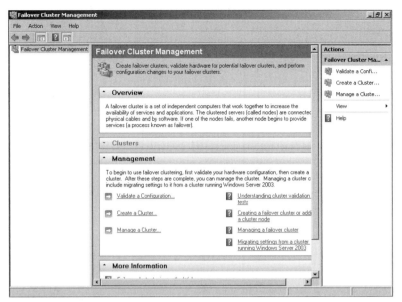

Figure 39-14 Failover Cluster Management.

Validating a Configuration

Before creating a failover cluster, you should run validation tests to determine whether the servers, attached storage, and network configuration are compatible with Windows Server 2008 and set up correctly to support failover. The tests are organized into several categories and include:

- Inventory tests that record the configuration of every important aspect of the server hardware from BIOS information to environment variables to hardware component configuration.

- Network tests that validate the network topology for clustering as well as the configuration of IP addressing and Windows Firewall.

- Storage tests that list all disks that are visible to servers you are testing, identify potential cluster disks, and validate storage performance parameters, including disk access latency, file system formatting, and disk arbitration processes. Disk arbitration processes allow a server to take ownership of a disk.

- System tests that validate the system configuration. These tests ensure that: all servers are part of the same domain and organization unit, only signed drivers are being used, all servers have the same operating system version, required services for failover clustering are running, the same processor architecture is being used on all servers, and that all servers have the same service packs and software updates.

Chapter 39

You can validate a cluster configuration by completing the following steps:

1. Start Failover Cluster Management. With the Failover Cluster Management node selected, click the Validate A Configuration link. This starts the Validate A Configuration Wizard.

2. If the Before You Begin page is displayed, read the welcome message and then click Next. You can hide this page in the future by selecting the Do Not Show This Page Again check box before clicking Next.

3. On the Select Servers Or A Cluster page, add the names of all servers to test. Alternatively, you can test an existing cluster by adding the name of the cluster or one of its nodes.

4. On the Testing Options page, select a testing option. Choose Run All Test to perform all tests.

5. Choose Run Only Tests I Select to select the tests to run. Click Next.

6. If you elected to choose the tests to run, you can now select the tests to run. All tests are selected by default. Clear the check boxes for the tests that you do not want to run and then click Next.

7. On the Confirmation page, review the testing options and then click Next to begin testing. The wizard displays the progress and status of each test as it works through the test list. When testing is complete, click View Report to view the report created by the wizard. If any test failed, review the detailed information carefully to determine what must be corrected.

Creating a Failover Cluster

You can create a new cluster in Failover Cluster Management by completing these steps:

1. Start Failover Cluster Management. With the Failover Cluster Management node selected, click the Create A Cluster link. Or right-click the Failover Cluster Management node and then select Create A Cluster. Either action starts the Create Cluster Wizard.

2. If the Before You Begin page is displayed, read the welcome message and then click Next. You can hide this page in the future by selecting the Do Not Show This Page Again check box before clicking Next.

3. On the Select Servers page, add the names of all servers that you want to be a part of the cluster (see Figure 39-15). To add a server, type its host name or IP address and then click Add. Alternatively, click Browse to select a computer to add. Click Next.

> **Note**
> You must add at least one server before clicking Next to continue. If the server you select doesn't have the Failover Clustering feature installed, you'll see an error regarding this and will need to install the feature before you can continue. You'll also see an error if the server you select is a part of another cluster or cannot be contacted as well.

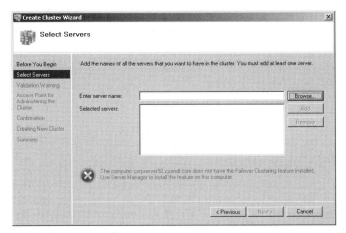

Figure 39-15 Specify the server or servers that you want to be a part of the cluster.

4. On the Access Point For Administering The Cluster page, shown in Figure 39-16, enter the host name for the cluster in the Cluster Name box. This is the host name by which the cluster will be known within its default domain. Because users will connect to the cluster using virtual servers, this is the name that administrators will use to work with the cluster. This name must be unique in the domain and must also not currently be in use.

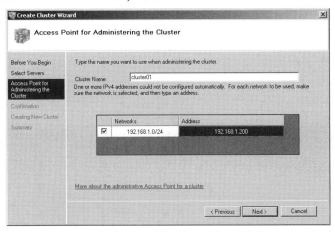

Figure 39-16 Set the host name and IP address of the cluster; this is the access point for administrators.

5. For each network to be used, make sure the network is selected. Then click in the Address box for that network and type the IP address to use for cluster administration. This IP address must be available and not currently in use.

6. When you click Next, the wizard validates the settings. If there are name or IP address conflicts, you'll need to make changes before you can continue. Otherwise, you'll see the Confirmation page when you click Next.

7. On the Confirmation page, review the cluster configuration and then click Next to create the cluster. The wizard displays the progress and status as it creates the cluster. When configuration is complete, click View Report to view the report created by the wizard. If any part of the configuration failed, review the detailed information carefully to determine what must be corrected.

Add Nodes to a Cluster

After you've created a cluster and added at least one node, at any time you can add other nodes to the cluster, up to a maximum of eight. Additional nodes automatically inherit the quorum and resource configuration from the initial host.

To add nodes to a failover cluster, follow these steps:

1. Start Failover Cluster Management, which can be started from the Administrative Tools menu or by typing **cluadmin** at the command prompt. If the cluster you want to work with is not listed, click Manage A Cluster. In the Select A Cluster To Manage dialog box, connect to the cluster you want to work with by typing the cluster name or IP address and then clicking OK. Alternatively, click Browse to browse the network and Active Directory for clusters.

2. In Failover Cluster Management, click Add Node in the actions pane or on the Action menu. This starts the Add Node Wizard.

3. If the Before You Begin page is displayed, read the welcome message and then click Next. You can hide this page in the future by selecting the Do Not Show This Page Again check box before clicking Next.

4. On the Select Servers page, add the names of all servers that you want to be a part of the cluster. To add a server, type its host name or IP address and then click Add. Alternatively, click Browse to select a computer to add. Click Next.

5. On the Confirmation page, review the cluster configuration and then click Next to add the node or nodes to the cluster. The wizard displays the progress and status as it creates the cluster. When configuration is complete, click View Report to view the report created by the wizard. If any part of the configuration failed, review the detailed information carefully to determine what must be corrected.

Managing Failover Clusters and Their Resources

After you create the cluster, you can specify the resources that you want to be highly available and configure the policies that you want to follow to administer those resources. You can, for example, specify how resources fail over and fail back as well as which nodes are the primary owners of resources.

Adding Storage to a Cluster

Currently configured storage is displayed when you select a cluster's Storage node in Failover Cluster Management. After you expose storage to a cluster, such as by changing LUN masking or zoning, you can add storage to the cluster by completing the following steps:

1. In Failover Cluster Management, expand the node for the cluster you want to work with by double-clicking it. If the cluster you want to work with is not listed, connect to it.

2. Right-click the cluster's Storage node and then click Add A Disk. Select the disk or disks to add to the cluster.

Modifying Cluster Network Settings

Currently configured networks are displayed when you select a cluster's Networks node in Failover Cluster Management. For each of the networks physically connected to the servers in a cluster, you can specify whether the network is used by the cluster. For configured networks, you can specify whether the networks are available to cluster nodes only or also to clients. If you use a network for iSCSI, do not use the network for cluster communications.

To modify network settings for a cluster, follow these steps:

1. In Failover Cluster Management, expand the node for the cluster you want to work with by double-clicking it. If the cluster you want to work with is not listed, connect to it.

2. Expand the cluster's Networks node. Right-click the network you want to modify and then click Properties.

3. Choose one of the following options and then click OK:
   - To allow only nodes in the cluster to use the network, select Allow The Cluster To Use This Network and clear the Allow Clients To Connect Through This Network check box.
   - To allow clients to use the network, select Allow The Cluster To Use This Network and select the Allow Clients To Connect Through This Network check box.
   - To prevent the cluster from using the network, select Do Not Allow Cluster To Use This Network.

Configuring Cluster Quorum Settings

Although you should change the default quorum configuration only to meet specific requirements, four possible quorum configurations are available:

- **Node Majority** This configuration is recommended for clusters with an odd number of nodes. Clusters in this configuration can sustain failures of half the nodes (rounding up) minus one. For example, a five node cluster can sustain two node failures.

- **Node And Disk Majority** This configuration is recommended for clusters with an even number of nodes. Clusters in this configuration can sustain failures of half the nodes (rounding up) if the quorum (witness) disk remains online. For example, a four node cluster in which the witness disk is online could sustain two node failures. However, if the quorum (witness) disk goes offline, the cluster can sustain failures of half the nodes (rounding up) minus one. For example, a six node cluster with a failed witness disk could sustain two node failures.

- **Node And File Share Majority** This configuration is recommended for clusters with special configurations. Clusters in this configuration use a witness file share rather than a quorum (witness) disk. Otherwise, this configuration works like the Node and Disk Majority configuration. Note that before a cluster in this configuration can start, one of the nodes must contain a current copy of the cluster configuration.

- **No Majority: Disk Only** This configuration is not recommended. Clusters in this configuration can sustain failures of all nodes except one (if the quorum disk is online). However, this configuration is not recommended because the quorum disk might be a single point of failure.

You can configure the quorum type to use by completing the following steps:

1. In Failover Cluster Management, expand the node for the cluster you want to work with by double-clicking it. If the cluster you want to work with is not listed, connect to it.

2. Right-click the cluster node, point to More Actions, and then select Configure Cluster Quorum Settings. This starts the Configure Cluster Quorum Wizard.

3. If the Before You Begin page is displayed, read the welcome message and then click Next. You can hide this page in the future by selecting the Do Not Show This Page Again check box before clicking Next.

4. On the Select Quorum Configuration page, select the desired quorum configuration and then click Next. If you select Node And Disk Majority, you must next select the witness disk to use. If you select Node And File Share Majority, you must enter the shared folder path to use as the file share witness resource.

5. On the Confirmation page, review the configuration changes and then click Next to apply them. The wizard displays the progress and status as it creates the cluster. When configuration is complete, click View Report to view the report created by the wizard. If any part of the configuration failed, review the detailed information carefully to determine what must be corrected.

Creating Clustered Resources

After you create a cluster, you can specify the resources that you want to be highly available. The Cluster service defines specific resource types that can be configured for high availability. The available resource types include the following:

- **Distributed File System (DFS) Namespace Server** Distributed File System (DFS) Namespace Server provides high availability for stand-alone DFS roots. As a stand-alone DFS root, you can share DFS roots that aren't configured to be fault tolerant. This is ideal when the DFS data changes frequently and you don't want to have to replicate changes to DFS replicas frequently.

- **DHCP Server** DHCP provides dynamic IP addressing in the domain. When you can run it as a resource of the cluster, you provide for high availability. For DHCP to fail over successfully, the DHCP database must be on the shared cluster storage. Be sure to use the full directory path and end the path with a backslash (\), such as **g:\dchp\data**.

- **WINS** WINS provides resolution of NetBIOS names to IP addresses. When you can run it as a resource of the cluster, you provide for high availability. For WINS to fail over successfully, the WINS database must be on the shared cluster storage. Be sure to use the full directory path and end the path with a backslash (\), such as **g:\wins\data**.

- **File Server** For file servers, this resource type provides for high availability of any shared folders. You can manage file shares in several ways. As a normal file share, only the top-level folder is visible as the share name. This is the most basic type of file share. As shared subfolders, the top-level folder and each of its immediate subfolders are shared with separate names. This allows you to create a large number of related file shares easily, such as those for users' home directories.

- **Print Server** For print servers, this resource type provides for high availability of network-attached print devices. Printers connected directly to print servers cannot be included because there is no way to fail over control to a different server. If a print server fails, all jobs that are currently spooling are restarted. Jobs that are in the process of spooling are discarded and must be respooled or reprinted to the Print Spooler resource.

- **Generic Application** The Generic Application resource type is used to manage cluster-unaware applications that can be failed over. Generic applications must use an IP-based protocol for their network communications and must be able to store their data in a configurable location.

- **Generic Script** The Generic Script resource type is used to manage Windows scripts as cluster resources. Only the most basic clustering functionality is provided. If the script is running, it is assumed that it is online.

- **Generic Service** The Generic Service resource type is used to manage Windows services as cluster resources. Only the most basic clustering functionality is provided. If the service is running, it is assumed that it is online.

When planning high-availability resources, you should list all server-based applications and services that will run in the cluster environment, regardless of whether they will need high availability. Be sure to look at applications and services running on front-end servers, application logic servers, and back-end servers. Afterward, divide the list into three sections: Support, HA, and Non-HA. The Support section should include all applications and services that run on severs that aren't part of the cluster and on which clustered resources do not depend. The HA section should include all applications and services running on the cluster servers that need high availability. This section should also include the resources these applications and services are dependent on. The Non-HA section should include all applications and services running on the cluster servers that do not need or do not support failover. Put an asterisk next to any items that need further research or discussion as a reminder that the deployment team should reexamine the items later.

Support applications and services often interact with clustered applications and services, and these interactions should be clearly understood and tracked. Failure of a support application or service shouldn't impact the core functions of the business system. If it does, the support application or service might need to be clustered or load balanced.

Applications and services in the HA section represent resources that should be allocated as high-availability resources. Applications and services in the Non-HA section represent resources that might not need to be allocated as high-availability resources. Before making the final determination, administrators should ensure that failure of a support application or service doesn't impact other applications or services. If it does, the application or service represents a dependency for another application or service—and all dependent resources should be made highly available. Failure of a support application or service shouldn't impact the core functions of the business system. If it does, the application or service might need to be clustered or load balanced. In the case of dependent services that don't support clustering, you might want to provide backup planning in case these services fail or might want to attempt to make the services cluster-aware by using Windows scripts.

To get a better understanding of dependencies, you can draw a dependency tree for each high-availability resource. This will help you understand not only which resources that an application or service is dependent upon, but also how those dependencies are interrelated.

You can configure a service or application as a high-availability resource by completing the following steps:

1. In Failover Cluster Management, expand the node for the cluster you want to work with by double-clicking it. If the cluster you want to work with is not listed, connect to it.

2. Select and then right-click the cluster's Services And Applications node. On the shortcut menu, select Configure A Service Or Application.

3. If the Before You Begin page is displayed, read the welcome message and then click Next. You can hide this page in the future by selecting the Do Not Show This Page Again check box before clicking Next.

4. Select the type of service or application you are configuring and then click Next. The subsequent wizard pages depend on the type of service or application you are configuring.

5. On the Client Access Point page, you'll need to set a host name and IP address for the clustered service or application. The name and IP address must be unique and available in the current domain.

6. On the Select Storage page, you'll need to select the storage volume or volumes that the clustered service or application should use.

7. On the Confirmation page, review the configuration and then click Next to create the high-availability resource. The wizard displays the progress and status as it creates the resource. When configuration is complete, click View Report to view the report created by the wizard. If any part of the configuration failed, review the detailed information carefully to determine what must be corrected.

Controlling the Cluster Service

By using the Cluster service you can control operations on a per-node basis. To stop the Cluster service on a node, right-click the node in Failover Cluster Management, click More Actions, and then click Stop Cluster Service. When you stop the Cluster service, you prevent clients from accessing resources on that node. If the node's failover policies are configured to move resources to another node, all resource groups on the node are moved to another node. If no failover policies are configured, however, clients cannot access the node's resources. To start the Cluster service again, right-click the node in Failover Cluster Management, click More Actions, and then click Start Cluster Service. The key reason for stopping and starting nodes is to repair a node. Here, you stop the Cluster service, make the necessary repairs, and then when you are finished you bring the node back online by starting the Cluster service.

You also have the option of using Pause and Resume. To pause a node, right-click the node in Failover Cluster Management and then click Pause. When you pause a node, existing resources stay online, but additional resources cannot be brought online. You can later allow new resources to be brought online by right-clicking the node in Failover Cluster Management and then clicking Resume.

Configuring Resource Failover and Failback

Services or applications that are part of a high-availability resource fail over and fail back according to the failover and failback policies set on the resource as a whole. Basically, the failover policy for a resource sets a threshold for the maximum number of times that the resource is allowed to fail over in a specified period before it is left in a failed state. If a resource fails over more often than the failover policy allows, the Cluster service leaves it offline. For example, if a resource failover threshold is set to 4 and its failover period to 2, the Cluster service will fail over the resource at most four times within a 2-hour period.

Chapter 39

You can set resource failover policy in Failover Cluster Management by clicking the Services And Applications node in the left pane, selecting the resource you want to work with in the right pane, and then clicking Properties in the actions pane. On the Failover tab, set the Threshold and Period options as appropriate for the resource.

For failback policy, you specify whether and how the resource is returned to its preferred owner. You set failback policy in Failover Cluster Management by clicking the Services And Applications node in the left pane, selecting the resource you want to work with in the right pane, and then clicking Properties in the actions pane. On the Failover tab, select either Prevent Failback or Allow Failback. If you click Allow Failback, set a preferred owner and a failback interval. Select Immediately to allow immediate failback, or click Failback Between and set the time interval during which it is permissible to fail back the group. Enter numbers between 0 and 23 to specify the beginning and end of the interval. These numbers correspond to the local time of the cluster group with regard to a 24-hour clock.

You can test failover and failback by completing the following steps:

1. In Failover Cluster Management, expand the node for the cluster you want to work with by double-clicking it. If the cluster you want to work with is not listed, connect to it.

2. Expand the cluster's Services And Applications node.

3. Right-click the service or application to fail over and then select Move This Service Or Application To Another Node.

4. As the service or application moves, the status is displayed in the main pane. Repeat step 3 to move the service or application to a new node or back to the original node.

Creating a Shared Folder on a Clustered File Server

You can create a shared folder on a clustered file server by completing the following steps:

1. In Failover Cluster Management, expand the node for the cluster you want to work with by double-clicking it. If the cluster you want to work with is not listed, connect to it.

2. Expand the cluster's Services And Applications node.

3. Right-click the clustered file server and then select Add A Shared Folder. This starts the Shared Folder wizard.

4. Follow the prompts to create the shared folder. This is the same wizard that you use with nonclustered servers.

Configuring Print Settings for a Clustered Print Server

You can configure a printer for a clustered print server by completing the following steps:

1. In Failover Cluster Management, expand the node for the cluster you want to work with by double-clicking it. If the cluster you want to work with is not listed, connect to it.

2. Expand the cluster's Services And Applications node.

3. Right-click the clustered print server and then select Manage Printers. This opens Print Management with a Failover Cluster Management interface.

4. Under Print Management ensure that the clustered print server or the cluster node is listed. If it is not, right-click Print Servers and then select Add/Remove Servers. Type the host name or IP address of the clustered print server and then click Add To List.

5. Right-click the clustered print server and then click Add Printer. This starts the Add Printer wizard.

6. Follow the prompts to create the shared printer. This is the same wizard that you use with nonclustered servers. After you've added the printer, you can manage it as you would any other printer.

Chapter 39

Ask three different people what their idea of a disaster is and you'll probably get three different answers. For most administrators, the term *disaster* probably means any scenario in which one or more essential systems, services, or applications cannot operate and the prospects for quick recovery are less than hopeful—that is, a disaster is something a service reset or system reboot won't fix.

To ensure that operations can be restored as quickly as possible in a given situation, every network needs a clear disaster recovery plan. In this chapter, I'm not going to mince words and try to explain why you need to plan for disasters. Instead, I'm going to focus on what you need to do to get ready for the inevitable, because worst-case scenarios can and do happen. I'm also going to discuss predisaster preparation procedures.

Preparing for a Disaster

Chapter 38, "Planning for High Availability," went into detail about planning for highly available, scalable, and manageable systems. Many of the same concepts go into disaster planning. Why? Because, at the end of the day, disaster planning involves implementing plans that ensure the availability of systems and services. Remember that part of disaster planning is applying some level of contingency planning to every essential network service and system. You need to implement problem escalation and response procedures. You also need a standing problem-resolution document that describes in great detail what to do when disaster strikes.

Developing Contingency Procedures

You should identify the services and systems that are essential to network operations. Typically, this list will include the following components:

- Network infrastructure servers running Active Directory, Domain Name System (DNS), Dynamic Host Configuration Protocol (DHCP), Terminal Services, and Routing and Remote Access Service (RRAS)

- File, database, and application servers, such as servers with essential file shares or those that provide database or e-mail services

- Networking hardware, including switches, routers, and firewalls

Use Chapter 38 to help you develop plans for contingency procedures in the following areas:

- **Physical security** Place network hardware and servers in a locked, secure access facility. This could be an office that is kept locked or a server room that requires a passkey to enter. When physical access to network hardware and servers requires special access privileges, you prevent many problems and ensure that only authorized personnel can get access to systems from the console.

- **Data backup** Implement a regular backup plan that ensures that multiple datasets are available for all essential systems, and that these backups are stored in more than one location. For example, if you keep the most current backup sets on-site in the server room, you should rotate another backup set to off-site storage. In this way, if disaster strikes, you will be more likely to be able to recover operations.

- **Fault tolerance** Build redundancy into the network and system architecture. At the server level, you can protect data using a redundant array of independent disks (RAID) and guard against component failure by having spare parts at hand. These precautions protect servers at a very basic level. For essential services such as Active Directory, DNS, and DHCP, you can build in fault tolerance by deploying redundant systems using techniques discussed throughout this book. These same concepts can be applied to network hardware components such as routers and switches.

- **Recovery** Every essential server and network device should have a written recovery plan that details step by step what to do to rebuild and recover it. Be as detailed and explicit as possible and don't assume that the readers know anything about the system or device they are recovering. Do this even if you are sure that you'll be the one performing the recovery—you'll be thankful for it, trust me. Things can and do go wrong at the worst times, and sometimes, under pressure, you might forget some important detail in the recovery process—not to mention that you might be unavailable to recover the system for some reason.

- **Power protection** Power-protect servers and network hardware using an uninterruptible power supply (UPS) system. Power protection will help safeguard servers and network hardware from power surges and dirty power. Power protection will also help prevent data loss and allow you to power down servers in an appropriate fashion through manual or automatic shutdown.

Implementing Problem Escalation and Response Procedures

As part of planning, you need to develop well-defined problem escalation procedures that document how to handle problems and emergency changes that might be needed. You need to designate an incident response team and an emergency response team. Although the two teams could consist of the same team members, the teams differ in fundamental ways.

- **Incident response team** The incident response team's role is to respond to security incidents, such as the suspected cracking of a database server. This team is concerned with responding to intrusion, taking immediate action to safeguard the organization's information, documenting the security issue thoroughly in an after-action report, and then fixing the security problem so that the same type of incident cannot recur. Your organization's security administrator or network security expert should have a key role in this team.

- **Emergency response team** The emergency response team's role is to respond to service and system outages, such as the failure of a database server. This team is concerned with recovering the service or system as quickly as possible and allowing normal operations to resume. Like the incident response team, the emergency response team needs to document the outage thoroughly in an after-action report, and then, if applicable, propose changes to improve the recovery process. Your organization's system administrators should have key roles in this team.

INSIDE OUT   Using and configuring a UPS

Putting in a UPS requires a bit of planning, because you need to look not only at servers but also at everything in the server room that requires power. If the power goes out, you want to have ample time for systems to shut down in an orderly fashion. You may also have some systems that you do not want to be shut down, such as routers or servers required for security key cards. In most cases, rather than using individual UPS devices, you should install enterprise UPS solutions that can be connected to several servers or components.

After you install a UPS, you can configure servers to take advantage of the UPS using the management software included with the UPS. You can then configure the way a server reacts when it switches to battery power. Typically, you'll want servers to start an orderly shutdown within a few minutes of switching to battery power.

In your planning, remember that 90 percent of power outages last less than 5 minutes and 99 percent of power outages last less than 60 minutes. With this in mind, you may want to plan your UPS implementation so that you can maintain 7 to 10 minutes of power for all server and network components and 60 to 70 minutes for critical systems. You would then configure all non-critical systems to shut down automatically after 5 minutes, and critical systems to shut down after 60 minutes.

Creating a Problem Resolution Policy Document

Over the years, I've worked with and consulted for many organizations, and I've often been asked to help implement information technology (IT) policy and procedure. In the area of disaster and recovery planning, there's one policy document that I always use, regardless of the size of the company I am working with. I call it the problem resolution policy document.

The problem resolution policy document has the following six sections:

- **Responsibilities** The overall responsibilities of IT and engineering staff during and after normal business hours should be detailed in this section. For an organization with 24/7 operations, such as a company with a public Web site maintained by internal staff, the after-hours responsibilities section should be very detailed and let individuals know exactly what their responsibilities are. Most organizations with 24/7 operations will designate individuals as being "on call" 7 days a week, 365 days a year, and in that case, this section should detail what being "on call" means, and what the general responsibilities are for an individual on call.

- **Phone roster** Every system and service that you've identified in your planning as essential should have a point of contact. For some systems, you'll have several points of contact. Consider, for example, a database server. You might have a system administrator who is responsible for the server itself, a database administrator who is responsible for the database running on the server, and an integration specialist responsible for any integration components running on the server.

> **Note**
>
> The phone roster should include both on-site and off-site contact numbers. Ideally, this means that you'll have the work phone number, cell phone number, and pager number of each contact. It should be the responsibility of every individual on the phone roster to ensure that contact information is up to date.

- **Key contact information** In addition to a phone roster, you should have contact numbers for facilities and vendors. The key contacts list should include the main office phone numbers at branch offices and data centers, and contact numbers for the various vendors that installed infrastructure at each office, such as the building manager, Internet service provider (ISP), electrician, and network wiring specialist. It should also include the support phone numbers for hardware and software vendors and the information you'll be required to give in order to get service, such as customer identification number and service contract information.

- **Notification procedures** The way problems get resolved is through notification. This section should outline the notification procedures and the primary point of contact in case of outage. If many systems and services are involved, notification and primary contacts can be divided into categories. For example, you may have an external systems notification process for your public Internet servers and an internal systems notification process for your intranet services.

- **Escalation** When problems aren't resolved within a specific timeframe, there should be clear escalation procedures that detail whom to contact and when. For example, you might have level 1, level 2, and level 3 points of contact, with level 1 contacts being called immediately, level 2 contacts being called when issues aren't resolved in 30 minutes, and level 3 contacts being called when issues aren't resolved in 60 minutes.

> **Note**
>
> You should also have a priority system in place that dictates what types of incidents or outages take precedence over others. For example, you could specify that service-level outages, such as those that involve the complete system, have priority over an isolated outage involving a single server or application, but that suspected security incidents have priority over all other issues.

- **Post-action reporting** Every individual involved in a major outage or incident should be expected to write a post-action report. This section details what should be in that report. For example, you would want to track the notification time, actions after notification, escalation attempts, and other items that are important to improving the process or preventing the problem from recurring.

Every IT group should have a general policy with regard to problem resolution procedures, and this policy should be detailed in a problem resolution policy document or one like it. The document should be distributed to all relevant personnel throughout the organization, so that every person who has some level of responsibility for ensuring system and service availability knows what to do in case of an emergency. After you implement the policy, you should test it to help refine it so that the policy will work as expected in an actual disaster.

Disaster Preparedness Procedures

Just as you need to perform planning before disaster strikes, you also need to perform certain disaster preparedness procedures. These procedures ensure that you are able to recover systems as quickly as possible when a disaster strikes and include the following:

- Backups
- Startup repair
- Recovery disks
- Startup and recovery options
- Recovery Console

Performing Backups

You should perform regular backups of every Windows Server 2008 system. Backups can be performed using several techniques. Most organizations choose a combination of dedicated backup servers and per-server backups. If you use professional backup software, you can use one or more dedicated backup servers to create backups of other servers on the network, and then write the backups to media on centralized backup devices. If you use per-server backups, you run backup software on each server that you want to back up and store the backup media on a local backup device. By combining the techniques, you get the best of both worlds.

With dedicated backup servers, you purchase professional backup software, a backup server, and a scalable backup device. The initial costs for purchasing the required equipment and the time required to set up the backup environment can be substantial. However, after the backup environment is configured, it is rather easy to maintain. Centralized backups also offer substantial time savings for administrators, because the backup process itself can be fully automated.

With per-server backups, you use a backup utility to perform manual backups of individual systems. The primary tool for performing per-server backups is the Windows Server Backup utility, which is discussed in Chapter 41, "Backup and Recovery." Because this tool is included with Windows Server 2008, there is no initial cost for implementation. However, because the backup options are fairly limited, the process may require more time than using centralized backup servers.

Using Startup Repair

Like Windows Vista, Windows Server 2008 has several automatic repair features. If the boot manager or corrupted system file is preventing startup, the Startup Repair wizard is started automatically and will initiate repair of the server. The Startup Repair wizard can be helpful if one or more of the following problems are preventing startup:

- A virus infection in the master boot record

- A missing or corrupt boot manager

- A boot configuration data store with bad entries

- A corrupted system file

Although Startup Repair typically runs automatically, you can manually initiate this feature using the Windows installation disc. For this reason, part of your recovery planning should include ensuring that a Windows installation disc is available for each hardware architecture used in your server deployments.

With a Windows installation disc, you can manually run Startup Repair by completing the following steps:

1. Insert the Windows installation disc for the hardware architecture and then boot from the installation disc by pressing a key when prompted. If the server does not allow you to boot from the installation disc, you may need to change firmware options to allow booting from a CD/DVD-ROM drive.

2. If Windows Setup doesn't start automatically, select Windows Setup (EMS Enabled) on the Windows Boot Manager menu to start Windows Setup.

3. On the Install Windows page, select the language, time, and keyboard layout options that you want to use. Click Next.

4. When prompted, do not click Install Now. Instead, click the Repair Your Computer link in the lower-left corner of the Install Windows page. This starts the System Recovery Options wizard. Keep the following in mind:

   ○ If the boot manager is damaged, the wizard will repair it at this point to obtain a list of available operating systems.

   ○ If a server has only one operating system, click Next to continue.

   ○ If your server has multiple operating systems, you'll need to select the operating system to use and then click Next.

   ○ If a server has multiple operating system and the operating system you want to use is unavailable, click Load Drivers to load the drivers for your server's hard disks.

5. On the System Recovery Options page, click Command Prompt to access the MINWINPC environment. As discussed in Chapter 3, "Installing Windows Server 2008," the mini Windows PC environment gives you access to the command-line tools listed in Table 3-5 on page 90.

6. At the command prompt, enter **cd recovery** to access the *X*:\Sources\Recovery directory.

7. At the command prompt, enter **startrep** to run the Startup Repair wizard. Follow the prompts to attempt to repair the server and enable startup.

Getting Outside Help

As part of your disaster planning you should plan for scenarios where you or another administrator are unable to recover a server and need help. A key part of this planning includes the escalation procedures discussed previously, where you contact more senior administrators when necessary. When escalation fails and you need to get a server back online, you may need to turn to outside help. Windows Server 2008 includes a facility for obtaining diagnostic information during setup and recovery, and then delivering this information to Microsoft Product Support. This diagnostic information comes from the Windows diagnostics and troubleshooting logs and can help diagnose problems that are preventing installation or recovery.

To share troubleshooting information about the server with Microsoft Product Support, follow these steps:

1. Insert the Windows installation disc for the hardware architecture and then boot from the installation disc by pressing a key when prompted. If the server does not allow you to boot from the installation disc, you may need to change firmware options to allow booting from a CD/DVD-ROM drive.

2. If Windows Setup doesn't start automatically, select Windows Setup (EMS Enabled) on the Windows Boot Manager menu to start Windows Setup.

3. On the Install Windows page, select the language, time, and keyboard layout options that you want to use. Click Next.

4. When prompted, do not click Install Now. Instead, click the Repair Your Computer link in the lower-left corner of the Install Windows page. This starts the System Recovery Options wizard. Keep the following in mind:

    o If the boot manager is damaged, the wizard will repair it at this point to obtain a list of available operating systems.

    o If a server has only one operating system, click Next to continue.

    o If your server has multiple operating systems, you'll need to select the operating system to use and then click Next.

    o If a server has multiple operating system and the operating system you want to use is unavailable, click Load Drivers to load the drivers for your server's hard disks.

5. On the System Recovery Options page, click Command Prompt to access the MINWINPC environment. As discussed in Chapter 3, "Installing Windows Server 2008," the mini Windows PC environment gives you access to the command-line tools listed in Table 3-5 on page 90.

6. Insert a floppy disk into the server's floppy disk drive or a USB flash drive into a USB port. This ensures that the disk or flash drive is available when you start the wizard.

7. Change directories to *X*:\Sources\Recovery by typing **cd recovery**.

8. Start the Microsoft Product Support Service wizard by typing **psswiz** at the command prompt. When the wizard starts, write down the contact information provided, including the support phone number. This information is different depending on your locale.

9. Select the drive letter of the floppy disk or flash device and then click Next to save the data. Remove the floppy disk or flash device.

10. On another computer that is started and connected to the Internet, insert the floppy disk or flash device and then contact Microsoft Product Support. Follow the instructions given to you by Microsoft Product Support.

> **Note**
>
> You don't necessarily need to deliver this information to Microsoft Product Support. You can just as easily deliver this information to a senior administrator or a skilled technical expert on staff who is not in the office currently or is located at another office. On the floppy disk or flash device, the diagnostics files are created as standard text files. You can open these files in any text editor or easily add them to an e-mail message.

Other Windows Recovery Environment Features

As long as the CPU architectures are the same, you can use any Windows installation disc to recover any server running Windows Server 2008. Once you access the Windows Recovery Environment by selecting the Repair Your Computer option, you can access the following tools:

- **Windows Complete PC Restore** Allows you to recover a server's operating system or perform a full system recovery. With an operating system or full system recovery, make sure your backup data is available and that you can log on with an account that has the appropriate permissions. With a full system recovery, keep in mind that existing data that was not included in the original backup will be deleted when you recover the system. This includes any volumes that are currently used by the server but were not included in the backup.

- **Windows Memory Diagnostics Tools** Allows you to diagnose a problem with the server's physical memory. Three different levels of memory testing can be performed: basic, standard, or extended. The basic memory tests are: MATS+, INVC, and SCHCKR (cache enabled). The standard memory tests include all the basic tests, plus LRAND, CHCKR3, WMATS+, WINVC, and STRIDE6 (cache enabled). The extended memory tests include all the basic and standard tests, plus ERAND, CHCKR4, STRIDE38, WSCHCKR, WSTRIDE6, WCHCKR3, CHCKR8, MATS+ (cache disabled), and STRIDE6 (cache disabled).

> **Note**
>
> When memory diagnostics starts, you can press F1 to access the Options menu. You can then select the test mix as Basic, Standard, or Extended. Using the Tab key on the Options menu, you can set the Cache and Pass Count options. Cache controls how caching is used with the memory tests: Default uses the default settings as listed previously, On turns the cache on for all tests, Off turns off the cache off for all tests. Pass Count sets the total number of times the entire test mix will repeat. The default setting is 2, meaning each test in the selected test mix will be performed twice. To return to testing from the Options menu, press F10 to apply your changes or Esc to cancel your changes.

You can also access a command prompt within the mini Windows PC environment (WinPE). This command prompt gives you access to the command-line tools listed in Table 3-5 on page 90 as well as to these additional programs:

- **On-Screen Keyboard (*X*:\Sources\Setuposk.exe)** Allows you to enter keystrokes using the On-Screen Keyboard. This means you can use a mouse or another pointer device to type commands or enter key combinations. Function keys are provided as well as letters, numerals, and the following special characters: ` - = , . / [ ] \

Chapter 40

- **Rollback wizard (*X*:\Sources\Rollback.exe)** Normally the Rollback wizard is started automatically if Windows Setup encounters a problem during installation. You can use this wizard to subsequently attempt to restore the previous version of Windows. If the Rollback wizard is successful, the previous version of Windows is completely restored. If the Rollback wizard is unsuccessful, the server typically is left in an unbootable state and you must either perform a full restore of the previous operating system or a clean installation of Windows Server 2008.

- **Startup Repair wizard (*X*:\Sources\Recovery\StartRep.exe)** Normally this tool is started automatically on boot failure if Windows detects an issue with the boot sector, the boot manager, or the boot configuration data (BCD) store. You can use this wizard to initiate a startup repair. If the repair is successful, you should be able to start the server and log on. If the repair is unsuccessful, you'll need to use another recovery technique to restore the server.

- **Startup Recovery Options (*X*:\Sources\Recovery\Recenv.exe)** Allows you to start the Startup Recovery Options wizard. If you previously entered the wrong recovery settings, use this wizard to restart the System Recovery Options wizard so that you can provide different options. Note that you cannot change the language or time options. You can, however, change the keyboard layout and selected operating system.

You can recover a server's operating system or perform a full system recovery by using a Windows installation disc and a backup that you created earlier with Windows Server Backup. With an operating system recovery, you recover all critical volumes but do not recover non-system volumes. If you recover your full system, Windows Server Backup reformats and repartitions all disks that are attached to the server. Because of this, you should use this method only when you want to recover the server data onto separate hardware or when all other attempts to recover the server on the existing hardware have failed.

Setting Startup and Recovery Options

As part of planning for the worst-case scenarios, you need to consider how you want systems to start up and recover in case a stop error is encountered. The options you choose can add to the boot time or they can mean that if a system encounters a stop error it does not reboot.

You can configure startup and recovery options by completing the following steps:

1. Click Start and then click Control Panel. In Control Panel, click System And Maintenance\System to start the System utility.

2. In the Tasks pane, click Advanced System Settings. This opens the System Properties dialog box.

3. On the Advanced tab, click Settings in the Startup And Recovery panel. This displays the dialog box shown in Figure 40-1.

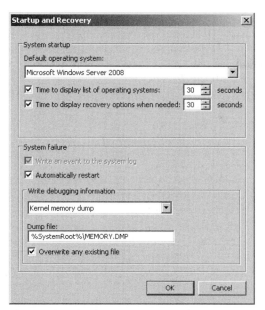

Figure 40-1 Configuring startup and recovery options.

4. In the Startup And Recovery dialog box, you configure the settings as follows:

○ If a server has multiple operating systems, you can set the default operating system by selecting one of the operating systems in the Default Operating System list. These options are obtained from the boot manager.

○ When multiple operating systems are installed, the Time To Display List Of Operating Systems option controls how long the system waits before booting to the default operating system. In most cases, you won't need more than a few seconds to make a choice, so reduce this wait time to perhaps 5 or 10 seconds. Alternatively, you can have the system automatically choose the default operating system by clearing this check box.

○ When you want to display recovery options, the operating system uses the Time To Display Recovery Options When Needed setting to determine how long to wait for you to choose a recovery option. The default wait time is 30 seconds. If you don't choose a recovery option in that time, the system boots normally without recovery. As with operating systems, you won't need more than a few seconds to make a choice, so reduce this wait time to perhaps 5 or 10 seconds.

○ Under System Failure, you have several important options for determining what happens when a system experiences a stop error. By default, the Write An Event To The System Log check box is selected so that the system logs an error in the system log. The check box is dimmed, so it cannot normally be changed. The Automatically Restart check box is selected to ensure that the system attempts to reboot when a stop error occurs.

Chapter 40

> **Note**
>
> In some cases, you may want the system to halt rather than reboot. For example, if you are having problems with a server, you may want it to halt so that an administrator will be more likely to notice that it is experiencing problems. Don't, however, prevent automatic reboot without a specific reason.

○ The Write Debugging Information options allow you to choose the type of debugging information that should be created when a stop error occurs. In most cases, you will want debug information to be dumped, so that you can use it to determine the cause of a crash.

> **Note**
>
> If you choose a kernel memory dump, you dump all physical memory being used at the time of the failure. You can create the dump file only if the system is properly configured. The system drive must have a paging file at least as large as RAM and adequate disk space to write the dump file.

○ By default, dump files are written to the %SystemRoot% folder. If you want to write the dump file to a different location, type the file path in the Dump File box. Select the Overwrite Any Existing File check box to ensure that only one dump file is maintained.

5. Click OK twice to close all open dialog boxes.

Backup and Recovery

Way back in Chapter 1, I provided a detailed discussion on the support architecture in Windows Server 2008. As I discussed, Restart Manager, Problem Reports And Solutions, Startup Repair Tool, Performance Diagnostics console, and Windows Memory Diagnostics are all a part of this support architecture, and when things go wrong, they can really save the day. That said, it's fitting to end this book with a look at what you must do to ensure that you can recover your servers, your applications, and your data in case the worst happens because the worst can and usually does happen.

Every Windows Server 2008 system on your network represents a major investment in time, resources, and money. It requires a great deal of planning and effort to deploy a new server successfully. It requires just as much planning and effort—if not more—to ensure that you can restore a server when disaster strikes. Why? Because you not only need to plan and implement a backup for each and every server on your network, but you also need to perform backups regularly. You also need to test the backup process and procedures to ensure that when disaster strikes you are prepared.

Developing Backup Strategies

Backups are insurance plans, plain and simple—and every administrator should see them that way. When disaster strikes, your backup implementation will either leave you out of harm's way or drowning without a life preserver. Trust me: you don't want to be drowning when it should be your moment to shine. After all, if you've implemented a well-thought-out backup plan and practiced the necessary recovery procedures until they are second nature, a server that has stopped working is nothing more than a bump in the road that you can smooth out even if you have to rebuild a server from scratch to do it.

Creating Your Backup Strategy

So where to start? Start by outlining a backup and recovery plan that describes the servers and the data that need to be backed up. Ask yourself the following questions:

- How important is the role that the server is performing?
- How important is the data stored on the server?

- How often does the data change?

- How much data in total is there to back up?

- How long does each backup take?

- How quickly do you need to recover the data?

- How much historical data do you need to store?

- Do you have the equipment needed to perform backups?

- Do you need to store backups off site?

- Who will be responsible for performing backups?

The answers to these questions will help you develop your backup and recovery plan. Often you'll find that your current resources aren't enough and that you'll need to obtain additional backup equipment. It might be one of the ultimate ironies in administration, but you'll often need more justification for backup equipment than for any other type of equipment. Fight to get the backup resources you need and do so without reservation. If you have to make incremental purchases over a period of several months to get the backup equipment and supplies, do so without hesitation.

Backup Strategy Considerations

In most cases, your backup strategy should involve performing some type of backup of every server daily and full backups of these servers at least once a week. You should also regularly inspect the backup log files and periodically perform test restores of the data to ensure that data is being properly written to the backup media.

> **It's All About the Data**
>
> Much of your backup strategy depends on the importance of the data, the frequency of change, and the total amount of data to back up. Data that is of higher importance or frequently changed needs to be backed up more often than other types of data. As the amount of data you are backing up increases, you will need to be able to scale your backup implementation. If you are starting out with a large amount of data, you will need to consider how much time a complete backup of the data set will take. To ensure that backups can be performed in a timely manner, you might have to purchase faster equipment or purchase backup devices with multiple tape drives.

Plan separate backup strategies for system files and data files.

- *System files* are used by the operating system and applications. These files change when you install new components, service packs, or patches. They include system state data.

> **Note**
>
> For systems that aren't domain controllers, the system state data includes essential boot files, key system files, and the COM+ class registration database as well as the Registry data. For domain controllers, the Active Directory database and System Volume (Sysvol) files are included as well and this data typically changes on a daily basis.

- *Data files* are created by applications and users. Application files contain configuration settings and data. User files contain the daily work of users and can include documents, spreadsheets, media files, and so on. These files change every day.

Administrators often back up an entire machine and dump all the data into a single backup. There are several problems with this strategy. First, on non-domain controllers, system files don't change that often but data files change frequently. Second, you'll typically need to recover data files more frequently than system files. You recover data files when documents are corrupted, lost, or accidentally deleted. You recover system files when you have serious problems with a system and typically are trying to restore the whole machine.

Look at the timing of backups as well. With earlier releases of Windows, you are often concerned about the time that backups are performed. You want backups to be performed when the system's usage is low, so that more resources are available and few files are locked and in use. With the advances in backup technology made possible by the Shadow Copy API built into Windows Server 2008, the backup time is less of a concern than it was previously. Any backup programs that implement the Shadow Copy API allow you to back up files that are open or locked. This means that you can perform backups when applications are using files and no longer have to worry about backups failing because files are being used.

Selecting the Optimal Backup Techniques

When it comes to backup, there is no such thing as a one-size-fits-all solution. Often you'll implement one backup strategy for one system and a different backup strategy for a different system. It will all come down to the importance of the data, the frequency of change, and how much data there is to back up on each server. But don't overlook the importance of recovery speed. Different backup strategies take longer to recover than others and there may be differing urgencies involved in getting a system or service back online. Because of this, I recommend a multipronged backup strategy that is optimized on a per-server basis.

Key services running on a system have backup functions that are unique. Implement and use those backup mechanisms as your first line of defense against failure. Remember that a backup of the system state includes a full backup of a server's Registry, and that system configuration includes the configuration of all services running on a system. However, if a specific service fails, it is much easier and faster to recover that specific service than to try to recover the whole server. You'll have fewer problems, and it is less likely that something will go wrong.

Specific backup and recovery techniques for key services are as follows:

- With Dynamic Host Configuration Protocol (DHCP), you should periodically back up the DHCP configuration and the DHCP database as discussed in "Saving and Restoring the DHCP Configuration," on page 734, and "Managing and Maintaining the DHCP Database," on page 735.

- With the Windows Internet Naming Service (WINS), you should periodically back up the WINS database as discussed in "Maintaining the WINS Database," on page 836.

- With Domain Name System (DNS), your backup strategy will depend on whether you are using Active Directory–integrated zones, standard zones, or both. When you are using Active Directory–integrated zones, DNS configuration data is stored in Active Directory. By default, when you are using standard zones, DNS configuration data is stored in the %SystemRoot%\System32\DNS folder and backups of zone data are stored in the %SystemRoot%\System32\DNS\Backup folder.

- With Group Policy, you should periodically back up the Group Policy object (GPO) configuration as discussed in "Maintaining and Troubleshooting Group Policy" on page 1268.

- With print servers, you should periodically back up the printer configuration as discussed in "Preparing for Print Server Failure" on page 912.

- With file servers, you should implement Volume Shadow Copy Service (VSS), as discussed in Chapter 10, "Using Volume Shadow Copy," for all network file shares. This makes it easier to restore previous versions of files. In addition, you should back up all user data files on the file server regularly.

The disaster preparation techniques discussed in Chapter 40, "Disaster Planning," are your next line of defense. Take the time to develop plans and procedures that can help you through everything from a power outage to the worst case scenario. Don't forget that BitLocker locks a computer until you provide the necessary recovery password. When a computer is locked, you must use the recovery password from a USB flash drive, or use the function keys to enter the recovery password. F1 through F9 represent the digits 1 through 9, and F10 represents 0.

Finally, you will also need to perform regular backups of both system and user data. Most backup programs, including Windows Backup, which is included in Windows Server 2008, support several types of backup jobs. The type of backup job determines how much data is backed up and what the backup program does when it performs a backup.

INSIDE OUT **How backup programs use the archive bit**

Most backup operations make use of the archive attribute that can be set on files. The archive attribute, a bit included in the directory entry of each file, can be turned on or off. In most cases, a backup program will turn off (clear) the archive attribute when it backs up a file. The archive bit is turned on (set) again when a user or the operating system later modifies a file. When the backup program runs again, it knows that only the files with the archive attribute set must be backed up—because these are the only files that have changed since the last backup.

Understanding Backup Types

The basic types of backups include the following:

- **Normal** A normal backup is a full backup of all the files and folders you select, regardless of the archive attribute's setting. When a file is backed up, the archive attribute is turned off.

- **Copy** A copy backup is a full backup of all files and folders you select, regardless of the archive attribute's setting. Unlike a normal backup, the archive attribute on files isn't turned off by the backup. This means that you can use a copy backup to create an additional or supplemental backup of a system without interfering with the existing backup strategy.

- **Incremental** An incremental backup is used to create a backup of all files that have changed since the last normal or incremental backup. As such, an incremental backup is a partial backup. The backup program uses the archive attribute to determine which files should be backed up and turns off the archive attribute after backing up a file. This means that each incremental backup contains only the most recent changes.

- **Differential** A differential backup is used to create a backup of all files that have changed since the last normal backup. Like an incremental backup, in a differential backup, the backup program uses the archive attribute to determine which files should be backed up. However, the backup program does not change the archive attribute. This means that each differential backup contains all changes.

- **Daily** A daily backup uses the modification date on a file rather than the archive attribute. If a file has been changed on the day the backup is performed, the file will be backed up. This technique doesn't change the archive attributes of files and is useful when you want to perform an extra backup without interfering with the existing backup strategy.

As part of your backup strategy, you'll probably want to perform normal backups on a weekly basis and supplement this with daily, differential, or incremental backups. The advantage of normal backups is that they are a complete record of the files you select.

Chapter 41

The disadvantage of normal backups is that they take longer to make and use more storage space than other types of backups. Incremental and differential backups, on the other hand, use less space and are faster because they are partial backups. The disadvantage is that recovery of systems and files using incremental and differential backups is slower than when you only have to perform a recovery from a normal backup. To see why, consider the following backup and recovery examples:

- **Normal backup with daily incremental backups** You perform a normal backup every Sunday and incremental backups Monday through Saturday. Monday's incremental backup contains changes since Sunday. Tuesday's incremental backup contains changes since Monday, and so on. If a server malfunctions on Thursday and you need to restore the server from backup, you would do this by restoring the normal backup from Sunday, the incremental backup from Monday, the incremental backup from Tuesday, and the incremental backup from Wednesday—in that order.

- **Normal backup with daily differential backups** You perform a normal backup every Sunday and differential backups Monday through Saturday. Monday's differential backup contains changes since Sunday as does Tuesday's differential backup, Wednesday's differential backup, and so on. If a server malfunctions on Thursday and you need to restore the server from backup, you would do this by restoring the normal backup from Sunday and then the differential backup from Wednesday.

Using Media Rotation and Maintaining Additional Media Sets

As part of your backup strategy, you might also want to use copy backups to create extended backup sets for monthly and quarterly use. You might also want to use a media rotation scheme to ensure that you always have a current copy of your data as well as several previous data sets. Although tapes traditionally have been used for backups, more and more organizations have been using disk backup instead of tape backup as disk drives have become more affordable. With disks, you can use a rotation schedule similar to the one you use with tapes.

The point of a media rotation scheme is to reuse media in a consistent and organized manner. If you use a media rotation scheme, monthly and quarterly media sets can simply be media sets that you are rotating to offsite storage. Consider the following media rotation scenarios:

- **Media rotation with three weekly media sets and one monthly media set** In a 24/7 environment, you use a total of 14 tapes or disks as a media set. Seven of those tapes or disks contain your normal weekly backups for a set of servers. The other seven tapes or disks contain your daily incremental backups for that set of servers—one tape or disk for each day of the week. Three weekly media sets are maintained on site. Once a month, you rotate the previous week's media set to offsite storage.

- **Media rotation with three weekly media sets, one monthly media set, and one quarterly media set** In a 9 to 5 environment, you use a total of 14 tapes or disks as a media set. Nine of those tapes or disks contain your normal weekly backups for a set of servers. The other five tapes or disks contain your daily incremental backups for that set of servers—one tape or disk for each workday. Three weekly media sets are maintained on site. Once a month, you rotate the previous week's media set to offsite storage. Once a quarter, you rotate the previous week's media set to offsite storage.

Backing Up and Recovering Your Data

Many backup and recovery solutions are available for use with Windows Server 2008. When selecting a backup utility, you'll need to keep in mind the types of backups you want to perform and the types of data you are backing up.

Windows Server 2008 includes Windows Server Backup and backup command-line tools. Windows Server Backup is a basic and easy-to-use backup and recovery utility. When the related feature is installed on a server, you'll find a related option on the Administrative Tools menu. The utility is also added to Server Manager. A set of backup and recovery commands is accessible through the Wbadmin command-line tool. You run and use Wbadmin from an elevated, administrator command prompt. Type **wbadmin /?** for a full list of supported commands.

You can use Windows Server Backup to perform full, copy, and incremental backups on both local and remote systems. You cannot use Windows Server Backup to perform differential backups. Windows Server Backup uses the Volume Shadow Copy Service (VSS) to create fast, block-level backups of the operating system, files and folders, and disk volumes. After you create the first full backup, you can configure Windows Server Backup to perform either full or incremental backups on a recurring, scheduled basis automatically.

When you use Windows Server Backup, you will need separate, dedicated media for storing archives of scheduled backups. Although you cannot back up to tapes, you can back up to external and internal disks, DVDs, and shared folders. Support for backing up to DVDs is new functionality. Although you can recover full volumes from DVD backups, you cannot recover individual files, folders, or application data from DVD backups.

Windows Server Backup automatically manages backup disks for you. You can run backups to multiple disks in rotation simply by adding each disk as a scheduled backup location. After you configure a disk as a scheduled backup location, Windows Server Backup automatically manages the disk storage, ensuring that you no longer need to worry about a disk running out of space. Windows Server Backup automatically reuses the space of older backups when creating newer backups. To help ensure that you can plan for additional storage needs, Windows Server Backup displays the backups that are available and the current disk usage information.

Chapter 41

You can use Windows Server Backup for recovery in several ways. Rather than having to manually restore files from multiple backups if the files were stored in incremental backups, you can recover folders and files by choosing the date on which you backed up the version of the item or items you want to restore. You can recover data to the same server hardware or to new server hardware that has no operating system.

Using the Backup Utility

To perform backup and recovery operations, you must use an account that is a member of the Administrators or Backup Operators group. Only members of these groups have authority to back up and restore files regardless of ownership and permissions. File owners and those who have been given control over files can also back up files, but only the files that they own or the files that they have permission to access.

The Windows Server backup and recovery tools are available for all editions of Windows Server 2008, including both 32-bit and 64-bit editions. Although you cannot install the graphical components of these utilities on core installations, you can use the command line or manage backups remotely from another computer.

You install the Windows backup and recovery tools using Server Manager. In Server Manager, select the Features node in the left pane and then click Add Features. This starts the Add Features Wizard. On the Select Features page, select Windows Recovery Disc and then select Windows Server Backup Features. When you select Windows Server Backup Features, the Windows Server Backup and Command-Line Tools options are selected. Click Next and then click Install.

When the wizard finishes installing the selected features, click Close. From now on, Windows Server Backup will be available as an option on the Administrative Tools menu and the Create A Recovery Disc option will be available on the All Programs\ Maintenance menu.

The first time you use Windows Server Backup, you'll see a warning that no backup has been configured for the computer as shown in Figure 41-1. You clear this warning by creating a backup using the Back Up Once feature or by scheduling backups to run automatically using the Backup Schedule feature.

> **Note**
>
> When you start Windows Server Backup, the utility connects to the local computer by default. This allows you to easily manage backups on the local computer. If you want to manage backups on a remote computer, click Connect To Another Computer in the actions pane or on the Action menu. Select Another Computer and then type the server's name or IP address. Alternatively, if network discovery is enabled, click Browse, choose the remote computer in the dialog box provided, and then click OK. Finally, click Finish to establish a connection to the remote computer.

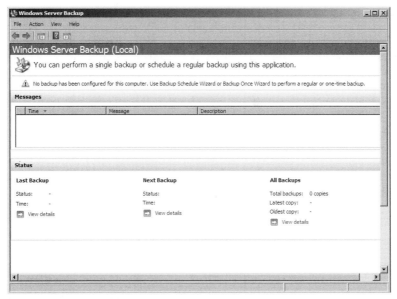

Figure 41-1 Getting started with Windows Server Backup.

When you use Windows Server Backup, the first backup of a server is always a full backup. This is because the full backup process clears the archive bits on files so that Windows Server Backup can track which files are updated subsequently. Whether Windows Server Backup performs subsequent full or incremental backups depends on the default performance settings that you configure. You can configure the default performance settings by clicking Configure Performance Settings in the actions pane or on the Action menu, doing one of the following, and then clicking OK:

- Select Always Perform Full Backup to perform full backups of all attached drives.

- Select Always Perform Incremental Backup to perform incremental backups of all attached drives.

- Select Custom and then, from the option lists provided, select whether to perform full or incremental backups for individual attached drives.

After you've configured the default performance settings, you can start a full or copy backup by selecting Backup Once on the Action menu or in the actions pane. You can configure a backup schedule by clicking Backup Schedule on the Action menu or in the actions pane.

Chapter 41

INSIDE OUT **Performing backups at the command line**

Wbadmin is the command-line counterpart to Windows Server Backup. After you've installed the Backup Command-Line Tools feature as discussed previously, you can use Wbadmin to manage backup and recovery from an elevated, administrator command prompt.

Wbadmin is located in the %SystemRoot%\System32\ directory. When you are working with Wbadmin, you can get help on available commands. To view a list of management commands, type **wbadmin /?** at the command prompt. To view the syntax for a specific management command, type **wbadmin *CommandName* /?**, where *CommandName* is the name of the management command you want to examine, such as **wbadmin enable backup /?**.

Most Wbadmin commands use the *-backupTarget* parameter. The backup target is the storage location you want to work with, and can be expressed as a local volume name, such as D:, or as a network share path, such as \\BackupServer05\Backups\Server24.

Backing Up Your Data

As part of your planning for each server you plan to back up, you should consider which volumes you want to back up and whether backups will include system state recovery data, application data, or both. If the Windows Firewall is enabled and you are trying to work with a remote computer, you might need to make an exception to allow backup and recovery operations.

As part of the backup process, you also will need to specify a storage location for backups. Keep the following in mind when you are choosing storage locations:

- When you use an internal hard disk for storing backups, you are limited in how you can recover your system. You can recover the data from a volume, but you cannot rebuild the entire disk structure.

- When you use an external hard disk for storing backups, the disk will be dedicated for storing your backups and will not be visible in Windows Explorer. Choosing this option will format the selected disk or disks, removing any existing data.

- When you use a remote shared folder for storing backups, your backup will be overwritten each time you create a new backup. Do not choose this option if you want to store multiple backups for each server.

- When you use removable media or DVDs for storing backups, you can only recover entire volumes, not applications or individual files. The media you use must be at least 1 GB in size.

When you create or schedule backups, you will need to specify the volumes that you want to include and this will affect the ways you can recover your servers and your data. Back up just critical volumes if you want to be able to recover only the operating system. Back up just individual volumes if you want to be able to recover only files, applications, or data from those volumes.

Back up all volumes with application data if you want to be able to recover a server fully, along with its system state and application data. Because you are backing up all files, the system state, and application data, you should be able to fully restore your server using only the Windows backup tools.

Back up all volumes without application data if you want to be able to restore a server and its applications separately. With this technique, you back up the server using the Windows tools and then back up applications using third-party tools or tools built into the applications. You can recover a server fully using the Windows backup utilities and then use a third-party utility to restore backups of application data.

Scheduling Backups

To automate the backup process, you can create a scheduled task that runs Windows Server Backup for you. For Windows Server 2008, the task creation and scheduling processes are integrated into Windows Server Backup. You can schedule automated backups using Windows Server Backup. Click Backup Schedule on the Action menu or in the actions pane to start the Backup Schedule Wizard. After scanning the available disks, Windows Server Backup starts the Backup Schedule Wizard. Click Next.

On the Select Backup Configuration page, shown in the following screen, note the backup size listed under the Full Server option. This is the storage space required to back up the server data, applications, and the system state. To back up all volumes on the server, select the Full Server option and then click Next. To back up selected volumes on the server, click Custom and then click Next.

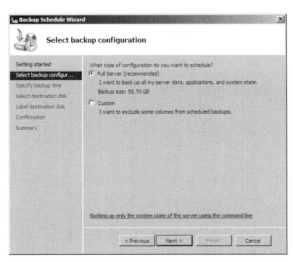

If you selected Custom, the Select Backup Items page is displayed as shown in the following screen. Select the check boxes for the volumes that you want to back up and clear the check boxes for the volumes that you want to exclude. Only locally attached disks formatted with NTFS can be included in scheduled backups. Volumes that contain boot files, operating system files, or applications are included in the backup by default and cannot be excluded.

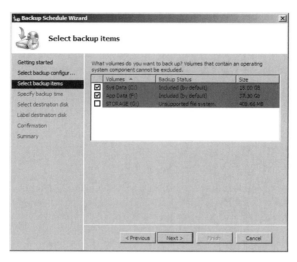

On the Specify Backup Time page, shown in the following screen, you can specify how often and when you want to run backups. To perform backups daily at a specific time, choose Once A Day and then select the time to start running the daily backup. To perform backups multiple times each day, choose More Than Once A Day. Next, click a start time under Available Time and then click Add to move the time under Scheduled Time. Repeat for each start time that you want to add. Click Next when you are ready to continue.

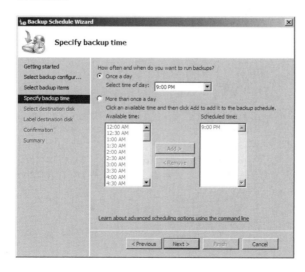

On the Select Destination Disk page, shown in the following screen, select the external disk that you want to use for scheduled backups. If the disk that you want to use is not listed, click Show All Available Disks. Then select the check box next to the disk that you want to use to store the backups. Each external disk can store up to 512 backups, depending on the amount of data contained in each backup. You can select multiple disks. If you do so, Windows Server Backup will rotate between them.

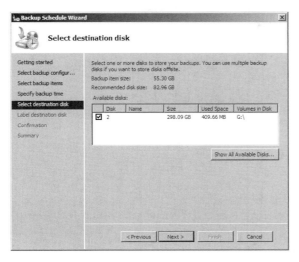

When you click Next, you'll see the warning prompt shown in the following screen. This prompt informs you that the selected disk will be formatted and any existing data will be deleted. Click Yes.

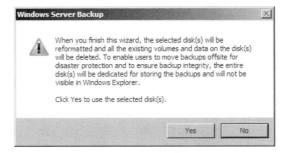

On the Label Destination Disk page, shown in the following screen, the disk that you selected is listed. A label that includes the disk type, server name, the current date, the current time, and a disk size is assigned to the disk. If you need to recover data from the backup stored on the disk, you will need this information to identify the disk. There-fore, be sure to write down this information. With external disks, you might want to attach a printed label containing this information.

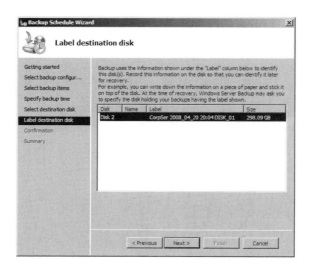

On the Confirmation page, review the details, and then click Finish. The wizard will then format the disk. The formatting process might take several minutes or considerably longer depending on the size of the disk. When this process finishes, the Summary page should show that you've successfully created the backup schedule as shown in the following screen. Click Close. Your backups are now scheduled for the selected server. You'll need to check periodically to ensure that backups are being performed as expected and that the backup schedule meets current needs.

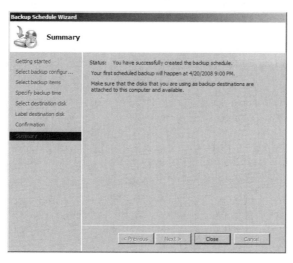

On the Scheduled Backup Settings page, shown in the following screen, you have two choices. You can select Modify Backup if you want to add or remove backup items, times, or targets. Or you can select Stop Backup if you want to stop the scheduled backups from running. Stopping backups releases backup disks for normal use. However, backup archives are not deleted from the backup disks and remain available for use in recovery.

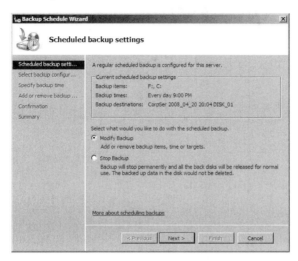

If you want to modify backups, you'll continue through the scheduling process as discussed previously with one important change. After the Select Backup Configuration page, the optional Select Backup Items page, and the Specify Backup Time page, you'll see the Add Or Remove Backup Disks page, shown in the following screen. Here, select Do Nothing if you do not want to modify the currently selected backup targets. Otherwise, do one of the following:

- Select Add More Disks if you want to add one or more backup targets. On the Select Destination Disk page, select the check box for the disks you want to use as backup targets. When you click Next, you'll see a warning prompt informing you that the selected disk will be formatted and any existing data will be deleted. Click Yes. On the Label Destination Disk page, each disk that you selected is listed. Note the label—you will need this information. Click Next.

- Select Remove Current Disks if you want to remove one or more currently selected backup targets. On the Remove Current Disks page, select the check box next to each disk that you want to remove from the disks used to store backups.

Chapter 41

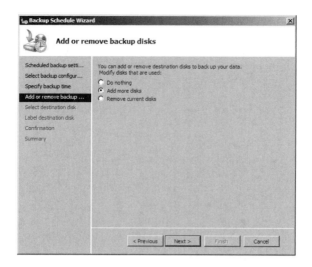

Performing a One-Time Backup

Regardless of whether you want to back up data using a recurring schedule or perform a manual backup, the techniques are similar. In this section, I am going to discuss manual backups so that you know how to perform backups manually. You can perform a manual backup using Windows Server Backup. Click Backup Once on the Action menu or in the actions pane to start the Backup Once Wizard.

After scanning the available disks, Windows Server Backup gives you the backup options shown in the following screen. If you want to back up the server using the same options that you use for the Backup Schedule Wizard, select The Same Options That You Used In The Backup Schedule Wizard For Scheduled Backups, click Next, and then click Backup to perform the backup. Otherwise, select Different Options, click Next, and then continue through the wizard pages to perform the backup.

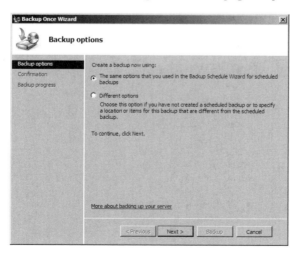

On the Select Backup Configuration page, shown in the following screen, note the backup size listed under the Full Server option. This is the storage space required to back up the server data, applications, and system state. To back up all volumes on the server, select the Full Server option and then click Next. To back up selected volumes on the server, select Custom and then click Next.

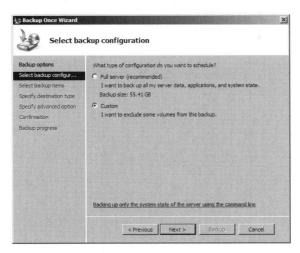

If you selected Custom, the Select Backup Items page is displayed as shown in the following screen. Select the check boxes for the volumes that you want to back up and clear the check boxes for the volumes that you want to exclude. If you want to back up the system state and all critical operating system volumes, select the Enable System Recovery check box. Note that any external disk being used for scheduled backups is excluded by default, but these and other external disks can be included in the backup set. Click Next.

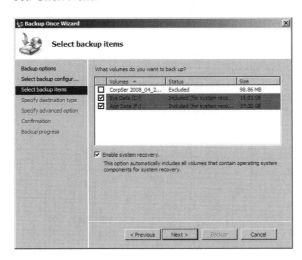

On the Specify Destination Type page, do one of the following:

- If you want to back up to local drives, select Local Drives and then click Next. On the Select Backup Destination page, select the internal or external disk or DVD drive to use as the backup target. Backups are compressed when stored on a DVD. As a result, the size of the backup on a DVD might be smaller than the volume on the server. If the backup target is a removable media drive, the backup is verified automatically after the wizard writes the backup data. Clear the Verify After Writing check box if you do not want to verify the backup. Click Next.

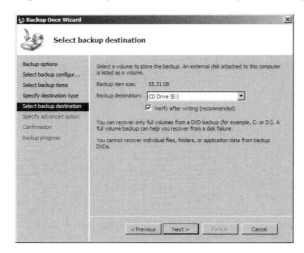

- If you want to back up to a remote shared folder, select Remote Shared Folder and then click Next. On the Specify Remote Folder page, type the UNC path to the remote folder, such as \\BackupServer06\Backups\Server21. If you want the backup to be accessible to everyone who has access to the shared folder, select Inherit under Access Control. If you want to restrict access to the shared folder to the current user, administrators, and backup operators, select Do Not Inherit under Access Control. Click Next. When prompted to provide access credentials, type the user name and password for an account authorized to access and write to the shared folder.

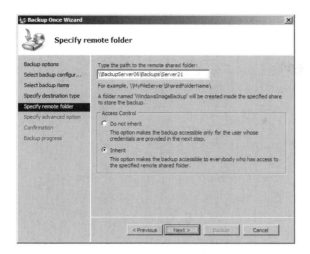

On the Specify Advanced Option page, shown in the following screen, specify whether you want to perform a VSS copy backup or a VSS full backup. Choose VSS Copy Backup if you are using a separate backup utility to back up application data. Otherwise choose VSS Full Backup to back up the selected volumes fully, including all application data.

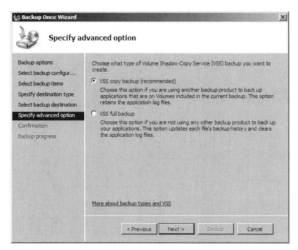

Afterward, click Next and then click Backup. The wizard starts by creating a shadow copy of the selected volumes. When this process finishes, the wizard will then try to write to the media you selected. If you are backing up to DVD, you'll be prompted to insert media as shown in the following screen. Note the disc label, which includes a time and date stamp as well as a unique identifier for each disc in the backup set in sequential order. To help you keep track of your disc, you should write the label on the disc before inserting it in the DVD drive.

The wizard displays the progress of the backup on the Backup Progress page, as shown in the following screen. You'll see the status of the backup process for each disk drive that you are backing up. If you click Close, the backup will continue to run in the background.

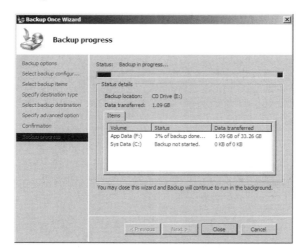

Tracking Scheduled and Manual Backups

Whenever Windows Server Backup backs up a server, it writes related events related to the Windows event logs. You'll find events related to shadow copies in the Application log and all other backup events in the Microsoft\Backup\Operational log as shown in Figure 41-2. By looking through the Operational log, you can quickly determine when backups were started, when they were completed, and reasons for failure, such as when backups were cancelled by another administrator or there was not enough space on the backup target. By looking at the time difference between when a backup started and when it completed, you can also determine how long backups are taking.

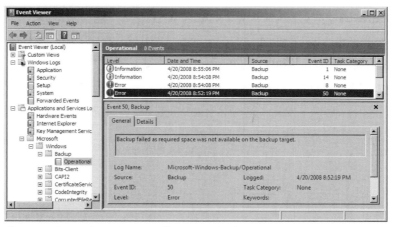

Figure 41-2 Windows Server Backup writes backup events in the event logs.

As shown in Figure 41-3, Windows Server Backup provides summary details regarding backups as well. In the Messages pane, you'll find information regarding completed, failed, and currently running backups. In the Status pane, you'll find details on the last backup, the next scheduled backup, and all available backups. Click the View Details links to determine what volumes were backed up, the backup type, and more. In the Details dialog box, you can track errors that occurred during the backup on the Errors tab.

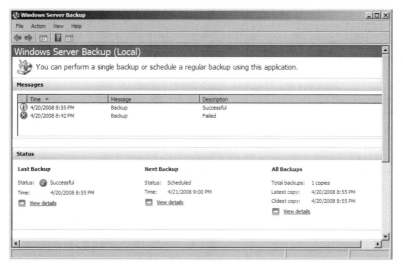

Figure 41-3 Review the backup status in Windows Server Backup.

Recovering Your Data

Windows Server 2008 provides separate processes for system state recovery, full server recovery, and recovery of individual volumes and files and folders. You use the Recovery Wizard in Windows Server Backup to recover non-system volumes and files and folders from a backup. For example, if Mary loses a spreadsheet and there isn't an available shadow copy of the file, you could recover the individual file from the backup archive. If John accidentally deletes an important folder, you can recover the folder and all its contents from a backup archive.

Before you begin, you should ensure that the computer that you are recovering files to is running Windows Server 2008. If you want to recover individual files and folders, you should ensure that at least one backup exists on an external disk or in a remote shared folder. You cannot recover files and folders from backups saved to DVDs or other types of removable media.

You can recover data in two ways. You can recover data from the server to which you are currently logged on. Or you can recover data from another server. As these are different procedures, I'll discuss them in different sections.

Recovering Data from the Current Server

To recover non-system volumes, files and folders, or application data, start Windows Server Backup. Click Recover in the actions pane or on the Action menu to start the Recovery Wizard. On the Getting Started page, select This Server as shown in the following screen and then click Next.

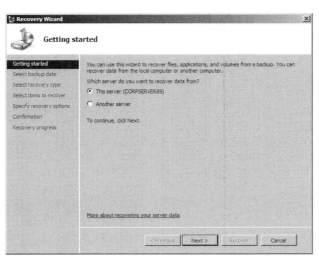

On the Select Backup Date page, shown in the following screen, select the date and time of the backup you want to restore using the calendar and the time list. Backups are available for dates shown in bold. Click Next.

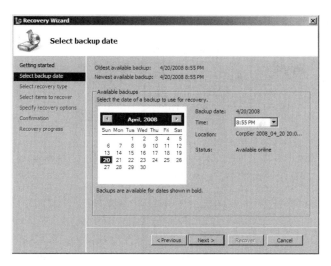

On the Select Recovery Type page, shown in the following screen, do one of the following:

- To restore individual files and folders, select Files And Folders, and then click Next. On the Select Items To Recover page, under Available Items, click the plus sign (+) to expand the list until the folder you want is visible. Select a folder to display the contents of the folder in the adjacent pane, select each item that you want to restore, and then click Next.

- To restore non-critical, non-operating system volumes, select Volumes and then click Next. On the Select Volumes page, you'll see a list of source and destination volumes. Select the check boxes associated with the source volumes that you want to recover. Then select the location that you want to recover the volume to using the Destination Volume drop-down list. Click Next.

- To restore data from applications that have been registered with Windows Server Backup, select Applications and then click Next. On the Select Application page, under Applications, click the application that you want to recover. If the backup that you are using is the most recent, you will see a check box labeled Do Not Perform A Roll-Forward Recovery of the application databases. Select this check box if you want to prevent Windows Server Backup from rolling forward the application database that is currently on your server. Click Next. Because any data on the destination volume will be lost when you perform the recovery, make sure that the destination volume is empty or does not contain information that you will need later.

Chapter 41

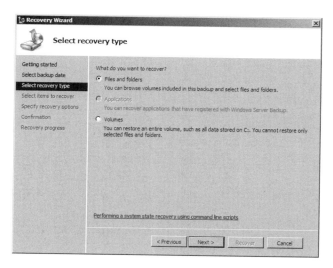

On the Specify Recovery Options page, shown in the following screen, specify whether you want to restore data to its original location (non-system files only) or an alternate location. For an alternate location, type the path to the desired restore location or click Browse to select it. With applications, you can copy application data to an alternate location. You cannot, however, recover applications to a different location or computer.

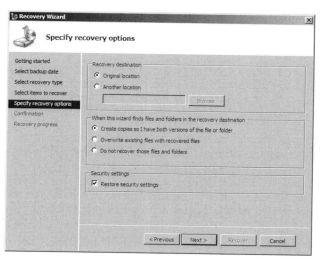

Under When This Wizard Finds Files And Folders In The Recovery Destination, choose a recovery technique to apply when files and folders already exist in the recovery location. You can create copies so that you have both versions of the file or folder, overwrite existing files with recovered files, or skip duplicate files and folders to preserve existing files. By default, the Recovery Wizard restores the security settings. In most cases, you'll want to use this option. Click Next when you are ready to continue.

On the Confirmation page, review the details, and then click Recover to restore the specified items. The wizard displays the progress of the recovery on the Recovery Progress page, as shown in the following screen. If you click Close, the recovery will continue to run in the background.

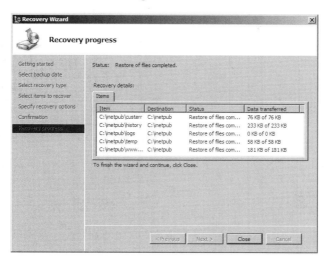

Windows Server Backup provides summary details regarding recovery in the Messages pane. You'll find information regarding completed, failed, and currently running recovery operations. Windows Server Backup also writes related recovery events to the Windows event logs. You'll find events related to shadow copies in the Application log and all other recovery events in the Microsoft\Backup\Operational log. By looking through the Operational log, you can quickly determine when recovery operations were started, when they were completed, and reasons for failure. By navigating through the recovery-related events, you can also find an event that provides the location of a log file that lists all files restored in the recovery operation. Figures 41-4 shows an example.

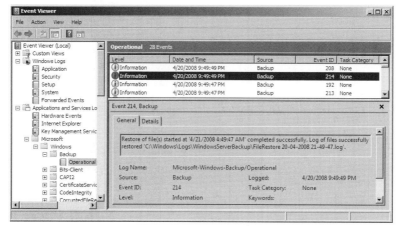

Figure 41-4 Windows Server Backup writes tracking events for recovery in the event logs.

Recovering Data from Another Server

To recover non-system volumes, files and folders, or application data, start Windows Server Backup. Click Recover in the actions pane or on the Action menu to start the Recovery Wizard. On the Getting Started page, select Another Server, as shown in the following screen, and then click Next.

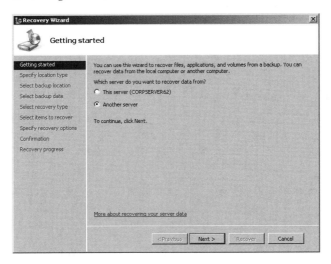

On the Specify Location Type page, shown in the following screen, specify whether the backup that you want to restore is on a local drive or in a remote shared folder, click Next, and then specify location-specific settings.

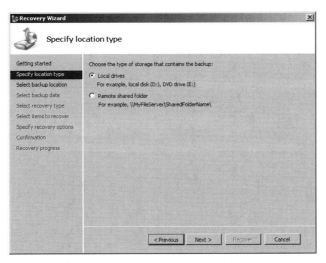

When you are recovering from a local drive, on the Select Backup Location page, select the location of the backup from the drop-down list. Any external disk attached to the server is listed as a volume. You can recover only full volumes from a DVD backup. If your backup is on a DVD and spans multiple volumes, insert the last backup of the set.

When you are recovering from a remote shared folder, on the Specify Remote Folder page, type the path to the folder that contains the backup, such as \\FileServer07\ Servers\Server18Backup. If you are prompted to provide your logon credentials, enter the user name and password for an account with owner or co-owner permissions on the shared folder.

The rest of the recovery operation is the same as discussed previously, starting with the Select Backup Date page.

Recovering the System State

On Windows Server 2008, there are over 50,000 system state files and these files use 4 to 6 GB of disk space. The fastest and easiest way to back up and restore a server's system state is to use Wbadmin. With Wbadmin, you can use the Start SystemStateBackup command to create a backup of the system state for a computer and the Start System-StateRecovery command to restore a computer's system state.

> **Note**
> When you select a system state restore on a domain controller, you have to be in the Directory Services Restore Mode. To learn how to restore Active Directory, see "Backing Up and Restoring Active Directory" on page 1409.

You can back up a server's system state by typing the following at an elevated command prompt:

```
wbadmin start systemstatebackup -backupTarget:VolumeName
```

where *VolumeName* is the storage location for the backup, such as G:.

You can restore a server's system state by typing the following at an elevated command prompt:

```
wbadmin start systemstaterecovery -backupTarget:VolumeName
```

where *VolumeName* is the storage location that contains the backup you want to recover, such as G:.

You can use other parameters for recovery operations as well. Use the *-recoveryTarget* parameter to restore to an alternate location. Use the *-machine* parameter to specify the name of the computer to recover if the original backup location contains backups for multiple computers. Use the *-authorsysvol* parameter to perform an authoritative restore of the Sysvol.

Chapter 41

Restoring the Operating System and the Full System

The Startup Repair Tool can recover a server in case of corrupted or missing system files. It can also recover from some types of boot failures involving the boot manager. If these processes fail and the boot manager is the reason you cannot start the server, you can use the Windows Server 2008 installation disc to restore the boot manager and enable startup.

When the Startup Repair Tool and other support tools fail to recover normal operations, you can recover a server's operating system or perform a full system recovery by using a Windows installation disc and a backup that you created earlier with Windows Server Backup. These two operations differ in fundamental ways:

- With an operating system recovery, you recover all critical volumes but do not recover non-system volumes. A critical volume is a volume that has files the operating system needs during startup and normal operations and includes both the boot volume and the system volume (which might or might not be the same volume). You should use this method only when you cannot recover the operating system using other means.

- With a full system recovery, Windows Server Backup reformats and repartitions all disks that are attached to the server and then sets about recovering the server's volumes. Data that was not included in the original backup will be deleted when you recover the system, which includes any volumes that are currently used by the server but were not included in the backup. You should use this method only when you want to recover the server data onto separate hardware or when all other attempts to recover the server on the existing hardware have failed.

Before you begin, you should ensure that your backup data is available. You can recover a server's operating system or perform a full system recovery by inserting the Windows installation disc into the DVD drive and turning on the computer. If needed, press the required key to boot from the disc. The Install Windows Wizard should appear. You'll need to specify the language settings to use, and then click Next.

Click Repair Your Computer. Setup searches the hard disk drives for an existing Windows installation and then displays the results in the System Recovery Options Wizard. If you are recovering the operating system onto separate hardware, the list should be empty and there should be no operating system on the computer. Click Next.

On the System Recovery Options page, click Windows Complete PC Restore. When the Windows Complete PC Restore Wizard starts, select Use The Latest Available Backup (Recommended) and then click Next. Or select Restore A Different Backup and then click Next. If you chose to restore a different backup, on the Select The Location Of The Backup page, do one of the following:

- Select the computer that contains the backup that you want to use, and then click Next. On the Select The Backup To Restore page, select the backup that you want to use, and then click Next.

- Click Advanced to browse for a backup on the network, and then click Next. Browse the network to select the backup to restore, and then click Next.

On the Choose How To Restore The Backup page, do the following optional tasks, and then click Next:

- Select the Format And Repartition Disks check box to delete existing partitions and reformat the destination disks to be the same as the backup.

- Click the Exclude Disks button and then select the check boxes associated with any disks that you want to exclude from being formatted and partitioned. The disk that contains the backup that you are using is automatically excluded.

- Click Install Drivers to install device drivers for the hardware to which you are recovering.

- Click Advanced to specify whether the computer is restarted and the disks are checked for errors immediately after the recovery operation is completed.

On the Confirmation page, review the details for the restoration, and then click Finish. The Windows Complete PC Restore Wizard will then restore the operating system or the full server as appropriate for the options you've selected.

Backing Up and Restoring Active Directory

Backing up Active Directory is easy. Recovery of Active Directory itself, however, is different from recovery for other types of network services. A key reason for this involves the way Active Directory data is replicated and restored. Because of this, let's look at backup and recovery strategies for Active Directory, and then look at various restore techniques.

Backup and Recovery Strategies for Active Directory

Domain controllers have replication partners with which they share information. When you have multiple domain controllers in a domain and one fails, the other domain controllers automatically detect the failure and change their replication topology accordingly. You can repair or replace the failed domain controller from backup. However, the restore doesn't recover Active Directory information stored on the domain controller.

To restore Active Directory on the failed domain controller, you use either a nonauthoritative or authoritative approach. A *nonauthoritative restore* allows the domain controller to come back on line, and then get replication updates from other domain controllers. An *authoritative restore* makes the restored domain controller the authority in the domain, and its data is replicated to other domain controllers.

In most cases, you'll have multiple domain controllers in a domain, giving you flexibility in your disaster recovery plan. If one of the domain controllers fails, you can install a new domain controller or promote an existing member server so that it can be a domain controller. In either case, the directory on the new domain controller is updated automatically through replication. You could also recover the failed domain controller, and then perform a nonauthoritative restore. In this case, you would restore Active Directory on the domain controller and obtain directory updates from other domain controllers in the domain.

Chapter 41

In some cases, you might need to perform an authoritative restore of Active Directory. For example, if a large number of objects were deleted from Active Directory, the only way to recover those objects would be to use an authoritative restore. In this case, you would restore Active Directory on a domain controller and use the recovered data as the master copy of the directory database. This data is then replicated to all other domain controllers.

The disaster recovery strategy you choose for Active Directory might depend on whether you have dedicated or nondedicated domain controllers, for the following reasons:

- When you have dedicated domain controllers that perform no other domain services, you can implement a very simple disaster recovery procedure for domain controllers. As long as you have multiple domain controllers in each domain, you can restore a failed domain controller by installing a new domain controller and then populating the directory on this new domain controller. You can do so through replication or by recovering the domain controller using a nonauthoritative restore. You should always back up one or more of the domain controllers and their system state as well, so that you always have a current snapshot of Active Directory in the backup archives. If you need to recover from a disaster that has caused all your domain controllers to fail or Active Directory has been corrupted, you can recover using an authoritative restore in the Directory Services Restore Mode.

- When you have nondedicated domain controllers, you should back up the system state whenever you perform a full backup of a domain controller. This stores a snapshot of Active Directory along with the other pertinent system information that can be used to fully recover the domain controller. If a domain controller fails, you can recover the server the way you recover any server. You then have the option of restoring the system state data and Active Directory to allow the server to resume operating as a domain controller, by using a nonauthoritative restore in the Directory Services Restore Mode. If you need to recover from a disaster that has caused all your domain controllers to fail or Active Directory has been corrupted, you also have the option of using an authoritative restore in the Directory Services Restore Mode.

When planning backups of Active Directory, you should also remember the tombstone lifetime. As you might recall from Chapter 33, "Implementing Active Directory," Active Directory doesn't actually delete objects when you remove them from the directory. Instead, objects are tombstoned (marked for deletion) and the tombstone is replicated to all the other domain controllers. By default, the tombstone lifetime is 60 days, meaning that a tombstone will remain in the directory for 60 days and then be deleted. To ensure that you don't accidentally restore objects that have actually been removed from Active Directory, you are prevented from restoring Active Directory if the backup archive is older than the tombstone lifetime. This means that, by default, you cannot restore a backup of Active Directory that is older than 60 days.

Other system information is contained in the system state besides Active Directory. So, any restore of Active Directory includes all that information, and that information will be restored to its previous state as well. If a server's configuration changed since the backup, the configuration changes will be lost.

Performing a Nonauthoritative Restore of Active Directory

When a domain controller fails, you can restore it the way you restore any other server except when it comes to Active Directory. With this in mind, first fix the problem that caused the server to fail. After you've restored the server, you can then work to restore Active Directory.

You recover Active Directory by restoring the system state on the domain controller, using a special recovery mode called Directory Services Restore Mode. If you have made changes to Active Directory since the backup, the system state backup will not contain those changes. However, other domain controllers in the domain will have the most recent changes, and the domain controller will be able to obtain those changes through the normal replication process.

When you want to restore Active Directory on a domain controller and have the domain controller get directory updates from other domain controllers, you perform a nonauthoritative restore. A nonauthoritative restore allows the domain controller to come back on line and then get replication updates from other domain controllers.

Schedule a full server backup of a domain controller to ensure recovery of the server operating system and application data in the event of a hardware failure. Schedule a separate backup of critical volumes to ensure timely recovery of Active Directory. To guard against unforeseen issues, schedule backups on at least two different domain controllers for each domain and schedule additional backups on any domain controller with a unique application partition.

A full server backup is a backup of every volume on the server. You can use this type of backup to recover a domain controller onto new hardware. On a domain controller, critical volumes include the boot volume and the volumes that contain the following data:

- Operating system files
- Registry
- Active Directory database and log files
- Sysvol folders

You can use critical-volume backups to restore Active Directory on a domain controller. Critical-volume backups can also be restored and copied to transferrable media to install a new domain controller in the same domain.

The procedure to perform a full server or critical volume recovery of a domain controller is the same as for any server. When you do this, you will also be performing a nonauthoritative restore of Active Directory. After the recovery is complete, restart the domain controller in the standard operations mode and then verify the installation. When you restart the domain controller, Active Directory automatically detects that it has been recovered from a backup. Active Directory will then perform an integrity check and re-index the database. From that point on, the server can then act as a domain controller and it has a directory database that is current as of the date of the backup. The domain controller then connects to its replication partners and begins updating the database so that any changes since the backup are reflected.

Chapter 41

After you log on to the server, check Active Directory and verify that all of the objects that were present in the directory at the time of the backup are restored. The easiest way to confirm this is to browse Active Directory Users And Computers, Active Directory Domains And Trusts, and Active Directory Sites And Services.

Performing an Authoritative Restore of Active Directory

An authoritative restore is used when you need to recover Active Directory to a specific point in time and then replicate the restored data to all other domain controllers. Consider the following example: John accidentally deleted the Marketing organizational unit (OU) and all the objects it contained. Because the changes have already been replicated to all domain controllers in the domain, the only way to restore the OU and the related objects would be to use an authoritative restore. Similarly, if Active Directory were somehow corrupted, the only way to recover Active Directory fully would be to use an authoritative restore.

When performing authoritative restores, there are several significant issues that you should consider. The first and most important issue has to do with passwords used for computers and Windows NT LAN Manager (NTLM) trusts. These passwords are changed automatically every seven days. If you perform an authoritative restore of Active Directory, the restored data will contain the passwords that were in use when the backup archive was made. If you monitor the event logs after the restore, you might see related events or you might hear from users who are experiencing problems accessing resources in the domain.

Computer account passwords allow computers to authenticate themselves in a domain using a computer trust. If a computer password has changed, the computer may not be able to reauthenticate itself in the domain. In this case, you may need to reset the computer account password by right-clicking on the computer account in Active Directory Users And Computers, and then selecting Reset Account. If the reset of the password doesn't work, you might need to remove the computer account from the domain, and then add it back.

NTLM trusts are trusts between Active Directory domains and Microsoft Windows NT domains. If a trust password has changed, the trust between the domains may fail. In this case, you might need to delete the trust, and then re-create it as discussed in "Establishing External, Shortcut, Realm, and Cross-Forest Trusts," on page 1035.

Another significant issue when performing an authoritative restore has to do with group membership. Problems with group membership can occur after an authoritative restore for several reasons.

In the first case, an administrator has updated a group object's membership on a domain controller that has not yet received the restored data. In this case, the domain controller may replicate the changes to other domain controllers, causing a temporary inconsistency. The changes shouldn't be permanent, however, because when you perform an authoritative restore, the update sequence number (USN) of all restored objects is incremented by 100,000. This ensures that the restored data is authoritative and overwrites any existing data.

Another problem with group membership can occur if group objects contain user accounts that do not currently exist in the domain. In this case, if group objects are replicated before these user objects are, the user accounts that do not currently exist in the domain will be seen as invalid user accounts. As a result, the user accounts will be deleted as group members. When the user accounts are later replicated, the user accounts will not be added back to the groups.

Although there is no way to control which objects are replicated first, there is a way to correct this problem. You must force the domain controller to replicate the group membership list with the group object. You can do this by creating a temporary user account and adding it to each group that contains user accounts that are currently not valid in the domain. Here's how this would work: You authoritatively restore and then restart the domain controller. The domain controller begins replicating its data to other domain controllers. When this initial replication process finishes, you create a temporary user account and add it to the requisite groups. The group membership list will then be replicated. If any domain controller has removed previously invalid user accounts as members of these groups, the domain controller will then return the user accounts to the group.

You can perform an authoritative restore by completing the following steps:

1. Perform a full server or critical volume recovery of the domain controller. After you've repaired or rebuilt the server, restart the server and press F8 during startup to access the Windows Advanced Options menu. You must press F8 before the Windows splash screen appears.

2. On the Windows Advanced Options menu, select Directory Services Restore Mode (Windows Domain Controllers Only). Windows will then restart in Safe Mode without loading Active Directory components.

3. You will next need to choose the operating system you want to start.

4. Log on to the server using the Administrator account with the Directory Services Restore password that was configured on the domain controller when Active Directory was installed.

5. The Desktop prompt warns you that you are running in Safe Mode, which allows you to fix problems with the server but makes some of your devices unavailable. Click OK.

6. Click Start, click Run, type **cmd** in the Open field, and then click OK.

7. At the command prompt, type **ntdsutil**. This starts the Directory Services Management Tool.

8. At the Ntdsutil prompt, type **authoritative restore**. You should now be at the Authoritative Restore prompt, where you have the following options:

    o You can authoritatively restore the entire Active Directory database by typing **restore database**. If you restore the entire Active Directory database, there will be a significant amount of replication traffic generated throughout the domain and the forest. You should restore the entire database only if

Chapter 41

Active Directory has been corrupted or there is some other significant reason for doing so.

- You can authoritatively restore a container and all its related objects (referred to as a *subtree*) by typing **restore subtree** *ObjectDN*, where *ObjectDN* is the distinguished name of the container to restore. For example, if someone accidentally deleted the Marketing OU in the cpandl.com domain, you could restore the OU and all the objects it contained by typing the command **restore subtree ou=marketing,dc=cpandl,dc=com**.

- You can authoritatively restore an individual object by typing **restore object** *ObjectDN*, where *ObjectDN* is the distinguished name of the object to restore. For example, if someone accidentally deleted the Sales group from the default container for users and groups (**cn=users**) in the cpandl.com domain, you could restore the group by typing the command **restore object cn=sales,cn=users,dc=cpandl,dc=com**.

9. When you type a restore command and press Enter, the Authoritative Restore Confirmation dialog box appears, which prompts you to click Yes if you're sure you want to perform the restore action. Click Yes to perform the restore operation.

10. Type **quit** twice to exit Ntdsutil, and then restart the server.

> **Note**
> Every object that is restored will have its USN incremented by 100,000. When you are restoring the entire database, you cannot override this behavior, which is necessary to ensure that the data is properly replicated. For subtree and object restores, you can override this behavior by setting a different version increment value using the Verinc option. For example, if you wanted to restore the Sales group in the cpandl.com domain and increment the USN by 500 rather than 100,000, you could do this by typing the command **restore object cn=sales,cn=users,dc=cpandl,dc=comverinc 500**.

Restoring Sysvol Data

The Sysvol folder is backed up as part of the system state information and contains critical domain information including GPOs, group policy templates, and scripts used for startup, shutdown, logging on, and logging off. If you restore a domain controller, the Sysvol data will be replicated from other domain controllers. Unlike Active Directory data, Sysvol data is replicated using the File Replication Service (FRS).

When you perform a nonauthoritative restore of a domain controller, the domain controller's Sysvol data is not set as the primary data. This means that the restored Sysvol would not be replicated and could instead be overwritten by Sysvol data from other domain controllers.

When you perform an authoritative restore of a domain controller, the domain controller's Sysvol data is set as the primary data for the domain. This means that the restored Sysvol would be replicated to all other domain controllers. For example, if someone were to delete several scripts used for startup or logon and there were no backups of these scripts, these could be restored by performing an authoritative restore and allowing the restored, authoritative domain controller's Sysvol data to be replicated.

You can prevent a restored, authoritative domain controller's Sysvol data from overwriting the Sysvol on other domain controllers. To do this, you should back up the Sysvol in the desired state on another domain controller prior to performing the authoritative restore. After you've completed the authoritative restore, you can then restore the Sysvol in the desired state to the authoritative domain controller.

Restoring a Failed Domain Controller by Installing a New Domain Controller

Sometimes you won't be able to or won't want to repair a failed domain controller and may instead elect to install a new domain controller. You can install a new domain controller by promoting an existing member server so that it is a domain controller, or by installing a new computer and then promoting it. Either way, the domain controller will get its directory information from another domain controller.

Installing a new domain controller is the easy part. When you've finished that, you need to clean up references to the old domain controller so that other computers in the domain don't try to connect to it anymore. You need to remove references to the server in DNS, and you need to examine any roles that the failed server played. If the failed server was a global catalog server, you should designate another domain controller as a global catalog server. If the failed server held an operations master role, you will need to seize the role and give it to another domain controller. Let's start with DNS and roles.

- To clean up DNS, you need to remove all records for the server in DNS. This includes SRV records that designate the computer as a domain controller and any additional records that designate the computer as a global catalog server or PDC emulator if applicable.

- To designate another server as a global catalog server, see "Designating Global Catalog Servers" on page 1012.

- To transfer operations master roles, see "Design Considerations for Active Directory Operations Masters" on page 1044.

To clean up references to the failed domain controller in Active Directory, you are going to need to use Ntdsutil. You must use an account with Administrator privileges in the domain and should run Ntdsutil on a computer running Windows Server 2008. The cleanup process is as follows:

1. Click Start, click Run, type **cmd** in the Open field, and then click OK.

2. At the command prompt, type **ntdsutil**. This starts the Directory Services Management Tool.

Chapter 41

3. At the Ntdsutil prompt, type **metadata cleanup**. You should now be at the Metadata Cleanup prompt.

4. Access the Server Connections prompt so that you can connect to a domain controller. To do this, type **connections** and then type **connect to server** *DCName*, where *DCName* is the name of a working domain controller in the same domain as the failed domain controller.

5. Exit the Server Connections prompt by typing **quit**. You should now be back at the Metadata Cleanup prompt.

6. Access the Select Operation Target prompt so that you can work your way through Active Directory from a target domain to a target site to the actual domain controller you want to remove. Type **select operation target**.

7. List all the sites in the forest by typing **list sites** and then type **select site** *Number*, where *Number* is the number of the site containing the failed domain controller.

8. List all the domains in the site by typing **list domains in site** and then type **select domain** *Number*, where *Number* is the number of the domain containing the failed domain controller.

9. List all the domain controllers in the selected domain and site by typing **list servers in site** and then type **select server** *Number*, where *Number* is the number of the server that failed.

10. Exit the Select Operation Target prompt by typing **quit**. You should now be back at the Metadata Cleanup prompt.

11. Remove the selected server from the directory by typing **remove selected server**. When prompted, confirm that you want to remove the selected server.

12. Type **quit** twice to exit Ntdsutil. Next, remove the related computer object from the Domain Controllers OU in Active Directory Users And Computers. Finally, remove the computer object from the Servers container for the site in which the domain controller was located, using Active Directory Sites And Services.

Troubleshooting Startup and Shutdown

Troubleshooting startup and shutdown are also part of system recovery. When problems occur, you need to be able to resolve them, and the key techniques are discussed in this part of the chapter. As part of your troubleshooting, you might need to refer to the extensive startup troubleshooting techniques discussed in "Managing Startup and Boot Configuration" on page 383 as well as "Troubleshooting Hardware" on page 237.

Resolving Startup Issues

When you have problems starting a system, think about what has changed recently. If you and other administrators keep a change log, access the log to see what has changed on the system recently. A new device driver might have been installed or an application might have been installed that incorrectly modified the system configuration.

Often you can resolve startup issues using Safe Mode to recover or troubleshoot system problems. In Safe Mode, Windows Server 2008 loads only basic files, services, and drivers. Because Safe Mode loads a limited set of configuration information, it can help you troubleshoot problems. You start a system in Safe Mode by completing the following steps:

1. If the system is currently running and you want to troubleshoot startup, shut down the server, and then start it again. If the system is already powered down or has previously failed to start, start the server again.

2. Press F8 during startup to access the Windows Advanced Options menu. You must press F8 before the Windows splash screen appears.

3. On the Windows Advanced Options menu, select a startup mode. The key options are as follows:

- *Safe Mode*–Starts the computer and loads only basic files, services, and drivers during the initialization sequence. The drivers loaded include the mouse, monitor, keyboard, mass storage, and base video. No networking services or drivers are started.

- *Safe Mode With Command Prompt*–Starts the computer and loads only basic files, services, and drivers, and then starts a command prompt instead of the Windows Server 2008 graphical interface. No networking services or drivers are started.

- *Safe Mode With Networking*–Starts the computer and loads only basic files, services, and drivers, and the services and drivers needed to start networking.

- *Enable Boot Logging*–Starts the computer with boot logging enabled, which allows you to create a record of all startup events in a boot log.

- *Enable Low Resolution Video*–Starts the computer in low resolution 640×480 display mode, which is useful if the system display is set to a mode that can't be used with the current monitor.

- *Last Known Good Configuration*–Starts the computer in Safe Mode using Registry information that Windows Server 2008 saved at the last shutdown.

- *Debugging Mode*–Starts the system in debugging mode, which is useful only for troubleshooting operating system bugs.

- *Directory Services Recovery Mode*–Starts the system in Safe Mode and allows you to restore the directory service. This option is available on Windows Server 2008 domain controllers.

- *Disable Automatic Restart On System Failure*–Prevents Windows Server 2008 from automatically restarting after an operating system crash.

Chapter 41

○   *Disable Driver Signature Enforcement*–Starts the computer in Safe Mode without enforcing digital signature policy settings for drivers. If a driver with
an invalid or missing digital signature is causing startup failure, this will
resolve the problem temporarily so that you can start the computer and
resolve the problem by either getting a new driver or changing the driver
signature enforcement settings.

4.   If a problem doesn't reappear when you start in Safe Mode, you can eliminate
the default settings and basic device drivers as possible causes. If a newly added
device or updated driver is causing problems, you can use Safe Mode to remove
the device or roll back the update.

5.   Make other changes as necessary to resolve startup problems. If you are still
having a problem starting the system, you might need to uninstall recently
installed applications or devices to try to correct the problem.

Repairing Missing or Corrupted System Files

Windows Server 2008 enters Windows Error Recovery mode automatically if Windows
fails to start. In this mode, you have options similar to those you have when working
with the Advanced Boot menu. For troubleshooting, you can elect to boot the system
in Safe Mode, Safe Mode With Networking, or Safe Mode With Command Prompt.
You can also choose to use the Last Known Good Configuration or to start Windows
normally.

If you can't start or recover a system in Safe Mode, you can manually run Startup Repair
to try to force Windows Server 2008 to resolve the problem. To do this, complete the
following steps:

1.   Insert the Windows installation or Windows Recovery disc for the hardware
architecture and then boot from the installation disc by pressing a key when
prompted. If the server does not allow you to boot from the installation disc, you
might need to change firmware options to allow booting from a CD/DVD-ROM
drive.

2.   With a Windows Recovery disc, select Windows Setup (EMS Enabled) on
the Windows Boot Manager menu to start Windows Setup. With a Windows
installation disc, Windows Setup should start automatically.

3.   On the Install Windows page, select the language, time, and keyboard layout
options that you want to use. Click Next.

4.   When prompted, do not click Install Now. Instead, click the Repair Your
Computer link in the lower-left corner of the Install Windows page. This starts
the System Recovery Options wizard. If the boot manager is damaged, the wizard
will repair it at this point to obtain a list of available operating systems.

5.   On the System Recovery Options page, click Command Prompt. At the command
prompt, enter **cd recovery** to access the *X*:\Sources\Recovery directory.

6. At the command prompt, enter **startrep** to run the Startup Repair wizard. Follow the prompts to attempt to repair the server and enable startup.

Resolving Restart or Shutdown Issues

Normally, you can shut down Windows Server 2008 by clicking Start, and then clicking the Shutdown button, and restart Windows Server 2008 by clicking Start, pointing to the Options button, and then clicking Restart. Sometimes, however, Windows Server 2008 won't shut down or restart normally and you are forced to take additional actions. In those cases, follow these steps:

1. Press Ctrl+Alt+Delete. The Windows Security screen should be displayed. If the Windows Security screen doesn't appear, skip to step 4.

2. Click Task Manager, and then look for an application that is not responding. If all programs appear to be running normally, skip to step 4.

3. Select the application that is not responding, and then click End Task. If the application fails to respond to the request, you'll see a prompt that allows you to end the application immediately or cancel the end task request. Click End Now.

4. Try shutting down or restarting the computer. Press Ctrl+Alt+Delete, and then click the Shutdown button. As a last resort, you might be forced to perform a hard shutdown by holding down the power button or unplugging the computer. If you do this, run Check Disk the next time you start the computer to check for errors and problems that may have been caused by the hard shutdown.

Index to Troubleshooting Topics

Topic	Description	Page
Active Directory schema	You cannot change an attribute even though you are a member of the Administrators group	1016
Defragmenting disks	Be careful when defragmenting	592
Drag and drop	I'm unable to drag and drop items	135
Dynamic disks	Dynamic disks have limitations	430
Hardware configuration	RAM and CPUs are incompatible	99
Hardware interrupts	Check the device slot configuration	241
Joining computer to domain	The computer won't join the domain	1227
Network interface	Get separate views of bytes received and sent for troubleshooting	323
Network interface performance	Compare network activity to disk time and processor time	363
Network user class	Class ID problems	726
Printer spooling	Check permissions on the spool folder	881
	Clear out stuck documents	909
	Running out of space may indicate a deeper problem	913
Processor performance	Rule out processor affinity as an issue on multiprocessor systems	359
Remote monitoring	Try the IP address if you can't connect	355
Shadow copy	Shadow copy relies on the Task Scheduler	596
Shortcut menus	No shortcut menus appear when I right-click	135
Storage area networks	Detecting SAN configuration problems	410
System processes	Isolate 32-bit or 64-bit processes	315
Virtual memory	Be careful when setting or moving the paging file	308
WINS replication	Resolving WINS replication errors	828

Index

Symbols and Numbers
.NET Framework 3.0, 188
64-bit computing, 7–8. *See also* Itanium-based servers

A
access control
    access permissions for files and folders, 571–578
    Active Directory related features, list of, 989–990
    entries. *See* ACEs (access control entries)
    lists. *See* ACLs (access control lists)
    systems, physical, 1315
    user account control. *See* UAC (User Account Control)
account policies. *See also* Group Policy
    Account Policies, editing with default GPOs,
        1247–1249
    configuring user policies, 1169–1170
    Group Policy objects. *See* GPOs (Group Policy objects)
    Kerberos policy settings, 1169, 1173
    local user accounts, 1169
    location of, 1169
    lockout policy, 1172, 1247
    password policy enforcement, 1170–1171
    password settings object creation, 1173–1176
accounts
    Accounts: Rename Administrator Account policy, 1248
    Accounts: Rename Guest Account policy, 1248
    Administrator. *See* Administrator account
    authentication of. *See* authentication
    built-in capabilities of, 1178
    contact accounts, 1168
    creating user accounts, 1184–1187
    default user accounts, 1168
    domain. *See* domain user accounts
    expiration options for, 1192
    Guest account, 1168
    InetOrgPerson. *See* InetOrgPerson accounts
    local. *See* local user accounts
    membership in groups, 1178
    naming accounts, 1168
    OUs, placing in, 1136
    permissions of. *See* permissions
    policies for. *See* account policies
    RODC password replication policies, 1148, 1158–1159

user. *See* user accounts
user account control. *See* UAC (User Account Control)
ACEs (access control entries), 1188
ACLs (access control lists)
    Active Directory, role in, 988
    RODCs, for, 1158
ACPI (Advanced Configuration and Power Interface),
    379–382
ACPI BIOS, 240–241
Act As Part Of The Operating System privilege, 1178
activation of Windows Server 2008
    process for, 88–90
    viewing status of, 126–127
Active Directory
    administering. *See* Active Directory Users And
        Computers snap-in
    architecture of. *See* Active Directory architecture
    attribute management, 1014–1016, 1076
    authoritative restores of, 1412–1414
    backup strategies for, 1409–1410
    backups for installation media creation, 1127–1128
    bridgehead servers role, 58. *See also* bridgehead
        servers
    building blocks, logical, 1053
    business requirements for, 1053–1054
    changing structure of, 1061–1062
    classes of objects, 1014
    client connection requirements, 1111
    compatibility issues, 1016–1020
    Computer objects, 1014
    configuration containers in a forest, 1055
    Contact objects, 1014
    counters for, 1303–1304
    CPUs, requirements for, 1108
    creating domain controllers for existing domains,
        1114–1122
    data store architecture, 995–997
    delegation of administrative rights, 1064–1065,
        1136–1139
    designing systems of. *See* Active Directory system
        design
    DHCP authorization, 689
    DHCP set up with, 696, 698, 701